OUR FAITH-FILLED JOURNEY
TO THE ENDS OF THE EARTH

# Unlikely

# RICK RENNER

Harrison House

WWW.HARRISONHOUSE.COM

*Unlikely*
*Our Faith-Filled Journey to the Ends of the Earth*
ISBN: 978-1-68031-787-9
eBook: 978-1-68031-788-6

Copyright © 2021 by Rick Renner
P. O. Box 702040
Tulsa, OK 74170-2040

Published in Partnership:
Harrison House
Shippensburg, PA 17257-2914
www.harrisonhouse.com

Rick Renner Ministries
Tulsa, OK 74170

1 2 3 4 5 / 25 24 23 22 21

Editorial Consultant: Rebecca L. Gilbert
Cover Design: Jennifer Grisham
Text Design: Lisa Simpson, www.SimpsonProductions.net
Photo Layout: Debbie Pullman, Zoe Life Creative Media,
www.ZoeLifeCreative.com

# DEDICATION

As I finished writing this autobiography and prayed about to whom I should dedicate it, I felt it was right to dedicate this book to the various kinds of partners who have played influential roles in different seasons over many years of our lives and ministry.

My English dictionary says that a "partner" is one who *is associated* with another; a person with whom one *shares* a relationship; either of two persons who *dance* together; one of two or more persons who *play* together in a game against an opposing side; one who *is a member* of a partnership, especially in a joint venture; one of the heavy timbers that *strengthen* a ship's deck to support a mast; or, simply, one who *is a sharer* in something with someone else.

In the following paragraphs, you will see that I describe six categories of partners who *have been associated* with us in some way: those who *have shared* some level of influential role or relationship with us at different times; who have *danced* with us closely through some interesting seasons; who *have played, worked, and strategized* with us against opposing forces of darkness so we could take new territory for God's Kingdom; who *have been real-life members together* in our joint venture; who *have been like a heavy timber of strong support* whose prayers, gifts, and lives have strengthened our spiritual masts so we could keep sailing; and who *will share eternally* in the fruit that has been reaped over the years by this ministry.

*First and foremost*, I dedicate this book to my most important partner in life — *Jesus*. It was Jesus who called me before the foundation of the world; who separated me from my mother's womb; who saw to it that I was raised in a godly home and church; who saved me and baptized me in the Holy Spirit; who directed every step of my earlier life; who led me to the right places at the right times; who gave Denise to me as a treasured lifelong partner; who blessed our lives with three godly sons, three godly daughters-in-law, and eight godly grandchildren; who has healed, delivered, and set me free more times than I can remember; and who led our family to the far side of the world to help us swing the "harvest sickle" for an amazing end-time ingathering.

As Paul said in First Corinthians 3:7, I, too, can say that we have planted with others and have worked very hard — but God, *our Chief Partner*, is the only One who could give the increase. To Him be all the glory.

*Second*, I dedicate this book to those who influenced me along the way in life. There are so many that I cannot list them all. But I'm talking about family, friends, church members, pastors, co-workers, teachers, and the list goes on and on. Each of them made significant contributions that helped fashion who I am today. From those who first held me in the nursery of the church to those who influence and inspire me today, I am so thankful.

*Third*, I dedicate this book to our parents, to our families, to Denise, and to our sons. Denise and I were both blessed with marvelous and godly parents who taught us many important lessons that prepared us for life and ministry. Like planting seed, they poured themselves *and the Word of God* into us, and all that we have done over the years is in part due to our parents' influential roles in our lives. Our families likewise have always been supportive voices as we have done our best to do what God has called us to do. Their *agape* love for us is a treasure that we do not take for granted.

Of course, I am eternally thankful to God for my wife Denise, a true lifetime partner, who has stood at my side in every season of life and who has fought every battle alongside me and our sons as we have given our lives for God's call. And Paul, Philip, and Joel are not only birth sons, but they are our *spiritual* sons and co-laborers in the vineyard. I am so thankful for the call of God on their own lives and for their willingness to do whatever Jesus has asked them to do in the ministry.

*Fourth*, I dedicate this book to our partners who have given sacrificially over many years to help us fulfill God's mandate on our lives and ministry. Denise and I, our sons, and our team were willing to do the work on the front lines, but our faithful partners have sowed their prayers of faith and their finances for this remarkable work to be done. Every line of this story is underscored with the financial gifts of people who generously and consistently gave their hard-earned money as offerings for this ministry to take place. We have literally worked hand in hand with them, and they are "partners" with us in the truest sense of the word. When we stand before Jesus, our partners will be richly rewarded for the fruit that was produced as a result of their giving.

*Fifth*, I dedicate this book to the team members who have faithfully served alongside us. For everything that has been accomplished, there has been a team of God-called people who have stood with us also embracing God's call on our lives. They have been right at our sides to fight every battle we have faced, to charge the enemy when needed, to advance by faith to take new territory, and to stand in faith and prayer with us through every step of this journey. God has enabled us to do a lot, but we have not done anything without them at our sides.

*Sixth*, I dedicate this book to believers who suffered in years past or who gave their lives in the USSR for the Gospel. In John 4:38, Jesus said, "I sent you to reap that whereon ye bestowed no labour: other men laboured, and ye are entered into their labours." Before our time in the lands of the former USSR, there was a generation of persecuted believers who sowed the first seeds for this move of God with their prayers and, for many, in the giving of their very lives. Those seeds eventually produced the harvest we are experiencing today. As those previous generations lay in prisons and even died, they stood in faith and prayed for a day to come when the Gospel would be freely preached. We are standing in the manifestation of their prayers and faith. In this sense, we have been "partners" with those heroes from the past who have taken their seats in the grandstands of Heaven.

Hebrews 11:39 and 40 refers to those who believed for something to come to pass that they never saw, but because they stayed in faith and refused to relent, others later stepped into the harvest of what they believed would come to pass. It says, "And these all, having obtained a good report through faith, received not the promise: God having provided some better thing for us, that they without us should not be made perfect."

These verses perfectly describe the persecuted Church in the days of the Soviet Union. Those saints sowed in the hardest season of all, but God received their faith and their lives as seeds for a future harvest. Then He allowed us to be sent into the field as reapers of the precious seed they sowed. Although many of them died without seeing the results of their believing, they died with a good report, as they never relinquished their faith. And today, we have been a part of the manifestation of their prayers and in the sacrificial giving of their lives. Indeed, we are partners with God, and we are also partners with them.

# CONTENTS

## Chapter 12

# ACKNOWLEDGMENTS

This autobiography has been on my heart for years, but I was waiting for the correct time to write it. Then suddenly the Holy Spirit prompted me that it was time to begin interviewing what turned out to be fifty-plus people whose memories, comments, and testimonies would be vital to our amazing story. When I finally sat down to write, the pages of this book literally flowed from my heart, mind, and fingertips, and I wrote the majority of my autobiography in the space of about six months.

Although I have written this book, and it bears my name as the author, many contributed to this "unlikely" story and have participated in this adventure of God's amazing, *abounding* grace. The *New Living Translation* of First Corinthians 3:7 says, "It's not important who does the planting, or who does the watering. What's important is that God makes the seed grow."

Many people have played important roles in the story of our lives and ministry, but God is the One who deserves a standing ovation, for only He had the ability to make all of this unlikely story come to pass. However, because many played a vital role in planting and watering along the way, I want to acknowledge some of them.

*First*, I want to acknowledge Denise and our three sons Paul, Philip, and Joel. My story is also *their* story. Denise and I started our lives together in the ministry and have lived every moment of this adventure together with our sons, who have faithfully been with us every step of the way. Our sons are not only our birth sons, but they are our *spiritual* sons and our most cherished friends and co-laborers in this ministry that God has entrusted to our family. I am also forever thankful to relatives, friends, and long-time staff members who have also been a key part of this amazing journey.

*Second*, I want to acknowledge the more than fifty people who took the time to be interviewed so we could capture their perspectives of the various phases of our story. Each of the following were interviewed, and their interviews combined produced nearly *two thousand pages* of transcripts that contain their personal insights and memories of the events recounted in the pages of this book.

These interviewees include (but are not limited to): *Denise Renner, Paul Renner, Philip Renner, Joel Renner, Erlita Miller Renner, Melita Miller Davis, Ronda Renner Roush, Trula Roberson, Bonnie Brown, Kathy Packell, Phyllis Crawford, Joella Crawford Davies, Terry White, David Grosse, Pam Grosse, Janey Spencer, Eddie Graber, Linda Graber, Tom Harkness, Teresa Smith, Gina Smith, Carolyn Hoopaw Stephens, Mark Carter, Roy Beebe, Barbara Beebe, Bob Yandian, Robb Thompson, Tony Cooke, Wayne Boosahda, Stephanie Boosahda, Walter Gorman, Cindy Duvall, Ray Taucher, Lois Taucher, Duane Vander Klok, Terry Young, Terri Young, Adele Alexander, Sharmon Adams, Andrey Chebotarev, Anita Busha Vavilova, Alexander Dovgan, Yuri Ruls, Andrey Vasilyev, Leonid Bondarenko, Maxim Myasnikov, Nikolai Kulakevich, Renata Kulakevich, Alexei Ledeyev, Bishop Nikolai Gribs, and Bishop Sergei Ryakhovsky.*

*Third,* I want to acknowledge Becky Gilbert, the chief editor in our ministry, who did all the interviews with the people listed and whose editorial hand was so vital to make this book sparkle for God's glory. Becky is a fabulous editor and creative writer. When I started this project, I knew she would be the editorial partner to make this book what it needed to be. In the many years that Becky has worked with us, she has never disappointed, and once again in this book, she has shown her gifts and her excellence. With a position in our ministry that is already substantial, she nonetheless took this assignment with grace and tenacity. Becky's touch, along with the help of her fabulous editorial team, is on every page.

I am so thankful to the entire team (Debbie Townsley, Beth Parker, Lisa Cowerd, Lisa Simpson, Susan Woodrow, and Loretta Yandian), whose attention, care, and input were so valuable — and to Michelle Gilbert for her contributions to the Glossary and to Mica Olinghouse for her work on footnote research. Debbie Pullman did a *marvelous* job on the photo sections, for which I am so grateful. I am immensely thankful to Sergei Bagretsov, who invested significant time to brilliantly translate the original text into Russian at a miraculous rate of speed. I'm grateful to Anton Kruglikov for his important commentary on various parts of the book — and to Anton and to Alexander (Sasha) Dovgan for their invaluable help locating photos.

Lastly, I wish to thank Maxim Motyavin, who meticulously recorded every word of the audio book for many hours.

*Fourth*, I want to acknowledge a group of special people who read the manuscript before it was sent to be printed. I felt it was important to choose a handful of thoughtful, serious, and spiritual people to read it for impact and accuracy. I carefully selected people who would be honest and forthright in their feedback and whose eyes were connected to their hearts and minds. These deeper readers included *Denise Renner, Paul Renner, Philip Renner, Joel Renner, Ronda Roush, Adele Alexander, Beth Parker, Lisa Cooke, Tony Cooke, Lisa Cowerd, Danyelle Lee, Loretta Yandian, Hannah Cowart, Teresa Smith, Gina Smith, Barbara Beebe, Jon Blume, Jane Blume, Michelle Gilbert, Andrey Chebotarev, Yuri Ruls, Maxim Myasnikov, Sergei Bagretsov, Anton Kruglikov,* and *Andrey Vasilyev.*

*Fifth*, in addition to the people I just mentioned, I want to acknowledge other people, places, and organizations that have made indelible influential marks on my life. I am so thankful to each of them for the roles they played in my life. These whom I wish to acknowledge are *David and Pam Grosse, Jim and Tanya Farmer, Ann Noel, Doug and Sharon Graham, Jim and Anne Frease, Bishop Sergei Vasilyevich Ryakhovsky, Pastor Bob Yandian,* and *Wally and June Blume.* Organizations and ministries I wish to acknowledge are *Glenwood Baptist Church (Tulsa), Sheridan Road Assembly (Tulsa), Kenneth Hagin Ministries, Grace Fellowship (Tulsa), Oral Roberts University, First Baptist Church (Fort Smith, Arkansas), Fellowship of Believers (Fort Smith, Arkansas), Calvary International (Jacksonville, Florida), Kenneth Copeland Ministries, Joyce Meyer Ministries, the Latvian Pentecostal Union, POCXBE,* and thousands of *partnering churches and other faithful organizations* that have graciously stayed with us as associates, friends, and partners for the many years of our ministry.

Everyone mentioned here has played some key role in our unlikely story and in the writing of this autobiography. There are many more, but I want to say thank you to each of these and also to those unnamed who have been used mightily by God in our lives and ministry.

# INTRODUCTION

# *YOU* HAVE AN 'UNLIKELY' STORY TOO

*A* lone shepherd unrolls his mat on a knoll overlooking a valley filled with livestock. Weary from his day's journey, he stretches out on his bedding made of lion skins stuffed with wool, reminded of God's faithfulness as he takes in the glorious view of the stars in a twilight sky. Nearby, other shepherds are bedding down in makeshift huts — and the sheep, well-fed and free from agitation under the shepherds' care, also begin to settle down, their shaggy images dotting the field like a blanket of fleece.

Far enough from camp to be undistracted by the conversation of the day's events, the teen-aged shepherd draws out his rugged, worn lute. His fingers gliding deftly upward across the strings, he plays softly the tunes that are ever familiar to his companions in the field, both animal and man.

Before he finally lies down to sleep, the shepherd looks wistfully into the sky once more and dreams, his heart filled with worship and wonderment as he anticipates God's plans for his future. In his lowly assignment

**Left:** *Rick and Denise Renner, Moscow, Russia.*

1

*in the fields, the young shepherd is often overlooked and disregarded, even by his own family. Pondering his situation, a pang of rejection strikes unexpectedly against his soul. But little does he know what open doors lie ahead — with an adversary to greet him far greater than any he has faced before.*

*David closes his eyes and rests in the arms of his own beloved Shepherd. Shivering in the cold in that distant field — a sleeping, unsuspecting world around him — lies a king.*

Just as He did in David's "unlikely" story, God has a way of using the experiences of our early days — even our very bad experiences — and redeeming them as only He can. He forges them into a glorious purpose for our lives and uses our seasons of obscurity, loneliness, brokenness, clumsiness, and even *failure* to weave together a plan so *unlikely* that only He could bring it to pass. Our future doesn't lie in our own impressive resume or grandiose list of accomplishments, but in our faithfulness and consistency day to day as we walk with God and build a "resume" of accomplishments, exploits — *and even godly character* — with Him.

You are about to read my own unlikely story. As I reflect on my life and ponder what God has enabled my family and me to do over these many years, it is clear how very *unlikely* it seemed that He would call me from a small town in Oklahoma to take the Gospel to the farthest parts of the world. In fact, the odds were so against this possibility that I have chosen to entitle my autobiography, *UNLIKELY — Our Faith-Filled Journey to the Ends of the Earth.*

As I consider the unlikelihood of what God has done in my life, my thoughts turn to the apostle Paul's words in First Corinthians 1:26-28, where he wrote: "For ye see your calling, brethren, how that not many wise men after the flesh, not many mighty, not many noble, are called: But God hath chosen the foolish things of the world to confound the wise; and God hath chosen the weak things of the world to confound the things which are mighty; and base things of the world, and things which are despised, hath God chosen...."

This passage so well describes me that I'd like to share more about it with you before we dive into my story. (Perhaps those words describe you too.) If any verses in the Bible could describe me and my family to a "T," it is *these* in which Paul described how God especially delights in choosing those who are *unlikely* to do something significant.

If you see yourself as feeble, weak, unskilled, or undeveloped — and if that has been your excuse for why God couldn't possibly use you — you're about to discover that from the beginning of time, God has delighted in choosing the most *unlikely*.

Very few whom God has called have been the "cream of the crop" when He called them. Again and again, Scripture shows that God chose those who were ill-esteemed in the eyes of the world when He has needed a candidate or a group of people to do a special job. God has always used "common people" to build His Kingdom. In other words, He doesn't primarily choose famous movie stars or the royalty and nobility of the world to fulfill His plans and purposes. God's requirements are different from the criteria of the world. As He states in Isaiah 55:8, "...My thoughts are not your thoughts, neither are your ways my ways...."

For example, when God chose Samuel to lead the nation of Israel as the prophet in the land, Samuel was just a young boy. That was certainly an *unlikely* scenario. When God looked for someone to kill a warrior giant, He chose a young shepherd boy named David. That was *unlikely* too. When the fullness of time had come and the moment arrived to send His Son to this earth, God chose a young girl named Mary to give birth to the Savior of the world. That was an *unlikely* choice as well. The world probably wouldn't have chosen any of these three people who have become such a significant part of our spiritual history and heritage. But God *delights* in choosing those who are *unlikely* in the eyes of the world.

Also, when it was time for Jesus to choose disciples, He didn't go to the theological institutes or seminaries of the day. Rather, Jesus chose disciples who knew more about fishing and tax-collecting than about the Scriptures. All of those disciples were *unlikely* choices. And when God searched for someone He could use to write the majority of the New Testament, He chose an *unlikely* man named Saul — later known as the apostle Paul, who had been one of the meanest Christian-killers of all time!

God has historically shown up in places where He was not expected. Consider the location where Jesus was born — in a lowly shepherd's stall. This was certainly not the place anyone would have expected the King of kings to be born. After all, wouldn't it have been more fitting for such a King to be born in a majestic hall gilded with gold, with trumpets announcing His birth?

So if you've ever thought you weren't good enough for God to use, it's time to change your thinking! God is looking for people no one else wants or deems valuable. When great victories are won through ordinary folks, there's no question about who should receive the glory. As First Corinthians 1:29 says, "That no flesh should glory in his presence."

### You Are a 'First-Pick' in God's Mind

As you get started on this book, don't discount the possibility that God may be using these very words — *and this book* — to point His finger at *you*. The very things that disqualify you in your mind may actually be what make you a *first pick* in God's mind. *Keep reading!*

And think about it. Would *you* have selected Samuel, David, Mary, or Paul? How about Jesus' disciples? Yet those were the people *God* chose to use in mighty and powerful ways. They may have been flawed, but they had hearts that qualified them for God's use. In fact, the Old and New Testaments are filled with illustrations of people *God wanted,* but *the world rejected.*

God's choice is not based on beauty or ugliness, talent or lack of talent, education or lack of education, a diploma or no diploma. If a person has *a right heart* toward God, he or she is qualified to be used by Him. No passage teaches this principle more clearly than the one in First Corinthians 1:26-28, which we have read.

Before we get into my story, I want to delve a little deeper into these verses to understand exactly how God is in the habit of choosing those who are *unlikely* in the eyes of the world. I want to give you scriptural proof that this is God's way of choosing people. And then I'll give you *experiential* proof — because I have *lived* these verses of Scripture!

## Whom God Does and Doesn't Use

In First Corinthians 1:26, Paul said, "For ye see your calling, brethren, how that not many *wise* men after the flesh…." As Paul began to write his list of those whom God *does* and *doesn't* use, he started by stating that God *doesn't* use many who are considered wise by the world's standards. The word "wise" is from the Greek word *sophos*. It refers to a person who possesses *special enlightenment* or *special insight*.

The word *sophos* was often used in ancient Greek culture to portray highly educated people, such as scientists, philosophers, doctors, teachers, and others who were considered to be the *super-intelligentsia* of the day. These belonged to a class of individuals the world would have called *clever*, *astute*, *smart*, or *intellectually brilliant*. The term *sophos* was reserved only for those considered to be *super-impressive* in society or *a cut above* the rest.

But Paul said, "For ye see your calling, brethren, how that *not* many wise men after the flesh…." Paul was informing us that most of the people God calls don't fit into this category of the *super-intelligentsia*. In other words, God doesn't specialize in calling those who are *especially clever*, *educated*, *astute*, *smart*, or *eminently enlightened*. Those traits are not His criteria!

I would be remiss if I overlooked the fact that over the years, many intelligent men and women who loved God have made a great impact on the world. Paul himself was a part of this elite group before he came to Christ. Apollos, Paul's friend who later pastored the church of Corinth, also came from this intellectual "upper echelon" of society. But Paul and Apollos were not typical of the First Century Church.

In fact, it was predominantly the *sophos* who scorned and ridiculed Paul when he preached in Athens. The philosophers of Athens — the Epicureans and the Stoics — derided him and made him a laughingstock. But Paul said that "not many" are called who fit into this *sophos* category. Of course, God's call is to all men, but the fact is, "not many" from this category actually *respond* to God's call.

If you take a close look at the Early Church, you'll see that it was primarily composed of servants, slaves, and poorer people who heard the Good News of the Gospel and believed. *It was an army of common people who became mighty men and women of faith God could use.* Although there were a few elite in the Church, they were the exceptions rather than the rule.

As we continue in First Corinthians 1:26-28, you will see that God specializes in calling people from a much lower class in the world's view. And if you take a close look at the Church today, you'll see that God *still* specializes in calling common people. That's good news because it means God wants to use you and me!

I'm certainly not debasing education. I believe people should get as much education as possible. But school-issued pieces of paper are not the criteria that impress God and get His attention. There have been many educated people whom God could not use. Although they were brilliant according to the flesh, they were not worthy of being chosen because their hearts weren't right. Educational degrees may help you get a good job and positively sway the opinion of men in your favor, but Paul made it very clear that God is not looking for people who are *"especially bright"* (*sophos*) according to the standards of the flesh.

When God does call people who are intellectually impressive, such as Moses or the apostle Paul, He usually has to empty them of themselves before He can use them. When they lean on their own understanding or their talents, they are unable to accomplish what God wants them to do. But when they lean wholly upon *God*, He is able to perform miracles through their lives.

The psalmist David wrote, "Some trust in chariots, and some in horses: but we will remember the name of the Lord our God" (Psalm 20:7). The best technology of David's time was used to develop the chariots of that day. Men's greatest intellectual powers were employed to make those chariots faster, stronger, and safer. In addition, horses represented natural power, strength, and might. Therefore, David was essentially saying, "Some trust in man's mind and his great achievements; others rely on their own natural power and might. But we will rely upon the name of the Lord."

Perhaps you're one of those people who says, "God can't use me because I don't have many gifts or talents. I haven't been to college. I don't even have a Bible-school degree." If you are, it's time to change the way you're thinking and talking. It's time for you to start seeing yourself the way *God* sees you.

If you feel inferior to others, remember that God regularly calls unskilled and uneducated people, such as the majority of the apostles Jesus hand-picked to serve at His side and to lay the foundation of the Church. Those "unlikely" apostles were fishermen, tax collectors, and common people — *not* theologians.

God is looking to build a strong, powerful army for His Kingdom — and He has designed a place for *you* in those ranks! He doesn't necessarily need the super-intelligentsia of the world to get the job done. In fact, common people are often God's first choice because they are already equipped to a certain degree to face the challenges and difficulties of life without complaining or quitting.

So if you want to be used by God, it's time to quit confessing that you're not as smart or sharp as someone else. Where does the Bible ever say God is looking for brains? He's looking for hearts that are willing to follow Him. *If you have that kind of heart, you are exactly the kind of person God wants to use.*

### Not Many 'High and Mighty' Are Called

Then in First Corinthians 1:26, Paul added, "For ye see your calling, brethren, how that not many wise men after the flesh, not many *mighty....*" The word "mighty" is translated from the Greek word *dunatoi*, plural of the Greek word *dunamis*, which refers to *power or ability*. But the word *dunatoi*, as it is in this verse, refers to people who have *political power or might*. It carries the idea of a person who is *"high and mighty"* in the world's view.

When you are in the presence of people who possess "political might," a tangible atmosphere of power and influence is usually present. For example, that power can be felt as you walk through the hallowed hallways of notable governmental buildings. It can also be experienced when the motorcade of a president, vice-president, king, queen, ambassador, or other high-ranking official passes by on a road or highway, flanked by law-enforcement vehicles that escort them. This political "might" can also be felt when a plane carrying dignitaries lands at an airport, and the runway is lined with special security forces, policemen, and local dignitaries who have come to greet the arriving guests.

But God's Kingdom doesn't depend on the statesmen, diplomats, bureaucrats, or politicians of the world. Certainly it would be dramatic and impacting if a famous politician came to Christ, but this rarely happens. From the beginning of the Church age, God's people have been, for the most part, common folks who worked regular jobs and lived normal lives.

You don't have to be "high and mighty" to get things done for the Kingdom of God. All you need is the anointing of the Holy Spirit and to respond to God and His plan — to *His* story — for your life. With that spiritual equipment, you can move Heaven to action and push hell out of the way. So if you perceive yourself to be a plain, common type of person — rejoice! *You are exactly the kind of person God wants to use.*

## God Delights in Using Ordinary People

In First Corinthians 1:26, Paul continued, "For ye see your calling, brethren, how that not many wise men after the flesh, not many mighty, not many *noble*...." The word "noble" is from the compound word *eugenes*, which portrays people who are *well-born* or who have *excellent genes*.

In ancient Greece, the word *eugenes* meant *men of high descent,* such as sons of kings, politicians, or others from the upper crust of society. It referred to *individuals whose ancestors had been powerful, wealthy, rich, or famous.* These were high-born, blue-blooded, cultured, refined, courtly, pedigreed, aristocratic people who sustained their lofty positions in society based on their birth.

Examples of this class of people would be members of royalty, who held their exalted positions in society whether or not they personally merited those positions. They were *born into* the upper crust and stayed there simply because of their family name or relations.

Modern examples of *eugenes* are sons and daughters of kings and queens, who retain their royal posts simply because of the blood that runs in their veins. Other examples would be the sons and daughters of famous politicians. Although the offspring themselves may have not accomplished anything significant, their famous last name has sealed their notoriety and their place in society. They were born with a "name" that gives them certain guarantees and privileges that are not available to common people with unknown names.

So the word *eugenes* for "noble" in First Corinthians 1:26 describes both kinds of people: those born into famous families who enjoy the inherent privileges of their last name — and it can also depict those who carry a streak of genius, talent, or "superiority" in their genes. People in both of these groups comprise the upper crust, the ruling class, or the aristocracy of the world.

*But Paul said that God hasn't specialized in calling these groups of people either!* Take a look at world history and you'll see that God *hasn't* primarily specialized in using kings, queens, royalty, or famed politicians, scientists, philosophers, writers, movie stars, or other celebrities to advance His Kingdom. From the beginning of time, He has instead reached into the hearts of *ordinary* men and women. These are the ones who most often accomplish mighty feats on earth by God's grace and power.

Since God isn't looking for the upper crust of society, He must be looking to the "lower crust" — *to the ordinary, regular, routine, run-of-the-mill, standard, typical kind of people* — people like you and me.

## God Delights in Using
## Those the World Calls Foolish

Paul continued in First Corinthians 1:27, "But God hath chosen the *foolish things* of the world to confound the wise...." The word "foolish" is a translation of the Greek word *moraino*. The word "moron" also comes from this Greek word. My thesaurus gives these synonyms for a "moron": *idiot, imbecile, halfwit, numskull, dimwit, dunce, blockhead, dope, ignoramus, lamebrain, jerk,* or *twerp*!

The truth is, no one is an idiot in God's view. But the world often views people whom He chooses as being *nitwits, lamebrains,* and *idiots.* The word *moraino* was used in Paul's time to depict people whom the world scorned, made fun of, and treated with contempt. But truly, God looks at the heart, beneath the surface, and doesn't see things like we see them (*see* 1 Samuel 16:7; Isaiah 55:8,9).

Paul said, "...God hath chosen the foolish things of the world to *confound the wise...*" (1 Corinthians 1:27). The word "confound" in Greek means *to put to shame, to embarrass, to confuse, to frustrate, to baffle.* The word "wise," again, refers to *those who are naturally brilliant, intellectually sharp, or especially enlightened.* Paul was saying that God calls people whom the world considers *morons* in order to put to shame, embarrass, confuse, frustrate, and baffle those who think they're so smart. So if anyone has ever called you an idiot — if you've ever been called a stupid imbecile, a jerk, or a twerp — it's time for you to rejoice! This makes you a candidate for God's "first pick"!

First Corinthians 1:27 goes on to say, "But God hath chosen the foolish things of the world to confound the wise; and God hath chosen *the weak things* of the world to confound the things which are mighty." The word "weak" is the Greek word *asthene,* and it refers to something that is *weak, base, feeble, puny,* or *powerless.* It describes something that is so substandard, second-rate, low-grade, and inferior, it's almost laughable.

This makes me think of David, who was but a young boy when God called him. He was so young in age and immature in physical development that the Bible says, "And when the Philistine looked about, and saw David, he disdained him: for he was but a youth, and ruddy, and of a fair countenance" (1 Samuel 17:42). Goliath took it as a joke that David was sent to fight against him. The giant *laughed* when he saw whom God had chosen.

The Bible tells us Goliath said, "...Am I a dog, that thou comest to me with staves? And the Philistine cursed David by his gods" (1 Samuel 17:43). Who would have dreamed that God would select a young boy like David, inexperienced in war, to bring this giant down? It may have looked laughable in the eyes of the world, but this youth who fearlessly faced Goliath in battle was *the exact person* God had chosen.

When Paul wrote First Corinthians, the Church was the laughingstock of the Roman Empire, and Christians were viewed as a weak, puny, powerless religious group. The world views the Church today in much the same way. This perception is nothing new; it has always been this way.

The world didn't understand the incredible power God had placed both inside the Church and at the Church's disposal. The Church may have looked low-class compared to the rich ruling class of Romans who dressed in luxurious attire and held positions of authority and notoriety in the community. But the Church of Jesus Christ was vested with power and authority from on High — and this *unlikely* band of believers had marching orders to take the world for Christ!

Paul warned, "...God hath chosen the weak things of the world to confound the things which are mighty" (1 Corinthians 1:27). Again, the word "confound" means *to put to shame, to embarrass, to confuse, to frustrate, to baffle.* The word "mighty" describes *people who have political power or clout.*

When you keep in mind that it was the political arm of the Roman Empire that was trying to wipe out the Early Church, you realize this verse packs a powerful message! Paul was saying, *"God has chosen those whom the world considers to be puny and powerless — even laughable. These are the very ones God will use to confuse, frustrate, and baffle the political powers of the world."*

It took a while for the Early Church to *put to shame* all the evil forces that had come against it. But in the end, that's what happened! The Church eventually emerged in power and changed the face of history. The common, regular, run-of-the-mill people God had chosen were so mighty and powerful in the Lord that they "conquered the world" for Christ during their day.

The world may view you differently, but quit seeing *yourself* as someone who is substandard, second-rate, low-grade, or inferior. You are filled with the Spirit of God and have the call of God on your life. Who cares what the world thinks? Even if your gifts and talents seem small in comparison to what others possess, that doesn't mean you're eliminated from God's list of candidates. Your feelings of weakness and inadequacy — committed in trust and dependence to Him — actually qualify you as a candidate in God's service.

First Corinthians 1:28 continues to tell us God delights in choosing the "*base* things of the world." The word "base" in Greek is the word *agenes*, which is the exact opposite of the word *eugenes*; it describes people of *low birth* or with *bad genes.*

This may be an accurate description of the kind of people they were *before* God called them. But after they received the nature of God and were washed in the blood of Jesus, they became so powerful in the Spirit that God used them to confound the whole world! You see, *what you were in the past does not determine who you are today or who you will be in the future.*

If you have been feeling ordinary and not too special, guess what! Your "ordinariness" qualifies you to be used by God. You are *very* special. Your standing in God's eyes is extremely high. In fact, *you are exactly the kind of person God wants to use!*

## God Delights in Using
## Those Who Have Been Disregarded by Others

First Corinthians 1:28 goes on to say, "And base things of the world, and things which are *despised*...." The word "despised" in the Greek means *to make light of, to despise, to treat with contempt, to disregard,* or *to neglect.* It pictures *someone so low and detestable that he is hideous, disgusting, despicable, and nauseating to the viewer.* This outcast is so low, he isn't even worth recognizing.

The force of this Greek word is very strong. It indicates that the terrible opinion I just described has always been and will continue to be the prevailing opinion of the world concerning the Church. In other words, as long as it lies in the grip of the enemy, the unbelieving world will not even consider believers worth mentioning, no matter how much they try to do what's right.

Since this is the case, why should it surprise us when the world doesn't jump up and down about what you and I are doing in the earth? The Bible clearly teaches that "...the god of this world hath blinded the minds of them which believe not, lest the light of the glorious gospel of Christ, who is the image of God, should shine unto them" (2 Corinthians 4:4).

Hasn't the world always been harsh and bitter toward God's people? From the beginning of time, the lost world has ridiculed, made fun of, sarcastically accused, and debased the people of God. There is nothing new about this at all. Remember that Jesus was also "despised and rejected of men" (Isaiah 53:3). You are in good company with Jesus!

So if the world makes light of you or treats you with contempt — if it disregards, neglects, and overlooks you — *take heart.* You are exactly the "unlikely" kind of person God wants to use!

The *Renner Interpretive Version* of First Corinthians 1:26-28 says:

**For you see your calling, brothers, how not many of you were especially bright, educated, or enlightened according to the world's standards; not many of you were impressive; not many came from high-ranking families or from the upper crust of society. Instead, God selected people who are idiots in the world's view; in fact, the world sees them as imbeciles, jerks, and real twerps. Yet God is using them to utterly confound those who seem smart in the world's eyes.**

**God has chosen people whom the world finds laughable, and through them, He is confounding those who think they are so high and mighty. Low-class, second-rate, common, average, run-of-the-mill people — those so low that the world doesn't even think they're worth the time of day — these are the ones whom God has chosen....**

God has big plans to use you as a demonstration of His almighty power to the unbelieving world. How will you respond to Him?

Rather than complain that you're too feeble, it's time for you to throw up your arms and shout for joy! Your lack of skill may be the very thing that makes you usable to God! That way, when people begin to glory over what has been achieved through your life, you can truly say, "Anything good that has been done in my life has all been through the grace of God!"

By choosing "regular" people, God has made sure that when a victory is won, everyone will know it is due to His glory and grace. Paul said, "...According as it is written, He that glorieth, let him glory in the Lord" (1 Corinthians 1:31).

When I think back over the years, it is clear that what has happened in my life is completely *unlikely.* Nevertheless, the unlikely *has* occurred. Though the odds were against it...

- God enabled this *unlikely* boy from Sand Springs, Oklahoma, to write approximately fifty books, to date, in the U.S. and in the former USSR that have been translated into multiple languages and distributed by the millions all over the world. Several, at the time of this writing, are bestsellers.

- He graciously called and equipped me to preach before multiple thousands of people gathered in single events; in small, underground meetings in nations where the Gospel is prohibited; and to accumulated millions of people worldwide in public ministry and over the Internet and airwaves.

- He equipped me to build a TV network in the Soviet Union and to have a media ministry that is viewed by people all over the world.

- He not only chose Denise and me to start and to lead several significant churches in various countries, but He has also allowed us to travel to a long list of nations ministering to pastors, ministers, and the saints all over the world.

Denise and I have ministered from lecterns in governmental auditoriums to some of the largest churches in the world — and to churches just getting started. And God has given us precious friends in the ministry over the years as well, many whose names and faces are known to the majority of the Church today. I am deeply grateful for those relationships.

As I survey the blessing of those God has given us to minister to — and of those He has given to minister *to us* — I can assuredly tell you that God *delights* in taking the "unlikely" and blessing them for His glory.

You were not assigned to do what Denise and I were called to do, and you should not compare your God-given accomplishments with those of anyone else. Nevertheless, God can use you to do things that are important to Him and crucial to His plan, regardless of your background or how unqualified you've felt in the past.

### What if You Never *'Just Start'*?

The Bible talks about small beginnings that yield endings that are *filled* with increase (*see* Job 8:7). And Zechariah 4:10 (*NLT*) says, "Do not despise these small beginnings…." Jesus affirmed this principle in Luke 19:17 when He said that if you're faithful in *little*, He will grant you responsibility for *more.* Throughout the Scriptures — including what we read about David's beginnings as a lowly shepherd defending his father's flocks — we see this principle again and again. When we put our hand to the plow that God has placed in front of us, and we do it with all our might, He always gives increase, making us fruitful in our endeavors and entrusting us with more.

Just as God blessed Moses' rod, Gideon's sword, and David's shepherd's sling — He will bless what He places in *your* hands to work with in obedience to Him. In my own case over the years, God placed within me the call to teach and the ability to learn the Greek language and to minister on camera. And He has entrusted me with the mandate to forge into new territories previously darkened *for decades* in order to bring the light of the Gospel into those spiritually bleak places. He also put a "pen" in my hand, prophesying His blessing on my writings as I put my hand obediently to that assignment as well.

But what if I hadn't started? What if I hadn't prepared my first message as a teenager when my pastor asked me to minister in the Wednesday night service at our church to a congregation of adults? What if I'd leaned to my own understanding and said no to attending the university God led me to, where I learned how to read the Greek New Testament?

And if I'd never utilized our out-of-date camera equipment to film my first teaching program in the Soviet Union against a crude backdrop, I may never have been used to begin the first-ever Christian television network in that vast region of the world.

Certainly, God grants us second chances and new starts, and He helps us redeem the time. But we shouldn't try to hold out for something big when an opportunity is right in front of us, no matter how small — or how difficult or daunting — the task may seem.

Although it was an *unlikely* scenario indeed, God graciously enabled Denise and me and our three sons to minister in the Soviet Union in *unimaginable* conditions at a most *unimaginable* moment in history. Stepping "back in time" to Jelgava, Latvia, a city still scarred by a war that ended almost fifty years earlier — and then *shredded* by the collapse of the Soviet Union — we made the decision to obey and to *just start.*

Those were our own small beginnings that God Himself would grow into a ministry that would span an entire region of spiritual barrenness and brokenness. And the verse He had given Denise and me for our ministry, Romans 10:18, began to unfold in ways we'd never dreamed: "…Their sound went into all the earth, and their words unto the ends of the world."

All of this happened because we *started.* We learned to speak Russian, began the first Christian TV network in the former USSR, planted several Russian-speaking churches in that vast territory, led an influential ministry region-wide, and produced books, TV programs, and various media that reached around the world.

We also gained three Russian daughters-in-law and eight Russian grand-children, increasing our family of five in 1991 to *sixteen* family members at present — along with a whole crew of team members in the United States and in our international offices who are called alongside us to help facilitate the work God has assigned us.

God delights in taking people from unlikely places and situations and enabling them by His grace to do what they could never do by themselves. And God has a plan He designed for *you* to thrive in as you pursue His purpose for your own life. He will divinely enable *you* to do what you could never do on your own.

If anyone could claim to be *unlikely* for such a huge assignment, it's me. Just *how* unlikely is what you will learn as you read this book. But when God's Spirit called out to me, He also enabled me to say *yes* to His divine invitation. Once I said yes, He threw open the door, rolled out the red carpet that welcomed our entire family into His divine plan, and empowered us to miraculously step forward to fulfill His specific destiny for each of our lives.

The events you're about to encounter in my story have not been embel-lished. The whole account has been read by others who were *there* and can personally testify to its accuracy. I write about my calling and about my hesitance to obey at times — as well as about the transitions, tests, *and even the fiery trials* as my family and I were often challenged by hell to give up and quit on our journey.

But we adamantly refused every opportunity to quit. God had ordained and commanded it, and we had reached a point of no return in our obedience to Him. We endured threats by the Russian mafia, betrayal by some who were close to us, and the constant danger in the early days of being beaten or killed for just a few dollars. Our will swallowed up in His, there was indeed no turning back.

Revelation 12:11 tells us that our testimonies are powerful. It says, "And they overcame him by the blood of the Lamb, and by the word of their testimony; and they loved not their lives unto the death." My story is my testimony. It is a demonstration of what Jesus Christ has miraculously done in my life. I share it because I want you to know that if you're willing to do *whatever* God asks, He can do something significant with your life. Whether you're *twenty*, *forty*, or *eighty* years old, if you're willing — even if you feel that you are *unlikely* to be used — you can experience your own "adventures in God"!

If you are crying out for God to use you and you're willing to push aside the fear of risk and the unknown to follow Him wholeheartedly, get ready for a life that's filled with adventure! He *will* release His power to enable you to do what you naturally would be *unlikely* to accomplish on your own.

As you read on, you'll understand why it seemed so very unlikely that God would choose me. But since God could use my family and me as He has, He can use anyone — and, yes, that includes *you*. You are about to discover that what you think eliminates you from running and finishing your spiritual course *may* be the very thing that makes you just right for the assignment in the mind of God.

Let's proceed to our story.

'I truly learned from my family that people
are the biggest treasure on earth. It's not oil hidden
in caverns, but rather our friends, our neighbors,
and the members of our own house — those "hidden"
in plain sight in our day-to-day lives.'

# 1

# MY UNLIKELY ROOTS

I lived as a young boy in the 1960s in what some say was a poorer area of west Tulsa. My family and friends congregated regularly at softball games and church potlucks in a happy blend of hard work and social gatherings that defined our lives. Our lives were *so* well-defined, in fact, that our community was nestled *smack-dab* between two sets of railroad tracks. Those tracks were the markers that identified our sheltered, predictable world.

Except for occasional family vacations, I never as a child traveled outside a ten- or fifteen-mile radius from home. I traveled the world in my mind, however, only to snap out of my daydreaming on a dusty street near the ball field or outside Redbud's market, where my friends and I could buy a Coke with ice formed inside the bottle for 10 cents apiece.

I was born in this town — Tulsa, Oklahoma — a city built in the middle of what was once known as Indian Territory. Like all cities, Tulsa has its unique stories to be told, some pleasant and to be proud of and some very sordid and shameful. Before I get into my own story, I want to tell you a little about Tulsa and its surrounding areas where my life — my family's Oklahoma roots — began.

In 1830, the U.S. Congress had just passed the Indian Removal Act, a reprehensible law that was signed into law by President Andrew Jackson on May 28 of that year. It authorized the government to forcibly remove Native Americans from their ancestral lands and relocate those tribes. As this shameful law was enforced, Native Americans were *evicted* from their homes and lands east of the Mississippi River. This embarrassing chapter in American history resulted in the forceful eviction of Cherokee, Chickasaw, Choctaw, Creek-Muscogee, Seminole, and many less-populous tribes — and their resettlement via what infamously became known as the "Trail of Tears." From their ancestral homelands, these tribes marched to newly assigned lands, *Indian Territory*, that would later become the State of Oklahoma. (Other tribes affected by the Indian Removal Act included the Kickapoo, Lenape, Potawatomi, Shawnee, and Wyandot tribes.)[1]

More than sixty thousand tribal members traversed the arduous Trail of Tears before reaching their new home in Indian Territory, also known as Oklahoma Territory. Along the way, they suffered exposure, disease, and starvation, and more than four thousand Native Americans died before they reached the new territory.[2] The journey ended beneath the branches of what became known as the Council Oak Tree — a mighty oak located on a hill east of the Arkansas River in what later became downtown Tulsa. Using coals they had carried on their journey, tribal chiefs lit a ceremonial fire and established a marked-off area where council business would be conducted and as a gathering place for tribal ceremonies, feasts, and games. They named this new village *Tallasi* or "Old Town," but nicknamed it "Tulsy" — and the name stuck. It was from this epithet that the name "Tulsa" finally emerged[3], and that landmark tree and memorial can be visited in this same location today.

## A Story 'Out of the Tears'

As it turned out, exactly where the Trail of Tears ended is where our walk of faith began when Denise and I moved back to Tulsa from Fort Smith,

Arkansas, in 1985. (It was a critical part of our journey, or *mis*-journey, that I also write about in this book.) In that year when Denise and I started our itinerant ministry, we lived in a rented apartment just across the street from the Council Oak Tree that had been a memorial for those displaced Native Americans. Every time we exited our apartment in downtown Tulsa, that lone majestic oak was in full view, as if mounting a protective guard over that otherwise insignificant plot of real estate.

Admittedly, we didn't fully realize at the time the national disgrace it represented because of a crime perpetrated against those tribes approximately 150 years earlier. But as I look back today, it's interesting how the roots of that enormous tree are entrenched beneath the surface — sprawling the entire breadth and length of that ceremonial plot — as if to speak for those tribes of old, *We will not be uprooted again.*

And to show how God works, among those dislocated Indian families was a family whose last name became known as Roberts. In the not-so-distant future, two of them — Ellis Melvin Roberts and his wife Claudius Priscilla (Irwin) Roberts — would produce a fifth and youngest son named Granville Oral Roberts, born in a little log cabin fifteen miles northwest of Ada, Oklahoma, on January 24, 1918.[4]

Years later, a young Oral Roberts would be stricken with tuberculosis. After feeling death hover over him for sixty days at the age of seventeen, he was taken by car to a Pentecostal tent meeting where he was prayed for and was completely healed, a fact that dramatically affected the course of his life.

The Roberts family was of Choctaw descent. In fact, years later when Oral was interviewed on the Larry King talk show as a minister of the Gospel, he testified that he was a card-carrying member of the Choctaw Nation of Oklahoma — one of the tribes tragically evicted from their homeland who walked the Trail of Tears to their new territory in Oklahoma.

My great-grandmother Faulkner — one of my six living grandmothers during that time due to rampant divorce in my family — actually lived close to the Roberts family in Ada when Oral was a small child. As a young man, I distinctly remember this grandmother, who never gave any indication she knew the Lord, disparagingly telling me, "I don't know how Oral Roberts ever ended up on TV when he came from such a poor beginning. Our family was poor, but that family was poorer than us. They were just a bunch of poor ol' Indians." (This grandmother was a very dark character I will tell you more about in a few pages.)

Oral Roberts was a descendant of those displaced tribes. But as God would have it, he emerged as a Native American televangelist and was considered to be one of the founders of the modern Charismatic Movement. He was one of the most recognized preachers worldwide at the height of his notoriety. *And* he founded Oral Roberts University! Also, as unlikely as it seems, his son, healing evangelist Richard Roberts — who also has a mighty healing ministry — later became a cherished friend.

God really does delight in choosing those who seem unlikely!

## A 'No-Man's Land' Infested With Gangs and Criminals

Even before the Native Americans arrived in what later became the state of Oklahoma, that territory was infested with notorious criminals who used the area to hide from U.S. Marshals that were stationed at Fort Smith, a federal outpost that was built on the east bank of the Arkansas River in the state of Arkansas.

Then after the Civil War, the number of outlaws in Oklahoma Indian Territory had substantially grown, and they were wreaking havoc among the tribes that had relocated there. Because the proliferation of crime in this "no man's land" was raging out of control, the U.S. government appointed Judge Isaac Parker to preside over a federal court in Fort Smith, situated directly across the river from the gang-infested territory to the west.

By the time Judge Parker arrived in Fort Smith to commence his duties as federal judge, Indian Territory had become a nest for criminals who thought the law didn't apply to them. Judge Parker's court was the only federal court with jurisdiction over Indian Territory for 21 years, Isaac Parker served in this capacity as a federal judge. In those years, he tried 13,490 cases, in which 8,500 defendants either pled guilty or were convicted. Of that number, 160 were sentenced to death — and 79 of those were executed by hanging on Judge Parker's famous gallows erected directly behind his courtroom at the Fort Smith settlement.[5]

Because of these *on-the-premises* executions, Judge Parker became known as the "Hanging Judge" of the American Old West. Parker also presided over a jail in the basement of that federal courthouse that was so legendary among gangsters and criminals that they referred to it as "Hell on the Border."[6]

Indian Territory — which became the state of Oklahoma in 1907 — had become overrun with bank robbers, gangsters, and rogue criminals, some of whom became quite legendary in American history. Because it was a "wilderness," it attracted considerable numbers of famous lawbreakers, such as Belle Starr, Jesse James, the Dalton Gang, the Marlow Brothers, Fred Tecumseh Waite (who famously came to be known as "The Outlaw Statesman"), Bonnie and Clyde, Pretty Boy Floyd, Machine Gun Kelly, and Kathryn Thorne, just to name a few.[7]

Despite his reputation for bringing the "long arm of the law" to a land terrorized by robbery and violence, Isaac Parker made other invaluable contributions toward ensuring a civil society in newly settled Indian Territory. He championed the rehabilitation of non-violent offenders, reformed the criminal justice system, and advocated for the rights of Indian tribes. His goal, in his own words, "to create the moral force of a strong federal court," was largely achieved. And his motto to "do equal and exact justice" made him both honored and feared across that entire region.[8]

## Tulsa's Greenwood District and 'Black Wall Street'

When the Civil War ended, Indian Territory became a wide-open space for growth, with numerous opportunities and few restrictions. By the time Oklahoma was incorporated as a state in 1907, it already boasted a sizeable black community. Traveling by train, horses and wagons, and even on foot, this community of people came in hopes of building a wall against the system of racial degradation and segregation known as Jim Crow. Oklahoma represented the hope of change and the opportunity for African Americans to walk away from the haunting memories of racism they had experienced before the war.

Tulsa in particular seemed the ideal place for a new beginning, and many of the newly freed slaves began streaming to this city to form one of the fastest-growing black communities in the United States. In fact, so many freedmen immigrated to Tulsa that some began referring to north Tulsa as "Little Africa."[9] North Tulsa eventually became known as the famous Greenwood District, and by 1921, it was home to approximately ten thousand black residents, many of whom had become educated and affluent professionals, including doctors, dentists, lawyers, business owners, real-estate developers, and clergy. Greenwood was a thriving commercial district with businesses, grocery stores and other retail businesses, banks, libraries, newspapers, movie theaters, nightclubs, and numerous churches — it was one of the most affluent black-American sectors in the country and was even referred to as "Black Wall Street."[10]

But all of that was disrupted in the days just before the summer of 1921. After rumors of an alleged incident between a young black man and a white woman in a downtown Tulsa elevator (a story that was eventually debunked), sparks began to fly between the white and black communities. Emotions were charged and, seized with inconsolable rage, mobs of white residents attacked the Greenwood District and its residents and businesses — an event so horrific that it has been called one of the single worst incidents of racial violence in American history.[11]

In the early morning hours of June 1, 1921, white rioters rampaged streets in Greenwood and neighborhoods, killing people and looting and burning stores and homes. The Oklahoma governor declared martial law, and National Guard troops were summoned to gain control of the violence. By the time it was over, thirty-five square blocks of the Greenwood District lay in charred ruins and more than eight hundred people were treated for injuries. Local historians postulate that as many as three hundred people may have been killed. More than six thousand people from Greenwood were rounded up and held at the Convention Hall and Fairgrounds for as long as eight days. Nearly ten thousand people of color in this community were left homeless, and property damage amounted to multiplied millions of dollars even in 1921.[12] As you can well imagine, many survivors quickly left Tulsa forever in the aftermath of this tragedy.

This horrific event has been called the Tulsa Race Riot, the Tulsa Race Massacre, the Greenwood Massacre, and the Black Wall Street Massacre. But this tragic episode was largely omitted from local, state, and national history books for decades. It was so buried that neither Denise, myself, nor any of our siblings were taught about it when we studied Oklahoma history, a required course, in our respective high schools.

The fact is, I didn't know about the Tulsa Race Massacre until I was nearly fifty years old. I vaguely recall one of my grandmothers telling me as a child that something terrible happened between the black and white communities when she was younger. She didn't elaborate, and what she said didn't register with me at that young age. Other than that incident, I'd never heard a word about it growing up. It seems "the powers that be" in Tulsa at the time did all they could to erase that event from our blemished history.

## Tulsa, the Oil Boom, and Life's Biggest Treasures

After the Civil War, Tulsa's economy began to take off as rapidly as its population when underground caverns filled with oil were discovered west of "Old Town" in 1905. When news of that underground reserve began to circulate, men with ambition were drawn to Tulsa like metal to a magnet. As a result, this territory that was once filled with outlaws became home to oil barons, such as Robert M. McFarlin, Harry F. Sinclair, Charles E. Page, J. Paul Getty, William Skelly, Waite Phillips, Thomas Gilcrease, and W. K. Warren, whom I worked for as a teenager at his estate in Tulsa.[13]

Palace-like estates adorned the streets of exclusive neighborhoods adjacent to shopping districts laden with prosperity where these oil magnates called home. The booming oil industry affected the entire city as Tulsa's infrastructure began to loom large to accommodate the economic growth even in pre-statehood days. More than fifty years later when I was born in 1958, Tulsa was still buzzing with life as the "Oil Capital of the World."

This is the city where I lived as a young boy — a city of treasures and tragedy. I was blessed growing up to enjoy the treasures of Tulsa, though my family was by no means wealthy in terms of money. Yet we were rich in faith and friendships — and we understood that the biggest tragedy in life was to waste it seeking happiness outside of God.

I truly learned from my family that *people* are the biggest treasure on earth. It's not oil hidden in caverns, but rather our friends, our neighbors, and the members of our own house — those "hidden" in plain sight in our day-to-day lives.

There's a saying that life is a circus, filled with a lively mixture of laughter, tears, and unexpected moments — some pleasant and some not so pleasant that take your breath away. But beyond that philosophical view of life that could apply to all of us in one way or another, I learned as a young man that *I actually descended from a line of professional circus members!* And I can hardly wait to tell you about that.

### The Miller Family Arrives in the Great Plains After a Rendezvous With the P. T. Barnum Show

You may be wondering, *How did your family end up in Oklahoma?* That story begins with my great-grandfather Nathaniel Clinton Miller, my mother's grandfather. As a young man in his twenties, he left his home in Kentucky to attend Valparaiso University and the Indiana School of Music, where he was educated in fine arts and music and became a notable musician with a dazzling reputation as a band and orchestra director.

Nathaniel moved west to Texas where he taught music for about seven years. During that period, he met an adventuresome young woman named Louella Hestand, who eventually became his wife and my great-grandmother on my mother's side of the family. Also during that period, news of Nathaniel and his talent somehow came to the attention of a traveling circus begun by the legendary showman P. T. Barnum. Nathaniel was hired by that circus as their traveling bandmaster, and for almost two decades, he traveled extensively with the P. T. Barnum show before beginning his own circus, band, and comedy troupe on the Oklahoma plains.

In 1883, Louella had traveled west with her family in three covered wagons from the state of Tennessee, and they settled on the range. The Hestand family were frontier people, raising sheep, horses, and cattle. Their daughter Louella, right from the start, had a pioneer mindset. She was filled with such gusto, zest, and a spirit of adventure that even as a twenty-year-old woman, she had the audacity to take part in the historic Oklahoma Land Rush of 1889 — a feat practically unheard of for a young woman at that time.

## The Oklahoma Land Rush

In 1889 Congress announced that the Unassigned Lands of Indian Territory — about two million acres — would be opened for the Oklahoma Land Rush, also known as the Land Run.[14] The run was filled with adventure-seeking people who would ride like mad on their horses to stake a claim across that vast acreage. For anyone who had the guts to stake a claim and be willing to meet the criteria for settling on his or her parcel of land, this was a once-in-a-lifetime opportunity for the taking. Those who were first to stake a claim could take up to 160 acres if they were willing to live on the land and improve it. Well, my great-grandmother had guts, and she successfully staked her claim in that land run!

In 1942 when the then *Tulsa Tribune* newspaper heard that a survivor of the land rush was alive and still mentally vibrant, they asked to interview Louella Hestand Miller to capture her memories of that historic event in print. In the interview, my great-grandmother Miller said, "There had been a lot of talk of opening up the land in Oklahoma and everybody seemed interested in trying to make the run…. My father was in bad health and he couldn't make the run and my [older] brother decided he would not attempt it. I had ridden my horse up from Texas and on the day the run was to start I got a front position on the line near El Reno. My 13-year-old brother, Bedford…was on his horse beside me."

She added, "I was determined to make it on my horse 'Baldy,' whether anyone else in the family did or not."

In the interview, Louella also remembered how she found herself positioned on her horse in front of a large cavalcade of riders on race horses, and she feared that when the guns sounded, she would be overridden. So she shrewdly changed positions with a man behind her. She laughed as she remembered, "That got me out of the way of those race horses."

She recalled that the signal guns sounded at high noon, and thousands of men and, yes, some women, had lined up on the borders, poised to thunder ahead at the sound of those guns. It was "the birth-throes of a new empire that is the Oklahoma of today."[15]

Recalling that moment, my great-grandmother said, "I remember passing a man — I think it was the one I had given my place to — and he had staked a claim with his spade sticking in the dirt. He waved at me as I went by. My brother and I didn't know where we were going — just running ahead until we could find a likely piece of land."[16]

My great-grandmother also related that she saw another girl about her age who had been thrown from her horse. The girl's nose was bleeding and she was struggling to control her steed so she could remount. "At another place I saw a new spring wagon that had lost a wheel. The driver had abandoned it and apparently jumped on his team and rode ahead. The funniest sight and rather tragic one, however, was a buckboard whose wheel had come off and the axle had caught in the rocks and ground. The team [of horses] was running around in a circle."[17]

But Louella and her brother managed to keep up and rode many miles. She said, "We finally stopped at a place where there seemed to be no one near. We staked our claim and sat down to rest. Soon we heard voices…and two men came up with a chain. They were surveying the claim. I told them to stay off our claim that we had staked it. They didn't say a word but picked up their stuff and walked away." In her old age when she gave this interview to the *Tulsa Tribune*, she confidently announced, "If I had my life to live over I would ride in that run again."[18]

It was sometime after the Land Run that Nathaniel and Louella were married and began raising a family and making a life together. And it was there that Nathaniel began to note that this wide-open territory with its wide-open opportunities didn't have a circus, and his mind began to turn like a Ferris wheel about how his talents and experience might fill that entertainment void.

## Life Really *Is* a Circus — and the Miller Family Had an Elephant To Prove It!

Because of my great-grandfather's time traveling as the bandmaster for P. T. Barnum, the circus was alive in him still. Most would have never attempted such an enterprise because Oklahoma Indian Territory was still unpredictable and filled with lawlessness. Nevertheless, Nathaniel had eyes to see that this "no man's land" held vast opportunities for anyone with guts. And his imagination and entrepreneurship went to work to stake his own claim in this vast territory.

With the eyes of both pioneer and entrepreneur, Nathaniel obtained a circus tent and he, his wife Louella, and their children — all of whom played musical instruments or performed as clowns or comedians — set out to make a name for themselves as a traveling circus and comedy troupe. They had a variety of animals, including an elephant named Mena that was so mean that it once tore up the circus tent completely. They eventually had to sell that untamable elephant, and story has it that years later, my mother was with her father Earl — Nathaniel's son — at a circus-type event, where they spotted Mena. They were shocked to observe that the elephant remembered Earl!

For years, the Miller family traveled with the "Black Top Tent" and a smaller tent in which they performed comedy shows as the Miller Comedy Troupe. This pioneer family from the plains began traveling the entire region as a circus family and gained quite a bit of renown, though they never attained the notoriety of larger circuses, such as Barnum's show, or even of some of Nathaniel's contemporaries who were also bitten by the circus-entertainment bug. It is also interesting that Nathaniel was also credited as being the first to ever show a "moving picture" in Indian Territory.

Nathaniel was known for his intelligence and creative talent. He sang light opera in a thousand-voice choir and once won a scholarship for his painting entitled, "Shakespeare's Tomb." Friends and family remembered him as even-tempered and as a man who didn't drink. He was loved and admired by all who knew him. One of his sons, Earl Miller, recorded his own fond memory of receiving $25 a week for playing the trombone in his father's band when the show was on the road. Earl would later play a significant role in our family, as we will see.

Truly there was never a dull moment in the Miller family house. Nathaniel's remarkable sense of humor and Louella's wit were passed to their children along with their contagious love for life. People said you couldn't be around them for long without laughing. To the Nathaniel Miller clan, *life really was a circus!*

## Pentecostal Long Before Topeka or Azusa Street

I'm pointing out the high points, but reality is that life in Oklahoma Indian Territory in those days was rough. When the Nathaniel Miller family started there, they lived in dugouts, traveled by horse, carriage, and buggy, combated disease and death, fought wild cougars, and even befriended gangsters that held celebrity-like status in the annals of American history. There were few doctors and few medications available, so if anyone got sick, the situation could quickly escalate. This made learning to pray prayers of heartfelt faith paramountly important.

Great-grandmother Louella Miller was a staunch Bible believer. Even more, she had a Pentecostal encounter with the Holy Spirit long before the later historic outpourings that occurred in Topeka, Kansas, in 1900 or at Azusa Street in 1906. Even before those events, out on the frontier range, she had an encounter with God that changed her life, and she became known to many in Oklahoma Indian Territory for her raw faith in the healing power of God.

Louella's prayers were accompanied by so many miraculous manifestations that people came by horse and buggy from all over that territory to have her pray for those stricken with sickness and disease. It was generally known that if they could get to Louella Miller quickly enough, her forceful faith would drive out demons, heal the sick, and move mountainous problems out of the way.

Family members recall that Great-grandmother Louella was almost as forceful in personality as she was in her faith — and nearly impossible to sway once her mind was made up about something. If something she heard couldn't be found in the Bible, she wasn't interested in hearing it. People called her "bodacious" — a popular term on the plains to describe someone who was bold and daring.

That was the positive side of Louella Miller's stern, immovable personality. But those same characteristics manifested a weak side of Great-grandmother Miller as well. In fact, she was so committed to divine healing that when her husband Nathaniel cut his hand on a barbed-wire fence and developed blood poisoning, she wouldn't allow a doctor to attend to him (he later died from that blood condition). When she fell and broke her hip later in life, she wouldn't let doctors set her broken hip. They sandbagged her hip while she was in the bed, and she just lay there and withered away. She refused to have an operation because she wanted to be healed only by God's power.

But *wow* — what a heritage of faith Louella Hestand Miller imparted to our family. She passed into Heaven in 1958, just three months after I was born. But she left a fabulous spiritual legacy that impacted many in her family line. However, as it so often happens, one particular son of her six children, Earl Raymond Miller, unfortunately chose to go a different direction than the faith-filled path she had paved for him so well.

One can only guess why Earl went a different way that was so contrary to his mother's faith. Some speculate that he'd become weary of Louella's strong spiritual influence and he simply rebelled against it. Others conjecture that being exposed as a young boy to wild living on the Oklahoma frontier affected him. Because the Miller family traveled Indian Territory to perform under the big top, in saloons, and any place that would allow them to "set up shop," they constantly rubbed elbows with gangsters and low-level life on the plains that may have wrongly influenced Earl. Still others suspect that his time as a soldier in World War I affected his mind, and he never resolved his inner turmoil in his civilian life *post-war*.

Regardless of *why* his life was so wayward, Earl Miller, who became my mother's father and my grandfather, chose early in his young-adult life to walk a very crooked path.

## Grandpap Earl's Weekend in Jail

My mother's daddy, whom we grandkids later called Grandpap Earl, didn't amend his ways until much later in life and ended up living a raucous and rowdy lifestyle as a traveling musician. He had what some call "wanderlust" — the urge to keep wandering and to never stay put in the same place for very long — probably influenced in part by his upbringing in a traveling-circus family.

Many years later, after he had finally recommitted his life to Christ, I sat down with him and asked him to tell me about his life as a young man in Oklahoma Indian Territory. He'd been a heavy drinker, and I knew of his past drunkenness, so I was not surprised when he began to tell me about an incident in which he and one of his brothers were arrested and thrown in jail for public intoxication in Fort Sill, an Army post near Lawton, Oklahoma, in the southwestern part of the newly formed state.

As Grandpap Earl elaborated, he told me about an event that sounded like something out of an old western movie. But it was not a fabrication. It was a real-life happening in the "wild west" of those days. I was fascinated by my grandfather's recollections of life in that uncivilized territory, including the incident of that arrest in Fort Sill.

As he related the story, I looked deeply into his eyes, noting his expressions as he recalled each detail. As I held his gaze, I also noticed a face aged by years of unrestrained living and wrong choices. Finally, as he entertained me with his story of wild living on the plains, he exclaimed, "*Rick!* Can you guess who we spent that weekend in jail with?"

Of course, I couldn't, and I waited in curious suspense for my grandfather to clinch his story with a fascinating grand finale.

Pausing, as if for an imaginary drumroll, he blurted out, "*Geronimo!* My brother and I spent a whole weekend in jail with *Geronimo!*"

Geronimo may be one of history's most famous Native Americans. He was from the Apache tribe and was arrested and imprisoned on multiple occasions, predominantly for his role in a territorial conflict between the tribe and the United States government. Geronimo died at a military hospital in Fort Sill in 1909 and was buried alongside the graves of other Apache prisoners of war.

As a kid, we grew up yelling *"Geronimo!"* as a part of some of the games we played. But this was no game. My grandfather was telling me he actually spent time in jail with Geronimo when he was a young man!

I remember thinking, *What kind of family am I from!* As I quickly processed the whirl of images going through my head, my grandpap Miller said it again: "Yep, I spent the weekend in the same cell with Geronimo. It was him, me, and my brother for the whole weekend." Then he added, "And, Rick, Geronimo was one of the nicest men I've ever met in my life."

I enjoyed my time with my grandfather that day as he took me with him on his wistful and nostalgic walk down memory lane. He had become a man filled with God's peace, and the grace of God upon his life in those later years was so evident. However, Grandpap Miller's earlier years were wayward and very hurtful to many around him. During those years, he not only drank recklessly, but he also *married* recklessly, marrying and divorcing two times *before* he married my grandmother Juanita — Grandma Ettie, as we later called her — and Juanita would not be his last wife.

Although certain members of my family made wrong decisions through-out their lives that didn't reflect the heart and mind of God, He was with us through it all, His own will and plan unchanging as He waited for *someone* to pick up the baton, don the mantle, and agree to His divine purpose.

The same is true of every family. God's plans and purposes do not change. He simply searches "to and fro" (2 Chronicles 16:9), looking for a man or woman who will respond to His will completely, *on His terms.*

As you will see in the next chapter, my mother Erlita Miller Renner said *yes* to the Lord wholeheartedly. She had no way of knowing where her response would lead, but what a 'snowball' it was that began to roll headlong into the future as a result of her decision, picking up momentum and strength, and transcending *generations.* Her *yes* forever altered — *realigned* — people's courses and lives to make earth's "unlikely" a reality and Heaven's plans pros-per and succeed.

*Hang on.* My "unlikely" story gets more interesting still.


## Marriage, Divorce, and the Love of God in the Renner Family

If you can imagine it, we kids — my two sisters and me — had six living grandmothers at one time! Two of them were great-grandmothers, and two of them came into the family due to divorce and remarriage. Nonetheless, we knew them all as our grandmothers. Ronda and I actually had a seventh grandmother, Great-grandmother Louella Miller, who preceded some of these other grandmothers. But she passed away three months after I was born, as I said previously.

I've written about this briefly in my book *Sparkling Gems From the Greek, Volume Two* because the fact we had six grandmothers really was a big deal to us because of the great value we placed on family. My parents had a desire to honor their elders and to make everyone feel included — a part of something bigger than themselves — because for some of those family members, their later years became very lonely, isolated years.

My sisters and I were raised in this culture of honor because of my parents' love and respect for God and His Word and their desire to embrace the "pure religion" that pleases Him in visiting the lonely and afflicted (*see* James 1:27). This noble desire became a daunting logistical challenge at times, however, especially on Christmas Day. On Christmas morning, we kids knew that as soon as our gifts were unwrapped and enjoyed for a precious few minutes, we would all be piling into the family car to begin making the rounds to visit each grandparent, including great-grandmothers.

I joke as an adult that our very long Christmas Day felt like rigorous geriatric ministry! For hour after hour, we'd drive from house to house to demonstrate our love — and, most importantly, the love of God — to our various grandparents. I didn't particularly enjoy spending all that time going from place to place in one day, but looking back, I'm not sorry at all that we did it.

It's hard to fathom, but as I calculate all the divorces and remarriages that happened in the lives of only four of my grandparents, it comes to *fourteen* divorces and, in every case, remarriages that followed. As a child, it was difficult for me to keep all my grandmothers straight in my young brain. But I have a better perspective today, so let me tell you a few interesting things about my six grandmothers.

### Six Living Grandmothers at One Time!

As we move forward together, you'll see that I write about, in order:

- Grandma Bagley (*Gertrude Bagley*, mother of Juanita Mock Miller, who was my mother's mother; Grandma Bagley was my great-grandmother)

- Grandma Ettie (*Juanita Miller*, mother of Erlita Miller Renner, who was my mother; Grandma Ettie was my maternal grandmother)

- Grandma Jo (*Jo Miller*, fourth wife of Earl Miller, who was my mother's father, after his divorce from my mother's mother Juanita; Grandma Jo was my step-grandmother)

- Grandma Cora (*Cora Allison*, mother of Juanita's second husband, Buddy Allison, after her divorce from Earl; Grandma Cora was my step-great-grandmother)

- Grandma Faulkner (mother of Ethel Tate Renner, who was my father's mother; Grandma Faulkner was my great-grandmother)

- Grandma Renner (*Ethel Renner*, mother of Ronald Richard Renner, who was my father; Grandma Renner was my paternal grandmother)

My mother's mother, the second daughter of Gertrude Bagley, was Juanita Mock. We grandkids never called her Grandma Juanita due to the fact that my older sister Ronda couldn't pronounce her name correctly when she was a little girl. So as kids often do, Ronda made up a name for her — Grandma Ettie. After that, all of us Renner kids called her by that name.

## Great-Grandma Gertrude Bagley

Grandma Ettie's mother, of course, was our Grandma Bagley. She was one of the most precious grandmothers in our complicated array of six. Grandma Bagley was a simple woman of little means who had a lot of faith. She had lost two husbands and two children to influenza, but she always retained unflinchingly her reverence for God and her trust in Him.

As a young boy, I loved to visit Grandma Bagley at her tiny house that sat right next to the train tracks in a poorer part of west Tulsa. Her house was so close to the tracks that when the trains roared by, her entire little frame house *shook*, and the glass that was so loosely fitted in the sills of her windows rattled in synchrony.

Often the train would stop nearby and transients who had lifted a ride on a rail car would emerge and roam the area. My grandmother would try to feed as many of them as she could on what little provisions she had. Some of those "hobos," as we called them, were regulars at her house. Once a man was run over by a train and the impact completely severed one of his legs. He dragged himself in his weakened state to my grandmother's house, where she immediately tied off the upper part of what remained of his leg and administered first aid until emergency care arrived. Blood was *everywhere*, in both her yard and in her house, and older members of my family talked about that incident for *years*. But she saved that soul's life. Truly, in a world where society had shunned or forgotten those transients, they knew they had a friend in Gertrude Bagley.

Grandma Bagley always made us grandkids the most wonderful lunches. But when I would ask for seconds, she usually reminded me that she was a poor woman and didn't have enough for seconds. She would gently encourage me to be satisfied with what I had — and that was good enough for me. I could eat later at home — my visits with Grandma Bagley were the real treat.

I have such vivid memories of our times together, grandmother and grandson. In fact, I was at her house on December 21, 1968, when the Apollo 8 was launched as the first crewed spacecraft to orbit the moon and return safely to Earth. Enthusiastically, I watched the live airing of that rocket launch on her modest black and white TV. I sat comfortably squeezed into her tiny living room crammed with too much furniture and stacks and stacks of old newspapers, magazines, and ministry letters she had saved that were sent to her by the Oral Roberts Evangelistic Association.

I remember the musty smell of old newspapers fused with the aroma of something wonderful my grandma was always cooking up in her tiny kitchen. Some of my fondest childhood memories are of moments spent with my Grandma Bagley and all the wonderful sights, smells, and sounds in her humble house by the tracks.

Grandma Bagley made other impressions on my young heart that stayed with me through the years, and one of those impressions was her generous heart toward God. I vividly recall once watching her write the name "ORAL ROBERTS" on an envelope with painstaking care and then attentively write the address underneath. When she was done, she inserted a worn one-dollar bill to send to that ministry so she could take part in the work of God. Licking the seal, she folded the envelope shut, carefully pressing down the edges to secure her treasure within. Then she held that envelope to her heart, prayed over it quietly and purposefully, and walked it outside to her mailbox.

That offering my grandma gave was not a mindless, hurried act that others might consider "busy work" as if they were paying bills. It was a very holy moment that I will never forget. It was as if Jesus was physically present, beholding the entire scene. She gave that money with all her heart. The Lord knew it, and I knew it.

It reminded me of the time in Scripture when Jesus observed the gifts being given into the temple treasury. He saw the rich giving their gifts, and then He noticed a poor widow putting in only "two mites." Jesus said, "…Of a truth I say unto you, that this poor widow hath cast in more than they all: For all these have of their abundance cast in unto the offerings of God: but she of her penury hath cast in all the living that she had" (Luke 21:3,4).

Jesus was so impressed with the enormity of that widow's faith and the size of her gift compared to what she had to give that He stopped everyone and drew attention to what the woman had done. It didn't take very much faith for the others to give offerings from their great wealth, but it took *great* faith for that poor widow to cast into the treasury all that she had. She was fully entrusting herself to the care of God, believing He would supernaturally meet her needs. The amount that woman gave was small, but the faith required to give it was large indeed.

Just like that poor widow Jesus described, my Grandma Bagley gave all she could give to support Oral Roberts' ministry. It was a monumental act of her faith to place that special offering into the envelope for the postman to collect. And just as Jesus watched the poor widow, He was watching my grandma — as He watches *all* who sacrificially give with a heart of faith.

What I witnessed that day at my Grandma Bagley's is indelibly etched in my memory, and it has impacted my thinking about the sacrificial gifts people give to God. That one dollar was such a significant amount for her to sow into that ministry. My grandma was not rich financially, but she was rich in faith, and my respect for her grew even greater on that unforgettable day.

Oh, how I loved Grandma Bagley! As a young boy, I would often sit next to her on Sunday mornings in the pew at our church. I would take her hand in mine and run the tip of my index finger along the veins that bulged like a network of tangled cords from her aged hands. I was amazed at how I could push those veins from side to side and how easily they moved beneath her crinkled flesh. I was equally fascinated by the liver spots that dotted her hands and stood out so vividly against her fair skin.

Hands tell stories. They so often tell the story of one's life. And I know by remembering her hands that my grandma's life was not an easy one.

As I shared previously, Grandma Bagley was twice widowed and she also lost two young children earlier in her life. She had two living daughters — Juanita, who became my mother's mother and whom I knew as Grandma Ettie, and an older daughter named Marie, whom we kids knew as Aunt Marie (she was our great-aunt). Aunt Marie was a godly woman, too, who raised a daughter who surrendered to be a foreign missionary and a son who became a pastor. In every way, Aunt Marie was a committed Christian and was instrumental in my own mother, her niece, coming to Christ.

## Grandma Juanita Miller (Grandma Ettie)

I'll tell you a bit about my mother Erlita's less-than-ideal upbringing later — an "unlikely" story in itself — but first I must talk about the marriage of Juanita, Grandma Bagley's second-born, to Earl Miller. (Earl and Juanita were my mother's parents.)

There is no doubt that Grandma Bagley's life had been visited with multiple tragedies, but she had an indomitable spirit that refused to give up or quit on God. The fact that she couldn't read or write well hindered her from getting a good-paying job, and she was a widow besides. Nevertheless, she had two daughters to feed and clothe, and she worked hard as a janitor, a housekeeper, and a cook to try to make ends meet for her small family of three.

Grandma Bagley was very devoted in her faith, but because of her low level of education, she didn't understand a lot of the deeper doctrinal truths of the Bible — and her lack of basic Bible knowledge and her naivete often made her gullible to people with insincere motives. For instance, she wanted to know God's will desperately, but did not know how to find it by herself, so she once volunteered to clean house every week for a fortune-teller. Because of Grandma Bagley's lack of Bible knowledge, she didn't understand that this woman was involved in something forbidden by the Lord. In her simplicity, my grandma believed the woman had a gift from God to help people know the future.

Because Grandma Bagley had suffered so many tragedies in life, she longed for some hope for the future and craved assistance to help her navigate what was left of her life. I always wondered if her visiting a fortune-teller opened the door to perpetuate some of the hardships she endured.

When Juanita was fifteen years old, thirty-six-year-old Earl Miller showed up in their lives looking for a new wife — Juanita would be his third. His second divorce had just been finalized, and when he appeared on the scene, my precious, uneducated, and very simple-minded grandma, Gertrude Bagley, became impressed with him because he was older and had made some money in life. She surmised that God had perhaps sent him to marry her Juanita.

The Miller acreage was located adjacent to Gertrude Bagley's homestead. Juanita was a gifted acrobat, so she was naturally attracted to Earl's circus background. (In fact, Juanita — Grandma Ettie — never lost her acrobatic skills, and even in her sixties and seventies, she would entertain us kids with backflips, cartwheels, and walking on her hands! She was so much fun to be with!)

The newly divorced Earl Miller quickly proposed to Juanita, and her mother Gertrude convinced her young daughter to marry him, a man more than twice her age. So at the tender age of fifteen, Juanita became Mrs. Earl Raymond Miller.

This kind of arrangement would be illegal today, but in those days, it was not unusual for girls to marry young and to marry older men. Gertrude Bagley wanted desperately for this arrangement to be the blessing she'd hoped for. But life with Earl Miller would be anything *but* the dreams Gertrude had for her young daughter.

Earl was a drinker and caroused regularly with his drinking buddies. If he came home at all, he usually came home late — or he'd show up at home at odd hours with a gang of musicians for Juanita to feed and play host to. Because Earl had grown up in pre-statehood Oklahoma Territory, he had rubbed elbows most of his own growing-up life with mobsters and other criminals. For some reason that I do not know, he once even got into some sort of a dilemma with an infamous gang. There is disagreement among older members of the family about which gang it was. One says it was a remnant of the infamous Dalton Gang and another says it was Pretty Boy Floyd.

My own mother told me that her father once took her, her siblings, and their mother and hid them all in a secret location because he was worried that they would be murdered. My mother was very young at the time and retained only vague recollections of their environment in hiding for the period of time it took Earl to either resolve his "dilemma" or determine it was safe for them to return home.

For a short time, Earl tried to tone his wilder side by getting a "normal" job so that he could be at home every night instead of playing music gigs. But his idea of a normal job led him to the arid plains of Dalhart, Texas, in the middle of *nowhere*. Just to give you an idea of what I mean by "nowhere," this town was 491 miles from Austin, 458 miles from Lincoln, 434 miles from Topeka, 375 miles from Cheyenne, 289 miles from Denver, 281 miles from Oklahoma City, and 201 miles from the closest major city, Santa Fe.

In the late 1930s when Earl moved his family to Dalhart, it had become the epicenter of a devastating drought that had decimated a large swath of the central plains of the United States from 1931 to 1939. That drought was called the "Dust Bowl" because it reduced so much of the country to dust, blowing in huge dust storms that would completely blacken the sky and block the sun. By the mid-1930s, the Dust Bowl had so devastated the area that it forced thousands of families to leave in search of life elsewhere. This American tragedy is depicted in John Steinbeck's famous 1939 novel *The Grapes of Wrath*.[19]

So the time when Earl moved his family to Dalhart was exactly the time when others were leaving — *fleeing* — to live somewhere else! But their "vacancies" also meant there was new opportunity, and that's why Earl Miller packed up his family and moved to Dalhart in the western panhandle of Texas. At about that same time, Dalhart also became host to cowboys who came from far and wide to participate in huge rodeo events. In the aftermath of the damage caused by the Dust Bowl, Dalhart was becoming the perfect "wild west" atmosphere complete with horses, cowboys, and all the familiar trappings.

My mother told me when they lived in Dalhart, their family lived in a house in an arid plain so covered with rattlesnakes that the kids were never allowed to go outdoors without adult supervision. Dust *invaded* the air like a marauding army, and tumbleweed danced wildly about as fierce winds blew almost constantly on their lonely prairie homestead.

Mother also told me of a time she went into town with her father and saw horses tied up to real hitching posts along the central street of the town. She said she remembers her father reaching out to pet a white steed when a man came bursting out of the saloon nearby, drawing his gun and warning Earl to back away from his horse. Her description of that chain of events conjured images of a Hollywood movie set. But it was no movie — that was where Earl Miller had moved his family to enjoy a more "normal" life!

Soon afterward, the Millers' chapter in Dalhart ended, and the family moved back to Tulsa, where Earl and Juanita's marriage grew more and more strained. The marriage was like a roller coaster — there were constant upheavals, Juanita's "sucker-punched" feelings of grief and distress, and other ups and downs too numerous to recount. Eventually Juanita's emotions began to deteriorate, and she filed for a divorce in hopes of offering her children some stability in what remained of their growing-up years. But her hopes were to be dashed again.

### Grandma Cora Allison and Her Son 'Buddy'

Grandma Ettie was always respectful as she spoke of Grandpap Earl to the family, because he was the father of her children. But it was evident that life with him had been very painful for her. However, their union produced three wonderful children — Erlita, Melita, and Raymond, whom I would later know as Mother, Aunt Melita, and Uncle Raymond.

Eventually my Grandma Ettie married a man named Harold Marquis "Buddy" Allison. Everyone called him Buddy because he didn't like his real name. We kids simply knew him as Buddy when we were growing up. We knew he wasn't our biological grandfather, but he had been married to Grandma Ettie since before any of us grandkids were born, so we lovingly called him Buddy and viewed him as our grandfather.

Buddy descended from the Cherokee Indian tribe. His family had also come to Indian Territory in about 1838 when the Indians marched westward on the Trail of Tears. As I tell you my story, I am amazed at the influence the Trail of Tears had on my circle of friends and family. If you can imagine it, even Denise is part Native American. She is so much Indian that Denise and her siblings could register on the official roll of the Otoe tribe. Her father's mother, Denise's paternal grandmother, was a full-blooded Otoe Indian. In family photos that show this grandmother at a younger age, her long black braids make her look so traditionally Indian that it could appear she'd just walked out of a teepee!

Buddy's family settled on a piece of land just outside of Westville, Oklahoma. That huge piece of property teemed with deer and all sorts of wildlife, and hosted a beautiful crystal-clear river filled with fish that ran right through the middle of it. Buddy's mother, my "Grandma Cora," lived on the land in an old house that had been in her family for a long time. When I was a boy, my father would occasionally take me there to go fishing. I remember walking a trail from Grandma Cora's house that led steeply down to where the river flowed. That water was so clear I could see the bottom as if I were looking through glass. My Grandma Cora was part Cherokee. I remember her as a stoic woman who showed little emotion, but everyone who knew her well remembered her as very gracious and kind.

During the war years, Buddy had served in the Navy on a minesweeper vessel and had been stationed at Pearl Harbor. In fact, he was present on December 7, 1941, when Japanese fighter planes descended on the base and destroyed or damaged nearly 20 American naval vessels, including 8 battleships, and more than 300 airplanes. More than 2,400 Americans died in the attack, including civilians, and another 1,000 people were wounded.[20] President Franklin D. Roosevelt called that event "a date which will live in infamy."

When his ship was attacked that day, Buddy saw many of his friends blown to pieces, and it dramatically affected him. In fact, it seems he could never get past that moment. When I was a boy, he told me about the attack multiple times. Looking back, I see now that he was still trying to process that traumatic event, even years after the fact. And by the manner in which he conducted his life, it was doubtful he was effectively moving forward from that horrific, tragic experience.

When Buddy returned to Oklahoma, he met Juanita Miller — Grandma Ettie — and they married on Valentine's Day in 1948. Right from the start, it was a tumultuous marriage. Grandma Ettie was still recovering from her marriage to Earl Miller, and Buddy was affected by what he had experienced at Pearl Harbor, and he was not saved. It was a troubled marriage with non-stop arguing and fighting. Buddy even once broke Grandma Ettie's arm in one such fight.

Not only was Buddy abusive toward Grandma Ettie, but the children — Erlita, Melita, and Raymond — also felt the brunt of his abusive words and behavior. Buddy was simply an unsaved man who had grown up fighting prejudice against him because he was Native American — and he was filled with trauma from what he witnessed at Pearl Harbor. He carried all of that in a very broken and embittered soul. On top of that mental and emotional agony, when Buddy married Grandma Ettie, he immediately became stepfather to three children, and his patience with children was very low.

I recall being terrified of Buddy when I was a child because he was filled with so much anger, and he expressed rage at me when I didn't behave like an adult. Once I had to stay with Buddy by myself, and I remember being fearful to be alone with him. I had seen his rage vented at my Grandma Ettie so many times and felt the impact of it myself. The truth is at that time, he wasn't a very nice man.

But all of that changed in the early 1970s. After experiencing a severe heart attack, Buddy was rushed to the hospital where he was admitted into the ICU. While there, he had a second massive heart attack that blew out virtually half his heart. As that second attack occurred, he said he saw Jesus step into the hospital room. Grandma Ettie was in the room when it took place, and she said Buddy sat upright in his bed and began to converse with Jesus as the Lord began to speak to him about his life and what he was to do with the balance of it. Suddenly, Buddy collapsed back onto the bed, his eyes rolling back into his head. A doctor and a nurse rushed in and said there was no pulse, and they were certain he was dead.

In a sense, they were right, for in that moment of his encounter, Buddy had given his life to Jesus, and the old Buddy Allison, whom we all feared, died, and a new man emerged. In that split-second decision, Buddy became a new creature in Christ as his spirit was reborn (2 Corinthians 5:17). And as he was resuscitated by the medical personnel that had surrounded him, life sprang back into his physical body!

I've seen a lot of people saved in my life, but that was singularly the most radical conversion I have ever witnessed. Buddy literally became a new man. He was so "new" that we all had to become reacquainted with this new person whose lips, once filled with rage, were now filled with the name of Jesus. Buddy loved his Bible and devoured Christian television and any teaching material he could get his hands on so he could learn more about the things of God and satisfy that deep spiritual hunger that had been birthed in him. *What a changed life we all witnessed in Buddy Allison's new birth!*

### Grandma Jo Miller

In the meantime, my Grandpap Earl Miller also married again, a fourth time, to a widow from Indiana who was well-to-do and whose married name became Josephine Miller, but we kids called her Grandma Jo. About this time, Grandpap Earl also recommitted his life to Christ, and as a result, he and Grandma Jo remained in their marriage to the end of their lives. He was married to Jo so long that none of us grandkids could ever remember when he was not married to Jo.

Our parents insisted that we honor Grandpap Earl by calling his wife Grandma Jo. But the truth is, we Renner kids didn't like her very much. She never had children of her own, and she had *zero* tolerance for little kids. Since we were little children, that meant she had no tolerance for *us*! Her husband previous to my grandfather had been a business owner of a higher-class department store, and she had a lot of fine things left over from her prior marriage — expensive porcelain, sculptures, paintings, and other exquisite home-decor items. She was a pampered lady whose first husband left her quite well-off. She had very beautiful things and she didn't want any of the kids to bother them. We loathed going to their house because we would get in trouble if we even *accidentally* touched or bumped into any of those things that she loved so much.

But because Grandpap Earl and Grandma Jo lived right next to a lake on their property that swarmed with water moccasins, my sisters and I couldn't roam around outdoors because our parents were concerned about the snakes. So for what felt like endless hours each time we were at their house, Ronda, Lori, and I sat on their living-room sofa like statues.

*Ugh!* I really disliked going there! We could feel the tension in the room from Grandma Jo because she was uptight and concerned that we might touch one of her objects or leave a fingerprint on her coffee table. When Dad would finally announce that it was time to get in the car to leave, we would breathe a sigh of relief and inwardly rejoice that it was time to end that miserable experience and go home! Finally, the torturous silence was over — that is, until the time came for our next visit.

## Bird Creek and Dead Man's Lake

Grandpap Earl and Grandma Jo lived on a large parcel of land located just outside of Tulsa. Almost right in the middle of this land was a small lake that the locals called Dead Man's Lake because a dead body had been found at the bottom of it many years earlier. The water in that lake was muddy red because the entire lake bed was comprised of layers and layers of Oklahoma red clay. I can remember fishing with my grandfather on the banks of that lake, thinking with great distaste that we were actually going to eat the catfish we pulled out of that filthy water.

Dead Man's Lake was fed by a small river that was equally disgusting called Bird Creek, where debris could constantly be seen floating in its waters. Not only was Bird Creek known for being muddy, just like Dead Man's Lake, but it was also well-known for the oversized water moccasins that would slither over the branches that lined its banks. Bird Creek was so close to my grandfather's property that my family had to cross the Bird Creek bridge every time we drove to his house.

Nearly every spring during Oklahoma's tornado season, the waters of Bird Creek would rise during the heavy rains. They would rise and rise until, finally, those filthy, stinking waters would spill over the banks of the river and flood the entire local area. Of course, whenever the waters of Bird Creek rose, they would also rush into Dead Man's Lake on my grandfather's property. Those muddy red waters would then flood out of the banks of that lake and slime my grandfather's entire property with gunk and goo.

As a boy, I thought it was fun when my grandfather's property was flooded because it meant we'd have to get into our boat, pull-start the motor, and start our ride across highways covered with water in order to reach Grandpap Earl's house. He and Grandma Jo would be standing on the porch waiting as we pulled up to the house in our boat to rescue them.

The mess left by a flood is always a dirty sight. When the waters would finally recede from the Miller property each time, the fun was over, and it became time to clean up the mess left by the flood. Everything in sight had been polluted by those invasive muddy waters. We would all pitch in to help so Grandpap Earl and Grandma Jo wouldn't have to do it alone.

We were family, and of course we were there to help. Truthfully, it seemed both my father and my mother "came alive" when a need arose in their community that they could help meet. I feel so blessed that my parents consistently modeled this kind of servanthood to my sisters and me. I'm thankful for it to this day. My parents served the Lord by serving others, and they did it "in season and out of season" — in times that were good and in times that were *not so good*, including those not-so-good times during Oklahoma tornado season when the floodwaters rose at Bird Creek.

### The Floodwaters of God's Grace

Over the years I have often thought of those floodwaters at Grandpa Miller's when I read Romans 5:20, which says, "…But where sin abounded, grace did much more abound." The words "much more abound" describe *something that is growing out of measure, beyond proportion, and out of its banks to a far-stretched extreme* — just like a river that's being flooded with waters from upstream. Those waters coming downstream are flowing so fast that the river can no longer hold the raging current within the confines of its banks. Its waters *rise, rise, rise* until they finally begin "growing out of measure," pouring out of the river's banks until they affect everything in sight.

Romans 5:20 could actually be interpreted, "For wherever sin exists in abundance and is multiplying and constantly expanding, that is precisely the time and the place where grace is poured out in a far greater, surpassing quantity." That water-covered land at Grandpa Miller's place visually helps me remember that regardless of how bad a situation is that we're facing, the grace of God is flowing downstream to lavishly pour forth in abundant measure and to completely cover — *flood* — our circumstances!

In fact, it is impossible for us to measure the amount of divine grace God is sending our direction. No banks can hold the flood of that grace! It isn't just *a lot* of grace. It's *a flood* of grace — *grace, grace, and more grace*!

Over the years, Denise and I have been in some hard places in the ministry. Many times, I've said to her, "God's grace abounds in hard places, so let's believe for abounding grace to inundate our lives and our situation right now!" Because of what I knew from Scripture and what I'd seen so many times when Bird Creek overflowed, it helped me release my faith for a flood of grace to come into all those hard places and completely cover them!

Well, I have introduced to you the Millers, my mother's side of my family, and their heritage of faith — *and I've told you a bit about four of my six grandmothers!* Although the Millers were imperfect vessels, as we all are, and they took many missteps in life, they participated with the grace of God in varying degrees from generation to generation. (I write in greater detail about my mother, Erlita Miller Renner, in the pages to come.)

But now we'll move to my father's side of the family, beginning with my immigrant grandfather, Paul Richard Renner, from southern Germany to the northeastern shores of the United States.

### Grandfather Renner Arrives in America

Grandpa Renner — Paul Richard Renner — was born on September 22, 1905, in Stuttgart, Germany. He was one of the sons of Eduard Hermann

"Hermann Sr." Renner and his wife Karoline Antonette Sophia Pelke, who were my great-grandparents. Together Eduard Hermann and Karoline produced five children, including Paul, Hermann Jr., Alma, and Henryetta — the latter we kids lovingly called "Aunt Henny." There was one more sibling, a brother, whose name I can't remember, but my Grandpa Renner told me he immigrated to America and settled in Houston, but was later killed in a gun duel. Hermann Jr. also immigrated to the U.S. along with my Grandpa Paul and the third brother, but it appears all three brothers each left Germany separately.

Ronda, Lori, and I never met Aunt Henny, our great-aunt, face to face, but she often wrote us letters from her home in Germany when we were young. We were always so thrilled to receive a letter from Aunt Henny written in long-hand in German and often accompanied by small trinkets from her area of the country that absolutely delighted us. We would huddle eagerly around Grandpa Renner as he would methodically unfold her letters, so perfectly creased, and read them to us — translating them from German to English, of course. His animated expressions and thick German accent made her words *leap* from the pages to elate us with her stories from abroad and, of course, her warm thoughts of us kids whom she'd never even seen.

Grandpa Renner's brother Hermann settled in Henryetta, Oklahoma. Hermann and his wife Mary had a son named Charles, whom I remember very well. He was my Grandpa Paul Renner's nephew, my first cousin, once removed — but my siblings and I just referred to him as our second-cousin. After Hermann passed away, Charlie would come to Tulsa from time to time to see my grandparents with his elderly mother Aunt Mary Renner, my great-aunt by marriage. It was nice to know Mary Renner because she was the only family member I'd ever met besides my grandparents and my immediate family whose last name was also Renner.

For many years, reactions were hostile toward German immigrants because of what happened during World War II. Because of all the hatred and bias against Germans after the war, my cousin Charlie changed his surname from Renner to *Rennar* in an attempt to make his name sound more French than German. I always enjoyed seeing my older cousin Charlie when he came to visit us, even if he didn't exactly share our last name.

I know very little about the background of my Grandpa Paul Renner (our oldest son Paul is his namesake). It seemed he'd wanted to keep something about his life in Germany hidden. I did my own genealogical research and learned some basic information — for example, that my Grandpa Renner's parents Eduard Hermann and Karoline Renner were hardworking people from Dusseldorf. Grandpa Renner came from a long line of family members who had worked as master dyers, store managers, school directors, and even Lutheran ministers. But *his* father owned a machine and metal shop. His father was also a Lutheran, which would be expected in Protestant Germany, and he was a man of good reputation in his community.

There is one possible exception to our strong Lutheran lineage — my great-grandmother Karoline. Her maiden name was Pelke, a distinctly Scandinavian-Jewish name. A professional genealogist I once hired to help research our genealogical records could not find birth records for her in the Lutheran church, so he suspected she was a Jew who converted to Lutheranism at the time she married Eduard Hermann.

Since we didn't have a lot of concrete information about the history of our family, I took a DNA test years ago to learn more about the family line. When the results arrived, it genetically affirmed that we are European (German) with a noticeable trace of Jewish blood. *However*, there was another trace in our genetic makeup that we would have never dreamed — *those markers show that we are part Russian!*

### A Stowaway, Ellis Island, and the Statue of Liberty

Why my father's father, Paul Richard Renner, left Germany to immigrate to America as a stowaway is a complete mystery. But in 1927, he secretly boarded a passenger ship as a stowaway and set sail from Hamburg, later arriving at the port in New York City. Once his ship arrived at New York Harbor, he was guided with all the other new arrivals through the immigration processing center at Ellis Island.

Ellis Island had processed approximately twelve million immigrants who'd left their homes in the Old World for various reasons in search of greater opportunity in America. Many left their homelands because of drought and famine or for political and religious reasons. But after an often arduous voyage by sea, immigrants would arrive at the harbor, where they were tagged with information from their ship's registry. Then they waited in long lines for medical and legal inspections to determine if they were fit for entry into the U.S.

Because of the Immigration Act of 1921 (the Emergency Quota Act) and the Immigration Act of 1924, including the National Origins Act, by the time Grandpa Renner arrived in 1927, smaller numbers of immigrants were being processed from ships that arrived at Ellis Island. But when Grandpa Renner arrived, he was among those who gained entry. He later told me that he was nearly overcome with emotion when he read the words inscribed on the towering Statue of Liberty — words that felt reassuringly as though they were written just for him.

*...Give me your tired, your poor,*
*Your huddled masses, yearning to breathe free,*
*The wretched refuse of your teeming shore.*
*Send these, the homeless, tempest-tost to me,*
*I lift my lamp beside the golden door.*

"Nearly overcome with emotion" was pretty good for a man of typical stoic German demeanor!

## A Family Mystery

Even when I was a young boy, I was inquisitive about our family history. My sisters didn't seem interested in genealogy, but I was deeply interested in our history, so I asked a lot of questions of my Grandpa and Grandma Renner about our lineage. One day I dug really deep with my Grandpa Renner about his growing-up years and what his life in Germany was like before he boarded that ship as a stowaway in 1927.

He told me about his training as a violinist, which explained why my father had an old violin that had belonged to my grandfather. My grandpa had brought it on board with him from Germany. Grandpa also revealed that he had fought as an amateur boxer, which explained his flattened nose. And I was spellbound when he told me about the short time he had spent in prison in his native country and how he learned to communicate with the men in the adjoining cell by tapping on his cell wall with a pencil in code.

But when I asked him why he'd been in prison, his answer seemed vague, and I could tell that he didn't want to go any further into that conversation. In fact, it *always* seemed to me that there was something about his life in Germany that my grandfather wanted to keep hidden.

I also asked him, "Of all the places you could have moved, why did you choose Tulsa?" That's when I discovered that his brother Hermann had previously immigrated to America and lived in Henryetta, which is near Tulsa. Yet there remained parts of my grandpa's history that seemed shrouded and mysterious. My son Paul was once in Dusseldorf and located my Grandpa Renner's elderly niece. She agreed to visit with him, and he asked her why Grandpa Renner left Germany. She responded that she didn't know much about him, but that she'd always assumed that he and his two brothers wanted to escape the economic instability of Germany at that time — the aftermath of World War I and the precursor to Hitler's rise to power before World War II.

Some family members speculate that at the time when Hitler first began to gain popularity and influence in his party in the mid 1920s, Grandpa Renner had been called on to train in a "special" police force. These relatives claim that my grandfather, discerning that something was amiss with the new force, underwent his training, but then refused to serve and was jailed for a period of time because of that violation.

The truth is, no one knows exactly why Grandpa Renner left his homeland. But his niece who agreed to talk with my son Paul clinched in our minds that whatever that reason was, he didn't want to disclose it. Her lack of knowledge of her uncle and her sparse answers to my son Paul's questions were a real wake-up call that my grandpa was for all intents and purposes forgotten once he left his native country — almost as if he were a "black sheep" of the family. The only member of his family who stayed in touch with him was his sister, our Aunt Henny.

When my Grandpa Renner left Germany, he left *everything* behind — his family and his history. The wiped slate he brought to this side of the world was not just a clean slate to us, but rather an empty page in his life's story. We would have to live with that and let life go on — for my grandfather's sake and for all of us who knew and loved him.

As an immigrant, Grandpa worked hard to make a new life as a good, godly man. But much of his previous life in Germany was *not* discussed. Even my father didn't know much about his father's past — it was considered to be an off-limits conversation. It was simply the truth that there was something about my grandfather's past that he did not want to disclose.

## I Kept Digging and Learned
## a Valuable Lesson

Approximately ten years after Grandpa and Grandma Renner passed away, an elderly friend of Grandma Renner's called my mother and said, "I want to tell you something confidential about your father-in-law, Paul Renner, that you have a right to know. It's something that you don't know concerning his life in Germany before he came to America. Please meet me and I will tell you what it is."

But before my mother could meet this elderly friend of the family, the woman unexpectedly passed away! And when she died, she took with her whatever it was that she knew and wanted to tell my mother about Grandpa Renner. Many years have passed, and I *still* know almost nothing of the history of our Renner ancestors or what happened in my grandfather's life in Germany.

Over the years, I've wondered what it was about my grandpa's past that he so meticulously hid from the rest of us. I tried to unearth information about his life when I hired a genealogist to research our family history. But no matter how hard I tried to find information about a "secret" that may have occurred in Grandpa's earlier life, the information was simply not available. Whatever the big mystery was, it is something that my family will likely never know. The last possible link was Grandma Renner's friend, who took that information with her to the grave. When her grave was closed, it seems that case was forever closed too.

## A Family Sea of Forgetfulness

After years of frustration, hitting wall after wall as I tried to dig up whatever I could find about our family's secret history, I realized one day that God didn't *intend* for us to know that hidden information from the past. Why should I be seeking it out, anyway, since Grandpa Renner didn't want us to know it? He had become a Blood-cleansed believer in Jesus Christ, and God wasn't holding his past against him — whatever "that past" may have been.

Micah 7:19 declares that once God has removed our sins, He throws them into a sea of forgetfulness. The "sea of forgetfulness" is clearly where Grandpa Renner's past ended up. Whatever it was that he wanted forgotten, it had been *irretrievably removed* from God's memory and, by all appearances, from any physical records or remembrances as well.

In my fevered search to learn what Grandpa was hiding, I finally came to understand the power of redemption reflected in my inability to discover or discern it. Since God had put the past away, I needed to put it away, too, just as I would want my own past mistakes and regrets put away and forgotten. It was an invaluable life lesson — one that I carried with me into the ministry as I learned to deal thusly with others endeavoring to live godly in their new lives in Christ.

So as determinedly as I began my search into my precious grandfather's life in Germany, I *ended* it and closed the book on my questions once and for all, never to open that book again.

## An Immigrant's Hard Life

When he arrived in America, my Grandpa Renner spoke absolutely no English. In fact, he was so unversed in English that I don't know how he managed to navigate from New York City to Tulsa. The only surviving photo we have of Grandpa from those first few days in Tulsa pictures him walking somewhere downtown looking upward at the buildings that formed an imposing skyline overhead. He'd made his way to Tulsa in 1927 — a mere twenty years after Oklahoma's statehood. It was a prime moment in the state's young history that was filled with opportunities.

In old Tulsa archives, I found a file documenting that when Grandpa arrived, he rented a room in a cheap boarding house downtown. Even though it was cheap, it wasn't free, and he also needed to eat. So he immediately set out to find a job.

But how do you find a job when you don't speak English? Although it's certainly possible, it is the challenge every immigrant faces who is making a new life in a new country.

In the fall of 1991 when Denise and I traveled to the Soviet Union to rent a house in Jelgava, Latvia, I was confronted with that very same kind of challenge. Although we had done our homework, we were still only limitedly familiar with the language, culture, and customs in a Russian-speaking world. We had to learn life all over, in a sense, in order to adapt to our new surroundings and build our new lives halfway around the world from home.

That period of transitioning in our lives, which did not occur just over-night, gave me an appreciation and compassion for anyone who ventures out to "start over" again as an immigrant. Our own experience gave me pause and caused me to reflect on what Grandpa Renner's early days in Tulsa must have been like. It was a land of great opportunity on one hand — every step filled with uncertainties and challenges on the other, challenges that he would have to work hard to overcome.

Denise and I and our sons had interpreters and new friends we'd made to help us in our new country of Latvia. But my grandpa, like most arriving immigrants to the United States, did not have those luxuries to help him adjust to life in a foreign land. Nevertheless, my grandfather quickly got his first job as a janitor at the Mayo Hotel, which had opened just two years prior in 1925. This Tulsa landmark was built by two Mayo brothers who wanted to create a world-class hotel in the heart of the Oil Capital of the World. Over the years, its guests included notable people, such as Charlie Chaplin, Charles Lindbergh, and even U.S. Presidents. Famous oilmen J. Paul Getty and Waite Phillips even took up residency there for a time. Famous historical oil deals were brokered by the greatest oil barons of the time in the opulent lobby of this fabulous structure.

Because my grandfather could speak no English, the best work he could get was janitorial, so he diligently cleaned various rooms of that plush hotel.

We have an old photo of him dated in 1927 showing him standing next to the huge sign "MAYO HOTEL" that stood on the very top of the building. After proving himself faithful as a janitor, his next job there at the Mayo was washing dishes in the kitchen, stocking the kitchen shelves, and even working as a cook.

While he worked in the kitchen, he found a way to start learning English. Because each can of vegetables bore a photo that described the content, he figured he could compare the wording likewise to begin expanding his English vocabulary. So step by step — can by can — he slowly built his vocabulary and began acting on that hard-won knowledge by speaking broken English every chance he could. It was told that his heavy, thick, German accent endeared him to those around him who loved him from the start.

### Paul Richard Renner Marries Annie Ethel Tate

After a time, my grandfather began his next job, also as a janitor, in the Philtower Building, newly constructed in 1928. The Philtower was built by renowned oilman Waite Phillips, founder of Phillips Petroleum Company. It was originally built as a high-rise office building with 24 floors and was 323 feet tall, which made it the tallest building in Tulsa at that time. The design was Gothic Revival architecture that featured an illuminated sloping tiled roof. Waite Phillips ultimately deeded the building to the Boy Scouts of America, along with most of his Philmont Scout Ranch and his Villa Philmonte. The Philtower in downtown Tulsa is so historic that today it is listed in the National Register of Historic Places as a part of the Oil Capital Historic District.[21][22][23]

My Grandpa Renner's job at the Philtower was to clean and maintain a certain floor of that exclusive building. On the floor directly beneath him another janitor worked — a newly divorced woman whose name was Annie Ethel Tate. They met and eventually married and began their family that would include my father Ronald Renner, their only child.

I must add that my Grandma Renner hated the name Annie Ethel and changed it, albeit not legally, to Ethel Ann. She said she hated the name Annie Ethel because it reminded her of Annie Oakley, the female

American sharpshooter who starred in Buffalo Bill's Wild West Show. I'm sure if it were possible — *and I'm glad it's not!* — she would crawl out of her grave to slap me if she knew I was telling you her real name! She was always called Ethel by her dearest friends, so that is how I will refer to her in the remainder of my story.

## Great-Grandmother Faulkner

Ethel Tate Renner was the middle daughter to my Great-grandmother Faulkner. Grandma Faulkner had an older daughter, Wilma, and a younger daughter, Velma — and each one of those daughters was from different marriages. Grandma Faulkner, as we called her, was a controversial and truly scary character, to say the least. She had been married five times by the time we buried her when she died in her nineties. Those five marriages are all we *knew* about, at any rate.

At the time Ethel, my Grandma Renner, was born, her mother — Grandma Faulkner — was married to a man who was surnamed Tate, and she had two children from that marriage, a son and a daughter. I only met Ethel's brother once, as he lived in another state and didn't visit very often.

Truthfully, my Great-grandmother Faulkner had a terrible reputation in our family. My own father's childhood was filled with memories of his grandmother being dishonest, scandalous, and mean. Grandma Renner told me that when Tulsa was just getting started, her mother opened and operated a nursing-home type facility in Tulsa near the Third Street Bridge. But Grandma Faulkner didn't start it because she cared for the elderly — she did it because she said it was so easy to steal from old people who were too senile to know they were being robbed.

When my Grandpa Renner died in December 1976, I was in the room when I overheard an unforgettable conversation between Grandma Renner and her younger sister Velma. I actually heard Velma say, "I'll never forgive Mother for giving my kids arsenic that time she was so mad at me.... If I had not caught on to what she was doing, she could have killed my children."

*Arsenic? You have to be kidding!* I thought. My great-grandmother gave her grandchildren arsenic a little at a time, until she was caught, to get back at their mother, her daughter Velma.

## A Real-Life 'Ma and Pa Kettle'

I always adored my Aunt Velma, Grandma Faulkner's youngest daughter and my Grandma Ethel Renner's baby sister. Even as I write Velma's name now, precious memories flood my mind of times I spent with her when I was young. My sisters and I were thrilled every time we were able to visit Aunt Velma and her husband.

Velma was a large, roundish woman who wore blue-jean overalls with straps — and an engineer's cap to conceal the fact that she was nearly bald. She lived in a primitive house on a farm just outside of Claremore, Oklahoma — in a tiny town called Foyil. Many Native Americans lived in the area, and there was actually a totem pole erected a couple of miles from Aunt Velma's house.

Velma was married to Leon, a full-blooded Indian, but I'm not sure what tribe he was from. When we would visit Aunt Velma and Uncle Leon, we always felt like we were stepping into the lives of the main characters in the TV series "Ma and Pa Kettle"! Someone suggested it was like visiting "Green Acres," but *Green Acres* may have been too sophisticated to represent Leon and Velma's simple but happy lives in Foyil.

Their tiny house was built on a foundation of dark stones that they'd collected from their property, and I was always told to be careful walking around the house because sometimes copperhead snakes slithered in and out of those stones along the sides of their house.

They had no indoor toilet and no normal indoor plumbing for water. In Velma's kitchen, in place of a sink, there was a metal trough with a hand-operated pump that was sometimes referred to as a pitcher pump. Such pumps were usually installed over outdoor water wells, but Velma had one in her kitchen. To get the water into the house, she had to pump and pump until, finally, water would begin to gush into that trough. Most of their water was hand-drawn from a rock-lined well located near a barbed-wire fence that lined their property. But I can still hear the grinding sounds of the rusted pump handle in Aunt Velma's kitchen as she would vigorously maneuver water from beneath the earth into her simple basin.

Leon and Velma didn't have a normal indoor-heating system either. Leon had constructed a homemade system in their tiny living room that was covered like wallpaper with cardboard and old newspapers. The heating system was a large discarded oil drum that sat right in the middle of their room. He had cut a hole in the bottom front to serve as an opening for stocking with wood. He cut another hole in the top to install a flue that went from the barrel through the roof of their house. Flames *blazed* inside that drum, which was blistering hot to touch! They kept a kettle filled with water on top of that drum, so they had hot water at all times.

Velma and Leon maintained a large garden and ate off the land. Also on their land were *piles* of old, abandoned cars with seemingly the meanest dogs in the world chained to each one.

Leon didn't believe in banks, so he put all his money in Mason jars and hid them in those junk cars that were protected by those ferocious dogs. There was a well-worn path encircling the cars where Velma and Leon walked, just beyond reach at the end of the chains that held those "killer beasts" at a safe distance. I can remember walking that path, praying that the chains wouldn't break that held those scary dogs. They would lunge at me as I passed them, snarling and baring their teeth, and then suddenly be *jerked* back as the chain became taut and they could proceed no farther.

Velma smoked, but she didn't buy store-bought cigarettes because they were too expensive. Instead, she rolled them herself. I can still see Velma opening the flap of a new cigarette wrapper, jiggling tobacco out of its sack onto the paper's surface, licking its thin edges, and rolling it up. After her cigarette was smoke-ready, she'd take that limp cigarette into her mouth. But rather than protrude straight from her lips like a store-bought cigarette, it repulsively drooped onto her chin. It was a *ghastly* sight!

Also interesting was the fact that Leon — and my Great-grandmother Faulkner too — chewed tobacco. Leon would sit on a padded metal chair in his tiny living room and chew thoughtfully. Then with robotic aim, he would spit that black tobacco refuse into a trusted spittoon that he kept nearby. I can still hear the distinct *splat* of wet tobacco echoing inside that can — I would practically cringe with each spew.

Next to dodging vicious guard dogs, watching these "tobacco" scenarios unfold each time was my least favorite part of my visits there. But all that aside, I found being in the company of these two precious people enthralling, and the times I spent with Aunt Velma and Uncle Leon — *"Ma and Pa Kettle"* — make up some of my best family childhood memories.

Sadly, the same could not be said about any time I was forced to spend with my Great-grandmother Faulkner. From my earliest childhood memories, she was always a scary sight to behold. Her face was creased with the deepest wrinkles my young eyes had ever seen. She always looked much older than her age — a real outward manifestation of the spotted, wrinkled, and wayward life she'd chosen for herself, which you have already discovered in part, but there's more.

Grandma Faulkner wore large, heavy earrings that hung from her stretched-out earlobes like giant clusters of grapes from a drooping vine. The pupils of her eyes were glazed over with cataracts that covered her eyeballs like a milky-white veil spotted with iridescence in the sunlight. And she reeked of mildew and heavy dime-store perfume. It was simply a challenge for a boy my age to keep a straight face and maintain my composure in her presence. But unlike Aunt Velma with her signature "drooping" cigarettes and non-existent sense of fashion, Grandma Faulkner was not a very nice woman, and I think that contributed to my impressions of her as very garish in appearance.

As I described previously, Grandma Faulkner was a very selfish woman who lived only for herself. Watching her as a young boy and later as a young man, I observed the negative effects of a self-absorbed life. Grandma Faulkner lived in downtown Tulsa in various hotels that were dilapidated at the time. Today those old hotels have either been demolished or marvelously renovated as Tulsa landmarks. But back in those days, she moved from one run-down, derelict hotel to the next. When we would go to see her, first we'd have to figure out which hotel she was living in that week. One week it might have been the Tulsa Hotel — next the Adams Hotel or the Ambassador Hotel or one of a sundry of other broken-down hotels to which she was constantly moving.

Sometimes we'd see our great-grandmother walking the streets in downtown Tulsa — she was easy to spot in one of her large floppy hats that she always wore. But because her eyesight had grown so dim, when we would stop to speak to her, she would sometimes shoo us away. "Get away from me! I'm not sure I know you!" she'd screech. Believe me when I tell you, she was not warm, kind, appealing, or grandmotherly in any way toward us kids. We approached her nervously and were always relieved to leave her presence.

But for some reason, Grandma Faulkner liked me, and that is why my parents always seated me next to her at family lunches at Grandpa and Grandma Renner's house. I was just a kid, but I had a reputation as one who could carry on a conversation with just about anyone. However, the challenge was difficult to both eat and look into Grandma Faulkner's eyes at the same time as she spoke to me. My glass of milk on the table and those milky-white cataracts that slipped around in her eyeballs as she looked at me were simply incompatible. That may sound harsh, but in that same spot as a young kid, you would have probably felt the same way.

## Great-Grandmother Faulkner's Last Husband and His Sudden Death

When my Great-grandmother Faulkner was in her late eighties, she married one last time. I had no idea she'd remarried, but one day Grandma Renner said, "Ricky, come with us — we're going to see my mother and meet her new husband."

Even that trip was not a simple venture. We arrived at the last-known hotel where Grandma Faulkner resided, only to discover she no longer lived there. So we had to search for the new location she was sharing with her new husband.

Finally, we found her new home, and it was *terrible*. We walked up a flight of dirty stairs to the top floor of an old building and then down a dreary hallway with no light to the last door at the very end. We knocked, the door opened, and there stood Grandma Faulkner. And on the couch behind her was a terrible-looking old man we had never seen before, who was her new and last husband. She wasn't married to him very long because he died suddenly under strange circumstances.

Years later as Grandma Faulkner was dying in her nineties, she told her daughter, my Grandma Renner, that she wanted to make a confession and "get something off her chest." She then proceeded to tell my grandmother that the reason her last husband died so unexpectedly was, she had given him an overdose of his medication to kill him because she figured he had a little money.

That was my great-grandmother on my father's side of the family. Sadly, she typified a greedy life with seemingly no thought given to the life to come. And we were all sad witnesses of what catastrophic and ruinous consequences accompanied *on earth* the kind of life she chose to live.

## An Unforgettable Funeral

Regardless of the evil my Great-grandmother Faulkner perpetrated in her lifetime, she somehow always got away with it without being held accountable. On the day of her funeral, no one showed up for the service but us — members of the family — which wasn't surprising.

My own father, her grandson, didn't want to attend the funeral and only went because it provided an opportunity for us to all see Aunt Velma, and we wanted to support her and her sister, my Grandma Renner. I sat next to Daddy in the service. As it started, I heard him mutter, "Let's get this over with as quickly as possible." Then when the hired minister stood to give the eulogy, Daddy leaned over to me and said, "*Good grief!* What good could he possibly say about her?"

Lying there in her casket, Grandma Faulkner looked like an old gypsy or fortune-teller with a glittery shawl wrapped around her head and shoulder. One by one, the family walked past the coffin to give their last respects. Soon it was Velma's turn (her youngest child whose own children her mother had tried to kill by arsenic poisoning). Aunt Velma walked up to the coffin and leaned over, *glaring* into her mother's face. We all watched as Velma stuck her finger right into her mother's face and scowled, "*Mama, you're not getting out of this one!*"

Well, it was true — Grandma Faulkner was finally in a fix she could not escape!

I realize Heaven will be full of surprises — who is there and who is not there — but let me say I would be *very* surprised to see my Great-grandmother Faulkner in Heaven. I realize no one likes to think about it, but Heaven and hell are real places. What we *do* or *do not do* with Christ in this life determines everything in eternity.

Yes, my great-grandmother was created in the image of God. But the life she chose was in stark contrast to the one He had designed and purposed for her to live. Her life was a lesson of the dangers of resisting God and going your own way, and I took that deeply to heart in my observations of my great-grandmother's life.

## When God 'Closed the Casket' on Our Sin

When I read Romans 6:6, I often reflect on that moment when Velma pointed her finger into Grandma Faulkner's face and said, "Mama, you're not getting out of this one!" That verse says, "Knowing this, that our old man is crucified with him, that the body of sin might be destroyed, that henceforth we should not serve sin."

The words "old man" refer to who we used to be before we committed our lives to Christ. The word "old" in Greek depicts something *old, worn out, outdated*, and *no longer relevant*. The word "sin" describes all our identities and activities before we surrendered to the lordship of Jesus, including our rebellious sinful nature that we were born with and all of its actions and behaviors that were contrary to God.

But this verse explains that Christ died "…that the body of sin might be destroyed…." The word "destroyed" means *to render inoperative and to make inactive*. This means Christ's work on the Cross literally put our old man in the grave! In God's mind, that old man — that is, who we used to be — is just as dead as any corpse in a morgue or dead body being buried in a cemetery. Its life is gone, and it is nothing more than a hull. Nothing can resuscitate it; no one can breathe life back into it; and there is nothing that can stimulate it into action again — because it's *dead*. The life of that old man has been *terminated for good* — PERMANENTLY.

Think how glorious it is that when we came into Christ, God rendered our old identity powerless over us. That's why Romans 6:7 goes on to say, "For he that is dead is freed from sin." That word "freed" depicts a divine justification so complete that it has permanently *taken us away* and *separated us from* who we used to be. That means our old man has irreversibly been dealt a death blow by the cross of Jesus Christ — that is an inescapable fact!

The day I gave my life to Jesus, my old man — with all of its rebellious nature and ugly behaviors — was permanently buried with no ability to ever escape that death blow! Just as Velma pointed her finger into the face of her mother and said, "Mama, you're not getting out of this one," I can just imagine Jesus pointing His finger into the face of my old man and saying, "Old man, you have tried to get out of everything to escape accountability — but you're not getting out of this one! I'm rendering you inoperative, and you'll never breathe life again!"

I'm so thankful for what Jesus did on the Cross and in His resurrection to permanently slam shut the "coffin lid" as He rendered our old man inoperative forever! That is the best news in the world — and that is where my thoughts always go when I reflect on that day when the lid was sealed once and for all on Grandma Faulkner's casket.

### Our Connection to the Declaration of Independence

On a more positive note concerning Grandma Faulkner's life, my great-grandmother was very proud that, on one side of the family, we were descendants of Charles Carroll, who was known as Charles Carroll of Carrollton, Maryland, the wealthiest man in the United States during the time he lived. Carroll was elected to the Continental Congress on July 4, 1776, and remained a delegate until 1778. He arrived too late to vote in favor of the Declaration of Independence, but was present to sign the official document that survives today. In fact, his signature is listed just four signatures below John Hancock's ubiquitous autograph. After both Thomas Jefferson and John Adams died on July 4, 1826, Charles Carroll became the last living signatory of the Declaration of Independence. Grandma Faulkner was so proud to say he was one of our early ancestors in the United States.

## Life on 'the Other Side of the Tracks'

So far, I've talked about my mother's genealogy — the colorful Miller family — and about my Grandpa Paul Renner, my father's father, who immigrated from Germany. We also know that he married Ethel Tate, and her mother was Grandma Faulkner, whose first name I do not know — nor do I know very much about my Great-grandmother Faulkner except what I already wrote. But I'll tell you a little more about Grandma Renner — Ethel Tate Renner, wife of Paul Richard Renner — the last one in my list of six grandmothers in this chapter.

Ethel Tate had previously been married to an abusive husband that we know little about because she didn't like to discuss the situation. She and my Grandpa Renner were married in 1932 in Sapulpa, Oklahoma, five years after he'd immigrated to the United States. Sapulpa was a small town west of Tulsa named after a Creek Indian leader, James Sapulpa, who established a trading post there in about 1850.

After one year of marriage, Paul and Ethel celebrated the birth of their son in 1933, Ronald Richard Renner, my father. In that day, Paul and Ethel, in their late twenties, were considered to be "older" parents, so Ronald turned out to be their only child. His birth was significant because it initiated a new branch of Renners in the United States — a branch that would only be perpetuated if he had a son to carry on the name. Well, that was *me*!

## Our Renner Roots at the Sand Springs Line

Paul and Ethel moved to an area of Tulsa called the Sand Springs Line, so called because it was nestled mainly between two sets of railroad tracks — one set for industrial trains and the other set for trolleys that carried passengers back and forth between Tulsa and Sand Springs. Charles Page, a wealthy oil magnate who founded Sand Springs, invested money in 1911 to construct the almost nine miles of track for these lines. Later the trolley system was abandoned because cars became popular. But the unused trolley track is still there today, and a road was built right alongside it called Charles Page Boulevard in memory of the city's founder.

While parts of Tulsa were marvelously adorned with sprawling palaces of oil barons and sumptuous homes, life was not like that in northwest Tulsa on the Sand Springs Line. In the truest sense of the word, the Sand Springs Line was literally on "the other side of the tracks" — from an idiom that usually depicts a part of a town that is undesirable. The word "tracks" refers to railroad tracks, which were often used as lines of demarcation to separate lower economic areas of a town.

The biggest part of the neighborhood where Paul and Ethel Renner moved was nestled on a relatively small strip of land that lay between the two tracks. To the farther side of one set of tracks, a levee had been constructed to stop the floodwaters of the Arkansas River. Then there was a smaller neighborhood squeezed between those tracks and the levee. It's kind of funny when I think of it now, but anyone who lived in that entire area lived on some side of a track — between the tracks, on the other side of one set of tracks, or even worse, butted right up next to the levee.

People moved to the Sand Springs Line because the homes were smaller, generally older, and much less expensive compared to homes in other parts of Tulsa. Few in that neighborhood were professional people, and few had higher education. If they did, they may not have made it known because others there may have seen them as being snooty if they disclosed that kind of information. But to be sure, it was a less desirable part of Tulsa where good ol', down-to-earth, common folks lived. And that is where my grandparents lived with their newborn son Ronald in the mid-1930s.

Nearly all our relatives and friends lived in that area around the tracks. Grandpa and Grandma Renner lived there; Grandma Bagley, on my mother's side of the family, lived there; Grandma Ettie and Buddy were there; Aunt Melita and Uncle Howard lived there; Uncle Raymond and his first wife lived there; and virtually all of our friends were there.

Perhaps most importantly, Glenwood Baptist Church was there. That church was the very center of our lives — and, by the way, it was built right alongside the tracks as well.

As I was remembering our early life one day with my older sister, we both realized that in our growing-up years, we lived practically unaware that life existed beyond the Sand Springs Line. Everywhere we went — to church, school, sports events, stores, and places to fellowship with friends — fell in between or just on the other side of the tracks! As a young boy, I played on the tracks, walked on the tracks, crossed the tracks, searched for snakes at the tracks, and even played games where we would count the wooden ties on the tracks. Our lives were entrenched around those tracks so entirely that I thought everyone lived near tracks!

Back in the mid-1930s when my father's parents moved there and as they raised their small family, the elder Renners faithfully attended Glenwood Baptist Church with Ronald. As a young man, Ronald walked the aisle to the altar of that church to give his heart to Christ. Years later his children — Ronda, Lori, and me — would all make the same commitment at the very same altar.

But Glenwood Baptist Church became a "saving grace" to my father in other ways too. *Let me explain...*


### Challenges Between Immigrant Parents and Children

As you now know, my father's father was a German immigrant. He came from the Old World and struggled in the early years to assimilate in a new culture in America. Culture determines so many things in our lives — our names, what foods are normal or desirable to us, how we dress, what we believe in, how we interact with others, and an endless list of other things. If a new culture is vastly different from our old one, assimilation can be a difficult process. Anyone who has immigrated to a new country will tell you that such transitions can be challenging and hard.

Immigrants usually move to a new country to seek a better life and because they dream for their children to have more opportunities to thrive. But for immigrants to learn a new language, get a job (usually lower-paying jobs due to their lack of language skills), and adapt to so much that is different from everything they have previously known creates a huge strain mentally and emotionally. The unintentional result is that often even good immigrant parents become so absorbed in their own struggle to assimilate that they become less available to their children.

Often there's also a communication breakdown between immigrant parents and their children because of language. You see, immigrant children almost always begin speaking the new language quicker than their parents. And often the children don't want to hear or speak their native language because it hinders them as they're assimilating *themselves* in classrooms and with a new set of peers. Making matters more complicated is that the parents often don't know how to say things correctly in a new language, so they lean on their children to be their mouthpiece and even ask them to bear responsibilities beyond their years. This puts a strain on the relationship between the parents and the children, who also deeply struggle with identity issues in the new country.

Immigrants' children usually want to let go of the past to become integrated and have a sense of belonging in their new environment. They discover quickly that if they live and think like they did in a past life, they will never thrive in the new setting. So on one hand, they want to please their parents by honoring the past, but they feel the constant tug to move on.

My father told me this is what he felt growing up with an immigrant father. An example is that my father had zero interest in learning to speak German. My grandpa was frustrated with that fact, but my father rightfully questioned, "Why should I learn to speak German when I will only use it to speak to my father who *needs* to start speaking English?"

Grandpa Renner embraced America proudly, but he was nonetheless German, and America was notably different from the place where he grew up. He was trying to leave a world behind him, embrace a new one in front of him, get established, learn a new language, make an income, and be a husband and father at the same time. That's a tall order for *anyone* to fill!

All of these factors can lead to distancing, misunderstanding, and disconnection between immigrants and their children — and that disconnect is what my father felt between him and his father. But Glenwood Baptist Church became a "saving grace" to my dad because there he found a rich social life and emotional and spiritual support from his church-going friends.

Glenwood Baptist Church really was a lighthouse on the Sand Springs Line — literally a hub of activity that attracted young families with babies and children as well as youth, young adults, and even older singles. The church teemed with life as it provided Sunday School, Training Union, church services, bowling leagues, softball teams, Girls Auxiliary for young girls, Royal Ambassadors for young boys, Vacation Bible School, and youth camp every year. It was the coolest place to be on the Sand Springs Line. It was filled with life, friends, good preaching, a love for the Bible, and a commitment to reach souls — *just the way church ought to be*!

Ronald and his parents remained faithfully connected in that church — in fact, Glenwood Baptist is where my dad Ronald Renner met my beautiful mother Erlita Miller. They were children when they first met, and years later they were married in the church sanctuary. Nearly our whole family attended Glenwood Baptist Church for generations.

Although they did not have Bible-school diplomas or even come off as being deeply spiritual, my dad's parents never missed church unless someone was sick or inclement weather made it hard to get there. I can even tell you where they sat years later after I came into the picture and actually sat with them or with Grandma Bagley every Sunday. They sat on the second to the last pew on the left side of the auditorium, always right in front of Elder Wilkins, whose family was another faithful family in the church.

Actually, I can tell you where each family member regularly sat in the auditorium during my early childhood years. As I noted, Grandpa and Grandma Renner sat on the second to the last pew on the left side, usually with my younger sister Lori and me. Grandma Bagley sat about six or seven pews in front of them, but a little further to the left, usually right next to her friend Mrs. Wilson, who was the church pianist.

Ronda was older than Lori and me, so she sat with other kids and teenagers on the right side of the auditorium. Daddy and mother were longstanding choir members, so they were always seated in the choir — Dad was almost always seated in his place at the center of the back row, and mother in her place in the middle of the first row. My church memories from childhood are very vivid and pleasant memories that I will always hold dear.

### A Chicken Coop and a Satchel of Candy —
### My Own Mother's Early Days

Because the elder Renners lived on the Sand Springs Line, my father Ronald grew up at Glenwood Baptist Church and learned to serve the Lord there. And not far from Glenwood — just down the street and across the tracks — was a newly divorced Juanita Miller, who was getting settled in the area with her three children Erlita, Melita, and Raymond.

Divorced and with nowhere to go, Juanita turned to her precious mother, my Grandma Bagley, whose house as you might recall was located right next to the railroad tracks. On the backside of Grandma Bagley's house was a large chicken coop where she had raised chickens. Because Juanita and the kids needed somewhere to live, she went to work cleaning the chicken debris out of the coop and remodeling it into a tiny house.

From the outside, everything about that small house looked like a chicken coop, including its typical slanted chicken-coop roof. But inside, Juanita had transformed it into a home where she and her kids could live in those early years as they started life over without Earl Miller. Juanita's sister Marie, along with Marie's husband, also lived nearby. It was the perfect place for Juanita to live — near family who could help her with the children while she went to work to earn a living for her own family of four.

Just a few houses down the street from that chicken coop lived a woman who was aware of Juanita's situation, and she knew Juanita's kids needed to know the Lord. So that year at Christmastime, she invited Erlita to attend a special service at Glenwood Baptist Church — with the enticement of a satchel of candy that would be given to each child who attended that particular service.

A satchel of candy might not sound like much today, but when my mother was eight years old, World War II was an ongoing reality, and sugar, among other commodities, was a scarcity. This made candy a *very* rare treat. When my mother heard that candy was going to be given to each child who attended the service, she asked her mother for permission to go. Not only did her mother say yes, but she even accompanied her daughter to that event.

That night, my precious mother not only received her small satchel of candy, but she also heard the Gospel explained to her for the first time. Later that same night at home, she bowed down on her knees with her Aunt Marie and surrendered her life to Jesus Christ. *This amazing miracle all started with the lure of a small satchel of candy!*

## Candy as a Catalyst To Reach a Child and *the Nations*!

When a young Erlita Renner returned home from that service full of questions about eternity, she told Aunt Marie what she had seen, heard, and felt in her heart. That is when Aunt Marie knelt with my mother and prayed with her to receive Christ. It is amazing to me that something as simple as a gift of candy brought my mother to the feet of Jesus — and so much fruit has resulted from my mother's salvation! She continued strong in her Christian walk, little knowing that she would bear a son one day whom God would call to impact Russian-speaking nations with the Word and the power of God. Because of her deep commitment to Christ, my mother delivered a spiritual legacy to both of my sisters and me — and to her grandchildren and great-grandchildren — that will speak for all eternity.

And to think that it all started with a neighbor's invitation to attend her church — Glenwood Baptist Church — with the offer of free candy to be given out at Christmastime. I am stunned when I think about what a catalyst that small satchel of candy was in reaching millions of people for Christ over ensuing decades.

Juanita had been deeply impacted by the vibrant faith of Earl Miller's mother, her former mother-in-law Louella Miller. Louella was the pioneering legend who ran in the 1889 Oklahoma Land Rush and who prayed with miraculous results for the sick who came for healing from all over Indian Territory. I recall as a boy sitting next to my Grandma Ettie as she told me amazing stories about the miracles that my Great-grandmother Louella witnessed as she used her faith to minister to the sick. Grandma Ettie had been miraculously healed of a serious kidney ailment due to Great-grandmother Louella's prayers, and that miracle dramatically impacted her. But Juanita herself, in a rough season after her tumultuous marriage and divorce from Earl Miller, did not regularly attend church.

Juanita deeply loved God, but in those "emotional-rollercoaster" years after Earl Miller, she didn't regularly attend church because she was trying to earn money to raise three children. Also, whether it was true that it was happening or not, she felt "judged" by church people for her divorce. It was rare in those days to hear of a Christian going through a divorce. In fact, I can only remember two couples who divorced in my entire growing-up years. It was simply shocking to all of us to know a Christian who went through divorce.

But whether it was true that others were judging her — or it was self-condemnation that Grandma Ettie felt herself — she *perceived* it to be the former, so she was never really excited about going regularly to a place where she felt looked down on. But she knew her children needed to be there, so she made sure that Erlita, Melita, and Raymond attended Sunday School and services regularly at the church.

So my Daddy and Mother were kids who both attended Glenwood Baptist Church, and they became childhood friends. They would both attend Vacation Bible School, Sunday School, Training Union, and youth group. They were always together in multiple choirs, at softball games, at the bowling alley, and so on. Daddy attended Sand Springs High School and Mother went to Central High School in downtown Tulsa, but their church life was like a glue that held them together. By the time Daddy turned eighteen and Mother seventeen, they were madly in love and walked the aisle at Glenwood Baptist Church on February 28, 1953, to be joined in holy matrimony.

### My Mother Lived in That Chicken Coop *Again*

When Daddy and Mother got married, they were young and had little money to rent a house. So with Grandma Bagley's permission, they moved into the remodeled chicken coop that was located on Grandma's small property next to the train tracks. But it wasn't long until Daddy got a better-paying job at American Airlines.

In high school, Mother developed secretarial skills when she worked at the Tulsa Country Club, so in the early years of their marriage, she used those skills at Warren Petroleum Company where she worked as a secretary for the oilman W. K. Warren at his downtown Tulsa office. (When I was a teen, I, too, worked for W. K. Warren.) Later, after Ronda was born, my mother worked part time as the pastor's secretary at Glenwood Baptist Church.

Eventually Daddy and Mother earned enough money to move out of Grandma Bagley's chicken coop into a very small house right next door to Grandpa and Grandma Renner on 46th Street. That is where they lived when Ronda — that is, Ronda Marie Renner — was born on February 10, 1954, and that is where they lived when I, Richard Raymond Renner, was born early in the morning July 21, 1958.

After some time, our family moved two blocks away to 44th Street, and that is where we lived when Lori, our youngest sister, was born. Early one morning, Daddy woke Ronda and me and told us it was time for the baby to be born. Grandma Renner was ready to come at a moment's notice to take care of Ronda and me. Since Grandma lived only two blocks away, it took her just minutes to get to the house. We watched as Daddy walked Mother out the door to the car to drive her to the hospital. After a day or so, they returned, Mother carrying in her arms a precious little gift, Lori Ann Renner, who came into the world on February 24, 1963. When Lori arrived, *it completed our family of five.*

Fruit that is hidden for a season
is fruit just the same.

NATIONAL
BANK
OF TULSA

# 2

# MY UNLIKELY SURVIVAL
# AND EARLY YEARS

Early in the morning of July 21, 1958, I was born in the old red-brick wing of St. John Medical Center and Hospital in Tulsa. Interestingly, that is the only part of the old hospital that remains of the fabulous newer structure today. My father, Ronald Richard Renner, was a faithful employee at American Airlines and a young twenty-four years old at the time of my birth. My mother, Erlita Marie Renner, was a stay-at-home mom who was barely twenty-three when I was born. Their first child, my older sister Ronda, was four years old when I entered the world.

But I could have exited the world as quickly as I entered it. In fact, the delivering doctor grimly forewarned that I would not likely live to see the end of my first day.

Late into my mother's fourth month of pregnancy while she was teaching Vacation Bible School at Glenwood Baptist Church — *suddenly*, in the

**Left and Above:** *Tulsa, Oklahoma, 1950s. © Tulsa Historical Society & Museum.*

77

middle of one of her classes, her water broke. She was rushed to the doctor, who ordered her to go straight to bed and warned her that if she got up to do anything at all, the baby could be born prematurely and would probably die. Obeying the doctor's charge, Mother went straight to bed and stayed there.

Her sister Melita later said, "Erlita's body started trying to lose Rick about five months into her pregnancy. I remember going there to help wash her hair in a basin while she lay in bed because she was not supposed to get out of bed at all. I know it was the enemy trying to steal the gift of God she was carrying in her womb. But Erlita told me that she and Ronald never doubted that Rick would be born without a problem."

All seemed well for weeks and weeks of total bedrest until Ronda developed chicken pox and needed to see a doctor. That is when Mother got up, got dressed, put Ronda with her on a city bus, and took her to downtown Tulsa to the doctor's office. Then just as her own doctor had predicted, Mother's body went into labor. She was rushed to St. John's, where I was born at thirty-seven weeks, barely at the premature mark.

## The Stubborn Faith of My Father

Perhaps due to Mother's water breaking so early in her pregnancy, I'd experienced some oxygen deprivation and was born as what was termed a "blue baby." Mother said, "You were small and so cute, but you were also so blue when you were born that the doctor said, 'You have a little boy, but don't name him and don't expect to keep him.'

"I just let those words go and never gave them another thought," my mother related. "And when we brought you home from the hospital, you never had a moment's problem. All the negative things the doctors said were not true. But we *did* do a lot of praying."

I was born with Blue Baby Syndrome, and my skin tone was, of course, "blue" as a result. My fingernails and toenails were so bluish in color that they were undetectable. My condition was so fragile that even after I survived my first day, the doctor insisted to my father that they make no birth announcement to family or friends for a few days. Initially believing I wouldn't live beyond that first day, the doctor was still concerned that I would not survive my condition and that I would die in that hospital.

But in typical Ronald Renner style, my dad ignored the doctor's grim pronouncement and went out and bought a box of knock-off Cuban cigars. Then he called his buddies together and handed out those cigars to celebrate the birth of his son.

Daddy had a faith that refused to heed bad news. It was a stubborn faith that marked his whole life. He didn't know it was faith, but that's what it was.

For example, in his later life, my father faced a serious kidney condition and was placed on dialysis for more than two years with no medical hope of his kidneys ever functioning again. One day he belligerently announced, "I've had all of this I'm going to take. I'm tired of this, and I'm not going for another dialysis treatment! *My kidneys will just have to start working!*" My mother begged him not to stop, but he shrugged it off and answered, "I'll be fine."

*And guess what?* He *was* fine. Against all medical odds, the *very* day he stopped his treatment, his kidneys instantly kicked into operation and worked normally the rest of his life.

I would never suggest that someone just end his or her medical treatment as my father did — but my father simply had a "gut" kind of faith that refused to accept a bad report. In his case, he wouldn't have explained it as "faith for healing." Nevertheless, he possessed a type of stubborn faith that got results.

It was that same faith operating in him on that July morning in 1958, the day I was born. While doctors waited for me to die in the newborn ICU at St. John's, my dad threw a party with friends to celebrate that he and his wife had a new little boy.

Daddy and Mother named me Richard Raymond Renner. I was called Richard after my Grandpa Renner and my own dad who both shared Richard as their middle names. The name "Richard" is a Germanic name that means *ruler* or *mighty*. And my parents gave me the middle name Raymond after my mother's father and her younger brother who both shared Raymond as *their* middle names.

The name "Raymond" is also Germanic, and it means *advisor* or *protector*. I am certain Mother and Daddy hadn't studied the meaning of those names prior to naming me. They simply named me after loved ones. But it was pretty amazing that they gave me *those* names. I was so close to death that it was a far-fetched, *unlikely* dream that I would ever be a mighty ruler, advisor, *or* protector.

There's even more to my name that I believe is *really* significant.

The name "Renner" is from a Middle High German word that meant *runner*. It is actually from the word "rennen" — which was an occupational name for *a messenger*, normally *a mounted and armed military servant*. It described specially trained men who ran across battlefields with messages for troops who were engaged on the frontlines of battle.

Although my parents didn't realize it at the time, the name they gave me, Richard Raymond Renner, was actually quite prophetic considering the assignment God gave me to be a strong Christian leader, an advisor to younger leaders, a protector of biblical truth, and one called to run with the message of God's Word across battlefields to the frontlines of conflict.

### A Newborn and a Nursery Worker

My parents were *really* committed to serving God by being faithful to our church, so as soon as it was possible, they loaded me into the car with Ronda, and we headed to church as a family for the first time. It was a true miracle that I was alive in spite of the doctor's first prognosis. It was so miraculous that Daddy wanted to film that historic moment, so as he often did in the years that followed, he pulled out his Brownie 8mm movie camera to document their little boy "attending" church for the first time. I was eight days old!

All of us Renner kids started our church lives in the nursery. I can *actually* remember being in various rooms that comprised the nursery up to about two and half years of age! All the women who served there were kind and they really cared for us. I'm talking about women like Nina Reeves, a tiny woman who worked for years like *a fixture* in that nursery. She was among the first to take me in her arms at church, and she stayed with me in those earliest years as I grew and graduated from one room to the next.

Nina's job might have seemed insignificant to some, but it wasn't insignificant to God. Oh, how she impacted my life and the lives of many others in the more than *sixty years* she spent working in that nursery as unto the Lord! Over that period of time, she held *hundreds* of babies, including my sisters and me and all my friends. Just before Nina went to Heaven at the age of eighty-four, *she was still serving every week* in the same nursery where she had cared for me as an infant.

When I think of Nina Reeves — and other faithful people in any church — the word "pillar" comes to mind. To think that Nina forfeited her right to sit in Sunday-morning church services for sixty-plus years so parents could be in the sanctuary to receive the teaching of the Word. That is simply amazing to me. Surely there must have been times when Nina felt that her ministry was unimportant — just caring for babies in the most isolated room of the church. I'm sure there were moments when the devil or even her own mind would tell her, *You're just a nursery worker.* But the fact is, Nina's service ultimately impacted the lives of countless people for eternity. Part of the fruit of my own ministry, I'm sure, will be credited to Nina Reeves. She was a pillar *indeed* who helped support the house of God — the local church — in our small community of believers.

I'm telling you this because it's important to recognize the vital roles each person plays where he or she serves God in the local church. And we need to remember those who have been a blessing to us because *everyone* is important. And when someone lays down his or her life in obedience to the Lord and for the service of others, that person is *doubly* important in the mind of God!

## From Vanquisher of Shoe Scuffs to Slayer of Evil Powers

Our family didn't just attend church services once or twice a week — our *entire lives* revolved around the activities of Glenwood Baptist Church in Tulsa. My parents were both in the choir — a volunteer commitment that entailed countless hours in rehearsals at the church, always with kids in tow. Choir rehearsals for us as children meant playtime with friends as we wandered the church hallways — our pastor often doling out dimes so we could buy Cokes at the gas station and family market across the street (and so that we would vacate the auditorium during those rehearsals).

My father loved the church, and he was a well-liked friend to many in our larger church family. Daddy also cleaned the church building every Saturday, with me dutifully at his side. At just four or five years old, my job was to scrub scuff marks off the linoleum-tiled floors in the classrooms and foyers.

That experience became a lesson in persevering until a job was done *and done correctly.* I never wanted to miss a spot and fail my father's meticulous inspections at unpredicted intervals. That early experience served me well in my adult life as it instilled in me the need to always do my best at whatever I do for Jesus.

My mother taught Sunday School, and when I wasn't scouring floors with my father, I was helping Mother set up her classroom, a task that held the greater appeal for me. With rapt enthusiasm, I'd help her decorate bulletin boards, organize chairs, and stack mimeographed lessons, with pencils and pens, in preparation for her teaching of God's Word the following morning.

In my own classroom each Sunday, I would sit *captivated* by our lessons from the Bible. With relished delight, I'd listen to every word, scrutinizing each detail of the colorful illustrations our teacher showed us as she taught. Fueled by my vivid imagination as she read those Bible stories, I regularly traveled back in time as the young warrior David, felling the wicked giant Goliath — or as faithful Daniel, beholding God's power clenching the jaws of lions as He protected me in that awful den.

From vanquisher of shoe scuffs to slayer of the dark powers of evil, each of my biblical time travels found me perfecting those heroic feats with every debilitating blow I dealt to God's enemies.

## Kool-Aid Klatches and Tempera Paint —
## Sights and Sounds of My Childhood at Glenwood

In those classes, I eagerly participated in classroom activities, such as coloring, painting, and waging glitter wars with my preschool friends. I remember the *thrilling* bitter tang in the air as teachers opened old bottles of tempera paint and prepared our palettes and brushes. Those were the beginning moments when I realized I possessed such a deep love for art.

I can still picture the small, Formica-topped tables where we sat two by two, busily creating our refrigerator-door masterpieces. Hollow metal legs made moving the tables easy, with just minimal friction, and we'd glide them noisily across the floor to gather for Kool-Aid klatches and brisk four-year-old conversation. I can still recall the taste of Saltines mixed with our berry-flavored drinks as we washed those crackers down, melting them in our mouths for the entertainment portion of our snack-time experience.

Like all the kids at Glenwood Baptist, I eventually graduated to another part of the building where the kindergarten and grade-school kids attended Sunday School. Like my older sister before me, I joined the children's choir and became a "Sunbeam" (for preschool through kindergarten ages) — an endearing term that anyone who grew up in the Southern Baptist church will remember.

In my Sunday School class every Sunday, I sat at tables well-stocked with art supplies to draw colorful pictures of whatever Bible story we were studying that week. From the faces of my teachers to the colorful images on the posters that lined our classroom walls, those precious memories are so vivid to me today that they will be cemented in my mind for the rest of my life.

## A Household of Favor Through *Faithfulness*

The Renner household was so committed to church attendance that whether or not we went to church was never a discussion. Torturous moments in my young life were Sunday nights when, every week, *The Wonderful World of Disney* program came on TV just as it was time for us to return for Sunday-night church activities. I can remember seeing Tinker Bell fly over the Disney castle and *ping* the top of it with her wand as fireworks magically exploded into the air. Then, as if that tiny fairy was *pinging* on cue, we had to turn off the TV and pile into the car for church.

So many times, I prayed, "God, just once, please let me stay home and watch *The Wonderful World of Disney*." It was a prayer that was never answered because my parents were *committed* to teaching us that serving God was our highest priority. I'm so thankful that Daddy and Mother instilled that in us, as it became a solid foundation for my entire spiritual life.

Our family of five was involved in every facet of church life for as long as I can remember. We gave offerings, attended services, volunteered, and reached out to those in need. We faithfully attended revival meetings, diligently volunteered wherever there was a need, and dutifully showed up for weekly visitation, where we'd reach out both to visitors and the lost. We worked alongside our friends on special projects, befriended the surrounding community, and stood behind the pastor — oh, how we loved our pastor and his family. We gave our best, dressed our best, and did our best where the house of God and the people in it were concerned. We carried a deeply felt awe concerning our service to God — a sentiment that seems to have dissipated in much of the Church today.

Because church was our priority, a lot of careful preparation went into the way we conducted our lives on Saturday in order to honor church attendance on Sunday. Mother made sure our clothes were laundered and pressed. Daddy made sure his shoes were polished, and he taught me to make sure my shoes were polished too. Our Sunday-afternoon meal was usually prepared in advance so Mother wouldn't have to think about it while we were focused on our serving at church.

I cannot fail to mention that we kids always read our Sunday School lesson — which was "required reading" in our home — in preparation for Sunday School. Granted, we were sometimes still reading it in the car on the way to church, but we *for sure* had the lesson read before we arrived! It wasn't just required reading by the church. My mother was a Sunday School teacher — and even a Sunday School director for a while — so she made certain we read our lesson whether we wanted to do it or not!

But I had another motivation for reading my lesson. Back in those days, the Southern Baptist Convention (Southern Baptist was the name of our denomination) gave every church member a small multi-colored box each quarter that contained three months' worth of offering envelopes. The envelopes contained a line to write our names on and multiple little squares we could mark to indicate our level of faithfulness each week.

For example, you could check a box to show you'd attended Sunday School, Training Union, Wednesday-night service, visitation, or that you gave your tithe and offering for the week. But for me, a very important box to check was the one that indicated I'd read that Sunday School lesson from our denomination's quarterly publication. I truthfully thought the lessons were boring, but I was not going to miss a week without putting a check in the appropriate box because I wanted to be *faithful*!

### You Can Be Just the Person God Is Searching For!

Why is faithfulness so important to God? Just for a moment, let me share a verse that demonstrates why I wanted so badly to be faithful as a young boy. First Corinthians 4:2 says, "Moreover it is required in stewards, that a man be found faithful."

According to this verse, it is *required* that anyone who serves God be found faithful. The word "required" is a Greek word that means *to seek, to search, or to look very intensively for something*. In history, it was used as a legal term to denote *a judicial investigation*, and it could even refer to *a scientific investigation*. It was not a mere surface investigation. Rather, it depicted an intense and thorough searching for accurate, concrete facts. The verse could be interpreted, "Moreover, God is making *a concentrated, exhaustive, and thorough search* in pursuit of stewards who are faithful."

Because that particular Greek word is used here, we know that the kind of steward God is searching for is not abundant in His House. In fact, these kinds of people are so uncommon that God must *search exhaustively and thoroughly* to find those who show respect for spiritual principles and who are faithful. That is why Second Chronicles 16:9 (*AMPC*) says, "...The eyes of the Lord move to and fro throughout the whole earth to show Himself strong in behalf of those whose hearts are blameless toward Him."

"Moreover it is *required* in *stewards*, that a man be found faithful" (1 Corinthians 4:2). Let's also look at the word "steward" in this verse, a compound of two words — the Greek word for *a house* and a Greek word that means *to dispense* or *to administrate*.

The first word that depicts *a house* includes within it the idea of a real physical residence where a family resides. Then included in *that* is the idea of not only the residents, but also the furniture, the finances, the property, and all the household items, activities, and components connected to that particular family and home — and it is often translated as "household."

The second word in the compound word for "steward" means *to dispense* or *to administrate*. It is derived from a word that means *law* and refers to anything *laid down, ordered, established,* or *made into law.* It depicts *standards, norms, or laws that are firmly established, publicly accepted, and categorically expected.* Simply put, these are rules that are to be respected and followed.

When these two words are compounded, the new word for "steward" means *the rule or management of a house.* It was the very word used to depict leaders who were so trusted by the king or by the state that they were appointed to administrate entire departments or even nations. They were to set the supreme example of honoring the law in their private lives — in their personal affairs and households — as well as in their public offices.

The word "steward" could also designate *gatekeeper, chief concierge, head janitor, head cook, chief accountant,* etc. These were not mere laborers, but rather those who had oversight and responsibility and who were accountable for the areas entrusted to their care. They knew, respected, and followed the rules set forth by the one in authority over them — and they made sure others in the household followed the rules as well.

This is fascinating to me because the word "steward" literally describes the faithfulness my Daddy and Mother demonstrated in their responsibilities over their family and household — *and* over the house of God, Glenwood Baptist Church. And they were putting it deeply into their children what it meant to be faithful.

At a very early age, my parents taught me that if God found me faithful, a new assignment would soon be arriving at my door. Of course, so much of my training began at home with my assigned duties to wash, dry, or put dishes away after family dinners. I was also charged with making sure the yard was clear of dog droppings each weekday after school after my daddy had meticulously mowed, edged, and weeded with such care the weekend before. Everyone in my family knew how to contribute to the success of the whole household, *as it should be*, and I am forever grateful for that fact.

I share First Corinthians 4:2 with you because it is an integral part of my story. My parents instilled in me the necessity to be found faithful in everything I set my hand to do in the service of God. They taught me that He was watching me and that He expected to find me faithful. And I assure you that God is watching *you* to see if He can trust you with more too.

### Our Sunday Life — *'Everyone to the Car!'*

Our home life blended seamlessly with church life at Glenwood Baptist. After a busy week of work and school — pleasantly interrupted by Wednesday night's church supper and service, as well as some other church activity as a rule — *finally*, Sunday morning came.

*And we were ready.*

A typical Renner family Sunday included the early morning busyness of preparing a family of five to leave the house to arrive at church *on time*. My daddy had a lot of German blood in his veins, and in typical German fashion, he was disciplined, which meant he was *prompt* — on time and never late for anything. It didn't take long for my father's disciplined, "on-time and never-late-for-anything" attitude to be passed on to me. I am so thankful for it because it has helped me to be *on time* with the responsibilities God has entrusted to me over the years.

Daddy and Mother especially had to be on time because they each had responsibilities at church every Sunday. Like clockwork, at 8:45 every Sunday morning, Daddy would yell, *"Everyone to the car!"* It was a call to action that sparked a lot of movement as we all quickly fell into our places inside the family automobile — a black '57 Chevy with white, stainless-trimmed

fins that gleamed in the sun like angels' wings. Inside, the vinyl seats —
scorching-hot or freezing-cold to the touch in Oklahoma summers and
winters — were ample and more than roomy enough for Ronda, Lori, and
me *and* Grandma Bagley, whom we picked up at her tiny house near the
tracks almost every Sunday.

When church was finished, we would pile back into the car and head
home. There was no air conditioning in many cars before 1968, so in
warmer months, we would be *sweating* by the time we arrived home. Often,
I'd fall asleep in the car and stay there for a short nap while the rest of the
family changed clothes and prepared to eat lunch. We could have predicted
with nearly one-hundred-percent accuracy what we were going to eat. On
Sundays, it seems Mother always served us roast with potatoes, carrots, and
onions — and string beans as a side. If we had dessert, it was pineapple
upside-down cake.

Later that afternoon, it would be time to start the process all over. At
about six o'clock, Daddy would yell again, *"Everyone to the car!"* Sunday
nights were time for Training Union — a one-hour-long pre-service class for
those who were *really* committed to be Christ's disciples.

And we Renners were *committed*! So we attended Training Union every
Sunday night along with most of our closest friends. At the conclusion of
that class, we'd race down the steps in the educational building and dash
toward the auditorium for our Sunday-night service. I loved Sunday-night
services because that was when the youth choir sang, and I thought their
talent was so upbeat and amazing.

### Breaking Bread From House to House

When the evening service was over, things were just getting started for
us because every Sunday night after church, we'd gather at someone's house
for fellowship, where there was always coffee, dessert, and a smorgasbord of
finger foods to enjoy. Parents played cards and board games while we kids
huddled in a back room to watch a weekly Sunday-night program called,
*Fantastic Theater*, an old television show in black and white that featured
scary movies. Although we were serious about Christian service, friendships, and

respect for the Bible — we were pretty ignorant about the devil and spiritual warfare. So without a thought in the world that we might be doing something harmful, we watched those horror films with hysteria and delight — an occasional shriek escaping our hideout, usually followed by one of the parents peeking in to remind us to tone it down.

When those Sunday-night fellowships were held at our house, Daddy would often buy large sacks of uncooked peanuts, which he would then pour into cake tins and cook in the oven until they were toasted and piping hot. When they were done, he'd pull those baking tins out of the oven and, using oversized oven mitts, carry them into the main room of the house, where he had spread newspapers all over the floor. He'd pour the warm peanuts out onto the paper, and we would all begin the process of cracking them open. Piles of empty shells would soon cover the newspapers as we gobbled up the peanuts one by one!

On some Sunday nights, someone might bring tacos — the next Sunday night, we'd enjoy an array of desserts. It was exciting to anticipate what special treat we would share with friends from house to house each week.

When I think of these precious times that we spent fellowshipping within our circle of church friends, I am reminded of the Early Church and how they were committed to the same quality of fellowship with one another. Acts 2:46 says, "…Breaking bread from house to house, [the believers] did eat their meat with gladness and singleness of heart."

But they didn't just fellowship. They also "did eat." Food has always had a role in the fellowship of the saints, *both then and now*! Early believers enjoyed each other from house to house and shared food as a part of their fellowship. This is *exactly* what it was like on Sunday nights when I was a young boy!

This kind of fellowship is lacking in many churches today. I think more people should host a houseful of people from church for generous evenings of food, fun, and fellowship. Such times build relationships and make your spiritual union as a local church body stronger.

If you're considering this, but the thought of it intimidates you, I want to encourage you that you don't have to serve an eight-course meal to step out and start a warm tradition among fellow believers. Just throw some peanuts in the oven and bake them until they are ready — or have tacos, chili, or something inexpensive and easy to make. The food helps pull everyone together, but in the end, it's really not about the quality of the food. *It's about the fellowship!*

## Bobbie Jo's Biscuits

Wednesday nights were also special at our church, and they always began with a supper in the basement of the Rock Building.

The Rock Building was an old rock structure that was decrepit, but those who were my parents' age really loved it because that is where they all went to church as children themselves. By the time I was a kid at Glenwood Baptist Church, that building was basically unused except for the church kitchen located in the basement where Wednesday-night suppers were served.

Those Wednesday-night suppers included servings of ketchup-covered meatloaf, creamy mashed potatoes with heavy brown gravy, and cherry or apple pie. But for me, Bobbie Jo's biscuits were the "grand slam" of everything on the menu. These were not ordinary biscuits. They were large, fluffy, butter-covered biscuits, and they were served *every week* at the church's supper before our midweek service.

To a young Rick Renner, no food in the world compared to Bobbie Jo's light-golden biscuits, and I was always trying to sneak an extra one before or after dinner. Although it has been many decades since I've eaten one, I can still hear Bobbie Jo yelling, *"Ricky Renner* — KEEP YOUR HANDS OFF THE BISCUITS!"

Bobbie Jo's biscuits were terrific. But even those fluffy, buttery biscuits couldn't compare to the fellowship, encouragement, and love that was exchanged across tables as people ate a family meal together every Wednesday night. It was truly a weekly *love feast*, just as the Early Church experienced regularly during their times together. That kind of fellowship among our family of believers was the *real* reason I loved Wednesday-night suppers at our church so much.

You might wonder, *Why was a simple dinner that important?* The people who gathered there each Wednesday were pillars in our local church whom we could depend on — people who we knew really loved us. I am not exaggerating when I say that around those tables of fellowship, men and women spoke *strength* into each other's lives. The church members who gathered at Glenwood each Wednesday night were real "troops" — *comrades-in-arms* — who encouraged each other to live for Christ to the fullest. And if someone "disappeared" from church attendance, we looked until we found them! We weren't going to let them fall out of fellowship simply because they were discouraged! *That's when they needed us the most!*

These families and the men and women who led them were examples of faithfulness, consistency, and stability to me as a young boy. Much of what I believe about church fellowship today was formed in those Wednesday-night suppers. Although decades have passed and people have either died or moved away to various other places, many of these church members remain in touch with each other and deeply love one another today.

*Fellowship.* What a gift from God it is to you and me and to our local churches!

## My Mother, My Mentor

My sisters and I, from *infancy*, received the Gospel message in our young lives — from both our church and our parents. My mother remembered that from a very early age, I possessed a voracious spiritual appetite, asking questions about God, the Bible, and spiritual things that were well beyond my years. I'm not at all saying that others my age didn't have a deep love for God too. But from the beginning of my life, the call of God was already beginning to show up. And, thank God, my mother recognized it.

For example, my mother has described to me and others over the years an unusual experience she had one day as a young Baptist mother feeding her infant son in his highchair. What to her was a very mundane instant of spooning a small bite of food into my mouth became a profound moment in which, in a second of time, she "saw" the call of God on my life. She related that as she looked into my eyes that were to her "as crystal blue as the sea," in that swift moment, she knew she was looking into the eyes of a prophet.

My mother didn't have many experiences like that one, but she was a very spiritual woman nonetheless who paid close attention to the things she saw and perceived in her heart. And what she saw in me that day so greatly impacted her that discipling me, pouring her spiritual life into mine, became one of her great quests in life. She was truly my spiritual mentor who schooled me in Scripture and in the faith and helped lay a timeless foundation beneath me that would support me in the work I am doing today.

As I grew a little older, Mother would lie by my side every night when it was time for me to go to sleep, and she would read me stories from the book *Hurlbut's Story of the Bible*. Oh, how I loved that time with my mother. It was the highlight of every day and the perfect ending to both good days and bad days that was filled with spiritual comfort.

Mother also purchased a set of record albums of *Hurlbut's Story of the Bible* for me so I could listen to those stories on our family hi-fi. I can still visualize those shiny black vinyl records with deep-blue labels containing the titles of the Bible stories on each side of the record. When I'd arrive home from school every day in my early elementary years, my mother and I would pray, eat lunch, and listen to those Bible stories together. I played those albums over and over and over, listening *literally* for hours at a time.

I was simply filled with wonder and awe of God's Word, and a profound love for the Bible was nurtured in me by my mother. She would sing Christian hymns, songs, and choruses to me and talk to me about the things of God in every facet of life. For example, we would walk outdoors, simply picking up leaves from the ground, and she would show me the veins in the leaves and explain that God made everything perfect and with painstaking detail. I was eager to learn everything I could about the Lord, and I held on tightly to her every word.

My mother personified God's solemn instructions to His people to "…teach them [His words] diligently unto thy children" (Deuteronomy 6:7). The rest of that verse says, "…And shalt talk of them when thou sittest in thine house, and when thou walkest by the way, and when thou liest down, and when thou risest up." *That was my mother and me!*

I want to encourage you that if you didn't have a mother like mine, don't think you can't fulfill every bit of God's calling on your life. He is more than enough and will send you the right mentors, teachers, and trainers to help you if you'll draw near to Him and determine to stay on the right path. Just keep your eyes on Jesus!

At about this same time in my life, my parents bought me an old iron bed that was covered with several layers of paint, and they'd planned to eventually refinish it. Every night, Mother lay at my side and the two of us would meticulously pick the paint off that bed. As we would flake off that paint with our fingernails, Mother would talk to me about Jesus, the Bible, and my need for salvation. It didn't take long for me to understand that I was lost and that if I died without Christ, I'd go to hell.

At the "ripe old age" of four, I told my mother, "I need to walk the aisle at church and give my heart to Jesus." My mother had prepared the soil of my heart and even though I was only four, I fully understood what it meant to be lost and to be saved, and I felt deeply my need to respond to Christ. Each week during the altar call, as our congregation sang, "Just as I Am," I could feel my heart pound in my chest in response to the conviction I was feeling. I knew I was as yet unsaved and that I needed to give my heart to Jesus.

At first, Mother was hesitant because I was so young. She wanted me to really understand what I was doing, so she asked me to wait. So I waited… and waited…*and waited*. Week after week, I wanted desperately to respond to the altar call so I could finally cinch my eternal salvation as I yielded my heart and life to Christ.

And night after night, I'd crawl into bed under the covers and lay my head on my pillow, thinking about Heaven and hell and eternal salvation. I did that every single night. I truly feared dying unsaved.

Of course, I hadn't committed any horrendous sins. After all, *I was four years old!* But I did understand that I wasn't dead in sin because of sinful actions — but rather because I was *born* a sinner. So you can imagine my eagerness to be *re*born.

My mother had poured the Bible into me — and the sound preaching in our church reinforced those transforming truths within. And at the tender age of four, I understood all of it, and I *knew* I needed to give my heart to Jesus Christ.

Never think your children or grandchildren are too young to understand spiritual things. If you nurture their hearts, children can easily understand basic spiritual truths. I have seen many parents make the mistake of thinking their children will get around to inquiring about spiritual things on their own when they get older. But often, when they are older, it can be too late because they are already distracted, disinterested, or spiritually hardened. It's better to start talking to children about spiritual things when they are young so they will come to Christ at an earlier age when their hearts are tender.

Denise and I started early with our own sons about their need to be saved, and all three of our children gave theirs hearts to Jesus at young ages. This was years ago, of course, but they have followed suit in raising *their* children, who have all come to the saving knowledge of Christ as Lord early in their lives.

## Riveted by the Flames

When I was five years old, our pastor announced that we were going to have a week-long revival meeting in our church. Today when people speak of "revival," they're usually referring to a mighty move of God coming to a city or an entire nation. But back in those days, the word "revival" was generally used to describe a week of meetings with special preaching designed to reach the lost, touch the hearts of those who needed to rededicate their lives to Christ, and stir the local church to be more committed. That is what we meant when we said we were going to have *a revival.*

In advance of these services, our pastor urged our church family to pray and to invite unsaved or backslidden family and friends to that special week of meetings. As was the custom back then, the evangelist preached fiery messages every night. One night, he preached on the Second Coming of Christ, and the next night about the fatal effects of sinful living — and so on. But on the final night that week, he preached powerfully about *hell.* That sermon was so compelling that I can still mentally *see* it and it *hear* it today.

As that evangelist preached, he described the white-hot swirling, twisting flames of the fires of hell itself. As he spoke, I could picture those flames arching fiercely upward to engulf and consume sinners caught eternally in their scorching grip. The minister's message was so graphic and vivid that I could see that fire in my mind and feel the heat of the flames swirling nearer and nearer. That message reached all the way from the pulpit into my heart and grabbed hold of my soul.

Frankly, I was deeply disturbed by that message, but I was "disturbed" in a way that would lead me straight into the arms of a loving Savior, who was and is the only way of escape from such a devastating, irrevocable eternal punishment.

I knew the Bible taught that anyone who died in sin would be consumed in that eternal torment. Since I was unsaved, I *trembled* at this man's words, gripping the pew in front of me with my five-year-old fingers lest I slip into eternity at that very moment unprepared!

Oh, how I wanted to rise from my seat, step out into the aisle, and run to the altar to make my commitment to Christ that night. But because my mother wanted me to wait, I held myself back and refrained. After that week of meetings concluded, night after night, I shuddered in my bed at thoughts of what would happen if I died in my sleep. And every night, Mother looked into my eyes and my heart as I spoke to her about it. She was attempting to comprehend the depth of my understanding at five years of age concerning Heaven and hell and choices concerning eternity. Did I really understand what it meant to be unsaved and about my own need to be saved?

*I really did*, and soon, everyone in my circle of family and friends would know it.

### 'Just as I Am'

During our next regular Sunday-morning service, I was seated with my older sister Ronda in our church auditorium about midway between the pulpit and the back of the church. When the pastor finished his sermon, the church rose and began to passionately sing, "Just as I Am"[1] as we did every Sunday.

But on that day, I simply could not resist. I felt the tug of the Holy Spirit on my heart as strongly as I ever had, so I quickly slipped out of the pew into the aisle before I had time to think about refraining myself and waiting for a more opportune time, perhaps until the age of six or so, to be saved! Carefully, with deliberation in every step and my heart trembling inside my chest, I made my way to the altar of the church.

Our pastor, Brother Post, always stood at the altar to welcome anyone who came forward to make a decision for Christ. So he met me there, my daddy and mother in the choir loft behind him focused intently on their five-year-old son. Brother Post reached out to take my hand. He leaned down and gently asked me, "Ricky, why have you come today?"

"Brother Post," I answered in a whisper, "I want to give my heart to Jesus."

Theda Paddock was an altar worker in the church whom I'd always called "the clipboard woman." She appeared at my side just seconds after Brother Post seated me on the front pew in the auditorium. One of her duties was to record why people responded and came forward to the altar. We Southern Baptists were masters at keeping records, so even before I prayed, Theda had already recorded the reason I'd come forward and marked the date of my salvation, which I do not remember, but I can relive that day and that moment as if it happened yesterday.

After Theda marked her clipboard, my Sunday School teacher Jerry Sloan slid into the seat next to me and said, "Ricky, let's get on our knees right here and pray."

We both knelt at that pew, and he led me in a prayer as I gave my heart to Jesus that bright and brilliant Sunday morning in 1963. Then my parents slipped down from the choir loft to join me on the front row as my pastor presented me before the church so I could make my public profession of faith in Jesus Christ.

That was the morning I was gloriously saved!

That same afternoon, Brother Post came to visit me at our home. He said I needed to be baptized in water. In those days, if someone was saved on Sunday morning, he or she was automatically scheduled to be water-baptized that night during the evening service. But because I was only five years old, Brother Post wanted to make sure I had genuinely been saved that morning. When he saw that I really understood what I had done, he proceeded to prepare me for water baptism in the evening service.

I was so small as I was water-baptized that night, and Brother Post worried that no one in the auditorium would be able to see me in the baptistry. So he set up a metal folding chair for me to stand on. I walked down the steps into the baptismal waters, and he helped me up onto the folding chair. Suddenly, I could see all the people in the congregation and they could see me. Then I heard Brother Post say, "I baptize you in the name of the Father, and of the Son, and of the Holy Spirit." With that, he held my nose tightly shut and baptized me under the water.

## Hell Is a Real Place

That evangelist's message on hell just days before was the final push that caused me to respond to the altar call on that unforgettable Sunday morning. Today people rarely speak of hell, almost as if it no longer exists. But hell is a real place, and people go there every minute of every day.

The mere thought of a friend, relative, co-worker, or acquaintance going to hell should motivate us to do something to prevent that person from his or her eternal fate. That's why it's so imperative that the doctrine of hell be taught and preached from the pulpit. A revelation of hell puts a fire in believers' hearts to pray for the salvation of the unsaved and to ask God for opportunities to share the Gospel with them.

Jesus was so convinced of the need to convey hell's reality to people that He spoke about it in the four gospels *three times more* than He spoke about Heaven! And His apostles, after learning about hell from Jesus, passed on this painful truth to others as the Church was being established. As a result, the doctrine of hell is one of the central tenets and earliest creeds of the Church that we must hold fast to today.

Jesus taught so plainly about hell that this Bible doctrine became a driving force motivating early Christians to reach others with the life-changing message of the Gospel. Their belief in hell was deeply embedded in their hearts because *Christ Himself* planted it there! And as a result of Jesus' profound and revelatory teaching on hell, the early believers embraced a responsibility to "go" with the Gospel to rescue the unsaved — to do all they could to keep them from passing into eternity in a lost state.

Since Jesus spoke so explicitly about hell and since scriptures throughout the Bible do the same, how is it possible that this vital and eternal subject is so ignored? I am convinced this subject is ignored because the thought of hell is so horrific that people feel uncomfortable talking about it. People would rather talk about Heaven than hell because thoughts about Heaven are much more pleasant to contemplate. But we need to be reminded that hell is a real place and that family and friends will go there if they do not receive Christ.

That message on hell didn't hurt me. God used it to bring me to the altar!

## A Glorious Beginning and an Unfortunate Ending — a Minister Commits Suicide

I was gloriously saved at the age of five in 1963 just a week after that revival meeting concluded at our church. That was the pivotal moment when I knew I had to come to Christ. As a result, the question of eternity was forever settled for me. God used that evangelist and his fiery message to give me *a glorious beginning*!

But the evangelist who so dramatically affected my life became despondent years later because he felt he had little lasting fruit to show for his ministry. As he slipped deeper into depression, he was consumed with thoughts that his life had been of no consequence. In tormented despair, he tragically chose to end his life because he wrongly thought he had not borne any real fruit in his life's work.

But I was a part of that man's fruit! I was just a child when I got saved — *but children don't remain children!* I grew up, answered the call of God, and received His miraculous touch on my life to touch the nations of the earth with the Gospel and the teaching of the Bible.

Yet that man ended his life thinking his ministry had been fruitless. No doubt, he had brought others to Christ who continued in the faith, their eternities also sealed and their lives lived as wonderful testaments of a God who saves. But I know for certain that my life is fruit credited to this man's account, and it is fruit that *remains*.

## The Holy Spirit the Marvelous Reminder

I'm sharing this because I want you to hear something very important. There are moments when we all question whether our lives have been worthwhile. Often the devil torments us and tempts us to believe the lie that we have lived in vain. I am very aware that many people combat hopeless thoughts that they haven't made a difference in anyone else's life.

If that describes you, don't move too fast and judge yourself wrongly. If you'll wait, in time you'll see fruit that you are unaware of right now. You have touched more people than you realize. You may not be able to see it right now, but the fruit is out there nonetheless. I am an example of what I am telling you. Fruit that is hidden for a season is fruit just the same.

That minister believed that his life had no lasting fruit. But in the annals of Heaven, my salvation and the fruit that has been reaped in my own ministry will partially be attributed to *his* ministry. I am so thankful for his fruit that was reaped in my salvation and, subsequently, in my life and ministry. But that man ended his life thinking he had no fruit to show for it! Although I'm sure he had a lot of fruit besides me — because he touched so many people — if I was the only fruit he ever reaped, it made his life fruitful in the eyes of God.

Hebrew 6:10 (*NLT*) says, "…God is not unjust. He will not forget how hard you have worked for him and how you have shown your love to him by caring for other believers, as you still do." In times when you're tempted to overlook or forget what God has done through you, that's a good moment to ask the Holy Spirit to show you what Heaven remembers! You may be having a memory problem right now, but God never forgets. He is the Marvelous Reminder, and He will reveal it to you — *just ask Him!* He'll give you a brighter picture of your life than the one the devil is trying to show you.

## Grandpa's Garage and 'Gossip Central'

News of suicide would visit our family again, closer to home this time, and I write about that in Chapter Four. But right now, I want to talk about early life with my extended family, in particular, life with Grandpa and Grandma Renner. In words and deeds, these grandparents sowed into my life and character in my formative years, making impressions on my young soul that would last forever. In a very real sense, I was their fruit too.

Although we were not perfect, our home and family life was one of stability, security, and love. In those earlier years, our family of five lived two blocks away from Grandpa and Grandma Renner, and almost every day, I'd go visit my precious grandparents on my father's side of the family.

When I'd arrive at the back gate, I'd always yell out, *"Grandpa!"* — knowing he was probably somewhere in the backyard or in his garage doing something interesting and fun. When he heard my voice, Grandpa would always appear from seemingly nowhere to cheerfully open the gate so I could follow him to see what he was doing. I loved to sit with my grandpa on the back porch of their house eating homemade ice cream and listening attentively to stories of his own childhood in Germany.

Grandpa always seemed to be working on something new in his meticulously laid-out garage — a wonderland of treasures unlike any garage I'd ever seen. He had a rock collection he kept there, and I remember that he gave his favorite rock a whimsical name that I can't remember, but I thought it was fun that he did that. He had all kinds of other collectibles — and an impressive array of tools besides! The memories of times spent in that garage were warm, but would become bittersweet as we will see in Chapter Four.

Grandpa was a master with his hands, and he was always making something for someone. When Ronda was a teenager, he built her a phone booth that was quite impressive. He also built a second-story addition to their house by himself. He was a woodworking *"wonder man"* to me — it seemed there was *nothing* he couldn't do.

Grandma Renner was a master seamstress who could sew anything without a pattern. You could just show her a picture and tell her what you wanted and she could make it. She was also an amazing cook. Often on

Sundays, we'd all go to their house for lunch after morning church services. She always served lunch on fine china that was creatively set up on an exquisite tablecloth.

Grandma was an immaculate housekeeper, and inside their home, the familiar saying held true that you could have eaten off the kitchen floor! My grandparents were both such people of order, and they worked hard for the lives they were blessed to enjoy, though they were never very rich.

When I'd visit Grandpa and Grandma nearly every day, our routines were predictable, yet enthralling nonetheless. Grandpa would be busy in his yard or garage, and Grandma would be busy inside sewing or cooking — *or* talking on the telephone.

Grandma and Grandpa Renner had a beige rotary telephone that sat right next to a notebook filled with the names and phone numbers of Grandma Renner's friends. I remember her spinning that dial around clockwise several times with her pencil and then waiting patiently for someone to answer on the other end. She'd say, *"Hello, _____ — this is Ethel…,"* and within a minute or two, it began sounding like "Gossip Central."

Grandma Renner was a sweet woman, but she gossiped about everyone in the neighborhood and in the church. It was something Grandma seemed as committed to as Grandpa was to woodworking! As soon as one phone conversation ended, she'd pick up her pencil, put the eraser end into the circle openings on the rotary dial, and begin dialing the next girlfriend on the list to start the whole gossipy conversation over again.

There was Grandpa working contentedly in the garage minding his own business while Grandma was in hot pursuit of knowing everyone else's business! As much as I loved Grandma, it was just a fact that she was continually repeating what she had just heard from someone else and expressing her opinions about people's personal issues that were really none of her business.

Because of my decades in the ministry and my experiences in life, I shudder to think how many people's reputations have been stained, jaded, or even *ruined* because of information spread person-to-person by those who didn't know what they were talking about or who really had nothing to do with the matter. Even if those loose-tongued individuals thought they had good "inside information," it was none of their business, and it was wrong to spread that information to others.

In Second Corinthians 12:20, Paul used the word "whisperings," which is from a Greek word that depicts these whisperers as *gossipers*. They "whisper" behind closed doors — or in Grandma Renner's case, on the telephone while no one else was watching — because they inwardly know that what they're doing is inappropriate. They whisper tidbits of information in secret because if they did it publicly, they know they would be corrected or earn themselves a bad reputation. That is why the Holy Spirit in Second Corinthians 12:20 calls a gossip a "whisperer."

I can still hear kindhearted Grandpa Renner saying, "Ethel, come on. That's enough!" That whole scenario that played itself out time and time again really affected me, but it affected me *positively*. It positively caused me to determine that I would not be guilty of gossiping in secret about things that are none of my business or about things that I do not have the power to change. If I'm not invited by the person involved in the situation to discuss it or share it with others, why should my tongue wag about it? That's a pretty good philosophy to live by — and it is thoroughly rooted in Scripture!

Grandma Renner was a wonderful grandmother with many marvelous traits, but this habit of gossiping wasn't one of them. But I loved both Grandpa and Grandma Renner so much! I usually went to see them every afternoon, spending endless hours talking to Grandma about our family history or to Grandpa as he told me stories from his days in Germany.

Then on Sundays, Lori and I would usually sit with our grandparents on their pew at the back of the church. My precious Grandpa Renner gave his life to Christ after he came here from Germany, and he loved to attend church. *And* he loved to sing hymns! I always got a kick out of how he would belt them out with all his German heart!

As I've talked to other people over the years, I've come to realize that our long list of grandparents is unusual compared to other families. Most people didn't grow up with *six grandmothers* and *three grandfathers*. For example, Denise only knew *one grandmother* that she was only able to visit one weekend a year. And Denise never met any of her grandfathers. But we Renner kids had *a whole slew* of grandparents!

Grandpa and Grandma Renner, Grandma Ettie and Buddy, and Grandma Bagley all lived within minutes of us. My mother's father Earl and his fifth wife, Grandma Jo, lived about an hour away. Grandmother Faulkner lived in various hotels in downtown Tulsa, as I already shared, and we almost never knew what hotel she was living in at the moment. Buddy's mother, Grandma Cora, lived in Westville on her large piece of Indian acreage. Most of our grandparents lived nearby, so we saw a lot of them every week.

Eventually Grandpa Renner got a job as the chief building engineer at First Baptist Church in downtown Tulsa — the biggest church in Tulsa back in those days, and it was a very prestigious church. First Baptist Church was growing so much back then that it needed space for growth, but in the downtown area, there was no available space. So the church purchased the Wells Hotel, which was an old hotel built during the oil-boom days that shared a common wall with the church property. Not only was Grandpa Renner placed in charge of that building, but they moved him and Grandma Renner into the big penthouse with an elevator that opened right into their living room!

When First Baptist church bought the old Wells Hotel, as a part of the renovation process to turn it into Sunday School space, they had to get rid of most of the hotel's furnishings. So Grandpa loaded his truck and moved the exquisite furniture, books, and art that the church gave him to their home in west Tulsa, which they kept while simultaneously residing at what had been the Wells Hotel. Among those furnishings were remarkable antiques, including a hand-carved hutch dating to 1762, a hand-carved desk, library bookshelves, original paintings, and three hand-carved throne chairs with pedestaled feet and leg and arm pieces made of swirled wood.

Because Grandpa and Grandma Renner had just built a new second-story addition to their house on the Sand Springs Line, Grandpa used those "throwaways" to decorate the entire second floor. Grandpa and Grandma's home became such a fascinating museum of beautiful handmade furniture, exquisite needlework and crafts, and antiques, including antiquated books, which I especially loved. I loved Grandpa Renner's office the best and relished every moment I spent there examining *and re-examining* his hand-carved desk and all the other treasures he had on display there.

What good memories we Renner kids also had of Grandpa and Grandma Renner's time in the penthouse at the Wells Hotel! The property had a full-time elevator operator, an African American man named Leslie, whom I loved — and he loved me. The elevator was one of those old ones with a lattice gated door that he could push open or shut, and it had a hand-operated lever he would switch back and forth to direct the elevator to the floor of choice. He sat on a tall stool, dressed like a gentleman, and would give Ronda and me extended rides *up and down, down and up* as if it was his full-time job to entertain us on that old elevator!

## Divine Order Prepared Me for My Divine Call

I spent so much time with my Grandpa and Grandma Renner that I couldn't help but observe and learn from their lives, and I'm so thankful for every minute I could spend with them.

One thing I observed was that the discipline and order so characteristic of my Grandpa and Grandma Renner could not help but influence and pass its way to their son, my father, who in turn passed it on to *his* children — my two sisters and me. It was no accident indeed that our own household, with my father at the helm, was marked by these very traits. For example, our yard always looked carefully manicured. Our front yard was a smooth carpet of green that beckoned a lot of attention in the neighborhood, and our back yard could claim that same integrity and workmanship.

Even Christmas mornings were orderly in the Ronald Renner household. Before the first gift was ever opened by Ronda, Lori, and me, Daddy and Mother's morning coffee had been percolated, its bold aroma traveling down the hallway to our bedrooms like a silent alarm clock summoning us to the living area where gift-opening would soon begin.

Oversized trash bags, along with scissors for cutting tightly knotted ribbon from our presents, were set in place around our decorated tree that was shrouded with icicle tinsel like a fuzzy aluminum cape. Of course, Daddy's Brownie 8mm camera was on hand to film the entire event.

*Then we would begin.* One gift was unwrapped by one child, documented by Daddy's movie camera for posterity, and then all the paper was properly placed in the trash before the next sibling would have his or her turn, repeating the process with logistical precision, but thrilling delight nonetheless. My daddy orchestrated this otherwise chaotic Christmas-morning event with the skill of a tenured engineer. Order was simply the Renner way.

These are memories I *cherish*. I learned doctrine from my mother that placed a solid foundation beneath my feet. But this trademark characteristic of order that I observed from my father prepared me to labor effectively in the ministry God has given me today.

My parents' example provided me the wherewithal to build a life that eternity promises to crown with reward. I'm not saying that those who weren't privileged to grow up as I did can't travel this same blessed path, for through their submission to divine authority — to the governance of God and His Word — indeed they can. I'm simply saying with deepest gratitude that, *together*, my mother and father groomed my sisters and me all our young lives to live for Christ and to follow His plan with excellence.

Without doubt, I am the byproduct of all that my family poured into me.

## Stopping the Rampage of Divorce!

But that's not all my parents did for my sisters and me. They also — and perhaps most importantly — broke the horrible cycle of divorce and division that "haunted" our family line for *generations*. As you've already discovered, our family was historically *riddled* with divorce.

- Grandma Renner was married two times.

- Grandma Faulkner was married five times.

- Grandpap Miller was married four times.

- Grandma Ettie was married two times.

Add it up and you'll see there were thirteen marriages between these four grandparents — and besides these, there were divorces and remarriages in other parts of the family too.

As a child, I could still feel the traumatic effects that divorce had on my mother and her siblings. Even I could sense moments of tension between various combinations of grandparents who used to be married to each other, but who now each had different spouses. As grandkids, we were careful about what we could say, what we couldn't say, telling where we had been, whom we had visited, where we were going, or whom were we going to see.

Sometimes as a child, I even got confused about who was a "real" grandparent and who was not. And those who were not original grandparents, but rather grandparents by second marriages, etc., what *were* they? And why did I have to call them Grandpa and Grandma?

For example, was Buddy my grandfather, a friend, or just my Grandma Ettie's husband? Who was he?

Or how about Grandma Jo? We kids didn't like her very much, but she was my Grandpap Miller's fourth wife, so she was *someone* to us — but *who*?

Then there was Melva, my mother's step-sister from one of her father's marriages prior to Grandma Ettie. How did she fit into the picture? And was my mother's step-sister's son my cousin — or who *was* he to me in the grand scheme of things?

*Such confusion!* And then there was the shock of finally learning that the parents of Grandma Renner's first husband — her ex-in-laws — lived just one block from the home of her and Grandpa Renner! That we drove right past that house every day for the longest time without knowing who lived there made it an even more shocking discovery.

What a mess all of it was. But it hit home the hardest to know how negatively the divorce of my mother's parents, Grandma Ettie and Grandpap Earl, affected my mother and her siblings when they were children. They rarely saw their father. And for a time, my mother was even separated from her sister and brother and moved to Texas where she lived with her Aunt Marie. Although my mother's Aunt Marie taught Mother so much about Christian service — hospitality, follow-up, and other pastoral skills — it was nevertheless a painful time of separation. The pain and brokenness that go along with divorce and all its endless ripple effects are simply devastating.

These childhood memories — with the confusion that came with visiting all those grandparents, especially around the holidays — helped me understand people who are from broken homes and are confronted with the realities of brokenness during the holidays. It's just a fact that holidays are not always easy to celebrate for people who have fragmented families.

This also makes me think of one aspect of Jesus' ministry that brings healing to those who deal with these kinds of painful memories. In Luke 4:18, Jesus said, "The Spirit of the Lord is upon me, because he hath anointed me to preach the gospel to the poor; he hath sent me *to heal the brokenhearted*, to preach deliverance to the captives, and recovering of sight to the blind, *to set at liberty them that are bruised*, to preach the acceptable year of the Lord."

I emphasized the phrases "to heal the broken hearted" and "to set at liberty them that are bruised" for a big reason: *Jesus is a Healer of those who have been brokenhearted and bruised in life!*

But what do these words really mean? The word "brokenhearted" is from a Greek word that described *the crushing of grapes* or *the smashing and grinding of bones into dust*. It depicts *people who have been walked on by others, who have been crushed by others,* or *who feel they have been smashed to pieces by life or relationships*. So the "brokenhearted" describes those who are emotionally shattered and smashed.

The phrase "set at liberty them that are bruised" is also so very important. The words "set at liberty" are translated from a word that describes *a release* or *a dismissal,* but in this case, it indicates *a permanent release from the detrimental effects of a shattered life*. The Greek here speaks of a permanent release from the destructive effects of brokenness.

The word "bruised" means *to crush* or *to break down*, and it depicts *a person who has been shattered or fractured by life* or *one whose life has been continually split up and fragmented*. It is the exact same Greek word where we get the word "trauma." By using this word, Jesus clearly said that he came to set at liberty — *to give permanent release* — to people who have been traumatized by life.

Divorce and its rippling effects cause people to feel brokenhearted and "bruised." Those who have been through divorce themselves — and the children and relatives of divorce — often feel like they have been walked on, crushed, or smashed to pieces by life. They are shattered and fractured, as if their lives have been split up and fragmented because of broken relationships.

## Jesus Healed Our Broken Family

That was precisely the catastrophic effects this rampage of divorce wreaked in our family for so long. These two phrases in Luke 4:18 well describe the situation I saw in my family when I was growing up. But in the end, Jesus healed every broken heart and bruised soul just as He promised He would do!

Maybe you are from a divided family. If so, these words could describe you and the shattered emotions you may be dealing with in the aftermath of a broken relationship. The anointing that is on Jesus is more than enough to release you from the adverse effects of your experience. Even though you were once broken by life, the Holy Spirit has the power to *release* you from this captivity that has held you in emotional bondage and to *restore* you to a healed and whole emotional state.

Although our own family was *filled* with the brokenness of collapsed relationships, God's powerful presence was enough to restore us amidst those failed covenants. There was no hate that I can remember, and people who were once at odds with each other eventually became congenial toward one another, even during the holidays. It was a true miracle of God's grace. It didn't fix the relationships and put them back in their original order, but the grace of God made them peaceable and livable for everyone.

But *finally*, the rampage of divorce in the Miller and Renner families came to *a grinding halt* when my daddy and mother got married — and when my mother's sister and her husband got married. It stopped because these two sisters, Erlita and Melita, "drew a line in the sand" and said, *"No more!"* Salvation had come into their families and marriages, and their families became ordered according to the Word of God. And that divine order brought divine blessing — deliverance, healing, and wholeness — to our families once again.

My mother's brother never completely recovered from the brokenness that afflicted his life due to his parent's divorce. But my mother and her sister — and their husbands, my daddy and my uncle — stood resolved to have godly marriages free of divorce, and it literally halted the rampage in our lineage. That does not mean their marriages were perfect, but these souls were committed to breaking the curse of divorce on our family. And they did it. *It was BROKEN!*

## Training by 'Doing'

As I shared earlier in this chapter, Mother was a Sunday School teacher, a department director in the church, and she sang in the choir. Daddy was involved in the choir, in church team sports, and he even served as the church janitor for a season. As I shared, my first "official" job was helping my father clean the church on Saturday. He paid me 25 cents a week, and for that big salary, I was privileged to scrub all the scuff marks from the linoleum tiles on the second floor of the educational building.

Almost every week as Daddy dispatched me up the stairs to get me started scrubbing those tiles, he'd say, "Ricky, this place is where God's people come to learn, serve, and worship. We need to make sure it looks the very best for them. We're doing this for the Lord, so put as much *elbow grease* into it as you can and make those floors shine for God's people when they show up on Sunday morning!"

Those were formative moments in my life that still have an effect on me today. From that early age, my dad instilled in me that what we do for God should be the best we can do. Nothing second-class or second-best for Jesus will do. It reminds me of Colossians 3:17 where Scripture commands us, "…Whatsoever ye do in word or deed, do all in the name of the Lord Jesus…" — and also Colossians 3:22 that tells us not to serve "…with eyeservice, as menpleasers; but in singleness of heart, fearing God."

Both of our parents taught Ronda, Lori, and me from a young age that serving Jesus in the local church was *a priority* and *a privilege* in life. They also taught us — and the church taught us too — that the Great Commission was God's personal charge to each of us and that we were to use our lives to influence others for Christ and to bring people to the saving knowledge of Jesus.

My parents didn't use "lip service" when they talked about being faithful. They *showed* us what it meant to be faithful by never allowing us to even entertain a thought of missing church and by teaching us to keep our word to do whatever we had promised to do for the Lord.

Our life was literally in the church — in Sunday School, Sunday-morning services, Training Union, Wednesday-night services, visitation, evangelism, softball, football, basketball, bowling, Sunday-night services, and fellowships at various homes. And all of us Renner kids attended youth camp and Vacation Bible School every summer as well. This was the only life we knew.

All the foundation of my spiritual life was formed at home and at the church. I learned to respect my pastor. I learned to respect spiritual authority. I learned to respect the authority of the Bible. I learned to love the lost. And I learned there was nothing more important than serving God. Most of who I am today is the result of what I learned from my parents and my local church.

### How To Train a Child's Spiritual Taste Buds

What parents establish as a priority in the lives of their children when they are young will stay with them when they are older. The Bible confirms this truth in Proverbs 22:6, where it instructs parents to "train up a child in the way he should go: and when he is old, he will not depart from it."

In the Hebrew language, the word "train" is connected with one's *taste buds*. Specifically, it depicts parents who start their children out early eating foods that are healthy, such as fruits, vegetables, whole grains, and lean meats. When those kids are full-grown, they will return to eating those same nutritious foods. On the other hand, if parents train their children's taste buds with junk foods, when those kids are grown, their appetites will continually be drawn back to those same nutrient-deficient foods they were conditioned to eating when they were young.

So when God says, "Train up a child in the way he should go: and when he is old, he will not depart from it," He is actually saying, "Give your children healthy spiritual taste buds at a young age. Give them an appetite for the things of God when they are young, and when they are older, they won't depart from it." What you condition their spiritual taste buds to eat when they are young is what they will continually be drawn to when they are older.

If you make regular church attendance important to your children when they're young, it will be important to them when they are older. Likewise, if you make reading the Bible, praying, giving tithes and offerings, and serving in the church a priority, these practices will likely be the focus of their lives when they're grown and start families of their own.

I also encourage you to read illustrated Bible stories to your children or grandchildren from the time they are toddlers through the growing stages of their lives. It is one of the most rewarding habits you can develop with them. Throughout their lives, they will remember the colorful images they saw, the foundational truths they gleaned from every story, and the time they spent with you learning and growing.

In the same way, creating a library of godly entertainment — books, music, and video — that is filled with God's Word can help instill His Word deep in their hearts that will continue to "play in their ears" throughout their adult lives. That is what my mother did with me, *and it really worked.*

Every verse of Scripture, every Bible story, and every song of praise and worship your children hear will help hide God's Word in their hearts and give the Holy Spirit truth to draw from to teach them throughout their lifetime. Concerning His Word, God said it "…shall not return unto me void, but it shall accomplish that which I please, and it shall prosper in the thing whereto I sent it" (Isaiah 55:11). If you consistently plant the Word into the hearts and minds of your children or grandchildren, it will produce a harvest in every area of their lives and in the lives of those they touch.

It is the parents' job to create an environment conducive to training up their children in the ways of God. If you're in the stage of life when you're raising children, I encourage you to take them to church regularly. Start reading the Bible to them when they are very young and teach them to read it for themselves when they are older. Have family devotionals that are age-appropriate and relevant to what they are experiencing in their lives. Encourage them to develop their closest friendships with other Christian kids.

Left to themselves, children are not going to choose to read and study the Bible, go to church, or serve others. On the contrary, they will naturally gravitate toward a self-centered life absent of God. But if you consistently educate your kids in spiritual matters and do your best to connect them in a personal relationship with Jesus, you are setting them up for success in every area of their adult lives.

I'm thankful for the spiritual foundation my parents built underneath me through consistent training that I could build my adult life upon. My life was certainly not perfect, and Satan set his sights on me to tear down my life before God even began to use it, as you will see. But I did not have to tear out a weak foundation later, as many do, and start all over spiritually.

Thank God, wherever a person is in life, he or she *can* start all over and redeem the time. But if you have the opportunity to invest in your children's lives *right now*, make the most of that divine opportunity to train their "taste buds," lay the groundwork for their future, and set them on the right spiritual course.

## Something Was Missing in My Life

Not only were we Renners serious about being Christians, we were also seriously committed to the Southern Baptist Convention — the denomination to which we belonged. I can honestly say *we were Baptist to our bones!* We lived our lives by the Bible and by our doctrine — that is whatever was written in the "Baptist Faith and Message," the Statement of Faith of our denomination.

Every Sunday as I was growing up, I saw my pastor, Brother Post, faithfully preach the Gospel of Jesus Christ. Each week with great conviction, compassion, and boldness, he unflinchingly proclaimed the death and resurrection of Jesus. His presentation of the Gospel was no-nonsense, unapologetic, clear-cut, compelling, and persuasive. It not only dramatically affected me at a young age, but it still has a formidable influence on my thinking and my philosophy of ministry today.

It is unfortunate that the preaching of the Cross has become more and more a rare occurrence in the local church. I thank God that I had a pastor who faithfully drove the truth of the Cross into my heart and soul, helping me to cherish the Cross and the great price Jesus paid for me. Brother Post's commitment to preach this never wavered — indeed, it is the most important message the world will ever hear. As a result, when I was growing up, I saw many people genuinely repent and come to a saving knowledge of Jesus Christ at the altars of our church.

It has been many decades since I sat under the ministry of my childhood pastor. But I would be remiss if I didn't express how thankful I am that God used this precious man to teach me that leading a soul to Christ is the most important eternal act I can do.

As I have stood before audiences in meetings around the world, it has now become *my* responsibility to call sinners to repentance and the backslidden to recommitment. As I do, I often remember how my pastor stood before us to give his altar calls. I can still hear his voice as he would walk the aisles and passionately beg people to make their hearts right with God. And God used one of those altar calls to beckon me to salvation.

There is no doubt that today, at least in part, I mirror the example my pastor lived before me as I grew up in our church. I know that when we all stand before Jesus, much of what has been accomplished through my life and ministry will be credited to my pastor's account because he was so instrumental in helping form who I am and what I believe today.

However, the official position of our denomination in those days was that the gifts of the Holy Spirit that were a part of the Early Church in its formative years had passed away with the death of the first apostles. Because we didn't believe in the manifestations of these spiritual gifts in this present day, we basically deemed the whole lot of Pentecostals and Charismatics to be doctrinally off-base. We believed that whatever it was that they were claiming to experience, those experiences were merely foolish, made-up works of the flesh based on bad doctrine and a mishandling of Scripture.

The word "charismatic" was pretty new in those days. Those people were largely still called Pentecostals. And to my young brain, Pentecostals were people with long dresses, long sleeves, long hair, buns on their head, no makeup, no joy — *yet* who occasionally swung on chandeliers and rolled in the aisles. From everything I had picked up from the attitude of our spiritual leaders, they were just unstable people promoting bad doctrine.

I picked up this same attitude toward Pentecostals because of all I'd ever heard about them. And just around the corner from Glenwood Baptist Church was the Glenwood Full Gospel Church, which, of course, was Pentecostal. I remember thinking how much I wished they would drop the name "Glenwood" so no one would associate us with them!

When our family drove past that Full Gospel church on our way to church on Sundays, I felt pity for that congregation of believers because I had been given the impression that Pentecostals were a lesser-class group of Christians, and I believed they were doctrinally uneducated, spiritually unstable, easily beguiled souls — *with weird hairdos*!

But eventually a time came in my spiritual journey when my heart began to yearn for more. My heart was established on God's Word, but deep within, my heart also yearned for a deeper encounter with Him. Yes, I could have passed a doctrine test, but I was becoming hungry for God in a brand-new way. Something was missing from my life, and my hunger and search for that "something missing" led me to an unlikely encounter that changed my life completely and set me free from the inward isolation and *torments* of childhood that I share about in the last sections of this chapter.

### All Was Not Well — I Was a Child
### Who Was Struggling Inwardly

The memories I hold dear from my childhood at Glenwood are truly warm memories of some of the very best times I experienced in my young life. But as I grew older, still in my elementary-aged and junior-high years, all was not so well with little Ricky Renner.

In fact, an inward struggle began in my life that was quite serious, and the torment I experienced as I wrestled with mental and spiritual bombardment was almost intolerable.

Because I was just a child and didn't know how to express what I felt, *or to whom to express it*, thoughts that I was a misfit and out of place — unaccepted at best and rejected at worst — *plagued* my mind continually. "Plague" is a good word because those thoughts swathed *widespread* across my mind and continued their onslaught in wave after wave, for years, until I was almost too weak to withstand them or fight back.

### Fitting Into My Father's World

What I am about to describe to you in the following pages is about *me* and is not a commentary about my precious daddy's fathering skills.

My daddy did the very best he could to be a fabulous father. In retrospect, I can see he didn't want the disconnect between himself and me that he'd experienced with his own father. So naturally, he wanted to involve me at an early age in the things that were dear to him — and two of those things were sports and fishing.

Our church hosted *a lot* of extra-curricular activities that included softball games, football games, basketball games, and even a church bowling league. In essence, my daddy loved every sport that revolved around a ball. For example, Daddy was a master at bowling, and every week, he and Mother participated in the church bowling league. My memories at the bowling alley start so early that I can remember when Lori and I played in the bowling-alley nursery while Daddy and Mother bowled with their friends. From the nursery, we could hear bowling balls crashing against the pins and then being recovered to the ball return and racked into place for the next bowler. Howls of joy and laughter would erupt each time someone bowled a strike — and strikes were regular occurrences when my daddy was at the top of his game.

Really, my father was a consummate athlete who excelled in every sport he put his hand to. From any kind of sport *involving any kind of ball* to fishing and almost anything pertaining to the outdoors, my father's athleticism was true giftedness — he was *a natural*!

Besides his prowess at the bowling alley, Daddy was the pitcher on the church softball team, and they played every week during softball season at New Block Park on Tulsa's west side. Every week, all five of us in our family — along with our dearest friends from church — would march through the ivy-covered gate at the softball field, our water coolers and bags of snacks in tow. Then we'd make our way up into the bleachers and take our regular seats to watch husbands and dads play their games. We'd scatter all over the bleachers to settle in, sitting on blankets and eating our snacks. Wives yelled at the top of their lungs as they rooted for the guys on their team. And we each held on to our numbered tickets and waited with anticipation to see whose number would be called to win a free gallon of Borden's Ice Cream each week!

As a child, I spent countless hours at that softball field watching our men's team practice and play — *and practice and play some more*! I was so disinterested during practices that I spent most of my time looking for frogs or lizards under the bleachers, the boisterous exchanges of camaraderie between my dad and his teammates faintly echoing in my focused, treasure-hunter brain.

The men at our church didn't stop with bowling and softball. They also played football and basketball, both of which included similar rituals of their family of fans tagging along as cheerleaders at those weekend games. Indeed, there was no rest from sports in our small community as one season seemed to flow right into the next.

I now know it wasn't true, but in my very young mind, it appeared that a boy's masculinity was proven by his participation in sports. After all, that's what all the men around me did. Even when we weren't at a game, it seemed all the guys were watching some kind of sports on TV or talking about some game they had seen — everyone, that is, but me.

I never liked sports. Actually, I didn't just *dislike* sports; I *hated* sports. I detested being dragged into any game that required my participation to throw, catch, hit, kick, carry, or bowl a ball. Of course, I know now that not every young man enjoys sports — and that the love of sports is not a requirement for manhood. But every spring, summer, fall, and winter, all my young mind knew was what it saw — softball, football, basketball, and bowling. So in my ignorance, I had no valid argument against the accusing thoughts that were penetrating my beliefs that, *Ricky Renner, you are so WEIRD!*

I can't begin to express what a conflict this created inside me in such a sports-loving context — and I felt *out* of context. I wondered, *What is WRONG with me? Why do I not like what all the other guys like? Where do I fit in?* And, unfortunately, I would answer myself: *Nowhere at all. You don't fit in anywhere.*

This wasn't a one-time conversation I had with myself. These thoughts pounded mercilessly at my young brain like pelting rain on a tender young plant. I felt like such a misfit because of this looming, *gargantuan* issue of sports, which seemed to dominate our lives at Glenwood Baptist and life on the Sand Springs Line.

Because I wasn't even mildly interested in any sport and began to feel more and more isolated from all the boys my age who *were* interested and involved in these activities, the devil began to launch a full-scale attack against my life — against my soul and my identity. *What IS wrong with you?* I'd hear over and over again in my mind, and I could not make it stop.

I didn't know at the time that it was the devil attacking me. And I certainly didn't know how to stand against him. Instead, I wrestled internally, and over time, I embraced — *truly believed* — that there was something defective within me. And there hiding in the shadows, behind the scenes, the devil was obliged to tell me I was right.

As I already noted, in my growing-up years, people were fairly ignorant of the devil and the reality of spiritual warfare. And it wasn't just our family and our church — it seems *all* people (at least all the people I knew) were ignorant of this subject in those days. Just to give you an idea of how spiritually illiterate we were on this topic, on Halloween each year, our parents dressed us up as spooks — witches, monsters, and goblins — and we walked the streets to knock on doors and say, "Trick or treat!" with no thought that dressing up like the devil might not be a good idea.

Halloween was such a time of celebration for us that in the weeks leading up to this dark holiday. I would draw jack-o-lanterns, witches, and other popular Halloween figures and cut them out of colorful construction paper — but mostly black, especially for the screeching black cats and the witches poised for flight on their brooms. Then I'd carefully Scotch-Tape those images all over our big living-room window that faced our street so the whole neighborhood could enjoy my handiwork.

On Halloween night, my sisters and I would excitedly don our costumes — I was usually a black-and-white skeleton or a red devil complete with pitchfork and tail — and we'd set off anticipating a big night of fun. With huge brown-paper grocery sacks in hand, we'd walk the neighborhood along with what felt like an ocean of neighborhood kids. Systematically, we'd move door to door shouting, "Trick or treat!" as neighbors dropped generous helpings of candy into our bags. When our bags were filled, we'd head home to empty them and rush right back out to start over again.

Looking back on those times, I am simply amazed that we thought dressing like the devil and demons was funny. *But we truly never even considered it.* Of course, we would never do that today because we know the devil is *not* funny. But, as I said, most people didn't have a revelation about the devil or the seriousness of spiritual warfare in those days.

When you were a kid, did you walk the neighborhood on Halloween? Would you let your kids or grandchildren do it today? Probably not, because now most of us know better! Nevertheless, it was all sort of a joke to us in those days.

If anyone ever did talk seriously about the devil when I was a young boy, we dismissed that person as having a mental issue. I distinctly remember a woman in our church saying she was being mentally tormented by the devil. Rather than pray for her, we laughed and told jokes about it, assuming she was crazy. And some even suggested she see a psychiatrist!

My point is, we were so ignorant of these things that when the devil began to silently pound my own mind, I never imagined that it was him who was assaulting me and my identity. But it was a *brutal* assault intended to stop me and take me down before I ever really got started in life.

## Awkward and *'Different'*

Others around me back then may argue today that it wasn't true, but I always felt different from the other kids in our church. Although I ran and played boisterously with other children around the church grounds and along those railroad tracks that were such a big part of our lives, I inwardly felt awkward and out of place. I had a few close friends who were really dear to me, but generally I didn't feel like I fit in. I don't think it was anyone's fault in particular — I just felt different from the rest of the gang. And to me, "different" could only mean one thing: *Something was wrong with me.*

Some of the differences between my peers and me stemmed from my spiritual hunger that preoccupied me at times to the exclusion of everything else. But by far, the biggest struggle with my self-image was over the issue of sports — an issue that made me feel isolated from my friends and that tormented me endlessly. I also felt like a constant disappointment to my father because of my complete lack of interest. Every sport captured my father's interest and *no sport* captured mine. By involving me in all his activities, my father was trying to bridge with me the disconnect he felt with his own father as he grew up — but he built that bridge with a ball and a bat! Our failure to connect through sports was discouraging to him, I'm sure — but, although he in no way intended it, it was *devastating* to me.

I simply wasn't fashioned that way. Trying to interest me in sports was like forcing the proverbial square peg into a round hole. With every stroke of the "hammer" — or in my case, with every sound of a ball contacting a bat, a glove, or a bowling pin — attempts to coax or convert me were awkward and painful. My interests were in fine art, antiques, and museums. I liked to draw, paint, listen to classical music, and visit museums of almost any kind.

And I liked history — I *really* liked history!

But what "normal" boy from my part of the world liked all these things and favored them over spending long days and evenings at the softball field, bowling alley, or gym? I felt like the things I loved and leaned toward were out of sync for kids growing up between the tracks where we lived.

As I grew older, I'd go to the Philbrook Museum of Art every Tuesday night because the watercolorists would set up their easels so that visitors could come and watch them paint. I could hardly wait to get there each week! I would watch in wonder as they turned a blank canvas into something magnificent. I'd walk from easel to easel, not wanting to miss a single masterpiece that so brilliantly came to life from these artists' imaginations every Tuesday night.

No one ever intended to make me feel it, but I really felt like a "weirdo" among most of my friends. I'd try to tell my buddies how much I loved to go to the Philbrook or Gilcrease museums, two world-class museums in Tulsa that were filled with fine art, sculpture, and history. But when I would express my elation, they seemed puzzled and would sort of stare at me — at a loss for words — as if I were from another planet. I knew they liked me, but I often felt like they didn't know what to do with me. As a result, I felt often tolerated rather than appreciated and enjoyed.

I deeply related to the animated character Rudolph in the Christmas television classic *Rudolph, the Red-Nosed Reindeer*, which first aired in December 1964 — I was just six years old at the time. But even at that early age, I so identified with Rudolph as the *odd man out* among his peers that I not only felt sympathy as I watched, but — right along with that "anomaly" of a reindeer that struggled with his identity — I felt a personal pang of rejection as the movie's plot poignantly unfolded before my young eyes. Even today, if I watch that classic movie, I still feel the tinge of anguish that I felt as a boy at being so misunderstood, disregarded, and unesteemed for who I truly was at my core.

To confirm my misbeliefs and my worst fears that I'd be an outlier for the rest of my life, if my parents let me go to the museum or attend a concert event, I was usually dropped off *alone*. And that "aloneness" became another voice that told me silently — and yet ever so loudly — that something was very wrong with me. The devil used people and circumstances to pound away at my mind, injecting a stream of thoughts that made me desperately wonder, *Why can't I be like everyone else?*

When I asked my parents if I could take oil-painting lessons, Daddy's face told me he was horrified that I would want to do such a thing. If I was misreading what I saw in his countenance with my eyes, my ears actually heard him tell Mother he didn't think it was "normal" for a boy my age to want to sit around the house painting. But Mother swayed Dad to let me take lessons twice a week, so soon I began taking private painting lessons.

*And WOW!* When a canvas was in front of me — with paint brush in hand and a palette before me to mix colors — I felt like fresh air and new life was being breathed into me! I felt so alive in that creative atmosphere. My teacher saw my desire, so she really focused as she taught me to paint. Soon I was painting landscapes, still life, and even portraits — and I relished every moment.

I also became very interested in antiques. While my friends were playing team sports or pick-up games of basketball or tag football, I was spending every free minute at the local antique shop that everyone else called the junk store. It, too, was located by the railroad tracks. I would go there to look for old Mason jars to add to my large collection. Glass jars were what I could afford, and I just loved them. I had blue ones, green ones, and if I could find amber — those were rare — that was a good shopping day! I loved everything about art and history.

Daddy, however, would not give up hope that he would turn me into a sportsman. He tried hard to draw me into some sport I might enjoy or learn to like. When he was a young man himself, he dreamed of playing professional baseball for the St. Louis Cardinals. He never fulfilled that aspiration, and he once told me he hoped that *I* would one day play for the Cardinals in fulfillment of his lifelong dream.

The added pressure of those words landed hard on top of my hatred for sports, and it further fueled my feelings of inadequacy and rejection. My father's dream became my nightmare. But I really wanted to please him, so I kept trying to manufacture a desire to play ball like all the other "normal" guys at church. But the desire never came. I only wanted to paint, visit museums, attend symphonies downtown, or do something of a creative nature.

My sister Ronda noted, "Even at a young age, Rick was a dreamer. He had big dreams and he'd tell us what they were. Even when he was ten or twelve years old, he was already having such big dreams. Because he loved to draw and paint, he would capture with his talent what he saw in his mind. He was actually doing this when he was still using crayons!

"Rick was constantly nurturing his dreams — speaking them out and finding ways to visually remind himself that they would come to pass one day. Principles of faith that we now understand were working in his life very early."

### My Dad Deserved an 'A' for Effort!

If anyone should get an "A" for effort, it would have been my dad! He kept trying and trying to help me be "normal" like all the other guys on the Sand Springs Line. I'm sure Daddy thought that one day, it would all "kick into gear" and I would love sports, so he kept putting me in sports league after sports league.

But when I played baseball, no one really wanted me on their team. They knew I wasn't interested. I can't count how many outfield balls I missed because I was looking for four-leaf clovers instead of paying attention to the game. When it was time for me to bat, I always struck out. I can imagine how frustrating this must have been for my dad who was a premier athlete and softball pitcher — and who had such dreams for his son to play professional baseball!

On defense, I'd grab my glove and take to the outfield looking for worn patches in the grass so that between plays I could slip in some art practice with my fingers in the sand. Glove in one hand and nature's brush in the other, I'd execute my master strokes with transported delight, oblivious to everything else around me. I could hold my own in the realm of brushing and blending, but my skills as a right-fielder were woefully inadequate.

When my father saw that his professional-baseball aspiration would be twice denied, he decided to give me a try at basketball to see if I'd do better there. Now, I don't want to offend those who like this sport, but as a kid I thought basketball was the stupidest game ever conceived. I remember thinking, *What fun could possibly be found in a bunch of sweaty guys screaming and chasing a ball in a stifling, air-tight gym?*

While waiting every week at the recreational center for basketball practice to start, I couldn't help but notice the art and pottery classes that were offered in an adjoining room to the gym where we practiced. I'd linger there at the window of that classroom as long as I could each week, peering in as the teacher taught students to marvelously transform primitive pieces of lumpy clay into beautiful pottery. Now *that* was impressive! But that wasn't what I was supposed to be impressed with, and the guys would have to practically drag me away from the window into the stinky gym where I didn't want to be.

The following year in the fall, Daddy decided to give me a try at football to see if I would show any interest in that sport. But the whole idea of football was abhorrent to me, and I dreaded every practice. I remember thinking to myself, *Who could possibly think it's fun to chase a pointed ball around a field and to hit and slam each other to the ground to the point of injury?* I know Americans are nuts about football, but from the very start of my young life in sports, I loathed it. To get out of playing football as quickly as possible, I performed as poorly as I knew how so Daddy would take me out of that sport. *I would have preferred a smelly gym where I couldn't breathe!*

Ronda later said, "Daddy never dreamed he would have a son not interested in sports. He was, like, *What is the world coming to if your son doesn't like baseball?* But years later when Rick started having success in the ministry, it got Daddy's attention, and he became very proud of Rick."

But in those early years, though my daddy dearly loved me, I am sure he didn't know what to do with me.

## An Attempt To Turn Me Into a Fisherman

I didn't make it in sports, but never one to concede defeat, Daddy thought he could turn me into a fisherman! My father *loved* fishing! He bought camping gear and would load it into his truck, hook up the boat, and off we'd go to the lake for a few days or a whole week with the guys from the church. I had to fight thoughts like, *How could anyone find it fun to sit in a boat in all kinds of freezing, raining, or blistering-hot temperatures for hours on end, hoping a fish will swim by and bite a hook with a worm or a minnow on it?*

Sure, it was fun if the fish were biting. But on our fishing trips, they usually were *not* biting. We would sit for hours in Daddy's boat in freezing temperatures in the winter or in the sweltering heat of Oklahoma summers.

Daddy would exclaim from time to time, "Isn't this great! Is there anything better than being out here on the water in the middle of nature?"

I didn't dare tell him what I really thought — not because I was afraid of him, but because I knew he wanted me to like fishing as much as he did, and I didn't want to disappoint him again. So the fact that I would have rather been visiting a museum or participating in some art class never came up in conversation.

One day when I couldn't bear the thought of sitting miserably for long, boring hours in a boat any longer, I did *the unthinkable* in a fisherman's world — something that *really* made me look like a freak in the eyes of the guys. Before one upcoming fishing trip, I brought a special bundle with me containing my canvas, paint brushes, oil paints, and turpentine! I even packed an easel to set up in the boat! While the other guys cast out their lines and lures hoping a bass would strike, I captured the scenery on canvas with equal excitement and anticipation of a great artistic "catch."

I'm certain those guys thought I was an oddball, and I don't blame them. That's what I thought about *myself*. I felt like such a misfit — that no matter how hard I tried, I simply didn't fit into the mold of "normal" for guys in my world.

Although my father dreamed of long afternoons fishing at the lake with me or playing catch at the softball field, it proved to be an elusive desire that I lacked the grace to fulfill. I was clumsy at every sport involving a ball, and although I tried to like fishing, my disdain for this activity couldn't be hidden or denied. I simply was not prone to be a sportsman *or* fisherman like Daddy wanted me to be.

If those guys in our sports and fishing groups from church read this book today, they may be taken aback to learn what a struggle all this was for me at that age in my life. But it was deeply what I felt. I want to encourage you that if you have a child who is a little different from his peers, if you'll ask God, He'll show you how to help that child find his way without making him feel he is wrong or "less than" for being different.

So often, young children struggle silently because they are not mature enough to understand what they are feeling, or because they do not know how to express it. This is why parents and grandparents need to pray for spiritual sensitivity to discern what is happening below the surface in the lives of children under their care.

Everyone sparkles a little differently in life, but everyone *does* sparkle, given the chance. It is God's design. So find your child's gifts and strengths and practice magnifying those things. It's all right if your child is different from you. He or she can have your same heart and same basic beliefs, but God fashioned and destined that child for a future that will be different from yours. Hence, He has gifted your child uniquely to be able to fulfill that divine call.

## My Daddy's Heart

Although the whole issue of sports drove me to such emotional despair, perhaps my precious daddy was also visited by despair. Not only was he trying so hard to deflect in our relationship the kind of disconnect he'd experienced with his own father, I'm sure he also genuinely wanted a fishing buddy and a sports pal, and he wanted that "buddy" and "pal" to be me.

In retrospect, I wonder at times if Daddy was a frustrated father because he could not instill in his only son a love for sports. Although he never completely recognized or grasped that I had other interests and talents that fell outside the boundaries of his world of sports, I think my lack of fondness for any sport whatsoever was as hard on him as it was on me. What disappointment and feelings of failure may have beset him to see other fathers having no such struggles. While their children happily participated in sports, my father must have sensed the great loss of the dream he'd held in his heart for the two of us. A father and son on the same team is a powerful experience that we both fell short of and missed out on although we loved each other dearly.

In my own heart, I knew Daddy really wanted to help me fit in with the other guys. But regardless of his "A" for effort and my trying so hard to please him with sports, I failed miserably each time. It caused me to struggle inwardly for years, doubting my worth. My father simply had a son who marched to a different drummer. God had given me the inner makings I needed for what I would be doing later in life — and, in hindsight, *none* of my future would be connected with sports *or* fishing. And nothing was wrong with me at all.

As much as I'd like to say my torment was short-lived, I cannot. My inner struggles didn't last for just a short season and then suddenly resolve themselves. Instead, the war that raged within — telling me that I was a complete misfit — assailed for years, giving me no hope of escape. In my mind, I would forever be the *unlikely* "Rudolph the red-nosed reindeer" in his rejected and unwanted condition, and that was all there was to it.

Because we didn't possess a great understanding of the enemy's plots and schemes in those days — and because I was young and didn't know how to express my fears and struggles — it became *a perfect storm* of the devil's attack on my life. Those storm winds got worse before they got better, and I would have likely succumbed to them if Jesus, by the power of the Holy Spirit, hadn't rescued me. I talk about that next!

'Just as Clark Kent would enter a phone booth
as a normal man, but astoundingly emerge as Superman,
I, too, was instantly *changed* into a new young man. Of
course, Clark Kent and Superman are fictional characters,
but nothing about what happened to me was fictional.
God's power literally manifested as the force of an
army to sweep over enemy lines and reclaim
the territory — *me and my mind* — that
had belonged to Him the entire time!'

# 3

# AN UNLIKELY ENCOUNTER

In 1969 my dad decided to upgrade our living conditions, so he moved our family of five away from the Sand Springs Line to a small town west of Tulsa, also called Sand Springs.

Almost ten miles from the only home I'd known in Tulsa, Sand Springs was a small town of about eighteen thousand people at that time, a veritable Mayberry like the beloved community in the old *Andy Griffith* television series. Sand Springs had a small but thriving town square that boasted a monument of the suburb's oil-wealthy founder and benefactor Charles Page. From shops and sculpted landscapes that lined the square to the red-brick walkways that weaved their way through downtown, Sand Springs was a peaceful community with all the colorful makings of a Norman Rockwell creation, neatly tucked away in northeastern Oklahoma.

---

**Left:** *Charles E. Page Memorial at the Sand Springs Cultural and Historical Museum. Photo credit: Ed McConnell.*

Sand Springs was also filled with wonderful people who were so dedicated to their hometown that they proudly called themselves "*Sandites.*" Most intended to live there for the rest of their lives — even a small move down the road to Tulsa would have been an unthinkable leap. It was truly an idyllic "Small Town, America," drawing families into its borders who sought to build lives for themselves and their children — and their *children's children* — for generations.

## Why Sand Springs?

Sand Springs was also a very hospitable town, and for a good reason. It was started with the wealth of oilman Charles Page, a philanthropist in every sense of the word who began the small city for the noblest of causes. I think you'll find those causes very interesting because Charles Page was a strong believer, and his causes were biblical in nature, as you will see.

Charles' father died when he was young, and he witnessed firsthand the struggles his mother experienced as she labored to the point of exhaustion to care for him and his siblings. As a young man, he got a job working in the oil industry and soon worked his way up to entering the drilling business for himself. He hit his first oil gusher in 1905 when he was forty-five years old — one that eventually produced more than two thousand barrels of oil per day.[1] Soon Charles hit another gusher — then another and another. It wasn't long until this son of a poor widow became immensely wealthy at a relatively young age.

Because he was so affected by his mother's financial struggles after his father died, Charles chose to devote the bulk of his fortune to helping widows and orphans. In 1908, he purchased land west of Tulsa and began construction of what became Sand Springs, Oklahoma. This is the town where I lived with my family during my late grade-school, junior-high, and high-school years.

Charles Page dreamed that this city would become a hub for his *real* dream — the Sand Springs Home, a well-financed orphanage that would care for orphans until adulthood. To assure the future of these young people, the philanthropist strategically constructed a city around this home, negotiating with steel, glass, and porcelain industries to establish themselves there, successfully providing employment opportunities to the "sons and daughters" his foundation cared for so thoroughly and generously.

In addition to the Sand Springs Home, Charles also built a widow's colony on an expanse of land that held forty houses for widowed women with children who could live there freely at his expense.[2] At that time, it was the only widows colony in America.

All these benevolences were provided because Charles Page remembered the burden of poverty that his own family carried when his father died unexpectedly.

I am very familiar with this story because my Grandpap Earl Miller, my mother's father, was hired by Charles Page to lead the orchestra and band for the Sand Springs Home. Through my grandfather's connection to Page, my own mother and her sister spent many days and weekends at the home as young girls, where they witnessed how generously this amazing man treated the children who lived in the home.

Although those children lived together in a large home for orphaned and abandoned children, they were Charles' "kids," and he treated them as such. In effect, they were no longer orphans at all.

When I entered high school, I, too, became aware of how well the children from the Sand Springs Home were treated. The orphans who attended the Charles Page High School were well-dressed and well-groomed, and at Christmastime they received what seemed like mountains of gifts that were provided by funds held in trust after Charles' death. If the young men and women did well in school, funds were also provided to help them go to college or university.

What this man did for those orphans — including the long-term planning he did to ensure their future well-being — was fatherly, godly, compassionate, and remarkable. He gave those people his heart and in so doing, the giving of his resources followed closely behind.

## Pure Religion, Undefiled

Charles Page's life and legacy has impacted thousands of people for the better since he put action to his dreams more than one hundred years ago in 1908. He founded the town of Sand Springs with the express purpose of helping those who were neediest and most vulnerable. His belief in human value and potential motivated him to do something tangible to make a difference in *people* — the world's most valuable resource. With his own resources of wealth and his tireless perseverance, he made his dreams *and theirs* a reality.

I think of Charles Page every time I read James 1:27, which says, "Pure religion and undefiled before God and the Father is this, To *visit* the *fatherless* and *widows* in their *affliction*...." Because of what I know about this verse from the original Greek, it is difficult for me to proceed without letting you know that, in effect, it denotes extending a deliberate helping hand toward those *forgotten by society, but never by God* — the orphaned, abandoned, afflicted, and struggling who find themselves crushed by life, often through no fault of their own.

That word "visit" doesn't mean just to wave hello to someone in passing. The Greek word means *to look upon, to physically visit*, or *to provide help for* those in need, and it was even used to denote *the provision of medical care*. But James then specified the target of *whom* we are to care for: "...the fatherless and the widows in their affliction...."

The word "fatherless" is the very Greek word from which we get the word "orphan." In early New Testament times, it described not only children left without a parent, but it also included the idea of *abandonment*. Perhaps the parents were still living, but the children were abandoned and left to themselves with no parental care or guidance. For all intents and purposes, children in this condition are fatherless, motherless, or *both*.

The word "widows" describes widows in the traditional sense of the word. James used the word "affliction" to describe the condition of this category of women. It depicts *pressures* that make it difficult to cope with life. Their hardships may include struggles to provide housing, food, medical care, or other physical needs — struggles that leave a person hard-pressed to get up and face each day. According to James 1:27, we have a God-given responsibility to reach out and do what we can to help widowed women who are struggling due to the loss of a spouse.

I realize we live in an age when insurance pays death benefits, and the government often assists women who have lost spouses. Many widows today are not suffering financially as they did years ago. But there are still many widowed women who suffer great financial and social needs when their spouse dies, and God commands us to do whatever we can to be a blessing to them in their times of suffering. Much of what we do today in our ministry in Russia is geared toward caring for orphans and the needy — those who are widowed, poor, sick, or shut in.

We don't have to be wealthy like Charles Page in order to obey this verse in the first chapter of James. In fact, Charles made the decision to do these things *before* he struck oil. It was as if he consecrated his resources to do God's bidding before he even *had* resources.

The reason I'm telling you about Charles Page is so you'll know that Sand Springs was a wholesome place from its earliest beginnings — a town *built* on charity. Even now, people from Sand Springs remain wonderful down-to-earth people who stay close to the home front, and it's no wonder why. The city was built on a great foundation, and it's still a great place to live today.

But as wonderful as Sand Springs was, I felt out of place there growing up. Something inside was calling me to do something elsewhere and on a scale that was different from a quieter life in Sand Springs. That "something" inside me, I learned later, was *Someone* inside me — in my spirit. It was the Lord Himself, as "deep crying to deep," letting me know that Sand Springs would not ultimately be my home.

People in Sand Springs do great things, no doubt, but I knew deep down that God had a special plan for me that would reach places larger than our happy community of eighteen thousand people. As precious a town as it was, I could not see my destiny being fulfilled in Sand Springs. And what I "saw" was right. The Lord had plans for me that I deeply sensed, but could not have completely fathomed at my young age — plans that would take me, along with a family of my own, a vast ocean away from Sand Springs, Oklahoma.

## Notable Others Who 'Sprung' From Sand Springs

It just so happened that years later, after I moved away from Sand Springs, I discovered there were others who ministered in Sand Springs who dreamed of venturing out to touch the world with the Gospel. One was a young preacher by the name of Oral Roberts, who ministered on the streets of Sand Springs in the mid-1930s. And while ministering there, he was visited by another young man whose name was Tommy Lee Osborn, otherwise known as T. L. Osborn, who later brought the Gospel message to millions as a worldwide healing evangelist.

But in those early days, T. L. was volunteering to help Oral with his evangelistic meetings. He later told the *Tulsa World* newspaper, "Oral did the preaching, and I did just about everything else."[3] One of T. L.'s duties even included playing the accordion for the musical portion of the meetings.

Eventually both Oral Roberts and T. L. Osborn launched into their respective worldwide ministries. Who would have imagined that such "spiritual dynamite" as Oral Roberts and T. L. Osborn ministered on the streets of little ol' Sand Springs, Oklahoma! But when God orchestrated that early putting together of those two men in that small town, it resulted in the Gospel being propelled *literally to the ends of the earth*! How unlikely that three of us ministers whom God has used to touch the world on a large scale would have in common *Sand Springs, Oklahoma*, of all things!

Sand Springs was an amazing small town with a lot to attract families, small businesses, and, apparently, even ministers of the Gospel! But when Daddy decided to move there, his focus was *family* and his dream was to build a brand-new house for his wife and children. It was a daring step because, as far as I can recall, none of our friends had ever attempted to build a new house. But Daddy sold our house in Tulsa for a whopping $12,500 and proceeded to the bank to qualify for a loan to build a new home in Sand Springs.

When the bank told him how big a loan he could get, my father chose a lot and a builder, and began constructing a new house for our family in Sand Springs. Daddy was thrilled to think we would actually own a *new* home! When he returned home from work every evening, we'd pile into the car and head to the construction site to see what had been done that day on the new house. We watched workers pour the slab, erect the frame and walls, put on a roof, install the kitchen and bathrooms, do finishing work and painting, and lay the tile and carpet. The house even had *a fireplace*! That was amazing to us because no one among our friends had a fireplace. But my daddy was in hot pursuit of a dream to upgrade our lives.

## A Broken Dream and a Broken Heart

Eventually the house was near completion, so my father returned to finalize the loan at the bank. But when the bank saw that the construction costs had slightly exceeded the amount he had prequalified for, they backed out of the deal and denied the loan. I watched as Daddy pleaded with the officers at the bank, but no matter how much he pleaded or promised that he would make the payments, they refused him. So after months of dreaming about this new house and watching the dream daily unfold before our eyes, the house was finished, but our family never occupied it.

The loss was monumental and a deep disappointment to my father. The builder was stuck with a house with no buyer, so he put a "For Sale" sign in the yard — and in just a short time, another family bought and moved into our dream house. Daddy's heart was broken.

When I think back on that experience and how it affected my father, my mind goes to Proverbs 13:12, which says, "Hope deferred maketh the heart sick...." A "sick heart" is exactly what I saw in my father when that happened. It *crushed* both Daddy and Mother.

I have never forgotten the way that event affected my father. Seeing his disappointment — and feeling it right along with him — was another moment God has used over the years to help me minister to others. I developed a real compassion for those who have been disappointed and hurt by life — and a heart to minister truth, freedom, and hope to them concerning their better days to come.

In true Renner fashion, Daddy pulled himself together after this huge letdown and said, "Erlita, let's go find a house we can afford." The search was on, and soon they chose a red-brick, three-bedroom house on Garfield Street. The front of the house faced the street and at the edge of our backyard, a slope descended into a neighborhood park with slides, swings, and a huge, effervescing water fountain that cascaded onto the sidewalk around it. Children would be splashed by the overflow, and that fountain was especially fun to play in during hot summer months.

Living in Sand Springs meant Ronda, Lori, and I would be starting school in the fall in a brand-new district. I felt afraid to start the sixth grade because I didn't know anyone in my new, unfamiliar setting. Barely twelve years old, I felt a bit like a young immigrant to another country!

Every child handles change differently, and for me, this change in schools was a real struggle. Every weekday, I'd awaken with an ominous, foreboding heaviness in the pit of my stomach. With every action of getting ready for school — brushing my teeth, putting on my socks and shoes, etc. — I would mentally push my way through as best I could. By the time we had to leave the house, I'd worked up sufficient nerve to walk out the front door without showing emotion. But it was an exhausting struggle so early in my mornings.

I never told Daddy or Mother what I felt because I could have almost guessed that my father would tell me it was a good growing-up lesson and that I would "get over it." So every day, for the better part of that first entire year, I did my best to grit my teeth and show no emotion as I headed to school with an unshakable sense of unease.

## My Job at the Cemetery —
## Life Is Not a Game

My father was very disciplined and strict with his own life — and the strictness he imposed on himself, he also required of me. He was easier on the girls — I think dads *are* generally easier on their daughters than on their sons. But Daddy was always very strict with me. Today I am very organized and productive in my ministry and also personally, and I believe it's partially because my dad instilled in me the characteristic of order and a great work ethic.

That work ethic came into play about the time I received my Social Security card as a young man of twelve. When that card arrived in the mail, my father said, "Rick, it's time for you to get a job and learn what it's like to earn a living." Like other boys, I had started to mow lawns to earn a little money on the side. But now that I was twelve, Daddy felt it was time for me to get a "real" job. Since I wasn't old enough to drive, I had to look for someplace to work that was within walking distance, and the only place that fit that description was the local cemetery.

Daddy said to me, "I want you to march right over and apply for a job at the cemetery." The cemetery was right up the street, so I walked over and knocked on the door of the front office. Soon the cemetery director, a tall, elderly man wearing a cowboy hat, opened the door. He was a big, gruff-looking guy who had run that place for many years. Nervously, I stated my business — that I was there to inquire about a job that might be available for a twelve-year-old boy.

He sat me down immediately for an interview and hired me that day as a lawn boy to mow the grass over the graves, edge around the tombstones and grave markers, weed the flowerbeds as needed, and remove wilted flowers from the graves.

Every weekday after school, I walked down the street and passed through the huge arched entry to the cemetery to begin my shift. I pulled the giant industrial lawnmower out of the shed and went busily to work mowing, edging, trimming, and ensuring that my assigned areas were as *ship-shape* and beautifully manicured as I could make them.

So for my first fully paying job — every day after school, five days a week — I found myself working among the dead. I didn't realize at the time that the Lord was teaching me, but He was imparting many spiritual truths to my heart during my time there.

For example, in the two years I worked at that cemetery, I can't recall a single instance in which a corpse crawled out of his grave because he was tired of being dead! Once the person was dead and buried, it was permanent. When goodbyes were spoken at gravesites, they were always final farewells. Those present were well aware that the person they were honoring would never be seen alive in their lifetimes again.

As I look back over the years, as with so many events in my life, I see that even my job at the cemetery was divinely orchestrated to occur at that moment in my development. As I mowed the cemetery lawn and edged the grass around the stones every day, *literally walking among the dead*, I found myself asking questions about life and death. *Who was this person?* I'd ask to myself as I'd glance at the names on the markers. *What did he do with his life? What kind of impact did he make on the world around him?*

Because of my love for history and antiquities, I especially liked one old section of the cemetery where what was written on the tombstones had been worn away by years of weather and wear. I'd strain to see if I could make out the epitaphs on those old sandstone markers, but most often, my attempts were frustrating. It seemed to me that even the tombstones didn't remember who was buried beneath them. I became *gripped* by thoughts of a never-ending eternity, knowing that we would each be remembered for how we stewarded our relatively short time here on earth.

God used this moment in my young career to make me seriously think about eternity and about my own life. It saddened me to think that people could live, die, and be forgotten — especially if they never contributed anything to the world or to those around them with the time they were given on earth. I just knew I didn't want my life to be lived for naught or to be forgotten after I was gone. God used my job at the cemetery to teach me that life is not a game and to encourage me to make the quality decision that I would not live a frivolous, purposeless life with no lasting fruit.

Another part of my job at the cemetery was to help lower coffins into graves after gravesite rites were finished and everyone had left the cemetery. When we would lower those coffins into the graves, I was again gripped with the utter finality of the moment. I couldn't seem to shake the thoughts that there were many who wasted their talents and cheated the world *and themselves* of books that were to be written; symphonies that were to be arranged; masterpieces that should have been painted; cities, states, and nations that were to be led in government; and scientific theories that could have been developed as breakthroughs in science.

Yet many died *unknown* with no credit to their name for having accomplished anything concerning God's foreordained plan for their lives. Their coffins were placed into freshly dug graves, and clods of dirt crashed down like rain on the surfaces where they lay entombed, hiding them from view forever. The act was so permanent and final — and either a great celebration or an immense tragedy took place at that moment that would not be reversed or changed.

The tragedy was the unanswered callings and the grim fact that now *permanently buried* was a book never penned, a symphony never written, a song never sung, a leader who never emerged, an answer for medical science never discovered — in short, a life wasted by failing to respond to Heaven's destiny and calling.

I'm not saying that everyone is called to have his name in lights, as it were, as a famous author, painter, actor, etc. The fulfilling of destiny for many is to faithfully raise their children, nurture their families, and serve faithfully in their jobs or careers and in their local churches — making a difference for all eternity in the lives of those around them that they loved and served well.

But as just a twelve-year-old boy, I thought, *Nothing could be more immoral or wrong, and no crime more tragic, than a person who was gifted and called and who could have made a difference…but DIDN'T.* I didn't want that to be my story, and it was in that season that I solemnly determined I would fulfill divine destiny for my life.

But while I was struggling emotionally to adjust to my new school surroundings — simultaneously surrounded by the dead for five afternoons per week — our family's transition from west Tulsa to Sand Springs continued otherwise uneventfully. Of course, one element of our lives remained constant, and that was our commitment to Glenwood Baptist Church. We had moved almost exactly eight and half miles down the tracks, but our service and involvement at the church never waned.

It is no exaggeration to say that our *whole lives* were enmeshed in Glenwood Baptist Church. Our spiritual service, our social life, our family relationships, our lifelong friendships, and our Bible-loving pastor — all of that was there at our home church. We may have relocated geographically, but spiritually and emotionally, our hearts never left Glenwood church for one second.

### I Faked a Call to the Mission Field

While life in Sand Springs was sheltered and predictable, I longed for something my soul could not express that would *rock* me from my world of predictability and light me *ablaze* from my life of smoldering constancy.

Our cousins, David and Lorna Daniel, were Southern Baptist foreign missionaries who had already been serving in Mexico City for many years at that time, and when they came to the United States on furlough, they would always visit us, bringing with them trinkets from the mission field that thrilled my heart. They also showed us slide presentations of what they were doing, who they were reaching, and the places near Mexico City where they were ministering. I found all of it *thrilling*!

One summer, our cousins invited Ronda, who was sixteen at the time, to Mexico City for a summer experience on the mission field. Ronda and I were very close, so it upset me to think I'd be left behind the whole summer without her. But she went, and every single week, she sent me a letter to tell me the fun she was experiencing besides ministering with the missionary family. She wrote about her visits to volcanoes, the Teotihuacan pyramids, the local market, and even the beaches of Guadalajara. Every letter made me salivate with jealousy to be with her. Although I was barely twelve at the time, I begged my parents to let me fly to Mexico City to join her. Since Daddy worked at American Airlines, I could fly on a non-revenue status for just a few dollars.

But my request was not favorably received. Instead of Mexico City, youth camp at Falls Creek in Davis, Oklahoma, was to be my summertime destination.

Falls Creek Baptist Youth Camp was and still is an amazing summer camp for young people. However, at that time, being hunkered down with thousands of Baptist kids for a week was a far cry from Ronda's exciting summer of nonstop adventure in another country. Every day at that camp I thought, *Ugh! I can't believe I am suffering in the heat in the middle of nowhere, with thousands of other kids, while Ronda is visiting pyramids and volcanoes!*

On the last night of camp, the legendary Andrae Crouch was present to sing for us and to lead us in a song. Then the special speaker ministered, and as he did, he addressed the need for some in the crowd to surrender to God's call to foreign missions.

As I listened to this minister in my increasingly disgruntled state of mind, I began to hatch a plan that I hoped would put me on a plane to Mexico City to join Ronda for the rest of the summer. I thought, *If I walk the aisle and pretend to be called to missions — and go home to tell my parents the news — they'll be so moved that their son surrendered to the foreign field that they'll WANT to send me to join Ronda so I can confirm God's call on my life.*

It sounded right to me, so when the altar call began, I slid out of my seat and into the aisle to begin my walk to the front to "surrender" to foreign missions. I remembered the tug of the Holy Spirit on my heart when I was five as I took the sacred step forward in my church to give my heart to Jesus. This time, I felt no tug and no call at all. But I was desperate — I *needed* to get to Mexico *right away* to see those pyramids and volcanoes!

When I finally reached the altar, a counselor met me. I gulped nervously, my throat parched and dry. I should have turned around and returned to my seat, but I was determined to go through with the plan. I stuttered at first and then spoke so quickly that I'm surprised the counselor could make out a word I'd said: "I'm here because I…feel…*the Spirit tugging on my heart to surrender to foreign missions. I feel called to be a missionary to MEXICO!*"

He must have understood me, because before I knew what was happening, a group of counselors and teens rushed me into the nearby McBurney Chapel where the counselor there began to take my name and address and record my "call" to missions.

*It was official.* Ricky Renner had yielded to God's plan to use him in foreign missions in Mexico. It said so right there in the books of the Falls Creek Baptist Youth Camp in Davis, Oklahoma!

When camp was over and I returned home, with a tone of seriousness and sobriety, I asked to sit down with Daddy and Mother so I could tell them about my decision to be a missionary to Mexico.

*I was really feeling the moment.* My plan was proceeding successfully just as I had hoped. Next, I was *sure* to hear my parents share in my joy and celebrate my decision with the words, "Oh, Ricky, that is so wonderful! We want to send you to Mexico to be with Ronda for the rest of the summer so you can confirm your call."

Instead, I heard them say, "Ricky, we weren't born yesterday. We know this is a scheme to get the trip to Mexico you've been asking for, and you can just forget it. If God has called you to be a missionary, He'll confirm it for you right here in Sand Springs."

## *God's* Secret Plan Began To Unfold

My foreign-missions conversation with my parents ended almost as abruptly as it had begun. My plan had *failed*. But, in fact, God was working a plan of His own, and it would be one that ultimately would *not* fail.

Because my "decision" at camp had been so well-documented, the Southern Baptist Foreign Mission Board began sending me *boxes* of maps to highlight the places all over the world where missionaries were desperately needed. I thought they would *never* stop sending me maps! *Maps, maps, and more maps* kept showing up at our house to assist me as I prepared to answer my "call."

Until that time, I'd never given much thought to other places in the world where the Gospel needed to be preached. But when those maps would arrive, I'd pull them out, lie across them on the floor as I studied them — and I would dream about what life must be like in other parts of the world, well beyond the borders of my small town of eighteen thousand people.

Because I had a very vivid imagination, as I lay on those maps, learning the names of various cities and nations, I began to imagine what life was like not just in Mexico, but in Cuba, China, western Europe, *and even the Soviet Union*. I thought, *Oh, what a horrible place the Soviet Union must be.* To my young mind, the USSR was a massive prison expanse where people had few freedoms and Christians suffered for their faith. As I lay across the territory of the USSR and saw the vast size of it, I wondered what it was like for Christians who lived in *all* communist countries. It was during those times of imagining — a menagerie before my face of interestingly shaped countries with swirls of lines denoting borders, rivers, and highways — that God began to put *wonder* in my heart for the foreign field.

I thought I had worked a secret plan to try to get a vacation in Mexico that summer — but God was the One working a plan. Through my conniving, He began to put maps into my hands — maps that would make me think seriously for the first time of His work in other parts of the world.

That is literally how God dropped missions into my heart and mind at the age of twelve. I was becoming not just aware, but *keenly* aware, of other parts of the world that needed the Gospel. I also became deeply respectful and reverential toward individuals who dared to accept the call to leave the comforts of their familiar surroundings for the sake of the call.

## The Demonic Attempt To Destroy Me
## Continued as a Three-Year-Long Nightmare

As I shared in the last chapter, I *really* wrestled with my self-image. The devil tormented me endlessly with thoughts that there was something inherently wrong with me because I was so different from the other young men at church. Those thoughts *hounded* and *harassed* me continually. But if that wasn't agonizing enough, this demonic attack on my soul was turned up several notches when I entered junior-high school in Sand Springs.

Our junior high was flooded with kids from a number of different elementary schools. On the first day of classes, I felt lost in a flurry of new faces. My father was elated that he attended classes as a young teenager himself in the very classrooms where I would be sitting each day. However, that time for me was *not* exciting. I had barely survived sixth grade emotionally. Now, unbeknownst to me, I was about to embark on a three-year-long nightmare that started midway through the school year when I was diagnosed with a terrible case of mononucleosis.

My case of mononucleosis was so severe that our family doctor ordered me to bed for several months. So in obedience to the doctor's orders, my parents took me out of school and put me to bed. While I lay in bed at home for most of my days during that time, life went on at school without me. More importantly, classes and subjects continued to progress to greater and greater degrees of difficulty, each level building on the last. They were levels I was clueless about as I lay convalescing in a different world, academically stagnant, trying to recuperate from my illness. And by the time the doctor released me to go back to school, I was still mentally on subjects that the other students had left months before.

Although my mother had been in communication with the school over the course of my illness, no one there had been assigned to help me catch up. When I finally returned to class, I was far behind in subjects like grammar and mathematics, and I had no idea what my teacher was talking about as she taught on topics like subject-verb agreement, prepositional clauses, adjectives, adverbs, and other parts of speech. She might as well have been speaking a foreign language into my ears! That was intimidating enough, but when she shifted to math, it became *really* scary for me. I might have recognized a familiar phrase here and there in English, but I was *completely oblivious* to what she was discussing in math because I had missed so much classwork.

Because no one at the school helped me catch up to the rest of the class, every day I sank deeper into confusion. Instead of recognizing my plight for what it was — that I had simply fallen behind — I remember so vividly just thinking I was hopelessly stupid because I could not grasp what the other students were learning. I struggled in silence, badgered by devilish, nonstop thoughts of worthlessness. Now, on top of being pounded with thoughts that I was weird because I didn't like sports, a new word tried to make itself at home in my life — "*STUPID.*"

## A Devilish Whisper Became a Roar
### and the War Was On

Most of what I know about spiritual warfare I learned through the school of experience as I eventually thwarted this attack that the demonic realm had launched against me early in life. The devil was bombarding my mind because he wanted me to believe there really was something inherently wrong with me. That's why he pounded so relentlessly in his early attempt to take my mind, *and my life,* completely captive.

I understand firsthand what Peter was talking about when he wrote First Peter 5:8, which says, "Be sober, be vigilant; because your adversary the devil, as a roaring lion, walketh about, seeking whom he may devour." Of course, I didn't know it at the time, but that word "roaring" depicts *a nonstop howling or roaring.*

This verse perfectly describes the nonstop barrage of lies that flooded my ears and my mind during the devil's early assault in my life. At first, the attack started as an insinuation — just a whisper of a suggestion. But then as time passed, those insinuations got louder and louder until they became a full-blown roar in my head that practically consumed my thinking and my beliefs that there was something very defective about me.

The devil knew that if he could get me to believe his lies, he could use them to drag me deeper into a place where he could completely "devour" me. The word "devour" in First Peter 5:8 doesn't mean *to eat* or *devour*, as in the devouring of the carcass of a dead animal. It is actually the Greek word meaning *to slurp*. It pictures the dead animal, all right, but it's the animal whose meat is already gone and all that's left are the juices. The lion pictured in this verse is so bent on consuming the animal's remains that it hungrily *slurps up the juices* with the intention of leaving nothing at all behind of that dead animal.

Peter used this word to tell us what the devil wants to do to you and me. He wants to mess you up — maul you, victimize you, and take you down — not just to chew on or even eat you, but to so totally consume you that there's nothing left but "juices." Then his intention is to *slurp up* what remains so as to completely liquidate you.

That is why verse 9 says, "Whom resist stedfast in the faith…." That means God gives us the ability to stand against the enemy's attacks and to put him to flight!

I don't want to glorify what the devil tried to do to me — I am simply sharing this personal part of my story because I want to help you recognize how the devil may attack you or someone you know or love. In retrospect, I see that the devil wasn't interested in just devouring me in the traditional sense of the word. Instead, he wanted to "slurp me up" until there was nothing left of me on this earth to make a mark or impact that would bless others and glorify God.

But I was too young — and too untaught about how the devil operates — to realize this was a spiritual attack. I thought the roar in my head was simply harsh self-realization — my coming to terms with the fact that I was stupid. In reality, it was the plan of the enemy to destroy me.

## Mounting Evidence
## To Support the Enemy's Claims

Because my seventh-grade teacher liked me, she didn't want me to fail a grade and be held back a year, so she gave me the lowest possible passing grade so I could move into the eighth grade the following year with my classmates. But I wondered, *If I didn't understand grammar and math in the SEVENTH grade, how am I going to survive grammar and math in the EIGHTH grade?*

But straight into the eighth grade I went — *unprepared*. Once again, I failed test after test after test. But also once again, my teacher liked me, so she gave me the lowest possible passing grade in order to promote me to my freshman year with the rest of my class.

In those two years in seventh and eighth grade, I had combated bombardments as best I could at my vulnerable adolescent age of twelve and thirteen. Mental accusations that I was stupid assaulted me *rapid-fire*. I vividly recall especially hard times when I stood in front of my bathroom mirror to brush my teeth and comb my hair. Looking at my reflection, I'd berate myself, *You are stupid, stupid, stupid! Why can't you understand anything the teacher tells you? Everything about you is wrong. You're not like other guys and you're terrible at math and grammar. What is wrong with you? You're a misfit and a mistake, and you're hopelessly STUPID!*

In reality, there was nothing wrong with me academically that a good teacher couldn't have helped fix, but that help never manifested. In the meantime, I sank deeper into feelings and, later, *strong beliefs* that I was inherently stupid.

### Mrs. Sparks and the 'Last Straw' To Push Me Over the Edge

I'd almost learned to live with the continual, nagging thoughts of worthlessness that were more and more becoming a part of my consciousness. The enemy used them to construct his tower of lies, from which he intended to reign over my life as a cruel tyrant. But when I entered the ninth grade, those mental assaults escalated to a nearly unbearable point of completely breaking me.

As I already shared, the enemy's goal was not just to knock me down or even to *keep* me down, but to trample and *destroy* me. The objective of his attacks was *annihilation*. Looking back, I can just imagine him licking his chops in anticipation of slurping up the juices of my life and leaving me "dead," empty, and completely useless.

Although I had been passed from the seventh and eighth grades, the truth is, I had failed math and English during both of those school years. And now, how in the world was I going to survive math and English in the ninth grade, especially *ninth-grade algebra*!

Almost every student was at least a *little* nervous as he or she moved from grade to grade — those feelings were normal jitters that come during seasons of change. But I was a walking bundle of fretful, knee-knocking, sick-to-my-stomach nerves — it was a combination of nervousness and insecurity *on steroids*! All the same old attacks and accusations screamed in my ears at once until they became one large, deafening sound inside my head. Like breaking ocean waves in a furious storm, those crashing thoughts had become so all-consuming that I couldn't think a rational thought about my situation if I wanted to!

Then I stepped inside the classroom of *Mrs. Sparks*.

Mrs. Sparks was a legend in our "Mayberry" town. She had taught algebra in that school, *in the same classroom*, for so many years that she had even taught my daddy in that classroom when *he* was a teenager! Mrs. Sparks was a tough woman, who dressed sharply and wore stiletto heels with straps that wrapped fashionably around her ankles. Her name "Sparks" was completely appropriate because sparks would *fly* if anyone rubbed her the wrong way!

Her fiery temperament was legendary and few dared to take on an argument with this woman. She had the tongue of a viper and knew just how to inject the right dose of venom that could knock even the bravest, strongest, and most confident souls off their feet. Anyone reading this who ever had her as a teacher will probably laugh out loud and remember at least one tempestuous experience with Mrs. Sparks.

Like all the other students, I entered Mrs. Sparks' classroom that first day of school looking for a desk that would be mine for the entire year. I selected one in the back of the room, where I felt safer, and waited for her to call the roll for the first time.

Mrs. Sparks began at the beginning of the roll, reading off each name alphabetically. I waited anxiously as she progressed…M, N, O, P, Q, R… reading each name as if she already couldn't stand each one of us. Finally, I heard her say, "Ricky Renner," and I responded with the required, *"Here!"* What happened next is no exaggeration and is nothing short of outrageous.

*Suddenly*, Mrs. Sparks stopped in a long, cold moment of silence. Glaring over the top of the half-moon glasses she wore, as if seized with disgust, she just stared at me. Her icy stare shot like an arrow, piercing me through even at the back of the classroom.

Placing the palms of both hands on her desk with deliberation, as if indignant that *I* had disrupted her roll call, she arose and clicked angrily on those stilettos to the front of her desk. With the roster of names still in her hand, she leaned back on the desk and crossed her arms like a ranking officer in the Gestapo about to render condemnation and doom.

I could feel the uneasiness among the whole class as they were no doubt wondering about me and what I could have possibly done to anger Mrs. Sparks so intensely on our first day of school. We were all breathless with uneager anticipation, bracing ourselves for the impending attack.

Then in a brutally forceful tone, she snapped, "Is your father Ronald Renner?"

Barely able to swallow, much less talk, I temporarily forgot all about my fear of algebra as my fear had now officially shifted to Mrs. Sparks. Nervously, I managed to answer, "Yes…ma'am."

I watched as her face reddened, her eyebrows crinkling and her eyes closing to a squint. It seemed as if all the air in that room had been suddenly sucked out by some tornadic force, leaving us all holding on tightly to our last breath. Mrs. Sparks then screeched out the most unthinkable words an adult could say to a young teenager she'd never even met.

*"STUPID!"*

Mrs. Sparks continued seamlessly. *"Stupid, stupid, stupid.* Any child of Ronald Renner is just *stupid*! And in this class, your name will be *Stupid Renner!"*

Nearly four decades previously, my dad had apparently lit a cigarette and smoked it in the back of Mrs. Spark's classroom — in the very classroom where I was now seated — and I had inadvertently chosen a desk in nearly the same spot where my dad sat when he defied and disrespected his math teacher. Mrs. Sparks had neither forgiven nor forgotten my father's dishonoring act. Hearing my name triggered her wrath and unleashed her fury on me *just as if I were Ronald Renner smoking a cigarette in class*!

When I could collect my scrambled thoughts, I remember thinking, *All I did was walk in, take my seat, and answer, 'Here.' And I've just been ASSAULTED for it!*

But true to her word, from that day to the end of the ninth grade, every day as Mrs. Sparks called the roll, when she came to my name, she said, "Stupid Renner," and I'd say, *"Here,"* just as I was expected to answer.

Furthermore, if I raised my hand to ask a question, Mrs. Sparks would reply, "Yes, Stupid, what do you need?" On days that she was particularly irritated, if I raised my hand for assistance, she would say, "Can someone please help Stupid with his stupid question."

I'm certain that if this all transpired today, Mrs. Sparks would never get by with such despotic behavior. But back in those days, it was laughed off by the administration as, "That's just the way she is." Even when I told my dad, he told me to laugh it off and not press my luck by challenging her. Absolutely no one wanted to tangle with Mrs. Sparks, so her verbal abuse was tolerated at my expense.

That whole classroom of ninth graders, *or most of them*, thought it was funny that Mrs. Sparks called me stupid. So one by one, they began to forget that my name was Ricky and began to use my new name — *Stupid*!

Yes, my nickname throughout my ninth-grade year was "Stupid Renner." As I walked the hallway each weekday, I'd hear the echoes of fellow students chanting, "Hello, Stupid," "How are you, Stupid?" and, "Where are you going, Stupid?"

Kids can be cruel, and those kids had no idea what their words were doing to my mind and my life, nor that they were being used as instruments of evil to help further a plan to knock me out of my spiritual race and my divine destiny.

In retrospect, I can see exactly the strategy of the enemy to set up circumstances, use people's weaknesses and ignorance to attack me, and then lie to me that "it must all be true." He railed on me day after day, telling me that I was a sorry excuse for a human being and that I had no business setting the soles of my feet on the earth to do anything meaningful or worthwhile. And for a long season, I bought into the lie that I was one huge, bumbling mistake in life — that I wasn't just a square peg trying to fit into a round hole, but that there was no place for me to fit *at all*.

No one knew that I had wrestled all my young life with anxiety over the fact that I did not like sports — *or* that my sixth-grade year at a new school was a perpetual struggle and one that I never got victory over. Nor did anyone realize my discouragement in the seventh grade over being seriously sick for half a school year — and the fear and sadness I faced when I returned to that classroom completely lost academically.

Now *once again*, Ricky Renner was a misfit among his peers.

It was as if the devil had brought in reinforcements as affirming evidence that I didn't just *feel* defective and inferior, but that I really *was* defective, inferior — and now STUPID. A whole demonic choir had harmonized with those accusations, and from every direction, the same song was being sung in my hearing that this was the harsh truth about me. I had picked up the tune in my own heart and my resistance was weakening to the point of wholehearted agreement with this lie.

It is amazing to me, but somehow I liked Mrs. Sparks in spite of her treatment of me during that school year. When she would get particularly ugly in the classroom, I'd wonder what had happened in her life to make her turn so harsh, vindictive, and cruel. It seemed that she didn't like *anyone* and that she was deeply dissatisfied with every aspect of her life. I wondered what had perhaps transpired with her children or in her marriage, and what kind of life disappointments she'd encountered to cause her to act the way she did.

It's just a fact that when people are deeply disappointed in life and do not have a mature relationship with the Lord, they often show it in their contempt for others. But somehow, the Holy Spirit produced love in my heart for this woman. Years later after I was an adult, I saw her in public and stopped to speak with her. I could actually see the wounds of brokenness in her eyes. Although my self-image was deeply affected by my experience in her class, God miraculously enabled me to keep my heart clear of any ill feelings toward Mrs. Sparks.

### Doomed Dreams and a Prison of Failure — the Attack Was Ramped Up One More Time

That same year, schools in Sand Springs gave job-placement tests to help ninth graders think about their future occupations or the educational plans they should choose upon high-school graduation. Every ninth grader was required to take the test and then sit down with two professional job-placement counselors who would go over the students' results and encourage them concerning what they should do with their lives.

The day came for me to meet those professional counselors. Feeling anxious, as I did after taking almost every test, I walked tenuously down the steps into the cafeteria to meet them and to talk about my results. I felt so insecure, yet I held out hope that they would say something positive and encouraging to me. I pulled up my chair, introduced myself, and waited for them to speak.

The first counselor to speak said, "Ricky, we have looked at your results, and we feel we must simply speak honestly and directly to you about your test." Then the other counselor chimed in and began the actual evaluation, saying rather bluntly: "Ricky, our advice is that you never go in the direction of college, university, or any level of higher education because you mentally don't have what is required for that."

Then he said, "Our professional recommendation is that you choose some form of manual labor in which you can work with your hands — such as digging ditches, pouring concrete, paving roads, etc."

I'm certainly not belittling manual labor as I rehearse to you what happened during that session. Where would our world be without these professions — without people with these technical skills and trades? We would have no plumbing, no electricity, no homes or buildings, and no roads — *we would be in a mess!* The contributions of these men and women are *essential* to our lives. Furthermore, many of these people are handsomely paid for what they do.

But that was simply not my dream. And I felt woefully bound to a life of unfulfillment because I was simply too unqualified to do the things I dreamed in my heart of doing. Working in one of those technical trades was a far cry from my goals of venturing beyond Sand Springs to explore the world as I obeyed and served God. Would I ever be free from this prison of failure and doomed dreams — before I ever had one chance to fulfill them?

But that was nearly word for word what I heard from those counselors in the cafeteria that day: *You just don't have what it takes*. And I *believed* them! After all, they were professionals. It was like the ceiling of my life stopped just over my head in the ninth grade and forbade me to go any higher or further. Those counselors might as well have said, "Your dreams are dead — *done!* You're just going to have to accept what we're telling you and be happy about it."

The words I heard that day were like a death knell to my dreams. I should have perhaps shaken off their words, but I had fallen victim to a perfect storm of assaults that were mercilessly battering the ship of my life, and I was lost at sea. I already felt like an *oddball* because I didn't play sports; that I was *inferior* because I couldn't seem to master math and English; and *stupid* because Mrs. Sparks said so. And now *this*. To me, it was *a sign*: just one more piece of evidence to support the claim that I was weird, inferior, and stupid — and that my struggles would never end until I simply resigned myself to the fact that every word was true and that I would never live a life of destiny and fulfillment.

The evidence was mounting that I had no future worth living for — that I was destined for a routine life in a small Oklahoma town. If I'd ever had a dream for anything bigger — and I *had* — it looked like it was finally time for me, at the tender age of fourteen, to put it away and accept that mine would be a life void of fulfillment. Those counselors finished jerking the rug from under my feet, sending me tripping into a dark abyss of hopelessness with no chance of recovery.

As I look back on it now, I see that the devil must have perceived the call of God on my life. And he brought out all his best ammunition to shoot me down so that I'd never step into Heaven's plan. But as you will see in the pages to come, all of those attacks were ultimately foiled by the power of the Holy Spirit. And to the glory of God, I can say definitely that I'm *not stupid*!

## My Aunt Melita as God's Emissary
## To Rescue Me

Just two blocks from my home, my Aunt Melita, my mother's sister, lived unaware of my torment and struggles. One day during that awful time in my life, I dropped by her house after school for a surprise visit. But on that day, I had a surprise encounter of my own that started a chain of events that eventually turned my captivity and changed the trajectory of my life. But before I tell you about that encounter, I'll tell you a little about my Aunt Melita.

Melita also grew up between the tracks on the Sand Springs Line and had attended Glenwood Baptist Church in her childhood years with her sister Erlita, my mother. But as Melita grew older, she became hungry for more spiritually and ventured out on a quest to find the power of the Holy Spirit and to satisfy her spiritual hunger. In the process of her searching, she received the baptism in the Holy Spirit.

Melita probably wouldn't have called herself Pentecostal, but we in the Ronald Renner household sure did! She and her husband and children began attending a Pentecostal-type church where the congregants claimed that the gifts of the Holy Spirit were in operation.

Back in those days, Southern Baptists were prone to be *cessationists* — a term that means we believed the gifts of the Holy Spirit ceased when the age of the first apostles ended. So if anyone claimed to operate in the gifts of the Holy Spirit in our day, we most assuredly believed he or she was deluded. We generally regarded people who spoke in tongues as gullible types who were easily led astray. To us, Pentecostals were a fringe group who were overly influenced by their emotions. We sincerely believed Pentecostalism was *heresy*.

And now, Melita and her husband Howard had become *Pentecostals*! But Melita wasn't the first Pentecostal in our family. As I told you in Chapter One, my great-grandmother Louella Hestand Miller, Grandpap Earl's mother, had a Pentecostal encounter with the power of God even before the outpourings in Topeka, Kansas, or at Azusa Street in California.

Great-grandmother Louella Miller passed that Pentecostal influence to her daughter-in-law, Juanita, whom we called Grandma Ettie and who was the mother of Erlita (my mother) and Melita. When Grandma Ettie married Grandpap Earl, she would sit at the feet of her mother-in-law and listen for *hours* as Louella related stories about divine interventions, deliverances, healings, and angelic encounters she and her family experienced on the range in Indian Territory before Oklahoma became a state.

Grandma Ettie was seeking for more to satisfy her own spiritual thirst, and because of Great-grandmother Miller's influence, including those *riveting* stories of faith, Grandma Ettie had her own Pentecostal encounter. She even received a dramatic healing in her body as a result of Louella's prayers.

My mother Erlita testified that Great-grandmother Miller's faith and spiritual life affected her positively too. But she and Daddy were such staunch Southern Baptists, and our denomination drew a well-demarcated line between Pentecostals and Baptists. We thought whatever Pentecostals were claiming to experience was simply bad doctrine, which, of course, we vehemently shunned.

My home church, Glenwood Baptist Church, was fabulous in so many ways. Much of who I am today is because of what I received at Glenwood Baptist Church, including the amazing Bible teaching of my pastor. Over the years, more than one hundred people from that church have gone into full-time ministry. Eventually, the Glenwood church merged with another church. But the long-lasting fruit of Glenwood Baptist Church can still be felt all over the world — *and I am a part of that fruit.*

I would never want to give the impression that people in my church deliberately tried to restrict the moving of the Holy Spirit. But what I eventually experienced as a teenage boy was outside of the range of what they believed was acceptable back then. Regardless, that church was my spiritual birthplace and the people in it were my spiritual family whom I love with all my heart to this very day.

## Spiritual Misery and Then Breakthrough

Everyone destined to grow in God eventually comes to a place of dissatisfaction in his or her spiritual life. Jesus said, "Blessed are they which do hunger and thirst after righteousness: for they shall be filled" (Matthew 5:6). Such people are blessed because their spiritual hunger and thirst starts them down a path that leads to a new encounter with God — and as they yield to that encounter, He *fills* them.

But the season of spiritual hunger and thirst that precedes this infilling can be one of the most uncomfortable, unsatisfying periods a person can ever experience. Amazingly, it is in this state of spiritual misery that a person is driven to a position where God can reveal Himself to him or her in a more meaningful, personal, and powerful way. That is exactly the season I found myself in as a young teenager.

Doctrinally and intellectually, I understood a lot about the work of the Holy Spirit. In our church, we were taught the truth about His working as the Agent of the new birth and His working to produce the character of God and the fruit of the Spirit in us, conforming us to the image of Jesus Christ. That teaching was superb, but it was primarily taught and received in the mental realm. It never put me in touch with the Holy Spirit's power in a tangible, experiential way.

But in the years 1972 and 1973 I began to wonder, *Surely there must be more to the Christian life than what I'm experiencing. Is this all there is, or is there something I'm missing?* It was as if there was a hole in the pit of my stomach, and I yearned for God to fill it up with Himself. I searched here and there, looking for someone who could help me find this deeper place in God that my heart longed for.

When I dropped by Aunt Melita's house unannounced on that sunny afternoon after school, what I encountered set me on a determined path to find what my heart had been craving to know. As I pushed the door open without knocking and stepped into her living room, I could hear she was listening to a Bible teacher on a reel-to-reel tape. I loved Bible teaching so before I yelled out to let my aunt know I was in the house, I paused to listen. Suddenly the speaker began to deliver a public message in tongues. I remember thinking, *TONGUES! This must be tongues! I can't believe I'm actually listening to a man who is speaking in tongues!* Soon, another speaker began to interpret the message that had been spoken out in tongues.

Just then, Aunt Melita strolled around the corner, not aware yet that I was in the house. When she saw me and realized I'd heard the message delivered in tongues, she froze and a panicked look filled her eyes. Melita *knew* that Daddy and Mother did not want me to be exposed to Pentecostal or Charismatic experiences. Years later, Melita told me that if she had known I was coming to her house that day, she would have put that reel-to-reel tape away out of respect for my parents.

But it was too late. She wondered, *Should I cut the tape off? What should I do?* But after she quickly prayed, on the inside, she said she felt she should leave it on. And am I ever glad she did! What I heard on that tape reached into the depths of my spirit, latched hold of me, and would not let me go — and in turn, I would not let *the Holy Spirit* go.

Today many Pentecostal and Charismatic churches have backed away from the operation of the gifts of the Spirit. The unspoken implication is that it's not popular or culturally acceptable to be known as people who speak in tongues or to associate with people who operate in those spiritual gifts. They say they're concerned that the gifts of the Spirit will scare people away. But I can tell you the gifts of the Holy Spirit did *not* scare me — and if you've had an encounter with the power of the Holy Spirit, they probably didn't scare *you* when you were first exposed to them.

In fact, at the moment I was exposed to that message in tongues at Aunt Melita's house, it felt like my spirit suddenly "stood to attention." I was like a radio receiver that finally found the signal it had long been searching for. That day I embarked on my own quest for the power of the Holy Spirit.

I was so serious about this quest that I began to drop by Aunt Melita's house every afternoon to probe what she knew about the Holy Spirit — I had so many unanswered questions. Every day, she knew I would be stopping by, so she began to prepare for my visits. Melita later said, "Rick was really seeking God. As a good, solid Baptist boy, he was earnestly seeking the truth."

Every day Aunt Melita answered my questions, but I learned later that she did it with fear and trembling because she didn't want to offend my parents. Yet she recognized that God had set a hook in my heart and had brought me to her to help me experience this divine encounter.

There are multitudes of Christians who really love God, but they haven't walked in this deeper place I'm describing. They strive to please God and to do what is right, and they go to church week after week, wondering why they feel so powerless and empty as believers. They faithfully keep up the pace, hoping that somehow, someday, it will all begin to "click" for them. Meanwhile, they feel guilty about the way they feel, and they dare not share their frustrations with anyone else.

If you've ever been in this condition, you know there's nothing more miserable and defeating than to be a Christian, sincerely trying to live the Christian life, without really knowing the power of the Holy Spirit. If this describes you, God wants to bring *you* into a deeper place that has been waiting for you for a long time.

Eventually, every hungry Christian reaches this turning point — a time when the heart is no longer satisfied and seeks for more. That is when God's

Spirit beckons that person and draws him or her closer — to enter a deeper relationship with Him. That's what was happening to me in 1972 and 1973.

### An Epiphany in the Summer of 1972 — and I Actually Traveled Outside of Sand Springs!

For my fourteenth birthday, I asked my parents for a two-day trip to New York City with my older sister Ronda. My dad's employee benefits at American Airlines meant we could fly with special passes for very little cost. I was stunned when Daddy and Mother said yes to my request. They actually let us two "kids" who'd practically never stepped outside of Tulsa County — a fourteen-year-old boy and an eighteen-year-old girl — get on a plane and go to the Big Apple.

When Ronda and I arrived in New York City, we wasted no time and immediately began pounding the pavement looking for big-city adventure. We went from Wall Street to Fifth Avenue on foot. By the end of the first evening, we both had swollen ankles from miles of walking. But we knew our experience wouldn't be complete without a Broadway show, so Ronda said, "Let's buy the cheapest tickets available to see the original production of *Pippin*," a musical based on a legendary tale of Emperor Charlemagne's son. The cast included Ben Vereen, Jill Clayburgh, Irene Ryan (who was so endearing as "Granny" from *The Beverly Hillbillies*), and John Rubenstein, who played the role of Pippin.

The story unfolds of Emperor Charlemagne's son Pippin who felt trapped by duties thrust upon him as he inherited a kingdom he didn't want in a world where he didn't fit. At a critical moment in the story, Pippin opens his heart and begins to passionately express his feelings about living in a world where he feels he doesn't fit in. The song he sings, "Corner of the Sky" was written by renowned lyricist and composer Stephen Schwartz, and in the play, the lyrics unfold Pippin's profoundest, deepest sense of feeling out of place and "out of time." Pippin was ahead of his time as he reached in his heart for a season not yet upon him — one in which he *would* fit in, find purpose, and "fly free" in his own unique *corner of the sky*.

"There's a time for every season…" My mind wandered to Ecclesiastes 3:1, where the writer, in essence, communicated those very words: *There is a season and a time for every purpose.* Hope began to well up in my heart that my dreams of doing something significant in life were not just daydreams that would never materialize. They would come in their season, and I would fulfill my God-ordained purpose.

The words to that song gripped my soul during my epiphany moment that day. It was another *unlikely* encounter. Scarcely aware of Ronda sitting next to me — or of any of my surroundings that day in the Imperial Theater on West 45th Street — I sat dumbstruck in my seat, the words sung by the Pippin character turning over and over in my mind. That song had become indelibly etched in my heart, magically transporting me to another world.

Watching the Pippin character on stage in that Broadway production, I suddenly saw the stage of *my* life. Pippin was a young man, as I was, with loving parents and a family just like mine. But like Pippin, as precious as my family was to me and as wonderful a town as Sand Springs was to its contented residents, I knew deep down that I was born for something different.

I walked out of that production with a newfound determination that I would find exactly what God had designed for my life and that I would fulfill it. The words in Pippin's song resonated with me like chords in my heart strumming a tune that was finally on key. Although I was still hounded by the dark choir that tormented me regularly, I now had a hopeful song I could embrace and call my own.

Today when I hear a recording of John Rubenstein singing this song from that old production, I am still moved to tears — so great was the work of the Holy Spirit in my heart that day in New York City.

At fourteen, I was finally grasping that God was calling me elsewhere to do something beyond anything I could ever imagine. Whatever it was, I didn't know it at the time — it was imperceptible to my mind. But I inwardly understood that my path would lead me on a very different route from the one that was familiar to my family and friends — and that it would likely lead me far away from my surroundings in Sand Springs. I was ready to let the adventure begin.

Decades have passed since that summer day in New York, but my heart still cries with the same earnest desire to do God's will — to go wherever I must go to fulfill it and to never settle for a life that's just long. I simply must be where God's Spirit can run free in and through me. Maybe that's the song of your heart too.

## Kathryn Kuhlman's Ministry
## and an Unforgettable Miracle Service in Tulsa

Back in Tulsa from New York, still in fervent seeking mode concerning the things of the Spirit, I was flipping from one radio station to the next one day when, suddenly, I was drawn into an unusual program that simply *captivated* me. Over those radio waves, I heard a woman named Kathryn Kuhlman speaking about miracles and her relationship with the Holy Spirit.

I had heard of Kathryn Kuhlman earlier as part of my ongoing spiritual search. But that day as I sat in the kitchen near our radio, my ears were tuned to every word as she described a continually growing, intimate relationship with the Holy Spirit. My heart nearly beat out of my chest! I was so excited to hear someone speak about that deeper place in God I desperately longed for.

At the beginning of each program, the announcer would come on and say, "And here she is — that young lady you've been waiting for — *Kathryn Kuhlman!*" Kathryn's first words on each broadcast were always the same: "Hello, there — and have you been waiting for me?" Although this was her usual way of addressing her listeners every day, it seemed as if she was always speaking to me personally. Well, I *was* waiting for her to teach me how to cultivate my relationship with the Holy Spirit that I was learning He wanted me to have.

I had never heard anyone speak about the Holy Spirit the way Kathryn Kuhlman did. My heart was completely captured — *mesmerized* — by what I was hearing about actually experiencing a relationship with the Holy Spirit. I wanted to experience the intimacy with Him that Kathryn Kuhlman obviously knew and lived.

When she once read from Second Corinthians 13:14, "The grace of the Lord Jesus Christ, and the love of God, and the *communion* of the Holy

Spirit be with you all," that last statement dropped into my heart with a thud, and I wondered, *What is the communion of the Holy Spirit?*

It was apparent to me that, *whatever* this communion with the Holy Spirit was, Kathryn Kuhlman had it. For one, I knew it by the way she spoke so naturally about Him and by her relationship with Him. She spoke as though He were a real Person, a real Friend with whom she shared her mornings, her afternoons, and her evenings — her *life*.

Each Friday on the broadcast, she would play actual excerpts from miracle services she was holding all over the United States. Then when she announced she would be holding one of those miracle services in Tulsa, I knew I had to be there. I mentioned to my Aunt Melita that I wanted to go, and she immediately suggested, "Rick, let's join the volunteer choir so we'll have some of the best seats in the auditorium near the stage!"

Soon Aunt Melita and I were attending choir rehearsals at First Methodist Church of Tulsa for the upcoming Kathryn Kuhlman miracle service! The actual meeting was to be held at the Mabee Center auditorium on the campus of Oral Roberts University. On the Sunday the meeting was to be held, I excused myself from my church's Sunday School a little early and drove across Tulsa to ORU to get prepared for that afternoon's miracle service.

When I arrived on the ORU campus, I couldn't believe my eyes! A sea of people *surrounded* the massive Mabee Center. The streets and parking lots were jammed with buses and carloads of people who had driven hundreds of miles — even more than a thousand in some cases — to get to this service.

I had never seen anything like it. I was grateful Aunt Melita had coaxed me into singing in the choir, because choir members were taken right into the auditorium through a back-door entrance so we could begin a final rehearsal for the service. As I made my way in, I wondered, *Why have all these people come from so far to hear this woman preach?* It wouldn't be long before I understood.

The entire back half of the auditorium's bottom floor had been partitioned off for the critically and terminally ill. A huge crowd was standing outside, but the ushers were allowing those who were debilitated to enter that special area so they wouldn't have to compete with the crowds. From where I sat in the choir, I could see scores of people in wheelchairs, with oxygen tanks, IVs, and crutches, and even on stretchers. There were also doctors and nurses in attendance with them. It looked as if an entire hospital ward had been emptied and brought to the service! Some of the critically ill had been transported by family members. Others were so close to death that they had been brought to the meeting by ambulance.

One hour before the service began, the main doors to the auditorium were opened. The crowd rushed in as fast as their feet could carry them. That sea of people poured into the seating area like swelling torrents through an open dam. They *flooded* into the aisles and then scrambled to get a seat as close to the front as possible. Soon the auditorium was filled, and those still remaining outside were diverted to an overflow area where they could watch the service by closed-circuit television. An overwhelming air of excitement and faith filled the auditorium and could be felt in the atmosphere around us.

I couldn't help but look in curious wonderment at the section reserved for the wheelchairs and stretchers. The people in that section were so sick. I knew that many of them had come to the meeting out of desperation. This was their last hope. I found myself praying quietly, "Oh, Lord, please don't let them be disappointed today."

The ushers walked up and down the aisles offering various booklets that contained testimonies of those who had received medically confirmed miracles in other services with Kathryn Kuhlman. I reached out and chose three of the booklets and read them as I waited for the choir director to come on stage. What amazing testimonies they were! By the time I had finished reading that third little booklet, I could sense my faith rising to a place it had never been before.

Moments before the service began, a crusade spokesman came to the microphone and announced that miracles had already occurred even while people were waiting for the service to begin. Once again I could sense my faith and the corporate faith of that massive congregation rise in expectation. It was so buoyant and strong, it seemed as if it could have lifted the building right off its foundation!

Then the choir director appeared before us, beckoning us to stand to our feet and to get ready to sing. The huge throng stood with us as we sang and worshiped the Lord. Thousands of voices — Southern Baptists, Methodists,

Catholics, Episcopalians, Presbyterians, Lutherans, Greek Orthodox, Pentecostals, and Charismatics — were all joining together in the adoration and worship of God.

Then the entire crowd began to sing the song, "How Great Thou Art." As we did, Kathryn Kuhlman came out on the platform to sing with us. It was my first time to see her in person. Dressed in a long white gown, she moved gracefully back and forth on the stage. In her deep, contralto voice, she sang out, "Then sings my soul, my Savior God, to Thee: How great Thou art, how great Thou art…."

When the music and instruments stopped, Kathryn Kuhlman welcomed the people and then led us as we all sang the chorus, "Alleluia." I remember thinking, *This must be what Heaven will be like.*

After more worship, Kathryn Kuhlman approached the microphone to speak. One hour passed like seconds. Being in that auditorium on that afternoon was like being invited to publicly view the private, dynamic, and intimate relationship between this woman and the Spirit of God. It was truly remarkable to experience. Here a human was engaging in intimate fellowship with the Holy Spirit right in front of us. Although I had grown up in church all my life and had been saved as a young child, I had never seen or even heard about what I was witnessing that day. Watching this woman relate to the Holy Spirit was more dramatic and impacting to me than any sermon that could have been preached. It was the most moving thing I had ever seen in my life — wonderful beyond words.

Interrupting her own message at one point, Kathryn pointed her finger toward a section of seats at the top of the auditorium and said, "Someone right up there has just received a miracle. Stand up and claim it!"

At the same time, a whirlwind of power *rushed* through the auditorium, and miracles of healing started taking place throughout the congregation. Soon people were lining up near the stage to testify about what had happened in their bodies. Paralyzed people got up from their wheelchairs and stretchers and walked — and blind eyes and deaf ears were opened.

For about three hours, I watched in amazement as the supernatural power of God continued on full display. Everything I'd ever dreamed — everything

I'd ever wanted to believe in — was happening right before my eyes. If any lingering question about God's miracle-working power had tried to hide in my soul, it was utterly dissolved as I watched those wheelchairs and stretchers being emptied and people who had been unable to walk or move now walk — and even run — from one end of the stage to the other. Soon the entire front of the auditorium and the aisles on the bottom floor were jammed full of people who had come forward to give their lives to Christ.

*What a powerful meeting that was!* Not only did I see multiple miracles of the human body, but I also saw miracles of salvation for the human spirit! All my denominational teaching that miracles no longer occurred was stripped away by the end of that service. And no one could accuse Kathryn Kuhlman of taking glory for herself, because *no one* received the glory that day except Jesus Christ.

But the thing that struck my heart even more than the miracles was the vibrant, intimate relationship between the Holy Spirit and a human being that I'd witnessed during those three hours. It was something I had only dreamed was possible. How remarkable it was to watch Kathryn Kuhlman flow in the gifts of the Spirit and respond to the Holy Spirit's gracious, gentle leading that yielded powerful, *fierce* manifestations of healings and deliverances from bondages that were afflicting God's crowning creation. This was no oasis mirage in the desert. Surely God had brought me to this place to see the kind of relationship He wanted *me* to have with the Holy Spirit. Surely He would not leave me disappointed.

From that moment on, it was my heart's passion to become an intimate, cherished friend with the Holy Spirit. My heart and soul longed to discover the secret place in God I had witnessed that Sunday afternoon on the campus of Oral Roberts University. I wanted to know the real-life communion of the Holy Spirit.

## A Confrontation by My Pastor

Because I was completely intrigued by what I was learning at Aunt Melita's house every day, I began to pose questions to my Sunday School teachers about the Holy Spirit. Since that was an off-limits topic, it didn't take long before my pastor got wind of it and called me into his office for a face-to-face confrontation. There he rehearsed to me several appalling stories about Pentecostals. He was talking about people who were not perfect, no doubt, and although they loved God, there were those who indeed did not represent Him in the best way possible. And it had a negative effect on "outsiders" looking curiously into their experience.

In that confrontation in my pastor's office, he also elaborately detailed to me all the flawed points in their doctrines and expressed freely his certainty that many of "those Pentecostals" were mentally deranged. He sincerely believed the gifts of the Holy Spirit were no longer in operation and didn't want me getting caught up in something that would negatively affect me.

I am one-hundred percent positive my pastor had my best interests at heart as he talked to me that day. He loved me and didn't want to see me go in a spiritual direction that he believed was wrong. I'm also sure he thought he'd put the subject to bed when I walked out of his office. But it was too late. I had already been exposed to a new realm of God, and I was in hot pursuit to know for myself this new dimension of the Holy Spirit.

When my pastor finally realized that I would not let the matter rest, from the pulpit, he began to publicly say things like, "We have a boy in our church who's been going to some strange meetings, and I advise you to be careful of him." Also because of me, he launched a seven-week series on Wednesday nights called, "The Errors and Excesses of the Charismatic Movement." The entire series was designed to convince *me* that I was headed in a wrong direction — but as he addressed me, of course, the whole church got to hear the series!

Week after week, he pounded the message into our minds that anyone who believed in the gifts of the Holy Spirit was silly and childish. And every Wednesday night I took detailed notes of everything he said — and then the following day, I'd head to Aunt Melita's house with notes in hand to see how she would respond to his allegations. My aunt was right — I *was* a good Baptist boy who was in vehement search of truth!

I am amazed that Melita took all that time to patiently answer my many questions about the Holy Spirit. I was just a teenage boy, but because she could tell that I was genuinely hungry for a deeper experience with God, she made time with me a priority. Like my mother, my aunt perceived that God had a special plan for my life, and she had yielded herself to God to be a part of it.

We must always be available to those who are sincerely seeking answers from God's Word. Melita could have said, "Ricky's just a teenager. I'm too busy for this." But instead, she set aside time every afternoon to meet with me and answer my questions. Those afternoon meetings eventually led me into the power of the Holy Spirit. And the power of the Holy Spirit is how I became enabled to have the ministry that God ultimately entrusted to me. I am so thankful Aunt Melita invested that time in me!

Melita actually typed out answers to the charges my pastor brought against anyone with a Pentecostal or Charismatic experience. I still have those worn, typewritten notes today, and from time to time, I take them out to reread them. They are so precious to me because they represent the time she took with me to teach me invaluable truths from God's Word that I cherish and live by to this day. Line-by-line, point-by-point, and verse-by-verse, she intelligently answered every question I posed with solid answers from the Bible.

In First Peter 3:15, we are told, "But sanctify the Lord God in your hearts: and be ready always to give an *answer* to every man that asketh you a reason of the hope that is in you with meekness and fear." The word "answer" in this verse is the very word used to depict a trial where one position is defended against accusations or allegations from a differing position.

That is exactly what Aunt Melita did for me. She was always ready to give an answer as she biblically defended every point of accusation concerning the legitimacy of the baptism in the Holy Spirit and the manifestations of His power.

And that was just what I needed. I wasn't interested in just hearing about someone's experience, although that intrigued me. I wanted *biblical answers* to satisfy my heart and mind. And the Lord used Melita Davis to provide those answers for me.

Many people are regrettably unable to intelligently explain what they believe from the Bible. But it is important that each of us studies to be able to provide *biblical answers* for any person who is sincerely seeking God and His Word. So I must ask you — can *you* defend what you biblically believe?

As I've written many books over the years, I've kept Aunt Melita in mind as I've done my best to craft intelligent responses to questions I hear people asking. I want them to *really* know what the Bible says concerning these serious questions. Remembering Melita's example and the command in First Peter 3:15 to give a ready answer, I have endeavored to answer people's questions about the Bible intelligently and with meekness and reverential fear.

### A Wonderful, Unlikely Encounter With God's Power

Seeing that I was Baptist to my bones, it seems *unlikely* that it could happen, but on January 11, 1974, I received the baptism in the Holy Spirit. On that Friday after school, I dashed to Aunt Melita's house because I knew I was ready be filled with the Holy Spirit. Huffing and puffing, as I literally ran to her house from school, I burst through the front door exclaiming, "Today I want to be filled with the Holy Spirit! I am ready for it right now!"

Melita looked at me practically spellbound. "Rick," she started slowly. "I've never asked the Lord for anything for my birthday before. But today, for my birthday, I asked that you would be filled with the Holy Spirit as a gift to me."

We wasted no time kneeling right there at her coffee table in her living room, Aunt Melita on one side and me on the other. She reached across the table to lay her hands on the top of my head as she prayed for me to receive the baptism in the Holy Spirit. She prayed in tongues, she prayed in English, and she even prophesied over me. It felt like liquid fire descended from the top of my head all the way to the bottom of my feet.

When she finished praying, she looked into my eyes to see what had happened to me. Right in front of her was a young Rick Renner so filled with the Holy Spirit that I didn't know if I could contain any more!

### I Was Instantly Set Free
### From the Torment of the Past

When I received the baptism in the Holy Spirit, a divine power was released inside me. In a flash, the insecurities and struggles that hounded me since childhood *disappeared*! It wasn't a slow transition that took place over a period of time — not that it couldn't happen that way in a person's life. But what happened to me was instantaneous. In a mere "second" of time, I was completely *freed* from the harassing, tormenting thoughts that had pestered, pounded, and pummeled my soul for as long as I could remember.

In the blink of an eye, a torrent of power had come upon me that drove all the shadows of evil away.

In Acts 1:8, Jesus described this power when He said, "And ye shall receive power after that the Holy Ghost is come upon you...." I find it so interesting that word "power" in Acts 1:8 is the identical Greek word used to depict *the full force and might of an advancing army*. By using this particular word, Jesus promised that when the power of the Holy Spirit is finally released in a person's life, it's like an army of God's power that drives away darkness, brings the light of God, and ministers delivering power to anyone who is bound.

That mighty army of power is what came upon me that day in Aunt Melita's living room. That is *exactly* what happened! And when the power of God was "detonated" inside me that day, it exploded upon my soul to drive out and obliterate all those inner struggles from my life. And it all happened in a spectacular flash of time!

- I had been filled with inner turmoil, but now I was filled with peace.
- I had been filled with timidity and insecurity, but now I was filled with courage and confidence.
- I had been filled with fear, but now I was filled with faith.

Everything that Satan intended for evil in my life was wiped away in one moment of time.

Second Timothy 1:7 reveals that it is God's desire to, by His power, give us a "sound mind" and to eradicate those things that once captivated us. And that's what He did for me. The power of God blasted through that evil, and

God Himself by His Spirit delivered unto me *a sound mind — a completely delivered brain*!

What happened to me that afternoon after school was nothing short of miraculous. It was like one young man existed just seconds earlier, but a brand-new man emerged seconds later to take his place. The cowardice, hang-ups, self-consciousness, struggles, and inner turmoil that had completely controlled my self-image and run my life instantly melted away. Just as Clark Kent would enter a phone booth as a normal man, but astoundingly emerge as Superman, I, too, was instantly *changed* into a new young man.

Of course, Clark Kent and Superman are fictional characters, but nothing about what happened to me was fictional. God's power literally manifested as the force of an army to sweep over enemy lines and reclaim the territory — *me and my mind* — that had belonged to Him the entire time!

It's interesting that all these years later, God has exponentially grown my ministry as a Bible teacher to the Body of Christ around the world. In my books that have been published in many languages, several of which are bestsellers — and through public meetings, television, and the Internet — God has graced me over many decades to exegete New Testament Greek. Many see me as a gifted writer and intelligent thinker — not as a "stupid" misfit who's unqualified to lead or to serve the Church as a teacher and communicator of truth from God's Word.

What I'm doing today in the international Church community is *exactly opposite* the enemy's plans to derail me and destroy me from the inside out with his vicious attacks on my mind. He used broken, weakened people — often those in positions of authority — as his mouthpiece to "authenticate" his accusations and to hurt me. But *God* strategically set people in place in my life to *help* me! And by His Spirit, He set me completely free.

Today I see so clearly the schemes and machinations of the enemy to destroy me. They are absurd when I think of them after all these years. But I didn't see it as a malevolent plot back then when I was just a child and the fight was unfair.

One of the most valuable lessons I've taken from this horrible experience in my life that lasted many years is that our words are more important than we've realized — words we say to ourselves as well as to others. The Bible has much to say about the power of what emanates from our heart and our mouth into the atmosphere around us. This topic would make a good Bible study for any serious disciple of Christ and His Word. But simply put, as believers, our words are to minister grace and edification, not corruption and destruction, to those around us (*see* Ephesians 4:29).

## My Transformation Was Visible

I was so completely transformed by the Holy Spirit as a fifteen-year-old boy that people around me knew something had happened. I began carrying my Bible to school every day and to boldly witness to others, even standing on a ledge in one of the long hallways in the high school to preach to students as they walked by on their way to class. I even started a club that met before school called, "Alive in Christ" in which students could gather to pray, study their Bible, and allow the Holy Spirit to move among us. Many students got saved and were filled with the Holy Spirit through that group.

The change in my life was so visible that the high-school drama teacher could see it and said to me, "Rick, whatever has happened to you, I want it to happen to me too." Soon afterward, I laid hands on him there at the school to receive the baptism in the Holy Spirit. And He was gloriously filled and began to speak in tongues!

Through my experience, we had a real visitation of the Spirit of God at Charles Page High School in Sand Springs!

## I Had Become Charismatic and Now I Had To Get Past the Weirdness

Because I didn't personally know a lot of people outside my church, I didn't know very many people who had been baptized in the Holy Spirit, as I had just experienced. So in the early months of 1974, I decided to venture beyond the walls of my denominational church to make some Spirit-filled friends who could help take me deeper in my relationship with the Holy Spirit.

Pentecostals were the only group I knew about that really understood the supernatural power of the Holy Spirit. But I was afraid of them because of all the things I'd heard over the years. I'd heard stories about their wild meetings, in which they swung on chandeliers and even rolled in the aisles in their churches. Over my many years since I've been baptized in the Holy Spirit, I have never seen anyone swing from a chandelier. But that was the rumor I'd heard over and over, and that's why I was leery at this early date about diving unbridled into this new experience.

Also, as a young boy, my friends and I laughed at the way Pentecostal women looked. The men always seemed to wear beautiful suits, but their poor wives looked as if they had been stored away in a dusty closet and were only occasionally brought out for the public to see. The way Pentecostal girls dressed also made a bad impression on me. They wore long sleeves, buttoned-up blouses all the way up to their collars, dresses or skirts down to their ankles, and beehive hairdos. I wondered how they got so much hair to stand on top of their head and, because I knew they weren't allowed to cut their hair, I imagined just how long their hair would be if they took the beehive down. That was my mental image of Pentecostals.

## My First Charismatic Meeting

When I began my search for those who could lead me spiritually deeper, I didn't want to find it among traditional Pentecostals because that wasn't attractive to me at all. So I looked for a more refined kind of Pentecostal that had begun to emerge in those days — *Charismatics*.

Charismatics were those who had received the baptism in the Holy Spirit, as I had, but who were from every denominational background. In those days, there weren't as many large churches as there are today, but all over the country at that time, Spirit-filled believers were meeting together in home Bible studies to listen to teaching tapes and to learn how to move in the gifts of the Spirit. I decided to take a step in that direction, so I located a group like that in our town and found out what time the next meeting would begin.

*Finally the day came.* I was both excited and scared. I was excited to encounter the power of the Holy Spirit, but scared because of everything I'd heard from fellow Baptists about wild emotionalism. So with tentativeness and apprehension, I went to that first meeting to see what I would experience. I nervously knocked at the door and was greeted by the very friendly and welcoming homeowner. I placed my Bible on a seat and went to the kitchen to get a cup of coffee before the meeting started. There were doctors, nurses, teachers, housewives, and lay preachers in this home meeting that night. Although I still remembered some of my pastor's words, I began to relax a little because these people seemed very nice and normal to me.

When it was time for the meeting to begin, I returned to my seat full of expectation. The meeting started quite normally with an opening prayer and a few testimonies. Then the group began to sing praise choruses, some of which I'd heard before. But then that very quickly moved into singing in the Spirit.

This marked the first time I had ever heard anyone sing in the Spirit. *It was the most beautiful sound I had ever heard in my life!* It sounded as if the angels of Heaven had descended into the room and were singing the praises of God with us. I was *enraptured.*

## Charismatic 'Flippers'

But then, with no warning at all, the woman seated in the chair next to me suddenly threw her body back in her chair and "went rigid" as if she was caught in some kind of convulsion. I looked at her as she bore down on the arms of her chair with her forearms and then gripped the corners of the arms with her hands and arched back, almost violently, into her previous rigid position. It looked like she was convulsing and simultaneously lapsing into some sort of trance.

Then in a high-pitched tone, she started shrieking, her eyelids fluttering and twitching, *"Ooh! Ooooh! He's h-e-e-e-r-e!*

I could see the veins in her neck bulging as her voice rose to a crescendo, then descended, and then rose again. I was so alarmed by what was happening, but I was even *more* alarmed that no one else in the room seemed to notice!

Careful not to startle this woman or do more harm than good as I tried to assist her, I leaned in cautiously and whispered, *"Are you all right? Can I help you?"*

As if she was responding to me for all the room to hear, she shrieked again, *"He's here! He's here RIGHT NOW!"*

I couldn't figure out who she was talking about and didn't know how she could possibly know someone was there, because her eyes were closed. I leaned in again and asked her, *"Who's here?"*

Between shrieks, she had to come up for air. Stammering to get the words out, she said, *"He...He...He..."* Then, finally, she burst through the stammering, proclaiming to all, "He's *here* — the Holy Spirit is *HERE*!"

Adrenaline surged through my body, as this was just what I'd been hoping to see — *a supernatural manifestation* of the Holy Spirit.

Just then the woman started groaning. *"Oh, oh, o-h-h!"* she cried. But I could not be distracted from my mission to see a supernatural sign of the Holy Spirit's presence. By this time, I felt I had some rapport with the woman, so once again, I whispered, *"Where? Where* is the Holy Spirit? And how do you know His power is here right now?"

As quick as a flash, she unbuttoned the cuffs on her sleeves and rolled her sleeves up above her elbows. *"There!* Do you see these goose bumps on my arms? That is how I know the Holy Spirit's power is here! These goose bumps are the witness of the Holy Ghost!"

I stared down at her arms. Sure enough, they were covered with tiny little chill bumps.

Now my mind was reeling. I wondered why she thought those chill bumps were the witness of the Holy Spirit. But never in my entire Christian life had I encountered Holy Spirit goose bumps in the Baptist church. I wondered, *Was this a legitimate spiritual manifestation, or was this the wild emotionalism that the Baptists had been warning me about all these years?*

But because I was so hungry and wanted to believe so badly, I reached down, unbuttoned my cuffs, and rolled up my sleeves to see what was happening on *my* arms.

Sure enough — *goose bumps!* However, I was disappointed, and certainly not convinced, because I knew my goose bumps were due to the extremely cool temperature in that house.

My goose bumps were just plain old, everyday, ordinary goose bumps. There wasn't anything supernatural about the chill bumps on my arms. A small adjustment to the thermostat, and they would disappear as quickly as they came.

The whole incident seemed very strange to me. I walked away from that first meeting trying hard to believe I had encountered something wonderful and marvelous — but all I walked away with was "Holy Spirit" goose bumps!

However, as strange as the lady in the chair next to me was — and as turned off as I was by the goose-bumps ordeal — I couldn't get away from the marvelous presence and power of God I felt when we were singing in the Spirit together in that home meeting. Although I was genuinely freaked out by that woman's exclamations of spiritual goose bumps, I had also genuinely been touched by God in a tangible way in that meeting. And I was in desperate pursuit of Him, willing to go anywhere necessary to learn more about His Spirit's power and presence.

## I Took My Sunday School Teacher To See 'Elvis'

A short time after that, I heard that a radio preacher from another city was coming to hold a series of meetings in Tulsa. Word was circulating around town that great miracles and healings occurred in this man's services.

I decided that this would be the perfect opportunity to convert some of my Baptist friends to the "deeper" life of the Spirit. My first convert would be my Baptist Sunday School teacher. I told him about the meeting and invited him to join me. I knew if I could just get him to a meeting, he would leave gloriously filled with the Spirit of God. So after a little coaxing, I convinced him to go.

My anticipation at this larger, more organized meeting was at an all-time high. As we waited for the service to start, I kept looking over at my Baptist Sunday School teacher, thinking, *You are going to see things today that you've never seen before.* It was to be a horrifyingly accurate prediction that I would later regret.

When that radio evangelist came to the platform, I could hardly believe what my conservative, small-town, Baptist eyes were seeing. I had only heard this man on the radio, so this was my first time to see him in person. *I was in shock.*

The minister walked slowly across the stage dressed in a white tuxedo with shiny satin lapels. A bright red carnation in his lapel matched his red oxford shirt with French cuffs that peeked out of his coat sleeves like the sharp plastic curl of a child's pinwheel. The evangelist's coiffed jet-black hair was stacked high upon his head, combed backward into a shiny, seamless wave. His hair stood as stiff as my stunned countenance that was now frozen forward, not daring to look my Baptist Sunday School teacher in the face.

As the evangelist walked closer toward the edge of the stage, I could see the lavish gold chains that hung from his wrists and the multiple diamond rings that adorned his fingers on each hand. The minister's gait suddenly turned to a bit of a swagger as he strolled the length of the platform in four-inch, patent-leather platform shoes that he'd had plenty of practice wearing or I'm certain he would have tripped and fallen. I practically held my breath in fear that at any moment, he would begin performing an Elvis Presley number right there on the stage during his Holy Ghost meeting.

Under his arm, this minister carried the biggest white family Bible I had ever seen. At that point, I had been holding my composure decently well considering the circumstances. But when I finally gained the nerve to turn toward my Sunday School teacher sitting beside me, I saw in his face *horror*, and I grimaced in mental pain of my own as I sunk lower into my seat, wishing the meeting would end.

But that meeting was just warming up. The radio preacher walked back and forth on the stage as he welcomed everyone to the meeting. Then with no warning whatsoever, I watched in amazement as he threw his body into the wildest contortions I had ever seen. I didn't know the human body could go in so many directions at the same time. It was one of the freakiest things I had ever witnessed. I went from grimaced to *aghast* as he flipped his back *this* way, then *that* way, then *this* way again. He was yelling the entire time, *"There He g-o-e-s! There He G-O-E-S!"*

Because of the home meeting I'd attended, this was not language I was unfamiliar with. Only instead of the Holy Spirit *"coming here"*—this time, apparently, He was *going somewhere*. I looked to see if I could perhaps tell where the Holy Spirit was going when, *suddenly*, the minister clarified the Spirit's whereabouts for the audience.

"There He *g-o-o-o-o-e-s!*" the evangelist continued. "The Holy Ghost is running up and down my backbone! *WHEW!*"

I shut my eyes and reopened them slowly, hoping I was just dreaming. But when I opened my eyes, the speaker was still flopping back and forth on the stage — and by this time, most of the crowd around us had lapsed into the same frenzy. A woman seated in front of us was wearing a back brace, and I kept thinking, "If this poor woman keeps flopping back and forth with that back brace on, she is going to break her body in half!" Another woman across the aisle from us fell on the floor in a spasm.

Of all the meetings to bring a Baptist leader to, this was the worst one I could have chosen. All my hopes of introducing him to a deep and meaningful walk with the Holy Spirit dissipated right in front of me as these sincere, but emotion-driven believers equated goose bumps on the arms and chills down the spine with a move of the Spirit of God.

### 'To Be or Not To Be' Charismatic — That Was My Question

As a Southern Baptist, I was taught to make no room for emotion. But here I was, surrounded by what I considered to be *a sea* of emotion. I was beginning to understand why our denomination had dismissed this

Charismatic business. Today I understand from a different perspective much of what I saw in those meetings. But back then, I was disappointed in what I'd witnessed so far in my journey. Surely there was more to the supernatural walk of the Spirit than what I was seeing. It seemed that Charismatics were completely driven by emotions — goose bumps and chills down the spine.

I soon found myself in prayer, asking the same question Shakespeare's Hamlet asked in his dilemma: "To be or not to be?" Here I was, already at a crossroads concerning my involvement with others who'd been baptized in the Holy Spirit — *and I had just gotten started!* While I had experienced a new realm of God when I was filled with the Holy Spirit, I was shocked by what I was seeing in Charismatic circles. I honestly didn't know what to do. I asked, "Shall I go on with these people whose spiritual lives appear to be no deeper than a goose bump, or shall I return to my denominational church, which lacks power but at least has a sound mind?"

In all fairness, it is absolutely true that when the power of the Spirit manifests, unusual things can happen. In my own meetings across the world, I have seen God do some very unusual things. And remember that when the Holy Spirit was poured out upon the Church on the Day of Pentecost, the disciples' behavior was so unusual that people assumed they were drunk. So we simply cannot eliminate the possibility of spiritual expressions that are different from what we are accustomed to experiencing.

The Charismatic Movement of the 1970s was a real outpouring of God's Spirit that by divine enablement spawned many of the worldwide ministries we know today. But in the first months of my experience, it felt to me like Charismatics depended on wild emotions to determine whether any power was present. Because I had been taught not to base my relationship with the Lord on my feelings, this was a far cry from the deeper life I was pursuing.

## My Current Thoughts on the Charismatic Movement

I'm sharing with you my honest first impressions of Charismatics when I was a young man just having experienced the baptism in the Holy Spirit. Today I can handle with joy all the various ways people respond to the moving of the Spirit. But back then, I thought a lot of it was weird, and for a time, I had a bit of dilemma on my hands after my encounter with God's power — whether or not I would be a part of the Charismatic Movement and the fellowship of the saints who'd had that same encounter.

But as I said, my baptism in the Holy Spirit is what enabled me to be effective in the ministry that God would ultimately entrust to me — a ministry that would reach around the world and penetrate the deep darkness of atheism with the glorious light of Christ and His Gospel. I'm glad I didn't dismiss the whole experience just because I'd witnessed a few incidents I didn't understand!

It's obvious that any reservations I'd initially had have now been completely resolved. I unequivocally view the Charismatic Movement as a supernatural move of the Holy Spirit that is desperately necessary to advance the cause of Christ to the ends of the earth. It is a God-sent movement to energize the Church with His own power and might so that we can accomplish our Christ-commissioned task of reaching the world for Him before His return. *I am so thankful to be a part of it!*

## The Ministry of Derek Prince: Intelligent Teaching *and* a Supernatural Experience

At long last, I found a home Bible study that was attended by Spirit-filled people who were madly in love with solid Bible teaching. It was held in the home of a dentist, Dr. Robinson, who lived on the far end of Sand Springs. He and his family — him, his precious wife, and all their children — had also been gloriously filled with the Holy Spirit. Dr. Robinson was a strong man spiritually who had a sound approach to the Bible and to the work of the Holy Spirit.

The Robinsons owned something very rare in the early 1970s — a *tape duplicator* that could duplicate six cassette tapes at a time! Plus, they had a massive collection of teaching tapes tucked away in a cabinet that was a real-life treasure chest filled with precious spiritual riches. When I opened that cabinet and looked at all those marvelous master cassette tapes with so many various themes, they beckoned me to dive in and dig deep!

Among that massive collection of teachings were a lot of teachings by a group of men, referred to as the Fort Lauderdale Five, who had aligned themselves with each other to bring intelligent, balanced, Bible-based, Spirit-filled ministry to the Body of Christ. The five men were Charles Simpson, Don Basham, Ern Baxter, Bob Mumford, and Derek Prince. All of them had marvelous teaching gifts, but the teaching ministry of Derek Prince stood out to me above them all.

Derek Prince (1915–2003) was born in India to British parents. Educated as a scholar of Greek and Latin at Eton College and Cambridge University, England, he also held a fellowship in Ancient and Modern Philosophy at King's College. Additionally, he studied several modern languages, including Hebrew and Aramaic, at Cambridge University and the Hebrew University in Jerusalem. His years at Cambridge brought him into contact with some of the luminaries of the age, and he devoted himself to studying philosophy, reading every word that Plato had ever written in the original Greek. He also wrote poetry in Latin and Greek and had earned a solid reputation in his field. Still, he confessed that he was confused and frustrated with this world and longed for "something that was real."[4]

In the 1940s when Derek Prince was drafted into the Royal Army, he realized he would not have room in his kit for books, so he tried to think of one large, engaging volume that he had never read before that would last him for months — something that would make him a better philosopher. When he settled on the Bible, he bought himself a large black *King James Version*, the first Bible he'd ever owned. He began to study it, and he experienced a life-changing encounter with Jesus Christ as a result. Out of this encounter, he formed two conclusions: first, that Jesus Christ is alive; and second, that the Bible is a true, relevant, up-to-date book.[5]

These conclusions altered the whole course of Derek's life, which he then devoted to studying and teaching the Bible. His main gift of explaining the Bible in a clear and simple way has helped build a foundation of faith in millions of lives. At the end of his life, Derek spent much of his time in Jerusalem, where he died in 2003 and where he is buried today. More than 80 books are accredited to him, along with 600 audio teachings and 110 video teachings, many of which have been translated into more than 100 languages. His daily radio broadcast continues to touch lives around the world.

But it was in that early moment at Dr. Robinson's home when I learned of the ministry of Derek Prince. The first time I heard him teach — from one of those cassette tapes from the Robinsons' spiritual treasure chest — I was *captivated*. It was the first time I had ever heard anyone teach from the original language of the Greek New Testament. When I heard him teach with nuances from New Testament Greek, something "clicked" in me and set me on a course that would affect my own teaching ministry in the years to come. It was as if the Spirit of God reached into my heart and mind to say, "This is a taste of what I want you to do in your ministry."

Although I didn't agree with all of Derek's teachings on demonology, I nonetheless found his intellectual and historical approach to the Bible to be liberating. It is impossible to exaggerate how greatly God used Derek Prince's influence to help determine the course of my own ministry. Later in his life when he conducted several large events in the territory of the former Soviet Union, it was my honor to send our TV crew to film those events for him, and I still cherish several letters he wrote to me from Jerusalem in the later years of his life.

## My Miraculous Healing in 1974
## at a Kenneth E. Hagin Meeting

In the mid-summer of 1974 I was hospitalized due to a severe kidney infection that was caused by a condition I was born with called horseshoe kidney, or renal fusion.

As a baby develops in the womb, the kidneys move into position — one on each side of the body — but sometimes the kidneys fuse together at their base, forming a "U" or a horseshoe shape. In essence, they are conjoined much like Siamese twins. This uncommon condition can produce chronic kidney obstructions, kidney infections, kidney stones, kidney cancer, and even problems with the heart, blood vessels, nervous system, reproductive system, urinary system, digestive system, and bones.

In severe cases, doctors can even recommend the kidneys be surgically separated. Because I had persistent kidney obstructions, my urologist wanted to surgically separate my kidneys. But in the mid-1970s, this was considered to be a high-risk surgery. So my parents decided to see if medication would remove the obstruction so we could avoid a risky surgery.

That summer I was on fire for God and in fervent pursuit of knowing the power of the Holy Spirit. I heard that Kenneth E. Hagin was going to hold a meeting at the Sheridan Road Assembly in Tulsa. It was Kenneth E. Hagin whom I'd heard on that tape at Melita's house — and I had also listened to him on his daily radio program. I found comfort in listening to him because everything he taught was so solid and rooted in the Bible. He was also from a Southern Baptist background. Knowing that he and I had a similar doctrinal foundation gave me a sense of trust when I listened to him on the radio.

So I decided to attend those meetings in July 1974. I was astonished my parents gave me permission to attend the services because that kind of teaching was outside the scope of what we believed. It was a historic week of meetings filled with the power of God — with signs and wonders and other supernatural happenings.

During that week, Brother Hagin preached a message which is still well-known by many called, "El Shaddai." The packed auditorium was *"electric"* as the anointing of God moved across the crowd. All of a sudden, Brother Hagin leaped from the stage and began running around the auditorium — for sure, this was something I had never witnessed in my denominational church. I watched as he prayed for people with uneven limbs and their legs grew out right in front of all of us! Tongues, interpretation of tongues, and prophecy flowed in each evening service that week. The power of God erupted, and every night more and more people packed into that space to experience a divine encounter with the anointing of God.

So many key people were there that week, but at that time, they were all relatively unknown. For example, a young man named Kenneth Copeland was there and he prophesied. A young woman named Vicki Jamison sang prophetic words over the crowd. Buddy Harrison and Vep Ellis led worship. Kenneth W. Hagin made the announcements and was responsible for the introductions. His wife Lynette played the organ. An unknown young man named Bob Yandian recorded the services on audiotape. An unknown man from California named Fred Price testified of being healed of a tumor. A singer named David Ingles played the piano and sang by the Spirit. Kenneth Copeland's daughter, Terri, had brought her boyfriend to meet her dad, Kenneth, in that meeting that week too. Today they are lovingly known as Pastors George and Terri Pearsons at Eagle Mountain International Church, located at the headquarters of Kenneth Copeland Ministries in Newark, Texas.

Many of these people eventually became well known in the Charismatic Movement, and they are my friends today. But I was also there in that meeting — a young teenager so hungry for the power of God.

On July 24, 1974 — during those same meetings — Brother Hagin preached a message called, "A Man Full of Faith and Power" from the example of Stephen in Acts chapter 8. I still vividly remember that message. He described Stephen as a common man who had surrendered himself, and as a result became a man of faith and power whose life was marked with mighty signs and wonders. At the end of the message, Brother Hagin asked people to come forward for the laying on of hands if they felt called to surrender to God's service.

I had known I was called to the ministry, but on that night, my heart and spirit were tugged to move out of my pew to go to the front for the laying on of hands to receive a divine impartation of the anointing for full-time ministry.

However, because this whole atmosphere was unfamiliar to me, I hesitated. I lingered until Brother Hagin had nearly reached the end of the line as he prayed for those who had gone forward. I desperately wanted to go to the altar, but trepidation held me back. Finally, I broke free from the grip I had on the pew in front of me, and I moved to the altar to receive prayer. By the time I got into place, Brother Hagin was sitting on the platform to rest before continuing. So I stood, along with a few others and waited...*and waited...and waited.*

Brother Hagin descended from the platform to finish laying hands on the last of us "stragglers" who had come forward. When he passed in front of me, he spoke quietly in tongues as he reached out to touch my forehead with a single finger. When he touched me with the mere tip of his finger, instantly, I felt a wave of God's power flood over my whole being and I found myself falling onto the ground! My legs literally collapsed from under me, and I crumpled to the floor. I could feel the power of God radiating from one end of my body to the other end.

Minutes later when I stood to my feet, I had received a special empowerment for service, but I had also been *completely healed* of the kidney obstruction. I inwardly knew God had touched my kidneys. When I returned to see the doctor to be checked, my physician verified that I had been healed — and in the decades since that event occurred, I have never had a single reoccurrence of that obstruction. I was *supernaturally* and *permanently* healed by the power of the Holy Spirit when I fell to the floor under His mighty power that eventful evening in the summer of 1974.

### Why Do People Collapse Under the Power of God?

People often wonder why people collapse when they come in contact with a supernatural flow of God's power. But as you study the Old and New Testaments, you'll find there were *many* who fell to the ground when they encountered the strong presence of God.

- Genesis 17:3 records that Abram *collapsed* when God spoke to him.
- Joshua 5:14,15 tells us that Joshua *collapsed* when he experienced the presence of God.
- Ezekiel 1:28 and 3:23 say that Ezekiel *collapsed* when God's glory appeared to him.
- Daniel 8:17 and 10:15 state that Daniel *collapsed* when he encountered the glory of God.
- Matthew 17:6 records that when God's glory was manifested to Peter, James, and John, all three of these men *collapsed* to the ground.
- Acts 9:4 and 26:14 reveal that Paul *collapsed* to the earth when he saw Christ on the road to Damascus.
- Revelation 1:17 tells that the apostle John *collapsed* at the feet of Jesus at the beginning of his vision on the island of Patmos.

So if you hear of someone crumpling to the floor in the presence of God, don't be too surprised. There are a lot of scriptural examples of people falling or collapsing when they come in contact with God's supernatural power. I encourage you to look at each of the examples I just shared and search this truth out for yourself. This "falling" may not be a common event in your church, but it has scriptural precedence and it still happens. As I noted, it *undeniably* happened to me.

If you're standing in a prayer line to receive prayer, and you feel the strength go from you — surrender to it and let the Holy Spirit perform a divine operation in your life. This may even happen in the privacy of your own home. For me, the experience of collapsing in God's presence was *real*, and it resulted in a permanent healing in my body. God has used such moments in other people's lives to remove bitterness, hardness of heart, and to perform all kinds of "spiritual surgeries." Be assured — His power is not just for display, but for *purpose* so He can work in your life in ways that you can't work on your own.

### Grandma Ettie Also Stepped in To Help Me

After that experience in the Kenneth E. Hagin meeting, my pursuit for the deeper things of God was turned up a notch and, really, that desire began to burn inside me like an insatiable spiritual fire. My precious mother, my Aunt Melita, and others had been such a God-given help to me — used by Him to guide me along my path of divine destiny, even when that path at times cut straight through dark storms of opposition. Now I was searching high and low for meetings I could attend where I would learn to go deeper with the Holy Spirit. And during that time, it seemed God's hand came upon my Grandma Ettie to step up to the plate to help me. She was thrilled that I had received the baptism in the Holy Spirit, and she began loading me up in her small car as the two of us would head out to all kinds of Spirit-filled meetings.

Every month I attended meetings of the Full Gospel Businessmen's Fellowship International. In those large meetings, my heart was thrilled to hear special speakers like T. L. Osborn, Norvel Hayes, Terry Law and the Living Sound, and so many others. Once a week, I even participated in a small prophetic intercessory prayer group that was led by a notable prophetess named Jeanne Wilkerson. Inside the walls of a tiny little church in Broken

Arrow, Oklahoma, Mrs. Wilkerson led a group of about twelve of us every week in prophetic intercession.

### Another Unforgettable Kathryn Kuhlman Service in Tulsa

The first Kathryn Kuhlman meeting I attended was in September 1973, just prior to my baptism in the Holy Spirit in January 1974. Later that year, I heard Kathryn Kuhlman was coming to Tulsa again, in September 1974, to conduct another big miracle crusade. I learned from my previous experience that those in the choir had the best seats near the stage, so once again, I joined the Kathryn Kuhlman choir. This time, I was baptized in the Holy Spirit — but just as before, I was rendered *speechless* at the power of God I saw manifested in that meeting!

As in the previous meeting, the Mabee Center at Oral Roberts University was packed, overflowing with people from across the nation in need of miracles. And on that day, miracles again happened before my eyes! In that service, I remember feeling a whirlwind of power pass through the auditorium — and with my own eyes, I saw miracles manifesting all around me. People were being miraculously healed right in front of me — *here*, *there*, and *everywhere*. Before long, people were lined up near the platform waiting to testify about what God had done in their bodies. Wheelchairs were emptied; paralyzed people got up from their stretchers and walked; blind eyes were opened; deaf ears were unstopped; and the mute began to speak!

God's miracle-working power was on clear display as I watched people who had been brought in on stretchers and in wheelchairs walking *and even running* from one end of the stage to the other. Soon, just as in Kathryn Kuhlman's previous meeting in Tulsa, the entire front of the auditorium and the aisles were jammed with people who had come forward to give their lives to Jesus. God's power was on display, liberating the diseased and infirm and beckoning the lost to come to Christ!

Those experiences with the power of God changed my heart and mind, and they forever impacted me concerning the ministry of the Holy Spirit. There is nothing like a firsthand encounter with the power of God to alter one's way of thinking and believing. Often we preach and try to appeal to people with all the right words, but we stop short of the one thing that will put an end to all doubts: *one outstanding demonstration of God's power.* A real miracle or a healing demonstrated before the eyes of doubters can have a greater impact than years of coaxing and begging.

*The fact is, there is NOTHING more gripping than an actual, personal encounter with the power of God!* When we allow God to "show off," that supernatural manifestation drives the message deeper into people's hearts and makes a far greater impact than we could ever achieve with just words.

When the apostle Paul first started preaching to the Corinthians, who were deeply pagan and immersed in gross darkness, he knew words alone would never do the job. To reach them, he would need a confirming demonstration of God's power. In First Corinthians 2:4, he reminded them about the manner in which he first preached to them. He said, "And my speech and my preaching was not with enticing words of man's wisdom, but in demonstration of the Spirit and of power."

In the next verse, Paul continued to tell them the reason he wanted them to see a demonstration of God's power: "That your faith should not stand in the wisdom of men, but in the power of God" (1 Corinthians 2:5).

Just as I was so deeply impacted by the miracles I saw in that Kathryn Kuhlman meeting many years ago, the apostle Paul knew that miracles, healings, and other displays of God's power would have a great impact on his own listeners. If all he offered them were "enticing words of man's wisdom," they could argue, disagree, or debate with him about the message he preached. But if an unquestionable miracle happened right before their eyes — *a demonstration of supernatural power that literally knocked them off their feet* — they would know that God Almighty was behind the message Paul was preaching!

I'll never forget what one great man once told me about the power of God. He said, "You can't win an argument with a man who has had a supernatural experience." This is true! When people have an encounter with the power of God, it puts an end to all speculation and all arguments about whether God is active in the affairs of men today.

Paul knew that a display of God's power would have a great influence on his audience, so in addition to carefully crafting a message that would touch their hearts, he took it one step further and made the choice to allow the power of God to do its unparalleled work. Paul knew God's power would melt away every doubt and put an end to all debate, so he stepped aside and allowed God to show off and thus confirm that the message Paul preached was indeed the truth!

Of course, Paul later told the Corinthians the reason he took this approach: "That your faith should not *stand* in the wisdom of men, but in the power of God." (1 Corinthians 2:5). The word "stand" in this verse is the little Greek word *en*, which simply means *in*. As used here, this word describes the medium in which faith is *rooted*.

It could be translated, "I took this approach so your faith would not be rooted in the wisdom of men...." Then Paul continued, "...but *in* the power of God." This verse lets us know that Paul wanted his listeners' faith to be rooted deeply not in the wisdom of men, but *in* the power of God.

The word "power" in this verse is the Greek word *dunamis*. This well-known, often-used word denotes *the mighty power of God*. First Corinthians 2:5 is not merely talking about power, but about *tremendous power*. This word *dunamis* denotes God's supernatural power, which is *explosive*, *mighty*, and *awe-inspiring* to those who see or experience it.

Paul's words in First Corinthians 2:5 could thus be paraphrased: *"I took this approach so your faith would not be rooted in the wisdom of men, but that your faith would be steadfastly rooted in the power of God."*

We must not make the mistake of taking only a mental approach when we preach the Gospel or share the Word with people. Of course, we must use our mind to its maximum capacity. God gave us our mind and expects us to use it as we share Christ and His Word with others. But we should always get quiet in our heart first and ask the Holy Spirit what *He* would like to do in those moments. What needs in the lives of our listeners would He like to step in and meet supernaturally to reveal His great love for them? He'll lead us each step of the way if we'll stay sensitive to Him.

And if you ever come to a standstill in a conversation — when it's your word against another person's — that may be the golden moment when you need to step aside and allow God to step in and do what only *He* can do! Give His supernatural power an opportunity to intervene and *confirm* the truth you are attempting to drive into that person's heart.

When you come to one of those moments when the greatest efforts of your mind seem futile, yield to the power of God that resides within you and allow the Holy Spirit to do what you could never do by yourself. When the Spirit of God is finished confirming the Word with supernatural demonstrations of power, all arguments will cease, the case will be closed, and the person you are trying to reach will be *convinced*!

## Oral Roberts' Influence
## and 'The Holy Spirit in the Now'

Not long after this big Kathryn Kuhlman meeting, I heard that Oral Roberts was teaching a class called "The Holy Spirit in the Now" every Tuesday night on the campus of Oral Roberts University. It would be held in the Mabee Center, and it was a required course for all students at ORU.

Oral Roberts taught this class from his personal experience and from more than thirty years of prayer and his study of the Word. Oral said, "During my ministry, I have personally laid hands on over a million people in prayer, thousands of whom had been given up because there was no known medical cure. And I am convinced that no disease is hopeless — none is incurable — for God can heal all sickness. His power has no limits or barriers when we center our faith in Him."

By the time I attended Oral's class on the campus of ORU, his ministry was already enormous in influence, as he had become the leading voice of the Charismatic Movement. Because I was a senior in high school, I had to get special permission to attend the class because I wasn't a university student yet. I'd *assumed* that when I graduated from high school, I would attend Oral Roberts University. It seemed logical that a young man with the call of God on his life would attend this amazing university. So I obtained permission to attend Oral's class, understanding that when I enrolled as a student a year later, the course would be applied to my credits at the university.

Every week, Grandma Ettie and I attended that class taught by Oral Roberts himself, and I sat on the front row hanging on to every word he said. Grandma Ettie would meet me at my parents' house in Sand Springs, and we'd make the drive to ORU each Tuesday night. We always arrived early so we could get a seat on the front row directly in front of Oral Roberts. Sometimes as he taught, he walked so close to where I was seated that I could have nearly touched him. He was *right there* in front of me every week!

I didn't want to forget a word that Oral said in those classes, so I bought a small tape recorder from RadioShack to take with me each week to class along with a blank cassette tape. Just as Oral would begin the lesson, I'd press "play" and record every word he spoke in those classes. Somewhere deep in my archives, I still have a few of those old cassette tapes, and they will always be precious to me.

But when each of these special meetings was over, I'd head back home to Sand Springs where I lived with my parents and my sisters. Without a doubt, Sand Springs really was a nice place, but I knew I did not "fit" there. My interests had always been so different from my friends at Glenwood Baptist Church. And now my spiritual life had totally changed, and my receiving the baptism in the Holy Spirit put even more distance between me and them.

I was elated and grateful for my new experiences and the knowledge of the Holy Spirit that I was gaining. I knew God was giving me what I needed to get me started in my own ministry in the future. But that wasn't all He was giving me — He was giving me back my dreams. The baptism in the Holy Spirit had delivered me and transformed me, opening doors of learning that I would desperately need later for forging into new spiritual territory in a communistic, atheistic region of the world.

The enemy had tried unsuccessfully to slam the door shut on me early in life to stop the plan of God. His strategy was an assault on my mind to trap me, as if in a dark prison, and never let me escape. But the God of hope was not done with me yet. Possibilities of dreams fulfilled were emerging again like seedlings poking their heads from the dark soil that had previously held them captive. Pieces of a puzzle that each revealed a part of God's grand plan for my life were beginning to snap into place to disclose their secrets that my dreams were *not* futile wishes that would go continually unrealized. I'd held those "puzzle pieces" — my secret dreams — close to my heart, dreams that the enemy of my soul had almost convinced me to abandon.

But now things were beginning to come together for me. They were starting to make sense where, before, they made *no* sense in my misfit world that spanned only the breadth of a small town in northeastern Oklahoma. In the following chapter, I'll share where God led this "misfit" next — to a place where I would find my niche in the Body of Christ as a Bible teacher and begin to discover where I perfectly fit in His *unlikely* plan.

'God does not rush to promote anyone
into the next phase of life. God surely wanted me
to fulfill my dream of studying New Testament Greek,
but first He wanted to establish me in the basic principles
that I needed in order to do that. He let me do what
I *wanted*, but He first made me do what I *needed*.'

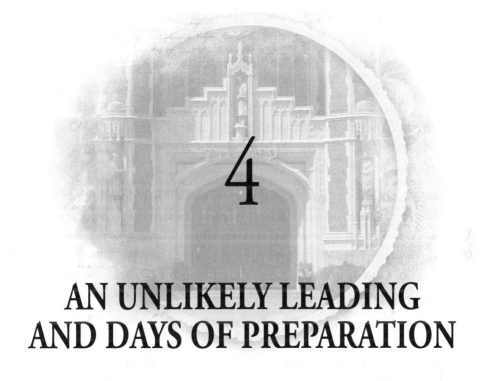

# AN UNLIKELY LEADING
# AND DAYS OF PREPARATION

Finally the time came for me to graduate from high school, and I eagerly anticipated attending Oral Roberts University full time in the fall. I already had three credit hours under my belt, and I was ready to pursue my ministry calling by way of a degree from ORU. However, one day as I was praying about my future, the Holy Spirit spoke to my heart and actually *forbade* me to attend ORU!

I was *stunned*. I thought, *What now?* — as if my only possible pathway to successful ministry had just been sealed shut.

"Why don't You want me to go to ORU, Lord?" I asked incredulously. "There's no better place for a young man like me than ORU." The Holy Spirit answered, *There are things I want to teach you that you can only learn somewhere else. You'll be in a good environment at ORU, but you'll miss the greater things I want to impart to you that are important for your future.*

---

**Left:** *Bizzell Memorial Library, University of Oklahoma, Norman, Oklahoma.*

When I consider how the Holy Spirit worked with me as I faced the decision about which university to attend, I am reminded of Romans 8:14, which says, "…As many as are *led* by the Spirit of God, they are the sons of God."

The word "led" in this verse is from a Greek word that was used in both the *agricultural* and *athletic* worlds. In agricultural terms, it described *a person who led an animal that was held at the end of a rope.* Wherever the farmer led, the animal was *to follow.*

But interestingly, in athletic terms, this word "led" in Greek is where we get the word *agonidzo*, which in history described *the intense struggle of a wrestler as he fought an opponent.* From this Greek word, we derive the word "agony." So in this context, the word "led" can depict the struggle — or the wrestling — of two opponents who are fighting furiously to pin the other to the mat in defeat.

Romans 8:14 is telling us that the Holy Spirit wants to *lead* us about, but often there is a *wrestling* that occurs between our flesh and our spirit. The Holy Spirit leads in one direction, but because the flesh doesn't understand the leading of the Holy Spirit or doesn't want to obey, it throws us into *an agonizing struggle.* The Holy Spirit is willing to lead us — He can make sure we are in the right place at the right time — but we may have to overcome the flesh in order to follow and claim this "right place, right time" promise.

I'm sharing this with you because it was a very big struggle for my mind to yield to the leading of the Holy Spirit to forego attending ORU and to attend a secular university instead. But as difficult as that decision was, I *knew* in my heart that I needed to follow the Holy Spirit's direction and to give up my plans for ORU.

I made the "agonizing" choice to obey the Lord and to enroll at a state university located a couple hours away from my hometown. After a period of wrestling with this leading of the Holy Spirit, I'd successfully "pinned my soul to the mat" of obedience to God's plan. And although I felt disappointed at first at my being *pinned*, I ended up the decisive winner by His grace. I would learn in the days to come that it *always* pays to obey God. The "prize" in life always goes to the obedient!

## America in the Years Leading Up
## to My College Days

My packing up to finally leave my small hometown was such an interesting period in U.S. history, so I want to give you an overview of that moment as a backdrop to the early beginnings of my adventures in God as a young adult. Some who read this will receive quite the education about the events of the time — while others will remember this period all too well.

In the fall of 1976, at the age of eighteen, I loaded my car with my few belongings and drove two hours away to move into student housing at the secular university where I'd enrolled as a student. America had gone through a tumultuous fifteen years before I graduated from high school and set out to take my place among the ranks of those seeking higher education.

I was born in 1958 when Dwight D. Eisenhower was President of the United States. After President Eisenhower followed the presidencies of Kennedy, Johnson, Nixon, and then Ford, who became president after the resignation of Richard Nixon in 1974.

But much earlier than that, in 1963, in a wake of national heartache and confusion, President Lyndon B. Johnson assumed the presidency immediately after President John F. Kennedy was assassinated on November 22 of that year. Many who read this book will remember that exact moment — where they were and what they were doing — when the news of this tragedy broke.

I was a mere five years old when it happened, but I remember it very well because my mother made sure I watched the daily news reports on television so that I would never forget that historic moment. I watched as Jacqueline Kennedy walked with her children behind President Kennedy's flag-draped casket carried on a horse-drawn caisson wagon. I was mesmerized by the gravity of the moment as our President was transported along Pennsylvania Avenue to the U.S. Capitol where he would lie in state.

President Johnson's presidency ensued — but it both began and ended in turmoil. It was marked with the wounds of assassination and wounds from the Vietnam War. As a youth, I recall sitting in front of the news every evening as my father watched Walter Cronkite report about the military actions taking place in Vietnam. It marked the first real-time news reporting of a war. Those grisly images were so graphic that it tore the hearts of dads, moms, brothers, and sisters of soldiers as these loved ones sat night by night watching the bloodshed that was happening on the warfront.

## The Vietnam War and the Hippie Movement

The Vietnam War gave rise to discontent in the hearts of young people across the United States, and that discontent helped produce the "hippie" counterculture of the late 1960s. The "hippie movement" reached its height during the escalation of the Vietnam War. Most in the movement resented the war — they were also opposed to the "pressure" to conform to traditional standards and lifestyles of middle-class America, which they viewed as being dominated by materialism and hypocrisy.

Alienating themselves, they developed alternative lifestyles to mainstream society. They advocated nonviolence (in defiance of the war) and "love." In fact, the mantra, "Make love, not war" became popularized during this period. Participants of this movement — *hippies* — wore long hair, beads, braids, and a relaxed Bohemian style of dress. They drowned themselves in folk, rock, and heavy-metal music and famously experimented with psyche-delic drugs. They also adopted a belief in free love, or promiscuous sex.

Hippies claimed to be "open-minded" and "tolerant," so they threw off the shackles of past moral norms to engage in open sexual relationships, frequently living in non-traditional family groups, or communes. They explored new forms of spirituality that lay outside the boundaries of Judeo-Christianity, usually in the form of Eastern religions and the occult. In fact, astrology was so popular among hippies that they even referred to their movement as the "Age of Aquarius."[1]

As I mentioned, these young people freely promoted the recreational use of hallucinogenic drugs, particularly marijuana and LSD. Many saw hallucinogens like these, as well as peyote, "magic mushrooms," and DMT (also known as "the spirit molecule") as a way to open themselves to new "spiritual" experiences. Timothy Leary, a notable figure in this movement encouraged others to use LSD to expand the consciousness "and find ecstasy and revelation within."[2] This newly formed movement was an *anti-God* expression that protested the powerless mainstream church of that period, which was largely steeped in hypocrisy.

It wasn't long before the new Hippie Movement spread its tentacles into nearly every university campus across America and began to have a presence in every major U.S. city. Hippies also moved to communes in rural areas and joined disaffected political radicals and Vietnam draft-dodgers, often participating in demonstrations and public sit-ins.

## Woodstock — an Event That Became Synonymous With the Movement

Imagine rain-soaked fields, a mix of mud, urine, vomit, and other filth, where *hundreds of thousands* of young people gathered for "peace, love, and music." Mostly oblivious to the lack of food, clean water, and sanitation, these festival attendees came *and stayed* for this notorious days-long event just for the experience. Nudity, illicit sex, and psychedelic drugs were prominent among the sights, sounds, and smells of this sixty-plus-hour concert experiment that remains unparalleled in U.S. history, although some events have come close in more recent times. Of course, I am talking about *Woodstock.*

Public gatherings, usually in the form of music festivals, were an important part of the Hippie Movement. And the music festival I just described, known as Woodstock, was a big one. Held in rural New York state in 1969, this event drew an estimated 400,000 people. Woodstock became synonymous with the entire Hippie Movement, attracting hundreds of thousands of people who lived for those three to four days in sporadic rain, in mud, and with disgusting bathroom setups, unmanageable trash and debris, food shortages, drug overdoses, and indiscriminate sex and nudity. In an editorial published in the *New York Times,* one reporter wrote, "…Woodstock was a spectacle of spaced-out, skinny-dipping, promiscuous hippies cavorting in squalor…."[3]

I would be remiss if I didn't also mention some of the music associated with the Hippie Movement that emerged in the late 1950s and 1960s and seemed to resonate with the movement and flourish in those troublesome years. I'm talking about the music of Alice Cooper, the Allman Brothers, Joan Baez, the Beach Boys, the Beatles, Black Sabbath, Chicago, Eric Clapton, Joe Cocker, Judy Collins, Creedence Clearwater Revival, Jim Croce, Crosby, Stills, and Nash, Deep Purple, the Doors, Bob Dylan, Fleetwood Mac, Peter Frampton, the Grateful Dead, Arlo Guthrie, Iron Butterfly, Jefferson Airplane, Jethro Tull, Jimi Hendrix, Janis Joplin, Carole King, Led Zeppelin, Lynyrd Skynyrd, the Mamas and the Papas, Melanie, Joni Mitchell, the Moody Blues, Procol Harum, Rolling Stones, Linda Ronstadt, Santana, Simon and Garfunkel, Sly and the Family Stone, Rod Stewart, James Taylor, Three Dog Night, the Who, Yes, Neil Young, ZZ Top…and the list goes on and on.

A lot of that music had no appeal to me, but my older sister and I really enjoyed the music of the Beatles, the Carpenters, Judy Collins, Elton John, Carole King, Joni Mitchell, Simon and Garfunkel, and James Taylor. As I look at the longer list, it is heartbreaking to see the personal devastation that occurred in the lives of many of those musicians who were affected by disastrous lifestyle choices that were so prevalent during that time.

## Political Scandal in Contemporary History

The Vietnam War continued throughout the presidencies of Johnson and Nixon. During Nixon's administration, the nation continued to be affected by the burgeoning Hippie Movement and the culture of nonconformity.

But the scandal of Watergate in the Nixon administration shook the nation even deeper. For months, the Senate held public hearings about the Watergate break-in that were broadcast into our homes. When it became apparent that Nixon would be impeached, he tragically became the first President to resign in disgrace. Vice-President Gerald Ford was quickly sworn in as President, and as one of his first acts in office, he pardoned Nixon of all crimes. That pardon stirred tremendous bitterness, offense, and even greater resentment among much of the younger population in the United States.

Also during that time period, gay rights, women's liberation, and other activist movements gained prominence, as well as radical political ideologies that were openly anarchist and communist. The drug culture remained epidemic, and it was as if "Pandora's Box" had been opened never to be closed or contained again. Parents' hearts were broken all over America by the deaths of untold numbers of young people who overdosed on drugs or who brought ruin upon themselves as a result of disastrous lifestyle choices.

Eventually the Hippie Movement waned as the Vietnam conflict drew to a close. But before it ended, the civil-rights movement began tumultuously with its own heroes and villains emerging from that sad time in our nation. Many good changes resulted from that movement, but the country remained scarred by the blight of racial discrimination that had gone practically *unchecked* before that period of great reform.

## The Jesus Movement

In the midst of this whole period in American history that brought so much devastation among our youth, God did not sit still to watch the enemy devour lives. God never misses an opportunity to make grace abound over sin and to demonstrate His mighty power in response to the cry of hungry hearts. At the very same time the devil was wreaking havoc in the lives of countless young Americans, God began to pour the Holy Spirit out upon the Church — giving birth both to the Charismatic Movement and to another spiritual upsurge that was called the Jesus Movement.

God began to move mightily among young people all over the nation during that same time. What became known as the Jesus Movement began on the West Coast in the late 1960s and early 1970s, and it quickly spread throughout North America. The participants in that movement were often called *Jesus people* or *Jesus freaks*.

The Jesus Movement sought to return to the original life of the early Christians. The movement called for a return to simple living and had a strong emphasis on the Bible, faith, prayer, healing, signs, wonders, miracles, evangelizing the lost, and other supernatural works of the Holy Spirit.

Perhaps the longest-lasting effect of the Jesus Movement was its music. Singers, musicians, and notable groups became recognized leaders in the movement. In my geographical region during that time, some of the big names in the emerging Christian music market were Debby Boone, Pat

Boone, Stephanie Boosahda, Ralph Carmichael, Paul Clark, Terry Clark, Cynthia Clawson, Kenneth Copeland, Andrae Crouch (and the Disciples), DeGarmo and Key, Phil Driscoll, Evie, the Gaithers, Amy Grant, Keith Green, Janny Grein, Honeytree, the Imperials, Phil Keaggy, Lamb, Randy Matthews, Barry McGuire, Larry Norman, the Rambos, Reba Rambo, Resurrection Band, Second Chapter of Acts, Randy Stonehill. Noel Paul Stookey of Peter, Paul, and Mary, Sweet Comfort Band, Russ Taff, John Michael Talbot, and B. J. Thomas.

Before I ever arrived at the university, Christians my age all over the nation were coming alive to fabulous contemporary Christian music that was erupting on the scene. The music was simple, pure, and powerful.

Also during that remarkable time, notable Charismatic publications began to emerge, such as *New Wine* magazine and *Charisma* magazine. *New Wine* was a potent, influential, and beneficial resource dedicated to Christian growth. Regular contributors were the "Fort Lauderdale Five" I mentioned in Chapter Three — Charles Simpson, Don Basham, Ern Baxter, Bob Mumford, and Derek Prince.

After *New Wine*, *Charisma* launched in 1975. Jamie Buckingham, a noted and respected author who played a monumental role in the Charismatic Movement, was a regular columnist. His books sold more than forty million copies during his lifetime, yet he was probably best remembered for his column in *Charisma*. Before his death Jamie personally corresponded with me and wrote glowing reviews for two of my earlier books. Those book reviews were among the greatest honors I've ever received as a writer because Buckingham's voice was trusted and his opinions ranked so highly with many across the nation.

In addition to these magazines, Charismatic book companies were also started during those years. Among them were notably Whitaker House, which started in 1970, Chosen Books, which started in 1971, and Harrison House, which started in 1975. These publishers began distributing Charismatic books by the millions to spiritually feed the burgeoning Charismatic Movement in the Church and those involved in the Jesus Movement, which continued to grow across the nation.

That was also the season when Christian television networks were born. The first to be launched was CBN, which was started by Pat Robertson in 1960. The second was TBN, which was started by Paul and Jan Crouch in 1973 followed by PTL, which was started by Jim and Tammy Faye Bakker in 1974. Eventually there were others, but in the 1970s, all three of these networks showcased the outpouring of the Holy Spirit in the Church, the move of God among the young people in the Jesus Movement, the new Christian music that was birthed in that movement, and emerging Charismatic faces and their books.

What I'm sharing in this chapter as an introduction to my *unlikely leadings* are some of the historical events and times surrounding the period, some of which played into my own story of "coming of age" and discovering where I fit in the world. In one way, it was a good time for the Church because the Holy Spirit was mightily moving. But the United States was still trying to recover from years of nonstop events that produced instability and shaking in the nation. The ramifications of the last big event, the resignation of Richard Nixon, were still reverberating nationwide.

### Jimmy Carter

When I enrolled in 1976 as a student at the university, Gerald Ford was still the President of the United States. A new election was coming up and he was to run against a former Democratic governor from Georgia, a peanut farmer whose name was Jimmy Carter.

Because Americans were disillusioned with the executive branch of government due to the Watergate scandal, Jimmy Carter marketed himself successfully as an outsider to Washington politics and, as a result, he won the Democratic nomination in the summer of 1976. People really liked Carter because he seemed to be so "down-to-earth." Making him even more likable was the fact that he was a good-ol' Southern Baptist who taught a Sunday school class every week in his small hometown church.

Even more, his sister, Ruth Carter Stapleton, was reputed to be involved in a specialized Christian healing ministry that involved the healing of memories. Baptists were thrilled to have one of their boys on the ballot to become

President, and Charismatics and Pentecostals were elated that someone close to him seemed to have Charismatic leanings. This put him in a very popular category with believers, including me.

During my first fall semester in 1976, Jimmy Carter held a big campaign rally on our campus. I attended it with my sister to show my support for his candidacy. Eventually, he won the race against President Ford, whom many viewed as "clumsy" both literally and figuratively. They could not forgive President Ford for pardoning Richard Nixon and soon afterward, Jimmy Carter — the Southern Baptist peanut farmer from Georgia with a Charismatic-leaning sister — was sworn in as the thirty-ninth President of the United States.

But from the inception of Carter's presidency, he was met with formidable challenges — including a major energy crisis, skyrocketing inflation, the highest gasoline prices anyone had ever heard of, and the highest unemployment in recent memory. Carter opened U.S. relations with China in 1979 and, just a year before that, in 1978 made great strides as a broker of peace in the historical Egypt-Israeli conflict. But these events quickly faded from his list of efforts late in his presidency due to an upsetting development that occurred in Iran.

The Shah of Iran had ruled from 1941 until 1979 when he was finally deposed in the Iranian Revolution. The Shah had initiated a series of reforms that sparked opposition from Islamic religious scholars, and among his opponents was the Ayatollah Khomeini. Nationwide demonstrations erupted against the Shah all over Iran. Khomeini led the opposition, and eventually emerged as the foremost opponent to the Shah, bringing charges of bloodshed and torture against the Shah and his dynasty.

At the very time I arrived at the university, opposition to the Shah was visible — in front of me nearly every day — as I observed large groups of Iranian students regularly gathering to demonstrate against the U.S. government and to burn effigies of the Shah along with the American flag because the United States had stood firmly by this leader.

Then in 1979, the Iranian Revolution erupted, the Shah was ousted from power, and he and his family fled to take up life elsewhere. A group of college students in Tehran who participated in the Iranian Revolution — and who resented Washington D.C.'s support for the Shah — forcibly seized control of the U.S. Embassy in Tehran and held fifty-two American diplomats and citizens as hostages for 444 days.

From November 4, 1979, to January 20, 1981, President Carter tried to obtain their release, but he was incapable of mitigating the crisis and, in fact, it *escalated*, spiraling more and more out of control. U.S. diplomats and citizens were retained in Tehran as hostages, and America watched these events on television, feeling *helpless* and *humiliated* by it all. As a result, President Carter experienced a massive loss of public confidence and lost his reelection bid to a former actor and Governor from California whose name was Ronald Reagan.

When I arrived on campus in the fall of 1976, America had been in upheaval for about fifteen years, during which time we experienced:

- President Kennedy's assassination
- President Johnson's increased participation in the Vietnam War
- burgeoning counterculture movements, including the Hippie Movement
- the "follow-up" assassination of Senator Robert Kennedy
- the assassination of Martin Luther King Jr.
- President Nixon's scandalous resignation
- President Ford's pardon of Nixon
- skyrocketing inflation and a catastrophic economy during Carter's presidency
- the civil-rights movement and racial unrest nationwide
- Carter's impotence in solving the hostage crisis in Tehran

All of this happened within a relatively short time frame — some of it occurred simultaneously — and it dramatically shook the nation. Compounding the national shaking and ensuing trauma was a Hippie Movement steeped in rebellion, disrespect for parents and all types of authority, dangerous use of illicit drugs, and wild sex that cumulatively produced ravaged and ruined lives among America's youth. The whole country was shaken to its core and was trying to regain its equilibrium.

## 'Ready or Not' — My College Education Began

As a young college student, I could feel the compounded negative effects of those experiences among the faculty and student population where I attended school. A spirit of unrest was in the air, and it reverberated throughout the student body, manifesting itself in as many different ways as there were political and religious beliefs and ideologies — in other words, in *numerous* ways. It was a first taste of the "real world" for a young Rick Renner from Sand Springs.

As I shared, this was my first time to be away from home. To be very honest, all of these converging ideologies made me feel apprehensive in my new surroundings. In our more modern, progressive world of agitation and turmoil, I was vitally aware that I had left the safety, quiet, and predictability of life in Sand Springs far behind me. My heart had craved a life of adventure outside of my hometown, but suddenly I was faced with the stark reality of a society spinning out of control — through no fault of my own on the one hand, yet with the charge of adulthood on my shoulders on the other hand, demanding something of me to help change it.

Little did I know that the past fifteen years of confusion in the world around me would practically pale compared to what the next fifteen years of life held for me personally. In little more than a decade and a half, I would be saying good-bye to my life in the U.S. altogether and moving — *with a wife and children at my side* — to a nation halfway around the world. How's *that* for a life of adventure!

As a college freshman, one thing I could focus on amidst the swirl of worldly confusion was my studies. I was confident from the very beginning about the type of education I needed in order to fulfill the dream of ministry God had placed in my heart. In my first semesters of study, while many students wandered from course to course and meandered from major to major, I had clear direction from the Lord and knew what I needed to learn while at the university.

Because of the brilliant way Derek Prince exegeted from the Greek New Testament and the impact his teaching ministry had on me, the hook for New Testament Greek had been set deeply in my heart. I simply *knew* that I needed to study the original Greek language of the New Testament. So it was easy to reason that ancient Greek should be the first class I should enroll in.

God had also made it clear to me that a part of my future ministry would include writing books for Christians who wanted to dive deeper into the study of God's Word. I was so confident that God wanted me to write that I had attempted my first book when I was fifteen years old. I still have those old typewritten pages of that first manuscript — typed on my Smith-Corona typewriter — on the subject of the power of God. Since I knew God had called me to write, it was clear right from the start that I needed to also enroll in the School of Journalism to develop this gift.

## God Has a Specific Plan for *You* — Prepare To Fulfill It!

God knows your future, and if you will listen to Him, He will direct you as to what you are to do, how you are to study or train, and where you are to go in your own life's adventure. God created you, and He has a plan for your life. There is nothing He doesn't know about you, and He certainly knows how to direct you and prepare you to fulfill His divine plan.

Psalm 139:15,16 declares that God's eyes were fixed on you, not only when you were in the earliest stages of formation in your mother's womb, but *even before you were conceived.* David said concerning himself, and this is true of you, too, "My substance was not hid from thee, when I was made in secret, and curiously wrought in the lowest parts of the earth. Thine eyes did see my substance, yet being unperfect; and in thy book all my members were written, which in continuance were fashioned, when as yet there was none of them."

According to these words, God knew all about you when you were in the earliest stages of being formed in the womb. God was so intricately aware of you that He took note as your arms, hands, fingers, legs, feet, and toes were developing. In fact, this verse says He even knew you "…when as yet there was none of them."

Think of it! Long before you were conceived, God already knew you — and by faith, He could see you being conceived, formed in the womb, and born into this world. This means there isn't a single human being on the earth who was a surprise to God — and that includes *you*!

Paul added to these amazing truths in Ephesians 1:4 when he wrote, "According as he hath *chosen* us in him before the foundation of the world...." The word "chosen" in Greek is a compound of two words. The first word means *out*, and the second word means *I say*. Together these words literally mean, *Out, I say!* It means *to call out, to select, to elect,* or *to personally choose.*

In other ancient Greek writings where this word is used, it depicts a person or a group of people who were *selected* for a specific purpose. For example, this word depicted the *selection* of men for military service. It denoted soldiers who were *chosen* to go on a special mission or to do a special task. In every case where this word is used, it portrays the *election* or *selection* of individuals to do something significant.

So when Paul said that God "...hath *chosen* us in him before the foundation of the world..." (Ephesians 1:4), he was explicitly telling us that God looked out to the horizon of human history *and saw you and me*. And when God saw you and me, His voice echoed from Heaven and said: *"Out, I say!"* In that flash, our destinies were divinely sealed! We were separated by God from a lost and dying world, and He called each one of us to be His own and to fulfill a specific task or assignment.

Paul furthermore said that God's plans for us were developed "...before the foundation of the world...." The word "foundation" is a Greek compound of two words — the first word means *down*, and the second word means *to hurl* or *to throw*. When these two words are compounded, it means *to hurl something down*. It refers to *the very first act of creation*. Thus, before God ever spoke the earth into existence — before His booming voice ever called out for the first layers of the earth's crust to be put into place — He had already spoken our names! He selected and elected us *before* the very first layers of the earth were created. And He had a plan for us right from the start!

In light of these Greek meanings, Ephesians 1:4 could be phrased to read: "When God saw us, He said, *'Out, I say!'* In that moment, He separated us from the rest of the world and enlisted us in His service. And think of it! He did all of this before He ever hurled the first layers of the earth's crust into existence...."

So if your flesh ever tries to tell you that God doesn't have a special plan for you, you need to take authority over your flesh and tell it to shut its mouth! Then you need to declare, "God chose me, and He planned a great future for me. I'm not going to listen to this foul garbage from my flesh and unrenewed emotions. I have an awesome destiny — in fact, I'm a significant part of God's plan!"

God has chosen *you* and has called you to step into the glorious calling He has placed on your life! No matter how large or small the task — no matter how big or tiny the assignment — joy and satisfaction will become yours when you start accomplishing what God brought you into this world to do. God didn't bring you into the world so you would live an inconsequential life! He has a plan and a purpose for your life. He wants to use *you*!

I'm so thankful that the Lord directed my steps right from the beginning so that I didn't have to struggle to try to figure out what to study at the university. And, friend, I'm convinced that if you will set your heart to hear the Lord, He will also show you what He has called and gifted *you* to do! Even if you missed your "right from the start" moment, God knows where you are now, and His plan for you is unchanging (*see* Romans 11:29). If you'll ask Him to use you, He will begin to teach you what you need to know, show you what you need to see, and prepare you for His divine assignment for you — even concerning the next steps you need to take to get there!

## My First Greek Class With 'Dr. Pain'

I sincerely committed my way to God, and He was in charge of my every step at the university. Because I was at a secular university, the focus of the Greek department, where I'd enrolled in my first class, was a much more ancient kind of Greek, not New Testament Greek.

Among our studies, we even briefly considered an even rarer form of ancient Greek writing called *Boustrophedon*. The word "Boustrophedon" is a compound of two Greek words that depict an *ox* and *a turn*. It pictures the action of an *ox turning* at the end of a row that a farmer is plowing to begin plowing in the opposite direction on the next row. A farmer plows one row, then drops down to the next row and plows in "reverse," in the opposite direction. This ancient form of writing called *Boustrophedon* thusly flips back and forth on alternate lines to create a bi-directional text. As hard as it is to fathom, the lines of writing were flipped, or reversed, with reversed letters so that even the individual characters were reversed, or *mirrored*.

These various older forms of Greek were not the New Testament Greek I was longing to study, but I had to start somewhere, and God wisely made sure I was given a solid foundation in more ancient texts before I finally got to my studies of New Testament Greek.

There are several well-defined periods of ancient Greek in history that are distinct from each other. However, one builds on top of the next.

- The first period is Archaic Greek, which is Greek that dates from the Eighth Century BC to the Fifth Century BC.
- After that is Classical Greek, which dates from the Fifth Century BC to the Fourth Century BC.
- Then after that is Hellenistic Greek, which spans the years from the Fourth Century BC all the way to the period of the First Century BC.

Hellenist Greek is the period that gave rise to what is called Koine Greek. The word "koine" means *common* and describes the Greek that was spoken mostly by common people in history and is much simpler than Classical Greek. Sometimes Koine Greek is referred to as Alexandrian Greek because it was the vernacular used by the troops of Alexander the Great, and his troops spread it to the regions of the world that Alexander the Great conquered.

As a result of the conquests of Alexander the Great and his generals who succeeded him, Koine Greek became the first truly international language. For the very first time in human history, a large swath of the civilized world could speak and read a single form of verbal and written communication.

Consider how English is read and spoken around the world today, and it will help you understand the role that Koine Greek played in the First Century. It was spoken almost everywhere in the Roman Empire, irrespective of the native dialects that might have been used in the privacy of one's home. Many ancient writings are in Koine Greek, including the writings of Plutarch and Polybius, who were Greek philosophers, writers, and historians.

But, most importantly, the New Testament is written in Koine Greek. Learning that Greek form was the prize I had my eyes on as I embarked in my collegiate studies.

The Classics department at the university focused primarily on Archaic, Classical, and Hellenistic Greek, so in my first years in Greek classes, that was the focus. My first Greek professor was a man named Dr. Payne. To me, he was truly so *painful* to deal with that I inwardly changed his name from Dr. Payne to *"Dr. Pain."* Maybe other students did well with him, but to me, he seemed to come from some other planet in the cosmos.

I was later relieved to discover I wasn't the only student who wrestled mentally to understand "Dr. Pain." I struggled so much that I decided to repeat that class the next semester because I wanted to get a good foundation as I really began studying the language. Several other students likewise decided to repeat the class with a different professor so they, too, would have solid, sure footing in the basics of Greek before moving upward to more difficult readings from ancient texts.

## Dr. Wallis — a Giant Mind in a Frail Body

My next teacher was Dr. John S. Catlin, a brilliant, down-to-earth, humorous man that I really enjoyed. But after that, I studied with a professor who profoundly affected me. His name was Dr. R. T. Wallis. He had originally come from England and was regarded as one of the world's top authorities on the subject of Neoplatonism because he had published the first scholarly, full-length study of Neoplatonism that had been written in more than half a century. Having Dr. Wallis as my professor was one of my greatest honors, but I had to learn to overlook his physical appearance in order to learn from him.

Dr. Wallis was a small, crumpled, *hunchback*-looking man with twisted, uneven hips that caused him to wobble lopsided when he walked. His deeply wrinkled face was so contorted that his glasses sat crooked across his face. His hands were knobby, and his hair always looked to me like it was uncombed and tousled. These were my nineteen-year-old impressions of this physically afflicted, frail man with a mind that I deeply respected.

Dr. Wallis also had a difficult time breathing — no doubt due to his physical form. I felt compassion for Dr. Wallis because he struggled so much with his brittle health. Every week as I sat across the table from him and looked at his frail body, I was dumbfounded that such a *giant*, brilliant mind could be confined in such an unimpressive, diminutive package. In many ways, Dr. Wallis physically reminded me of Stephen Hawking except that Dr. Wallis was not bound to a wheelchair. But in spite of his infirmed outward appearance, he was positively *a genius* when it came to Greek, Latin, and ancient philosophy.

After concluding that year with Dr. Wallis, he took me and a handful of other "daring students" into a private classroom where we took turns reading out loud the ancient Greek writings of antiquity's greatest writers. I say "daring students" because our task was to read materials from all periods of Greek history, including selections from Homer's *Illiad* (Eighth Century BC), Aristophanes' *Clouds* (423 BC), Plato's *Apology of Socrates* (399 BC), and *Crito* (360 BC). *Whew…* reading those ancient texts was absolutely *not* for the faint of heart!

I agonized reading page after page those ancient texts, all the while wondering, *Why am I studying the writings of Homer, Aristophanes, and Plato when what I REALLY want to read is the New Testament in the original Greek!* Reading the New Testament in its original language was my objective, but in the process, I was required to start with very difficult writings from ancient antiquity.

That older form of Greek was simply painful to read! Oh, how I wanted to ditch those ancient texts and finally dive into the Greek New Testament! But as is true in my own story, *every step we take in life prepares us for the next step for our future.* Those days of studying difficult forms of Greek were necessary to enable me to do later what God wanted me to do with the Bible in my teaching ministry.

If you're able to follow the Greek roots, it makes it easier to understand the development of many New Testament words. Those who study Koine Greek without studying the historical background may lack the foundation behind many words and concepts in the New Testament. My time spent in class studying these more ancient forms of Greek was a difficult undertaking, but I later understood its importance and became thankful that this was where my studies began.

### Dr. Catlin and the Break I Needed
### To Study the Greek New Testament

When I concluded my classes with Dr. Wallis, I asked to meet with Dr. Catlin, the same professor whom I enjoyed so much and who taught me the basics of ancient Greek when I'd repeated the class from my first term with Dr. Payne. By then, Dr. Catlin had been promoted to Director of the Classics and Letters Department. I really liked him — *plus*, it meant a lot to me to know he had taught New Testament Greek in the past. That let me know he had a very strong grasp in this aspect of the language.

I sat down with Dr. Catlin and began to express what I sensed about the call of God on my life — that I knew God had called me to exegete and teach people from the rich treasures of the Greek New Testament. I felt the call to help Christians who had spent much of their time merely skimming the surface of God's Word and never discovering the profound treasures of truth that lay hidden below the surface. My dream was to help God-lovers dig deeper into the untold riches locked away in the New Testament.

Listening attentively as he sat across his desk from me that day, Dr. Catlin leaned back in his office chair as I finished, as if quietly digesting everything I'd just said. I could see he *really* heard what my heart was saying. He was the first among the faculty I'd felt comfortable enough with to express my calling, my passion for the Word of God, and the wonderment I felt for the language of the Bible.

Although the university's specialization was in Classical and Hellenistic Greek, Dr. Catlin said, "Rick, here's what we'll do. I'll give you private classes — directed readings — in the Greek New Testament. This kind of class is not offered here, so I'll offer it personally." He needed a few days to contemplate how to proceed, so he said we'd meet again the following week to discuss a course of action.

One week later, I returned to his office, eager to learn just how we'd proceed. With a tone of excitement in his voice, he said, "Rick, I want you to translate and interpret the gospel of Luke from the Greek New Testament!"

My assignment was settled and our agreement sealed. My order from Dr. Catlin was to read the gospel of Luke in the Greek, translate it and interpret it into English, and then bring my work to him each week for review in our private classes. I was *elated*!

Day by day, I began to hover over the gospel of Luke in the Greek New Testament. The Greek text came *alive* to me. It felt like the strings of my heart had become an instrument that the Spirit of God had begun to skill-fully play as I studied and labored meticulously over each word.

I was thrilled when Dr. Catlin said he was impressed with my translation abilities and that he especially enjoyed how I not only translated word for word, but added freer interpretive descriptions to the translation. That entire year he regularly met with me and encouraged me to dive deeper to mine the depths of those rich New Testament words.

## First Things *First* — Don't 'Get the Cart Before the Horse'

My experience in the Greek department at school taught me the importance of not skipping vital steps in life. Almost everyone wants to find a shortcut around things that are difficult, but shortcuts often don't pay off and therefore tend to be more expensive in the end. Perhaps I didn't enjoy reading those ancient texts of Homer, Aristophanes, and Plato — *I didn't*.

But the mental muscle I put into those texts — and the depth of history I discovered layered inside each word — became so vital for me to be able to do what God called me to do with the New Testament.

The skills I gleaned from this discipline of extracting definitions from the Greek profoundly affected my life. My approach to studying began to be completely reshaped, which laid the foundation for my teaching ministry that would touch the lives of many thousands of people across the world in the years to come.

In fact, after studying the writings of Homer, Aristophanes, and Plato, the New Testament seemed like *a breeze*. I'd finally "graduated" from those laborious texts to the deeper study of the New Testament, and it was as if my wings had been unclipped so I could fly! But that would not have happened then had I skipped those earlier, preparatory stages. Those previous levels of learning, although difficult, paved the way for me to have a firm, historical grip on the words of the New Testament. Because I persevered in the bumpy, challenging places, I was on a smooth highway now, moving at a rapid speed.

It was also during this very fulfilling time in my life that I realized that I had a special knack for remembering words. The vast catalog of New Testament Greek words that I retained *quickly* was uncanny, and I am amazed by this touch of grace on my life to this day. I may not always remember where I read something, but if the material "enters my eyes," it simply doesn't go away. Therefore, my vocabulary in Greek grew remarkably in those early days, and my foundation in that language became deeper and wider *quickly* as I learned to unearth treasures from the New Testament that had previously been "locked away" from me.

It seemed life was moving at a fast, smooth pace, with the kiss of Heaven upon my life to study Greek and Journalism at that university. But that old phrase that says, "Don't get the cart before the horse" certainly applied to my time in the Greek department at the university. I had been in such a rush to get to the Greek New Testament that I was tempted to bypass much of my studies in the more ancient texts. But God was careful in His plan to make sure I had a firm foundation in the language before I ever got to the New Testament where my heart longed to be. Because He could establish me there as I studied those ancient texts patiently, the pace on my path was accelerated later as my vocabulary of the Greek language grew broader and broader.

This reminds me of Second Corinthians 1:21, where the apostle Paul wrote, "Now he which stablisheth us with you in Christ, and hath anointed us, is God." Most everyone wants the anointing, but look at the order in this verse, which tells us how to position ourselves for a greater operation of the anointing in our lives. It tells us that God's order is making sure we are first *established* — and only *then* does a greater anointing follow.

The word "established" in Greek means *firm, durable, dependable, steadfast, trustworthy*, or *reliable*. By using this word, Paul was telling us that God wants to "establish" us — to make us *firm, durable, dependable, steadfast, trustworthy*, and *reliable* — before he takes us to a higher level.

But there is another meaning to this Greek word for "established" that is significant. In history, it was also a term used to depict the lengthy and intensive investigative process to validate whether a document was *trustworthy* enough to be relied upon.

In the ancient world, documents were written by hand, and if those who wrote the documents were not careful, mistakes could be made of great legal consequence. Because these often-occurring mistakes caused documents to be flawed, it was not wise to give final approval to a document until it was proven *trustworthy.*

If a document was found to be valid, a contract could be quickly concluded. But if a document had errors in it, those errors had to be corrected *before* the papers were signed and the seal of approval would be pressed into the hot wax to finally validate the contract. To approve a document without first validating it would have been an act of foolishness.

When you apply that meaning to what Paul said in Second Corinthians 1:21, we learn that God does not rush to promote anyone into the next phase of life. God surely wanted me to fulfill my dream of studying New Testament Greek, but first He wanted to establish me in the basic principles that I needed in order to do that. He let me do what I *wanted*, but He first made me do what I *needed*.

You see, God is not interested in helping anyone skip steps that are vital to his or her success at a later stage of life. I wanted to rush into fulfilling my dream, but God knew I needed a foundation to undergird my studies in the Greek New Testament.

Never forget that God is always faithfully doing His investigative research to ensure that you are ready to move into the next phase of your calling. God loves you so much that He is more concerned about your being established and firmly grounded than meeting your schedule requirements.

So I advise you that in the process of reaching out to seize what you are dreaming for, do not take shortcuts or skip important steps that are essential to keeping you solid along the way. Get established in the basics so God can know you are ready for Him to put His hand on you and move you to a greater assignment. *First things first!*

## The School of Journalism
## and My Professor's Ministry Legacy

Besides calling me to public ministry, God also called me to write, so in addition to heading straight to the Greek department, I'd also enrolled in the university's School of Journalism. I knew I would especially need to understand advertising and marketing. Many great authors have privately published their books with no plan about how to get those books in front of the public. As a result, some of the best books ever written have been stored away in boxes in authors' garages. Due to a missing advertising and marketing plan, those life-transforming books have never gotten into people's hands.

I didn't want that to be my story. So the day I entered the School of Journalism, I enrolled with an emphasis in advertising.

When I arrived as a student, I also knew one of my first steps was to find a place where I could worship and serve God while at school. My older sister Ronda told me about an exciting Christian fellowship that I could attend while I was at university studying. Ronda lived in the same city with her new husband John Roush. John had attended the University of Oklahoma and played as a starting offensive guard for the Oklahoma Sooners football team. He was a member of the 1974 team coached by Barry Switzer that completed an 11-0 record that season and won the national championship. He was a consensus first-team selection to the 1974 College Football All-America Team. He was also an Academic All-America selection in 1974.

After college, John played professionally for the Ottawa Roughriders in the Canadian Football League and then became a full-time staff member of the Fellowship of Christian Athletes. A decade later, he was named to the Big Eight All Decade Team for the Big Eight Conference. Later in 2019,

John's 1974 championship team at the University of Oklahoma was voted the number-one team in the history of the OU football teams.

That is quite an impressive resume! And John is an "all-star" brother-in-law today, whom I love very much. It was a blessing to have my older sister and her husband living in the same town as me during those first college semesters.

Ronda was the first in our Renner family to attend a university, so when I started school, I followed in her footsteps. Taking her advice, I began to attend the fellowship she recommended. That was when I learned the pleasantly surprising news that my advertising professor had originally started that fellowship in his home as a Bible study. Over time, it had grown so large that the group purchased a building on the outskirts of the city, and it had become a thriving college church. My advertising professor at that secular university was saved, filled with the Holy Spirit, and had a thriving ministry on the side. That professor's name was Frank Heaston.

Professor Heaston had been a long-time advertising professional who, over the course of his career, had assisted in the introduction of Duncan Hines cake mixes, Purina Dog Chow, and Carlton cigarettes — and had significant roles with other national accounts. He had been the creative director of one of the largest advertising agencies in New York City, and he was credited with the development of the Media Area Concept (MCA), which began the allocation of advertising dollars by media coverage rather than geographic locations.

But most notably, this man was recognized in the advertising industry as the original creator of "white space" in print advertising — a revolutionary concept at the time, originated by our own Professor Frank Heaston.

But after he was radically saved, he relocated to the university where he became a highly regarded professor in the School of Journalism and Mass Communication. I relished the creative nature of his classes, and I excelled in the courses I took under Professor Heaston. I developed ad campaigns and learned to write text for articles as well as advertising copy. The principles I learned from this man are still at work in my writing today. What I learned from him was just what I needed to prepare me for writing the books that God would later put into my heart to write.

### More 'Right-Place-Right-Time' Days of Preparation — This Time in the Form of *a Job*

My parents were doing all they could to pay for my education, but I needed a job to also help pay the bill. I applied and was accepted for a job at the university newspaper — a student-produced newspaper staffed by journalism students who worked as paid student labor under the direction of faculty and a professional newsroom director, back-shop supervisor, and an offset pressman.

First, I worked in the newsroom as a writer. The newspaper had just entered the computer age with an archaic system that used video-display terminals and a scanner to read typed copy. Today I call it archaic, but it was top-of-the-line technology at that time.

I worked that year as a writer and even did a bit of editing of articles by other writers. And because those terminals were available to me after hours, I began to write my second full-length book on my own time. Along with my unpublished book on the power of God that I wrote at fifteen, I still have this early unpublished book called *The Perfect Gift*, a book about Christ's gift of the fivefold ministry to the Church.

I also wrote numerous brochures and tracts for friends to give to people who were hungry to grow deeper in their knowledge of the Bible. It was my first real attempt to put into print things that were deep inside my heart.

After I'd spent some time as a writer, I asked to be transferred to the back shop of the newspaper to work as a typesetter. I not only wanted to learn textbook material in the classroom, but I also wanted hands-on experience in every aspect of writing and publishing. I had the perfect job on campus to equip me in those areas!

For what seemed like endless hours, I sat in front of a brand-new Linotype machine that was considered to be "breakthrough" typesetting equipment. After text was set, it was taken into the camera room to be photographed. Then it was printed out on photo paper. I had to cut it up, put it through a messy paste machine, and then carefully lay each piece into place on every page of the newspaper.

That phase in my education was so important. It taught me about type-setting and text design, a lesson that has been such a benefit to me as my own books began to be typeset and published. In fact, I am so picky about text design that part of every publishing contract I sign, I ask for the right to inspect and change the way a book has been typeset if I don't approve of it.

After school and often very late into the night, I also worked in the press room so I could learn the processes involved in printing newspapers and different kinds of books and magazines.

But that wasn't all…to get hands-on experience in every single facet of this trade, I felt I needed to also work in the advertising department.

So soon I moved from the back shop to the advertising department, where I became a sales representative. My job was to visit potential retail advertisers to present advertising ideas to them. I had to pre-design ad campaigns and then convince the retailers why they needed to purchase space in our newspaper and use the campaign I'd created for them. It required a lot of creativity and guts to face those retailers on cold calls. But in my time in that department, God blessed me, and I became one of the highest-selling sales reps during that period of history of the newspaper.

When it was time for the newspaper to produce and print the annual magazine that was published for incoming students, the editor of that magazine appreciated my graphic-design abilities, so she asked me to join her department's team to design many pages of that magazine. I illustrated a lot of the graphic images, including the cover of the magazine.

As if that wasn't enough extracurricular activity in my life, in addition to my involvement in the university church, my weekends were free, so I applied for a job at the local Christian bookstore to further my preparation for the call of God that awaited me. To be sure, that was also a strategic part of my education.

Because it was the only Christian bookstore in the city, there was a non-stop flow of Christians in and out of those doors. I loved working with the Christian community that flooded that store on most days. I intentionally studied the interests of the Christian world to observe what they liked and disliked and what subjects were of the greatest interest to the Christian market. Because Whitaker House, Chosen, and Harrison House were new to the market, their books were really exciting, with content that was filled with dynamic testimonies of how God worked miracles in people's lives.

Top-selling books in those days were those written by Dennis and Rita Bennett, Corrie ten Boom, Merlin Carothers, Kenneth Copeland, Billy Graham, Don Gossett, Kenneth E. Hagin, and a long list of others. Many of those names that I stood in awe of at that young moment in my life became very meaningful friends later. What an unlikely scenario that I could have never imagined as a college student standing behind the counter and ringing up sales at the cash register.

All my jobs and studies — Greek and advertising classes, reporting in the newsroom, typesetting text in the back shop, working the presses, serving as an ad rep, designing graphics and illustrations for a magazine, and working at the Christian bookstore — were a strategic part of God's plan to train and equip me for future assignments He would give me. Again, everything was in place and right on time to equip me for my future.

## Embrace Your Days of Small Beginnings and Make the Most of Each Season

I was in a period of testing and training — of being *established*. Many times I wondered, *What am I doing working all these secular jobs when my heart's desire is to take people deeper into the Bible?* But over and over, the Holy Spirit would bring Zechariah 4:10 (*NLT*) to my mind: "Do not despise these small beginnings...." The Holy Spirit also regularly reminded me of Job 8:7, which says, "Though thy beginning was small, yet thy latter end should greatly increase."

I want to encourage you not to lament what "small thing" you may be doing right now as being too tiny or unimportant. Romans 8:28 says, "And we know that all things work together for good to them that love God, to them who are the called according to his purpose." God loves you so much that if you'll cooperate with Him, He'll see to it that everything you're learning right now will help in your future assignments. Believe me when I tell you that nothing is being wasted in what you are doing right now. God is *committed* to training you now so you can be a success in the future!

Everyone has a small beginning, so I also feel I should encourage you that you will not be the exception. But instead of perhaps bemoaning the fact that you feel so far away from doing what God has placed in your heart, *thank* Him for the precious time you're in now to grow, mature, and prove you are worthy of greater responsibilities — of being able to handle those responsibilities for His glory. God needs to see this growth process in you.

And you need to know for *yourself* that you are mature enough to move on to the next level. If the next job assignment is too big and comes too quickly, you won't have peace as you enter it — or you may not be able to be *sustained* so you can remain in that job or position. It's God's will to *get* you there and *keep* you there!

So learn to appreciate the stage of life you're in right now. You are on *God's* schedule; He's not on *yours*. Rather than contesting your present assignment and complaining about it, jump in with both feet forward! Do the best you can and give it everything you've got! Show God that your attitude is right, your heart is willing, and your desire is fervent to be faithful with the level of responsibility you have right now.

If you'll follow this advice, God will begin the process of promotion that you've been seeking. So just do what God has put in your hand to do! Prove yourself responsible, and God will see to it that you'll be given more responsibility. That's what promotion and authority entail, after all: *responsibility* and *stewardship* of the tasks He assigns to us, the relationships He blesses us with, and the people He gives us to lead.

### The Power of Words — *The Perfect Gift* and the *Not-So-Perfect* Book Review

I mentioned that after my work hours at the school newspaper, I wrote and typeset my first book, *The Perfect Gift*, as a college freshman. After it was all done, I decided to send it to a noted prophet to ask him to give me his feedback. I really didn't think he would do it, because he didn't know who I was, but I thought I'd give it a shot.

One day I received a letter in the mail from him that said he wanted to speak to me as soon as possible about my manuscript! I was ecstatic and nervous at the same time. My heart pounded wildly in my chest as I dialed the number he'd given me in his letter. I swallowed hard as he answered, clearing my throat so I could enunciate as clearly and as professionally as possible. I was in the "presence" of a notable man of God who had read my manuscript and was now giving me even more of his time and attention, and I wanted to make a good impression.

After our formal introductions and initial exchanges on the phone, this minister immediately began to *rave* over my manuscript! He actually went on and on, telling me that he thought it was the best book he had ever read on the subject of fivefold ministry.

I couldn't believe what my ears were hearing. I was only eighteen years old, and I had written a book on the weighty subject of fivefold ministry that had impressed a notable prophet.

Then the minister asked me, "Rick, how old are you?" I answered, "Sir, I am eighteen years old."

When he heard my response, the whole tone of the conversation abruptly changed. As quickly as he had given my manuscript his rave review, he suddenly began to reprimand me. I heard him say, "How *dare* you attempt to write a book on such a serious subject when you are only eighteen years old. Who do you think you are to attempt such a feat with no years of experience behind you. You should be *ashamed* of yourself!"

In one moment, this minister said my manuscript was the greatest thing he had ever read, and in the next moment, he chastised me and said I should be ashamed of myself for attempting such a book at my age.

I can't describe the dejection that enveloped me as he finally finished with me and we managed our awkward good-byes before I hung up the phone. My hand still glued to the phone as I carefully replaced the receiver in the cradle, I sat motionless, unable to move for many seconds. I was completely stunned by this man's words. His words cut so deep into my soul, in fact, that I laid that book aside — *The Perfect Gift* — and said to myself I would never try to write another book again.

Once again, I was woefully reminded of the powerful effect of a person's words upon the lives of others. In one moment, this man's words had encouraged me, but in the next moment, all that encouragement was bitterly swept away and *erased*. His words had such a negative impact on me that it literally shut down my gift for writing for years.

I fully intended never to put the words of my heart and mind to the printed page again. But, as you know, that's not how my story ended. Almost a decade later, Pastor Bob Yandian in Tulsa, Oklahoma, encouraged me to put a message I'd taught into print — and I did it! Accepting Pastor Bob's encouragement helped launch me into a prolific season of traveling and ministering in churches *and of writing again*. That book I wrote at Pastor Bob's suggestion was the first of *many* to come in the years ahead.

Although I was deeply affected by the negativity of that other minister's words, God did another amazing thing. Many years later after God had begun to use my books around the world, the same man who had lambasted me asked me to help him in his ministry, which I gladly did. I learned from that whole situation not just the power of words, but the power of trusting everything about our lives to the Lord so that He can redeem the negative circumstances that assail us to His own honor and glory.

### Discovering My 'Niche' in the Ministry — More Light for My Path at the University

As my time at school progressed, it became apparent that by attending this secular institution, some doors were beginning to open that might otherwise have been left shut had I attended a Christian university. For example, it was in this environment that I first began to get deeply involved in the ministry.

My earliest experiences teaching the Bible publicly took place in the off-campus university church. And because I was also constantly surrounded by unbelievers at school, I had plenty of opportunities to share Christ with others. Where sin abounds, God's grace much more abounds, and where darkness is great, His light *shines* (*see* Romans 5:20). And the need for light on that campus was great. These experiences emboldened me and familiarized me with the academic community's objections to the Gospel, which in turn sharpened my ability to be an effective witness for the Lord.

Never forget that your environment — *the surroundings and conditions in which you live and operate* — is important! Being in the right place at the right time according to God's plan for your life is *crucial* as you seek to find and fulfill His will for your life. God will use people, places, and the opportunities around you to shape you, sharpen your gifts, and prepare you to do what He has planned for you to do.

All of this makes me want to ask, "Are you where God has directed you to be?" It might be that where you are right now is outside your comfort zone, and you wish you could escape to somewhere else far away. However, if you know in your heart that God has spoken a word over your life, don't second-guess Him — *trust* Him. Trust that He is working to fully develop the gifts He has placed within you so that you can fulfill your divine mandate. *He knows exactly what you need!*

As I continued studying Greek and getting more deeply involved in the campus ministry, it wasn't long until believers in our young church began to approach me if they had a question about the Greek New Testament. Through these interactions, I began to see how I could fill a vital niche in the Body of Christ. By utilizing what I was learning about New Testament Greek, I could open up Scripture in a way that listeners could gain new insight about the Word of God. Exactly as I had been so impacted by Derek Prince, I saw that what I was learning from my own studies could bless and enrich others.

I am very thankful for the Lord's wisdom, guidance, and instruction to have me be at the right school in His plan for my life — *the right place* at *the right time.* This was true in my Greek studies, and it was certainly true of my time in the university church that He also joined me to.

I'll never forget the first service I attended there. I was so excited to be a part of a congregation filled with young people who were also excited about the things of God. What a group that was! Many of the young men and women who called that church their spiritual home came from "colorful" backgrounds, to say the least. Remember, this was the 1970s. Quite a few were former hippies who used to smoke marijuana and support a myriad of radical political causes. Having grown up in a denominational church surrounded by denominational Christians, I was definitely *not* in the church environment I was accustomed to!

One thing I really loved about this church was the diversity of backgrounds on the one hand and the uniformity of spiritual fervor on the other hand. They were all so open to the work of the Holy Spirit. They were simply *on fire* for the Lord! Very few of them had grown up in church or had any sort of religious background whatsoever. They had come to college to party, smoke dope, and join any radical cause they could find. But then, unexpectedly, someone shared the Gospel with them, and they received Jesus Christ into their hearts.

When these young people came to Jesus, they brought the same passion to the things of God that they had previously held toward their lives in the world. They earnestly wanted to evangelize, preach, pray, prophesy, and experience spiritual dreams and visions from the Lord. When I first walked into that church building, I witnessed a congregation exploding with life. When it was time to prophesy, people would often line up to give their words from God. It was the most exciting environment I had ever been in!

In addition to the young people who had little or no religious upbringing, God had also strategically placed a few people in the group who had a solid foundation in the Word of God — including me. The denominational church I had grown up in placed a strong emphasis on sound doctrine, and because of that, I had been taught the Bible all my life.

As I've already written, my daddy and mother imparted the Scriptures to me when I was still a young child, and our pastor was a profound Bible teacher who taught the principles of the Word in a balanced, thorough manner. Even though the church I grew up in didn't allow the gifts of the Holy Spirit to operate, overall I was given a solid, scriptural foundation upon which to build my life and ministry. I am so thankful for that spiritual upbringing!

So there were the free-spirited new believers in our university church — sitting right next to a number of folks like me who had a strong background in the Bible. Having more seasoned believers alongside the enthusiastic new believers and those who fervently pursued spiritual manifestations made for a powerful mix in our congregation. In that environment, my Bible education and study of ancient Greek proved to be an important ingredient in our young college church. I learned how to move freely with the Holy Spirit and to blend that supernatural work with a solid, intelligent exposition of the Bible.

Those among us who were well versed in the Word of God were able to discern what was doctrinally sound and what was contrary to the teaching of Scripture. This became extremely important as the church began to move into new realms of the Spirit. God had created the right balance to keep the church healthy, vibrant and forward-moving.

It's so easy for me to see now that as I yielded to God and His plan for my life, He always put me in the right place to prepare me for my next step. Remember, God knows what you need and is working a plan to fully develop the gifts He has placed in you. However, you have to allow Him to place you in the environment that *He* knows is best.

It might be that God has asked you to go somewhere you hadn't planned to go, or to do something you hadn't planned on doing with your life. You might be struggling with where you are right now, and you may be asking, "Lord, why in the world would You want me here?" But never forget that the Bible teaches: "Man's steps are ordered by the Lord. How then can a man understand his way?" (Proverbs 20:24 *AMPC*).

Maybe the church you're in right now is your "Holy Spirit University," just as that college church was for me. It may not be your final destination, but perhaps it is a needed step for you to be able to fulfill your destiny. Once again, it could be your spiritual training ground for the crucial days ahead. You need to learn the art of getting quiet on the inside, even in the midst of chaotic circumstances and external noise, so you can discern accurately what the Holy Spirit is trying to get across to you and so you can learn all you can from where you are right now.

### A Terrible Emotional Setback —
### Suicide in the Renner Family

I was seriously on track to fulfill the will and plan of God for my life. And I continued to experience freedom from my years of bondage to Satan's attacks on my mind in my younger, junior-high-school years. My experience of the baptism in the Holy Spirit had delivered me from the devil's stronghold, and because of that and my increasingly intimate relationship with the Holy Spirit, I'd also become freshly invigorated by God's plan for my life and ministry. Although the ministry He had called me to — as I understood it at the moment — seemed far off in its fulfillment, I was on an accelerated track to prepare for it, and life was exciting and fast-paced for me in my early college days.

But then our family hit a sizable bump in life's road — a really big one. During a Christmas break from college when I went home to be with my family, I learned that my Grandma Renner had been hospitalized with a heart condition and that my wonderful Grandpa Renner had been at home alone for several weeks. Everyone in our family had noticed over that period of time that he had begun to act strangely, but they simply attributed it to the medication he was taking for severe arthritis. He seemed to be thinking irrationally a lot, lost in the fog of his imagination while he was home alone and Grandma was in the hospital. I had no idea about this development.

One night while I was at home on Christmas break, I dreamed that my beloved grandfather died. I woke up immediately and tried to shake it off. But when I went back to sleep, I dreamed it again. Once again, I awoke and I tried to shake it off. I fell asleep again and dreamed the exact dream a third time. By the time the next morning rolled around, I felt it was a God-given dream to prepare me and my family that Grandpa Renner may be close to death. I shared it with my mother, not understanding his recent odd behavior, nor realizing that she had been very worried about it. So naturally, my dreams deeply disturbed her.

My grandfather was a smart man with a sound mind and a kind soul, but later in life he suffered terribly with arthritis. Over time, he became so debilitated with this disease that he was taking medication regularly to reduce the inflammation and mitigate the pain. Grandma had always helped him with his doses, but during the time when she had to be hospitalized for an extended period, Grandpa Renner was left to administer his own medication. We later learned that he had begun overdosing on the medication, becoming more and more confused and distraught. My father had been calling on him every day — in person or by telephone — and became suspicious one morning when my grandfather didn't answer his phone.

On that morning, my father said to me, "Grandpa doesn't answer the phone, and he hasn't been to the hospital to see Grandma today. She's worried about him, and it's not normal that no one has heard from him. Let's go over there so we can make sure everything is all right."

Without going into all the horrible details, I'll tell you that everything was *not* all right. Daddy and I drove to Grandpa Renner's house and tried to enter the front door, but it was locked. We actually forced open the door, but could not find Grandpa, so we ventured outside to look.

We went straight to the detached garage where Grandpa and I had enjoyed each other's company so often as he would make small conversation with me while working thoughtfully on various wood projects. As we approached the garage that sat adjacent to my grandparents' house, I tried to gulp down the knot that was quickly forming in my throat, feeling sick to my stomach at what I instinctively knew we would find. Slowly, Dad and I rolled up the garage door. Warm puffs of exhaust from Grandpa's running car engulfed my face in a suffocating mask, causing me to choke. Holding my breath, I watched as Dad rushed to open the driver-side door, reaching in over my grandfather's slumped-over body to turn off the ignition.

Because of the three dreams I'd had several days before, the Holy Spirit had prepared me for this ordeal so that I could be a supernatural support to my father in that moment of intense shock. The Holy Spirit filled me with such a tangible sense of His power as my father and I stood helpless over Grandpa Renner's stiffened body. I'll never forget the great grief that I saw completely overwhelm my father. I watched as the man who'd been a rock for me all my young life became *stricken* by heartache and bewilderment. It was he who needed me at that moment, and I was not going to let him down.

Dad stayed with Grandpa's body and asked me to call our pastor. Within minutes, Brother Post rang the doorbell to announce his arrival. Soon afterward, medical workers arrived in an ambulance to examine my grandpa's body and transport him to the morgue. As if that day had not already been difficult enough, Daddy and I then had to go to the hospital to break the sorrowful news to Grandma. When we told her, she and Daddy simply held each other and cried — it was a sight I will never forget as long as I live.

That day at my grandparents' house, I experienced in the midst of trauma a greater peace than I had ever known — and a strength that was not natural or that could be conjured just by human will. Although at one moment, I thought my own knees would give way beneath me in despair, in the next moment, I was infused by the Holy Spirit with a strength not my own that I desperately needed — I needed it for my father too.

God was with us in a powerful way throughout that time. His grace was simply upon us — comforting us, strengthening us, and helping us move forward with no great, *crushing* grief. It was truly miraculous to see how God faithfully worked to help us through what could have been an unbearably hard time in our lives.

## Back at School as Life Rolled On

After my grandfather's funeral, my grandmother was left to heal from her own grief and to adjust to her new season of life bereft of the man she'd known for the last forty-plus years. My dad was back at work at American Airlines, and my mother resumed her work at an allergy clinic in Tulsa. Time continued to move forward as the family resumed their routines and their places in the world, still deeply affected by what happened.

I headed back to school to pick up where I'd abruptly left off pursuing the plan of God for my life and my "corner of the sky." Back at school, our college church was filled to overflowing with students who were absolutely on fire for God. So many signs and wonders happened among those students that I felt like I was living in a real-life mini-version of the book of Acts.

By the fall of 1977, I was seriously devoted to studying Greek, still working in various departments of the newspaper, and still working extra hours at the Christian bookstore. But even with all of those activities, I never missed a single service or event at the church. As it had been in my childhood, church was still the *very center* of my life!

Not only did I want to grow educationally, I wanted to grow spiritually during this season of my life. So that year, I purchased multiple copies of large blank art notebooks that contained nothing but empty pages. Instead of using them for art as they were intended, I turned them into journals. Every day I sat at my desk in my dormitory and listened. I was giving my all to learn how to hear the voice of God.

Day after day, I wrote, "The Spirit of the Lord would say to you…," and I'd begin to write what I heard in my spirit. That was important because it taught me how to discern the voice of God — that still, small inner voice — that is speaking to us all the time. Today I still have those old journals, and the prophetic words I wrote were very accurate. Much of what I prophetically wrote way back then is still being fulfilled today.

In addition to being a college church, our fellowship had a "coffee-house ministry," a particular kind of outreach that was popular in those days because of the lingering effects of the Jesus' Movement. Every Saturday night, we packed the place with students who sat around at tables drinking coffee and listening to whatever group we had invited to minister to us that weekend.

A lot of music ministries were just getting started in those days, so it was pretty easy to get people to come and minister. Everyone was seeking an opportunity to share the love of Jesus through music, and nearly everyone felt the passion of God to reach the lost. On Saturday nights, we had names like Stephanie Boosahda, Ferrell and Ferrell, David Stearman, and others who stood on our small stage to minister the message of Jesus and the power of the Holy Spirit to the lost we brought to hear them. God moved, people were saved and filled with the Holy Spirit, and healings always abounded. It's interesting to look back at those days realizing that many of those "start-up" music ministries eventually became known nationwide.

### Footprints and Coffee Stains — a Lesson in Humility

I knew that God had called me to teach the Bible, and because I was studying the Greek New Testament, I was filled with new insights that I was eager to share. So I asked for an appointment to meet with the elders of our university church. They gave me a date to meet with them, and I boldly went into the meeting to tell them about God's call on my life to teach!

Nearly everyone in our church was a young university student. There were a few exceptions, but only a handful. Even the elders of the church were about twenty-five years old on average. Most of them were former hippies who had come to Christ, but hadn't grown up in a strong denominational church that was established in doctrine, as I had. They were good men. They knew how to move in spiritual gifts, how to pray for the sick, how to cast out demons, and how to lead the lost to salvation. But the majority of them were unschooled in biblical foundations.

So a young Rick Renner proceeded to boldly tell them that God's hand was on my life and that He had sent me to them as an answer to set them and the rest of the fellowship on a good biblical foundation. I let them know that as soon as they were ready to use my gift, I would be available to teach publicly at a moment's notice!

They sat silently and listened as I told them I was God's answer to help them. Finally, I finished, and the leader said, "Well, Rick, we didn't realize such a highly anointed person was sitting right here among us. We see the call of God on your life, but we need to pray for wisdom as to how your mighty gift can be used in our midst. Give us a week to pray and then let's meet again next week to see how we can maximize your anointing in our church."

I was elated that they could see the anointing of God on my life. So I eagerly awaited the next meeting where I imagined they would tell me, "Rick, we are so humbled that God has sent someone like you to us. We want you to start teaching your deep insights to us and help set us on a strong biblical foundation. Please, begin your public teaching ministry as soon as possible!"

I went to the meeting with the elders where I expected them to hand me the pulpit of the church to teach that week. I was stunned when I heard the leader say, "Rick, we definitely see the call and the anointing of God on your life. There is no doubt that you are called. So to help you start releasing your gift, we believe the Holy Spirit wants us to give you a prominent place of ministry in the church."

I was thrilled! But then he explained: "Starting next Sunday morning, we believe God wants you to begin vacuuming the auditorium carpet that is pretty dirty after our Saturday-night coffee-house fellowship. People always spill their coffee, and there are a lot of stains. But we know you'll do a marvelous job vacuuming and getting those stains out each week before our main Sunday afternoon meeting starts each week."

I was dumbfounded. Here, I surmised, they had a great gift of God sitting among them, and they were asking me to vacuum the carpet and to scrub away coffee stains from the previous night's coffee fellowship! I swallowed hard and willfully thanked them for giving me this wonderful opportunity to serve. Then the next Sunday I headed out early to the church, pulled out the vacuum cleaner, and began to vacuum. That carpet was old and spotted with what seemed like *years* of coffee stains. It wasn't cleanable — not completely, anyway — but every week I'd get on my hands and knees and *scrub, scrub, and scrub*, doing my very best to remove those stains.

At first, I admittedly resented what they had asked me to do. But God got hold of my attitude, and I decided if they wanted clean carpet, I was going to give them the cleanest carpet they had ever seen. So I *scoured* that carpet. And since I was in such close contact with that carpet, anyway, I thought I'd go ahead and pray in tongues as I labored over it, interceding for every person who would walk across it to their seats in the Sunday meeting. Just as my father had trained me as a child scrubbing scuff marks off linoleum floors at our church, I became *passionate* about that carpet because God's saints would walk on it!

Even today, I am finicky about the carpets and the tile foyers in our ministry facilities. Those early days put it deep into me that the way ministry facilities are maintained is important. Some may laugh to hear it, but even with the greater responsibilities God has entrusted to me, when I walk into a ministry building, my eyes still immediately scan the carpet and examine the grout between the foyer tiles to see if it smacks of excellence or shows a lack of care.

The weeks and months passed relatively quickly so that it seemed that in "no time," the elders called me in for a review. They said, "Rick, we've seen the work you've done on the carpet at the church. It has never looked better.

In fact, we're so impressed that we know that God is saying it's time for you to step up into the next phase of your ministry."

My heart skipped a beat in my excitement. By now I'd been studying the Greek New Testament for nearly a year, and it felt like my spirit was jam-packed with treasures that I longed to share in a public forum. So with great trepidation, I asked them, "How would you like me to proceed with my ministry?"

I was shocked when I heard the leader say, "You have proven yourself so faithful with the carpet that we next want to give you the responsibility of setting up the folding chairs for the meeting." I silently thought, *You've got to be kidding. You want me to set up metal folding chairs? Have you any idea what a great gift is sitting in front of you? God's hand is on my life, and you're asking me to set up chairs? THAT'S the next exciting phase of ministry you're offering me?*

I thanked the elders once again and walked out of that meeting feeling humiliated. But I decided to embrace my new assignment. So in addition to vacuuming the carpet and scrubbing coffee stains, I began to set up all the chairs in the auditorium as they had asked me to do. I was so serious about it that I began to experiment with how to get maximum seating capacity in the room.

One week, everyone would arrive at church and find the chairs facing one direction — and the next week, they would arrive to find the chairs facing the opposite direction. Then the following week they would find them in a completely different formation as I worked and worked to provide the most excellent seating arrangement I could give them. And I was so meticulous about how those chairs were set up that it looked as if I'd used a measuring tape to make sure they were all correctly spaced and that every row lined up perfectly. *Nothing was out of order in Rick Renner's assignment of preparing the carpet and chairs for the saints to congregate!*

By the time I was done with that chair-setting-up season, I had become a "pro" when it came to maximizing seating capacity. And just as my eyes still scan carpet and tiles, when I enter an auditorium today, I still automatically examine the way chairs are arranged. Over the years as we've moved from facility to facility, this "expertise" has proven so helpful. If someone tells me that no more people can be seated in a sanctuary, my natural instinct is to show them how it can be done!

Since I was putting every chair in its place each week, anyway, I thought I'd stop a moment and pray in tongues for every person who would be seated in each chair at that university church. I prayed fervently for the anointing of God to touch each person. I passionately prayed they would all leave transformed by the Word of God and the power of the Holy Spirit. So chair-setting-up ministry also became a time of intercession for others.

But something else was happening while I cleaned that carpet and set up those chairs. My flesh would silently rail against my being assigned such demeaning tasks. No one but God heard the ugly thoughts that passed through my mind, but God revealed this very ugly blemish in my attitude that needed to be eradicated. I needed to understand I was not *entitled* to ministry. When the day came that I would be invited to minister publicly, it would be because God found me *faithful* and because I allowed His fire to remove impurities from my character and attitude that were unacceptable. When I finally figured out that God was watching my attitude, I quit focusing on what I hadn't been asked to do and focused on what I *was* asked to do — and I did it "as unto the Lord and not as unto men" (*see* Colossians 3:23).

Most ministry begins by vacuuming the carpet, setting up chairs, cleaning the restrooms, and so on — with the seemingly "small things." God doesn't promote people instantly. He often requires that they go through a period of training first. For me, this lesson in faithfulness was absolutely vital. God was watching both my attitude and my performance to see if He could trust me with the next phase of my ministry.

*Finally*, my long-awaited day arrived when the elders said, "Rick, it's time for you to publicly teach the Bible in our church. You have proven yourself faithful at everything we've asked you to do and you've done it with excellence. Now we are ready to receive your public teaching gift. Next week the pulpit is yours, so give us your best!"

That week I prayed and studied incessantly. I wanted to give my best when I stood in front of the church. I prepared a message called, "God's Kings and Priests" that was about the authority Christ has entrusted to every believer. When I stood in front of the fellowship, I think everyone was as excited as me because it was generally known that I really wanted to get started using my teaching gift and sharing what I'd been learning from my studies of the Greek New Testament. Most people who speak publicly the first time quickly run out of material, but I taught a whole ninety minutes the very first time I stood to teach at that fellowship!

The response of the crowd was thrilling to me. Fellow church members expressed that it was some of the best teaching they had heard in a long time. From that moment on, the leadership began to ask me to speak from time to time — those were the earliest beginnings of my teaching ministry. I spent countless hours exegeting entire texts from the Greek New Testament — writing down every single Greek word with its most original meaning and then typing out near-perfect notes. I still have those early notes stored in my files today.

## The Blessing of 'Waiting'

I waited and waited for that opportunity, but all that waiting was *good* for me. You may be wondering about your own life, *God, how long am I going to have to wait for that promotion I've worked so hard for? Is there a reason that the promotion I want keeps getting delayed? What is happening in my life, Lord?*

It seems we are always trying to make things happen faster than they're supposed to happen, but God doesn't work in the same time frame we do. There are some things that are more important to God than giving us a promotion when we want it or making sure we get recognized as quickly as we think our time and efforts merit.

To ensure that we're really ready for our next big assignment, sometimes it takes a little longer than we might like before God promotes us. It's hard on the flesh while we wait, yet it is actually the mercy of God at work. You see, during that time of waiting, the imperfections that could potentially ruin us are exposed so that God can remove them. Then He can move us up into the new position with no concern that a hidden flaw will cause us to fall flat on our faces.

I think there is no clearer example of this than the apostle Paul himself. We know from Acts 9:20-25 that when Paul first became a Christian, he tried to barge right into a public ministry. But he wasn't ready for that yet and therefore created some problems and a lack of peace in the Early Church. Although saved and called, he simply wasn't ready for a visible position of leadership. It was going to take some time for God to prepare Paul for the kind of ministry and anointing he was going to carry in his life.

Paul referred to this process when he wrote to the Thessalonians. He said, "But as we were allowed of God to be put in trust with the gospel, even so we speak; not as pleasing men, but God, which trieth our hearts" (1 Thessalonians 2:4). This verse is packed full of insight regarding Paul's own experience of being prepared, tested, and finally promoted into his own public ministry.

Notice first that Paul said, "But as we were allowed of God...." The word "allowed" means *to test, examine, inspect, scrutinize, or to determine the quality or sincerity of a thing*. It means that because the object being scrutinized has passed the test, it can now be viewed as *genuine* and *sincere*.

This was the very Greek word used to illustrate the tests to determine real and counterfeit coinage. After a scrutinizing test was performed, the bona fide coinage would stand up to the test and the counterfeit would fail. This Greek word was also used to determine the quality of metal before it was used in a building. First, the metal was placed in a fire that burned at a certain degree of heat; then it was placed in a fire burning at an even higher degree; and finally, it was placed in a blazing fire that burned at the highest degree of all. Three such tests were needed in order to remove from the metal all the unseen impurities that were hidden from the naked eye.

From just the viewpoint of the naked eye, the metal probably looked strong and ready to be used prior to those tests. But hidden defects resident in the metal would have shown up later as a break, a fracture, or some kind of dangerous malfunction. Before a builder could be assured that the metal was free of defects and thus ready to be used, these three purifying tests at three different degrees of blazing-hot fire were required. The fire was hot and the process was lengthy, but the tests were necessary in order to achieve the desired result.

Because Paul used this very Greek word, he was telling us about the fires he went through himself before God promoted him. The Greek actually means. *"It was a lengthy process, and I went through a lot of refining fires to get to this place, but finally I passed the test and God saw that I was genuinely ready...."*

I tell you this because I don't want you to be discouraged if it takes time for you to get the advancement you believe belongs to you in God. He never gets in a hurry, because godly character is more important to Him than gifts, talents, or temporary success in the eyes of other people. He wants to use you, but He also wants you to be ready to be used.

Like a young Rick Renner at that college church so long ago, it could possibly be that you need some time to prepare, change, and grow. Don't despise this time. By taking time to make sure you're ready, when God finally does promote you, you'll have what you need both naturally and spiritually to stay in that God-ordained position as you fulfill your assignment with excellence!

## I Was an Eighteen-Year-Old Elder

The elders had watched me serve and noted my teaching gift. I was deeply grateful for every opportunity that was extended to me to teach. And rather than think I was entitled to it, I saw it as a gift from God. But to my surprise, the elders eventually asked me to join them as one of the spiritual leaders of the fellowship. Because it was a university church led by university students, nearly all the leaders were young. But I was eighteen, almost nineteen — the very youngest among them.

On a Sunday afternoon in March 1977, hands were laid on me and I was installed as one of the leaders of the fellowship. So in addition to being a student and working at various jobs while studying at the university, I also assumed spiritual responsibilities alongside other leaders in the church. I remember feeling odd every time I was called an elder because I was so young, but I embraced this as a serious responsibility that was given to me by the Lord, and to the best of my ability at that time, I served the people in that university church.

A long-time friend who was there when I first began to teach said, "Rick is such a consistent personality. Since college, I don't think his personality has changed a whole lot. He has always been stable, serious — and also humorous. And as a leader in our fellowship, he possessed a calmness about him, and it always felt like he spoke with authority."

He added, "I was actually present that first time Rick taught the Word in our fellowship. We could see he had a depth that most young people didn't have in the '70s. We thought, *Wow, he can really teach.*

"But what I always loved most about Rick was his commitment to stick with the Bible. I've watched him all these years, and he has been consistent and stable with what he believes and what he teaches."

### 'Write, Write, Write...'

I was so thankful to the Lord for finding me faithful and opening the door for me to minister and have some influence in that university church. But deep in my heart, I knew that God wanted to use me to take the deeper revelations of the New Testament to *many* Christians who were famished for truth. And I prayerfully kept in mind the other facet of what I knew God had called me to do — and that was to *write.* So despite my disheartening experience with the older minister who had chastised me for writing that book, I kept studying New Testament Greek and working to improve my skills as a writer.

I intensely focused on how to exegete words from the Greek New Testament and explain them on paper in a way that was easy-to-understand and that people could apply to their personal lives. My prayer was that God would enable me to take people into the New Testament to see it, feel it, and experience it as never before. As I look back on those days, I realize those early writings as a university student were the first beginnings of what would later become known as my devotional series called, *Sparkling Gems From the Greek.*

One day as I focused on how to write these Greek word meanings in an easy-to-understand form that had practical application, I began to feel weary. I prayed, "Lord, will anyone ever read what I am writing? Is this really what You've called me to do, or is this just a figment of my imagination?

Why would You choose me to do this when there are others who are more gifted than me? Are You sure this is what You want me to do in life?"

Abruptly, I heard the Holy Spirit speak from deep inside. He commanded me:

*Write, write, write. I will prosper what you write. You say, 'I've never written a book before.' Did I call you because of your own abilities? No, I called you simply by My divine purpose. You'll never understand or comprehend it. I don't ask you to understand. I ask you to obey.*

That word from the Holy Spirit encouraged me to keep digging deep into the original language of the New Testament and to learn how to put all of those insights on paper for future readers. I had no clue how to proceed as a writer or how to speak to a publisher — or why any publisher would ever be interested in what I had to write. But I had a word from the Lord. He had said, "Write, write, write. I will prosper what you write."

I held on to that word and took it as a mandate for what I was to do in terms of the printed page. I testify to you today that God has prospered the books I have written as they have been distributed by the millions around the world in multiple languages. God is always faithful to do what He says. But I had to do my part, which was to *"write, write, write."*

When no one knew my name, I sat alone at tables with my computer and with books stacked all around me. And I gave myself to what God had instructed me to do. He'd said, "Write, write, write" and that He would prosper what I wrote. My part was to write and God's part was to do the prospering. I was well aware that I would never experience the prospering hand of God unless I first did my part. So I yielded my heart, mind, hands, and fingers and became a writer at the Lord's command. And the prospering part was miraculously manifested by His own hand over many years.

But that didn't stop me from fulfilling my new responsibilities as a church elder. In fact, I began to understand that *everything* I was doing in that season was preparation for future seasons, and I was determined not to miss my mark, nor to miss a step of preparation along the way.

Our university church had always been committed to evangelism and our congregation *blazed* with a burning heart for souls. As a result, a nonstop flow of unsaved people was coming into the Kingdom. In fact, the members of our fellowship were engaged in *many* types of evangelistic outreaches to bring people to a saving knowledge of Jesus Christ.

The earliest leadership of the church, including my advertising professor Frank Heaston, exhorted us regarding our responsibility to reach the unsaved, urging us to reach people who did not know Jesus Christ. As we reached out to the lost, the power of God showed up in that church — *it was simply a spiritual powerhouse!* The whole church burned with the fire of God. Oh, how I cherish the memories I carry of that church in those early years. It was *overflowing* with the power of the Holy Spirit!

Those who regularly attended that church could hardly wait for the next service time to come because they knew they would experience something amazing and rich of the presence of God. They *expected* the gifts of the Spirit to manifest with miracles and healings and other notable signs. Decades have passed since then, and many of the people who were there in those early years have since struggled to find a place to worship God that matched what they experienced in that university church so many years ago.

## A Melodic Voice From the Back Row

During one Sunday afternoon service as we worshipped at our college church, a still hush came over the crowd as the Holy Spirit moved among the congregation with His deep peace. After what felt like a couple of minutes, from the back of the room, someone on the very back row began to spontaneously sing one of the most beautiful songs in the Spirit I had ever heard. The prophetic nature of the song gripped my spirit, but it was the *voice* that overpowered me.

I thought, *What a voice! Whose voice could that be?* It was full, powerful, and rich, and the vibrato was something that I would have imagined to be sung by an angel.

I slowly turned to see who was singing on that back row, and I saw a young woman with dark hair whom I had never met before. She had been attending the church all this time, but I'd never taken note of her until she stepped out to obey the Holy Spirit that Sunday afternoon to sing that prophetic song.

If you know my family, you've probably already figured out the woman I saw that day was Denise Roberson, whom we all now know as Denise *Renner*. And the many twists and turns of our early beginnings together, as well as Denise's own small beginnings, are what I'm excited to share with you next.

'The path in front of Denise would not always
be easy for her, but it would always be bright with the
light of God's favor and grace upon her life. Like Mary
who waited at Jesus' feet while Martha strove busily
with what was mundane, Denise had chosen
"that eternal, good part," which would not
be taken away from her.'

# 5

# AN UNLIKELY RELATIONSHIP —
# RICKY RENNER AND
# DENISE ROBERSON

Before I go into how Denise and I met — how we briefly began our relationship...quickly disconnected...and then picked up our relationship again, finally aligning ourselves with the will of God — I need to tell you a little bit about my Denise.

In this chapter, I will share with you where Denise is from, what kind of family she was raised in, how she and I ended up in the same university church together, and how we became "betrothed" *multiple times* to be husband and wife! It was an *unlikely* encounter and a lesson in the importance of being led by the Holy Spirit.

---

**Left:** *Lincoln Center, New York City, New York.*

## More Indians in My Life and History!

Denise Roberson was born and raised in northeastern Oklahoma in a small town called Miami, so named after an Indian tribe called the *Miami* Indians. Her father, David Roberson, was Indian to his bones. His mother, Denise's grandmother, was a pureblooded Native American Indian from the small Otoe tribe that had relocated to Oklahoma nearly a hundred years earlier — in the late Nineteenth Century — when Oklahoma was still Indian Territory.

After Denise and I were married, I happened upon an old photo of Dave's mother. I knew Denise had a little Native American ancestry, but I didn't know *how much* until I saw the photo of her Otoe Indian grandmother. That photo of her grandmother perfectly depicted an Indian girl from pre-Oklahoma Indian Territory — she looked like she had just walked out from under the flap of a teepee! She wore long braided, black hair, beads, and leather clothing with fringes and more beads. I was nearly speechless when I realized I had married a real-life Otoe Indian!

Denise's father Dave was the seventh child to be born to his parents. Their family started in Texas, but relocated to southeastern Oklahoma where the majority of Dave's growing-up years took place. They were a simple family who lived off the land and who suffered many financial hardships during Dave's childhood. Those early events deeply impacted his life. All his life, through adulthood, he struggled with a fear of being without.

To alleviate his fear that he might end up without money, Dave secretly carried $700 at all times that he wrapped around his ankles under his white socks every morning. Once when I saw that money with my own eyes, I asked him why he did it, and he told me, "I know what it is to have nothing, and I'll never be left destitute in my life again." Obviously, $700 couldn't have gone very far in a serious crunch, but knowing he had cash hidden so close by seemed to help him have peace.

Dave joined the Marines as a young man and was soon shipped off to war. Every Marine in his particular group was killed in action on the frontlines, but Dave never made it to the battlefront because as he disembarked his ship to report for duty, he tripped on his way down the plank and broke his leg. That broken leg stopped him from going to the battle lines, and to his demise, with his buddies. God is certainly not in the business of breaking people's legs, but Dave's relatively small injury was undeniably a life-saving blessing to him in the long-run.

In our family archives, we have a tattered photo of Dave in his wheelchair in a military hospital. And who would you think was photographed at his side? It was Eleanor Roosevelt, wife of President Franklin D. Roosevelt, who had preceded President Harry Truman in office. Eleanor Roosevelt had gone on a mission to visit Marines who had been injured in military service. Dave was among them and he met her that day.

Dave returned to the U.S. and he married Nora Stamps in 1946. Nora (Denise's mother) was a twenty-eight-year-old young woman who had grown up in southeastern Oklahoma with nine brothers and sisters in her family. The Stamps were a family of Gospel singers, some of them professional singers. If you've ever heard of the famous Stamps Quartet, which was begun in the 1920s, that is the family line Denise's mother was born into.

I can vividly remember Nora, "Buck," and Margarete — Nora and two of her sisters — as they would stand around a piano to belt out Gospel songs. Even though they were getting older, if anyone just struck a key on the piano, they would jump into place and start harmonizing. I'm certain that heritage has something to do with Denise's gift for singing.

Dave and Nora were not equally yoked when they got married. Nora knew the Lord, but Dave did not. Nora's father was a choir director in some of the old-time brush-arbor meetings that were held in southern Oklahoma. But although Dave was not saved when they married, not long afterward, he had a radical conversion. Denise told me, "My dad came under conviction, got radically saved, and started to diligently serve the Lord."

In all the years I knew Dave, I was impressed with his tender heart for the Lord. As he got older, he would sit in his chair and watch countless hours of TV preachers — and he was mesmerized by anyone who taught on the end times. When Denise and I would go there to visit, he'd say, "Rick, sit down and let me tell you what I've been learning about the end times." His magazine-and-book rack was filled with ministry publications and books he'd ordered from various television ministries.

Eventually Dave and Nora moved to Miami, Oklahoma. Denise was born in Miami at the Baptist hospital in 1952 — a mere seven years after World War II ended in 1945. And for the rest of his life, her father worked as a salesman for Electrolux vacuum company.

Denise's older sister Trula recalls that Dave was pretty detached as a father because he worked so hard knocking on doors to sell Electrolux. He was so relentless in his career that Nora once exclaimed in exasperation, "I swear, *that man will sell an Electrolux on his deathbed!*" Well, her words turned out to be prophetic, because as Dave lay on his deathbed, barely able to breathe he pulled himself together for one last sales pitch and sold an Electrolux to his doctor just moments before that same doctor had to pronounce him dead.

In addition to Dave's career as a vacuum-cleaner salesman, he and Nora opened two local businesses in Miami — *Dave's New and Used Furniture* and *Nora's Draperies*. Nora was an excellent homemaker and a fine cook, committed to serving her family nutritious food — and she also had a gift for sewing. Nora had learned how to sew fine draperies, and so many people commented on them that she decided to start Nora's Draperies.

Dave and Nora purchased a vacated department-store building on a prominent corner of their Main Street in Miami. In the front part of the building was a small room designated for Nora's Draperies, which was right behind the section of the store where Dave sold reclining chairs. Nora's shop was filled with bolts of fabric and drapery materials that she used to make special-order draperies for people who came to her from all over northeastern Oklahoma.

The rest of their store was filled to the point of clutter, with new furniture mingled with old furniture, real antiques, and a hodge-podge section in the very back of the store of knick-knacks, ornaments, figurines, and novelties — what to me seemed like leftovers from people's garages. To my eyes, it looked like a bunch of junk, but that section of the store stayed busy all the time with people digging through those items, hunting for treasures they could take home to enjoy.

Both of Dave and Nora's businesses were successful. Even when they were at retirement age and didn't need to work anymore, they continued to work for several more years. Nora would stand for hours putting up drapes when she could have been sitting at home living on Social Security benefits. And Dave, even in his mid-seventies, was loading furniture into his truck by himself to deliver to buyers who had shopped at his store.

Denise's father was *passionate* about health products! Denise might not describe it that way because she is a lot like her daddy. But in Dave's kitchen — *whew* — outside of a drugstore or health-food store, I'd never seen so many bottles of supplements in one place in my life. Their cabinets contained shelves *filled* from the front to the back with vitamins and other supplements. Dave took handfuls of them several times a day.

Dave regularly read multiple magazines that explored alternative kinds of medical treatment. He was very attracted to what seemed to me to be really weird ways to heal the human body — like putting an ice cube on your big toe when you have a headache. He even visited an "eye reader" who looked into people's irises to sort of "prophesy" what happened in their physical bodies all the way back when they were babies. To me, it all kind of bordered on the edge of *eccentric*. Nevertheless, Dave was a precious man and a good man — and he was a *healthy* man!

## The Robersons and Their Dutiful Lives

The Robersons faithfully attended a Baptist church in their small town. When I later visited the church myself, I felt it to be a rather "stiff" atmosphere that lacked warmth. Maybe it wasn't *really* that way, but for certain it was unlike the atmosphere I grew up in at Glenwood Baptist Church. But the Roberson clan of five — Dave, Nora, Trula, Denise, and their younger brother David — all faithfully went to church every Sunday morning, Sunday evening, and Wednesday night.

Like all dedicated Southern Baptists, Denise graduated from the nursery up to preschool and then to kindergarten class, etc. — and participated with certificates of completion in every class that was offered by their church, including Sunbeams and G.A.s (Girls in Action). She memorized Scripture, wrote to missionaries, and, *can you believe it*, even signed a commitment card in which she pledged never to marry a Catholic! Like the Renners, the Roberson clan was Baptist to their bones too!

And like most Southern Baptist churches at that time, the First Baptist Church of Miami was cessationist in its beliefs about the gifts of the Holy Spirit. Like us, they believed the gifts of the Spirit ceased at the end of the apostolic age, so they were opposed to any type of Pentecostal experience.

Whereas my family had loads of close friends and nonstop fellowship in our church experience, Denise's parents had very few close friends. Maybe it was because they were twenty years older than my parents and lived with vivid memories of struggling through the Great Depression, having experienced multiple tragedies and losses in their childhoods that had a lasting impression on them. The effect of it all caused them to have a dutiful mindset about working that included little room for friends or relationships. There was not even much room in their minds for fun. Life was a duty. Going to church was a duty. Pretty much everything was a duty. And Dave and Nora were very good at fulfilling their duties. But they truly loved God, and they deeply loved their children.

There was also so little room for vacations in the Roberson family that they never took one that Denise can remember. Once a year, they did drive five hours to Idabel in southern Oklahoma to see one of Nora's siblings and her children — Denise's aunt and cousins — and Denise's grandmother, Nora's mother. They stayed two nights, went to church on Sunday with the family, and then loaded back into the car to drive five hours back home to Miami. Those three days once a year was the only semblance of a "vacation" that Denise can recall from her entire childhood.

When Denise was six years old, Dave and Nora decided to purchase an old farmhouse on the outskirts of town. The house sat at the end of a long driveway and had been built nearly in the middle of their five acres of land. During Denise's growing-up years, her parents always planted an enormous garden each year where they grew tomatoes, green beans, cucumbers, squash, okra, and watermelon. They also had chickens, cows, and a horse. Denise even had her very own pony that her father bought her. It was a very simple life. Oh, yes, they also played Dominoes!

Every night in her clean but cluttered kitchen, Nora served them dinner at the round table that could barely accommodate their family of five. She always fed them right from the garden — their meals included fresh vegetables and homemade cornbread. After washing the dishes, they'd all head to the living room to watch TV from six to nine o'clock. Then the kids would head to sleep for the night. Life was routine and predictable and consisted mostly of eating homemade cornbread and fresh vegetables from their own garden, fulfilling their duties to go to church, and being responsible neighbors.

It's no exaggeration that the scope of Denise's life experiences from the age of six until she left home was pretty limited to the five acres of land where their family lived. A big highlight for her was taking a short drive to the fairgrounds once a year to see a rodeo. And because Nora was from the Stamps family and Gospel music flowed in her veins, every once in a while, she'd take the kids to a Gospel music concert in Joplin. That was huge because Joplin, Missouri, was a whole, whopping twenty-nine miles away and it was *across the border in another state.* For them, that was like a trip to another country!

## When Denise Met Jesus

Just as I had done at the age of five at Glenwood Baptist Church, Denise walked the aisle of her home church at the young age of seven to give her heart to Jesus. That same day, she was water baptized.

Right from the start, Denise had a tender heart toward the things of God. Oh, how she loved Jesus and wanted more of Him. But in our churches in those days, we didn't know *how* to have more of Jesus. The altar seemed to be the place where serious spiritual decisions were made. But in our churches, there were really only four decisions that could happen at an altar. You could walk the aisle to get saved, you could go forward to rededicate your life, you could surrender to full-time service, or you could surrender to be a missionary. That was about it.

Every week during the altar call, Denise would hear her pastor say, "If God is touching your heart and you feel the need to come to the altar, please come. Don't hesitate or hold back if God is dealing with you." Well, Denise *always* felt God touching her heart, so in simple childlike obedience and faith, she'd make her way out of the pew to walk the aisle and go forward to rededicate her life — *and she did that almost every week!* I'm sure when the pastor gave the altar call, he probably thought, *If no one else responds, we know Denise Roberson will come forward to rededicate her life again.*

Finally, Nora told her, "Denise, please stop going forward every week. You don't have to rededicate your life every single week!"

Yet Denise's heart longed for more. Girls in the Southern Baptist Convention were not allowed to preach at that time, but they *could* serve as a missionary. In retrospect, the whole idea that you couldn't do one, but you *could* do the other doesn't make much sense. But at the age of fifteen, Denise surrendered to be a missionary while at youth camp. The mere thought of going to a foreign country was a far reach for a small-town girl who only knew life on those five acres of cornstalks and fresh vegetables.

As I told you, my childhood memories of growing up in Glenwood Baptist Church were mostly fond — spotted with oppressive thoughts in my early life that I was a misfit. Those spots grew and grew the older I got, and they eventually tainted my adolescent and young teenage years before the Lord gloriously delivered me.

And Denise's childhood memories at her church were not all sweet either. Like me, she, too, was a little different as a child. She was more pure and simple than most girls — what others may have deemed as "Pollyanna" and naive. In fact, the other girls at church scorned her so much that they even formed an "I Hate Denise" club. While Denise yearned to be accepted, she was nevertheless shunned and ostracized by others. It was as much an attack on her mind by the devil as what I similarly experienced as a young man.

Making matters worse was, at the age of twelve, Denise developed a severe case of cystic acne — a severely painful and disfiguring disease. It begins when pores in the skin get clogged and bacteria gets trapped in it, which causes the infected area to become excessively red and swollen. In Denise's case, the cysts that formed were so severe that they went deep into all five layers of the skin on her face and neck. When she or a doctor tried to remove them, it left permanent scars on her face and neck that were rough and uneven.

Cystic acne is not only very painful, it is emotionally distressing and often affects the self-esteem of those who struggle with it, especially young people. They are often shamed, shunned, and rejected by others. Those who struggle with cystic acne often obsess to try to find ways to hide the ugly indentations and scars. They wear longer hair to try to cover them or use excessive amounts of makeup to try to hide the blemishes. The marred appearance of those who suffer with this excruciatingly painful and disfiguring disease causes them to experience a lot of shame as a result. *That* is what attacked Denise when she was twelve years old.

Denise struggled for thirteen years with this damaging disease. For a period of time, Nora drove her to Tulsa to see a doctor who would give her solid carbon-dioxide, or cryotherapy, treatments, which were terribly painful. In those days, doctors took a block of "dry ice" and rubbed it across the part of the face and neck affected by acne to "burn" a layer of skin off the face. It was an attempt to smooth out the indentations. But after the treatments, Denise's face and neck would become covered with deep, crusty scabs — which were equally repulsive to other young people at church and school. The scabs added more pain, embarrassment, shunning, ridicule, and rejection.

### *'Rollin', Rollin', Rollin'* — Denise's Unlikely Beginnings on the Path of God's Plan for Her Life

Denise discovered she had a gift to sing when she went to see the movie musical *Oklahoma* that starred the acting and singing talent of Shirley Jones. Denise was so enamored with the singing of Shirley Jones that her mother bought her the soundtrack of the movie. Every day, Denise would stand on her vanity stool in front of her mirror in her bedroom and sing along with Shirley. That was the earliest moment Denise says she began to realize she could sing!

In those days, there was also a TV program called *Rawhide*, a popular western series starring a young Clint Eastwood that aired from 1959-1965.

If you're older, you may remember watching *Rawhide*. The Renner family never missed an episode because Daddy was an avid *Rawhide* fan. And the Roberson family were fans too.

If you ever watched this program, you no doubt recall that in the opening theme song of the series, a male singer sustains the last note for quite a long time. He begins, *"Rollin', rollin', rollin'…*and of course ends with the word, *"RAWHIDE!"* Denise would sing along and eventually figured out she could hold that note even longer than the man singing the song on the program! *Whew…*if she could hold the last note of *that* song, she really had a special gift to sing!

Denise was trying to find her musical niche. First, she became Shirley Jones in *Oklahoma*. Then she was the singing cowboy in *Rawhide* — then she attempted to become Barbra Streisand in *Funny Girl*.

Denise got her first public job working behind the counter of the concession stand at the Coleman Theater, where she sold soft drinks and popcorn to moviegoers. While she worked there, the Coleman Theater showed *Funny Girl*, of course, starring Barbra Streisand. Denise went to the movie and came under the "spell" of Streisand's voice. She was so enthralled that she saw *Funny Girl* three times — and purchased that soundtrack so she could sing along and learn all the songs.

Barbra Streisand captivated her so much that Denise not only learned every note, but also every physical gesture Streisand used as she sang. When her high school announced it was having a talent show, Denise stood on the stage and belted out Barbra Streisand songs as if she were the famed diva herself. These multiple experiences with a musical, a TV series, and a movie were all a part of the process of Denise coming alive to her own voice.

Denise remembers, "One minute, I was singing in front of the mirror as Shirley Jones, and the next minute, I became the cowboy singer on *Rawhide*. Then I'd become Barbra Streisand. I must have been diligently searching for my identity because I eventually memorized every single song on the *Funny Girl* album and could imitate Barbra Streisand really well."

Because Nora could see Denise's talent and was a "Stamps" girl herself, she was just *thrilled* at the thought of having a singing daughter. So Nora went straight to the choir director at the First Baptist Church to ask if he would give Denise private voice lessons.

Soon Denise began taking voice lessons from him, and when he scheduled Denise to sing her first public solo at the church, she performed, "What a Friend We Have in Jesus." She was so nervous about standing in front of people that when it came time for her to sing, she cleared her throat all the way through the song.

Realizing what she'd done, she cringed with embarrassment as her performance ended and vowed never to sing again. She said, "I cleared my throat throughout the entire song. I was so embarrassed that I walked off the stage, went back to the choir room, looked in the mirror crying, and said out loud, 'I will never sing again.'"

But two little grandmothers who were at the church service when she sang sent Denise cards to express their thanks for how she was using her voice for the Lord. Those women's cards really encouraged Denise to keep trying. What a gift the words from those older women were to the aching heart of a discouraged, deflated young girl. We must never underestimate the power of encouragement!

But then came the era of beauty contests. I well remember that beauty-pageant phase in my house growing up, because my older sister Ronda also participated in those kinds of contests. Ronda was such a super-achiever — if there was anything to compete in, *she was in it!* I will never forget sitting through *hours* of monotonous spelling-bee competitions that Ronda entered in Tulsa. She was a masterful speller, which meant she lasted every time to the very end of the competition. I remember sitting there in my jacket and bowtie, "burning up" because it was so hot and stuffy in that auditorium. Privately, I would plead, *God, please, please, please... let Ronda make a mistake so we can get out of here!*

But Ronda also participated in beauty competitions. For the talent segment, one year she'd play the piano, and the next year she'd twirl machetes or fire batons. Oh, how I detested those competitions, but Lori and I sat silently, side by side with our parents, to watch Ronda perform year after year onstage among all the other beauties.

In Denise's pageant phase, she got involved because it was the thing to do back in those days. She might not say it, but Denise was very beautiful even back then. However, she well knew that she could not win a beauty competition because of the condition of her skin. But those contests gave her opportunities to use her voice and to sing, so Denise started her season of competing in pageants. First, it was "Junior Miss" in her small town and she went from there to participate twice in Miss Grand Lake. Out of the three competitions, she was awarded the "Miss Congeniality" prize twice — which explains why she *loves* to watch the movie *Miss Congeniality* so much!

## Denise's Spiritual Hunger Began To Stir Even More — Along With Her Vision for Her Future

When Denise was a freshman at a community college, Northeastern Oklahoma A&M, a guest speaker came to First Baptist Church who seemed to have something that was "different" from anyone else she had ever heard preach. That was the first time she realized there was "something deeper" in the Lord that she had never experienced, and it caused the spiritual hunger in her heart to be stirred even more.

Campus Crusade for Christ then came to her college and Denise attended some of their sessions. In one session, they talked about the need to be filled with the Holy Spirit. That was a radical new idea to the ears of this Baptist girl. But because her heart was drinking in every word they spoke, she ended up attending their meetings on campus every evening.

On the last night of those meetings, Denise left the service early in deep turmoil because she felt an almost unbearable ache in her heart for something more. She sat on a curb just outside the campus and cried out, "Lord, please cleanse me of every sin." She then named every sin in her life she had never confessed. She recommitted her life to the Lord *yet again*, and right on that curb, she prayed to be filled with the Holy Spirit. But the leader of Campus Crusade had never said a word about speaking in tongues, so Denise had no expectation for anything like that to accompany her being filled with the Holy Spirit.

Later she was asked to sing a solo at a Charismatic conference that was also held on campus. Bob Mumford was the special speaker that night. He was one of the ministers in the "Fort Lauderdale Five" I mentioned in Chapter Three. After Denise sang, she seated herself toward the front of the auditorium to enjoy the rest of the service. But, suddenly, people all about the auditorium began praying in some "foreign language" — it was *tongues*! For the first time Denise was hearing people speaking in tongues.

As a Southern Baptist cessationist, Denise had previously thought people who spoke in tongues were psychologically nuts! And on the night of that conference, she wanted to get out of that auditorium as quickly as possible — she thought the people were crazy, and she was shocked by what she saw and experienced. She excused herself from the meeting to flee that environment, but in the weeks that followed, she couldn't deny that the Holy Spirit was tugging on her heart to return to that Charismatic church to experience more of what was happening there.

Denise later expressed, "I was afraid because in my home church growing up, we'd never heard anything about the Holy Spirit. The subject of the Holy Spirit was just swept under the carpet in our church."

After months of crying out to know the deeper things of the Spirit, Denise came to a moment when she was ready to receive whatever God had for her — even if that meant "tongues." One night, alone in her bedroom, she opened her heart and cried out for God to move mightily in her life and to even give her tongues. She remembers that she had been praising Him in English and at one point extolling Him as "stupendous." It was then that she realized there weren't enough words in the human vocabulary to worship and praise Him as He deserved. She knew she needed to embrace that heavenly language to exalt Him and give Him all the honor due His great name. She opened her heart, and the Holy Spirit met her, giving her that heavenly language of prayer and praise.

Once Denise experienced the baptism in the Holy Spirit, like me when I had this same encounter, she was so changed that she began to visit and pray for the sick at the hospital even though she didn't personally know any of them. Her heart was *ablaze*, and she cried out to do the works of Jesus. And somehow, along the way, she began to perceive it was God's plan for her *to marry a preacher and go into the ministry with her husband*! She visualized marrying a preacher — having kids and a big dog and living in a little white house with a white picket fence.

Well, she got the preacher, the kids, and even a dog — but even she agrees that the little white house with a picket fence must have just been her imagination!

The leadership of the First Baptist Church back home in Miami became deeply concerned about Denise's mental state because she had stepped across the "forbidden line" to have a Pentecostal experience. In fact, when that Baptist church launched a mission church closer to her parent's house, the new local pastor there warned churchgoers to stay away from Denise Roberson "because she was *crazy*"!

## Denise's Own Unlikely Leading

After finishing her schooling at the Northeastern junior college, Denise transferred to Oklahoma Baptist University to continue pursuing her higher education. OBU had given her a full scholarship to study in their music program. But before she ever moved to OBU, she already knew on the inside that it was not God's will for her to attend there. However, her parents really wanted her to go because it was a Baptist school and because of the full scholarship.

Denise knew right from the start that she was supposed to attend another university in the state. And after enduring almost a year of weepy, sleepless nights of problems with multiple roommates and general feelings of unhappiness, Denise heard the Holy Spirit say to her one day, "You can stay here and I'll bless you. But if you do, you'll *NEVER* know what it was that I wanted to show you."

So after attending OBU for just one year, she called her parents and told them it was God's will for her to relocate to the state university. She didn't know it at the time, of course, but in just two years, she would be meeting me there at the new school.

In 1974, Denise finally enrolled at the university where the Lord was directing her and continued her education in vocal performance. God carefully arranged the perfect voice teacher for her. His name was Thomas Carey — a well-polished, dignified, elegant, yet warm and jolly African-American man who was renowned for his baritone operatic voice. When Mr. Carey entered a room, his personality was so huge and his presence so captivating that he seemed to *engulf* the whole place and everyone in it.

In his younger years, Mr. Carey's voice opened doors to sing on operatic stages around the world. However, it wasn't considered acceptable in those days for a black man to have a leading role on America's most prestigious operatic stages. At the peak of his career, Mr. Carey was offered a position as an eminent faculty member at the university, and he became one of the school's first black faculty members. He was married to Carol Brice, another celebrated African-American opera singer.

Mrs. Carey, known professionally as Carol Brice, was a contralto singer who attracted considerable attention for her ground-breaking roles as one of the first female African-American opera singers in the world at that time. She sang on stages around the world and performed leading roles in various Broadway musicals. But as it was with Mr. Carey, because she was African-American, she was prohibited from getting leading roles on many of the most important American stages. She moved to the university where she spent the rest of her life teaching students to sing, and she also co-founded a small student-run opera company that provided students opportunities to grow as performers. I remember Mrs. Carey so well. She was the epitome of dignity and grace.

When Mr. Carey saw Denise's talent, he and Mrs. Carey took Denise under their wings almost like a daughter. Mr. Carey believed that Denise had major talent, so he began to teach her technique, lyric theater, operatic literature — and he even introduced her to important competitions that she began to win one after another. She became the "diva" at the university and stood out as a gift among all the other students. On one hand, Denise was *thrilled* to be recognized for her vocal abilities — but on the other hand, singing opera was no longer her dream. She wanted to marry a preacher and use her gifts for the Lord. However, because no preacher had materialized as yet, she kept pressing forward to improve her gifts and talents in the world of opera.

Soon Mr. Carey suggested that Denise take a leave from school to move to Houston for one year to become a member of the chorus at the Houston Grand Opera. He felt it would give her the additional experience she needed before hitting the big stage on her own. So Denise moved to Houston to become a member of the chorus, and that year she was on stage with Beverly Sills, Kiri Te Kanawa, Jerome Hines, and other world-class singers.

But something much more important than this huge operatic experience happened in Denise's life that year in Houston — *something that eventually radically changed her life*!

### 'You Are Healed by the Stripes of Jesus!'

While driving to work each morning in her car, Denise noticed a new radio preacher she had never heard of before whose name was Kenneth Copeland. She was so intrigued that she started tuning in every day to listen to him. Listening to Kenneth Copeland, she heard for the first time that Jesus' paid the price for her healing when he took those stripes on His back. Over and over, she heard Brother Copeland say, "You *are healed* by the stripes of Jesus!"

According to Mark 5:25, the woman with the issue of blood had been sick for twelve years — and at that time, Denise had been sick for almost *thirteen* years! The woman with the issue of blood was deemed unclean and was shunned all the years of her infirmity — and Denise had similarly been shunned by others all the years of *her* affliction.

Mark 5:26 tells us the woman with the issue of blood had "…suffered many things of many physicians, and had spent all that she had, and was nothing bettered, but rather grew worse." And for the past twelve years, Denise had visited doctor after doctor who'd tried all types of remedies to cure her incurable condition. Yet Denise "was nothing bettered," but rather seemed to be getting worse.

But Mark 5:27 and 28 finally tells us when the woman with the issue of blood "heard of Jesus, [she] came in the press behind, and touched his garment. For she said, If I may touch but his clothes, I shall be whole." Likewise, when Denise heard the good news that Jesus heals, her faith reached out to "touch Jesus' garment" so His healing power could flow into her diseased face.

Denise asked the Lord, "Does this mean even *I* can be healed by the stripes of Jesus?" It seemed so incredulous to think that after living trapped with her disease for thirteen years, she could actually be healed. Most people who are chronically sick learn to adapt to their disease, and that is what Denise had done. Whether she liked it or not, all the evidence told her conclusively that this was to be her lot in life. But her faith began to connect with the messages she'd heard on the radio that were taught from the Word of God.

Every morning when Denise looked into the mirror to dress for the day, she'd look at her deeply affected face and declare by faith, "By His stripes I am healed." In the evening when she washed off her makeup and prepared to go to bed, she'd look into the mirror at her pitted face, swollen neck, and facial bruises, and she would adamantly declare, "By the stripes of Jesus I am healed."

Day by day, Denise's faith grew in the promise of divine healing. She would call her mother to jubilantly say, "Mother, did you know the Bible says I'm healed by the stripes of Jesus? I believe I am healed." Nora did not rejoice in those phone calls, as it seemed to her that Denise was embracing a delusional, false hope that her face would one day be free of her incurable condition. Nora would try to calm her down and talk her into being "sensible" — but it was too late, because the word of faith had gone into Denise's heart, and she *knew* healing belonged to her!

## 'Do You *Really* Want Your Life Back Again?'

When the healing did not come quickly, Denise did wonder why, however. One day she heard the Holy Spirit ask, "Denise, do you *really* want to be healed?"

The question the Holy Spirit posed to Denise reminds me of the event that took place in John 5 at the pool of Bethesda. One day Jesus came walking into the area around the pool of Bethesda — a wretched place filled with porch after porch of unclean and critically ill people who were waiting for the supernatural moving of the water so they could be healed. John 5:6 tells us that the day Jesus came to the pool, He fixed His eyes on one man who had been there for thirty-eight years. The verse says, "When Jesus saw him lie, and knew that he had been now a long time in that case, he saith unto him, Wilt thou be made whole?"

Interestingly, that was nearly the same question the Holy Spirit was asking of Denise.

The Scripture says that when Jesus knew the man had been sick a very long time, He asked him an all-important question: "*Wilt* thou be made whole?" Jesus was, in effect, saying, "Do you really want to have your life back again, or do you want to stay the way you are?"

At first, it may seem strange for Jesus to ask this question of a sick man — but, in fact, it was quite wise. It was a question with great ramifications. For example, if this man was made whole — and really got his life back — it would mean he'd have to leave the pool of Bethesda. He would have to find new friends. And he would need to get a job and start working. Because he hadn't worked in thirty-eight years, it meant he might even need to receive some kind of education or training before he could be hired. And, lastly, he could no longer be an object of "pity" as he had been for those many decades. If Jesus healed him, all of that would have to change.

Because Jesus knew that radical changes would be brought about in this man's life, He wanted the man to count the cost and be absolutely sure he was ready and willing to embrace those changes before Jesus healed him. And later, in the 1970s, the Holy Spirit was asking Denise that very same question!

That probing question penetrated Denise's heart and soul deeply as she pondered why the Holy Spirit would ask her such a thing. And her eyes began to be opened to see something that she would have otherwise never seen by herself.

In all those years that Denise's mother drove her back and forth to Tulsa for "dry ice" treatments — as painful as those treatments were — it created moments when she received special attention and "pity" from her mother. Nora was very supportive of Denise in those hard days. *(To be continued on page 261.)*

# Photos Corresponding to Chapters 1-5

**Above:** At the time I was born in 1958, the city of Tulsa was already home to famous oil barons and known far and wide as the "Oil Capital of the World." Photo: © Tulsa Historical Society & Museum.

**Above Left:** The infamous "Trail of Tears" ended beneath the branches of an oak tree, known as the Council Oak Tree. This historical landmark was once designated for tribal ceremonies, council business, and cultural feasts and games.
**Above Right:** Native American tribes arrived and settled in an area they called "Tallasi" — a name that later became "Tulsa."

**Above:** Tulsa's economy took off rapidly when underground caverns of oil were discovered west of "Old Town" in 1905. When news of that reserve began to circulate, men with ambition were drawn to Tulsa like metal to a magnet.

**Above:** After the Tulsa riot that started in the early morning hours of June 1, 1921, more than six thousand African Americans were rounded up and held at the Tulsa Convention Hall and the Tulsa Fairgrounds for as long as eight days.

**Above:** The Greenwood District in Tulsa was one of the most affluent African-American sectors in the country, often referred to as "Black Wall Street." This photo shows the charred remains of an African American man from Greenwood after the massacre associated with the riots.

**Above:** White rioters rampaged streets in Greenwood, killing people and looting and burning stores and homes. Some historians postulate that as many as three hundred people were killed.

Photo: © Courtesy of Library of Congress.

**Above:** Nearly ten thousand people of color were left homeless, and property damage amounted to multiplied millions of dollars even in 1921.

Photo: © Tulsa Historical Society & Museum.

**Above and Below:** In 1889, Congress announced that the Unassigned Lands of Indian Territory would be opened for the Oklahoma Land Rush. My great-grandmother, Louella Hestand, was one of the few women who rode in that Land Run.

Photos: © Courtesy of the Oklahoma Historical Society.

**Left:** In 1942, when the then *Tulsa Tribune* newspaper heard that a survivor of the Land Run was alive and still mentally vibrant, they asked to interview my great grandmother, Louella Hestand Miller, to capture her historic memories.

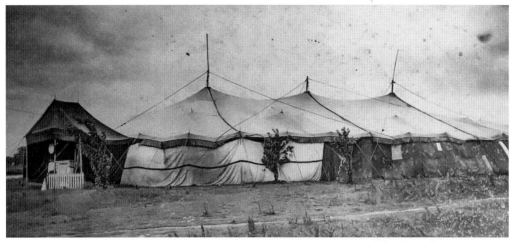

**Above:** Our pioneer circus family from the plains began traveling the entire region with their "Black Top Tent" and gained quite a bit of renown.

**Above:** Our family traveled by horse, carriage, and buggy to perform under the big top, in saloons, and any place that would allow them to "set up shop" across Indian Territory.

**Above Left:** Indian Territory had become overrun with bank robbers, gangsters, and rogue criminals, some of whom became quite legendary in American history. These photos picture our family comedy troupe on stage and Grandpap Earl playing the trombone on top of a piano. Earlier in life, he lived a raucous lifestyle and once spent a weekend in a jail cell with Geronimo, one of history's renowned Native Americans.

# P.T. BARNUM & CO'S GREATEST SHOW ON EARTH

P.T. BARNUM.

GREAT JUMBO'S SKELETON

JUMBO

THE COLOSSAL PRODIGIOUS FRAME of the LARGEST & NOBLEST Animal that ever lived. The ONLY ELEPHANT SKELETON ever publicly exhibited. A STRANGE & AMAZING SHOW WITHOUT A PARELLEL. MOUNTED BY PROF. HENRY A. WARD, THE DISTINGUISHED NATURALIST & SCIENTIST OF ROCHESTER, N.Y.

**Above:** My great-grandfather had previously worked as bandmaster for P. T. Barnum's famous traveling circus. But after moving to Indian Territory, he obtained his own circus tent and he, his wife, and their children — all of whom played musical instruments or performed as clowns or comedians — set out to make a name for themselves as a traveling circus and comedy troupe. Photo: © Courtesy of Library of Congress.

**Above Left:** My grandfather, Paul Richard Renner, left Germany to immigrate to America as a stowaway in 1927. He secretly boarded a passenger ship that arrived at the port in New York City famously known as Ellis Island. **Above Right:** When my Grandfather Renner arrived in America, he made his way to Tulsa in 1927 — a mere twenty years after Oklahoma's statehood — and became a naturalized citizen of the United States. This is a photo of his naturalization document from 1934.

**Above Left:** I was born prematurely with Blue Baby Syndrome on July 21, 1958, at St. John's Hospital in Tulsa. Doctors thought I would die in the hospital and encouraged my father not to make a big birth announcement to friends.
**Above Right:** In this photo, the house to the left is where my Renner grandparents lived, and the house to the right is where my parents and Ronda lived at the time I was born in 1958.

**Above:** Our Renner family photo from 1963. Pictured here are my parents Ronald and Erlita Renner, my older sister Ronda, me, and my younger sister Lori, whose new arrival completed our Renner family of five.

**Above:** My mother remembered that from a very early age, I possessed a voracious spiritual appetite, asking questions about God that were well beyond my years. She poured the Bible into me, and at the age of five, I gave my heart to Jesus one Sunday morning in 1963.

**Left:** That is me on the last row on the right in a ballcap. I really tried to embrace sports, but I honestly detested any game that required me to throw, catch, hit, kick, carry, or bowl a ball. That's when the devil began to launch a full-scale attack against my life. *What's WRONG with you?* I'd hear over and over in my mind, and I couldn't make it stop.

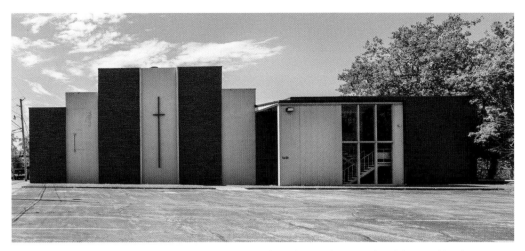

**Above:** Our home life was blended seamlessly with church life at Glenwood Baptist Church (pictured here). Our spiritual service, family relationships, lifelong friendships, and Bible-loving pastor — all of that was there at our home church. Much of who I am today is because of what I received at Glenwood Baptist Church.

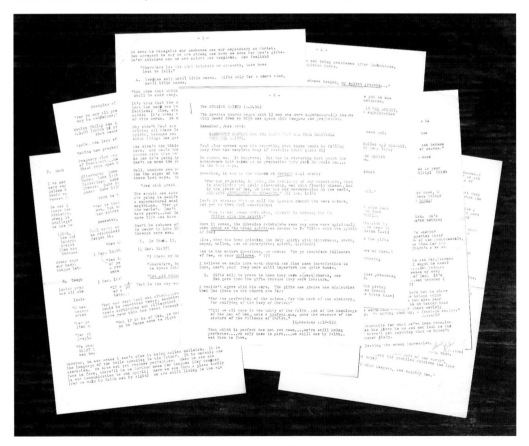

**Above:** Pictured here are the original notes my Aunt Melita typed out for me to answer the charges my pastor brought against anyone with a Charismatic experience. These worn notes represent the time she took to teach me invaluable truths from God's Word that I cherish and live by to this day.

**Above:** The Kathryn Kuhlman miracle service on the campus of Oral Roberts University. The entire back half of the auditorium was partitioned off for scores of people in wheelchairs, on stretchers, and with oxygen tanks, IVs, and crutches. It looked as if an entire hospital ward had been emptied and brought to the service!

**Above:** It was remarkable to watch Kathryn Kuhlman flow in the gifts of the Spirit and respond to His gentle leading that yielded powerful manifestations of deliverances from bondages that were afflicting God's crowning creation. I learned so much about the kind of relationship God wanted me to have with the Holy Spirit.

**Above:** In the spring of 1973, I heard a recording by Kenneth E. Hagin that exposed me to a deeper work of the Holy Spirit. My spirit suddenly "stood to attention," as if I was a radio receiver that finally found the signal it had been searching for. Photo: © Kenneth Hagin Ministries / used by permission.

**Above:** When I received the baptism in the Holy Spirit at fifteen, in a moment, a divine power was released inside me, and the cowardice, insecurities, self-consciousness, struggles, and inner turmoil that had hounded me since childhood disappeared!

**Above:** As Kathryn spoke, it felt at times like a whirlwind of the Holy Spirit's power would rush through the auditorium, and miracles would begin taking place. Wheelchairs and stretchers would be emptied, and people who had been unable to walk or move could walk and even run!

Kathryn Kuhlman photos: © Douglas D. Grandstaff / used by permission.

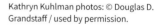

**Left:** I attended Kenneth E. Hagin's Campmeeting at Sheridan Road Assembly in Tulsa on July 24, 1974. At the end that service, I went forward for prayer. As Brother Hagin touched my forehead, God's power flooded my whole being. Minutes later, I realized I'd been supernaturally healed of a serious kidney condition.

**Left:** I attended Oral Roberts' class called, "The Holy Spirit in the Now," held weekly at ORU. Grandma Ettie and I always arrived early so we could get a seat on the front row as Oral taught a large crowd.

**Right:** Listening to Derek Prince was the first time I'd ever heard anyone teach from the original language of the Greek New Testament. That's when something "clicked" in me and set me on a course that would affect my own teaching ministry in the years to come.

**Right:** Oral Roberts personally taught his class "The Holy Spirit in the Now" from his own experiences and from more than thirty years of prayer, his study of the Word, and ministering to the sick around the world.

**Above:** Because I didn't want to forget a word Oral said, I took a small tape recorder and a blank cassette tape with me to class every week, and I recorded every word he spoke.

**Above:** This blurry photo shows me sitting on the front row of Oral Roberts' class "The Holy Spirit in the Now." As he taught, he sometimes walked so close to where I was seated that I could have nearly touched him.

**Left:** Me in the fall of 1976 in a dorm room at the university where I studied. As a college freshman, I was confident from the very beginning about the type of education I needed in order to fulfill the dream of ministry God had placed in my heart.

**Above Right:** A photo of me at the age I became one of the elders in the university church where I began to get my earliest experiences publicly teaching the Bible.

**Above:** Besides enrolling in Greek language studies, I also enrolled in the university's School of Journalism, where I studied print media and marketing. Here I am pictured at the school newspaper, where I worked as a writer and in the advertising department.

**Above:** After I'd spent some time working as a writer, I asked to be transferred to the back shop of the newspaper to work as a typesetter. I wanted hands-on experience in every aspect of writing and publishing to prepare me for my calling as an author.

**Above:** I'm pictured here with my Greek New Testament, which I carried nearly everywhere I went. During this time, I realized I had a special knack for remembering words. My vocabulary in Greek grew remarkably in those days as I learned to unearth treasures from the New Testament that had previously been "locked away" from me.

"And Ye Shall Receive Power"

1. Acts 1:8. δύναμις -power, strenght, power, abilily.
2. John 20:19-22. Actarist. ίχυν -toabili ity. to iate.
   Receive-λάβετε -you receive, as in an immediate actance.
3. Acts 1:1-3. In the early days of the ministry of the Lord Jesus He
   proclaimed that the kingdom of God was at hand, and now in the
   last days of His ministry He continues proclaiming that the
   kingdom of God was nigh, even upon them. Matthew 4:7.
4. Marie 24:44-53. Endued-ενδύσησθε -to put on, to be clothed with, to be
   invested with. Invested with spiritual gifts, graces, or
   character.
   Whereas the Lord breathed into them the Holy Spirit in John
   20:22, He now was clothing them with the power of the Spirit.
5. Acts 1:8. "... after the Spirit is come upon you...".
6. Acts 2:1-4. Filled-επλήρωσεν -to pervade with an influence, to lavluence
   fully, possess fully.
   Acts 2:15-18. The fulfillment of prophecy.
7. Luke 4:18. Anointed-ἔχρισεν -to anoint, by way of instituting to a dignity,
   function, or privilege. The same word is used in Acts 10:38,
   "How God anointed Jesus...".
8. Act. 4:18. Filled-πλήθεις -to fill, fill up, become full of, satisfied
   enough of.                                                    have
9. 1 Corinthians 4:20. The word power is the same word used in Acts 1:8.
10. Mark 5:30. Power-δύναμιν -power, strenght, ability.
11. Luke 17:20-21. The kingdom is within you. έντος is taken from έν .
12. Ephesians 3:7. The working of His power within us. ένέργειας from δύναμιν .
13. -22. 14:16-17,26. The comforter in us. παρακλήτον -one called for to assist
    another.
14. 1:8. 8:4-8. The signs of power which accompany the proclaimed Word.
15. F17ins 15:19. Signs and wonders by the power of the Holy Spirit.
16. 11 1orinthians 1:21. The power of the Lord to establish us in the gospel.
17. John 15:1-8,16. The fruit of Jesus Christ produced within us by the Spirit
    of God.
18. Ephesians 2:10. We have been ordained unto good works, fruit of the Spirit.
19. Matthew 28-17, 20. Power-έξουσία -delegated power, authority to do anything,
    permission, license.
20. Mark 16:20; Hebrews 2:4. God, by His Spirit will do the works and will make
    us steadfast.

**Left:** Original notes I publicly taught from as a student at the university church I attended. As I continued studying Greek and getting more deeply involved in the campus ministry, I began to see how I could fill a niche by utilizing what I was learning about New Testament Greek. I discovered that I could open up Scripture in such a way that listeners could gain new insight about the Word of God — and that what I was learning from my own studies could bless and enrich others.

**Above:** Denise (left) and me (in blue) at a church picnic — so close in proximity, but we didn't know each other yet.

**Above:** *His Highway House* was the student church where my earliest experiences in publicly teaching the Bible took place. When I first walked into that church, I witnessed students who were exploding with life. It was one of the most vibrant spiritual environments I had ever been in.

**Above:** On the back row, fourth from left, is Denise Roberson. I am in a blue shirt to the right of Denise, separated by one person. The group had gone to a lake for a baptismal service and picnic. Denise and I were standing nearly side by side. We didn't know each other yet — but God had a plan!

**Right:** Pictured here is Denise as a baby, who was welcomed into the Roberson family on December 22, 1952. Her younger brother, David, was later added to the family, making it a family of five.

**Below Middle:** Here Denise is pictured at the age of five. She walked the aisle of her church two years later to give her heart to Jesus, and she was water-baptized that same day. Right from the start, Denise had a tender heart toward the things of God.

**Left:** Pictured at left is Denise with her older sister Trula and her younger brother David. Including their parents, Dave and Nora, the Roberson family faithfully attended the First Baptist Church, at least three times per week, in their small town of Miami, Oklahoma.

**Above:** As a freshman in college, Denise realized there was "something deeper" in the Lord she had never experienced. After crying out to fulfill this longing, one night she opened her heart for God to move mightily in her life, and she was gloriously baptized in the Holy Spirit.

**Above:** Pictured here is Denise just returning from Houston where she'd moved to become a member of the chorus at the Houston Grand Opera. Later Denise traveled to New York where she auditioned at the New York City Opera and the Metropolitan Opera. After her audition at the Met, the assistant of the renowned James Levine wrote in her appraisal: "Tall, impressive, MAJOR TALENT."

**Above:** Denise pictured with a well-polished Mr. Thomas Carey — a dignified and elegant, yet warm and jolly man, who was renowned for his baritone operatic voice. At the peak of his career, Mr. Carey became an eminent faculty member at the university, and one of the school's first black faculty members. As a teacher and fatherly figure, he poured much of himself into Denise to help develop her vocal gift.

And in a certain way, Denise relished those trips for "dry-ice" treatments because it put her in the car alone with her mother for two hours in each direction. In that recollection, the Holy Spirit revealed to Denise that all the attention she'd received made her feel "valued," and it was for that reason the disease lingered, even though she was boldly proclaiming the promise of divine healing.

When Denise saw this, she immediately repented of enjoying the pity she had received for years as a result of her sickness. At that moment she said, "I want to be healed and I don't want anyone's pity anymore!" Denise then really understood that acne was an assault of the devil to scar her face, and she never, ever again saw it as a means of obtaining pity. That was a vital, internal work of the Spirit in Denise's soul that had to transpire before her healing would manifest.

Soon Denise's year-long stint at the Houston Grand Opera came to a close, and she packed up her belongings and returned to the university in Oklahoma to continue her vocal studies with Mr. Carey. All the while, every morning and evening, she continued to look into the mirror and boldly declare, "I am healed by the stripes of Jesus" — still with no visible changes to her face.

No one can exactly explain the process in the walk of faith — of how the seed of God's Word is sown in the human heart and begins to germinate and grow, pushing its way upward from the dark soil of the unseen to the realm where faith becomes sight. And it's difficult to completely fathom how that one day, the circumstances of a person's life can look stubbornly identical to the way they've appeared for days, weeks, months, and even years — but then on another day, completely without warning or fanfare, that person tangibly receives into his possession what he'd taken ownership of in his heart long before.

That's what happened for Denise as she heard the Word about healing and embraced it, nurtured it, and held fast to it in her heart and her mouth — in her confession and her confident expectation that results would be forthcoming. Then on one "usual," ordinary day, her miracle took place!

Denise went to the bathroom one evening to wash her face as she did every night. Her precious face was covered with disease, deep bruises, and scars — but as she had been doing so faithfully, she declared boldly and confidently that she was healed before finally going to bed and falling asleep.

Denise awoke the next morning and went to the mirror, and her face was absolutely clear of those cysts! The bruises were gone and the swelling had already begun to recede. Her miracle had come to pass! Before, it was excruciatingly painful to even lightly touch her face with the tip of her finger. But at that moment, she began to excitedly slap her face and exclaim, "I'm healed! I'm healed! And I am *beautiful!*"

Immediately, Denise ran to the phone to call her mother with the joyous news. "Mama, I'm *healed!*" she proclaimed. "I don't know how God did it. I went to bed last night with cystic acne just like I've done for thirteen years — but today it's gone. I don't know if Jesus took the whole night to work on me — or three minutes or three *seconds*. BUT HE DID IT! When I woke up this morning, my face was completely clear!"

Nora didn't believe it, so Denise held the receiver close as she slapped her face for her mother to hear. Denise's previously swollen face was so changed that some people who saw her after her healing thought she had lost ten pounds. Jesus had stepped out from the pages of the Bible and had become Denise's personal Healer!

## The New York City Opera and the Metropolitan Opera Company — a Long Way From Home

Denise's deepest dream was to marry a preacher, but no preacher had yet come into her life. So when Mr. Carey said, "Denise, I think it's time for you to audition with the New York City Opera and the Metropolitan Opera Company," Denise agreed to travel with Mr. Carey and a pianist, and the three of them flew to New York City to audition with these prestigious opera companies.

In a matter of days, Denise Roberson, a little farm girl from Miami, Oklahoma, who thought driving twenty-nine miles to Joplin was a big deal, found herself standing on the grand stage of the New York City Opera to audition before Beverly Sills herself. *That is as unlikely a scenario as they come!*

Denise wrestled with fear before going to her audition. She remembered: "I was in the practice room at the Juilliard Conservatory warming up, and the Lord said to me, *Denise, I own everything. I gave you your mind, I gave you your voice, I gave you the legs you're standing on, I gave you the brain to memorize the music, and I gave you the gift to sing it. I gave all of it to you.*

With that comforting word resonating in her heart, she walked onstage for her first audition where she stood before the legendary Beverly Sills. Sills asked her, "What are you going to sing?" Denise confidently answered, "Puccini's 'Vissi d'arte' from *Tosca*."

To sing for Beverly Sills — known as "Bubbles" to her fans — was amazing because at that time, she was among the most famous face of opera for millions of opera lovers around the world. Sills' voice brought her to international distinction as a performer and made her a celebrity. But now, the little Baptist girl who had cleared her throat all the way through her first solo was onstage in front of this woman of prominence. Denise was a *long, long* way from home!

The following day, Mr. Carey accompanied Denise to the Metropolitan Opera Company, commonly referred to as *the Met*. The Met is one of the world's most famous opera companies and has historically engaged the world's most talented singers, conductors, composers, musicians, stage directors, designers, visual artists, choreographers, and dancers from around the world. Denise was escorted into a small auditorium where she auditioned for a committee and for the assistant of James Levine, who was the legendary principal conductor of the Met. Denise sang for them Mascagni's "Voi lo sapete" from *Cavalleria Rusticana* and her number from *Tosca* that she'd performed for Beverly Sills.

When Denise finished performing, the committee and Levine's assistant gave Mr. Carey a document on which they had written their appraisal of Denise and her performance. It said: "Tall, impressive, MAJOR TALENT. We want her to come back one year from now to audition again for James Levine himself in the main house and sing from the arias of 'Lady Macbeth' from Verdi's *Macbeth*."

*Tall...impressive...MAJOR TALENT.* What an amazing review!

### *Direction and Dreams —*
## God Spoke and Changed Everything

During the next year, Denise threw herself into her vocal training to get ready for her return to the Met for her next audition. She was determined to sing those arias like a true diva. Mr. Carey was elated because his prized student had been labeled "major talent" by the most important people in the opera business. If those leaders at the Metropolitan Opera believed Denise was major talent, he knew it meant Denise was headed to the big stage as a serious opera singer with a fabulous career in front of her.

But the big stage was no longer Denise's dream because her heart was fixed on marrying a minister and fulfilling a life of destiny with him in obedience to the will of God. Mr. Carey hadn't counted on that.

In the course of that year, Denise remembers, "I continued learning all those incredibly difficult arias, and I worked really hard, taking part in other competitions too. I was really doing well — I was even teaching voice at another college.

"And then one day, I heard the Holy Spirit sweetly tell me, 'I never called you to aspire to the Metropolitan Opera Company. My plan for your voice has always been the praises of God to the glory and honor of Jesus.'"

Denise had already been sensing a divine shift in the dreams of her heart for what she would do for the Lord with her life and the talents He'd given her. But on that day, *at that very moment*, Denise's life took a radically different turn. Although she had scholarships lined up for further studies in Europe and had already scheduled her return audition at the Metropolitan Opera, she knew she had to go to Mr. Carey immediately to break the news to him that his dreams for her life were not to be.

"Mr. Carey," Denise started slowly in her meeting with her mentor and friend. "I've heard from God about my life, and I need to talk to you."

Denise continued, "You know it was God who told me to come to this school and who put me with you so I could learn from you and train under you. But He has made it clear to me that it is not His plan for me to go to the

Metropolitan Opera. I'm supposed to use my voice for Him. I know I have the call of God on my life and that I'm to be in the ministry."

Mr. Carey was furious and brokenhearted at the same time. He pleaded with her, "Denise, there is no better place to use your voice for God than at the Metropolitan Opera." But Denise said, "No, Mr. Carey, I'm supposed to dedicate my voice to sing God's praises and not operatic literature."

As a teacher and father figure who had poured so much of himself into her, Mr. Carey genuinely felt she was throwing a once-in-a-lifetime opportunity down the drain. Others would have given their "right arms" to have the opportunity that was being offered to Denise. Mr. Carey also saw it as his personal loss. After he had invested so much of himself in her — teaching her, building her confidence, and giving her amazing opportunities — he naturally longed to see the fruit of his efforts standing on stage at the Metropolitan Opera. But those dreams would not be fulfilled. God had decidedly spoken to Denise Roberson *and that was that.*

The direction of Denise's life took an unexpected turn, but it would be a turn for the better because she was following *His* plans for her life. She was allowing *Him* to guide her on the path of destiny that He had preselected and designed just for her. Denise would not be an opera star, but she *gleamed* in the Kingdom of God for her determination to make whatever sacrifice necessary to do His will.

The path in front of Denise would not always be easy for her, but it would always be bright with the light of God's favor and grace upon her life. Like Mary who waited at Jesus' feet while Martha strove busily with what was mundane, Denise had chosen "that eternal, good part," which would not be taken away from her (*see* Luke 10:42).

Denise's decision was final, and Mr. Carey knew it, although it is unclear as to whether he ever completely resigned himself to Denise's big life choice. But, truly, Denise was done pursuing a career in opera, and from that moment forward, she set her heart to follow God in the ministry.

In the last chapter, I wrote about my first awareness of Denise Roberson when she stepped out to sing that prophetic song in the Spirit from the back row of our college church. That was the fall of 1976, and I had just arrived at the university as a college freshman. As I look back over our journeys, it's plain to see that God's Spirit directed both of us to that place, where we would each receive vital instruction, but most importantly, where we would meet each other!

Neither one of us had wanted to attend that school. I wanted to go to Oral Roberts University and Denise had been on a course to attend Oklahoma Baptist University. But God had a different plan. Psalm 37:23 says, "The steps of a good man are ordered by the Lord...." The *New Living Translation* says, "The Lord directs the steps of the godly...." And the classic edition of the *Amplified Bible* (*AMPC*) says, "The steps of a good man are directed and established by the Lord...." Just as He had promised, God was ordering, directing, and establishing our steps to supernaturally put the two of us together in the same place at the same time. God was about to give birth to a marriage-ministry team that He would equip to impact nations.

I had already met Denise briefly before she left the university for a year to work and train in Houston. In fact, Denise went from the state university to Houston, back to the university in Oklahoma — and from there, she traveled to New York City to audition at the Met. Then she returned to school, where she made the decisive move to stop her pursuit of an operatic career.

Throughout all this time and movement, our paths intersected at various intervals as we both "zigged" and "zagged" in diligent pursuit of God's will for our lives. It took some time, but He granted us success to discover the *right* path for our lives — the straight and the right way we were to go — according to the mind of God.

The following is a chronological retelling of the story of Ricky Renner and Denise Roberson.

### Our First Meetings, Thoughts, and Impressions

Denise was honestly one of the sweetest people I'd ever met. She was so sweet that some people wondered if she was genuine. But she was genuine to her toes! One long-time friend interviewed for this book said, "When I first met Denise, I would watch her and wonder if she was real because she was *so* nice. But she *was* absolutely real — and she is the same today as when I met her at the university decades ago."

It is remarkable to me that the first thing Denise and I ever did together was evangelize the lost. Volunteers from the church met on Saturday mornings and everyone was paired randomly with someone else to either knock on doors, hand out tracts, or visit nursing homes. One day Denise and I both showed up for evangelism. Although I had become deeply enmeshed in the fabric of our local church at that time, she and I had only seen each other from a distance and had never spoken — although I knew her as "the voice" on the back row in church.

But on that day, we were randomly paired to be a two-member team that would visit a local nursing home. At the nursing home, Denise and I dutifully traveled from room to room to share the Gospel with the elderly. The last room we entered was occupied by a brain-cancer patient who was in his very last stage of life. He had a huge horseshoe-shaped scar on the side of his head where brain surgery had been performed. His speech and motor skills had been damaged by the surgery. Denise and I shared the Gospel with him and led him to the Lord! She and I were practically strangers to each other except for the fact that I'd heard her sing that prophetic song. But in our first moments of being together, a man's life was eternally saved.

Neither one of us had the slightest inkling about it at the time, but that man's salvation was the firstfruits of our future lives when God would call us to be husband and wife, fellow ministers, and "heirs together of the grace of life" (*see* 1 Peter 3:7).

But our relationship didn't begin to evolve and blossom during that first spiritual venture — *far from it.*

## A Tragic Spiritual Miscalculation by Church Leadership

Visiting nursing homes and evangelizing on the streets in our college town were routine activities that our fellowship of believers engaged in regularly. And as we did, the church continued to explode with growth and the vitality of the Holy Spirit. As I wrote in the last chapter, we lived *in the book of Acts* in our local university church! Our young but vibrant congregation was ablaze with the fires of the Spirit and a passion for the things of God, including reaching the lost.

But a regretful moment came when the main leaders of that church began to emphasize discipleship among the congregation above winning the lost. In fact, reaching out to the unsaved was put on a complete pause "just until" the shift inward — toward discipleship — could be established.

The truth is, both emphases are right — evangelism and discipleship — and maturing the believers should have gone hand in hand with reaching the lost. But outreach was shelved so that a new focus on growing the saints could be developed. The leadership's position was that once a greater level of maturity was achieved, the church would then return to reaching the lost. This was a fateful decision, however, for when a church turns inward, it greatly reduces the need for God's power to be manifested, and that usually produces catastrophic results after a period of time.

In the case of our student body of believers, it was only a short period of time before everything that had made our church powerful and vibrant *evaporated* right before my eyes. As the congregation began to focus only on themselves, numbers began to dwindle until it became nothing but a shadow of the glorious place it had once been. I felt that the church slowly began to lose the life-giving position of influence it once held in the community. Maybe others didn't see it that way, but that is what I observed to be happening to our precious church.

I am confident that the leadership was sincere about their desire to help believers reach greater spiritual maturity and to develop a system of spiritual accountability. The motives behind their decisions were clearly pure, but it was a grave miscalculation to draw back from reaching the lost, and that decision resulted in painful consequences.

It wasn't long before I began noticing that the gifts of the Holy Spirit stopped flowing in that church, and the once joyful atmosphere seemed almost *engulfed* by a spirit of heaviness. It was clear to me that the Holy Spirit was deeply grieved, and all His brilliant attributes that were so marvelously manifested in the past began to recede. In my view, a powerful church that had *blazed* with the fire of the Spirit became a hollowed-out shell of what it once had been.

I am thankful for the indelible mark that early experience made on my life. I witnessed firsthand the regrettable pattern that develops when any believer or church retreats from Christ's Great Commission to His people to take the Gospel to the lost.

I began putting distance between myself and the church because of the decisions that were being made. Even though I was among the leaders there, my influence was not strong enough to effect a change in the new direction. I could see that what had once been a burning inferno was morphing into an inwardly-focused group that was losing its vision. As much as I was thankful for the role that church played in my life, these spiritual miscalculations had put the church on a new trajectory that I was sure would eventually produce spiritual loss.

Although the circumstances would eventually necessitate a peaceful parting of the ways between me and that church, the Lord Himself had already begun guiding my steps in a different direction. From a young age, I had been on fire for God and single-minded about pursuing His calling on my life. I had never had a girlfriend and had already settled on the fact that I would probably be celibate in order to fulfill His plan. Not only had I never had a girlfriend, I felt no need to have one now — let alone *a wife*! I never planned to marry, *ever*. My only dream was to focus on the Lord for the rest of my life.

### I Was Only Being Polite

But soon Denise returned from her year-long stint at the Houston Grand Opera. I was working in Tulsa during the summer break from school, and she and I experienced another unlikely encounter in Tulsa at the summer wedding of a mutual college friend.

Denise and I bumped into each other during the wedding reception. She recalls that moment: "I saw Rick across the room in a cream-colored suit, and I remember thinking how handsome he looked. When our eyes met, he approached me and we talked for a few minutes before he looked at me and said, 'Well, come see me in Tulsa sometime.' And he walked away to mingle with other guests."

When I said to Denise, "Come see me in Tulsa sometime," I never dreamed she would take my offer seriously. In my mind, we were just making "small talk" at a wedding reception, and I was ending a conversation by being polite. If I had known she would really come to see me, I never would have said those words to her. When I walked away from her that day, I never dreamed I'd get a call from her the very next week telling me she was coming to see me!

But sure enough, my phone rang, and I heard Denise's voice on the other end of the line, saying, "Ricky, this is Denise Roberson. You invited me to come see you, so I'm coming to see you this weekend. Can you pick me up at the place where a friend driving me to Tulsa will drop me off?"

I was *speechless*! How could she have taken me so literally? Why in the world did I ask her to come see me when I really didn't mean it? How was I going to entertain Denise Roberson for a whole weekend? Where would we go and what would we do for two whole days?

*And what would we talk about?* I kept thinking, *That is the LAST time I'll ever say words I don't mean for the sake of being polite!*

I was totally taken off-guard and unprepared for the moment. But I had indeed invited her, albeit insincerely, so I pulled myself together and drove to the predetermined location where her friend would be dropping her off. To say I felt uneasy and uncomfortable is an understatement. I was going to have to improvise as we went — I *still* had no idea what we were going to do for a whole weekend!

### 'Denise Is Your Wife!'

That weekend in the summer of 1978 will live forever etched in my memory. Denise and I drove around Tulsa the whole time talking, praying, singing songs and hymns, and sharing about spiritual things. It was actually a marvelous time. And as we drove around Tulsa for hours doing all these things, I became keenly aware in my heart that *my wife* was sitting with me in the passenger seat of my car!

On the last night of her short trip to Tulsa, I heard myself propose marriage to Denise. *What?* When that proposal came out of my mouth, I immediately wished I could retract the words. What had I done? Did I really just spontaneously propose marriage to a woman nearly six years older than me? *Had I lost my mind?*

I was *shocked* I had asked Denise to marry me, because this short week-end was the only time we'd ever spent together except for that solitary trip to the nursing home a couple of years earlier. I barely knew her and my only attraction to her was her spiritual life. I knew she was deeply committed to the Lord. I kept thinking, *A twenty-five-year-old and nineteen-year-old? You've got to be kidding.* Yet the Holy Spirit told me and *kept* telling me, *Denise is your wife!*

Denise asked for a few days to think it over. During the few days she was thinking over this very serious proposition, I became so gripped with panic at the whole idea of marriage that I called her to cancel it. Here I was — a nineteen-year-old who never wanted to get married — and I'd just proposed to someone older than me that I hardly knew! My heart said this was right, but my head went *tilt!* I couldn't reconcile the fight between my heart and my head, so I called Denise and said, "I have a favor to ask of you. I need for you to pretend like I never proposed to you. I'm not ready for this, so can we please forget it and move on as though nothing happened?"

Denise was put off by my erratic behavior, so when I returned to the university that fall to continue my studies, she naturally tried to steer clear of me. Even when I attempted to be friendly with her at church, she would try her best to avoid me. I inwardly knew Denise was to be my wife, but I was not ready for that idea and I ran from it, trying my best to ignore it and shake it off. But I *knew* that she was supposed to be my wife.

Denise was understandably hurt, confused, and annoyed. Nevertheless, she loved the way I taught the Bible, and she was there every time I was scheduled to speak at the church so she could receive from the teaching of God's Word that I brought to that congregation. As she sat and listened, she would radiate such passion and excitement as long as I was teaching. But the moment the service was over, she'd distance herself from me again. I honestly couldn't blame her for how she felt because I knew I had been a jerk in her eyes.

Our pre-marriage story is complicated, but in short, I'll just tell you that over the next couple of years, I passed in and out of Denise's life almost like a ghost.

## A Modern-Day Apostle Paul in Arkansas

Somewhere during that time frame, I drove three hours to Fort Smith, Arkansas, to spend a weekend with my sister Ronda and her husband John. They asked me to join them at their church that Sunday morning before I drove back to Oklahoma. To be honest, I didn't want to go because I'd had enough of the denominational church. I had zero interest in visiting what I figured would be a stiff traditional church. But Ronda and John pleaded with me and kept exclaiming that it was "different" from other Southern Baptist churches. Because it was important to them, I hesitantly agreed to join them that Sunday morning before I headed back to the university.

Fort Smith's First Baptist Church was famous in the Southern Baptist Convention. It had previously been led by J. Harold Smith, a dramatic, evangelistic-type pastor whose preaching caused both sinners and saints to shake in their boots. During the time he led the church, the church had been the leader in the Southern Baptist Convention in salvations and water baptisms. But the present pastor was Dr. Bill Bennett, a brilliant man who was a scholar and had an earned doctorate in Theology. But what made him unique to me was that he read New Testament Greek.

For the first time since I had been exposed to Derek Prince, Dr. Bennett deeply impacted me in his handling of the Greek New Testament. The way he mixed doctrine, Greek, and the anointing of the Holy Spirit was amazing to me. It was a blend of brains and anointing all gloriously blended to produce some of the most powerful preaching I'd ever heard.

What also made Dr. Bennett exceptional was that he had been reared in a Pentecostal home as a child. His own father had been a Pentecostal pastor. Dr. Bennett himself did not speak in tongues, but he had been exposed to enough of the gifts of the Spirit in his life to believe in it all. It was the first time I had ever seen a notable Southern Baptist who *was not* a cessationist.

That weekend when I heard Dr. Bennett preach, he delivered a masterful sermon on the Great Commission that Christ gave the Church. It especially stirred me because at that time, I was still deeply troubled by the retreat by our university church from reaching the lost. As I listened to Dr. Bennett, it was like the mighty blade of God's Spirit cut to the depths of my heart to give me the conviction that even if no one else in our university church continued to reach the lost and untaught, I would accept Christ's command to do it.

On my drive back to the university, I privately began to work on a strategy about how to start reaching out to the lost and to the untaught. Since my gift was teaching and I was so eager to share what I had been learning from the Greek New Testament, I decided I would launch my own Bible study on campus. I studied and prepared lessons on First Peter — exegeting every verse from the Greek, laying it all out perfectly on paper, and I even typeset the material because typesetting equipment was available to me at the newspaper where I was still working.

The big question was where to hold my Bible study. I began to search on campus for a location, and I finally chose a conference room that was on the second floor of the Library in the very center of the campus. The conference room had a large conference table that was surrounded with executive-type chairs and could seat approximately twenty people. Yes, it was small, but I was just getting started, and I had no idea how many people would show up for the classes I was about to teach on First Peter.

I began to verbally share with fellow church members that I would be teaching First Peter at 10:00 a.m. on Tuesday in the conference room at the Library. The leadership of the church wondered what in the world I was doing since they were in a mode of withdrawing from reaching out to new people. But no one hindered me, so I proceeded to hold my first self-sponsored teaching of the Bible in the heart of the campus. Every day I prayed for God to send me exactly the right people to teach — those He had chosen who were hungry to dive deeper into the Scriptures and to mine the treasures that could be found there.

Finally the day came for my first teaching session. I arrived early to make sure everything was in order. I brought along all my study notes with my perfectly typeset handouts that I would give to attendees. I waited for the room to fill. I watched the clock as I lingered — 9:45, 9:50, 9:55…wondering finally if anyone at all would show up.

Then at 9:59 a.m. — exactly one minute before my study was to begin — who do you think walked through the door and took a seat to join me for that very first Bible study? *Denise Roberson!*

I looked at Denise and thought, *What in the world am I going to do? I'm going to be sitting in this room for a full hour with Denise. After all the proposing and waffling and abandoning of our relationship that I've done, what am I going to do now?*

I felt trapped. I kept wondering why she showed up because I knew she was generally disgusted with me as a person. But the truth is, she loved the way I taught the Bible, so she put all her negative feelings aside to come and receive from the Lord through me. I asked God to send me exactly the right people, and He sent Denise to dive deeper into the Scriptures with me that day. I can't say that I was thrilled. In fact, I wondered, *Why Denise?*

I struggled to overlook that Denise and I were sitting in the same room together after all the awkwardness that had transpired between us. Very formally, I asked her to please open her Bible to the first chapter of First Peter, and then I handed her my typeset handout for that session. Focusing as hard as I could, I began expounding on First Peter 1:1 and 2 as a part of my introduction.

Finally, I got to the end of verse 2 where Peter writes, "…Grace unto you, and peace, be multiplied…." I began to open the Greek meaning of the word "multiplied," and as I did, Denise began to weep. She said, "Oh, please, tell me that one more time. I want to get it deep into my heart how much grace and peace God wants to multiply in my life!"

Denise was like a sponge as she soaked up every word that I was teaching. I could see that she was really getting a lot out of my message, but I kept thinking, *If she's the only one who's going to show for these classes, I am done. No more classes after today if Denise Roberson will be my only student.*

It is true that Denise was put off with me personally, but she loved my teaching gift. I greatly respected her spiritual commitment, but I was embarrassed by my unstable behavior in our relationship. I felt such conflict inside as I tried to teach that day. When that hour-long session came to a close, I said, "Denise, I realize this class today was the first session, but it's also the last session."

"Why?" she asked. I answered, "Because no one showed up." She retorted, "What do you mean no one showed up? Who am *I*? *I* showed up!"

Then on a more comforting, encouraging note, she added, "Please don't stop, because this is the best Bible teaching I've ever heard!" But regardless of her pleading, I insisted it was the first and last session I would teach in the library — that one student was simply not enough for me to keep renting the room. So that was the end of that Bible study — interestingly, it had been another outreach with Denise Roberson at my side.

After that Bible study with Denise and me, our lives rarely intersected. I was so relieved and I had learned my lesson never to repeat the embarrassing mistake again of proposing marriage to someone I barely knew. Denise and I were polite toward each other when being present together in the same room was unavoidable. But, *whew — finally*, I was done with the subject of Denise Roberson. Yet deep in my heart, I knew Denise was my God-chosen partner and that I was running from what I knew.

## A Sad Ending and Parting of Ways
## With the Local Church Fellowship

Dr. Bennett's message about the Great Commission continued to echo in my heart and mind. I knew that even if our church was retreating from reaching others, I had to continue reaching people in any way I could. I went to the leadership of the church and asked if I could use the church building on Sunday mornings to teach the Bible to anyone who was hungry for more of the Scriptures.

Because their focus had already changed and they weren't interested in reaching new people, they were not too excited about my idea. But, finally, they couldn't see the harm in letting me do it, so they gave me permission to begin holding teaching sessions every Sunday morning. The regular church services were held on Sunday afternoons, so the main hall was free on Sunday mornings for me to teach anyone who showed up.

Since the leadership gave me permission to teach in the main hall on Sunday mornings, I put all my advertising skills together to produce a marketing campaign to attract people to my teaching sessions. I prayed in tongues and sought the face of God for His wisdom to reach new people — and for the anointing of God to change every person who showed up. As part of my marketing strategy, I wrote, designed, typeset, and printed flyers that I could pass out to the local neighborhood near the church. By myself, I knocked on doors and invited nearby neighbors to come.

I knew it was time for me to step out in faith, so I thought, *I'm going to launch my teaching ministry. It's time for me to do it. I've got all this Greek in me, and I'm ready to do it.* So I began exegeting the book of First Corinthians and knocking on doors. I prepared pages and pages of notes, which I still have, and there is hardly a thing from the Greek I'd correct even after decades of deeper study. I still use those Greek studies to this day.

The day came for my first Sunday morning session. I'd gone through every chapter of First Corinthians to exegete what I deemed to be the most significant words in the Greek New Testament. I typeset them into a beautiful format to give to anyone who came to the study. I determined this time that no matter who did or didn't show up, I would teach these tiny Bible studies as if there were ten thousand people there.

The first person to walk through the door was, once again, *Denise Roberson.* But, thankfully, this time, others showed up too. It wasn't a huge crowd, but it grew little by little every week. I had the deepest satisfaction knowing that even if our church ceased to reach new people, I was doing my little part to fulfill the Great Commission. The crowd was small, but I knew something significant was happening. My teaching gift was beginning to be "unpacked" in those meetings. And, yes, though the crowd was small, I did teach like there were ten thousand people in attendance. *I gave it my best!*

One day, the leadership asked me to speak at the main mid-week service. By this time, the services were beginning to dwindle, and I felt it was time for the church to be scripturally reminded about the Great Commission and about the power of God that accompanies those who go to the lost and unreached.

Any study of Church history shows God's power goes hand in hand with the Spirit-led efforts of any person, church, or organization committed to proclaiming the Gospel to the lost. But when God's people withdraw from Christ's command to reach the lost, His divine power begins to slowly wane — and that is what was beginning to happen in our church.

I asked everyone to turn to Matthew 28:18-20, where Jesus not only gave the Great Commission, but also a promise of supernatural power to anyone who would obey and fulfill it. Jesus said, "...All power is given unto me in heaven and in earth. Go ye therefore, and teach all nations, baptizing them in the name of the Father, and of the Son, and of the Holy Ghost: Teaching them to observe all things whatsoever I have commanded you: and, lo, I am with you always, even unto the end of the world. Amen."

Opening my Greek New Testament, I explained the tense for the word "go" in Matthew 28:19 means *to go and to keep on going*. I wanted that church to remember God's expectation for us to continually take the Gospel to the lost — and that those who obeyed this command were guaranteed supernatural power to fulfill the appointed task. Matthew 28:20 clearly promised divine power to those who *go and keep on going*. That night, I pleaded that they not forget this Christ-given commission that belongs to every church and to every Christian.

Toward the end of my message, I asked them to focus with me on Matthew 28:20 where Jesus said, "...And, *lo*, I am with you always, even unto the end of the world. Amen." I explained that in the Greek, the word "lo" is an exclamatory promise to anyone who will "go" with the Gospel to the lost and unreached. That word "lo" is so powerful that it would be better translated, *"And, WOW, will I ever be with you — even to the ends of the earth!"* In essence, Jesus was saying, "If you will go and keep on going — doing all you can in every way possible to preach and teach the Gospel — *WOW, I promise that you will experience My amazing presence in the doing of it!"*

As I came to my conclusion, one of the leaders of the church stood to his feet and furiously pointed his finger at me and said very sternly, *"That's enough!* We are done with reaching the lost. We are moving into a phase of focusing on each other. Shut up and sit down. You're finished here!"

I was stunned. Everyone else in the room was stunned. But before I sat down, I thanked everyone for listening, picked my Bible up from the podium, and sat down as commanded.

That was a pivotal moment. Although that church was filled with precious and sincere people, from that moment forward, it was never the same again. And that was the last thing I ever did in that church. As much as I loved them, I knew it was time for me to move on.

## An Angelic Visitation: 'God Has Given You an End-Time Ministry'

I knew my time at the university and that church was coming to a close, and I had really begun to seek God's direction for my life. Sometime during that time before I left the university, I had an experience in the middle of the afternoon one unexpected day that dramatically impacted me. After spending time praying in tongues one afternoon, I decided to take a nap. I lay down on the sofa to sleep, but before long I began to feel like there was an unseen presence in the room with me. I reached up and turned on the lamp, sitting straight up to see if someone was there. But I saw no one.

The sense that someone else was there persisted, so I continued scanning the room to try to put the matter to rest. Sitting upright, my mind fully alert, I saw no one, but I wondered, *Why do I feel there's a presence here with me?*

Then, *suddenly*, before my eyes, a man literally *materialized* in that room about eight feet in front of me. I was seeing this with my *opened* eyes. Although I've never gone into detail about it with anyone, to this day, I can tell you exactly what he looked like. His eyes were so captivating and deep, it felt as if I could look into them *forever*. The look on his face was one of indescribable purity. One would think that such an experience would be alarming, but I was not alarmed in the least.

I thought to myself, *Who is this?* Right at that moment, the man answered me, but with God as my witness, he never opened his mouth. In other words, I *thought* a thought, and he *heard* it. Then *he thought* a thought, and *I heard* that thought! It was non-verbal communication the entire time.

As I thought, *Who is this?* he answered, *I am from the presence of the Lord.* I was having an experience with an angel. An amazing peace filled my heart, and I was certain this was an encounter with an angel just as real as those that I had read about in the book of Acts. I knew this angelic being had come to deliver a message to me.

Suddenly the angel held up his hands in front of him, as if he was holding something that was stretched between his two hands. There was something there that I could not see. Instantly, the words of Jesus from John 6:63 were brought to my mind. In that verse, Jesus said, "My words — 'they are spirit.'" Then I understood that stretched between the angel's hands were the words of a spiritual text. Immediately, I felt the words of that text leave his hands and *enter* into my chest. It was the words of First Peter 1, where Peter writes about "sojourners."

In a split second, I instantly understood the angel's message that my ministry would be a "sojourning" ministry — and that I would be a stranger much of my life and would live in places that were not original to me. When that text came into me, it *filled* my chest. Then the angel held his hands up again with a second text. It was the words of Isaiah 53 that describe the suffering Savior. Suddenly the words of that text left his hands and also entered into me, *filling* me. I actually felt the suffering of Jesus on the Cross — and I felt the suffering of people who had suffered for their faith all over the world. In some way, I instantly knew that my sojourning ministry would take me to lands where God's people had been persecuted for their faith.

Then a map of the world — a map so big that it filled the whole room — appeared in front of the angel. The map filled the entire space in front of him and began to violently shake. As every corner of that map shook, I heard the angel say, "You're going to live through times where you see *violent episodes* all over the world. The world is going to literally be shaken in the last days. God has given you an end-time ministry, and you must not be disturbed by the shaking you will see as time goes forward."

As quickly as the angel came, he left. And when he disappeared, I found myself sitting upright on my sofa with my hands in my lap, staring across the room at the space where the angel had stood. That is when the impact of it all hit me and I realized that I'd had an angelic visitation.

The words of First Peter 1 entered me, and I understood my ministry would take me to places that were not original for me. The words of Isaiah 53 entered me, and I *felt* the suffering of Jesus, and a love for people who had suffered for their faith also entered me. My ministry would be focused on those people. And when I saw that map of the earth *violently* shaking, I also understood there would be world-shaking events in my lifetime that would occur as a part of the scenario of the last days. I knew God wanted to use me to help prepare others everywhere for victorious living in perilous end times.

I have rarely recounted this story to others because I haven't wanted people to think I was strange. Although I didn't grasp the full breadth of it all at that time, as I look back on my life, I can see how accurate that early foretelling was about my life and ministry. My life has been spent sojourning in parts of the world that were not original to me. The greatest bulk of our lives and ministry has been in places where believers once suffered tremendously for their faith. And God has given us the task of equipping His people everywhere to live victoriously in the last days.

I was young when this visitation occurred, and I was really seeking God's will for my future. He answered me in a way that I would have never expected and did not fully grasp at the moment. As it so often happens, sometimes the things God shows us when we are younger only come into clearer view the longer we walk with the Lord.

But I knew my life was not to be forever in the state of Oklahoma. Before me was a ministry that would take me into regions beyond — to places where others had not recently labored before me. And deep inside, I knew I could not take this "regions beyond" journey alone — yet I *still* had not made the shift in my willingness to obey God concerning Denise Roberson and the whole subject of marriage.

## A Well-Timed Trip to West Virginia

Because of the upsetting circumstances in my life and church in that university city, I felt the need to get away to clear my mind. In my previous summers, I had worked to earn money for the fall semester, but a dear friend named Richard Shaw invited me to his home in West Virginia to visit him and his family that summer, and I accepted his invitation.

The Shaw family lived in the lovely historical city of Lewisburg. As I started my drive eastward to see him and his family, I stopped in Fort Smith, Arkansas, to stay overnight with my sister and her husband. Again, Ronda asked me to join them for the Sunday service at First Baptist Church the following morning before continuing my trip on Monday.

Their pastor, Dr. Bennett, always preached the main service at the church, but he additionally taught a large non-denominational "Pastor's Class" each Sunday at 8:30 a.m. in the main sanctuary. His class was attended by more than a thousand people who came from every denomination. Ronda and John really wanted me to experience this amazing Sunday School class, so we went early that day to attend it. I didn't know that "Pastor's Class" was the largest Sunday School class anywhere in America in those days. If you can imagine, it was a Sunday School class with three thousand students enrolled and more than one thousand in attendance every week. It was truly remarkable.

I sat on the right side of the auditorium close to the front as I listened to Dr. Bennett teach the Bible in the power of the Holy Spirit. My jaw nearly fell open. I was dumbfounded — *awestruck* — at the anointed revelation that poured from his lips. I was speechless. I found myself thinking, *Surely this must be what it was like for those who were privileged to hear the apostle Paul two thousand years ago.*

As I had been captivated by the teaching of Derek Prince years before, I now found myself equally captivated as Dr. Bennett expounded brilliantly and powerfully from the Greek New Testament. For five years, I had given myself to studying the Greek New Testament with the dream of exegeting it like a master to feed hungry hearts. Now Dr. Bennett was doing precisely the very thing *I* dreamed of doing — and with a powerful anointing of the Holy Spirit. I saw in his ministry that my own dream was possible.

When "Pastor's Class" was finished, we stayed for the main service and I listened intently, watching Dr. Bennett's every move. At the conclusion of his message, the altar filled with people who responded to the most intelligent presentation of the Gospel that I had ever heard in my life.

The next morning, I told Ronda and John good-bye and started my drive to West Virginia. With every mile I drove, I became more convinced it was time for me to uproot from the university and relocate to Fort Smith to sit under this mightily anointed man of God. If it was really possible for a person to find what his heart had been dreaming of, it was just then happening to *me*. In listening to Dr. Bennett, I found the ministry model and mentor I had been looking for all my life.

During the almost two months I was in West Virginia, I continued to ponder my decision to leave the university. I knew that if I left, it would break my parents' hearts because I was only about eighteen credit-hours away from graduation. Ronda had been the first in our family to graduate from college, and Daddy and Mother so looked forward to my being the next Renner to graduate. They worked so hard to put me through school, and I worked really hard, too, at all kinds of jobs in my college years.

I logically wondered, *Should I really leave right now when I am just eighteen hours short of graduation?*

But because of the deteriorating situation at the church — and because I was so entrenched in relationships there — I inwardly knew that if I stayed, it would be difficult for me to be unaffected by what was taking place there. The call of God on my life was beckoning me onward. He was daring me to step out by faith into a new adventure beyond my wildest imagination. I knew if I stayed at the university, any step of faith I endeavored to take would be frowned upon and discouraged by the leadership of the church.

So while I was in West Virginia — far away from the toxic environment, where the fog in my mind could clear and I could think more soundly — I made the decision to pack up my belongings, uproot from the university, and move to Fort Smith to sit under Bill Bennett's ministry. Although I had never even shaken his hand, I inwardly knew God wanted me to study under this man. I was so sure of it that I was willing to lose friends, forfeit my graduation, and run the risk of disappointing my parents whom I loved so much.

When I returned to the university and informed the leaders I was going to move to Fort Smith, they saw it as a betrayal. Consequently, people were told to avoid me because I was going against their spiritual leadership. In fact, I was not going against their leadership at all. I could no longer agree with their leadership, so it was right for me to remove myself. But more importantly, I was breaking free of spiritual bondage to follow the supernatural leading of the Holy Spirit — *His* leadership. Now more than ever, I was convinced He was leading me to Fort Smith and was about to put me in a spiritual environment that would positively impact me for the rest of my life. Although I was stepping away from and forfeiting my graduation, God knew that what I would receive in Fort Smith was far greater than what any diploma could ever give me.

I'm not advocating that, as a rule, it's wisdom to walk away from a college degree one semester before graduation. But let me also assure you that you never lose when you obey the Lord. Even though I left before graduation, I continued my studies, and over many years I've written books that some consider to be doctorate-level materials. Later, I was able to use all my studies to graduate from a Christian university with a bachelor's degree, a master's degree, *and* a doctorate in theology. It didn't happen earlier when my parents wanted it to happen. But eventually, it happened. The Bible says God will not withhold any good thing from those who are obedient and walk uprightly (*see* Psalm 84:11).

The day I prepared to drive out of that university town, no one told me goodbye or came to express thanks for the five years I served faithfully in that local church. I literally packed my car and drove away with no emotional good-byes or fanfare, leaving that sad situation behind me forever.

## Proposal Number Two

As I drove away from that school for my next step — Fort Smith, Arkansas — I thought I was leaving the troublesome subject of Denise Roberson behind me as well. I was focused on the fact that in front of me was an unlikely mentor, Dr. Bill Bennett, who would make a lasting, life-changing impression on my ministry, and I did *not* want to be distracted! But God would not leave me alone on the matter of marriage to Denise. I kept hearing the Lord's voice deep within me saying, *Denise Roberson is to be your wife!*

It was like the "Hound of Heaven" — a term some refer to concerning the Holy Spirit and His dealings — was on my trail and would not be called off this assignment. And I *knew* I was running away from God's plan. So I finally relented and summoned the nerve to contact Denise and ask her to meet me for breakfast on a particular Saturday. I drove from Arkansas to meet her for breakfast, where I resolved I would start the marriage conversation again.

Denise remarkably agreed to meet me. At the restaurant, I sat across the table from her and began by saying, "Denise, I realize I asked you to forget my last proposal. It was very hurtful to you, and I know I haven't looked very stable in your eyes. But deep in my heart, I know it is God's will for you and I to be married. I don't understand it all, but I know for sure that this is God's will. He has a plan for you and me *together*. So I'm asking you to forgive me for my erratic behavior and to please be my wife."

With tears streaming down her face, Denise answered, "Ricky, this doesn't make any sense. There's a lot for me to overcome due to the way you disregarded your past proposal. If you and I were just spirits and didn't have to deal with flesh and blood and mental doubts, I would say *yes* right now to be your wife. I believe this is the will of God, too, but I need time to adjust in light of your past behavior."

After our very serious conversation concerning marriage, we joined hands and prayed together. *And then I walked out and did it again!*

When I left the restaurant that day, I once again panicked, and I didn't contact Denise again for months. I kept thinking, *You did it again. You proposed to marry a girl you hardly know and who is so much older than you!* I froze at the very thought of it. And as you can imagine, Denise was confused by my odd behavior. I was so embarrassed to ask Denise to forget my proposal *a second time* that I opted to just "disappear" and act as if we'd never met for that breakfast that day. In fact, I disappeared so well that I never even called to cancel this second proposal!

As far as I was concerned, *that was it.* It was officially settled and over. I was done with Denise Roberson and the whole idea of marriage forever. Although I knew God told me to marry her, I did *not* intend to obey!

## The Leading and Timing of the Holy Spirit

All our talk of marriage was premature in those earlier moments, but God had supernaturally begun to link Denise and me together and then commence a divine plan for us to eventually unite as husband and wife and to live a lifetime of ministry together. In spite of the difficulty I had at first obeying God's plan for Denise and me, I eventually did obey, wholeheartedly coming in line with His will for our lives. I'll share the details in the next chapter, but you no doubt already know that it all worked out wonderfully. After two premature, failed marriage proposals, the third would result in our union as husband and wife!

Regardless of all the ups and downs of our pre-marriage relationship, the Holy Spirit faithfully worked to direct us over the years to find and fulfill His plan for our lives. We give Him all the glory for leading us and helping us get on track with His plan, because we weren't smart enough in ourselves to be at the right place at the right time. But the Leader we were each following knew exactly where we needed to be *and when we needed to be there.*

Denise and I ended up at the same university, at the same church, at almost the same time because of an *unlikely leading* in each of our lives by the power of the Holy Spirit. Although Denise and I didn't know each other before then, God knew us both and had marvelous plans for us *together.* And because we were endeavoring to follow Him every step of the way, He was able to lead us to each other, and He has led us to victory in our lives since then time and time again.

I want to encourage you that when *your* journey of faith begins, you will not likely have all the answers you would like before you take your first steps. As wonderful as it would be to see the whole picture *before* we get started, the Holy Spirit usually leads us one step at a time *after* we get started. This has certainly been true in the lives of Denise and me.

This is why I've found Romans 8:14 to be so encouraging: "For as many as are led by the Spirit of God, they are the sons of God." Notice, it doesn't say, "For as many as are *forced* by the Spirit of God...." That's why I encourage you to pay careful attention to the gentle "tugging" and "pulling" of the Holy Spirit in your heart. He is a Gentleman and does not *force* you to obey Him. He prompts you, tugs on your heart, and pulls on your spirit to get your attention. Sometimes His tugs can be so gentle that you can miss them if you're not sensitive to them. But if you'll develop your sensitivity to the Holy Spirit, He will gently lead you exactly where He wants you to go with your life.

And don't demand that the Holy Spirit tell you the whole story first before you obey Him! *Trust Him!* Remember that Jesus called the Holy Spirit the "Spirit of Truth" (John 16:13) to help you understand that the Holy Spirit and His leading can be *trusted*! Since He is the Spirit of Truth, if He is leading you to do something, you can know He has a good reason for it. He sees and knows what you cannot see. If you'll follow Him, the Holy Spirit will take you exactly where you need to go and help you reach your maximum potential in life.

Our *unlikely leadings* led Denise and me to our *unlikely encounters*, and you'll see the details in the next chapter of how they worked out beautifully, finally culminating in marriage. As I reflect today on all that has happened to us throughout our years of courtship, marriage, and ministry together, I see that our testimony is really one of being led by the Holy Spirit.

Because of the Holy Spirit's leading, I ended up in God's place for me to learn New Testament Greek and to learn how to write and then to market what I wrote. I also gained experiences in a church unlike any I'd experienced in my life. In that church, I learned what to do and what *not* to do — every experience and lesson would prove vital to me throughout my ministry.

Most importantly, because we were led by the Holy Spirit, Denise and I met each other at the university. And Denise ended up with the perfect voice teacher to train her, build her confidence, and give her amazing opportunities she may have never had at Oklahoma Baptist University.

All of this happened because two young people were willing to be led. Although we missed it at times along the way, we repented and got back on track. It is impossible to exaggerate the important role the leading of the Holy Spirit has played in our lives — both then and in our lives and ministry today. He *has been*, *is*, and *will always be* the Leader for our family and our ministry. Wherever He leads, we are committed to follow.

I urge you to make the decision to let the Holy Spirit be the Leader in every area of your life. Let Him take you by the heart and give you a little "tug" to lead you in the right direction. And when He does, *respond to Him!* Say, "Lord, I sense that You are tugging on my heart, and I'm ready to let You lead me where You want me to go."

At the close of my years at the university, the Holy Spirit was leading me away from Oklahoma, across the Arkansas River, and into the state of Arkansas — to the place where God would give me what I needed for the next phase of my life. And the subject of Denise Roberson was *far* from being closed. God really is a Matchmaker — and He had a plan for Ricky Renner and Denise Roberson! In the next chapter, I will share more about that and about more of God's dealings with me concerning the ministry He had called me to — a ministry He would surely prepare me for in a most *unlikely* classroom.

# 6

# AN UNLIKELY CLASSROOM

In the fall of 1980, I made my move to Fort Smith, Arkansas, eager to follow the leading of the Holy Spirit — in everything except the topic of Denise Roberson and marriage, that is. On all fronts, in so many ways, Fort Smith would be God's classroom to teach me things I needed for my future ministry and life. It was there during those long years that I learned what I *should do* and, woefully, what I *should never do*.

Never in a million years would I imagine that I would live in Arkansas, but there I was. The Holy Spirit led me there to put me in a God-created classroom that I desperately needed so I could be sustained and *effective* in the things He'd assigned for me in the years ahead.

*Life itself* can be a classroom if we'll sell out to God and His plan for our lives and choose to learn the valuable lessons of the heart He will inevitably teach us along the way. These practices of conforming to Him establish us in

---

**Left:** *Garrison Avenue, Fort Smith, Arkansas.*

the places He calls us to so that we don't forfeit His grace or fall short of His calling — of fulfilling His preordained plan for our lives.

How many people, possessing a glimpse of the divine will for their lives, fall short of fulfilling it because they fail to obey those gentle tugs of the Holy Spirit. They choose in so many instances and at so many junctures in life to have their own way instead. It may feel harsh to hear, but there is a real danger of forsaking the leading of the Lord so often that one becomes hardened, sidetracked, and even derailed from God's big-picture plan for that person's life. In some cases, only strong repentance and miraculous acts of God can restore someone to his or her Heaven-ordained path and destiny.

And, of course, we all know people who missed it irrevocably because they resisted those leadings of the Lord and refused to learn in the classrooms of life He placed them in to prepare them for the future. I certainly didn't want that to be my story. Yet if I had known all that awaited me in Fort Smith as just a young man of twenty-two, I may not have been so eager to pull up stakes in Oklahoma and to boldly move across the border with all my belongings for the "adventure" that awaited me on the other side.

But I did leave Oklahoma for Arkansas and eagerly began studying the history of my new city. As I described in Chapter One, due to Fort Smith's strategic location just across the Arkansas River from Indian Territory — later joined to the Territory of Oklahoma before Oklahoma became a state — the federal government decided to establish a military presence in Fort Smith to control criminal developments.

Indian Territory had become infested with outlaws and gangs who had used the area as a hideout because it was beyond the reach of the law across the border from Fort Smith. But the government decided that a heavy hand was needed in Fort Smith to deal with the criminal activity, and their solution was Judge Isaac Parker, who presided as the U.S. District Judge from 1875 to 1896.

Judge Parker was known as a righteous man, but he is mostly remembered as the infamous "Hanging Judge" of that wild-west frontier. As you read in Chapter One, hanging gallows stood behind his courtroom, where many whom he sentenced were executed "on the spot." And, of course, in the basement of Parker's courthouse was a jail, known as "Hell on the Border," that overflowed with outlaws who were captured by U.S. Marshals and brought to Fort Smith to stand trial before Judge Parker. When visitors today tour Parker's re-created courtroom, they can read a plaque that states, "…More men were put to death by the U.S. Government [here in Fort Smith]…than in any other place in American history."[1]

Fort Smith boasts a more interesting history than many cities its size — due in large part to Judge Parker and the city's role in taming that wild-west territory before neighboring Oklahoma became a state. The oldest neighborhood in Fort Smith is called the Belle Grove Historic District, an area of the city adorned with whimsical houses and buildings that pre-date the Civil War. Actually, there are parts of the old downtown district of Fort Smith that look very similar to how they looked in the days of Judge Parker. It was not a modern city by any means, even in the early 1980s, but Fort Smith was to become my home for the next five years.

As you read in the last chapter, my first visit to Fort Smith was to see my sister Ronda and her husband John. They were attending the city's historic First Baptist Church, which I'd attended with them on previous visits. Hearing the pastor, Dr. Bill Bennett, rendered me speechless every time because I had never heard such genius in the pulpit. Not only was Dr. Bennett brilliant, but he understood the anointing. So in front of me was a man who had *Spirit* and *brains*. And I was *hooked*!

Dr. Bennett had earned a Doctor of Theology degree from New Orleans Baptist Theological Seminary, a Master of Arts and a Master of Divinity from Duke University, an undergraduate degree from Wake Forest University — and he was a twelve-year trustee of the Sunday School Board of the Southern Baptist Convention. Dr. Bennett was truly brilliant, and as I listened to him, I knew beyond a shadow of a doubt that I needed to sit under his ministry because the combination of Spirit and brains that I saw in him was the epitome of what I longed for in my own ministry.

I had been driving to Arkansas from Oklahoma whenever possible to experience this man's ministry. Because I knew the situation at the university church wasn't going to get any better, I'd sought the Lord and felt the Holy Spirit telling me to get out of that situation before it negatively affected me spiritually. There was no doubt that He was leading me to move to Fort Smith to start the next chapter in my life, so I made my move.

As I also shared briefly in the last chapter, the people at the university church were convinced I had lost my mind because I was going to relocate to a denominational church — so much so that *no one* showed up to say good-bye as I left. I drove away from almost five years of my life there without a single farewell. But God has a way of using all the pieces of our lives so that nothing is wasted, so I considered my time at that church well-spent, and I left grateful for everything I'd experienced and learned.

I arrived in Fort Smith for the sole purpose of sitting under the ministry of Dr. Bennett. My heart was filled with hope that I might serve one day on staff at First Baptist Church in some capacity. I wanted to get as close to Dr. Bennett as possible so I could learn for my own ministry how to mix intelligence with the anointing of God.

Derek Prince's earlier impact on me had been very important, but I knew that Dr. Bennett was the man who could practically help develop and take me to a new spiritual dimension in preparation for the next phase of my ministry. Never did I ever dream that I would return to a Southern Baptist Church, but I was hot on the trail of pursuing ministry training and so "smitten" by Dr. Bennett's ministry that I didn't pause for *a second* to consider whether I should return to a denominational environment to learn in this unlikely classroom.

At the university, I had done my part to learn how to read the New Testament in its original language. And at the university church, I'd also learned to move in the gifts of the Holy Spirit. But knowing how to *mix* intelligence and anointing was what I still didn't quite know how to do. I really needed Dr. Bennett. This amazing man read New Testament Greek and was a theologian, a scholar, and the most masterful Bible teacher I had ever heard. I needed him, and God was about to use him mightily in my life.

When I moved to Fort Smith, Dr. Bennett didn't even know I existed. But I was so convinced I needed what this man had to offer — and that God was leading me — that even though I had no promise of a job to work for Dr. Bennett, I relocated to this new city to sit under his authority and anointing. My purpose was to get as close as I could to this man of God for the sincere motive of learning everything I possibly could from him.

## Life Gets Started in Fort Smith

My first Sunday in Fort Smith, I walked the aisle to join the church and then immediately began to serve in the small single-adults class that met in a little white house at the far end of the church property. The married couple who led the single-adult ministry were friends of Ronda and John, so that made it easier to get to know this couple. These ministry leaders knew I had a strong call of God on my life, so they asked me to join them in helping lead the single-adult ministry.

In a few weeks, this couple had asked me to begin teaching the class of nearly forty single adults every Sunday. It certainly wasn't the opportunity I was dreaming of — I wanted to work alongside Dr. Bennett. But I knew that if I was faithful to use my gifts, the Lord would use it as an open door to lead me in His plan to work closely with that man of God. So I gave my very best as I began to teach those single adults.

The class was comprised of people who were either widowed, divorced, or had never married — and a number of them looked like they had been completely broken by life. The location of the class in that little white building stuck at the far end of the property communicated the message that these were the "outcasts" of the church — and I was soon to learn that was exactly how quite a few of them felt as well. For years, I'd been studying at the university and I was "trapped" intellectually in my head. But in that singles class, I really learned how to minister to people — people who were precious and not outcasts at all in the sight of God.

Ronda and John had graciously allowed me to move in with them in my early months in Fort Smith. Ronda and I had always been close, and she wanted to help in any way possible. But at that moment, I had no promise of any position at First Baptist Church, so I began to search for a job where I could earn enough to pay my bills and use every other spare minute to volunteer in the single-adult department and to ultimately draw nearer to Dr. Bennett so that I could be mentored by this man of God.

## Visions and Callings That Are Yet To Be — *Wait for Them!*

It was while I was living with Ronda and John for that brief time that God specifically showed me in a vision that a day would come when I would start and lead multiple churches. That vision was so real that it felt like, surely, this was something that would happen quickly in my life. But it was a vision that would be fulfilled much later.

That experience taught me the need to discern the timing of what we see from the Lord. Often we see something by divine revelation that is correct, but it's for a later time. That is when I really laid hold of the words of Habakkuk 2:3 that read, "For the vision is yet for an appointed time, but at the end it shall speak, and not lie: though it tarry, wait for it; because it will surely come, it will not tarry."

I include this in my story because often people see things correctly, but the time for the manifestation is not yet. When people don't see a quick manifestation of what has been shown them, they tend to dismiss it or think they misunderstood what God revealed. But remember, even Joseph had an authentic God-given vision for his life that was not fulfilled for many years. Psalm 105:19 says Joseph endured a lot of obstacles and waited a long time for his dream to come to fruition. That verse says, "Until the time that his word came: the word of the Lord tried him." As often is the case when God gives someone a glimpse of his future, what Joseph saw was right, but the *timing* was for later.

I can avow that many things God showed me at that early stage in my life were correct, but only came to pass decades later. You see, sometimes "the vision is yet for an appointed time." It may take a while to come to pass, but wait for it in faith, trust, humility, and preparedness, because in time, it will come to fruition.

In those early days in Fort Smith while I was waiting for an opportunity to work alongside Dr. Bennett, I got a job working as a substitute teacher at the city's junior-high and high schools. *Whew…*that was an enlightening experience! Let me tell you that no salary can compensate for what a substitute teacher goes through at the hands of students who disregard and disobey him or her because they know that teacher is temporary and has no lasting authority.

But that experience was important because it taught me how much disdain for authority had already developed in families across America. Our Renner household had always been a place where governance was respected, so for me it was quite shocking to see that disregard for authority was so widespread. That was in the fall of 1980, and this trend was "juvenile" compared to the disdain for authority that has spread its toxic poison throughout society today.

Working as a substitute teacher was hard for several reasons — primarily, because of the mistreatment I suffered from students. But it was also challenging because it was not a stable job. I was only called to work if a full-time teacher got sick and couldn't report to work. So there I was — a young man who believed in divine healing and that it was God's will to heal everyone — hoping someone would get sick so I could go to work! I was so conflicted about this that I soon began to look for another job.

Eventually I found a job at a Christian bookstore, my second job in retail Christian book sales. The manager of the store, a godly divorced woman, cared for me and gave me a schedule that would allow me to volunteer as much as possible at First Baptist Church. Working at that store was good for me because it further put me in touch with the Christian market, and I learned even more about what kind of spiritual materials people needed and wanted. It was part of God's classroom experience that would benefit me for the rest of my life.

But in my off-work hours, I was at the church doing anything and everything that needed to be done. I never said, "I can't" or, "That's not my calling" when a request for help was made. If it needed to be done, I was the one to ask because I wanted to prove myself faithful both to God and to the leadership at the church who was watching me.

## A Spiritual Interrogation

When the married couple who led the single-adult ministry saw me serving so wholeheartedly, they told me it was their intention to turn their whole department over to me. And soon afterward, they indeed asked me to take the helm of the class. By that time, the class of forty had grown to nearly one hundred every Sunday morning. In fact, the little white house could no longer contain the class, so interior walls were moved, and the space was enlarged to accommodate my growing Sunday School class! News of the class's doubling made its way to Dr. Bennett. He was so impressed that he asked to meet with me.

Dr. Bennett's office looked more like a library than a pastor's office. Every wall was lined with mahogany bookshelves that held more than eleven thousand books that were alphabetically arranged by the Dewey decimal system of that day. When I went to meet Dr. Bennett, I was stunned by the size of his library and asked if he had really read all those books. He gave me a scowling look that I would even ask such a stupid question and proceeded to tell me he had read every word in every one of them. He even told me to walk to any shelf, pick up any book, flip it open — and that there I would see his handwritten notes written all over the margins. I decided to take him up on his offer, so I did as he suggested. When I opened a random book, I saw pages filled with his handwritten commentaries about what was written by the authors.

In my first face-to-face appointment that day with Dr. Bennett, he *interrogated* me like a prosecuting attorney who examines a witness on the stand. He probed deeply about my spiritual life. He inquired about my salvation experience and questioned me on non-negotiable doctrines of the Bible. When he discovered I could read New Testament Greek, he plunged headlong to see what breadth of a Greek vocabulary I possessed. But when he asked me what I believed about the Holy Spirit and I told him I spoke in tongues, he then became *fascinated* with me! And he began to probe deeper and deeper into my spiritual experience.

Although he wasn't a Charismatic, Dr. Bennett liked to live close to the edge of the Charismatic Movement. His openness even caused a lot of people with a Pentecostal experience to attend First Baptist Church with the false hope that one day it would swing all the way to becoming a full-fledged Charismatic Baptist church. In the Southern Baptist Convention itself, Dr. Bennett was recognized as one of the leading authorities on the present-day ministry of the Holy Spirit. Because of Dr. Bennett's impeccable education and various degrees — and because of his openness to the work of the Holy

Spirit — Oral Roberts once even offered him the position of Dean of the School of Theology at Oral Roberts University.

Oh, how Dr. Bennett relished the fact that Oral Roberts himself had offered him that job! In fact, Dr. Bennett reminded me often that he could have been the Dean of Theology at America's leading Charismatic university.

At the conclusion of our first meeting together, Dr. Bennett was satisfied that I was serious about working with him and being in submission to his authority, so he decided to take the conversation one step further. In a matter of mere minutes, I found him beginning to make *requirements* of me. I didn't realize it, but an intense period of testing had commenced in my life that would go on for several years. Dr. Bennett's first requirement was that I would begin meeting him *every morning* at 5:30 a.m. at a local restaurant for an hour of discipleship with him.

*Wow…*this is what I'd prayed for, so my heart jumped for joy when he gave me this requirement. But I was actually stepping into a classroom where I was about to be intensely tested by fire beyond my imagination. However, at that moment, his requirement looked like the opportunity I had prayed for, so I rejoiced!

The very next morning I got up early and rushed to the designated restaurant for my 5:30 a.m. meeting with Dr. Bennett. When I walked through the door, I scanned the tables to see where he was seated. When I finally found him, I eagerly walked toward him to sit down, but noticed his eyes were fixed on his watch to see if I was on time or a mere few seconds tardy. I did not realize yet what a strict disciplinarian Dr. Bennett was, because our mentor-disciple relationship was just getting started. But in the days to come, I would realize that if I was even a *few seconds* late, I would regret it. I can still hear him saying, "Well, I guess you wanted to sleep a little more than you love Jesus." If I was late even *seconds*, Dr. Bennett would scold me for being undisciplined. But I needed a tough mentor. And believe me when I tell you that Dr. Bennett could fill the bill!

I responded well overall to the requirements he made of me, and, as I said, it was what I needed at that time in my life. Diamonds don't shine until after they're put under pressure. I am sure God was using Dr. Bennett's incessant pressure to make me shine better. But few survived the rules that

Dr. Bennett imposed on those who wanted to follow him as a serious disciple. I was determined that I would be one who would — and that I would shine better and more brightly for my endurance.

In retrospect, others have since told me that Dr. Bennett was ruthless in his expectations of me. But he really wasn't singling me out; he treated everybody the same. It is true that he was very hard on me because I was young. At times he could be crushing. But it was good for me because I needed someone to make me realize that brains were not everything. He taught me the need to have order in my life and to be disciplined — and I was grateful for every admonishment, exhortation, censure, correction, criticism, dressing-down, or lecture that he directed toward me — at least I was grateful *at first.*

My head overflowed with the Greek New Testament, and my heart burned with passion to be used by God — but I was fairly ignorant about a lot of practical areas of life. Dr. Bennett not only helped me think through scriptural issues, but he taught me wisdom in practical things that I desperately lacked. He waded right into every area of my life to bring the correction he felt I needed. And he never hesitated to really let me have it if he perceived an area where I was undisciplined. He required me to study doctrine, to read deep material, and to submit my personal finances to the treasurer of the church, who helped me learn how to manage money. No area of my life was off limits to Dr. Bennett's examination and correction. I needed it, so I was thankful, *most* of the time.

In those days, I wanted to be at Dr. Bennett's side, so I volunteered to serve him in any capacity needed. I vacuumed his car, polished his shoes, raked the leaves in his yard, carried his books, and traveled with him to meetings when he provided me that opportunity. I would do anything to be near him and I relished every minute of that season because Dr. Bennett spent time speaking to me from the Word of God and helping me establish my thinking in sound doctrine. Being at his side and serving him in any way possible was the greatest honor God had ever given me to that moment. *I was living my dream!*

## Death Appeared at the Foot of My Bed

In 1980, ships carrying approximately 125,000 Cuban refugees arrived in the United States on the shores of southern Florida. President Jimmy Carter's administration was challenged to find places to house them. Crowded conditions in immigration-processing centers in Florida forced federal agencies to move many of those refugees to military bases across America — including Fort Chaffee, a base located on the outskirts of Fort Smith.

By October of that year, Fort Chaffee was a designated Cuban refugee resettlement center with more than nineteen thousand Cubans present. But it was soon discovered that many of the refugees at Fort Chaffee (and at other bases as well, I'm sure) were Cuban criminals who had been released from prison by Fidel Castro. Castro cleverly emptied Cuban jails and mental-health facilities and sent the prisoners and the mentally ill to America in the guise of refugees. So Fort Chaffee was filled with serious Cuban criminals, the mentally ill, and those with tropical diseases. The situation spun out of control as the detainees rioted, destroyed barracks, and fought with State Police officers. Soon Fort Chaffee became like *a prison*, encircled with miles of razor-sharp wire and two thousand heavily-armed federal troops.

Dr. Bennett, a formidable believer in the Great Commission that was given to us by Jesus in Matthew 28:18-20, felt that since these Cubans had arrived in our city, it was our opportunity to reach a foreign world right on our own doorstep. So he led First Baptist Church in a significant evangelistic effort to visit the newly arrived Cubans at Fort Chaffee. He and members of the church held church services and Bible studies and performed all kinds of humanitarian work at Fort Chaffee in their effort to share Christ with the burgeoning population of criminals and the sick and mentally ill who were detained at the base.

I was volunteering everywhere at the church where help was needed, so when I saw a need for people to share Christ at Fort Chaffee, I joined one of the teams that regularly visited the detainees. I remember being amazed at how Castro had cleverly disguised thousands of thugs as refugees and how we threw open our arms to receive them, not realizing that we as a nation were embracing some of the worst criminals in the world!

One day during that period, I became strangely ill. Regardless of what medications I took to try to mitigate my symptoms, I couldn't seem to shake whatever it was that was afflicting me. As the sickness lingered — for *days* — I became weaker and weaker. Then one night something happened that I will never forget. In fact, I remember it almost as if it happened last night.

As I lay in bed very sick, in the very middle of the night, my little dog Skittles that had been sleeping at my side unexpectedly jumped up, stood at the foot of the bed, and started growling, then viciously barking at something, as if there was an intruder in the room. I knew no one was there except me, so I kept calling her to calm down and come back to sleep. But regardless of how much I tried to calm her, she kept viciously growling as if something foul was standing at the foot of my bed.

When I finally sat up to see what the dog was growling at, I was stunned to see a dark hooded figure step out of the darkness and stand at the very foot of my bed. As I write this, I can still see it there with its gruesome and dreadful cloak and hood. I leaned toward the foot of the bed to take a closer look. When I did, the hooded figure stepped even closer to me. But rather than see a face with eyes looking at me from inside the hood, there was no face. That space inside the hood was filled with blackness and death.

I understood that a spirit of death had come for me. That spirit did *not* come from God — it had come to try to steal my life. I immediately began to take authority over that foul spirit in the name of Jesus and commanded it to leave. And soon, just as it had stepped out of the shadows, it retreated back into the shadows from which it had come. But when it left, it left *without me*!

I could hardly sleep the rest of the night. When I saw that death had come to take me, I realized just how sick I really was. I have to say that I was also stunned that my dog had seen that evil spirit before I did. I had always heard that animals could specially perceive spiritual things, but that night I was a witness that my dog saw that spirit before I saw it.

When I woke up the next morning after a night of fitful sleep, I went to the bathroom to brush my teeth. As I looked into the mirror at my reflection, I could hardly believe what I saw. My entire face looked like it had been burned, and deep wrinkles and creases covered so much of my face that I looked like a very aged, old man. I reached for a bar of soap to wash my face, and as I did, I saw that all the skin on my hands had peeled off during the night due to the flaming-hot temperature that had afflicted my body. I was literally burned all over — and I was so sick and still stricken with fever that I dressed and as quickly as I could in my weakened condition and drove myself to the emergency room at St. Edward's hospital.

When I walked into the emergency room, the medical workers looked at me in shock and quickly rushed me into a room where doctors encircled me because of my condition. Before I could hardly grasp what was happening, they checked me in as a patient and I found myself in a hospital bed at the very last room at the end of a long hallway.

Doctors ran multiple tests to see what the source of the fever was that had gripped me and burned me so badly. I was flabbergasted when they gave me their diagnosis. They asked if I had been to any tropical country where I could have contracted a tropical disease. Of course, my answer was no. But I *had* been going to Fort Chaffee where there were thousands of prisoners, many of whom had tropical fevers. The doctors finally concluded I had picked up a deadly tropical fever while I was volunteering with our evangelism teams at Fort Chaffee.

I was in the hospital for days with a mysterious tropical fever that belonged in some tropical climate and not in Fort Smith, Arkansas. Medical workers hovered over me to help me recover. It also felt so strange that maximum-security armed guards and soldiers continually walked the hallway outside my room. I soon learned that a Cuban mass-murderer was also in the hospital, in the room directly below me on the next floor. Apparently, he was so dangerous that armed guards walked the hallways to make sure everything was in order. It was such a strange, surreal experience all around that I will never forget.

## My Personal Disobedience Opened the Door

What in the world was happening to me? How had this door been opened for this horrible attack to happen? Think of it. I had been sick for weeks, death had come to take me, I was deeply wrinkled and looked like an old man, the skin was burned from the palms of my hands, doctors diagnosed me with a deadly tropical fever, and now I'm in a room directly above a mass murderer on the floor below me! I wondered, *How did all of this happen to me?*

It was then that I heard the Holy Spirit say, *Rick, your personal disobedience has opened the door for the devil to attack you in this way. It is your own disobedience that has put you in this terrible position.*

I was completely mystified by the Holy Spirit's words because I was earnestly trying to do God's will with my life! So I asked, "What disobedience? Please tell me how I've been so disobedient that I could put myself in a position to be attacked like this? Tell me so I can repent!"

All sickness is not due to disobedience — there are many causes of sickness. But in this case, the Holy Spirit told me that *my personal disobedience* had opened the door for that attack. The Holy Spirit responded, *You've been disobedient in regard to Denise Roberson. I clearly told you that she is to be your wife, but you have been disobedient in this matter. And it's your disobedience about this that has opened the door for these things to happen to you.*

I really thought that when I moved to Arkansas, I buried the question of Denise forever. But I could never completely shake the knowing I had that I was supposed to marry her. Deep down, I knew it was absolutely God's will for me to marry Denise Roberson. God's plan was for her to be my wife and lifelong partner in ministry. I knew that at the very root of my being. So when the Holy Spirit told me I had been disobedient in that matter, it didn't take me but minutes to acknowledge my disobedience and to repent. Then I immediately picked up the phone in my hospital room and called Denise!

I dialed quickly to act on this revelation from the Lord as to why I'd been so severely attacked. But I was apprehensive in my mind to call Denise because I had already canceled two marriage proposals, and I didn't know how happy she would be to hear my voice. But when she answered the phone, I could hear that Denise was weeping. I asked what was wrong and she opened her heart to tell me how heartbroken she was because Mrs. Carey, her voice teacher's wife, was dying of terminal cancer. I felt the need to comfort her, and in that moment, Denise leaned on me for strength. During the course of that telephone conversation, God supernaturally wiped away years of confusion in our relationship, and we started all over again on a brand-new foundation.

Denise said, "I was surprised to receive a phone call from Rick because I had not heard from him at all after his second marriage proposal. But his call came at a moment when I was feeling so vulnerable because of Mrs. Carey's health, and I needed someone strong to lean on. In my past, anytime I'd leaned on a male figure, it always seemed in vain — it seemed that there had been no substantial, enduring strength I could rely on. But when I told Rick about Mrs. Carey, I felt a strength on the other end of the telephone, and it was at that very second that I really fell in love with Rick."

In a split second, God erased the slate of the past, and Denise and I launched into a new relationship. It was a long-distance telephone relationship because now we lived in different states, but it started that day in my hospital room in the very moment I repented for being disobedient about marrying her. Within days, my fever disappeared, and I was dismissed from the hospital. And after that initial phone call from my hospital room, Denise and I began to talk every day by phone.

## A New Beginning as God Wiped the Slate Clean

From the very beginning, our relationship was unusual. I was too young to get married when I first perceived that Denise was to be my wife, and she wasn't ready either. While I accurately perceived she was to be my wife, we didn't know each other very well because we had never spent any time together. We knew each other only from a spiritual perspective — and we knew we were spiritually on the same page. But now, even if it was by telephone, we were getting to know each other in other ways.

In the following months, I invited Denise to visit me in Fort Smith to see where I was living and serving so she could experience First Baptist Church and the ministry of Dr. Bennett. While on that visit, she attended my single-adults class and could see God was moving in my life. She even sang a solo in a Sunday morning service, and people were awestruck to hear such a powerful, operatic voice!

Denise returned to Oklahoma, and our relationship continued to develop long-distance over the telephone. We were growing closer, and we were really learning to enjoy each other. After several months of talking to Denise every day by phone, I knew it was time to move back to the subject of marriage. So one day I called to ask her for the *third time* to marry me. This time I was sure — this was the point of no return.

If "the third time's a charm," this was to be our charming moment! Denise asked for a few days before she answered. At the agreed-upon time, I called her for her answer, and she said, "*YES!* I'd love to marry you!"

Because I was in submission to Dr. Bennett's spiritual authority, I involved him in what was happening in our relationship. I told Dr. Bennett I wanted to marry Denise and he said with his notably southern drawl, "*Rick…*do you love her?" I answered, "Dr. Bennett, I love her and I know she's to be my wife."

He suggested that Denise move to Fort Smith so she and I could continue to get to know each other better. I also needed to ask her parents for permission to marry her, so I went to Miami, Oklahoma, to ask them for her hand in marriage. In about a month, Denise had packed up her belongings and moved to Fort Smith so we could really engage our courtship before we walked the aisle to become husband and wife.

Denise recalls the moment when Dr. Bennett met with the two of us to probe deeper to determine if he would approve our marriage. With his deep voice coupled with his southern accent, he asked, "Denise, why do you want to marry Rick and spend the rest of your life with him?"

Denise answered, "Dr. Bennett, if I turned down this opportunity, it would be like turning away millions and millions of dollars. There's such a treasure in Rick and in our relationship, and I want to spend the rest of my life with him. We'll be a great team that God will use to do great things. It will be my honor to support him and stand beside him in marriage and ministry."

Denise had moved in with a wonderful couple named Ben and Janey Spencer. Janey was Dr. Bennett's secretary, a precious woman of God with a deep prayer life, and she was a big supporter of mine in those days. It didn't take long before Janey and Denise became dear friends, and Janey and Ben graciously helped guide Denise and me forward in our relationship as we prepared for marriage.

When Janey was interviewed for this book, she remembered, "Rick Renner was so hungry to know the Word, its deeper meaning, and what God wanted him to do with it to help others. That's why he followed Dr. Bennett around. He felt that Dr. Bennett was a great teacher of the Bible, so he just followed him around."

Those were the redemptive developments that occurred for Denise and me in the latter days of our lives as singles, just before our union as husband and wife. Things began to smooth out after I became obedient to God's plans for our lives together and had matured to become ready for marriage. But the earlier days of our relationship were so extremely unconventional that if our own sons had proceeded toward marriage as Denise and I had done it, it would have deeply concerned both of us as their parents. Nothing about the way we got started was traditional. As I look back on it, all of it was so *unlikely*, but God supernaturally brought us together to live a blessed life together in His service. It just took us a while to get on track!

We set the date of October 3, 1981, for our wedding. When Dr. Bennett learned that we had set a date — and realized I was becoming more valuable to him because my part of the ministry was rapidly growing — he offered me a full-time position with the church. I would be his personal assistant as well as leader of the single-adult ministry. My salary would be a whopping $50 a week, but the church would also allow me to move rent-free into one of the old houses that was situated at the far end of one corner of the church parking lot.

The house was so dilapidated that it had a staircase that leaned dangerously to one side, and that was just one of the many strange intricacies of this house, as you will soon learn. But the rent was free, and I was thrilled to have it because on my $50 weekly salary, I could not afford to pay rent elsewhere. In the months before Denise and I married, we went to work to improve the sad interior of that house, and little by little, we transformed it into a *cute* little dilapidated house!

Then just one month before Denise and I were married, Dr. Bennett realized it was impossible for a newly married couple to live on $50 a week, so he gave me a generous salary increase. Before Denise and I met at the altar to become husband and wife, I was raised to a gargantuan $100-a-week salary!

### Rick Renner Marries Denise Roberson

Finally, October 3 arrived, and at one o'clock in the afternoon, Denise walked the aisle to meet me at the altar of First Baptist Church, where we became husband and wife. Denise wore a beautiful white gown made by her mother, and I was dressed in a white tuxedo with tails. A packed auditorium watched as Dr. Bennett officiated our marriage. And as part of our ceremony, Denise sang a song, and I knelt on the floor with a tub of water and washed Denise's feet to symbolically declare that I would serve her for the rest of our lives.

Before God, the angels, the spiritual realm, and the Body of Christ, Denise and I made a commitment that we would serve God together for the rest of our lives and that we would do whatever He would ask us to do and go wherever He would ask us to go. Little did we know that the will of God would "ride" on that vow like a train on a perfectly laid track of commitment from which there was no turning back. It would be a powerful train of fierce intensity that would take us as its passengers right out of the United States and into a land of sojourners, indeed, where people had suffered for their faith — *just* as I'd seen in that angelic visitation. And it would be a place where I would lead churches, as I had also seen.

I had no way of knowing just how God would do all of that, and I didn't *need* to know. Our jobs were simply to obey Him from our hearts every step of the way, and He would certainly do the rest. But our first stop would be ministry to singles in Fort Smith — and what a *privilege* it was to serve God and those precious people to whom we'd been assigned.

After our wedding ceremony, Denise and I drove the next day to Crested Butte, Colorado, for a week-long honeymoon where we stayed in a condo provided by a member of the church. Afterward, we drove back to Fort Smith to move into our dilapidated house and to start our lives together as husband and wife in full-time ministry. Denise also taught voice lessons to students who wanted to study with a serious singer. Although we had little materially, we had each other, we had the call of God on our lives, and we had a ministry to single adults. And we were thrilled beyond our ability to express it.

While most couples struggle in their relationship in their first years of marriage, we had no struggles at all. We were blissfully happy together. We were absolutely passionate about drawing people together and bringing souls into the Kingdom. The single-adult department started growing exponentially — in fact, it *boomed*! A hundred and fifty people were coming within a few months. It was really remarkable to watch, and we were seeing people getting saved all the time.

As I said, our group consisted of the widowed and divorced and those who had never married. Divorce was less common in those days, and this group especially seemed to be at the very bottom of the list of classes if a "class system" were to be put in place in the church. But our hearts were wide open to anyone from any class of society!

## Murder Threats From a Motorcycle Gang — Starting Our Married Life and Ministry!

From the very first week of our new life together in Fort Smith, Denise and I began opening our home for a weekly Bible study, and it seemed single adults were in our house nearly every other evening of the week as well. We loved those singles and they loved us. And because many of them had free evenings with no children at home, we were with them almost all the time.

In time, people began streaming to our house nearly every night of the week for fellowship and Bible study. It started with one study a week, then a second, then a third until we were holding Bible studies in our house almost nonstop! Then on Saturdays, we were conducting all kinds of activities for singles with children. Denise and I were giving all our hearts to what we were doing, and the singles in response were giving their hearts right back to us.

In addition to all the wonderful people who came to our dilapidated little two-story house in those early days of marriage, a few strange people came as well. Denise and I were so young and naive that we threw open the door to anyone — including one rough-looking character who showed up at our home one evening for one of our Bible studies. He was a member of a notorious motorcycle gang that had committed murders in the state. I didn't realize it at the time, but the devil had covertly brought something sinister right into our living room and had launched a plan to distract us and redirect our attention from what God was remarkably doing among us.

Never forget that anytime you're doing something significant for the Kingdom of God, the devil will try to thwart the plan God wants to accomplish through your life. What Denise and I experienced at that early moment taught us that spiritual warfare is most definitely a reality we must all learn to face at some point in our lives. We learned that the devil, who is a very cunning strategist, seeks ways to sidetrack us to prevent us from doing any real damage to him. He often sets up distractions when we are on the verge of a major breakthrough. Denise and I witnessed this *through personal experience*.

The first night this gang member came into our living room, what unfolded felt like pure drama. He claimed that he wanted to repent of his life of sin and give his heart to Jesus Christ, and he wept and wept in front of everyone. But deep inside, I was suspicious that it was all just that — *drama* — and that his conversion was insincere.

But when Dr. Bennett heard that a member of this notorious gang had been "saved" in our living room, he eagerly announced the good news to the whole church. I'd privately warned Dr. Bennett that I did not believe his conversion was real, but Dr. Bennett reprimanded me for being suspicious when he thought I should be supportive of this man's conversion. Dr. Bennett even publicly told the church that this man's conversion was a real-life "apostle Paul" type of conversion — perhaps the greatest single conversion he had ever witnessed in his ministry. Still, I knew deep inside something was very wrong, and I simply wasn't buying the story.

In the weeks and months to come, I watched as doctors, lawyers, and wealthy members of the church surrounded this so-called "convert" in their attempts to help him transition from a world of crime to a new life in Christ. One person purchased him a car. Someone else put him up in an apartment and paid his rent, while others put together money to dress him in brand-new clothes. But all along, I had a sinking feeling in the pit of my stomach because I felt it was nothing more than a scam to take advantage of sincere people.

In the end, I was correct. With the skills of a journalist, I began to dig deeper into this gang member's past to see what I could find out about him.

In the process, I unearthed information that he had done the exact same thing at other churches where he was also regally taken care of by people who were sincere, yet lacked discernment.

Even more, I figured out that he was collecting money to funnel it to the motorcycle gang. He was a top-of-the-line *charlatan*! I went to the church leaders to expose the fraud so he would be stopped in his taking advantage of people. When the so-called "convert" realized he had been caught and exposed by me, he called me on the phone and said, "Rick Renner, you will regret what you have done. You have stepped across a dangerous line. You're not just dealing with me anymore. Now you're going to answer to the gang itself. When you least expect it, they will show up to take retribution on you and your wife in that lonely little house of yours at the end of the parking lot."

That "lonely little house" where we lived was so old and decrepit that no window in the house had working locks. Anyone could open a window anywhere in the house with no problem whatsoever. And the back door didn't even have a lock! We locked the front door every night, always hoping that if an intruder ever tried to get in, he would only try the front door — because he could easily enter the house from any window or through the back door. So when this gang member told us that we were going to be attacked by the motorcycle gang, Denise and I were aware that we were living in a precarious place where it would be very easy to get to us.

We decided to ignore his threats, which we did, until one late night when we physically felt the house shaking by the deafening sounds of motorcycles outside. We rushed to the window to see what all the noise was — and we saw about twenty members of that notorious gang riding their motorcycles in endless circles around our lonely house at the end of the parking lot. They drove around and around, screaming atrocious and threatening words at us as we peered out the window.

That gang member had forewarned me that they would take retribution against us, and he was not kidding when he made that threat. But on that night, they apparently came only to give us a good scare, perhaps planning to return and make good on their words *next* time.

### From 'No Locks' to 'Fort Knox'!

Because it was well-known that this notorious gang had committed heinous crimes and even murder, the church felt I needed to contact the police department to tell them what was happening. So I did that, feeling certain the police would tell us not to worry. But instead, they told me that we needed to worry, because if this group said they were going to murder us, it was likely that they would really try.

Because First Baptist Church needed more parking space, they had already decided to tear down the dilapidated house we were living in to make room for more parking — so at that critical moment, an executive decision was made to go ahead and move the newly married Renners directly across the street into a house with doors and windows that actually locked.

Very soon afterward, we moved into a remodeled carriage house that had been constructed before the Civil War to hold horse-drawn carriages. That house was so perfectly preserved from its pre-Civil War status that the rock wall under the staircase still had the original corncobs in it that were used as filler between rocks in the wall. The building had been converted into a small two-story house with walls that were about two feet thick and all the doors and windows locked securely. That house was so secure that it felt like we had moved into Fort Knox!

Nevertheless, the threats from that gang continued relentlessly. Denise and I felt trapped inside the house with no way to escape if the gang chose to attack us. So to help alleviate our fears, we decided to purchase a guard dog that would protect us from intruders. We were told the best dog for this purpose was a Doberman Pinscher, so we purchased a male Doberman, which Denise named Jerome after the famous operatic bass singer Jerome Hines, who performed at the Metropolitan Opera in New York.

There was one problem, though. Jerome was the kindest, stranger-loving dog I'd ever owned. One night when the motorcycle gang actually pounded on our front door and our hearts trembled with fear — while we hoped Jerome would protect us, he instead postured himself at the front door, wagging his knobby Doberman tail with glee because visitors had come!

For months, the motorcycle gang continued to harass us. I called the Police Department regularly for help. In fact, I called so often that when they heard my voice, I didn't even have to identify myself. The operator would say, "Brother Renner…are they back again tonight?" To their credit, the police began to make hourly patrols each night in our neighborhood to make sure we were all right. And after months of living with this unending harassment, it ended just as suddenly as it had started.

## Resist the Devil and He Will Flee From You!

The devil had tried his best to scare us off, but it didn't work. It was all nothing more than a demonic tactic designed to chase us off and to divert our attention from the ministry we were doing that was so rapidly growing. That early experience turned out to be a lesson that helped us many times over in our future years of ministry. As I said, we learned from this incident that Satan always tries to distract and divert attention at key moments of breakthrough and growth. We also learned that even if demonic forces try to scare us off, if we refuse to be moved, Satan would be the one who would eventually retreat.

James 4:7 says, "…Resist the devil, and he will flee from you." We may not have done it perfectly from the very beginning, but eventually Denise and I decided we would not surrender to these attacks on our lives. Instead of living in fear, we decided to "resist" what the enemy was trying to do to us. The word "resist" in James 4:7 demonstrates *the attitude of one who is fiercely opposed to something and therefore determines that he will do everything within his power to resist it, to stand against it, and to defy its operation.*

This word "resist" means you have to be determined to stand against any assault the devil tries to wage against you. You have to dig in your heels, brace yourself for a fight, and put your full force forward in Jesus' mighty name to drive him back and out of your life. Your stand against Satan must be firm, unyielding, and steadfast if you want to successfully resist his bombardments.

James 4:7 promises the devil will "flee" from you — and that word "flee" means *to take flight.* It is the very word used to depict *a lawbreaker who flees in terror from a nation where he broke the law.* The reason he flees so quickly is that he wants to escape the prosecution process. Remaining in the nation would most assuredly mean judgment. So rather than stay and face the consequences, the lawbreaker flees for his life.

Knowing this meaning of the word "flee" tells us that the devil knows he is a lawbreaker and that if a believer stands against him — in other words, if the believer resists him by using his God-given authority — the devil will eventually withdraw and look for a way to escape prosecution. That is precisely what James means when he says the devil will "flee" from you!

An expanded interpretation of James 4:7 is as follows: "Stand firmly against the devil! That's right — be unbending and unyielding in the way you resist him so he knows he is up against a serious contender. If you'll take this kind of stand against him, he will tuck his tail and run like a criminal who knows the day of prosecution is upon him. Once you start resisting him, he'll flee from you in terror!"

Through that early experience in our marriage and ministry, Denise and I learned the lesson that if we would dig in our heels and refuse to surrender to the devil's attacks, eventually his diversions and distractions would dissipate. In many years of ministry — including later, in the lands of the former Soviet Union — we knew that if we would remain steadfast and refuse to surrender, the devil would inevitably tuck his tail and run!

That first lesson was an emotional one for Denise and me, but it was one that has stayed with us our whole lives.

## 'Singled Out' — a Ministry for Single Adults

When those ludicrous attacks ended, Denise and I were able to really focus on our ministry. And because I was now making a mammoth salary of $100 a week, I stopped working at the bookstore and devoted my attention fully to the single-adult ministry at the church. The singles were *thrilled* to have attention and willingly gave themselves wholeheartedly to what God was doing among them.

The enthusiastic crowd of singles packed the little white house at the far end of the church parking lot. Every week the class grew larger and larger until it could no longer be contained within the walls of that structure. Dr. Bennett was elated with the growth, so he approved our single-adults class to move to the original fellowship hall of the old education building across the street from the main sanctuary.

I decided it was time to put my advertising and marketing education to work in order to make the single-adult department grow even more. The ministry needed an official name — a "branding" that would give it distinction not only in the church, but in the whole city. Many felt the singles at the church had been looked upon as second-class citizens — and that's why they met in the little white house at the far end of the parking lot. Because they were widowed, divorced, or had never married — and the original group had quite a number of troubled people in it — the church generally didn't know what to do with them. And as is often the case with singles in some churches, many of those single adults felt like the "misfits" in the church.

Churches at that time had respectable singles classes for "College and Career" ages, but only a few had significant outreaches to other single adults who were older or who had been hurt by life. One staff member from First Baptist Church recalled, "That was in the early 1980s, and during that decade, a singles outreach would have been frowned upon. But Rick had a certain boldness about him to start things, and because God had called him to start it, he did it."

I wanted to get rid of that "single" stigma forever, so in 1981, I renamed the singles ministry "Singled Out" and even designed a logo to match the name of the ministry. It was my intention to let every single adult know — whether younger, middle-aged, or older — that they were not misfits in God's Kingdom. I remembered my own struggles of feeling like a misfit and out of place as an adolescent. It was a feeling I would never want another human being to experience no matter *what* his or her age or status in life.

Weekly I pounded into these singles' minds that they had been "singled out" by Jesus Christ! Rather than let the name "single" be something negative in their eyes, Denise and I set out to turn their singleness into a positive message that they were "singled out" by Jesus to do something significant. We watched singles from all over Fort Smith come to take part in the "Singled Out" ministry as it began to exponentially grow and *explode*.

But singles wanted more than just the time allotted during one Sunday School class on Sunday mornings. Actually, Sunday School classes on Sunday mornings felt religious, stuffy, and unattractive to our singles. So in addition to starting the "Singled Out" outreach, Denise and I launched *home groups* for singles within the "Singled Out" ministry.

Home-group ministry was a novel idea at that time because most churches were so focused on a traditional Sunday School structure. I knew I was taking chances within the existing structure of our church, but deep down, I felt singles would respond well to home groups, so we launched them. One staff member from that time recalled, "In the eighties, small groups had not yet evolved, but Rick basically pioneered these small groups for our singles."

One of our single-adult leaders from those days said, "Rick's forte was getting out there on the front lines and forging ahead into unknown areas. God used him in incredible ways like that even from his early days. He always had a kind of apostolic mantle upon him, and he wasn't afraid to forge into new areas. And Rick's God-given characteristics were such that people wanted to be associated with him and to help him. There was just a genuineness about both Rick and Denise that attracted people. Another thing that really made me want to draw near to Rick was his humility, wisdom, and insight in the Word."

The singles loved the concept of home groups because it felt more intimate and gave them more opportunities to serve in various roles. To train leaders, Denise and I opened our carriage house to the top home-group leaders, and every Tuesday night, they gathered in our living room for a time of worship and teaching. Then they would replicate everything we did in our group in all their respective groups around the city.

A large group of singles were learning the Word of God, and I had taken ten or twelve leaders as my own disciples. We were teaching them in our home and showing them how to move in the power of the Holy Spirit. God's hand was on Denise and me and on the work that was growing all around us. One man from that time recalls, "We were hootin' and hollerin' in the Baptist Church...God had shown up and people were even falling under the power of God in our meetings." He added, "But even then, Rick was teaching us deeply from the Greek New Testament. What he taught us at that time became the spiritual foundation for so many people's lives."

Janey Spencer recalled, "Rick and Denise reached out to all kinds of people that our church didn't know how to reach. The Renners lived close to the church, and their home became a gathering place for people who were seeking the Lord. It was a place where people could go to fellowship and learn. Rick's personality and his zeal for the Lord really attracted people. A love for the Word was the strongest thing about Rick, and he really desired to follow that *and* the Lord, wherever He would lead him."

The noise of this newness in this department in the church caused singles from every nook and cranny of the city to participate in our ministry. What started with a sad-looking group of forty individuals had morphed to several hundred single adults — *and we were just getting started!*

## 'Starting Over' — a Divorce Recovery Program for the Newly Single

God was undeniably moving in "Singled Out" at our church, but I felt we had not done our part to bring healing to people who had gone through the trauma of divorce. The topic of divorce was a touchy one in our church and to the Church at-large back in those days. Nevertheless, I felt called to help people who had gone through this traumatic event.

As Denise and I counseled divorced people, compassion for them in our hearts began to grow. We saw how they had suffered relational disruptions that affected them, their children, and their incomes — and that they often didn't know how to "fit" in the church after their marriages dissolved. I personally began to wake up to the fact that a huge part of the city's population that was divorced didn't know how to connect with the local church after their marriages ended. The Holy Spirit was opening my eyes to an area of ministry that needed our compassionate attention.

So I began to read book after book on the subject of divorce and how to recover from it. Denise and I were newly married and so excited about getting started in life together, but a lot of our private conversations revolved around how to minister to people who had suffered personal loss in their marriages. The word "divorce" was practically taboo back in those days, and Dr. Bennett and his pastoral team were a little worried about too many divorced people being in the church. But I pressed forward because I knew God was calling me to learn all I could in order to know how to minister to those who were newly single.

I finally received permission to launch yet another outreach that I called, "Starting Over — a Divorce Recovery Program for the Newly Single." I rented a ballroom at a Holiday Inn just a few blocks away from the church, and I once again put my advertising and marketing education to work as I designed an advertising campaign to reach this group of people who generally felt unwanted by the majority of churches in Fort Smith. As we prepared to launch this new aspect of our ministry, I continued studying materials about the trauma of divorce and how recovery from it was possible. I prayerfully began to write pages and pages of materials that I divided into weekly classes.

When I announced to our singles that they were going to help start this new aspect of our ministry with us, many of them were skittish about it, especially those who had experienced the pain of divorce. For some of them, it had been years since they'd been married and they felt trepidation about meeting other divorcees. Some *newly* divorced women expressed concerns about being taken advantage of by predators who were on the prowl for lonely and hurting women.

These were legitimate concerns for people who were still fractured in their souls and in pain.

So Denise and I assembled the very best leaders from "Singled-Out" who had been through the pain of divorce themselves but had recovered. As a team, we committed to welcome every single hurting person with open arms and to assure them that our meetings were a safe environment. To get the attention of the divorced community, we sent multiple mailings to our burgeoning mailing list and placed advertisements in the newspaper in the days before our first meeting was to be held. Then we waited to see who would show up on that first night.

Denise and I and our team arrived early to set up the room and to make sure everything looked warm, hospitable, and professional. About a half hour before the meeting began, a few people began to wander into the room. I could see they felt scared to be there, so Denise and I welcomed them, hugged them, offered to get them a cup of coffee, and helped them find a place to sit. More and more people wandered into the room until, finally, when it was time for the meeting to start, the ballroom was filled to maximum capacity. I was *elated* and *stunned*, as the size of the crowd was much larger than I'd anticipated. When I stood to publicly greet them and get started, I felt a desperate need for the Holy Spirit's anointing. Here I was, a man newly married who had never been through divorce, addressing a room full of brokenhearted people.

I kept hearing the devil say, *Who are you to think you can minister to these people?* But I knew God had asked me to do it, so I shoved those thoughts aside and dove headfirst into that first session. In retrospect I'm sure many of them also wondered who I was, a newly married man who had never been through divorce, addressing them or daring to try to minister to them.

But our compassion compensated for any mistakes we made. And because they felt embraced by our compassion, those singles, many who were *newly* divorced, kept coming back week after week. The first full round of sessions was eight weeks long, and during that time, not a single person dropped out. By the time those eight weeks concluded, some of them had given their lives to Christ and had begun to attend our "Singled Out" ministry at the church.

That year we conducted "Starting Over" five times. Within a year and a half, more than 1,100 divorced people spent eight weeks with us in our five courses held at the Holiday Inn. As I've told you in previous chapters, there was a lot of divorce in my own family. Four of my grandparents had been married thirteen times cumulatively. I already felt no judgment for people who had been through divorce, but working so closely with these hurting people gave me compassion for them beyond what I knew was possible. And it wasn't long until a flood of them had joined us in our "Singled Out" ministry.

### An Outpouring of the Holy Spirit at First Baptist Church

From the very outset, I had been honest with Dr. Bennett about my relationship with the Holy Spirit and the fact that I prayed in tongues.

Although he personally did not speak in tongues, he honored my experience as a legitimate one.

So when the single adults began to ask questions about the gifts of the Spirit and tongues, I proceeded to tell them what I believed the Bible taught on these subjects. As a result, scores of single adults began to be filled with the Holy Spirit. Although speaking in tongues publicly was not permitted because Dr. Bennett did not allow it, in their private lives and fellowship with each other, our ever-growing single-adults ministry began to abound with the life of the Spirit.

One particular week, Dr. Bennett asked me to preach the Sunday night evening service. I was humbled and thrilled. That night I preached a message called, "Where Is the Power of God?" In my message, I called the church back to the power of God as it was experienced in the book of Acts. That night, the altar filled with people weeping and crying out for a fresh outpouring of the Holy Spirit upon the church. Even Dr. Bennett was deeply moved.

But while Dr. Bennett could accommodate the moving of the Spirit himself, more traditional church members stood firmly against what they perceived to be Charismatic excess, and they raised their voices that "their" church had been invaded by rabble-rousers who spoke in tongues!

Those more traditional members were offended by my message. Plus, some of them were already not too thrilled to have so many "misfits" in the church who had never married or those who *they* felt had failed in marriage. For some, it was already difficult to see so many singles, but to have them speaking in tongues on top of that was just too much for them to bear.

Some prestigious members of the church, led by the chief of the deacons, began to exert pressure on Dr. Bennett to shut the whole deal down before it got out of control. It made me think of the crippled man who was healed at the Pool of Bethesda (*see* John 5:5-15). After being crippled for thirty-eight years, he was healed by Jesus and was walking again. But the religious people couldn't rejoice in his transformation because it was done in a way that disturbed their religious standards and rules.

Denise and I had already learned that the devil, when resisted, would flee from our lives and ministry with his distractions and lies. Now this new experience was teaching us that when God touches a person's life, not everyone rejoices about it. I thought surely everyone would be delighted at what God was doing among the single adults. Those who had been emotionally crippled were "walking" again! But instead, it felt to me like an all-out war was being launched to put an end to the moving of the Spirit in our department. I'll never forget the words of one of the most revered members of the church, who said, "Rick, I can see that you, with your rebels and rejects, are trying to take over the church!"

I was flabbergasted! How could these precious souls whose lives were being transformed by God and brought to the knowledge of Jesus be depicted as rebels and rejects?

But in all fairness to both Dr. Bennett and to the traditional members, they simply hadn't anticipated that what was happening would ever happen in their church! On one hand, Dr. Bennett was elated with the growth of our department and how it was boosting overall church attendance. But he knew if he allowed it to continue, he would have to go to war with some leading members of the church who were staunch Baptists that were opposed to such workings of the Holy Spirit.

As I look back on it, I can see what a difficult position Dr. Bennett was in — and that it made him feel the need to play politics to accommodate both wings of the church. But playing politics in church isn't a strategy that normally ends very well.

### The Problem of Old and New Wineskins

I've met many people over the years who have held on to the hope that traditional churches will be visited by the power God and be miraculously renewed. On rare occasions, it happens, but it is truly rare when tradition moves out of the way for a new move of God. This is why in Luke 5:37 and 38, Jesus said, "And no man putteth new wine into old bottles; else the new wine will burst the bottles, and be spilled, and the bottles shall perish. But new wine must be put into new bottles; and both are preserved."

History and experience show us that it is hard for an old wineskin to become flexible enough for a new infilling with stronger wine. Our singles ministry seemed like a new wineskin, but it was strangely contained inside the older wineskin of that church. Our singles were flexible and not fettered by religious traditions of the past. God was miraculously using our department to bring much-needed vitality to the church. I do not intend to give the impression that the more traditional folks didn't love God or want to experience more of Him, but some who represented a more traditional way of doing things were not too thrilled about what was happening because it disrupted their religious pattern.

Often earlier generations are born in the power of the Spirit, but over time, the fires grow dimmer — *unless* the church and its members are unrelenting in their commitment to retain it. It is tragic, but true, that often a church that began like a spiritual inferno and once possessed vibrancy and excitement for the things of God later allows those things to slowly ebb away. Churches that once experienced the power of God can be reduced to spiritual drudgery and their experience can become a monotonous, religious routine. Often what begins as a new wineskin that was filled with the joy of the Holy Spirit turns into an older wineskin that loses its flexibility for God to use it as He was once able to do.

God's best plan is for a church to age gracefully and to increase its capacity for more of Him as it matures. I feel absolutely no sense of judgment for those who have fallen into the rut of tradition. I cannot think of a single Christian leader who hasn't had to fight the tendency to fall into this pattern. In my own life, I've had to intentionally determine to stay pliable in God's hands and not to get stuck doing something a certain way just because it's the way we've always done it. It takes great commitment for a church, ministry, or person to remain pliable. I'm thankful for the many assignments God has given me that have never allowed me to remain stagnant very long. *I never want Jesus to call me an old wineskin!*

But in the midst of the challenges that the more traditional members of First Baptist Church were leveling against us, God nevertheless continued to give unprecedented growth to our ministry in the context of that church. We outgrew the old fellowship hall in the old education building and moved into the newer fellowship hall on the main campus because it could hold hundreds of people.

Later, when we outgrew that space, the only other space to accommodate us was the main sanctuary — and that space was off limits on Sunday mornings because that was where Dr. Bennett conducted his "Pastor's Class" every week. So the search was on to find an off-campus location nearby where we could move the "Singled Out" ministry to hold our weekly services.

After diligently searching, we found a nearby location that was large enough to accommodate the growth we were experiencing. As I think back on it, I am amazed to think I moved the entire ministry with hundreds of single adults into the highly ornamented auditorium of the Masonic Temple, which was just two blocks from the main campus of the church!

The auditorium of the Masonic Temple was completely adorned with masonic symbols and emblems — including Egyptian pyramids, sphinxes, and gargoyle-like figures that were suspended from every corner of the ceiling in the auditorium. As we lifted our heads and hands in worship, we had to ignore demonic-looking statues and figures that glared down at us. But even there, God moved and we grew even more in that spiritually dark location.

Soon we needed to move again because we were outgrowing the various spaces at the Masonic Temple. The only space we could find large enough to seat the growing ministry was the main sanctuary of the church. But since that space was occupied on Sunday mornings by Dr. Bennett's large class of more than one thousand people, I came up with a concept that I called *Saturday Night Singles*. The concept was that of a Saturday night Sunday School class advertised especially for those who were widowed, divorced, or who had never married. This was really anti-traditional, but Dr. Bennett didn't know where else to move our growing ministry, so he permitted us to move into the main sanctuary on Saturday nights.

### *Saturday Night Singles* and *Wide Awake With Rick*

Soon we had our own praise-and-worship teams, ushers, and counselors — a full-fledged service for the single adults in the "Singled-Out" ministry of the church. News of this growth began to spread through the church and others hungry for more of the Holy Spirit began to show up even if they were not single. This further angered the more traditional members of the church, and I sensed that even Dr. Bennett felt a bit threatened by their attending *Saturday Night Singles* services instead of the main services on Sunday morning.

At times, up to eight hundred singles were in attendance, and it looked like there would be no end to the growth in front of us. We had tapped into a large segment of the population of the area that needed to be touched, and single adults were starting to drive to our meetings every Saturday night from all over northwestern Arkansas.

My secretary from those days, Teresa Smith, said, "We started having our meetings on Saturdays and hundreds of singles started coming. There really was nothing else for Christian singles in town to do and no place for a Christian to go. Our meetings had a draw for Christian singles to come meet other Christians, and those services became our nucleus."

She continued, "We had a lot of singles that might have been Lutheran, Methodist, etc. So, they'd go to their own church on Sundays, but on Saturday nights, we would fill the auditorium with hundreds of people from everywhere."

She concluded, "Rick and Denise are the two people who've made the biggest impression on me ever, and their ministry truly changed my life. Rick and Denise were there for anything we needed. They really had the biggest influence on us, introducing us all to something that has stayed with us and laying the foundation that would get us through the rest of our lives."

We moved into the main auditorium of the church, and the single-adult ministry just kept growing. It took off like wildfire, in fact, and many of our members were speaking in tongues. God's power was "falling" in the auditorium — manifesting His presence — on many Saturday nights.

But some of the older members of the church who were died-in-the-wool Southern Baptists — and they were also the "powers that be" of the church — were offended. They called us radicals, lowbrows, outcasts, renegades, and rebels. But all we wanted was to follow God. Those older members of the church were struggling with our growth, but the fact is, our singles ministry *was growing* — so much so that the Southern Baptist Convention asked me to write an article for their main magazine because their research showed that we were the eighth fastest-growing single-adult ministry in America.

About that time is also when I embarked on my own first daily TV program that I called *Wide Awake With Rick.* It was broadcast Monday through Friday at 6:55 a.m. on a local TV channel just before the morning news. Every Monday, Denise and I would drive to the TV station, I would take my place on the set, and we'd begin to film a week's worth of my program, *Wide Awake With Rick.* People began to tune in every day to hear the broadcasts.

Everywhere we looked, Denise and I could see God was blessing us, and it was an exciting and magnificent time for newly married Rick and Denise Renner.

### Paul Richard William Renner Is Born

It was during this time that Denise and I became the proud parents of a nineteen-inch-long, seven-pound, eleven-ounce little boy who was born at Sparks Regional Medical Center in Fort Smith on September 14, 1983. We named him Paul Richard William Renner. He was named *Paul* after the apostle Paul and my Grandpa Renner whose name was Paul Renner. And he was named *Richard* after me, my dad, and other Richards in a long line of Renners. He was named *William* after Dr. Bill Bennett, whose name was actually William Bennett. Because nobility are given three names at birth in addition to their last name, we decided to give all of our children three names as our way of communicating right from the start that they were nobility in God's eyes and ours.

I loved Dr. Bennett so much that I wanted our first son to bear his name *William.* But by now Dr. Bennett was inwardly conflicted about how to handle the political mess emerging between various factions of the church — those who wanted to remain traditional Southern Baptists and those who wanted to be Charismatic. It was a terrible tug-of-war.

Denise and I knew that Dr. Bennett and his wife, Doris, loved us deeply. Their door was always open to us. They'd had us to their home often for lunch on Sundays and tried to keep us close to their sides. And even though my responsibilities had grown in the church, I still happily served him in any capacity that was needed. He felt the incessant need to keep me humble, so in order to do that, he kept requiring me to do menial tasks like vacuuming his car, polishing his shoes, and even raking the leaves in his yard.

He was an invaluable blessing to my life as my mentor, but he was heavy-handed in his leadership style. Truthfully, Dr. Bennett was hard to serve because he was so demanding. As I prepared for writing this book, I spoke with a former youth pastor and preschool minister, who recalled, "Dr. Bennett only expected his staff to work a half a day, and he did not care what twelve hours you chose to do it! He was a taskmaster, and 'enough' was never enough for him. He was probably the toughest person I ever worked for in my life — but I'm the person I am today because God used him to ground me in my faith and my theology. Later in life, Dr. Bennett was much more relaxed and became a different leader in that season. But earlier, even though he was so demanding, we all recognized that when he stepped into the pulpit, the anointing of God came upon him."

Whether it was true or not, at that time, I felt some of the pastoral staff resented me because I was young, because I received a lot of special attention from the pastor, and because I did not have a seminary degree. At times I felt like the eyes of some on the staff were on me, scrutinizing me to see if I was "worthy" of the attention I was getting. And the lack of a seminary degree was definitely deemed by some to be a strike against me.

Another former staff member recalled, "Even when Rick was a young man, there was an anointing on him. He was young and he was learning, growing, and developing — and our pastor at that time was probably in his mid-sixties. Dr. Bennett was an amazing man of God who had memorized most of the Bible. And we could also see that Rick had brilliance running in his veins. Because Dr. Bennett was a genius himself, he was able to recognize that Rick's capabilities were not normal, and he just fell in love with Rick. When the two of them connected, it was like a hand and glove that fit together perfectly."

He continued, "Rick had a great heart, and he was humble and normal; he ran with the rest of us. Rick was so authentic, and he was earnestly seeking to do God's will. I think that even today, Rick would never admit to being brilliant. He'd probably say, 'Oh no, I'm just pretty average.' But I can tell you that Dr. Bennett recognized his potential and poured himself into him. And the growth in Rick was exponential. Much of what Rick Renner is today is a product of Dr. Bill Bennett's influence in his young life."

Before I continue my story, I have to say it is amazing to me that anyone would *ever* say that I am brilliant. I'll never forget how assaulted my self-image was as a young man, how Mrs. Sparks called me stupid for a whole year, and job-placement counselors also basically told me I was stupid. If God has done anything with my brain, I give Him all the glory, because the devil definitely waged an early war on my mind to try to bring me to naught and to keep any God-given gift or calling from manifesting and helping one single person, much less *nations*.

### Dr. Bennett Began To 'Double Down'
### With His Demands

Although I originally felt privileged to attend Dr. Bennett's pastoral-staff meetings as a department head at such a young age, in time, I began to feel they were becoming torture sessions. He was so tough that he would go around the room in those meetings to ask how many people we each would have coming to the altar the following week to commit their lives to Christ. He wanted to know how many "visits" we were going to make before the following Sunday too. I became so terrorized by those meetings that I would go to the local shopping mall and just shake hands so I could say I'd made a visit. I didn't want to look in Dr. Bennett's face and say I hadn't reached my quota.

But in those staff meetings, one by one, each of us would go around the room to also give a report about what was happening in our various departments. I was always eager to share the good news of what our department was experiencing, and I naively believed everyone else would rejoice with me. But my glowing reports were often met with disdain from a few of the pastoral team who didn't like the fact that a non-seminary graduate was leading a major department of the church.

As I said, because Dr. Bennett wanted to see people saved every week, he actually gave a few of us who were over certain departments a weekly quota for people to be saved — and that included me. He held me personally accountable for how many singles I was responsible to have walk the aisle each week to be saved or to join the church. If I failed to meet my quota, I knew that I would be reprimanded in that staff meeting. *Wow…that's why I say those meetings could be* torturous!

But I was completely sold out to see the single-adult department grow. I did visitations several nights a week, and I even had a self-imposed rule that no week would pass without my personally calling two hundred people by phone. Week after week and month after month, I met that goal. But as we approached weekend services every week, I would nearly get hives as I wondered whether or not I would meet my altar quota. If I fell short one person, I trembled to think what would be said to me at the pastoral-staff meeting the following morning.

In fact, I was so given to work that once I ended up in the hospital with a bleeding ulcer. The doctor sat on the edge of my bed and said, "Rick, it is not normal to work like you're working. You're going to have to slow down if you don't want to die early in life." I told him, "But you don't know what it's like to work for Dr. Bennett! He calls on me day and night and expects me to perform at the same level he has performed in *his* work." But because I loved Dr. Bennett so much, I didn't really see this as negative; I was thrilled to be serving alongside him in the work of the ministry!

Dr. Bennett also had no sense of time when it came to when to call or *not* to call people. He could call at five o'clock in the morning or at midnight with no thought whatsoever that it might be too early or too late to call. He didn't intend to be rude — he truly had no sense of time. He was such a genius that he lived on a different plane from the rest of the planet. Because he was always on duty, he assumed every good Christian should always be on duty too. If I wanted to take a day off, he would ask me, "Do you think Jesus would take a day off while the rest of the world slips into eternity unsaved?"

And although Denise and I were newly married, he continued to require me to meet him every morning at 5:30 a.m. for those one-on-one meetings in which he taught me doctrine, lectured me about personal disciplines and finances, and challenged nearly everything I believed. He wasn't challenging my beliefs because he didn't agree with them — he just really wanted me to be able to theologically defend my faith. It was tough, but it was very good for me at that time in my life. I needed a strong hand to develop me, and Dr. Bennett was that strong hand.

But as it often happens, as I got closer to Dr. Bennett, I began to see flaws that I hadn't previously seen. As I've told you, he could be *very* demanding, and he corrected me *harshly* even when it wasn't needed. But I was so thrilled to be at his side that I was willing to take a little abuse to stay there. I rationalized that everyone has issues, which is absolutely true, so I chose to ignore cracks in his character. I practically adored this man of God.

But as time passed — and the pressures began to mount from the traditional Southern Baptist quarters of the church that wanted to shut us down and kick us out — things began to turn sour. I think Dr. Bennett finally realized that a war was about to take place on his turf that could be very expensive. Instead of fighting, he surrendered to the pressures leveled by the chief deacon that was ordering him to shut down the move of the Spirit "or *else*."

### A Suicide Among Our Singles

One Sunday Dr. Bennett decided he would teach his Pastor's Class on the subject, "Can a Christian Who Commits Suicide Go to Heaven?" The question intrigued people, so that week, his class was especially packed with people who came to hear the answer.

Among the thousand-plus people who attended his class that Sunday was a struggling divorcee from our single-adult department — a precious woman that Denise and I really loved who had been deeply wounded by her husband's philandering. In spite of the fact that several years had passed since her divorce, she had never recovered emotionally from the trauma she experienced at his hands. At times she would seem to come around, but overall, she deeply struggled with hurt and brokenness. Because Denise and I felt great compassion for her, we had often reached out to make sure she knew how much we loved her.

But when she walked away from Dr. Bennett's class that day, for some reason, she apparently left with the belief that it would be all right to end her life and her sadness — that she would still go to Heaven. And so the next day when she was home alone, she took out a shotgun and killed herself.

Janey Spencer, Dr. Bennett's secretary, called to let me know that this woman had committed suicide. Because the woman's entire family attended the church, Dr. Bennett decided to go to the scene of the suicide to join the grieving family. Because she was in my department, he also felt it was right that I go with him. He asked me to ride with him in his car to the site where the suicide occurred so we could console her parents. When we arrived, I saw her dead body still lying in a pool of blood in the kitchen. Her parents obviously struggled to get a grip on themselves, and Dr. Bennett and I joined hands with them to pray for the Holy Spirit to comfort them. It was a heart-rending emotional ordeal.

I learned from that experience that every spiritual leader needs to really think through every statement made from the pulpit. One never knows who is listening and what people are perhaps hearing you say that you never intended. Of course, Dr. Bennett never intended to give the impression that suicide was all right, but that woman no doubt walked away believing she had some kind of clearance and that Heaven seemed like a better option than the trauma she couldn't seem to recover from.

This makes me think of James 3:1, where we are warned that those who teach will be more strictly judged. That experience early in ministry impacted me with the need to be very careful about statements I make when I preach or teach.

## A Regrettable Conversation in a Poorly Timed Moment

As Dr. Bennett and I drove away from the house on that tragic day, a very regrettable conversation commenced. In the car on our way back to Fort Smith, he decided to take the opportunity to say, "Rick, don't think too highly of yourself. I know you think you're mightily anointed, but you're not as anointed as you think you are. And don't *ever* get the idea of starting a church or another ministry in our town. You can't do it because you're not that anointed. You'll never succeed without me."

But that wasn't the end of it. Nearly the whole way back to Fort Smith, he chided me for all the troubles he was experiencing with the chief deacon.

To be honest, he was frequently chiding people for various reasons, but on that day, it was my turn to be challenged.

As Dr. Bennett continued his rebuke of me, in essence, he continued to verbally lambast me as he said, "Rick, you are too high and mighty for a man your age! Let me remind you that you don't even deserve your position because you've never been to seminary. The only reason you're on this staff is, I opened the door and gave you an opportunity. No one else wanted you to be a part of this team. You're only on this staff because of me and you should never forget it. And should you ever have the smallest inkling to leave me and go off to do something yourself, just forget it, because you'll never be able to do anything without me."

Perhaps a lot of what Dr. Bennett said that day was true. For example, he *had* given me an opportunity that few on staff wanted me to have. And it was true that I was not a seminary graduate. And perhaps it was even true that I thought too highly of myself at times. But because I felt so completely *assaulted* by him after I'd served him night and day — and because we'd just walked away from a rough emotional moment in which a dead woman was lying in a pool of blood — I allowed my emotions to rule me and I spoke disrespectfully to him for the first time. Anger erupted from deep inside me as I reminded him that Jesus was my Savior, *not him*, and that God called me into the ministry, *not him*!

Instead of putting on the emotional brakes and refraining from saying more, I continued when I should have simply stopped talking. I heard myself say, "Based on your words, it's clear you think I could never do anything without you. So, Dr. Bennett, to my ears, it sounds like *you're* the one who's thinking too highly of himself."

But I didn't even stop there. I continued, "I might add that it would be nice if you stopped occasionally to show a little gratitude for people who serve you night and day. And may I also remind you that I serve you like a slave for $100 a week. My department is responsible for more souls getting saved than any other department in the church. In fact, if it were not for what is happening in my department, this church wouldn't have the accolades you're getting for having the largest number of salvations in a Southern Baptist church in Arkansas each year!"

Even if there was some truth to what I had just blurted out in pain and anger to Dr. Bennett, I was wrong to speak so disrespectfully to this man I had so admired and respected. But it's also true in life that any one of us can be wronged by another and then respond poorly to the offense. In other words, we can be in the right and yet so very wrong at the same time if we don't hold our calm and bridle our tongue!

And I'd just responded poorly to what, in truth, was an egregious assault on me that day by Dr. Bennett. I was right in one sense, but I was *oh, so wrong* in my ugly and disrespectful rebuttal of his harsh rebuke. It was true that Denise and I were living off "a nickel and a dime," and living on so little had been really tough. We were just newly married, and we had this wonderful group of single people whom we cared for night and day while we were just barely scraping by. We really should have been paid better, which is why to this day, I believe in paying people correctly for the jobs they do in the ministry.

But even though living like that was tough financially — and dealing with Dr. Bennett could be really tough — it had never been an issue with me until that day in the car when I allowed myself to be offended by him!

That afternoon, Dr. Bennett and I were both on edge because we had just walked away from that emotionally charged atmosphere with that woman's corpse still present at the scene. Truth be told, it was the wrong place and wrong time for a serious conversation. But so often the door for the devil is opened when people try to have serious conversations when they are weak, tired, or unusually susceptible to their emotions.

## Satan Tried To Turn Me Into a Betrayer

After that horrible incident between Dr. Bennett and me, the devil flooded my mind with disapproving, cynical, mocking, sarcastic, and disparaging thoughts about this man whom I'd considered a model, mentor, and friend. Now the flaws that I had previously overlooked came *raging* to the forefront of my mind.

That string of negative thoughts should have been a warning flag that Satan, the accuser of the brethren, was trying to wedge his way into my mind and emotions. If I had spent some time getting quiet before the Lord and allowing Him to give me *His* perspective of the situation, I probably would have let it all go. But, instead, I gave place to the devil and allowed him to accuse Dr. Bennett to me continually.

You see, I became *offended* in the car that day. After all the opportunities Dr. Bennett had given me, I allowed Satan to wedge his way between us, and we were never quite the same again after that time. The devil had been waiting for the perfect opportunity to attack my mind and to try to ruin our relationship. And because I gave place to offense, I became his *perfect prey.*

The incident in the car became a major issue in my mind. I didn't realize that I was allowing this over-exaggerated issue to become an open door for the devil. Isn't it amazing how quickly a dart of the enemy can be thrown into your heart? Equally amazing is the speed in which just one of his evil darts can change your perspective of someone you previously honored and respected!

In a matter of hours, my view of Dr. Bennett completely soured. Like the pounding of a battering ram against a barred fortress, the devil began to repeatedly strike my mind with accusations against Dr. Bennett. Although I didn't completely recognize these thoughts as the accusing voice of the enemy, I heard that voice whisper:

- *Dr. Bennett is so arrogant and proud!*
- *If other people saw what you see, no one would attend this church.*
- *He doesn't really love his people!*
- *He doesn't appreciate you.*
- *He doesn't deserve to have you serve on his staff. LEAVE HIM!*
- *The people in this city need a pastor who really loves them.*
- *It's time for you to leave and start your own church!*

Never forget that the devil is a master at embellishing real or imagined offenses in people's minds until they become inflated and "larger than life." He knows just when to spring an attack. He watches for the right timing and then strikes. He waits until you're tired, weary, or exasperated. Or perhaps you woke up in a bad mood, someone gave you a "look" you didn't like, or you just started your day off on the wrong foot. Then suddenly someone does something totally unexpected that you don't like — something that takes you off guard and by surprise — and negative thoughts begin to deluge your mind. That is usually a sign that Satan is trying to ensnare you and cut you off from the people you need most in your life.

There is no such thing as a perfect person and everyone has flaws — *including you.* If you are going to get upset every time someone says or does something beneath your expectations, you are going to live your life constantly bothered and frustrated. If you lose your peace every time someone doesn't do what you expect of him or her, you are going to end up living an up-and-down, roller-coaster existence.

Rather than focus on the flaws and faults of others, I have found it is much smarter to look in the mirror so the Holy Spirit can deal with *me* about *my responses* to situations that trouble me.

Although it was true that Dr. Bennett's treatment of me was excessive, that event showed something ugly about *me.* When I allowed a seed of offense to take root in my soul against him, it exposed my level of maturity that needed to be changed!

Could it be possible that recurring situations are actually exposing something inside *you* that needs to change?

## From Gratitude to Discontentment to Resentment

As the months passed, the offense in my soul started screaming that Fort Smith needed a loving pastor — a pastor like *me*! It was as if someone put a special set of glasses on me that wrongly colored everything I saw about Dr. Bennett.

God had given me incredible favor with this man by allowing me into his inner orbit. Dr. Bennett had graciously allowed me to shadow him almost everywhere he went. Every opportunity that presented itself, I was with him. I regularly and sincerely told people how much I loved and respected him and how great he was as a man of God. And like a mirror that can reflect someone else's glory, I began to shine in the eyes of others as I drew closer and closer to my pastor.

I was provided an environment where my teaching gift could begin to grow and flourish. It was absolutely amazing to see how God's gift in me began to flourish when I was allowed to come alongside that precious man who had taken me into his orbit — his sphere of influence.

But after that conflict, that offense began to worm its way into my heart. I forgot that I was becoming recognized and had started to shine because I was in my pastor's orbit. Instead of being grateful for the phenomenal opportunity that had been gifted to me, I began to think that the reason I was shining so brightly was that *I* was so amazing!

But the devil seized that moment to tell me, *Just look at all you are doing in comparison to everyone else.* Before long, I began comparing what I was doing with what others on the pastoral staff were doing. And when I realized I was being paid much less than the others, the devil began to additionally hit me with thoughts in the first-person, such as, *They're making five times more money than I'm making, and they're touching only a fraction of the people I'm touching. Surely I deserve more than I'm making!*

## A Hotel Room and a Chinese Fortune Cookie

As this pattern of thinking progressed, my gratitude turned to discontent and then to resentment. The devil constantly whispered negativity in my ears. He would say, *You are so abused! You are underpaid and unappreciated. The church keeps talking about its amazing growth, but no one has mentioned the fact that it's because of YOU!*

Again and again, I heard the hiss of this serpent inserting its venom into my mind. I didn't recognize the source of those thoughts then or realize what was happening, but the devil was using the open door created by my offense to insert his poisonous thinking into my mind: *Your pastor treats you like a slave. You carry his books, transport his luggage, mow his grass, clean his car — and for what? No appreciation and a meager salary! You are being so abused by this man!*

Before long, I lost my sense of gratitude for the position I had been given. Dr. Bennett — whom I'd so loved and respected — became the focus of my resentment. He had taken the risk of bringing me under his wings, had spent hundreds of hours with me personally discipling me, and had taught me what I needed to know to excel in ministry. But eventually I began to think, *I am more anointed than this man, and I deserve so much more than this.* I began to regularly ponder, *Maybe it's time for me to move on and start my own church.*

I finally told Denise, "I need to get away for a few days to be quiet and sort out how to deal with all the abuse I've endured at the hands of Dr. Bennett." Denise didn't think it was wise for me to do it, but I nevertheless decided to get a room at a hotel to be alone and try to really process everything I was thinking and feeling.

On my way to the hotel, I decided to stop for lunch at a Chinese restaurant. When the waiter brought me the bill, it came with a fortune cookie. So just for fun, I broke it open to read its contents. In that raw, emotional moment, I read, "You are about to receive a brand-new set of clothes."

It embarrasses me to tell it now, but I want you to understand the nature of offense and its destructive path. I normally would have *never* taken something seriously that I read in a fortune cookie. But in my offended state, it said exactly what I wanted to hear! I read it like this: "God is about to put a new pastoral mantle on you. You are about to receive a brand-new anointing to pastor your own church. If you leave Dr. Bennett, God will equip you with clothes — a new mantle — to start your own work!

It was ridiculous that I would believe such nonsense — that God would speak to me through a fortune cookie. But I was about to learn the hard lesson that when offense is working in a person's mind, it opens him to all kinds of deception. People who are deceived look for anything to affirm their feelings of offense — and that was what was happening to me! This is why James 3:14-16 says, "But if ye have bitter envying and strife in your hearts, glory not, and lie not against the truth. This wisdom descendeth not from above, but is earthly, sensual, devilish. For where envying and strife is, there is confusion and every evil work."

Once in my hotel room, I proceeded to write Dr. Bennett a nine-page, single-spaced letter to document everything I perceived to be wrong about him and why I felt he was not fit to be the pastor of his church. After he had poured his life into me, even if he hadn't been the easiest person to get along with and even though others thought he abused me, I still had no right to tell him all those things that I wrote in that letter. Among other things, I said, *"Dr. Bennett, you're like King Saul; you've lost the anointing and now God is looking for a David to take your place!"* No one deserved to be on the receiving end of what I wrote to him.

But because offense and deception had taken root in me, I couldn't see that I was the one who didn't deserve my position because of my attitude. I told him, "I'm leaving you!" Then I boldly announced that when I left, I would be taking all my people with me to start a new church!

When I recall what I put in that letter, it embarrasses me to this day. *What arrogance.* How could I ever think it was acceptable for me to address an older man of God in such a disrespectful tone? After all he had done to help Denise and me, I gave way to a "self-righteous" attitude and even inwardly justified that *someone* needed to confront his arrogance! If no one else was willing to do it, then I convinced myself that God wanted it to be *me!*

I am sure *some* of what I wrote in that letter was factual, but it was *not* my place to say it. And it was certainly ungodly to say it in the bitter, spewing, vitriolic manner in which I communicated it. The deacons of the church should have taken me behind a barn to whip me for what I wrote in that letter. I'm so glad I didn't save a copy of it.

### 'Demoted' to a Different Kind of Classroom

I didn't realize it, but I was about to be transferred to a different kind of classroom to learn the most humiliating lesson in my life to that moment. God wanted me to pass the test with Dr. Bennett, but I allowed my offense to remove me from the place of blessing.

There I was — a twenty-four-year-old young man with very little experience in the ministry who had been given a great opportunity by the man I was accusing — and *I* was reprimanding *him*. He had been serving as a pastor for forty years, and I had taken it upon myself to teach *him*! I was clueless that offense was blinding me to my own arrogance. This is why today I feel compassion toward younger people who do similar foolish things to their leaders. I did it when I was younger, and I personally know the consequences of such stupid actions.

I hadn't counted on the fact that I was missing it by a mile to write that scathing letter and to leave Dr. Bennett in such a wrong manner. I also hadn't counted on the fact that I had more than met my match by tangling with Dr. Bennett!

Dr. Bennett told me he wanted to tell the church of my intentions to leave and asked Denise and me to attend the service in which he would make the announcement. We sat on the front pew and listened as he told the entire church how we had slipped into pride and rebellion. I nearly wilted. Then he called us up to the pulpit. Paul was a baby, and Denise held him in her arms as we stood in front of the congregation. Denise and I stood behind the pulpit with him, and he prayed a prayer filled with rebuke and humiliation. Because all heads were bowed, I whispered to Denise, "Let's leave while he's still praying and no one sees that we are walking out."

So as he wrapped up his prayerful rebuke and repudiation of our actions, I took Denise by the hand, and with Paul in our arms, the three of us exited the side door of the auditorium — never to return there for many years.

### An Anguishing Experience With a Church
### God Never Told Me To Start

When we left the church, Denise and I took a small handful of single adults with us to start our own church, which we called *Fellowship of Believers*. We didn't know it, but starting our little church was the exact time that Denise and I stepped out of a classroom of real ministerial training into a *new* classroom where God would teach us some of the hardest lessons we had learned up till that moment.

We struggled to survive financially as we attempted to give birth to this new church. In the meanwhile, Dr. Bennett and First Baptist Church did wonderfully *without me*. I found myself pastoring a small group of people in a broken-down building in a poor part of town.

But for many who attended Fellowship of Believers in those years, that experience was like a slice of Heaven. God did many wonderful things in people's lives, yet it was an "Ishmael" experience for me because, even though God did marvelous things in people's lives, He never called me to start that little church. Yes, God did wonderful things in the church and lives were enriched. But like Abraham, who gave birth to Ishmael out of God's will and experienced all kinds of heartache in his life as a result, I was trying to do something God never asked me to do.

I want to make it absolutely clear that our misstep didn't mean that good things didn't happen in that small church. In fact, looking back, we can see that a lot of lives were changed during those years at Fellowship of Believers. People were saved, filled with the Spirit, healed, delivered — and many of the people from that church are still precious friends whom we love and who will be in our lives forever. And today there are people serving in ministry because of what God did in their lives in that little church. In God's economy, good was wrought because *God* is good. And He had a plan for those people's lives and wanted to teach them, bless them, and use *them* to point others to His loving plan for their own lives.

Wherever God is, great things come right along with Him, and He certainly showed up to manifest His greatness in our midst at Fellowship of Believers. So when I speak of veering off my personal course with the Lord because of my wrong actions and the wrong attitude of my heart, I am not at all overlooking the good that He did in those years. Nevertheless, it was a very difficult time for Denise and me.

## My Dark Personal Atmosphere of Disobedience and Offense

We started that little church in a strip mall in an abandoned location that had formerly been a school of cosmetology. It was in a dumpy part of town and had nearly no parking. It had a low ceiling, and scads of electrical outlets were scattered intermittently across the floor where cosmetologists had worked at their stations. We tried to dress it up, but it was really in a very sad condition.

I was embarrassed to invite people to come to church there, and often when I met newcomers at the door, I would immediately start apologizing for the dreadful condition of the interior of our building. The stage was only one step high, the back wall of the platform was covered with cheap burgundy material, the best we could afford to buy, and we had to set up our second-hand metal folding chairs in a certain pattern so people wouldn't trip over electrical outlets that were sticking up out of the floor everywhere. The rooms for the children's department on the backside of the building were separated by particle boards that we covered with small carpet samples that we got from Denise's parents' store in Miami, Oklahoma.

The offerings were barely enough to pay the rent on the building, let alone any salaries, so there was little money to pay anyone for their work. Our precious full-time team members worked so hard for hours and hours with little to no pay.

Furthermore, when Denise and I walked away from First Baptist Church, it also meant we had to leave our lovely little carriage house where we had been living for two years. We found ourselves moving from one rent house to the next — including one that had no heat. We had so little money — and a little baby boy that needed to be fed — that one dear man who felt sorry for us regularly brought groceries to our house so we would have something to eat. I usually put only one dollar's worth of fuel at a time into the tank of our gas-guzzling car — my biggest faith-filled prayers had become that we could drive on fumes until I got another dollar to put more gas in the tank. And my faith didn't work too well in that regard. One week I ran out of gas *five times* and had to call on others to help me!

Denise and I eventually moved into a two-story house with a basement in the historic district of Fort Smith. That house was so old, built right after the Civil War, that it still had a carriage step near the street that former own-ers had used to get into their carriages.

A precious couple from our church, who are still our dear friends, had come forward to help us purchase this "historic" house. They believed in us and wanted to help us. But the condition of the house was pretty atrocious.

The house had windows with scads of tiny triangle-shaped panes, and when we first moved into it, many of those panes were either broken or missing! So to try to stay warm during our first winter and protect ourselves from the wind and elements, Denise and I stuffed clothing through all those broken panes.

Even worse, the window frames were so eaten by termites that the mere pressure of the tip of a finger could shatter those wood frames completely. The whole wooden frame of that house was so devoured by termites that the brick fireplace in the central room on the first floor "leaned" significantly. The termite damage in the basement had caused the wooden beams between floors to decay and crumble, which is what caused the fireplace to tilt.

Our first winter there, the kitchen had no heat whatsoever. But Denise and I were thankful for that because we couldn't afford to purchase a refrigerator. So in the first year we lived there, we lived without a refrigerator and never had food products that needed refrigeration. But when winter came, the kitchen was so cold, we could finally buy goods that needed to be refrigerated. We simply put them on the kitchen shelves because the room was literally *freezing*.

This was a problem on especially cold winter mornings, though, because the milk we needed for our little boy was frozen solid in the kitchen cabinets, and we'd have to warm it up on the stove in order to feed him. One night it got so cold in the kitchen that the pipes in the house broke. We were unaware of it because we were sleeping on the second floor. In the morning, I heard our little dog yelping, so I rushed downstairs to see what all the commotion was about. As I entered the kitchen, I started to slide across the room because the kitchen floor was completely covered with a sheet of ice! The dog, too, had come running into the room and had similarly slid across the room, slamming into the wall on the other side. By the time I arrived, the dog was shaken up and shivering in the corner of the kitchen!

It seemed even our toilet was cursed. It had somehow been connected to the hot-water tank, which meant it was filled with steaming hot water. That was good news for Denise and me because the second floor of the house didn't have much heat. The toilet was the only place where Denise and I could get warm, so we went to the toilet often — not because we needed to, but because it was the only place where we could get warmed up! But because the toilet was connected to a limited supply of hot water in the hot-water tank in the basement, after a couple of flushes, the tank was emptied! We'd have to wait for the hot-water tank to refill and reheat the water before we could go back to taking turns sitting on the toilet to warm ourselves.

*Whew...* I shiver with amazement just remembering the conditions we were living in at that time!

We moved into that house hoping we could restore it. But it was delusional to think that house could be restored on the meager money we had to live on at that time. Even the back wall of our closet on the second floor had no wall — yes, it was completely exposed to the climate! I hung heavy plastic across the exposed portion to keep snow and rain out of the closet and therefore out of our bedroom. If you can recall the old TV program *Green Acres* and how one part of their house on the farm had no wall, you can picture what our open-air closet looked like!

The house was actually a safety hazard. All the termite-infested baseboards, window frames, and window sills were covered with lead paint so dangerous that social workers came to see what the city could do to help. Finally, city authorities approved us for a grant to remove the lead paint from the entire house and to repaint those areas.

We had nearly no money for food, clothes, or toys and necessities for our little boy. When we finally scraped together enough money to buy a gift for Paul's second birthday, we were only able to buy a used toy at a downtown secondhand store that was really a charity-run store to help poorer people.

My sister Ronda and her husband John had moved to Tulsa by this time. They came back to visit us once so they could see where we were living and to experience our little church. When Ronda walked into the house, she wanted to sound positive as she told us the house had a lot of potential, but I noticed she kept secretly wiping away tears from her eyes. She later told me that she was stunned to see us living in such destitute conditions.

## Poverty, Brokenness, and Our 'Blended' Church Family — Reality Was Setting In

When I say that we had a "menagerie" of people — from business owners to social outcasts — attending our church, I am not exaggerating. While we love everyone as Jesus commands us to do, it would have been nice to have a few more "normal" folks in addition to the growing category of atypical people who felt called to be part of our church family.

Every week we waited to see who would show up — some really excited us and some nearly made me despair. A few professional folks joined us, including a hospital administrator, a car-dealership owner, a realtor, a lawyer, and an accountant. Those folks were so supportive as we tried to launch our little church. They became some of our best friends and we are still in relationship with them today. There were also some singles who really loved us and came with us from our department at the First Baptist Church, and some of those became cherished friends as well. *Then* there was the category of those who were considered social outcasts. I'm talking about extremely poor people and even quite a number who were demonized and mentally ill.

We thankfully had some really solid people, but we also had some who were so filthy dirty that they stank — *badly*. Denise and I felt so sorry for a few of them, and we took them into our home for a while to teach them how to shower and wash their clothes. But as soon as they left our house, it looked and smelled like they returned to living like a walking pigpen. I wish I was embellishing as I share this part of my story, but this is absolutely the way it was back in those days.

Denise and I slowly began to make friends, some of whom happened to be in as bad a financial shape as we were. On weekends when none of us had enough food to feed our families, we would call each other to see what leftovers each family had — then we'd meet at one of our homes so we could mix all our leftovers together into some kind of soup. We'd eat together with thankful hearts because we had something to eat.

It seemed the madness of it all would never stop! Denise and I were learning firsthand yet another lesson in the classroom of life — that *poverty is a curse!*

We made some precious friends during that time in our lives. They were God-sent people who were bright spots for us amidst the dark backdrop that Denise and I were experiencing. We shared some good times and had many moments of fun and laughter together. They were beloved team members who were real lifesavers to us, unbeknownst to them. They needed us as spiritual leaders — but truth be told, we needed them just as much as they needed us.

What made all of this even harder for me personally was, our dilapidated house was on the same street as First Baptist Church, which meant I had to pass that church every time I drove home. When I passed that magnificent church building and realized that it had gone marvelously on without me — and that we were suffering financially beyond what I could have ever imagined possible — it was like torture in my soul that never ceased. I remembered the blessing I'd walked away from when I allowed that seed of offense to grow in my heart toward Dr. Bennett, and I wondered, *Is THIS the ultimate plan of God for our lives?*

Well, I am convinced it *wasn't* the plan of God for our lives. And Denise and I were not blessed due to the fact we had stepped into a wrong place in ministry that had been born in a season of my resentment and offense. I urge you that if you are ever tempted to leave a place of blessing because you're offended, *don't do it!*

### More Threats Against Our Lives — We Had To Go Into Hiding!

One day a newcomer at church asked for an appointment to discuss her struggling marriage. I met with her in the presence of our church secretary, and she told me that her husband had said that when he came home that evening, he was going to kill her. As she talked, I heard her tell me that he had already stabbed her in the back with a butcher knife. She said he had tried to kill her on *multiple* occasions, but she'd never pressed charges because she loved him and wanted the marriage to work.

But now she was asking me, "Knowing that my husband stabbed me with a butcher knife not too long ago, and he has told me that he is going to shoot me tonight, do you think I should go home and hope for the best, or would it be better for me to go stay with my mother tonight?" I answered her, "Well, based on his past actions, you might be better off to let him know you will be staying with your mother tonight."

I was shocked when she walked out of my office, picked up the church telephone, called her husband, and said to him in my hearing, "Rick Renner told me to divorce you and make sure you never see our son again!"

I never said anything like that, but when he heard what she said, I heard him screaming through the receiver, "Hand Rick Renner the telephone so I can say something to him!" Before I could tell him I didn't tell her those things, he was so out of control that he yelled, "Mr. Renner, you're going to be sorry you met with my wife today because now I'm going to use my gun to kill you, your wife, *and* your little boy!"

That event started a months-long drama in our lives. This man called me hundreds of times to make death threats against me and my family. He would call during the day, during the evenings, and in the middle of the night. The phone rang so often — and was filled on the other end of the line with so much of his wrath, rantings, and ravings — that I feared to answer the phone at night.

After the phone would ring twenty-five times or more, with my not knowing if it was a church member in trouble or this stalker, I would finally answer to hear his voice as he laughed like a madman. He'd say, "What's wrong with you tonight, preacher? Seems like you're afraid to answer the phone. I'll be over to see you in a few minutes. And, by the way, I'll be bringing my friend with me — a shotgun that I'm going to use to kill you and your family. See you soon!"

I called the police department time and time again for help, but every time they repeatedly told me, "Mr. Renner, we can't take any form of action until he actually tries something!" I said, "*What?!!* When he tries something, it may be too late!" But they stood firm that they could take no legal action until he actually tried to harm us. So Denise and I, along with Paul, moved out of our house for a time and went into hiding in a friend's basement in a nearby town.

But this madman found us *even there*!

We decided this was so serious that we needed to begin recording his phone calls. We filled many cassette tapes with his threatening calls. Finally, I told him, "I'm recording these calls, and I'm going to the District Attorney to discuss what you're doing." He answered, "Tell the District Attorney I'm going to blow his head off too!"

I threw all those cassette tapes into a brown paper sack and went to see the District Attorney in downtown Fort Smith to once more plead for help. The District Attorney told me what the police had said — that there was nothing they could do until he actually tried to harm us.

Exasperated by his seeming unwillingness to help, I turned that paper sack upside down and dumped all twenty cassette tapes onto the top of his desk. I said, "I'm not leaving until you listen to one of these tapes to see what we are dealing with every day of our lives."

I watched as the District Attorney randomly selected one of the tapes and slipped it into his tape machine. To my amazement, he chose the very tape in which the man had said, "Tell the District Attorney I'm going to blow his head off too!"

What would be the odds that this DA would randomly select that very tape and start it at that very moment? But when he heard that, he said, "Now *this* is prosecutable. It is a felony to threaten to murder a District Attorney! By threatening me, this changes everything." Soon the man was apprehended and placed in jail, and the whole test and trial came to a grinding halt.

During this entire period we called our "Ishmael" experience, nutty things happened to us, it felt like we had no protection, and we experienced little financial provision. And I had a serious wake-up call when I realized that it was my offense that had driven us into this terrible, two-year wilderness.

I called a dear friend in Canada and told him our desperate condition. He asked me to come visit him for a week. I couldn't afford a ticket, so my daddy got me a non-revenue ticket with his benefits at American Airlines, and I went to see my friend in Canada for a week. While there, far away from the mire of our lives, the fog cleared in my mind, and I really woke up to the fact that I had wronged Dr. Bennett — that when I left him, I left offended, that I was living in disobedience, and that it was time for Denise and me to get back into God's perfect will for our lives.

When I came home, I told Denise, "We should have never started this church. I don't know what we should have done, but the way I left Dr. Bennett was wrong and I should have never started this church. I don't know how to get back into God's plan, but I have to resign and take some time to clearly hear what God's next step is for our lives. I'm not making another serious mistake like this one again."

## The Hardest Phone Call I've Ever Made

God began to deal with me about contacting Dr. Bennett to ask for forgiveness. But sometimes there is a lapse between knowing what you're supposed to do and actually doing it. I can testify to that fact because it took me a long time to contact Dr. Bennett even though I knew it was what I needed to do.

During that lapse of time when I knew that I needed to contact Dr. Bennett, I was in a Christian bookstore one day looking at books on a back row in the store. I heard the front door of the shop open, and whose voice do you suppose I heard? *Dr. Bennett's.* I had not seen him for two years and now I was trapped in the same space with him. I was *terrified.*

Instead of going to him right then to ask for forgiveness, I looked for a place to hide. I found an empty shelf under a row of books and crawled under it so he wouldn't know I was in the store with him. I sweated with perspiration, fretting that he might see me hiding. *If he saw me hiding under a row of books, what would I look like to him? What would I say to him if he saw me there?* I waited as he looked at books until, finally, he bade the manager of the store farewell and left. I crawled out from the bookshelf shaken, embarrassed, and disappointed by my ridiculous behavior.

I heard the Holy Spirit whisper, *How long are you going to hide from what you need to do? When are you going to repent and tell Dr. Bennett you're sorry?* More time passed — and then one day the Holy Spirit spoke loud and clear: *Your ministry is ON HOLD until you make things right with Dr. Bennett!*

Overwhelming embarrassment and humiliation gripped my heart as I dialed Dr. Bennett's phone number to start the conversation. I wondered, *How will he respond when he hears my voice? Will he hang up on me? How will he respond to my request for forgiveness?* I can tell you that as much as I wanted to be unburdened and freed to move on with my ministry, nothing in me really wanted to make that call. But I knew that calling Dr. Bennett was essential if I was going to move on with God's plan for our lives.

When he answered, I blurted out the words, "Dr. Bennett, I have so wronged you. I sinned against you and the entire church. I'm so sorry. I am repenting for it. I am asking you to please forgive me."

He immediately answered, "Rick, I forgive you." Then he continued, "I forgave you when it happened because I loved you so much. Rick, I did more for you than I've ever done for anyone else. I believed in you and gave you opportunities I've never given to anyone. I treated you like a son and you paid me back by hurting me more than anyone has ever hurt me. But I forgave you long ago."

What he said was true — he had loved me like a son. Yet I had allowed offense to affect me so much that I actually led an insurrection against this gracious man who had allowed me into his orbit and mentored me. I did what *Absalom did to David,* what *Judas did to Jesus,* and what *Lucifer did to God.* But by the grace of God, I not only asked for his forgiveness and received it, but our relationship was so restored that we remained precious friends and we financially supported him to the end of his life. I loved him like a father, and I will be forever thankful for all this precious man poured into me — and I look forward to being with him forever in eternity!

One staff member from that time in our lives said, "When so many people rebel against authority, they never come back to ask for forgiveness and make things right, but Rick apologized and ended up having a beautiful relationship with Dr. Bennett until the end of Dr. Bennett's life."

My heartfelt repentance and apology to Dr. Bennett was about doing the right thing and getting unstuck in life so we could proceed with what the Lord wanted Denise and me to do for Him. But my making things right with the man I'd so wronged also witnessed to others of the grace of God and made a lasting positive impression on them as well. And it brought restoration to my relationship with Dr. Bennett, a relationship that God had given to me and that I had foolishly forsaken.

I found it interesting that Dr. Bennett never apologized to me. However, I never seriously grappled with that. It was all right with me because all I'm certain of is that God was dealing with *me* about *my* attitude. In other words, that phone call was not about Dr. Bennett's apologizing to me. It was for the sole purpose of my apologizing to him because I needed to get things right with him. Most importantly, I needed to do what God was asking me to do. To this day I am convinced that if I hadn't humbled myself to make that call and ask for forgiveness, Denise and I would have stayed stuck in one place and never moved into God's blessing and the fulfillment of our divine destiny and calling.

Never forget that if you've missed the mark in some area and deviated from God's plan, He requires you to do what is right before you can move to the next phase in your life.

I share this experience only because I want you to know the toxic ramifications of offense. I can personally testify that if *you* have been ensnared by offense, it will have terrible ramifications. As is true in my story, God offers forgiveness to you or to anyone who acknowledges the wrong he or she has done. If you're willing to repent and seek forgiveness from those you've wronged — *regardless* of what wrong they've done — God is so gracious that He can bring healing and restoration into even the most breached relationships. He will likewise help you get back on track with His plan for your life.

## We Stepped Out of Our Black-and-White World
## Into a Full-Color Spectrum

In those years at our little Fellowship of Believers church, *God used us in spite of us!* But Denise and I were *not* blessed in the way we were living. We were miserable and poor beyond my ability to exaggerate. It may be difficult for you to believe that we actually lived in such dire, destitute conditions — but we *did*. And it wasn't just us — our team who started the church with us was in the same plight!

But we learned that if you ever get so far off track that you don't know how to get back on track, God will help you if you'll ask Him and then obediently follow His leading as He redirects you. I finally woke up to my misstep and repented for making it. *But what next? What should we do now?* I asked. *Prolong our misery by staying there? Resign? Go somewhere else so our minds could clear and hear God's Spirit speak a new directive? What were we supposed to do next?*

If we left, I wondered what would happen to the people we loved in our little church. We didn't want them to feel abandoned, yet we began *to know* it was time for us to leave Arkansas. Those five years in Arkansas were a classroom that taught us *what to do* and *what never to do* in ministry. But now it was time to go somewhere else and start over. So Denise and I stood in front of our church to resign and appoint another pastor. Then we started the process to move. But we didn't know where to go — except *home to Sand Springs!*

I called my parents and we had a heart-to-heart conversation. I asked if we could temporarily move into their house with them. I had left Sand Springs at the age of seventeen — and now I was returning at the age of twenty-seven with a wife, a little boy named Paul, and another baby, *our middle son Philip*, on the way! Daddy and Mother were gracious as always and welcomed us to come home!

What began as wonderful in my Arkansas journey turned dark and difficult, and our final years there were really tough. Still it was hard to say goodbye to our friends and to start over somewhere else. When our precious friends asked us what we were going to do, we couldn't clearly answer them. Every answer we tried to give them sounded uncertain and inadequate because we simply weren't sure yet. We simply knew it was time to make the break and start over again. When we finally left Fort Smith, we had learned a lot of hard lessons — and we purposed never to step into that particular kind of classroom ever again!

Although Denise and I knew we were supposed to leave Fort Smith, leaving was hard to do, which is why I understand how difficult it is for people to step out in faith to obey God. Even if they're living in not-so-good conditions, those conditions are what they know and are familiar with. Breaking free to do something new means they must release what they have and what they've been surrounded with. Some are so afraid to let go and move on that they stay stuck for the rest of their lives. I was determined that was not going to happen to us.

I am so thankful that God enabled Denise and me to do whatever was needed in order to hear His voice for the next phase of our lives and ministry. The leap of faith He was requiring us to take was certainly not the last bridge He would take us over in the course of our lives. But if we had not been willing to cross *that* bridge, we would have never been able to touch the countless lives that have since been impacted by our ministry. Seeing God's faithfulness as we crossed that difficult bridge encouraged us later to obey Him when He would ask us to leave the United States to move our family to the Soviet Union!

The day finally came when we attached our tiny U-Haul trailer to our car to start the 120-mile trip from Fort Smith to Sand Springs. We didn't have many belongings because we'd had a yard sale to raise money for our big move to Oklahoma. We sold nearly everything, including all but one of our wedding gifts — a casserole dish, which we still have today. We left Arkansas with nearly nothing — just me, Denise who was pregnant with Philip, and Paul. We ventured into our new life with our gas-guzzling car that pulled a small U-Haul behind us. That was everything we had, plus a few dollars to pay for gasoline and tolls to get to Sand Springs.

I've been talking about figurative bridges that take us from one place to another when God is leading us into the next phase in His plan for our lives. But when Denise and I physically drove across the bridge from Arkansas into Oklahoma, something interesting happened. The split-second we passed the Arkansas-Oklahoma border — which is right in the middle of the bridge over the Arkansas River — it was like the heavens opened for us. We both sensed something lift from us — *we left a black-and-white world and entered a full-colored spectrum!*

In a flash, Denise and I both felt things breaking off of us. I turned to her right in the middle of that bridge and said, "Sweetheart, God has instantly changed me. He is going to open doors to use us and bless us — and we are entering a new phase of life that is going to be marvelous! And I will be an excellent money manager from this moment forward!"

## A Question Never Answered

A logical question could be asked, "In retrospect, how do you think you *should* have left the First Baptist Church?" The short answer is, I have no idea. But my lack of an answer has never been an issue for me because one day when I see Jesus, He'll show me how I should have done some of those things differently.

But one thing I know for sure is that my offense opened the door for a two-year wilderness that God never planned for our lives. And along with Denise and Paul, I took several hundred precious people along with us into that wilderness.

I want to reiterate that God did wonderful things in those two years at Fellowship of Believer's Church. But that doesn't change the fact that I know it was not God's will for me to make all those mistakes. Yet over the years, I've realized that the experiences in that classroom in Fort Smith have been beneficial to us and to our ministry. And I'm certainly grateful for the relationships we had there, as well as everything we learned from that time in our lives.

Even those who attended Fellowship of Believers mostly remember good times. While preparing to write this book, we interviewed many of them. They still relish their memories from those years. We still love each other and hold our relationships as dear. Janey Spencer, Dr. Bennett's secretary, was interviewed in her elderly years, and she only recalled a precious relationship between Dr. Bennett and me.

The blood of Jesus is so powerful. Once His blood was applied to that situation, it washed the slate clean, and people generally remember the good times and not our many mistakes.

Sometimes people are paralyzed by not knowing answers to issues of the past while God is endeavoring to simply give them the grace to move forward. Someday God will show all of us how we could have done some things differently.

So don't be disturbed if you don't always know the reason for everything that happens or what should have been done differently. What's important is that if you have made a mistake and you've gotten off track, repent and get back on track again.

My own testimony is that at a young age, I moved to Fort Smith, Arkansas, to sit under the finest, most anointed teaching from the New Testament I had ever heard. My heart was hooked, and what I learned there became the foundation for my teaching ministry today. It was there that I also married my beautiful bride Denise Roberson Renner, who has fulfilled this calling alongside me ever since. I simply could not have realized the success in ministry that I've experienced without her love and respect, her constant belief in me, and her own heart of complete surrender to God's will.

As Denise and I crossed that Arkansas River Bridge, heading to Oklahoma with our little boy Paul, we were filled with faith and vision for the future. We had been trained in the classroom of life and were ready to follow Jesus wherever He would lead us — *with* a right heart as we were doing it!

But during those years in Fort Smith, we had been totally out of contact with the rest of the Charismatic world. Because we had been limited in our exposure, we really didn't know anyone beyond that small sphere and, similarly, no one knew us. While the odds said it would be *unlikely* that our lives would turn around, God was about to show us how the odds can be beaten when you obey Him.

We were about to experience an *amazing* turnaround in our lives!

# 7

# AN UNLIKELY TURNAROUND

The split-second Denise and I and our son Paul passed the Arkansas-Oklahoma border on our way "home" to Sand Springs, it was as if all of Heaven opened to us. It felt as if we had left a black-and-white world and entered a full-colored spectrum. It was a spiritual experience in which we were instantly changed, as I described in the last chapter. The Spirit of God breathed upon us anew on that beautiful spring day in 1985, and *we came alive!* There was such a newness about us — we were filled with fresh hope for the future, *whatever* that future entailed in God's master plan for our lives.

As I also shared, my parents graciously allowed us to move into their house for a time as we regained our footing on God's path for Denise and me and our growing family. When we arrived in Sand Springs at the home of Ronald and Erlita Renner, we received a warm, open-arms welcome and quickly put most of what remained of our belongings in their garage.

---

**Left and Above:** *Downtown, Tulsa, Oklahoma, 1980s.* © *Tulsa Historical Society & Museum.*

As we began settling in, my parents were curious and of course asked us, "What do you plan to do now?" Although I was so filled with hope and confidence concerning the future, I didn't know how to answer them because the next step was not clear to me yet. So I asked them to give me some time to pray about it. While we waited on the Lord extensively that first month, we began attending Grace Fellowship Church, Tulsa's largest church at that time, which was pastored by Bob Yandian.

In those days, there were not a lot of large influential churches like there are today. A church of five hundred people was considered very large back then, but Grace Fellowship had several thousand members and was one of the most strategic hubs for believers in that region of the country at the time. My sister Ronda and her husband John had already moved to Tulsa from Fort Smith and attended and served there, so Denise and I decided we would join them for services every Sunday and Wednesday.

Pastor Bob was a masterful Bible teacher, and he stood out among other pastors because of his remarkable teaching gift. Like me, Bob was also a Tulsan. As a child, he attended a Pentecostal church with an emphasis on grace. His wife, Loretta, also grew up Pentecostal and attended a church that was minutes down the street from where we lived on the Sand Springs Line when I was young. Her pastor actually lived in a house directly across the street from ours. At that time, Tulsa was inundated with ministers moving there because of the influential role of Oral Roberts University and Rhema Bible Training College. But Bob and Loretta were among the few who were "homegrown," and because of that, I felt drawn to them.

It's interesting to note that years earlier, I had gone to Pastor Bob for counsel about how to handle difficult moments with Dr. Bennett — and now we were back in the Tulsa area sitting under him as our pastor. I was especially drawn to Pastor Bob's style of verse-by-verse teaching from the Bible. He dug deep into every verse and extracted marvelous truths that fed his congregation well. The growth of Grace Fellowship was proof that people were hungry for that type of teaching. Every week, Denise and I came with wide-open hearts as we searched for God's next directive for our lives. We were determined not to make a single move until it was clear what He wanted us to do next.

### *Finally* — New Direction

One Sunday, a special speaker named Ed Dufresne spoke at the church. Because Denise and I had been living remotely in Arkansas for several years, we had never heard of Ed Dufresne. But our thoughts were that if Pastor Bob felt the church needed to hear him, we wanted to be there to receive whatever he had to impart to the congregation. I honestly cannot tell you the whole message Ed ministered that night, because he made *one statement* that shot to the very core of my being and stayed there! I heard him say, "If you don't know what to do, it's time to return to the original call God first gave you."

That statement gave me my directive. I was to return to the original call God gave me to exegetically teach from the Greek New Testament to hungry hearts everywhere. When we walked out of the meeting that Sunday night, we knew God had given us what we needed to start moving forward. Returning to my parent's house that night, I told them we were going to start traveling in a teaching ministry. My daddy said, "Son, that's great. But since no one has a clue who you are, how do you intend to get started?" His question didn't bother me because it was also my question — yet I knew that somehow God would open doors for us and make a way.

In the following weeks, Denise and I officially joined Grace Fellowship so we'd have a home church for our family, plus accountability to a spiritual leader. I asked for an appointment to meet with Pastor Bob, and he graciously made time for me. At that appointment, I told him of our plans to start a teaching ministry that we would call *Rick Renner Ministries*. He asked me nearly the same question my daddy had asked me, "Since no one knows who you are, how do you intend to get started? Do you have any idea how hard it is to get into traveling ministry when you're unknown?"

I asked if he would consider writing a letter of endorsement for me. He reluctantly said he would do it. I say "reluctant" because he had never heard me teach before. But because he knew and loved my sister and brother-in-law, he decided to write me a letter of recommendation. Pastor Bob later said, "Rick asked me to give him a recommendation, but it was very hard to do because I really didn't know him. I'd known his sister for quite a while, so because *she* recommended him, I decided to write the letter based on what I knew about her and not about him."

When I received his letter of recommendation, I could see that it said almost nothing about me. But, really, what *could* he have honestly said? He didn't have any experience with me.

I'll paraphrase how that letter read:

> Today I am writing this letter on behalf of Rick Renner. I don't know him very well, but his sister and brother-in-law are outstanding members of our church. His sister is the pianist in our music ministry. As a couple, John and Ronda are in good standing with the church. They are faithful in everything they do, and we love them very much. Rick is Ronda's brother. — *Pastor Bob Yandian*

When I received his endorsement letter, I realized that I had put him in a tough position in asking him to write a letter for me when he really didn't know me and had never heard me teach. But I was grateful for his clumsy, albeit honest, attempt to recommend me. Looking back on it, if I had been Pastor Bob, I would have *never* written that letter. But he did it — and he did it as well as he honestly could — because I was Ronda's brother.

### The Earliest Meetings of Rick Renner Ministries

I knew that in order to venture out as a valid ministry, we needed to be legally registered, so I contacted a Tulsa attorney to register the name "Rick Renner Ministries." The cost of registration was $500. That amount was a mountain to me, so Daddy offered to pay the bill. It was a huge contribution for him and Mother, and I was thankful that they believed in us and wanted to pitch in to help us.

Registering Rick Renner Ministries was the first step in our new season of ministry. Then Kenny and Tracey Taylor, old friends from Glenwood Baptist Church who had also ventured out to find more of the Holy Spirit, heard that Denise and I were starting our teaching ministry. So they called us to ask if we would be willing to speak to a group of people in their living room one evening.

Of course, we were going to step through every open door, and that meeting was an open door. So on the night of our first small meeting, we swung by and picked up my Grandma Ettie and took her with us as we drove to the very first meeting of our brand-new ministry called Rick Renner Ministries.

The crowd that night consisted of Kenny and Tracy, Grandma Ettie, and Denise and me — *a whopping crowd of five!* I taught on the Holy Spirit and then we all spent time praying together. The Taylors handed us a check, which I *think* was for the amount of $25. It was the first official offering ever given to Rick Renner Ministries!

Denise said, "I had made the commitment to follow Rick anywhere, and I was serious about that commitment. Paul was small, I was pregnant with Philip, and we had no income. I didn't know how God was going to provide for this new ministry. Although I was committed in my mind to follow Rick, I wanted my heart to be all in as well. So I went to the Lord and said to Him, 'You have to help me because I am afraid.'

"A few days later, I was in a worship service in Tulsa, and as we all prayed together in the Spirit, I happened to look down at my feet, and right then, the Holy Spirit spoke a *rhema* word to me. He knew the fear that was coming against me, and He responded to it by saying, *I do direct the steps of a righteous man.*"

Denise responded quickly, "All right, Lord, I receive this word into my heart." She said, "It was in that exact moment that all fear left me, and I was not only following Rick with my head, but my heart was now one-hundred-percent involved to help him develop this new ministry that God was leading him to start. The role of a wife is very important for the success of her husband. She can either 'make him or break him' with her support or her *lack* of support. I was determined to support Rick as he followed the voice of God."

Soon afterward, another invitation came, and we were invited to speak at a home Bible study and, of all places, it was back in Arkansas! Denise and I drove to a small town called Danville and ministered to a handful of people — again, in someone's living room. But in that small group was a minister named Walter Gorman, who pastored a church about thirty miles away in Booneville, Arkansas. After I taught, Pastor Gorman said, "That teaching was amazing! Can you guys come minister at my church in Booneville? I'd like you to do two Sunday services and then stay to do a Monday-night service too." Denise and I were *thrilled* for another open door, and we joyfully said yes to his invitation to do those three meetings.

Two weeks later, Denise and Paul and I drove from Sand Springs to Booneville for our meeting. Because I was embarrassed for anyone to see this "faith preacher" driving such a horrible car as ours, I decided we'd arrive one hour early and park the car far enough away that no one would see us getting out of it. But we were so early that no one was at the church when we arrived, and the doors were still locked, so when people arrived, they saw us sitting in the parking lot in our embarrassing car. So much for trying to hide the vehicle we were driving!

Denise and I poured ourselves into that little church for three services. Denise sang as if she was standing on the stage of the Metropolitan Opera Company in New York City. I taught as if I was on the platform at a huge convention. Since they had tape-recording equipment, I seized the opportunity to produce our first recorded series — a three-part series on "Spiritual Armor." For three services, I exegeted nearly every word from Ephesians 6:10-18. The early messages in those services eventually became the primitive materials that I later developed into my bestselling book *Dressed To Kill — A Biblical Approach to Spiritual Warfare and Armor.*

At the conclusion of the Sunday morning service, I called people to the altar for the laying on of hands for healing and for a fresh touch of God's power. Denise and I ministered to them together, side by side. The Holy Spirit moved and people were healed, delivered, and filled with the Spirit. Gifts of the Spirit operated, including unusual words of knowledge that were so accurate, it electrified the crowd. Because of what happened in the prayer line in the first meeting, the Sunday-night crowd nearly doubled — and by Monday night, the place was almost packed.

Pastor Gorman encouraged me, "Rick, you have an amazing gift to teach and you need a teaching-tape ministry. I want to encourage you to start putting your messages on tape so you can make them available to people. There aren't many ministers out there teaching from the Greek like you're doing, and these teachings on tape will really feed people."

Pastor Gorman is in Heaven now, but I credit him as the one who encouraged me to make my teaching materials available in audio form. God really worked in that little church in Booneville, and today our teachings have gone into all the world as a result.

Seeds of strength and encouragement were being sown into our hearts through this precious man of God — and through our own hands as we began to distribute my teachings via cassette tape. It was a small beginning, but it was a crucial time of ministry in our lives. Booneville, Arkansas, was a significant event in our journey for which we will always be so grateful.

Soon we received an invitation to speak at a small church in Vinita, Oklahoma. I couldn't believe we were going to be ministering there, because Vinita was the notorious location of Oklahoma's biggest psychiatric hospital. When we were kids, if anyone behaved strangely, we'd tease him or her by saying, "We're going to send you to Vinita!" Now Denise and I were really headed to Vinita, not to the psychiatric hospital, but to a small church that was hungry for the deeper teaching of the Bible and a move of the Holy Spirit.

Because Vinita was only a few miles from where Denise's parents lived in Miami, we stayed with them and drove back and forth from her parents' home to the meetings. In those five meetings that ran Sunday through Wednesday, I taught a series called, "How You Can Heal the Sick." I went through all the Gospels and exegetically taught from every place where the word "healing" was used. Although that was in the earliest stages of our traveling teaching ministry, we still use those early principles of healing as we pray for the sick today.

Success in the plan of God for one's life often happens through a series of small breakthroughs — and sometimes through even more subtle changes that can be almost undetectable at times. Denise and I were simply grateful for *everything* — for every blessing in our lives, big and small. At every small turn, we acknowledged Him and His goodness in our lives, and we were just so thankful every single day.

Then a big breakthrough occurred when the pastor of the First Assembly of God Church in Miami, Oklahoma, asked us to minister in their Sunday morning and evening services. Gerald Baser had been the pastor there for years and knew Denise because she had grown up in Miami. When he heard we were starting a teaching ministry, he asked us to come do a day of services. First Assembly had about five hundred people in regular attendance, and to us, this was a huge open door. It would be the biggest crowd we had ever ministered in front of at that time. Denise and I arrived at that meeting with fear and trembling because we were going to be ministering to such a huge church.

In those two services, I preached the message, "The Communion of the Holy Spirit" based on Second Corinthians 13:14, and Denise sang like an anointed diva. At the conclusion of the morning service, I called for people to come forward who wanted a new touch of the Spirit in their lives. Denise and I were *speechless* at the response because it looked like the whole church had come to the front for the laying on of hands. Pastor Baser was ecstatic!

When the services concluded that day, Pastor Baser gave us an offering of $500! It was the largest offering we had received in our new ministry.

### 'Though Thy Beginning Was Small,<br>Yet Thy Latter End Should Greatly Increase'

That offering of $500 enabled us to move from my parents' house into our own apartment — a small three-room apartment on the second floor of a large old house located directly behind the old headquarters of Oral Roberts Evangelistic Association (OREA) in downtown Tulsa. Our rent was $350 per month, but because that amount was too much for us to pay at once, our landlord worked out a deal for us to pay it in two monthly payments of $175 to make it easier to manage.

Although OREA had moved to Oral Roberts University by that time, every day when I'd drive past that old OREA building, it reminded me that even Oral's ministry had a smaller beginning. The Holy Spirit regularly brought to my remembrance Job 8:7, which says, "Though thy beginning was small, yet thy latter end should greatly increase." Our beginning seemed really small, but I was convinced we were doing what God wanted us to do and that He wanted to use us mightily.

Our three-room apartment had a *tiny* kitchen, a *tiny* living room, a *tiny* bedroom, a *tiny* bathroom, and a *tiny* porch! But having that *tiny* apartment meant we could move out of my parents' house. It was *our* apartment, and we were so thankful for it! We had no furniture, but a few people pitched in to give us some second-hand furniture. We used the enclosed porch as Paul's bedroom, but it was too small for a bed, so he slept on a folding cot.

Because we were starting a teaching-tape ministry, my Aunt Melita offered to give us her tape-duplicating machine that duplicated three cassette tapes at a time. I was so excited to own a tape duplicator and was thankful to Aunt Melita for giving it to us. But we needed a typewriter to type the tape labels, so I figured out a way to finance a $500 typewriter, which we purchased and kept on a desk in our small living room. I duplicated cassette tapes on the kitchen counter and typed labels in the living room.

By that time, I was already duplicating *hundreds* of teaching tapes because people who attended our meetings were starting to request my teaching materials. We couldn't afford to hire employees, so I was the *secretary* who typed all the letters sent to pastors who requested information about us. I was the *production person* who duplicated cassette teaching tapes with labels.

And when we began to publish our first two-color magazine, I was the *writer* who wrote every article — and the *designer* who designed every page. Then I stapled it together and, as the *order-fulfillment person*, I mailed it to our small, but growing mailing list. Denise supported me diligently and faithfully, but because she was so busy with a small child and a second child on the way, the logistical, hands-on help for our ministry at that time consisted of *me*.

### Philip Richard Reinhard Renner

It was while we lived in that little apartment in downtown Tulsa that our second son, Philip, was born at the City of Faith hospital at Oral Roberts University. When we brought Philip home from the hospital, we had to creatively squeeze his baby bed into that tiny apartment!

We named our new little boy *Philip Richard Reinhard Renner*. Before anyone knew Denise was pregnant, a prophetess had laid her hands on the area of Denise's stomach and said, "The baby in your womb will be named Philip because he will carry the Gospel to others." So in response to that prophetic word — and in memory of Philip the evangelist of the Bible — we gave our second son the name *Philip*. His second name was *Richard* after me, my daddy, and Grandpa Renner. And the name *Reinhard* was in honor of the evangelist Reinhard Bonnke. We believed Philip would carry the message of the Gospel to others, so we gave him a name to match that calling. And that is Philip's mission and calling today!

### Two Encouragers Re-Enter Our Lives

Wayne and Stephanie Boosahda were pastors of Jubilee Christian Center in Tulsa. Wayne lived to serve the Body of Christ and was doing a top-notch job at his church. Stephanie had been a part of the World Action Singers, which worked closely with Oral Roberts. She then traveled with Anita Bryant, and she had top-selling records of her own with various record labels. Stephanie had even been co-host on the CBN television program the *700 Club* with Pat Robertson. The Boosahdas were quite a celebrity couple and well connected with people all over the nation.

Denise and I first met Wayne and Stephanie before we were married when they ministered in our coffeehouse ministry at the university church we attended. Denise and I were both so impacted by their ministry, so we decided to ask if they would be willing to meet with us. Soon we sat at a restaurant table, where Denise and I shared our vision to have a national teaching ministry. Wayne was openhearted and willing to help in any way possible and even asked us to minister at his church. Stephanie said, "I'll give you my entire list of pastors that have had me in to minister, and I'll even recommend to them that they have you minister in their churches."

Over time, Wayne and Stephanie became our dear friends. They realized every breath we were breathing was a step of faith, as we were stretched financially to get our teaching ministry started. So they said, "Please give us your monthly long-distance phone bill because we want to pay it for you as you begin to call all those pastors for meetings. It takes a lot of money to make all those long-distance calls, and we want to cover that expense for you as a seed into your ministry."

In addition to Pastor Bob Yandian and other men and women of God, the Lord really used Wayne and Stephanie Boosahda to build confidence in us as we got started in our new ministry. Stephanie said years later, "Rick and Denise were hungry for more of the Lord. God had so anointed Rick as a teacher. All the Greek he knew just made the Bible come alive. Rick and Denise wanted to get that knowledge of the Bible out there to others, and we wanted to be a part of it."

Pastor Bob also lovingly kept an eye on us and regularly checked in with us to see how we were doing. At that time, Grace Fellowship overflowed with notable ministers who were members there, so Pastor Bob and Loretta held a monthly luncheon for those ministers. If we were in town, Pastor Bob always made sure Denise and I were included in those lunches. We were so honored to sit at the same table with those ministers of such renown. They would share what God was doing in their ministries, and they always wanted to hear what was happening in our ministry too. They showed great interest in us even though we were just getting started.

Pastor Bob and I personally met every month so I could give him a report about our ministry. I believed in being accountable, so for me it was important that he knew everything we were doing. Our ministry was minuscule compared to the other "legends" in the faith who attended his church, but Pastor Bob always treated us like we were just as important. Every month, I showed him our calendar so he would know where we were scheduled to minister and how many services we would be conducting. I'd show him what kind of materials we were distributing, and he would listen carefully to my questions and concerns. He became a real voice of encouragement to me at that formative time in our lives and ministry.

Pastor Bob later said, "I watched to see what would happen with Rick and Denise's ministry. And I was shocked to see Rick develop it in such a short time. I'd never seen anyone do what he did that fast. It seemed like in no time they were booked nonstop in churches. I kept wondering, *How has he done this? It takes YEARS for a teaching ministry to get established with a track record and to really start growing.* What happened with Rick and Denise was truly amazing. Their ministry took off *fast.*"

Of course, we know that it is God who ultimately gives the increase to the work we put our hands to in Him. But I knew it was going to take hard work to do what God had put in our hearts, so I gave it my best efforts right from the start. Ronda later said, "Rick worked very hard — I've never seen a harder worker. Anyone who has known him for very long knows you can't outwork Rick Renner."

When I think back at how God used Pastor Bob and the Boosahdas to encourage us in those "small-beginning" days, there is simply no way I could exaggerate how much it meant to us that they were in our lives. To this day, we are grateful that God put them in our path to help us move steadily forward.

## A Ring of Fire

Until that time, our meetings were all in small towns within a radius of about 150 miles of Tulsa. Denise and I, along with Paul and Philip, traveled to these churches as often as they would have us. I often thought of First Samuel 7:16, which says, "And he [Samuel] went from year to year in circuit to Bethel, and Gilgal, and Mizpah...." I remember thinking we were like Samuel the prophet, who kept returning to the same place over and over again. I also thought of Jesus' circuit-type ministry. Luke 9:6 tells us that Jesus "...went through the towns, preaching the gospel, and healing every where."

Yet I knew our ministry was to reach believers all over the nation and not just a small geographical area with churches we'd return to time and time again. I just didn't know how to break free from that little circle to take our ministry to a wider audience. Then one day as I was praying in tongues, the spirit realm opened in front of me, and I saw in a vision a map of the United States with fire burning from Tulsa all the way up to the northern border of the nation. I watched as the fire turned westward and burned all the way to the Northwest Coast, then south to California. Then the fire burned along the southern border of the country all the way back to the East Coast and up to the New England states.

Before the vision ended, I had seen *a ring of fire* burning all along the perimeter of the continental United States. Then I heard the Holy Spirit say, "I am showing you how to take your ministry to the next phase. I want you to follow the ring of fire you have seen in this vision. As you go, I will ignite spiritual fires in hearts as you teach the Word and minister. You are to go on 'a ring of fire' around the perimeter of the United States."

I told Denise, "We don't have many contacts beyond our tri-state area, but today the Holy Spirit has shown me that we are to go on a *ring of fire* around the perimeter of the continental United States. This is how we are to launch out to begin a teaching ministry that will eventually touch places all over the nation."

Because Stephanie Boosahda had given me a list of pastors' names, Denise and I began to call pastors in the areas of the nation where I had seen the fire burning. I followed the vision explicitly. We started calling churches in the central part of the country — all the way up to the northcentral border of the U.S. Then we began to call on churches as we headed westward to the Northwest Coast, then south to California, and so on. Just as I had seen in the vision, we focused only on the perimeter of the country where the fire burned.

At the time, we had about twenty-five partners who sent offerings to the ministry every month. One was a dear man named Charlie whom we had met at our very first meeting in Booneville. He was so touched in our services that he wanted to partner with our ministry. He faithfully sent *a single dollar* every week. That weekly gift meant so much to us because we knew he was giving it sacrificially. Denise and I prayed fervently for him as if he had given our ministry a million dollars. I can attest that from the very beginning of our itinerate ministry, Denise and I have been grateful for every hard-earned cent people have given to help us fulfill our heavenly assignment.

We felt we needed to inform all our partners that we were going on a ring-of-fire ministry tour around the nation, so I wrote and asked them to consider giving a special gift to help us as we launched out by faith. We knew that we couldn't take a big trip across the country in our broken-down car, so we purchased a tiny Isuzu to start our journey. The interior and trunk were so small that it couldn't accommodate Denise, me, Paul, and Philip, plus all our luggage. So we attached a luggage rack to the top where I could strap on all our suitcases. When we finally did start on that big first trip, our car looked like the Leaning Tower of Pisa on wheels! The luggage on top was almost longer than the car and everything on that rack leaned treacherously to one side as we drove!

## A Visitation That Took Me Off Guard

Before we started our big trip across the country, we first accepted an invitation to minister for a few days again in Booneville, Arkansas. After those meetings ended, we stopped at Fort Smith to stay the night with friends on our way back to Tulsa. That night, something unexpected happened that dramatically affected our lives and ministry.

To be honest, I was filled with fret about *many* things at this point in our traveling ministry. I wondered, *Will we be able to schedule enough meetings to keep us busy and pay our way as we start our traveling ministry across the nation?* Denise tried to encourage me, but I found myself eaten up with worry nevertheless that we would not be able to schedule enough meetings to keep us busy or that we would run out of money along the way on the first big leg of our new faith adventure.

That night at our friends' house in Fort Smith, I couldn't sleep because I was so consumed with worry. I tossed and turned until about two o'clock in the morning. I took authority over restlessness and commanded worry to leave. Finally I decided to get up and spend some time in prayer. I walked to the back of the house where there was an enclosed porch that had been converted into an in-home office.

I began to walk back and forth in that room as I prayed in tongues. I surprisingly soon found myself pressing very deep into the Spirit. In fact, I began to pray so deeply in other tongues that I felt *lost* in tongues. I remember thinking that I was going into a spiritual place that was deeper than I had ever experienced.

After a time of prayer, I opened my eyes and saw that I had stepped across the very thin line that separates the natural realm from the spiritual realm, and I found myself in another dimension. I could not see the room anymore — it was *gone*. If someone had come into the room at that moment, perhaps that person would have seen me, but I would not have seen him or her because my senses and spiritual sight had been shifted to another realm.

To my sight, it looked like this spiritual dimension stretched around me "forever" into eternity. Then suddenly in the far distance, I saw a very small light. As I focused on it, it drew closer to me and grew stronger and brighter. When it finally reached me, I saw Jesus — and when I saw Him, I dropped to my knees and bowed my head.

When I lifted my head to look again, Jesus was seated on a throne before me. He reached out and took one of my hands, placing it in a layered fashion between His two hands. Then He did the same thing with my other hand, placing one of His hands, palm side up, directly under my hand — and His other hand, palm side down, on top of my hand so that my hand was sandwiched between His.

The Lord spoke and said, "See today, I give you an anointing of love mixed with hate."

## Two Elements That Release
## the Flow of Divine Compassion

I had never heard of that, so I asked, "What is an anointing of love mixed with hate?"

I heard the Lord answer, "It is a flow of divine compassion. Divine compassion is divine love mixed with divine hate. When these two mingle together, they flow like a river of love toward people: divine love for the individuals mixed with a divine hatred for what the devil has done in their lives. As the two of these mingle together, it creates a divine flow that brings deliverance and healing."

Again, I heard him say, "Today I'm giving you an anointing of *compassion* that will bring deliverance into people's lives."

Anyone who has had an experience in the spirit realm knows it's difficult to explain spiritual experiences, but I will try to tell you what happened next. All of a sudden, I saw myself walking through what looked like the ward of a *hospital* — a very unusual hospital that was filled with people who wore clothes like I had never seen before. They wore old, tattered clothes that were grayish in color. I saw that the people in that hospital ward were those who were hurting — who had suffered in life — and that they were crying out for God to move in their midst. It was clear that these were not physically sick people, but they were hurting people, nonetheless, who really needed special care and attention.

In Chapter Five, I wrote about my experience with an angel when I was in college, in which it was revealed to me that I would one day minister to people who had suffered for their faith in difficult parts of the world. But in *this* vision in Fort Smith, I saw myself walking through the midst of that same people group with an anointing of compassion, and I understood again that God would eventually call me to take His compassion and power to a people who were not my people, but who had suffered much and needed God's special care and attention.

## Fullness of Ministry and Finances

As I told you at the first of this section, I worried that no one would want us to minister in their churches and I worried incessantly about finances. I would frequently ask Denise, "How are we going to schedule meetings when we are unknown, and how will we pay for this ministry as we're getting started?" That is why the following episode that also occurred during his visitation was so impactful to me.

Suddenly, I heard the Lord say, "Behold, I give you fullness of ministry — so much ministry that it is already amassing more ministry for your future."

In an instant, I received into my heart the words of Jesus and understood that it would never be a problem for us to have something to do in the ministry. Jesus was giving us ministry that was already *amassing* more ministry — and that's the word He used: *amassing*. Instantly and supernaturally, I knew it was going to mean greater, greater, and *even greater* responsibility as the years passed.

Then just as quickly, I heard the Lord say, "And behold, I am giving you finances for your ministry. It is wealth on a measure that is already amassing more wealth for you to fulfill your ministry assignment."

Jesus was giving us finances that were already *amassing* more finances. And, again, that's the word He used: *amassing.* Those words also entered into my spirit, and in an instant, I *believed* God would provide financially for us. I instantly understood that He would massively provide for any assignment He ever entrusted to us. I knew that even though I couldn't see or touch those finances at the moment, God was providing finances that were already *amassing* more finances so that we could do any job He would ever give us to do.

In a matter of mere seconds, I felt fullness of ministry and fullness of finances enter me. Then just as Jesus had come, I saw Him walk back into the distance. I closed my eyes for a moment, and when I opened them, I was once again "in the room" where I had gone to pray.

The room where this occurred was an office with a typewriter on the desk, so I immediately put a piece of paper into the typewriter and typed out everything that had just happened to me. I still have that piece of paper that I finished writing within *minutes* of this experience. I wanted to be sure that I would never forget a single word of what Jesus said to me that night.

This vision was so vivid that I clearly understood Jesus had given us fullness of ministry and fullness of finances. It was such a pivotal experience in my life. In moments when I've been tempted to wonder, *Can I financially do what God is asking me to do?* or, *Where will the money come from to do what God is asking us to undertake?* I have remembered that night. Most important are the promises in the Bible that God will provide everything we need — but in addition to these precious Bible promises, God had given me a divine encounter that became a *rhema,* a spoken word of revelation from Heaven, that has encouraged me over and over through the years.

Today our ministry touches people all over the world, and God really did specially call us to people who once suffered terribly for their faith and who needed special care and attention. When God called our family to the Soviet Union, He connected us to the very type of people I had seen in that hospital ward in my vision. And He sent us with divine compassion to bring them healing and deliverance.

## The 'Ring of Fire' Begins

Before we started on our trip to follow "the ring of fire," I scheduled one last appointment with Pastor Bob to let him know what we were doing. I gave him a cassette tape of my most recent teaching because he had never heard me speak publicly. I said, "Pastor Bob, I know you have a lot to do and people probably give you all kinds of things to listen to, but if you ever get an opportunity to listen to this, I think you might enjoy this teaching." He eventually listened to it, but I'll get to that part of the story in a few more pages.

The day finally came when we began our long-awaited "ring of fire" trip around the perimeter of the continental United States. We started on the road to our first meeting at a large Assembly of God church in Kansas City, Missouri. I packed our luggage, a tape duplicator, a typewriter, and boxes of blank cassette tapes into the car so we'd have them on hand to duplicate from church to church. Our vehicle was so small that there was nearly no room left in it for *us!*

Our first meeting far exceeded our expectations. In fact, the pastor asked if we could prolong the meetings for a few days. So Denise and I ministered for several days there, and every night we watched people load up with our teaching materials as they left the building. It thrilled us to see people leaving with our materials because we really wanted the teaching to get into people's hearts and affect their lives for a long time to come.

After we ministered in Kansas City, we drove to the next meeting in Minneapolis. While we stopped to gas up at a filling station, someone stole my wallet. *Ugh!* What were we supposed to do now? I had no wallet, no driver's license, no credit cards. We only had the cash that we had from the product sales at our Kansas City meeting. But we refused to be moved because we knew we were on track with God's plan. I had always heard, "Where there's a will, there's a way." So we got creative and figured out how to keep moving with no credit card, and *we did it.*

After we experienced a great meeting in Minneapolis, we then drove to our next meeting in Janesville, Wisconsin. I called the pastor to let him know we had arrived and asked if Denise could do a sound check in preparation for singing on Sunday morning. He sent someone to pick her up for a sound check while I sat with the boys at the hotel. Denise went to the platform with a microphone in hand to rehearse, and when the pastor heard her sing, he said, "If your husband preaches anything like you sing, we're going to need to extend this meeting a few more days. Can you guys stay a few days longer?"

Those meetings, *too*, turned out fabulous. The pastor asked us to stay and do morning and evening meetings every day for a full week. We were thankful for the opportunity and for everything God was doing on our first big trip!

When we wrapped up those meetings in Wisconsin, we started out to our next meetings in western Canada and in the states of Washington, Oregon, and California. A huge blizzard hit the northern states en route, so we had to drive at a snail's pace through blizzards and snow drifts.

After we closed out our meetings in Canada, we ministered near Seattle at a church that would become a hub for Denise and me in the years to come when we would travel often to the West Coast to minister. The people we met in that first meeting became friends and partners, and they are still friends and partners to this day.

From Washington, we drove to the Oregon cities of Portland and Seaside, where we conducted multiple day-long meetings. We finally came to California for meetings, where we saw the power of God do remarkable things — including perform several major healings. On that trip, we particularly enjoyed the meeting in San Francisco for a Filipino congregation. They were wonderful people filled with faith, and the church was packed completely full for that meeting. Denise and I viewed that meeting as the icing on the cake for our whole trip!

*Wow*…what we were experiencing was wonderful beyond description!

## A Big Break in Tulsa

By this time, our family of four had been on the road in our small Isuzu for two full months. Because we had a short pause in our calendar before the next meetings started, we decided to drive back to Tulsa to rest for a few days. Back then, mobile telephones didn't exist, so I stopped at a filling station just outside San Francisco to call home to let everyone know where we were on our journey and to give a report about what was happening in the meetings. That's when I heard my mother say on the other end of the line, "Bob Yandian is urgently looking for you and needs to speak to you today."

I wondered what Pastor Bob would urgently need, but I put a quarter into the pay phone and dialed his number. When he answered, I said, "Pastor Bob, this is Rick Renner. Are you looking for me?"

He said, "*RICK!* I just listened to that teaching tape you gave me, and I am speechless. I had no idea what kind of teacher you were. This Sunday I cannot be at my church, and if you are available, I'd like to ask you to speak in my place in the Sunday morning and evening services."

It was my turn to be speechless. Did Bob Yandian just say he was impressed by something *I* had taught? And did I really hear him say he wanted *me* to speak in his pulpit at Grace Fellowship?

We were about 1,700 miles from home, and I knew it would take us thirty-plus hours to get to Tulsa if we drove nonstop. The call with Pastor Bob happened on a Thursday afternoon, and I knew if we started immediately and drove nonstop, we could arrive in Tulsa in time to do the meetings on Sunday. So I said, "Of course, I'm available, Pastor Bob. I'm so honored that you would ask me. You can count on me to be there this Sunday *on time!*"

When I hung up the pay phone, I rushed to the car and told Denise about my conversation with Pastor Bob. She said, "Rick, we've got to get moving *right now* if we're going to get there on time to do that meeting." So we put the car in drive and drove nonstop to Tulsa. I knew we would need to have teaching tapes available for people, so when we finally arrived home, I worked fervently to duplicate teaching tapes for the people who would be in the meetings.

Finally, Sunday came. Denise sang and I ministered in the Sunday morning and evening services and taught a two-part series called, "Walking in the Spirit" that was based on Galatians 5:16. At the end of the evening service, we laid hands on hundreds of people and went home to our tiny apartment in downtown Tulsa. There, we unloaded everything we'd taken to the meetings — then I vomited for two days because of physical exhaustion!

## A Suggestion That Reignited a Call and
## Changed Our Ministry *Again*

Soon Pastor Bob was on the phone with me again, but this time, he said, "Rick, I just heard the messages you preached while I was away. This is some of the best teaching I've ever heard on the subject of walking in the Spirit. I had no idea you knew New Testament Greek so well. I'd like to schedule you to do a four-day meeting at our church. I want to start on a Sunday morning and run it to the following Wednesday night so you can have five services to teach a whole series."

That first time at Grace Fellowship, Pastor Bob was away ministering somewhere else, but this second time, he and Loretta were on the front row for every meeting. He sat there with a pen and a pad of paper and took notes almost like a student listening to a teacher. I was amazed at his humility and openness to learn. I was stunned to see someone like *him* willing to sit, listen, and learn from someone like *me.* But it showed his hunger and his love for the Word of God and the teaching of the Bible. I was deeply impressed with this man of God before that, but now I was even more moved.

In those five meetings in four days at Pastor Bob's church, I taught a brand-new series that I called, "Seducing Spirits and Doctrines of Demons." It was based on the kinds of spiritual error the devil would try to smuggle into the Church at the end of the age. I also addressed the New Age movement, which was growing in popularity at that time. For four days, I poured my exegetical studies into the hearts of the people who attended those meetings. Many walked away with armloads of my teaching tapes. But for me, it was most important that when those services concluded, Pastor Bob and I had become friends and we remain cherished friends to this day.

But then I heard Pastor Bob say something that would radically affect the future of our ministry. He said, "Rick, I believe the messages you preached this week are so important that you need to put them into written form. People everywhere will be helped if you'll write a book on this subject."

Then he added, *"If you write the book, I'll write the foreword for it."*

I was momentarily stunned. But in another flash of a second, I was mentally transported back in time to my younger years when I'd written my first book called, *The Perfect Gift.* And I felt a pang of emotional hurt almost as sharply as I'd felt it more than a decade before.

In 1978, I had heard the Holy Spirit say, "Write, write, write, and I'll prosper what you write…." But if you'll recall from Chapter Four, a national prophet had reprimanded me for attempting to write a book on the subject of fivefold ministry at such a young age. That encounter was so traumatic that I allowed it to "swallow me up" in my emotions and completely shroud the sacred instruction from God Himself that I'd received. And after that terrible experience, I exclaimed to myself that I would never attempt to write another book.

But now Bob Yandian was telling me to write! In fact, God was speaking to me *through* him, ordering me to return to the call He had placed on my life years earlier. Bob Yandian was my pastor, so I told him I would do as he recommended. But because of my previous bad experience, I *reluctantly* agreed to take the message "Seducing Spirits and Doctrines of Demons" and put it into book form.

However, in order to do it, I had to overcome a spirit of fear about writing because the stinging words of that prophet still vividly echoed in my memory. Although I was trained to write and I surely could have written the book myself with no problem, instead I searched for a writer to help me craft my first book. After months of wrangling with that writer's style, which I never liked, I finally agreed to a finished manuscript and sent it to the printer along with Bob Yandian's foreword. Many years later, I let the book go out of print, but not before I mined the treasures of its pages and expanded on them to use in other books — especially relating to end times — including *How To Keep Your Head on Straight in a World Gone Crazy.*

But what a turnaround of events! Pastor Bob's first letter of recommendation had been based entirely on my sister and brother-in-law's reputation. But now Pastor Bob wrote the following foreword for my first published book:

Rick Renner preached this series at Grace Fellowship. I am pleased to see it being published in a book. It was one of the most timely messages I have ever heard, and it has impacted many of my sermons since. This book is an accurate insight from Paul's letter to Timothy of the day we are living in. Rick paints a clear picture of Satan at work in the world today in the New Age movement, imitating the role of the Church. He also tells of Satan's attack in the Church itself to lure believers away from the foundation of the Word of God and chase only after miracles and the supernatural. Rick brings a balanced truth to those who long to hear the Word of Truth rightly divided. It is a pleasure to recommend Rick Renner as an able minister and my friend.

Before I go any further, I want to say how thankful I am for Pastor Bob Yandian's encouragement in my life years ago and for his continued friendship over many years. God used this precious man to play a vital role in my life and in the expansion of our ministry. Knowing what he did for me has made me want to return the favor by being helpful to others over the years. Small words of encouragement put a lot of gas in the tank of people's lives that strengthens them to keep going!

Because I believed in giving my best to whatever I'm called to do, I decided that if I was going to put a book into print, I also wanted to give my best efforts to see it get into as many hands as possible. Many authors write books with no marketing plan, and their books sit in boxes in their garages and never reach the people who need them. I didn't want that to happen to my books, so I searched for a way to get *Seducing Spirits and Doctrines of Demons* in front of potential readers.

In those days, one of the best ways to advertise any Christian product was to run an advertisement in *Charisma* magazine. So we took a leap of faith and purchased a full-page ad to run in *Charisma* for two months. Purchasing books online didn't exist at that time, so to place an order, buyers had to cut out a little coupon usually positioned at the bottom of a page, fill it out with the correct address and contact information, and mail it to the ministry with a check. It was a long process that could take weeks. The advertising department at *Charisma* warned me not to expect big results because I was a new author and people were not familiar with me or my books.

But those who predicted low results were completely wrong. In one month, more than ten-thousand orders arrived, which surpassed my wildest imagination! My book became a hot topic, and the advertisement was designed in such a way that it really captured people's attention. So before the first month passed, we already needed to place a second order for another twenty-thousand books! Then *those* twenty-thousand books sold quickly, and within three months, we were already into the third printing.

By 1988 standards, *Seducing Spirits and Doctrines of Demons* was a bestseller — and it was my *first* book to be published and marketed. And when those thousands of books started arriving in homes and churches, the phone began to ring off the wall from pastors who wanted to invite us to come minister in their churches and conferences all over the country.

In those years, Denise and I did all we could to minister in as many churches as we could physically get to. We were laying hands on as many people as possible in those services, and we were flowing in the gifts of the Spirit. I was teaching with an emphasis on the New Testament in its original Greek language, Denise was giving her all as she ministered in music, and God was touching lives in our meetings.

We didn't realize it at the time, but we were also building relationships with churches and pastors that would stay with us for decades. We ministered in large churches, middle-sized churches, and small churches. It didn't matter what size the church, we walked through any open door because we wanted to minister to people. Although it's not physically possible to accept every ministry invitation we receive these many years later, we have that same attitude today.

## Put Your Light on a Lampstand

For a moment, I want to refer to the words of Jesus in Matthew 5:15 about letting your light shine so that it can affect other people. Jesus said, "Neither do men light a candle, and put it under a bushel, but on a candlestick; and it giveth light unto all that are in the house."

In this verse, Jesus is exhorting us to let our light shine. He strongly admonishes us to keep our gifts, talents, and influence out in the open where they can be seen, where they can grow, and where they can provide light to others.

Why would God give you something to benefit others and then have you hide it where no one can see it or appreciate it? God never intended for you to conceal your gifts or to hide your influence. *He wants your light to shine brightly!*

Many people hear the devil's voice whispering that what they have to offer falls short in comparison to others whose gifts and talents shine especially bright. But you have to come to a time when you decide you're going to quit hiding in the shadows. *You have what it takes to be a success!*

To be the phenomenal success God knows you can be for His glory, you have to choose to step out of the shadows! As you seek His face, you'll know when it's time to come out from under that bushel and let the Holy Spirit light your wick with a fire that will cause you to shine for Him. But if you refuse to bring your gifts and talents out from "under wraps," no one will ever know what God has put in you.

In Matthew 5:15, the word "candlestick" depicts *an elevated stand* that was used so that a lamp could give maximum light. During the time of the early New Testament, it was customary for homes, palaces, businesses, and public buildings to place brightly burning lamps on *pedestals* because those higher positions provided superior light that could illuminate the entire environment. The higher the lamp, the greater the light that would be present and the lesser the darkness. So when Jesus said, "Neither do men light a candle, and put it under a bushel, but on a candlestick...," He was telling us that we must lift our lamps — *our gifts, talents, and personal influence* — as high as possible. When these elements are elevated in a highly visible position, God can use us to "give light unto all that are in the house."

If you keep your light at just a table level, you'll illuminate the people around the table with you. If you keep it in the corner, you'll illuminate people who are in the corner with you. And those things are certainly not wrong to do; *wherever* you find yourself in life, you should be encouraging, strengthening, and influencing for good the people who are around you.

But if you lift that same light high, elevating it and making it visible by putting it on a pedestal, it will illuminate *everyone* in the room or environment, whereas it previously touched only a handful. The amount of light given is the same, but the elevated position of the light makes the light much more effective.

I share this verse because of my own story about publishing books. I knew God wanted me to write books that would be read around the world. I thought and dreamed about it constantly, but I would also second-guess myself. I would occasionally think, *Who am I to think people would read something I wrote?* But the day came when the Holy Spirit spoke to my heart through Pastor Bob and told me that it was time to start actually using my God-given gifts — *elevating them and believing in them* — so they could become a blessing to people.

### 'The Book You've Been Waiting For!'

I shared earlier that I'd placed an advertisement for my first book *Seducing Spirits and Doctrines of Demons* in *Charisma* magazine and that the ad was designed in a way that it really captured people's attention. Well, I designed that ad, and I wrote the headline to read as follows: *'The Book You've Been Waiting For!'*

You may have heard me tell the story, but after I submitted all the content for that ad, my head began to scream at me, *What did you just do! Did you really say that your book was THE book everyone was waiting for?* I cringed with embarrassment at my boldness, but my embarrassment was short-lived when orders began to pour in and books began to fly out of our office to fulfill those orders!

You see, if I had never dared to promote and *elevate* what I had written, it is doubtful that you would have ever discovered the book you are holding in your hands right now. For my dream to come to pass, I had to accept that my light was needed in the lives of other people, and I had to elevate it out of the shadows and allow God to use it in His perfect timing to edify and bless others.

The truth is that there are many "unknown" writers who are more talented than I am, but they're not known because their gifts are hidden under a bushel and, therefore, they have not reached a larger audience with their writings. Although their skills are tremendous and loaded with power, they *remain* unknown and will probably remain unknown unless they are willing to do whatever is required according to the Lord's instruction to elevate those gifts and put them on a lampstand where they will be seen and appreciated. Only then will they begin to affect more than the small handful gathered around the table or the few who are sitting in their corner.

If *your* light is going to be a blessing to the world, you must dare to lift that light high and put it on a pedestal where people will see it and be affected by it. Once you've silenced intimidation and made that bold decision, you can begin to fulfill your dream of reaching and illuminating a larger audience.

The believers who have influence in the world — such as those who write the songs you sing, the books you read, or the sermons you hear preached on TV — are not necessarily the most gifted, talented, or anointed people. But they had the nerve to step out by faith and obedience to elevate their God-given abilities. Regardless of how good or seemingly inferior their abilities were, today they are renowned and influential because they had the guts and gumption to get their light out from under a bushel and to *let it shine*. A great part of their success is due to their willingness to step out from obscurity to let their light begin to shine to others.

So I want to ask you: Are your gifts, talents, abilities, and influence giving light to the people around you in all spheres of your life, such as your home, your work, your school, or your church? God has given you everything you need to make that kind of difference in the lives of other people, but *you* are the only one who can decide to put that light out on a lampstand where it will be a blessing to others. No one can make that decision for you.

So what are you going to do — keep your gifts, talents, and potential influence a secret, or put your light on a pedestal so it can give light to everyone in the house? One thing is sure — the success in God you dream about will come as a result of your willingness to step out from obscurity and *let your light begin to shine!*

## Our First Full-Time Employee —
## My Mother Erlita Renner!

At the time these thousands of book orders were pouring into our Post Office box, we only had one full-time employee — *me*. But because of this overwhelming and unexpected response to my book, we fell into such an "emergency mode" to fulfill orders that I quickly called my mother to come help me. Mother had been working at a doctor's office for twenty years at that time. But on that day, I said, "Mother, can you please ask the doctor if you can be free to help me today? It's urgent."

Within hours, Mother was in our one-room office behind our only desk to help me figure out how to process the mountain of orders that were piling up every day. At the end of that day, she said to me, "Rick, it looks like you need your mother full time. If it's okay with you, I'm going to turn in my resignation and come work full time to help my son with his ministry!"

That day my mother became our first full-time employee, besides me, and she stayed with us until the time of her retirement more than three decades later. In all those years, my mother corresponded with pastors, scheduled meetings, arranged the delivery of teaching materials, ministered to partners, and eventually led our entire Partner Care outreach as Rick Renner Ministries grew.

*Think of it.* My mother was instrumental in leading me to Jesus. She taught me the Bible and mentored me in the things of God in my child-hood. She later became our first full-time employee, eventually leading our Partner Care ministry, working alongside Denise and me until the time of her retirement! *What a gift from Heaven to my life, who brilliantly let her own light be lifted up to shine!*

When *Seducing Spirits and Doctrines of Demons* hit the bookstores, every-thing in our ministry began to exponentially grow. Orders began to pile into our office for my tape and video series, and orders for my book kept coming and coming with no pause. Within a short period of time, we had received nine hundred invitations to minister in all kinds of church meetings, confer-ences, seminars, and other events.

Then another event happened that catapulted things even further. Grace Fellowship at that time was indisputably *the* leader in praise and worship in the nation. They annually hosted a Local Church Music Seminar that was led by Daniel Amstutz, the worship leader at Grace Fellowship, and Daniel asked me to be one of the speakers at the event. Several thousand ministers attended the event, and scores of them heard me minister at the conference. As a result, even more doors began to open as more invitations began to pour into our small office.

Now rather than praying for opportunities to open up for us, we found ourselves in a new position where we were praying for wisdom about which opportunities to accept. Ministry was *amassing*, just as Jesus had spoken. It's hard to fathom, but as we added up all the morning and evening services we were doing in multiple-day meetings and conferences, we were ministering in 450 services a year!

### Ours Was Truly a Family Ministry

When I arrived home from those meetings, I always did my best to focus on my family. Philip Renner recalled that time, saying, "We never had the understanding that it was Dad and Mom's ministry — it was always *the family's* ministry. And although Dad was gone on ministry assignments sometimes every week, I don't have a memory of an absentee father. When Dad got home from a trip, we were his first priority. Even if he had to go to the office, we went to the office with him, and he tried to take us along to as many events as possible."

It's true that all three of our sons have worked in the ministry in some capacity from the time they were each old enough to do so. They helped me carry my Bible and study books, unpack boxes of books and teaching materials, set up and manage book tables, help distribute offering envelopes, straighten chairs, and work in the sound booth, etc. At every age and season, they grew in their skills and abilities, and they loaned those God-given talents, *with* a heart for service, to the Lord and His work — and, in particular, to Rick Renner Ministries.

Today each of our sons, Paul, Philip, and Joel, have callings from God on their lives for ministry, and they are each functioning at a high capacity in those roles. *Denise and I* didn't call them; *God* called them. But their mother and I always included them in whatever we did for the Lord. They never resented the ministry — it was our ministry as a family, and we explained to them repeatedly that God had called all of us together. Instead of resenting the ministry, Paul, Philip and Joel all saw the value in our obeying God and serving Him to meet the needs of others.

We had fun together doing what God had called us to do as a family. We worked as a unit, not as individual parts. We shared victories together and lots of laughs! And in hard times, Denise and I always pointed our sons to Jesus and shared our faith with them that He would take care of us, giving us the wisdom we needed and meeting our *every* need. They saw our ministry in motion and our faith in action — and all the fruit that accompanied our obedience over the years. When it came time for each of them to begin stepping into their individual roles, they knew how to embrace the grace of God and how to walk with Him personally for themselves.

Denise and I take no glory for ourselves that our sons carried into their adult lives a fervent desire to serve and please the Lord. We simply endeavored to obey God and His Word concerning our ministry and our family so that His blessing could come upon our obedience in every way. No family is perfect, including ours. The blessing of God simply makes all the difference in a person's life and in his or her family no matter who you are in the Kingdom!

Over the next few years, we moved from one office to the next to accommodate the needs of our growing ministry. Everything was growing at an exponential rate of speed — our number of meetings, our number of employees, and the distribution of our teaching materials.

My books were selling so fast that I decided to start our own book company, which I called *Pillar Books*. In a relatively short period of time, the company began to take off and we were even publishing and distributing books for other authors. I wrote *Life in the Combat Zone*, and it seemed like we couldn't print books fast enough to keep up with the orders that kept pouring into the office.

One day *Charisma* magazine sent me notice that Jamie Buckingham wanted to write a book review for my new book *Life in the Combat Zone*. At that time in the 1980s, there was no Christian Charismatic leader more respected widespread than Jamie Buckingham. Jamie was an internationally renowned best-selling author, columnist, and conference speaker, and he was a friend to nearly every significant Christian leader in the Charismatic Movement. He was author of more than forty-five books, and he was a regular columnist for *Charisma* and *Christian Life* magazines. He also served as senior editor for *Ministries Today* magazine until his death.

When Jamie wrote that glowing book review that was published in several publications, things turned up a notch again. Over the years after that, Jamie wrote several reviews for my books, each one positive, and this was another encouragement to me to keep writing!

## The Fulfillment of a Personal Heart's Desire as We Were Growing

Denise and I were completely committed to building our U.S.-based teaching ministry. We had moved from an apartment to a rental house, but we dreamed to one day own our own home.

Soon an opportunity came along that enabled us to purchase our first home, a lovely two-story house near the Southern Hills Golf Course in Tulsa and just a few blocks from the homes of Kenneth E. Hagin and Buddy Harrison — also not too far from Oral Roberts.

When we moved into that house, I reminded Denise of our crossing that bridge leading out of Arkansas into Oklahoma just a few years before — how we'd left a black-and-white world for a fresh, new life filled with color. God had given us such a supernatural turnaround. Just a few years before, we were living in an embarrassingly dilapidated, *unfixable* house — with no potential and little market value — but now God had given us a beautiful house we could truly call home.

In fact, as we diligently sought, obeyed, and trusted the Lord, it looked like everything we touched was blessed. It was totally amazing. What was happening to us was like something you would read in a fairy tale. But this was no fairy tale — this was *really* happening in our lives and ministry!

### Joel Richard Daniel Renner

While we lived in that beautiful house in Tulsa, another amazing event took place in our lives. Our third son, Joel, was born. We named him *Joel Richard Daniel Renner.* We named him *Joel* after the prophet Joel and also after a marketing executive in New York City, a dear friend who also was on the Board of Directors for the *700 Club*. We gave our youngest son the second name of *Richard* after myself, my daddy, and my Grandpa Renner. We gave him his third name *Daniel* after Daniel Amstutz, who was the worship leader at Grace Fellowship and who had been a real comrade to me in ministry. When Joel was born, our family was finally complete! The Lord gave us our sons as gifts who would become instrumental partners with us later in the ministry.

Among all the marvelous blessing and excitement in our lives amidst this season of divine turnaround, a difficult season came for us as a married couple in the ministry. Paul and Philip needed to start school, and I understood that it was time for Denise to stay at home with our three sons while I traveled alone without them.

Although this was a logical decision, this was a first for us, and it was emotional and heartbreaking for Denise. Up until that time, we had done everything together — traveled together, ministered together, and prayed together at the altar for people who came forward for prayer. We literally did everything together. The mere thought of us not being together was heartbreaking for Denise, and it was also very hard for me.

When I knew I had to talk to Denise about this change of season, it was difficult for me because I didn't want to hurt her. But we got past it and grew through it. Because of that experience, Denise has been able to help many wives concerning the various "seasons" that come in their own lives. Many people resist new seasons that simply cannot be circumvented or sidestepped. But when these unavoidable seasons are resisted, it only makes our adjustments to them more difficult.

# BUSINESS REPLY MAIL
FIRST-CLASS MAIL    PERMIT NO. 9316    TULSA, OK

POSTAGE WILL BE PAID BY ADDRESSEE

RICK RENNER MINISTRIES
PO BOX 702040
TULSA OK 74170-2040

# CLAIM YOUR FREE RESOURCE!

As a way of introducing you further to the teaching ministry of Rick Renner, we would like to send you free of charge his teaching CD, "How To Receive a Miraculous Touch From God."

In His earthly ministry, Jesus commonly healed *all* who were sick of *all* their diseases. In this profound message, learn about the manifold dimensions of Christ's wisdom, goodness, power, and love toward all humanity who came to Him in faith with their needs.

Simply complete the section below to receive this powerful teaching. Or complete online at **https://renner.org/claim-your-free-offer/**

YES, please also email me Rick's FREE monthly Teaching Letter!

Name:

Address:

City:                                    State:              Zip:

Email:                                   Phone:

How To Receive
a Miraculous Touch From God
Rick Renner

RENNER

CD36

**R** www.renner.org      **f** www.facebook.com/rickrenner

▶ www.youtube.com/rennerministries

◉ www.instagram.com/rickrenner

Denise said, "One day when I was home with the boys, the Holy Spirit told me I needed to embrace that particular season of our lives. He said, *You have two different things you can embrace: You can embrace resentment, jealousy, anger, and depression because you're not traveling with Rick — or you can embrace being thankful and proud of your husband, and you can have grace and a positive attitude.*

"A choice had been put in front of me. So I said, 'Okay, Lord, I'll do my very best to turn from my struggles and embrace this season.' I probably didn't do it perfectly, but I knew God was asking me to make an attitude change in my heart, and He helped me do it as I agreed with Him."

Although welcoming that new season was hard for us, we both knew what we'd decided was the right thing to do. Denise accepted it by God's grace and actually flourished in it. And because she had time on her hands while the boys were at school, she began to teach a ladies' Bible study in our home every week. That Bible study for women became the seed for Denise's future massive outreach to women that would later be developed in the lands of the former USSR!

## A Supernatural Visitation With Jesus Concerning My Family and Ministry

I continued our ministry on the road alone, and God's blessing continued to rest heavily on us. But at times, I became concerned about being away from my family.

Then one day while I was on a ministry trip in Canada, I awoke very early one morning to see Jesus standing at the foot of my bed! When I realized the Lord was standing right in front of me, I sat straight up in my bed and listened as Jesus began to speak to me once again about my life, my family, and our future ministry.

Denise and I were young parents at the time, and because I was often away ministering, I found myself concerned at times about the negative effect my absence might have on our children. From time to time, I really felt tormented with thoughts that I was a poor father because I was gone so much of the time.

But as Jesus began to speak to me about our future, I suddenly saw Paul, our oldest son who was still very young at that time, appear in the vision. He ran to Jesus and jumped up into His arms. Right in front of me, I saw Jesus at the foot of my bed with my son Paul in His arms!

In that moment, the Lord looked at me with a smile in His eyes and said, "Don't worry about your children. I'll take care of them. I have *all* your children in My arms." In one instant, I understood that our children were secure in the arms of Jesus, and I was comforted that our ministry would never negatively affect our sons. It gave me such peace.

Then in the vision, I heard the sounds of an airplane almost as if I was seated on a plane right above the engines.

To be honest, at that point in my life, I had no desire to go "into all the world." My dream was to reach the United States with my teaching ministry. But I heard Jesus say, "See, I'm sending you forth into the world." And then He added, "And I will provide everything you need to do what I've called you to do."

Then just as quickly as the Lord had appeared, He was gone.

This vision happened right in the thick of a burgeoning teaching ministry that was thriving and "busting at the seams" with growth and even greater possibility than we'd imagined. But what Jesus shared with me in that vision was intended to prepare me for yet another changing season that lay shortly ahead for Denise and me and our family.

### A Seed That Would Come Back
### to Us in an Unlikely Way

In the following years, a mission organization called *Calvary International* had become familiar with my teaching ministry. Some of their missionaries had gotten hold of my teaching tapes, and the organization wrote to ask if we would be willing to donate twenty-four thousand teaching tapes to their missionaries who would attend at their next annual convention in Florida.

I believed in the Great Commission, but I was so focused on building our ministry in the United States that I didn't have missions on my mind at all for Denise and me and our boys. But because I knew that God's heart is for missions, I felt I needed to sow the twenty-four thousand cassette tapes into the lives of those missionaries at the convention in Florida.

I thought, *If I do this, I'll be done with missions, and I can keep focusing on our U.S.-based ministry.* But that obviously would not be the end of our commitment to missions *at all*! Those thousands of teaching tapes would be seed that would come back to us in the not-so-distant future as a harvest transcending *nations*, moving us from our comfort zone to answer our calling halfway around the world.

After we sowed the twenty-four thousand teaching tapes into the lives of those missionaries, they wanted me to be one of their speakers at the following annual conference. I was so busy doing other meetings that I really didn't want to do it, but how could I say no to a group of missionaries who were blessed by my ministry. So I reluctantly accepted the invitation and soon found myself agonizing in the suffocating humidity of Florida at that conference.

When I walked into the first meeting, my attitude couldn't have been worse! I did not want to be there, but there I was — trapped for a whole weekend with a room full of missionaries I did not know. They were excited to see me, but I was not excited to see them.

As the first service began, I sat with my head down, looking at the carpet during the whole worship portion of the service, asking God to please help me adjust my attitude so that I could minister to the people with a happy heart. As I was having this conversation with the Lord, I happened to look to my left, and I saw someone's Bible on the pew next to me. I picked it up and flipped through the pages to see what kind of notes were scrawled in its margins. When I began looking through this Bible, I realized it was a Russian Bible.

*Hmm*...I had never seen a Russian Bible. But I was captivated because I could instantly phonetically read much of it. *What were the chances of my phonetically reading Russian the first time I ever looked at it?*

What I didn't completely realize at the time was that the Cyrillic alphabet (the basis for the Slavic and Russian alphabets) originated in Greece. In the

Ninth Century, two brothers, Saint Cyril and Methodius, born in Thessalonica, were sent as missionaries to the Slavs in the East. The two brothers began the task of devising an alphabet for the Slavs and for translating the Bible into their languages, and that alphabet became the basis for the Russian language.

Because Cyril and Methodius were Greek, the alphabet they devised had many characteristics that were similar to Greek. Since I could read New Testament Greek, this explained why I could phonetically pronounce a lot of the Russian words the very first time I saw them.

When I realized I could phonetically read the Russian Bible, I was mesmerized by it. When they called me to the platform to minister, I didn't hear them call my name the first time because I was so engrossed in the fact that I was phonetically reading the Russian Bible.

When I finished ministering that night, I returned to the front row of seats to look at that Russian Bible again. Curiosity had gotten the best of me, so I casually slipped that Bible on top of mine and carried them both in my arms through a side door nearby. I saw no harm in "borrowing" it for the night — so I took it to my hotel room and read it voraciously for several hours before I finally fell asleep.

I returned the Russian Bible the following morning to the same row of chairs where I'd found it. It belonged to a man named Peter Kulakevich, a native of Ukraine and Estonia most of his life before immigrating to the United States. He and his brother Nikolai were both a part of a small team that was planning to move to the Soviet Union in January 1991 to help train Russian-speaking people to fulfill their ministry callings. When I heard that these brothers had fled the USSR in 1988, only to be moving back with a small group to train young men and women for ministry, I thought, *These must be some of the bravest people I've ever met in my life.*

But while I was at that meeting in Florida, I was having an "accidental" encounter with people I would later work with half a world away. Certainly, I couldn't have known at the time that Nikolai Kulakevich would one day become my interpreter and that he would work closely with me for many years in my own ministry in the former Soviet Union. *(To be continued on page 389.)*

# Photos Corresponding to Chapters 6-7

Fort Smith, Arkansas (1942), © Library of Congress.

**Above:** The original site of "Fort Smith" was built in 1817 on the eastern side of the Arkansas River because the U.S. government needed a "fort" to serve as a western frontier military post. Eventually, Fort Smith became a bustling boom town that was full of brothels, saloons, and outlaws. Also noted for fur trading, it became a place of convergence for those with a pioneering spirit who wanted to help settle this "wild, wild west."

**Right:** Pictured here is First Baptist Church and my pastor Dr. Bill Bennett. The historic Fort Smith First Baptist Church was pastored by Dr. Bennett, a brilliant man who was a scholar and had an earned doctorate in theology. But what made him unique was that he read New Testament Greek. The way he mixed doctrine, Greek, and the anointing of the Holy Spirit was an amazing blend of brains and anointing all gloriously blended to produce some of the most powerful preaching I'd ever heard.

Judge Isaac Parker

**Above:** Pictured here is an original photo of Judge Isaac Parker's courtroom. The federal government decided a heavy hand was needed in Fort Smith to deal with the criminal activity in Indian Territory, and their solution was Judge Isaac Parker, who presided as the U.S. District Judge from 1875 to 1896.

**Right:** This is an illustration of Judge Isaac Parker's famous gallows. For 21 years, Judge Parker tried 13,490 cases, in which 8,500 defendants either pled guilty or were convicted. Of that number, 160 were sentenced to death — and 79 of those were executed by hanging on Judge Parker's famous gallows erected directly behind his courtroom at the Fort Smith settlement.

**Photos:** Judge Parker, Courtroom, Gallows (detail) © Fort Smith National Historic Site.

**Above:** In my off-work hours, I was volunteering at the church doing whatever needed to be done. I never said, "I can't" or, "That's not my calling" because I wanted to prove myself faithful both to God and to the leadership at the church who were watching me.

**Above:** A younger Rick Renner teaching in the single-adults ministry. For years, I'd studied at the university, "trapped" intellectually in my head. But in this ministry, I really learned how to minister to people — people who were precious in the sight of God.

**Above:** Pictured here is Denise at about the time we knew God had called us to be husband and wife. She was everything I needed and more — and together, God was creating us to be a team that would take God's Word to the ends of the earth.

**Left:** On her first visit to see me in Fort Smith, Denise could see God was moving in my ministry. She sang a solo in my single-adults class — people were awestruck to hear such a powerful, operatic voice!

**Right:** Dr. Bennett not only helped me think through scriptural issues, but he taught me wisdom in practical things that I desperately lacked. No area of my life was off limits to Dr. Bennett's examination, correction, and instruction.

**Left:** Our wedding on October 3, 1981. Denise met me at the altar of First Baptist Church in Fort Smith, where we made a commitment to each other and to God — to go wherever He asked us to go and to do whatever He asked us to do.

**Right:** Pictured is Dr. Bennett officiating our wedding. A packed auditorium watched the ceremony, which included Denise singing a song. I knelt on the floor with a tub of water and washed Denise's feet to symbolically declare that I would serve her for the rest of our lives.

**Above:** Our single-adults ministry grew until it could no longer be contained within the walls of the little house where it started. Dr. Bennett was elated with the growth, so he moved us to the original fellowship hall of the old education building across the street from the main sanctuary.

**Above:** I'm pictured here leading the first session of "Starting Over," a divorce-recovery program for the newly single, which we conducted five times in a year and a half with more than 1,100 participants. When I stood to greet our first group, I felt such a desperate need for the anointing. There I was, newly married and never having gone through divorce, addressing a room full of brokenhearted people.

**Left:** This is me in the fellowship hall to the left of the column, wearing a dark suit. When the single-adults ministry outgrew the old fellowship hall in the education building, we moved into the newer fellowship hall on the main campus that could hold hundreds of people.

**Above:** Pictured is me speaking in the church's main auditorium. Our ministry took off like wildfire and God's power was "falling" in the auditorium, manifesting His presence, on many Saturday nights.

**Above:** After we outgrew the fellowship all, we moved to the auditorium of the local Masonic Temple, adorned with pyramids, sphinxes, and gargoyle-like figures suspended from the ceiling. As we lifted our heads in worship, we had to ignore those demonic-looking figures that "glared" down at us. But God moved, and we grew *more*, even in that spiritually dark location.

**Above:** I was completely sold out to see the single-adults department grow. I went on visitation several nights a week, and I even had a self-imposed rule that no week would pass without my personally calling two hundred people by phone. Week after week and month after month, I met that goal.

**Above:** The single-adults ministry was experiencing a real outpouring of the Holy Spirit in that historical auditorium in the First Baptist Church. Dr. Bennett was elated with our department's growth, but he knew if he allowed it to continue, he would have to go to war with some leading members of the church who were opposed to what was happening.

**Above:** Our *Saturday Night Singles* group had its own worship team and ushers — and a full-fledged service for those in the *Singled Out* ministry. News of this growth began to spread through the church, and others who were hungry for more of the Holy Spirit began to show up for our services — *even if they weren't single*!

**Above:** I taught the Bible in our single-adults ministry, believing for a greater move of the Holy Spirit. Many were thrilled to see what God was doing — we were the eighth fastest-growing single-adults ministry in America. But some of the older members of the church called us *radicals*, *renegades*, and *rebels*.

**Above:** Denise and I are pictured at a dinner for the leaders of our single-adults ministry. I led the ministry and Denise taught voice lessons. We had little materially, but we had each other and the call of God on our lives. We were thrilled beyond our ability to express it.

**Above:** While many couples struggle in their relationship in their first years of marriage, Denise and I were blissfully happy together and absolutely passionate about drawing people together and bringing souls into the Kingdom.

**Above:** We held Bible studies in our house almost nonstop in those days. And on most Saturdays, we conducted activities for singles with children. Denise and I gave all our hearts to what we were doing. Those singles, in response, gave their hearts right back to us.

**Above:** Denise and I became the proud parents of a baby boy born in Fort Smith in 1983, whom we named Paul Richard William Renner. Because nobility are given three names at birth in addition to their surname, we gave all of our children three names as our way of communicating from the start that they were nobility in God's eyes and ours.

**Above:** Here I am speaking at Fellowship of Believers that we started when we left First Baptist Church. It was a time when we stepped out of a classroom of real ministerial training into a *new* classroom, where God would teach us some of the hardest lessons we had learned up till that moment.

**Above:** For many who attended Fellowship of Believers, that experience was a slice of Heaven. God did many wonderful things, yet it was an "Ishmael" experience for me because God never called me to start that little church.

**Above:** Pictured are Denise and I praying for people at the altar. Wherever God is, great things come right along with Him, and He certainly showed up to manifest His greatness in our little church. Nevertheless, it was a very difficult time for Denise and me.

**Above:** Here I am ministering to a precious soul during a time of prayer. The platform was only one step high, the back wall was covered with cheap material, and our folding chairs had to be set up in a strange pattern so people wouldn't trip over the electrical outlets sticking up out of the floor.

**Left:** In Fort Smith's historic district, we lived in a two-story house with a basement, built right after the Civil War. It still had a carriage step that owners long ago used to get into their carriages. The house was in atrocious condition, and we were in no position to notably improve it.

**Above:** Our Fort Smith house had windows with scads of tiny triangle-shaped panes, many of which were broken when we moved in. To stay warm during our first winter, Denise and I stuffed clothing through the broken panes.

**Above:** Our house was actually a safety hazard. All the termite-infested baseboards, window frames, and window sills were covered with lead paint so dangerous that social workers came to see what the city could do to help. We were approved for a grant to remove the lead paint and to repaint those areas.

**Right:** The instant Denise and I passed the Arkansas-Oklahoma border — which is right in the middle of the bridge over the Arkansas River — we both sensed something lift from us, and we knew we were entering a new phase of a life of obedience that was going to be marvelous.

**Left:** Pictured here are Pastor Bob Yandian and his wife Loretta. Pastor Bob regularly checked on us and showed great interest in us even though we were just getting started. He with met me every month and became a voice of encouragement at that formative time in our lives and ministry.

**Right:** It didn't matter what the church size, we walked through any open door because we wanted to minister to people. Although it's not physically possible to accept every ministry invitation we receive these many years later, we have that same attitude today.

**Above:** In the very beginnings of Rick Renner Ministries, we walked through every open door and were grateful for every opportunity to minister to God's people. I taught from the Greek New Testament, Denise ministered in music, and the gifts of the Holy Spirit flowed.

**Above:** The day finally came when we began our long-awaited trip across the continental U.S. I packed our luggage, a tape duplicator, a typewriter, and boxes of blank cassette tapes to duplicate from church to church. Our vehicle was so small that there was nearly no room left in it for us!

**Above:** Our first teaching meetings turned out fabulous. The people we met became friends and partners, and they are still friends and partners today. We saw the power of God do remarkable things — including perform several major healings. It was wonderful beyond description.

**Right:** Pictured here is our newborn second son, whom we named Philip Richard Reinhard Renner. Today Philip is a bold, Spirit-filled man with a wonderful ministry that is taking the Gospel across the world with the help of his wife Ella and their two beautiful daughters.

**Left:** Pictured here is Denise, Paul, and Philip in our little car that we drove nearly nonstop across the U.S. to any church that invited us. Our two young sons lived that part of their lives in that tiny car as we traversed the nation to get to those meetings.

**Right:** Pictured here is our newborn third son, whom we named Joel Richard Daniel Renner. When Joel was born, we knew that our family was complete. The Lord gave us our sons as gifts who would become instrumental partners with us later in the ministry.

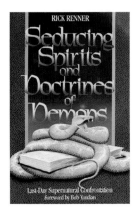

**Left:** Pictured is my first published book *Seducing Spirits and Doctrines of Demons*. By 1988 standards, it was a bestseller with more than twenty thousand copies selling in the first two months. Within a short time, we received nine hundred invitations to minister in all kinds of churches, conferences, seminars, and events.

**Right:** Pictured here is the original version of my book *Dressed To Kill*, which I wrote to help believers have a biblical understanding of the devil — of our Christ-imparted authority over him and our divinely empowered weaponry to use against him. *Dressed To Kill* became my best-selling book that has been published in multiple languages around the world.

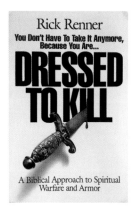

**Right:** Pictured here are a few of the cassette tapes we gave to a missions organization that asked if we would donate 24,000 teaching tapes to their missionaries. Those tapes would be seed that would come back to us as a harvest that would transcend nations, moving us from our comfort zone to answer our calling halfway around the world.

**Left:** Paul, Philip, and Joel at approximately eight, six, and two when I first agreed to visit the Soviet Union. Denise and I always included them in whatever we did for the Lord. Today our sons each have their own families and are our closest comrades in the ministry.

**Above:** In January 1991, a series of uprisings occurred in Riga, and Soviet military troops moved into the city with tanks and armored vehicles. All of this occurred at the moment that team of missionaries arrived to begin the first above-ground Bible school in the history of the Soviet Union. Photo: © National Latvian Library / used by permission.

**Above:** Over the following days of the outset of the Riga demonstration, six people were killed, several were wounded, and others were beaten by military forces. Photo: © National Latvian Library / used by permission.

Nikolai later said, "Russian is a very complicated language. Although we who are from the USSR learned it for ten years in school, even we have a tough time mastering it. Really the language is a challenge for any foreigner, but Rick was very determined, and his grasp on Greek gave him an amazing start at learning Russian."

I was dumbfounded by the bravery of that group of souls who were going to move to the lands of the USSR in January 1991 — just a few months from the date of that conference. To think that some of them had fled that region, and now they were returning! This was just amazing to me. It was such a tumultuous time in the Soviet Union, and there were deficits of every imaginable commodity. *Plus*, the USSR was the great enemy of the United States. I wondered what would happen to these brave missionaries.

But God used that weekend to sit me on a pew next to a Russian Bible. And when I saw that I could phonetically read it, He set a hook in my heart! When I returned to Tulsa, I purchased a Russian textbook, and with no teacher to assist me, I began to devour the Russian language and to teach myself how to read it. Of course, I was not a master by any stretch of the imagination, but for a reason I couldn't explain, I was obsessed with learning Russian vocabulary.

When I was at home in Tulsa between meetings, I would lie in bed at night before Denise and I fell asleep and would study my Russian vocabulary. One night I said to Denise, "Dobraye ootra." Denise said, "Rick, please stop reading Russian and go to sleep." But I kept saying out loud, "Do-braye Oo-tra!"

Finally, Denise said, "What does *'do-braye oo-tra'* mean?"

I answered, "It's Russian for 'good morning.'" She responded, "Can you please learn to say *'good night'* and go to sleep? Please turn out the light and go to sleep!"

God knew I needed to know Greek so I could teach from the Greek New Testament. But in giving me Greek, He was also giving me a language so similar to Russian that making the leap when He later called us to move to the USSR would not be hard for me. I didn't know it at the time, but God was helping me get a jump-start on Russian before I ever knew I would need to really learn this language.

## Revolt Against the USSR in January 1991

In January of 1991, that brave group of missionaries I met at the missions conference boarded their plane to move to the USSR. They arrived the morning of January 13, 1991. Their plane landed in Riga, the capital of the Latvian Soviet Socialist Republic, which was a part of the Soviet Union, and they could not have chosen a more volatile moment to arrive.

Due to a series of uprisings in Riga, Soviet military troops moved into the city with tanks and armed vehicles. Soviet efforts to restore power culminated in several violent incidents. Barricades were built throughout the oldest parts of the city, and over the following days, six people were killed, several were wounded, and others were beaten by military forces. All of this was occurring at the very moment that team of missionaries arrived in Riga to begin the first aboveground Bible school in the history of the Soviet Union.

Denise and I sat in our living room in Tulsa watching the news of those horrific, tumultuous events in Riga and thinking of the brave souls I'd met in Florida who had just moved there. I wondered what was happening to that group of missionaries who were right there in the middle of it all. We later learned that some of them actually got caught in the gunfire that killed people on the streets of Riga. Fortunately, no one on that missions team was injured.

## Dressed To Kill

At about this same time, all over America there seemed to be a new rage about spiritual warfare. A lot of what I heard being taught seemed like unfounded, unbiblical ideas about the devil. In fact, what I heard many people teaching was so disturbing that I sensed the Lord wanted me to bring a balanced approach to the subject of spiritual warfare.

All of that spiritual error and excess was a crazy season of extremes that brought erroneous doctrine to God's people. I felt that if believers did not have a solid, biblical understanding of the devil — of our Christ-imparted authority over him and our divinely empowered weaponry to be used against him — it could leave them wide open to all kinds of wrong thinking and unfounded methods of opposing our enemy.

So I decided to write a book about spiritual armor with a biblical approach to spiritual warfare. That book became my best-selling book called *Dressed To Kill* that has now been published in multiple languages and is read all over the world. As I said, the material in that book reached back in origin to our first public meeting in Booneville, Arkansas!

For months in 1990, I was writing that book, exegeting every possible word from the Greek New Testament that had anything to do with the subject of spiritual warfare and spiritual armor. I was speaking at churches and conferences all over the country and enjoying the hard-earned success we were beginning to experience as a ministry. We were so thrilled at the remarkable turnaround in our lives since we'd left Fort Smith, and we were totally focused on obeying the Lord and establishing a teaching ministry in America.

Notable Christian leaders began calling me for help on key words they were studying from the Greek New Testament. One prominent leader flew to Tulsa to spend an entire day with me so I could sit with this minister and go over every single usage of a certain Greek word in the New Testament.

I truly felt that Denise and I were making a difference and having a significant impact in the lives of many through my books, our book-publishing company, and our public ministry across the United States. But God was about to lift our lampstand even higher to shine His light through us *around the world*, even as He had shown me.

## A Ministry Meeting That Brought Me *Full Circle* Back to That USSR Missions Team

In the immediate days after the tumultuous uprisings in Riga, I was invited to speak at a large church in Michigan that was pastored by Duane Vander Klok. Duane and his wife Jeanie had served as missionaries in Mexico for seven years before assuming the pastorate of their church, and they really had a heart for missions. In fact, Duane was a member of the Board of Directors for Calvary International, the missionary organization that had held the conference where I'd ministered at in Florida — and that had sent those missionaries to the USSR during what turned out to be a tumultuous and potentially very dangerous moment.

I was excited to be scheduled for those meetings in Duane's church in Michigan, and the services that weekend were wonderful. But it was something that occurred just *prior* to the Sunday morning service that became monumental, leading to an unexpected turn in our ministry.

In the pastor's study just before that service, I sat with Duane who was on the phone with another minister whose name was David Duell. I'd walked into Duane's office to greet him before the service and saw that he was on the telephone, so I lingered just outside the door. But when he saw me, he said, "Rick, come on in here. Dave and I have something we want to talk to you about."

With Dave on speaker phone, the three of us talked enthusiastically for a few minutes about the things of God. Then Duane got around to what he *really* wanted to talk about. He said to me, "Rick, we want to ask you to do something with us at the end of April."

I knew I was in trouble if Duane Vander Klok and Dave Duell were teaming up to ask me to do something. Dave had been an auctioneer at one time, and he could talk an Eskimo into buying a bag of ice! And if the two of them were ganging up to ask me to do something, I knew I was probably about to be "roped" into something I didn't want to do.

So with my defenses already in place, I asked, "What do you want me to do at the end of April?"

With Dave still on the speaker phone, they chimed in together and said, "Now listen to us all the way to the end before you answer. We're going to present you a deal like you've never had in your life."

I listened as the clincher came, and they said, "We're going to the Soviet Union to visit that first aboveground Bible school at the end of April — *and we want you to go with us!* We won't take no for an answer!"

This Bible school had been started by that same missionary group who had braved the early events of the collapse of the Soviet Union and had been caught in the crosshairs of violence on the streets just after their arrival. What Duane and Dave were proposing didn't sound safe to me, but even if it were a completely safe venture, I had no desire to travel halfway around the world through multiple time zones, even for a week or so. I didn't even have that much time free in my schedule, so I turned down their bold offer.

In fact, I said, "You guys are crazy. They are killing people on the streets over there this very week, and you want me to go there with you to teach in a Bible school? Have you guys forgotten that the new Bible school there is still technically illegal — and that they could all be sent to prison for what they are doing? No! I *won't* go to the USSR with you in April. *Never, never, never.* My answer is *NO.*"

They continued pleading with me, but I told them, "I am called to teach the Bible in the United States, and I'm working hard to get our ministry established here. I'm not going overseas — and I'm *especially* not going to the Soviet Union where we could be killed or imprisoned. I'm not interested, and I'm not going with you. So stop asking."

### 'Enjoy Yourself…While the Rest of the World Goes to Hell'

Because Duane and I were friends, he didn't mind resorting to friendly cajoling and coaxing to try to guilt me into making that trip. Duane looked at me sadly and said, "Okay, we'll go without you. But you will be missing the opportunity of a lifetime. Those students' parents spent time in jail for their faith and prayed for this day to come. We'll go in response to their cries and their prayers while you go ahead and stay here in the United States in your lovely house near the golf course." Then Duane sealed his sad discourse with the words, "You just enjoy yourself, Rick, while the rest of the world goes to hell."

I felt so "guilted" by those words that I heard myself say to them, "Okay, I'll go with you to the Soviet Union at the end of April."

*What! Did I really just say that? What had I committed to do?* I couldn't believe I let Duane Vander Klok and Dave Duell con me into saying yes — I actually fell for it!

Over a period of almost an hour in Duane's office that day, I'd gone from not considering this proposition at all to giving those two men my committed consent — not because I'd warmed up to the idea, but because I'd been cajoled and *practically coerced* into making this dreaded trip to, of all places, Jelgava, Latvia.

I can't say I was thrilled, or even happy at all, about what I'd just agreed to do. But because I am a man of my word, since I said I'd go, it meant I was going to go with them to the Soviet Union at the end of April.

Actually, I cannot begin to exaggerate how upset I was that I had been roped into a missions trip that I didn't want to take. I went home from that meeting and told Denise that I would be going to the USSR with Duane Vander Klok, Dave Duell, and a missionary based in Mexico named John Vereecken, whom I had never met. Denise could hardly believe that I'd agreed to go because she knew I did not have it in my heart to go anywhere overseas.

*However,* strangely enough, I'd been learning Russian for a couple of months, so I began to think this might be a chance to see how well I was coming along in my skills with this new language.

## The Plan Had Been Hatched

Right in the middle of all the wonderful turnaround developments we'd been experiencing in our U.S. ministry, I found myself preparing to get on an airplane to fly to the Soviet Union with Duane, Dave, and a man named John. Of all people, why was *I* going on a ten-day mission trip — especially one halfway around the world!

I continued watching some of the uprising and skirmishes in the USSR on the news. It was just terrible what was happening there. There were blockades, shootings, and confused attempts to quell potential uprisings and to prevent, or forestall, the inevitable collapse of the Soviet Union that was just around the corner.

What in the world was I doing planning to fly into the territory of the USSR — an unlikely place at a *most* unlikely time? I had no way of knowing what lay ahead for me and my family halfway around the world…but I was about to find out.

# 8

# ANOTHER *SURPRISING* WORD AND BRAND-NEW ASSIGNMENT FOR THE RENNER FAMILY

With my visa, passport, and plane ticket in hand, the time had come for me to make the trip overseas with my three traveling companions Duane Vander Klok, Dave Duell, and a man I hardly knew named John Vereecken. I had done my due diligence to prepare for teaching those young students from my knowledge of New Testament Greek. I understood the scheduled times that I would have with them, and I'd planned to do my part to lay a foundation underneath their lives that would hold them in good stead as they sought to do God's will. I was unschooled in working with an interpreter, so I did my best to prepare for that new experience as well.

I really didn't want to go on this ten-day missions trip, as I explained in the last chapter. But I'd agreed out of guilt to do it, and now, after many

---

**Left:** *Flag of the USSR, Union of Soviet Socialist Republics.*

exhausting hours over nine time zones, I was about to step foot on Soviet soil for the first time. Our plane was making its final approach to land in Riga, Latvia, and from my window, I could see the Riga airport just below.

As I peered out of the plane window, the images on the ground began to take vivid shape, and my first impressions that I'd been so eager to make were not very positive. Trashed and abandoned airplanes sat along the sides of the runway. The main terminal, which was quite small, looked like its entire marble exterior facade was falling off piece by piece. The name RIGA stood on top of the terminal in big letters, but parts of the letters were missing. The whole scene was dismal, like a movie scene in a war film, and the overcast skies, now above us, made it even more dreary and bleak.

As we exited the plane, Soviet soldiers with machine guns stood at the base of the airplane stairs to scrutinize all the passengers as they disembarked. The soldiers' faces were harsh-looking, worn by the hardness of life that they'd endured. The plane was parked quite a distance from the main building, but there was no bus to pick up passengers, so we walked from the airplane to the dilapidated terminal.

There, we were told to collect our suitcases, so we went to the baggage area to collect them from the luggage belt. However, the luggage carousel looked like it had been built in another era and was there only for show. Since it wasn't working mechanically, workers in the baggage area beneath our floor hurled all the suitcases into the air through a hole, where they all came flying upward and then dropping randomly onto the floor in front of us.

Once we located our suitcases, we proceeded to Passport Control for our passports and Soviet-issued visas to be checked. There, more soldiers sat in booths with glass windows that were so scratched from top to bottom, I didn't know how those officers could even see us to compare our faces with our passport photos. The booths were unpainted and every bit as dilapidated and broken down as the rest of the airport.

Passport officers in military clothing, with patches depicting the sickle-and-hammer emblem of the USSR, glared suspiciously at us as if we were enemies of the state. I'm not exaggerating when I say that if looks could kill, we all would have been left slaughtered on the floor before them! Believe me when I tell you, they did not look thrilled that we Americans had entered their territory.

Once we made it past Passport Control, we were greeted by a sweet woman from Texas with a southern twang who had just moved to the USSR in January with that missions group that I wrote about in the last chapter. Adele Alexander was serving on the team as the administrator for this first aboveground Bible school since the Bolshevik Revolution of 1917. Adele's warm and welcoming voice pierced the icy chill in the terminal, and we gladly followed her to a worn-out van that waited for us outside.

## More Impressions of the Soviet Union

We took our seats in the van and started our approximate twenty-mile drive from Riga to the city of Jelgava where the Bible school was located. The roads were poorly paved, and many of the buildings along the main road stood eerily burned out exactly as they had been at the end of World War II when they were bombed. Again, it felt a bit like we were touring a movie set where a post-war scene was about to be filmed.

Here we were, having barely entered the Soviet Union, and we were already speechless at what we were witnessing. I said to one of the other men, "Is this broken-down mess the Soviet Union we have been taught to fear all our lives?"

As we drove into Jelgava, I was taken aback by the dreariness of it all. I saw a towering statute of Lenin, the infamous leader of the Bolshevik Revolution, that stood prominently in the middle of the city's central square about a hundred feet from our hotel. All the buildings looked like they were crumbling and about to fall to pieces. I saw rundown public buses that were jam-packed with people wearing dark clothing and heavy coats as protection from the bitter winter weather they were still experiencing in April.

The city of Jelgava was established in 1265 and became known as Mitau by the Germans who once occupied that whole territory in those early centuries. I'll give a more detailed history of the city in the next chapter, but it's interesting that the city was again occupied by German troops during World War II. As a result, Soviet forces launched an attack against it in July

1944, and for three long months, Jelgava became the very front for battles between the Germans and Soviet forces. When the war ended, Jelgava was eventually rebuilt in typical Soviet style as part of the Union of Soviet Socialist Republics — the Republic of Latviskaya (Latvia) — and lost much of its Old World grace and charm.

When our small team arrived for our first visit in 1991, Jelgava simply looked like a neglected and broken-down city. I didn't realize how badly it had been devastated in World War II, and I thought it probably looked a lot like it appeared right after the devastation of that war. But that dejected little town, for the most part, *had been* rebuilt after the war. It was nonetheless terribly sad-looking, and everyone I saw on the streets looked hopeless and oppressed.

We checked into the hotel, the only hotel in the city, which was called the Hotel Jelgava. In those days, every hotel was under the control of the KGB, who were watching every movement of foreigners. The entire Hotel Jelgava looked derelict and abandoned. The walls and floors were a drab grayish color, and there was hardly any heat in the building. The reception desk was a tiny wooden desk that sat in the corner on the first floor — it reminded me of a little desk I may have put in one of our sons' bedrooms. As we walked up three flights of stairs to the floor where our rooms were located, I labored in my mind to grasp that this was actually a hotel, because its cold concrete walls felt more like the interior of a prison.

Dave Duell and I checked into room 201 on the second floor. The room was large with big windows, worn wooden floors, sparse amounts of furniture, and the wallpaper was an orange-brown color that I had seen in the hallways of most of the rest of the building. The two beds, each on opposite sides of the room, looked so much like coffins that Dave and I even joked that we'd be sleeping in caskets that week. Curtains covered the massive windows, so I reached up to pull them apart. But the material was so rotten that it ripped at the slightest touch. Those curtains literally came apart in my hands, so for that whole week, we slept in that room with no window covering.

When I looked into the bathroom, I couldn't believe my eyes. The tiles on the shower walls were falling off, exposing ugly tile mud beneath, and the rest of the walls looked like some kind of disease was growing on them. The sink, which was attached to the wall with screws, was nearly falling off — all of this for the bargain price of 25 cents per night.

I didn't know that this was a typical interior of a Soviet hotel at the tail-end of the Soviet Union. One morning while we were living in that hotel for the week, we were awakened very early by the entire building shaking. I jumped up to look out the window — and to my amazement, I saw a huge Soviet army tank rolling down the street. As that massive tank rolled along, it shook the entire hotel!

On our first morning there, our small group of four went to breakfast in our hotel before we started over to the Bible school. We had to walk out the front door and then back inside through another entrance and into a long, narrow room with old wooden tables that sparsely filled the dining area. The woman working there couldn't speak a word of English, so she pointed to a table with samples of food so we could choose the kinds of food we wanted to eat. For breakfast, the choices were a single slice of dark bread, a sugar-covered cookie, and a cup of coffee or tea. When they brought me my coffee, it was loaded with more sugar than coffee itself. My teaspoon stood straight up in the center of my cup, supported by all the sugar that had been poured into it! Despite all the shortages, that was just the way they prepared coffee in those days.

We were also shocked at the near-absolute silence in the cafe. Several tables were taken with local people who were drinking coffee, but they whispered among themselves as they spoke. Because people lived with fear that someone might overhear what they were saying and "inform" on them to the local KGB, they whispered and communicated in seemingly unintelligible tones. Duane, Dave, John, and I sat at our table and talked in normal tones, as Americans normally do, and others in the cafe stared at us in disbelief that we would dare to speak above a whisper.

After breakfast, the four of us were escorted on foot to the Bible school, which was about four blocks away. The sidewalks and streets were cracked and uneven, and the walls of the buildings we walked past were deteriorated and crumbling from years of neglect. People we passed on the sidewalks were all dressed in various dark shades of clothing. It felt like we were spectacles in a sea of drab, monotonous military-colored clothing worn by everyone else around us.

I also noticed that many of the people we saw were "humped over" as they walked. Years of oppression had taken a toll not only on their minds, but also on their bodies. They would also not look into our eyes as we passed them on the street. They lowered their heads and looked at the ground, almost as if they were afraid to look into our faces because we stood out so much.

No one had told me that for years, Jelgava had been a "closed city" because of a large Soviet military presence that was located in the very center of town. Residents had never seen foreigners in their city because no foreigners had been allowed. The people of Jelgava didn't intend to be rude and standoffish — they just didn't know how to respond to us. Many were fearful that if they spoke to us, it might get them into some kind of trouble with local authorities.

### Previously Underground Christians in an Aboveground Bible School

We approached the Bible school, which was located in a second-floor auditorium in a newer, Soviet-style building directly across the street from the local headquarters of the KGB. As we came close to the building, I saw scads of young people excitedly entering the main doors. They were some of the students who had come from all over the USSR to attend this first aboveground Bible school in existence in more than seventy years.

I later found out that a local man with strange contacts with the KGB had negotiated the renting of the auditorium to get the Bible school started. It was unthinkable that this happened right under the watchful eyes of the KGB, but God made a way for it to happen, and more than two hundred students were coming there daily to be trained for ministry.

The majority of those students were children and grandchildren of parents and grandparents who had spent time in prison for their faith. For seventy long years of the atheistic communist regime, their parents, grandparents, and their offspring prayed that a day would come when they could freely study the Bible and train for ministry.

*That day had miraculously come!* The fact that they were assembling to do these things publicly was almost unimaginable at that time, and I'm sure it felt surreal to most of them there who understood the persecutions of the past.

I must mention that before the communist regime came to Latvia and to the other nations of the USSR, those lands had a rich spiritual history. Latvia itself had been converted from paganism to Christianity, and Slavic-Russian-speaking peoples were officially converted to Christ when church tradition says the apostle Andrew carried the Gospel across the Black Sea into Crimea, where several thousand were converted to the faith. Later the apostle Andrew allegedly traveled north along the Dnieper River, where Kiev would be founded in the Fifth Century, and it's also said he eventually took the Gospel as far north as the future location of Veliky Novgorod. Nonetheless, paganism continued to dominate until Prince Vladimir initiated the Christianization of Kievan Rus in the year 988 AD.[1]

The extent to which Christianity previously influenced that enormous swath of land is a revelation that becomes more and more real to me the longer I live in the lands of the former USSR. But we know that when the atheistic Communist Party seized control in 1917, the Christian faith fell out of favor with the new authorities. To merely believe in God put individuals at odds with the new ruling class, and as a result, untold numbers of Christian believers were killed, sent to prison for their faith, or ostracized and penalized for their belief in God. Many of these Bible-school students' grandparents, parents, family, and friends were among the many who had been terribly persecuted for their faith.

So when I think back to that day when I first traveled to Jelgava to teach in that school, I am *still* mystified as to how God made it happen. The odds of a Bible school operating openly in the USSR — and across the street from the local KGB *and* being run by Americans — was practically nil. It was *impossible*, yet it was really happening. And I was there to capture a small glimpse of this history in the making. It was a surreal experience that I was privileged to witness and participate in.

From the start, I was profoundly moved by the dedication of the students in this school and the sacrifices they'd made to be there. They had very few possessions, and they'd left homes, parents, and siblings — some traveling enormous distances — to pursue their callings. They had placed themselves completely in the Lord's keeping, not knowing what the future held. For example, how long would this newfound freedom from communism last? Their very presence in that aboveground school marked their own points of no return — truly there was no turning back for them. But they saw it as a privilege and not a sacrifice. Those young men and women considered it a privilege to lay down their lives to make Christ's name known among the nations. Their faith was childlike, yet they possessed the vision of generals and the wisdom of sages. I felt privileged to be asked to stand before them, and the atmosphere was heavy with God's presence in each of our sessions together.

## More Divine Encounters That Led
## to Lifelong Connections and Friendships

*Andrey Chebotarev* was a young student in the school who would later become a part of my team and help me start our TV network, the first of its kind in this part of the world. And he eventually became my associate in Riga.

Andrey remembered, "Going to Bible school was a big dream. It was unheard of because such schools had been illegal in the Soviet Union. So when news about the Bible school began to circulate, everybody started calling their friends to say, 'There is a Bible school…do you want to come?' It was an opportunity that never existed before. Everybody was burning with spiritual passion, but we didn't have much systematic teaching, and we really needed that to move forward in our callings. That school was an awesome time for all of us. We were truly at the right place at the right time."

*Alexander Dovgan*, a student at the school who later became my TV producer and a leader in our ministry, said, "Most of the students already served in underground churches before they came to the Bible school. But they needed education to grow so they could return to their churches to raise up prison ministries, worship ministries, and youth and children's ministries. That's the reason most of them came to the Bible school — to raise their level of excellence and to return home to use it in their local churches. And most of the people who attended that Bible school are still in ministry today. It was really 'fruit that remained,' and it was marvelous."

*Anita Busha*, also a student at that time, said, "I was there for every lesson and every study. The atmosphere was filled with faith and the worship was awesome. It was just unbelievable because it was the first Bible school in the Soviet Union."

*Leonid Bondarenko*, another student who has worked with us in our ministry for decades, related: "I had just become a believer and when I came to Bible school, I knew I belonged there! Looking back, I'm amazed that God had so much mercy on me to get me into that school. But when Pastor Rick taught, something in me came alive…his teaching was different from what I'd heard from others. The whole atmosphere in the Bible school was electric and exciting."

Alexander Dovgan also related, "I was a believer in the underground church from my childhood. When I came to the Bible school, I was shocked to see so many people there because at that time, there were very few good telephone connections to even call people to tell them about the school. But so many people found out about the school, and they all came on time to get in on those first classes.

"It all started so suddenly. We were all concerned that the new freedom wouldn't last, so we wanted to use the opportunity because we thought that this time in history may not happen again. Everything in the USSR was falling apart, so we all wanted to take advantage of what was happening because we didn't know what would happen later to prevent us from studying the Bible in a formal setting."

Andrey Chebotarev added, "There was such a spiritual hunger in that school. We all tried to catch every word that was being taught. We had never heard such teaching, so we ate up everything we heard. We made notes from every word spoken from the platform, and we tried to use every minute wisely. My grandfather had been imprisoned for his faith, as were many believers in his age group.

"My father related to me the story of how my grandfather was arrested one day with no warning. They came in one night and took away all the believing men from our town…and later on, even the women and children. It was so devastating. My grandfather was sentenced for twenty-five years, but Stalin died in 1953, so my grandfather was released early and only served thirteen years.

"We students knew that could happen to us, too, so we took that time at the Bible school as a gift. It was a time to study — a divine moment — because we didn't know if such an opportunity would ever come again."

These students were bright, but they had never been allowed any kind of higher education because most of them were from a Pentecostal background — and in the eyes of the government, this was a strike against them. Thousands and thousands of Pentecostal kids were forbidden higher education because when officials opened their documents, big red letters across the top of their files read: PENTECOSTAL. In general, Christians were not allowed to obtain higher education. So to attend a Bible school was a dream come true.

## My First Time To Teach the Students

Adele Alexander, the sweet woman from Texas, met us at the front door of the Bible school that first morning to walk us upstairs and show us around. Adele herself had only been there for about three months, but she made us feel comfortable in our strange surroundings. She introduced me to Nikolai Kulakevich, the young man from the Florida missions conference, who would be my interpreter that week. I recognized several American team members whom I'd met at that missions conference several months earlier. Their plans then to move to the USSR had materialized, and now here we all were in the same room, embarking on something bigger than ourselves that I'm sure few of us comprehended at the time, least of all me.

Among that team were Nikolai and his brother Peter Kulakevich. Peter was the man whose Russian Bible I had "borrowed" for a night during the missions conference. He was serving as the co-director of the Bible school and as one of the interpreters that week, along with Nikolai.

Nikolai was my first interpreter in the Jelgava Bible school when we moved to the Soviet Union, and he ended up serving alongside me for years afterward. Commenting about the school and the students, he said, "I think the Bible school and its impact was the biggest of any Christian work in the Soviet Union at the time. The students who went out from there to start the churches still lead the biggest and most powerful churches in the former Soviet Union today. The Bible school was a huge work that still continues in the ministries of those students. *Hundreds* of churches across the land have been started because of that Bible school."

At the front of the auditorium, where I was about to take my seat, I scanned the auditorium as it began filling up with students for that first session in which I would minister. Words spoken in Russian were buzzing all around me, and I became abruptly aware of what a very different environment I was standing in at that moment — it was *electric*!

Then a team came to the platform to lead worship for a roomful of students who seemed filled with a strange mixture of faith and fear. I could feel the students' faith and their excitement that they were publicly studying the Bible — that they were actually experiencing the fulfillment of their parents' and grandparents' prayers and dreams. But their faith was blended with a sense of trepidation and urgency that this open door might not stay open for long and that they needed to maximize their opportunity before it could be suddenly taken from them — or before they were all sent to prison for studying the Bible publicly.

The truth is, those students' attitude of seizing the moment and stewarding their time is the way each of us as believers should live our lives every day, making the most of every minute and every opportunity we're afforded to proclaim God's Word, because the days are evil (*see* Ephesians 5:16). We must be "busy about the Father's business," preaching the Word when times are good and when times are *not* so good because none of us knows exactly how much time we have left.

As I peered over that auditorium into the faces of those students — all of them from the underground Church — I was gripped with the realization that they were standing in their moment, in the very time those who had gone before them had prayed for. I became emotional trying to take it all in — the sights, the sounds, the smells, *everything*. I could *feel* the uncertainty in the air as people wondered if this new freedom was going to last or be shut down, forcing them to retreat to their old way of life.

Although I had a lot of Bible knowledge, these students knew commitment beyond anything I had ever known in my life. They were willing to jeopardize their lives to be there. I kept thinking, *Who am I to teach THEM? They could be teaching ME what it means to be committed.* Yet I was there to teach, and I felt so humbled and honored to be there among them.

The worship further gripped my heart as I began to understand what a huge price those students were willing to pay to study God's Word aboveground. Andrey Chebotarev, the twenty-something year-old man on the platform leading worship would later become my assistant for years and eventually take my place as pastor of the Riga Good News Church when our family relocated to Moscow.

But at that moment, I didn't have the slightest idea that God would call our family to make the USSR our home and that my connection with the people in the room around me would continue beyond the teaching sessions that week. All I can tell you is that in that moment, I felt staggered, undone, and *dazed* by the emotion and the spiritual fervor in the atmosphere that swirled around me. I was standing in a prayed-out moment of my own, and it was as if my heart knew something my head could not grasp.

Soon an offering was received from the students. I watched as a worn-looking offering bucket passed in front of me. I looked in it and could see it was filled with *kopeks*. Each was less than a cent in value, but it was all the students had to give.

The students lived in a dormitory and were each given a monthly stipend of thirty rubles that was provided by the Bible school. At that time, *thirty rubles* was about the equivalent of *one dollar*. From that meager stipend, which was really only enough to purchase paper for classes and maybe a single pastry, those students gave as generously as they could into that offering every morning. When I saw those kopeks, I realized those students were not only jeopardizing their lives to be there, but they were also giving sacrificially of their substance to honor the Lord, support the work, and show gratitude for what they were receiving in that school.

After the praise-and-worship portion of the service and the morning announcements, I was called to the platform to introduce myself and greet the students with the help of my interpreter. That day, I'd planned to teach them from Ephesians 6 on the subject of spiritual warfare — even as I stood there wrestling with my own thoughts, *Who am I to teach them on this subject? They have lived it their whole lives!*

Standing behind a homemade pulpit, I looked into the eyes of the most spiritually hungry people I had ever seen in my life, and I have to honestly say that I was undone by their eagerness to know more of God and His Word. And now, they openly sat with Bibles in their laps and paper and pens in their hands. They were *ready* to take notes and to learn.

I inwardly felt humbled to stand before them. I had never undergone the persecution they had experienced in life, and I had never jeopardized my life as they had to serve Jesus. In one flash, I repented quietly that I had taken my faith for granted in our country where we simply had not experienced religious oppression as they had experienced and lived through.

### 'Welcome to Your New Home'

I tried to push my emotions out of the way so I could focus on teaching in that first session. But as I opened my Bible to get started, I was *jolted* to my core when I clearly heard the Holy Spirit say the words to me: *WELCOME TO YOUR NEW HOME.*

I was so dumbfounded by what I'd just heard that I stumbled verbally as I began to teach in that first session. I looked out into the eyes of those spiritually hungry students who sat before me in their tattered, Soviet-looking seats in that run-down auditorium all around me. And I forced myself to focus on my message, but with the words, *"Welcome to your new home"* pounding in the back of my heart and mind the whole time I taught.

No emotion could adequately describe my stunned shock as I heard and *felt* those unexpected words reverberate throughout my being. Although I'd given God my wholehearted *yes* to do with my life as He pleased, I had not seen this coming. I hadn't even *wanted* to go on this mission trip. I almost *didn't* go. I was very happy with how my life was going and was content to stay the course and give everything I had to traveling and teaching believers the Word of God — *in the United States.*

Was He *really* saying He was calling me to uproot my family from Tulsa in the United States and move them to Jelgava, Latvia, in the Soviet Union?

## What Would I Do With What I Had Heard?

The Bible-school meetings continued as if oblivious or indifferent to the mind-numbing words I had privately heard from the Lord. But those services helped my remaining time on the trip to pass quickly. The atmosphere in the school was charged with enthusiasm every day. Everything about the way those sessions were conducted was vibrant with God's presence — the praise and worship, the announcements, the teaching, the fellowship among the students — it was all so precious and filled with energy and vitality.

We were experiencing a visitation from the Lord in that place, and we were careful to embrace it. We were keenly aware that we were working with Heaven, and that Heaven was working mightily with us. The intermingling of those two realms was both sobering and exhilarating. We literally felt God's pleasure and His joy as we endeavored with all our hearts to yield to Him and allow Him to orchestrate His good plan for each meeting.

In my time in the Bible school that week, I realized that I had been drawn into a divinely timed moment — one that marked history in the making for that vast region of the former USSR. Yet nothing I experienced on that trip was as weighty as my own encounter with the Lord during my first session in the school. I knew it was the voice of the Holy Spirit, but my mind struggled to comprehend what I'd heard Him say.

For the remainder of the week, I surveyed the city of Jelgava with new eyes, imagining what it would be like to live in the midst of this broken-down and derelict city where stores were empty and void of nearly every essential product needed for life. Finally, one day in our room, I told Dave Duell what the Holy Spirit had spoken to me. Although Dave was known to be a man of faith, I was stunned to hear him say, "Don't do it, Rick! Why would you jeopardize everything you are building in America? You're living every preacher's dream, so I'm telling you to stay in Tulsa and simply make a missions trip here every once in a while. *Do not move here!*"

But in the depths of my being, I was confident that the Holy Spirit had told me this was to become our new home. When I wasn't in class sessions teaching, I roamed in and out of stores, where I saw shelf after shelf empty of nearly all products. There was no bread, no milk, no eggs, no flour, and no medical supplies at all. I kept thinking, *How could this be? All our lives, we were taught to fear the Soviet Union, and it is a completely broken system.*

In fact, it's difficult to describe just how broken the entire system was at that time. Except for the time of World War II itself, this was the worst economic moment in the history of the Soviet Union. It was *certainly* not a place where a loving husband and father would desire to move his family. Yet I knew the Holy Spirit had said, *Welcome to your new home.*

As that day passed, the Holy Spirit continued speaking to my heart. I'll summarize what I heard Him say, "There are many good Bible teachers in America, but I need you *here* to be a part of laying a scriptural foundation under the mighty move of the Spirit that is going to take place in this part of the world. What you are doing in America is good, but you are more needed here than there. I am calling you to move because the teaching gift I've put inside you is so needed in this part of the world. Because it was illegal for pastors and leaders in this territory to study the Bible, they do not have a grip on solid teaching, and I need someone like you to help lay a reliable foundation under them."

When Nikolai Kulakevich was interviewed for this book, he recalled my first sessions and the response of the students very vividly. He said, "The very first time Rick came to the Bible school to teach, he was a guest speaker for a week. The students were fascinated with his teaching and how he taught from the Greek. Right from the start, he was one of their favorite teachers. They were captivated by his knowledge of New Testament Greek and with his precise handling of Scripture."

It was true that I experienced an amazing connection with those students that week. I even began to experiment with the eight-hundred Russian words I had committed to memory. After each class, students flooded the front of the classroom to inundate me with so many marvelous questions. It was impossible that they could have enjoyed me more than I enjoyed them. As I said, I had never witnessed such spiritual hunger in my life. I longed to impart so much to them, but my trip was about to end and I would have to leave. Actually, the connection I felt with those students was a foretaste of what would come in the future. Meanwhile, I couldn't shake the words, *Welcome to your new home* that the Holy Spirit had spoken to me and continued to speak to me.

Each night in my hotel room, I had plenty of opportunity to deeply ponder what I had experienced in the pulpit during that first morning session. Although there was no way I could make sense of it, I needed to come to grips with what I'd heard the Holy Spirit say to me. *My new home?* Had I dreamed the whole thing? Past moments in which I'd received distinct direction from God confirmed that I had not dreamed it. Yet I was failing desperately to form a concrete thought about what to do next.

What *would* I do now? Far from a soldier receiving his marching orders and setting out to carry out his directive, I stumbled in my mind about what I would even say to Denise. I pictured her in my mind's eye waking the children up for the day, making them breakfast, and praying for me on my assignment at a foreign Bible school. She would be expecting me to return home to captivate her with stories about the meetings, about my time with Duane and Dave, and about the sights I'd seen in this still war-affected city halfway around the world. She would *not* be expecting to hear me say, "Pack your bags, Honey. We're moving to the USSR!"

In the dark silence of that hotel room, the thoughts even came to me that I could say nothing at all *to anyone* about what God had said. After all, I had not told a soul except Dave. I could easily keep quiet and act as if nothing happened. The temptation to draw the curtain between our present course and God's new direction for our lives was very real.

During our time on that first trip to Jelgava, besides spending time in the Bible school, we also went to some missionaries' homes. I saw the conditions they were living in — tiny little houses on horrible, muddy, rut-filled streets. When we went to stores in other areas of Jelgava, I was stunned by the lack of goods and basic supplies there too. *Everywhere* we went, we saw deficit.

Before we left Latvia on that trip, we had also held a public meeting in the Throne Room of a huge palace that had been built by Elizabeta Petrovna, the daughter of Peter the Great — and another meeting in an auditorium in Dobele, a town south of Jelgava where Soviet army tanks were kept in case they were suddenly needed. In those meetings, the power of God erupted and we saw amazing miracles of healings and deliverances take place that still dumbfound me to this day when I remember them.

By the way, Jelgava and Riga today simply *sparkle* with Old World charm and are delightful places to visit and even live. The cobblestone walkways in Old Riga are picturesque paths for tourists to travel on foot, and that beautiful part of the city is host to quaint artisan shops and eateries that tourists are thrilled to patronize — *and locals as well.* But back then, everywhere we went on that trip, our eyes and minds were filled with deficit and need on the one hand and with great manifestations of God's love and power on the other. And He was telling me this was my new home.

## A Trip to Moscow and a Vision of the Future

After almost a week of teaching in the Jelgava Bible school and in the public meetings, our team flew to Moscow, Russia, so we could experience the capital city and what had been the very heart of socialistic communism. President Ronald Reagan had referred to the Soviet Union as "the evil empire." Naturally, I was curious about what kind of conditions we would find in this vast city. But like everywhere else I'd been on this short missions journey, Moscow appeared tattered, torn, and worn out by years of Soviet neglect and atheistic communism.

But the city was *massive,* filled with unending streets lined with Soviet-style apartment buildings and factory smokestacks jutting over the top that billowed gray smoke into the air above us. In the distance, I saw more factory buildings that sort of melded together with apartment residences to form large shafts that mechanically shot blasts of dark smoke into an equally dark sky. It was an ominous, dismal sight to my eyes.

We stayed at the Izmailovo Hotel, a huge complex that had been built for the 1980 Olympics that were boycotted by President Jimmy Carter as a protest against the Soviet Union's invasion of Afghanistan. The hotel rooms were small and looked unkept, and the beds, like those at the Hotel Jelgava, reminded me of coffins. The telephones in the rooms looked like the oversized toy phones that my younger sister played with when she was a little girl.

The bathroom was startlingly deteriorated with water pipes that protruded from around fractured tiles that were falling off the walls. The soap on the sink had been used by many previous hotel guests and only a slither of it remained. The toilet paper contained so many wood grains that were visible to the eye that I wondered if I'd get splinters if I used it. The bath towel was the size of a hand towel and was so stiffly ironed that it felt more like cardboard than a towel.

Soldiers were everywhere on the streets and many were carrying machine guns. Because of the various uprisings that were occurring in different Soviet Republics, the air was tense with suspicion and authorities were on edge.

I scanned our surroundings, noticing that most people were dressed in unattractive, military-colored clothing just as I had witnessed in Latvia. And on that trip, I never saw a single foreign-made car. All the cars — and believe me when I tell you there weren't too many of them on the streets in those days — were all Soviet-made vehicles that looked like toys compared to American automobiles.

## It Happened at Lenin's Mausoleum

We finally made it to Red Square, which is situated right outside the walls of the Kremlin. My companions and I were *speechless* that we were in the Soviet Union and were actually standing right in the middle of Red Square!

We walked toward a red stone structure in the square that looked sort of like a stair-stepped pyramid with a small parapet platform on top. It was a mausoleum with the name ЛЕНИН (Lenin) inset in red granite in a belt of black granite wrapped around the top of the structure. I stood silently in front of this mausoleum and felt a cold chill shoot through my body as I pondered this leader of the Bolshevik Revolution of 1917, Vladimir Lenin, who became the founder of the Soviet Union that was birthed from that uprising.

Like many others, when I was growing up as a young man in America, I had seen films and photos of Soviet leaders standing in places of honor atop the parapet of that mausoleum to observe and salute military parades that marched through Red Square. I was quite taken in by this landmark standing in front of me that represented such a significant part of the Soviet Union's history.

Minding my own business as I focused on the monument and the name *Lenin* inset in granite, *suddenly*, the mausoleum and the walls of the Kremlin behind it "disappeared," and I found myself in the spirit. Now before me, in place of the mausoleum, I was seeing a vision of my future play out before me like I was looking at the stage of a play on Broadway. The "curtains" separating the actors from their audience suddenly *vanished* before my eyes as I looked onto this "stage" as a spectator, in amazement at what flashed before me.

First, I noticed an auditorium with seats positioned in a crescent-moon configuration, and *I* was on the stage! I instinctively knew that I was seeing into the future a church, and I was the pastor of that church — *in the city of Moscow*. I could even see the size of the church. I realized I was having another divinely granted experience — a brief view of my future in that part of the world. Instantly I knew that I would pastor a sizable congregation in this vast city of Moscow.

Then, just as suddenly as it appeared, it *disappeared*, and I found myself once again looking at the front of Lenin's mausoleum.

That was in April 1991. At that time, there *were* no large congregations in Moscow. In fact, because it was the end of the Soviet Union and barely the dawn of a new era, there was only one fairly large Protestant church in Moscow — a Baptist church — where evangelical believers could legally meet. During the seventy years of the Soviet period, it was necessary for the Soviet authorities to publicly assert that there was freedom of religion in the USSR, so they used this church as "proof" of such freedom.

Despite the fact that large Protestant church congregations were simply unheard of, somehow, God opened a portal for me — a window between time and eternity — and allowed me to see this very thing in my future.

On this short missions trip, I had already heard the Holy Spirit say to me, *Welcome to your new home.* From that word, I understood the Lord wanted my family and me to move to Jelgava. Then with the vision at Lenin's mausoleum, I also understood that Latvia would not be our final assignment. I'd gathered that we would eventually move to Moscow, Russia, where we would start a significant church. It was all very overwhelming to me and so much for my mind to take in.

Sometimes spiritual experiences like that one and moments in which God reveals something about your future can take you off guard as He allows you a small preview into what is to come. It's a "blip" concerning a time to come and just one piece of a larger, grander puzzle that doesn't provide huge answers for your mind, but it certainly gets your attention. The Lord uses those moments so you'll seek Him and hold yourself steady as He leads you straight into those future experiences, though it may take years to make the journey.

That's what happened to me that day at Red Square in 1991. *What a week!*

## But I Decided To Keep It All a Secret

When I finally returned home to Tulsa, I decided to keep quiet about what the Holy Spirit had said to me. As I wrote in the last chapter, we had recently purchased a house, and how we loved that house.

We had just recently settled into this haven we called home on a large corner lot in a quiet Tulsa neighborhood. It had served as our retreat between ministry engagements as I taught the Word of God and traveled across state lines from coast to coast. With all the invitations I'd been receiving to minister, those retreats had become fewer and further between, yet we'd never been happier nestled in our lovely home in Tulsa. Denise and I and our sons were as joyfully busy serving Jesus as we had ever been, and we were as prosperous and blessed as we had ever been.

I had hoped that being back home after my time in Jelgava would help me forget what the Holy Spirit had said to me while on that trip. But day after day — week after week — God's words, *Welcome to your new home,* lingered in my hearing, and were becoming lodged inside me and I couldn't get them out of my head.

In fact, I so wanted to forget what the Lord had said to me that almost a month passed and I hadn't spoken one word to Denise about it. My mind simply struggled to grasp and embrace what I had heard. In fact, my mind was *numbed* for the better part of those days as I processed my new assignment. I found myself just going through the motions of life — while reaching out to God in my heart with every bit of willingness to obey that I could muster.

To be truthful, even though God had clearly spoken to me, at that moment, I did not intend to obey it. I simply didn't *want* to move my family to the Soviet Union. And I knew that Denise would be terrified by the very thought of it.

I thought, *We're busy building our ministry in the United States and we're being blessed. If I just keep this to myself and disregard what I heard the Lord say to me, no one will know that I've been disobedient. So I'm not going to tell anyone.*

Please remember that it was 1991 and the Soviet Union was still fully in force. The Soviet hammer and sickle flew on Union of Soviet Socialist Republics flags throughout the vast expanse of the USSR's *eleven* time zones. Lenin's image loomed large over the geography in the form of monuments, statues, and paintings that could be found in almost every city, village, factory, and school. His face was even printed on the ruble so that every time someone pulled out money to buy food, the image of Lenin passed through that person's hands.

At that time, Gorbachev was still in power, and Soviet troops marched on the streets of many cities. The Soviet economy had crashed, and the government was rationing the most basic products, such as milk, butter, flour, and meat. Automobiles sat unused in garages because there was virtually no gasoline to purchase. It was an economic mess so terrible that it seemed only a fiction writer could have dreamed up so frightful a scenario. But millions of people were experiencing this nightmare as their everyday reality.

I shuddered with sadness as I considered this and pondered the idea of moving my family to the Soviet Union, which seemed *horrifying* to me. What man in his right mind would want to move his family into that kind of predicament? However, in my spirit, I knew God had to have something great in store for us or He wouldn't have wanted to move us there. Yet my mind *reeled* at the thought of obeying what He had put in my heart and all that it would mean for my family. I couldn't figure it out, and I was still in shock over the newness and the *strangeness* of it all.

You see, my spirit was willing, but my flesh was weak. My emotions interpreted God's call to the Soviet Union this way: "Leave everything you've worked for; abandon everything you've built; and follow My voice to a country where there is no money, nor any visible way to financially support your family or your ministry."

I thought, *At least when God called Abraham, he was called to a beautiful land.* The Soviet Union at that time didn't sound anything like the land of milk and honey that became Abraham's destination. Did God really expect me to leave our growing ministry and beautiful home in Tulsa, Oklahoma, and relocate to a country where everything had been dominated *and destroyed* by communism?

Little did I know what amazing wonders God had in store for our family and ministry — wonders far greater, richer, and more colorful and blessed than I could have imagined. When He first pointed His finger at me and said, *Get up, get out of your country, and follow Me to another place where I have wonderful things in store for you,* I couldn't have begun at that moment to fathom how miraculously He would use us on behalf of precious Russian-speaking people "a world away."

But *questions, questions.* There was still so much I didn't know; however, I *did* know that if I didn't tell anyone what God had said to me, no one but God and me would know if I disobeyed that divine mandate. (No one but God, me, and Dave Duell, that is, but Dave had flatly told me not to do it.) My flesh was tempted to do just that. It wanted to say, "No, thank You, Lord. I'm staying right here in good ol' Tulsa, Oklahoma, along with all my faith buddies, where I'm enjoying the sweet taste of success!"

I'd even tried to convince myself that I'd missed it and that my mind was playing tricks on me. But as loudly and clearly as I'd heard the message, I knew it *was* God's voice that I'd heard speaking to me.

After wrangling with God for two months, I was beginning to relent. If He wanted us and our ministry in the USSR, then that's where we'd go. But before I had completely thrown in the towel and surrendered, I would drive through our beautiful neighborhood and look at the lovely place where we were living — and I'd tried despairingly to tell myself, *God wouldn't ask you to leave all of this to move your family to an unstable situation in the Soviet Union. That's a dangerous place. Christians have been imprisoned and killed there for their faith. What will the future hold if you move your family there?* I struggled deeply as I thought about all we would be losing and leaving behind.

Finally, I realized that if I didn't say, "Yes, Lord, I'll do what You say to do and go where You tell me to go," the Lord would find someone else to do the job. I knew He wouldn't wait on me forever, so a deciding moment came when I would have to get with it or get out of the way so God could choose someone else.

That deciding moment occurred when I was again invited to speak at the annual conference for the missionaries from that same missions organization I'd ministered for before. Their annual conference was held in Florida again that year, and I went to the conference by myself while Denise stayed at home to care for the boys.

All those missionaries had gathered from all over the world, including from Russian-speaking parts of the world, and one by one, they all stood to give testimony of what God was doing in their parts of the world. As I listened to those from the Soviet Union testify about what God was doing, my heart was simply gripped. I absolutely *knew* that God had told me the Soviet Union was our new home, but I hadn't told Denise because I was hoping the tug in my heart would go away.

But as I sat in that service among all those missionaries who were testifying about what God was doing in the Soviet Union, I thought, *It's now or never. It's time for me to say yes to the Lord.* In the excitement of the moment, I succumbed and said, "Yes, yes, yes! I'll do what God is asking me to do!"

## I Said It and My Words Set the Plan in Motion

I walked to the front of the auditorium, asked for the microphone, and proceeded to publicly announce that Denise and I and our sons would be moving our family to the Soviet Union to work alongside the other missionaries. I told them, "I am surrendering right now to move Denise, myself, and our boys to the Soviet Union. I am committing to give one year of our lives to the emerging work there."

The leadership of that mission organization rushed forward to lay hands on me and rejoice that I was willing to lay my ministry aside to participate in the miraculous work God was beginning in the USSR.

I knew that good written material was needed for this mighty move of God, so I would join the team there and I would write materials for new, emerging church leaders. So I said, "We're willing to go if you're willing to take us." They clapped, they shouted, they laid hands on me, and they prophesied over me. It was such a wonderful night — until I went back to my quiet room, alone, and realized what I had done.

Because there was such a faith-filled atmosphere in that meeting, it was easy for me to make that announcement. But when I returned to my hotel room that night, the reality of what I had done really hit me. I berated myself, *Rick Renner, why did you make that announcement tonight? If you had kept it to yourself, no one would have known you were living in disobedience by refusing to go and by just minding your own business in your ministry here in the U.S. But now you've made a public announcement. If you don't keep your word, they will KNOW you're living in disobedience to God.*

But it was official. By my own lips, my destiny had been sealed. Like a locomotive in full throttle, my words themselves seemed to contain the power to move our lives in a brand-new direction. The plan, held secretly in my heart, had now been fiercely set in motion by my public testimony. We could choose to remain on board that train and experience where this wild ride would take us — on the adventure of our lives. Or we could disembark and choose to abandon the new direction God was taking us.

That night I called a dear friend, a well-known pastor who was also a financial supporter, to tell him about my announcement. When I told him, he said, "That's the dumbest thing you've ever done in your life. You're going to leave your ministry when you're experiencing what very few people get to experience? Let me tell you what's going to happen to you. First, you are moving your family to a land that is so unstable that there could be a revolution at any moment. You are endangering your family.

"Second, once you're off the road from ministering and out of sight, you'll be out of mind, and your partners will forget you. Then when everything over there crashes and you need to get out in a hurry, you'll be calling me to help you get plane tickets to get your family out of danger." He continued, "Rick, if you move your family to the Soviet Union right now while you are being so blessed in every aspect of your life, you are a fool."

That friend was usually very encouraging to me. But on that particular night, he *terrified* me. After that conversation, I *vomited* all night. I only left the toilet for moments at a time — mostly I held onto the toilet and vomited because that phone call upset me so much. But at the same time, it was a night when I was coming into alignment with the will of God. In spite of all my apprehensions and fears and my friend's horrible predictions, I was completely, once and for all, surrendering to God's will.

I felt so trapped because I knew God had told me to move my family to the USSR, but this new plan was *not* a part of *my* plans. And now, because I had made a public announcement, it seemed there was no turning back. And the pessimistic words of my friend echoed in my soul: *Out of sight, out of mind. If you disappear from the scene, people will forget you and stop support-ing you financially. When things get badly out of control in the USSR and you need to flee for your lives, you won't even have the money to buy a plane ticket. You'll be calling me to buy you plane tickets to get you out of a mess!*

But before I go any further sharing this unlikely turn of events leading to a brand-new season in our ministry, I want to let you know that my friend's words that night were *good* for me. They made me look really hard at what we were about to do. While his words greatly discomforted me, that con-versation caused me to seek the face of God and to dig my heels deeper into what He was asking our family to do as I became more and more convinced that we were on the right track.

That night I sought the face of God as I spent that entire night on my knees in front of the toilet *vomiting* and *vomiting* — not because God made me sick, but because my soul was waging an all-out war against what God had told me to do, and it was affecting me in my body.

That same friend remained a trusted friend to me throughout many years and stepped in at critical moments to help us and our ministry in important ways. When I think of him, my mind immediately goes to Proverbs 17:17, which says, "A friend loveth at all times, and a brother is born for adversity." He has been a friend who loved us at all times and has always been there in difficult moments in our lives and ministry.

## I Made the Announcement
## to Denise Over the Telephone

Since I had made a public announcement about the future of our ministry halfway around the world, I knew I needed to call and tell Denise about it. But how was I going to tell her?

Denise and I had grown up during the Cold War and we knew that believers in the USSR had suffered terribly for their faith. We could both remember evangelists in our youth who would ask audiences, "If communists came to America and arrested Christians for their faith, would there be enough evidence that you were a Christian for you to be arrested?"

Because of such comments, Denise was terrified of communists and even had recurring nightmares of running from communists. Because I knew Denise had a fear of communists and all things connected to communism, I wondered, *How am I going to tell Denise we're moving to the Soviet Union?*

But that night, I called Denise. She was at home in Tulsa with our three sons. Over the telephone — and not face-to-face — I told her, "Denise, I have to tell you what God said to me when I was in the USSR two months ago. He told me that the Soviet Union was our new home. I've silently struggled with this ever since God spoke to me when I was in Jelgava, but tonight, I said yes to the Lord and publicly surrendered to move our family to the Soviet Union for a one-year commitment.

I continued, "Sweetheart, this is the point of no return. We are moving to the Soviet Union for one year to help pioneer the amazing work God is doing there."

I'll never forget Denise's response. She said, "Well, I can't say I'm very excited about this right now. But if this is God's will for our lives, when we finally get on the plane to move there, I'll be a happy woman."

*Ugh.* The reaction I really wanted was that she would kick and scream and say, "*NO! I won't go!* How could you move our precious family into the heart of atheistic communism!" But instead, she surrendered and was immediately supportive of whatever the Lord wanted us to do. And isn't that exactly what we had committed to do as a couple when we were married at the altar of the First Baptist Church in Fort Smith, Arkansas?

Next, I knew I needed to meet with Pastor Bob Yandian to tell him what we were planning to do. I really hoped he would tell me I was making a disastrous mistake. Pastor Bob was level-headed, practical, and truthful, so I knew I could rely on him to tell me what he really thought.

Of course, I hoped he would say, "Rick, this is a bad decision. It's impractical that God would bless your ministry so marvelously and then tell you to walk away from it." If that would have been what he'd said, I would have canceled the whole deal. But instead I heard him say, "Rick, for some reason, I bear witness that this *is* God's will for your life. You're supposed to move your family to the Soviet Union."

With that, the engines were definitely warming up, and the train of our new calling was beginning to roll down an unfamiliar track into yet another new season in the lives of Rick and Denise Renner.

### A Talk With Our Three Sons
### That *Also* Didn't Go the Way I Wanted

Denise and I had discussed the goings on of the past several weeks since I'd surrendered to God's call to move the USSR. She knew I felt trapped by this decision and she herself was processing the sudden *and stark* change of direction — and she was doing as well as one could expect. But we had not talked to our children about this landmark event in our family that would significantly change their lives as well.

As I said, I really didn't want to move our family to the USSR, and I kept trying to find other voices to tell me that this was a mistake. But now, most everyone seemed to be on board with it and even agreed that it was definitely God's will. And the two well-meaning friends who said *no* riveted my attention only temporarily, as each time I wavered, the Holy Spirit swung into action to grip my heart so tightly that His dealings had become more and more difficult to resist.

I told Denise, "We are going to tell our sons about this, and if just one of them hints to us that this is a bad idea, I'm going to take it as a sign that we are not supposed to do it."

*Oh, how I wanted someone to tell me this was just a bad dream and I needed to wake up!*

We sat the boys down on our family-room sofa that seemed to engulf their small frames as they sat huddled in the dead center. They sat waiting with uncertain anticipation for our talk to begin. It was an otherwise cheery, sunny afternoon, but I was about to give them the bleakest, most solemn talk of their young lives.

Eight, six, and two years old, respectively, Paul, Philip, and Joel were accustomed to family discussions, as Denise and I had always included them in the work of ministry and made them feel an integral part of our family unit because they *were* such a critical part. But I'd let them know that this was a *big* one — the *queen mother* of serious family discussions. They were ready.

In my best storytelling voice, I began our "talk" by dramatically describing Soviet-era Russia and the treachery of socialistic communism with its dark effects on generations of people held captive under its rule. In somber tones, I related to them that this horrible place called the Soviet Union had historically imprisoned and killed Christians.

Then I asked, "How would *you* like to live there?" I continued, telling them, "I sense God is calling our family to move there, but I want to know what you think about it first." But before I allowed them to answer, I continued quickly to keep my momentum and provoke the negative response I was hoping for.

"If we go, you won't have the things there that you have here. You'll have to give up your friends. You will rarely see your grandparents, aunts, uncles, and cousins." Then, as if I couldn't leave well enough alone, I clinched my dramatic performance with the ultimate warning: "Your parents could be killed in this venture and you'd be orphans, with no father or mother to raise you. If that happens, it's entirely possible the three of you would end up living in an orphanage in the Soviet Union.

*"Or we could ALL be killed!"* I ended my speech with those horrifying words that would frighten even the most resilient among children.

*That should do it*, I thought, feeling satisfied with my performance. *The boys will be so frightened that Denise and I couldn't possibly pick up and move to that part of the world under such circumstances. After all, what parents would do such an emotionally cruel thing to the vulnerable minds of their own children?* (As I recount this moment, I am amused at my desperation and the depths to which I was willing to go to find a last-minute loophole in this new undertaking.)

I waited for the boys to respond and to see if they would cry and flail their arms and legs about, sprawling all over the length of that sofa and writhing in terror at what I'd just proposed. Instead, long, quiet seconds passed as they remained silent, still huddled together in the middle of that sofa.

Finally, I asked them, "Well, boys, what do you think about what I just told you?" Philip slowly raised his hand to speak as if hesitant to be the one to break the silence.

"Well…," Philip started. His forehead wrinkled in deep concentration as if he were choosing his words carefully while simultaneously processing his thoughts. "We're all going to die *sometime*, Daddy."

Then he straightened his shoulders a bit, seemingly bolstered in his convictions by getting out those first few words. "You've always told us to do whatever God says to do, at any cost. Someday we're all going to die, anyway," he reasoned more confidently, *"so we might as well die doing what the Lord told us to do."*

Before I could counter Philip's answer, Paul nodded his head vigorously in agreement, and Joel affirmed his brothers' unified response.

I could have sworn that at that moment, I heard the Lord laughing over our situation. With my clever storytelling skills, I had succeeded only at backing myself further into a corner. I could either come out fighting or I could wave my white flag of complete surrender to the will and plan of God.

But "come out fighting" with what? Despite my best efforts, I had just been disarmed by two elementary-school students and a toddler! It was time to start making our move.

By the time that conversation with our sons ended, I had fully embraced the fact that God wanted me to move our family into the deficit-filled, dangerous environment of the USSR. But I thought it was just a *one-year commitment* and then we'd be back in Tulsa to resume building our U.S.-based ministry.

It is God's mercy that at times, He doesn't tell us from the beginning the whole picture of what He has planned for us. If He had told me that the mission I was about to embark on was a lifetime commitment, I perhaps would have never obeyed. But moving for one year was something I could finally negotiate in my mind. Through that experience, I learned that sometimes God gets you in motion — and moves you well beyond the point of no return — before He shows you the full picture.

I later remembered that Jesus taught, "For *many* are called, but few are chosen" (Matthew 22:14). There are "many" who have had opportunity to do something great and significant, but because they wouldn't obey what God told them to do, they were not chosen to do it. I couldn't live with the thought that God would have to replace me with someone else. So, finally, I came to a place of complete surrender to His will and plan for my family and me in the Soviet Union — even if I *did* still think it would be for only a year.

### Next, We Had To Tell Our Parents

One particular day after this new, huge development in our lives, I was pondering how it had all come about, and I remembered those days at Falls Creek youth camp when I faked a call to the mission field. I had tried to manipulate my parents into sending me to Mexico to be with my older sister one summer. As I remembered that incident, I realized God was getting the last laugh with me once again.

As a teenager, I thought I was pulling the wool over my parents' eyes — and even fooling the mission board that sent me all those maps after I'd "surrendered" to foreign missions. But God would get the last laugh because even when I was faking a call to missions, He had a secret plan to move me, with my future family, to another part of the world in another season of my life. So, in retrospect, mine wasn't a fake calling after all!

But this time, I would need to have a different kind of conversation with my parents — and with Denise's parents as well.

The time had come for us to prepare logistically to make the move of our lives — from our beautiful home, precious family and friends whom we dearly loved, and everything that was familiar to us. My mind still raced wildly at times, concocting worst-case scenarios to fill the gap of my ignorance and the many questions I still had. But while most of my questions went unanswered for the time being, peace began to settle in as I labored in prayer concerning our life-altering move. As I entered that place of rest, I began to see the steps I needed to take to pull up our roots in Tulsa and replant them in the Soviet Union.

Of course, once we were confident that our decision was right, I knew we needed to break the news to both our parents and our other family members. My parents lived nearby, so we decided to start by telling them. Denise and I sat in their living room with them over coffee, and I began to tell them how God had spoken to me when I stood to teach in the Bible school in Jelgava and that we were going to be moving to the USSR for a year to help in the new move of God.

My dad looked at me as if I had lost my mind, but he and Mother were never negative. I actually can't ever remember a time when my parents were negative about any step of faith I felt led to take in the ministry. In my years in college to that present time, my dad had seen from my life that I really had been led by the Holy Spirit.

Mother was an employee at our ministry and had always been so supportive. But when my older sister Ronda learned about our plans, she said, "What? *What!* You're going to do *what*?!!" She was in total despair at first. My sister Lori said, "Rick, are you sure you're supposed to do this?" And Denise's sister Trula was so upset by our news that she lost her breath as she almost choked on our words. Regaining her composure, she asked, "Do you guys realize what the USSR is and what has happened to Christians there?"

Then it was time to go see Denise's parents in Miami, Oklahoma, so I could tell them that I was going to move my family to the Soviet Union. Denise and I knew this was going to be the hardest conversation to have because Denise's parents were twenty years older than my parents, and they vividly remembered the ruthless reign of Joseph Stalin over the USSR. Her parents remembered the days of concentration camps and *gulags* where believers suffered terribly for their faith.

So when I told Denise's parents that we were moving to the Soviet Union along with their three grandsons, it was a rollercoaster conversation that I will never forget. Denise's precious daddy, Dave, said, "Rick, you're moving my girl and grandsons over there to die. Why would you do such a thing when you know that is a dangerous part of the world?" As an older man, he had a lot of memories of Stalin's time, so I understood his concerns. I told him over and over that I was at peace that this really was God's plan for our family.

### Five 'Barley Loaves' in the Hands of Jesus

We had been staying at the Robersons' house for a few days because we were ministering in a nearby town for a few services. On the last night of our meetings, Denise's mother Nora decided to go to our last service with us. That night, I preached on the little boy in John 6 who surrendered his five crackers for Jesus to use however He wished. You know the account, of course, that once those five crackers entered the hands of Jesus, they were multiplied to feed a giant multitude.

As I ministered that night, the Holy Spirit spoke to Nora and said, "Rick and Denise and their boys are your five crackers. Are you going to hold on to them, or are you willing to release them into My hands? If you will release them to Me to do with them as I wish, I'll use them to touch more people than you could ever imagine."

Before we got back to Denise's parents' house that night after the meeting, Nora had released us to do God's will and let us know that she would be supportive. But Denise's dad still struggled with our decision to move to the USSR.

On the day we left Miami, Oklahoma, to head back to Tulsa, we finished our conversation about the big move, said our good-byes, and Denise and I and Paul, Philip, and Joel got into our car to leave. Denise's daddy and mother stood on the back porch, as they always did, to wave goodbye. But this time, her daddy stepped off the porch and moved toward us, waving for Denise to roll down her window because he wanted to say something to her before we drove away. His tall frame towered over our little car as Denise rolled down the window and he leaned in to speak to his baby girl.

"Yes, Daddy," Denise said. "Did you want to say something?"

Very solemnly, he answered her: "Take a good look at me right now… because when you drive off today, I'm probably going to die of a heart attack. You'll end up killing me if you go through with this decision."

*Wow.* That was heavy for me to handle, but Denise shrugged it off and said, "Oh, Daddy, you're going to be fine and live a long time. And God is going to take care of us in the USSR." With that, she said one last good-bye and rolled up the car window. And Denise was right — we had many more visits and conversations with both Dave and Nora before Dave died years later, and Nora passed away many years after that.

## Preparing for the Big Move

Back in Tulsa, we began preparing for our big year-long adventure to the Soviet Union. I began to call friends and pastors to tell them we were moving to the USSR. Every pastor I called and every church we told was just stunned. *Everyone*, for the most part, was speechless when they heard the news. One after another, they asked, "Who in the world would leave all the great things that are happening in your life?" They were genuinely shocked that we were going to walk away from it all — and potentially jeopardize our lives — to do what God had asked us to do.

However, everyone who knew us well understood what a turnaround we'd experienced in our lives after leaving Arkansas. So they understood that, after all we had been through and all that God had restored unto us, we would not be making such a drastic change in direction unless God had ordained it.

I really can't over-dramatize it. What was happening in our lives was remarkable, and everybody knew it was remarkable. Just think of it. For us to walk away from the extraordinary success we were experiencing touched people so deeply that they said, in effect, "We want to be a part of this by becoming your ministry partners."

In addition to the nonstop invitations to minister that we were getting, as well as our burgeoning book sales, we had also recently gone on fifty radio stations across the U.S., and those broadcasts were well-received. We were beginning to have a really good response to those radio programs. Yet in spite of that and the fact that we were selling a lot of my books and teaching materials, we really didn't have a big group of financial partners. But *suddenly* people began to sign up to support us while we would be living and ministering in the USSR.

Then in August 1991, the coup took place in Moscow that eventually led to the complete unraveling of the Soviet Union. People all over America sat in front of their televisions to watch the news of military tanks rolling down the streets of Moscow. Gorbachev was arrested, a new committee took control, and Boris Yeltsin seized the reins of power. It was a total collapse that took place in front of a watching world. It was a time of demonstrations, revolution, and it was volatile beyond description. And I was about to move my family into the middle of it all. No one could predict if what was happening there would be a good or bad development — whether the new freedom would be long-lasting or *crushed*.

During that time, my phone began to ring nonstop as pastors and churches asked, "Are you still going to move with all that's going on there right now?" But I knew we were on track and that God was not surprised by any of these developments. So I assured each concerned caller that we were still going and that Jesus would show Himself to be Lord over our lives there.

As a part of preparation for writing this book, several people were interviewed to capture how they felt about our giant step of faith at that time. A long-time friend named Tom Harkness recalled a phone call that we'd made to him and his wife Laurel as we prepared to leave the U.S. He remembered, "Rick and Denise called us and said, 'We just wanted to call and make sure we contacted you before we moved to the USSR. We don't know what's going to happen to us when we get there because it's so precarious there and we may never talk to you again. So before we leave, we want you to know how much we love you.'"

My sister Ronda recalled, "It was dangerous in the Soviet Union. So I thought, *What are you doing? Are you kidding me! What are you thinking? Have you forgotten that the USSR is our enemy — that it's an atheist nation and you'll be wasting your time?*"

Ronda expounded more on her raw feelings at that time by telling me, "People in America love you, Rick. Why would you leave at the very moment your ministry is taking off? Your own country needs you, and you are going to move to the Soviet Union?"

Ronda also related, "But, deep down, no one in our family would ever want to hold Rick and Denise back from what the Lord wanted them to do. And I'd learned from Rick when he was young that if he heard God's voice telling him to do something, he was going to do it regardless of the cost. But I honestly cried a lot during that time, and I kept thinking, *This can't be happening.*"

Ronda continued, "But because we all had 'a one-year commitment' in our minds, we thought, *Okay, there's an end in sight, so we can do this for a year.* But if we had known up front it would be for the rest of their lives, it would have been so much harder. I think it was God's mercy to let us all think they were going there for just a year. Still, it was a journey for all of us to walk through and to discover along the way all that God had planned. It turned out well, of course, but let's face it, the Soviet Union was a dark and really scary place back then."

When I asked my mother how she felt about our making that move to the Soviet Union, she said, "I knew if it was God's will for you to move there, then it had to be my will too. I always prayed that my children would follow God. And I knew that you and Denise had a special calling on your lives. So I wouldn't have done a thing to try to keep you from going. I was all for it. When your father expressed concern, I didn't feel concern at all. I just felt like if God was going to lead you there, He would take care of you there."

Mother related to me, "But your father was so sad about your leaving America. I encouraged him that if God has called you and Denise to do this, it was simply what you and your family had to do. It took him a while to adjust, but when he began to see the fruit of what God was enabling you to do in the Soviet Union, he became calmer, and he was really proud of you."

## Our Partners Quickly Got Behind Us

I had been passionately motivated by the grace of God to minister in 450 meetings a year. But I was beginning to see that the Lord had been working a plan all along that I was not aware of. I didn't know that those years of going to *church after church* was a part of His plan to help finance our ministry when He would send us to the USSR. Most of these churches would eventually become our partners to graciously support our new ministry in the Soviet Union!

Denise and I were simply being obedient one step at a time, and a foundation was being laid by God Himself onto which we would be able to step out and obey His larger plan. Of course, I didn't know for a long time what was happening. When I was doing those 450 meetings a year, all I knew was that we were being obedient to what God had asked us to do at that time — but that step of obedience was laying the groundwork for future steps of obedience.

Friend, never minimize what you are doing *right now*. It is likely that God has not shown you the full picture yet of what He will ask you to do in the future. But what God has asked you to do right now is critically important for your future success. Every single step of obedience builds upon previous steps of obedience. If you don't obediently do what God has assigned to you right now, you will not be prepared for things He will ask you to do in the future. All those pastors, churches, and friends that we ministered to nonstop would become a part of God's provision to support our ministry in the lands of the USSR. But all we knew was that we loved God and His people, and we longed to share the life-transforming truths of His Word with all we could as He opened the door for us to do so.

My first step to prepare for our move overseas had been to call pastors and churches where we had ministered and let them know about our new development — our next big step to move overseas for a year. Because we didn't know what kind of income we'd have after we made our big move to the Soviet Union, my second step was asking our growing staff to economize in every way possible.

I told them, "When you pick up the newspaper on your front porch every morning, please save the rubber-band and bring it to the office so we don't have to buy rubber bands. If someone sends us a letter that has a paper-clip on it, please save the paperclip so we don't have to buy paperclips. If you print something on the printer, please turn it over and use the other side of the paper for what needs to be printed next. It's time for us to *economize, economize, economize*. We have to be extremely careful so we can do what God is asking us to do."

## Denise's First Impressions of Moscow

In late September 1991 — just one month after the historic coup in Moscow in August of 1991 — Denise and I flew together to Latvia to bring our first load of belongings there as a part of our preparation for our family's arrival in January 1992. It was Denise's first trip to what had been the Soviet Union, and October 3 would be our tenth wedding anniversary.

When I took Denise to the Soviet Union on her first trip there in the fall of 1991, it was for all practical purposes still the Soviet Union. In other words, nothing had visibly changed at that point. Soviet troops were still visible everywhere. So Denise's first visit was quite a startling "waking up" to where we were moving our family. She was stunned at the living conditions and the gloom that seemed to hover in the atmosphere like low-hanging smoke in a room of people. But true to her words and her heart, Denise was committed to doing whatever God asked of us, so she was fully on board although *shocked* by all the sights she was taking in.

On that trip in the fall of 1991, Denise and I purchased our first Soviet-made car due to the generosity of two couples who were partners with us and gave a financial gift so we could buy it. That gift was huge to us, and it was a God-sent encouragement that He would financially provide for all our needs. The car we purchased was a small cherry-colored Lada with doors that never closed properly. We also officially rented our first home in Jelgava on that trip, which is why I've always counted October 1991 as the time of our official move to the territory of the former Soviet Union.

On that trip, I took Denise from Jelgava, Latvia, to Moscow, Russia, to see the capital city since it was the heart of the former Soviet Union. Remembering our arrival at the Moscow Sheremetyevo airport, Denise said, "When we walked off the plane and into the airport, it was dark inside the terminal. Half the lightbulbs were out, and the only people I saw were men in black leather jackets and they all looked angry. There wasn't a woman in sight anywhere. Finally, we went through Passport Control, and the passport officer looked at me as if she hated me. Then in broken English, this female officer began to ask, 'Do you have any cigarettes…how about blue jeans… do you have any Kotex?'"

Passport Control back in those days was a little bit like a shakedown. Because there were deficits of all those items, the passport officers would use their leverage to get incoming foreigners to surrender those kinds of items to them. American cigarettes, blue jeans, and Kotex were like luxury items. Jeans…people would nearly do anything for a pair of blue jeans. And Kotex…those kinds of feminine products didn't even exist in the Soviet Union. So when you'd go through Passport Control, it was not unusual for passport officers to shake you down to see what they could get from you before stamping your passport.

Once we collected our suitcases, we started our drive to the massive Izmailovo Hotel with its multiple towers that had been built as dormitories for the athletes of the 1980 Olympic Games. As we drove, Denise was taken aback by how dark and dreary everything looked. She said, "I cannot exaggerate how dark the streets looked to me. It was like a city with no lights. I was totally freaked out by what I was seeing."

And even though the Soviet Union was unraveling at that moment, there were Soviet soldiers all over the place and big red Soviet flags were still flying everywhere. And the hammer-and-sickle emblem of the USSR was also visibly present. The USSR was in an ongoing state of collapse, but it would be two months before the Soviet Union would be formally dissolved. At the time Denise and I were there on that trip, instability and uncertainty were simply all around us.

We finally arrived at the Izmailovo Hotel where we would be staying that week — the same hotel where I'd stayed on my trip in April of that year with Duane, Dave, and John.

I want to paint a broader picture of that hotel for you at that time — October 1991. As I told you, it was built for the 1980 Olympics as a dormitory for athletes, not as a hotel, and at the time it was built, it was the largest housing complex in the world. After the Olympic games were over, it was converted to a hotel, and from 1980 up to the time we stayed there in 1991, it had become a popular hotel for foreigners.

Denise recalled, "We drove into the parking lot of the Izmailovo Hotel, and there were no lights on there, either. Huge, dirty trucks filled the parking lot — it was a very dingy, ugly sight. Then we walked into the hotel to find, again, that many lightbulbs were out in the hotel — I think less than half of the lights were working. I literally shook inside — I was *traumatized* by what I saw."

Denise continued describing her initial ordeal at the Izmailovo: "The floors of the lobby and hallways were covered with worn, dirty carpet. When we got to our tiny little hotel room, I couldn't believe how horrible its condition was. The two beds looked like little coffins with bedcovers that were red, green, and brown — and old, worn out, and rumpled.

"I went into the bathroom and was shocked to see about half the ceramic tiles on the walls were missing, and exposed pipes ran up and down the walls like a power grid. I reached for toilet tissue and couldn't believe my eyes. The roll of toilet paper in that bathroom was held in place by a broken branch from a tree! And when I went to the sink to wash my hands, there was just a misshaped slither of used soap that had been used by previous guests!"

Denise added, "The sheets on the bed and the bath towels in the bathroom were ironed like cardboard. The bath towels were so tiny, they were actually more like hand towels, and absolutely nothing matched. Even where they had tried to replace ceramic tiles that had fallen off the walls, the replacement tiles were mismatched. I was shocked and appalled at every turn in that room. I slept in my clothes every night!"

The next morning, Denise and I went downstairs for breakfast — if you could call it breakfast. It consisted of a single hot dog and a few green peas. Denise was given an apple and she was thrilled — that is, until she bit into it, and a worm that had been living inside that fruit was "staring" back at her.

That morning at breakfast, a Christian brother from the underground Church met us to give Denise and me a tour of some of the bigger sites in Moscow. All of the teeth in that dear brother's mouth were either missing or they were gold-plated, which was a status symbol back in those days. He was a tall, bony guy whose gold teeth went in all different directions. But he spoke perfect English and was very joyful, smiling almost nonstop the entire time we were with him.

Denise remembers being taken aback by this man as well. Then at one point, he looked at her from across the table and said, "Sister, I think you need some joy. You need to pray in tongues!" Denise answered him, "You're *right* — I *do* need joy." And, immediately, she started to pray in the Spirit.

One evening, Denise and I tried to eat in one of the few restaurants we could find. But eating in restaurants was a very interesting experience because they usually didn't have any of the food listed on the menu. Deficits of food were felt everywhere, so when the waiter handed us a menu, at first it looked huge and filled with pages and pages of delicious-looking choices. But when we began pointing to the menu to show the waiter what we wanted, she would over and over say, "Nyet" ("No"), and then explain in Russian that they were out of that particular item.

We'd point to items on page after page on the menu, and the waiter would answer, *"Nyet, Nyet, Nyet...."* Finally, we learned to simply ask, "Tell us, what do you have available in this restaurant?" Although we had menus loaded with choices, most of them didn't exist because of food deficits. Usually, the only thing we could really count on to order was Russian borscht, black Russian bread, and maybe a meat and pea dish mixed with mayonnaise.

The whole time we were in Moscow, Denise struggled with our surroundings because it was totally foreign to our way of living and seemed so dark, dreary, and bleak. Remember I told you about recurring nightmares Denise had experienced in which she was chased by communists. Because soldiers with machine guns were so visibly present almost everywhere we went, she was tempted often to lose her nerve. Here I was, elated and excited for the new adventure we were about to embark on as a family, but Denise was in a state of shock.

But then something happened that changed everything for Denise *in a split second.*

## The Power of a Smile in Any Language

On our last day in Moscow, our guide took us to Arbat Street, which at that time was just about the only place where foreigners could buy souvenirs. Arbat Street was a long walking street lined with vendors selling all kinds of Russian-made knickknacks — Russian black-lacquered boxes, Russian nesting dolls, military hats, military paraphernalia, lots of Russian fox pelts and hats, and so on. Because capitalism was illegal, the vendors on Arbat Street were illegal, but they were tolerated because tourists needed somewhere to buy souvenirs.

The whole length of the street — from beginning to end — was filled with little folding tables that were covered with souvenirs. Also on the sides of the street were artists who would sketch your portrait for a few bucks, and there were men carrying parrots and Polaroid cameras for anyone who wanted to pose with their exotic birds. And because the economy of the USSR was in such a state of collapse and stagnation, there were many grandmothers standing at the sides of the street selling items from their homes or shawls they had woven as a way to get a few rubles to buy food. They lined streets by the thousands *all over Russia* to sell things from their homes just to pull together a little money. But there on Arbat Street, you saw a little of everything. It was astounding what Arbat Street looked like back in those early days compared to its contemporary flair today.

As Denise and I walked along Arbat Street looking at all the items, she noticed an elderly woman standing over on the far side of the street selling handmade shawls and beautiful black fox-fur hats. Denise said, "Rick, I want to go look at her handmade items and hats."

When she approached that elderly woman, the older Russian woman smiled at Denise with a warm and welcoming twinkle in her eye. In that flash of a moment, this elderly woman's smile melted Denise's heart and the two of them connected. Although they could not speak each other's language, they traded smiles, they hugged, and they laughed and laughed together. In that moment, all of Denise's apprehensions simply fell away, and she began to enjoy not only where she was at the moment, but also her new adventure.

*Oh, the power of a smile and a twinkling eye!*

## Preparations Back in the United States and God's Financial 'Covering'

Denise and I returned to Tulsa from our first trip to the USSR together after we'd said yes to God's call to help His Church in that part of the world. Because we still had three or four months before leaving the U.S. for one year, I had time to minister in more meetings across the country.

Everywhere I went, people were *stunned* that we were leaving our ministry in America to take the big leap across the Atlantic, beyond the Iron Curtain, and into the very lands of the Soviet Union that seemed so unpredictable and dangerous at that time.

In one of those last meetings, I was ministering in a church conference in Tacoma, Washington, along with several other speakers that week. They were all talking about our big move to the Soviet Union. Privately, I'd been wondering how we would financially cover all our expenses while living in the USSR and not conducting meetings where we would be given offerings. But I kept my concerns to myself and kept telling the Lord that I trusted He would meet our needs, even as He had already enabled us to rent a house in Jelgava and purchase a car.

On the last night of that conference, two of the other speakers who were ministering asked me to come forward so they could pray over me about our family's next big step. As they laid hands on me, I felt the power of the Holy Spirit come upon me as my legs buckled under me and I fell to the floor. On the floor, I could tangibly sense the power of God moving all over me. This was already a wonderful experience, but then something totally unexpected happened as I lay there on the floor.

People all over the auditorium began to simultaneously move out of their seats and walk to the front of the room where I was lying on my back on the floor. With absolutely no prodding from any of the special speakers, people lined up to walk past me and to lay cash on top of me! One by one, they walked by dropping cash on me, and more and more money began to be piled on top of me until I was *covered* with a mountain of cash.

As I lay there, I was a little embarrassed and surprised by what was happening. I kept wanting to get up, but the Holy Spirit kept impressing me to lie there. Then suddenly He spoke clearly to my heart and said, *Let this be a sign to you that you do not need to worry about financial provision. This is My sign to you to let you know that I'll see to it that your financial needs are COVERED.*

God did not have to give me a sign that night. He could have just required me to trust Him with no special outward sign. But in His mercy, He gave me this visible illustration to help my faith. I knew from that point onward, God was going to somehow supernaturally meet all our needs and that we would be financially covered.

### Kenneth E. Hagin Ministered
### From My Book Manuscript

But something else important was happening in our concluding months before we left the United States. I was finishing my newest book called *Dressed To Kill*. As I mentioned, it contained biblical teaching on spiritual warfare and armor that I wrote to refute some of the silly teachings that were growing in popularity in some Charismatic circles. For months, I had lugged my big desktop computer onto planes with me, set it up in hotel rooms, and between meetings typed and typed until I finally finished *Dressed To Kill*.

Because we lived only a few blocks from Brother Hagin, I decided to drive over and put the manuscript in his mailbox with a note asking him if he would be willing to read it. I had never personally met Brother Hagin. My only personal contact with him had been when he laid hands on me at Sheridan Road Assembly in Tulsa in 1974 when I was supernaturally healed of a serious kidney condition. But I thought, *What would it hurt to simply ask if he would read it?* So I drove to his house, put the manuscript into his mailbox, and drove off, not knowing whether I would ever get a response.

A couple of weeks later, I received a phone call from Brother Hagin's associate, Tony Cooke. I heard him say, "Brother Hagin has read your manuscript and really likes it. He wants to know if you would be willing to let him use a portion of it at his upcoming Winter Bible Seminar at Rhema Bible Church, where he will be addressing some of the off-balance issues of spiritual warfare that are so popular in some parts of the nation right now."

I was *flabbergasted.* I said, "Mr. Cooke, as far as I'm concerned, Brother Hagin can do whatever he wants to do with my manuscript. I am so honored that he would want to use any of my materials."

Wow…Kenneth E. Hagin was a living legend to me. I couldn't imagine a greater honor than for him to minister from something I had written. I had hoped Brother Hagin would read my manuscript and perhaps make a simple comment to me about it. But now he was asking to use it as part of his teaching for one of his annual conferences! As you can imagine, I was *elated.*

When he was interviewed about his memories of that moment, Tony Cooke said, "Brother Hagin liked Rick's manuscript and asked about permission to use it at the Winter Bible Seminar in 1992. Brother Hagin liked a lot of the verbiage Rick used. His manuscript was consistent with the same kinds of things that Brother Hagin was teaching, and because he liked Rick's wording, he decided to utilize it pretty heavily, incorporating multiple sections of the book that he read over the course of the meeting. It was pretty rare for Brother Hagin to take somebody else's book and read sections of it… that was just not something he commonly did."

Brother Hagin's Winter Bible Seminar was to be held just a few days after our family boarded our plane to move to the lands of the former Soviet Union. But Brother Hagin read extensively from my book in that meeting. In fact, when I got the cassette tapes and heard how much of my book he used, I was blown away by it. He even told the attendees at the seminar — and the multiplied thousands who heard the cassette tapes later — that he was quoting from my book and that they should go out and buy it.

The reason I'm telling you this part of my story is, I want you to see what God was doing in our lives right up to the moment we departed the United States. Up to the last minute before we left, we were experiencing amazing blessings from God and a phenomenal turnaround in our lives and ministry that was simply unending.

So when we moved to the USSR, we were not running from failure. In fact, it felt like we were walking away from what we had dreamed for all our lives. Here we were building our ministry and had such a bright future ahead of us, by all accounts. But it wasn't our ultimate destiny. God had merely been getting us ready for the biggest assignment of our lives. And our future would be bright *still*!

Just a short time before we left the United States, we realized we would be leaving just four days before Joel's third birthday, so we decided to use his birthday as a moment to gather the whole family at our house to celebrate his special day together and to spend time with them for the last time before we departed for a year. We didn't want Joel to miss celebrating his birthday with his cousins, so in the midst of our last-minute preparations to move across the world, we reached across town to extended family and threw together a party for Joel that was also a private good-bye party for us with our family members.

## JANUARY 27, 1992 — A Monumental Day
## in the Renner Family

A few days later, our immediate family stood outside our boarding gate at the Tulsa airport to bid us farewell. They really thought we were only going for a year, which made our good-byes a little easier. But we were moving to an extremely volatile region of the world, so they had to put aside their worries and trust that God would take care of us during that one year.

Denise's sister Trula remembered that day at the airport very well. She said, "I was shocked and so upset when they went to Russia. I was so devastated that I bawled and bawled, and so did Rick's dad. He and I made spectacles of ourselves at the airport — we were just ridiculous! But for me, it was a really sad day. I mean, they were moving *to the SOVIET UNION,* for heaven's sake!"

It was true — we *were* moving our family to a *very volatile* part of the world at the time. But because of the experience I'd had with the Lord a few years earlier, I was sure our sons were safe in the arms of Jesus and that they would be just fine. I also knew that *somehow* God was going to be faithful to provide every dollar we needed to do the job He was assigning to us.

*But wow…* all of this was so *unlikely* for a boy from Sand Springs and a girl from Miami. We knew no one else from our small towns who had moved their families to the USSR, of all places! When we crossed the bridge from Arkansas into Oklahoma a few years before, it had been a huge leap of faith and obedience that caused a real turnaround in our lives. But now we were crossing a bigger bridge, one that would lead us to another continent and from a free world to a world devastated by communism — from a land of prosperity to a land of utter brokenness.

In the pages that follow, I will share the details of how we transitioned as a family from living in our beloved home in Tulsa to living in rented houses and apartments with little or no heat in sub-zero temperatures during long, harsh Russian winters. In many ways, those inconveniences were the least of our difficulties, as we had to scale with endurance many other mountains of challenges — or retreat to a valley of mere existence outside of God's plan. There would be no in-between.

Whether you know me and my family or not, you can probably guess that we scaled those obstacles, overcame the challenges, and passed our tests — and we *remain* committed to stay the course of obedience to Jesus for the rest of our days. Because we sought God diligently to obey Him and to hold fast to what He had spoken to our hearts, this unlikely family from Tulsa would soon be privileged to witness the transformation of *nations* over three short decades since the fall of communism in this part of the world.

But at that moment, everything that's now history was still a mystery to us — a mystery we found the courage to step into and start walking out so God could bring more light. I'll share next the unlikely details of that light that burned so fiercely into the darkness that also awaited us an ocean away.

'From Tulsa to Riga, it seemed as if we
had been supernaturally led into a very dark alley
in terms of our new spiritual surroundings. But we
never felt abandoned there for one minute! In fact, I felt
strangely invigorated by our dismal new environment. My
gifts and calling to start things never done before and
to forge into previously impenetrable territories
were gathering unprecedented steam.'

# 9

# AN UNLIKELY MOVE
# IN THE AFTERMATH
# OF THE SOVIET UNION

O ur family of five departed for the Soviet Union in the early morning on January 27, 1992. As I shared in the last chapter, before
we boarded our plane for takeoff, relatives from both sides of the
family gathered at our departing gate of the Tulsa International Airport to
send us off for what we all believed would be a year-long adventure on a
foreign field.

It was a tearful departure in many respects, but the fire of anticipation
*burned* in my heart, and I was fiercely motivated by God's grace to move
forward and not look back on the decision I'd made to invest ourselves in the
Bible school in Jelgava. Having lived all our lives in Oklahoma and Arkansas,
Denise and I, with our children, were forging into unknown territory both

---

**Left:** *People waiting in line for bread, an unfortunate development that occurred
toward the end of the USSR. Photo used by permission of ITAR-TASS.*

naturally and spiritually. It was an apprehensive and exhilarating moment at the same time.

We pulled ourselves away from our precious family and waved farewell as we, along with our God-sent nanny, Sharmon, walked down the airbridge to board our first flight en route to our "new home" for a year. Family members remained dutifully at our gate, following us with fastened gaze until we were out of sight and ready to board our plane.

Stepping over the threshold from the airbridge to the cabin of the plane, Denise suddenly turned to me, just *beaming*, and said, "*Rick,* we really did it!" All the praying and preparing we had done — and the gut-wrenching agony we'd experienced as we struggled with God's new direction for our lives — had brought us to this place of actually stepping out to do His will half a world away.

Finally, the last passenger boarded the plane and the door to the cabin was sealed. The high-pitched sounds of the engines starting *thrilled* us as we tucked away our baggage and buckled up for the trip of a lifetime. Paul and Philip were seated with Sharmon in the row in front of Denise and Joel and me. Joel was not quite three years old, but he vividly recalled, "I remember looking outside the window to see that it was still dark, and the crew was defrosting the airplane. I was seated next to Mom and Dad, and I wasn't at all afraid of anything."

### *'I Am Sending You Forth Into the World'*

I was thirty-three years old when my family and I boarded that plane in Tulsa. Even at our younger ages, Denise and I had already seen God do so many wonderful things in people's lives. But now, we were ready for what lay ahead. The Lord had given us such a sense of excitement and accomplishment that we were really doing it — launching out to help establish a new move of God in the lives of hungry believers who were eager to fulfill their own divine destinies.

The whirr of the massive engines drowned out most of the conversation around us and the plane began its taxi down the runway, preparing for takeoff. The craft shook as it picked up speed and the engines began to roar.

At that moment, my spirit became *gripped* by the words of Jesus as He stood before me in the vision a few short years earlier when I was in Canada. He'd held Paul in His arms and lovingly talked to me about my sons. But then, in that vision, I'd also heard the distinct roaring of jet engines — *exactly* as I was hearing them now. And the Lord had said, *See, I am sending you forth into the world.*

That moment on the runway was riveting as I played back the vision and Jesus' words in my mind, embracing them anew in my heart, for this was a moment of divine fulfillment. I turned to Denise and said, "Sweetheart, do you hear the roar of those engines? They are exactly the same engines I heard in the vision when Jesus appeared to me and said He was sending us forth into the world. What we are doing right now is the beginning of what Jesus told me in that vision."

Then...as I was still speaking those words to Denise, so completely enthralled and gripped with the profundity of that moment, I heard the Lord say, *NOW YOUR MINISTRY BEGINS!*

I was shocked to suddenly realize that although Denise and I had accomplished so much in our ministry by the grace of God, everything we had done to that point was simply preparation for *this* moment.

Our ministry was really just getting started.

### Blessed Are Those Who Wisely Choose God's Plan

The long flight to the former USSR was uneventful, yet exciting for the adventuresome young spirits of Paul, Philip, and Joel Renner. By the time we landed in Riga — more than five-thousand miles from Tulsa and nine time zones away — it was mid-morning on January 28, almost a full twenty-four hours later, and the boys' excitement had turned to exhaustion.

There in Riga, we were entering a totally different world filled with political uncertainty, which we had already anticipated. But we could *not* have anticipated all the ways that uncertainty would manifest in the lives of millions of people in that region of the world, now including *us*! The economic nightmare we witnessed and experienced there was simply beyond anyone's ability to embellish or exaggerate. There could not have been a worse moment in time to move one's family to that part of the world, nor could there have been a *better* moment.

*I'll explain.* Life was truly so dark and dismal there at that time that most people were searching for ways to escape the territory of the Soviet Union. Yet as unlikely as it seemed, God called our family to move right into the middle of that unimaginable chaos *at that exact time.*

Shambles created by the total, sudden collapse of the USSR were difficult to navigate day by day and very hard to bear. At the same time, this was also the amazing moment when God's power was being unleashed like a torrent to wash across those old Soviet wastelands. It is eternally true that God's timing is perfect and that the Holy Spirit, as our infallible Guide, knows every path and alleyway down which to perfectly lead us to His desired destination for our lives. This was never more true for the family of Rick Renner than on that day in late January of 1992 when we arrived in Riga, Latvia.

From Tulsa to Riga, it seemed as if we had been supernaturally led into a very dark alley in terms of our new spiritual surroundings. *But we never felt abandoned there for one minute!* In fact, I felt strangely invigorated by our dismal new environment. My gifts and calling to start things never done before and to forge into previously impenetrable territories (or places where no one wanted to go) were gathering unprecedented steam. The motivation, inspiration, strength, and ability of God Himself was with me in a mighty way.

And that supernatural "might" was exactly what was needed! What lay ahead for us in starting the first Christian TV ministry in that part of the world — and in constructing the first Protestant church building there in more than half a century — would be a rocky road to traverse. But it would take place relatively quickly despite both the physical and spiritual odds against us. Those things would *need* to happen quickly. After all, we would be here for only one year — two *at best* — or so I thought. *There was no time to waste!*

Indeed, Denise and I wasted no time from the moment we landed in Riga, Latvia, in the Soviet Union. We rolled up our sleeves to begin our work there, intent on making the most of our time in order to do the work God had commissioned us to do.

Isn't it true that each one of us in life is responsible for how we spend the time God has given us — not just on the assignments He has called us to fulfill, but in our everyday lives? Every day when we wake up, we are stewards, or managers, of our resources of *time, money,* and *energy*. Whether we commit those resources to God and live our lives accordingly, or we squander them in any manner we feel is right at the moment, is up to each of us. *But blessed are those who choose wisely!*

This is a commitment Denise and I made to the Lord early in our lives together — to yield our resources to His command — and we endeavor daily to live by that commitment in life and ministry today.

## An Abridged Russian History Lesson

Because our calling was to Russian-speaking people, in this chapter, I'm going to talk to you about our very early moments in the Soviet Union. But first I want to share with you about the history of Russia and the former USSR so you'll better comprehend the dire aftereffects of communism's fall in these lands.

The word "dire" is such an understatement that later, President Vladimir Putin called the collapse of the USSR the greatest tragedy of the Twentieth Century.[1] In just a few pages, I think you'll understand the reason why. Many Western pundits railed against Putin for making such a statement, but you're about to see that what he said was true. It's hard for Westerners to understand what happened when the Soviet Union collapsed the way it did, because they have never experienced anything like it.

Anyone who lived in the territory of the Soviet Union at that time and experienced what happened in its total collapse knows full well that it was indeed a tragedy beyond anything any fiction writer could create. Because our family was there and we lived through that period, we are living witnesses to exactly what President Putin meant when he said he felt it was the greatest tragedy of the Twentieth Century.

I realize the unlikely Russian history you are about to read may seem like a diversion from my own story. But I feel that I must share an abridged history of the lands to which God called my family and me because that part of the world has been such a big part of our lives. I want you to understand as my reader just why there was so much chaos in the territory of the USSR when we arrived there on January 28, 1992. So I'll give you a condensed narrative that led to the anarchy, chaos, and pandemonium that existed in the Soviet Union at the time our family moved there.

But to do that, I'll need to go all the way back to the Russian Revolution in 1917.

In 1917, Nicholas Romanov — Nicholas II — was czar (tsar) of Russia and all its vast territories. His family's dynasty, the House of Romanov, began their rule three hundred years earlier when Michael Romanov became the first Romanov czar in 1613.[2] Throughout its three hundred years of rule, the House of Romanov had many famous rulers, including Peter the Great, Catherine the Great, and Alexander I, among others. But the last czar to rule Russia was Nicholas II.[3]

Let me help you get a perspective of Russia's long history. When the United States' Declaration of Independence was signed in 1776, the Romanovs had already been ruling Russia for 163 years. In fact, Catherine the Great had already been on the throne for fourteen years. The multi-century rule of the Romanov dynasty was such an integral part of Russia's heritage that no serious leader in Russian lands during that time frame in history could imagine a Russia without Romanovs.

As time progressed, Russia became powerful and even had one of the strongest currencies in Europe before World War I. But in the years *before* Nicholas II took the throne in 1894, a simmering discontent was percolating among the lower classes that had been lingering from the time of his grandfather, Czar Alexander II.[4]

Alexander II was most notably known for his emancipation of Russian serfs in 1861 (among many other reforms), which earned him the title *Alexander the Liberator.* He was responsible for the new judicial system, setting up elected local judges, abolishing corporal punishment, promoting local self-government, instituting universal military service, ending some privileges of the nobility, and supporting university education.[5] But in spite of these radical reforms that he introduced to Russia to help the poorer classes, rabble-rousers would not be appeased and made several assassination attempts against him.

On March 13, 1881, while en route to the Winter Palace in Saint Petersburg, Alexander II's carriage was attacked by a bomb that had been planted to detonate as his carriage rolled by. The carriage was only slightly damaged, and the emperor emerged from the carriage shaken but unhurt. A nearby awaiting terrorist hurled another bomb that exploded at the feet of the emperor, which shattered his legs, and blood began to profusely pour from his body. Alexander II was quickly carried by sleigh to the Winter Palace to the very study where he had previously signed the Emancipation Edict, freeing the serfs twenty years prior in 1861.[6] Because the czar was bleeding to death, members of the Romanov family were rushed to the scene, and at 3:30 in the afternoon on that day, the flag of Alexander II was lowered, announcing his death.

Within just forty-eight hours of that tragic event, Alexander II had planned to release even greater reforms on behalf of the Russian people. But following his death, the new czar, his son, Alexander III, abandoned those proposed reforms — reforms that would have given greater freedoms to his father's assassins — and the new czar pursued a policy of greater autocratic power. Alexander II's bloody assassination triggered suppression of civil liberties by Alexander III, and police burst back into full force after they had experienced some restraint under the reign of the younger Alexander's father. The spectacular Church of the Spilled Blood in Saint Petersburg was ordered to be constructed on the site where Alexander II was assassinated and dedicated to his memory.[7]

The death of Alexander II was witnessed first-hand by his grandson, Nicholas II, who would become the future emperor. Nicholas II vowed he would not suffer the same fate, but his future, of course, would prove otherwise. History has well documented the house arrest of Nicholas II's entire family after he had come to power and the brutal execution of every family member that ensued.

But Alexander III began ruling in 1881 in the aftermath of that horrific assassination and died unexpectedly in 1894 at the relatively young age of forty-nine. When he suddenly died, his son Nicholas II ascended to the throne sooner than anyone expected. As a result, one of the largest countries in the world, in a rather difficult historical period, was headed by a man who did not have any serious managerial talent or the required breadth of views to act as a trained ruler.

Nicholas II quickly married Alexandra, the granddaughter of England's Queen Victoria, and within weeks he was coronated as the new czar of Russia. Nicholas and his wife Alexandra were private people, living in the shadow of assassinations and premature deaths. As a result, they tended to avoid public appearances except when necessary. They produced four daughters — Olga, Tatiana, Maria, and Anastasia — and one son, Alexei, who was next in line to the imperial throne after his father.

But early on, his parents became rudely awakened to the fact that Alexei was a serious hemophiliac.[8] To hide that the heir-apparent carried a deadly disease in his blood, they moved into the Alexander Palace some fifteen miles from Saint Petersburg and lived in relative seclusion, only occasionally making public appearances. The general population didn't understand why the royal family lived in seclusion, and it was generally perceived that the czar was an absent, aloof leader.

Nicholas II was essentially a good man, a sincere believer in Christ who loved his family and his country. But, unfortunately, he was not a very good leader. He failed to devote enough time to serious state issues and was not popular among the elite of society, the army, *or* ordinary people.

In addition, Nicholas II's period of rulership was further plagued by political and social unrest. Due to what was perceived as his unsuccessful handling of the Russo-Japanese War of 1904-05 and to the uprisings of Russian workers in 1905 that were filled with widespread accusations of police brutality, many came to view Nicholas II as a weak and indecisive leader.[9] Because of these and many other factors, discontent began to grow even more among the working classes of Russia.

In an attempt to bring peace, Nicholas II issued his *October Manifesto* — a manifesto to guarantee civil rights, the creation of a Russian constitution, and the establishment of a parliament.[10] While the reforms appeased a segment of the population, another segment had already been poisoned by anti-czarist leaflets that were being printed *en masse* and were being distributed by revolutionaries who claimed that Nicholas II had done too little, too late.

It's also important to note that it was Nicholas II who issued a decree on religious tolerance in 1905. Until that moment, the official religion was Russian Orthodox. Catholic and Lutheran churches were very limited in Russia, and all evangelical churches — Baptist, Pentecostal, Adventist, and others — were *outlawed*.[11]

It's interesting that a weak leader in many other respects brought that nation freedom of religion. It would not be until the end of the Twentieth Century, after about seventy years of the atheistic communist regime (1917-1991), that religious freedom would return to the land. And the Renner family was there to see it and to catch the early waves of that freedom that have continued to this day.

As Russia entered World War I in July of 1914, social tensions escalated even more, and Saint Petersburg (then called Petrograd) found itself filled with soldiers and disgruntled workers who were exhausted from fighting on the war front.

At this moment, the crisis of leadership was particularly evident as a significant part of the population dreamed of getting rid of the autocracy, and that sentiment contributed to the unrest in the country. It is also worth noting that at this time, the authority of the established church was seriously weakened due to spiritual compromise and the close ties they had formed with the royal family. Also, people were looking for answers to life's questions — but not from the Bible; therefore, fascination with cultic spiritualism became widespread. As it often happens when people turn away from God, society seems to go mad as a result. We can still see this phenomenon today.

During this period of Nicholas II's reign, mobs began to fill the streets, pulling down statues and monuments and attacking police precincts. Nearly every visible authority figure was targeted by mobs, including judges, policemen, government officials, army officers, priests, teachers, employers, landowners — even *parental* authority became a target of disdain. In place of the Russian tricolor flag, these mobs, fueled by Bolshevik revolutionaries, began to fly red communist flags and call for the overthrow of the monarchy.

The upper classes doubted that the unrest would lead to much, and they generally felt it would pass and that life would return to normal. But these disgruntled political revolutionaries grew more powerful, thoroughly intending to overthrow the Romanov dynasty. Among these political movements was the Bolshevik movement, which would eventually be led by a revolutionary named *Vladimir Lenin.*

As World War I raged, Nicholas II decided to take personal command of the Russian Army on the front lines of the war. Departing on a train for the war front, his absence from Saint Petersburg — mixed with burgeoning discontent among the working classes — continued to grow. Russians were rapidly losing confidence in the czar's ability to rule, and making matters even worse was the suffering Russian economy due to the cost of war.

Finally, Czar Nicholas knew he had to return to Saint Petersburg to try to bring order to a society that was in chaos and reeling out of control. But while on a train back to Saint Petersburg, his train stopped at a rail station near Pskov, and he was confronted by members of his government who urged him to abdicate in order to save the country. Although it was unthinkable that it could happen, a document of abdication was placed before him on March 2, 1917, and the emperor placed his signature upon it.[12] In that surreal moment, three hundred years of the Romanov dynasty abruptly came to an end.

This momentous act was strangely in sync with the overthrow of monarchies that were occurring all over Europe at that same time. But the overthrow that occurred in Russia would turn out to be the bloodiest of them all.

## Vladimir Lenin

A short-term provisional government in Saint Petersburg took power over Russia, but it was quickly overthrown by revolutionary forces who stormed the Winter Palace on October 25, 1917. Mobs pulled down visible symbols of the monarchy, including emblems, coats-of-arms, the double-headed eagle of the Russian State, and other statues and monuments. In the first days of the revolution, even many expensive, elaborate interiors of the

Winter Palace were carried into the Palace Square to be burned in a huge bonfire.

A revolutionary with a Marxist philosophy who intended to create a new communist Russia, *Vladimir Lenin*, seized power and, with him, a new police state emerged at the helm. Soon the new government began to confiscate private property and take retribution against authority figures from the Czarist years. The White Army stood by the Czar, and the Red Army stood with Lenin's new communist regime, resulting in a bloody civil war that continued until 1922 and claimed the lives of millions of Russians.

As a result, millions faced starvation, factories stopped working, the railways were destroyed, and the country was thrust into even deeper crisis. Those who had ruled for hundreds of years never believed such events could happen in Russia. But *quickly*, the Russia that *once was* no longer existed, and Lenin and his comrades were freed to move forward to create a new communist state.

The strength of the Bolsheviks was the outwardly attractive idea of making a new, honest world. In a country where there had been great social inequality, this captured the hearts of people. However, the diabolical nature of this idea was manifested in a complete denial of God, so Lenin's new state had an atheistic ideological objective to eliminate religion along with the *extermination* of all religious people.

Lenin issued a decree for the nationalization of all church property on January 20, 1918, which resulted in cathedrals, churches, church properties, including all church grounds, being seized.[13] To abide by one's faith was so dangerous that it could result in a death sentence. Clergy and believers were arrested, sent to labor camps, and executed. Seminaries were closed and religious publications were prohibited.

The Russian Orthodox Church was the first to be persecuted since it was essentially part of the state power during the reign of the autocracy. The evangelical churches, on the other hand, had a short period of freedom in the first, early years of Soviet rule. While the new communist regime was busy retaining and consolidating power, evangelical believers preached the Gospel, and churches were established all over the country.

No matter how troubled the times are in a nation, the Lord will always act — and sometimes it's true that in the most difficult times, He acts the most powerfully. It was certainly true during this politically tumultuous period in Russia that Pentecostal and Baptist churches spread in Russia.

However, having sufficiently strengthened their power, the Communist Party eventually began to work against believers of all faiths. The persecution reached into the scientific and educational spheres as well. The new ideology demanded the eradication of any views that did not fit into the new communist narrative. Governmental special forces began to monitor the entire population with a kind of "thought control." Those who refused to modify their words or behaviors to match the new political agenda would often *disappear*.

By the time of Lenin's death on January 21, 1924, in that span of six or seven years, unthinkable numbers of people had been arrested, sent to prison, shot, or otherwise mercilessly executed as a part of the plan to eradicate a czarist past and build a new Soviet world where the communist regime ruled as supreme.

## Joseph Stalin

When Lenin died, another revolutionary eventually replaced him as leader — *Joseph Stalin*. Lenin had warned others that he had bad premonitions about Stalin and his obsessive hunger for power.

As a young man, Stalin had attended seminary, but left before he took final examinations, which could have qualified him to be a priest. While at seminary, Stalin became familiar with Karl Marx's political ideas and chose to leave seminary to become a revolutionary. But even years later in revolutionary circles, some referred to Stalin as "The Priest" because of his earlier theological studies.[14]

But as evil as Lenin was, he was concerned that if Stalin obtained power, it would be to the detriment of everyone because he considered Stalin to be dangerous. Nevertheless, Stalin was elected the General Secretary of the Central Committee, and quickly after Lenin's death in 1924, he began to promote himself as Lenin's heir. And by the end of the 1920s, Stalin had become the undisputed leader of Soviet Russia, and he retained that control for twenty-nine years until the time of his death in 1953.

In his first years as leader, Stalin instigated a series of five-year plans to turn the USSR into a great modern industrialized country. These five-year plans were ruthlessly enforced, and factories were given strict goals that were impossible to fulfill. Those who failed to achieve Stalin's objectives were treated as saboteurs and they were imprisoned or executed as enemies of the state. Because agricultural lands had been owned primarily by small land-owners, Stalin initiated a plan of collectivization — the seizing of all farms and lands to be "collectivized" and owned by the state. When landowners and farmers resisted, they were killed or imprisoned.

Stalin idealized himself as the benevolent "father" of the Soviet Union, but he employed secret police to strictly enforce "Stalinism" — which is now historically referred to as *the cult of Stalin*.[15] When people refused to participate, others were encouraged to "inform" on them to the secret police, and as a result, countless numbers of people were accused by friends and neighbors of opposing Stalin and his idealogy, and those accused were sent to labor camps or executed.

In 1939, just before the start of World War II, Joseph Stalin signed a non-aggression pact with Adolf Hitler, and they agreed to carve up Eastern Europe between themselves.[16] In June 1941, Hitler violated the agreement when German forces entered the Soviet Union, and by December of 1941, German troops had nearly reached Moscow. Stalin called on his army to resist, which they bravely did. But the turning point in the war occurred in Stalingrad when German troops were defeated there and were driven all the way back to Germany, where they were ultimately conquered by Allied forces.

Although the Soviet army suffered *many times over* compared to other Allied armies, Stalin played a very decisive role in Germany's defeat. As a result, large portions of Eastern Europe fell under the ever-enlarging shadow of Soviet forces and entire countries became satellite states of the Soviet Union. This is why Winston Churchill in 1945 so ominously warned that "an iron curtain has descended across the continent" — a clear reference to the influence of the USSR in the Eastern Bloc countries of Europe.

It is impossible to exaggerate the horrific impact that World War II had on the people of the Soviet Union. No nation lost more lives than the USSR, as nearly twenty-seven million people in the Soviet Union died as a result of the war.[17] That event was so tragic that it affected in some way literally every family across that vast territory. Nearly every family either lost an immediate or distant family member or friend. In Belarus alone, which was a predominant war front, some say nine out of every ten men were killed, leaving an entire generation to be raised with no father and putting the full responsibility of earning a living and raising a family on the women who remained after the war. It was a nation devastated by the war, and they lost a significant number of their population.

I can confidently say that at the church Denise and I eventually started in Moscow, every member of our large congregation, *without exception*, has a horrific story about someone they knew who was lost in World War II. To this day, that war remains a painful memory, and this is the reason Russia still commemorates May 9 as "Victory Day," the day the war ended in 1945. Even in recent years, an important part of this holiday has become a moment when hundreds of thousands of people take to the central streets with their children and carry photos of their ancestors who fought in World War II — which in the lands of the former Soviet Union is referred to as the Great Patriotic War.[18]

Many Westerners accuse Russia of being a war-mongering nation, but Russians have deeply experienced the tragedy of war, and they did not want it. They despised it. Over the nation's long history, it has faced invasions from Mongolians, Teutonic Knights, the Polish-Lithuanian Commonwealth, Sweden, France, the Austro-Hungarian Empire, and Germany, just to name a few. It is hard to fathom, but during World War II, Saint Petersburg was under siege for more than nine hundred days — and because there was no food, people ate sawdust, wallpaper, and leather. At times, some even resorted to eating the corpses of those who had died of starvation.[19]

These lands were so affected by war that even when our three sons were growing up in our small town in Latvia, it was not unusual for them to find a rotting German helmet or shattered pieces of ammunition in the dirt that still remained in a field near our house. The horrible effects of World War II are felt to this very day.

In 1953, Stalin finally died after ruling the Soviet Union for twenty-nine years. In his final years, he continued purges against enemies within the Communist Party and anyone he deemed to be his enemy or an enemy of the state. Untold numbers of Christian believers languished in prisons all over the Soviet Union during Stalin's era. Even so, on March 5, 1953, the Soviet Union went into great mourning because of the death of Joseph Stalin.

Although millions had been incarcerated or killed at his hands, Joseph Stalin had led the USSR into a period of great euphoria after the German defeat. In the wake of that euphoria, the Soviet people felt they had triumphed under Stalin's leadership and made great industrial progress. Buildings, sky-scrapers, and educational institutions were built. As a result, the people of the Soviet Union really embraced the dream that a utopian communist state was attainable, and they were committed to work together to see that dream come to pass in their lifetimes.

## Soviet Leaders From 1953-1985

After Stalin, five more men served as leaders before the USSR was finally dissolved in 1991. The next to rule the USSR after Stalin was *Nikita Khrush-chev*, whose rule was also quite authoritarian, and persecution continued against Christian believers or anyone who held a view that did not fit the socialist-communist narrative.

Special forces continued to exert "thought-control" on the population, and many were sent to labor camps who did not fall in line. Industrialization continued, and rebuilding after the war was at an all-time euphoric high. In spite of the renowned Cuban Missile crisis of 1962, Khrushchev worked to have a more peaceful co-existence with the West.

At the same time, it was during the reign of Nikita Khrushchev that the evangelical churches experienced another strong wave of persecution. In fact, the persecution of believers of all faiths unfolded on a new level, and feature films and "documentaries" were made that presented believers as dangerous people.

During this period, several court trials were held in which a number of pastors and bishops were wrongfully convicted. Among them was Vasily Ryakhovsky, whose son, my good friend Sergei Ryakhovsky, is the bishop of the group of churches to whom our churches in Russia belong. Vasily Ryakhovsky went to prison the first time in 1950 for "wrong religious thinking" and for "slandering the Soviet regime."[20] He was sentenced to ten years behind bars.

Soon after his release, in 1961, my friend's father, a factory worker who also pastored an underground Pentecostal church, was sentenced again — this time to three years in prison — for proselytizing. Then in 1972, after Khrushchev had left power, Ryakhovsky had another run-in with the state because of his faith. But this time, no sentence ensued. Instead, he was fined twenty percent of his wages for one year.[21]

Nikita Khrushchev finally left power in 1964, and he was followed by *Leonid Brezhnev.*

Leonid Brezhnev was known for his heavy eyebrows and a style of speech that was so difficult to understand that many rightfully or wrongfully assumed he was a drunk. By 1977, Brezhnev became the most powerful man to rule the USSR since Joseph Stalin. During his ruling period, persecution continued against Christian believers, and those who held views that did not fit the communist narrative were punished. Brezhnev's years were marked with a national disease of alcoholism and economic stagnation. The unattainable dream of communism began to become obvious as economic stagnation and decline paralyzed the nation. Finally, when Brezhnev died in 1982, he was followed by *Yuri Andropov.*

Yuri Andropov was another old communist hardliner who had previously been the head of the KGB since 1967. Andropov's rule was relatively short due to his age and sickness, but it was very eventful nonetheless. He worked feverishly to reignite the stagnant Soviet economy and attempted to curb the rage of alcoholism that was on the rise in the Soviet population.

Andropov was dedicated to the ideals of communism and seethed against the anticommunist diplomacy of Ronald Reagan. The relationship between the Soviet Union and the United States became so strained that Soviet diplomats ended negotiations for reductions in Intermediate Range

Nuclear Forces and the Strategic Arms Reduction Talks, otherwise known as START.[22] Andropov's leadership ended abruptly when he died of illness in 1983. He was quickly replaced by another communist hardliner whose name was *Konstantin Chernenko.*

Konstantin Chernenko was elderly and sick when he was appointed to be leader of the Soviet Union. Chernenko's time of leadership was noted for a return to the more hardline policies of the Brezhnev period and for pulling back from economic and political reforms that had been initiated by Yuri Andropov. Soviet foreign policy took on a harsher tone during his brief tenure as leader. Due to his declining health, Chernenko made few public appearances and he finally died on March 10, 1985. That is when *Mikhail Gorbachev* was chosen to be the new — *and the last* — leader of the USSR.

## Mikhail Gorbachev, the Last Leader of the Soviet Union

Mikhail Gorbachev was deeply committed to Marxist-communism, but he and his wife, Raisa, brilliantly gave a new, more friendly face to communism that appealed to people in the West. He departed from past Soviet policies and instigated dramatic social and economic reforms called *Perestroika* and *Glasnost.*[23][24] Because he wanted to bring about radical political and economic reforms, he found himself opposed by hardline communists.

In 1985, *Boris Yeltsin* moved to Moscow to run that city's Communist Party machine. Yeltsin had previously been the Secretary of the Communist Party in Sverdlovsk — which today is called Ekaterinburg, the original name of the city when the Romanov family was held under house arrest and shot there in 1918. Once in Moscow, Yeltsin soon came into conflict with communist hardliners, but also fell out of favor with Gorbachev and was removed from his position of running the Moscow Communist Party.

But Yeltsin did not disappear. After that, he was elected to be a deputy in 1989 for the Congress of People's Deputies and thereby found himself with a national platform, which he used to attack Gorbachev, the Communist Party, national corruption, and the slow pace of economic reform. Though Gorbachev bitterly opposed him, Yeltsin was elected president of the Russian Parliament, and he soon became the raging antagonist of Gorbachev.[25]

Mikhail Gorbachev had launched what he called *Perestroika*, which in Russian means *restructuring* or *rebuilding*. The goal of *Perestroika* was to make socialism work more efficiently to better meet the needs of Soviet citizens. But the implementation of *Perestroika* created shortages, along with political, social, and economic tensions within the Soviet Union. Instead of streamlining the system as Gorbachev hoped it would, it gave rise to new production bottlenecks and hurled the Soviet Union into an unimaginable economic crisis, and deficits of every imaginable product abounded everywhere.

The new policies were implemented so fast that the system became irretrievably broken. Stores became emptied of even the most basic food products. There was no fuel for cars, and there was even a shortage of rubles. People who worked at factories were no longer paid in cash, but were being paid in whatever good or commodity they produced.

The country generally moved into a barter system of exchange that was embarrassing and humiliating. Unrest and turmoil could be felt across all eleven time zones of the USSR. The economy was not just failing — it was failing at a galloping speed and racing toward total collapse. The USSR's economy was sinking so fast that rationing was introduced for even some of the most basic food products.

Simultaneously, Gorbachev launched *Glasnost*, which is derived from a Russian word that means *openness*. This was his attempt to open up the political system to overcome inertia in the system's structure — and he believed that this attempt at economic and social recovery required the inclusion of people in the political process who were outside of the old "hardliner" structure. The launching of *Glasnost* also permitted the media more freedom of expression, so editorials began to appear for the first time that described depressing economic and social conditions and the government's inability to correct them.

A defense budget of nearly twenty-five percent of the Gross National Product was also crippling the country. At this same time, the USSR was involved in a prolonged war in Afghanistan, which was the equivalent of America's Vietnam War. But the immense defense budget required cuts in education, social services, and even medical care — in fact, the skyrocketing defense budget was one of the main causes of the Soviet economic decline.

Meanwhile, Gorbachev traveled extensively and was very successful in convincing foreigners that the Soviet Union was no longer the international communist threat it had previously been. There is no question that Gorbachev's changes in foreign policy contributed to the end of the Cold War. But in spite of his widespread appeal in the Western world and friendships with Ronald Reagan and Margaret Thatcher, his policies weakened the hold of Soviet ideology, and old communist hardliners in Moscow were furious at him. In fact, these hardliners so despised what they felt were actions that were *crippling* the whole nation that they decided to act to stop it.

While on vacation at his state dacha in Crimea, Gorbachev and his wife were put under house arrest by special orders of these hardliners. Soviet tanks and troops were ordered onto the streets of Moscow, and an ill-conceived and poorly executed coup took place August 19-21 in 1991.[26] The whole world watched in shock as army tanks rolled down the Tverskaya Street toward the Kremlin. Thousands of Moscovites watched the tanks roll by and uncertainty filled the air as people wondered what would happen next.

And what happened next was *Boris Yeltsin* — a man who seized the moment to project himself as the next leader of Russia. When army tanks rolled up to the Russian Federation building on August 19, Yeltsin climbed on top of one of those military tanks and delivered a riveting speech intended to dismantle the Communist Party.[27] Many soldiers who were opposed to opening fire on unarmed citizens chose to stand with Yeltsin. In a few days, the coup collapsed, and Yeltsin banned the Communist Party and ordered all of its property to be seized. Finally, when Mikhail Gorbachev returned to the city of Moscow from his house arrest in Crimea, he discovered his nemesis had the reins of power in his hands.

When that coup by the old Communist Party leaders failed in Moscow, various Republics of the USSR saw it was their moment to break free from the grip of the Soviet Union.[28] On August 27, 1991, Moldova declared its independence, followed by Azerbaijan and Kyrgyzstan, then Estonia, Latvia, Lithuania, Tajikistan, Armenia, Turkmenistan, and finally Ukraine. The mighty united front of the Union of Soviet Social Republics was literally coming apart at its seams as these newly independent states began to quickly erect new borders to officially divide themselves from the once far-flung Soviet Union.

## A Momentous Unraveling

Allow me to explain just how this momentous unraveling occurred. As I described, the process of disintegration of the USSR actually began in the second half of the 1980s with the beginning of *Perestroika*. One of its driving factors was the desire of the Soviet Union republics to have political and economic independence from Moscow. Then in 1990, the so-called "Parade of Sovereignties" took place when all the Union republics adopted declarations of state sovereignty, establishing the precedence of their laws over the laws of the USSR.

The official document that brought about the collapse of the USSR began with the signing of the Belovezhskaya Agreements on December 8, 1991, at a government hunting dacha in the center of the Brest region of Belarus. The agreement was signed by senior officials and heads of government of the three union republics: Stanislav Shushkevich and Vyacheslav Kebich from the Republic of Belarus; Boris Yeltsin and Gennady Burbulis from the Russian Federation (RSFSR); and Leonid Kravchuk and Vitold Fokin from Ukraine. I find it so interesting that these were the exact countries that signed the document first establishing USSR on December 29, 1922.

On December 8, 1991, this newly signed document stated that "the USSR as a subject of international law and geopolitical reality ceases to exist." At the same time, the participants agreed to form the Commonwealth of Independent States (CIS). The official seat of the coordinating bodies of the Commonwealth was established in Minsk, and the activities of all bodies of the USSR in the territories of the member states of the new Commonwealth were terminated.

The special forces of the Ministry of Internal Affairs were aware of what was happening, and they informed Gorbachev, who was ready to arrest the participants who had gathered at that dacha to sign the Belovezhskaya Agreement. However, Gorbachev never gave such a command. According to Gorbachev, he never gave the order because he was worried that such a decision could lead to bloodshed.

The next stage of the collapse of the USSR was the signing of the Alma-Ata Declaration, which spoke about the goals and principles of the CIS. The declaration confirmed the Belovezhskaya Agreement, indicating again that with the formation of the CIS, the USSR ceased to exist.

Soon, on December 21, 1991, in Alma-Ata (Kazakhstan), the leaders of eleven of the fifteen former Soviet republics signed the Protocol to the Agreement on the Establishment of the CIS, which had been dated December 8.

Then on December 25, 1991, Mikhail Gorbachev announced the termination of his activities as President of the USSR and signed a final decree that transferred control of strategic nuclear weapons to Russian President Boris Yeltsin. In the evening of the same day, the state flag of the USSR was lowered from the flagpole of the Kremlin and the state flag of the Russian Federation was raised.

Also on that day, Gorbachev personally called President George H. W. Bush to inform him that he had signed the papers to transfer all powers to Boris Yeltsin and that the USSR was officially gone. In our unlikely story, I refer frequently to December 25, 1991, as the date it all officially came to an end because on that day, Mikhail Gorbachev and Boris Yeltsin together signed documents to dissolve the Union of the Soviet Social Republics (USSR).

Accordingly, on December 26, 1991, the Council of Republics of the Supreme Soviet of the USSR (the Upper House of the Soviet Parliament) abolished the post of President of the USSR and all union bodies, which marked the final recognition of the termination of the existence of the USSR.

*So with the swipe of a pen*, the USSR — a seventy-year experiment in socialism and communism — was officially gone. The former Soviet Union had been birthed in the bloody revolution of 1917 that killed the House of Romanov and obliterated Russia's glorious past history. Mikhail Gorbachev was the last official leader of the Union of Soviet Socialist Republics. When he resigned, he did so as the last President of the Soviet Union, and Boris Yeltsin became the first President of a new Russian State.[29]

With just two signatures, seventy years of Marxist-communist leadership died. But the *way* it died had tragic ramifications, hurling more than 300 million Soviet citizens into a state of bedlam and confusion for a number of grueling, backbreaking, exacting years.

Indeed, there may have been a new Russian state, but that new state was headed on a treacherously hard road ahead toward building a free-market economy after seventy years of being committed to and enslaved by a communist dream. In one moment, a new Russia had exited a failed system, but at the same time, it entered a state of disorder and even greater economic chaos.

## We Arrived in the USSR at That Moment

That is *exactly* when our family entered this bleak picture. In fact, one month after we arrived, Denise and I happened to be at the Kremlin *at the very moment* one of the last flying red flags of the USSR there was being lowered for the last time. We even took a photo of it to document that remarkable, historic event. Only God could have put us there at that exact moment. That day when Denise and I "just happened" to be at the Kremlin, we literally saw *old* history go down and *new* history come up.

Amazingly, I was also on-site when the city of Moscow removed the remaining parts of the towering statue of Felix Dzerzhinsky that had stood for decades in front of the central headquarters of the KGB. Dzerzhinsky had been the founder of the modern KGB (*Komitet Gosudarstvennoy Bezopasnosti*).[30] The statue was enormous. As workers labored to remove it and demolish its granite base, I ran over to them and asked, "May I please take a piece of the broken granite from the base of this historical monument?" And today I still have that piece of granite in our ministry offices.

## Our New Life and Surroundings in the Soviet Socialist Republic of Latvia

As noted in the first paragraph of this chapter, our family of five arrived in Riga on January 28, 1992, to begin our new life there. When we arrived, it was only thirty-four days *after* Gorbachev called President George H. W. Bush on December 25, 1991, to inform him he had resigned from his position — thus the reason all the passengers that exited our plane at the Riga airport were greeted by Soviet soldiers with machine guns.

Although the Soviet Union was officially dissolved, the reality was that the Soviet Union was still, in practice, very much in place and standing all around us. In Riga, everyone still spoke fluent Russian in their daily business, signs on streets were in Russian, the Soviet ruble was still the currency, and several hundred thousand Soviet troops were stationed in Latvia. Furthermore, all our travel documents bore the emblems of the hammer and sickle of the USSR stamped all over them. For all practical purposes, it was *still* the USSR.

Both *euphoria* and *fear* filled people's hearts at the time our family arrived in that atmosphere. Those in former Soviet states were euphoric that they were finally on their own, but the future was filled with fear and uncertainty. People wondered, *Would this new freedom last? How will we survive financially? What does the future hold for us as free nations?* The level of apprehension that gripped these new nations could be felt in the air around us and was nearly suffocating. They didn't know how to navigate the freedoms they had abruptly attained, and most wondered if it was real or if it was just a mirage that would dissipate in a short time.

### *Confusion, Hysteria,* and *Pandemonium* — How People Experienced the Early Days of the Soviet Collapse

What I am about to tell you may be hard to comprehend, and you may even be tempted to think I'm being sensational or overdramatic, but you are about to read the *true* story of what happened to millions of lives in the USSR after it dissolved on December 8, 1991.

I'm not borrowing this scenario from some dystopian novel — rather, I'm giving you my firsthand observations of the *startling* changes in governments and economies that raged across national borders, affecting every living soul in this territory once controlled by an atheistic communist regime.

As I said, in a situation that many who lived in this part of the world wanted to escape, we were thrust headlong into by God Himself. Our family was there to see and experience the consequences of the fall of socialistic-communist ideology that I am about to describe. I want you to get a glimpse into the madness that resulted from the sudden collapse of the USSR so you'll better understand why President Vladimir Putin called this situation the greatest tragedy of the Twentieth Century.

Because the former communist regime of the Soviet Union wanted the massive conglomerate of its fifteen republics eternally tied together, they had intentionally interconnected those republics so that it would be hard for any one of them to break free from the whole conglomeration. However, in 1991, one by one those republics began to declare their independence and each straightaway began to erect their own distinct national borders to become separate from the whole. These actions were implemented so quickly that it had catastrophic consequences for millions of people who had previously lived united as one nation.

To help you comprehend exactly what it was like, try to imagine the bedlam and utter chaos that would develop if overnight, the United States of America suddenly dissolved, and all fifty states, one by one, began to declare themselves to be new independent nations. What kind of confusion would ensue if overnight, these fifty states erected distinct national borders between themselves and all their neighboring "countries" (states)?

## The Fictional 'Nation' of Oklahoma

Because I am originally from Oklahoma, let me use the state of Oklahoma as an example of this ludicrous scenario. If Oklahoma suddenly declared itself a free and independent nation, it would need its own independent constitution, president, congress, and courts — and an army to defend itself from neighboring state-countries. It would need ambassadors and embassies in all other states for widespread representation — and consular offices to issue visas to people from neighboring states who wished to visit friends and families in Oklahoma.

Since Oklahoma in this case would be a brand-new country bordered by the other newly declared nations of Colorado, Kansas, Missouri, Arkansas, Texas, and New Mexico, visas would then be needed for anyone in the "country" of Oklahoma who wished to drive into *any* of those bordering "countries" that he or she could have visited freely before each state became an independent nation.

And because it happened practically overnight, what would happen to Oklahomans who happened to be in other states when the new borders were suddenly announced and erected? If they had no Oklahoma passport to prove Oklahoma citizenship, would they be able to freely cross the border to get home? Or would they find themselves trapped with no ability to get back to their homes and families? Since it all happened so quickly, no one would know where to go to get an Oklahoma passport — or where to find a consular office to get an Oklahoma visa.

And who would qualify for Oklahoma citizenship so they could obtain an Oklahoma passport? What would be the criteria for citizenship? Would you be required to have been born in Oklahoma to have citizenship? Could you even become a naturalized citizen if you weren't born there, but you lived there before it became an independent nation?

In this hypothetical scenario, what if citizenship in the "country" of Oklahoma could only be obtained if you were native to Oklahoma, proving lineage from Oklahoma's inception as a state in 1907? How would you have to prove you were a "pureblooded" Oklahoman? What about those who had lived there all their lives, but could not trace their lineage to Oklahoma's beginnings? If you couldn't prove your "nationality" as an Oklahoman by the prescribed criteria, would you be a second-class person in Oklahoma — treated as a non-citizen — with fewer legal rights, such as the right to vote and receive social benefits?

As an Oklahoman, if you wanted to drive into a neighboring state that also just declared itself to be a new nation, would your driver's license work there or would you be required to get a foreign driver's license or a permit that would allow you to drive in that former state? And what about your medical, life, and car insurances — would those policies be accepted in new neighboring countries? If you experienced a health crisis across the border, would you gain hospital admittance or be denied because you were not covered there? Would you need to purchase travel insurance before you crossed borders to visit your friends and relatives?

And what about money? Because all fifty of the new independent countries wanted their own currencies, the dollar would be abandoned and each new country would then print its own currency and means of exchange.

Would there be any guarantees that the other countries would accept your country's currency?

Imagine the herculean task required to produce each country's new currency and to formulate protocol on how to interact with the currencies of all the other countries. What would be the impact of this on financial markets?

Making matters even more complex in this fantastical development, what if all fifty states had their own languages and each chose to abandon the mother tongue of the conglomerate United States and resort to their provincial languages? To implement the use of all fifty provincial languages in each respective new nation, what if new language laws were enforced that made it a punishable act to speak the former, mother tongue that citizens had spoken all their lives? What if people didn't *know* the new local tongue because it had not been spoken fluently in their lifetime? Yet now they are not permitted to speak the only language they really know.

Even worse, what if the new language laws said citizens could not work if they couldn't speak the local provincial language — and all state documents were printed in a language they didn't know how to read? If people wanted to cross the border into a neighboring country where language laws were being enforced, would they be able to communicate with immigration and customs officials at border crossings?

In this mad scenario, everyone who previously carried a U.S. passport, was confident of his citizenship, and knew his national flag and anthem. But now there are new national flags for all fifty states — and what would be their fifty new national anthems? Such a development would produce societal confusion resulting in political, economic, and social chaos.

No body of leaders in a right state of mind would ever attempt such a feat without a long-term plan for a smooth transition. Disconnecting nations, setting up national borders, creating new currencies, and abandoning a single national language with no long-term plan in place for a peaceful transition would be pure insanity.

An overnight development of that magnitude would be utter madness that would produce a nightmare of the greatest magnitude for people to navigate. The breaking apart of a huge conglomerate into independent sovereignties would require a massive infrastructure and more money to build it than is imaginable. It would take years and years to develop a plan for this kind of dissembling to occur in order to avoid sheer chaos.

## Yet This Really Happened in the USSR, and People Were Decimated, Devastated, and *Displaced*!

All of this madness I just described to you is *exactly* what happened nearly overnight in 1991 when, one by one, former republics of the Soviet Union began to declare independence at *meteoric* speed. The immediacy of this stark action — with little advance planning — produced traumatic, catastrophic results in the lives of millions.

Immediately upon the formal end of the communist regime in the territory of the USSR, the various republics that comprised that Soviet expanse hurriedly declared independence, set up their own national borders, abandoned their old currency, and enforced new language laws. In one sense, it was an exciting moment when smaller nations were captured with emotional euphoria to declare their independence. And an onlooking world largely viewed it that way as well.

But few outsiders saw that the way this reorganization was conducted resulted in the devastation of millions of lives. Actions were implemented with no realization of long-term consequences and, overnight, people who were not original to where they'd been living all their lives suddenly found themselves *aliens* in "new" countries with languages they could not speak. Their passports became useless — and their money became just paper with no buying power whatsoever. In one instant, they became impoverished and displaced, refugees inside a new country that had strangely been their lifelong homes.

In a very literal sense, *they were men and women without a country*.

If this wasn't tragic enough, if people were away on business or visiting friends or family in some other part of the USSR when all of this suddenly occurred without warning, they frequently found no way to return home because they didn't have passports to prove citizenship in the land where they had homes and family waiting for them to return. I personally witnessed long-time residents who were forcibly kicked off trains as they tried to return to their homes after they had been away to see friends or were away on business when the new borders were erected "overnight."

I was personally present to witness people sobbing as they were thrown off trains, and customs and passport people would open every compartment in the train wagons looking for people hiding under the beds and in the ceilings of the rooms. I can still hear them screaming in agonizing distress as border officials dragged them and their belongings from trains that then sped away with them left standing on the side of the tracks *stranded* — bewildered, helpless, and confused, like an abandoned pet in that they often helplessly didn't know how to return home. It was a gut-wrenching sight-and-sound picture that I will never forget. As I witnessed what was unfolding before my eyes, I began to understand even more Jesus' words to me that we would be sent to minister to a hurting people who needed God's love, attention, and special care.

Also, very often, if a Russian tried to speak to the Latvia border officials in the Russian language, those Latvian soldiers answered only in Latvian even though they all spoke Russian fluently. There were many challenges with languages during that confusing time. One of my earliest team members, Anita Busha, said, "During the Soviet years, the Latvian language was suppressed and the Russian language was the dominating language. But when times changed, many Latvians wanted to show that they were the real lords of their land and also to communicate to Russian-speaking people that 'it's now *our* time, and you can just go back to your native country.' The times were tense and filled with unfathomable hardship."

As I said, I'm not writing about this based on something I read or heard or saw on the news or even in a history book or documentary that chronicled the time. This is my own testimony of what I saw and experienced in those years of traumatic change. We were right there to witness the complete disarray that took place, affecting so many people at that time. It was as if God gave us front-row seats to observe it for ourselves so He could show us the depths of people's needs and give us insight on how to best meet these precious people at their point of need and give them the Gospel.

## A Close-to-Home Example of This Tragedy

Because our family had just moved to Latvia in January 1992, we indeed personally witnessed the early unraveling of the Soviet Union and its devastating consequences on the people. I'm sharing all this because it's such an important part of our story as we watched the unfolding of these events occur at such lightning speed. And what I'm describing didn't occur to a handful, but to *millions* of people who lived in the territory of the USSR.

And, please, as I relate these heart-wrenching memories, remember that our family lived for nearly a decade in Latvia, and we love that country very much. What I will share with you may come across as if I'm "picking" on Latvia, but I'm not. In fact, what you are about to read happened to some degree in all fifteen of the former Soviet republics.

If you were to ask locals about those difficult years of transition, they would tell you it was a traumatic time for them as well. To break free from the massive conglomeration of the USSR and transition out of it was profoundly difficult for *everyone* in every part of that far-flung collapsed empire.

During the time of all these tumultuous changes, Denise and I were serving as pastors of the Riga Good News Church, which we founded — a large church primarily comprised of Russian-speakers, but which also had a large number of Latvians, who also predominantly spoke Russian. But due to the fact that our family had moved to Latvia at a time when the Russian language and Russian ruble was still the main language and currency, we had focused entirely on "everything Russian" at the time of our arrival. Like many Russians who lived there, we didn't know the Latvian language. Because we were so entrenched in the Russian-speaking community, we were very familiar with the challenges that the Russian-speaking community faced at that turbulent time.

At the time Latvia declared its independence from the Soviet Union, nearly fifty percent of its population was comprised of ethnic Russians who had lived there for decades. Some argue that ethnic Russians should have never been there in the first place. But they were there, and they had helped build the Republic of Latvia for decades, right alongside native Latvians, in the ravaging aftermath of World War II.

Like everyone else in the former USSR, when communism fell, the people who lived in Latvia were citizens of the former Soviet Union, carried a Soviet passport, used the same mother tongue of Russian, and shared the ruble as the common currency. But in one fell swoop, the USSR ceased to exist and all of those things, along with the "powers that be," became relics of the past.

Those who were native Latvians were instantly qualified for Latvian citizenship. But how would the massive Russian population be assimilated into the citizenry of the new country? Most of them had lived there all their lives, so would they be granted the same rights as others, or would they be treated as aliens in a "new" nation where they had lived for so many years?

Just as I described in my fictional scenario in which all fifty of the United States declared themselves to be independent countries, a process immediately began to be implemented in Latvia to determine who would be given passports. The final decision was that passports should be given only to those who could trace their heritage to that nation. Those who could not prove this status were denied citizenship and were issued documents that identified them as *aliens* in a land where they'd lived all their lives.

Having "alien" passports was humiliating for ethnic Russians. This perplexing problem meant they were no longer citizens of the USSR because it ceased to exist — yet they weren't granted citizenship in Latvia, either. So just who *was* that fifty percent of the population that appeared to belong nowhere and to no one?

Due to the fact that ethnic Russians didn't have the new Latvian passports, even if they wanted to travel to Western countries, first, would they be received as Latvian "aliens"? Second, it was likely they would not be able to return "home" to Latvia afterward because they didn't have proper documentation to re-enter the country. Hence, they felt *trapped* and *in a state of dilemma* beyond their wildest imagination. They had only old, defunct Soviet passports that no longer worked. In a country where they had been born, raised, and had lived all their lives, they now felt stranded, without rights — like second-class citizens — and with few legal protections.

## Language Difficulties and Challenges

Furthermore, they had spoke Russian in a newly declared nation that now wanted Latvian to be the primary language. For years, Latvians were forced to speak Russian. It was understandable that they wanted the new national language to be Latvian. The newly applied language laws demanded that Russians begin to speak Latvian — which they largely did not know — or they would jeopardize their employment.

Soon the new national language laws required everyone who worked in stores and in all public places to speak only Latvian, and financially penalized those who were caught speaking Russian, even behind the counter between employees. Nearly fifty percent of the population did not know how to communicate well, and many began to lose their jobs because they could not publicly speak well enough to comply with the new laws.[31]

Finally, a time came when we saw all public semblances of the Russian language disappear. Street signs, shop signs, and all official documents were changed into the Latvian language. And nearly fifty percent of the population found themselves linguistically crippled by an ever-deepening language crisis.

The goal of public schools was to begin teaching in the Latvian language. This created family problems for parents who spoke only Russian, but whose children were now being educated in Latvian. The language barrier began to find its way into families' homes and it caused a disconnect between parents and children in many ways, including the inability of Russian parents to help their children with school work.[32] Our own sons attended a public Russian-speaking school, and they personally witnessed this difficult transition.

The challenges with a new national language were not only difficult for Russian-speaking parents and children, but it also wreaked intellectual and emotional stress for public-school teachers who taught in Russian-speaking schools that were slowly transitioning to Latvian. For many of these teachers, it was a language they spoke, but it was not their native language. Could they continue their careers teaching fluent Russian speaking students in a language that was in many cases awkward to both teachers and students?

Because the nation had been a Soviet Republic, many Russians held notable positions in Latvian government and business as well. One member of our church had been a member of the Latvian Politburo, which was the highest-ranking body of the Communist Party in Latvia.

When Latvia declared its independence, this church member had been serving as the official Latvian Minister of Commerce. He and his family had seen our TV programs, come to Christ as a result, and faithfully attended our church. But regardless of who they had been in the USSR, they were now outcasts in the new Latvia — in one fell swoop removed from their positions because they were not native-born Latvians and did not speak the Latvian language.

Adele Alexander recalled: "I so vividly remember a prayer meeting in the building we were meeting in for church — a building that Stalin had built. One woman cried almost continually because the new independent nation of Latvia was making Latvian the official language, and her family could not pass a 'level-two' Latvian language exam. Therefore, they were losing their jobs in local stores.

"Oh, how I hurt for this woman and her family! Hopelessness was written all over her. The same was true for another woman in the prayer meeting whose husband worked in the railway yard. He would be required to pass a 'level-one' Latvian language exam or lose his job. Feelings of bewilderment and uncertainty concerning the future were heavy in that room on that day."

This scenario was repeated *thousands of times* as those who were not natives were removed from positions they'd held for years. Again, some may argue that they were never entitled to their positions as non-Latvians to begin with. Nevertheless, I hope you can see how the abrupt nature of these changes brought chaos to people's lives on a massive scale. This was no small inconvenience that they could endure for a few months before resuming once again the lives they lived before. This clashing of political eras caused almost irreparable devastation to many in that part of the world, where the chaotic transition dragged on for *more than a decade.*

Because our family was there when all of this happened, we felt the difficulty of this change right along with the Russian population. We had learned Russian and had begun to pastor a large Russian congregation, and we walked through many of these changes and challenges with them.

Of course, it was natural for people to want to speak their country's language, but to enact such stringent, enforceable language laws meant nearly half the population found itself linguistically crippled. And what we saw was not unique, as this occurred in nearly all fifteen of the former Soviet republics.

## Currency Difficulties
## Leading to Financial Decimation

Language difficulties were just the beginning of the terrible transitional period that occurred in those years. For example, what currency should now be used? That question became a huge quandary. The entire USSR had functioned on the Soviet ruble since its earliest beginnings. In fact, when we moved to Latvia in January 1992, the Soviet ruble was still the currency in use.

But soon that changed right under our own noses, and we felt the brunt of the ruble's near collapse along with all those precious people we'd been sent to reach. Again, what I'm describing occurred in nearly all the old Soviet republics, not just one or two.

Because the nation was still using the ruble when we arrived there, on our first day in that country, I changed our dollars into rubles, and the exchange desk gave me a bunch of fifty-ruble notes. But when we woke up the next morning, those fifty-note rubles had been officially canceled during the night. The other denominations held their value, but not the fifty notes. So we had fifty-note rubles that were reduced to mere pieces of paper.

Even worse — those who were lucky enough to have saved rubles in the national bank woke up one morning to find the ruble so devalued that their bank accounts were worth next to nothing. One night, people went to sleep thinking they had money, and the next morning, they woke up to realize their life savings were virtually gone.[33] Their money was worth very little compared to its old value.

Although the Soviet ruble continued for a significant length of time, it was eventually replaced with a currency that looked like something from a board game of Monopoly. The first new currency was a multi-colored currency called the Latvian *coupon*. On the international market, it had absolutely no value, and it was barely accepted in Latvia. Once on a trip to Scandinavia, I asked a currency-exchange desk if they exchanged the Latvian coupon for dollars. The person behind the desk laughed out loud and said, "You've got to be kidding! Who would want that piece of trash? It's worth nothing!"

The temporary use of this currency served to "disconnect" the newly declared nation from the international community. They could do almost no buying, selling, or trading with that measly piece of paper that had little or no value.[34]

This issuing of new currencies was a problem in nearly all the former Soviet republics that had quickly broken free from the conglomerate of the USSR. I'll never forget how horrible the Ukrainian coupon looked back then. It was so ugly and worthless that it made the Latvian coupon look like an artful masterpiece!

This currency tragedy was bigger than life. I wish I was exaggerating, but countless lives were destroyed by the seemingly never-ending devaluation of the ruble, skyrocketing inflation, and newly emerging currencies with no value. And since we lived there, we saw it when nearly fifty percent of the population in Latvia who were ethnic Russians had no currency to use when they traveled back east to see friends or family in Russia. The Latvian coupon was nothing more than paper in Russia.

In addition to all of this madness, there were hundreds of thousands of ethnic Russians who were at retirement age and who were living on "social security" that previously had been provided by the USSR. Who would pay their social benefits now that the Soviet Union no longer existed? Thousands of retired Russian military personnel lived there and had received benefits that had been paid to them by the Soviet Union. Who would pay them their retirement salaries now? Would the new government pay benefits to the former military of the USSR who lived there? The fear and uncertainty in this chaotic mix was stifling and oppressive.

## Nationality Difficulties
## Leading to More Grief and Humiliation

And what would be the new national flags of all these fifteen newly declared nations? What would be their new national anthems? Do you recall when the athletic team from the dissolved Soviet Union participated in the Olympic games of 1992? When it came time for announcers to introduce their teams, what would they be called? Who *were* they as a nation, or *nations*? Seven of the fifteen former republics participated in the Winter Games in Albertville, France, and twelve of the republics joined the Summer Games in Barcelona, Spain — where they were all simply called the *Unified Team*.[35]

And when some of them won in their categories of competition, the crisis of national identity — or a *lack* of identity — became truly humiliating. In the Winter games, fabulous athletes walked away with *gold* medals for cross-country skiing, figure skating, ice hockey, and the biathlon. They won *silver* medals in cross-country skiing, figure skating, freestyle skating, and the biathlon. And they earned *bronze* medals in cross-country skating, figure skating, short-track speed skating, and biathlon.[36] (In the Summer games, they won 112 medals in twenty sports, including artistic gymnastics, wrestling, swimming, shooting, and fencing.[37]

But after each event in which they medaled, as those proficiently trained athletes stood on their respective platforms to receive awards, they stood in a momentary vacuum of humiliating silence *because there was no national anthem to play in their honor.* Then Beethoven's "Ode to Joy," queued up to play in lieu of their former nation's anthem, would begin to blast over the sound system — a beautiful song, but a tearful reminder that they stood apart from their competitors as men and women without a country of their own.

I think the lyrics for "Ode to Joy," translated here into English, are very interesting and speak of people turning in thanks to God for freedom, peace, and unity — something that really was happening in the former Soviet Union at that time, but the times were difficult, nevertheless.

> *O friends, no more of these sounds!*
> *Let us sing more cheerful songs,*
> *More songs full of joy! Joy! Joy!*
> *Joy, bright spark of divinity,*

*Daughter of Elysium,*
*Fire-inspired we tread*
*Within thy sanctuary.*
*Thy magic power re-unites*
*All that custom has divided,*
*All men become brothers,*
*Under the sway of thy gentle wings....*

*Gladly, like the heavenly bodies*
*Which He sent on their courses*
*Through the splendor of the firmament;*
*Thus, brothers, you should run your race,*
*Like a hero going to conquest.*

*You millions, I embrace you.*
*This kiss is for all the world!*
*Brothers, above the starry canopy*
*There must dwell a loving Father.*

*Do you fall in worship, you millions?*
*World, do you know your Creator?*
*Seek Him in the heavens;*
*Above the stars must He dwell.*[38]

I haven't even begun to cover the depth of tragedy that occurred as a result of the radical breakup of the USSR. Please understand — I am *not* lamenting the breakup of a godless, socialist-communist regime. I simply want to show you the other side of what happened to millions of people in all fifteen former republics of the USSR that you may have never considered before. But we remember it very well because we were there and experienced it along with everyone else *firsthand.*

I know it all sounds crazy, but what I'm sharing only scratches the surface of the devastation that was wrought when the USSR collapsed. It would take a whole book to tell the complete story. To get a *hint* of the widespread impact of the sudden collapse of socialistic communism — and the tragic repercussions people were challenged with *overnight, without warning* — just multiply the scenarios I'm describing by the millions of people and households who lived through it. What happened in this part of the world was simply staggering, nearly beyond belief.

## Problems Deeper Still — the Total Destruction of Infrastructure

Because all the former republics of the Soviet Union were interconnected with all the other republics, factories everywhere were reliant on sources and services that were located in other republics. In other words, all the parts and materials needed to produce goods weren't located at one source, but rather came from various parts of the USSR. Because of the new borders, customs were now required in order to receive those materials across those lines. However, procedures to process goods across borders had not been established. As a result, factories with no supplies coming in began to close all over the territories of the former Soviet Union with an astounding number of lost jobs that naturally followed.

I'll give you just one example from Jelgava, Latvia, the city where our family moved in 1992. Jelgava had been home to one of the largest automobile plants in the Soviet Union and employed tens of thousands of local workers in a city of seventy thousand people. That automobile plant fabricated the physical car bodies for a particular well-known Soviet minivan. But its other parts — the motor, chassis, brakes, dashboard, and wheels — were all made in other parts of the former USSR. Because new borders had been so quickly erected, essential parts could no longer be shipped across the border to reach the Jelgava factory. So once the parts on hand were used, that massive plant closed because it had no supplies to finish out the minivans.

Immediately, tens of thousands of people had no employment and no income. Even worse was the fact that the factory also produced the local heat for all the apartments where the factory employees lived nearby. When the factory closed its doors, it not only stopped making cars, it stopped producing the heat that those tens of thousands of people needed to stay warm in their apartments in sub-freezing winter temperatures.

In the former Soviet Union, large industrial plants were the main places of employment for the Soviet worker. These plants also provided basic social services, such as child care, medical care, and even housing in some cases. When the factories began to close like dominoes all over the former USSR, it meant a whole array of social services and benefits were also eliminated. The loss of these benefits created a massive tragedy. The factories that attempted to remain operational struggled to pay bills because of the huge disconnect in the system. In those cases, it became commonplace for workers to go months without being paid.

Finally, those struggling factories that were barely staying afloat began to resort to paying employees in whatever goods each factory produced. For example, if a factory produced tires, it paid workers with a few tires at the end of the month. If a factory produced stuffed toys, it paid its workers with a few stuffed toys at the end of the month. If a factory produced dishes, it paid its workers with a few dishes at the end of the month. The problem with that is that a person can't feed his or her family with tires, toys, or dishes — so you can well imagine the hardship this thrust upon hundreds of thousands of factory workers.

As a result of this bizarre development, it seemed as if most of the former Soviet Union moved into a barter-driven economy as people tried to trade their products for food and other goods they needed for living. Even highly skilled workers, company directors, professors, teachers, and doctors had to stand on the streets to barter and sell their goods to try to bring in enough cash and provisions for their households.

But even the money brought in so they could shop for food was frustratingly useless most of the time because grocery-store shelves were nearly always bare. It became a humiliating, heart-breaking, and *desperate* time for a once-proud Soviet people.

Later when I began to travel nearly nonstop by train to negotiate for TV time and to hold large TV meetings all over the lands of the former Soviet Union, I was regularly confronted with this sad state of affairs. When our train would make stops in various cities, I would look out the window to see hundreds of people lined up outside holding dishes, towels, tires, crystal vases, silverware, and stuffed toys that their factories had given them in place of salaries — hoping that someone on the train would jump off long enough to pay cash for something they were offering to sell.

It was heartbreaking to see these hard-working people trying to sell the goods their factories had given them in lieu of salaries. Many of them were highly educated Soviet citizens who were now standing on the streets, nearly begging for cash to survive.[39]

I wish I was exaggerating when I tell you that streets in every city were lined with tables where people stood to sell or barter their goods. The inflation rate was skyrocketing and people were so strapped for cash that they began taking personal items from their homes — even prized, valued possessions that included family heirlooms — to sell on the streets. Grandmothers, grand-fathers, fathers, and mothers, including higher-ranking professionals — and young people as well — tried to sell anything they could find to get cash for survival. It was as if the entire former Soviet Union had become a huge flea market.

As I shared, the very day our family arrived in January 1992, the economy was so crippled that store shelves everywhere were literally empty. Meat markets had no meat, bread stores had no bread, and pharmacy shelves had no medications. In an effort to jumpstart a free-market economy, President Yeltsin ordered the removal of nearly every price control on the most basic food goods.

That one act triggered such unbelievable inflation that on our very first day in the former USSR, inflation actually went up five-hundred percent on basic commodities. That's right — *in one night*, bread, sugar, flour, eggs, and milk cost five-hundred percent more than the day before!

And this was just the tip of the iceberg because inflation was about to take off like no one ever imagined possible. The runaway inflation became a constant worry for people as their salaries and purchasing power declined daily while prices for even the most basic goods rose higher and higher — literally, *by the hour.*

And deficits of *all* goods, not just food, abounded. Products of every kind were very difficult to obtain. When Denise and I needed to purchase a couch for our house in Jelgava, the store, which was a true Soviet-style store, was filled with all kinds of *samples* of furniture, but you had to place an order for the item you wanted to purchase. So we chose a couch and asked the store manager when it would be delivered if we bought it that very day.

The manager looked at his calendar and wrinkled his forehead as he pondered our question. Then we heard him say in almost a positive tone, "Well, if you pay for it today, it can be delivered to you about *two years* from now"!

We were trying to order the couch because Denise and I both knew within just a short time of arriving in the former USSR that the word "home" the Holy Spirit first used as He spoke to me about coming here literally meant *home*. We'd discovered that we were here to stay — and we needed a couch! Friends told us we were blessed to have such a quick delivery because in the final days of the Soviet Union before the collapse, people would often have to wait *five years* for their furniture items to be delivered to them. But if we had not purchased our couch on that day, the fact is that the system was so broken down at that time, a couch would not — *could* not — have been delivered to us at all during this period of recovery and reform.

### Black-Market Trade and the Emerging Mafia

The whole socialistic, economic system was broken across the board. The waiting list for a car could easily be five years *or more*. In fact, nearly all such purchases required a multi-year waiting list. It was in this frustrating environment of weary and worn consumers that a Soviet Russian type of "mafia" began to appear on the scene to provide black-market goods to those desperate to have even their most basic needs supplied.

I once happened to be seated on an airplane next to an FBI agent who told me that he and his buddies at the agency had never encountered criminals like the new mafia that was emerging in the lands of the former USSR. I asked him what he meant and he said, "We've dealt with the Italian mafia for years, but at least the Italian mafia grew up Catholic and have a sense of guilt for doing wrong. But this new Russian mafia grew up atheistic with no belief in God or in eternal consequences — it seems they have no conscience or guilt whatsoever for anything they do. They do worse things than we've ever encountered." Then he added, "They are so heartless, they'll cut your heart out for a hundred dollars."

That period of time in the early 1990s was so dominated by the Russian mafia that referring back to that time even now, my team members will often say, "Oh yeah, I remember the nineties. It's a miracle any of us survived those days."

During that time, it truly *wasn't* uncommon for someone to be killed for as little as a hundred dollars. In fact, many people were killed back in those days. Sometimes it was random killings or car bombings and at other times, it was hits ordered by someone who wanted to get rid of competition.

I am still amazed at how God's grace protected our lives in some foul situations in which we could have been eliminated by some really bad people. As we go on in my story, I'll share some riveting stories of God's miraculous provision and protection over our lives as we carried out His plan to see the Gospel proliferated in spiritually dry, parched lands.

The Russian mafia situation was so dangerous and so prevalent in those early days after communism's collapse that when our middle son Philip was a little boy, he once asked if the whole world was run by the mafia. If our sons had grown up in good-ol' Tulsa, Oklahoma, they would have never been mindful of mafia surroundings or asked such a question. But our sons grew up in the former USSR, where they were constantly aware that there was a sinister community of unscrupulous characters always lurking not too far away. On one hand, we knew to keep a distance from it, but on the other hand, we also knew the "black market" was the only way certain goods and services could be purchased that wouldn't take *years* to receive.

## Our 'Serious Mafia Covering'

At that time, it felt like everything was up for grabs. State assets were being privatized, businesses were forced to pay for protection against the influence of local mafia, and swarms of gangsters *mushroomed* in the community at large. Religious and non-profit organizations were not immune from the corruption.

After we started our church in Riga, a local mafia boss approached us to tell us we had to pay him a protection fee for our church or suffer the consequences. My associate wisely told him, "We are already under someone else's covering." He didn't tell him that he was referring to "the Shadow of the Almighty" that covers those who walk with God as referred to in Psalm 91!

That mafia boss left, but returned after a few days to talk to my associate again. He said, "My higher boss told me not to touch you because your covering is very serious. He says if I touch you guys, I'll get into trouble. So you're lucky. We're backing off and leaving you alone."

To this day we have no idea just what his mafia boss told him — but, for sure, the "Shadow of the Almighty" was covering us very well that day. I tell you this to show you how this criminal environment was touching every imaginable kind of organization and business — *even some churches*! But God's touch was so much greater in the midst of such depravity.

This criminal mafia was seemingly *omnipresent* — pervasive everywhere — in those former republics. And that corruption seemed to especially thrive just after the collapse of the Soviet Union. Life became not only devastatingly difficult in terms of the scarcity and lack, but it seemed a little like the *wild, wild west* in an environment where violence was prominent — and where trade was concerned, there was an underworld mindset of "anything goes."

## Even Business With Local Banks
## Could Be a Challenge

I know it's hard to fathom, but there were nearly no computers and relatively few commercial banks in those early years. So as our ministry was getting started there, we were thrilled to hear a new commercial bank had opened in Riga where we could do wire transfers. But we were soon warned to be extremely careful doing business there. We heard of one occasion of bank clients who were pulled over in their cars to be robbed, and one person was shot to death by mafia who had been tipped off by insiders at the bank.

So when our own ministry had to make large cash withdrawals for ministry purposes, our employees who took the cash worked meticulously with our drivers to plan alternate and previously unused driving routes to confuse those who may have gotten a call from inside the bank to hit us after we left. I meant it when I said that living there in those days was a little like living in the *wild, wild west*. But this was simply the cost of doing ministry in a collapsed and dangerous system that emerged during that critical moment in history.

It was truly a system that was out of control. In Russia, when President Vladimir Putin later came to power, he began to rein in that darkness and restore civility to society. He just seemed to clean things up for everyone and make life feel safer again, and this is one reason Russia has esteemed his leadership for so many years. Many who are older vividly recall life before Putin, and it was not a life that any knowledgeable person would ever want to return to.

So when President Putin stated that the collapse of the Soviet Union was the greatest tragedy of the Twentieth Century, he was lamenting *the way* it ended. Those who lived in the USSR understood him *exactly* and knew what he meant as he recalled the total collapse that resulted in three-hundred million people's lives becoming destitute, abandoned, stranded, handicapped, and at times permanently crippled. The repercussions were simply textbook *devastating*. Health institutions, educational institutions, governmental institutions, and every branch of the military seemed to be in disarray during that sad time as the former USSR attempted against all odds to get its footing in a new era.[40]

Later when China studied the wreckage of those years at the close of the Soviet Union, they took note of the mistakes and took a decidedly different approach to move more slowly into a free-market economy. They sought to avoid the catastrophe that was thrust on the Soviet people by what began as Gorbachev's ambitious plan to quickly reform the system.

It was for all these reasons that Mikhail Gorbachev, who was deeply revered and loved in the West, was not widely lauded at home in Russia. The Western world also loved the new, weak version of Russia that was led by President Boris Yeltsin before Putin came to power. The West looked on through the lens of a camera on the evening news, no doubt thankful for the fall of communism, but at the same time, they were left in the dark concerning the millions of lives that were in shambles.

That is what life was like when we moved our precious family of five to the lands of the former USSR *just thirty-four days* after official documents to dissolve the Soviet Union were signed by Mikhail Gorbachev and Boris Yeltsin in the Great Hall of the Kremlin Palace on December 25, 1991.

## A Brief History of Jelgava, Latvia —
## the Place of Our New Home

When our plane arrived in Latvia on January 28, 1992, our family was greeted by Soviet soldiers with machine guns who stood at the bottom of the stairs as we disembarked. As we walked down those plane stairs into the midst of soldiers, right in front of them all, we got on our knees as a family, held hands, and prayed together — right on the tarmac — that God would put this land deep into our hearts. The soldiers tried to rush us along to leave the area and to enter the terminal, but I was determined. I'd already decided that when our feet touched the pavement, we would drop to our knees and kiss the ground of what I thought would be our new home for one year.

I wanted to outwardly demonstrate our determination to open our hearts to God so He could put a love in our hearts for that place and its people. Although Denise and I *thought* we would be living there for a one-year period, we intended nonetheless to pour ourselves into the work for that span of time, and we desired to be filled by God in our hearts with love for these precious souls.

Those soldiers watched us cautiously as I led my family in dropping to our knees. We joined hands and leaned down together to literally kiss the ground! Then I led us in a prayer of committal for protection and provision, and I earnestly asked God to put a love in our hearts for this new part of the world and the people who lived there.

When we prayed that prayer, we did not fathom how profoundly God would answer us! We really believed this was a mere one-year commitment to help the new move of God get started, but we were thoroughly committed to that year to give it everything we had to give. So we kissed the ground and prayed. And, of course, God had something altogether different in mind for us than a one-year commitment.

Remembering that precious moment on the tarmac, our son Philip recalled, "When we got off that plane in Riga, I was just six years old, but it's something I remember very clearly. All of us carefully got on our knees and held hands to pray. And Dad said, 'Let's kiss the ground and ask God to put this land and its people into our hearts.' I remember looking around and thinking how dirty the runway was. But together we all kissed the ground and prayed right there outside the airplane."

When the five of us finally stood to our feet, those soldiers with machine guns had nearly encircled us. I'm sure they had never seen anything like that before. Using their guns to point the way, they directed us toward the terminal, and we understood that it was time for us to get moving. But that time of bowing to the ground on our knees in prayer was such a divine moment for our family. We were embracing God's call and asking for His favor to do what He had commissioned us to do with power and grace.

Inside the airport, the luggage belts were still broken, so suitcases and boxes were being thrown upward through a hole in the floor into the luggage area as I had seen months earlier on my first visit to the Soviet Union. We had brought suitcases plus thirty-two boxes, many of which were filled with breakable items. I ran as quickly as I could to try to catch our boxes as they were being hurled into the air. I'm sure it looked a bit like a circus act as I ran to catch one box and try to lower it carefully to the ground in time to catch the next box as it came sailing through the air — and the next one and the next one, etc. But we eventually secured all our things and incurred only minimal damage.

Just as on my previous trip in late April of 1991, our family was greeted outside Passport Control by Adele Alexander, the sweet woman from Texas who served as administrator in that first aboveground Bible school where I would be teaching the students.

As before, Adele's warm and welcoming voice comforted and cheered us as we followed her to the same worn-out van that had transported me months earlier to our hotel in Jelgava. Denise, in obedient step behind Adele with the rest of us, was speechless, although this was her second trip to Latvia. We had moved into a world unlike anything we had ever known before — even in our dim home surroundings in Fort Smith. But the look on our three sons' faces let me know they were elated for the adventure that certainly lay before them!

As we headed from the Riga airport to our new city of Jelgava, the road wound through a section of Riga still paved with ancient, unevenly laid cobblestones — some parts literally from the Thirteenth Century. Our minivan bumped and jostled on the street as we passed houses that looked like they hadn't been touched since the devastation of World War II. We continued our choppy journey in silence as we viewed from our seats what looked eerily like scenes from the war-torn 1940s.

As I look back on it, I realize that if our family had not dropped to our knees immediately and surrendered our lives to this new place, we could have become quickly discouraged. But instead, we found each challenge invigorating and fun. When we discovered that the grocery stores were practically void of food and that finding basic necessities would be a serious challenge, we didn't let it discourage us. Instead, every day turned into an adventurous scavenger hunt!

God amazingly filled our hearts with rejoicing, and every difficulty became an opportunity for another joy-filled experience as He met us at every turn. We certainly weren't living in the lap of luxury — far from it. But He graciously met our basic needs and, more importantly, filled our hearts with His own joy.

Adele, who had been there from the very beginning of the Jelgava Bible school, observed, "The whole country looked like it had suddenly stopped at the time of the war and had never gone forward. At that time, even though communism was lawfully out, its presence was still very strong — it wasn't exactly romping out of the picture at a great rate of speed!"

Jelgava was some twenty miles south of Riga, the capital city that was officially founded in the Thirteenth Century by Bishop Albert following the Crusades. The history of Riga actually goes back to the Second Century, but Riga's prominence grew after 1282 when it joined the Hanseatic League. Due to its location by the Baltic Sea between Russia and the Nordic countries — and due to its strategic port — Riga became desirable to many foreign powers for centuries to come. Following German rule during the Sixteenth Century, Riga was largely ruled by Poland — then in the Seventeenth Century by Sweden.

Later Riga was ruled for more than two hundred years from 1700 to 1918 by the Russian Empire. Even today, the scenes of Riga's Old Town are a stunning testament to the city's tumultuous history of being tossed around by many powers that held it captive at various periods.[41]

## About the Once Elegant City of Jelgava...

Because our family moved first to Jelgava (and later to Riga before we finally moved to Moscow), I want to tell you about Jelgava so you'll picture the tragic place where God moved our family and where the grace of God was to be poured out richly on us and our ministry as we got started in the lands of the former Soviet Union.

When we moved to Jelgava, we learned that it was a rebuilt city that had been established in 1265 and reconstructed by Soviet forces after World War II. Parts of the city still stood in ruins from the war, "frozen" in history almost five decades after its decimation by the fighting that raged there. For hundreds of years, Jelgava had been an elegant, prestigious city on the idyllic Lielupe River. But during World War II, it became a front for the war for three long months, rendering it decimated.

During the past when Jelgava was ruled by the Russian Empire, it was even the site of a massive and magnificent palace built by Rastrelli, the same Italian architect who constructed palaces for the Empress Elizabeth and who was most noted for his fabulous creations of Peterhof and the Catherine Palace near Saint Petersburg.[42] The magnificent Jelgava Palace incurred heavy damage in World War II, and although the exterior was reconstructed, the interior was never restored to its original beauty. Today the palace houses faculty and administration of a prominent Latvian university.

## Hitler's Plan To Extinguish Latvian Jews From That Region

Damage to structures was not the worst of the destruction that occurred in this Baltic country during World War II. When German forces entered Latvia and Nazi troops and tanks first rolled into the region from Lithuania in 1941, Jelgava was the first city they occupied. In the wake of that invasion, on the fateful day of June 29, 1941, the Nazi regime publicly announced its plans to exterminate as many "undesirables" as possible. Of course, as we know today, those undesirables were the approximate two-thousand-person Jewish population of the city of Jelgava.[43]

Within two or three days after Germans captured Jelgava, the beginnings of a Nazi holocaust in Latvia began. First, Nazi troops seized the central Jewish synagogue, and it was burned by Germans who used hand grenades and gasoline to inflict that disastrous blow. As the fire burned, the building was surrounded by German soldiers to prevent any attempts by citizens to intervene. It is reported that the chief rabbi refused to leave the synagogue, and as a result, he and other Jewish leaders who joined him were burned to death inside while others were brutalized outside. Jelgava residents stood helplessly by, watching the synagogue burn.

The date for the extermination of the Jelgava Jews cannot be determined, but it seems that it occurred on the weekend of either July 25-26 or August 2-3. Supporting an August 2-3 date for the murders is a published directive from a German commander on August 1, 1941, which read: *I order all Jews living in Jelgava city and the district to leave the limits of the city and the district by August 2 at 12:00 noon. Those guilty of non-compliance shall be punished in accordance with the laws of war.*[44] The edict was issued so fast that no one had time to pack up and flee, plus Jelgava had been their home for generations. It was hard for anyone to fathom what was about to occur.

The killing site for the Jews was a former shooting range for the Latvian army that was located about 2 kilometers (1.24 miles) south of Jelgava near a highway to Lithuania. According to witnesses, men, women and children were brought out to the shooting range over the course of 2 days, where on each day they were forced to dig a pit about 20 to 50 meters (about 66 to 104 feet) long and 2 meters deep (more than 6.5 feet) — a massive human gravesite.[45]

After that traumatizing event of digging their own graves, the victims were ordered to remove their outer clothing and surrender any valuables they were carrying. They were then led to the pits by policemen carrying rifles and wearing armbands. Eight to ten Jews were killed at a time by shooters who used bolt-action rifles. After being shot, some victims fell in the pit, others collapsed along the edge. The Nazi commander who gave the command to shoot walked among the victims and shot with his pistol at close range those he found still alive. Rapid-file, more victims were then brought to the trench — in terror, no doubt — shot, and pushed into the grave. When the pit was full, local residents were ordered to cover the victims up with dirt.

Virtually the entire Jewish community of Jelgava was killed during the course of these massacres. Afterward, Nazis posted signs at the entrance to the town of Jelgava which announced: "JELGAVA IS CLEANSED OF JEWS."

When we moved into our first house the day we arrived in Jelgava, we were unaware that we had moved into the very shadow of the site (a nearby forest only a half mile from us) of the horrific Jewish extermination that occurred almost exactly fifty years before. We were *literally* living in the "shadow of death" and didn't even know it.

At that time, the massacre site was still not commemorated — and it was just one of many locations where Jews had been exterminated in Latvia by Nazi troops. As hard as it is to fathom, it was just "a place over there" on the other side of our creek that no one wanted to remember.

The city of Jelgava was a sad and dilapidated city in January 1992 when our family moved there to make it our home for what we thought would be one year. The effects of World War II could be felt everywhere. Parts of the city remained in ruins, as it had been bombed in war. The main tower of the city, a large gutted and burned Orthodox church, and bombed walls of other buildings stood as visible reminders of the close conflict between the Germans and the Allied Russian troops that occurred there for three solid months.

Jelgava was so decimated by the bombings of World War II that when Joseph Stalin ordered a movie to be made about the infamous fight at the city of Stalingrad (*The Battle of Stalingrad* — Russian: Сталинградская битва), he chose Jelgava as the city to depict Stalingrad because it lay in such realistic ruins from the war. Of course, movie directors re-bombed the ruins in certain parts of Jelgava and set them on fire again so that they depicted a war scene. But when the movie was released in 1949, it looked so authentic that the people of the USSR assumed much of it contained actual footage from the war.[46]

The burned-out city of Jelgava retained but a remnant of its former glory. The old city hall still stood with a majestic bell tower, and a Lutheran church and a Catholic church from former years had also been restored. But besides that, there was not much left remaining of the elegant ancient city that was once so marvelously appointed that French nobility fled there to live after the French Revolution.

In place of the ancient city was a rebuilt city that had been constructed by the hands of German prisoners of war after the signing of the German Instrument of Surrender in 1945.[47] The main street of Jelgava was lined with a combination of typical German- and Soviet-style construction from that period. As I described previously, there were a handful of government-run shops scattered throughout the city that were basically unstocked due to the economic stagnation that had existed for years preceding the end of the Soviet Union, and was now only worsened.

As people crossed the main bridge into Jelgava, they passed the Jelgava Hotel, a decrepit old building I had some familiarity with because of my first missions trip with Duane and Dave in April 1991 — and it was also the hotel where Denise and I stayed on her first trip the following October. In the backside of that hotel was a restaurant that had almost no food to serve, and in the front of the building was a coffee shop that was also nearly bare.

Because the USSR was socialistic and communist in objective, it had no private enterprise. When we arrived, nearly all the shops were government-owned and were poorly run and poorly stocked. For example, across the street from the hotel was a grocery store with shelves that were empty of goods except on rare occasions when a handful of products "showed up." There were a few bread stores that were often flocked with long lines of people waiting to purchase bread.

Passing a little deeper into the city, one could see a dish store that also had vacant shelves, a "jewelry" store that occasionally also had a few plates or dishes to sell, and a large store located in the center of the city, which only had products once per month when the delivery of a particular type of commodity arrived, and those items did not last long in the store!

A typical delivery in a big central store might be shoes one particular month and something else the next month. When shoes would be delivered — mountains of shoes, actually — every single shoe was the same *identical* color. The color was determined by what kind of dye was available at the also sparsely supplied factory that made them.

Once Denise and I jumped into a long line at that store so we could get in to see what everyone was so excited about. To our amazement, we walked in to find in front of our eyes *purple* shoes in every shape and size imaginable — sandals and high heels for women, men's loafers, etc. — all in the same identical hue of purple. But people buzzed about with so much excitement when a delivery was made to this big store that long lines of people formed around the block just to see what showed up to be purchased.

Before the Soviet Union collapsed, the city square in the center of Jelgava hosted a massive iron statue of Vladimir Lenin, who, of course, was the founder of the Soviet Union. His image loomed over most cities in the Soviet Union, including Jelgava, until it was removed in 1991. When we arrived in Jelgava, the city square had three government stores — and one of those stores was an electronics store. This was ironic since by the time we arrived in 1991, all stores were nearly bare of electronics in the USSR.

In fact, there were so few electronics in Jelgava that stores didn't even have cash registers. Instead, cashiers used archaic beaded abacuses to tally customers' purchases. The other two stores on the square were for plumbing parts and school supplies, respectively. And these stores were also empty of products most of the time.

And, of course, there was the furniture store — the one I told you about where Denise and I later purchased a couch and were put on a two-year waiting list to receive it.

To the far right side of the city's square was a *Dom Kultury*, which in Russian means a House of Culture. It was the equivalent of a civic center with an auditorium that would eventually become the place where the Gospel would be preached and proclaimed in that city with signs and wonders following. I'll share more about that later.

Jelgava had only two gas stations, neither of which usually had any fuel to sell. The fuel situation was so critical that to a newcomer, it looked like there were no cars in the former USSR. But the problem was not a lack of cars — it was a lack of fuel. As a result, most cars were parked at home or in storage units.

We owned a tiny Russian-made Lada automobile, but it was difficult to find fuel to drive it. Then finally someone put me in touch with a local man whose job was to fill Soviet army tanks with fuel. He was siphoning some of it and selling it on the "black market" for $20 a gallon! If it hadn't been for him in those early days, we would have almost never had fuel for our car. Twenty dollars a gallon may sound outrageous, but since that was the only way to get fuel, we were willing to pay it.

And, really, the only way to purchase food was to visit the open food market in the city or go to the main open market miles away in Riga. Neither of them were socialist-communist, government-run entities. Rather, they were the early models of a free market that was re-emerging in a new environment of free enterprise.

Our family loved to go to those markets because we saw things there we had never seen before, like gorgeous multi-colored vegetables from Central Asia and raw meat of every imaginable kind that hung on hooks in the open air. Our sons loved to go so they could try to guess what kind of meat was hanging in front of them. By looking at the feet or hooves, they guessed what they were looking at — skinned rabbits still had fur on their paws and pork had hooves, etc. Men behind the counters would chop beef into smaller pieces with giant axes. They would swing down *hard* into the meat that had been placed on tops of sawed-off tree trunks that they used for tables. When we would buy that meat, we sometimes had to pick the splinters out before we cooked it!

Trips to the open-air market were simply a blast for our family. Those trips were important to us in those days because those markets had food to sell and because it was so adventuresome for our family to see what we would find there on our shopping expeditions.

But local people referred to the open-air markets as the "black market" because any form of capitalistic business was still considered to be evil by most people. Socialistic communist ideology was so rooted in people's consciences that many really believed it was immoral to buy and sell to make a profit. Because it was the only easy option for our family to have food, we patronized those markets. The only other options were the government-run stores with bare shelves. The fact is, the socialistic, government-run system had miserably failed, as it will always do — and as a result, the earliest beginnings of capitalism were starting to bloom all over the former USSR in open markets like the ones in Jelgava and Riga.

*We were simply thankful for them, because our family needed to eat!*

Philip and Joel especially loved the Riga market. Joel said, "That market was a blast. We would go there and see huge tree stumps used as tables, with men swinging axes to cut the meat right in front of us. When you ordered your piece of meat, they would lay it on that stump, take out an ax, and start cutting it, even through the bones."

Philip remembered, "The meat market was our favorite! It was fun because everywhere we looked, we saw scores of pig heads, and that was awesome!" To young boys, the sights of an outdoor, post-revolutionary butcher shop were simply fascinating!

The Riga market was so much bigger than the market in Jelgava — like a flea market for selling food. It was technically illegal, as in the Soviet Union, everything had to go through government stores. Yet it was somehow allowed to operate. Everywhere we looked, we were surrounded with heads, arms, and legs of various animals that people bought to cook and enjoy as delicacies and as sustenance. That part of the market looked and felt like a world of "cannibalism" — certainly not like the sanitary stores back in the United States. Those images were so vivid to our eyes and our minds — it was as if we were stepping back in time each time we went there.

## Ordered Steps Amidst the Chaos

This was where our family had just moved in January 1992 in obedience to God's call on our lives. Naturally speaking, we were living in the middle of chaos, deficit, and hardship. But in the chaos, our all-knowing, everywhere-present and powerful God was perfectly ordering our steps. He had a plan to use our family of five to pierce the darkness of Soviet communism with the fires of the His Spirit and the light of His love.

Certainly, there were those who thought I had lost my mind moving my precious family halfway around the world to adapt to this strange new culture — and to a people in transition who were deeply struggling for identity and, really, just to survive. But we knew it was the call of God, so we pushed aside all fear and concern and charged forward by faith.

We had no idea what this "one-year commitment" would entail, but God had been preparing us all our lives for this moment, and He was getting ready to launch us into the unchartered territory of Christian TV in the Soviet Union. We just wanted to build a foundation under a few hundred Bible-school students who had the anointing on their lives to *themselves* turn the world upside down. But God had His sights set not just on hundreds, but on *millions* who would be eternally impacted by the teaching of His Word — right in their living rooms through the medium of television.

If the black-market buying of meat and vegetables and fuel for our car had seemed risky at certain moments in our journey, we were barely scratching the surface of "risky" as we ventured into the next rocky stage of our ministry. We were about to start a Protestant church and construct a church building that would be the first of its kind in five decades. And through the airwaves — *with a blast* — we were about to penetrate a vast swath of the population in the former USSR with the Gospel of Jesus Christ.

'Suddenly I heard the Holy Spirit speak
to my heart, *Now I'm going to tell you why I REALLY
brought you to this part of the world. The move of God that
will happen here is so huge and will transpire so fast that
there isn't enough time to train all the leaders necessary
as quickly as it needs to happen. As a part of your calling
here, I am asking you to take Sunday School by
television to all the people of the entire eleven
time zones of the former Soviet Union.*'

# 10

# WHY GOD *REALLY* MOVED US TO THE FORMER SOVIET UNION

With my assignment to teach in the Bible school in Jelgava planted firmly in my heart and mind, we had embarked on our "one-year journey," having prepared ourselves to live in a new country in the very best way we knew how to do it. We were ready for the small twists and turns of daily life that we would have to adjust to as they came.

However, as you step out to obey God's plan, nothing *completely* prepares you for some of the bigger curves the enemy will invariably throw your way to try to stop you or get you off track. But God will faithfully assist and guide the willing and obedient.

In this chapter, I will share with you an enlightening moment when the Lord revealed more of His plan — *a lot more* — that we had not seen coming, the *big* reason He'd relocated my precious family of five from the

**Left:** *Riga, Latvia, 1991.*

United States to Latvia. Then right on the heels of that revelatory moment, as is so often the case, we encountered our first big "curve" — betrayal and treachery on a scale we'd not experienced before. I'll write about that in these pages, and just for fun, I'll describe some of our more minor twists and turns as well.

*Buckle up* for our "ride" into Jelgava, Latvia, and our odyssey into the world of TV as, over the airwaves, we penetrated the spiritual darkness that had held sway in the Soviet Union for so long.

### Getting Settled in Our New 'Home' of Jelgava, Latvia

As I shared in the last chapter, when our family arrived at the Riga airport on January 28, 1992, a driver was waiting for us to take us to our house in Jelgava — a house we had rented, sight unseen, with the help of some of the Bible-school team. Denise and I had rented *another* house when she and I made the trip together in October 1991, just four months earlier. But less than one month before we left Tulsa, the owner reneged on our lease, and the deal on our rental agreement fell through.

From the Riga airport, we took a rural route and rode *for miles* on a monotonous country road before finally arriving at the entrance of our new neighborhood. Entering the neighborhood in this broken-down city of Jelgava, we drove past a house that looked more like a chicken coop than a house. A woman was outside with her head down, diligently working among *chickens, chickens,* and *more chickens.* She would be our new neighbor.

The driver turned left to access our street, but the street was so full of wintery sludge that the only way to proceed without getting stuck was to "gas it" and drive really fast. As he approached our house, he had to *really* put on the gas. Our van slid through the mud as if we were in a high-powered action movie. Suddenly, the driver hit the brakes, causing the van to slide into a breathtaking half spin that amazingly "fishtail" landed us right in front of our house.

We unloaded all our luggage and the thirty-two boxes from the vehicle, and we waved good-bye to our magnificent stunt driver as he exited our "driveway" practically the same way he'd come in. Having carried everything into the house, we quickly discovered the house that had been found for us had no heat. And this was during a *very* cold Latvian winter. We were *freezing* in that ice-cold house. We were so cold during those first nights that all five members of our family crammed into one tiny bed to try to stay warm.

Our youngest son Joel remembered, "I remember that it was really cold. It was so cold that first winter in Latvia that my hands started cracking and bleeding — Philip's too. The cold was indescribable."

That tiny house had a kitchen that was so decrepit, when you pulled open the door to the oven, it made ear-piercing, squeaky noises that could be heard all over the house. And the inside of the oven was completely black with grime and filth. The bathroom was on the other side of the kitchen on the first floor. The threshold between the two rooms was never finished, so it was just exposed raw ground. To go from the kitchen into the bathroom, we had to step over the threshold so we didn't get dirt on our feet.

The bathroom was covered with broken tiles that dotted the walls — the rest had fallen off. The bathtub was an old Soviet-style tub made of metal. It was functional, but lacked any kind of aesthetics whatsoever. Just as we had witnessed at the Jelgava Hotel and at the Izmailovo Hotel in Moscow, all the pipes and plumbing ran externally, *exposed*, up and down the bathroom walls. It looked like a maze of pipes — even figuring out how to turn the water on for the first time was a great endeavor.

Upstairs, at the top of the steps to the left, was our bedroom. It had a bed in it that was about the size of a large card table. Down the small hallway, there was a room that belonged to the landlord that we couldn't use because it was where he put all his belongings. Our sons' nanny, Sharmon, had a really uncomfortable couch in one room, and our three boys would be sleeping together on a fold-out couch in another room that had a television in it. They were excited about the television until we discovered it didn't actually work.

### Our Homebuilder Came Knocking on Our Door... *That Night*

Before we'd made our move to the Soviet Union, the American director of the Jelgava Bible school had contacted me and gave me what I thought at the time was some very wise counsel. He told me that if I had *even the slightest inclination* we might be in Latvia for more than a year — even just a *little* more than a year — we should be prepared to build a home there. He let us know that it could be done at that time for about $11,000 because the economy had crashed and the dollar was king in that part of the world. Because he was the spiritual leader I would be working under, I chose to take his recommendation. Although there were shortages of everything there, prices *were* very low at that time, and his advice sounded reasonable.

On the heels of communism's sudden collapse, the transition to capitalism in that entire region did not happen nearly as suddenly. The economy had already become sluggish and then nearly stagnant from 1965 to 1985. Then when Mikhail Gorbachev came to power, the economy further plummeted until the time of the total collapse of the Soviet Union. The Soviet economy was in a tailspin when Denise and I and our family arrived there, and the American dollar had a lot of purchase power.

Additionally, under a socialistic economy, everything had been basically "free." The average person didn't have very much, and everything he did have was government-issued. For example, in almost every apartment, one would see the same kind of sofa, the same kind of kitchen table and chairs, the same kind of dishes, etc. — down to the color and minutest detail in design. Individualism was frowned upon and collectivism was king. When that system suddenly changed, people were at a loss to know what to charge for things that in the past had been free. For example, the price of a train ticket from Riga to Moscow was about 25 cents *roundtrip*. To get a flight from Riga, Latvia, to Murmansk, Russia, was pennies on the dollar compared to costs for the same services today.

So when the Bible-school director counseled me to construct a house in Latvia if I even *remotely* thought our stay might go beyond our one-year agreement, I came to the former USSR prepared. A partnering church had, in fact, given us the money to build a home, money that we carried with us on the plane. Denise and I thought that if we did build a house there, when it became time for us to return to the U.S., we would give the house away, perhaps to a minister and his family. So we traveled from Tulsa to Riga to Jelgava with $11,000 in cash on our persons, with the almost-certain intention of buying real estate at an optimal time in Latvian history to do so.

Our first night in this new country was January 28, 1992. We'd settled into our "ice-box" house as best we could. Sharmon was getting the boys ready for bed for the evening, and Denise and I were also preparing to go to bed when we heard a loud knock at our front door.

Thinking it was perhaps someone from the Bible-school team greeting us at a rather odd time of night, we opened the door to see a very shady-looking man in our doorway wearing a black-leather jacket and introducing himself as the contractor for our new home. He also quickly informed us that he was there for the cash in order to build it.

This man was the son of the man who had negotiated the contract for the building where the Bible school was being held — the younger man was recommended to us as a homebuilder by the American director of the school, who had vouched for both the man and his father.

It was pitch black outside, the streets were blanketed in knee-deep snow, and we were exhausted from just having traveled halfway around the world. The whole scene was very strange. We'd barely agreed to use this man's son as our contractor — and he showed up out of the blue late in the evening on our first night in the former Soviet Union. *And* he wanted cash from us so he could build our new home!

The man spoke very broken English, but I asked him, "You're already here to collect the cash for our new house? We don't even know anything about the house yet."

Very confidently, the man said, in effect, "No worries. I have it all under control. Put on your coats, get in my car, and I'll drive you right now to the land where I am going to build your new house."

Denise was very uptight about the way this was unfolding because the man looked like a bona fide criminal figure — plus it was practically the middle of the night. But because we were brand-new arrivals, I thought, *This is certainly not the way things are done in the United States, but we are not in the U.S. anymore. So we'll just go with the flow and get in the car with this man to see what he has to show us. Besides, our leader at the Bible school told me to give him the cash to get things moving.*

So Denise and I got into the car with this man. On our first day as a family in the former Soviet Union, there Denise and I were, riding in the backseat of a car with a complete stranger, in the middle of the night, on a road filled with mud and chickens. This "stranger" said he was taking us to see the land where he would be building our new home.

Our new contractor drove down several very dark roads, *left, right, then right again* — I couldn't keep up with what direction we were actually heading. Denise and I had no idea where we were or where this man was taking us. Then to make things really exciting, he was driving without headlights!

Back in those days, there weren't a lot of cars on the road, and there weren't a lot of car parts available with which to repair a car. So unless it was absolutely necessary, people drove at night without headlights — or they drove with their lights on low beam — because if their headlights burned out, they could not buy replacements.

Granted, there were very few cars on the road that night, but every once in a while, an oncoming car flew past us in the opposite lane like a cloaked phantom. Denise held tightly to my arm and flinched with surprise at the cars traveling full speed in our direction *without lights*. But our driver seemed oblivious to this wild roadway scenario.

A few long, almost breathless minutes later, the man finally pulled the car onto a parcel of land that was covered with heaps of snow. I became momentarily excited until I saw huge blocks of concrete already on the property that were so large, they looked like they could be used to build a bomb shelter. Our builder squared the vehicle in that direction and flashed on his headlights so we could see the lot.

"This is your house!" he said proudly, waiting for my gleeful response.

I was not gleeful — I was shocked. Referring to the huge concrete structure, I asked him, "How is there a foundation already here when I haven't even paid you yet?" In really bad, broken English that I barely understood, he said, in effect, "Well, we were already building this house for someone else, but this one is going to be ideal for your family, so it will be your house."

It seemed very weird to me, but it *kind of* made sense. In those days, it was not uncommon for new-house construction to be performed outside regular channels. Plus, I'd had the guarantee of the American Bible-school director that this was a man I could trust. So I pushed my trepidations aside, handed him the cash, and we went home on our first night in the former Soviet Union to sleep in our freezing-cold house that had no heat.

*And that was it* — our home would be built by this stranger while life and ministry for the Renner family would pick up speed rapidly, beginning the very next morning.

## Reconnecting With the Bible-School Students

The next day, I woke up early and I quickly dressed to head to the Bible school to teach my first lessons. The amazing connection I'd felt with the students less than a year before was still there, and I fell in love with those Soviet students. I felt like I had stepped into the book of Acts as I taught them the Word of God. It was energizing to both them and me. God's hand of blessing was on us as I began to fulfill what we had come to do.

There would be more for my family and me to do that He had chosen not to disclose. But we would soon discover it, and that's what I am going to share with you in this chapter.

My first day of classes with the students was Wednesday, January 29. Then on Friday, January 31, just three days after we arrived, we threw a *second* birthday party for Joel — on his actual third birthday. Several missionaries' kids came to that freezing-cold house and gathered in that grungy kitchen — *near the stove so they could be warm*! We served modest treats — whatever we could quickly gather from markets that had almost completely bare shelves.

Then, not to be outdone by our already fast-paced life, three days after *that*, in an attempt to turn on the heat in our rent house, the garage became *flooded* with the oil used for the heating system. The fumes and the smell throughout the house were almost unbearable. By the grace of God, we found another house on the outskirts of Jelgava, and our family moved out of that first house into a second one while we waited for our permanent home to be constructed by the *Mafiaso* builder who gave us the creeps.

*Whew.* We started our new lives in Latvia in a way that was anything but smooth. But our sons never once complained that life was difficult in those early days — and Denise and I were never sorry that we had brought our family to this part of the world. Each of the day-to-day challenges we faced, we turned into a fun learning experience. As a result, we fell in love with all of it — with the people, the land, *and even the problems and the challenges*, if you can imagine that.

That moment of kissing the ground on the tarmac and consecrating this new season of our lives to the Father had really accomplished a work of grace in our hearts. Regardless of how broken and neglected everything around us seemed to be, we quickly fell in love with the nation of Latvia and the people who lived there.

## Bathing in the River

Within approximately a week of touching down in the nation of Latvia, we were already settling into a second house — and not long after that, there was a *third* rental house. That one was heated with coal. Every morning, Paul put on his blue denim coat lined with nappy wool fleece and would go to the front yard to shovel buckets and buckets of frozen black coal to put into the stove in the back hallway.

Paul would dig through the freshly fallen snow to reach the coal and then load up pails of coal to dutifully carry into the house. As I write, I can almost smell that coal burning in our furnace, and I can still see Paul's little face covered with black soot from shoveling it into the burner.

That house was also really sad. The only toilet was in an enclosed space on the front porch, and there was no heat in that part of the house — which meant the toilet froze in those extreme temperatures. That produced a real dilemma because we had nowhere else to go to the bathroom. When we lifted the lid to look into the toilet bowl, we often saw a solid slab of ice.

Do you know anyone whose toilet freezes solid like that? *It's hard to go to the bathroom on a slab of ice that you cannot flush!*

The bedrooms were on the second floor, and the staircase was more or less a ladder. It was so treacherously steep that we had to be careful going up and down so we wouldn't slip and fall. Try to imagine living in an "improved" little shack with a ladder to the second floor, and perhaps you'll understand what that house was like.

When that first winter passed, we were so thankful that things began to warm up. But then we ran into another unexpected dilemma. Because that house was on the outskirts of town, it was not connected to the city's water system. Our water came from a well on the property. But little by little, the well had begun to run dry. Every day Paul, Philip, and Joel would go to the well to draw water, but one day, it finally ran completely dry. We put our heads together to find a way to get enough water to cook and to clean the dishes with each day — small bucketfuls of rationed water. Once Denise even colored her hair and had to rinse out the color with just a bucket of water! That was an ordeal in itself, but Denise was always a trooper and never complained about any lack of convenience in our early days overseas.

However, the small amount of water we were able to bring home every day didn't solve our problem of how we would take baths. But eventually we came up with a solution for that as well.

That rented house was built on a piece of land right next to a little river on the backside of the property. So Denise and I decided that because there was no other option, our family would go to the river behind our house to bathe.

Joel remembered, "Because the house was right next to the river, we took baths outside when there was no water inside. We gathered our soap and towels and went out to the back of the property, through the rickety back gate, and down the short path that led right to the river's edge."

That river was crystal clear with ice-cold water that was filled with massive pike fish. I can remember our being in the water and watching those big pike swimming in circles all around us. Denise got in and out as fast as possible because the water was so cold and because she didn't want to be touched by a fish. *And who could blame her?* But the boys would always linger and have fun on those bathing adventures until I would make them get out and dry off to go back inside.

After regularly bathing in the river for several months, something strange started to grow on Joel's skin on his chest. It was a black growth that looked like a spider spreading its long tentacles across the front of his torso. We had no idea what it was, but then we discovered that upstream from where we were bathing was a military base from which chemical poisons were being dumped into our little river. Those chemicals had flowed downstream and had gotten caught in a little crook in the river — almost exactly at the spot where we were bathing. Somehow those chemicals affected Joel's skin, and a hideous growth on his chest was the result.

When a partner of our ministry heard about this attack on Joel's skin, he abruptly took authority over it in Jesus' name and commanded it to leave. God is our witness that within days of that prayer, that hideous growth fell off Joel's body — but that was the end of our bath-time adventures in the river.

## One Phone Call to the States
## Was a Three-Day Wait

Besides problems with heat and water, life in general was technologically fifty years behind at that time. Even placing an international phone call was quite a complicated task.

First, all international phone calls had to be *scheduled*, or *ordered* in advance, through the telephone company. And all international calls were still monitored — and they knew exactly when each international call was being made.

In Jelgava, it took three days after ordering a phone call to get through to someone in the United States. We would call the operator, tell her we wanted to place a call to America, and provide her with the number of the person with whom we wanted to speak. The operator would usually respond, "Your call will come in three days. We will call you at some (undisclosed) time in three days to place your call."

She could, of course, not predict what time that call would come. So on that third day, we didn't dare leave the house for any reason, because the call could come at any moment, and to miss it meant another ordered call and another three-day wait.

Also, if the call came through from the operator and the number of our party was busy, which was sometimes the case, we couldn't simply say, "Can we try another number?" That call was our only chance! If the line was busy, we had to schedule *another* call and wait *another* three days.

When we actually got through to the person we were calling, the connections were so bad that we often had to yell in order to be heard. Once Denise reached her father after trying to call for many days. The connection was so terrible that Denise screamed at full volume, hoping her father could hear her. Finally, he said on the other end of the line, "*Rick*...is that you?" Dave could not distinguish the voice of his own daughter!

Connecting to the States was so difficult. Finally, someone suggested that we purchase a satellite phone with a gigantic antenna, so we did that. Satellite phones were nearly unheard of in those days. Ours was enormous and heavy. I would dial the call on a huge black box, and Denise would stand in the yard simultaneously holding a gigantic antenna and pointing it *this way and that way* toward the sky, trying to figure out an optimal position so we could get the best possible connection to the right satellite.

That antenna was *huge*. Denise and I must have looked like quite a sight in our front yard — me with my black box and Denise wildly waving a giant, umbrella-shaped antenna that was as tall as her! We went to amazing lengths to connect with friends and loved ones in the United States in those days.

## The *Stench of Smoke*
## After the Fire of Communism Died

We learned to live with the fact that we were being watched and monitored in our new home in a foreign land. Adele Alexander, a missionary from that momentous period who eventually became an integral part of our team, recalled, "The KGB followed us all the time in those early months. Everywhere we went, they were somewhere nearby. We were told not to ever let them know that we figured out which one was following us, because they would just assign a new person to surveil us, and we'd have to start all over learning to spot the new agent.

"We often joked with each other about our 'constant-companion' followers. We'd say, 'I see your guy watching you, and, *look*, there's my guy over there watching *me*.'"

Socialistic communism was centrally controlled, so everything around us was still essentially controlled by the government. The level of control by the socialist-communist system before the collapse was *so* intense that it made everything imaginable that was "normal" and enjoyable become completely joyless, lifeless, and stagnant.

Adele Alexander added, "Living in the former USSR at that time, you really saw the effects socialistic communism had on the people. It was so dismal that people didn't smile much. But something wonderful happened where we were when Rick and Denise came along. They began to teach and sing about the Lord, and people began to smile. It may not sound like a big deal to a Westerner who's never lived in such a dismal state over a prolonged period, but when people began to smile again, it was a *huge* deal."

Adele also recalled the unspeakable economic conditions that existed when we all arrived and started there. She said, "The first time I changed dollars into rubles, I had fifty U.S. dollars, and the stack of rubles I got for that fifty dollars was quite large. And it seemed like those rubles lasted forever because there just wasn't much available to buy."

She added, "When I was a little girl growing up in America during the time of World War II, everyone had war-ration coupons that they had to use in order to buy things because of all the hardships of the war. Living in the USSR in those early days felt like I had been transported back in time to my childhood. Because there was such a scarcity of products, everyone had to have government-issued coupons to purchase even basic things. You even had to have a special stamp to buy butter, sugar, and flour. Most stores were pretty empty, anyway, but even if they had products, you were not allowed to just walk in and buy any of them. You had to use your monthly allotment of coupons to buy those goods or you were out of luck.

"Also, coupons were for citizens, not for people like us. So the members of our team who were Latvians helped us buy what we needed in order to live."

Adele also remembered, "People wore such bleak-looking clothing. Because it was cold, women basically wore heavy wool skirts. Women didn't wear pants as we think of pants. They wore leggings that had feet in them, and most women knitted them themselves because buying them was largely out of the question due to supply, yet they desperately needed them to stay warm. Men's clothing looked like something we would have seen back in the 1940s. And we almost never saw clothes that were colorful. They were mainly military colors — grays, browns, and greens — and just very dingy looking."

Our nanny, Sharmon, recalled how primitive life was when we arrived in Jelgava. She said, "There were no modern conveniences. We didn't even have a washer and dryer. We had to take our clothes to a local place to have them washed. They put everything through an ironing press, and all our things would come back ironed — underwear, towels, you name it. And they were ironed so stiffly that everything felt like cardboard when we got them back.

"And because there was a deficit of buttons and the place that cleaned our clothes was afraid they might break a button that we couldn't replace, they would take all the buttons off Rick's shirts and give them to us in a little bag along with the perfectly cleaned and stiffly pressed shirts. Of course, that meant I had to sew all his buttons back on his shirts every time they were cleaned."

Day-to-day life was difficult enough to navigate after years of communism and then its sudden collapse. But receiving medical treatment was *an ordeal*. Even though medical doctors were compassionate and brilliantly educated, the socialist-run medical facilities they had to work in were atrocious.

Medical services were provided for free as a part of the overall socialist-communist programs that were centrally controlled by the state. But those facilities were horrible beyond one's ability to describe. People dreaded even receiving basic medical care because it was such a terrible, traumatic ordeal. Well-trained doctors worked in state-run clinics that were dilapidated with tiles falling from all the walls and ugly exposed mortar everywhere. Light bulbs were nearly nonexistent, so doctors worked in dark and dreary rooms.

But the worst part was not the facilities, but rather the actual lack of supply of medication and equipment to properly treat the sick. For example, there was such a deficit of the medicine used for anesthesia that simply going to the dentist was a traumatic event for people. Everyone basically had dental work done with *no pain-killer*!

I'll never forget when our sons' nanny needed a root canal. Sharmon knew it would be performed without any pain-killer, so she put it off as long as possible. Finally, when she couldn't put it off any longer, she went to the dentist in fear and trembling because of the pain she would have to endure. When she arrived back home hours later, she was still in tears, her jaw was swollen, and the excruciating pain was still lingering.

As the days passed, her mouth pain persisted. As much as she didn't want to do it, she returned to the dentist to see why — only to discover that, because of inadequate x-ray equipment, they had done the root canal *on the wrong tooth*! She had to do the whole procedure over *a second time*! Believe me when I tell you, although those procedures were probably done "textbook" perfect and with excellence, she was *traumatized* by her experiences with the dentist and socialized medicine.

### My Trip to the Hospital

This part of our story is a little out of sequence, but it further illustrates some of our basic challenges in our early years in the former USSR. Denise and I had sometime later been invited to minister at three European conferences in Austria, Switzerland, and Germany, and we decided to bring our sons along with us to give them the experience of ministering in Europe. When the day finally arrived for our long-anticipated trip, things got a little hectic at home, to say the least. The clock was ticking and it was time for us to depart to the airport so we wouldn't miss our flight.

However, instead of getting ready, the boys were just poking around, and Denise hadn't even finished packing. I knew that if we didn't leave on time, we'd miss our flight and have problems rebooking and being at the meetings on time. So in the midst of it all, I began to yell and threaten everyone to get downstairs immediately and pile into the car or I was going to leave without them!

Our administrator had agreed to house-sit for us while we were gone and had just arrived at our house with her beautiful Golden Retriever who had never encountered our St. Bernard that lived outside in our yard. But that all changed in a moment's time! When I couldn't seem to get my family together to leave on time, I became upset that they were jeopardizing our flight — and in that emotional moment, I threw open the front door to carry a few suitcases to the car. But as I threw open that door, that Golden Retriever *darted* out the door ahead of me — and in a split second, the two dogs started attacking each other viciously.

I watched in horror as our St. Bernard wrapped its jaws around the neck of the other dog and clamped down. I thought, *Oh, great, not only are we going to be late for our flight, but our dog is going to kill our administrator's dog!*

I was already worked up into a frenzy over my family's "tardiness" — and now we had a very ugly dogfight happening in our driveway. So in a moment when I was upset, I jumped into the middle of the fray to try to pull the dogs apart from each other. I attempted to open the jaws of our St. Bernard to remove his sharp teeth from the neck of the other dog. As I did, I inadvertently stuck my hand right into my dog's mouth, and in a startled instant, he bit down hard on my finger. *I'd been bitten by my own dog.*

The pain was so intense that I momentarily forgot all about our flight and our tight ministry schedule. Quickly, I lifted my hand to see how badly I'd been bitten, but all I could see was blood pouring from the tip of my right ring finger. I managed to stop the dog fight before rushing into the house to wash my hand to assess the damage. Looking down into the water in disbelief, I saw that *the entire tip* of my finger had been bitten off, and blood *continued* to pour out of my finger like an open hydrant.

Now, everyone needs the ten fingers God gave him, but I'm a writer — *I really need my fingers.* When I saw that the tip of my finger was missing, I realized how serious a situation this was. My family was finally ready to go to the airport, but I said to Denise, "We're not going to the airport — we're going to the hospital!"

With my hand wrapped in blood-soaked towels, we arrived at the hospital, and I was immediately admitted into the emergency room. After examining me, the doctors on duty decided to check me into the hospital for the night. Denise and I walked down a cigarette-smoke-filled hallway to my assigned hospital room, which was another dismal sight. A single light bulb dangled precariously from a wire in the ceiling of this nearly defunct hospital room. The sink was barely bolted to the wall and looked like it could fall off at any moment. The wallpaper was peeling off the walls, and the glass in the windowpanes was cracked.

And there I was — wounded, flustered, and wearing a tattered hospital gown for an overnight stay in this decrepit hospital. Denise graciously called the pastor in charge of the first conference to say we'd be a day late, while I waited for the chief physician to pay me a visit.

When the doctor in charge finally arrived, he asked me a question I didn't anticipate. "Mr. Renner," he said, "I understand that you were bitten by your own dog. Has your dog had rabies shots?" When I answered no, he replied, "Well, I regret to tell you that in this country, if you are bitten by a dog that has not had rabies shots, *you* must have rabies shots. That's the law of the land."

I lay in my hospital bed *speechless* as I realized that this doctor was preparing to give me the first of a series of rabies injections. He continued with some slightly better news, saying, "We used to give *thirty* of these shots in the stomach, but the French have come up with a new, stronger rabies vaccine that requires only seven injections — and we are going to give you your first injection right now."

After instructing me to turn over so they could give me an injection in my backside, the doctor casually said, "There's just one downside to this particular form of rabies vaccination. Once you start these injections, you have to take the following six injections right on schedule, or you will actually *develop* rabies." I thought, *That's just great. If I'm a day late, I'll end up as a rabid preacher, foaming at the mouth!*

The next day, the nurse administered another rabies shot and then gave me a packet containing five more doses of the vaccine along with a packet of syringes — and she firmly reminded me *not* to miss a single dose at the scheduled time or I would develop rabies. Being dismissed from the hospital, my finger stitched and bandaged, I went home to gather my family and we flew to Europe where the three conferences still awaited us.

At every conference where I ministered, I had to ask the pastor, "Excuse me, but do you have a nurse in your congregation who could give me a rabies injection?" I felt horribly humiliated by the entire ordeal, as I had to meet with a nurse in a pastor's office or study for five days in a row to receive an injection in my backside so I would be spared the more awful experience of contracting rabies.

I learned a big lesson from that experience. Strife throws open the door for the devil to attack in ways we never would have imagined. Ironically, if I hadn't allowed strife and anger to get me all worked up that day, I never would have thrown open the front door of my home in such a thoughtless manner. The guest's dog never would have run out before me, and the ugly dogfight never would have happened. That moment of emotion resulted in my being bitten and having to endure the debacle that followed.

I'm sure you can think of a time when strife caused a situation in your life to quickly spiral out of control. That's what happened on that fateful day at our house as we were preparing to travel to a ministry meeting. And it only took *seconds* for it all to happen!

After losing the tip of my finger, I realized that I was personally responsible for the chaotic events of that day because I allowed an angry attitude to have a place in our home. God was gracious, and the end of my finger *miraculously* grew back! But my family and I resolved from that day forward, we would have a "no strife" policy in our home. We learned the hard way that strife-filled attitudes can open the door to *painful, chaotic confusion* that results in hurtful consequences. It's far better not to allow strife to rear its ugly head than to give in to it like I did, let it mushroom to its full-blown, ugly conclusion, and then have to repair the damage left in its wake.

That experience in Jelgava's bleak, dimly lit, cigarette-smoke-filled hospital let us all know firsthand we were not living in a place where good medical care was available. In fact, what we experienced there was quite shocking. Medical conditions were simply miserable in Jelgava. But since that was where God had called us for that time, we knew His power, provision, and protection were available to us — *if we would keep the strife out*. So Denise and I put on our happy faces and chose to move onward, not dwelling on what we could not change.

But, unfortunately, this would not be our last experience in a government-run hospital in the former Soviet Union.

### Joel Had To Have an Appendectomy

We had another memorable encounter with socialized medicine when our youngest son Joel suddenly began to have pain in his right side that would not go away. We rushed him to the closest children's hospital in nearby Riga to try to determine the cause of his increasingly agonizing pain. This hospital complex was a series of disconnected, ruined yellow-brick buildings with rusted metal roofs and rotting doors and windows. It was *dreadful* — worse than the hospital where I had been previously admitted, if you can imagine that.

But this was the only hospital for children for miles — our only option for Joel to receive care as quickly as possible and to find out what was going on in his young body.

In the building we were in among that compound, we walked down a long, dark corridor, that had absolutely no lights on, toward a wing of the hospital where a doctor waited to examine Joel. After the examination, the doctor, who was very credentialed and qualified, but who worked in dismal conditions, said to us in Russian, "Your son is having an attack of appendicitis and needs to have his appendix removed immediately."

Denise nearly went into a panic because she saw how terrible the surroundings were. But the fact remained that Joel needed an operation immediately. No tests were taken, no documents were signed, and, in fact, no medical-history questions were even asked. Joel was taken into a hospital room where there were multiple beds and multiple patients. Denise and I accompanied him there to make sure he was going to be all right.

A little time passed before he was taken into surgery, during which we couldn't help but notice that the nurse, the cook, and the janitor were all the same person! That little woman carried a bucket of water into the hospital room and mopped the floor with the saddest-looking mop I'd ever seen. Then she reappeared moments later with a tray containing a meager bowl of soup for the patients to eat. Then when it was time for Joel to go into surgery, she physically picked Joel up, threw him over her shoulder, and carried him into the operating room, because the hospital had no gurneys with which to transport patients.

Denise and I waved at Joel as he waved calmly back at us from over the nurse's shoulder, and then they both disappeared through broken double doors into what must have been the operating room for his emergency appendectomy.

Denise was so totally in shock that she found a dark corner with a chair and sat there, praying in the Spirit so she could get into a place of faith for Joel's safety. I decided to go outside to pray. As I walked around the exterior of the building, I realized that I was standing just outside the operating room where the doctor would be operating on Joel. One of the windows to the operating room was so badly cracked and broken that a large piece of glass was missing, and I could actually look into the operating room from the street and see them as they prepped to perform surgery on Joel! I ran inside to get Denise. "Sweetheart, come with me — there's a big crack in the operating-room window — we can watch Joel's operation!"

Denise responded, "*Rick*, I am not going to watch Joel's operation. I'll just stay here and pray." So while Denise prayed in that dark corner inside the hospital, I stood on the street and watched Joel's entire surgery through the cracked window of the operating room. He made a full recovery from that ordeal, and Denise and I were strengthened in our faith, grateful to God for seeing us safely through that trying time in our lives.

Joel's appendicitis and surgery became yet another of our experiences with socialist-run medicine. Socialism and communism are systems that simply do not work. Anyone who doesn't understand that socialistic, communist-run ideas don't work has never studied history and the long-term effects of those repeatedly failed policies and philosophies.

But we saw the results of a state-run medical system firsthand, and we can testify of its gross inefficiencies and the diminished quality of care one receives under such a system.

## We Started Our TV Ministry
## With a Home Video Camera

As I told you in the previous chapter, the Bible school where I was teaching was the first Bible school to operate aboveground since the time of the Bolshevik Revolution in 1917. Other schools were starting in other places, but this was the first to start in many years since the Communist Party had become king.

This school had, oddly enough, been started under the covering of a local man with many curious ties to local mafia organizations. And his son was the building contractor for our home. These two men were father-and-son "movers and shakers" in the newly emerging nation of Latvia that had become a lot like the *wild, wild west*.

The father had been raised as an underground Pentecostal and now in his older years had developed a knack for doing the impossible, albeit usually with a serious lack of integrity, as we would soon discover. But due to his connections with the local KGB and underworld type of organizations, he was able to negotiate a contract with the city authorities to rent the building where the Bible school was held — a building across the street from the old headquarters of the KGB. What would be the odds of that happening in the USSR as it once stood?

Paul Renner commented, "It is amazing who was in that Bible school in Jelgava. We didn't know it at the time, but those students would become Russia's new spiritual leaders. Now, years later, it is not unusual for a notable national leader to come up to me at a conference and say, 'Do you remember when I stayed at your house in Jelgava in the early years of that Bible school?' One of the most prominent church leaders in Russia today once told me, 'Did you know I was one of the students who helped move all the furniture into your house?' So many of today's really anointed leadership were there with us in those early years."

### A Meeting Invitation and a New Assignment
### From God — This One Was *Big*!

After our first week of classes at the school, the mysterious local businessman invited me to speak at the national hockey stadium in Riga for a Sunday service. The idea of a public Gospel meeting was simply *outlandish* in that land where the communist regime had ruled with an iron fist. So I was quite excited to participate in this event.

When our family arrived, the national hockey team was still playing a game on the ice, so we had to wait for the match to end before we could use the auditorium for the meeting. After an hour or so, the hockey game ended, and the man's helpers rolled a strip of Soviet-looking red carpet onto the ice with a microphone positioned on a stand at the very end of the strip in the middle of the ice rink. Soon the doors opened to the public, and Denise and I and our sons watched as people began to take their seats in the bleachers that flanked the ice rink.

Everything about this man and his multi-membered family seemed dark and mysterious, but the American Bible-school director, whom I trusted, had told me to work with them, so I obediently did as I was told. We were new, and the Bible-school director had been working with this businessman for months. So we did what newcomers usually do, and we blindly obeyed whatever we were instructed to do.

At the hockey-rink meeting, a small group of musicians sang and then Denise was invited onto the strip of carpet on the ice to sing. Then I was called to the microphone to preach. My feet were *freezing* from the ice below the thin, threadbare carpet.

When I finished speaking, the man who'd invited us called on people to come forward for prayer. We watched with shock as people on crutches came walking across the barren field of ice to receive prayer for physical miracles.

I kept thinking, *These people are all going to need miracles by the time they get over here because they are going to fall on the ice!* But I couldn't help but notice the deep hunger in the hearts of the people who attended and their utter openness to receive God's goodness and power. It was the easiest thing in the world to minister to them — it was like we were under an open

Heaven as we prayed and God lovingly manifested His presence to each person.

As I've already noted, this man who'd invited me to speak had a lot of interesting connections. His office was located on a former military base and all around its perimeter were *stacks* of missiles and military equipment! The whole place was busy with men who looked shady and dangerous. They were busily up to *something*, and it felt to us like that "something" was *no good*. We later discovered that we were right.

But the man also had connections with the big TV station in Riga and had even negotiated a contract to broadcast Jimmy Swaggart from time to time. Those Jimmy Swaggart programs were the first Christian programs to be broadcast in the USSR, but there was no regular schedule for when they would air, so they were shown weekly at random, unpredictable times.

Because this man also owned TV equipment, he had filmed the service at the ice rink where Denise sang and I preached, and he informed us that the following day, it would be broadcast on national television from the big TV tower in Riga.

So the next day, Denise and I waited and waited to see our program on TV. Finally, after hours of seemingly endless waiting in front of an old Soviet television in our rented house, the program came on. There on Soviet television, Denise and I saw ourselves singing and preaching from the previous day's meeting! We were baffled that this was happening in a land that was still very dominated by atheistic, socialistic communists who ruled every part of the country.

Then, suddenly, I heard the Holy Spirit speak to my heart. I'll summarize what I heard Him say: *Now I'm going to tell you why I REALLY brought you to this part of the world. The move of God that will happen here is so huge and will transpire so fast that there isn't enough time to train all the leaders necessary and as quickly as it needs to happen. As a part of your calling here, I am asking you to take Sunday School by television to all the people of the entire eleven time zones of the former Soviet Union.*

I turned to Denise and asked, "Sweetheart, I just heard the Holy Spirit say something amazing to me. Has He said anything to you while we've been sitting here watching this program?"

To my astonishment, she had heard, *nearly verbatim*, the same words the Holy Spirit had spoken to my heart. We immediately joined hands — and invited our three sons to join us — and together we all prayed and dedicated ourselves to do whatever God was asking us to do on television. I had not had a TV program since that early program in Fort Smith called, *Wide Awake With Rick*. I hadn't *thought* of doing television again, and certainly not in the shambles of the former Soviet Union — in the Russian language, in a culture I didn't know, and, as I was learning, in a world filled with criminal activity.

Because the director of the Bible school assured me the businessman could be trusted, I leaned upon this curious person to help me learn how to get on television with the Gospel in the former Soviet Union. No one had ever succeeded in doing this except him — *no one*. If anyone had the ability to make it happen for us, I knew it would be him. So I began to talk to him about how to start a TV ministry in the former USSR. Technology was so limited and of such poor quality back then that even a simple American home-video camera was superior to the "high-end" cameras used at many of the TV stations.

So with the use of a home video camera, Denise and I adjusted our living room to become a makeshift TV studio, and we began to film the most primitive-looking one-hour programs for daily TV that you can imagine. In fact, looking at those early programs now is hysterical to me. It is remarkable that anyone was willing to broadcast them, but the low quality of our program was still superior to what was being produced at that big TV station — so on that network we began to go.

Adele Alexander recalled, "The interpreter would sit there with Rick in his house, and he would make TV programs with a home camera. The instant people heard Denise sing and Rick teach, there was a connection. It was such a treasure to see what God was miraculously doing as Rick taught on television. From the moment he greeted the TV viewers for the first time, he captured people's hearts. Rick wasn't just *called* — it's my personal opinion that he is the *most called* person from the United States to the Russian people. The call on Rick's life to the Russian people is special and deep."

Denise and I and our sons and nanny had come to the lands of the former USSR on an extremely limited budget — but we were prepared to minister in the Bible school to those hungry, God-called souls who were so eager to fulfill His plan for their lives. But I hadn't considered television, much less television across all eleven time zones of the former USSR, and I didn't know how we would pay for the broadcasts. Yet I knew the Holy Spirit had spoken to our hearts, so by faith, I signed a Russian-language contract to begin broadcasting *Good News With Rick Renner* every single day on the national TV channel at the big station in Riga.

The contract had no broadcast times listed, so from day to day, the program appeared at random times. The only way we could see the program was if we stayed in front of the TV all day long to see if we would catch it when it finally aired. The schedule was totally unpredictable, and it was impossible to know when the TV program would appear on the air.

In spite of the unstable broadcast schedule, people all over the new nation of Latvia were catching the program when it came on. It immediately created a sensation for several important reasons.

Television in the USSR had been off limits to Americans because Americans had been viewed as untrusted enemies of the state. Remember that the USSR had just officially dissolved on December 8, 1991 — and then just a few months later, an American suddenly began to appear on television almost every day for a whole hour. This was unheard of at that time. People were so mesmerized that an American was speaking to them every single day for an hour that they began to tune in to see what I was doing on television and what in the world I would be saying to them for a full hour every day.

The second reason the program mesmerized people was that I was speaking publicly about the subject of God and the Bible — subjects that had been taboo in the USSR. People wondered how in the world it was possible for an American to be on television speaking so freely about this previously strictly forbidden topic?

Because we were starting a television ministry, we rented an office we found in a socialist-communist-run bus depot and assembled a small staff of five students from the Bible school as our first employees. And we began filming TV programs! Those programs may have been embarrassingly primitive, but the effect was enormous on the viewers. And on those programs, I invited the people to write to me, with no understanding of the *mountain* of mail that was about to show up at our office.

Those students who first came to work with us were either newly saved or had grown up in the underground church and never dreamed they would live to see a Christian TV program on the air. Not only were we reaching large numbers of people on TV, but our small team was thrilled that they were witnessing for themselves a miracle in the former USSR. It seemed like a fairy tale that was coming to life right before their eyes. This was what their grandparents and parents prayed for as they languished in prisons for their faith during the hard days of the Soviet Union, and now their lineage was experiencing the answer to those tear-soaked petitions.

With our young team, we began to produce our primitive one-hour daily TV programs, but I was also teaching in the Bible school several times a week. Then as the mail began to flood in from a hungry television audience, it became quickly apparent that TV ministry was going to become our focus.

When it came time for the Bible school to graduate its first class, I asked Peter Kulakevich, the assistant director, to help advise me on which students I should invite to work full-time in our new TV ministry. He said, "We are primarily focused on starting churches, so whoever is not assigned to go somewhere are the ones I will recommend." Soon the day came when he said to me, "I have a group of graduates for you to talk to about joining your team."

One of those students, Anita Busha, said in an interview for this book, "I thought it was a great privilege to be invited by Pastor Rick to work for his ministry. Everything was so new. Of course, I agreed. Who would not agree to work for Pastor Rick? He had already connected with a large TV audience, who had written letters to the ministry, and he was responding to each one. There was so much to do from the beginning, and it was exciting!"

Soon that small group of graduates whom Peter Kulakevich recommended to me officially joined our ministry team. Among them were several that are still with us to this day. As the TV ministry continued to grow, others followed. Names like *Andrey Chebotarev, Leonid Chebotarev, Anita Busha, Leonid Bondarenko, Alexander Dovgan, Yuri Ruls,* and *others,* whom I will refer to and quote in this book, were there right from the start, and all but one remain with us decades later.

When we started our ministry office in Jelgava, it was just a small group of daring young people. But they eventually became mighty men and women of valor whom God uses today to lead entire parts of our ministry in Moscow, Russia; Riga, Latvia; and Kiev, Ukraine, and to help oversee our own Russian-speaking satellite network that reaches across the planet. Even now when we meet at various events, we cherish seeing one another. All of those students have an amazing connection to this day, and they are all the leaders of the modern-day move of God.

Actually, the Jelgava Bible school produced massive fruit. That school, although no longer operating, is still legendary. I would say that the students who attended that school are kind of an elite spiritual group of leaders in the former Soviet Union today, because in a divine slice of time, they seized their moments in that beginning move of God.

### '*Mountains* of Mail' Was No Exaggeration

Denise and I thought it was appropriate to encourage people who watched the TV programs to write to us and tell us about their prayer needs. And we promised that our team would *personally* read each letter and that we would *personally* write each person back.

Well, it sounded good and right at the time, but we had no idea that many hundreds of thousands of people would take our invitation to heart — *but they did.* We simply had no idea of the *mountains* of mail that would come so quickly into our office. Before we could hardly catch our breath, we had thousands of unread letters packed in boxes stacked on top of more boxes. An entire large room in our office was *filled* from floor to ceiling with boxes and boxes of unread mail that desperately needed to be read and answered *as promised.*

The fact is, we were overwhelmed by the response. Worse yet, our staff was so small that as hard as they worked to get through this mail, we simply had neither the staff, nor the equipment to answer such huge numbers of letters in an expeditious manner. We had only one computer for *mountains* of data entry, so the letters themselves would have to be answered by hand!

Later when we finally got more computers, it helped us speed up the process of answering mail and we never lost our momentum again. But that acquisition came much later — and when it did, we became the first office in Jelgava to have so many computers. In fact, our having computers made such a commotion in the city that people actually scheduled visits to see what they looked like and how they worked. Eventually, those computers were sabotaged, a story I'll tell you about in the next chapter.

As I said, I'd made a promise on TV that if people wrote to us, we would read and answer each letter. But *how* were we going to keep that promise with the mail growing by boxloads every day?

Then someone on staff suggested that we schedule a number of all-night, weekend "mail parties" — working all night long and simultaneously celebrating this great breakthrough of reaching so many thousands of TV viewers.

Well, it really *was* worth throwing a party in order to get it done because we were seeing a miracle before our eyes with each new huge box of mail that was carried into our office. People were responding to the program — to the teaching of the Bible — and to my invitation to write. So having a "party" to celebrate this miracle — and combining it with a team effort to catch up — seemed like a fun and great idea. We reasoned that if we put our whole effort into it, perhaps we could catch up on the mail.

A series of weekends were chosen, and *everyone* who served in any capacity on the team — workers in the mail department, our small team of TV producers, secretaries, and guards — participated in multiple all-night mail-party events. One group of people would open the letters, put data into the computers, and pass the letters on to readers, who read and answered each letter by hand. Once the letters were answered, they were passed on to a group who stuffed envelopes, licked stamps, and sealed the letter. Finally, the last group organized the thousands of letters into batches in order to fulfill the requirements of our local Soviet-style post office.

The work was exhausting, and everyone pitched in to lend his or her supply to the task. It took nearly one month to do it, but by being committed — and by every person doing his or her part joyfully — we were able to supernaturally answer all that mail and catch up with the new incoming mail.

That series of mail parties was one of the biggest catch-up operations I've ever witnessed. Throughout each overnight marathon, I encouraged the team from Ephesians 4:16 — a very powerful verse about team participation and supernatural energy to get a job done. That verse says, "...The whole body fitly joined together and compacted by that which every joint supplieth, according to the effectual working in the measure of every part, maketh increase of the body unto the edifying of itself in love."

I want you to especially notice the central section of this verse, where it talks about the whole body being "...fitly joined together and compacted by that which every joint supplieth, according to the effectual working in the measure of every part...."

What a picture of teamwork this is. That's why I chose to use it to encourage our team as we dove into that mountain of mail during each of our mail-party sessions.

Those letters from Soviet TV viewers were so precious to me that I never allowed them to be disposed of until *many* years later when I realized that we had a whole warehouse that was filled with tons of old mail from those early days. Each letter represented a precious soul, and it was so hard for me to let those letters go. When we finally did decide to dispose of them after so many years, it was all together *more than one-hundred tons of mail* that we shredded and burned. But to be honest, I kept several boxes as precious memories of a truly notable moment in the history of our ministry.

I want to ask you: What tasks do you have in front of you today that can only be accomplished if a team comes together to make it happen? Do you find yourself, as I did, with something that grew more quickly than you anticipated and it has nearly overwhelmed you?

Whom has God called to join with you with deep commitment? I assure you that if you find a team who will accept the challenge and who will cooperate together, it will release the divine energy of the Holy Spirit — and He will supernaturally supply whatever you need to get the job done!

Within a short time of our being in the former Soviet Union — from helping in the Bible school to hearing God's directive to bring Sunday School into people's living rooms through TV ministry — Denise and I and our sons began to realize that God had actually given us a *life commitment* to this part of the world, not a simple one- or even two-year engagement.

At the time of this writing, we have lived in the former Soviet Union for *decades* and have seen the Holy Spirit's supernatural fruit as hundreds of thousands have received Christ, grown in the Spirit, and found their places in local churches — many of which we helped start. *It has been the experience of a lifetime!* And our sons — now full-grown men in the ministry and with families of their own — grew up experiencing a book-of-Acts kind of childhood by living in this spiritual environment.

## God Is Your Most Valuable Partner

What has God called you to do that you never dreamed you would be doing? I've learned that as we walk with God as our most important Partner in life, we often find ourselves doing what we would have never thought possible.

In our own lives, just after relocating our family to live and minister in the former USSR in 1992, God miraculously opened that door for Denise and me to begin our television ministry that would transcend the eleven time zones of the former USSR. We didn't realize at the time that our step of faith to start that one program in our living room was actually the inception of what would become *the first Christian television network* in the territory of the former USSR.

Decades later, we are still broadcasting our own TV programs in addition to programs that we broadcast for other ministries. And as I mentioned, we now own our own Russian-speaking satellite network. Seven days a week, twenty-four hours a day, we broadcast to a viewing audience of millions of Russian-speaking people.

Over all these years, we have broadcasted *hundreds of thousands of hours* of Bible-teaching programs across this vast territory. I am thoroughly convinced that it has made a permanent impact on the spiritual environment of the former USSR, by the grace of God. So much teaching of the Bible has gone into homes that the Church in this part of the world will *never* be the same.

Since we started broadcasting in 1992, we have received millions of letters and correspondence from people whose lives have been changed by the teaching of God's Word via the airwaves and other forms of media. It is no exaggeration that several hundreds of thousands of people have come to Christ as a result of our television network. And books have been distributed free of charge by the millions.

We give all the glory to God for what has happened and for what will ensue, and we are thankful for the gifts of our partners who have worked hand in hand with us so we could establish, build on, and continue to fulfill this mighty work.

To do all of this has taken faith, courage, finances, equipment, a skilled technical team, and a group of giving partners who have stood by us through the years so we could consistently and professionally reach the multitudes who were in spiritual darkness.

In addition to the technical expertise needed, this assignment has also required a large team of dedicated employees who read and answer every single letter that is received from those who correspond in response to the programs. We still provide the same painstaking care that we did in those early days as precious Soviet souls took the time to sit down with pen and paper and write to us. *And we love doing it!*

Like so many other ministries, ours was no small undertaking, and it is a ministry today that requires a *"thousand-percent"* commitment from everyone involved — despite the obstacles and setbacks that invariably occur with such a monumental undertaking. Hell does not sit silent as you take Christ's life-saving message to those in darkness, so you must stand ready to combat spiritual enemies that come to oppose you.

But I'd be remiss if I didn't say that God's mercy and grace remain the most important factors in this mix. And we have experienced it all — spiritual warfare, overwhelming victories, *and lots and lots of mercy and grace*!

It's true that we can buy the finest television equipment, produce the highest-quality programs, and purchase the most coveted time slots available — but if God doesn't supply *His* part, it will all be to no avail. I am reminded of Psalm 127:1, which states: "Except the Lord build the house, they labour in vain that build it: except the Lord keep the city, the watchman waketh but in vain."

What Denise and I have experienced as we've given God our *yes* and stepped out to obey Him has been nothing short of amazing — we are running to keep up with what He is building with our hands.

### *But Wait... There's More!*
### Our First Big Public Meeting

As we caught up on our mountain of mail that poured into our office from all over the former USSR, we sensed we should hold a large meeting to see how many of our TV viewers we could minister to personally in a public venue. So in the late summer of 1992, I filmed a commercial inviting people to attend a meeting that we would hold in the same national hockey stadium where I had been invited to minister by the man who helped us get on television. The filming and airing of that single service early on brought our faces before the people God had called us to — through their television screens in their living rooms. That's how we were introduced to what was now becoming our growing family of TV viewers, precious Russian souls whom God Himself was reaching out to through us.

That hockey stadium — which today is demolished because it became so sadly dilapidated — was at the time the largest venue in the nation of Latvia. If all the bleachers and the main ice rink were used to maximum seating capacity, the venue could hold about eight thousand people.

## God Was About To Show His Loving Care
## to a Hurting People

Previously, I shared with you about what receiving medical treatment was like in that part of the world during those tumultuous times, and I related our personal experiences at Soviet-run hospitals and clinics.

But those were not isolated incidents. Everywhere you went, without exception, medicines and medical equipment were in short supply. Well-trained doctors could diagnose a patient's sickness, but that's where it ended most of the time and people remained unhelped because no medications were available to treat the sickness. Even basic medications, such as aspirin, were a treasure because they were so hard to obtain.

It was in the midst of this dismal state of affairs that I made the announcement that we were going to hold a series of miracle services in Riga, and I urged people to come if they needed a miracle of healing in their bodies.

Well, when no medications are available, the idea of a miracle becomes *good news* for those desperate to receive healing in their bodies. So for two weeks prior to those big meetings, we broadcast our advertisements for the miracle services many times a day on television. We had no idea what kind of effect the commercials would have, but we prayed people would come to the meetings to hear the Gospel, receive a miraculous touch from God, and personally come to know Jesus Christ.

The long-anticipated day finally arrived and we drove to the city to begin our series of meetings. As we drove on bumpy cobblestone streets that led to the venue, Denise and I saw *thousands* of people walking down the streets in one direction. We made our way through the crowds in our little Russian-made car, curiously commenting to each other, "Where are all these people going?"

When we finally arrived at the large auditorium — the hockey stadium we had rented — we were *stunned* to see *masses* of people in line, waiting for the doors to open. We had advertised this meeting and prayed that people would come — and didn't have a *clue* all the countless people we'd just driven past were headed to *our* meeting!

As Denise and I stood on the platform and looked out over the audience in that large hockey arena, we were shocked to see the place filled to capacity with *eight thousand* people! Many of them were sick people who had no means of obtaining desperately needed medicine and had therefore turned to the power of God as their only hope for healing.

And He did not disappoint them. Night after night, we witnessed mighty miracles occurring before our eyes. Blind eyes were opened, epileptics were healed, and deaf ears were unstopped. And the greatest miracle of all was the hundreds of people who came forward to give their lives to Jesus at the conclusion of the meetings each night! By the end of that week, the aggregate attendance was approximately forty thousand people — and of that number, *more than seven thousand prayed to receive Jesus as Lord!*

Yet there was one man who was obviously in need of a miracle, but had not received a healing touch for the duration of the meetings. He came each night after the service had started so he could get to his reserved seat without fighting the crowds that swarmed busily into the big auditorium as soon as the doors were opened. Because he came in late each evening, I couldn't help but notice him. His sad, desperate physical condition and the intense look of agony on his face were hard to ignore as he slowly made his way to his seat each night.

We learned later that nineteen years earlier, this man had become crippled from the waist down after falling from the roof of a house. On the first day of the meetings, he had hobbled toward the stage on his crutches to give his life to Jesus. On the second day of the meetings, he'd come forward to receive the baptism in the Holy Spirit. So we had noticed this man early on. Then on the fourth day, he showed up at the local swimming pool nearby where we were baptizing people, and he was water-baptized. If nothing else happened to this man, his life had already been completely transformed for all eternity by the power of God.

But for nineteen years, this man had used his crutches like legs. He would swing the dead weight of the lower part of his body on those crutches as he slowly moved forward one "crutch step" at a time. Once he finally reached his seat each evening, he would collapse into his chair, exhausted from his crutch walking. Because he had come in *after* the rest of the crowd was seated, many people had watched him come into the auditorium each evening and were aware of his extremely disabled condition.

That week, we had witnessed many instantaneous miracles. It was everything I had read about in the book of Acts, but it was happening *here and now* — in our meeting! Denise and I were speechless at the wonder-working power of God we saw in those services.

But now it was the last night. Oh, how I longed for that paralyzed man to receive a miraculous touch. As that last meeting concluded, I stood to dismiss the crowd and bid them farewell. Suddenly, I heard a great commotion to my left, and I turned to see what the disturbance was all about. I turned at the exact moment that man suddenly shot straight up from his chair and threw his crutches into the air!

Before I could even catch my breath, the man jumped and began walking — *free of the crutches*! The bottom half of his paralyzed body had suddenly come alive. This was the first time this man had walked in nineteen years without the assistance of his crutches. Like the lame man in Acts chapter 3, this man literally went "walking and leaping and praising God" all the way to the front of the auditorium, where he threw his crutches on the stage and then stood there *jumping* for joy!

This paralyzed man had released his faith and thrown his arms into the air — and as his crutches hit the ground, the lower part of his body was quickened. *Now he was standing before us all with his own legs to hold him up.*

### 'There Was Great Joy in That City'

Because of where the man had been seated, the entire crowd turned to watch as he grasped the truth of God's Word, seized it in his heart, and threw his hands upward in praise as a demonstration of faith. When his body became "quickened," or made alive by the power of God, he began to take his first steps in nineteen years. He took one step, then another, then another — and with each step, he moved faster and faster. Soon he was running back and forth in front of the vast crowd that was gasping with shock at the miracle they were witnessing.

*The entire crowd saw this miracle take place.* And, certainly, it was one of the greatest miracles we had ever witnessed in our ministry.

After that remarkable event, I gave an invitation for the lost to be saved, and more people gave their lives to Jesus Christ that night than in any of the other four days of services! Years later, people still recall that amazing miracle. As a result of that miracle and the other miracles that took place during those meetings, multitudes believed in Jesus. Many of those people hadn't previously believed in the existence of God at all — but because of these miraculous demonstrations, they gave their lives to Christ!

Our oldest son Paul said, "I remember arriving at those meetings and driving up to the back door of that huge venue. We sat on the bleacher chairs near the stage and I remember being there for all the events. When we left the building on the last evening, there were still people congregated outside. The meetings were over — everything was finished and done, yet there were still people outside looking for Dad and Mom so they could receive prayer."

That meeting was our first large public meeting ever conducted in the former USSR. Of the more than 40,000 people who sat in those seats over the course of that event, 7,000 people came forward to receive Christ, and 926 people received water baptism, which I will tell you about in a moment. But that week, we witnessed *scores* of healings, miracles, and deliverances.

That public meeting reminded me of Acts 8:5-8, which says, "Then Philip went down to the city of Samaria, and preached Christ unto them. And the people with one accord gave heed unto those things which Philip spake, hearing and seeing the miracles which he did. For unclean spirits, crying with loud voice, came out of many that were possessed with them: and many taken with palsies, and that were lame, were healed. And there was great joy in that city."

In those five days of meetings, the people literally "gave heed unto" the things that we preached, as we saw in Acts chapter 8. As a result, we saw *miracles* that week — including the expulsion of many unclean spirits that cried out as they were expelled from people by the delivering power of Christ. Many who had various types of sickness were healed, including the lame. And just as Acts 8:8 says, there was great joy as a result of all these happenings.

There was a crowd every night of approximately eight thousand people. But on that last night when they saw this miracle happen right before their eyes, hundreds *rushed* the stage for more prayer. Only God knows how many *more* people received miracles that night.

## 926 People Baptized in a Swimming Pool

As the meetings went on that week, those precious people didn't want to go away once they had been touched by God's power. And during those meetings, I was deeply disturbed by one very important fact — these new believers needed to be water-baptized!

In Matthew 28:19, Jesus proclaimed, "Go ye therefore, and teach all nations, *baptizing* them in the name of the Father, and of the Son, and of the Holy Spirit."

Jesus didn't tell us to just preach to them; He commanded that we baptize them and get them moving on the road to discipleship. Jesus treated baptism like it was important, so I knew I needed to find a way to get these new believers into baptismal waters.

Before I continue with my story, may I speak to you for a moment about the word "baptism" to see what it originally meant in the Greek? The word "baptize" is from the Greek word *baptidzo*, a very old word that originally meant *to dip and to dye*.

For instance, in very early cases, the word *baptidzo* described the process of dipping a cloth or garment into a vat of color to dye it, leaving it there long enough for the material to soak up the new color and then pulling that garment out of the dye with a permanently changed outward appearance.

In like manner, when a person comes to Jesus Christ, he can be likened to an old garment that needs to be dipped into a vat of dye so its color can be changed. The person isn't dipped into a vat of colored dye, but into the precious blood of the Lamb. This person is so totally transformed by Jesus' blood that he becomes a new creature. His countenance is so changed that he even looks different. You *could* say that this new believer has been "dipped and dyed." For me, this sheds such powerful light on the subject of baptism.

In Romans 6:4, Paul said, "Therefore, we are buried with him by baptism into death: that like as Christ was raised up from the dead by the glory of the Father, even so we also should walk in newness of life." Water baptism is a symbolic proclamation of the fact that believers have been buried with Christ and raised with Him. When a believer is placed in the baptismal waters, it symbolizes being immersed in one condition and coming out looking brand new. In other words, this pictures what happened to that person when he got saved. This outward symbol represents the fact that he has been dipped in the blood of Jesus and now his entire life has been newly colored and transformed to be like Jesus!

According to Paul's instructions in Romans 6, this is the act of officially burying the past and starting a new life in Christ. So at the time of those public meetings, I'd understood that Christ commanded us to lead people into the waters of baptism as a public declaration of what God had done in their lives — in addition to preaching and leading people in a prayer of repentance. But because so many people had been saved that week, we had to come up with a solution to baptize them.

To solve this problem, we rented a nearby public swimming pool for three afternoons, and I announced that we would make water baptism available to each new believer and that we would instruct them about water baptism around the sides of the swimming pool before they entered it to be baptized.

We thought it would be extraordinary if one hundred converts showed up to be baptized in a mid-afternoon service. Our team was ready to baptize ten people at a time to speed up the process. We thought that with all the getting in and out of the pool, we could handle a hundred people in one hour per afternoon if we really managed the process. We thought that if three hundred of the new converts showed up over the course of the three afternoons, it would be a fabulous turnout — so you can imagine how stunned we were when more than three-hundred people showed up *on the first afternoon.*

There were so many people that we could not fit them around the edge of the pool in one teaching session, so we decided to divide the afternoon into three different baptismal sessions that each accommodated about one-hundred people. And we successfully baptized a little more than three hundred people that afternoon!

Then on the *second* day, another 300-plus people came to the pool for water baptism — meaning the turnout had already exceeded 600 people! Then on the *third* day, we were stunned when an *additional* 300-plus people showed up to be baptized. By the end of those three afternoons, *we had water-baptized 926 people!* Our team was both *spiritually elated* and *physically exhausted* at the same time. And we still had one more evening service to preach, in which we knew more people would repent and give their lives to Christ. That meant even more people would need to be water-baptized!

When the auditorium authority said it was time to shut down the meetings on our last night of services, people didn't want to leave and had to be almost forcibly directed out of the arena and onto the street. People clung to us, asking for more prayer, but it was time to leave, so we quickly left the platform through a private back hallway and a door that opened right to our transportation. However, when we exited that exterior door, several hundred people had already surrounded our vehicle, wanting one more opportunity to receive a touch from God.

This series of events provided the answer to the question I was asked about why we saw so many supernatural signs and wonders in that big meeting. The crowd was *fixated* on every word we preached from that stage. And where the message of Christ is *really* heard, faith comes. That explains why miracles started occurring all over that vast auditorium. The people *heard, believed,* and *received.*

This shows how important it is that you *really listen* when the Word of God is being preached. If you're talking to your neighbor, writing notes, sending text messages, thinking of something else, or merely not listening, the Word can have *great* effect on the people all around you, yet have *no* effect on you.

If you want to experience the supernatural power of God working and manifesting, you *must* be totally focused on the message that's being preached, for faith comes by hearing — *really hearing* — the Word of God (*see* Romans 10:17). And when the message has been heard and embraced by a one-hundred percent hearing heart, the environment becomes right for the supernatural to take place.

On the last night of the meetings when so many people were getting saved and water-baptized, I felt the tug of the Holy Spirit on my heart and understood that He was asking me, *Now, what are you going to do with all these new believers? They need a church, and they need a pastor. What are you going to do about that?*

Indeed, it seemed our commitment to come to this land for one year was opening up into something much bigger and broader than we could have anticipated. The Bible-school director's suggestion to build a house if we suspected for a minute that our time here might surpass one year had been a good one, and it looked like we were going to be long-term residents in the former Soviet Union. As I shared in the last chapter, after Denise and I aligned our wills to make the commitment to move here for one year, God began to unveil His plan *rapid-fire*, but the fulfilling of that plan was going to be met with challenges.

### Deceived By 'Mine Own Countrymen' — The 'Christian' Mafia and the Bitter Lessons We Learned

In that last meeting in the hockey stadium, there was so much excitement in the air with the healing of the paralyzed man and the record number of people being born again as a result. But also during that last service, just about the time the service was finally being dismissed, a ministry team member walked up to me right on the stage and handed me a copy of the national newspaper's latest edition.

Turning my gaze from the crowd as the musicians played, I almost couldn't believe what my eyes were seeing in bold print on the front page of that newspaper. I turned aside for a few seconds to scan the article as the crowd continued to worship.

The feature story was about the unscrupulous Christian businessman and his mafia-looking son who was building our house in Jelgava! The son had strangely disappeared for the past couple of months, and construction on our house had been paused without explanation. But as I read that article, I began to understand what had happened — and why Denise and I had always felt there was something very dark about that family we'd become involved with and had trusted to help us.

The reason for the front-page article was that this man's son, our "house builder," had disappeared into Europe after having kidnapped a European businessman and demanded a ransom for his release! Interpol had captured and arrested him on charges of international kidnapping. The story in this paper was the unraveling of the full story of the family's criminal activities that they'd covered under the facade of doing "ministry."

If all of this wasn't strange enough, just steps away from me on the platform was this businessman! He was standing right on the stage with me! I looked at him and swallowed hard as my mind began to catch up with what my spirit had known all along — that there was something very dark and mysterious about this man who'd befriended me to "help" me.

Although he was a Christian, when the Soviet Union had just collapsed, he realized there was quick money to be made from Westerners who were new to the former USSR and didn't know the ropes. So he'd seized the opportunity to prey on their ignorance — including *my* ignorance. It was true that *many* people at that time were taking advantage of Westerners, and he likewise — though he was saved — had become seduced by the lure of money, and it had affected him.

What I was experiencing reminded me somewhat of the apostle Paul's plight in Second Corinthians 11:26, where he said he was "...in perils by mine own countrymen...."

I stared at this businessman from a short distance on the platform, still in the throes of shock and disbelief. *What a way to end a glorious week of meetings.*

## We Found Out Our New House Was Stolen Property!

When the meeting finally concluded and Denise and I made it home, I immediately called the American leader of the Bible school to ask him if he knew that his man and his family were involved in criminal activity.

What unfolded next was almost as strange as the revelation of this Christian businessman and his life of crime.

To my surprise, this American minister knew this man had been involved in criminal activity. I was devastated that I had trusted and followed this man's leadership when he had known of this businessman's criminal connections. Now Denise and I found ourselves in cahoots, as it were (*unwittingly*), with a criminal.

As I dug a little deeper, I soon discovered why the man's son first took us to see a foundation for a house that was already being built. The truth was, that house was being built by another family whom the man had threatened to *murder* unless they stopped building and surrendered the property to him!

While we thought we were building our own house, "our" house was actually being built on a foundation constructed by another family, who had been physically threatened and forced to walk away from what they had built.

Sharmon said, "They just kept taking money from Rick and Denise, saying, 'Here's your house. This will be a great house.' But it was never *really* their house. That man was taking Rick and Denise's money and completely scamming them while robbing the original property owner. It was a *disaster*!"

## The Enemy Was Trying To Undermine Our Fruitfulness and Abort Our Assignment

A glorious week of eternity-impacting Gospel meetings had seen thousands of people saved and hundreds water baptized. The people who attended those meetings knew us from the television programs we had produced and that had been broadcast right into their living rooms and homes. They *trusted* us. We'd said many times in those programs that we were here to stay. And in a world where their lives were anything *but* certain, those words meant something to them. And they meant something to us to say them.

Things were going so well, but I realized with this abrupt revelation that to guard my own integrity, I had to break off all relations with this businessman and his family. When I didn't know their activities were crime-infested,

God had blessed us. But now that I knew, I could not continue in a relationship with this businessman and expect God's blessing.

This decision would mean walking away from our house construction and losing everything we had invested in it — and also breaking the TV contracts we'd made to broadcast our programs for an hour every day. Walking away from the house and losing the money we'd invested in it was minor compared to the heart-breaking knowledge that our precious TV viewers would have no program to bring them the message of Christ and the teaching of the Bible. And it had been *in just the last week or so* that I'd told our viewers we were committed to staying on television and bringing them the Word of God.

Now it looked like I was a liar and my promise would not be kept. It broke my heart to think those untold numbers of viewers, who were tuning in to find spiritual answers that had been *taboo* for them for so long, would no longer have the program.

But in addition to the heartbreak of stopping the TV broadcast, when the man realized he was going to lose our TV-contract payments, he and his henchmen began to threaten me and trail me nearly everywhere I went in Jelgava and in Riga. If I took the trash out at night, I prayed first that no one would be hiding behind the corner of the house to attack or kill me. Also, we discovered that our phones had been tapped so this man could know all about everything we were doing.

It was such a traumatic moment filled with such intense danger that I decided to appeal to the U.S. Consul's office in Riga to ask for help. Latvia was so new as a country that it didn't even have an official embassy — just a Consular office that had been quickly set up to help a handful of Americans who were in Latvia. But when I met with the U.S. Consul to describe this onslaught of criminal activity against us, he told me, "Mr. Renner, there is absolutely nothing I can do to help you. You are living in a wild new country, and you are on your own to deal with this problem."

Although it was *years* before it happened, this man I'd done business with to get those TV contracts eventually "called off the dogs," as it were, and stopped harassing and threatening me. Perhaps it was our "serious 'mafia' covering" I spoke of in Chapter Nine that had also warded off those who tried to coerce us into hiring them for protection. Well, it *was* the Lord — the most serious Covering of all — who was supernaturally protecting and providing for us every step of the way.

### A Magic Marker and a Map of the Former Soviet Union — This Was Only The Beginning

I sunk into a horrible depression when I realized that I had been lied to by the Bible-school director, a fellow American whom I'd trusted, and now our family was in serious peril. The vulnerable position in which we found ourselves in a foreign country that barely had its footing was unsettling, to say the least. Even more, it seemed no one with legal authority could come to my aid to protect me and my family.

But what bothered me most deeply was the fact that thousands of people would soon turn on their televisions looking for my teaching of the Bible, but it would be gone. I also wondered, *How am I supposed to communicate to partners and supporters back in the States that we discontinued the television ministry because we were working with the mafia?* How could I possibly explain such a crazy situation?

The whole episode caused me to sink into a depression that engulfed my mind to a degree that I literally went to bed and stayed there for five days. I cried and cried as I thought about the insanity of this situation and the loss of ministry to people who needed the Word of God. Denise tried to reassure me that everything would somehow turn out all right, but I was deeply saddened and affected by the cruelty and injustice of it all.

But on the last afternoon that I lay in bed, God mercifully entered that room with me in a powerful, tangible way. In one miraculous moment, the dismal atmosphere evaporated, the spirit-realm opened in front of me, and I saw a map of the entire former USSR that filled the entire room before my eyes.

I'll summarize what I heard the Holy Spirit say when I saw that map open before me: *You thought you lost the TV ministry. But until now, you were only reaching a small, western part of the Soviet Union. Now I am going to give*

*ALL of this vast territory to you. I am giving you ALL of this massive region for the broadcasting of the Word of God.*

In a flash, an explosion of faith erupted in my heart, and I came out of the bed like Clark Kent emerging from his phone booth as Superman! I distinctly remember wondering if this is what Abraham felt in Genesis 15 when God called him out and showed him the stars of the sky, saying to him, "So shall your seed be." The divine mixture of seeing those stars and hearing God's words caused faith to come into Abraham's heart. And now the same thing was happening to me. By both *seeing* and *hearing*, faith came alive inside me, and I ran out of the bedroom exclaiming to Denise, "We have only *begun*. God is going to give the whole Soviet Union to us for the television ministry. This is not the end — *it is only the beginning!*"

Naturally speaking, this all seemed impossible, but God had quickened my heart to believe. Just as it seemed impossible that Abraham and Sarah would produce a child because they were too old, God made a promise to them, nevertheless — a promise and a vision that seemed too fantastical to believe — that they would give birth to a child in their old ages.

But Romans 4:20 tells us that in spite of the overwhelming odds stacked against them, Abraham believed what God had told him. It says, "He [Abraham] staggered not at the promise of God through unbelief: but was strong in faith, giving glory to God."

Abraham could have doubted the possibility of having a child — he could have easily convinced himself that this dream was impossible. But the Bible says that Abraham "...staggered *not* at the promise of God..." (Romans 4:20).

When I saw that vision and heard those words from the Spirit of God, I jumped into our little red Lada with Denise at my side, and we drove straight to our office to announce I had received a clear answer from Heaven that we were to launch out over all the lands of the former USSR. We didn't know how to do it, but *God* knew how, and He would direct us every step of the way.

Arriving at the office, I quickly pulled out a large folded map of the former USSR and unfolded it across the desk of my administrator. I pulled out a permanent marker and began to circle the regions where we were to start traveling to negotiate for our own TV contracts.

As if a divine hand was guiding me, I took that permanent marker and began to circle huge geographic areas where the Holy Spirit drew my attention. I knew the Spirit of God was instructing me to take the teaching of the Bible to these vast territories through our television ministry. There had never been a Christian TV network in the former Soviet Union, so we were breaking brand-new ground. Hence, I knew that *all* the areas where the Holy Spirit led me to circle were virgin territory for the broadcasting of the Word of God. It wasn't long before the entire divine strategy was laid out on the map before me.

The Holy Spirit guided my hand and the permanent marker as I circled one region, then another, and another — until a massive chain of connecting circles covered one side of the map all the way to the other far extreme. It reached all the way from Riga in the west, across the cities nestled in the Ural Mountains, all the way to Siberia, and over to Vladivostok in the Far East. Also circled were Estonia, Latvia, Lithuania, Belorussia (Belarus), Ukraine, Moldova, Georgia, Azerbaijan, Armenia, all the southern Muslim republics, and the vast territories in Russia's northwest lands.

When I finished, I looked at my team members, and they were astonished. They had just witnessed an entire vision supernaturally laid out before their eyes! That day, we all laid our hands on those circled areas and claimed them for the Kingdom of God. I even laid my whole body across that circled map and prayed for the anointing of God to open doors we didn't know how to open. There was no doubt that a major event — a television network that would span the breadth of the former Soviet Union — had been supernaturally birthed by the Spirit of God. It was conceived, put on paper, and already committed to the hands of God in prayer.

I took that large map, framed it, and hung it in the hallway of our offices. It became a reminder of the vision God had supernaturally given us — a reminder of where we were to go and what areas we were to tackle to get our programs on the air. I didn't realize it at the time, but to broadcast in all those areas would make our TV ministry the largest Christian broadcast in that part of the world — over a network of stations that would reach millions upon millions of TV viewers. And that is exactly what has come to pass in the decades ever since, and we broadcast teaching from the Bible across many of these lands today.

But that was just the beginning, because once the vision was conceived and put to pen and paper so others could see it, the work had to begin. That meant I would have to travel to all those regions. But first, God would have to make a way and open doors for me to meet with the top TV directors of the largest stations in those areas. Since most of them were atheistic communists who were opposed to the Gospel, this would take a miracle.

Step by step, God gave us appointments with powerful TV directors — and we watched as those huge, circled areas were seized by the Spirit of God for the broadcasting of our programs. In a relatively brief period of time, doors began to open, agreements were signed, and our TV programs were being broadcast all over the former USSR. It was a *first* for Christian broadcasting in the former Soviet Union!

In a few weeks, our son Paul, who had turned nine years old by that time, and Andrey Chebotarev, a man in his twenties and a Pentecostal team member who had grown up in a persecuted underground church in Ukraine, took off with me on our first big trip across the former USSR to negotiate for TV time on our own. God Himself was leading the charge, and we went by His might *full force* into those uncharted areas that had been long untouched by the Gospel message.

Although the fifteen republics of the former USSR were in the process of erecting borders, all the borders weren't up yet and people could still travel back and forth in many places relatively easily. I said to Denise, "I'm going to go on my first trip, and I'm going to come home with TV contracts in my hands."

I wondered, *What in the world am I doing? I don't know anything about buying TV time. I don't know of any Westerner or any major broadcaster who ever negotiated for TV time in the former USSR.*

Even Coca-Cola had never negotiated for TV time in the USSR — *no one* had done it. The whole idea that I was going to go negotiate for TV time was absurd, but this was clearly what God was instructing me to do.

That first trip took us to Saint Petersburg, Murmansk, Moscow, and Kuy-byshev (Samara) in Russia, Donetsk and Kiev in Ukraine, Minsk in Belarus, and back home again to Riga. When we went to purchase our plane tickets, selling commercial airline tickets in what was still a socialist-communist-run system was still so undeveloped that the ticket agent didn't know how to charge the three of us for flights. To negotiate the deal, we gifted her with a box of chocolates and she issued the three of us roundtrip tickets to all of these far-flung cities for a whopping $36!

Our first TV negotiations took place in Murmansk, which is the biggest city in the world above the Arctic Circle. We arrived at the building where the negotiations were to take place and walked up a dimly lit staircase to the office of the TV deputy. Of course, he was a communist, because everyone in top positions in those days were communist leaders.

Paul remembered, "Every TV deputy's office was set up almost exactly the same. Like all of them, he had a desk with a long conference table butted up against it. On the desk there were multiple telephones, because in those days it was a sign of power if you had many telephones on your desk. And there they were — a bunch of rotary phones with all kinds of buttons and gadgets. This was clearly a powerful man. And hanging on the wall directly behind the deputy's chair was, of course, a huge portrait of Lenin, the founder of the Communist Party."

The TV deputy in Murmansk said to us, "What can I do for you?" I remember thinking, *He's going to laugh his head off when I ask him to sell me TV time for a Bible-teaching program. FIRST, he's an atheist. SECOND, he's a communist. And THIRD, Lenin is hanging on the wall overseeing everything he says and does.* I finally worked up the gumption to say, "I'd like to buy airtime on your station."

This station had *never* sold airtime. They hadn't had a need to sell time. Like all stations at that time, it was a government station controlled by the state. He didn't even know how to determine a price for airtime. As I said, this was before Coca-Cola could buy airtime in this part of the world. Truly, no one had ever done such a thing before then.

### Our First TV Contract for the Gospel

I got a little bolder and looked across the table and said, "I want to teach the Bible on television, and this is the amount I can pay," at which time was $50 per program.

Fifty dollars didn't sound like a lot even then, but at that time when the financial system had totally collapsed in the former USSR, it sounded like a mountain of cash to his ears. When he heard my offer, he totally took me off guard when he said, "I think I can make this happen for you." To my total shock, we walked out of his office with a contract in our hands. It was our first TV negotiation and we walked out of that place victorious!

After that victory, I was ready to charge ahead, so we continued our herculean trip to all the cities on our itinerary. My interpreter, Andrey, who became one of the most faithful and long-term relationships in my life, had grown up in the Pentecostal underground church and was raised to believe watching television was a sin. Even with that victory in Murmansk, he was still skeptical that we would get those contracts. But then we went to the next city and *the next city* and *the next city*, and by the time we came home from that trip, I had five contracts in our hands to broadcast to a potential audience of thirty-six million TV viewers.

It was a massive victory for our television ministry — far greater than what we had previously lost. We even had a contract for Channel One in Belorussia (now Belarus). That was the "craziest" deal of all at the time because Channel One could be seen in every single home in the nation.

These were victories that were undeniably God-granted and Spirit-wrought, as no religious organization had ever broadcast regularly over the airwaves in the former USSR. Networks had been off-limits to foreigners and were under the ultimate control of the KGB. It reminded me of the prophetic word the Holy Spirit gave me as a teenager when He told me He would use my voice to affect principalities and powers in the air. We were pioneering territory over the airwaves that no one else had ever pioneered.

For all the decades that have passed since those days, we have worked with great effort to strategically maintain our relationships with those powerful

TV directors and stations. For that reason, it's possible no one else has the history in television in the former USSR that our ministry has had.

By the time we were finished with our TV negotiations, I had negotiated for television time in almost every region of the far-flung former Soviet Union. Because we went where no one had ever been, knocked on doors, asked questions, and negotiated for TV time before anyone else had done it, we learned the ins and outs of the industry — what you can do, what you can't do. As a result, I am confident when I say that there is probably no media company or ministry today that knows more about television in this part of the world than we do.

In the very beginning, all the traveling and negotiations were done by Andrey and me as we ventured across the former USSR. It was really hard to do business by phone in those days, so we went to every single station. Sometimes we sent telegrams to make initial contact because phone calls would not go through. But we did what was necessary to build relationships with those TV deputies and to get those contracts.

Throughout all these years — from those early beginnings of negotiating TV time — we have been faithful to keep our word to never get involved in anything political and to pay our bills on time. God called our ministry to bring teaching of the Bible to the nations, not to make political statements. And in the spiritual and political climate we were in halfway around the world from Tulsa, Oklahoma, it was especially important to maintain that focus and keep a steady gaze on our ministry calling. We took our relationships with those powerful TV directors seriously, and God has given us a good reputation with them as a result. People in high places know our ministry and the Renner name, and they believe from experience that we are "the real deal."

Paul commented, "Right from the beginning, God helped my dad make a wise decision to stay away from anything political in our part of the world. Because of his very neutral position about government issues, he has a great reputation with people in power. In fact, I was recently speaking to a government employee, and he told me he recommends that other churches study how our ministry has stayed neutral and respectful of 'the powers that be' to retain the favor of governmental authorities."

The reason I'm telling you this is, it is very important to stick with your ministry calling. We have been very focused on staying with exactly what God has called us to do and not to transcend the boundaries of our assignment by meddling in political affairs. Other people are mightily anointed to be politically involved, but God made it clear to me from the very start that I was to steer clear of it entirely, and I have been faithful to obey that.

Because of that, people in powerful positions never need to worry that our ministry will step across a boundary that should not be violated. They have their own reputations to protect, and we don't want to violate their trust in us in any way as they show us favor in their dealings with our TV ministry.

One of Russia's most revered spiritual leaders, Bishop Sergei Ryakhovsky, commented on those early days of our pioneering TV ministry in the former Soviet Union. He said, "Rick was one of those very unique people that God used mightily from the beginning. In the early 1990s, God even made a way for him to go on television stations of all kinds all over the former USSR. It was a rare open door that eventually became harder to find — but because Rick had seized the moment *at the right time,* the door was opened for him. It is still open to him today, and the rest is history."

Precise obedience to the will and plan of God — including His divine timing — is a huge key to successfully walking out His plans and bearing the fruit that He intends. Denise and I have purposed in our hearts — and we have postured our lives accordingly — to do God's bidding *exactly* for the rest of our lives on earth. Therefore, we have more history to make and adventures in God to seize and fulfill. God wants to "make history" with *your* life, too, and He can do it if you'll yield yourself to Him completely, and if you'll willingly give Him your *yes* concerning what He has created and called you to do.

I've given you an overview of how we started our TV ministry in the former Soviet Union. But getting those contracts was not always as easy as waltzing into a director's office and dancing right back out with an agreement. In fact, there were often many perils associated with getting our teaching programs on the air in nations that had once been hostile to the Gospel of Christ. I'll share some of those stories in the next chapter, as well as about our next big history-making assignment from God to pastor those souls who'd become born again under our ministry.

God had a plan for Rick and Denise Renner and our sons in this place He had called *our new home* — and He was wasting no time accelerating us on a path to fulfilling that plan very rapidly.

# 11

# PLANES, TRAINS, AND AUTOMOBILES — MORE OPEN DOORS AND ADVERSARIES

The apostle Paul wrote in First Corinthians 16:9 that a great door for the Gospel had been opened to him in Ephesus, where he needed to tarry in order to carry on the work. Then he said something very interesting: *"…And there are many adversaries."*

It's true that the enemy uses people to oppose every breakthrough in which he loses territory as the Kingdom of God *gains* new ground. And that was certainly true of what God had commissioned us to do — to go on TV to potentially *millions* of households in a land almost destitute of the Gospel. As I said in the last chapter, we had divine appointments, supernatural favor, grace, and many victories as we stepped out to negotiate our own contracts to purchase TV time. *But there were many adversaries.*

---

**Left:** *Trains at train depot in the USSR, 1991.*

God has granted our TV ministry astonishing success over the years as it has developed. But forging into the brand-new territory of Christian TV, where there had been no Christian TV, wasn't a walk in the park! In fact, at times, it was very dangerous. The former Soviet Union was just getting its footing as it was leaving a socialist-communist system of government and entering a whole new era in history. And as you know by now, for a long season, that disheveled transition negatively affected millions of people. Those millions of precious people needed the Gospel and a special touch from God so they could understand Him and the great compassion He had for them.

But in this new, un-pioneered system of emerging capitalism, those who were unsavory and uncouth also saw the transition as a money-making prospect — and their unwelcome presence quickly caused these lands to resemble what I've described as the *wild, wild west.*

After the mono-banking system of the Soviet empire had disintegrated, the new banking system was still developing in this part of the world, and without the availability of checks or credit cards, people everywhere carried their cash with them to do any kind of business — even *big* business. I shared with you in Chapter Nine about people inside the bank — one of the first-ever commercial banks in Latvia — tipping off the mob whenever large withdrawals were made. Oftentimes, those people who'd just done business with the bank were robbed of their cash before they ever reached home.

This presented an interesting predicament in our situation of needing to buy TV time, which gradually began to rise higher and higher in price. To negotiate those deals quickly and get the contracts we needed to move forward, we had to pay up front in cash. We carried large amounts of cash with us in areas that were not safe, and we regularly risked being robbed, *or worse,* as we couriered cash and tapes of TV programs from place to place to fulfill our new assignment.

The apostle Paul wrote in Second Corinthians 11:26 that he and his team had similar experiences of being in peril of robbers as they carried out their own divine assignment. Those risks were our daily concern as well.

Besides the opposition of brazen thieves that we resisted in prayer, there were also the former "hardliner communists" who were still vehemently opposed to Christianity and the Gospel. When the Lord instructed us to build a permanent church home for our Riga congregation of believers, besides its being a massive financial undertaking, we were opposed on every side by those hardliners — to the point of the government's once forbidding us to collect our containers as the ships were about to dock to unload tons of steel necessary for our next phase of construction. We were delivered by God, and I talk about that adventure later in the book.

To walk through those open doors in the early days, I started to travel by plane almost continuously across the eleven time zones of the former USSR to obtain contracts for the programs we would broadcast on television. Because of the continuing shortfalls and deficits, there were times when the pilot of the airplane would announce that our plane was landing at an alternate location because there simply wasn't enough fuel to reach our intended destination. In those situations, after we de-boarded, we then had to get very creative to figure out how we were going to get from where we were to the place we needed to be. It usually meant we had to travel by train or by car from that airport or landing space — and we often had very long distances still to go to reach our destination.

And then there was the issue with trains. Russian trains today are beautiful, and traveling by train is a delightful experience. But back in those early days after the fall of the Soviet Union, passenger trains were *filthy*. A person nearly needed waders to go into the restrooms because the urine was so deep on the floors of the toilet stalls. Drunks drank vodka like water on the trains; drunken people physically fought each other on the trains; gypsies roamed the cars and robbed travelers on the trains; and cockroaches scrambled across the floors *on the trains*! People even put their shoes under their pillows at night to keep the gypsies from stealing them while they were sleeping.

Also, the trains often did not run on schedule, which meant there was a strong chance you would show up late for whatever kind of meeting you were trying to get to. It only cost about 25 cents to take a train from Riga to Moscow back in those early days, but you more than paid for the inexpensive ride by having to put up with the inconveniences — the filth, the thieves, and the drunken fights. Add to that the delays, and it took hours upon hours in the most unpleasant conditions to reach your destination by this mode of travel. There were more decent trains on the central routes, like those between Moscow and St. Petersburg, for example, but the collapse of a centralized system of transportation was accompanied by a weakening of quality control, and the greater the collapse, the greater the mess — and the greater the corruption and violation of rules.

The difficulties of travel when we first moved to the former Soviet Union simply can't be exaggerated. For example, because the whole USSR was gripped with deficits in those days, people never knew if they'd be able to find gasoline for their car. In Jelgava, the town where Denise and I and our family lived, there was rarely gasoline at the gas station. Even if you found fuel, there was no guarantee you'd make it to your destination. You could be en route to some location with a full tank of gas at the outset — but along the way when you needed to refill, you could drive past gas station after gas station and see big signs at the pumps that read, "CLOSED: NO FUEL!" It was a definite challenge to travel by car!

Traveling by plane across such vast regions of the former USSR really was the best and most expedient mode of travel for what we needed to accomplish. Today Russia has world-class airlines that are a pleasure to fly on, but in the early 1990s, getting on a Russian airplane was *an adventure*! I actually experienced times when I would be seated next to someone who had a dog or goat on the plane with him!

Furthermore, airline ticket agents with few customer-service skills often oversold seats on planes. One time I was on a plane that was so overloaded, a nursing mother was seated in the cockpit, and the kitchen had people seated on the cabinet countertops and on the kitchen floor. My seat — which had been reserved and purchased in advance — was occupied by someone else when I arrived on board.

On that particular flight, the attendant said to us, "Just quickly find a place to sit." There were no seats anywhere. But she said to "just find a place," so I opened the door to the cockpit to see if there was an empty seat there, but it was already taken by that breastfeeding mother and her baby. So I went to the bathroom to see if I could sit on the toilet, but some-body was seated there too! The kitchen had a little cabinet that I thought I could sit on, but when I looked, people were already sitting on top of the cabinet. Andrey Chebotarev, who was traveling with me, sat on the floor in the kitchen, leaving me still wandering about trying to seat myself before takeoff.

The only place I could find to sit was inside the garment closet. It was full of coats, and on the floor were multiple pop bottles in a crate *and a rose bush full of thorns*! The flight attendant saw me open the closet and quickly directed me to sit down on the case of Pepsi bottles.

I sat on top of all those pop bottles for the entire flight. The rose bush kept scratching my face if I made even the slightest move. And I don't know if you've ever sat on top of glass pop bottles for hours on end, but let me tell you that it isn't very comfortable when those bottle tops feel like they're nearly piercing your bottom. That was the case with me, even with my jacket placed underneath me as a "seat cushion." Oh, how tempted I was to make better use of the other passengers' coats than to just leave them there hanging in the closet!

Plus, that garment closet had a fire extinguisher on the wall above my head that was barely hanging on the wall by a loose screw. When the plane hit turbulence, it rattled and shook like it was going to fall on me. With one hand, I was trying to keep the rose bushes from scratching my face, and with the other hand, I was trying to hold the fire extinguisher securely on the wall. All the while, those pop bottles were *ungiving* beneath me.

Then the attendant walked by and pulled the curtain closed, so I sat there in the dark juggling the rose bush and the fire extinguisher while trying hard not to be intruded upon by a pop bottle! By the end of that flight, my bottom felt sore from being poked by bottles, and my face and arms were scratched all over by the thorns on that rose bush. Both during and after that flight, I was a sight to behold!

Especially in those earlier years as I confronted horrible travel experiences in order to start our television ministry, I meditated often on the apostle Paul's words about his own travels in Second Corinthians 11:26, where he stated that he had been "...in *perils* of waters, in *perils* of robbers, in *perils* by mine own countrymen, in *perils* by the heathen, in *perils* in the city, in *perils* in the wilderness, in *perils* in the sea, in *perils* among false brethren." From this passage, we know that traveling as a Gospel preacher in Paul's time was not always a grand and glorious venture either. There were constant threats, which had to be staved off with faith and a determination to proceed regardless of the risks involved.

Back in those early days, the commercial banking system hadn't really gotten started, and the postage system was completely undependable. So after we obtained our contracts, in order to deliver tapes and pay for the programs, we developed a whole team of couriers who delivered the TV programs to the stations along with *cash* to pay for the broadcasts. This was at a time when criminal activity abounded and a person could be killed for less than a hundred dollars. Our couriers were literally putting their lives on the line to get the teaching of God's Word and those payments to all the various stations each month.

Yuri Ruls, one of our couriers in those days, said, "At that time, it was like we were all supernaturally energized by the Holy Spirit to do what we were doing. We were alive with the call of God to get the Gospel to those stations so people could hear the Word of God. The need was so urgent that we never stopped to ask, 'Is this wise? Is this common sense?' We were doused with God's grace to do what needed to be done at that time. We had a job to do and a vision from God, and we were giving our lives to step out to do it."

Marina Busheva, who co-directed the office at that time, said, "The couriers used to come to our Moscow office to get huge suitcases filled with cassettes, which they took to different cities everywhere. That's the way we got the program across the Soviet Union. And they carried all that cash.

"What they were doing was not simple, and it was very dangerous. It was not small money they were carrying — it was huge money. And their monthly travels took them into some very complex situations. But they did it month after month for years. We would duplicate the TV programs on tape — then we'd prepare the suitcases for the couriers. And every month, they would, essentially, jeopardize their lives to get that Bible teaching to those stations. That's just the way things worked at that time. And the TV ministry kept growing and growing and growing. We grew so much that we had to move from one office to another, and we kept adding more employees."

Marina added, "We received mountains of mail from so many whose lives were being changed. Because of the TV programs, the Word of God was going across this whole part of the world — and it was clear, understandable teaching that gave answers to people's questions. People came to Christ, and those programs helped to deepen their faith. The letters were coming so fast that they were almost uncountable. From the west all the way to the east, the effect was so huge, it simply wasn't measurable. Thousands upon thousands of people were being touched, and we were receiving mountains of mail."

In the early years of traveling in the former USSR, we faced our share of struggles to obtain those contracts and get the television ministry off the ground. I took courage from Paul's testimony in Second Corinthians 11:26. I am certain that many ministers of the Gospel over the past two thousand years have read these words and have similarly taken heart that their own particular struggles were not unique — and that if Paul could face such threats and go on to minister in God's power and anointing, they could do it too.

And today I want to assure you — you can do whatever God has told *you* to do. The devil may try to thwart God's plan for your life or hinder you along the way, but if you'll stay in faith and keep pressing forward, obstacles will move aside, and you will do exactly what God has asked you to do.

### 'A Bomb on the Plane!'

Over the years of traveling by means of dangerous kinds of transportation, I've learned a lot about the ministry of angels and how angels work to protect and deliver us in times of trouble. I learned that if we go in Jesus' name to carry the Gospel to parts of the world that are considered unsafe, God's power will protect us! We may not deal with the same problems early believers faced, but there may be times when we are required to fly on rickety airplanes, ride in trains that are unsanitary and unsafe, drive on dangerous or desolate roads, and pass through highly volatile areas when the only weapon to protect us is the Word of God.

But divine protection is activated in those of us who *believe* that God's promise of protection will work for us. When we enter dangerous territory in fear, doubt, and unbelief, we are likely to get in trouble. But if we will go believing and claiming that God's protection is ours and that the enemy can't do anything to hurt us, our faith in this promise will activate it and cause it to be manifested in our lives — it will even activate the ministry of angels to keep us safe!

Years ago, I'd long wanted to visit the city of Vorkuta, which is located above the Arctic Circle in Russia. It was one of the major cities where Joseph Stalin deported believers during a period of raging persecution. There, Christians were incarcerated in huge prison camps and forced to work deep under the earth in dangerous coal mines, where they dug the coal that fired the massive coal-burning factories and trains of the Soviet Union.

I sensed it was a divine assignment to visit Vorkuta at that time because I wanted to broadcast our programs into this region where believers had once suffered horribly for their faith. Because of its notorious place in history for Christian believers, I wanted to negotiate with the TV director of the station covering that large area in order to obtain a contract for broadcasting our program. I also intended to find out how many believers still lived there and what we could do to be of assistance to them.

I boarded my airplane to start my flight to Vorkuta and sat in my seat at the front of the plane near the flight attendant. From where I was seated next to a window, it was possible for me to see everything happening outside of the airplane. Also, my seat in that particular Soviet-made plane was located around a table in the aircraft. From the side of the table I was seated on, I could see the entire back of the plane, so I could also see everything that was happening inside the aircraft as well.

I watched as all the passengers boarded the plane, and then I watched outside my window as cargo handlers began to load cargo into the underside of the plane. I was shocked at the number of boxes, suitcases, and cargo they were putting into the cargo hold. In fact, it was so overfilled that when it came time to shut the doors of the cargo hold, it took several men to shut them, because the overflowing cargo was pressing so hard against them.

Meanwhile, from my seat, I watched as airport workers entered the plane and piled boxes, boxes, and *more* boxes into the tail of the plane, until the rear end of the plane — that is, the kitchen and the toilets — were no longer visible or accessible. After that, they began piling luggage and boxes into empty seats, and then they started stacking them from the back to the front of the center aisle of the plane. The extra cargo filled the cabin all the way from the very back to where I sat in the front of the plane!

Because I was seated close to the flight attendants, I could hear their conversation, and I overheard one attendant say to another, "I'm getting off this plane, because it's so severely overloaded that I'm afraid this plane is not going to make it."

But I *knew* I was supposed to go to Vorkuta, so *what should I do?* I bowed my head with those who were traveling with me, and we prayed, "Lord, if this plane is going to crash, please do anything needed to save us or to get us off this plane."

Not long after we finished praying, a flight attendant frantically yelled over the speaker system, "Everyone — as quickly as possible — get off this plane! *We just received a call that there's a bomb on the plane!*" People started fighting with each other and shoving their way to the airplane door, climbing over boxes in the overstuffed aisles. It was not a pretty sight!

At last when everyone was off the plane, and we were inside the terminal, a public announcement was made, which declared that the entire plane was being unloaded so the authorities could search for a bomb.

After hours of waiting and wondering what to do next, we heard another public announcement over the intercom, saying, "After searching the aircraft, we found no bomb on the plane. It was a false threat. However, we have decided that when we all re-board the aircraft, *no extra luggage or boxes* will be permitted. Only the suitcases of the passengers will be permitted on this airplane."

My companions and I stepped back into the plane and reseated ourselves in the same seats that had been assigned to us. People looked relieved, peaceful, and thankful that the plane was no longer overloaded. I heard the same flight attendant who had earlier threatened to get off the plane tell his colleague, "Now I feel good about this flight."

This leads me to share with you about the ministry of angels to protect us when we are on a God-given assignment. *Who do you think was that mysterious phone-caller who said there was a bomb on the airplane?* Who caused the airplane to be so quickly emptied, leading to the fortuitous decision to remove all that dangerous extra cargo? To this day, I am convinced *an angel* was the unidentified mystery caller.

Hebrews 1:14 declares, "Are they [angels] not all ministering spirits, sent forth to minister for them who shall be heirs of salvation?" According to this verse, angels are "sent forth to minister" on behalf of those who belong to the family of God. The word "minister" is the Greek word *diakonia*, a word that depicts high-level service. It is important to note that rabbis in early New Testament times used a very similar phrase to describe what they called "angels of service or ministry" — angels whom they believed were assigned to protect individuals and deliver them from harm.

We can be confident that part of the angelic ministry is to ensure our safety from dangerous and harmful things. Certainly, that day at the airport, something inexplicable happened that saved the lives of my team and everyone else who was on that airplane. I fully believe that event was some type of angelic intervention to spare our lives from tragedy.

## Machine Guns and a Cup of Tea

Beginning our Russian-speaking television ministry and traveling nearly nonstop to obtain contracts was a time when supernatural doors were *flying* open for TV ministry in nearly every corner of the former Soviet Union. But one particular area remained closed. Since it was a Muslim region, I had been strongly advised not to go there to negotiate for television time. Plus, that country was in a military conflict at the time. But despite what people were advising me to do, I sensed a strong leading of the Holy Spirit to go there. I simply *knew* that if I would put my feet on that land, God would open doors for us to broadcast the teaching of the Bible there.

We watched the news day by day to monitor what was happening with the military developments that were largely based around the capital city, where the largest TV tower in that part of the world was located. This tower was so huge, its signal covered not only that nation, but it also reached into a neighboring Muslim country. For a door of this size to open would definitely require the supernatural grace of God — and it would also require divine courage to go there in the middle of an escalating military conflict.

A single day came when a temporary cease-fire had been declared, so we quickly purchased plane tickets for two team members and me so we could leave that day. We called to set up a last-minute appointment with the director of the national TV station, and we raced to the airport so we could board our plane to fly to that country. Hours later, we landed — and after being vigorously searched at the airport, a private car picked us up and drove us directly to the broadcasting company of that nation.

When we entered the broadcasting building, we were escorted to a sitting area to wait for our meeting with the TV director. We were told that we would need to be patient because the cease-fire had been broken at almost that exact moment, and there was heavy machine-gun fighting all around the TV facility. At one point, a group of soldiers carrying machine guns ran hurriedly through the building, right past us, before disappearing through the door to an area outside where all the action was taking place. If you can imagine it, as all this action was taking place, a secretary offered us a cup of tea, and we sat drinking our tea listening to the skirmish outside, adjacent to the area where we sat.

Soon the door opened to the national TV director's office, and we were invited in for our scheduled appointment. To my surprise, the director was a woman. She held an unusual, very powerful position in a Muslim society. When I made my presentation about our TV programs, she responded, "Maybe you don't understand. This is a Muslim republic. Your Bible-teaching programs can't be broadcast here. Also, our signal reaches into another Muslim republic, and if we run your Bible programs, it would be considered offensive to our partners there."

But this broadcasting endeavor had been on my heart a long time. So rather than take no for an answer, I insisted, "We've come a long way today. Will you please just look at one of our programs?"

The director kindly consented. It just so happened that the random program she chose to watch was *part one* of a series I had done on what the Bible teaches about how husbands should treat their wives. As we watched, I could see the Holy Spirit was touching her heart with answers she had been seeking for her own marriage.

When that program ended, she asked if we had the second part of that series with us so she could watch that program as well. I could sense the programs about how a wife should be treated were deeply touching her, and by the end of the second program, the Holy Spirit had totally melted her heart.

She said, "How often would you like to broadcast these programs and what price would you like to pay?" Right before our eyes — *with machine guns firing in the background* — God opened a door that would not have opened if we had not had the courage to go to that place at that critical moment in history — during *a single-day* cease-fire agreement between warring factions.

That day I learned once again that it takes courage and confidence if you want to walk through a door that has never opened for anyone else. *It also takes the leading of the Holy Spirit.* It was the Holy Spirit who led us there *on that very day* — the day a great door flew open for the proclamation of the Gospel of Jesus Christ in a Muslim nation!

In Romans 8:14, we are promised, "But as many as are led by the Spirit of God, they are the sons of God." As we've already seen, the Greek word for "led" is the word *ago*, which simply means *to lead*. But it must also be pointed out that this word forms the root for the Greek word *agon*, which describes *an intense conflict, such as a struggle in a wrestling match* or *a struggle of the human will.*

This illustrates the fact that although the Holy Spirit wants to lead us, our human will doesn't like the idea of being led. It's the nature of the flesh to want to go its own way. Thus, when we choose to walk in the Spirit and let Him dictate our lives, His leadership over us can create a struggle of our will against our flesh. An example of this kind of intense struggle was that dangerous trip to that Muslim republic. The Spirit of God inside me was telling me, "Go *NOW* — there is an open door for you *TODAY*." But the flesh ranted and raved, "You're putting your life in danger! Don't do what the Holy Spirit is telling you to do."

Maybe that's how you've been feeling about your own life. You want to obey God and be led by His Spirit, but your flesh is interested only in self-preservation and going its own way. However, as a child of God, you must learn to walk with Him and stay in your place — *behind* the Holy Spirit and following His lead. If you really want to live a supernatural, Spirit-led life, you'll have to learn how to mortify and defeat the flesh, and allow the Holy Spirit to have His way.

I'm so thankful that on that day many years ago, God empowered me by His Spirit and gave me the courage to get on a plane to fly to that Muslim country. God knew what I didn't know — that a great open door was waiting for me. When we arrived and found that the cease-fire had been broken and the fighting had resumed and escalated, we could have turned around, gotten back on the plane, and headed home immediately. But we were *certain* the Holy Spirit was leading us. By God's grace, the fight with the flesh was won, and a great event occurred before our very eyes.

As we each do the will of God in our lives, we must listen to natural advice, but we must also never forget that the leading of the Spirit is the prime factor in bearing supernatural fruit and obtaining a heavenly outcome.

Over the years, I've seen many ministers and businessmen *pray and pray* for divine opportunities to come to them. They fasted, prayed, and waited for that golden moment to come — and at last, it came! A great door of opportunity stood directly in front of them, and it was time to act. But rather than seize the moment and walk through that door, they paused to pray just a little bit longer. God brought them *exactly* what they had been praying for, but they hesitated. When they finally got around to saying yes, it was too late and they missed their God-given opportunity.

The example of flying to that Muslim nation illustrates the point I'm making. When the TV officials in that nation invited me to fly to their city to meet with the director and talk about broadcasting our television program every week on national television, I knew the door was opened and that it was time for us to jump on the next available plane and to meet this powerful person who was willing to talk to us about TV time. I had already done my homework. I had studied the statistics of the station we were about to be offered time on. Then the moment came for me to step into that meeting with that television director. I was equipped for this long-awaited conversation, armed with information, supported by the prayers of our partners, and led by the Spirit of God.

The female Muslim director asked me, in effect, "How often would you like to broadcast your television program on our national channel and penetrate every single home in this nation?" I gasped as I realized the opportunity of a lifetime was presenting itself in the form of a television contract. I held my composure, not wanting her to know how excited I was at this chance to reach every home in that nation. But, of course, we responded, and we walked away with a successful contract and yet another open door through which we would step with the Good News of Jesus Christ.

I thank God that I had the spiritual guts and gumption to act at the right moment. I had already prayed and prayed. And as I sat with that director that day, I sensed that it was time to strike. Many people are afraid to obey what the Spirit puts in their hearts to do. Fearful that they will be led astray or that they will make a mistake, they sit on the sidelines and watch other people achieve success while they remain right where they've always been.

But let me tell you, you *can* trust the leading of the Holy Spirit. If you will let Him become your eyes and ears, you will never fail to recognize key moments and divine opportunities for your life, family, business, or ministry.

You and I are not brilliant enough to figure out the right timing for everything by our own logic. The timing of our actions must be directed by the Holy Spirit, not by us. If we learn to depend on the Spirit's leading, we will walk through many strategic doors at key moments. But it is imperative that we understand this: When He says *NOW*, He really means *NOW*!

### Traveling With a Large Squadron of 'Trained Forces'

As I ponder the risky, but faith-filled steps we took to establish our Russian television network, it is still totally amazing to me. *I could tell enough stories about it to fill a whole book by itself.*

One such amazing story occurred on October 3, 1993. That was our twelfth wedding anniversary. Denise and I had flown to Murmansk, Russia, which is located just north of the Arctic Circle, and it is also the place where Russian submarines are built. We had been ministering there in one of the largest churches in Russia at the time, and we were also negotiating for TV time on a station there. After several days of wonderful meetings and getting new TV contracts, we concluded our time there.

On the last evening — on October 3 — we returned to our hotel to begin preparing for our trip home the next morning. As we packed, we decided to turn on the television to see the late-night Moscow news. We sat nearly frozen in disbelief as we learned that there had been a major coup in the city of Moscow. The image of the Russian Vice President appeared on the screen before us. Looking disheveled, this man morbidly glared into the TV camera and stated that a coup had begun in Moscow and that Russia's newly gained democracy was about to be lost. We were stunned when we heard him "beckon" people to go into the streets to fight using whatever they could find from their homes as weapons to oppose the pro-communist faction — especially in the area near Red Square — that was trying to gain control.

While we were busy in Murmansk, a major conflict had broken out in Moscow. To consolidate his power, President Boris Yeltsin had dissolved Parliament in violation of the existing constitution. It was an enormous power struggle during which rebels forcibly seized control of the Russian White House, which was the official headquarters of the Russian Federation. They had barricaded themselves inside it, refusing to leave.

The Russian White House is located opposite the massive Novoarbatsky Bridge on the bank of the Moscow River. All that day while we were working in Murmansk, Boris Yeltsin was fiercely occupied with suppressing an uprising as army tanks lined up on top of the bridge to fire cannons at the Russian White House! By the end of the day, the tanks caused damage to the building, and some floors were burned out from the resulting fires. Despite the shelling, the rebels refused to give up their positions.

It was late at night, and Denise and I sat in front of the TV dumbfounded and perplexed about what we should do. There were rumors that the mayhem in Moscow might spread to other locations, and we didn't know what Moscow airports would be like the following morning while making our connection from Moscow to Riga. We didn't know if flights would be canceled — or even if there would be potential attacks at the airport. And God only knew what might develop in the nighttime as we slept!

So we arose early the following morning, took a car to the airport, and went inside to see if we could make our flight to Moscow en route to our home in Riga. When the time came for passengers to board the plane, Denise and I were strangely the *only two* passengers to embark the plane.

The airline attendants seated us in the very front row. Denise and I were somewhat amused and discussed quietly that it looked like we had the whole plane to ourselves as that large Russian aircraft took off from the runway and began to ascend.

To this day, we still don't know why we were the only two passengers to board that flight. We speculated that perhaps the person in charge knew us from our television program — or that we had received special treatment because of our American passports. All we could do was guess. But for the duration of that flight from Murmansk to Moscow, Denise and I sat alone on what looked to be an empty aircraft, musing over our strange situation.

That very large commercial airliner was completely empty — except for us and the flight crew. At least that's what we thought *until* it was time to disembark in Moscow. When we arose from our seats to disembark the plane, the flight attendant abruptly pulled back the curtain that concealed the whole back half of the airplane. To our complete amazement and shock, there stood in front of us a brigade of Spetsnaz — *Russia's highest-trained land-combat soldiers*!

What a scene that was! It looked like a battalion of "Rambos" standing there with machine guns hanging off their shoulders, handguns strapped to their waists, bandoleers containing hundreds of rounds of ammo draped around their necks, giant knives fastened to their boots — and their faces completely smeared with greasy black "war paint."

Denise and I stood there nearly paralyzed for what seemed like minutes. As much speculating as we had entertained about why we were alone on that flight, the thought never crossed our minds that we were *not* alone — and that we had flown all that distance to Moscow with the most dangerous Spetsnaz (highly trained special forces of the Russian Armed Forces).

We soon were seated on an airport bus to transport us from the plane to the terminal, and we watched *spellbound* as the soldiers who had flown with us quickly disembarked the plane and re-boarded jumbo helicopters.

By the time we entered the terminal, we saw on TV monitors a squadron of soldiers being lowered by ropes onto what was left of the roof of the now *bombed* Russian Federation Building! By the end of that standoff, more than one hundred rebel soldiers had reportedly been killed and hundreds more had been wounded.

At times in life, it is likely that we've all been oblivious to something profound that was happening around us. Had Denise and I known we were flying with trained Spetsnaz soldiers that day, we may have experienced some apprehension about getting on that flight. But we *thought* we were the only two people on board. We actually enjoyed the experience, laughing and talking during the entire flight to Moscow. We only realized a whole brigade of "Rambos" were riding with us when it was time to disembark. By that time, it was too late to worry because we had already arrived safely at the airport in Moscow.

As Denise and I watched the monitors from the airport terminal and saw soldiers being lowered onto the roof of the Russian Federation Building, we hardly spoke a word. Even as we awaited our next flight, we sat quietly, pondering the events that had just taken place. It wasn't until we were securely on board our next flight that we finally began to talk again. Excitedly we began talking about the situations we all find ourselves in at times that we don't fully comprehend until later. And we particularly talked about the ministry of *angels* — that just as those soldiers had been dispatched to restore order and peace, God sends His angels on "covert missions" to oversee and protect us in times of danger and uncertainty.

### I Signed a Contract and a Major Door Opened

As I said previously, I could write an entire book on our Spirit-filled adventures as we forged into new territory to blast Christian TV and the message of Christ over the airwaves in that spiritually desolate land. Some doors opened easily; others did not.

For example, in the early 1990s, I worked very hard for an "open door" to Channel One in the nation of Ukraine — which was the premier TV channel that broadcast into every home in that country. Regardless of how hard I tried, it seemed access to this massive station eluded me. But one day, I received a phone call from a journalist in Ukraine who said he had an "inside" contact at Channel One and that if I would meet him at a certain location in Kiev, he would accompany me to the station and introduce me to the top leadership of that channel.

So at the appointed time, I met him — it was almost like a clandestine operation — and he did exactly as he promised. He walked me through the open door that I had been seeking for years. I soon found myself standing in an executive TV office with the two men who had the final say-so about which programs would or would not be broadcast on Channel One. After a few minutes of talking, they said, "We've reviewed your programs, and we're ready to accept them as part of our daily broadcast schedule."

*I almost lost my breath.* Did they *really* say what I just heard? Were these men actually offering me the possibility of broadcasting our TV programs to the *entire* nation *every* day of the week? As far as I knew, this opportunity had never been given to anyone else. But now the door had flung wide open and was standing *right in front of me* as open and as passable as it could be!

*This was a God-ordained moment.* I knew in my heart that God was beckoning me to trust Him and to walk through this door.

When they told me the cost per broadcast, I didn't have that kind of money or anything even close to it. But the door was open, and God was urging me to put my name on the "dotted line" of the contract. So I asked for a few minutes to be alone with Andrey, my associate. Once we were alone, we bowed our heads, clasped hands, and prayed for the courage to accept this step of faith.

I said to him, "I don't have the money to pay for this, but I know God has opened this door and that I am supposed to sign this contract. I don't know where the money will come from, but I *must* sign this contract and trust that God will speak to someone *somewhere* to help pay for this huge opportunity for the Gospel."

The cost was *much* more than we had imagined. In fact, when I heard the price, I felt a hesitation at first, a concern that we wouldn't be able to come up with the cash each month. It would be a miracle payment for us every month, but I knew it was worth the money, considering the fact that our program would be broadcast into every single home in the entire nation of more than fifty million people. I knew I was not being presumptuous, but rather that a divine door had been opened before me. Only God could open such an incredible door for the Gospel. There was no doubt that He was orchestrating the entire event.

When we had finished praying, I had deep peace that despite the fact that I didn't have the money to take this step, God wanted me to sign the contract. So when the men reentered the room and asked what we had decided, I boldly told them, "Of course, we are going to broadcast, so give me that contract, and I'll sign it!"

After reviewing the contract one final time, I took the pen into my hand, gulped a deep breath, and signed that piece of paper. It was a huge leap of faith for me, but I had the awesome inward witness that we were about to experience the supernatural provision of God in a measure we had never seen before. God was going to show Himself strong to us and provide every cent needed to broadcast on this massive TV channel. As a result, *every* person in *every* home in that nation where there was a television would be able to hear rock-solid Bible teaching *every day of the week*!

My head and logic said, *Don't do it*, but my spirit said, *DO IT NOW!* In my heart, I knew it was the moment to strike and seize this incredible opportunity. So I signed my name on the dotted line — and national television in Ukraine fell into my hands! Our programs would now be broadcast into the homes of more than fifty million people each week!

## The Divine Timing of God

Within days of signing that contract, politics in Ukraine radically changed, and I realized that If I hadn't seized this opportunity at that exact moment, I would have lost it. If I had hesitated even one week, the door would have been closed. But because we seized it *at the right time*, our television program was locked into a contract that the government had to honor.

As a result of acting at the *right time*, our ministry and television programs became one of the most powerful spiritual forces in that nation. Since those early days when we first walked through that door, we have been impacting Ukraine with the teaching ministry God has given us, and countless lives have been forever changed. But there's even more to this story of God's divine timing and open door of opportunity.

At the exact time I was signing that contract in Ukraine, a ministry partner in the United States — a widow who had faithfully given smaller offerings for many years — received surprise information that she had received a large inheritance. She had always told the Lord, "If You'll trust me with money, I'll use it to finance the preaching of the Gospel." God heard her, knew she was serious, and did exactly what she prayed. He supernaturally put a large sum of money into her hands. When she received that inheritance, she said, "Lord, I'm going to help Rick Renner preach the Gospel across the former Soviet Union!"

When we later looked at the calendar and compared the times on both sides of the world — we discovered that at the *exact* moment I was signing that contract, this woman was receiving the news about her inheritance! I signed the contract and, literally *simultaneously*, God put the money into the hands of a widow who had made Him a promise.

Before the first payment was due for that massive TV outreach, we had all the finances we needed to pay the bill. God had entrusted that widow with the money necessary to cover the cost of those first broadcasts — and she kept her promise to steward her finances for the preaching of the Gospel.

In fact, this woman supported our TV outreach for many years afterward. As a result, our Bible teaching programs went into every home in that nation every day. Over time, we received millions of responses from people who watched the programs, who gave their lives to Christ, and who began to regularly correspond with our ministry for help to develop their lives in Christ.

As I think back on this experience, I see how every person played such a vital role for this miracle to be brought to pass. I signed the contract, but didn't have the money to pay for it. God gave finances to a faithful widow and used her to supply the money to pay. Each time I ponder this experience, I'm reminded of what the apostle Paul wrote in First Corinthians 3:6, "I have planted, Apollos watered; but God gave the increase."

That was certainly the case here. We each had a part to play, but God opened the door and orchestrated the entire event!

## We Were To Start a Church in a Citadel of Communism and Atheism

TV ministry was a huge, but rewarding challenge, and we were making great headway in our assignment to teach the Bible and make disciples of Russian-speakers through the medium of television. But besides TV, there was the issue of starting a church to make disciples of all those precious converts from the large meeting we'd held in the national hockey stadium in Riga. From the time we'd held those five days of meetings, I'd understood that God was asking Denise and me to start a church to pastor those new believers. So as I traveled nearly nonstop on planes, trains, and automobiles through dangerous territories and in crime-infested atmospheres to start the television network, I also had a mandate from the Lord to start the Riga Good News Church.

*Wow*…it seemed like the world was swirling around me as all these new developments were happening at lightning speed. We had faithfully begun the TV ministry, and God's magnificent favor was manifesting before us at every turn and through every open door. Now it was time to start the church. But how do you start a church of former atheists who know nearly nothing about the Bible? Where do you begin? What do you teach them first? Since they know nothing at all about the Bible, what should be the place to begin for a group of people totally unfamiliar with the Word of God?

Our team planned how to get started. We decided to hold five weeks of meetings in a local *Dom Kultury* — a civic center that had an auditorium and that was located in downtown Riga near the train station. I had studied marketing and advertising as a university student, so in typical American fashion, I wanted to make the advertisement for the meeting really captivating. We received about 500 names from the 926 we water-baptized during those meetings.

Because of the dangers associated with the old Soviet rule, people were still terrified of what might happen if they were brought to the attention of the wrong people, and they were hesitant to provide us with their personal information. So it was really a remarkable thing that we received 500 names from among those converts.

I designed an ad campaign that invited those five hundred new believers to a series of "revolutionary" meetings that would be occurring in downtown Riga. By using the word "revolutionary," I, of course, meant *spiritually* revolutionary, but when my small team saw the word "revolutionary," they exclaimed, "No, you cannot use a word like that here. It's too reminiscent of the tragedies that followed the Bolshevik Revolution. If you use the word revolutionary, secret-security services will be scrambling all over the place to shut us down!"

I submitted to my team's wise counsel, so instead, we advertised that we would simply be conducting five weeks of a Bible study on Tuesday nights. And every week, we arrived to find the auditorium filled with people who were eager to learn what their new faith meant. Because they didn't have Bibles and there was nowhere to purchase a Bible, we provided them with New Testaments that were supplied to us by my dear friend, Terry Law, who had served the underground Church in the Soviet Union for many years.

We announced that when the five weeks of Bible study concluded, we would be starting the Riga Good News Church on Easter Sunday 1993 at the Central Movie House in the center of Riga. We were going to name it the Good News Church because when Jesus started his ministry, He announced that He was anointed to preach the *good news* of the Gospel (*see* Luke 4:18). Especially in the wake of the collapse of the USSR when there was so much bad news in this part of the world, we believed this name would signal the truth of what the Gospel really is and beckon people to seek it out.

## A Conflict With a Government Leader

Everything was moving along smoothly until the unimaginable struck — and we began experiencing an almost unbelievable attack as the devil tried to drive us out of the country!

A prominent government leader despised me because of my position on the Bible and because I was broadcasting the Bible on television, and he took a hard stand against us. Because we had TV equipment, it was even rumored that we were a CIA group sent to spy on the activities of the nation. They believed we were secretly using our TV equipment to document various sites in the nation. Thus, we were unwelcomed by many influential people who occupied high positions of authority.

But we *knew* that this was the place where God had called us to start our work and our church, so we were determined not to be moved by fear or to be bullied out of that nation.

Among the people in Latvia, dread also loomed large that former Soviet troops, now new Russian troops, would suddenly reappear to summarily take back the country's newfound freedom. Unsure of *what* to believe — that the end of communism was their new reality *or only a mirage* — it seemed the entire nation of Latvia was gripped with fear not quickly shaken off or cast aside. Still burdened by a collective looking-over-the-shoulder mindset, local people viewed foreigners with great suspicion. It only stood to reason that the Renner family and all those associated with us were high on the list of those to distrust.

As is often the case in a foreign country, living in Latvia required a visa. Because the man in charge of immigration was against us too — he would only issue us a visa that lasted *one day, three days, five days*, or maybe *a week* at a time! Then at the end of that very brief period each time, we had to start the entire visa process all over! It was like the devil was trying to wear us down and run us out of town. But we knew that we had been called to be there, and we would not give up.

There were several times when our visas expired, and we had to plead with officials to issue us another one. When they'd finally grant our request, the new visas would often be valid for a mere twenty-four hours! That meant we had only one legal day to breathe a sigh of relief before we had to initiate the difficult process all over again.

We were fighting for our lives, believing God to build the TV ministry, and we were also starting the church — *while* the government of Latvia was regularly trying to kick us out. I went to bed every night wondering if we would be expelled the next day or week.

In those early days in Riga, scarcity of everything caused many taxing inconveniences, but nothing we'd experienced up to that time said, "You're not welcome here and you're not going to stay" like being continually informed by immigration officials that they would do all they could to remove us.

Our oldest son Paul recalled, "I remember once when our visas ended, and Anita Busha was fighting to get us visas. This was after we had started full church services! But Dad stood on the platform and told the new church, 'I'll see you next Sunday.' We had no visa and no guarantee, naturally speaking, that we would be there. But Dad stayed in faith and refused to budge. Anita fought for us — and we got our visas and were there for the next church service...*and the next and the next!*"

Anita Busha (later, Anita Vavilova after she married) was our team member who spent almost every day at the immigration department for us. Anita was like an anchor. Even in the hardest moments, she said, "I know it looks impossible, but it will be all right." And every time Anita made the ritual trek to renew those visas — dutifully standing in line for hours *again and again and again* — the nonstop vexation of that season simply triggered God's grace on our lives and caused our resolve to grow ever stronger.

By the grace of God, we persevered through all those difficulties, from rationed food and shortages at the market to imposing mafia-type figures, incessant persecution by immigration officials, and the intimidating presence of the secret-security service. And the light of all God desired to establish there slowly began to displace those long shadows of opposition and the people's hopelessness of the past.

Denise and I still have our old passports from back in those days, and they are *filled* with pages and pages of Latvian visas. We had so many visas that we ran out of space in our passports several times, and the U.S. Embassy would sew in extra pages to make room for more visas! It was like we were living on borrowed time.

Every night when we went to bed, and every morning when we woke up, we were talking and praying about visas so we could stay where we knew God had called us. It was undoubtedly one of the biggest faith fights we had ever encountered — *and this fight continued, unabated, for several years!* Space prevents me from articulating how much pressure it put on us. While we were producing TV programs, starting a new church in Riga, and answering mountains of pieces of mail from TV viewers, this visa problem was constantly in the background hassling us, and it affected every area of our lives. By God's grace and the virtue of patience, we endured and outlasted the enemy's onslaught.

### Our First Church Service Was About To Be Canceled!

I often hear about churches and pastors that feel local resistance from city councils, but the efforts of this one government leader against us were particularly fierce. We had decided to start our church in the Riga Central Movie House, which was located right in the heart of the city. But because this individual was against us, the Riga Central Movie House refused to let us hold our first meeting there on Easter of 1993 as we had advertised and planned.

Making it *really* hard was the fact that they turned us away just *three days* before the first meeting was to occur. That meant we didn't have time to let anyone know the agreement for our venue had been canceled. Everyone was going to show up for a meeting at a location we couldn't use. Furthermore, we didn't know where we were going to start the new church now.

But Adele Alexander, the Texan who served as administrator at the Jelgava Bible school, sprang into action and began to search for an alternative location where we could start the new church. After being rejected by several locations that we had investigated as potential sites for our church, Adele discovered an old auditorium formerly used by the Communist Party that was available if we wanted to rent it.

Adele said, "That huge communist auditorium was filled with wooden seats that would flop down like theatre seats. On the arms, they had little four-prong electrical outlets that had been used for headphones when the Communist Party met there. When I saw that auditorium, I said, 'Rick Renner will love it — it's so Russian! He won't just *love* it…he'll *L-O-V-E* it.' I was right — he fell in love with the place because it was so full of Soviet history."

Within hours of receiving that information, I went to the auditorium to see if it would work as our new church building. There I was, surrounded by 680 communist-red, leather-padded, theater-style seats. An enormous chandelier hung from the ceiling, and gigantic, matching light fixtures lined the circular auditorium. The walls were adorned with emblems of the Soviet Union that included huge cameos of Marx and Lenin adorning the top left and right of the stage. The back rooms of the stage were filled with communist memorabilia — including flags of every republic of the USSR, a gargantuan bust of Lenin, and a huge copper emblem that commemorated one of the anniversaries of the Communist Party.

Adele recalled, "When we found that auditorium, Rick was like a kid attending a circus for the first time in his life. He was wide-eyed and excited to think the church would be started in this former Communist Party auditorium where regulations against the Church had once been passed by communist powers. Now the Good News Church was going to be starting there!"

Our rented space was the assembly hall of the Academy of Sciences. It's important to note that one of the main tasks of science during the Soviet era was to prove that there was no God. Yet it was in this citadel of communism and atheism that we started our local church. Because the director of that building didn't like the new government, he was willing to work with us. When I inspected the location and stood on that stage looking out at those empty seats, I understood that *this* was the location where Jesus wanted us to start the Good News Church. I was simply in awe — starting a church in that prestigious auditorium used in a former time by the Communist Party would be a great victory for Christ and His Church!

The new location was five blocks away from Riga's Central Movie House, so when people showed up on Easter morning at the canceled location, we had people in place to redirect them to the new auditorium five blocks away. We started late that day because of this inconvenience, but we started with an enthusiastic crowd and a full week of meetings in the new location. From the outset of those meetings, the power of God literally burst into that place and established the Church of Jesus Christ in that part of the world!

Paul Renner said, "The Academy of Sciences was a landmark building that everyone knew. Because it was a landmark location, it was very easy to invite people to it. And at that time, it was one of the tallest buildings in Riga. Even if people didn't know the name of the building, you could just tell them to go to the tallest building near the train station. Everybody could find it easily."

During that first week, every chair was filled, and each evening, people crowded the steps that flanked the auditorium. The auditorium was packed to maximum capacity until the number of people attending overflowed beyond the limitations set by the local fire department, and we had to begin holding multiple services each week to accommodate our burgeoning new congregation of new believers. In the middle of that location — where communist powers had once prevailed — *the grace of God was being poured out!*

That week, I couldn't help but be reminded again of the apostle Paul's words in Romans 5:20, where he wrote, "…Where sin abounded, grace did much more abound." Paul said that sin "abounded" — from the Greek word *pleonadzo*, which describes *something that exists in abundance.* However, Paul went on to use comparative language to tell us that regardless of how immense sin and its dominion was in a person's life, it is *nothing* in comparison to the working of God's grace.

When I looked over the faces in that old communist auditorium, I thought of how that building, like so many lives, was once dominated by a horrible working of sin. But regardless of what sinful decisions were made there, it was nothing compared to the grace that was now poured out on us! God's grace was being poured out in a measure that was *way above and beyond* anything that sin had ever dreamed of accomplishing in that place and in that land.

Paul said "grace did much more abound" — that was his inspired way of explaining the *profuse, lavish, bountiful,* and *overflowing nature* of God's grace! And that can be our experience regardless of the flourishing of sin in our past!

But what was also amazing to me is that the new auditorium located in the Academy of Sciences was a Stalin-style skyscraper that had been built between 1951 and 1961, and it had been constructed in the very shadow of the ghetto of Riga, where Nazi forces had incarcerated the entire Jewish community of Riga during World War II starting in 1941.

In 1941, on the dates of November 30 and December 8, Riga's Jewish community of about twenty-four thousand was organized into columns of one thousand people and were marched from the Jewish ghetto to Rumbula, an area east of Riga where pits had already been dug and where the killing would be done simultaneously.[1] All the able-bodied Jews went by foot from the ghetto to the liquidation site. Near the pits, they had to deposit their overclothes, which were eventually washed, sorted, and shipped back to Germany. Jews — men, women, and children — passed through police cordons on their way to the pits, where they were shot by German soldiers.[2]

Victims were also stripped of their valuables. The people were then marched down the ramps into the pits, ten at a time in single file, forced to lie on top of previously shot victims, many of whom were still alive, in order to save executioners the trouble of throwing bodies into the pits. With their automatic weapons set on single shots, the marksmen murdered the Jews from a distance of about two meters (between six and seven feet) with a shot in the backs of their heads. One bullet per person was allotted.[3]

One rare survivor recounted the sordid killings, saying that some of those already shot were still writhing and heaving, oozing blood, brains, and excrement.[4] As they neared the pits, some of the victims wept, others prayed and recited the Torah, and still others tried to comfort the small children. Handicapped and elderly people, many of whom were specially transported to the killing site, were helped into the pit by other, sturdier victims.[5]

From 1941 to 1944, similar actions were taken again against the remaining Riga Jewish community, along with Jews who had been transported there from all over Eastern Europe. From the same ghetto where we started our Riga church, those Jews were marched to Bikernieki Forest, where approximately 35,000 people were shot and buried in 55 huge pits.[6]

I write about all this because it seemed our family was indelibly connected to these horrific Jewish execution sites. Our first home in Jelgava was just a half mile from the first site of the Latvian holocaust. Second, our church was started at the Academy of Science in the shadow of where the entire Jewish population in that vicinity was incarcerated before their mass executions by Nazi troops between 1941 and 1944. Later when we constructed our Riga church building, we ended up purchasing land right in the middle of the Biekerniki forest — just on the other side of the woods from where the execution of the Jews occurred.

In addition to these two sites — Rumbula and Biekerniki — there was also Salaspils, a small town outside of Riga near Rumbula that was converted into a concentration camp where blood was drained from Jewish children to provide to wounded German troops. Some estimate that seventy thousand Jews perished in Latvia during those ghastly years.[7] But the Academy of Sciences — exactly where we started our church on Orthodox Easter Sunday, April 18, 1993 — was built on the site of the old ghetto where those notorious death marches started for Jews in World War II.

So you can see why I was especially reminded of Romans 5:20 in those early days in Riga: "…Where sin abounded, grace did much more abound." As I said, the Greek tense of the word *pleonadzo* ("abounded") denotes *something that exists in abundance* and describes *an abundance that is growing larger and more expansive with the passing of time.*

The implication is that wickedness and sin is never stagnant, but continually grows, increases, and expands. Romans 5:20 could be translated, *"Where sin exists in abundance and is multiplying and constantly expanding…."* It describes the growing nature of unrestrained wickedness and sin. But the verse goes on to gloriously say that "…where sin abounded, grace did *much more abound.*"

Those words "much more abound" are translated from the Greek word *huperperisseo,* which describes *something that is growing out of measure, beyond proportion, and out of its banks to a far-stretched extreme.* It depicts something like a giant river that is being flooded with waters from upstream. Those waters are coming downstream so fast that the river can no longer hold the raging current within its banks. Its water *rises and rises* until it finally begins pouring out of its banks and flooding everything in sight, much like the swelling river near the property of my Grandpap Earl Miller that I described to you in Chapter One. This is exactly the idea of the word Paul uses when he says, "…Grace did much more abound." This means Romans 5:20 could be interpreted, *"For wherever sin exists in abundance and is multiplying and constantly expanding, that is precisely the place where grace is poured out in a far greater, surpassing quantity."*

This means that regardless of where you live or what you're facing — regardless of how bad the situation looks to your natural eyes — the grace of God is flowing *downstream*, and He is lavishly pouring it forth in *abundant* measure! It is impossible to imagine, measure, or even dream of the amount of divine grace God is sending in our direction. No banks can hold the flood of grace God is sending our way! It isn't just *a lot of grace* — it is *more, more,* and *much more* grace! It's a *flood* of grace that will always far surpass the flood of wickedness, sin, and darkness!

## Those Who Do the Will of God *Prevail*

Satan tried to stop us from doing the will of God when we started the Riga church, but the enemy *cannot* prevail against anyone who yields to the Lord and refuses to budge from his or her position of obedience.

When you are obeying God wholeheartedly, you will find that God is supplying you with more than enough grace to match whatever the enemy is trying to do. If you will surrender to that divine grace, it will rise higher and higher until it eventually floods every area of your life. Instead of just seeing all the destruction of the enemy, you will see the awesome outpouring of the marvelous grace of God everywhere you look!

That was not only true of the location where our first church gathered in Riga, but it is also true of you. Sin may have once existed in abundance in your life, but the grace of God has far exceeded anything that the devil or any past sin ever attempted to bring to pass in your life. The grace of God working *in you* is higher, preeminent, unsurpassed, and unrivaled by any past rule of sin in your life. God's grace in you is simply *measureless* and *inexhaustible*! Just as the grace of God was poured out in that old communist auditorium, it is now being poured out abundantly, *without measure,* in your life. This is your time to gloat over what God can do in a person's life. There you are, a former temple of sin, and now you have become a place where God with all His miracle-working power is actively at work!

It should leave you *speechless* to consider what God has done and is doing in you! *Wow*...as I think back to what God did in that desperate, dark location where we started the Riga Good News Church, I am almost dumbfounded to this day. God liberally poured out his mercy and grace in abundance in the very spot where Satan tried to liquidate so many of the Jewish people.

But in the midst of all this victory we were experiencing with our young church, Satan attacked again in his attempt to abort our TV ministry as it began to touch millions of viewers in many nations. I share about that in the following pages.

In general, the front lines are where the greatest number of attacks occur. Out on the front lines — on the cutting edge — Satan hits hard and often, trying to drive back the Lord's brave soldiers who are storming hell's gates and taking new ground for God's Kingdom.

I can personally testify to many satanic attacks that have come against my family and me as we have pressed forward to take new territory for the Kingdom of God over the years. The enemy is always looking for ways to sabotage the life of a true frontline soldier. But we are not ignorant of Satan's wiles, or *methods of operation*, and we can stand guard, victorious, over every single one of those attacks!

### *Dream Thieves* and *The Point of No Return*

It was during this time in our ministry in Latvia that I sat down at my little Soviet-style desk and wrote my book *Dream Thieves — Overcoming Obstacles To Fulfill Your Dreams*. At that moment, it seemed like so many dream thieves were trying to chase us off and cause us to give up. Right in the midst of our own battles in ministry and our determination to stay put regardless of the obstacles that came against us, the words of *Dream Thieves* began to pour from my spirit through my fingers and onto the printed page. Every word of that book was born from my own commitment to refuse to let the dream thieves of life steal our calling from us. That is one reason why I love that book so much to this day.

*Dream Thieves* was also the first book we eventually printed in the Russian language and offered on television to our TV viewers. What a timely book it was for people in the lands of the former USSR who were just realizing they could begin to dream. It was like the cap was being taken off their imaginations and they began to dream that perhaps they could have a better future than their past.

Orders for that book came into our office *by the thousands*. We printed it again and again — not having the cash up front each time to do it, but believing God for every cent needed to pay for the printing and postage. We knew people really needed this message at that crucial moment, and most could not afford to buy it.

Not long after that, I sat back down at my Soviet-style desk and wrote *The Point of No Return — Tackling Your Next Assignment With Courage and Common Sense.* That book, too, was born out of our new experience in the lands of the former USSR. We were indeed tackling our new assignment with courage and with as much common sense as we could muster. The combination of courage and common sense enabled us to stay on track regardless of what the enemy tried to mount against us. And truly, there would be no retreating or turning back.

And if our almost daily struggle with expired visas wasn't challenging and exhausting enough, the enemy was getting ready to mount *a really bizarre* attack!

## Sabotage in the Ministry *With Death Threats*

As I've shared with you in previous pages, we were receiving mind-boggling amounts of mail from our TV viewers who were really responding to the programs and reaching out to us for prayer, encouragement, and more trusted teaching from the Bible so they could grow. This was exciting, but because there were virtually no computers yet in that part of the world, it meant all the mail had to be answered by hand and very slowly. Anita Busha recalled, "We were not ready for that much mail. In the beginning, we were answering by hand and by heart — reading every letter and writing back every answer by hand. But because we did not have computers, we were pretty slow. But then Pastor Rick bought computers. At first, we had to take lessons on how to operate them. No one else in Jelgava had computers, so this was really amazing."

We were finally making progress answering our mail with better speed and efficiency — still by heart, but not by hand! But then, at about that time, an event took place that none of us could have ever predicted, as it was so off-the-charts crazy. It was a real act of sabotage that the devil used to try to stop what we were doing in the TV outreach.

As I said, we were the first office in Jelgava to be equipped with computers. Our purchase of these computers was quite a sensation in our little town. Our team proudly worked on those computers every day, and our speed in answering mail had increased greatly due to this new development.

But one day I received a phone call very early in the morning from our office guard. Due to the widespread infestation of mafia and criminal activities in those days, it was normal to have guards in all places of business and commerce. That morning, our guard called me with a terrified sound in his voice and begged me to quickly drive to the office. We lived only a few blocks away, so I jumped in the car and sped to the office to see what the commotion was about.

When I walked in, the guard told me that he had walked away from his post for about thirty minutes, and when he returned, he found something deeply disturbing that had happened in his short absence. Someone who had undoubtedly been watching had come into the offices with long nails that normally would be used for constructing railroad tracks, and this person, or *persons*, had hammered those long nails all the way through the keyboards of all of our computers and had also destroyed most of the computer screens!

This was bad enough, but making matters even worse was, in the middle of every nail was a note containing a death threat for the person who worked at each computer. In essence, each note said, "If you continue to work in this ministry, you will be killed."

I collected the death threats, as it was just about time for the office to open, and our staff one by one began to come through the front door to report to work. They were living their dream working in our ministry. But on that day when they saw the destroyed computers and heard that death threats had been leveled against them, a spirit of fear began to spread its poisonous, *fierce* tentacles throughout the members of our entire team.

## Fear Tried To Divide Us

Everyone on our staff knew that only someone "inside" had access to the building. There was no sign of a break-in — which could only mean that whoever the perpetrator was had to be one of us!

Whereas we normally held hands and joyfully prayed in unity together each morning, people stood aloof, no doubt wondering who among us had done this dastardly deed. The destruction was immense, but the fear produced by it was worse. And over the months that followed — months of continual vandalism, destruction, and threats — the tension in our ministry was so thick, you could feel its suffocating grip on the minds of our team members. The camaraderie and unity previously enjoyed among us began to erode, and we could see the enemy's tactic in play to dismantle our ministry one fearful, suspicious employee at a time. Denise and I were dumbfounded by what we saw being played out before our eyes.

In the days, weeks, and months that followed, these evil deeds did not let up. Because we had many Americans on our team at that time who had young school children, we had started our own private school. One day when the children opened their lunch boxes to eat, they found similar death threats inside their lunch pails — and again, such a deed could have only been done by someone from inside our organization.

Finally, whoever the perpetrator was began to play havoc on staff members' homes while they were at work — *including OUR home*! Denise and I returned home one evening to find that whoever the perpetrator was had come into our house while we were away for the day and had pushed all of our dishes out of our kitchen cabinets onto the floor. They were broken and strewn all over the kitchen.

This was at a time when there were mass deficits of everything, and there were no dishes available to purchase to replace them. We were simply out of dishes.

As we looked deeper around the house that evening, we discovered that the person who was doing all this had also been in our bedroom and had poured buckets of white paint into our shoes and ruined them.

Again, because of the deficits, there were no shoes available for purchase to replace them. We were simply out of shoes.

Then when it was time for Denise and me to go to bed that night, we pulled back the covers of our bed and found that the perpetrator had also poured buckets of white paint into our bed and then remade the bed nicely so we wouldn't discover it until it was time to go to sleep that night. It totally ruined our bedding, including a quilt that had been handmade by Denise's mother as her wedding gift to us. We felt so grieved and violated — and now completely exhausted by the many months of this unabated attack.

But there's more to this story. At church, people were so excited to be a part of what God was doing in the Good News Church — but one Sunday, I heard people shrieking from their seats in the congregation. I looked into the crowd and saw a few people waving notes in the air, and I instinctively knew the perpetrator had struck again. This time the culprit left death threats in random seats throughout the auditorium, warning people that if they continued to attend the church, they would be murdered. Believe me when I tell you that sending death threats is not a great way to encourage people to keep coming to church!

This madness went on for many months. Everyone on our team fretted about who among us would do such a thing. Whoever the person was, that individual was so sneaky that he or she had never been caught. But every staff member talked about it incessantly. Denise and I talked about it in the mornings when we woke up, at night before we went to bed, and any other free moment when it came up in conversation. All our team members were consumed and distracted by it. The momentum we had gained as a ministry was being negatively affected by this unending assault.

Denise and I inwardly suspected who the perpetrator was, but it was very difficult to bring a charge on the basis of a suspicion, so we waited to see what to do next as the rampage continued. Finally, I decided to do something I never would have dreamed of doing in my life. *I contacted the local offices of the special security services to ask them for help!*

When we first moved to Jelgava amidst such harsh economic times, their department in our vicinity desperately needed new uniforms, but didn't have money to purchase them. As an act of good will, our ministry provided the funds for the new uniforms for those officers in our location. Then later when Jelgava wanted to construct a new statue of a local hero near the train station, our ministry provided significant funds for the construction of that statue. So knowing that we had done something for them and for our community, I decided to ask them for help.

After explaining the entire situation to them, they contacted the main secret-security offices in Riga for consultation about how to handle this drawn-out situation. An answer came back from the main offices in Riga, ordering us to collect all the death threats — a very large stack of them by that time — and to turn them over to the secret-security services who would give all of them to handwriting-analysis experts to be examined.

My staff was unaware that I had contacted the security services and that I had begun privately to cooperate with them for their assistance in this matter. But, finally, the director of the secret-security services called to say he wanted to meet with our entire team, along with a handwriting-analysis expert from the central office in Riga. I was hesitant to agree to do this because many of our staff's family members had been sent to prison during the difficult days of persecution by the old KGB of the former USSR. But I knew I needed to comply with their request so they could help us with the unbelievable drama that had been unleashed in our ministry.

So I called all of our approximately fifty staff members together to meet on a certain day, and I announced we would be having a couple of special speakers. I didn't know how to tell them it was two members of the state secret-security services.

The staff all gathered in their seats to wait for our "special speakers." I met the officers at the front door of our building and walked them back to the meeting room where our team had gathered.

When those uniformed men walked through the door of that office — with me at their side — people's mouths fell open in shock and dismay to see officers from this state organization among us. I introduced them and asked our entire team to cooperate with whatever they asked us to do that morning.

There was complete silence in the room as those two officers began to distribute white pieces of paper and pencils to every person and then to watch carefully as each person wrote his or her name at the top of the paper. I heard the chief officer say, "Now I'm going to dictate a note that I want you to write on your piece of paper with the pencil we have given you."

To my total shock, I listened as he dictated murder threats that matched the various threats we had collected over the past months. I leaned over to Denise and said, "What has happened to us? Now we're *all* writing murder threats!"

Then when everyone was finished, he instructed everyone to turn the paper over, put the pencil into the other hand, and do it all again with the other hand in case the perpetrator had tried to disguise his or her handwriting. Once all the notes were written, he collected them, and I walked with those men into the hallway as they headed out the door again. They told me, "We'll take these to the main office in Riga and compare them to all the original notes you turned over to us. We'll be able to tell you exactly who has been doing all of this to you and your organization."

That day, the attacks abruptly ended because the saboteur knew that the evidence collected was sufficient to prove who had done these horrible deeds. When the results finally came back, they showed that it was exactly the person Denise and I had suspected. I was infuriated when I discovered who it was, and I was prepared to press charges against the individual for the destruction, terror, and havoc that had been wrought among us for so many long, *exhausting* months.

As I prayed about what actions to take, the Holy Spirit confronted me with a very difficult question. I heard His tender voice ask me, *What is better — to prosecute a person who is obviously mentally challenged or to heal that person?*

Well, it was obvious the perpetrator indeed had serious issues or these crimes never would have been committed. And, of course, I knew the answer. It would be better to heal than to prosecute. But I wasn't feeling too compassionate about this person anymore and really wanted to prosecute to the fullest extent of the law!

But I was sensitive enough to understand the Holy Spirit was trying to give Denise and me a new assignment. Rather than prosecute, God was asking us to cover the identity of this individual and to never reveal it — a promise that we have faithfully kept. It was one of the hardest assignments He has ever given us, but that individual eventually moved on to another ministry — in a restored state — and is still active in ministry today. Nevertheless, these acts of sabotage were some of the most horrendous things we have ever endured.

### 'Roasting' Under Forty Sunlamps for Eight Hours!

With that string of assaults behind us, our minds began to rest and our momentum returned as we focused full-force on the work that was before us. As our TV ministry continued to grow, we realized we needed low-hanging, directional lights for our studio. Our staff was inexperienced back then, but they were all we had, so I sent them out to search for lights we could use to illuminate the studio where we were going to be filming our TV programs.

With great delight, they returned with forty big lights that they were sure would work to light up the studio. For a week, staff members carefully hung the lights in place and tested them. After being satisfied that the lights were exactly what we needed, they determined we could begin filming with the new lights.

I was excited that the studio was so well lit and that the low-hanging lights looked so professional. But our studio had no air-conditioning, which made the room very hot. To stay cool, I wore a dress shirt, tie, and suit jacket from the waist up — and from the waist down, I wore shorts and sat with my feet and part of my legs immersed in two big buckets of ice-cold water in an effort to cool down while we were filming. Even with my legs submerged in that water, sweat would pour from my brow, and I would have to wipe my forehead the whole time we filmed. However, on this particular first day of filming with the new lights, it felt especially hot — much hotter than usual.

After two hours of nonstop filming under those forty lights, I felt really hot, so I took my legs out of the buckets, untied my tie, unbuttoned my top shirt, and went outside to get some fresh air. Then I walked into the editing suite where the producers were working hard to adjust the colors on their monitors because my skin looked so red on the screens.

They twisted this knob and that knob, trying to get the color to look right. They were so focused on what they were looking at on the monitors that they never actually looked at me!

Eventually, I heard them say, "We think we've got it fixed. Pastor Rick, why don't you head back into the studio and let's film some more programs."

Once I resumed filming, I didn't stop again until I had filmed a total of eight hours of TV programs that day. It was a personal record for the most TV programs I had ever filmed in a single day. This time when I walked out of the studio, the producers looked at me to congratulate me for completing such a successful day, but when they saw me, they *gasped*. It was at that moment they realized the forty lights they were so proud of — and that I had been sitting in front of for eight hours — were *sunlamps*, not TV lighting!

My face was severely burned and red, almost beyond imagination. Try to imagine what you would look like if you sat in front of forty sunlamps for eight hours. To make matters worse, I had been sitting in shorts with my feet and legs in two buckets of water, and the radiation from those lamps literally scorched my legs.

But worst of all was what happened to my eyes. My eyes — not just my *eyelids*, but my *eyes* — were so burned that I could hardly see. Every time I blinked, it felt like pieces of shredded glass were being dragged across my eyes.

At that time, pharmaceutical products were still nearly absent in the former Soviet Union, so there were no medications or ointments to put on my burned body. Instead, a local doctor recommended that I be covered in sour cream and that I then be tightly wrapped in plastic wrap, like Saran Wrap, to keep the moisture trapped around my body.

So that night I lay on the couch as Denise literally doused me from head to toc in sour cream and then had me roll over and over so the plastic would tightly stretch around me. My arms were trapped under the plastic, and my legs were also bound. I was completely immobile. I remember telling Denise that I felt like a huge enchilada!

Hour by hour, the pain increased all over my face and legs — every place that had been over-exposed to the forty sunlamps. I cried because of the horrible pain in my eyes every time I blinked. We requested an emergency call to a doctor in the United States, and the local operator amazingly placed the call quickly, rather than making us wait the usual three days. On the other end of the line, the U.S. doctor warned that it was possible I would wake up blind the next morning because of the extended amount of time I had spent staring directly into the sunlamps.

Fear tried to grip my heart. Denise stayed right at my side the entire night to comfort me because of the pain that wracked my body and the fear that attacked my mind. The pain in my eyes was especially horrific. Denise prayed for me and comforted me, reassuring me that I would be able to see and that, by the grace of God, we were going to get through this ordeal.

Throughout that first night, I shuddered with pain every time I blinked, and fear tried relentlessly to sink its talons into my mind. To fight against that fear, I decided to meditate on Philippians 4:6 and 7. When the pain raged through my eyes, I would quote this verse and focus on the promise of God instead of on my excruciating condition. I quietly spoke that passage to myself probably hundreds of times as I released all my faith that my eyes would be all right, regardless of the pain that tormented me throughout that seemingly endless night.

Philippians 4:6 tells us, "Be careful for nothing: but in everything by prayer and supplication with thanksgiving let your request be made known unto God." Honestly, it took all of my determination that night not to worry about my eyes. But the verse commands us to present our supplications and requests to God with thanksgiving and to leave worry behind us. So that night, I cried out to God and made my request known, asking for my eyesight. Hour after hour, I expressed thanksgiving to the Lord and did my best to praise Him from a grateful, thankful heart in spite of the pain. Denise prayed with me and helped me continue giving thanks to God through the night.

I wish that I could tell you that night was my last experience with sour cream and plastic, but the doctor recommended that I repeat this treatment over the course of a few more days. As I lay trapped in that plastic during those long days — smelling like sour cream and suffering from tremendous pain all over my eyes, face, hands, and legs — I especially focused on God's promise in Philippians 4:7. That verse specifically held me in peace during that difficult time, because after we do verse 6, it says, "And the peace of God, which passeth all understanding, shall keep your hearts and minds through Christ Jesus." Inwardly I knew that the battle for my eyes was over and that they were going to be all right as that peace began to "keep" my heart and mind.

As I recovered from that dangerous eight-hour encounter with the sunlamps, I asked my team, "Who recommended those forty sunlamps to you?" And I found out it was the criminal I'd broken those TV contracts with after I discovered he was involved in illegal activity. That "mobster" had caused that serious, very dangerous problem with my physical health. He struck one last time in an effort to take revenge on us for walking away from him when we had discovered his crimes.

Later in life before that man died prematurely, he called together a group of ministers as he approached death and told them, "I've destroyed my life and my family's reputation because I was money-hungry. I've done terrible things to people. Now I'm about to die and I'm regretful for the many wrong things I did to so many." Then he told them, "Don't make the mistakes I've made and come to the end your life sorry for how you've lived."

In spite of that difficult season with this man and his many regrettable actions, it is a fact that God miraculously used that man to audaciously rent the building for the Jelgava Bible school and to help launch Christian TV in the Soviet world. Perhaps he began very pure-minded, but later veered off track because of money. Regardless, today that man is in Heaven, and one day when I see him, we'll embrace each other with joy.

Since the very beginning of our time in the lands of the USSR, our family has had plenty of opportunities to "tuck our tails" and run back home to the United States due to hardship and lack, religious persecution, and outright evil done to us by all kinds of characters. But because we had surrendered our lives to God — and because of that prayer we'd prayed on the tarmac, asking God to put this land deeply into our hearts — we *stayed*. Because we had pledged to do what He wanted with our lives in that part of the world, what could have been very difficult and burdensome challenges became a daily adventure that continues to enrich our lives today.

As Paul, Philip, and Joel look back on all those years, they each testify of how thankful they are that they grew up with life experiences that they would have never known had they been raised in Oklahoma. Sure, they were deprived of technology, electronics, movies, sports, and other American experiences in those early days. But they also grew up living in a book-of-Acts environment where they saw the Church established, the Gospel go forth, and signs and wonders wrought in people's lives. They truly lived lives of adventure that were constantly filled with intrigue.

Our sons also became multilingual and gained a worldview that has shaped them to be the men they are today. And now, each stands in his own God-called, God-anointed position and is impacting the world with the Gospel in ways that Denise and I can't. We are *each* putting our hands to the plow of the ministry as unto the Lord, and He is truly calling the shots and giving increase to the work of our hands, respectively.

### Do You Believe God Raises the Dead?

Speaking of experiencing real-life book-of-Acts occurrences, we also experienced what some might call a real resurrection of the dead. Let me tell you the story and then *you* decide if it qualifies as a resurrection from the dead.

While Denise and I were on a trip to minister in the United States, I received a phone call one day from our driver in Jelgava. When I heard his voice on the other end of the line, he was sobbing because his little daughter, about nine-years old, had drowned in a river in Jelgava. The story I am about to relate to you is nearly word for word what he himself told me after this whole story was gloriously ended.

Our driver and his family lived right near the banks of the Jelgava River just across from the Jelgava Palace that was built during the time of the czars. In the summertime, its picturesque banks and the river itself were plenteous with sunbathers and swimmers. On that notable day, our driver accompanied his daughter and niece, both of whom were about the same age, to the river to swim as they and so many others did often during that time of year. He turned to speak to someone, and when he turned again to check on his daughter and niece who had just gone into the river to swim, they had disappeared before his eyes!

Our friend's eyes darted vigorously in the vicinity, but he couldn't locate the girls anywhere. That's when he realized something was wrong. Quickly he dashed into the river to dive under the murky waters to see if he could find them. When others realized something terrible had happened, they, too, joined him in diving to the bottom of the river to look for the girls. After a number of minutes passed, someone yelled, "Here they are!" and their bodies were dragged out of the river onto the bank.

Apparently, as the two cousins walked into the river together, they inadvertently stepped into a hole in the river bottom that no one knew about, and that hole swallowed them. By the time their bodies were retrieved, they were no longer breathing. A local doctor happened to be on the banks sunbathing that day. He rushed over to where their bodies lay to perform CPR and chest compressions. After feverishly working on them, he was able to get them breathing again, but they were not conscious and it wasn't known if their brains were functioning or not.

Soon an ambulance arrived on the scene to pick them up, and the young girls were taken to the local Jelgava hospital where both were put on breathing machines. Monitors were attached to their heads to see if there was any brain activity. After monitoring them for a period of time, the doctor told our driver in a hopeless tone, "Your daughter and niece are only breathing because they are on breathing machines, but they have no brain activity. If this breathing machine were turned off, they would quit breathing and we'd pronounce them both dead."

But our driver refused to allow them to turn off the breathing machine. That is when he called to let us know what happened. He said, "Pastor Rick, what should I do?"

I asked, "What do you want to do?" He was a brand-new believer and didn't know much about the promises of God, but he said, "I want to ask God to raise her to life again." So as soon as he hung up, I called our ministry leadership in our Jelgava office and asked them to please go and pray over his daughter in the hospital.

Because he was holding on to faith that God would raise her up, he refused to let the doctors turn off that machine, and every day, our top leadership went to the hospital to lay hands on the girl's lifeless body and to speak life to it in Jesus' name.

Our driver's daughter and niece had been placed in the same room, his daughter on one side of the room and his niece on the other side of the room, both of them on breathing machines with no brain activity. For all practical purposes, they were dead, but because of the breathing machines, they both looked like sleeping beauties who were just waiting to be awakened.

Our driver was using all the faith he had to believe his daughter would be awakened to life again, but his brother, the father of the other girl, was an atheist who did not believe in God. However, as was often the case in the lands of the former USSR, this brother believed in the powers of psychics and witchcraft. In little villages all over the former Soviet Union, there were witches who used dark powers to do so-called healings or who would curse others for a fee.

So our driver's brother paid a local psychic to come to the hospital every day to perform her magic on the lifeless body of his daughter. It was like the sorcerers of Pharaoh who competed with the power of God that operated through Moses. On one side of the hospital room was our anointed staff who laid their hands on the lifeless body of my driver's daughter — and on the other side of the room was a witch trying to conjure up healing powers by appealing to a dark spiritual realm. Side by side in that room, day after day, a contest of supernatural powers was on display.

As time passed, our driver's niece began to change to a putrid color as her body began to die even though she was on a breathing machine. The powers of that witch had done nothing. But on the other side of the room was our driver's daughter, who was having the hands of Spirit-filled believers laid on her every day. His niece's body withered away and her limbs began to turn blue, purple, and then black, while our driver's daughter looked like she was beautifully lying there, as if in a deep state of sleep.

Finally, the breathing machine was taken off the niece, and she immediately quit breathing, was pronounced dead, and was buried. But the daughter of our driver kept living and breathing even though the doctor said she had no brain activity whatsoever.

Weeks passed, and our team kept going to the hospital every day to pray over this young girl's perfectly preserved body that had no brain activity. Then one day — all of a sudden — his daughter sat straight up in bed, fully awake and aware, and asked, "Where am I? Why am I here? Would someone please give me something to eat? I'm so hungry!"

It was just like the biblical story we read in the gospel of Mark that tells of when Jesus raised Jairus' daughter from the dead. Those verses tell us that Jesus spoke to the dead girl and told her to rise. Then Mark 5:42,43 says, "And straightway the damsel arose, and walked; for she was of the age of twelve years. And they were astonished with a great astonishment. And he charged them straitly that no man should know it; and commanded that something should be given her to eat."

The niece, whom a witch had attempted to resurrect with the powers of dark witchcraft, was long buried by that time. But now our driver's daughter was fully restored with no memory of what happened at the river that day. When we returned from our trip to the United States and our driver met us at the airport, he greeted us with his daughter at his side. I patted her head and looked into her eyes, realizing that I was looking into the eyes of a real-life Jairus-type story.

Years later, my driver went to Heaven, but I have seen his daughter on several occasions. Every time I see her, I look into her eyes with wonder that I am looking at a girl whose brain was dead and who was on a breathing machine for weeks and weeks — but after the intense, consistent, authority-filled prayers of our team, she sat straight up from the sleep of death with no lasting ramifications. She was completely normal.

So let me ask you: *Would this qualify as a resurrection from the dead?*

In those days, it was indeed like we had stepped into the gospels and the book of Acts. We saw healings, miracles, and deliverances from demon spirits. Massive growths disappeared from people's bodies, the paralyzed walked, and against all medical odds, the lifeless body of our driver's daughter came to life again.

This, again, is why I say that Paul, Philip, and Joel may have been deprived of movies, sports, and other American experiences that other children enjoyed growing up — but our sons really did grow up living in a book-of-Acts environment.

In First Corinthians 2:4 and 5, the apostle Paul reminded the Corinthians that when he preached to them, he didn't come to them with just words, but with a demonstration of the Holy Spirit's power — and for that reason, they had a faith that rested not just in man's wisdom, but also in the power of God. He said, "And my speech and my preaching was not with enticing words of man's wisdom, but in demonstration of the Spirit and of power: That your faith should not stand in the wisdom of men, but in the power of God."

Our three sons were hearing the clear teaching of the Bible — but they were also seeing demonstrations of the Spirit and of power. As a result, their faith was not rooted in mere mental messages, but also in the tangible power of God. This was better than any technology, electronics, movies, sports, or other American experiences they were missing by living in the former Soviet Union. They were gaining life-transforming experiences with God that took them into the realities of the Bible and the power of the Holy Spirit.

### The First Official Christmas in Latvia — Formerly a Forbidden and Forgotten Holiday

The first year that our church met in the Academy of Sciences building was also when Latvia decided to officially celebrate its first Christmas since the collapse of the communist regime. Christmas had been legally canceled since the time Latvia was incorporated into the USSR in 1940. Because the state was ruled by godless, atheistic communism that was anti-faith, for almost fifty years, there had been no official Christmas. Even if people knew there was a holiday called Christmas, the majority of people didn't know what it was about.

After the Bolshevik Revolution, the new atheistic leadership of the USSR entirely banned Christmas in 1928, and the holiday became a normal workday.[8] That was the year Christmas disappeared from the Soviet Union. It was at the time Christmas was banned that New Year's Eve became the chief celebration of the year. High-ranking officials convinced Joseph Stalin that the *yolki* — the Russian word for the "fir tree" — could be utilized for a secular holiday as a symbol of Soviet children's happiness and prosperity. These *yolki* festivities included a performance with Father Frost and the Snow Maiden, along with fun activities and sweets. The new tradition spread rapidly across the Soviet Union, but it had *zero* connection to anything religious.

Before the Revolution, Saint Nicholas was the patron saint of Russia, but Soviet leaders were opposed to any and all religious connotations. So Saint Nicholas was banished and replaced with a pagan and magical warlock called Father Frost who, along with his sorceress daughter the Snow Maiden, performed all kinds of magical feats.

The central activity of every *yolki* celebration was children richly dressing in costumes and Father Frost and the Snow Maiden suddenly entering the room with their magic wands in hand. Soviet children cheered when they appeared, waiting for the moment when father and daughter would touch the *yolki* tree with their magic wands. The moment they touched the tree with their wands was when all the lights of the tree magically turned on!

Years later in Moscow, our Moscow church hosted a huge *yolki* for children, but mixed it with the story of Jesus to present the Gospel to children and parents — many of whom were hearing it for the very first time. Afterward, when I stood outside to shake hands with parents as they left the auditorium, one parent very innocently asked me, "Can you please tell me what was the fairy tale we saw today about the birth of that little baby boy in a manger? I don't recall ever hearing that fairy tale when growing up."

Bible truth had been replaced in the former Soviet Union with fairy tales and fantasies by an atheistic government bent on socialist-communist control.

The USSR was filled with activities intended to replace outlawed faith-related events and celebrations. For example, people still had a hunger in their souls for a touch of God, but God had been banned along with all other expressions of religious beliefs. So to satisfy the spiritual longings of people, psychics were paraded on television every morning to psychically forecast events of the day and the future. In fact, one Soviet psychic was so nationally revered that people hung on to his words as if he was the Billy Graham of the communist world — a real "spiritual" authority to their hungry hearts. Every morning before people went to work, this psychic appeared on television and nearly hypnotized the nation as he psychically forecasted events of the times.

In pre-Soviet times, people had been very religious before the Revolution, so they were traditionally accustomed to having the established church bless their wedding ceremonies. And even though the church was now out of fashion, people still longed for something "church-like" at their weddings.

So Soviet authorities provided a substitute. In the USSR, every marriage was registered and performed at Zaks, a governmental department that registered and officiated weddings. It had all the appearances of a religious service. Officials performing the ceremony dressed in a gown similar to a religious garment, wore a long chain around the neck with the emblem of the USSR dangling on the end as a substitute for the traditional cross of Christianity, and stood in front of what looked like an altar. In nearly every respect, the whole communistic service had all the trappings of a church ceremony — *but it was completely without God.*

Funerals were another place where faith was replaced by an atheistic substitute. Instead of clergy officiating memorial services or graveside rites, when a funeral took place, an official led the funeral ceremony dressed in clothing similar to a priest, and read from a black, leather-bound book that looked much like a Bible. But instead of Scripture, he read Soviet literature, poetry, and other writings intended to sound like Scripture, but which were written by atheistic writers. All of this was a substitute to somehow satisfy the spiritual longings of the bereaved.

All of these substitutes just scratch the surface of the many replacements provided to swap out all religious activities for secular, communistic ones. But let's go back to Christmas…

In the Soviet years, if it was *just rumored* that a family privately celebrated Christmas, it led to grave repercussions for their children the next semester at school. Teachers were required to make lists of children who were from religious homes or who hinted of anything religious. Then those children were made an example to others as they were discriminated against and forbidden to participate in sports, drama, music, or any type of extra-curricular activities as they went through the school system. So even privately celebrating Christmas was a risk.

Keep all of this in mind as I tell you that it was *a big deal* when I announced to our team that we were going to celebrate Christmas in 1993. One team member who had been recently saved, innocently asked me, "What is Christmas? We've never heard of that holiday. Can you explain to us what Christmas is and how people celebrate it?"

I understand it may be hard for you to imagine growing up never having heard of Christmas, but millions of people who grew up in the Soviet Union didn't know of Christmas or understand what it was about. That day when the staff member asked me "What is Christmas?" it reminded me again that we were serving in virgin territory where people were completely unfamiliar with the Gospel. They didn't even know what Christmas was!

So before our church could celebrate Christmas on December 25 (Russian Christmas today is on January 7), I needed to explain Christmas to them. I took a whole month and taught about the birth of Jesus from Matthew and Luke and then concluded by saying, "The Western world is about to celebrate the birth of Jesus as they do every year, so let's join them this year and celebrate Christmas!"

Exchanging gifts was already done on New Year's Day because that is what Soviet people did. In fact, even today, people — including nearly all Christians in the former USSR — still give gifts to each other on New Year's Day because it was the tradition for seventy years during the Soviet regime. Nearly every Soviet family also had a tree at home during the days of the USSR, but it was not a Christmas tree. As I noted earlier, it was a New Year's *yolki* created to be a substitute for the banned Christmas tree. Even today, believers everywhere in the former USSR still have New Year's trees, not Christmas trees, in their homes, because that was their tradition growing up in the Soviet Union.

Few people during the days of the USSR openly and publicly celebrated Christmas itself, so our church members were excited to learn how Christmas should be celebrated. A few months before Christmas, I made a trip to the United States to take care of ministry business. Because I knew that I would be presenting the idea of Christmas to our church, I went to a large Christmas outlet store to purchase garland, wreaths, rolls and rolls of red ribbon, and marvelous ornaments to use in the first Christmas our church had ever celebrated!

I transported all those Christmas decorations and materials back to Riga and asked Adele Alexander to think about how to adorn our communist-style auditorium for the first Christmas in the history of the new nation.

Remembering that event, Adele said, "That year was the first year that Christmas was permitted on the calendar. Rick planned to introduce the idea of Christmas to our church, so while he was in America, he bought tons of Christmas decorations and brought them back to decorate our communist auditorium. He wanted an enormous Christmas tree, so we paid for one to be cut down in the forest. We were shocked when it arrived because it was *really* enormous, at least thirty feet tall or even more. That huge tree stood on the stage larger than life and simply couldn't be missed!

"And because Rick really wanted people to remember their first Christmas, he wanted there to be a lot of lights, so he brought back what seemed to be unending strings of Christmas lights to adorn the whole auditorium. People from the church got so excited that they wanted to get involved, so I began to teach them how to decorate for Christmas. Rick also brought rolls and rolls of red foil Christmas wrap so we could make enormous beautiful foil bows. I so enjoyed teaching those little Russian ladies how to make those bows, and we made enough of them to cover the walls and to adorn the molding all the way around the edge of the balcony."

"Rick even bought a large Nativity scene, like one you would see in someone's yard. It had a stable, Mary, Joseph, Jesus in a manger, angels, sheep, and even a goat or two. I kid you not when I tell you the stage was full, and the whole auditorium looked like it was wrapped in gorgeous foil red bows. Rick and Denise brought everything we needed to give those people a wonderful first Christmas memory."

I am telling you this story because I want you to understand how "virgin" the territory was where we were doing this work of God. But God's grace was mightily upon us to see darkness pushed back, the light of the Gospel go forth, and the Church of Jesus Christ established in Riga.

### The Night Soviet Troops Withdrew From Latvia

Several hundred thousand Soviet troops had been stationed in Latvia prior to the collapse of the Soviet Union. When those troops began to move out and relocate to other places where they were assigned, very late one night, I was awakened by the sounds of aircraft overhead. I got up and saw that the noise had also awakened Paul, so the two of us went out into our front yard to see the commotion. And if I hadn't seen it with my own eyes, I probably wouldn't have believed what we witnessed that night.

Right there, overhead, Paul and I watched what looked like hundreds of different kinds of aircraft and countless helicopters all flying in one direction like geese migrating in winter. The sky overhead was *almost completely full*. It was a mass exodus of former Soviet forces as far as the eye could see. We remained on our front lawn the rest of the night because we knew we were seeing history unfold overhead as those former Soviet forces pulled out of Latvian territory.

## The *Teach All Nations* Bible School

Because new national borders had finally been set up all over the former USSR, students from far-flung regions could no longer get to Jelgava to attend the school. Eventually the Bible school closed, and all the American missionaries left. But that didn't change the need for a good Bible school to train future ministers for the Baltic States of Latvia, Estonia, and Lithuania.

I felt we needed to fill in the gap that was left when the original Bible school closed. After much prayer, I decided to open our own school and call it Teach All Nations Bible School. In Matthew 28:19, Jesus commanded the Church, "Go ye therefore, and teach all nations, baptizing them in the name of the Father, and of the Son, and of the Holy Ghost." I took that phrase *"teach all nations"* to heart, and we opened our Teach All Nations Bible School.

But because all the missionaries had gone, it meant there were few qualified local instructors living in Latvia. So I took a huge step of faith and invited several Americans who had a gift to teach the Bible to move to Latvia with their families for a season to help teach the students in our Bible school. After all, that's how our own family had relocated to the former Soviet Union.

Denise and I were thankful that those families were willing to uproot and move all the way across the world to join us. I knew it was a great sacrifice — and it was a sacrifice for us, too, because we were committing to help financially support some of them, and we fully paid others. It was a huge step of faith for everyone.

None of the incoming American teachers spoke Russian or understood a thing about living in the former USSR. They couldn't go to the grocery store or buy food without an interpreter. So having them didn't just add *them* to our payroll — we had to add interpreters and staff in order to take care of them. And just as our family was constantly challenged to get visas to stay in Latvia, every one of those teachers, *and every member of their families*, also needed visas that were very difficult to obtain. We had one staff member who did nothing but go back and forth to the immigration office in Riga to negotiate for visas!

In addition, some of the teachers disagreed at times with local customs and traditions, and there were a few discussions with our local staff about whether we should do things the "American way" or the "Russian way." I had to spend some unexpected time mediating those disagreements. I simply never anticipated something like that would occur because our own family never had a disagreement with local people over whose way of doing things was best. Thankfully, there was a lot of love and unity among the whole team at the Bible school, so despite a few interruptions, we experienced a lot of joy, laughter, and camaraderie together.

None of us is perfect, and if Denise and I had to be perfect before we could be used by God, we would have never qualified. God used every one of the Bible-school staff, and although having a large staff of Americans required a lot of time and attention, those teachers strove diligently and with excellence to do what they came to do — to teach day after day in our Bible school. I will be forever grateful to each one of them for the sacrifices they made to invest themselves, their families, and their God-given gifts into the lives and future ministries of those students. *They have my respect!*

## Beginning Right So We Could Finish Strong — Cultivating Fruit That *Remains*

Many students attended Teach All Nations Bible School for several years. They were taught the Word of God and were given practical instruction about how to start and lead a church. And like that original student body in the Jelgava Bible school, the students who attended the Teach All Nations school are leading churches and ministries all over the Baltic countries of Latvia, Estonia, and Lithuania. They all look back on that time as one of the most special moments in their lives.

In John 15:16, Jesus said, "Ye have not chosen me, but I have chosen you, and ordained you, that ye should go and bring forth fruit, and that your fruit should *remain*...." In this verse, Jesus made it clear that He ordained us to "bring forth fruit." The word "fruit" is a translation of the Greek word *karpos*, which describes *luscious, delicious, healthy, beneficial, wonderful fruit.* This means that our lives — including our churches and ministries — should produce marvelous and overflowing fruit that is luscious, delicious, healthy, beneficial, and wonderful! However, it's not enough just to bring forth initial good fruit. Jesus said we glorify the Father best when we bring forth fruit that *remains.*"

I can remember my mentor Dr. Bill Bennett telling me, "Rick, a lot of people begin with a bang and end with a fizzle. It's not important that you make a big noise for people to hear when you get started. What's most important is that you build your life and ministry in such a way that it endures and doesn't fizzle out over time." *Wow*...those words of truth still ring in my ears!

That is actually what Jesus meant when He said we are ordained to bring forth fruit that "remains." The word "remains" in John 15:16 is a translation of the Greek word *meno*, which pictures something that *firmly endures, continues steadfastly*, is *unwavering, unmoving*, and *long-lasting*. In other words, it pictures anything that *lasts, persists*, or *endures* the tests of life and time.

When I analyze my life and my ministry, I always look to see if what I have done was something that "started with a bang and ended with a fizzle," or if it was something that has endured the tests of life and time. All fruit is good, but according to Jesus, having *"fruit that remains"* is what is most important.

When I look back at the Teach All Nations Bible School and analyze the fruit of it, I can thankfully say that there was not only initial fruit, but the long-term effect of that school can still be felt today. To the glory of God, it is truly fruit that remains!

Nikolai Kulakevich said concerning the school and *all* the Lord enabled us to do, "The impact the Renners made on the nation of Latvia is bigger than any other ministry I know of that worked in the former Soviet Union at that time. And I know the impact the Lord allowed them to have will be long-lasting — in fact, I think it will go on forever. It was and is an amazing work that is simply full of good, long-lasting fruit."

## When You Lose Your Life for Jesus' Sake

Over the years, we've learned that to do anything significant for Jesus requires a one-hundred-percent commitment. But in Matthew 10:39, Jesus promised us, "He that findeth his life shall lose it: and he that loseth his life for my sake shall find it."

I can personally testify that neither Denise nor I, nor our sons, ever really lost anything by saying *yes* to Jesus' call on our lives and by commit-ting ourselves completely, one-hundred percent, to doing whatever He has asked us to do. Our family learned that when you obey what Jesus asks you to do, it never *takes away* from you — instead, it *adds* to you, leading you into an unlikely and amazing life full of adventure!

Adele Alexander said, "I think that when we all get to Heaven, we're going to have days and days when God and Jesus are going to take time to tell us everything that happened in those early days of ministry in the for-mer USSR that we didn't even know about. I don't mean this frivolously…I really believe God will have us all come into a big banquet where He's going to tell us everything He enabled Rick and Denise and the boys to do in the former USSR because the far-reaching effects are simply immeasurable. But God knows."

To be clear, as a family, we have seen our share of tests *and even fiery trials* as we were challenged by hell to go home at almost every turn. But we adamantly refused every opportunity to quit. This *was* our home — what had been the Union of Soviet Socialist Republics. God had ordained and commanded it. And experience told me we'd reached a point of no return in our obedience to Him. And although dream thieves could challenge us, they could not ultimately stand in our way. Our will surrendered and swal-lowed up in His, there was indeed no turning back. We were here to stay.

By obeying God, we found abundant life as we had never experienced it before, even though we had enjoyed a wonderful life in our Tulsa home near the golf course and our very busy, fruitful teaching ministry in the U.S. But it was as if our obedience to relocate was a spiritual pick-axe that struck the *motherlode* of a treasure of souls in a world where we never dreamed we'd find ourselves.

We were enjoying many victories in our lives and ministry in the former USSR. Directly in front of us lay more challenges, but we would overcome those, too, by the power of the One who called us and sent us — especially as we were about to commence on an *unlikely* venture to construct the first new church building in Riga for nearly six decades!

'In comparison to the lands of the former USSR,
the Western Church was rich. Even crumbs that
fell from their tables were so much compared to what
existed in that part of the world — it was
enough to make a Gospel difference!'

# UNLIKELY BATTLES
# AND BREAKTHROUGHS —
# OUR LAUNCH
# INTO NEW GROWTH

For the Riga Good News Church to have longevity, I knew it needed to have its own permanent home. Long-term renting is never a smart move if a long future is the intention for a church. But in 1993 when the Riga Good News Church was started in that communist auditorium in the Academy of Sciences, it was the worst time possible to announce a building program. No one had ever even *heard* of a building program!

Keep in mind that this was the former USSR and it had been a communist state since Latvia was incorporated into the USSR in 1940 at the end of World War II. An entire generation had lived in Riga who had never seen a new church building constructed. Because Latvia had been an atheistic, Soviet state, churches had been strictly prohibited. Plus, because

---

**Left:** *Bulldozers moved dirt as prayers of faith moved mountains of opposition to construct the building of the Riga Good News Church.*

the whole economic system was in collapse and disarray, people barely had enough money to buy bread — let alone donate something financially to a church building program. To be honest, the whole idea of a building program was *ludicrous*.

The truth is, people in our church *wanted* to give to the Lord, but the economic system was in a terrible state of flux. Many people had lost their jobs due to the newly erected borders, which stymied businesses and brought in a new currency — in Latvia's case, a currency that nearly no one wanted to barter with. Businesses were brought to a complete standstill and factories closed right and left, leaving families jobless and destitute.

Many people began to move to their country dachas (little parcels of land where they grow food) because they could live off the land. Because they had little money to give, in lieu of cash offerings, new believers began to regularly bring a tithe from the flowers or vegetables they were growing in their dacha gardens. Eventually they began to give financially, but it took a long time before they had anything financially to give due to the economic collapse we were all living in at that time.

I have to stop for a moment to express my profound thanks to the partners and friends who have supported our work over the years. When we moved to the former USSR, there was no local money to support a new ministry because money was nearly nonexistent. As deeply moving as it was to see people bring a tithe of vegetables and flowers — *and God blessed them for it* — we couldn't pay ministry bills with a handful of vegetables or flowers.

But our partners rose to the occasion and sacrificially gave their hard-earned money at that critical moment to help us drive back the powers of darkness and establish the work of the Gospel in a newly freed country with its fledgling *and floundering* economy. And in all the years since, these faithful partners have stayed with us to help us fulfill our God-given assignments.

I often liken ministry to a car that is ready to go on a trip. But if there's no gas in the tank, that automobile is not going to go anywhere. It cannot move without fuel. Ministry is the same. We who are in the ministry can be prepared and ready to go, but if there is no money in the "tank" to enable us to do what we need to do, there can be no forward movement. Using this illustration, there must be both a car *and* fuel for the car in order to make progress — and in ministry, it takes the preparation and willingness of those who do the ministry *and* the "financial fuel" provided by faithful partners to see the Gospel advance.

Although we started with very little finances, God was enabling us to miraculously pay for a burgeoning Russian-speaking TV ministry and all the required equipment, staff, and nonstop travel required to get it established. This was already a monumental feat! So to start a building program at the same time seemed illogical, yet it was what we needed to do. I had already learned that if I would obey what God told me to do, my obedience would work like a magnet to attract the resources needed to do any assignment He gave us.

Just as God was step-by-step, day-by-day, and often minute-by-minute providing all the money we needed for getting the TV ministry established, I knew that if I'd get into agreement with God for a new building program, He would bring us the resources we needed to buy land and construct a church building. All of it would require miraculous provision from Heaven, which God faithfully granted through the sacrificial giving of our own church members and from the open hearts of our partners in the Western world.

### A Rich Promise To Those Who 'Stay by the Stuff'

I realize this book is about *our* personal testimony, but a big part of our testimony concerns those who put financial fuel in the tank of our ministry to make it all happen over all these years. None of it could have been accomplished if it were not for the giving of faithful people who believed in us and were behind what we were being called to do.

Our family may have been the ones physically present on the front lines, but God used givers to provide resources to make it happen. In fact, if those faithful givers hadn't done their part, we could have never done our part. But because they partnered with us, we started churches, a television ministry, conducted large evangelistic meetings, printed and gave away millions of Christian books and other pieces of literature, and made other spiritual inroads for the Gospel over many years. Literally *millions of lives* have been changed because of the dual efforts of our front-line work combined with the simultaneous giving of partners.

This cooperative effort reminds me of a story from the Bible that I want to briefly share with you.

In First Samuel we read that a city called Ziklag came under attack by the Amalekites, and in that attack, David's own family and the families of others were taken captive. But David went to battle with his front-line soldiers and recovered everything the enemy had taken. First Samuel 30:18-20 tells us, "And David recovered all that the Amalekites had carried away: and David rescued his two wives. And there was nothing lacking to them, neither small nor great, neither sons nor daughters, neither spoil, nor any thing that they had taken to them: David recovered all. And David took all the flocks and the herds, which they drave before those other cattle, and said, This is David's spoil."

It was right for David and his soldiers to be celebrated for their bravery and victory. However, when it was time to reward those who had fought on the front lines, some among the fighters only wanted to acknowledge the ones who physically stood eyeball-to-eyeball with the enemy in the heat of the fray.

David, however, never forgot those at camp who took care of details that freed the soldiers to focus on the fight up front. In fact, David was so aware that those people were worthy of acknowledgment that in First Samuel 30:24, he said, "…For as his part is that goeth down to the battle, so shall his part be *that tarrieth by the stuff*: they shall part alike." Wow. God made no distinction between those actively participating in a battle and those participating back at the home base.

I'm telling you this because I have never forgotten those who supported us while we fought the fight up front. God indeed sent my family to do battle on the front lines in virgin spiritual territory, and we report our victories thankfully. But out partners who "tarried by the stuff" and put financial fuel in our ministry tank are equally important to everything we did on the front lines. If they had not done their part, it would have been impossible for us to do our part, and we would have no story to tell. But as it stands, we *do* have a story to tell of God's amazing grace — and our story is their story too!

One day when we all stand before Jesus, our partners who willingly and obediently put fuel in the tank of this ministry will share in the reward for the many manifestations of God's grace and glory that took place in a land in desperate need of His touch.

## Crumbs From the Table

I want to share one more scripture to underscore the importance partners have played in the success of our ministry. In the gospel of Matthew, we read that Jesus was visited by a woman whose daughter was vexed by demon spirits. Although she was a foreigner, she asked Jesus for help. Jesus answered her, "It is not meet to take the children's bread, and to cast it to dogs" (Matthew 15:26).

This woman was smart enough to know that Jesus was correct, and she knew that she had no legal basis to ask Him for help. But she appealed to Him on the basis of His mercy, saying, "…Truth, Lord: yet the dogs eat of the crumbs which fall from their masters' table" (Matthew 15:27).

The word "dogs" in this verse is a translation of the Greek word *kunos*, a word that depicts what some would call a "mooch" that hung around the edges of the table to steal leftovers and crumbs that fell from the table. Imagine it — this is how this woman described herself and her daughter! It was the equivalent of her saying, "I know people think we're low-life moochers that don't deserve a thing. But even dogs get to eat crumbs from the table. Will You please have mercy on us and share a few crumbs of Your power and blessings with us? I realize we have no right to your overflowing blessings, but, please…Your table is so full. Is it possible for my daughter and me to have a few of the crumbs that fall from Your table?"

I share this story because when our family moved to the lands of the former USSR, some people in the Western world said, "The people of the former USSR deserve all the bad things that are happening to them. They've been an atheistic, socialist-communist system that stood opposed to us and sent Christians to languish in prisons and even to be executed. They have no right to ask us for anything!" Some even argued, "Why should we share our financial blessings with them? We've worked hard for our blessings, and they just want to mooch off us."

It was true that Western Christians did not *have* to lift one finger to help them, but God miraculously touched believers' hearts, and they generously opened their pocketbooks to give. God was moving mightily in the lands of the USSR, but the people who lived there had no funds to support this mighty move. But God sent partners who came on board to send monthly financial gifts, and those people began to give generously. In comparison to the lands of the former USSR, the Western Church was rich. Even crumbs that fell from their tables were so much compared to what existed in that part of the world — *it was enough to make a Gospel difference!*

Because partners were willing to share their resources with those who needed "crumbs," we were enabled to take the Gospel of Jesus Christ into a part of the world that desperately needed a merciful touch. And we needed a lot of "crumbs" to do the job because the work was escalating at an unimaginable speed on multiple fronts.

## The Power of God *Explodes* in Our Church — and I Almost Stopped a Revival

As I noted in the last chapter, our church started in the former communist auditorium at the Academy of Sciences in Riga on Easter 1993. Satan had tried his hardest to stop us, but the power of God pushed back those forces of darkness, and the church was born in the power of the Spirit. We saw signs, wonders, and mighty deeds as throngs of people came forward to get saved when we started the church. It was a real-life book-of-Acts scenario with every imaginable kind of miracle taking place!

But most churches at that time still operated underground because they had been illegal due to the atheistic regime that had ruled that part of the world for so long. So when we began to publicly announce our meetings and make a "commotion," it garnered a lot of amazing attention. What was happening in our church was being talked about in all the underground churches and even in the newspapers and TV news. But as things were getting rolling, something very ugly took place between another pastor and me in Riga that I am not proud of, but God used it to teach me an important lesson.

At that time, there were only a handful of "aboveground" churches in Riga because nearly all the others tried to conceal their church activities from the sight of the former KGB, now the secret-security services. One of those who dared to go "aboveground" started his own church and declared that he and his congregation were going to lead the way forward for the next generation of believers in Riga. About the time God instructed me to start our church, his church was the most progressive and boisterous church in Riga — they had made quite a noise within the newly emerging Christian community.

But there were things I didn't like about this pastor or his church. For example, some of the things he taught rubbed me the wrong way. And I didn't like what I perceived to be an arrogant attitude toward other churches in Riga. He had publicly bad-mouthed a lot of the underground churches. Hearing someone talk like that really irked me. It was true that some of the other churches were a little stuck in the traditions of their past; nevertheless their congregations were filled with good, faithful people, many of whom had spent time in prison for their faith. I felt they deserved respect.

And when Denise and I started our church, it seemed this other pastor wasn't very happy about it. We were on TV every day, giving voice to the Gospel in the nation where it *seemed* he wanted spiritual preeminence. When our church began to grow quickly, he may have felt threatened and protective of his own flock and his work in that virgin, aboveground territory that was the new Latvia. But one day he started a war of words with me, and I engaged the battle! Unfortunately, a verbal feud marked by raging carnality erupted between me and this other pastor.

Back and forth, we began to publicly rip at each other with our words. It was shameful and revealed immaturity in both of us. But I wrongly convinced myself that someone needed to stand up to him — and since no one else would do it — then that someone would be me! I was ready to keep up the fight till the end to "win" this feud. What ensued between him and me was so ugly that even today — decades later — people still remember the mud-slinging that took place between this pastor and me in those days. It was *really* nasty and ugly.

Then the Holy Spirit stopped me long enough to pose a question to my mind: *Rick, do you want to keep having a revival in your life and your church?* I replied, "Yes, Lord, You know I do." He asked me again, *Are you absolutely sure you want to keep having revival in your church?* I answered, "Yes, Lord, You know I do."

A third time, the Holy Spirit asked, *How badly do you want revival to continue in your church?* I answered, "Lord, You know how desperately I want to see revival continue in our church. I'll do anything You ask of me if it will bring a great move of God to the world." And that's when He answered me, *Then I am requiring you to deal with your wrong attitude toward this man, because this foul attitude in your heart will stop you from experiencing the move of God I want to give you.*

I argued, "*My* attitude? What about *his* attitude? Have You forgotten that he is the one who picked this fight, not me!" I even told the Lord, "My family gave up everything to move here, and he could have welcomed and supported me, but instead he has been ugly from the very start. He is the one who started this feud, not me!"

But then the Lord explicitly told me that I was to go to him and repent for my wrong attitude toward him. Persistent in my tone, I replied to the Lord, "And what about *him*, Lord? What are You going to do about all the wrong things he has said and done against *me?*"

I'll never forget what the Holy Spirit said to me at that moment: *I'm not talking to you about this man and what I'll require him to do. I'm talking to you about YOU. I will deal with him for what he has done to you, but right now I'm dealing with YOU for your immature reactions to him.*

I definitely wasn't ready for what the Holy Spirit said to me next. He instructed me to get in the car, drive across town, go into that pastor's office...*and GET ON MY KNEES IN FRONT OF HIM and repent for every ugly thing I had heard and believed and said to others about him.*

*Ugh!* That was the *last* thing I wanted to do, but I *knew* the Holy Spirit had told me to do it.

When the Holy Spirit asked me to go to this fellow minister and get on my knees in front of him, my first response was, "*NO, I WON'T DO IT!*

I'm *not* giving that man the gratification of seeing me on my knees in front of him. I don't want to give him the pleasure!" You see, I was *certain* that the moment I walked out of his office, he would tell everyone, "*RICK RENNER* has bowed before me today!"

For two months, I heard the still, small voice of the Holy Spirit asking me again and again, *Are you going to obey Me? Are you going to do what I've asked you to do? Are you going to go to that pastor, get on your knees, and repent for your attitude toward him?*

I argued with the Lord for two months about the matter, but He just kept saying, *Rick, do you really want to keep having revival or do you want it to stop? If you're going to really experience revival, you have to do what I'm requiring you to do.*

It got to the point that the Lord was interrupting my prayer time every day, saying, *Are you going to obey Me? Are you going to obey Me? Are you going to obey Me?* At last, I threw in the towel and said, "*Yes, yes, YES* — I will obey You!"

After telling my associate what the Holy Spirit was requiring me to do, I asked him to go with me for moral support, and I drove across town to this other pastor's office. As I sat across the room from the pastor, he and I uncomfortably talked about the weather, politics, and even about our children. I was trying to buy time, hoping he would apologize first. But, finally, when we didn't have anything else to talk about, I knew the time had come for me to do what I had come to do. At that moment, I had a choice. I could get up and leave that room with unfinished business and fail this assignment, or I could slip down on my knees and do what Jesus had requested me to do.

After breathing a deep sigh, I told this pastor, "I'm here today to do something that the Lord is requiring me to do." I continued with all the sincerity I could muster: "I've heard a lot of bad things you've said about me and I am deeply disturbed about some of your teachings that I believe to be very wrong. But I'm not here to deal with you. Today I'm here to deal with *me*, because I've sinned against you. You have offended me, and as a result of my offense, I have believed every negative thing any person has told me about you, and I have said unkind things about you. I've been wrong, and I have been a source of division. Today I'm here to ask you to forgive me."

My heart cried out to hear this man respond, "Well, Rick, I have said a lot of bad things about you, so I need to ask you to forgive me as well." But instead of apologizing to me or acknowledging that he had done anything wrong, he just stared at me with what felt to me like a look of glee in his eyes. At the time, it seemed to me that he was relishing every moment of my contrition.

Then I heard the Holy Spirit say, *Now it's time to get on your knees in front of him.* I inwardly argued with the Lord: *Please don't ask me to get on my knees!* But the Holy Spirit quietly spoke to my heart again, *Rick, you need to get on your knees in front of this man to properly ask for his forgiveness.*

### The Holy Spirit Said, '*BOTH Knees!*'

Hesitantly, I lowered myself down on one knee, thinking that if I did it halfway, on just one knee, it would be enough. But I heard the Holy Spirit say, *BOTH knees!*

I knew full well at that moment that if I wanted to please the Lord and to keep experiencing His power in our church and ministry, I had to fully obey Him no matter how humiliated I felt or how this man responded. I also knew that if I didn't get it right this time, I would have to come back a second time. God would *not* let me off the hook. So I slowly lowered myself down onto both knees and looked up at this pastor and said, "Brother, I repent before God and before you for the ugly attitude and words that I've fostered and perpetuated against you."

From that day forward, I didn't care anymore what this man ever said or didn't say about me. I had done what the Lord required of me, and I was free. Even more, I began to take steps to pursue peace with this pastor. Denise and I invited him and his wife to our home for dinners on multiple occasions. I also invited him to speak in our church, and I attended his church conferences. Later, this pastor also acted on what the Lord spoke to *his* heart to do in order to pursue peace with *me.*

Over many years, that pastor and I became cherished friends. Today when I go back to visit Riga, we meet for breakfast and share from our hearts with each other about life and ministry and what the Lord is doing in our hearts and lives. We have a mutual and genuine respect for one another. The devil had very different plans for our relationship — and for the Christian community in that city who would be ill-affected by our bitter feuding. But we chose to thwart those demonic plans by doing what God told us to do in order to pursue peace with each other.

When this pastor in Riga was interviewed for this book, I became even more thankful for how the grace of God can turn a bad situation into a good one. He said, "I have a very good relationship with Rick Renner, who is a very special person in my life." He remarkably added, "I don't remember one time when Rick ever argued with someone. In fact, people would think you were joking if you said to them that Rick Renner got mad about something."

Well, that's how I endeavor to live my life, but it certainly wasn't the case back then when I fell into the trap of offense and allowed myself to be drawn into a public *blitz* with a fellow believer and minister of the Gospel. But, oh, how the grace of God can make up for our bad attitudes and wrong actions. If we are willing to do what God requires, even the worst relationships can be turned around.

That pastor added, "I'm so proud of Rick and how he's broadcasting on so many channels every day all over the world. He's really an example to the younger generation of how to work hard, how to watch after your body and your health, and how to have a good physical presence — he's doing such a good job. Rick and Denise have been amazing and they are still amazing. I have great gratitude to God for my dear friend, Rick Renner."

Instead of that earlier spirit of competition in our younger years, that pastor amazingly stated, "When a star or professional comes to a stage, the stage quickly becomes small because of his or her presence. That's Rick. When he steps onto a platform, he brings the bigness of God's presence with him, and it fills not only the stage, but the whole auditorium. In fact, that 'presence' is so big that when he and his family left Riga and moved to Moscow, we who remained could feel his absence."

As I look back on that day when I knelt before that pastor in his office, I'd have to say that it was one of the hardest things I'd ever done in my life up to that moment. But I learned a priceless lesson through that experience — that is, if we will obey God by responding to an offense in humility and love, we'll not only dismantle the enemy's trap, but we'll also create a platform for God to move on both sides of the situation in a way that will honor Him and promote His purposes. If I had refused to humble my heart and repent for my own role in all that ugliness between us, my lack of repentance could have bottlenecked everything God wanted to do in our lives and ministries. He had *nations* He wanted to touch through both of us!

As soon as that issue was taken care of and I was beyond that spiritual hurdle, God poured more growth out on us. The church continued experiencing a divine outpouring; the TV network was expanding at a breathtaking speed; and tons of mail continued to arrive at our offices from viewers. In fact, by this time, our TV programs were being broadcast in most places across the USSR.

If I showed you a map of our coverage, it would quickly become clear that God had done the *impossible* through us. We were broadcasting on more than eighty large stations, middle-range stations, small stations, and in any area where a door opened. In fact, if a door opened, we automatically walked through it because we knew that regardless of where the programs were broadcast, we would be speaking to masses of people who had never heard the Gospel or the teaching of the Bible. Even though we didn't have the money to do any of it, we had a directive from Heaven.

Bishop Nikolai Gribs, one of the most respectable Russian bishops in all of Latvia, vividly recalled those early years when he said, "In those days when tons of mail were coming in from television, Rick and his team answered every one of those letters that came into his office. There were a lot of questions coming from people because they knew nearly nothing about God or the Bible. The people who wrote the letters were deeply affected by Rick's programs and by the fact that he really answered them and didn't forget about them — when people wrote to Rick, it wasn't just a letter they sent into 'outer space.' Oh, I remember those boxes and boxes filled with letters — stacks and stacks of letters from people with so many needs."

He added, "When the Iron Curtain fell, it provided an opportunity for different missionaries and missions organizations to come do work in the USSR. Over time, fewer and fewer came, but the most faithful stayed — and Rick and his family were the most faithful from those earliest years. Rick was a big blessing because he could speak to all kinds of people — to ministers, businessmen, and to lay people. His teaching was simple, but straightforward and strong. He wasn't trying to build a career and didn't have his mind on himself. His mind and focus really was on us. We watched as he gave us his life and experience, and he did it without any ulterior motives or strings attached. Most important was, we could see that the way Rick spoke was really the way he lived. His words and his actions matched."

Bishop Nikolai concluded, "Rick — he left everything he was building in America to come to us and was willing to do whatever God was telling him to do. What God did through Rick and his family encouraged all of us to do whatever God would ever ask us to do. By watching Rick, we learned how to do the work of the ministry honorably and correctly."

## More Obstacles and Hurdles

As I noted at the first of this chapter, no new church facility had been built in Riga for almost six decades. However, I knew we needed to have our own building if the church was to have a prosperous future. But how do you announce a building program in a country that has never even heard of such a thing?

Bishop Sergei Ryakhovsky, bishop of the *Centralized Religious Organization of the Russian United Union of Christians of Evangelical Faith* (POCXBE) and one of Russia's most revered spiritual leaders, said, "Back in the 1990s, no one even dreamed about having his own church building. We didn't even know that would ever be a possibility. Everything abruptly changed and we were all in the process of trying to figure out how to maneuver our lives amidst the radical new reforms that were emerging. I don't recall *anyone* ever thinking about purchasing land for a church or considering the notion of constructing a church building at that time. That was such a brand-new idea."

But how do you start a building program in a crashed economic system where people primarily bring tithes of vegetables and flowers to church? How do you convince them we needed our own land and building? Would I be able to persuade them to believe it was possible to purchase government-controlled land and use it to construct our own church building?

Because everything was still basically being run in the same old communist style at that time, it meant that most real estate belonged to the government and was still under state control. There simply wasn't much land to buy. Would we be able to find land when most of it was up for grabs by hordes of people getting in line to claim it was theirs before communism?

And what were the odds that the government would actually give us permission to build a church building? Since no church building had been constructed for nearly six decades, what kind of regulations would the government put on us or try to use against us? And what about the local mafia trying to get their fingers into the whole deal. How do we keep *them* out of our affairs?

So many things were happening simultaneously. I get a kick out of people who say, "Never do anything without a plan" because although we always carefully performed our "due diligence" in new ventures, we rarely had the luxury of taking a long time to make a plan. God was opening so many doors so fast in those days, I often only had minutes to decide how to forge ahead! It was truly a historical moment — similar to that which occurred in the book of Acts when God's power was unleashed on the pagan world. But in addition to everything else that was gloriously erupting all around us, I knew God was asking me to add a building program to my plate of activities!

## THE BIG ANNOUNCEMENT

I labored in prayer and thought and thought about how to make the big announcement that I was going to lead our church into a new building program. I knew it was insane, naturally speaking, but it was the impossible thing God was asking us to do. To a visitor's curious eye, it didn't look like anything much had progressed in that once idyllic city since the devastation of World War II. To construct a church building in a place so stranded in the past would surely provoke the powers of darkness to oppose us.

I privately shared my vision with Denise, then with our sons, and then with the top members of our team. Denise asked, "How will we ever pay for this? Will the government permit it? There is a deficit of everything here, so where will you find building materials to construct a church building?"

These were all good questions that I could not answer. Regardless, I knew I was on track with God's plan and needed to bring the vision to the church at one of our services in the old communist auditorium of the Academy of Sciences.

Finally, I decided "how" I would make the big announcement. While on a short trip to the United States, I went to a large light-fixture store to look for three massive brass chandeliers. Once I found the ones I liked, I purchased them — not even knowing how to get them back across the sea to Riga. But finally I returned to Riga with those enormous chandeliers.

One may ask, "Why didn't you just buy them in Riga?" Because *there WERE no chandeliers in Riga*. Riga's stores were still nearly vacant due to the economic collapse of the USSR.

*Chandeliers?* You must be kidding — we were grateful to find a regular supply of bread in those days!

Every week, our family arrived early for church services because Denise was the praise-and-worship leader in those days. But on that particular Sunday, we arrived especially early with the largest of the chandeliers in a big box in the back of our minivan. We rushed into the auditorium with that enormous chandelier and began to assemble it in the center of the stage beneath the gargantuan emblem of the USSR and two immense cameos that bore the faces of Soviet communist heroes Marx and Lenin.

When the brightly colored, lavish-looking chandelier was assembled, we then covered it with a blanket and left it in the middle of the stage. As people came in that Sunday, I could hear them questioning among themselves, "What is that huge covered thing in the center of the platform?"

Sunday service began as usual with praise and worship — then when it was time for me to speak, I invited Denise and our sons to come to the platform with me. With my family at my side, I said, "Today I have an announcement to make to you. I know many of you have been wondering about this huge object under this blanket in the middle of the stage. So let me show you."

I pulled the blanket off the chandelier, and I could hear people gasping in awe. Nothing like that existed anywhere — not in any store in Riga, not in the whole nation of Latvia. Compared to the few dismal, Soviet-looking products that could be found in a handful of stores, this looked like a shimmering diamond. The lights from the massive Stalin-style chandelier over the top of our communist-style auditorium caused the brass in our beautiful light fixture to gleam even brighter.

Then I said, "Church, I know you're asking why this gorgeous chandelier is sitting in the middle of our stage today. The reason is, this fixture will one day soon be hanging in the new building of the Riga Good News Church — the building that *we* are going to build!"

As I finished with my announcement about the church building that we as a congregation were going to build, I expected excitement and applause in response — but, instead, the entire auditorium fell eerily silent, with *no* excitement, *no* applause, *no reaction at all.*

There was such dead silence, I felt as if I could hear my heart beating in my chest. And when I looked into the eyes of that packed auditorium, rather than seeing faith, I saw *fear.* The people were looking back at me as if I had lost my mind to actually think we could buy land or build a building. I could almost hear them thinking, *Pastor Rick, have you forgotten where you are? This is a ridiculous idea!*

Joel Renner, barely four at the time, remembered, "Dad had the whole family come up on stage to help him announce the big news. The chandelier was on the platform as a part of the announcement. When the building was finally built, that very chandelier was hung in the new building, and they were excited *then*, but they were not so excited when they first saw it on the stage at the Academy of Sciences. But we as a family were very excited about Dad's wonderful announcement that day."

I wish I could tell you it got better over the course of that service but, indeed, it got worse. Some laughed out loud, and a few others got up and walked out. This idea was so new, so radical and unheard of, they simply did not know how to react. But I knew God had given me direction, so I pushed their negative images out of my mind and *pretended* they were excited, which is often what leaders must do in the face of opposition if they are going to lead the way into the future.

I took the entire service to say that a process of looking for land would begin, and that day, Denise and I made a financial commitment by pledging the largest single financial gift we had ever given in our lives to that moment. I felt that if we were going to ask people to give more than vegetables and flowers, we needed to set the example by sowing our entire life's savings into the project.

## It Was Official and the Search for Land Was *On*!

True to my word, the next day, the hunt was on for a piece of land to buy for our church. For several months afterward, it felt like we had transitioned into the real-estate business as we scoured the city looking for our new property. As I told you, it was not easy to buy land or property. Lands, houses, and apartments had been confiscated by the Communist Party at the end of World War II. There was hardly any private land anywhere — and if there was, long lines of people were trying to reclaim it as their own.

If you think the economic mess I described in previous chapters was bizarre and sad, it doesn't even *begin* to compare to how messed up property ownership was at that time. The communist regime had sent many property owners to Siberian prisons, and multitudes of Jewish property owners perished in the local holocaust — and nearly all the ownership documents from pre-Soviet years had been burned or otherwise destroyed.

Now in a frenzied state of trying to recoup what was lost, thousands of people were hunting for any shred of evidence to prove they were the previous legal owners so they could reclaim their real estate. Because documents had disappeared or had been burned, criminal rings emerged who were more than happy to take bribes to produce false documents for whoever was willing to pay the highest price. And people were literally being murdered over the issue of property.

*And now I was going to lead our church to purchase property!*

If I had understood the full complications of this process, I might have *also* thought I had lost my mind! It was a good thing I didn't understand it all. In retrospect, I can see that my ignorance of these complexities were a benefit to my faith. I simply didn't comprehend the hurdles we would need to surmount to purchase a piece of land to construct the first new church building in Riga in many decades.

After a relatively brief search for land, we located a large piece of empty land near the edge of the Bikernieki Forest. The five acres we found was situated on the far side of Riga and was considered to be an unusable piece of swamp land among a seemingly unending number of tall Soviet-style apartment buildings.

Purchasing swampy land was not ideal, but it was the only large piece of land that could be purchased at that time, so it was our only option. But what I really liked was the fact that the neighborhood was home to the largest Russian-speaking part of the city.

Our son Joel recalled in retrospect, "The land we bought was in the middle of the forest. It felt like it was in the 'boondocks' because it was on the far side of Riga. But after we developed it and moved in, it seemed the whole city began to migrate toward the church, and the surrounding community got a lot better."

I find Joel's comment about the city's moving in that direction very interesting because that is exactly what happened. Today if you visit the Riga Good News Church, you will find it is surrounded by fabulous new buildings and shopping malls. None of that was there when we bought that swamp!

Jesus promised in Luke 4:18 that when the Gospel is preached to people in abject poverty, their economic status will begin to change. The Gospel is so powerful and so filled with good news that if impoverished, poverty-stricken people hear and believe it, it really will change their economic status. We are witnesses that this is exactly what happened in the region where we built the Riga building. The whole area around the church literally changed after the Gospel began to be proclaimed there. We saw this in Riga and years later we saw it again in Moscow. *The Gospel is an economic game-changer!*

But after finding the land, we began to go through *mountains upon mountains* of documents to see who it belonged to before Latvia was incorporated into the USSR — to discover who had legal rights to it now.

Then I wrote to our ministry partners in America to inform them we were going to start a building program. I felt such trepidation about writing that letter because our family was still living in that country on a temporary visa, and we had many enemies in the government who wanted to kick us out. What if we started this whole process only to be deported to the United States by the Latvian government? Or what if someone in Riga paid a huge bribe to the system to get us evicted from the process? Also, this huge undertaking would be a trigger for the mafia to try to get involved. All of this was so difficult to explain to people from an orderly society in the Western world, but I knew we were to move forward, so I forged ahead by faith and wrote a letter to our God-given partners.

Our base of partners was not large, but those who were with us were *really* with us. I knew that even if they did their very best, it would take a far greater miracle than I could imagine to pay for this land and to construct a building. And with all the "unknowns" in that "wild, wild west" environment at that time, it was *predictable* that the *unpredictable* would happen somewhere along the way to skyrocket all the costs. So in an unstable, volatile environment like that, how do you present a fixed building cost to potential supporters?

But once again — in the same way that no one had ever pioneered a TV ministry in our part of the world — God was trusting me to do something no other church had done in more than six decades. And he was asking me to do it at the same time I was using my faith to build and pay for the TV ministry. As much as I knew God was calling us to do this — and as much as I believed all things were possible with Him — what He was asking us to do was no small task!

### How Does God Choose Whom He Will Use?

People frequently ask, "How does God choose whom He wants to use?" This is an important question to ask, and it's one that you *should* ask if you desire to be used by the Lord.

Since God has given me a number of assignments to accomplish things in the lands of the USSR, I, too, once asked, "Lord, why did You choose me?

You could have chosen many people who were more talented than me." That is when I heard the Holy Spirit answer, "I chose you because I knew you would obey what I asked you to do. You are right that there are people more gifted and more talented, but your willingness to obey is why I chose you."

As I look at those whom God uses in a significant way, it is obvious to me that He doesn't choose people simply because of raw talent or gifts. There must be another, higher reason that causes Him to reach out and lay His hand on an individual to use him or her in a special way. *What is that reason?*

In First Corinthians 4:2, the apostle Paul gave us *one answer* to this question that has meant so much to me. He stated this so categorically that it seems this quality is at the top of God's list of requirements for those who will do His work. Paul wrote, "Moreover it is required in stewards that a man be found *faithful.*"

The word "faithful" in this verse comes from the Greek word *pistos*, which is derived from the word *pistis*, the Greek word *faith*. However, in First Corinthians 4:2, the word *pistos* doesn't refer to faith as a spiritual force; rather, it denotes *a person who is faithful.* This is a person whom God has found to be *faithful, trustworthy, reliable, dependable, true,* and *unfailing.*

But how does God know if a person is faithful, trustworthy, reliable, dependable, true, and unfailing?

Paul wrote, "Moreover it is required in stewards that a man be *found* faithful" (1 Corinthians 4:2). The word "found" is the Greek word *heurisko*, which means *to find* or *to discover.* It is where we get the word "eureka," and it depicts a discovery made as a result of careful observance. It tells us that God is carefully watching our actions and reactions in life. He is watching to see how we treat people, how we respond to pressure, and whether or not we have the tenacity to stay on track when distractions try to thwart our obedience. Before He taps us on the shoulder to give us a new assignment, He carefully observes to see how well we have done with the last assignment. Did we do it as He expected? Did we finish it completely or did we leave parts of the assignment incomplete? Did we do it in a way that glorified the name of Jesus?

The word "found" emphatically means that God watches us over a long period of time and in many different circumstances to see if we are faithful, trustworthy, reliable, dependable, true, and unfailing. If you were looking for someone to use in a mighty way, wouldn't you first watch a person's character and actions to see if he or she was someone you could depend on for a big assignment?

Similarly, God wants to know if we are faithful, trustworthy, reliable, dependable, true, and unfailing. Rather than take a shot in the dark and simply hope for the best, He bases His decision on *discovery*. So what has God *found* about you? The answer to this question is so important that it may determine whether God gives you another new assignment!

There is nothing more serious than eternal business, so before God promotes someone to preside over greater matters, He watches to see if that person is *"found faithful."*

Since God is watching, you can see how vital it is that you take a serious look at yourself to see what He is finding as He watches what you do, the promises you make, and the seriousness with which you obey Him and His Word. Has God found that He can trust you, or would He be wiser to choose someone else? If you and I want to move into a higher realm of responsibility that holds more exciting and significant assignments in life, we must do everything we can to be found faithful in what we are doing right now.

"Faithful" before God was something I desired to be in His assignment to us in the former Soviet Union. And after finding that swampy land and doing our due diligence — working with one government organization after another — we were cleared to purchase those five acres in the middle of that big Russian-speaking community. With my assistant Andrey at my side, I met the seller at a legal office in downtown Riga to sign all the documents, and per our agreement, we paid the full sum for the land in cash.

Cash was the way everyone did business back in those days. There were only a handful of private banks, and the ones that were in existence were deemed very risky. As I told you in previous chapters, sometimes insiders in a bank tipped off local criminals when people made large cash withdrawals, so people generally stayed away from banks because they were considered dangerous.

When all the documents were signed, I handed the seller a large plastic bag filled with a mountain of partner-entrusted dollars, including the Renner family's entire life's savings. We watched as the seller pulled out all the cash and laid it on the notary's desk and counted it in front of us to make sure it was all there. Then we bade each other farewell, and we ended that day as official owners of the largest "swamp" in the city of Riga!

## Now I Was Being Called a 'Hypnotist' — and I Made Front-Page News!

That night, Denise and I and our boys went to bed with thankful hearts that the land deal was done. The next day, I went to buy a few groceries for our family. As I waited to pay at the register, I noticed a weird, *eerie* illustration plastered all over the front page of a national newspaper.

In fact, the entire front page of the newspaper was covered from top to bottom with a graphic of a man who had a huge hand, like a claw, that tightly gripped the top of another man's head. The fingernails of the hand were curled like claws and dug into the sides of the man's head and forehead. The man whose head was being gripped had eyes that were streaked with long root-like blood vessels that spread through the whites of his glazed eyes. The man whose mind was being gripped looked as if he had been hypnotized or was under some kind of mind control. The huge boldfaced headline above the full-page graphic illustration said: "DO WHAT I TELL YOU TO DO!"

I wondered, *What is this terrible-looking article?* But when I lowered my eyes to see what the article was about, I was stunned to realize it was written entirely about *me*!

The whole purpose of that front-page illustration and article was to allege that I was a *professional hypnotist* who used hypnotism to mentally control all the people in our Riga church. That claw-looking hand was supposed to be *my hand*, and the words, "DO WHAT I TELL YOU TO DO!" were supposed to be *my words*!

Someone who hated what we were doing gave the word for the newspaper to attack. This was a true-life case of "principalities and powers" trying to smear our name. But this ridiculous article was only a foretaste of many articles about me that would appear over the years.

This particular article was so lengthy that it continued to the center of the newspaper where it became a full two-page spread — all about me and my alleged hypnotic powers and my ability to control the people who attended our church. But in that spread, the photos and illustrations wickedly changed — from a graphical illustration of a crazed hypnotist to photos of Germans saluting Adolf Hitler, plus photos of Eastern-cult followers mindlessly following their cult leaders. And right smack in the center of that two-page spread was a huge photo of me, prominently positioned between Hitler and those cult leaders!

The article went on and on about how I was the new Latvian menace and should be feared by all. To be honest, I was stunned, but also found it to be quite hilarious — that is, until people began dealing with me differently.

Denise and I and our sons had given our *all* to move there and had gained nothing financially by relocating to this former Soviet land. We had faced challenges with mafia criminal organizations, withstood accusations that we were secretly working for the CIA, survived horrible acts of sabotage from a ministry insider, and emptied our personal bank account to help buy land for the church. Yet the article accused us of moving there for an easier life and to financially take advantage of people! It was unbelievable to me, but it was typical *fake news* that regrettably affects and influences a lot of naive readers.

### When Storm Winds Arise

Working on the front lines of ministry for most of my life, I learned early on that anytime you're in a leading position in battle and are doing something significant for the Kingdom of God, the enemy's attacks against your life will escalate. Even Jesus came under such an attack when He was preparing to cast a legion of demons out of the demoniac of Gadara (Mark 4:35-41). Violent and destructive winds seemed to come from out of nowhere to capsize Jesus' boat and drown Him and His disciples in the middle of the lake. Verse 37 says, "And there arose a great storm of wind, and the waves beat into the ship, so that it was now full."

The verse says, "And there arose..." The words "there arose" are translated from a form of the Greek word *ginomai*, which here describes something that happens unexpectedly or something that catches one off guard. This word contains an element of surprise. Mark 4:37 plainly tells us that these winds took them by surprise that night.

Remember that many of Jesus' disciples were fishermen before they were called into the ministry, so they knew the weather around the area of that sea and perfectly understood the weather patterns of that region. If a natural storm had been brewing that night, these men would never have taken their little boat out into the middle of the sea. Therefore, you can be sure that when they began their journey that night, it was a perfect night for sailing!

But suddenly and unexpectedly, "there arose" a great storm of wind. Notice Mark tells us it was "a *great* storm of wind." The word "great" is taken from the word *mega*, which denotes something of magnificent proportions. It is where we get the idea of "mega bills," "mega work," "mega tired," and "megaphone." But by using this word, we know that this was a *mega* storm!

And notice Mark doesn't say it was a thunderstorm or a rainstorm; he tells us that it was "a great storm of *wind*." The word "wind" is taken from a Greek word that describes turbulence or a terribly violent wind. Therefore, the storm that came against Jesus that night was an unseen storm. Though the storm couldn't be visually seen, one could feel the effects of it.

This was an attempt of the enemy to capsize Jesus and His crew before they reached the other side, because on the other side, in the country of the Gadarenes, Satan had a prized possession called the demoniac of Gadara. The devil probably worried that if Jesus' ship reached the other side, Jesus would perform one of the greatest miracles of His ministry, and the enemy would lose his prized possession, which is *exactly* what happened.

So when Jesus was on the edge of a breakthrough, an unexpected attack of violent and destructive turbulence came down upon Him and His disciples to stop them from reaching the other side. This was a preemptive strike of the devil to undo the work of God.

But this was a great opportunity for the disciples to learn that Jesus Christ is Lord of the wind and the waves! After He exercised authority over this unseen turbulence and spoke to the waves of the sea, the Word says that "...the wind ceased, and there was a great calm" (Mark 4:39).

The fact that this attack came just as Jesus was on the brink of a major miracle is not uncommon. This is normally the time when attacks occur. Since such attacks came against Jesus, we can be sure that the enemy will attempt to do this to us as well. Therefore, we must mentally and spiritually prepare ourselves to deal with attacks. We are to "put on the whole armor of God" (Ephesians 6:13) and take authority over the wind and the waves that come against our lives — our families, our businesses, our finances, and our bodies — just as Jesus took authority over the wind and the waves that came against Him.

## A Moment Ripe for Attack Is Precisely When You Need To Hold Your Position!

My experience in the Lord has shown me that when you are on the front lines, you must understand that one of the devil's strategies is to attack you at a *key moment.*

If you understand this, it will help you overcome his attacks and move forward to win fresh victories and take new territory for the Kingdom of God. If it gets tough where you are, you must overcome it and get the job done — even if it causes your life to be temporarily uncomfortable. *Nothing* that changes this lost world and drives back Satan's forces is easy.

I can tell you that our family had many opportunities to escape from difficult assignments by quitting and simply abandoning the call. But remember, *anyone* can quit — only the victorious persevere. And God's delivering power will always be yours if you'll take it. However, He asks that you stay at your post, refuse to give in to pressure, and stay steady to enforce the victory Jesus won for you.

Friend, a big lesson in our story that I want to get across to you is that the devil doesn't know how to overcome believers who refuse to surrender. If you'll refuse to give in to your emotions and determine to stay on track with God and His Word, doing what He has told you to do, every storm will eventually blow away. Never forget that Satan always backs up, backs off, and steers clear of the Word of God that you'll hold fast to in your heart and in your mouth.

That's what we did in the case of this public slander in the national newspaper. Instead of giving up, throwing in the towel, and surrendering to this public campaign against us, we said, "Let's throw a party to celebrate the purchase of our land and publicly dedicate it to God!"

## This Was God's Land — and God Never Forgets a Prayer or a Promise!

No one in our Riga church had ever heard of a building program *or* a property dedication, so about two thousand believers showed up to witness that historical event! Everywhere we looked at that celebration, we saw brand-new Christians worshiping and rejoicing in the Lord on our land. I think the experience must have been similar to what they felt in the Old Testament when the foundations of the temple were being put back in place again. No one had ever witnessed such an event — it was a truly historical moment.

In the days just before the dedication, we received a call that a very elderly man had something serious he needed to tell us, and I agreed to meet with him. As I sat with him, I was mesmerized as this very wrinkled gentleman from the early Latvian freedom years related his story and the purpose of our meeting.

He proceeded to tell me that before Latvia was absorbed into the Soviet Union, the earlier owners of our new land had an experience with the power of the Holy Spirit on that exact piece of property. Because God had mightily visited them there, they dedicated that land for God's purposes.

Over all the years that Latvia had been entrenched in atheistic communism, it seemed the prayers of those previous landowners would never be answered and that the land would never be used for God. Those who had dedicated it in prayer died without knowing that it would one day become the home of the Riga Good News Church. But they died in faith that one day God would answer their prayers and use the land that they had dedicated to His purposes.

Similarly, Hebrews 11 tells us about people who believed God to do something, but they never saw it come to pass in their lifetimes. Rather than despair that they hadn't seen the fulfillment of their prayers, they shifted their faith to believe the next generation would see it.

For example, Hebrews 11:21 tells us, "By faith Jacob, when he was a dying, blessed both the sons of Joseph; and worshipped, *leaning* upon the top of his staff." God made promises to Jacob that this patriarch never saw fulfilled in his lifetime, but rather than think God had failed him, he leaned on the top of his staff in his old age and prophesied that the fulfillment would come to the next generation. He died in faith even though he had not personally seen all of God's promise to him fulfilled.

I'm sure those earlier generations who had consecrated that five acres to God wondered at times if God had forgotten that they had dedicated this land for His use. But rather than give up, they, too, shifted their faith to believe that one day in the future, things would turn around and God would eventually use that piece of land. And without our having any knowledge of that fact until we spoke to the elderly man just days before our dedication, the Holy Spirit supernaturally led us directly to the land they had consecrated for His purposes.

*God NEVER forgets!*

## A National Convocation of Architects
## To Discuss Our New Building!

Once the land was dedicated, we began to search for an architect to help us design the new church building that we would begin soon to construct. God led us to a young and upcoming architect, but for that architect to work with us was a big risk for his career because notable governmental officials were against everything we were doing.

Many still believed we were secretly working for the CIA and they were so hostile toward us that for this young architect to work with us put his career in jeopardy. One day as he and our team were working together on our plans, God put a word in my heart for him. I prophesied that because he was willing to jeopardize his own career to help us, God would raise him up as a leader in the nation. That word was fulfilled years later when he was appointed the chief architect in the nation — and he never forgot the word that I prophesied over him.

Our architect was perplexed about what a modern church building should look like because the only church structures he knew of were the Middle Age cathedrals in Old Riga that dated back centuries. And soon the news of our plans to build a new church erupted into an uproar in the nationwide architectural community. Some architects were offended that the first such building was being constructed by a foreigner, while others who were atheistic thought we were a bunch of religious nuts. Believe me when I tell you that the architectural community nationwide was really stirred up by the news of what we were about to do. And backing them up were people in powerful positions who had long been opposed to us.

The architectural community demanded a national convocation of all the architects in the nation to meet in Riga to discuss the issue. I thought, *What? They're going to call together a national convocation to discuss our church building?* But that is exactly what happened!

As the days approached for the convocation, I wondered, *What is going to happen at this meeting? Why are they discussing our church when we never invited them to convene for a discussion? How much authority do they have over our building plans and over the building of the church itself?*

The day came for the big meeting in the Central House of Architects in Old Riga. I came early with Andrey and the man heading up our construction project. We were there to answer any questions the architects might pose to us. We sat in the stuffy atmosphere and waited for the meeting to begin. Finally, the nation's chief architect at that time opened the meeting with a statement and question. I'll summarize what I heard him say:

> Today we stand at a critical juncture in our history. We are here because Mr. Rick Renner has announced that he and his church are planning to construct a church building in Riga. This brings us to a serious dilemma because none of us in this room has ever seen or

participated in the construction of a religious building in our life-times. Today we must vote whether to permit this or not. If we give it our approval, we are obligated to discuss and debate what elements should be included in a modern church building. Since none of us knows the answers to these questions, I am now opening the floor for discussion and debate.

These fabulous, well-educated, brilliant architects didn't have a clue how to design a modern church building because they had lived under an atmosphere of godless atheism where the construction of churches had not been allowed. As I listened to their conversations, I realized again how miraculous it was that we were about to do something an entire generation had never seen done. And I was in awe of God who, through His own process of discovery, had found me faithful to lead this assignment.

These architects were particularly intrigued with what kind of elements needed to be included in a modern church. For example, since all that they'd ever seen or known were European cathedral-style churches, should the first modern church building in Riga be a cathedral? Since old European cathedrals had steeples with bells, should the first new modern church building in Riga need a steeple and bell?

And on and on it went. I even heard them ask, "Should it have a belfry? If it has a belfry, does it have to have bells? Do the bells have to be made of bronze? Can they be made of plastic? What should be in a church building in our generation?"

Nikolai Kulakevich, my interpreter and one of my associates at that time, corroborated my observations, saying, "For over sixty years, no church building had been built in the city of Riga. Only old existing churches were operating, but no new churches were being built. So when there was a question about what a church should look like, they had no answers. It was quite challenging for them."

I listened that day for *hours*, and it finally dawned on me that a part of their uproar was due to the fact that they did not want to be *excluded* from the process of something so historical. When we would finally build our building, it would be the making of a brand-new chapter in history, and these architects wanted a voice in the process so they could say they had been a part of it. When the meeting concluded that afternoon — after what seemed like an eternity of conversation — we walked out the door with their vote that we could proceed — *with* the stipulation that we would be sure to include a bell tower!

So with the approval of the architectural convocation in hand, we charged ahead to design the first church building to be constructed in almost sixty years. In retrospect, the convocation of architects was not an impediment to us and, in fact, the whole meeting and its outcome validated our young architect whom we had hired, and it provided him with a new level of credibility and respect that he had not previously enjoyed.

### The Renners Move From Jelgava to Riga

Until that time, our family's official residence had been in Jelgava — since the time we'd rented our first house in October 1991. But now that we were starting a building program and I'd have to be in Riga more often, Denise and I decided to relocate our family from Jelgava to Riga to be closer to our ministry offices and to the construction site. So we began to search for a new home for our family in Riga, which was about a forty-minute drive from Jelgava.

After searching for a residence large enough to suit our family, we found an old apartment in a once-elegant building constructed in 1898 that would meet our needs. This apartment was located in Riga's most prestigious neighborhood — that is, a neighborhood that *had* been prestigious, before the rule of communism.

Before communism, the walls of that apartment were covered with fine wallpaper, and magnificent chandeliers once hung from giant, hand-carved medallions in the center of the ceilings. The huge-sized crown molding that was wrapped around the ceilings of each room needed to be meticulously restored using instruments similar to those used by dentists.

Every room had intricately inlaid parquet floors, which we restored to match those that had existed before the Revolution. And the nine ceramic fireplaces — one for each big room, including the bedrooms — were the most magnificent features of the apartment. I'm sure that, originally, those fireplaces looked like they belonged in a museum. But now this apartment was abandoned and in such miserable condition that, really, it should have been condemned. It was a muddled labyrinth of mold, mildew, collapsed ceilings, and plaster falling off the walls.

In the earlier Soviet years, apartments like this one had been confiscated and converted into communal flats. And in the case of our apartment, this once majestic space had been divided into eight tiny apartments for eight families that shared one kitchen and one toilet! The people who lived there over a period of nearly fifty-five years had no respect whatsoever for this architectural treasure. Their total lack of care was most obvious in the bathroom. As men used the bathroom over the years, they had missed the toilet so many thousands of times that the acidic effect of the urine had literally burned a hole through the heavy flooring big enough to see straight through it into the apartment below!

It was shameful to see what had happened to this once-luxurious apartment where an elite class of people had formerly lived. This once-grandiose residence now only boasted of collapsed ceilings, crumbling plaster, and mold that had spread over large sections of the walls. To top it off, hooligans had painted derogatory words and nasty phrases on the walls throughout the apartment.

Because it was so trashed, the apartment was available for an unbelievably low price. Actually, no one else wanted it! But it was what we could afford, and we knew with work, it could be put back in order. Although dirt, grime, filth, and trash were heaped in huge piles in every room, we knew that this place was restorable if we would be willing to do what was necessary to bring it back to its former glory. So we purchased it and went to work restoring it at the same time we were building the Riga building — which meant we would be doing *more* parallel tasks!

No one from pre-Soviet years had ever come forward to lay claim to the apartment, and we'd wondered why. But as the restoration process took place and we began to peel fifty-five years of Soviet wallpaper back from decades of history, we made a discovery that took us off guard. When all the Soviet wallpaper was removed, we came upon nearly perfectly preserved Yiddish newspapers that were plastered over every inch of those walls. The papers had been used to level the surface before the next layer of exquisite wallpaper could be hung. When I saw those Yiddish papers, I understood that the original owners of the apartment had been Jewish — and the reason no original owners had ever come forward to claim the apartment is, they'd been exterminated in the holocaust. *Once again, it seemed like our destinies in Latvia were connected to the Latvian holocaust!*

City authorities told us a city-wide heating system would be connected to the building before winter, so we installed new pipes in the walls to carry the heat to every room. But as the weather turned cold and winter approached, it became apparent that the promised heat was not coming that year and that our family would be living in freezing temperatures inside that beautifully restored apartment. This was a serious problem because this was very far north, not far from the freezing winter breezes on the Baltic Sea, and the city became *very* cold in winter.

That's when we realized we'd have to use those ceramic fireplaces to provide heat for our family. But where would we get fuel to burn in them? Purchasing firewood and hauling it to our home would be difficult because of our location and unpredictable availability of gas for transportation.

Instead, our potential fuel for those fireplaces lay directly below us in another apartment that was abandoned and destroyed by years of neglect. It is impossible to exaggerate its horrible condition, and because no one owned it, it continued to deteriorate. In fact, it was the apartment with a hole in its ceiling because so many men in the apartment we'd purchased had "missed" the toilet bowl for so many years.

That empty apartment below us was so destroyed that *nothing* could be salvaged from it. Walls were half gone; fireplaces were destroyed and crumbling; windows were broken; and the winter wind was blowing through it, wreaking even more destruction. The broken window frames and shattered glass windowpanes were especially bad for us because our apartment was located directly above, and we could feel the effect of the freezing winter wind blowing through the apartment beneath our floor. Our building was constructed from brick and plaster, so our apartment held on to those freezing temperatures almost like it was a refrigerator — and we were really suffering from the cold inside it!

The floors of that apartment below us had once been covered with splendid, expensive parquet with all types of inlaid exotic woods and intricate designs. But now those floors were warped and ruined from water leaks and the long-term acid effects of urine. The parquet was bowed by water damage and was lying in irreparable, shattered sections all over that apartment.

One freezing early morning as Denise and I were pondering what to do about the cold temperatures that were getting worse by the day, our three sons suddenly jumped up, put on their coats, dashed out the door, and disappeared as if they were on an urgent mission. When they reappeared some time later, they walked through the door of the apartment with heaping armloads of hundred-year-old parquet flooring that they had gathered from the floor of the devastated apartment below us.

Denise and I watched as the boys piled that old parquet into our fireplaces and worked on each pile until a fire was blazing strong. That wood was so old and dry that it began quickly popping and burning — and soon the brick and plaster walls of that apartment began to warm up in every room, fueled by wood flooring from the apartment below that our sons had collected and used as fuel for the fire.

When the fire would start to die down and it felt like the temperatures were dropping, the boys would quickly put on their jackets, rush down two flights of steps to the abandoned apartment below, and rip up more flooring. Soon the boys would be back with more armloads of ruined parquet flooring. They would first break the dry-rotted parquet into smaller pieces; then they would shove the pieces through the fireplace doors into the fire, and almost immediately the house would start warming up again. So during that first winter when we moved to Riga, we kept our apartment warm by the blazing heat that was produced in our fireplaces, courtesy of the ruined antique flooring of that downstairs apartment.

## We Were the Proud Owners
## of the Biggest Hole in the Nation

While we were working on our apartment, architectural plans for the church were being approved. Soon massive bulldozers moved onto the land to prepare the ground for pouring the foundation for the new building. That's when we received news that the soil on our newly purchased property was so swampy that it would not be sufficient to support a foundation for a building our size.

The density of the existing dirt was similar to that of peat moss, so we had to hire *additional* contractors to excavate the soil completely so we could fill it back up with something substantial and suitable for what we needed to build. We had to dig and dig and *dig*, looking for something solid underneath all that peat moss that could serve as the base for our building's foundation.

Day after day, bulldozers dug deeper into the black soil to search for a solid layer of harder ground beneath the soft dirt. Finally, at a depth of twelve feet — and in some places even fifteen feet deep — we came to a solid bed of sand.

But then came the next hurdle to overcome: The building was going to be approximately the size of a football field, and we were going to have to remove all that peat moss twelve to fifteen feet deep!

I watched as the bulldozers came to excavate our soil. Then large trucks began to drive away *hundreds* of loads of rich, beautiful, black peat moss to dump it into the nearby river. We needed to remove all that peat moss so we could replace it with tons of durable, more stable material comprised of soil, sand, gravel, and rebar, which we of course had to locate and purchase.

After bulldozers had done their extensive excavation work, I climbed down into that deep depression and walked the length of it — almost the span of a football field. The light of the sun was eclipsed from my view as I made my way along the walls of that dark chasm. The smell of mold and decay seeped through damp clumps of soil that turned loose easily from the caverned walls as I raked my hand across the sides. My feet slipped in particularly damp places, breaking my stride so that I had to regain my balance to resume my small journey.

But I was never so proud of a hole in the ground! We were, in fact, the owners of the biggest hole in the nation! That hole was enormous and the job had been immense so far — time-consuming, challenging, and *expensive*.

The hole had been dug — now it was time to fill it with materials substantial enough to support our building's foundation. *But we were out of money.* The financial support we'd received to begin the project had been well-placed in a hole in the ground. We had been prayerfully led to that piece of property, and I had no misgiving about how the money had been spent, as it had been wisely managed and used exactly for that which it had been given. But what would people think now if we suddenly halted construction?

What others thought of me wasn't nearly as bad as my own thoughts that stalked me nonstop like a bloodhound in feverish pursuit of a scent. Mine was the scent of *feelings of failure.* I'd walk around that huge hole in the ground and I could hear the devil speaking to me, even quoting Scripture: *You're just like the man who began to build a tower, but didn't count the cost. You can't finish what you started.*

Continually, I was taunted with the thoughts, *The whole nation is going to laugh at you because all you have to show for all your efforts is a big hole. You've failed your family and your team. The people are going to say to you, 'See, we TOLD you it was impossible.' The dream is dead and gone, and you alone are to blame.*

### 'Saved' By the Snow

By the grace of God, I stood steadfastly in faith, and within just days after finally digging that massive hole, as magically as a movie plot dramatically unfolds, the winter season set in *quickly* in Riga, with blizzard-like ferocity, bringing with it an early freeze and *tons* of snow.

In fact, it snowed so hard and long that any phase of construction became impossible, so the work *had* to stop.

Most winters in our part of the world make the time frame for outdoor construction very short each year. But that especially hard snowfall brought the project to a standstill and provided a welcome reprieve for our beleaguered team. This time, it was the pause I needed at just the right moment because we had exhausted all of the money that had been designated for the project.

I had cried out to God for deliverance, and He answered me with snow! I was so thankful for that harsh winter weather because it was an excuse to explain why we stopped building. After all, you can't build when you have a big hole in the ground filled with snow! Not only did that snowfall make working impossible, it completely filled that excavated hole and made it a construction site in hiding.

But the snow didn't just cover *the hole* — it covered *us* and bought me time to invite the Holy Spirit into our dilemma to provide the help I needed. At the same time, it also prevented discouragement from setting into our small camp. For the rest of the winter, I continued praying to God for money to show up so we could begin building our foundation in the spring. As those sleepy winter months passed when no work could be done, it gave our God-called partners time to keep sending their gifts and offerings, and we were able to accumulate additional funds to proceed in warmer weather with the construction of the foundation.

By the time spring came, we had the money we needed, and the next stages of construction began. Trucks began to bring in hundreds of loads of soil, sand, and gravel to fill up that enormous hole to ensure a solid foundation for the building that was to come. Soon we proceeded to lay down the rebar in preparation for pouring the concrete foundation. By the way, this was the first time a slab foundation was ever used for a large building in Riga, so it was ground-breaking technology in that city.

Finally, the day came when the cement trucks came and cement began to flow out of those trucks atop the glorious preparation work that had preceded this phase of the project. To me, that cement looked like liquid gold because I was the one believing for all the money needed to keep the process moving forward. Every day I practically lived on that site, watching them smooth that concrete over the entire surface of the foundation.

Then the crew brought in the big grinders and began grinding the surface to make it smooth like silk. And when they were done, *oh, what a foundation it was.* I have to tell you honestly — I knelt down and kissed it. My life was in that slab, and I was so proud of it. As if I'd just finished the last stroke of a masterpiece painting, I would stand at one corner of the site and just gaze on the foundation, thinking, *My goodness! Look at how huge and PERFECT it is!* Then I'd walk over to another area to see what my foundation looked like from another angle. I studied that finished work from every direction. I was just so proud of that foundation!

Later, as contractors began to lay granite tile on top of all that rock, sand, rebar, and concrete that comprised that strong foundation, I have to tell you that I had mixed feelings about it because I didn't want anyone to forget what a labor of love lay hidden beneath that beautiful flooring. But with the foundation poured, we could move forward to actually build the church.

I savored our monumental achievement and marveled as I pondered the importance of a solid foundation beneath our *lives*. And as I watched the whole process of that old, weak soil being removed from the ground so something stronger could replace it, I thought of how the Holy Spirit has to excavate what is in us that is weak and unstable so that something strong, steady, and unmovable can be built in its place. He is a Master Builder who is constantly seeking to establish something solid underneath us so that from it, He can erect His own masterpiece — *a beautiful life that He has prearranged for us to live in His will and plan*!

## The Good News Pastors Association — *Another* Mammoth Assignment From Heaven

Right in the middle of the building program, along with the daily operations of our growing TV ministry, my team asked me to start a pastors association because pastors and ministers who watched our program were corresponding to ask for ministerial oversight of their churches and ministries.

Because I teach the Bible verse by verse, and my teaching is not fixed to any given denominational viewpoint, all kinds of pastors from every imaginable persuasion were asking me to be their pastor and requesting our ministry to serve as a covering for them and their churches. There were even some Orthodox priests who regularly watched my TV programs because they appreciated my approach to the Bible.

There were dedicated spiritual leaders in the underground church in the days of the USSR, but there were no Bible schools during the Soviet era, and there were very few Bibles. Moreover, even the road to secular higher education for believers was closed. Under socialist-communist rule, the inscription of "Baptist" or "Pentecostal" on one's personal file closed the door for that believer to attain any form of higher education. When the time of freedom finally came, young Christians had nowhere to go to receive a Bible education. That's why so many of them flocked to the aboveground Bible school in Jelgava in the early 1990s.

Those underground believers needed a biblical education to be able to effectually serve in the church in modern times. But they didn't even know what a church should be like in a free country, as they had never seen or experienced that before. God used my gift, and the gifts of many others, to help these up-and-coming ministers to know Scripture better, to study the correct structure of a church, and to learn how to conduct evangelistic outreaches. My own teaching was affecting millions of TV viewers, and it was also having an impact in the lives of large numbers of pastors and others in the ministry.

I often went back in my mind to the words the Holy Spirit spoke to me when He first called me to move my family to this part of the world. I'll summarize again what I heard Him communicate to my spirit:

*There are many good Bible teachers in America, but I need you HERE to be a part of laying a scriptural foundation under the mighty move of the Spirit that is going to take place in this part of the world. It's good what you are doing in America, but you are needed more here than there. I am calling you here because the teaching gift I've put inside you is so needed in this part of the world. Because it was illegal for pastors and leaders here to study the Bible, they do not have a grip on solid teaching, and I need someone like you to help lay a reliable foundation underneath them.*

I want to say that when everything changed and education *did* finally become available, Russian-speaking pastors soared in terms of spiritual education. Their inherent brilliance carried over into the spiritual realm, and they quickly became brilliant theological thinkers.

But the idea of starting a pastors association caused me to nearly tremble because I understood the additional responsibility this would add to our lives. I also comprehended that caring for pastors, their families, and their congregations was a colossal God-given task that should not be entered into lightly. Plus, our financial plate was full of huge responsibilities, and I didn't know how I would pay for one more thing!

I was hesitant to start a pastors association for all those reasons, yet I knew pastors needed solid teaching, so I came up with an alternative and started a "Video Club" that would, in essence, be my teachings on video *with* Greek words and added graphics — almost like what I do on television today, but this would be only for pastors and spiritual leaders. The Video Club pre-dated the association, and it was an immediate answer for the needs of pastors who could not go to Bible school. So I developed video series after video series, and our team distributed the Video Club to large numbers of pastors and leaders free of charge every month.

But at the urging of my associates, we did finally take the leap and launched the Good News Association of Pastors and Churches. We knew the TV program was influential and that if we opened this door, a flood of pastors and leaders would come streaming into our organization. It was an honor that they wanted to associate with me, but I trembled at the immense responsibility of such a commitment.

This period was both a good and bad moment for the Church in that part of the world. It was a good moment because Christians were coming out of hiding. It was a bad moment because the underground Church had functioned secretly underground for so long that they didn't know how to function aboveground.

Underground Pentecostals had gathered in the woods and in other secret locations for church, so for them, the idea of having a church building was unheard of and amazing. Some Baptists had buildings, but they were small and were usually on the outskirts of a city.

They simply didn't know what to do, how to legally do business, or even know how to rent a public auditorium. In the past, they would have gone to jail for such actions. But now that freedom had come, a new way of thinking was required. Our association was instrumental in helping pastors and spiritual leaders walk through those kinds of landmines that they didn't know how to navigate simply because of a lack of experience.

Remembering this time so vividly, Bishop Sergei Ryakhovsky recalled the impact that our teaching had on pastors and spiritual leaders from every imaginable Christian persuasion. He said, "Even other denominations listened to Rick because they knew him as a theologian and a specialist in the Greek language of the New Testament. The Orthodox put great value on intelligence, and even they widely appreciated Rick as a Bible specialist and as a theologian. He really was, and is, held in great respect. As a matter of fact, I can't even remember anyone *ever* arguing about any of Rick's theological positions. And his teachings and books are not just a recognized authority for Charismatics, but they are also recognized by other parts of the Protestant movement in our part of the world."

As pastors and leaders kept appealing to our ministry for help, I felt the strings of my heart being pulled, so I finally threw in the towel and surrendered. I didn't know how I could handle one more thing, but we started a small pastors association in Latvia. However, as I suspected, news of it quickly spread into Russia, Belorussia, Ukraine, and other parts of the former Soviet Union. Requests were coming in faster than I could have dreamed, and we quickly developed an interview process and a system of accountability for incoming pastors and churches. Soon we had hundreds of pastors and congregations that were a part of our Good News Association of Pastors and Churches and spiritually under our covering.

Paul Renner recalled, "Pastors were looking for some type of unifying body to help pull them together. It was the very early beginnings of churches in the former Soviet Union organizing into unified associations that exist today.

"But one of the major differences between what my father did and what everyone else was doing was, others began to organize and create bylaws and rules. Dad did his best to stay away from that. All he really wanted to do was to provide teaching and help with practical areas of ministry as he could. A lot of people gathered around that, and we were able to provide all kinds of teaching to help the pastors and churches in every imaginable way. We did master classes on how to organize children and youth ministry, how to conduct a church service, how to form a worship team, how to lead worship, and so on."

When we started the association, we had the photos of all the pastors, so in every city we traveled to, I memorized the names and faces of those pastors. When they walked through the doors for their first time with us, I knew them instantly by sight and was there to shake their hand and call them each by name. It stunned them that I knew who they were, but they needed God's love and special attention, too, so I was committed to memorizing those names and faces and to do my best to know them and serve them.

Also, I usually spent fifteen minutes with every pastor at every association meeting. If you were to put a pencil to it, you'd see that it was a monumental task to spend that much time with as many as three hundred pastors at those meetings. It took *days* to do it, but that is what was needed at that time. It started a relationship with them, and they would pour their hearts out to me.

Nikolai Kulakevich, who served as director of the association for many years, said, "Rick did so many different kinds of meetings for pastors and spiritual leaders. In addition to monthly meetings in lots of regional areas, he also held huge special meetings where pastors and leaders gathered in one place for several days at a time so Rick could teach them the Scriptures. Rick taught them how to build a church and a ministry, how to serve effectively as a pastor, how to handle finances with integrity, how to build children's, youth, and worship ministries, and how a pastor should serve and build his own family to make it strong."

He continued, "The association and what it was doing was so special because few were doing that at the time. And Rick's ministry even paid for the pastors' and leaders' travel, for their stay in the hotels, and for all their food. We rented huge venues in those days and filled them to the brim — every room — with pastors and leaders who had almost no money and could have never paid for it by themselves. It cost Rick's ministry a fortune to do it, but the impact will go on forever — not only in the lives of those pastors and leaders, but in their entire congregations and those *they* will impact in the future. Only Heaven knows the real impact; it was and is truly exponential."

Nikolai added, "Rick and his team traveled great distances by every means of transportation, sometimes on difficult roads, to get to those pastors. For several days at a time, we would fill entire hotels with those pastors and ministers, and Rick did most of the teaching unless we brought in a special guest. Because those hundreds of pastors and leaders ended up spending so much time together at those many meetings that they began to build long-term relationships with each other. The Good News Association of Pastors and Churches became a real support structure to hundreds and hundreds of leaders and their congregations."

Paul Renner well remembered the influence we were having on pastors and churches everywhere. He said, "At the time our ministry began here in the former Soviet Union, everyone that had previously been in ministry was looking for a ministry model. They needed a new way to do ministry, and it gave us the opportunity to do ministry and church the way we thought it should be done. There were no previous models, so the influence that was there in the very beginning was huge because no one had ever done church the way we were talking about doing church.

"Almost immediately, pastors began using the church-format model that we were cultivating, and it was multiplied all over that vast region. Even today, many churches are still modeling their services after what we do in the church in Riga and Moscow.

"But beyond church structure, Dad had a huge influence as a Bible teacher. First, he was a Bible teacher in the Jelgava Bible school, then he became a Bible teacher on television to millions of people — *then* he stepped into the role of a teacher to pastors. Even today when pastors are trying to solve doctrinal questions, they usually start with the thought, *What does Rick Renner say?* If pastors get into a theological debate, they'll often say, 'Well, what does Rick Renner say about it?' God made our impact huge, and it's difficult to measure the far-reaching, *eternal* effects."

### We Were on God's Timetable — and His Clock Was *Racing*!

That part of our story may seem like a bit of a diversion — we actually felt that way at times too — but the pastors association was unthinkably born *right in the middle of the Riga building program.* At the moment when we needed every available dollar to pay for the miraculous construction of the building, the Good News Association of Pastors and Churches was mushrooming in front of our eyes throughout the Baltic countries of Estonia, Latvia, and Lithuania, in Belorussia, in Ukraine, in the southern Muslim republics, and across all of Russia's eleven time zones. However, not only then, but over many years, our partners' giving enabled us to pay for:

- hundreds of association meetings that were attended by thousands of pastors and leaders — providing all the costs of transportation for them, as well as our team, to get to these meetings.

- offerings to the special speakers we brought in whom we believed the pastors needed to hear.

- all the production of our teaching materials that we gave away at every meeting to those thousands of pastors.

- churches that we helped start and get established.

- building programs of other churches who had a God-given dream, but needed financial and practical help to fulfill it.

- massive evangelistic crusades conducted from one end of the former USSR to the other.

- medical bills and even surgical procedures for pastors and their families because they didn't have the funds to pay for those life-saving operations.

- monthly financial support for more than six hundred pastors at that time because they were serving God and their churches in crashed economies where there was nearly no money and their churches could not support them.

Furthermore, when my team traveled to conduct these massive association meetings, we seized every opportunity to rent local public venues to hold meetings for our local TV viewers who lived in those areas. Those viewers loved Denise and me, and many of them had come to Christ through our TV programs while thousands more had just needed a nudge to completely commit their lives to Jesus.

So we held massive meetings in person, in all kinds of venues in cities and regions across the USSR. We simply wanted to look into the eyes of our TV viewers and love them with the love of Jesus. It was a very large expenditure, but if Jesus were physically on the earth in those post-Soviet lands, it is exactly what He would have done. We knew it was what we needed to do as well.

While being interviewed for this book, several staff members from the early years were asked, "When did it really dawn on you that Rick Renner was carrying a strong anointing and a heavenly assignment for this part of the world?" Yuri Ruls, who was there from the earliest years, answered, "I had worked for Pastor Rick and the ministry for some time, but it really hit me when we began to hold those big meetings in cities where we were broadcasting the programs — like when we traveled to Odessa, Ukraine, and had meetings in the symphony hall. When I saw all those people flooding through the doors to hear Pastor Rick minister in person and to personally meet Rick and Denise, I thought, *Oh, my goodness, this is bigger than I knew, and I'm a part of this big thing that God is doing!*"

We conducted public meetings for literally hundreds of thousands of people who regularly watched us on television. They flooded into those auditoriums; they walked the aisles to give their lives to Jesus Christ; they were filled with the Spirit; they were healed and delivered; and they received teaching materials free of charge that we had printed for them. And because those meetings were conducted in conjunction with our Good News Association of Pastors and Churches, we then turned all those new believers into the hands of our pastors and leaders in our association churches. It was a heavenly strategy *of the Chief Shepherd Himself* right from the start!

Paul Renner said, "My dad became a prominent leader in the move of God in the former Soviet Union. What happened here simply cannot be exaggerated. When the walls fell and the Gospel came, the size of the crowds and the response of the crowds were amazing. When Dad moved our family to the former USSR, it thrust us into what I believe was one of the greatest single moves of God in two thousand years of Church events."

I must also add that thousands of people were not only thrilled to hear the Word of God that we preached, but they were also totally taken by Denise when she sang on stage for them. The people of the USSR had been raised with classical music, and the opera performed on stages all over the Soviet Union was some of the best in the world. They were accustomed to the music performed on the stages of Moscow's Bolshoi Theater, Saint Petersburg's Mariinsky Theater, the Odessa National Academic Theater of Opera and Ballet, Riga's Latvian National Opera, and so on. So when Denise stood on the stage and used her operatically trained voice to sing the praises of God, it would nearly bring down the house as people shouted, *"Bravo! Bravo! Bravo!"* It brought a whole new level of dignity to the proclamation of the Gospel to have Denise and her impressive and powerful voice on the stage.

As I have expressed so often in this book — but it's true — we were experiencing the book of Acts before our eyes. And just like the book of Acts in the Bible, *it was the acts of the Holy Spirit among us.* What was happening in our midst — among our ministry team and those God sent to us to minister to — was marvelous to behold. It was a move of God that kept growing and gaining momentum and strength until it *burst* into spiritual flames that the darkness simply could not quench.

At the same identical moment we were contending with enemies in Riga as we pressed forward to construct the first church building in that city in decades, we were also expanding the TV ministry and our reach exponentially — *and* we were ministering to thousands of pastors and ministers throughout the former USSR! We ministered to them in person and with countless free teaching materials as quickly as our growing staff could produce them. We were fulfilling three huge assignments simultaneously, and it required phenomenal surrender and consecration from Denise, myself, our sons, and our entire team — and it required a lot of money to do it all as well.

As I also mentioned previously, before we left the United States, we had spent several years working very hard to establish our own book publishing company that was called Pillar Books. That book company was off to a strong start publishing my own books and the books of other authors. But the complete inability to regularly call the Tulsa office to help them make business decisions put the company in such a bad management position that I decided to sell the company to another publisher who wanted our authors and accounts.

It really wasn't in my heart to give up Pillar Books. I dreamed for it to become a significant publishing company. But Denise and I had made up our minds that we would consecrate and commit ourselves to do whatever we needed to do to obey God in the former USSR and to stay on course with that assignment without distraction. And if losing Pillar Books was to be a part of the price we needed to pay, so be it. I would pay that price to walk in obedience to God's higher calling on my life.

But just in those accelerated small beginnings in Latvia, God was already starting to recompense me for giving up that publishing company. And today, on both sides of the world, we are publishing books as fast as I can write them, and those books are being read in a multiplicity of languages all over the world.

*It always — without fail — pays to obey God.* Anything we think we're giving up to serve Him pales in comparison to what He will invariably give to us in return. I can testify that Denise and I are continually in awe of His abounding faithfulness to recompense us for all we left behind to follow Him. *And there is more in our future to be seen!*

### We Had Been Divinely Placed To Seize
### a Moment in History, and We Gave Our *All*

On three fronts, we were focused on the church construction, the TV ministry, and the pastors association. It felt naturally impossible to do it all, but that was the time when we needed to push forward with all the divine thrust the Holy Spirit was giving us so we could launch all these aspects of ministry at one time. We had been divinely placed in a moment in history that a whole generation of persecuted Soviet believers had prayed for. That time was now upon us — we were *there*!

We had pledged our wholehearted obedience — including every personal dime and dollar we could muster — so we could cooperate with the grace of God to accomplish the task before us. A mighty move of God was taking place as a result. *Millions* of souls were coming to Christ all at once due to the multiple efforts of many people. Those new believers needed the verse-by-verse teaching of the Bible as well as capable pastoral ministry to shepherd them. There is no doubt that the move of God through our ministry had become one of the strongest streams of the outpouring of the Gospel in the former USSR. For that, we were thankful and in awe.

After many had languished in prisons for decades for their faith and had prayed for God to move, *God suddenly moved!* Now it was time for us to be a part of the answer to their prayers, so we mustered all our spiritual, mental, and physical strength — and all the resources God provided — to grab hold of the mighty sickle of the Holy Spirit and swing it hard to gather the harvest into God's house. When I look back on that time, I see how only God could have divinely energized us to do it all at the speed that was required — but we had to seize the moment and make the most of the opportunity while we could.

Because there were few private banks, and no one had ever done a loan with a church *ever*, borrowing money from a bank was out of the picture. The whole project from beginning to end had to be paid for in cash, so in addition to covering the rising costs of TV and the many needs of precious pastors and ministers in our pastors association, we had to believe for several million dollars to pay for the church construction at the same time. But by the time we finished, God had miraculously provided nearly $4 million in cash to cover every bit of the cost — a total miracle by anyone's standards!

Remember, our partner base was small, so to do what we were doing was already touching the realm of the miraculous. Then to come up with millions of dollars to complete the building program in twenty-two months was a bigger financial miracle than I had ever witnessed.

But God had already taught me that obedience works like a magnet and attracts everything needed to do any God-given job. If I would be willing to say yes to Him and to stay on track with whatever He asked me to do, He would see to it that money and resources showed up to fulfill the assignment. That is *exactly* what happened to us in our heavenly ventures in Latvia, every step of the way. We started with a chandelier on stage and no money in our bank account. But twenty-two months later, a massive building was constructed *in the nick of time* — and it was paid for in cash with no other part of the ministry curtailed in the process.

### Shipping the Building From America!

I want to share a few of the twists and turns that happened along the way as we were constructing the Riga church building. Opposition often raised its head in brazen defiance of God and His plan, shouting in our ears that this project would fail and not come to pass. I think some of what I share with you will surprise you, as it surprised even us.

One surprise we encountered was that there were no more functioning steel companies in Latvia at that time because of the collapse of the USSR. The only nearby place to purchase steel was Russia, but we couldn't buy it in Russia because Latvia restricted products coming from Russia at that time. Nevertheless, soon it was going to be time to erect the metal for the building, so we needed to purchase steel for the project.

After diligently researching our options, we determined that the best place to purchase steel was in Tennessee at a company that specialized in church structures. I remember thinking, *Tennessee? You've got to kidding! That's six thousand miles across the Atlantic Ocean. How will we ever transport it across the sea on time to complete the building and meet our government-imposed deadline?*

It seemed like nothing we did was easy or normal since moving to that vast Soviet land. Now we were about to purchase tons of steel *in America* to ship to Latvia. I knew of no pastor anywhere in the world who had ever attempted such a deed. But this is what we needed to do, so we negotiated for the steel company to get started fabricating and cutting our steel to our building specifications.

I didn't have a clue how we were going to pay for the steel up front, so we asked for terms to pay it out over a few years. They agreed, so we placed our order. Because we only had a total of twenty-two months to complete the project — and that twenty-two months had begun the previous fall when the bulldozers started moving dirt — it meant time was quickly running out. The company in Tennessee did a "rush job," and in two short months, the steel was fabricated, cut to the specifications provided by our architect in Riga, and ready to be loaded into fifty-five giant containers to be shipped across the Atlantic to the port of Riga.

But, unexpectedly the steel factory in Tennessee announced that they were requiring the full payment of $325,000 *before* they would ship our steel across the ocean. We had already exhausted every available resource and were standing in faith for the full amount we needed to pay for the architectural fees and other parts of the process in Riga. We didn't have the cash to pay for the steel up front, and the clock was ticking!

But God had faithfully seen us this far, so I had no reason to believe He would fail to bring us to the completion of the project. Yet I didn't have an *inkling* about how He was going to provide this much money so quickly. Even though I had already seen Him miraculously provide, my insides *ached* as I wondered how we were going to come up with that much cash so quickly to pay the bill. Every night, I tossed and turned in bed, wondering, *God, how will we do this?*

One evening I lay in bed thinking about the tons of steel waiting to be loaded into those fifty-five containers. I tossed, turned, and couldn't sleep. I couldn't get away from the constant pressure that the clock was ticking and that if we didn't finish this project on time, the whole thing could be lost. If that happened, it would be a tragedy. So that late night, I called a dear pastor friend in the United States and asked for a few minutes of his time to open my heart about the things we were facing. As we talked, he asked for the dollar amount we needed to pay for the steel so it could be shipped.

When I told him what we needed, his response totally disarmed me as I heard him say, "Rick, let us cover it. We'll take care of that for you and the ministry there."

I was stunned. I had not called him to ask for money. It was not and has never been my style to call anyone to ask for money. That night I was only seeking the ear of a friend to hear what I was facing — I never even thought he had the resources to pay that bill in full. But God was faithful to see to it that we were completely covered. The next morning that precious pastor and his church wrote a check for $325,000 and provided all the money to pay for tons of steel so that it could be loaded into containers, placed on a ship, and sent overseas so that our building could be completed *on time*!

But it's important for me to tell you who that friend was. He was the very same friend I had called about my announcement to move our family to the Soviet Union, who had said, "Rick, if you move your family to the Soviet Union right now while you are being so blessed in every aspect of your life, you're going to miss it." In his sincere care for my well-being, he added, "Who in his right mind would walk away from what you are experiencing? Not only that, if you leave, it is sure that people will forget you — *'out of sight, out of mind'* — and your financial support will dry up when you need it most. Then when things get really badly out of control in the USSR and you need to flee for your lives, you won't even have the money to buy a plane ticket. You'll be calling me to buy you tickets to get you out of that mess!"

But when push came to shove, that friend was proud of what we had done by faith and was regretful that he had been so pessimistic at that early moment when I needed his encouragement. I tell you this because I want you to know that every negative voice in your life today might not *always* be negative. This dear friend cared about me, and he is *still* a dear friend to this day. Think of the rewards in Heaven that await him and his church because he stepped forward to sow that seed and pay that bill. He *and his church* will be richly rewarded in eternity for the countless numbers of people who have been saved in that building and entire families of believers who have grown up in that church and who will continue to be taught, loved, and discipled there. One day, a lot of that fruit will be credited to his account!

### Racing Clocks and Open Doors

Once the steel was paid for, it was quickly loaded into those fifty-five containers to start their long journey from the United States to the port of Riga. But as we waited, there was another occurrence that took us totally off guard. We suddenly got word that I had been accused of being a contrabandist — that I was conspiring to secretly smuggle tons of steel into the country. And they were forbidding us to receive our steel upon its arrival! I thought, *What is a "contrabandist," anyway?* So I looked it up and read that a "contrabandist" is one engaged in illegal smuggling.

I wondered, *How could anyone SECRETLY SMUGGLE fifty-five huge containers into a country unnoticed?* It simply made no sense. But explaining ourselves was fruitless as it became painfully obvious that someone in the higher ranks of the government didn't want us to build that church building. That high-ranking official was determined to stop our endeavors to advance the Gospel and the Kingdom of God in that part of the world.

We had experienced many attacks in those days, but this one was *really* intense. The heat had been turned up to a full-scale onslaught. Christ and His Gospel had come to this land, and the powers of darkness had risen to greet them. But as we will see in the story that unfolds, those obstacles that looked so formidable eventually bowed their knees to the King of kings and the mighty power of His Word. The Lord's plan to reach the precious souls in this nation would stand as *we* stood our ground and endured the test of time.

Before the steel was ever ordered, we had obtained all the proper permissions to receive the steel. Now it was in the middle of the Atlantic, headed across the sea to the port of Riga in fifty-five containers. We couldn't call that massive ship and say, "We changed our mind; please take it back to Tennessee." So what was I supposed to do? The fact is, the Latvian government in essence declared, "We refuse to let you receive the metal. You are out of luck — and good riddance!"

But as God would have it, while we were pondering this dilemma, a new U.S. Consul was appointed to the U.S. Consulate in Riga. He had heard of the work we were doing on television and that we were among the longest-residing Americans in Latvia. Curious and eager to assume his post with as much knowledge of the local conditions as possible, he'd asked to speak with me by phone. During our hour-long conversation, I was able to provide him with the insights he needed about the many developments that occurred in Latvia right after the collapse of the Soviet Union.

Then just as our conversation was coming to a close, he surprised me with a question that provided the open door for which I and my team had been searching. He asked, "Mr. Renner, you have been a big help to me today, so I'd like to ask you — what is your biggest need at the moment? How might I help *you*?"

Rocked by his words, I quickly recovered myself so I could begin telling him about our plight with the government calling me a "contrabandist" and forbidding us to receive our steel. Step by step, I walked him through the details of our supplies at sea and the government's sudden refusal to let us receive them.

I swallowed hard as my mind tried to process his unflinching reply: "I'll make sure that you receive all your steel." And before I knew it — just like *that* — I'd stumbled through another door thrown wide open to me by the mighty hand of God.

In a few days, the U.S. Consul called again and asked me to join him in an official visit to a certain government office to discuss the accusations leveled against us. The meeting was to be held in the top office of the Director of the Department of Religion, a department used in the past by the old-time KGB to monitor, control, and even shut down all religious activities in the nation during the days of the USSR.

When the U.S. Consul and I walked into that meeting, I could see that those authorities nearly trembled at the presence of the U.S. Consul. We took our seats around a long Soviet-looking conference table. Then I heard the U.S. Consul say, "If Mr. Renner is refused his steel, I will do everything I can to see that this country loses its funding from the United States of America."

At that time, Latvia was just emerging as a new nation, and it was dependent upon U.S. financial aid back then, so his threat was enormous. To say I was stunned is an understatement. I was totally taken aback — previous to our meeting, I had no idea what he was going to say. But by the time the U.S. Consul finished delivering his ultimatum, the governmental authorities on the other side of the table looked at us and said, "Of course Mr. Renner may receive his containers and his steel…and is there anything else we can do for Mr. Renner?"

By the time that ship arrived at the port of Riga with our freight, true to the Consul's word, all restrictions had been removed and no time had been lost in fulfilling our divine assignment. And not only that, when the government saw the power of the United States standing with us, it changed our strained relationship with that newly formed and fearful government. Not long after that, they even asked me to be the official organizer for a conference for religious leaders from the European Union who were gathering in Riga. Eventually, the director of that Department of Religion became my personal friend, and he and his wife often met with Denise and me for lunch or dinner.

There would be many more such wide-flung doors, each one a precious testament of God's grace on our lives to remain on the divine path in a land not our own where He Himself had placed us. Each one of those testimonies was *and remains* a treasure — they are treasures that I am delighted to unfold to you in this book.

God has similar riches, testimonies of His marvelous works, in store for *all* who give Him their yes — even the most *unlikely*, like me.

## Those Racing Clocks...

Although we ultimately received our steel without delay, we were still racing against the clock to finish the project within the unrealistic time frame we'd been given. If we missed the deadline, we could possibly be forced to forfeit ownership of the church's land to the government along with everything we had invested in the project.

But like a small storm picking up speed until it can no longer be ignored, there was a supernatural momentum of God's power moving us forward. Yes, we'd endured a long season of continual challenges — *counter-storms* — that attempted to destroy what we were putting our hands to. I would be untruthful to say I didn't feel the constant barrage of enemy fire attempting to provoke our surrender. But even a momentary retreat would have diminished our momentum and pushed us backward from progress we'd already made. Like the all-or-nothing rage the shepherd David must have felt as he hastened toward Goliath — I knew that kind of raging commitment was where my own triumph lay, and I was hopelessly committed to the prize of constructing that church building!

With contractors, equipment, and workers buzzing vigorously around the clock, the countdown was on. We worked like the exiles returning to Jerusalem under Nehemiah to rebuild city walls amidst hostile resistance. With our "tools in one hand and our weapons in the other," we put our hands very diligently to the plow of our heavenly assignment. Of course, we knew our enemies were not flesh-and-blood men in seats of government. Our battle was spiritual, and our victory would likewise be Spirit-wrought.

## Five Psychiatrists Were Assigned To Study Me

Right in the middle of the Riga building project, there was one high-ranking man who hated me so badly that he ordered a group of psychiatrists to begin attending our church services covertly so they could discover "how I was using hypnosis to control the people who attended our church."

The psychiatrists' combined prognosis was that my level of hypnosis was so developed that I could even manipulate and control people who read my monthly teaching letters that we sent to television viewers. Those doctors suggested that as people read my letters, an amazing hypnotic power dramatically "enveloped" the readers, causing them to *want* to do what I had encouraged them to do in my writings. Of course, we know it was the power of the Holy Spirit at work, but this was their secular interpretation of what they were observing in our church members and TV viewers.

These psychiatrists were gravely concerned about the level of "hypnosis" I was using to influence people's lives. Of course, these men in government knew nothing of the divine Influencer, the Holy Spirit, and the anointing and power of God Himself, so they had no ability to comprehend the level of transformation that was occurring in believers' lives through the preaching of the Gospel.

I was unaware that I was "the talk" of this group until we received a call from the Director of the Department of Religion. He informed me that five unidentified psychiatrists were covertly attending all of our church meetings for three months to study the method of "hypnosis" they believed I was using to control my entire congregation.

I was amazed by what this man disclosed to me. All I had done was teach the Word of God verbally and in written form — under the anointing of the Holy Spirit — and it was producing supernatural *but naturally unexplainable* results in people's lives!

I must tell you that when you know that five psychiatrists are somewhere out in the crowd, listening carefully and trying to find something against you so they can accuse you before the government, it can try to play with your mind. It tends to make you very self-conscious about what you say or do, lest it be misinterpreted.

At first, I found myself very guarded in nearly every statement I made, very aware of the psychiatrists who were somewhere in the crowd trying to "catch" me in something I said or did publicly. But then I remembered Jesus and the time when the Pharisees listened carefully to Him in order to try to "catch" Him in His words so they could bring an accusation against Him. Knowing that Jesus had experienced the same thing, I turned to the Master to learn how to deal with the situation.

Matthew 22:15 says, "Then went the Pharisees, and took counsel how they might entangle him [Jesus] in his talk." This tells us plainly that the Pharisees met together, agreed on a mutual course of action, and then proceeded to try to catch Jesus off guard and "entangle" Him in His words so they could find a reason to charge Him.

Reading this account helped me because it sounded so much like the five psychiatrists who were scattered throughout our congregation. I knew that if Jesus could stand successfully against the Pharisees, then the Holy Spirit could empower me likewise to stand strong and stable in the face of these psychiatrists whose sole purpose was to prove that I was controlling and damaging people with hypnotism.

Matthew 22:15 states that the group of Pharisees wanted to "entangle" Jesus in his talk. The word "entangle" is a Greek word that can be translated *to ensnare, to catch in a trap,* or *to acquire information about an error or fault with the purpose of causing harm.* It carries the idea *to catch off guard* or *to catch in a mistake.*

Once I had a deeper understanding of the way Jesus handled His situation, I knew that I needed to respond like He did. Rather than cower in fear because those psychiatrists were there, I decided to preach more boldly and more fearlessly than ever before. This wasn't a time for me to be self-conscious. I decided if those doctors wanted to know what kind of power was operating through me, it was time to give them a vivid demonstration!

For three months, I poured out the Word of God in power and with the conviction and anointing of the Holy Spirit. When the three months were complete, the psychiatrists left, went their way, and filed their reports of what they had observed.

I personally saw those reports. In them, they indicated that they could not explain either the boldness or the effect of my message — and they suggested that it was something that superseded the powers of hypnotism.

A few of them had been so helped during those three months that they continued to attend our church for a period of time to receive *more* help!

Oh, what I learned from that whole experience! I learned that, like Jesus, we are not to change the way we present ourselves, or our message, simply because of who is in the audience or whom we're talking to at the moment. We have no need to apologize for what we believe or for the power of God that works through us. If we shrink in fear, they will perceive it as weakness, but if we stand boldly and pour out what we really believe with the convicting power of the Holy Spirit, it will silence our critics.

Never forget that when you are true to the Word of God and your Spirit-inspired convictions of who you are in Christ, the Holy Spirit will be right there to empower you through every situation! The Spirit working through you will protect you and render your accusers silent — *and* leave them better off for having been with you!

### More Deficits as We Surmounted Construction Hurdles, Rounded the Last Corner, and Neared the Finish Line

Finally, the building was standing, and it was time to start working on the interior, but there were practically no materials available in the nation due to the complete collapse of the economy. And what *was* available had become astronomically expensive.

Nikolai Kulakevich remembered, "Because the USSR had collapsed, not only were there no materials available, but if you bought materials from abroad, it was challenging to get them through customs and to pay the duty tax. So finishing the interior of the building was quite hard. Really, nobody knew where to get what we needed to finish the job. Even local authorities didn't know where to get building supplies."

Because there were nearly no building materials to be had in Latvia at that time, an international scavenger hunt ensued to gather what we needed to finish building: sheetrock, wood, doors, windows, and so on from all over eastern Europe — and, of course, our steel had come from the state of Tennessee.

Just as we had set out across the former USSR to figure out how to get on television, now my assistant Andrey and I began flying to nearby nations to see if we could find building materials and to research whether Latvia would allow us to receive them from those particular places — restrictions that were changing almost constantly. We flew to Warsaw to a massive building-supply market. That market had become the largest building-supply center in all the Eastern Bloc countries that were trying to rebuild after the collapse of the USSR. But getting materials from Poland to Latvia would prove too big a challenge. We flew to Scandinavia to see what we could find there, but we hit another dead end there because of more border restrictions.

Through our unbridled persistence and the leading of the Holy Spirit, we ended up gathering what we needed from a hodgepodge of nations around us. And in the end, I can't tell you whether time slowed down for us or we simply worked under a heavenly spell of grace — but I *can* tell you that we beat our deadline by *days*. We'd held our position through every storm of imposing threats, political maneuverings, and seasons of lack, and the Riga Good News Church secured its permanent home.

Not only was the foundation of that massive Riga church built and blessed by God to last, but the interiors of that building were thoughtfully and impeccably prepared for God's people to occupy this new place with joy. One staff member from that time recalled, "The Riga church building was so amazingly done. We were in shock at how beautiful it turned out — I never dreamed a church could be like that. Seeing what unfolded there was one of the most special times in my life. Watching that building being built will always be a precious memory to me because it was such a serious moment in history for Christians in our part of the world."

Denise and I, our sons, and our team had invested countless hours in prayer, negotiations, meetings, and deliberations to finally realize this dream-turned-reality right in communism's backyard (*and* in the backyard of the dreadful Jewish killing grounds of the Bikernieki Forest). And payday had come. In the almost seven years since we'd arrived as a family from the United States, we were literally doing the unthinkable — we were dedicating a church facility we'd built from *beneath* the ground up, the first church building to be erected in *generations* in that city.

## The Grand Opening of the Riga Good News Church

After all we'd endured to see this project through, the day had finally come for the grand opening of the Riga Good News Church building. It was an especially gratifying time for Denise and me and our sons Paul, Philip, and Joel, who were fourteen, twelve, and eight years old at that time. In fact, we could hardly contain our excitement!

We had finally established a base that would provide Bible teaching through the church and through the television network; nurture families inside and outside the church; teach pastors and leaders in our association; and unite Protestant pastors and organizations in Estonia, Latvia, and Lithuania and all over the former Soviet Union. In the truest sense of the words, hell had been pushed back, and the building of this church facility marked a brand-new day for the people of the former Soviet Union and especially Latvia.

The parking lot filled quickly on the frosty November Sunday morning of our very first service in the new building. Church staff and volunteers bustled about to seat people in the auditorium and to receive children into nurseries and classrooms. During that first winter in the new building, the church had no heat, so few people removed their coats once inside. While the building protected us from the harsh elements outside, the temperature inside was like an icebox, and that first service was a bone-chilling cold event.

But the level of excitement in the building on Dedication Sunday was *electric*! Through the glass double doors that led into the church foyer, Denise and I caught sight of the activity as we drove up to the church. As we approached our new building from the walkway outside, we could see the foyer packed with hundreds of people who had gathered for this historic event. They were all walking across my foundation, and no one was saying *a thing* about it!

Welcomed eagerly by greeters at their posts both outside and inside the church building, we stepped through the doors into the foyer, where my eyes focused on the dark, rectangular slab of granite embedded in the floor beneath my feet.

To honor our role in laying a foundation for the move of God in the USSR and in building this historic structure in that part of the world, a memorial stone was inlaid in the entryway floor to commemorate the dedication of the building and our work. The following words were inscribed in both the Latvian and English languages:

**Pastors**
*Rick Renner and Denise Renner*

**Bishops**
*Emmanuils Prokopenko*
*Nikolajs Gribs*
**Architects**
*Juris Poga*
*Earl Coulston*

**Built for the glory of God with this church's offerings
and the help of Christians around the world.**

**Consecrated on November 1, 1998.**

I read those words that Sunday morning in reverent awe of what God had done through us, vitally aware of what was commemorated by that granite stone placed carefully in the floor beneath our feet. We had built this church on a solid foundation both physically and spiritually, and because of it, we'd secured permanent solid footing for the Gospel to affect this small nation and other nations of the former USSR. With this huge task behind us, we could now move forward with momentum engineered by Heaven itself.

After reading the words inscribed on that memorial stone, I stood upright and adjusted my collar, still shivering from the cold outside but also moved by the presence of God that I felt inside that building. In mere minutes, the official dedication service would begin, so I hurried to the main auditorium. Thinking of all the work we'd poured into that building and the immense amount of money spent just on laying its physical foundation, I had decided I would speak that morning on the subject of building correctly on the solid foundation of Scripture and the lordship of Jesus Christ.

Denise and I walked hand-in-hand with our three sons onto the platform before a jam-packed auditorium of people — many of whom came out of curiosity to witness the phenomenon of the first church building to be constructed in the nation in generations. For the newly emerging Church in the former Soviet Union, the plan of Heaven had come to earth in this historic moment. *Few — if any — had ever witnessed such an event.*

Denise and I stood on the stage and welcomed the people in the packed auditorium. Denise led worship, and I stood on the front row with dignitaries who had come from all over the world to participate in this historic event.

Soon it was time for me to speak, so I stepped up to the platform behind my large granite pulpit, opened my Bible, and started to speak. But I hesitated, my eyes scanning the auditorium thoughtfully in a spontaneous moment of reflection. I was so grateful to God to be a participant of *history in the making.* After resisting so many attacks of the enemy to stop the construction of this building — and after using our faith to believe for the finances to build it with cash and to build it on time — finally, it was done.

It was a moment to breathe a grateful sigh of relief.

### 'Move to Moscow and Do It Again'

As I opened my mouth to speak my first message in the pulpit of the new building, I heard the Holy Spirit *abruptly* speak a word to my heart that totally took me off guard. Right on that stage in front of several thousand people, I heard Him say to me, *This assignment is finished. Now move to Moscow and do it again.*

As the congregation sat with their Bibles in their laps listening eagerly for me to speak to them the Word of God, my mind stumbled as I struggled to grasp what I heard the Spirit say: *This assignment is finished. Now move to Moscow and do it again.*

Stunned, I wondered, *How can this be?*

My mind raced as my message flowed from my spirit through my lips to the congregation that morning. But silently, while I should have been enjoying the moment, I kept thinking about what I'd heard the Holy Spirit say to my heart. *Lord, why so soon?* I asked Him. *After everything we went through to build this building…why now?*

I recovered myself and was able to finish my message while my questions were yet unanswered. Soon Denise and I stood together at the altar to await those who would respond to my call to action for salvation, repentance and rededication, and the baptism in the Holy Spirit. Refreshments and fellowship followed the morning service and, all in all, it was a powerful first service that Sunday morning in *"our"* new church building.

But in addition to the official building dedication on that Sunday, we also had special services every night for a week. Then in the weeks that followed, God sent Kenneth and Gloria Copeland, Billye Brim, Marilyn Hickey, Joyce Meyer, Bob Yandian, Robb Thompson, Phil Driscoll, Wally and June Blume, and other friends who came to speak to the church and to share in the church's grand moment of celebration. And in just a short period of time, we watched as the new church facility became a *center* for the Christian community in Riga.

Kenneth and Gloria came and spoke for several days just a few weeks after the church dedication. It was already late November, very cold outside, and even though we were in the building, it still didn't have any heat. It was so cold that when Gloria spoke in the auditorium, we surrounded her with space heaters to try to keep her from freezing. Then Brother Copeland said, "Rick, let's get you some heat in here!" He authorized his associate, Barry Tubbs, to immediately give enough money for massive heaters to be purchased for the auditorium. We were so thankful to Brother Copeland for those heaters!

After I'd heard what the Holy Spirit said about our new directive, you might think I'd waste no time relaying that information to Denise, but I put off telling her what the Holy Spirit had said to me. I'd known since 1991 that a divine appointment awaited us in Moscow at some future time because of the vision I'd had in front of Lenin's mausoleum on my very first trip to the USSR — a vision in which I saw myself pastoring a large church in Moscow.

That vision was always in the back of my mind, but because Denise despised Moscow, I knew she would not be thrilled at the thought of moving there. Plus, we had fought so hard for every victory in Riga that I wanted to really enjoy our victory before moving to Moscow, and I didn't want to quickly uproot our family from Riga to move to Russia's capital city.

But the Holy Spirit urged me that it would soon be time to make the big move. I had to quickly relearn the valuable lesson in ministry *and in life* that we're to hold all things loosely but Jesus. The Riga Good News Church was *His* church, not mine, and my job as the Lord's under-shepherd was to be where He said to be and to do what He said to do.

From the time Denise and I were first married, we'd made the determination that we would fulfill our heavenly assignment regardless of the cost. Had we both not held that attitude of commitment in our hearts, we would have never been able to lay hold of the spiritual wherewithal to uproot our lives and move our family from the U.S. to Latvia in January 1992.

But Denise's impressions of Moscow were simply *not* favorable. It was a massive, "gray" city filled with pollution. And I told you in Chapter Eight of her negative experience at the Izmailovo Hotel and, really, everywhere we went in that oppressive city during that trip.

I felt I needed a strategy to break the news to Denise rather than just abruptly tell her we would be moving our family to Moscow. So I said, "Denise, I sense a change is coming and God is calling us elsewhere. What if we moved to…*London* to start a new church?"

She responded, "Oh, I like London!" Then I said, "Well, I don't really think it's London, so what would you think about…*Paris?*"

"Oh, I love Paris," she answered. Again, I said, "Well, I'm pretty sure it's not Paris. What about…*Rome* or *Copenhagen?*" And I heard her joyfully say, "Oh, I love Rome and Copenhagen!"

Finally, I worked up the nerve to say, *"How about Moscow?"*

"NO!" was her quick response. "I'm *never* moving there. I can't *stand* the city of Moscow!"

But eventually, I gently broke the news to her that God was indeed leading us to move to Moscow. And as always, her attitude was precious as she said to me so sweetly, "Ricky, I'm not excited about Moscow right now. But I am sure that I will be when we get there."

In typical fashion, Denise *quickly* adapted to our new God-given assignment. But she was not passively waiting for some magical change in her attitude toward this next phase of our lives and ministry. She *inwardly determined* that she would greet our next assignment, and our new city, with the bold determination to fulfill God's will and to do it with a willing spirit. She meant that with all her heart, and I knew it. She knew the feelings would follow — and they *did* follow in the days ahead.

## Two Years of Preparation for Moscow

During the two-year period in which we prepared to move to Moscow, I knew we needed to break the news about our move to our Riga leadership team, so I took them to a retreat center in the seaside city of Jurmala, Latvia, where for a full weekend, I began to share our plans to move to Moscow to start our next church.

At first, the team laughed at my announcement, as they thought I was kidding. They never dreamed our family would leave Riga. But it finally dawned on them that I was serious, so they listened quietly, albeit through a webbed veil of disbelief. The Renner family was so entrenched in Riga that *no one* ever thought we'd leave — our role there had become so cemented in the Christian community and in the nation.

Years later, Alexei Ledeyev, senior pastor of the New Generation Church in Riga, said, "When the Iron Curtain fell, multitudes of people came into the former Soviet Union to preach and to minister — missionaries, evangelists, *a lot of people.* It looked like hundreds of foreign preachers and missionaries came very quickly, but only a few stayed.

"Back in those days," he continued, "a lot of foreigners simply used the USSR as a photo opportunity. But Rick Renner was different. He came to build a real ministry base for the Kingdom of God. Right from the start, he was committed and serious about what he did, and for that reason, we immediately respected him. People in Riga wanted to be with Rick because he carried himself like a spiritual diplomat. And he *was*, indeed, one sent by God Himself. So when he announced he was leaving, we were shocked. We never dreamed he would leave Riga!"

But Denise and I had always thrown ourselves completely into whatever work God had called us to for the season — as if it were our *only* season.

We were completely enmeshed with our people and immersed in the plan of God in Riga. But I knew what I'd heard from the Holy Spirit, and although the process to move to Moscow was slow, I was going to stay on track with moving and with transitioning my long-time assistant Andrey Chebotarev to become the next pastor of the Riga Good News Church.

Convincing Andrey to take the helm of the Riga church was no small challenge. I had known him from my first visit in 1991. He was an original member of our team, and I'd trained him in the ministry. He likewise trained me in the culture of the Soviet Union. Andrey was a mere twenty-something years old at the time I met him at the Jelgava Bible school — and it's hard to fathom, but I was only thirty-three years old when all of this started.

Andrey and I had traveled the farthest reaches of the former Soviet Union together, bargaining for TV time and putting together what would eventually become our own television network, the first of its kind in the former USSR.

In those days, Andrey was experiencing a new life of faith and adventures in God as we stepped out, at times under dangerous circumstances, to obey what the Lord was instructing us to do. From Andrey, I learned the Russian culture. I also learned the ins and outs of how to interact with our contacts — with the wisdom of God, the wisdom of Andrey's upbringing, and his familiarity with those territories, including the people who lived there.

Andrey and I had enjoyed a lot of history together over nearly a decade of time, and now we would be living and ministering in two different countries. But God was in it all, and Andrey was ready for this moment whether he realized it or not!

It was amazing to see what God had done with our ministry when we lived in the United States, and now we had seen God do amazing things in Latvia with the TV network, the church, and the pastors association. I had embraced my new corner of the sky, but the Lord was about to widen that corner to include the farthest reaches of the former Soviet Union *and* *beyond.*

The directive the Holy Spirit spoke to my heart to move our family to Moscow took almost two years to execute — from preparing the necessary legal documents to fortifying existing leadership in Riga to assuring *and reassuring* Andrey and his new wife Zina concerning their new roles in the Riga church. We notified family; talked, prayed, and cried with our leadership team; and began strategically planning for our first church service in Russia's capital city of Moscow.

We'd already had a television-ministry office in Moscow for many years, but now we were making frequent visits there by train to get the staff in Moscow ready for the start of the new church in Russia's capital city.

With Denise and our sons at my side, I began to raise up new leaders for the new work, and Denise began to work with a small group who would form the first worship team for the Moscow church. We talked and prayed and began strategically preparing for our big move to Moscow, which we'd planned to make happen in January 2001.

One step always leads to another and can set a course for our lives — either a right course or a wrong one, depending on whether we are in step with God. This is why we've always taken our daily and even *minute-by-minute* decisions before God so seriously. Whatever doesn't line up with our calling and destiny, we view as a distraction that can potentially lead us off course.

All our steps in the former USSR thus far had started in Jelgava, where our family began when we made our move halfway around the world from Tulsa. Then God led us to start the work in Riga, and it was His blessing that preserved, protected, and prospered us while we were there.

During this time, the mail response to TV continued to come in from everywhere. *Also* by this time, other people on the team began to be involved in TV negotiations because I had a church and a pastors association that was growing. Plus, I was preparing and teaching in all the TV programs that we were broadcasting. God was expanding our base, and it was becoming stronger. But now it was time to relocate our family once again, this time to the nation of Russia.

## Singing for the Glory of God —
## the Serious Attitude God Takes Toward Our Gifts

Not only was our base getting stronger, but Denise and I, *individually*, were becoming stronger. Because of all that God had faithfully seen us through, our roots had gone down deeper than ever, and our spiritual foundation had become deeper and wider too. It wasn't just the church, the TV ministry, and the pastors association that were growing — Denise Renner was growing in her own talents and calling.

In fact, before I tell you about our departure from Latvia, I want to tell you how Denise really began to use her voice for the glory of God. As I noted in Chapter Four, before we were married, Denise was preparing for a serious opera career and had even traveled to New York City to audition at the New York City Opera and at the Metropolitan Opera Company.

At the New York City Opera, she auditioned for the world-renowned Beverly Sills — and at the Metropolitan Opera Company, commonly referred to as the Met, she auditioned for a committee that included the assistant of James Levine, who was the principal conductor of the Met. After that audition, Levine's assistant and the committee gave their written appraisal of Denise and her performance, which read: "Tall, impressive, MAJOR TALENT. We want her to come back one year from now to audition for James Levine in the main house and sing from the arias of Lady Macbeth from Verdi's *Macbeth*."

The reason I'm reminding you of this is that in all those years of getting established in the USSR, Denise continued to develop her vocal gift. One day, I said to her, "Denise, I think you should audition for the conductor at the Latvian National Opera!"

The Latvian National Opera was a world-class opera in a fabulous building in the center of Old Riga. At my suggestion, Denise made an appointment, and within a few weeks, I accompanied her to the Riga Opera House for an audition for the conductor. I sat near the conductor and watched as Denise performed. I overheard him say to his assistant, "Where did this woman come from? She lives here in Riga? This amazing voice has been living here, and we didn't know anything about it? How is that possible — this woman has an amazing voice!"

*(To be continued on page 677.)*

# Photos Corresponding to Chapters 8-12

**Above:** In late April 1991, Duane Vander Klok, Dave Duell, John Vereecken, and I disembarked our Aeroflot flight in Riga, which was the capital of the then Soviet Socialist Republic of Latvia.

**Above:** Duane, Dave, John, and I with Vasily Filimonov, a local man who negotiated the renting of the auditorium to get the Bible school started. This happened right under the watchful eyes of the old KGB. But God made a way, and more than two hundred students attended for ministry training.

**Above:** April 1991 was my first time to speak at the Bible school in Jelgava. The odds of such a school operating openly in the USSR (and being run by Americans) was impossible, yet it was really happening — an experience I was privileged to witness and participate in.

**Above:** I was moved by the dedication of the students in this school and the sacrifices they'd made to be there. They had few possessions, and they'd left homes, parents, and siblings — some traveling enormous distances — to pursue their callings.

**Above:** As I peered over that auditorium into the faces of those students, I was gripped with the realization that they were standing in their moment, in the very time those who had gone before them had prayed for.

**Above:** On that first trip to Jelgava, I spoke at a public meeting in the Throne Room of a palace built by Yelizaveta (Elizabeth) Petrovna, the daughter of Peter the Great. There we saw miracles of healings and deliverances, as well as large numbers of salvations.

**Left:** When we finally made it to Red Square, my companions and I were speechless that we were in the Soviet Union and were actually standing in Red Square. As I focused on Lenin's mausoleum and the walls of the Kremlin, the scene before me suddenly "disappeared," and I saw a vision of my future play out before me like I was looking at the stage of a play on Broadway.

**Right:** At eight, six, and two, respectively, Paul, Philip, and Joel were accustomed to family discussions, as Denise and I had always made them feel they were an integral part of our ministry because they *really were* such a critical part. I told them we were moving to a country called the Soviet Union, thinking it was for just a one-year commitment and then we'd be back in Tulsa to resume building our U.S.-based ministry.

**Photos Above and Next Two Pages:** The whole world watched as thousands of Soviet citizens filled the streets, carrying massive flags of a new Russia. The world wondered what would happen next. What happened next was, Boris Yeltsin seized the moment to project himself as the next leader of Russia. In a few days, the coup collapsed and Yeltsin banned the Communist Party and ordered all of its property to be seized.

Photos: © ITAR-TASS News Agency / used by permission.

Photo: © ITAR-TASS News Agency/Alamy Stock Photo / used by permission.

Photo: © Sputnik / used by permission.

**Above:** Boris Yeltsin stood on top of a tank at the Russian Federation Building to address the crowd as the old powers were overthrown. **Below:** When Mikhail Gorbachev returned to Moscow from his house arrest in Crimea, he discovered his nemesis had the reins of power in his hands. Tanks and troops had been ordered onto the streets of Moscow, and a coup took place August 19-21, 1991.

**Left:** In late September 1991, just one month after the historic coup in Moscow in August, Denise and I flew to Latvia to bring our first load of belongings there as a part of our preparation for our family's arrival in January 1992. On that trip, we officially rented a house (pictured here) as our first home in the USSR.

**Right:** As this older Russian woman on Arbat Street smiled at Denise with a welcoming twinkle in her eye, Denise's heart, as well as her apprehensions, were melted by this woman's smile. From that moment on, Denise began to enjoy not only where she was in every season, but she began to look forward to each new adventure with me in the former USSR.

**Left:** Czar Nicholas and Alexandra with their four daughters Olga, Tatiana, Maria, and Anastasia — and one son, Alexei, who was next in line to the imperial throne after his father. Three hundred years of the Romanov dynasty abruptly came to an end, and the bloody revolution of 1917 led to the executions of this Romanov family and obliterated Russia's glorious imperial history.

Photo: © Archive Pics/Alamy Stock Photo / used by permission.

**Above:** Mobs began to fill the streets, pulling down statues and monuments and attacking police precincts. Nearly every visible authority figure was targeted by mobs, including judges, policemen, governmental officials, army officers, priests, teachers, employers, landowners — even parental authority became a target of disdain. In place of the Russian tricolor flag, these mobs, fueled by revolutionaries, began to fly red flags and call for the overthrow of the monarchy. Photo used by permission: © Chronicle/Alamy Stock Photo.

**Above:** The upper classes doubted that the unrest would lead to much and generally felt it would pass and life would return to normal. But disgruntled political revolutionaries grew more powerful, thoroughly intending to overthrow the Romanov dynasty. Among these political movements was the Bolshevik Movement, which would eventually be led by a revolutionary named Vladimir Lenin. Photo used by permission: © akg-images/Alamy Stock Photo.

**Above:** For a period of time, millions faced starvation, factories stopped working, the railways were destroyed, and the country was thrust into even deeper crisis. Those who had ruled for hundreds of years never believed such events could happen in Russia. But quickly, the Russia that once was no longer existed, and the new authorities moved forward to create a new state. Photo used by permission: © Sueddeutsche Zeitung Photo/Alamy Stock Photo.

**Above:** Ideas presented by Lenin were outwardly attractive and captured the hearts of the people in a country where there had been great social inequality. However, the diabolical nature of these ideas was manifested in a complete denial of God, so the new state had an atheistic ideological objective to eliminate religion along with the extermination of religious people. Masses died in the 1917 revolution. Photo used by permission: © Pictorial Press Ltd/Alamy Stock Photo.

**Above:** As a result of the 1917 Russian Revolution, every semblance of czarist Russia was destroyed, and noble families either fled or were executed. Quickly, socialist, communist-Marxist policies were implemented, and the Romanov monarchy that had ruled for three hundred years came to an abrupt and tragic end.

**Above:** Vladimir Lenin was a revolutionary with a Marxist philosophy who intended to create a new Russia. He seized power and, with him, a new police state emerged at the helm. Soon the new government began to confiscate private property and take retribution against authority figures from the czarist years. The White Army stood by the czar, and the Red Army stood with Lenin's new Communist Party, resulting in a bloody civil war that continued until 1922 and claimed the lives of millions of Russians. Photo used by permission © Archive Collection/Alamy Stock.

**Above:** When Lenin died, another revolutionary eventually replaced him as leader. Joseph Stalin was elected the General Secretary of the Central Committee, and quickly after Lenin's death in 1924, he began to promote himself as Lenin's heir. By the end of the 1920s, Stalin had become the undisputed leader of socialist-communist Russia, and he retained that control for twenty-nine years until his death in 1953. Photo used by permission: © Heritage Image Partnership Ltd/Alamy Stock Photo.

**Above:** Pictured here is Mikhail Gorbachev speaking to the Communist Party leaders in Moscow. He was deeply committed to Marxist-communism, but he and his wife, Raisa, brilliantly gave a new, more friendly face to socialistic communism that appealed to people in the West. He instigated dramatic economic reforms called Perestroika and Glasnost. Gorbachev was the last official leader of the Union of Soviet Socialist Republics. Photo used by permission: © Sputnik.

**Above:** Perestroika hurled the Soviet Union into an unimaginable economic crisis. Deficits of every imaginable product abounded everywhere, and store shelves were nearly bare. Photo used by permission: © Sputnik.

**Above and Below:** The system became irretrievably broken, and people everywhere stood in long lines at stores that were nearly empty of the most basic products, including food, clothing, and other basic necessities.

**Left:** Widespread deficits were evident in grocery stores, and it became a humiliating, heartbreaking, and desperate time for a once-proud Soviet people.

Photo: © Sputnik / used by permission.

**Right:** This photo shows a grocery-store clerk checking a man's documents to ensure he had a right to purchase rationed products.

Photo: © Sputnik / used by permission.

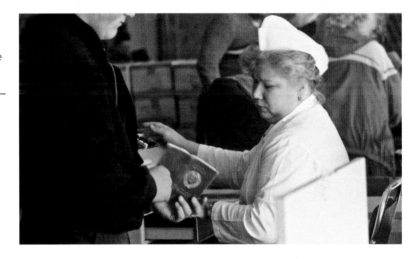

**Left:** On December 8, 1991, Boris Yeltsin along with the leaders of Belarus and Ukraine signed documents to officially dissolve the Union of Soviet Social Republics. With the swipe of a pen, the USSR — a seventy-plus-year experiment in socialism and communism — was officially gone.

Photo: © Sputnik / used by permission.

**Above:** The city of Moscow removed the towering statue of Felix Dzerzhinsky that had stood for decades in front of the central headquarters of the KGB. Dzerzhinsky had been the founder of security services that preceded the former KGB (Komitet Gosudarstvennoy Bezopasnosti). Photo used by permission: © Sputnik.

**Above:** During those dark days, people crammed into stores to see if any products were available. Streets in every city were lined with tables where people stood to sell or barter their goods. The inflation rate was skyrocketing, and people were so strapped for cash that they began taking personal items from their homes — even prized, valued possessions that included family heirlooms — to sell on the streets.

**Above, Below, and Next Page:** Grandmothers, grandfathers, fathers, and mothers, including higher-ranking professionals — and young people as well — tried to sell anything they could find to get cash for survival.

**Above:** I took this photo of our rubles the day our family arrived in the former USSR in January 1992. The USSR had functioned on the Soviet ruble since its earliest beginnings, and when we moved to Latvia, the Soviet ruble was still the currency in use. But soon we felt the brunt of that currency's collapse and the disastrous effects runaway inflation had on millions of lives in the former Soviet Union.

**Right:** On December 25, 1991, Mikhail Gorbachev called President George H. W. Bush to inform him of his official resignation as President of the Soviet Union and of the final dissolution of the USSR. When Gorbachev resigned, he did so as the last President of the Soviet Union, and Boris Yeltsin became the first President of a new Russian state. Photo: © ITAR-TASS News Agency / used by permission.

**Left:** Denise and I and Paul, Philip, and Joel — along with our nanny Sharmon — pose for a first "official" photo in the former Soviet Union. We departed for the former USSR on January 27 and arrived the following morning on January 28, 1992.

**Above:** Denise in our first Soviet-made car that we purchased in October 1991. The car was a small cherry-colored Lada with doors that never closed properly. We were able to purchase that car due to the generosity of two couples who were partners and who gave an offering to our ministry so we could buy it. That financial gift was a God-sent encouragement that He would financially provide for all our needs.

**Above:** On August 1, 1941, German commanders gave the order to exterminate all Jews in the city of Jelgava. Afterward, Nazis posted signs at the entrance to the town that announced: "JELGAVA IS CLEANSED OF JEWS." When our family moved to our first house in Jelgava, we were unaware that our house was in the very shadow of the site of the horrific Jewish extermination that occurred almost a half century before. At that time, there was no memorial erected to recall that event, but today a monument stands at the site — just a stone's throw from our first house.

**Above:** I fell in love with these Soviet students and cherished every moment with them. I felt like I had stepped into the book of Acts as I taught them the Word of God. It was energizing to both them and me, and God's hand of blessing was on us as I began to fulfill what we had come to do. We didn't know it at the time, but those students would become Russia's new spiritual leaders.

**Left:** The city of Jelgava was a sad and dilapidated city in January 1992 when our family arrived there to live. The effects of World War II could still be felt everywhere, as parts of the city remained in ruins since the time they had been bombed in war. The main tower of the city, a large gutted and burned Orthodox church, and bombed walls of other buildings stood as visible reminders of the conflict that occurred there for three solid months during the war. But this is where God called our family and where His grace was to be poured out richly on us and our ministry as we got started in the lands of the former Soviet Union.

**Above:** When our family first arrived in Jelgava, it was a broken-down and derelict city where stores were empty, and there were deficits of nearly every essential product needed for life. It was almost unbelievable to think a system could be so broken. There were deficits of all goods, not just food, and products of every kind were very difficult to obtain. Walls of stores were covered with broken tiles, meat freezers were empty, and people stood in line for basic goods that were being rationed. The whole socialistic economic system was broken across the board.

**Left:** Though the Soviet flag had officially been lowered and replaced by the flag of the Russian Federation in the fall of 1991, Denise and I were visiting the Kremlin on the day that the last remaining Soviet flags inside the Kremlin were being removed. I took this photo as Denise and I actually watched "history" occur when the last Soviet flag was taken away.

**Left:** After the collapse of the communist regime, Latvia celebrated its first legal Easter in 1992. When Latvia fell to an atheistic Communist Party in 1940, Easter had become outlawed. But on that first restored Easter day in 1992, our family celebrated it by going to church, and our sons hunted Easter eggs, a tradition no one in Jelgava had heard of before. That day, Paul, Philip, and Joel posed for this photo in our front yard to commemorate that historic Easter Day.

**Photos:** Just after we arrived in 1992, Denise and I walked onto a strip of Soviet-style carpet that covered the ice in the national hockey stadium so we could sing and preach. When we finished ministering, an invitation was given, and we watched as people walked across the ice to receive salvation. People on crutches treacherously traversed the ice to get to our side of the stadium to receive Christ and prayer for healing.

**Left:** With the use of a home video camera, Denise and I adjusted our living room to become a makeshift TV studio, and we began to film primitive-looking one-hour programs for daily TV. Those programs may have been embarrassingly simple — nevertheless, mountains of mail begin to pour into our office from viewers who were hearing teaching from the Bible for the first time in their lives.

**Below:** Pictured here is Riga and its huge TV tower. Television in the USSR had been off-limits to Americans because Americans had been viewed as untrusted enemies of the socialist-communist state. So when I began to appear on television every day, people tuned in to see what I was doing on television and what in the world I would be saying to them for a full hour each day.

**Left:** Our first TV studio had no air conditioning, so while filming I wore a dress shirt, tie, and suit jacket from the waist up — and from the waist down, I wore shorts and sat with my feet immersed in two big buckets of ice-cold water in an effort to cool down while we were filming. Even with my feet submerged in that water, sweat would pour from my brow, and I would have to wipe my forehead almost the entire time we filmed.

**Left:** When I asked TV viewers to write, I had no idea of the mountains of mail that would come so quickly into our office. Before we could hardly catch our breath, we had tons of mail packed in boxes and stacked on top of more boxes. An entire large room in our office was filled from floor to ceiling with boxes and boxes of mail from viewers that needed to be read and answered as promised.

**Photos Above and Next Page:** In the late summer of 1992, I filmed a commercial inviting people to attend a meeting that we would hold in the national hockey stadium. When the event began, Denise and I stood on the platform and looked out over the audience in that large hockey arena, shocked to see the place filled to capacity. Many of them were sick people who had no means of obtaining desperately needed medicine and had therefore turned to the power of God as their only hope for healing. Night after night, we witnessed mighty miracles occurring before our eyes.

Blind eyes were opened, epileptics were healed, and deaf ears were unstopped. The greatest miracle of all was the hundreds of people who came forward to give their lives to Jesus at the conclusion of the meetings each night. By the end of that week, the aggregate attendance was approximately forty thousand people — and of that number, more than seven thousand prayed to receive Jesus as Lord.

**Above:** These photos show the sequence of a paralyzed man in attendance receiving a miracle — healing and restoration in his useless limbs. Each night, he arrived after everyone else was seated so he could slowly make his way to his reserved seat without being overcome by a busy crowd. He had fallen from a roof nineteen years earlier, and his condition was desperate and sad. He used his crutches like legs to swing his lifeless lower body forward bit by bit as he walked. On the first day of the meetings, he came to the platform to give his life to Jesus. On the second day, he came forward to receive the baptism in the Holy Spirit. On the fourth day, he showed up at the local swimming pool where we were baptizing people, and he was water-baptized. If nothing else happened to this man, his life had already been completely transformed for all eternity by the power of God. But that wasn't all this precious man received from God during these meetings!

**Above:** At the end of the very last service, I heard a commotion in the crowd. Immediately, this man shot up from his chair and began walking — *crutch-free*! The bottom half of his body had suddenly come alive. Like the lame man in Acts 3, he leaped and praised God all the way to the front, where he threw his crutches on the stage *and left them there*! People flooded the altar to give their lives to Christ!

**Above:** We rented a government pool for three afternoons to baptize new converts. We thought that if three hundred of the new converts showed up over the course of the three afternoons, it would be a fabulous turnout — so you can imagine how stunned we were when more than three hundred people showed up *just on the first afternoon*.

**Above:** By the end of three afternoons, we had water-baptized 926 people. We were spiritually elated, physically exhausted, and still had one more evening service to preach, in which we knew more people would repent and give their lives to Christ! That meant even more people would need to be water-baptized!

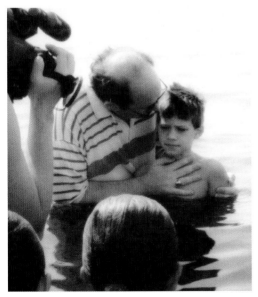

**Above:** Paul, eight, was water-baptized by me at the banks of the Daugava River in Riga in the early summer of 1992. In those early days there were no baptistries in churches, so people who came to Christ were water-baptized in rivers and lakes.

**Above:** Philip, six, was water baptized by me on the same day at the banks the Daugava River in Riga in the early summer of 1992. Because so many people were coming to Christ, we saw hundreds of people baptized that warm, sunny afternoon.

**Above:** The actual map of the USSR that I used the day I took a permanent marker and began to circle huge geographic areas where the Holy Spirit was instructing me to take the teaching of the Bible through our TV ministry. I knew that all the areas where the Spirit led me to circle were virgin territory for the broadcasting of the Word of God — He laid out on that map an entire divine strategy for my team and me to follow!

**Above:** Andrey Chebotarev and I preaching in a meeting on a trip to obtain TV contracts. He and I, and all our couriers, traveled almost continuously across the former USSR to obtain those contracts and to deliver the programs and payments to the stations.

**Above:** We placed flags on the map to track all the stations broadcasting our programs. Soon we watched those flags spread across vast regions of the former USSR. We were told it couldn't be done, but God was sending Bible teaching into people's homes via television.

**Above:** Whenever possible, I asked Paul, Philip, or Joel to join me as I traveled to negotiate for television time across the former USSR. I wanted them to experience the vastness of this region and to witness firsthand what God was miraculously doing in our ministry.

**Left:** Paul and Philip are pictured wearing Soviet military uniforms — something they loved to do when they were young. While friends and relatives in America were growing up in a Western world, our sons were growing up with a completely different experience that was equipping them for what they're doing today.

**Above:** The walls of the Academy's auditorium were adorned with emblems of Marxism and the Soviet Union, including huge cameos of Marx and Lenin adorning the left and right of the stage, and the back rooms were filled with Soviet memorabilia.

**Right:** The Academy of Sciences, where we started the Riga church, was a Stalin-style skyscraper built near the place where Nazis incarcerated the Jewish community during World War II. God poured out His grace in the very spot where Satan tried to liquidate so many Jewish people.

**Above:** Every week, every chair was filled, and people crowded the steps and lined the auditorium during each service. The auditorium was packed to capacity until the number of people attending "overflowed," and we had to begin holding multiple services each week to accommodate our burgeoning congregation of new believers. In the middle of that location — where the Communist Party had once prevailed — the grace of God was being poured out.

**Above:** The Academy of Sciences, where we started our church, had been constructed in the very shadow of the ghetto of Riga, where Nazi forces had incarcerated the entire Jewish community of Riga during World War II starting in 1941. This photo shows the barbed wire that marked off the Jewish ghetto in those dark days.

Photo: © Riga Ghetto Museum / used by permission.

**Above:** This original photo shows Jews being brought to the Jewish ghetto during the Nazi occupation of Latvia and were eventually liquidated during World War II. From 1941 to 1944, similar actions were taken against Jews who had been transported there from all over eastern Europe.

Photo: © Riga Ghetto Museum / used by permission.

**Above:** This photo shows Jews being arrested and executed in the Latvian city of Liepaja, but such atrocious acts were also being carried out in Riga and in cities all across Latvia during the Nazi occupation of World War II.

Photo: © Riga Ghetto Museum / used by permission.

**Above:** In 1941, on the dates of November 30 and December 8, Riga's remaining Jewish community of about 24,000 was organized into columns of one thousand people and marched from the Jewish ghetto to Rumbula, an area east of Riga where pits had already been dug and where the killing would be done. All the able-bodied Jews went by foot from the ghetto to the liquidation site.

Photo: © Riga Ghetto Museum / used by permission.

**Left:** The people were marched down the ramps into the pits, ten at a time in single file. With their automatic weapons set on single shots, the marksmen murdered the Jews from a distance of about two meters with a shot in the backs of their heads. One bullet per person was allotted.

Photo: © Riga Ghetto Museum / used by permission.

**Below:** One rare survivor recounted the sordid killings, saying that as they neared the pits, some of the victims wept, others prayed and recited the Torah, and still others tried to comfort the small children. Handicapped and elderly people, many of whom were specially transported to the killing site, were helped into the pit by other sturdier victims.

Photo: © Riga Ghetto Museum / used by permission.

**Above:** The Nazis operated another camp at Salaspils, a small town outside of Riga near Rumbula that was converted into a concentration camp. There, blood was drained from Jewish children to provide to wounded German troops. Some historians estimate that seventy thousand Jews perished in Latvia during those ghastly years.

Photo: © Riga Ghetto Museum / used by permission.

**Above:** The Jewish ghettos were empty after the liquidation of the Jewish community was complete. Our first home in Jelgava was just a half mile from the first site of the Latvian holocaust, and our church was started in the shadow of the location where the entire Jewish population was incarcerated before their mass executions by Nazi troops between 1941 and 1945. When we constructed our Riga church building, we ended up purchasing land right in the middle of the Biekerniki forest — just on the other side of the woods from where another horrific liquidation of Jews occurred.

Photo: © Riga Ghetto Museum / used by permission.

**Above:** About two thousand believers showed up to witness our historical land dedication. Everywhere we looked, we saw Christians worshiping and rejoicing on our land where we would build the Riga Good News Church. I think the experience must have been similar to what they felt in the Old Testament when the foundations of the temple were being put back in place. No one had ever witnessed such an event — it was a truly historical moment.

**Above:** Soon massive bulldozers moved onto the land to prepare the ground for pouring the foundation for the new building. That's when we received news that the soil on our newly purchased property was so swampy that it would not be sufficient to support a foundation for a building our size. Day after day, bulldozers dug deeper into the black soil to search for a solid layer of ground beneath the soft dirt. Finally, at a depth of twelve feet — and in some places even fifteen feet deep — we came to a solid bed of sand.

**Below:** After bulldozers had done their extensive excavation work, our Renner family climbed into that deep depression and walked the length of it — almost the span of a football field — and had a family photo made. We were now the owners of the biggest hole in the nation. It had been dug — and now it was time to fill it with materials substantial enough to support our building's foundation.

**Above:** Denise and I knew it was important to communicate with our partners about what was happening. We regularly filmed reports to keep these God-called partners abreast of all the developments so they would keep us in prayer as we proceeded.

**Above:** News about the Good News Association of Pastors and Churches began to quickly spread into Russia, Belorussia, Ukraine, and other parts of the former Soviet Union. Soon we had hundreds of pastors and congregations that were a part of our association and that were spiritually under our covering. With the financial help of partners, we held hundreds of association meetings that were attended by thousands of pastors and leaders, and we provided all the costs of transportation for them, as well as our team, to get to these meetings.

**Photos Above and Next Page:** We conducted public meetings for hundreds of thousands of people who regularly watched us on television. They flooded into those auditoriums; they walked the aisles to give their lives to Jesus Christ; they were filled with the Holy Spirit; they were healed and delivered; and they received teaching materials free of charge that we had printed just for them.

**Above:** Crusade photos from our meetings across the former Soviet Union.

**Above:** We dedicated our Riga church building in early November 1998. There was a long fight to finish this project, but we were grateful to be participants in history in the making. After resisting so many attacks of the enemy to try to stop the construction of this building — and after using our faith to believe for the finances to build it with cash and to build it on time — finally, it was done. Denise and I stood on the stage with our sons and others to thank God, our church, and our partners for what they did to make this miracle a reality.

**Above:** Denise was faithful to use her gift in whatever way she could, so God gave her platforms before audiences all over the former Soviet Union as we held our meetings and preached the Word to them. She sang to God's glory in front of thousands of people who were enraptured by the presence of God that was manifested as she used her voice and her gift. As Denise has sung on stage after stage, the anointing of God has released those who were bound and healed those who were sick.

That was such a victorious and encouraging moment for Denise, but she did not feel led to pursue anything further at the Riga Opera House. Instead, she began to schedule her own operatic concerts so she could sing classically and also include Gospel music in the mix because she wanted to use her voice for the glory of God.

At one time the great composer Richard Wagner had lived in Riga, and because of that, there was a fabulous concert hall in Riga called Wagner Hall, a part of the Richard Wagner Opera Theater House. From time to time, we rented that venue for Denise to give concerts, and when she performed in that hall, it was packed with believers who were so proud to see the Gospel proclaimed at such an esteemed venue.

Denise also gave concerts in the St. Peter and St. Paul Church, an Orthodox cathedral that had been built at the orders of the Russian Empress Catherine the Great. That gorgeous cathedral with blue and white interiors and gold-gilded features was filled time and again with believers who were elated to see Denise singing the Gospel on such a stage.

And because our Riga apartment had one room large enough to accommodate eighty seated people at one time, Denise also hosted private concerts in our home. Pastors, leaders, and even governmental leaders from Riga, came to our home for those amazing events.

Denise was using her God-given gift to the best of her ability, even if it *wasn't* on the stages of the New York City Opera, the Metropolitan Opera Company, or the Riga Opera House. But when Denise chose to walk away from those illustrious stages, she did not leave her gift behind. It went with her everywhere *she* went, and God expected her to use it to the best of her ability for His glory, as He expects *each* of us to use our gifts for Him.

In Luke 12:48, Jesus warned us, "…For unto whomsoever much is given, of him shall be much required…." In Matthew 13:12, Jesus also said, "For whosoever hath, to him shall be given, and he shall have more abundance: but whosoever hath not, from him shall be taken away even that he hath."

In both of these verses, we read that a person who has been gifted is expected to do something with that potential. Or as Jesus said, "much is required" of the one who has been given much. And even more, if a person is faithful to use what he has received, Jesus promises that more will be given to him. Hence, God is watching all the time to see how we are using and developing the potential He has placed within each of us.

Denise may not have sung on the world's most famous operatic stages, but she was faithful to use her gift in whatever way she could, so God gave her platforms before massive audiences all over the lands of the former Soviet Union as we held our meetings and preached His Word to them. She sang to God's glory in front of *tens of thousands* of people who were enraptured by the presence of God that was manifested as she used her voice and her gift. As she sang on stage after stage, the anointing of God was released, people who were bound were set free, and people who were sick were healed.

In later years in Moscow, God powerfully recompensed Denise by grant- ing her an open door to sing at the Moscow Kremlin Palace. Through a divine appointment and a series of God-orchestrated events, she was invited to sing with a hundred-piece orchestra at a gala affair on the prestigious stage of the Kremlin Palace — *and she performed fabulously!*

You see, God never overlooks our labors of love and the sacrifices we make for Him, and He specializes in giving us our heart's desires in a way that no man could devise or orchestrate.

## We Moved to Moscow in August 2000

Denise and I had planned to make the move to Moscow in January 2001, and we were already slowly moving our executive TV staff to join the rest of our TV staff there. But in the summer of 2000, we were suddenly made aware that our sons' English school teacher would not be returning to Latvia in the fall of 2000.

Paul, Philip, and Joel had been educated in Russian public schools, and they were fluent in the Russian language. But Denise and I wanted them to have an English education, too, so we had arranged for them to receive English education in Riga. Now we were searching to see if there was an English school in Moscow that our sons could attend. After finding a school that was about to begin its fall session the following week, on a Friday afternoon, I announced to our family: "Pack up! We've moving to Moscow this Tuesday — *you boys need an English education!*"

Denise and the boys began feverously packing belongings that we would need in Moscow — clothes, shoes, dishes, cooking utensils, a few lamps, rugs, small furniture items, and a television. We reserved two train cabins, and I wondered how we'd get all of those things into them and still have enough room for our family to endure the overnight train ride to Moscow!

I called Andrey to tell him that we were moving to Moscow on Tuesday morning, which was a full five months sooner than he had anticipated. He and everyone else understood that our sons needed an education, but that phone call nearly knocked the wind out of him. Looking back, I can see it was the mercy of God to do it this way so that this very emotional move wasn't prolonged over a five- or six-month period of time.

Tuesday morning came quickly. Our things had been packed into suitcases, sacks, boxes, and garment bags, and we needed to quickly cram everything into the two train compartments we'd reserved and then we would try to squeeze ourselves in!

After a tearful sendoff by Andrey and Zina and our Riga staff at the train depot, the train departed. We waved farewell to our precious team in Riga and our family spent an adventurous overnight ride in those cabins that barely had enough room for us because of all of our belongings. We crossed the border from Latvia arriving in Russia sometime in the early morning the next day — but *this* time, it was *to stay*.

For every bit of territory gained and victory won in our early experiences in Latvia, Denise and I and our small team had labored fervently and warred an almost constant spiritual fight. The vast shortages of everything in the early 1990s due to the sudden collapse of the Soviet system — from automobile fuel to food and medication to toilet tissue and other basic necessities — are events I am thankful our family experienced. When people from the former USSR describe those final days of the Soviet Union, we understand every word they share because we were living in that affected nation amidst those waves of turmoil, our own lives caught in the crashing foam.

In the pages that follow, I will share the details of how we transitioned as a family from Riga to Moscow. We were determined to scale every obstacle, overcome every challenge, and pass all our tests as we embarked on starting a church in yet more new territory in the former USSR. And we *remain* committed for the rest of our days to complete God's course for our lives. From Tulsa to Jelgava to Riga to Moscow — this *unlikely* family from two small towns in Oklahoma had been privileged to witness the transformation of *nations* over the short time since the fall of the Communist Party in this part of the world. And we were about to experience another move of God from our new base in Moscow.

'Less than a decade from the fall of the Iron
Curtain and the collapse of the communist regime,
these nations, and Russia in particular, were far
from over the struggles of the past, as we will see.
They needed God's special attention and care
more than ever. Moscow would be the place
from which God would gloriously
enable us to provide it!'

# 13

# AN UNLIKELY MOVE TO MOSCOW AS THE RENNER ADVENTURE CONTINUES

At about mid-morning, our train approached the Moscow train station with us in tow along with most of our earthly possessions. Some-what rested — having been awakened once in the night to show our passports when we crossed the border from Latvia to Russia — we eagerly headed to the nearest exit with as many belongings as our arms could carry.

Philip was in the U.S. visiting relatives at the time of our sudden move and would join us later. The rest of our family had spread out overnight between our two very small cabins, with all our luggage, bags, and household goods packed tightly around us. Squeezed into those tiny compartments along with our things, we were glad we were so close as a family and enjoyed each other's "close" company, or it would have been an even longer eighteen-hour ride! Now we were going to need lots of help to unload everything in a short span of time before the train would take off for its next destination.

**Left:** *The Kremlin Clock in the Spasskaya Tower of the Moscow Kremlin.*

In all the years I had been regularly traveling to Moscow by train, I'd never experienced a train overshooting the platform — but on that day, our train overshot the platform badly, and we ended up far from the truck and team awaiting us and our belongings. In fact, when we opened the train door to disembark, there was no platform at all. We were so high above the ground that we had to jump from the train. The boys jumped first, and after unloading our things, I jumped so I could gingerly help Denise down from where she stood, still inside the train, almost six feet above the ground.

No one was there to help us because our train was so far from where it should have stopped. So instead of being greeted by our awaiting team, we saw a pack of mangy dogs standing there, "greeting" us and perhaps looking for a handout of scraps. But they didn't bother us as we unloaded our jam-packed cabins — me standing six feet above the ground tossing suitcases, boxes, bags, and, *very carefully*, our television, to the boys who had positioned themselves below to receive them. After what seemed like a long time, we had everything unloaded and stacked into one big pile in the dirt. Feeling accomplished, but only partway done, one by one, we each picked up what we could and headed toward our transportation to let our team know we had arrived. We were *at home* in Moscow!

For many years, we'd already had a television office in Moscow that handled TV negotiations, answered mail from Russian television viewers, and conducted other TV-ministry business. They'd had three- or four-days' notice of our arrival, at which time, they speedily began the search for an apartment for our family. They found a newly renovated 750-square-foot apartment located downtown on the backside of a large military building near the Novokuznetskaya Metro, which our sons would be catching every morning to go to school.

The apartment, located across the street from a neighborhood market, was only about a two-minute walk from the Moscow River, and it was just across the Komissariatskiy and Bolshoy Ustyinskiy Bridges from our Moscow TV office, a mere twelve-minute walk from home to work.

Every morning, Denise and I walked together across those bridges to the office. The view of the Kremlin from our vantage point was simply breathtaking — the best view in the city of Moscow. In my mind, it was a panoramic view of one of the most spectacular sights in the whole world.

Oh, how we especially loved it in the fall when the sky was nearly lavender, and the gold-covered towers of the Kremlin glistened so brilliantly — the beautiful lavender-blue sky as their artful backdrop. A remarkable view in *every* season was ours to enjoy every morning and evening as we walked back and forth to the office — what a feast it was for our eyes and our souls.

Our office occupied the entire first floor of a stately old palace that had been seized by insurgents during the 1917 revolution and converted into an office building. Nothing of the palace interiors remained in our day, but the outside of the building had been beautifully restored with golden-yellow paint and multiple white, carved columns that adorned the front side of the building that faced the river. The building stood majestically on the bank of the Moscow River, and we enjoyed an easy five-minute walk from there to Red Square.

## The Grace of God was Abounding
## and Moving Us Along *Quickly*

In our earlier days in Riga, we'd had to lay a foundation for everything right from the beginning. But because our Moscow office and team had been functioning for nearly a decade, a foundation for our work here was already in place in this city, so the work could get moving faster.

Paul Renner commented, "The timing of our family's arrival in Moscow was amazing. The year we moved to Moscow, President Putin had just become President. During all the 1990s and up to the year 2000 — the Yeltsin years — things in Russia had been pretty crazy. But starting in 2000 when President Putin came to office, things began to quickly get better."

Paul continued, "The year we moved to Moscow, there had been internal problems in a couple of churches in Moscow, so there were quite a few people already looking for a church. The whole idea of a church with solid, Bible-based teaching and that had administrative order was the most necessary thing for people at that time. And we moved there with such a sense of hope and excitement. We really felt that 'things tomorrow were going to be better than today.' That kind of anticipation and expectation was present in everything we were doing."

Paul added, "When we moved to Moscow, everyone had told us, 'Moscow is a missionary-killer city. No one survives Moscow.' But when we moved here, it seemed so easy for us. The grace of God was *ABOUNDING*."

I can tell you that almost instantly, our family fell in love with Moscow. We loved the traffic, the industrial smells — simply everything about this city! Moscow had *grabbed* our hearts. I personally felt like an eagle that had been set free to fly. For the first time in nearly a decade, we were liberated from the competing Latvian language, and we could use Russian freely with no concern of offending anyone. It felt like our wings had been freed — and we were ready to soar!

Denise had previously deeply disliked Moscow because it was such a monster in terms of size. And at the very end of the Soviet era when we first moved to that part of the world, Moscow seemed gray, dirty, and just massively *bleak*. But when I told Denise we were moving there, she started confessing, "When I get to Moscow, I'll be the happiest I've been in my life." And because she made that her daily confession, of course, that's exactly what happened. She *quickly* fell in love with Moscow.

There was, of course, a divine purpose for why we were being transplanted to Russia's massively populated capital city. Our calling to the Russian-speaking world was about to be multiplied on new fronts as we willingly brought our supply so that God could disperse it from our new headquarters to the far-flung lands of the former USSR. Less than a decade from the fall of the Iron Curtain and the collapse of the communist regime, these nations, and Russia in particular, were far from over the struggles of the past, as we will see in the following section of this chapter. They needed God's special attention and care more than ever. Moscow would be the place from which God would gloriously enable us to provide it!

### Modern Terrorist Attacks — Russia Has Known Its Share of Terror

I wrote the following paragraphs to underscore the nationwide tone of uneasiness and fear that especially gripped Russia's capital, Moscow, at the time of our arrival. We all remember September 11, 2001, when the

United States especially felt the tragedy of terrorism associated with Islamic extremism when the Twin Towers of the World Trade Center were attacked and destroyed. Later when ISIS appeared on the world scene, practically the whole planet was awakened to wholesale terrorism in the nations' respective backyards.

But Russia felt the impact of terrorism much earlier and was, in fact, in the *throes* of widespread terrorism that was sweeping across that land when we arrived in the capital city.

One of the consequences of the collapse of the USSR was the weakening of the central government as evidenced by the fact that fifteen republics of the former USSR had quickly become independent states. Within Russia itself, there were also regions inside her borders that had considered becoming independent states.

One of these regions was the Chechen Republic, a significant part of the population of which suffered greatly during the Stalinist era. Unfortunately, their intense desire for independence was also accompanied by the presence of Islamic extremism. People who advocated Jihad against "infidels," along with experienced Arab militants, came to the Chechen Republic after the fall of communism. The main business was drug-trafficking, weapons, and kidnapping for ransom. But Russia could not allow the creation of a terrorist state on its borders, and the result was two Chechen wars.

A few months before our family moved to Moscow, a series of terrible terrorist attacks began to be carried out by Islamic terrorists from Chechnya. The first occurred on August 31, 1999, when an explosion took place in the Okhotny Ryad shopping mall right at Red Square that killed one person and injured forty others.[1] As tragic as that assault was, it was but a precursor to many attacks that were to follow, a few of which I will name.

## A History of Terror in Recent Decades

On September 9, 1999, the next terrorist attack was a massive bombing of a Moscow apartment building shortly after midnight local time. A bomb detonated on the ground floor of the building that was the equivalent to 660-880 pounds of TNT. The nine-story building was destroyed, killing

106 people inside and injuring 249 others. Nineteen nearby buildings were severely damaged. A total of 108 apartments were destroyed during the bombing. Russian President Boris Yeltsin ordered the search of 30,000 residential buildings in Moscow for explosives and took personal control of investigating the blast.[2] Within ten days during that month of September, several other terrorist bombings followed in two other towns in southern Russia. I'll tell you about three of those — those that took place on September 13, 16, and 22 — and give you a brief overview of the domestic terror that Russia endured all the way through the year 2017.

On September 13, 1999, four days after that devastating apartment bombing, a large bomb exploded in the basement of an apartment in southern Moscow, about 3.7 miles from the place of the last attack. This was the deadliest blast to date in the chain of bombings with 119 people killed and 200 injured. The 8-story building was flattened, littering the street with debris and throwing some concrete pieces almost a mile away.[3] On that same date, September 13, 1999, police found and successfully defused another bomb in an apartment block in Moscow.[4]

Apart from the police measures, citizen patrols helped foil additional bombings. At that time, people were so terrified that they began patrolling their own neighborhoods. They didn't ask anyone for permission, and there was no government initiative. People just decided that it was needed, so they did it.

Three days later, on September 16, 1999, a truck bomb exploded outside a 9-story apartment complex in the southern city of Volgodonsk that killed 17 people and injured 115. Surrounding buildings were also damaged.[5]

On September 22, 1999, police found sacks of white powder in the basement of a large apartment building in the city of Ryazan that were connected to a detonator and a timing device. Inhabitants of the apartment building were evacuated and residents of neighboring buildings fled their homes in terror. Nearly 30,000 people spent the night on the streets. Police and rescue vehicles converged from different parts of the city, and as many as 1,200 local police officers were put on alert. In an attempt to catch the terrorists before they fled the area, railroad stations and the airport were surrounded, and roadblocks were set up on highways leading in and out of the city — but the perpetrators were not caught.[6]

All of these attacks occurred in the months preceding our family's move to Moscow in August of 2000. Russia had not experienced many terror attacks like these, so people were quite on edge in that season, and that was the ominous tone of the whole atmosphere when we arrived.

If you count the lives lost in Russian terrorist attacks in 1999 alone, you will see that 243 people died in those attacks and 558 were injured. But this was just a portent of future chains of attacks that would tragically take the lives of almost a thousand people and injure over 500 more. The aunt of Joel's future wife died as a result of one such attack, so these events were felt very personally by the family of my future daughter-in-law Olya Renner.

But for the sake of our calling and our journey of obedience in the lands of the former Soviet Union, our family relocated to Moscow without fear or hesitation. And in this next section, I will recount for you notable terrorist attacks that occurred in Russia after our family had settled in our new home country.

### More Terrorism After Our Family Relocated to Russia

Of course, on September 11, 2001, America experienced an unprecedented terrorist attack that became known as "9/11" in which 2,977 people tragically perished in the collapse of the World Trade Center in New York City.[7]

Who could ever forget that heartbreaking day when so many lives were lost? I remember right where we were in Moscow when we received the horrific report and turned on the international news, watching *aghast* at what had demonically unfolded on American soil that fateful day. All of us who are old enough to remember it know where we were and what we were doing at the exact time that horrifying event occurred and the news of it reached our ears.

A little more than a year later, on October 23, 2002 — about two years after our arrival in Moscow — a horrible event occurred when Chechen terrorists seized the Dubrovka Theater in our city, where a performance of the fabulous Russian *Nord-Ost* musical was taking place. A short time before that siege, Denise and I had attended that performance in that building! And the very night before the tragedy occurred, several members of our Moscow staff had attended the performance there! They had been scheduled to be there the night of the attack, but due to schedule conflicts, they changed their tickets and attended the night before the siege. (I share more chilling stories of divine protection for us and our team in Chapter Fifteen, but don't turn there just yet.)

During the *Nord-Ost* performance on the evening of October 23, 2002, more than 40 armed Chechens entered the theater and took 850 people in the theater hostage. The attackers carried numerous explosives wrapped about their bodies, but the most powerful explosive devices were placed in the very center of the auditorium in this well-planned attack.

Special Russian forces enacted a rescue operation and were able to end the siege before more loss of life occurred. But by the time the crisis ended, 40 insurgents and as many as 204 hostages died, including nine foreigners.[8] It is not known exactly how many later died as a result of this horrific attack.

Then on February 6, 2004, a suicide bomber entered the Moscow Metro system and detonated a bomb that killed 39 people, whose bodies were blown to bits as the subway train exploded while in transit.[9] Members of our staff were in the adjoining subway car en route to work at the ministry that morning, but they were miraculously unharmed. In addition to those tragic fatalities, up to 120 people were injured in the attack. Again, a Chechen terrorist group claimed responsibility for the bombing.

About six months later, on August 24, 2004, explosive devices were detonated on board two domestic passenger flights that had taken off from Domodedovo International Airport in Moscow, causing the destruction of both aircraft and the loss of all eighty-nine people on board those planes. Subsequent investigations concluded that two female Chechen suicide bombers were responsible for the bombings.[10]

About one week later, on September 1, 2004, the first official day of public school when parents and children gathered to celebrate the beginning of the new school year, Chechen terrorists entered a public school in Beslan in North Ossetia, in southern Russia, and seized more than 1,100 hostages, including almost 800 children. This tragic incident is commonly referred to as the Beslan School Hostage Crisis or Beslan Massacre. The terrifying event lasted for three days and ended with the deaths of 333 people.[11]

Then on August 21, 2006, a terrorist bombing occurred when a home-made bomb made with more than two pounds of dynamite exploded at Moscow's popular Cherkizovsky Market that was frequented by foreign merchants. That bombing killed thirteen people and injured forty-seven others.[12]

On March 29, 2010, suicide bombings were carried out by two women terrorists. This particular terrorist attack happened during the morning rush hour at two stations of the Moscow Metro system — at Lubyanka and at Park Kultury — with roughly forty minutes between the attacks. At least forty people were killed and more than one hundred injured in that devastating attack.[13]

On January 24, 2011, a bombing occurred at the Domodedovo International Airport in Moscow. It was a suicide bombing in the international arrival hall of the airport. I remember it well because we had been in the arrival section of that airport just the day before. The bombing killed 37 people and injured 173 others.[14] I can gratefully testify that in all our years of ministry, Denise and I and our family have *lived* the Ninety-First Psalm — God's holy Word and His holy, covenant promise to all who dare to believe and act on it.

Less than two years later, on December 2013, two separate suicide bombings occurred a day apart that targeted the mass-transportation system in the southern city of Volgograd. One attack was carried out by a female perpetrator who had been converted to Islam by her husband. She detonated an explosive belt containing 500-600 grams of dynamite inside a public bus carrying approximately 50 people that resulted in the deaths of seven people and the injuring of at least 36 others.[15]

After that terrorist attack on the bus, people were terrified to travel, so we designed a beautiful, laminated tract with Psalm 91 written on it, and we called it *A Psalm of Protection*. Thousands of people eagerly received these cards and carried them everywhere they went. I kept one of these tracts inside my passport. Once as I was passing through Passport Control at the airport just after this terrorist episode on the bus, the passport officer saw my plastic-covered copy of Psalm 91. Instead of looking at my passport, she took Psalm 91 in her hands, read it, and said to me, "Excuse me, but I am really scared right now because of all these attacks. May I please have this?" People everywhere were on edge, and those copies of Psalm 91 brought great comfort to thousands of people. Of course, I joyfully gave that passport officer the tract.

The following year, on October 5, 2014, a terrorist went to the Grozny town hall where a celebration was taking place on Grozny City Day (Grozny is the capital of Chechnya). Police officers noticed him acting strangely and stopped him, and as the officers began to search him, the bomb he was carrying exploded. Five officers, along with the suicide bomber, were killed, and twelve other people were wounded.[16]

On December 4, 2014, a group of Islamist militants in three vehicles killed three traffic policemen after the officers had attempted to stop them at a checkpoint in the outskirts of Grozny. The militants then occupied a press building and an abandoned school that was located in the center of the city. Security forces launched a counter-terrorism operation with the use of armored vehicles and attempted to storm the buildings. A firefight ensued, and in the end, fourteen policemen, eleven militants, and one civilian were killed. Thirty-six other policemen were wounded in the incident.[17]

On October 31, 2015, a charter flight disintegrated above northern Sinai following its departure from Sharm El Sheikh International Airport, Egypt, en route to the Pulkovo Airport in Saint Petersburg, Russia. All 217 passengers and seven crew members who were on board were killed. Shortly afterward, an Islamic group claimed responsibility for the incident. The Russian Federal Security Service determined it was a terrorist attack caused by a bomb containing the equivalent of approximately 2.2 pounds of dynamite that detonated during the flight.[18]

On April 3, 2017, a terrible terrorist attack took place on the Saint Petersburg Metro system by an explosive device that was hidden in a briefcase. It was reported that seven people were killed instantly and eight more died later from their injuries bringing the total deaths to fifteen, with forty-five others being injured. Another bomb was detonated in Saint Petersburg on

December 27, 2017, in a supermarket, and that incident, also a terrorist attack, injured thirteen people.[19]

When President Putin was elected President of Russia, many considered his biggest achievement was stopping the disintegration of Russia. Putin immediately identified putting an end to terrorism as one of his main tasks. As a result of the counter-terrorist operation and diplomatic efforts, the Chechen Republic remained a part of Russia.[20] However, extremists periodically try to revive themselves with terrorist acts, which, fortunately, are incomparable in scale with those that were carried out previously.

### God's Special Care Amidst the Uprisings and the Fear

But from 1999 to 2017 in the former USSR, approximately 1,185 people were killed in terrorist attacks, and at least 1,067 were severely injured.[21] Because these nonstop attacks began just before and during the season when we moved to Moscow, people were generally fearful when we arrived in our new city. But when we arrived, our hearts were full of faith, and our whole family was ready to step into the new world where God was calling us to bring others into the knowledge of Jesus Christ, of His plan for their lives, and of His provision of peace, protection, and safety. Despite the horrific season of violent uprisings that were occurring in Russia, God was extending His special attention and care, and grace was truly *abounding* in that part of the world.

Our Renner family was under an amazing cloak of grace that was most unusual — it was a grace that enabled us to commit our lives completely to do God's work in this land. Decades later, as far as we can determine, we are the only family who came at the time of the USSR's collapse and consistently stayed here. And we're still here! Our sons married Russian women, and Denise and I have eight Russian grandchildren. All eight of our grandchildren are Russian-American citizens, and when we gather as a family, hardly any English is spoken. I must tell you that this is *not* the norm, and I know very well that our family received a special grace to be where we were and to do what we did.

## Our Sons' Disappointing
## Experience With Other Missionaries' Children

After our moving day to Moscow on barely three days' notice and being in Russia's capital city just one week, it was time for our three sons to start school, and we'd selected a school that had been established to serve missionaries' children. But over the years, the school had expanded and become quite large — now, in addition to missionary kids, it was attended even by children of some foreign ambassadors. It should have been a wonderful experience for our sons, but they didn't like it at all.

There was such a large number of missionary kids in that school, and it was nearly the first time our sons had spent much time with American missionary kids. Our sons' young lives had been lived almost solely among Russian-speakers. They attended a Russian-speaking church in Riga, and they mostly went to public Russian-speaking schools. We had a Russian-speaking staff, and we loved everything "Russia." Because our sons were eight, six, and two years of age when we moved to the former USSR, they had only spent a limited amount of time with other American kids and really didn't have many memories from America.

Being with those American missionary kids was a real wake-up call that, in general, left our sons disappointed with their experience at that school. For the most part, our sons *felt* the other missionary kids at the school did not like Russia, and it hurt them when the others made fun of Russian culture and Russian-speaking people.

Our sons felt the majority of those kids simply wanted to *escape* from Russia as soon as they graduated from school. Instead of embracing the adventure of living in the former USSR, many of them (not all) seemed only to dream and talk endlessly about going "back home" to attend college. Other kids couldn't wait to return home to the U.S. not just for vacations to visit family and old friends, but to escape Moscow and Russia because they detested it. Of course, many of those kids were older when their parents moved to Moscow. Those kids hadn't been immersed in the culture as our sons had. Nevertheless, those American students' unhappiness, though understandable, was disappointing to our children, who happily considered Moscow to be their home.

Joel said, "We really tried to integrate with the kids in that school. Philip tried to play basketball, I tried to play basketball — but it was a complete failure. We just didn't connect. Most of those kids didn't like Russia, and we had given our whole lives to serve God there."

Also, Denise and I were legendary as the "worst parents ever" in that school because we didn't make our kids participate in the school's extracurricular events. But we hadn't sent them there for extracurricular activities; we simply wanted them to be educated. And since the others there tended to make a lot of anti-Russian statements, we felt no need to make our sons spend time with them that wasn't essential.

I'll never forget when the principal of that school asked to meet with Denise and me to ask why our sons weren't involved in extracurricular activities at the school. We had to gently explain how our sons felt about the negativity from the other missionary kids. When school ended every day, the last thing our boys wanted to do was linger there at school, spending even more time in that environment. Instead, they ran to the TV office to be with our Russian staff, where they felt more comfortable.

What we witnessed in that school was really different for our sons who never wanted or asked to go "home" to America. As a matter of fact, at times when we all traveled to the U.S. for an extended trip, our sons did not particularly enjoy it because they had not grown up in America and they didn't understand American culture, which was so different from Russian culture. The only reason they ever wanted to go to America was to see their grandparents, aunts, uncles, and cousins — but besides that, they generally didn't find America as interesting as life in the former USSR. They, along with Denise and me, had been called to something different. We were God-called *as a family*!

I'm not at all saying this is true, but to *them*, America had very little adventure. In their eyes, every city seemed to have the same chain restaurants and big malls — and it *seemed* people had nothing exciting to do except go to the movies. Our sons felt like they had grown up with real adventure — deficits, shortages, scavenger hunts for everyday household needs, circumventing mafia organizations, experiencing political coups, and so on. And they really saw the power of God manifested in signs, wonders, and miracles. America seemed "routine" after growing up experiencing adventure as they had. Although Paul and Philip vaguely recalled some of the historic landmarks we'd visited in our U.S. ministry travels, going to an American mall or movie just didn't have any allure for our sons after all they had already experienced in life in the former Soviet Union. The grace of God to live in a land halfway around the world was upon our children mightily as well!

I also must tell you that for Paul, Philip, and Joel to visit some American churches really broke their hearts. All our sons knew was the fire of the Spirit they had experienced as God *unplugged* the power of Heaven and *swept* it over the lands of the USSR. Faith was so new and vibrant there, and every victory was so monumental that when they visited churches in America and saw what felt to them like a lack of passion, it left them feeling sad for the American Church.

Not only that, but our sons had embraced the Russian language. Paul, Philip, and Joel all fluently speak Russian — and sometimes they speak better Russian than they speak English. They almost exclusively speak Russian in their everyday lives, and they speak it so well that there were times when Russian friends have heard them speak English and, thinking of them as fellow Russians, have asked, "Wow, where did you learn to speak English so well?"

It wasn't that our sons disliked America; they were simply more Russian than American in their culture and lifestyle, and they simply didn't yearn to return to the U.S. They only went when we returned to the U.S. to minister or for various other reasons.

Later when our sons wanted their own Russian children to obtain American citizenship, all the rules for passing one's American citizenship to his own children had changed. For an American who had lived overseas most of his life to pass American citizenship to his children, he had to meet certain residency requirements, which meant being in the United States for a required length of time cumulatively. They eventually did it, but it was a real challenge for them to meet the necessary requirements because our sons had spent such little time in America when they were growing up.

So during their school days, when our sons encountered American missionary kids in that school in Moscow who talked about nearly nothing else but moving back to America — about fleeing the land our sons deeply loved — it stupefied them. They just couldn't understand it.

When our family kissed the ground in Riga and asked God to put the lands of the former Soviet Union into our hearts, He really put it deeply into our hearts. In fact, we were so "at home" that even calling ourselves missionaries seemed strange to our ears. We were not on a temporary assignment anymore, as this place had become *home*. Please believe me when I tell you that what our family felt was *not common* among others who had moved to the lands of the former USSR on a temporary assignment. This is not to diminish what other families had done, especially if they were only called by God to short-term missions in this part of the world. But the Renner family was under amazing grace to give our *lives* to do God's work in this land.

But in their younger days in Moscow, almost every day, Paul, Philip, and Joel would return from school and say, "It seems all the other kids do is mock Russia." Even at their young ages, our sons were beginning to question why those families were here, given their seeming disdain for all things Russian and their complaining, unpleasant speech at almost every turn. So rather than enjoy the other kids at their school, our sons shied away from them because of the negative attitudes of those kids.

Whether every impression our sons had was accurately perceived or not, I don't know. But Paul, Philip, and Joel loved Russia, its people, and Moscow, their city of residence. So they had little in common with their peers who didn't share that love they felt so deeply. Our sons' experience at that school wasn't a positive one, and, really, they just endured their time there. But the effect was that the negativity they dealt with at school drove their love for Russia even deeper into their hearts.

### 'We're Here, So Let's Get Started!'

When we arrived in Moscow, we enrolled the boys in school immediately and also immediately got started on the new church. We had planned to start in January of 2001, but I thought, *Why wait? We can get started right now!*

So Denise and I and the boys prayed together and decided as a family to launch the Moscow Good News Church on Thursday, September 7,

2000 — a date that, at that moment, was just a little more than two weeks away.

God was moving us along His path and plan for our lives in an accelerated fashion, but things back in those days still weren't happening super fast in Moscow. The whole system was still a maze of bureaucracy, so how were we going to push through all that red tape to launch a church in *two* weeks? We didn't even have a location chosen and we'd never made a public announcement that we were going to start a church on that date, so *how* were we going to start a church in this time frame?

Denise and I walked across the bridge to our office and asked the top leadership of our TV ministry to sit with us around the table in our conference room so we could make our special announcement to them. Our office staff here didn't know us on a personal, day-to-day level because we'd lived in Latvia for all those years. They were all still acclimating to the fact that their TV-personality bosses who had become well-known all over Russia had moved to Moscow. They knew we were planning to start the Moscow Good News Church in a few months because Denise and Paul had been traveling to Moscow every week for months to raise up a praise-and-worship team for the new church. But their jaws dropped with shock when they heard me say, "Hey, we're here, so we want to get started. I want us to start the new church in two weeks on Thursday, September 7."

I watched them gasp for breath and stutter as they asked, "*Where* are we going to start the church? Do you realize that is just two weeks away? *How* will we possibly have time to inform people that we are starting a church? The mail is really slow in Russia, so how can we get letters to people on time to let them know about it?"

Because of my public conflict with the preacher in Riga when we started the Riga Good News Church, I did not want a repeat experience of offending any Moscow pastors by our starting a church. I knew that we had an advantage because we had a mammoth list of names of people in Moscow from those who watched our TV programs and had received our books as gifts from our ministry. And I knew that if I inadvertently wrote to Moscovites who were possibly already attending other churches, it could anger a lot of pastors. We emphatically came to Moscow to be a blessing, not to anger pastors or to steal their people. So I had an alternate plan that I felt the Holy

Spirit had given me in prayer about how to inform residents of Moscow that we were starting a church — *without appealing directly to anyone in Moscow.*

I told our team, "I respect the other pastors in Moscow and do not want to offend any of them. So I do not want to directly invite anyone from Moscow to our church. Instead, I am going to send a letter to people who live in all the other time zones of Russia to inform them we are starting a church — and to ask that if they know anyone who lives in Moscow who needs a good church, would they be willing to let him or her know about it? This way, no one will ever be able to say we directly invited people from Moscow or tried to steal people from other churches. If Moscovites find out about the new church, it will be because family or friends contacted them, not us."

The staff said, "Do you know how long it takes to send a letter across all of those time zones? The mail system here is slow — we don't even know if people can possibly get a letter before September 7." They further stated, "To send a letter with information about the new church, we have to know where the new church is going to meet and we don't even have an address to put in the letter!"

I told them, "As of right now, finding a location to start the church is your most urgent assignment. I want to start the church as close to Red Square as possible — right in the heart of Moscow. As soon as this meeting concludes, I am releasing you into the city to find a place for the new church to begin on September 7. Remember, I want it to be as close to Red Square as possible. I believe you will miraculously bring me an answer by day after tomorrow!"

They looked at me in utter shock. They said, "This is Moscow! It's a massive city filled with red tape where it is hard to get anything done quickly. You are asking us for the impossible."

I answered, "If it's impossible, then 'the impossible' is what we need to be done! God is leading us to start the church *now*, so He will lead us to the right location. He will help us get mail to people in all those time zones on time so they can alert their family and friends in Moscow that we will be starting the church on September 7.

"*So now*…let's go find the place the Lord has chosen for the Moscow Good News Church to begin!"

### The Hotel Russia on the Edge of Red Square — Another Church Is Born in the Power of the Spirit

The very next day, our ministry administrator called to say, "It seemed impossible when you told us to find a location for the church, but I'm thrilled to tell you I think we've found the ideal location to start on September 7. If we'll agree to take it, they will bypass all the red tape so we can rent it immediately. *And it's right at Red Square!*"

When I heard it was at Red Square, my spirit leaped for joy! Our administrator explained, "We found an auditorium in the Hotel Russia, right on the edge of Red Square." Within minutes, I was in a car headed to the side entrance of the twenty-one-floor tower of the Hotel Russia so I could inspect this astonishing location where we would potentially start the new church in a mere two weeks.

Marina Busheva, a long-time team member in Moscow, recalled, "We knew Pastor Rick had received an assignment from the Lord to open a church in Moscow and that he wanted to start as close as possible to Red Square. So since Hotel Russia was right on Red Square, we went there to see if an auditorium was available to rent. When we found one there, we began to negotiate for a rate, and we got it! Everybody was shocked that we were really starting the church right on Red Square."

The gargantuan Hotel Russia opened its doors in 1967 and was the largest hotel in Europe at the time with three thousand rooms that could accommodate four thousand guests at one time. Its "Russia Concert Hall" was a place where many Soviet celebrities performed on stage. In all its years of service, the hotel accommodated more than ten million people, including two million foreigners and world-famous politicians.

But in April 2004, the government issued a decision to demolish the hotel because it had fallen into disrepair. And on January 1, 2006, the dismantling of Hotel Russia began. *But* before it saw its last days, it was the site where the Moscow Good News Church was born in the power of the Spirit on September 7, 2000.

Now that we knew where the church would begin, I composed a letter to all our TV viewers across all those time zones in Russia. Our Moscow staff worked feverishly to print it, stuff it into envelopes, stamp it, and deliver it to the central post office — praying and believing it would reach homes across Russia miraculously on time.

The fact that we had almost two weeks before the first meeting meant we had minimal time to prepare other materials for the grand opening. We printed beautiful song sheets, our Statement of Faith (what we believe), and prayer cards for people to fill out. We also prepared matching jackets for our staff to wear on opening night as they served as ushers. I wanted those Moscovites who attended that first night to see the excellence of Jesus Christ in everything we did. We were committed to being disciplined and organized and to making an impression on those who came that first night.

We also determined what kind of ministries we could immediately offer people, and I invited a very select group of foreigners to attend. Andrey Chebotarev, my assistant and the new pastor in Riga, Nikolai Gribs, our bishop from Riga, and leaders from our Good News Association of Pastors and Churches came from all over the Baltics and Ukraine. Altogether, about twenty-five special guests were invited to witness the opening of the church that first night. Besides that, we didn't have a clue how many people would show up. We were going to be thankful for anyone who came because we were starting on such short notice. If fifty people came, we would be thankful. If two hundred came, we'd be thankful for that too. We simply knew it was our God-appointed time to get started, so we were forging ahead.

## The First Night at the Hotel Russia

September 7 came quickly. Paul was the first in our family to go to the Hotel Russia that night because he was involved in setting up all the music equipment on the stage, including the drums, which he played. Next, Denise had to be there for praise-and-worship rehearsal. Philip and Joel went with her because Philip played his trumpet, and Joel sang on the worship team

701

that night. I was the last of the Renner clan to show up, and I arrived with other members of the team who dashed to our location inside the hotel to set up tables, prepare to hand out leaflets, and to make sure everything was in excellent order.

The doors were locked while we prepared, so I went to see how many were waiting outside in the entryway. Right outside the doors were slot machines and a cigarette-smoke-filled bar. We were sorry people had to stand there, but it was the only place to wait for the doors to open.

I was quite shocked to see the foyer completely full of people waiting for the doors to open! Finally, at 6:30 p.m., we unlocked the doors, and our staff who served as greeters and ushers began to shake hands, hug necks, and welcome all our new guests, many of whom had watched us on TV for years or had read our books distributed free of charge by the millions in the lands of the former USSR.

Against the odds, we discovered that our letters had indeed reached family and friends over all those time zones, and these Moscovites had received long-distance phone calls to tell them we were starting the church that night!

Denise led worship, Paul played the drums, Philip played the trumpet, and Joel sang with the backup singers on the worship team. The following week, Joel hilariously played the bass guitar. It was hilarious because he had never played a guitar in his life. But he wanted to be on stage with his mother and brothers, so that night, instead of using his wonderful voice to sing, he pretended to pluck those strings and to be playing music!

Bishop Sergei Ryakhovsky — one of Russia's most revered spiritual leaders in the nation, an advisor to the President, and my dearest friend among Russia's spiritual leaders — "loaned" us a few singers from his church to help us get started in the early months. Among those that Bishop Sergei sent to us was a lovely young Russian girl named Polina Shvenikova, who would later become the wife of Paul Renner and the mother of their four beautiful children. Many years later, Bishop Sergei joked affectionately that we returned all his singers and musicians except one. Although Polina had been practically raised in his church, he was thrilled to "lose" her to our ministry and, eventually, to our family.

The auditorium we'd rented was a hall used for lectures and only seated 225 people. That night, every seat was taken with people standing around the perimeters of the room. The people were stunned because they had never seen that much order and organization for something just getting started. People kept asking, "How can you be this organized just starting tonight?" Truly, that service was so highly organized that it felt like the church had been in existence for years. It was clear that the level of order and organization impacted people as much as the worship and even the ministry of the Word. Our prayer to do things right and with excellence was having great impact.

That first night, I welcomed everyone and asked how many of them had either seen us on television or read one of my books. Nearly every hand was raised in response to those questions. Then I laid out the vision for the new church and invited everyone back for all the following Thursday nights that we would be meeting in that location. The evening was so anointed and Heaven-kissed that it was "magical." God was there, and we knew something magnificent was unfolding before our eyes right on the edge of Red Square.

In fact, we were so aware that it was a historic night that we rented the restaurant on the twenty-first floor of the hotel's main tower for an after-event celebration dinner. Because many guests had traveled long distances, we wanted to honor their presence at a special dinner. The Soviet-style restaurant was located on the side of the hotel tower that faced the multi-colored domes of St. Basil's Cathedral and the Kremlin. The Kremlin with its own lighted towers in the night sky and the sprawling expanse of Red Square were all colorfully and glamorously visible before us. Guests commented endlessly about the stunning panoramic view before their eyes. It was simply surrealistic, but we were really there, and the church had really been born that night!

## The Day After

The following day, there was no time to rest. We began to make phone calls to thank each person in attendance for coming to be with us. Calling people was a brand-new idea in those days, and people were generally afraid to give their phone numbers. But because we asked, most of them *had* given us their numbers. So our team, who already had lots of regular TV work to do, focused entirely on calling every single person to personally express how thankful we were that they made time to come be with us. We wanted to know how we could serve them or pray for them.

Moscovites were unaccustomed to being called on in such a manner, but that was the beginning of our pastoral-care ministry — an important feature of our ministry even today. My mother, who helped lead me to Jesus, had taught me at a young age to love people and to care for them. Her influence is still at work today, and what she taught me helped me develop a pastoral-care ministry that soon became a role model for many Russian-speaking churches throughout the former Soviet Union.

As a result of those calls, the next week the auditorium was full again, but not as full as the week before because our international guests had gone home. But that is when the real work began, and in the weeks that followed, the hall began to be filled to capacity every week. Denise continued to lead worship, the boys played their instruments and sang as part of the worship team, and they helped in other ways as well. I taught, and our whole team excellently served.

In those first weeks, we laid the foundation for doing things excellently for Jesus. That level of excellence let people know this was going to be a serious and orderly church. That alone attracted people to stay with us. Still today, our church is known for its organization and discipline, which people believe to be a benefit because it does not waste their time. We value and honor the time and effort it takes them to get to church in a city of millions — two to three hours for some — and our staff of employees and volunteers are prepared and ready to receive them and minister to them each week.

Every week for several months, we met in that auditorium in the tower of Hotel Russia on the edge of Red Square. All of this was happening as I had dreamed — and just a few steps away from St. Basil's and the Kremlin. Before our Thursday service each week, we rented a sprawling room on the seventeenth floor of the tower that had a massive conference table that could seat twenty-four people. We invited new guests from every previous week to meet us there for coffee and tea for about an hour before time to prepare for service. During that time, we got to know them better and explained the vision of our church, and we personally asked them to join us. Many responded by quickly joining our ranks because they felt so embraced and included.

And week after week as I taught from God's Word, we saw people saved, filled with the Spirit, delivered, and healed. And they became regular participants in those services. When they began to call me "Pastor Rick," I knew that God was drawing them into our fold. We were there for several months when we began to realize there was no more room in that auditorium. At one point, we even crammed 400 people into that auditorium with 225 seats. We literally jammed the place until it could not accommodate another soul. So we began to look in downtown Moscow for another location.

### Going to Church With Russian Bears and Monkeys

We found a new location called the Kino Theater Mir. The Kino theater was a movie house with 820 seats located in downtown Moscow on Tsvetnoy Boulevard next door to Moscow's most famous permanent circus called the Nikulin Circus. We negotiated a deal to rent the theater once a week — at first, on Thursday evenings and later for Sunday afternoon services, including children's services. And, of course, we had to set up and tear down before and after our service each week.

In America, circuses historically travel from city to city, but during the Soviet years, nearly every major Russian city had a permanent circus that operated six days a week. The Nikulin Circus was the best circus in Russia and was even considered to be one of the best worldwide. From its inception in 1880, this central-Moscow circus had the best artists and attracted a nonstop flow of patrons. It was later renamed the Nikulin Circus after the legendary Yuri Nikulin, Russia's beloved clown who started his career there and later became its director before finally retiring — but the circus is in operation to this day.

Back then, the circular, one-ring circus seated two thousand people and featured a huge arena where the best clowns, jugglers, tightrope walkers, acrobats, horse riders, and animal trainers entertained spectators, plunging them into the magical world of aerial gymnastics and having them laughing *to tears* at the routines of clowns and pantomimes. Spectators marveled at the courage of trainers entering the arena with tigers, lions, elephants, and bears that had been trained to perform impressive feats.

The first half of the show was always devoted to acrobats and gymnasts doing elaborate somersaults, walking on their hands, standing on each other's heads, and lying down to twirl colorful objects with their feet. Tightrope-walkers danced along the wire with classical ballet movements, and acrobats twisted and tumbled in the air and did it all with a dancer's effortless grace. Clowns kicked each other in the pants and performed satire, sleight of hand, handstands on horseback, juggling, and fantastical cartwheels all the way around the ring.

After the intermission, a large troupe of bears would enter the ring to perform, and, incredibly, many of them did tricks like they were humans. The bears turned somersaults, carried dogs around, and walked on their front paws. One bear even climbed a ladder and stood on it on one paw. The bears rode trick bicycles and motor scooters, roller-skated, ice-skated, performed a staged boxing match, and even swung on trapezes. Other performing animals at the circus included monkeys, dogs, strange birds, and more.

Moscovites loved this circus so much that more than ten million people have patronized it over the years. Denise and I and our sons loved it too. Everyone who attends that circus is mesmerized by the wonder of it all. It is over the top in every way — *so typically Russian*!

But because this Moscow circus frequently had overflow crowds, they occasionally used the Kino Theater Mir next door to accommodate the overflow matinee audiences. That circus building was so close to the theater that performers and animals could walk back and forth to entertain overflow crowds that had been redirected to the theater. There were times when we arrived at the Kino Mir location to set up for church, and we had to wait for the circus to end and clear out after the afternoon matinee. There were also days when our paths literally crossed with Russian brown bears that were being walked out the same doors of the building that we were entering! When we arrived in the auditorium, there were also days when monkeys and colorful exotic birds were still in our auditorium as we were setting up for services.

I'm wondering…do you know another church that has had to wait for bears, clowns, acrobats, and monkeys to clear out of their space so they could start their service? For us, it was a real hoot — a genuine *barrel of monkeys* — to say the least!

Because this circus was known to all Moscovites, it was very easy to tell people the location where the church was moving. We simply told them, "We're meeting next door to the Nikulin Circus on Tsvetnoy Boulevard in downtown Moscow." That location was so well-known that people didn't even need an address because they had all been to that circus at one time or another in their lives.

## Children's Services in a Casino

The Kino Theater Mir had a dual purpose — it was a movie theater in the main auditorium, and it had a full-blown casino on the first floor. Back in those days, Moscow had a lot of casinos that were filled with criminal activities, and the first floor of our new church location was a cigarette smoke-filled casino with a full bar, pool tables, and walls that were lined with slot machines. For our people to walk up the stairs to the movie theater where our services were being held, they had to walk through the smoke-filled casino to get to the stairs that led to the auditorium. There were a lot of smokers in the former USSR, so this was not uncommon.

Each week, I stood downstairs in the casino to shake hands with and greet people as they came into the building. I watched people wave the cigarette smoke from their faces as they walked past people playing slot machines to make their way upstairs.

And what was really interesting was that there was no space in the building for us to have children's ministry, so the children's ministry was right in the middle of the casino! That's right, our children sat in tiny little chairs that we set up right in the middle of all the slot machines and pool tables next to the bar! But there was nowhere else to do it, so we made use of what space was available. And the only bathrooms in the whole building were also accessed through the casino. So anyone who had to go to the bathroom had to go through the casino, and then come back through the casino, of course, to get back to the service.

Once upstairs, people were welcomed again by another group of greeters. My attitude was that if people were willing to travel for multiple hours to get to church by the Metro and other public transportation — and then walk from there to the theater through all kinds of weather — I felt we had a responsibility to thank them for coming and to specially acknowledge their presence in a warm and welcoming way. It was a sacrifice for them to get there, and they needed to know we were thankful they came. And we always started on time because I wanted people to know we were not a sloppy organization and that we valued their time.

Denise led worship and did it *for years*. Paul played the drums and organized the stage and did that for years. He did it from such a servant's heart, and little did he know, it was part of his preparation to one day become the senior pastor of the church.

Philip played the trumpet and eventually led the youth ministry — and he did that for years as well. And Joel always did his part to make sure everything was done decently and in order, working on lighting, serving as part of the camera crew, etc. His duties were part of his preparation to one day lead the entire TV ministry — and, eventually, the entire U.S.-based part of the ministry. It may have looked like a small beginning for our sons, but everyone has to begin somewhere! That is why Zechariah 4:10 says we must "not despise the day of small beginnings." This is true for you and me — and it's true for our children too.

In our first service in that new location, about seven hundred people were there, but soon the auditorium — including the children's ministry in the first-floor casino — was filled to maximum capacity every week. But we knew this strategic location was important for people to be able to find us and access us easily using public transportation, so we kept meeting there for several more months. We even had our first Christmas services there. In the meantime, we regularly saw bears and monkeys on our stage and we could always smell the aroma of the circus.

Joel remembered, "One week, we were moving things into the auditorium and Philip said, 'Strange, it looks like that couch is moving.' I said,

'No, Philip, that's not a couch — it's a bear!'" But people regularly packed our new notable location, and they were saved, filled with the Spirit, delivered, and healed.

Also at about that time, property prices and rent for facilities began to *skyrocket* all over Moscow. The days of deficits were quickly passing, and prices were rising as Russia moved from a socialist-communist system to a capitalist market. I had never seen anything like it — our landlords kept demanding more and more money. In fact, in the six wonderful months we met there at the Kino Theater Mir, the rent went up *six times*. We were paying such an astronomical amount of money that we began to look for another venue that was less expensive and that would serve more people.

Remember that although we'd had an office in Moscow for nearly a decade, we had only moved to Russia's capital city in August, a few months earlier. We were learning so much about this megalopolis. And one of our discoveries was, surprisingly, that there were not many large theater-type venues in Moscow. Sure, there were massive auditoriums that seated 8,000 and even more, but it seemed that the ceiling for the type of venue *we* needed was only about 1,000 to 1,200 people at a maximum.

After searching and searching, we found a historic auditorium on the grounds of a Moscow university that could comfortably accommodate eight hundred people — a thousand if we really packed them into the room. The location was the concert hall of the Russian University of Transport. That theater-style auditorium was built in 1936 as a cultural center for the students and employees of this higher-educational institution. Over the years, famous opera singers, contemporary singers, and Soviet cinema stars performed on the stage in this concert hall. Today's famous opera company in Moscow called the New Opera was born on the stage of this grand auditorium.

This elegant old auditorium with a wraparound balcony was chosen to become the new temporary home for the Moscow Good News Church. But there was one problem we needed to overcome before people would go to church there. The main floor seated exactly 666 seats, and some Christians who had become familiar with the book of Revelation, said, "We're not going anywhere near a building that has anything related to 666." So to fix the problem, we negotiated with the building manager to have one seat removed so that the main floor would seat 665. The balcony could seat another 300 people.

God blessed us there and we continued growing — every week, it felt like the place was teeming with life. On some Sundays, the place was so full that it seemed people were practically hanging over the balcony. People walked the aisle to give their hearts to Jesus every week, and believers were filled with the Holy Spirit.

There was a massive red-velvet, Soviet-looking curtain that covered the equally massive stage that stretched across the breadth of the auditorium. The stage was also deep enough for an orchestra, so that nicely accommodated our praise-and-worship team, including our band. Before the service started each week, the band warmed up behind the curtain, similar to the way a symphony orchestra warms up before an orchestral event. Singers took their places at their microphone stands, waiting for the curtain to be opened on cue, for the congregation in the auditorium to stand, and for a time of joy-filled praise and worship to commence.

In my poignant remembrance of those days, I can still hear my son Paul lifting his voice behind the curtain: "*EVERYONE*, get in your places — the curtain is about to open!" Soon they'd pull on the big backstage ropes to open the curtain, and when it parted, there on the stage would be our choir and band with Denise and her team of worshipers. And the power of God would *erupt* in that auditorium. God moved in that place — those days were *magnificent*!

My pulpit was placed on the stage right above a sealed orchestra pit — and hidden in storage in that pit was an immense bust of Vladimir Lenin that had been used at communist events in that place in days gone by. Every Sunday when I preached, I was literally standing on top of Lenin, one of the premier leaders of the Bolshevik Revolution, who turned the lands of the USSR into an atheist state. Now we were worshiping God and teaching His Word in that amazing historical location. Our being there was a symbolic picture of the truth that God's power will *always* surmount evil and put it underfoot where His people yield to Him and obey His directives and plans.

## Then We Purchased an Entire Elementary School

By that time, our offices had moved to another downtown location into the top two floors of a six-story historical building that was a few-minutes' walk from the famous Bolshoi Theater. While we were there, we started the Good News Training Center, a school dedicated to training people for the work of the ministry — and over many years, it has trained more than one thousand people for ministry.

Pastors from the Good News Association of Pastors and Churches had been continually asking if they could send their people to us for ministry training. We'd never had space or a team to do it, but in that new location, we had more space and at the same time, God sent us a wonderful ministry couple who had a dream to start a ministry school. Working with us, Terry and Terri Young began leading the school, and it quickly mushroomed with students who were eager to be trained for ministry.

With the addition of the ministry school, once again, we were taking up every possible inch of our office space. We were so crammed into that space that I knew it was time for us to step out in faith to purchase our own office building so we could quit moving from place to place to rent facilities at such burgeoning prices. The increase in costs for rent was showing no signs of slowing down.

There was just one problem. We didn't have any money to purchase anything. What we were paying in various rents for church services and offices was so astronomical that we had never even finished the redecoration of our present office. Rent for the offices alone was thousands of dollars a month, and that didn't include the money we were paying for church rent on Sundays *or* for the auditoriums we were renting for our "Golden Age" ministry for the elderly every Monday. Altogether, we were paying colossal amounts for various rents.

My administrator had been asking to spend $100 to purchase baseboard materials to finish out the trim work in our office space, but we never had enough spare money to do that. So you can imagine the look on his face when I told him, "It's time for us to quit all this moving and renting — we need to purchase our own building!"

Respectfully, he said, "Purchase a building? Pastor, I've been asking for $100 for months to finish the baseboards in this office, and we haven't been able to do it. How do you think we are going to *buy* a building? Do you remember that property prices are skyrocketing? How are we going to come up with the money needed to actually *purchase* an office building in this market where building prices are going up daily?"

I answered, "I don't know where the money will come from, but I've learned over the years that if I'll get in agreement with God's plan, my obedience will work like a magnet to supernaturally attract all the resources needed to do anything He asks us to do. So let's not worry about money. Let's just go find an office building, get in agreement with God, and watch as He supernaturally provides what we need."

That day my administrator began to search for an office building large enough to accommodate the TV offices, church offices, and ministry training center. We were really growing, so we needed something significant. And since we had no money, we also needed God to "part the Red Sea" for us. And that is exactly what He miraculously did.

After a few weeks of searching all over Moscow, my administrator said, "Pastor Rick, we found an old, abandoned kindergarten on the other side of town. You won't like the location, but the building has possibilities. If it was renovated, we believe it would be sufficient to accommodate us for a while." But because Moscow is so enormous and traffic is horrible, before I went to see it, I first asked my entire executive team to go to the site and bring me word of what they felt as they looked it over. When they returned, in one accord, they all said, "You will not like the location, but if the building could be fixed up, it would work for us."

So Denise and I and our sons went to see it. My team was right about its not being in an ideal location, and the neighborhood was *really* ugly. After being downtown in the middle of the most powerful area of the city, this new neighborhood looked abandoned and desolate. But right in the middle of it was indeed a four-story derelict kindergarten that also had a full basement. As much as I didn't like the area, as I walked through the building, I could see its potential. If it was fixed up, it would be a nice home for all the departments of our ministry.

Because of the unsightly neighborhood, I knew no one was going to be negotiating against us. The price was $1.1 million — an astronomical sum for us since we didn't even have a spare $100 to purchase baseboards for our current office. But we never really had money to do *anything* God has asked us to do, so why let that bother us now? If this was God's plan, I had already learned that our obedience would bring us what we needed in order to do it.

So my administrator made an appointment with the seller, who was a devout Jewish man with a lot of property holdings in Moscow. But because this property was in such an abandoned part of Moscow, he really wanted to unload it because of its undesirable location.

Back in those days, newly emerging commercial banks did not give loans to churches or ministries, so the notion of getting a loan was off the table. Even the idea of a lease-purchase was nearly unheard of in those days. Nevertheless, my administrator asked the seller, "If we give you a good down-payment, would you be willing to let us purchase this property and pay the full amount out over time?" The Jewish man pondered the question for a few minutes and answered, "Well, I've never done this before, but if you'll give me a down-payment of $100,000, I'll give you one year to pay the balance. You can pay the balance any way you want to pay it, but at the end of that year, the entire amount has to be paid or it reverts to me, and you lose all your investment. But because I'm being gracious, the price of $1.1 million is not negotiable."

After a few days of prayer, I felt a green light in my spirit to proceed with purchasing this derelict kindergarten. When we had a gentleman's agreement, I knew it would still take time to work out the contract and that we also needed time to do our "due diligence" before we signed the final papers. So during that period, I prayerfully wrote a letter to our ministry partners to tell them of our plans and to ask if they would be willing to help as they had helped us in Riga years earlier. Once again, God touched their hearts, and our partners began to give. By the time we signed the final purchase contract, we had the money to make the down-payment.

But the full $1.1 million had to be paid in a year's time or we would lose everything. I knew we needed to get into that building as quickly as possible and stop paying the astronomical sums per month for our rented office downtown. But to get into that dilapidated building, first we had to renovate it. It was so dilapidated that the basement was filled with sewage. Everything in that building had to be fixed or replaced. The plumbing, toilets, kitchen, roof, and basement had to be replaced or renovated before we could move in. All of that was going to cost big money that we didn't have — but I knew if we would get our hearts in alignment with God, the money would come.

And that is exactly what happened. It didn't come all at once, but it came "on time" — in good time to keep moving forward with the renovations. But because I didn't want to pay any more rent, I asked my administrator to do the impossible. I asked him to have the whole interior of the building ready for us to move in within two months!

God graced his willing heart and his team's hearts and hands, and in two months, we were miraculously moving into that four-story elementary school that we had converted into our new ministry headquarters. By the time we moved in, we had spent a small fortune on renovations. Indeed, it was like the Red Sea had been parted, and we were already in our land of promise. But we still needed to conquer the real giant before us — and that was paying off the full balance on time before the end of our one-year deadline.

By that time, we had already paid $400,000 against the debt in addition to what we spent on renovations. But we still owed $700,000, and it had to be paid on time *or else!* Week after week, my administrator and bookkeeper would ask, "Pastor, do you have any idea how we are going to pay the full balance?" Everyone wondered how we would do it, and I wondered, too, but I refused to get into fear or worry. God had always paid for every project He put in our hearts, so why would I doubt Him now?

As we did each year, Denise and I made a summer trip to the United States to minister in various churches. On that summer's trip, we decided not to tell anyone about our financial need, but to simply quietly trust God to provide what was needed to finish the job. While we were ministering in Connecticut in a long-time partnering church, the pastor dropped his head while I was preaching and looked as if he was deeply shaken by something. In his office after the service, he asked me, "Rick, how much do you need to pay off that building in Moscow?" I said, "Well, I'd rather not tell you. I'm just trusting God to meet the need without my telling anyone how much we need to pay it in full. Denise and I agreed we would not tell anyone the amount, but that we would believe God to miraculously pay the bill."

When that summer trip in the States ended, Denise and I went back home to Moscow. As soon as we got home, I received a call from that same pastor, who said, "Rick, your Moscow church anniversary is coming up in September, and I believe the Lord wants me to be there." Because this pastor didn't travel internationally as a rule, I knew this was very unusual. We didn't know why he wanted to come, but we were delighted that he wanted to be with us for our celebration!

When he and his traveling companions arrived, Denise and I met them at the airport and, oh, how we cherished our time together! But during those days leading up to our anniversary Sunday, he kept insisting, "On Sunday, I need five minutes to say a word to your church. We've supported you and your ministry for many years, and I'd just like to tell the church face-to-face how much we love them and pray for them." I answered, "Of course you can do that!"

When Sunday came, we began with a great time of rejoicing at all that God had done in a few short years. After worship, I could see that my pastor friend was anxious about getting to the stage, so I said, "Church, today we are blessed to have a dear friend with us from America, and he has asked to speak a word to you." With that, I invited him to the stage and handed him the microphone. That's when I nearly fell to the floor in shock, as I heard him articulate what he had been wanting to say!

He said, "Church, we've been strongly supporting this ministry for many years. But recently, Rick and Denise were in our church, and while Rick was speaking, the Holy Spirit really shook me up with something He spoke to me. But what He said was so clear, I knew it was God speaking to my heart. And here it is…"

He reached into a pocket in his suit jacket, pulled out an envelope, looked at me, and publicly asked, "Rick, how much do you need to pay off your new building here in Moscow?" The congregation knew we needed $700,000 to pay it off, as we were all praying regularly about it. So I said, "I don't like to tell it, but we need $700,000 to completely pay it off."

### Our Entire Congregation Witnessed
### a True Miracle of Provision

My pastor friend smiled from ear to ear and said, "Well, that's why I'm here. That day you were preaching in my church, the Holy Spirit told me that you needed $700,000 and that our church was to give it so you could finish this project. Here is a check that was written more than a week ago." He handed the envelope to me, and when I opened it, there was a check for $700,000 — the exact amount we needed to pay off the building.

Think of it! I never told him what we needed, but the Holy Spirit that day had revealed to him our need and told him that his church was to pay off the balance on our ministry headquarters.

Do I need to tell you how nearly "berserk" our church responded at that moment? The place went wild — shouting, jumping, and dancing in celebration of this miraculous provision of God. I had been telling them that our obedience would attract what we needed and that we just needed to stay in alignment with God in our faith.

Now they had seen with their own eyes a true miraculous provision, and it impacted them more than any message they'd ever heard preached. The next time I told them God was leading us to do something and that He would provide, they believed it because they had already seen God do it. As a church, we were truly moving forward as one, and Jesus the Chief Shepherd was leading the charge. He had entrusted Denise and me as overseers of those precious people and the many "adventures in obedience" we would see and celebrate together in the days to come.

As time passed, other partners continued to give, and we were able to change the facade of that building as well. What started as a real "ugly duckling" piece of real estate turned out to be the sparkling gem in that region of Moscow that served us well for the next two years as we continued to grow as a ministry.

But in just two years, we had outgrown that facility, too, so we put it on the market, and very quickly, a major African embassy contacted us to say they wanted to purchase our building. We sold it to them for triple our purchase price. And because we invested our equity wisely, it grew and grew and became a large part of God's supply for the building we would eventually buy as the permanent location of our Moscow Good News Church. Jesus is truly Lord over all, and He will be *our* wise Master Counselor and Guide if we will individually submit to Him as Master and Lord.

### The Beginning of Golden Stars —
### the 'Golden Age' Ministry of the Church

For two years, I had searched for a way to reach the very large elderly population in Moscow. From the Soviet years, they were a generation that especially needed to be reached with the Gospel, but I had never found the key to touching them in large numbers. I knew there had to be a way to do it, but I didn't have a grasp at the time as to how it could be done. I had nearly bent my brain trying to think of how we could reach these lost souls in the sunset season of their lives on earth!

By that time, our family had moved to a different apartment, which was located on Tverskaya Street, the main thoroughfare that leads directly to the Kremlin. Our balcony on the backside of the apartment looked right into the windows of the State Duma, the lower house of the Federal Assembly of Russia. The Duma headquarters are located just a few steps from Red Square and the Kremlin, and its members are referred to as deputies. In fact, we were so close to the Duma that when our balcony doors were open, we could hear the announcers on loudspeakers calling for private drivers to come pick up Duma deputies after the sessions had ended. We often watched as Russia's most famous political leaders exited the building to get into their cars.

Every day from that balcony, we saw sophisticated, high-level guards dressed in black, who were assigned to protect those powerful politicians. Because our parking space was behind our apartment, and we regularly walked our dog back there, it was quite common that as we got into our car or walked the dog, we would come face to face with these legendary people.

The balcony on the other side of our apartment directly overlooked Tverskaya Street, where we enjoyed a marvelous view of the massive red-brick walls of the Kremlin and its mighty towers. In fact, we were so close to the Kremlin and Red Square that we could walk there in two minutes. When Paul McCartney gave a concert for thousands on Red Square, and the ticket prices were astronomical, we simply watched from our balcony. And on New Year's Eve, Victory Day, and other national holidays when the whole city celebrated, we had the best seats to watch tens of thousands celebrating on Tverskaya Street and all around the perimeters of the Kremlin. It was simply a remarkable place to live. Because we lived right there, our sons would head off to Red Square regularly, almost as if it was their backyard — in a sense, it very much *was* their backyard!

One day as I was looking out the window on the Tverskaya Street side of our apartment, I saw that there on the street that ran parallel to the Kremlin was a massive demonstration of pensioners and other elderly people who looked like they were having the greatest party of their lives. Some of them were carrying signs with communist slogans like they did in the old Soviet Union. Some even carried huge photos of Lenin and Stalin, waving them over the heads of the crowd.

I leaned out of our window to get a better glimpse and heard music from the Soviet era being played. I saw that many of those pensioners were actually dancing in the streets to the music. Although most people in the West remember communism as evil, these elderly people grew up in the USSR and remembered it as the time of their youth. They were reveling in the memories of earlier times when they were younger and life seemed easier than it had become in their old age.

I told Denise, "I want to go downstairs, get out on the street, and experience what those elderly people are experiencing." Within minutes, I was pressing the button on our elevator to take me down to the street. I eagerly *flew* out the door of our building to quickly join that big demonstration. My eagerness to join those pensioners wasn't because I agreed with communist dogma. I just wanted to share the experience with those thousands of lively elderly people — the very people I had been praying about how to reach with the Gospel!

When I stepped into the huge throng of senior citizens, I suddenly found myself engulfed by elderly people who were wonderfully behaving like youth.

All around me was a mass of white-haired senior adults who had seized the moment to step into their earlier memories of life in the USSR.

For hours, they "whooped it up" on that central street in downtown Moscow. It was so invigorating to see them *rhapsodic* in their memories that I lingered among them for several hours until the crowd finally began to dissipate. Large banners with Soviet slogans lay strewn on the ground in the quiet aftermath, and the air around me remained strangely electric with jubilation and levity that persisted in the atmosphere. I walked toward our apartment on confetti-covered streets, my mind enraptured by the faces of strangers that also lingered with me.

As I pondered the whole experience, I cried out, "Holy Spirit, please show me how to reach this elderly generation!" Before I reached the door to our apartment building, God had marvelously opened my heart and mind to a new idea about how to do it. Stepping back into the elevator, my mind was already brimming with revelation and a plan, finally, for how to reach this generation of people. When I would later act on that plan, God would breathe on it and enable us to establish one of the largest senior-adult ministries in the world.

I observed how those elderly people reveled in their golden memories of past Soviet years. They were living in a new Russia where they didn't particularly know how to fit in, so their memories of the past were precious to them. As I remembered how those senior adults were singing and dancing to old tunes sung by Soviet singers and celebrities, the Holy Spirit dropped an idea into my heart to create a special event and to call it *Golden Stars*.

The idea was to hold multiple concerts dedicated to elderly people, and to invite the most legendary Soviet movie stars, entertainers, singers, and performing artists to take part in our programs. We would invite seniors who reveled in their memories to a free concert with the legends they grew up in the old USSR watching in films and listening to in concerts and on radio and TV. At the conclusion of each concert, we'd give every one of them a bag of groceries, a bottle of vitamins, and a special invitation to attend a brand-new club that I would call *Vitamin Club*.

Because this vast elderly population lived on a meager pension, purchasing vitamins was often too expensive for them. So the idea was to hold a monthly concert — featuring famous Soviet stars that they would be thrilled to personally see and hear — and to afterward give each attendee a month's supply of vitamins. Then we would hold a monthly Bible study after the concert for those who wished to stay, with the goal of introducing these pensioners to Christ and to the knowledge of His Word. Since most of those pensioners had been raised in atheism, we knew they had never attended a Bible study. And because they were suspicious of strangers and especially foreigners, we were cautious. We didn't want them to feel we were using the concert event to manipulate them into the Bible study. So after each concert, we would simply offer the invitation to remain for Bible study — we completely gave them the choice to stay or to go.

With the help of a film star from the Soviet years who regularly attended our church, we set a date for the first Golden Stars concert — our huge kick-off event. We decided to do it in conjunction with the day that Moscow's Mayor Lushkov had designated to honor elderly people.

Then we began to explore which legendary performers would be willing to work with us. We decided to hold that first event at the Moscow Youth Palace (MDM), a famous location where millions of youth over many years had attended events, so it was very well known. Because the venue seated only two thousand people at a time, we had to repeat our gala event twice the first time to accommodate as many people as possible.

We invited legendary names to perform for the senior citizens — names unfamiliar to Western readers, but very familiar to Russian citizens of this era. Over the years, we invited:

- Mikhail Boyarsky
- Valery Zolotukhin
- Elina Bystritskaya
- Vladimir Zeldin
- Klara Luchko
- Lyudmila Kasatkina

- Zinovy Visokovsky
- Alexander Malinin
- Vasily Lanovoy
- Inna Makarova
- Vera Vasilyeva
- The Pyatnitsky Russian Folk Chorus

To help you understand how giant these names are, just imagine the impact of a church decades ago inviting American stars like Doris Day, Elizabeth Taylor, Richard Burton, Debbie Reynolds, Bob Hope, Bing Crosby, Danny Thomas, etc. — and all of them showing up at a church event at one time! Don't you think it would have been rare and historical to see those notable American personalities all on stage at once? *That is exactly what happened at our Golden Star event!*

Klara Luchko, a giant in Soviet films and a beloved star of the Soviet Union, was one of my favorites! She was one of the most humble and remarkable women I've ever met. I so enjoyed talking to her before she took to the stage. When our event was over, she went home — *and suddenly died that week*. Our stage was the *last* she ever performed on. When she died, she was posthumously honored as one of the most influential women in Russia's past hundred years.

And, oh, I'll never forget visiting with Ludmilla Kasatkina, a legendary star who became a dear friend to Denise and me. After performing for us, she regularly called us and even asked us to attend a special evening in her honor, in which she was honored as one of the most important actors to regularly perform on the historical stage of a building dedicated to the Soviet Army. We accepted her invitation, and she invited us backstage to ask us what we thought of her dress for that gala event.

And when actor and singer Mikhail Boyarsky showed up with his big black hat, I was shocked at what a simple and enjoyable person he was to work with. The legendary theater and cinema actor Vladimir Zeldin was also such a kind and humble man, who died at the age of 101 and acted until near the time of his death. The renowned Inna Makarova shocked me when she told me that she had been raised as a Methodist!

Acclaimed actor Vasily Lanovoi, a recipient of numerous awards in the Soviet years, performed for our events multiple times and was always such a gracious person and easy to accommodate. Many of these famous people have already passed into eternity, but they really performed at our events.

When I ponder that they all worked with us, I am still amazed. And to think, it all started with one God-inspired idea after a long afternoon of mingling with those Soviet senior adults and yearning for a way to reach them before they stepped out of this life and into the next.

But even though we knew the idea of reaching the elderly with these legendary stars was from the Holy Spirit, how would we invite the elderly population to such an event? We had very little contact information to be able to reach out to them. So, first, we started with what we had, which is really all anyone can do. We asked the senior citizens in our church to begin spreading the news that this remarkable event was going to take place and to help us distribute tickets.

When Mayor Lushkov's office heard we were assembling this unbeliev-able cast of legendary Soviet stars to honor the elderly on the day his office had designated to honor the elderly, he decided to endorse the event and asked us if *they* could invite senior citizens to come! *Wow.* We started out not knowing how to invite people — but we *started*. And we ended up with so many thousands asking to come that we had to limit the number of tickets we distributed and hold two back-to-back events to accommodate every-one and to extend our Gospel net as far as we could to reach this "golden" generation.

## Finally, the Big Day Came

Finally the day came for our first Golden Stars event, and Denise and I were so excited to be reaching this elderly population who so desperately needed the Gospel before they passed into eternity.

Because most of them had been raised in atheism, they had never heard the full story of the Gospel of Jesus Christ or held a Bible in their hands. Inviting them to a secular concert, then to Vitamin Club, and afterward to a Bible study meant a door would be opened for many of them to choose Jesus as Lord and Savior and to have a home in Heaven for all eternity. Because they were so elderly and close to eternity, this was truly an operation to "res-cue the perishing and care for the dying" before they passed from this life.

As several thousand senior citizens arrived at our large MDM auditorium on our big day, the air swelled with excitement. Expectation was high and the excitement mounted as our elderly guests were greeted with exuberant smiles and handed a playbill with the lineup of the afternoon's performances. Thousands of chattering voices blended into one vast sound as guests were seated, anticipating a performance that they would hold in memory for a lifetime.

That event was *enthralling* as the Soviet legends those elderly people grew up watching and listening to now stood on a stage right in front of them — and those stars had come just for this massive group of elderly honorees. The stars themselves were elderly, and as they spoke and performed, reminiscing with the audience of their glory days, they all connected in such an amazing, "magical" way. Such a specialized event for elderly people in Moscow had never occurred on this level before.

The two-hour-long concert seemed to go by in a flash, and audiences in both performances were so touched, they cried, *"Bravo!"* and wept as the love that had been extended to them flooded their souls and exuded from their faces. Then when they streamed out of the hall, we gave them bags with special gifts — and an invitation to our new Vitamin Club — they were overwhelmed, and they profoundly expressed their gratitude that we would invest all of that in them in one magnificent event *at no charge.*

Of course, this was the investment our ministry partners made into a harvest of souls that may not have been won to Christ otherwise. Although it was a concert to delight their imaginations — and vitamins and groceries to sustain their bodies — the eternal effect was the most important.

I cannot begin to tell you what I felt when I stood on the stage — with representatives from the mayor's office at my side and the leader of the Veterans Administration — to welcome the sea of elderly people who sat before me. I wanted to weep, but I contained my deep gratitude to God and my elation over what He was doing there by His Spirit, maneuvering people into a position to be impacted with the message of salvation. It was overwhelming beyond words. Really, it almost took my breath away to witness it all as it was finally unfolding before my eyes in those first huge concerts.

We anticipated that a lot of these precious elderly people would come to our first Vitamin Club after the concert, so we rented an auditorium for the first meeting that seated 1,750 people. Just as we had held those two initial back-to-back concert events, we planned two Vitamin Club events to accommodate the huge numbers that we expected to respond. And *just* as we expected, streams of senior adults flooded into that auditorium in *both* Vitamin Club meetings that day. The hall was completely full — more than 3,000 people combined attended those meetings. Afterward, we asked them to come to our Bible study.

Over the years, thousands of senior citizens have given their lives to Christ and have stepped into eternity with Heaven as their home because of those concerts and this God-inspired outreach. What began as an "idea" from the Holy Spirit morphed into a massive ministry to senior citizens in Moscow.

Eventually we held another concert for 8,500 people at Luzhniki Concert Hall — and then another big concert at the CSKA, a major Russian sports club that was a part of the Armed Forces sports society during the Soviet era, associated with the Soviet Army. That CSKA event was actually two back-to-back concerts attended by a total 16,500 elderly people in one day. Of course, when each of these events was over, we handed out tens of thousands of bags containing food, candy, Bibles, and an invitation to attend our Vitamin Club.

All these outreaches to the elderly were paid for by the Moscow church and the partners of RENNER Ministries. Because of our partners' giving, I am confident Heaven will be filled with thousands of Russians who otherwise would have never heard the Gospel before they died. How could I ever express my gratitude adequately to partners for every cent they've given for these outreaches!

Today we still have a massive outreach to senior citizens in Moscow. I am sure it is one of the largest concentrated ministries to the elderly in the world. There are so many elderly people involved in what has become known as our Golden Age ministry that we can't invite them to our regular church services because we can't physically accommodate them. So we designed a special service on Mondays that today is *packed* with seniors every single week. They have their own pastor, their own choir, their own ushers, and their own greeters and hospitality teams. This Golden Age outreach is a massive ministry for and, now, *by* senior citizens!

But it all began with an idea from the Holy Spirit that was birthed in my heart when I was not expecting it. That day when I looked out my balcony window and saw those thousands of elderly people marching in the street, I did not know God was going to give me the idea to reach them that I had been yearning for.

And not only did the Holy Spirit give me an inspired idea, He also injected me with the courage I needed to obey it. In one split second, I had both the idea and the courage to do what the Holy Spirit had shown me. Insight for the plan and the faith to act on it came simultaneously, and the outcome over the years since that moment has been truly profound.

Very often we think long and hard about how to do certain things that need to be done — when the Holy Spirit knows *exactly* how to do them. The Holy Spirit sees and knows everything. He knows the key to every heart. He knows the secret to every success, whether in ministry, education, family, or anything else. If we will listen to Him, the Holy Spirit will reveal exactly what we need to know for every situation we face in life. The question is — *are we listening?*

I will be the first to tell anyone that God has not blessed our ministry because we are so smart. If Denise and I have done anything right, it's that we have *listened*. We discovered that if we'll remember to ask the Holy Spirit for help, He will always be there to show us that which we're not smart enough to figure out on our own. I don't know what answer you've been seeking, but I know *who* has the answer! The Holy Spirit sees and knows everything — including those things your mind can never see or know on its own.

### The Broadway Musical 'Cats'

After we held our first Golden Stars event at the Moscow Youth Palace (MDM), I told my team, "This location is so fabulous, we should ask if they would allow us to rent it every week for church." So my administrator reached out to the management, and to our amazement, they agreed to let us rent it every Sunday for church services. So after being at the other auditorium for almost two years, we packed up the entire church and moved to this better location.

We were now meeting weekly in this celebrated auditorium, and it was *fabulous*! And because the Metro actually opened right into the building itself, it meant no one even had to go outside to walk to the location from the Metro. In snow, rain, and all kinds of foul weather, no one had to be exposed to the elements — they could simply walk from the Metro right into the auditorium. This contributed to even more growth!

But, unfortunately, we were only there for six months. While we were enjoying having up to two thousand people in a single service and were experiencing so many victories, we didn't anticipate that the Broadway musical *Cats* was coming to Moscow — nor that they wanted *our* stage for their show. Our stage really was the best in Moscow at that time, so as the producers of *Cats* looked over the city, it was decided that they needed our stage — and that *we needed to go!* On very short notice, we were informed that our time at MDM was over because *Cats* had come to town and would be taking our space!

But where would we go? We had grown considerably in the six months we were at MDM. But now we were told to move so quickly because the production crew for *Cats* needed to immediately start decorating the stage for their production. All we knew to do was to call the management of our last auditorium in the hall of the Russian university to ask if we could return. They graciously said *yes* — but this time, we would have to conduct two services to accommodate all our growth.

So on short notice, we packed up and moved back to our old location and ended up staying there for *five* years.

### Paul Renner Finds a Bride

Right from the start, even when Denise and Paul were traveling from Riga to Moscow to train a worship team before we moved there, a lovely young Russian girl named Polina Shvenikova had been encouraged to join Denise's new team of worshipers. Denise simply loved her, and it seemed the feeling was very reciprocal. So when Denise's women's ministry began to take off in Moscow and she needed an assistant to help her develop it, she longed for that assistant to be the precious Polina Shvenikova.

I really liked Polina too. Polina's father, who was an engineer and inventor — and who amazingly looked just like Vladimir Lenin — died of a heart attack when she was just a young girl. Her mother, who was a professional architect, was never able to recover emotionally from his death, so at a very young age, Polina became a "foster mother" to her younger brother Misha. At one point, her mother was so distraught and unable to care for her children that she sent them to live at a children's home just outside of Moscow for one and a half years. The care in that children's home was so terrible that Polina was planning to take her little brother and escape back to Moscow. But just before she could carry out her secret plan, her mother returned to retrieve them.

This was all happening to a very young Polina during the collapse of the USSR. Life was very hard for everyone at that time, but because of the fragile emotional condition of Polina's mother, their family really suffered in unspeakable ways. But God's grace intervened, and one day while searching for food to feed her brother and trying to find a way to stay warm and not freeze to death, Polina found a multi-colored tract on the street that got her attention. When she read it, she discovered the tract was about Jesus — *and that was the first time Polina ever heard the Gospel of Jesus Christ.*

To show you how connected life is, that tract was printed and distributed by my friend Terry Law, whose ministry headquarters was in Tulsa. When I was a teenager, Terry's international ministry and music group called *Living Sound* impacted me so greatly. Now on the other side of the world, his ministry was instrumental in bringing Paul's future wife, and our daughter-in-law, to Christ.

Paul began to notice Polina at the first meetings at the Hotel Russia. I once asked him, "Paul, have you ever considered dating Polina Shvenikova?" He answered, "Dad, I've noticed her, but I can't endure the thought of me and my wife being called *Paul* and *Polina*!" But the fact is that Paul *was* taking serious note of this precious Russian girl who by this time had become Denise's personal assistant.

Denise and I had a rule in our home that there would be *no dating* until after age eighteen. So when Paul turned eighteen, he and Polina began spending time together to get to know each other better. Denise and I could see that her young assistant was becoming Paul's girlfriend. Because Paul was always serious about life and didn't do much that was silly, we knew he was serious about Polina becoming his wife.

But our other rule was *no marriage* until after age twenty. So exactly four days after Paul's twentieth birthday, he and Polina, with our parental blessing, went to Zaks (the official Russian government agency that registers marriages in Moscow) to officially register their marriage. And exactly six days after Paul turned twenty, he and Polina were married in a church ceremony before God and the church. In God's sight, they were joined together in holy matrimony on September 20, 2003, and they became *Paul and Polina Renner.* Of course, Paul has since become accustomed to the notion that he and his bride are *Paul* and *Polina.*

Before their first wedding anniversary, Paul and Polina gave birth to their first child, whom they named William Richard Pavlevich (patronymically named after his father Paul) Renner, whom we lovingly call *William.* But in pretty fast succession, Paul and Polina gave birth to three more children, Anastasia Elisabeth Pavelovna (after her father Paul) Renner, whom we call *Anya*; Cohen David Pavlevich Renner, whom we call *Cohen*; and Abigail April Pavelovna Renner, whom we call *Abby.* In 2016, Paul officially became a Russian citizen, making him a dual American-Russian citizen, and Paul and Polina's four children also have dual citizenship.

### Singing in the Kremlin Palace

I shared briefly about it in the last chapter, but the state Kremlin Palace auditorium is the main stage of Russia and one of the most prestigious theatrical concert platforms in the nation. It seats about six thousand spectators and was built for political events, but in addition to political and educational forums, it also hosts concerts, cinema premieres, ballets, operas, and circus presentations. The most famous Russian stars and celebrities worldwide perform here.

In 2010, Denise was remarkably invited to perform on stage at the Kremlin Palace. A large group of American musicians and singers had come to Russia to perform Handel's *Messiah*. It was the first time it had ever been performed on the stage of the Kremlin Palace. The Russian conductor was a friend from Saint Petersburg. When he needed to find someone to sing between the first and second part of the performance, he thought of Denise and called to ask if she would be willing to sing that night.

First, the American orchestral members performed in Saint Petersburg, so we traveled there so Denise could perform with them. A few days later, the whole group arrived in Moscow to get settled and to prepare for performing on the stage of the Kremlin Palace. The day finally arrived for the performance in front of a packed auditorium. Nearly every one of those six thousand seats was filled with believers from every imaginable denomination who converged there for this monumental event.

When the first part of the program concluded, it was Denise's turn to stand center stage to sing, "The Lord's Prayer" with the accompaniment of a hundred-piece orchestra, as I also wrote in Chapter Twelve. People were *spellbound* as her voice and the orchestra filled that massive auditorium. She stood so regally on that stage that had once been dedicated to socialist-communist ideology. The crowd applauded over and over when Denise was finished. She wasn't singing on the stage of the Bolshoi Theater, but she was bringing glory and honor to God just as He had called her to do!

## More Ministry Expansion

Because we outgrew our wonderful "kindergarten" office building in two years' time, we sold it. Even though we nearly tripled our initial investment, the money wasn't sufficient to purchase the larger kind of facility we needed, so we invested it and let the investment grow while we believed for God to provide more funds. But in the meantime, we needed an office for the growing TV ministry, church, and Bible school, so we returned to renting offices at various locations over the next few years.

The TV ministry continued to rapidly expand and, in addition to broadcasting our own programs, we continued to add other God-sent broadcasters who we believed had something stable and trustworthy to impart to the Russian-speaking Christian community. And because of new national boundaries that made it difficult to receive all of our mail in Russia, we opened TV ministry offices with full staffs in Riga and Kiev, along with our office in Moscow. Now in addition to broadcasting in the Russian language, we also began to broadcast our programs in many other languages besides Russian — at various times in Ukrainian, Latvian, Estonian, Romanian, Armenian, Georgian, Azerbaijani, Uzbek, Tajik, Mongolian, Polish, French, Portuguese, and, of course, English. We were broadcasting across nearly all the republics of the former USSR —- and we continued to send books and literature free of charge to TV viewers across this part of the world.

Although the Gospel itself is free, it isn't free to get it to the people who need it. When I look back at how much money it has taken to do all of this ministry, I am amazed at how God has so supernaturally supplied everything we needed. People who observe from a distance often don't understand that it takes mountains of nonstop cash to purchase TV time; to pay employees who produce TV programs; to purchase and repair equipment; to print books and materials; to pay for envelopes, packaging, and postage; to pay rent for office space, etc. These types of expenses were also simultaneously needed for the church and the Bible school.

Over the next several years, God continued to send us an avalanche of response from our precious TV viewers. But responding to the multitudes who were reaching out to us required my team and I to stay in faith for every cent to pay for it all. We were experiencing every ministry's dream, but the dream was *really* expensive. And it wasn't a one-time project that needed a one-time injection of cash. It was an ongoing financial need that never let up. But God amazingly provided every cent needed to do the ministry He had called us to and that *He* was building. We never missed a beat.

God is so faithful — indeed, *GREAT is His faithfulness!*

In addition to that huge outlay of monthly expenses, we sowed unending hours into the work God had called us to. We knew we had connected with Heaven in a divine moment, and we weren't about to withdraw our hand from the plow of our service to God and these precious Russian-speaking souls.

But I could also never forget that in 1978, the Holy Spirit had said to me, "Write, write, write, and I'll prosper what you write." So even with everything else that we were doing, I continued to write books in obedience to the word the Holy Spirit had spoken.

In all the years we had been living in the former Soviet Union, books have *flowed* from my fingertips as I've held on to that word and to another prophetic word that had been spoken over me, which said, "If you will write, God will speak through your fingers." I embraced that word, too, so I kept my fingers on the keyboard and always sensed the anointing of God flowing from my mind and spirit onto the printed page as I've written book after book after book.

As I look back, I wonder how I wrote all those books in the midst of launching our ministry to the former USSR — building a Christian TV ministry; starting a new Protestant church in a city of millions; training those called to ministry in a Bible school; and writing books filled with the teaching of the Bible. There had been the first aboveground Bible school in Jelgava, and other Protestant churches were started by brave, equally God-called pastors. But much of what we were doing was a pioneering work and required so much of us to build it from the ground up — and that included building and training *people.*

All of these outreaches and ministries demanded my fullest attention. But I knew that writing was a major part of God's calling on my life, so I devoted myself to putting into book form what I felt the Holy Spirit wanted me to write about. The Spirit of God had worked such discipline into my life, and the long-term effect of my father's influence was also at work in me. Both he and my mother ingrained it in my character to be responsible with any assignment entrusted to me.

But during that busy season, I felt stretched even beyond my normal limits of "stretched" as the Holy Spirit began urging me to write the first volume of *Sparkling Gems From the Greek.* The idea for it had percolated in my heart for years. But suddenly the breath of God was upon me to write it, so I began to "write, write, write." For hours I would sit in front of my computer as those Greek word studies poured from my mind and heart. When I began to count how many actual days I worked on that book, I was speechless to see that I had actually written that 1,046-page book with more than 1,000 Greek word studies in *60 days*. Even as I write this, I wonder, "How was that even possible?" But the first *Sparkling Gems From the Greek* really was written in a matter of *two months*!

Because of the visibility of the TV ministry and the Moscow Good News Church, and because my books were in believers' homes all across the nation, my visibility as a leader continued to grow. It is so humbling to think God would use me that it is difficult for me to even write this about myself — but God really did begin to use my influence, because it was *His* influence — the influence of His Word and His Spirit.

Already we had been in this part of the world so long that solid, stable, long-term fruit was being produced by our ministry, and people even in high places took notice. Also, other spiritual leaders began to study our ministry and our lives personally — even the way Denise and I were raising our sons, doing ministry as a family, and training our children to take their places in God's plan for their own lives.

Paul Renner said, "To understand my father's influence in Russia, you have to step back a little bit in time and remember that millions of his books had already been handed out in the Russian language all over the former Soviet Union. Almost every Protestant in this part of the world has either seen Rick Renner on TV or has a book by Rick Renner in his or her home. I think it's pretty safe to say that the majority of Protestants have *more than one* of his books in their homes. They definitely know Dad's name.

"If you look back to when the TV program began," Paul continued, "everything was just opening up, and most pastors were trying to figure out what to do. But it looked like Rick Renner knew what he was doing. He was sure of God's plan and was so bold, determined, and resolute. So other spiritual leaders watched him. Many of them had little ministry training and no idea how to lead a church aboveground in a free world. So in their eyes, Dad was an expert. What he was doing in obedience to God was bearing undeniable fruit, and all eyes were on him, studying his every move. It was humbling, but it brought with it so much responsibility to stay the course of God's plan so that he wouldn't let them down. And by the grace of God, he *didn't* let them down."

Paul added, "Pastor Rick is a very fatherly figure here because of his track record of faithfulness, consistency, and fruitfulness. He has set such an example and has had such a unifying effect on spiritual leaders that many look to him as a spiritual father. It put him in a very reputable position. Really, God *thrust* him into that position, but Dad added hard work to the grace of God on his life. That divine cooperation made the difference, and, now, what my father teaches is practically a gold standard."

*Wow* — it was overwhelming and humbling to hear those words from my son!

Because of our established ministry in the former USSR, as my son Paul stated, Sergei Ryakhovsky — the bishop of the union of churches to which we belong and someone I consider to be the most visible Protestant leader in Russia — asked me to serve as one of his executive assistants in our union, the *Centralized Religious Organization of the Russian United Union of Christians of Evangelical Faith* (POCXBE). This church organization brings together nearly thirty different church associations, some of which are former underground churches. Other churches were founded by missionaries who came to Russia after the collapse of the USSR. But since its foundation in 1997, this union has been headed by Bishop Sergei Ryakhovsky. Subsequently, he is known as one of the leading bishops in Russia.

Bishop Sergei and I became connected when our family first moved to Moscow. I had heard of him for many years, but we never had the opportunity to personally connect until we moved to Moscow. Right from the start, he was so kind and accommodating that he actually once asked to pick me up at the airport and take me to my hotel so we could have time to get to know each other. It was the beginning of a very valuable friendship that I deeply cherish.

As I shared in Chapter Nine, Bishop Sergei's father was himself a bishop of the underground Russian Pentecostal Church and spent almost eleven years in prison for his faith — seven years during the Stalin era, three years in the time of Khrushchev. Then for three years, he was under house arrest during Brezhnev's time. As a child, Sergei learned the price that had to be paid for serving God in the Soviet Union, and he himself accepted the calling.[21]

So when the USSR collapsed and everything began to change, Bishop Sergei had been prepared by God to lead an entire movement and thousands of Russian churches in the newly emerged Russia. Today he is the main bishop of our union of churches. In addition, he is a member of the Civic Chamber of the Russian Federation, which exists to improve interaction between the authorities and society, a very serious representative organization. Also, Bishop Sergei is a member of the Council on Interaction With Religious Associations. In short, Bishop Sergei is our God-sent Joseph — what a blessing he is to the whole Christian community of Russia!

Bishop Sergei and I are nearly the same age, we have both been married about the same number of years, our wives both have vision for ministry, and we each have multiple sons who are called into the ministry with us. Because he and I have been involved as leaders in Russia longer than many of the current leaders, we mutually knew many of the Pentecostal leaders of the past in this region of the world. All these factors — and the fact that we dearly love each other — were used by God to lead the two of us into a treasured covenantal relationship.

Bishop Sergei had asked me to be one of his executive leaders, and I counted it a great honor. Because I had volunteered to serve with him, I found myself traveling to minister even more. Mainly by myself, but sometimes with Denise, I traveled to more than eighty cities across the former USSR to speak in churches and conferences. When I looked back to count how many cities we have been in to minister, I am stunned to see that, in the midst of all our other work in Moscow, God had enabled Denise and me to do it all.

### The Emerging Influence of Our Son Paul

In Moscow, Paul Renner has stepped forward as an emerging leader in our church, ministry, and the Christian community. He had been working alongside me since that first meeting in Booneville, Arkansas, when, as a four-year-old, he began learning how to set up the product table as we were just starting out. Paul was young, but his whole life had been spent working in this ministry, and he was well prepared for what he was now stepping into in terms of greater responsibility and visibility in leadership. No one knew our hearts, our philosophy, or commitment better than Paul.

At times when we've hosted all the top Protestant leadership of Russia at our Moscow church building for special meetings, although Paul is in charge, I have occasionally attended the meetings at Paul's side to welcome those leaders to our building. These leaders have greeted me respectfully and officially as if they were greeting a statesman. But Paul is so dearly loved by them all that when they see him, they exclaim, *"Paul!"* and hug him warmly!

What a joy to see Paul so embraced and respected. He has really become a significant and respected leader whom people love. It doesn't matter where I go in Russia, the Protestant leadership know and love Paul. He attends as many of their meetings as possible, spends time with these fellow leaders, and has built a strong relationship with them. I am blessed and overjoyed at how Paul has stepped forward to lead.

## Philip Also Stepped Into His Calling

Denise and I watched as Philip, too, began to step forward into his calling. After our youth pastor moved away, Philip became the youth pastor for the Moscow Good News Church and also began to write worship songs that would eventually be sung in Russian-speaking churches all over the former USSR.

Amazingly, Philip had also connected with many of Russia's top pop singers and musicians — some of the biggest names in the Russian-speaking world. Because of his wide-open heart, they fell in love with him and even began to hire Philip to help them transform their Russian lyrics into English for the international market. At times when Philip and I were at home together in those days, he'd say, "Dad, let me show you something," and he'd turn on the TV to the channel that showed Russia's equivalent to the American show *MTV*. One music clip after the next, I'd hear Philip say, "Dad, I'm working with that person, that duo, that group," and on and on he went. It was totally amazing to see the famous personalities Philip was helping with lyrics — and a little at a time, he was introducing them to Jesus.

Not only that, because Philip was a gifted singer and songwriter himself, he decided to compete in Russia's equivalent of America's *Star Search* — and he won it! As parents, Denise and I were thrilled that such an opportunity had been given to Philip, and we knew it was a door opened to him by the Lord. What especially elated us was that he sang a song in the finals that he had written, entitled, "Two Thousand Years Ago, There Was a Man From Galilee." It's a powerful song that declares the life of Jesus Christ in a contemporary format.

On the night of that grand-finale event, Denise and I arrived at the auditorium and walked into the building where the competition was to be held. We were immediately *shocked* at what we saw! The word "dark" doesn't even begin to describe what we saw and felt. It felt as if we had stepped into a cesspool of depravity! Through the years, we've been in a lot of difficult spiritual environments, but this one took the prize! We were taken aback by the darkness that abounded all around us.

Walking up the stairs to the hallway that led to the auditorium where the stage performances would be held, dim lights barely pierced through the cigarette smoke that filled the air. The smoke was so thick that we had to wave it out of our faces so we could see where we were going. Once we were seated, through the smoke, we could see prostitutes walking among the tables where the audience had been seated. The prostitutes flaunted themselves to advertise their wares and to alert potential customers that they would be available for business after the show. Then I looked over at the bar where drinks were being served. All the bartenders — young, handsome, muscular Russian men — had on *very* little clothing as they stood behind the bar showing off their toned bodies!

As I looked around the room that night, I told Denise, "This is a pretty grim place to be singing a song about the Gospel. I can't imagine the spiritual opposition our son must feel here. Do you think there is any chance he can win a competition in a place like this?"

Just before Philip went to the stage to perform, he came to our table and sat with us. Denise and I encouraged our son to sing boldly and without compromise. Soon his name was announced, and we watched as he walked confidently onto that stage. In that very dark, wicked atmosphere, Philip picked up his trumpet and with his band playing behind him, he belted out his song, "Two Thousand Years Ago, There Was a Man From Galilee."

Denise and I were stunned by Philip's boldness — and equally stunned at the response of the crowd. The people applauded and applauded *and applauded*. In fact, Philip was given a longer ovation than anyone else who performed that night! Our son's boldness, courage, confidence, and refusal to be ashamed of what he believed knocked his listeners off their feet!

To our further delight and surprise, Philip walked out of that building that night as the *WINNER* of that national event! As a result of what happened in that very spiritually dark, sinister place, phenomenal doors of opportunity began to open up for Philip. The acclaim he obtained that night opened the door for him to preach and sing in places he never would have dreamed possible!

The biggest reward for winning that contest was a recording contract with one of Russia's biggest labels. But the contract was so strict that if Philip signed it, he and his voice would be completely regulated by that recording company. According to the deal, he couldn't sing anywhere without their permission. When he realized the contract would not even allow him to sing in church, he said, "I realize this contract could really take me somewhere, but I am not going to be told when I can and can't worship God with my voice in church." So he made the decision to walk away from it.

### Philip Marries a Wonderful Russian Girl

At the time Philip was serving as our youth pastor, he met an outstanding young girl in our youth group named Ella Goncharova, who had been saved in one of our meetings in the earliest days at the Kino Theater Mir.

Ella was born and raised in Stavropol, a city in the southern region of Russia's Ural Mountains. Her father was a trained acrobat, and her mother was a school teacher. But Ella's parents were not active believers, and Ella had not been raised as a Christian. But after she gave her heart to Jesus, she became one of our most active youth.

In World War II, Ella's grandmother on her mother's side, from Ukraine, had been captured by Nazis in her younger days and was forced to walk with other POWs all the way to Germany. Once in Germany, her grandmother was so frail that it appeared she died, so her body was taken to the morgue. Just as those in the morgue were getting ready to do away with the corpses, a German woman who worked in the morgue heard a whimpering sound. She searched to see where it was coming from and discovered that Ella's grandmother — then a young woman — was still alive.

Remarkably, that German woman secretly nurtured her back to health. But when Ella's grandmother returned to Ukraine and it became known that she had been in German hands, she was unthinkably accused of being a spy, which added more trauma to her already very painful situation. Tragedy befell so many people by all the confusion and mayhem surrounding the war. But in the years just before her death in old age, that particular grandmother became a believer.

In 2001, Ella planned to go see her other grandmother on her father's side who also lived in Ukraine. That grandmother, whose name was Esther, had been one of our regular TV viewers for years, so Ella decided to take a video to show her of one of our church services. Her grandmother was a serious Spirit-filled believer and was known to be prophetic. As Ella and her grandmother sat on the sofa and watched that video together, her grandmother suddenly turned to Ella and said, "Ella, you're going to marry the Renner young man who is playing the trumpet in this video."

Ella was stunned because although she knew Philip from a distance, they had never really connected. So Ella said, "Come on, Grandma, are you sure?" Her prophetic grandmother insisted, "Ella, that Renner boy playing the trumpet is your husband."

Ella never forgot that prophetic word her grandmother spoke over her that day. And in time — just as her grandmother prophesied — Philip began to notice Ella. But we had that same rule in our home that there would be no dating until after age eighteen. So when Philip reached eighteen, he and Ella began to see each other to get to know each other better. And it was clear to them, and to Denise and me, that they were falling in love.

But we had that other rule, too, that there would be no marriage until after age twenty. Finally, in 2007 — with our parental blessing — they went to the official Russian government agency that registers marriages before the government. Their marriage before God and His Church occurred on May 19, 2007. In God's sight, that was the day they became *Philip and Ella Renner.*

After several years of marriage, Philip and Ella gave birth to two wonderful daughters, Emilia Daniella Philipovna Renner, who is called *Mia*, and MakKeila Berri Philipovna Renner, who is called *Mika*. Both of these precious girls are dual Russian-American citizens, and Philip and Ella are fabulous traveling ministers whose current place of residence is the United States.

## I Began To Set My Sights on Kiev

After those very intense first years in Moscow and the marriages of our two oldest sons, I began to feel a tug on my heart to start a church in Kiev, Ukraine. Literally tons of mail had come to us from every corner of Ukraine in response to my Bible teaching on television. We had distributed mountains of books free of charge to every "nook and corner" of that country, and Denise and I had regularly held large TV meetings for viewers all over Ukraine as well.

We once even took a whole team on a bus trip across Ukraine and stopped at every city along the way to minister to auditoriums filled with our TV viewers. When I was preparing to write this book, I asked my team to calculate the approximate amount of money we invested to take the teaching of the Bible to all of Ukraine by television. I nearly lost my breath when I heard the number. Only God could provide such a miraculous supply!

Our organization called the Good News Association of Pastors and Churches was bigger in Ukraine than anywhere else, and it continued to mushroom in size. Churches of all sizes were members of our association. Some of them were legally affiliated with us — others were more loosely affiliated. But we held meetings in various parts of Ukraine to gather all those pastors and leaders regularly for teaching, training, and fellowship. And our ministry paid the entire bill for all those years.

A typical meeting was held in Yalta on the Black Sea. We often went to Yalta because old Soviet hotels along the seacoast were large enough to accommodate the 400-600 pastors and their wives who attended. We literally rented every room in the facility, along with the biggest auditorium in the hotel, and we provided breakfast, lunch, and dinner for all those association members.

On top of that, our ministry covered all expenses to bring in top-notch names we believed had something significant to impart to the pastors. Denise held large meetings for pastors' wives who otherwise rarely received attention. Oh, how they cherished the love they felt from Denise, and she gave all those women special gifts to take home with them.

Before those events concluded, we handed the pastors gift bags full of books, videos, and other materials to take home. When pastors expressed their frustration that they didn't have DVD players to play the videos we gave them, I told Dave and Joyce Meyer about it, and to our delight, Joyce Meyer Ministries pitched in significantly to help us give DVD players to every pastor and church in the association.

Also while preparing to write this book, I asked our team to calculate the approximate amount of money our ministry invested in all those pastors in our association over all those years. *Wow* — we poured millions and millions of dollars into those pastors and churches! But at that time, it was very urgently needed because the harvest was ripe, and those pastors needed teaching and training so they could help those in their spiritual care take their places in society as robust believers in Christ.

I imagine it was similar to churches suddenly emerging in the book of Acts that needed oversight. It was the "now" moment to do it. Even though we didn't know how we would pay for it all, we said *yes* to the Lord and watched as He provided every cent needed along the way. If all that money had been needed at once, it would have been overwhelming, but God faithfully provided it over the years until it amounted to a massive investment in those pastors and churches.

And we weren't just doing that in Russia and Ukraine. We were simultaneously doing the same thing in churches in the Baltic states. In fact, our Good News Association of Pastors and Churches became so large that we ended up with full-time association staffs in Latvia, Russia, and Ukraine. We even had staff members whose jobs were to travel nonstop to visit association churches to assess their conditions and learn how we could better serve them.

There were many organizations trying to help pastors and churches in those days, but I was accountable for *ours*, and we took this charge very seriously, pouring everything we could into them to provide teaching, training, and pastoral care for pastors and their families.

## The Kiev Good News Church

But because this influence in Ukraine had grown so strong, I privately longed to start a church in Kiev, but didn't know how to do it because we did not live there and we were leading the TV ministry and church in Moscow.

As I percolated in my heart the idea of starting a church in Kiev, I realized that because we already had staff there who received and answered TV mail, they could assist us in starting a church. So at least, in part, we had staff who could help us. I finally shared the idea that Denise and I would be starting the church. It would be the third church we would start that bore the name Good News Church. The first, of course, was the Riga Good News Church. The second was the Moscow Good News Church. And the third would be the Kiev Good News Church.

Denise and I figured we could fly back and forth between these two mega cities every week — spending half our week in Moscow and half our week in Kiev. That way, we felt we could provide oversight to both churches. We had no idea how physically and emotionally challenging this lifestyle would be when we first laid out our plans.

Flying to Kiev every week was a huge undertaking. It meant driving up to three hours in horrendous traffic to get from our Moscow home to the airport — then standing in long lines for tickets and more long lines at Passport Control. Then after standing in *more* long lines for customs, we'd wait two hours for our flight to depart. Once our flight arrived in Kiev, we stood in more long lines at Passport Control and customs and then fought horrific traffic to get from the Kiev airport to our offices downtown. Even though we left Moscow in the mid-morning each time, it would take us all day to finally arrive at our Kiev offices. By the time we arrived, we were physically and mentally drained.

We started the Kiev Good News Church in the years following the Orange Revolution in Kiev, which occurred in the aftermath of the run-off vote of the 2004 Ukrainian Presidential election. That election was accompanied with massive public demonstrations in downtown Kiev, and when we started the church, the city of Kiev was still full of demonstrations that were so huge, it was mind-boggling. Tens of thousands of protesters were demonstrating everywhere.

So when Denise and I would eventually arrive in our area of Kiev, we had to also fight our way through thousands of demonstrators to get into our apartment. Almost every week, our car couldn't even get close to our apartment because of the masses of demonstrators. The driver would drop us off a considerable distance away, and on foot, Denise and I would make our way to our apartment, with our suitcases, through crowds of frenzied, mostly drunken demonstrators.

Because we were only in Kiev for a short time each week, we tried to make use of every minute we were there. We usually went straight into meetings with our emerging Kiev pastoral staff and with volunteers who were helping us start the church.

Denise and I went through this grueling process every single week to get to Kiev for our Wednesday afternoon staff meetings on time. All of that was *after* we had already had services, staff meetings, and filmed TV programs the entire first part of the week in Moscow. Denise and I could hardly find a spare minute for ourselves because we were attempting to live in two worlds at the same time.

Our Moscow team also began to travel regularly by train between Moscow and Kiev to help us train children's workers, youth workers, worship teams, and to develop a brand-new system of pastoral care. It was a massive endeavor to do this, and it took a huge financial investment. Our collective goal was that the church would be fully up and running from the day of the first service. With the sacrificial gifts of our precious ministry partners, we purchased all the sound equipment and other supplies that were needed to give the church a strong start. Then we began to inform people in Kiev — and all over Ukraine — that the Kiev Good News Church would be holding its first services.

The day finally came for the grand opening — Saturday, March 17, 2007. That was such a momentous event that Denise and I, our three sons and some of their family members, and the whole music ministry from Moscow traveled to Kiev to participate on that big day. More than 1,500 people packed into the auditorium where those first services were held, and many became part of the church. It was truly glorious.

For nearly two full years, Denise and I went back and forth every week between Moscow and Kiev. Then we finally shifted our focus back to fulfilling our mandate in Moscow. Today a wonderful church is thriving in Kiev, which we turned over to a pastor who is doing a marvelous job at leading that congregation. *Jesus truly is Lord over all!*

### Joel's Diligence in the Work of the Ministry

Joel had always been practical-minded and loved anything to do with business. He had "order" at the very core of his being. From the time he moved to the lands of the former USSR at the age of two, he had grown up here and therefore, of our three sons, he remembers the least about life in America *except* for the memories he had from our summer trips to the United States. But Joel really longed to be excellent in business and finances, and it seemed he was always working on a plan for the future.

Once when Joel was twelve years old, Denise and I noticed he had slipped into a state of somberness that seemed to hover over him for weeks. One night, I pulled him aside and asked, "Joel, what is going on with you? You seem so heavy and concerned about something." He said, "Dad, I'm concerned about whether I'll have enough money for retirement when I get older." He was so forward-thinking that at the age of twelve, he was already seriously thinking about how he would live when he reached retirement age!

I told him, "Joel, since you are twelve years old, you have a little time to think about it, so how about if you give it to the Lord, lighten up, and enjoy your life right now?"

But that was Joel's character. Even at eleven and twelve years old, he was always strategizing about the future and devising sound plans for what lay ahead in his life. We couldn't have foreseen it, but this was a part of Joel's character that would become a great blessing to our ministry in years to come.

As you might have guessed, schooling was a difficult situation in the lives of our kids. They had lived in three countries and had gone to school amidst three different languages. They'd had tutors and were enrolled in many different schools — more than ten in their young lifetimes. There were times in their early years when I'd wonder if they would end up being able to read and write in *any* language.

This was difficult for Denise and me to deal with. We were Americans in a Soviet world, and we didn't know if our kids should get an English education or a Russian education. In short, you could say the academics our children received were rather scattered, but the other lessons they were getting while we were building the ministry were invaluable and couldn't have been taught in any classroom. School was a big challenge in our family, but regardless, God doesn't look at education to decide whom He's going to use. God primarily looks at the heart.

When Joel was in his teens, he expressed a desire to pursue higher education. When I heard this, I was excited and knew exactly where I wanted him to get that higher education. But because his schooling was so messed up, he first had to get a certificate showing that his Russian language skills were good enough to study at a Russian university. Attending university-level classes in Russia would require the highest-level of knowledge of the language. So for two years, Joel was tutored at Moscow State University. Both Paul and Philip spoke excellent Russian, but neither of them had ever attempted this.

It had always been my dream that one of our sons would study at Moscow State University because it was such an impressive university. Russia does not have Ivy League schools as in the United States, but Moscow State

University has that kind of reputation. Joel knew I had always wanted one of our sons to study there, so when he decided to obtain a high-level certificate in the Russian language, he expressed a desire to go to that university to get it. And because Joel was so dedicated to excellence, he gave his all to the huge challenge before him.

Moscow State University was founded in 1755, and from the very beginning, its graduates became renowned alumni — famous Russian scientists and scholars. The sprawling university with its mighty central tower is located on Sparrow Hills just above the Moscow River. It not only has a rich academic history and an ongoing commitment to provide outstanding teaching, but its scholarship and research have remained the same for centuries. The brightest students have convened there from all over the vast Russian empire, the Soviet Union, and now the new Russia to study, to research, and to press into new frontiers of knowledge and learning.

I was impressed when Joel decided that he would attend Moscow State University to obtain a certificate in the Russian language. In my view, it was quite a bold step. And I was so proud of him and thrilled for him when he obtained that cherished certificate!

Joel was eleven years old when we moved from Riga to Moscow, and from "day one," he did almost every job thinkable — filming services at church, setting up equipment, running the lights, serving as an usher, singing in the choir, running the information table, and more. He was always doing his part to help build the church and the ministry.

Like his brothers, Joel had grown up working in our ministry and had *many* jobs in RENNER Ministries. At age eleven, he worked in the mail department during the summer. Then at age fifteen, he worked part time as a member of the grounds crew that maintained our ministry property. Then at eighteen, he joined the team full time, back in the mail department. Later he was placed over that department and also over the graphic designers — and later, he began to have the oversight of the office secretaries. Joel is a gifted leader who faithfully discharges his duties as Chief Executive Officer of our ministry to this day.

## Joel Marries a Remarkable Russian Girl

On March 8, 2002, Denise held a major event for women on Russia's Women's Day at the Kino Theater Mir. International Women's Day became a recognized public holiday in Russia in 1918, and it was one of the most important of all celebrations in the former USSR. It is comparable to Mother's Day in the United States except that it celebrates *all* women: mothers, sisters, grandmothers, and so on. Women's Day celebrates all women in general, but it also highlights women's achievements in the personal, business, and political spheres.

Women's Day is a holiday that is deeply ingrained in Russian history and culture. On that day, people celebrate important women in their lives by giving them flowers and gifts. Chocolates are also a hugely popular gift on this holiday — and that "gift of chocolate" leads to my telling you about a young girl named Olya Smolyanitskaya.

Hundreds of women packed the Kino Theater Mir on March 8, 2002. A woman named Ludmilla Smolyanitskaya brought along her unsaved daughter named Olga, whom we lovingly call *Olya* today. Later, Olya said the only reason she came that day was that her mother told her the church would be giving away chocolates. Oh, how powerful is the lure of a little candy!

Olya's grandfather was a full-blooded Russian Jew. In fact, he was so Jewish that his Soviet passport said "JEW" in big letters on the page that identified his bloodline. During World War II, Olya's Jewish grandfather commanded artillery troops. After the war, he became a member of Moscow's intelligentsia and one of the famous restaurateurs in Moscow who ran the Lira Café in the very center of the city on Pushkin Square. In its place, the first McDonald's in Russia opened in 1990. And what is also amazing to me is that one of Olya's grandmothers had roots that went all the way back to the family of the great Russian writer Leo Tolstoy.

But letting people know you were Jewish wasn't the smartest thing to do in the days of the USSR because Jews had been persecuted from the time of Nicholas II. So even though Olya was a Jewish girl on her father's side of the family, it hadn't meant a lot to her because her family had never celebrated their heritage. Like so many Jews from that difficult period, her family even tried to conceal it to avoid discrimination from those who did not like Jews.

Olya's Jewish father, Vladimir Mikailovich Smolyanitsky, was the cinematographer who worked at the Gorky Film Studio and who filmed nearly all the legendary Soviet films directed by Leonid Iovich Gaidai, including *Bootleggers*, *Obsession*, the *The Diamond Arm*, and *Twelve Chairs* in the 1960s and 1970s. In the Soviet Union, Gaidai's fame as a movie director was even bigger than America's Alfred Hitchcock.

Olya's mother, Ludmilla, was the first in the family to come to our church after the death of her eldest son. On the advice of her sister, who had immigrated to the United States and served there in a Baptist church, Ludmilla began to attend our church.

Because of the lure of chocolate, Olya accompanied her mother to Denise's big Women's Day celebration in 2002. That day she received her chocolate, but most importantly, she heard the Gospel and received Jesus as her Lord and Savior. Olya was so radically saved that she immediately began to regularly attend our church and became very involved in our youth ministry. After two months as a youth in our church, she learned that Joel Renner, the pastor's son and also a youth, was in the group, but the two of them never really got to know each other until three years later.

Denise and I still had that rule in our home that there could be no dating until after eighteen and no marriage until after twenty. So Joel honored our rule and waited until he turned eighteen to begin to pursue a relationship with Olya. Joel was always so serious-minded about everything he did and always had a long-term plan, so when he began to pay attention to Olya, Denise and I knew he was really, seriously thinking about her becoming his wife. Denise and I were thrilled because we were really impressed with Olya Smolyanitskaya.

Then in 2009, after Joel turned twenty, he and Olya, with our parental blessing, went to Zaks to officially register their marriage. Then on July 11, 2009, they were joined together in holy matrimony before God and the church, and they became *Joel and Olya Renner.*

After a few short years of marriage, Joel and Olya gave birth to their first son Daniel Ryan Joelevich Renner, whom we call *Daniel,* and later to their second son Mark Richard Joelevich Renner, whom we call *Mark.* Joel proudly tells people that his family and sons are Russian Jews!

By that time, Joel had also become co-director of our Russian media company, Media Mir, that was responsible for the management and expansion of our TV ministry. He co-led it with another director for ten years. And during that ten years, he and his co-director traveled the world to develop strategic ministry relationships with international ministries and to help me continue expanding our TV ministry in the territory of the former USSR.

Then in 2012, after years of proving himself faithful, Joel became the CEO of RENNER Ministries worldwide. In 2015, he was ordained into the full-time ministry and today, he serves God with his family alongside Denise and me in our worldwide ministry. In 2018, Joel officially fulfilled his dream to become a Russian citizen, making him an American-Russian citizen, and their two children also have dual citizenship.

### Denise's Ministry to Russian-Speaking Women Flourishes

In addition to serving alongside me right from the start in Moscow, Denise passionately developed a women's ministry for the women who attended our Moscow Good News Church. She dreamed to help as many women as possible. And to help *her*, God graciously brought her an amazing team of women who have worked with Denise to build one of the strongest ministries to women anywhere in the former Soviet Union. I realize that I am her husband, but I am telling you the objective truth when I say that the significance of what Denise has done with women in Moscow cannot be exaggerated. And beyond Moscow, the same is true all over the Russian-speaking world!

There are *tens of thousands* of women involved in some way in Denise's women's ministry, and there is no end in sight as to how many women will eventually be involved. But it all started with Denise's vision for women whose lives have been wounded to become healed and to become God's healing instrument to other women still struggling in their self-images and marriages. There are no better healers than those who have been healed, so Denise began to put forth effort to see her first group of women brought into wholeness in their lives — then that group of women would become God's hands to bring healing to other women. And that is exactly what happened!

## Two Big Strikes Against Marriages
## in the Former USSR

During the days of the Soviet Union, the subjects of marriage, intimacy, and other family matters were taboo. Those things were simply not publicly discussed, and it was considered to be improper if someone tried to publicly discuss them. Because communism had outlawed the teaching of the Bible, it meant what the Bible had to say about marriage and family — the roles of husbands and wives and the biblical way to raise children — was basically unknown. As much as people wanted to do well at home in their marriages and with their children, they had zero instruction on what the Bible had to say on these issues.

The impact of World War II was also devastating to marriages and families. Because millions of husbands in the Soviet Union perished in World War II, it meant women were forced to become the heads of their homes and the breadwinners for their families. Because of a statistically *striking* shortage of men all over this part of the world back then, women worked construction jobs, paved roads, and did all kinds of manual labor that had previously been done primarily by men, plus they were trying to raise their children. All of this eliminated tenderness for many women, and many women became hardened.

Because so many men died in the war, a whole generation of children were raised in homes where there was no father. Later when boys and girls grew up and got married, millions of them had no examples of marriage to follow as a guide because they had grown up in a single-parent household. Because of a lack of fathers, many boys whose fathers died in the war struggled with their self-images and turned to vodka as young men. When they got married, they carried problems of alcoholism into their marriages. Their new wives — who had grown up with female-dominated homes — took charge as their mothers had done after the war. All of this resulted in even more pain, brokenness, and dysfunction in families, and a maze of confusion over the roles of husbands and wives — *with* a rampage of divorce as a result.

The need to teach women what the Bible had to say about marriage and family was desperately needed. So Denise began to develop a series of six-week classes that she called, "The Art of Being a Wife." It was a seminar designed to strengthen women in their self-images and marriages and to give them a vision of having a strong marriage and a home that's built on biblical principles. Over the years, Denise has taught more than three hundred of those sessions that have been attended by several thousand women who have sat face-to-face with her and her helpers.

These women soak up Denise's teaching like sponges as they hear for the first time in their lives what the Bible has to say on these vitally important subjects. As a result, vast numbers of women have been saved, filled with the Spirit, delivered, and healed. Their husbands and families have gotten saved, divorces have been canceled, and marriages have been restored. And because women began to show respect to their husbands, their children likewise began to demonstrate respect to their fathers. There have also been reconciliations between spouses who got divorced. Once they learned what the Bible had to say about marriage, they returned to each other and remarried.

And I must mention again Denise's huge celebration on Women's Day, which falls on March 8 on Russia's calendar each year, but is celebrated on that day in most of the world. For *years* on that important holiday, Denise has hosted a conference for women in Moscow attended by nearly a thousand women. On that day, she invites guest ministers who give seminars throughout the day, and there is music, dances, skits, and even high-end fashion shows — all designed to touch the hearts of Russian-speaking women. Notable special speakers from around the world also join Denise to teach and to minister.

Because Women's Day is such an important Russian holiday, Denise has wisely used this event to minister to women and to make this holiday a celebration that's all about them. Life for many Moscow women is hard. They live in a city of millions where the vast majority of them use public transportation, walk to and from the grocery store with armloads of groceries, live in relatively small apartments, and do their best to take care of their husband, children, and elderly parents. Denise worked hard to make Women's Day *their* celebration in which she thanks every woman for all that she does for others and makes each woman feel like a queen for a day, even blessing them with gifts. And in those annual Women's Day meetings, many women have been saved, filled with the Holy Spirit, encouraged, and physically and emotionally healed and transformed.

Then there is Denise's weekly *School of Cinderella* that is based on her book entitled, *Who Stole Cinderella? The Art of 'Happily Ever After.'* This is an online event that has thrown open the door for Russian-speaking women around the planet to join Denise every week for two solid hours. But you may ask, "Why does Denise call it the *School of Cinderella?*"

So many little girls, even in the Russian-speaking world, have read or seen in other forms of media the fairy tale of Cinderella, in which Cinderella marries Prince Charming. These young girls carry in their hearts the dream that one day they, too, will experience a fairy-tale marriage. Then when they get married and life goes by and disappointments set in, they experience pain and hurt. But because every woman is precious in the eyes of God, this school has been designed to help them re-discover that they really are precious and that God wants them to flourish as a woman and wife.

Denise's women's ministry reaches tens of thousands of Russian-speaking women worldwide. Every woman who registers for her online classes is assigned a qualified personal counselor who stays with that participant for all the weeks she "attends" the class. The counselors primarily communicate by email and online chats as the participants pour out their hearts — their hurts, questions, and prayer requests — and every question is answered by their counselor.

Also, tens of thousands of women receive a special invitation to be a part of her special weekly session called, *Time With Denise Renner*. She also has a weekly evening program called, *Questions and Answers*, in which she answers questions that are sent to her by female viewers around the world. Women testify, "I've heard different marriage materials, but I've never heard this kind of teaching that is so loving and so candid."

Denise's women's ministry has touched women in difficult situations all over Russia and Ukraine. And the women whose lives have been changed want to help and heal other women, so they have visited many women's prisons, where they've provided concerts and given gifts of soap, shampoo, feminine products — and Bibles and Christian books when they're permitted to do so. For years, Denise's women have regularly ministered in women's drug-and-alcohol hospitals and other kinds of rehabilitation centers. The women in these rehabilitation centers have been so dramatically changed that doctors who preside over these centers have asked Denise and her group of women to return again and again.

Denise recalled how she felt about all these remarkable outreaches. She said, "I want to strengthen women so they can strengthen other women. My vision has been to raise up women who would minister to other women in prisons, rehabilitation centers, and orphanages. I had all this benevolent ministry growing and blossoming inside of me, and God opened the doors to enable us to do it."

For years, Denise and her women's teams regularly went to girls-only orphanages, where they have taught abandoned and orphaned girls about self-dignity, sexual purity, personal hygiene, the power of forgiveness, and matters of etiquette that includes such things as how to dress, how to set a table, how to prepare for a job interview, and how to manage a house — things that these girls otherwise know little or nothing about.

We have learned that when a woman is strong, it results in her marriage and entire family becoming stronger in every way. This is not a sideline ministry, but for us, this is a powerful ministry that is essential for the strength and restoration of women, marriages, and families. Those women who have been healed themselves feel a responsibility to reciprocate God's healing touch in their lives by becoming God's healing hands to others. And it is simply magnificent to see these *thousands* of women's lives touched and transformed as a result.

As miraculous and wonderful as our accomplishments were so far in Moscow, there was unfinished business that needed to be completed concerning the church. Like the church in Riga, in order for the Moscow church to have longevity, it needed a permanent home — its own facility. God did it for us in Riga, but now we needed God to do it again in Moscow, which had become one of the most expensive cities in the world to live.

The price of real estate was skyrocketing, but if God wanted to use us and our partners to do it again, we were willing to say *yes* to His plan. That was the word I'd received as we dedicated the church in Riga: "Your assignment in Riga is done. Now go to Moscow and do it all over again." But it would take another big miracle in this next leg of our journey as well.

'Moscow was a city where God wanted His presence
to be known and the influence of His Word to be felt
in a greater, new way — not just in this city of millions,
but *from* this city to the nations of the world. He was already
using so many ministers of the Gospel as influencers
in Russia's capital, where a vast majority of the population
still needs to be evangelized. And He had planted our family
here to play our unique part in that divine plan.'

# 14

# CHRISTIAN INFLUENCE
# IN THE HEART OF A NATION

Within the official city limits of Moscow, there is a population of more than twelve million people at the time of this writing. But if you were to add the "unofficial," unregistered numbers in the entire region of Moscow, the population exceeds twenty million.[1] In a recent speech by Moscow's mayor, he said that on a daily basis, there are some thirty million people in transit in the city of Moscow — more people than in the whole state of Texas!

To give you some perspective on that number, the population of the entire nation of Latvia was about two million people at the time we left there. Just one neighborhood or community in Moscow can have three million people in it — that's bigger than the population of the Paris, France, city limits! Where Denise and I presently live is an area considered very small because it only has a population of about a half million people. But just our

---

**Left:** *Red Square and the magnificent towers of the Kremlin, Moscow, Russia.*

"countryside" neighborhood is bigger than our original hometown of Tulsa, Oklahoma.

Moscow is among the top twenty-five most populated cities in the world, the second-most populated city in Europe, and the largest city by area on the European continent.[2] Moscow is so huge and covers so much geography that it makes cities like Chicago, Houston, London, Rome, and Paris seem small to our Renner eyes. Only a relatively few cities in the world fit into Moscow's super-mega category. Some of those cities include Tokyo, Delhi, Sao Paulo, Mexico City, Cairo, Beijing, New York City, Buenos Aires, Istanbul, Manila, Lagos, and Los Angeles.

Because Moscow is the headquarters of the Russian government — and millions moved here in search of work after the collapse of the USSR — its population has skyrocketed and continues to rise even in the years since we moved here. When our family relocated here in the year 2000, Moscow had a metroplex population of about ten million. But since then, that population has more than doubled in size. No city can proportionately grow its infrastructure to accommodate such astronomical growth in such a relatively short period of time.

It seemed that nothing was static in those days, not for one moment — not the exponentially growing population and all the shifting and adjusting to accommodate it, and not the plan of God for our lives, which seemed as fast-tracked as a subway train speeding *breakneck* to its next stop. We had been stretched in Latvia as we started the TV network, the church, the pastors association, and then the Bible school with barely a pause from one God-ordained venture to the next. It was like God's Spirit had been loosed, and He was *vigorously* carrying out His long-ago devised plans in those spiritually desolate lands.

Now we were doing it again in Moscow. Isaiah 54:2 says, "Enlarge the place of thy tent, and let them stretch forth the curtains of thine habitations: spare not, lengthen thy cords, and strengthen thy stakes." If Denise and I and our team thought we had been stretched in Latvia, we were about to be stretched and increased beyond all our past experiences. God was expanding our capacity for ministry in ways that surprised even us. But we had given Him our yes and had passed our point of no return long ago. What choice did we have but to run with the vision?

Everything in this part of the world was changing, radically and *quickly*, in the decade since the collapse of the USSR on December 8, 1991. But it seemed this was especially true of the city of Moscow, and it had a profound impact on every sphere of life. It affected traffic — the increased time spent driving and insufficient mass-transit systems. And it affected families — the cost of living, skyrocketing property prices for renting or buying, and not enough schools to accommodate growing numbers of children. Moscow's *enormous* population growth had affected individuals and families, and it was even affecting churches, as I will talk about in this chapter.

But Moscow was a city where God wanted His presence to be known and the influence of His Word to be felt in a greater, new way — not just in this city of millions, but *from* this city to the nations of the world. He was already using so many ministers of the Gospel as influencers in Russia's capital, where a vast majority of the population still needs to be evangelized. And He had planted our family here to play our unique part in that divine plan.

## Moscow, the 'World Capital of Traffic Jams' — Just One Reason Why Our Church Needed a Permanent Home

Currently, Moscow and the surrounding area combined have eight million cars registered and an unknown number of cars that come from extended surrounding areas. Because of this, in a report by an automotive analytics company, Moscow has been dubbed the "world capital of traffic jams, and in the year 2013 was ranked the worst in the world."[3] In the years leading up to the purchasing of our church property, the astronomical increase in population became critical. There were times we were in a car for up to *five hours* during rush hour, trying to go from our home to our church facility at the time, where we were paying equally astronomical rent.

At some point during this outrageous surge in Moscow's population, the network of roads in the city reached its maximum capacity, but the number of people in transit kept growing (and *keeps* growing). The situation has become so serious that in a worldwide rating system, Moscow edged out other global cities renowned for traffic congestion, including Sao Paulo, Mexico City, and Istanbul.[4]

People from smaller cities may think an everyday commute to and from work of 30-40 minutes each way is long. But Moscovites' typical commute can be anything from 1.5 to 4 hours due to traffic.[5] So a 1-hour commute each way is considered a "charm"; 1.5 hours is thought of as normal; 2 or more hours is enough to merit complaining about to friends or whomever will listen; and 4 or more hours, according to some psychologists, is simply mentally and emotionally unhealthy. In fact, psychologists in Moscow have made this finding their official statement — and the stress added to navigating this level of traffic due to late arrivals to work, missed meetings, and even missed flights only adds to people's feelings of emotional *dis*-ease.

Once when our family had planned to catch a flight to Kiev, because of the terrible traffic situation, we left home five hours earlier than the time we needed to be there. But on that day, the traffic was so bad that we "drove" — mostly sat in traffic — for eight solid hours en route to the airport! By the time we arrived, the flight had departed and there were no other flights we could get that day. So we turned around and drove another eight hours in bumper-to-bumper traffic to get home. We spent sixteen hours in traffic that day *and we never got anywhere!*

Long hours stuck in traffic can be non-productive and stressful, but research has linked traffic to other negative mental-health outcomes, such as depletion and exhaustion. You can imagine the overall negative consequences Moscow's traffic can inflict on those who regularly travel roads and highways to maneuver around in this vast city.

Due to improvements in mass transportation, plus the increased number of people who work from home, commuter traffic has become better in recent years; nevertheless, it remains a serious factor in the way we live our lives in Moscow. If Denise and I want to go out to get a hamburger, we think about it seriously before proceeding. To get that hamburger may mean sitting in traffic for two hours to get there and another two hours to get back home. When you know you're going to invest that many hours for a burger and fries, you think really hard about it before jumping in the car.

Once, just before the New Year holiday when Moscow's streets are the most congested, Denise wanted the two of us to go to downtown Moscow for an end-of-the-year lunch to celebrate what a great year we'd just experienced. We chose our location, calculated how much traffic there would be, and allotted ourselves four hours to get to the restaurant. Then on our big celebration day, we left our ministry office on our journey to enjoy this special lunch.

Six hours later and only halfway to our destination, we finally gave up and stopped somewhere else for a quick bite so we could get back on the road to drive another six hours back home. The traffic was frustrating, but it was even more disheartening to spend that much time in the car, never having made it to our destination.

Traffic can be so bad that when we need to fly to another city, getting from our house to the airport at times is the longest part of the trip! The actual flight is often *short* compared to the multiple hours it takes us just to get to the airport so we can board our plane.

You can guess that weekly trips to church, where we were having to set up and tear down each week in a rented facility, turned into an entire-day-long event, with some church members traveling up to two and three hours to church *one way*!

## The Moscow Metro

The Moscow Metro, Moscow's subway system, is an underground museum famous for its art, murals, mosaics, and ornate chandeliers. In addition to being fabulously decorated, it is considered one of the safest subway systems in the world. The Moscow Metro first started operating in 1935 and immediately became the centerpiece of Moscow's transport system.

But more than that, it was a Stalinist device to awe and reward the population and give them an appreciation of Soviet realist art. The artwork of the thirteen original stations is so fabulous that it enjoys national and international renown, and the Metro was once touted as sort of a Soviet "cathedral" of engineering.

Even though the Moscow Metro has a reputation for its architectural splendor, it can be quite intimidating because of its enormous size and congestion. At the time I'm writing this book, the Moscow Metro has 238 stations and is one of the deepest subway systems in the world. Also, its tracks run underground for 254 miles, which makes it the fourth longest in the world and the longest outside of China. It serves about 9,000,000 passengers daily, which equals an approximate cumulative number of 2,500,000,000 passengers every year.[6] In case all those zeroes throw you off, that number is *two billion, five hundred million* annual passenger rides. I realize such numbers are mind-boggling to many, but because the city has grown so much faster than anticipated, even this massive metro system is overcrowded.

Those who travel via the Metro during rush hours must be prepared to push and to be pushed, as there will be a lot of jostling and shoving by what looks like an endless sea of people shuffling quickly along to make their connections. Even those who are normally cultured and polite find themselves pushing and shoving to get on and off the trains or to fight their way up or down the lengthy and seemingly endless escalator rides.

The constant pushing and shoving can be so serious that when mothers in our Moscow church give birth to a baby, it usually means we won't see that mother for two years or more because they do not want to risk their babies being "crushed" by the masses of people on the Metro. We always rejoice for the birth of a baby, but we also know that the birth of a child probably means we won't be seeing that mother for an extended period of time.

Because extending the influence of the Bible across old Soviet lands was in the heart of God, He had planted church expansion in my heart long before we had our permanent building. I knew He wanted people ministered to and cared for, so even before we instituted our more than two hundred Home Groups held in homes throughout the city each week, I'd seen the vision *and the need* for having affiliate, satellite churches planted in key locations all over Moscow.

But it was Moscow's congested traffic and the extensive metro system that inspired us to begin aggressively planning for the opening throughout the city of other campuses for our church. It was unreasonable for church members, including elderly people and parents with children and youth to travel every Sunday for two to three hours *one way* to church and then repeat the same number of hours traveling to get back home. This eventually led us to plant our various campuses, which today are *filled* with congregation members and are teeming with the life of the Holy Spirit. I'll share more about that later.

## Moscow Is One of the Most Expensive Cities in the World

As I said, it seemed everything was changing *rapidly* in Moscow since the collapse of the Soviet Union, including the cost of living, which radically changed for Moscovites since the time our family moved here years ago. How much money one needs to live depends largely on his or her lifestyle, but even if a person lives minimally in Moscow, the fact remains that several surveys have identified Moscow as the most expensive city in Europe in relation to salary. In 2019, a worldwide research firm studied 144 cities across six continents and measured the comparative cost of more than 200 items in each location, including housing, transportation, food, clothing, household goods, and entertainment.

That particular survey is considered to be the world's most comprehensive cost-of-living survey and is used to help multinational companies and governments determine compensation allowances for their expatriate employees. It stated that Moscow has replaced Tokyo as the world's most expensive city. Seoul came in second place with Tokyo moving down two positions to take third place, followed by Hong Kong. With New York as the base city with a score of 100 points, Moscow scored 123.9 — nearly 24 points higher than the cost of living in New York City.[7]

Due to the mushrooming population, property costs have also escalated so unbelievably that Moscow now ranks as one of the world's most expensive cities for real estate. Like most cities, besides the size and type of property, location largely dictates the price. For example, the center of Moscow fetches the highest prices, but areas outside the city's center can also demand very high prices.

Prices for apartments vary based on economic trends, but one can expect to pay $4,000 on average per square meter (about $372 per square foot) on the outskirts of the city and $6,500 to $12,000 per square meter (about $604 to $1,115 per square foot) in a prestigious district. However, the price may exceed $40,000 per square meter ($3,717 per square foot) for a luxury apartment. So smaller, one-room apartments with about 50 square meters (538 square feet) begin at about $200,000, and a more luxurious apartment with 100 square meters (1,076 square feet) in the center of Moscow costs as much as $4,000,000 or even more. For this reason, Moscow is currently ranked as one of the most expensive cities in the world for purchasing property, and real-estate experts predict property prices will continue to escalate as the city's population grows.

## A New Russia Had Emerged Before Our Eyes

As you know, our family moved to the Soviet Union on the cusp of communism's collapse. Although we saw firsthand and experienced ourselves the horrible deficits and other traumatic occurrences that happened in the aftermath of that historical event, we were privileged to witness history changing right before our eyes. Drastic economic reforms prior to the collapse of communism, and then the dissolution of the USSR, had destroyed the existing economy. Traditional factories and enterprises were either completely ruined or were in a difficult situation in which workers couldn't be paid wages for six months or more. Nations were rebuilding *from the ground up*.

Then in the 1990s, most Russian cities were experiencing the wildest form of capitalism — from dire scarcity to massive supplies of everything. A huge chasm between dearth and plenty had been *shut tight* during that time, but that period was not without its problems.

I'll try to give you an idea of how erratically the economy ebbed and flowed — like a *tsunami* — in those days, when we first moved to the former USSR. Prices back then were so low as people were learning how to transition to a market system versus a state-run system. But it wasn't long before the prices of everyday commodities, such as bread, milk, flour, and sugar went up *nearly 500 percent*! Think about where *you* live — if a loaf of bread cost $2 and the cost of that bread went up 500 percent, you would have to pay *$10* for the same bread you had been buying for only $2!

Also, it was against this background that crime grew so dramatically. And the police, acting in situations in which there were a lot of gaps in legislation, could not adequately hinder organized-crime groups. The scope of law enforcement's new authority had not been clearly defined as a new Russia was emerging, and justice slipped between the cracks in many cases as those with the lowest forms of morality and scruples swooped in to make the most of a confusing time.

This capital city eventually became a symbol of success. Trade in Moscow developed and apartments, buildings, and roads were built. But at the same time, the urban structure of the city continued as a symbol of corruption. Eventually, however, a mayor was elected who carried out reforms in the fields of transportation and construction and who significantly renovated the city center and gave Moscow its current look. Today the Russian capital is in no way inferior to other European megalopolises and in some ways, it surpasses many of them.

My point is that Moscow today is nothing like the Moscow that existed at the end of the Soviet Union. But all these changes — most of them good — have also produced dramatic effects on churches and ministries. I could give you example after example, but let's just focus on one: the costs of renting various properties so a church can function. I'm talking about offices, auditoriums, and storage spaces. I think you'll be *flabbergasted* by what you read.

## Our Nonstop Search for a Permanent Home

As is always true, any church plant has enormous expenses to get started, and especially at the beginning, there are usually very few among that church's congregation who tithe. The majority of people who started to attend our earliest services had never heard what the Bible says about giving and tithing. Many of them didn't even know there was such a thing as a tithe. Because they were only hearing about it for the first time, they were just learning to tithe and to give. The result was, in the beginning, the income of our new church was minuscule at the same time that our expenses were enormous.

As I told you in the last chapter, we'd had a TV office in Moscow for many years before our family relocated here. So when our ministry first started in Moscow many years earlier while we were still in Riga, we were able to rent office space for a relatively small amount of money. They were not especially nice office spaces, but they were large enough to accommodate our rapidly growing ministry.

By August 2000, our TV offices had moved into a historic building on the banks of the Moscow River, about a five-minute walk from Red Square and across the bridge from where our family lived in a modest apartment.

Our ministry occupied half of the first floor of that building at first, but because we were rapidly outgrowing that space, we ended up renting the entire floor. Compared to today's prices in that same building, our monthly rent at that time was inexpensive. But soon we outgrew *that* office space, so while our TV offices remained at the location on the river, our church offices moved to another downtown location that was just around the corner from the renowned Bolshoi Theater.

The new church-office location was a six-story building, and we rented the top two floors to accommodate the new staff of the Moscow church. It was while we were there that we also launched our Bible school, after which we were utilizing every inch of that two-story space. After a lot of negotiations with the owner, we were able to rent the space for a surprisingly inexpensive price per month, but by this time, rent for both locations had more than doubled.

We were also renting the Kino Theater Mir for our weekly church meetings. But because the economy in Moscow was roaring, the rental price changed almost by the week. Within two months, the price for meeting once a week had doubled. It was really expensive for a brand-new church with very little income. And because we knew the price was going to keep escalating, we began a search to look for another location where we could hold services.

Soon we moved to the concert hall — a "Dom Kultury" (cultural hall) — at a local university in Moscow. The cost there was expensive for a new church, but it was stable, so we made the move there. But soon our church outgrew that location, so we moved our services to a big theater called MDM, which I described in the last chapter as the location people could access right from the Metro. That facility was large enough to accommodate us, but it was a huge financial leap to pay multiple thousands of dollars per month for one service per week. And in addition to that, we were also still paying rent for our offices downtown. So at that time, the brand-new church was already forking out a small fortune every month for various rents, and that didn't include what we were paying for storage in another part of the city.

We soon outgrew our downtown offices, so we began to search the real-estate market again, and we discovered that prices for office space were going up so fast, it was scary. Yet I knew we needed to anchor ourselves in a stable place, so I asked our administrator to search for a building we could possibly purchase and renovate. And, as you know, we lease-purchased a four-story abandoned kindergarten, including the basement that looked like a dump when we bought it. After we negotiated a year-long payout plan and God supernaturally gave us the funds to pay it off, He enabled us to transform that dump into a diamond.

In the last chapter, I shared about that step of faith and how God miraculously provided for us to buy that building that cost $1.1 million. But after being there for a short two years, we also outgrew that building. After much prayer, my team and I decided to put our building up for sale. The real estate market was growing so fast that we were able to sell that building for triple our original investment. It was a remarkable increase on our investment, but it wasn't enough cash to purchase a building large enough for our TV ministry and church. So we invested that money, waiting for our divine moment to own our permanent church building. And we went back to renting space for our burgeoning offices and staff.

While we sought God's direction about what to do next, to save money, I decided that our ministry offices would move into an office on the far side of Moscow that was so terribly dilapidated, I was embarrassed to ask our employees to come to work there. But they knew we had invested the church's money and that we were trying to save so we would be able to eventually purchase something permanent and stop having to move from place to place.

Then as I also told you in the last chapter, the MDM auditorium where we were holding weekly services was suddenly rented out from under us by the Broadway musical *Cats*. We had become accustomed to moving by now, but my countenance fell when they told us we had to be out in *two weeks*!

We were paying sky-high prices for rent in unstable locations because we didn't have enough cash to purchase something big enough for our TV ministry and church offices. But constantly moving from place to place was beginning to wear away at me and the rest of our team. Our faithful staff kept a great attitude, but every time we had to move, it became harder.

Plus we had to keep changing all our advertisements because the church address kept changing. We were spending another small fortune sending out regularly updated information to church members and potential visitors.

One day with resolve, I announced to our team, "As long as we rent, we are at the mercy of landlords and escalating rent prices. This is our season to buy!" God had commissioned us in Riga to "go to Moscow and do it all over again," and I now had my sights *lasered* on permanent church ownership.

But we had to be out of the MDM in two weeks. Where were we going to go? We returned to the Dom Kultury at the university in downtown Moscow where we had previously been, and we began conducting multiple services there each Sunday *for five years*. We occupied every spare bit of space in that building.

At the end of five years, our TV ministry and church offices had moved to the other side of Moscow into a huge Soviet-looking building with enough space to nicely accommodate all of us along with our growing Bible school. If we counted all the cumulative people who came to those offices for the Bible school, the pastors association, the church, and the TV ministry, *thousands* of people came in and out of those offices during the time we were there.

When we started there, the rent for that office space was expensive, and the church also moved from the Dom Kultury to an auditorium across the street from the offices that was also quite expensive. That auditorium had been abandoned for years and had to be renovated before we could hold services there. The rent was enormous for that building, but we were growing so quickly, and we were consistently conducting five church services there every weekend as well. But it was wonderful because it was "our" building every day of the week — this was the first time in our journey as renters that we didn't have to set up and tear down each week before and after services. We actually had designated space for a full-fledged Sunday School and a room for counseling new believers. Really, it was an amazing breakthrough for us — but between that auditorium and our offices across the street, we were paying a fortune in rent every month.

It's also important to note that the Russian congregation was largely paying for this. And while prices for everything in Moscow were skyrocketing, people's salaries had generally not caught up with the accelerating cost of living all around them.

But we were watching God supernaturally supply all our financial needs to pay for what seemed like endlessly rising costs to do ministry. And because we had been constantly either moving or searching for yet another new location, it really felt like we were in the real-estate business! I can't remember a time during those years when we weren't keeping our eyes open for a building we could afford to buy and renovate.

In the meantime, our various monthly rents continued to grow larger until, finally, we were paying unthinkable amounts for all those rents. When our team and I looked at this mountainous expense, we longed for that money to be invested into something permanent — into our own building — instead of into the hands of other property owners. But the fact was that although we had invested a large amount of money from the sale of that kindergarten building, and that investment was beginning to grow, it still wasn't enough to buy a building big enough to accommodate our church and ministry.

Finally, because property prices were escalating at what seemed like lightning speed, our top ministry team, under my leadership, decided to use the money out of our investments to purchase a piece of land. Instead of looking for a building to buy, we were going to *build* a church building from the ground up.

But where should we buy? Moscow was a huge city with so many options.

## The Importance of 'Laying Low' at Key Moments and 'Spying Out the Land'

Over our years in ministry, I have discovered *timing* to be extremely important. I have certainly found it to be true that we need to act quickly when favor is obviously on our side. But let me also say that wonderful opportunities that aren't *God*-opportunities can also come packaged with difficult, unnecessary challenges if we act on them and miss the mark.

Knowing exactly which opportunities to take — and which ones to let pass us by — has been one of my personal challenges in the former Soviet Union. One day, I was seeking the Lord about several opportunities that were presenting themselves, and the Lord said to me, *If you're going to survive and do what I've called you to do in this part of the world, you'll have to learn to think like a snake.*

At first, these words caught me off guard. But immediately, Matthew 10:16 came to my mind: "Behold, I send you forth as sheep in the midst of wolves: be ye therefore wise as serpents, and harmless as doves." In this verse, Jesus commanded His disciples, as He is commanding us today, *"Be as wise as serpents."*

The word "serpent" is the Greek word *ophis* and it simply describes *a snake of any type,* but it is used here as a sign of *cunning* or *cleverness.* Matthew 10:16 had always perplexed me because I had previously thought of a serpent as being only evil. But as I meditated on this verse more deeply, I began to gain new insight about what Jesus was saying. He was saying serpents are "wise," and we need to take a lesson from them!

If you're a little squeamish about the subject of serpents or snakes, just stay with me for the next few moments so you don't miss the full impact of what Jesus was telling us. He is the One who chose to use a serpent to make His point!

Let's consider the behavior of serpents to see how Jesus' statement about these creatures in Matthew 10:16 relates to *timing.* First, serpents blend into the environment when they move into a new territory. Rather than announce their presence, they lay low, stay quiet, and blend into their surroundings. In fact, you could walk right past a snake and not know you're close to it!

Most snakes have the ability to be nearly invisible because they were designed to be *camouflaged.* This camouflage serves as a protective "covering." Even the fiercest aggressor could pass by, but the serpent would not likely be noticed because it blends so well into the landscape.

The camouflage gives the serpent latitude to find its way around new territory — to move about freely while "evaluating" a new situation. Serpents will assess a situation to identify places of shelter so they can settle in a new environment. They find hiding places to protect themselves from attack. They also observe where to find the easiest prey. When all of these assessments are made and the facts are assimilated, the serpent is ready to act. But this "settling in" is a key time for a serpent.

Can you see the parallel between the behavior of a serpent and Jesus' strategic plan for us when we are entering new territory for Him? *Jesus said there's wisdom to glean from such a study!*

As I carefully pondered the behavior of serpents, I began to understand exactly why Jesus used this example. This analogy applies to all of us in regard to our families, businesses, ministries, or any opportunity God places before us in which we must implement His strategies in order to establish His victory on the earth.

When God calls us to do something new — to move into a new territory or seize a new opportunity — it is wise for us to move slowly and carefully into that new phase of our lives. A common mistake is to act too quickly. Acting hastily, before all the facts are gathered and assimilated, often leads to mistakes in decision-making. In fact, one serious mistake can cause us to lose out on an opportunity altogether. Better to *lay low, stay quiet, blend into the environment for a while*, and *learn from the facts we observe.*

## We Began Our Search Like a Snake!

That is our exact testimony in Moscow as we searched for a permanent church location. Jesus' illustration of the "wisdom of a serpent" served Denise and me well when we launched out to begin our search for land on which to build the Moscow church.

When we decided to buy land in Moscow, we took time to really learn the layout of the city before we acted. Although we immediately saw opportunities, we decided to gain as much knowledge of the environment and the circumstances as possible before we took action. In retrospect, I can assure you that, for us, acting too fast would have certainly meant making some poor decisions that we would have greatly regretted down the road.

Because of all our experience in renting and in the purchase of the kindergarten, which we sold for a profit, we were already becoming near experts in the field of real estate. So we began a scouring search throughout the city. Before I made any grand announcement that we had found our land, I first wanted to know something about a particular area of the city where we were looking. It is very unwise and a waste of Kingdom resources of both money and time to start fantastic projects without first understanding the challenges and risks involved. Many people have been hurt because someone got in a hurry and acted too quickly.

We knew that moving slower may take more time initially, but in the end, it would produce more stable, serious, and lasting results. So we made the choice to move "slow and steady" — to gather all the facts we could, analyze the accumulated information, and then seek the Lord in prayer, listening for what He had to say to us through those facts. Only then would we make announcements concerning our plans. I can't emphasize it enough: To move ahead more quickly than we did in those days would have proven a harmful mistake!

Most mistakes in forging new territory for the Gospel are avoidable. God is a strategic Planner who delights in giving you the wisdom you need in *whatever* venture you're undertaking for Him. Your part is to move forward by His grace and guidance. As you do, you will well secure the victory He has planned for you in that new territory and season.

I advise you to take as much time as you possibly can in any new venture for Jesus — and be sure of the actions you take. Before you act on any opportunity publicly, first "learn the landscape" of your new environment. Take time to really understand the opportunities and possible problems around you. Make sure you are completely informed of all the pertinent facts about your new environment — facts that will help you move forward smoothly in fulfilling your new assignment without unnecessary delays or detours. Then pray diligently about the information you gather and seek the Lord's wisdom on how that information applies to your assignment.

This is one of the reasons Jesus told us to be as wise as a serpent — that is, to emulate the strategy of the serpent and use wisdom before "settling" on a decision. Then when the right moment comes and opportunity strikes, you can seize your divine moment with the grace and favor of God.

Land prices were escalating faster than our investments were growing, so we knew the value of any land we purchased would also grow. The land we chose to buy was right around the corner from the Izmailovo Hotel, a very dear location to me, as that is where Denise and I stayed in the early days when we regularly visited Moscow as we traveled Russia's eleven time zones to establish the TV ministry. The Izmailovo was also where I'd stayed when I came on that first missions trip with Duane Vander Klok and Dave Duell to teach in the Jelgava Bible school.

Our tract of land measured one acre, which may sound small to you, but imagine if you could find a single acre of land in Manhattan. It would be pretty remarkable to find an available piece of land even that small. That is how rare it was to find empty land in Moscow in those days. So we took the money out of our investment account and purchased that *one acre of land* for what many would consider an immense sum, but it was relatively inexpensive by Moscow standards.

We hired an architectural firm to see what we could design to fit on an acre. After a lot of discussion, our architect presented us with a plan for a ten-story building on that acre of land. The suggested plan included a tower of ten floors with an auditorium that had two wraparound balconies and two levels of underground parking. The rendering he showed us was so beautiful that it was breathtaking. But when the architect gave us the projected price, I knew it was too big a project to undertake, so I put on the brakes.

So once again, our team began to earnestly search for a building we could renovate to become a permanent home for our church and ministry. The land was ours and continued to increase in value as we continued our journey toward securing a permanent church building and ministry headquarters on this side of the world. Actually, the investment in that land was one of the wisest investments we ever made — it increased that rapidly in value.

### *Finally* — a Building That Would Be Our New Church Home!

One day, my administrator came to me and said, "We have found a building in a miserable, destroyed condition. It's so horrible that it's not usable at all in its present state. But because of its derelict condition, it's on the market for only $5.3 million. If we renovate it, it would be large enough to accommodate our church for many years."

Since some luxury apartments downtown Moscow could cost more than that price, I asked him, "What's wrong with the building and where is it located?" He answered, "Its interior is totally gutted to bare bricks, but it is the former auditorium for a scientific institute where lectures were held years ago for the staff and leadership of that organization." Then he added, "The institute and this gutted building are actually still connected by a shared space."

This particular organization had earlier sold the building to another organization that gutted it with the intention of converting it into a massive entertainment center that would have contained a bowling alley. But for some reason, they dropped the project. The gutted interior of the building was the reason it was being offered at such a low price. It was 3,600 square meters, or 39,600 square feet. To think we could buy anything that large anywhere in the city for such a low price was astounding.

At first, I was thrilled, but then I realized the condition of the building must be *really* scary for a building that size to be offered at such a low price. I kept asking my administrator, "What is wrong with that building? Its condition must be really bad if the owners are selling a building that big for $5.3 million."

After prayer, I told my administrator, "I want to go see that building." So Denise and I, our sons, and our executive staff all loaded into cars and drove to the location to walk through it. Never mind that it was gutted — the *exterior* was so terrible, it looked like it hadn't been occupied in years. Windows were boarded up and exterior tiles were falling off the sides of the building. But what we saw on the outside would seem *nice* compared to the mess we were about to find inside. *Whew* — the interior was *devastated*. It was so ruined that it looked hopelessly destroyed.

As I walked through the building, I heard the crunching of crumbling concrete flooring under my feet, and we wore construction hats to protect ourselves from falling rubble from the collapsing ceiling. All around me I saw broken floors, falling ceilings, and bare brick walls. That building was in an appallingly desolate state.

Paul Renner remembered, "The first time we looked at that building and saw its terrible condition, we said *no* to buying it. But we kept looking at it and finally decided to negotiate for it. But the seller said they would need a down payment of $500,000 if we came to an agreement. All of our money was invested in the piece of land we had just purchased, and we were already using what remained of our previous investment to cover the astronomical rent we were paying each month. So we didn't have $500,000 in cash because it was all in the land.

But one of our most faithful partners said, 'If you can get a contract for the building, we'll give $500,000 to seal the deal and get you started.' We were stunned and so grateful that they wanted to do something so generous. That's when serious negotiations began."

Andrey Vasilyev, our church administrator, remembered the first conversation that took place between us and the seller. Andrey said, "The seller said, 'If you don't have money to move forward, tell us now, so we don't waste our time.'

"Instead of telling the seller we were trusting God for the money, which they would have never understood, Pastor Rick didn't directly answer their question. Instead he wisely told them, 'We don't have a problem with money.' It was true that we had no problem with money — we just didn't *have* any! But his simple answer satisfied the sellers. They never asked another question about our financial resources, and negotiations proceeded. As we came to the conclusion of the last negotiation meeting, we boldly asked the sellers for one year to make the final payment and they surprisingly agreed."

Paul summed up the payment plan: "First, we had to make the down payment of $500,000. Then the seller fixed a halfway point at which one half of the full sum ($2.6 million) had to be paid. If we didn't make that payment at the halfway point, the deal would be over, and we would lose the $500,000 down payment. Making the halfway mark was critical. And according to the contract, we could not begin any renovations until we successfully reached that halfway point."

Paul added, "We knew that if we could sell our land, it would give us what we needed to meet the halfway deadline. But our land didn't sell at that time. In spite of that, we watched the Lord graciously do many miracles to get us all the cash needed to meet that halfway-point deadline. The same partners who gave the first $500,000 gave much more and, cumulatively, partners all over the world gave sacrificially to help us. But it wasn't just foreign money that helped. A really big miracle was the sacrificial giving of our Moscow church. What they gave — compared to what they had to give — was so huge that it was a sign and a wonder.

"And if you can imagine it, while we were trying to come up with all that cash to meet our deadlines, we were simultaneously paying mountains of money every month for our rented office space and for the auditorium where our church was meeting. And we had also begun to pay architectural fees. Doing all of this *in chorus* was huge. But when we reached the halfway deadline, God had enabled us to miraculously make the payment.

"Now we could start renovating the building. All the while, we were praying for our land to sell quickly so we could pay the final balance within the following six months."

But when the land still didn't sell, God nevertheless enabled us to miraculously pay for the building *without* the sale of our land. Now the building was paid for in full, and we still had a big asset to sell that would provide us the money to proceed with the reconstruction.

Finally our land was purchased by a Russian oligarch who had made his money in the gold business. He wanted to build a high-rise apartment building in that part of Moscow. Even though our land was a mere acre, it was large enough to accommodate the building he wanted to erect. After long negotiations, we sold him the land for a significant profit, which meant our church had profited by wisely making the investment in that piece of land. That Russian oligarch built a luxury high-rise apartment building that today stands majestically on our former piece of land.

But that sale meant we had the cash to continue renovations on the exterior and interior of our building. It certainly was not enough for the whole project, but we watched as God continuously provided every cent we needed as we reconstructed and renovated that massive building — our permanent church home!

Soon it was time to finish out the trim work inside the building and to begin installing auditorium chairs and other fixtures. Because we wanted to be good stewards of the funds God had given us, we began to search worldwide for the best materials at the least expensive prices. As a result, the material for our building came from around the world. The tiles came from Italy, the carpet from Belgium, the chairs from South Korea, the furniture from the United States, and the light fixtures from China. We completed our beautiful world-market interior, and soon it would be time to dedicate the newly reconstructed building.

Because I knew that many people would be visiting our facility who had never been in a church building before, I wanted our building to look and feel serious. Large numbers of unbelievers would be coming for all kinds of social events. For example, we regularly give clothes to the needy. We also minister to children and parents from the area surrounding our church. For most, when they attend events like these, it's the first time they've ever entered a church building. They needed to know we were not scary and that we could be trusted, so we meticulously finished the interior with decorations that would mean something special to Russians and make newcomers feel welcomed.

As we wrapped up the building renovations, I asked our administrator to give me an accounting of all the associated costs of purchasing and renovating the building from beginning to end. My team sat around the table to look at his final report, and we were speechless when we saw that our church and ministry had invested millions from beginning to end into the project and our transition to the new facility, including all the rents we still had to pay throughout the building process.

Please remember that we are talking about a Russian congregation of people who had moderate incomes — an *unlikely* congregation to be undertaking such a momentous project. And when we started the whole process, we had *no cash* on hand. All we had was a word from Heaven to get started. But I had learned years earlier — and it has been proven time and time again to be true — that if we will get into agreement with God's directives and obey whatever He asks us to do, like a magnet, our obedience will supernaturally attract all we need to do any job He ever asks us to do. That's what happened in Riga, and that is exactly what happened *again* in Moscow.

## God Had Done a 'Quick' Fourteen-Year Work!

Against all odds, the building had been purchased, renovated, and finished with no outstanding debt whatsoever. Over all those years, we had invested our funds wisely and had been good stewards of God's resources. And miraculous large gifts and countless other gifts were given along the way by our partners around the world as well as by the members of our church.

I share this because, although our journey to establish a permanent home for the church took fourteen years, it was a momentous, supernatural accomplishment. We take no credit or glory for what God did in our midst. This was *His* plan and *His* doing, and it was indeed marvelous in our eyes (*see* Psalm 118:23). We heard the command to do it and were charged with seeing the plan through to completion. We leaned hard on His wisdom, grace, and strong arm of protection and provision every step of the way. This was not our achievement alone. It was the Lord's and ours to share and to enjoy — *and it was our partners' achievement and victory too!*

Earlier, I shared all the natural challenges of having a church in a city of millions — the highways, roads, and transportation system in a city where the population is growing *aggressively* even as I write! Many people were hard-pressed to get to church, participate in a service, and return home in less than eight to ten hours of their day. Then many of those would begin their commute before daybreak the following day, the first day of a new workweek, and start their commuting nightmare all over again! When those psychologists claimed that this kind of nonstop lifestyle provoked mental and emotional stress in people, they were not exaggerating one bit.

I also wrote about the obstacles to church ownership — the swelling property values that made even smaller, derelict properties become completely out of the grasp of most people. And the cost of living was also growing while people's salaries largely were *not* — and I didn't even go into the fact that the ruble was regularly revaluing and people faced uncertain economic times on an almost daily basis. It was simply a reality that they could wake up on a given morning, and find that their rubles were worth *half* the value they held just the day before.

As a matter of fact, just *days* after we moved into our new church building in Moscow, the value of the ruble fell so drastically that people were having to live on a little more than *half* their net income from just days before. We finished that building "under the wire." Had we waited any longer, this situation could have been a crisis in the making.

Our people eventually recovered from that sad turn of events, but had it happened sooner, even the most willing, generous, and able congregants would have been hard-pressed to sustain the level of giving they'd committed to in order to see the building project through.

Even a prosperous mega-church in the West would be hard-pressed to come up with that much cash for a building project. *That* is exactly my point: Though less likely to accomplish such a feat than a work in some other parts of the world, little by little and through a myriad of sources and circumstances, this *unlikely* congregation made it. God miraculously provided everything we needed so that we could undertake the project and so that we could conclude it debt-free. *To God be all the glory!*

It is impossible to exaggerate the significance of this "building victory" for our church and the Protestant movement in Russia. A building represents stability and permanence and says *we are here for the long haul.* Our permanent facility was a visible declaration that we were here to stay and that our church family of believers were a credible part of the community. It was a victory indeed for which we were and are so thankful.

## An Unforgettable Building Dedication

Nearly fourteen years had ensued of broken rental agreements, surprise displacements, false starts, and at times, discouraged dreams as we'd attempted to buy building after building across this city of millions. But, finally, on December 7, 2014, the day arrived for the grand opening of the permanent facility of the Moscow Good News Church.

This was a historic event for the entire Protestant movement in Russia, which was recognized even at the federal, state, and local levels of government. Among the guests of the ceremony who came to congratulate us were clergymen not only from Moscow, but also from other cities in Russia, as well as guests from abroad. And since the consecration of one of the largest, most beautiful and modern church buildings in the country was taking place in the

Russian capital, this event was not ignored by the officials of the Presidential Administration of the Russian Federation, the State Duma of the Russian Federation, and the Moscow city government.

The consecration ceremony itself was conducted by my good friend Bishop Sergei Ryakhovsky. Together with him, I, my dear son Paul, and my faithful and reliable assistant Andrey Vasilyev, performed a very important spiritual rite of anointing the building with oil. This joyful and solemn moment was preceded by a symbolic cutting of a red ribbon. The sobriety of that moment — and at the same time, the deep elation and joy — was a profound time that Denise and I and our family will hold in memory forever.

The speeches the government officials gave during our dedication ceremony were very warm, informal, and friendly. And just imagine — a high-ranking official from the Kremlin quoted the Bible during his speech! This was in the same country where a little more than thirty years ago, we could have been sent to prison for publicly reciting any passage from the Holy Scriptures. *My, how everything has changed.*

Also on that day, Sergey Melnikov, the Executive Secretary of the Presidential Council for Cooperation With Religious Associations under the President of the Russian Federation, publicly recalled that it is recorded in the gospel of Matthew that the Lord is present where two or three are gathered in Jesus' name (Matthew 18:20). Then he added, "But you are not two or three — you are many *more!*"

Indeed, there were many more of us. More than 3,500 people attended that day of festivities in person, and thousands more watched the opening ceremony through an online broadcast.

Stepan Medvedko, who represented the State Duma of the Russian Federation — and who is the head of staff for the Committee for Interaction With Public Associations and Religious Organizations — in addition to delivering official congratulations from the head of the committee, unexpectedly sang a Christian hymn. It was absolutely incredible that a top person from the State Duma sang in a Protestant church, but we saw and heard it ourselves.

With his beautiful voice, that official could have adequately complemented any choir. It was wonderful to see such high-ranking government officials standing in the pulpit of our new church to really celebrate with us. And the presence of these important and respected people clearly showed that we are in the good graces of the Russian government at the highest level. It was such a joy to be a part of God's great plan and to see how it was being carried out with so much of His favor and presence. God's favor and presence were with us, indeed!

When our family first moved to this part of the world, I could never have imagined that I would see this happen in the former USSR. Throughout our time of ministry in Moscow, we tried to be as open as possible to city authorities, carrying out a number of serious charitable projects that have borne much fruit. We not only received all the necessary permits for the reconstruction and operation of our building in Moscow, but an official representative of the Moscow government attended the opening ceremony of the church, read out a congratulation from the head of the city's Department of Interregional Cooperation, Ethnic Policy, and Relations With Religious Organizations — and on his *own* behalf expressed many good wishes to us as a church.

Interestingly, one of these senior speakers spoke about the Russian government's views of "Rick and Denise Renner." Although I had never met this person before, he knew so much about us that I whispered to Denise, "I think this person has more information about us than we know about ourselves." Then I added, "Denise, we have always wondered what they know about us...now we know!"

Secular media, including the largest Russian news agency, RIA Novosti, and the official state news agency, ITAR-TASS, posted reports about the opening of our church building. Also information about the event was posted on the official website of the Department of Interregional Cooperation, Ethnic Policy, and Relations With Religious Organizations of the City of Moscow. Bishop Sergei Ryakhovsky said that no evangelical church in Russia had ever been opened with such a serious representation of officials and with such attention from the secular media. Denise and I were *blown away* by his comment and were truly grateful to God for the great things He was doing through our ministry for Russian-speaking people in this part of the world.

### It Was a New Beginning, Even for Me

The events of that day of ceremony and celebration were colorful and lively. They included songs performed by the Golden Age senior-adults choir, well-rehearsed skits acted out by the children of the Moscow Good News Church, and cultural dance routines that were professionally presented by other young people in the church.

The moment was dreamlike — my head swam with the activity of the day and the many details I needed to attend to, but my heart beat steadily with the peace of God and His "joy unspeakable." What a moment in the Kingdom of God when faith was turned to sight and God's own dreams were being realized on earth, in our part of the world, as in Heaven.

Truly the Gospel light had penetrated the darkness of earth's spiritual powers. Those dark years when communism held sway had been peeled back, and now God was going to have *His* way. And the Moscow Good News Church had been commissioned to play its part among a Heaven-sent cast of others whom I was privileged to call brothers and friends. I felt light on my feet that day of our grand opening, but I was about to be visited with a serious reminder of the gravity of the moment as well.

When it was my turn to finally approach the platform and stand behind the pulpit, thoughts began to flood my mind of the thousands of messages I'd ministered over the course of my ministry — the tens of thousands of people I'd preached before in rallies and crusades; the millions I'd reached over the airwaves as I recorded broadcast after broadcast in front of a television camera and crew; and even those first messages I'd taught before a small congregation of my peers at the university when I was just getting started.

Yet as I stood before that assembly in Moscow that day — my congregation and the Lord's as the Chief Shepherd of His sheep — I felt suddenly shaken. Many of the precious people in our church had been with Denise and me for *decades*, having come with us from Jelgava, Riga, and other parts of the Soviet Union. I had taught some of them in the first aboveground

Bible school in Jelgava just after the collapse of the USSR. We had mentored them, married them, and been present when their children were born. We'd walked with them through deaths in the family, news of tragedy, and diagnoses of disease — as well as divine healings, miraculous interventions, transformed lives, and the knowledge of a present Savior who rescues, delivers, and intimately knows their lives and their needs.

Our church family knew us and we knew them. But standing there to minister that Sunday morning, all that familiarity left me momentarily like a bird in flight. I felt disarmed and tenderly vulnerable before the Lord and before His people. A wave of holy awe swept over me and my knees shook as if they would cave beneath me. My heart pounding, I began to inwardly rehearse my commitment to Christ's solemn charge to lead His flock and never to *mis*lead them — and to feed them with sound doctrine and with a well-nurtured, well-studied heart and mind personally, by His grace.

My family and I had willingly given *our lives*. But in that instant, it was as if God was asking me to give my life again. It was an unexpected summons to renew my vows, as when a husband and wife reaffirm their love and fidelity, though their many years together never hinted of a notion to the contrary.

Jesus had given me the calling and authority to lead these precious Russian-speaking souls, but He had also charged me with *responsibility*. I swallowed hard as He powerfully reminded me of that in those few captivating seconds of His manifested presence. Humbled and trembling, I gasped inwardly in awe of Him and His faithfulness to miraculously bring us to this wonderful new property. Then, as I had done so many times before, I stepped forward and said to my waiting congregation, to that Presidential delegation, and to visitors who had joined us that day, "Open your Bibles to…" And I began to deliver the word of the Lord.

In that outwardly ordinary instant, I had stepped through a new season and a new door.

## The Responsibility of Speaking for God

Our Moscow church waited many years to have its own building, and when that moment came and we finally moved in, it's an understatement to

781

say it was a time of great rejoicing. The building had been constructed debt-free, and it was one of the few church buildings of its kind in all of Russia. I was so awestruck by what God had done that when I first approached the pulpit to preach on our dedication day, I found myself *trembling*. Because of my upbringing, I'd always carried in my heart a deep fear of God, a reverential awe of the Lord. But on that day, His manifested presence *shook* me, and all I could do was worship Him in His great majesty, might, and glory.

I have always felt comfortable speaking to people from the pulpit. However, when our congregation moved into that new facility, I understood that the transition held more significance than a simple change of venue. The whole scope of our ministry had been elevated, and our influence would increase. I had a palpable awareness that I was being held to a higher level of accountability.

Every word that I uttered from the pulpit on that dedication Sunday had to be accurate, to the best of my ability, because it would be widely disseminated on television and the Internet, and the effect would be great. Because serious people from the government, including the State Duma, would be present at the event to convey their congratulations to us, I knew my words must be carefully chosen for this momentous day.

In the week prior to the official move, I was gripped by a sense of almost *electric* anticipation. I poured over my notes again and again, trying to discern if there was one last truth that I needed to share from the pulpit on Sunday. When our big day finally arrived, I rose up early in the morning, reviewed all of my notes again, drove to the church building, and entered the main auditorium with the full knowledge of what God was expecting in my delivery. Stepping up to the platform, I could literally feel myself *tremble* as I approached the moment when I was to step behind that pulpit and speak as the oracle of God to our church congregation and to others who were listening intently to every word.

Speaking for God is a great responsibility for any preacher of the Gospel, and the older I get, the more aware I am of the magnitude of this responsibility. I do not always tremble when I speak, but there are certainly moments when I do. The apostle Paul must have felt similarly at times, because he referred to a "great trembling" that he experienced as he prepared to preach to the pagan audience in the city of Corinth. In his first epistle to the

Corinthian believers, Paul reflected, "And I was with you in weakness, and in fear, and in much trembling" (1 Corinthians 2:3).

When Paul first stood up to preach before that crowd of pagans, he was about to begin his public ministry in Corinth — a city rife with paganism, immorality, and demon spirits. Paul knew that he was totally dependent on the power of God and would have no success in Corinth without it. He was overwhelmed with a sense of *utter dependence upon God*.

Paul actually said that in that moment, he experienced "much trembling." This is a translation of the Greek phrase *en tromos polloo*. The word *en* is translated "in" and describes the state of being that he was "in" when he began his ministry to the Corinthians. The next Greek word, *tromos*, means *to shake, to quake*, or *to tremble*. Paul even told us the extent to which he was trembling by adding the word *polloo*, which describes *a large magnitude* or *a great quantity*. Together these words emphatically tell us that Paul literally "shook" as he stood up to preach to the Corinthians.

What would make Paul feel such a great trembling? He had stood in front of large audiences and preached the Gospel on numerous occasions throughout the Roman Empire. So why did he feel such a strong inner shaking then?

Paul had just come from Athens, where his success as a preacher of the Gospel had been limited (*see* Acts 17:32,33) and where it is likely he felt that he had failed there. He was also very aware of his own shortcomings, even as an eloquent public speaker (*see* 2 Corinthians 10:10). Knowing that refined oratory skills were important to a Corinthian Greek audience — but that his skills alone would not summon the power that would convict their hearts and save them — Paul may have felt overwhelmed by his inadequacy of speech as he remembered his experience in Athens and was preparing to now publicly do it all over again and declare the Gospel to the Corinthians.

And as if these feelings were not enough, Paul was very aware that enemies were present in the crowd, lying in wait to attack him over the slightest verbal misstep. Any of these factors may have contributed to the "great trembling" he felt that day.

But in spite of the emotions or sense of fear and awe that tried to engulf Paul at that pivotal moment, he made a decision that proved to be key to the outcome of his entire ministry from that moment onward. He determined he would know nothing among the people except the simple message of Jesus Christ crucified for them (*see* 1 Corinthians 2:2) — and then he went on to preach in the power and demonstration of the Spirit (v. 4). In the end, the apostle's ministry in Corinth was an amazing success that led to the establishment of one of the most important congregations in the Early Church. His feelings of inadequacy produced an utter dependence upon the power of God that resulted in a message that was accompanied by supernatural manifestations — which proved far more successful than any eloquent oratory skills.

Over the years, I have come to realize that if such a powerful apostle like Paul felt weakness and trembling from time to time, others who are called to do something significant for God may also feel such emotions when it is *their* moment to stand up and be counted. That was precisely what I felt when I stood in the pulpit of our new Moscow church building during those first weeks — totally insufficient without the power of God assisting me.

But in spite of that tangible sense of my own natural deficiencies in His presence — and of my no-turning-back commitment to fulfill His calling and charge — I have also sensed an increased level of God's power manifested every time the Gospel is proclaimed from the platform of our new church building. *To God be the glory — it is all for Him and His purposes!*

When you are called upon to do something new — something that seems bigger than you or outside of your capabilities, yet you *know* it is your assignment — that is the moment for you to push aside those feelings of deficiency and turn to the sufficiency of the Holy Spirit. Prepare as well as you can, but when the time comes for you to stand, to speak, to sing, to witness, or to testify, lean upon the Holy Spirit and His power.

Always train and prepare as much as you can, but make room for the Holy Spirit to do *His* part — the part that only He can do. You may feel "great trembling" at that moment, but if you'll make room for the power of God to operate, you'll see Him work with convincing proof that is far more effective than anything you could do on your own. I've been utterly amazed at the things God does through those who surrender to Him in such moments!

### A New Venue for Protestantism in Russia

That church building will serve generations to come and stand as a testimony to the faithfulness of God and to the generous giving of partners and church members who gave to establish it as a permanent Church presence in Moscow. In commemoration of this monumental victory, we placed two bronze plaques in the foyer of the Moscow Good News Church — one written in English and the other in Russian — that will forever read:

### DECEMBER 2014
### SPECIAL DEDICATION OF THIS HOUSE OF WORSHIP
### MOSCOW GOOD NEWS CHURCH

**Pastors Rick and Denise Renner**
**Associate Pastors Paul Renner and Andrey Vasilyev**
**RUCEF (P) Bishop Sergei Ryakhovsky**

**We are so grateful to those
who with their resources, prayers, and gifts
partook in the realization of this dream.
A heartfelt thanks to the members
of the Moscow Good News Church
and to the partners of Rick Renner Ministries.
A special thanks to Wallace, June, Jonathan, and Jane Blume.
Your Christ-honoring sacrificial contributions
helped achieve this dream that will serve
God's people for generations.**

*We are a worshiping, Bible-believing people
who are called to present every man
perfect in Christ Jesus.
(Colossians 1:28)*

From that date — December 7, 2014 — to the present, the Moscow Good News Church has lived in its own permanent home and has become a regularly used venue for the Protestant movement in Russia. We knew going into the reconstruction project that just as it happened with the Riga church, the Moscow church would have a unifying effect on churches and ministers throughout the city *and beyond*, and God would use it to multiply the influence of the Bible in our nearby world, Moscow, as well as to the ends of the earth (*see* Romans 10:18).

For example, several times a year, the building is used to host the meetings of the advisory council of the heads of the Protestant churches in Russia, which includes practically all Protestant denominations. Then almost every year, clergymen of ROSKhVE churches (Russian Union of Christians of the Evangelical-Pentecostal Faith) from all over Russia also gather in our building to participate in the main convocation of the year. It is a special conference during which decisions are jointly made about how churches should respond to the challenges that modernity presents to the Church.

I am especially pleased that Paul Renner has often been the organizer of this conference. Among the guests are those representing government and ecclesiastical entities, including bishops and pastors of thousands of Russian churches. God is truly multiplying *His own* influence in the lives of Russian-speakers from diverse segments of society and culture!

Recently, I asked my son Paul to compile a list of the other various activities that our church building is used for *almost around the clock — 24/7*! The following is what he provided:

- Moscow Good News Church services, including Golden Age, and special conferences
- The Internet Good News Church
- Other churches that use our building weekly for their services
- Fund-raisers for local orphanages
- "Russia Without Orphans" annual conference
- Civic New Year's event for needy families
- Christian-school graduations
- Russian Pentecostal Church Union conventions
- Conferences for drug-and-alcohol rehabilitation centers

- Council of Russian Protestant Churches meetings
- "Russia Shall Be Saved" conference
- Inter-church youth prayer events and *'Hallelu-ween'*
- Weekly meals for the homeless and hungry
- Conferences for those who work with the homeless
- Easter and Christmas events for the homeless
- Weddings and water baptisms

Denise and I, our sons, and our team witnessed so many lives transformed by the Gospel, from the first meeting we held in that hall in the Hotel Russia to services in the Kino Mir Theater, the Dom Kultury, the MDM, the Dom Kultury *again*, and the last large, expensive auditorium we rented before God graciously established us in our own facility. *Every* place the Gospel is preached, God's Spirit and power are present to save, deliver, heal, and set men's hearts and courses aright from any blight of their past.

Although the path to building ownership for the church seemed long, we were privileged to obey God's directive in Riga to come to Moscow to "do it all over again." And ever since the Moscow church secured its permanent home, the glorious unfurling of God's grace during that fourteen-year journey has been *multiplied* as He continues to build His house and to watch over it. Denise and I, Paul and Polina, our associate staff, our congregation and team — *and our faithful partners around the world* — are His co-laborers in the work. We are all sharers together with Him of His manifold grace.

The fruit of our labors and the increase God has wrought cannot adequately be told in the pages of this book — it would take *volumes*. But, to date, in the permanent facility of the Moscow Good News Church, *thousands* have walked the aisles to be saved and to become members of the church — solid, strong believers and disciples of Christ in a city of millions that is still largely unevangelized. The church services and Sunday School are filled to overflowing with people who call the church their home. Also in this building, thousands of people attend our concerts for the elderly and other charitable events at which food and clothing are distributed to those in need. Because people find out about these outreaches and come to be ministered to, they learn about the church, and countless numbers have become saved and connected as members of MGNC as a result.

The church dedication in 2014 was a profound moment in the history of our ministry and its work that we continue to build on. It was the end of one part of our journey, but at the same time, it marked a brand-new beginning for all God has planned and desires to accomplish among millions of Russian-speakers on whom He has set His heart and His sights. What a memorable and unforgettable day that was — December 7, 2014. But there would be many more remarkable memories for my family and me in Moscow, Russia, as God proceeded to make new history for the lands of the old Soviet Union, as you will see.

### Luther's Reformation Celebration at the Pashkov Palace

October 31, 2017, marked one such event so memorable that I feel this book would not be complete if I excluded it. The sights and the sounds on that cold, crisp afternoon live indelibly in my memory, and I will attempt in the following paragraphs to convey the picture to you, as well as the profound significance of this date in history.

On that date, Paul Renner and I attended an event hosted by the Presidential Administration in the nearby renowned Pashkov Palace that stands on Vagankovsky Hill in Moscow. Today that palatial interior is used for Kremlin ceremonial functions and also houses the Manuscripts Department, Music Department, and Maps Department for the Russian State Library.

On this especially memorable day, there was a buzz in the room that resembled a crowd of eager reporters awaiting a dignitary to finally greet them. The sounds of musical instruments straining for the right tune fused with the commotion as a full orchestra seemed equally astir with anticipation. I recognized many familiar faces among the approximate 250 spiritual leaders gathered from around the world, and I spent those first exhilarating minutes greeting my brothers in the faith. After numerous handshakes and hellos, I took my seat, less attentive to the activity around me as a stream of thoughts began to ferry across my mind.

This was the five-hundredth anniversary, *to the day*, since the flames of Luther's Reformation had been ignited. Protestant, Catholic, and Orthodox ministers, representatives of other religions, and senior officials from the government of the Russian Federation, the administration of the President, and the State Duma were all gathered in the most picturesque setting imaginable in the center of Moscow to celebrate Luther's historical defining of the Christian faith.

I was surrounded by heads of denominations from all over the world, something that would have been *unthinkable* just thirty years previously during the time of the Soviet Union. Even since that time, that such an event would draw the participation of representatives of the state was such an unlikely occurrence in a city where many had only a vague understanding of modern-day Protestantism.

Completing this dream-like moment was the presence of my son Paul at my side. I looked at him, barely thirty-four years old, so confident and calm as he stood among those select invitees. I was mindfully aware that he had been positioned in his emerging leadership role by God's providence and foresight, and I began to quietly reflect on Paul's own days of small beginnings.

When we moved from Tulsa to Jelgava, Paul was a lanky eight-year-old child, but from the very beginning, he had been my faithful assistant. At that young age, he had set up chairs in the Bible school, organized books and teaching materials, and did whatever was asked of him to help. Even before we moved from Tulsa, Paul exhibited a servant's heart in our ministry as a family. Over the years, it had been gratifying to witness his gradual, but consistent transition to church leadership. And as I watched Paul at the summit that day, grown up and dressed in a perfectly ironed suit and polished shoes, I couldn't help but feel proud and a little emotional.

I reflected on my own past and the fact that I'd spent most of my childhood and young adulthood in a small town on the outskirts of Tulsa — a place I never ventured from until I was fourteen years old. That small community of precious friends and family was my whole world during my wonderful growing-up season. But now, after a little more than forty years, I was, by special invitation, present at the Pashkov Palace among more than two hundred spiritual leaders of *nations*.

Truthfully, I was *spellbound* in the moment. Mesmerized by the falling snow on the Kremlin turrets in my view to the south, I stirred myself from my recollections and gulped down an emotional response to this unlikely moment not just in my life, but in Russian history. As I continued to process my surroundings, I was simply filled with gratitude to God for His amazing plans for the lands of the old Soviet Union, of which He had entrusted me to be a part.

Still taking in the palace setting, I noticed the bright light refracting from the many-faceted crystal pendalogues that hung from the chandeliers high above me. Spilling over the brilliantly white concert hall to the golden parquet floors at my feet, the light cast an amber glow across the room. Scrolled columns stood guard around us like a colonnade of angelic hosts, and a massive, ornately wrapped window directly in front of me provided a fitting portal to the world outside where the Kremlin towers also stood at attention in perfect view.

Before the presentation portion of the ceremony began, an elegantly adorned choir sang Martin Luther's "A Mighty Fortress Is Our God" in perfect harmony and pitch. With each caroled verse filled with warfare and praise, listeners stood silently engaged, no doubt lost in the gravity of the experience we were sharing together half a millennium later. Truly, the costly message of grace through faith had forever sliced open the dark doctrine of works with its honed sword of truth. And through that gaping breach of divine illumination, Christ's Church had reformed, revived, and leaped centuries forward to nations near and far, beckoning my family and me and countless others like us as guardians of truth and light. That same truth and light had reached through time, extending even to the grand room of that palace in Moscow where Paul and I sat on that snowy afternoon.

The moment was poignant and profound, not just because of the exquisite beauty that surrounded me that day and the weighty significance of the Reformation itself — but because this was the first time in modern history that the Russian head of state had acknowledged not only the Reformation as a historical event, but in a letter *thanked* Protestants for their significant and multifaceted contribution to the development of Russia! We were witnessing history taking place — but more than witnessing it, I became gripped by the fact that my entire family and I had been enabled by God to be a *part* of this history in the making.

On that day, there were also *countless* guardians of the faith who were not in the room with us, but their impact was felt, nonetheless. I'm talking about those who in earlier years languished in prisons or died for their faith.

In John 4:38, Jesus said it so aptly, "I sent you to reap that whereon ye bestowed no labour: other men laboured, and ye are entered into their labours." Certainly, those of us who were present that day had worked very hard as ministers of the Gospel. But before us had been a generation of persecuted saints who sowed the first seeds for this move of God — with their prayers, and often with their very lives — for a harvest that would occur in our time. As they lay in prisons and died, they released their faith that a day would come when those hard times would be recompensed with change — *reformation*. I was soberly aware that we were standing in the manifestation of their prayers and their lives of faith. Many of those men and women may never be known by name, but we were standing there in the Pashkov Palace because of their prayers and their lives.

Hebrews 11:4-40 refers to people who believed for something that they never saw, but they stayed in faith till the end. And as a result, *others* stepped into the manifestation of what they believed to see come to pass. I think these verses well represent the persecuted Church of the past, especially where it says, "And these all, having obtained a good report through faith, received not the promise: God having provided some better thing for us, that they without us should not be made perfect" (vv. 39,40).

So you can see, it would be wrong for me to refer only to those of us present for that Reformation celebration in Moscow. Those who lived before us — who gave their lives for Jesus *and for us* — were in large part responsible for all of us who were commemorating Luther's Reformation together in that marvelous palace. Our predecessors sowed in the hardest of times, and God has sent all of us, including *you*, in this day as reapers of their precious seed and harvest.

That Reformation anniversary event was and will always be for me a surreal experience frozen in time, its images captured indelibly in my mind. Over decades of ministry, a full thirty years of those in the former Soviet

Union where I call home, I'd experienced a few times like that before —- poignant moments that occur without warning, like rushing waters, as God powerfully visits you with His presence or thunders an unexpected word through your spirit that shakes you to your core. That is exactly what I felt that day in the historic Pashkov Palace with my oldest son at my side.

## The Moscow Good News Church's Own Harvest of Emerging Light and Influence

With the help of my family and our team, the church and all its departments and outreaches were up and running in the new building, and we wasted no time taking steps toward God's vision for the church that He had placed deep in my heart from the beginning. I alluded to this earlier in the chapter, but my heart had always "broken" for church members — especially adults with children, singles traveling alone, and elderly adults — who were commuting every Sunday for *hours* to attend church.

Over time, we began to note that some of them stopped coming so regularly. Some were traveling two to three hours every week one-way to get to church. To put this in relatable terms, a person can leave Tulsa and drive 257 miles to Dallas in about the same time some of our Moscow people were traveling to and from church with their families each week.

Ezekiel 34:16 commands us as pastors — shepherds — to seek out the flock and to "…bring again that which was driven away…bind up that which was broken, and…strengthen that which was sick…." So we began to reach out to ask why some of those who lived in the farthest reaches of Moscow weren't coming to church as regularly as they had been. They communicated honestly that they wanted to be faithful, but the weekly travel was beginning to wear away at them.

Of course, our pastoral team, who understood the growing population of Moscow and the city's infrastructure and challenges with travel, knew this was a legitimate problem that needed to be fixed. So after much prayer, we decided it was time to begin opening our satellite campuses in various parts of Moscow so people would not spiritually drop off the radar. They simply needed a Good News Church location closer to where they lived. And that's when the plan to open seven additional campuses over a period of years began to commence.

But to start multiple campuses, we needed local campus pastors, worship teams, counselors, and of course a location where each of the campus churches would meet. This would take a huge investment of manpower, lots of training, and a mountain of money because renting venues for campus churches, even much smaller ones than those we'd previously rented for the main church, was going to cost a lot of money. Of course, as always before, we didn't have the cash to do it, but that never stopped us from doing what God was telling us to do. So we charged ahead with the faith that God would miraculously supply everything we needed to expand and to accommodate every single existing church member and those who desired to have MGNC as their church home.

We had been holding Home Groups throughout the city for many years, so we focused first on areas where a large number of congregants lived and where a significant number of Home Groups were operating, and we would use those Home Groups as a base for starting the new works.

Once we determined which areas we would target for openings over a period of time, we began to decide where the first campus would be started so we could begin our search for real estate that was available to rent. Everything we could afford needed to be renovated before we could use it. But because the socialist-communist system had built so many identical buildings all over Moscow, we chose one particular building plan we liked that would accommodate a small church and began to look for that same building style in every region of the city we had mapped as a future MGNC campus location.

We designed an interior plan that included space for everything a church needs — an auditorium, a large foyer for fellowship, children's Sunday School spaces, and offices. And because we wanted our people to feel "at home" in these new locations, we decided to decorate each location in the same style as the central Moscow Good News Church. The paint, the wall trimmings, the tiles on the floors, the light fixtures — even the way the children's ministry was decorated — was a "copy" in miniature form of the central church. And because we were using the same building plan in various parts of the city, it meant once we designed the first layout, all we had to do was duplicate it at all the other locations. It was the wisdom and provision of God for our expansion.

Today campuses for the Moscow Good News Church are proliferating across Moscow. To accomplish this, God enabled our team to raise up new campus pastors, teams for worship, counselors, greeters, Sunday School teachers, and children's and youth workers. Everything is "live" in every affiliate church until it's time for the teaching and preaching of the Word of God. Huge screens are set up on every stage, and the preaching is perfectly timed to appear on screen at the same time in every affiliate church.

Although people are seeing the message I preach on screen and not "live," they shout, clap, and rejoice as if I (or whomever is speaking) is on the platform in their presence. There is such a sense of community among each smaller congregation and yet no sense of disconnection from the central church. After the message, each campus pastor gives his own altar call, and the responses have been tremendous in these smaller environments that are teeming with life and the Spirit of God.

We didn't know how we would pay for all this, but God raised up partners and church members who generously gave to help us make this Gospel advancement. Oh, how I wish I could just "pick up" partners and faithful givers and bring them to see firsthand the impact of their giving. They have given into a work their eyes will probably never see firsthand, but their giving is changing thousands of lives. I am so grateful to each and every person who has sown into this work with his or her finances and prayers.

Because of our affiliate campuses, what began as a problem getting to the central church consistently because of where people lived in the city has become a huge blessing. People who once attended the central church whenever they could are now spiritually rooted in our affiliate congregations. Today MGNC's physical presence is growing across the almost one thousand square miles that geographically comprise the city of Moscow.

We saw a great need and addressed it by a manifestation of God's grace — but, as I said, multiple church campuses had been His plan the entire time.

## Pastor Paul Renner

All along, I had privately been telling my top team that one day Paul Renner would step into the position of senior pastor of the church, and I would become the overseer, or bishop, over our group of churches and ministry branches in multiple nations. Paul was well prepared for such an assignment, as he had served so faithfully his whole life at my side. No one knew the ministry or our vision better than Paul. Denise and I knew God had placed His hand on Paul to become the next senior pastor, so for a few years, I turned my focus toward helping Paul step into a more visible position in that new role.

As I followed the Lord's leading in this years-long season of transition, I repeatedly thought of John the Baptist's comments about Jesus' emerging ministry. When John saw Jesus come forward in the ministry, John 3:30 tells us that John the Baptist responded, "He must increase, but I must decrease."

As much as possible, I would continue to preach regularly in our MGNC church services. But Paul would begin to actually take the helm of our staff and the management of the church. I took on an overseer position to guide and to correct as needed, but I knew that I needed to give Paul space to begin stepping forward. So I backed up and Paul stepped forward to lead all staff meetings and to even lead the top team at the church.

Little by little, people began to recognize that Paul was emerging into a visible leadership position, and they could see that my role was changing too. I knew it could be challenging to follow in my steps, but Paul received grace to increase, and I received grace to back up and to decrease as needed so Paul could step forward. Both of us needed special grace for our increasing and decreasing roles, and God provided what we needed so that it was not difficult for either of us.

Paul's stepping forward was timed by God for all of these changes to occur, and today he is marvelously leading the Moscow Good News Church as overseer with Polina at his side.

Commenting on this transition of leadership, Paul said, "Big changes for the Church in Russia only started around 1991. Because so many churches in Russia are still relatively new, there are few churches that have made a transition from a founding pastor to the next pastor. At the point we started making our transition, the older churches in our part of the world were only about twenty-five years old. The transition of passing church leadership to the next generation was something that no one knew how to do. But eyes had been on my dad, our family, and our church and ministry for three decades, so now the eyes of leaders everywhere were watching again to see how this transition would occur. Once again, our family had a God-given opportunity to teach by example how a peaceful, godly transition can take place."

## Church Online — the Internet Good News Church

At that same time, I was ready to forge ahead with my dream to design a full online church called the Internet Good News Church that would reach believers all over the world. My heart was ever yearning to reach Russian-speakers scattered across the planet, many of whom had no local church to attend. They needed a church, a pastor, and Bible teaching they could trust.

All over the globe were people who had once lived in the former USSR and who had gotten saved watching our TV ministry. They'd fed on my teaching in the past, so there was a special connection between me and large numbers of Russians who were now living in various nations of the world. Our top team had received Paul at the helm at the physical church, and now I knew God would raise up a team to help fulfill the vision to design a full online church that could reach Russian-speakers worldwide.

There was no such thing as a *full-fledged* Internet church anywhere in the Russian-speaking world as I wanted it to be. Sure, there were online Sunday webcasts, but that didn't qualify as church in my mind. "Just a service" fell short of the mark of really pastoring people. I was dreaming about something more involved than a webcast.

Of course, there is no way an Internet church can ever replace a local church — but it is estimated by some that there are 37,000 small towns and villages in Russia alone with no church of *any* kind. There is no way we can raise up enough pastors and leaders and build enough buildings to reach those 37,000 small towns and villages — *and* all the other places around the world — where believing Russians live with no church. In cases like this, the Internet church is God's answer to meet a need and to provide a pastoral voice to people who desperately need it.

Remember, I was raised by Erlita Renner, a mother who cared for people and who taught me that providing pastoral care for people was very important in God's sight and one of the greatest honors in life. That foundational belief is why our partner-care ministry has been so serious and exceptional over the years. Taking care of people is not a second-priority issue; it is the *highest* priority. So I knew a mere webcast would fail to hit the mark of pastoring Russian-speaking people. My heart was beating to reach beyond the walls of our physical church across all of Russia and every nation of the former USSR — and into every continent of the earth — to become a pastoral voice in the lives of Russian-speakers everywhere.

But to fulfill that vision, I needed a deeply committed team to help me pioneer and apostolically plant the kind of online church that was in my heart. I'm talking about a full online church with a full online pastoral staff, a full online children's Sunday School, a real online youth ministry, online women's and men's ministries, lots of online counselors to pray with people, a full online Home Group ministry, and even a Bible school online so Russian believers across the world could study the Bible more deeply with us.

We'd been studying and planning how to do this for years, but as Paul began to take the helm of the Moscow Good News Church, I felt an urgency that the time was right for us to strike.

I was sure the Holy Spirit was telling me it was time to launch an online church to reach Russian-speakers around the world. But before I go into this part of the story, I want to briefly return to Jesus' words in Matthew 10:16, where He told us to be "wise as serpents." Besides "laying low" and understanding the lay of the land, as we saw, there is another important point in this verse that I want to revisit, and that is *right timing*.

## More Lessons From a Snake

Earlier in this chapter, I shared insights about being "wise as serpents." But as I discuss the timing of starting our online church, I feel the need to share a little more about "serpents," because there is more truth to glean from what Jesus said to us about this. The word "wise" is a translation of the Greek word *sophos*, and as Jesus used it in Matthew 10:16, it depicts *special insight* and *a wise approach* to a matter. According to Jesus, serpents are "wise" in the way they do things, and there is something we can learn from their actions.

For a serpent, *timing* is key to its very survival. When prey passes before a serpent, that serpent instinctively knows when it's time to strike. If it waits too long, the opportunity will pass irretrievably, and the serpent will go hungry. So we can learn from the serpent that when it's time for *you* to act, you must put aside all fears, emotions, and second-guessing — and *seize the moment!*

I have seen so many people fast, pray, and wait for a golden moment of divine opportunity to come to them. Then at last, that time arrives! A great door of opportunity stands directly in front of them, and it's time to act. But rather than seize the moment and walk through that door, they pause to pray just a little bit more. God brought them *exactly* what they'd been praying about for so long, but because they hesitated, they lost the opportunity. When they finally got around to saying yes, it was too late.

*Let me give you a personal example of this truth from our own lives.*

The year 1992 was when I was seeking God earnestly to start television ministry all over the former Soviet Union. That is when I was granted that historic meeting with the top directors of a national television station that I told you about in Chapter Eleven. I was asked to fly to Kiev so I could meet with them and talk about putting my program on national television in Ukraine. My associate and I booked the next available flight and flew to meet those two powerful men in their offices.

My heart was filled with anticipation as the plane carried us to that meeting. *Was this the opportunity I'd prayed for? Was it actually happening? Was God really answering my prayer?* I had a sense that something great and awesome was about to transpire, and I could hardly wait to arrive at the meeting to hear their proposal.

I had already done all my homework because I had been praying for that door to open. I had studied the statistics about the reach of the TV channel on which they were about to offer me time. I spoke with pastors and churches throughout the region to find out what they thought of that channel. I was equipped for this long-awaited conversation.

Armed with information and supported by the prayers of our staff and partners, the meeting began. Those directors asked me, "Would you like to broadcast on our national channel and penetrate every single home in the nation with your program?"

This is exactly what I had been praying for and waiting to see happen! The opportunity of a lifetime was in front of me in the form of a TV contract. The cost was astronomical, but I knew this was an open door that had not been offered to anyone else. I didn't know how we'd pay for it, but I thank God that I had the spiritual guts to act at the right moment. I had already prayed and prayed, and now it was time to act.

Certainly, there is a time to "lay low" — to study and prepare for whatever it is God is calling on you to do. But there will also come a moment when it is time to seize the moment and *strike*! Surely, this is a key part of what Jesus meant when He told us to *"be wise as serpents"* (*see* Matthew 10:16).

You may be asking, "But how do I know when it's a time to lay low — or a time to take action and seize the moment?" The Holy Spirit will lead you and cause you to know — if you will be sensitive to follow His leading. And believe me, if you will listen to and follow Him, He will *guide you past every obstacle, camouflage you from every attack*, and *show you exactly when to take action* in your family, your business, your church, or concerning any assignment God has given you.

Romans 8:14 is a profound verse that has been critical in my life to know how the Holy Spirit leads us. It says, "...As many as are led by the Spirit of God, they are the sons of God." Again, that word "led" is the Greek word *ago*, and it means *to be gently led about*. It was the same word used to describe a man leading his cow about on a rope. The farmer is the leader, and the cow is merely the follower. The cow doesn't argue with the farmer; the animal simply trusts and follows. This is how we are to follow the leading of the Holy Spirit.

Many people are afraid to obey what the Holy Spirit puts in their hearts to do. Fearful that they will be led astray or that they will make a mistake, they sit on the sidelines and watch other people achieve success while they remain right where they've always been. But let me assure you from personal experience: *You can trust the leading of the Holy Spirit!*

In John chapters 14-16, Jesus called the Holy Spirit "the Spirit of Truth" four separate times. It seems that Jesus thought this was a truth worth repeating! Jesus was emphatically assuring us that the Holy Spirit *will not* lead us in a wrong direction. He is "the Spirit of Truth" on whom we can rely. So if the Holy Spirit is prompting you to take action *now*, it's because He sees and knows something you may not see. Let the Holy Spirit become your eyes and ears in key moments of your life, family, business, or ministry.

### Hearing and Obeying — That's How Denise and I Did It

*Timing* has been a major key to the success of our ministry, and it is the key to your success as well. Denise and I are not brilliant enough in ourselves or by our own reasoning to figure out the right timing or the right strategy for everything we've been able to do. We give God all the glory because we know our timing has been directed by the Holy Spirit and not by us. Denise and I have depended on the Holy Spirit's leading through the years, and as a result, we have walked through many strategic doors at key moments — divine appointments and opportunities. We've learned that when He says, *"NOW!"* — He really means exactly that!

When God calls any of us to do something new — to move into a new territory or seize a new opportunity — we must prepare as much as we can, but if we take too long to respond when our opportunity is right in front of us, that mistake can cause us to lose out on an opportunity altogether. This leads me back to Jesus' words that we need to be "wise as serpents." Serpents know when an "opportunity" is in front of them, and they strike before it gets away.

Think about how many people prepared — studied and prayed — for something wonderful to happen, and then when that door flung open before them, their fear caused them to hesitate. They may have said, "Let me pray a little bit more." But they've already been praying; now it's time to *act*. That's why we need to take a lesson from the serpent and learn to lay low when it's time to observe and prepare — and to "strike" when the time is right.

I knew the timing was right for us to launch the online church because the Holy Spirit kept tugging at my heart and saying, *Start the online church now!* I still had a lot of unanswered questions because we had never developed a full-fledged online church. But I had stepped out to do *a lot* of things I didn't know how to do in the beginning — like build a Christian TV network in a part of the world where it had never been done before.

Just as obedience is like a magnet to attract the finances necessary to do His will and plan, obedience also attracts all the other resources you need, including the brains to do the job He gives you to do! So I knew concerning this massive online-church outreach that if I would simply get in alignment with God and what He was asking me to do, He would bring me all the knowledge, information, and any other resources I needed to launch this Internet church.

So I told our top team, *"It's time to strike!"* And together, we began to assemble a group of committed Russian believers to work with me on our Internet church.

Some scoffed and said that developing an online church was "anti-local church" because it would take people away from the *physical* local church. But I'd given my life for the local church and would never do anything that was *anti*-local church. My heart was to reach those who lived in places where there *was* no local church.

Nevertheless, some said that an online church was unnecessary. But I knew God was leading us to do it, so we pressed ahead past the accusations and insinuations that we were *"anti"* anything the Lord had instituted or was doing in the earth. I remembered that when we started the TV network, naysayers also said it couldn't and shouldn't be done — so voices of opposition don't really affect me *if* I am confident God has really given me a directive. *And I was confident about His will concerning the online church!*

I was also very aware that there are thousands of small towns all over Russia where there is no Protestant church at all. As I said, there is no way to raise up enough pastors and start churches fast enough to touch those multitudes in this late hour. Although an online church can never replace a local church, if there *is* no local church, then an online church becomes *an amazing* alternative — a spiritual lifeline to those with no pastor and no sound Bible teaching, but with spiritual hunger and questions about God and their own lives. With an online church, we could enter nearly all of those churchless cities very rapidly and help meet a great spiritual need.

I could lead the charge, but I knew that this technological development would need lots of anointed brains all around me to do this. Little by little, God began to lead people to me who had those anointed brains. A key member of our Moscow Good News Church pastoral team who had been with us from the very beginning and who had an engineering kind of mind, said, "Pastor Rick, I believe I am the one to help you lead this!"

He was right — Andrey Vasilyev was the one to help lead this project forward. This man had been our church administrator for years and was the one who had overseen the total reconstruction of our building from its gutted-out beginnings to the fabulous structure that stands on Schelkovskaya Street today. He was not only a faithful employee, but a brother, friend, and real soldier whom God had placed in my life.

First Corinthians 4:2 says the most important quality a person can have is faithfulness. There are plenty of smart, talented people in the world today whom God cannot use because they are not dependable. But Andrey was intelligent, talented, and had proven himself to be completely faithful over the years. And he was a spiritual man who knew the leading of the Holy Spirit. I fully believed he was indeed the man to help me lead the new project, so he and I began to pray together for other members of the team to appear.

It wasn't long before we knew who the first team members would be for the development of our Internet Good News Church. As a group, we began to put our spirits and brains together to see how to design a full online church with a full online pastoral staff, a full online children's Sunday School, a full online youth ministry, and full online women's and men's ministries, etc.

Since we knew of no one in the Russian world who had done exactly what we wanted to do, it meant we had no mental barriers to tell us what could or couldn't be done. We were like a blank slate that the Holy Spirit could write on. And as He began to write on the slates of our hearts and minds a vision for how to do this, ideas began to *explode* within us!

Day after day and month after month, we sat around the conference table to discuss what we needed to do in order to build a full online church — and what would be the most excellent, God-pleasing way to do it. The white board in our office was scribbled over with ideas and suggestions on how we would proceed. Our team built systems and programs to support our vision. Even though we didn't know where we'd get the money to pay for it, we began to hire a staff of full-time and part-time team members to put all the pieces together.

Over the years, we've never had money up front to start any project God has given us. It is just remarkable to me that when God has given us an assignment, He has never based that assignment on how much we had sitting in our bank account. But if we're really hearing from God — willingly doing what He says to do *when He says to do it* and refusing to budge from our task — He will richly provide *everything* we need to get the job done.

### Staying in a Place of Faith

Hebrews 11:6 says, "But without faith, it is impossible to please him [God]...." Because of the way this verse is translated, people generally think this verse pictures a censure for someone with a lack of faith. But that is not what the Greek means at all.

The word "without" is the Greek word *choris*, a word that means to be *outside* of something — like *outside* the city limits or *outside* the house, as opposed to *inside* the city or *inside* the house. It should actually be translated, "But *outside* of faith...." It describes faith as a "location" — a place where you can live *in* or live *out of.* The Greek literally means, "But *outside* of the place of faith, it is impossible to please Him...."

And the word "please" in this verse is the Greek word *euarestesai,* a compound of the words *eu* and *arestos.* The word *eu* means *well* — and the word *arestos* means *enjoyable* or *pleasing.* Together it describes *the pleasure one feels from seeing something that is especially excellent or delightful.*

But when all these different meanings are taken into account, Hebrews 11:6 can be translated: "Outside of the realm of faith, it is impossible to bring delight and pleasure to God...." When you are living *in* a place of faith — that is, if you are where God has called you to be, doing what God has called you to do — you bring pleasure to the Lord.

For Denise and me to "stay put" and refuse to budge from what God has asked us to do has required us to have faith. And when God calls *you* to do something — that calling is your own place of faith. But many who are called to do something get under pressure and move *out of* that place where God has called them to be obedient. Many times, we've faced that same temptation to move from a place of faith, but we decided to stay *in* the place of faith until the assignment was accomplished. Regardless of how difficult the task was or how long it took us to do it, we knew we had to be committed to stay *in* the place of faith until the job was done.

According to Hebrews 11:6, God has been observing all of us — and as long as we stay "*in* faith," or "in the place of faith," it brings delight and pleasure to His heart. I don't know about you, but that has been our great motivation to stay *in* our place of faith!

Anyone who wants to fully follow God's plan for his life must find out where God wants him to be and then not budge from that assignment. That means you must get in alignment with God's call and stay there until the task is fulfilled. It is only from this position of solid, unequivocal alignment with God's will that you can know you are pleasing God!

But Hebrews 11:6 goes on to say that "...He [God] is a rewarder of those who diligently seek him." That word "diligently" means it takes real diligence to stick with what God has called you to do. In other words, for you to stay *in* a place of faith that pleases God, you have to give it your best effort. You have to be completely committed to pressing forward all the way until you have fully accomplished the assignment. For this, you need *diligence* to stick with your assignment and to stay in your place of faith.

The words "diligently seek" are a translation of the Greek word that means *to zealously seek for something with all of one's heart, strength, and might.* It conveys the idea of being *hard-working, attentive, busy, constant, and persistent in one's devotion to what he or she is doing.*

If you and I take our life assignments lightly — approaching them with a casual, easygoing, take-it-easy, relaxed attitude — we'll never go far in the fulfillment of our calling. It takes hard work to achieve anything worthwhile, and complaining about how hard it is won't make the process any easier.

I always say, "Live like a slug, and you'll eat dirt the rest of your life." So unless we want to "eat a lot of dirt," we have to make the decision to get up and put our hands to the plow of what God has put in front of us to do! If you and I are serious about obeying God, we must adjust our level of commitment and get to work. Being a hard worker is a part of being *diligent*.

A casual approach to any God-given assignment will never get you to the triumphant end of the race God has placed before you. You have to give a hundred percent of your focus and energy to press through the barriers that will invariably stand against you to keep you from making it to the finish line. Diligence and all that it entails is a requirement for you to get to a place of victory. With this in mind, Hebrews 11:6 could read: "God is a Rewarder of those who are *hard-working*, *attentive*, *busy*, *constant*, and *persistent* in their pursuit of seeking Him."

If you and I want to see our dreams fulfilled, we must give our *full attention* to what God has called us to do. It must have our full consideration, our undivided attention, and our full mental and spiritual concentration. Ceaseless, around-the-clock, nonstop devotion is essential in order to be *diligent*. To remain diligent, we must be engrossed, totally absorbed, and fully engaged. We must immerse ourselves in faith, prayer, and meditation regarding God's call on our lives. All of this takes a hundred percent of our focus and effort if we are going to accomplish what God has placed in our hearts.

Being constant and consistent is also an essential quality needed to *diligently* pursue your God-given dream. Fickle, flighty, erratic behavior will never produce the fulfillment of God's will in your life. It takes consistency and determination to push aside the powers of hell and obtain the victory you desire. If you and I constantly fluctuate in faith — wandering back and forth and in and out of faith — we will never reap anything enduring for the Kingdom of God. To produce powerful results, we must be *constant* in our commitments. We must be "steady-as-she-goes" — fixed, unchanging, and steadfast. It's all part of being *diligent*.

Persistence is also a key to remaining *diligent*. When a person is persistent, he refuses to relent. He is tenaciously immovable, even in the face of opposition. He is *unbending* until his objective is achieved. Withstanding opposition, braving adversity, and overcoming challenges are just a part of the walk of faith. In order for any of us to resist attempts to abort our dreams, we must be *persistent*.

I'm sharing this from Hebrews 11:6 because when we decided to launch the Internet Good News Church, it wasn't just a "try" at something new. We weren't just toying with our own ideas. It was a Heaven-given assignment, and if we were going to please God in this matter, we had to dig our heels in and "stay put" and refuse to budge until it became what God wanted it to be. There were certainly times when we didn't know if our ideas would work — and there were times they *didn't* work. But God never asks us for perfection. He asks us to hear His voice, get in alignment with His will, and stay *in* that place of faith.

If any of us is going to please God, as Hebrews 11:6 says, we must dig in and determine not to move off any assignment He entrusts us with.

And you won't be in it alone! Since God rewards this kind of diligence, it means if you're diligent, He will join people to you who are also diligent in order to help you in your endeavor.

### The Fruit of Our Faith and Dreams Realized

So with this in mind, we dug in and decided we would not surrender until the Internet Good News Church was up and running, and an online pastoral voice was ministering to Russian-speaking believers all over the world *at the highest level of excellence possible.*

After months of conversation, preparation, and doing all of our groundwork, the Internet Good News Church was born on April 12, 2015. It was time to announce IGNC to people all over the Russian-speaking world.

The response was *enormous* — that's what we had anticipated in our hearts from the beginning. But looking back, those first huge results were *minuscule* compared to the vast numbers of worldwide Russian-speaking believers God has brought us since that time to become a regular part of our Internet Good News Church. We started with an astounding 30,000 participants in our online church. At the time of this writing, there are approximately 200,000 people around the world who are a regular part of this online outreach.

And we really do have a full online pastoral team, children's and youth ministries, women's and men's ministries, and almost two hundred online counselors who pray with people who reach out to us from their personal phones and computers. We also have on board professional Christian psychologists to help people with marriage and family problems and other sensitive issues. And last but not least, God's dream has been realized for an online Home Group ministry and a Bible school for Russian-speaking believers around the world!

We have received thousands of testimonies from those who are a part of our Internet Good News Church family. Here is one testimony that is typical of so many testimonies we hear that are almost just like it:

> My life has totally changed because of the online church. Because of the truth I have received, my heart began to clear of deep-seated resentment and anger, I was able to forgive all the insults I'd received for several years, and my heart is clearer and I can feel it. I have become calmer, more balanced. Thank You, Jesus, that You prompted me to go to the website of the Internet Good News Church. It has turned my life around.

### More Ministry Is Amassing

Obedience to God's instruction to move from Riga to Moscow began to bear fruit quickly as we stepped out confidently that He would provide all the resources we needed — of finances, ideas, constant guidance and direction, favor, and even strategies for averting trouble. His goal all along had been a permanent facility for the Moscow Good News Church. And I must tell you — the half-circle-shaped interior of our auditorium is exactly what I saw in the vision in front of Lenin's tomb in 1991 when I visited Red Square with the gentlemen I was with on my *unwilling, unwitting, UNLIKELY* missions trip to teach those students in the Bible school!

And since establishing a permanent home for the Moscow church, ministry has *mushroomed* with the campus-church expansions and The Internet Good News Church. The church's facility is debt-free and serves the congregation, the poor and needy in our community, and other spiritual leaders and organizations in the greater Christian community. And one of the associate pastors leads the Internet Good News Church that reaches and ministers to hundreds of thousands of Russian-speakers each year.

There will always be fruitfulness at the end of your journey of obedience and faith. The God who gives the increase will see to it! In our case, His own dreams for this part of the world were realized — and are *still* being realized — through our willing hearts *and our busy hands and feet*! I've said so many times before, and it's no exaggeration, that Denise and I, our sons, and team really *do* run to keep up with His vision for our ministry. The vision is ever expanding — it is a mighty Gospel net that is sweeping in a harvest of precious souls *at rapid speed* in this late hour of the age.

Although fruitfulness follows faithfulness, Heaven's answers and outcomes don't just "fall" on us with no cooperation on our part. The path to the fulfillment of dreams is often fraught with difficulties, challenges, and even outright opposition. But at the end of every struggle is a breakthrough if we're doing God's bidding and staying unflinchingly in our place of faith.

In the next two chapters, I want to share with you some of the stories we're often asked about of the supernatural protection and provision we've experienced in our God-given assignments over the years. I trust you will be inspired by my accounts of protection and provision graciously and powerfully granted by God to enable us to fulfill this remarkable ministry He has given us to do. Denise and I and our team have experienced a phenomenal level of protection to do this job, and we have lived in a wellspring of God's provision as well. When I confidently tell you that our God is a protecting and providing God, I am speaking both on the authority of Scripture and from our own testimonies of rescue and deliverance on the front lines of ministry.

*I can hardly wait to share these stories with you — let's get started!*

'I am convinced that every single one of us will hear
of accounts in Heaven of times we were protected
and we averted great disaster, completely unaware
of what was happening in the realm of the spirit
at the moment.'

# 15

# UNLIKELY, *TRUE* STORIES OF SUPERNATURAL PROTECTION

There isn't enough space in this book to tell you of all the instances of divine protection our family has experienced in our years of ministry together — those instances are truly too numerous to tell. I'm talking even about times when a deal didn't go through, and that "failure" averted a financial disaster for us personally. I don't know about you, but when God intervenes to prevent us from being robbed in our finances — that's divine protection!

You already read in Chapter Thirteen of incidents in which we were at an airport or other public settings just days before a disaster occurred. And you no doubt also remember that, once, members of our Moscow team had tickets to see the *Nord-Ost* musical on the night of the infamous Chechen hostage-taking of 850 patrons and employees — but at the last minute,

---

**Left:** *God has promised His powerful presence to those who travel near or far to obey the Great Commission.*

our team members changed their plans and saw the performance the night before, on an "ordinary" night that was without incident or fanfare.

I am convinced that every single one of us will hear of accounts in Heaven of times we were protected and we averted great disaster, completely unaware of what was happening in the realm of the spirit at the moment. This is not a chapter to teach or explain why good people encounter difficult or treacherous circumstances in life. But I do know that the Holy Spirit has never misguided or misled anyone yet, and He's not about to guide anyone into error and disaster in the future. It becomes our responsibility, then, to learn of Him and to submit to the will and plan of God for our lives, where protection, provision, and empowerment become blessings we can count on, even in the midst of danger and trouble.

In our own lives, Denise and I have discovered that confidence in uncomfortable or even scary situations came when we gave God our *yes* and then believed with conviction and courage that He would defend us and see us through any challenge that tried to oppose us. Those challenges *will* come in life — *to all of us* — but we have the power to withstand those forces and to put them to nought.

Over the years, Denise and I, our sons, and our ministry, have faced a lot of truly bizarre obstacles and challenges as we have followed the call of God on our lives. We learned that the devil is a real enemy who never wants the Kingdom of God to advance and often tries to thwart the plan of God at every turn. That's why anyone who dares to obey God and forges into new territory must determine that he or she is going to get the job done, regardless of the opposition.

Before I get into our stories of God's delivering power, which are just amazing to me even now as I remember them, I must tell you that when I think about all we have been through, my mind immediately goes to the various perils that the apostle Paul said he encountered in his own ministry, but which did not have the power to stop him.

When I read about the hardships Paul faced — troubles that he wrote candidly about in Second Corinthians 11:23-27 and in other places, I have even thought, *If I recount everything we've been through, I think we might be able to add a few things to Paul's list!*

The events Paul endured would have shattered a normal man, but because he used his faith and kept his focus on the prize before him, he was able to *override* the system and *supersede* each act of aggression that Satan engaged against him. The devil simply wasn't able to stop Paul because Paul had made a commitment to be *unstoppable*. That needs to be our commitment today — yours and mine — if we are going to fulfill *our* divine destiny as Paul certainly fulfilled his destiny and completed the race God had given him to run.

For sure, our family has lived an unusual and adventurous life. But through it all, we have laid claim to God's promise of protection, and we have experienced it on an amazing level. Our assignment has required us to travel on dirty trains, rickety planes, and unsafe automobiles. I can't even count the times in the earlier years when we had to stop short of our destination because there wasn't enough fuel in the automobile we were in to get us all the way to where we needed to go — and we have regularly been "stranded" in risky places where enemies awaited us.

### God Is With Us!

In Matthew 28:18-20, Jesus made an astonishing promise to any believer, church, or ministry organization that will "go" — *go and keep on going* — with the Gospel to reach those who are nearby and those who are abroad. Jesus said, "...And, *lo*, I am with you always, even unto the end of the world. Amen" (v. 20). Those who take this promise to heart and obey it will be ignited and *remain* ablaze with the power of the Holy Spirit as they, too, "go" with the Gospel of Christ!

The word "lo" in this verse is actually an exclamatory promise that Jesus makes to anyone who will in any fashion "go" with the Gospel to those who have not heard it. I often say in my teachings that the "lo" in this verse belongs to those who "go." In Greek, the word "lo" would better be translated, *"And, WOW, will I ever be with you — even to the ends of the earth!"* In essence, Jesus was saying, "If you will go and keep on going — doing all you can in every way possible to preach and teach the Gospel — *WOW, I promise that you will experience My amazing presence in the doing of it!"*

Jesus promises that His powerful presence will be experienced by all believers who are committed to go to the lost with the message of salvation. That means *if we want to experience the power of God, we must act on what triggers its release* — and in this verse, Jesus promised that His supernatural presence would accompany all who will do their part to take the Good News of salvation to others!

As Denise and I and our family have pressed forward to obey the Great Commission, we have experienced this amazing power that Jesus has promised. Even on multiple occasions when the enemy tried furiously to stop us, we have experienced God's preserving and delivering power.

I want you to see in this chapter that because we've exercised faith in the name of Jesus and the promises of God's Word — and we've proceeded with the promise of His powerful presence with us — we have seen many victories and received the supernatural ability to keep pressing ahead.

Be encouraged, friend — this can be your story too.

## Special Promises We Have *Claimed* and *Experienced*

Before I share some of the amazing stories of divine protection that we have experienced, first I want to share a few of the promises of protection we have personally claimed over the years. Jesus gave certain promises of divine protection for those who preach the Gospel in places where its light is dim. I'm talking about verses like Mark 16:18, where Jesus said those who "go" to preach the Gospel will "...take up serpents and if they drink any deadly thing, it shall not hurt them...." This verse sounds strange until you understand what Jesus was referring to as He addressed His disciples.

The word "serpents" in this verse is the Greek word for *snakes*. Snakes, both then and now, can be dangerous and life-threatening creatures. But in the First Century when those who carried the Gospel began to go into all the world to preach it, the road system was undeveloped in many places, and this meant people often had to "blaze their own trail" to get to some cities or remote places. Hiding in the rocks or grasses were dangerous and poisonous snakes that frequently bit travelers, causing premature death. These snakes were a constant concern to all travelers, especially to those traveling by foot.

This issue of snakes was so real for travelers that Jesus referred to snakes again in Luke 10:19, where He said, "Behold, I give unto you power to tread on serpents and scorpions, and over all the power of the enemy: and nothing shall by any means hurt you."

In Mark 16:18 and Luke 10:19, Jesus gave promises of protection to those who would go into the harvest fields of the world to reap the souls of men. Since they needed to take roads with rocks and ruts that were filled with snakes, they needed divine protection to withstand those serpents that came against them — as well as anything else the enemy might try to use to stop or hurt them.

Snakes were a real threat to travelers in those days, and in Mark 16:18 and Luke 10:19, Jesus literally gave a promise of protection against snakes and also against *any* situation that would try to "strike" those who carry the Gospel to other places.

### Protection From Situations That 'Sting'

Notice in Luke 10:19 that Jesus also added "scorpions" to the list. Scorpions in the Middle East were feared because they were *loaded* with deadly poison. One sting from a scorpion, and a person could be permanently paralyzed or possibly even killed. When people took journeys by foot, the prospect of encountering a scorpion was just as worrisome as coming across a snake. Like snakes, scorpions, too, hid in rocks and ruts in the road. This meant that sitting on a wrong rock or accidentally stepping on the wrong spot in the road could result in disaster.

But in this verse, Jesus' promise of divine protection meant that even *if* they accidentally walked right over a snake or scorpion, they need not worry because He was giving them supernatural protection against such dangers. This was a supernatural promise of divine protection for *anyone* journeying long distances or through rough terrain to take the Gospel where it needed to go.

And to make sure total protection was provided, Jesus added, "…And *nothing* shall by any means hurt you." In this verse, the Greek sentence structure uses a triple negative. It literally says, "…and nothing [first negative], no [second negative], by no means [third negative] will injure or harm you." Jesus was speaking in the strongest language available to assure His followers — and you and me — that we will be divinely protected from all forms of evil when we go into all the world to preach the Gospel.

Jesus *never* said snakes or scorpions wouldn't *try* to harm those who "go." Of course, those things would be encountered along the way because they simply go with the territory. A perfect example can be found in Acts 28:3-6 when the apostle Paul was bitten by a deadly viper. Paul simply shook off the viper into the fire and went away unharmed. That is exactly what Jesus promised — divine protection from anything that tries to sting, harm, hurt, injure, or stop us along our path of obedience to His plan.

## Protection From Bad Food and Toxic Chemicals

But wait…there's another promise of protection Jesus gave in Mark 16:18 that Denise and I and our sons have claimed over the years. In Mark 16:18, Jesus added, "…And if they drink any deadly thing, it shall not hurt them…."

The word "deadly" describes the effects of drinking or eating something that is *deadly or fatal.* Jesus was promising that if any believers ever unintentionally drink or eat anything fatal while on a God-sent assignment, that fatal substance "shall not hurt them." Jesus' promise literally meant: "*And if they consume anything that would normally be fatal, or anything that would usually make a person sick, it will have no effect upon them.*"

The Lord knew that His disciples, both then and in the times to come, would be going to the farthest ends of the earth to fulfill their assignments, and many would be eating foods they had never eaten before. For them to take the Gospel to new places meant they would have to eat "mystery food" — not knowing where it came from, who killed it, how long it had been dead, who cooked it, how clean or dirty the kitchen was in which it was cooked, or what effect the food was going to have on their stomachs.

As one who has spent much of my life traveling worldwide, I can tell you that sometimes it is difficult to eat what is set before you. But when "mystery food" has been set before me, I've claimed Jesus' promise in Mark 16:18.

Denise and I and our family learned that if we were going to take the Gospel to the ends of the earth, *we must be ready to eat the food that's prepared at the ends of the earth!* But in Mark 16:18 we have this fabulous promise that if we unintentionally drink or eat anything deadly or sickening while we are conducting His business, it will have no harmful effect on us.

Jesus has assured us of divine protection as we take the Gospel to the ends of the earth, so we have claimed that promise — *and we have experienced the fulfillment of this promise of God!*

### 'Those Who Believe'

Someone might ask, "Well, what about those who went to preach the Gospel in other parts of the world who did *not* experience God's protection?"

I cannot answer the question of what happened in those cases, but I can tell you that Denise and I and our family chose to release our faith in these promises and to believe Jesus' power would protect us as we followed His call to the ends of the earth.

It's important to note that Mark 16:18 says these promises of divine protection are only activated in "those who believe." The Greek actually says, *"in those who are believing."* This means these promises of protection are activated only in those who are believing for them to work for them. In other words, the promises are not automatic; they must be embraced and believed, and faith in those promises must be *activated.*

Years ago when our family went to "the ends of the earth" in the former Soviet Union, we aligned ourselves with these promises and released our faith that we would have supernatural protection. Although the enemy tried to strike us repeatedly with what would normally be deadly situations — or to put his "stinger" into us to harm us along the way — none of those things ever had any long-lasting effect because we refused to move from Jesus' promises of protection in these verses, and we refused to move from His divine call.

I'm telling you this *before* I get into my stories because it is a fact that God called us to take the Gospel to parts of the world that were considered to be unsafe. Especially as we were getting started, we have flown on rickety airplanes, driven on dangerous roads, passed through highly volatile areas, faced attacks by "powers that be" who were hostile to Christianity, received treatment in hospitals that were broken down and under-supplied, and navigated a mafia-type, criminally infested world. But on every step of our journey, we laid claim to God's protection, and His marvelous promises have been very active in the lives of our family and our team.

In the next paragraphs, I will share what I consider to be amazing stories of dangerous situations we've found ourselves in as we've obeyed the call of God — and how His promises of protection have been with us as He has delivered us and kept us at every stage of our journey.

### Flying With an Engine on Fire — *and* on a Plane With a Broken Door!

One freezing winter morning many years ago, my associate and I flew east to the Siberian city of Neryungri, a remote city in the Sakha Republic about 3,100 miles east of Moscow. This sparsely populated region, also known as Yakutia, is the largest in Russia by square miles — four times the size of the state of Texas! Although Neryungri was the second largest city in Yakutia, it was a small city of only about 100,000 that had been established because of a huge coal basin located nearby.

But the town was so isolated that it was only accessible in the summers by a dirt road. If there was ever any rain, the dirt road was hideously transformed into impassable mud so deep that it often swallowed smaller vehicles whole! When the nearby river was solidly frozen in winters, it was temporarily transformed into a winter highway that cars and trucks actually used to travel back and forth to the Siberian railway.

We were traveling to Neryungri because I'd been invited by a church to speak at a special conference there. After flying east for hours, we finally arrived at the city's tiny airport and were picked up by our contact and driven to where we would be staying during the conference.

The multiple-day meetings were filled with believers who packed the auditorium's main floor and balcony. A city that remote doesn't have many special speakers because of its difficult geographical location, so the believers in attendance that week were thrilled to have me as a guest.

Throughout the conference, I ministered in smaller meetings to pastors and leaders who had traveled difficult dirt roads and even along the river highway from across the region in order to attend. One minister was a pioneering missionary who would disappear into the remote wilderness for months at a time, where he was giving his life to reach the Eskimos and indigenous peoples from that region of Russia.

Because indigenous peoples there were wary of outsiders, that brave man would go into the wild to live, distancing himself from outside civilization. He ate the bark from trees and moss from the ground, just as *they* did, and did all he could to become one of them so they would embrace him and open their hearts to hear the Gospel. What an honor it was to meet and minister to this heroic brother in the faith.

When the meetings finally concluded, my associate and I returned to the airport to board our flight to Yakutsk, where we were scheduled to make a connecting flight that would take us back to Moscow. Yakutsk is the capital of the Sahka Republic. Located about 280 miles south of the Arctic Circle, Yakutsk is known for having the coldest winter temperatures ever recorded in any city in the world. The lowest temperature recorded in Yakutsk was *minus* 83.9 — while the average temperatures there during winter average minus 37.5.[1] This causes the ground around that place to stay in a continuous state of permafrost — and we were there right in the middle of those freezing winter temperatures.

As our plane was in flight from Neryungri to Yakutsk, I began to smell heavy smoke. Alarmed, I immediately asked my associate, "Where is that smoke coming from?" He said, "I don't know. But don't spend too much time thinking about it. We're already in flight — even if something is on fire, there's nothing we can do about it now."

Well, in a sense, he was right, so I tried to put it out of my mind. But the longer we flew, that smell of smoke became stronger and stronger. When we finally landed in Yaktusk without a catastrophe, I was thankful. But I wondered what had been the source of the smoke that I smelled during the whole flight.

When the door to that older Soviet-made aircraft opened, I saw workers from the Yakutsk airport quickly climbing onto the top of one of the wings of the airplane, and they were ripping off the cover of one of the plane's two engines to extinguish a fire that was burning wildly on the left side of the plane. That's when I understood we had flown all the way from Neryungri to Yakutsk with one of the plane's two engines on fire for nearly the duration of the flight. As we descended the steps to the tarmac in the coldest temperatures I have ever felt in my life, I couldn't help but fix my eyes on those airport workers who were working feverishly to extinguish a fire that was still burning inside the plane's left engine.

At the time the USSR collapsed, many cities and Russian states claimed as their property whatever aircraft were sitting in their airports, and as a result, nearly four hundred new airlines had suddenly emerged — mostly with outdated aircraft and no budget for keeping them in operating condition. Those regional airlines frequently didn't have the money, manpower, or equipment to keep those planes in working order, but they kept flying them nonstop nevertheless. They just kept flying those old planes almost like a car overloaded with a million miles that had seen better days.

Today the lands of the former USSR have fabulous new fleets of airplanes that are simply magnificent. But years ago, that wasn't the case, and flying anywhere was simply a risk, especially on smaller planes flying to and from regional airports. And in the case of that flight from Neryungri, that plane should have been out of service for maintenance, but obviously, the owners of that plane saw it differently, and we all lived to tell about it without even a hint of difficulty *except* for the alarming smell of smoke we endured for the entire flight!

Seeing that airplane engine on fire was quite a shock, but the shock wore off really fast as we were quickly thrown in another state of shock by sub-freezing temperatures and cutting winds that greeted us harshly on the tarmac where we had to stand as we waited to retrieve our own luggage to board our next flight.

Before I continue, I need to tell you that I simply love the winter season — it's my favorite time of the year! In fact, it has to get really cold for me to even wear a coat outside unless I know I'll be in the elements for an extended period of time. Cold weather simply doesn't affect me like it does most others — I *love* cold weather! But Russian winters can be harsh, and the freezing temperatures are not just uncomfortable for many — they can be dangerous without the right kind of layered clothing for protection.

On that day on the tarmac, our heavy winter coats offered little protection from the freezing Siberian winds belting fiercely against us. There was no cargo transportation to retrieve our bags and transfer them to the next plane and no bus to transport us to the terminal. We had to stand outside the plane and watch as the crew worked on the fire in that engine — the same crew that would need to open the cargo hold of the plane for us as soon as they weren't so "occupied" with the issue of putting out a fire!

When the fire was finally extinguished, we could see that the engine of that plane looked completely charred. The workers quickly scrambled down from the wing to open the cargo hold so we could grab our bags and haul them across the icy tarmac to the terminal to be tagged for the next leg of our trip.

Those blistering subzero winds were unlike anything I had ever felt in my life. As we walked across the frozen tarmac to the terminal, I could no longer feel any extremity of my body as my legs, feet, and hands lost all feeling due to the cold. I moved my legs by faith as we walked! My brain was giving my feet the signal to move, but I couldn't feel my feet, nor the concrete ground beneath me, as I marched quickly toward the welcomed sight of that terminal.

After waiting several hours inside the airport, it was finally time for us to go to our next plane that would take us to Moscow. Once again, there was no bus to transport us, so along with everyone else on the flight, I bundled up, taking a deep breath and bolstering myself for the walk back outside into the elements to board our next plane. When we reached that plane, the doors to the plane were still shut so we stood outside and waited — *and waited and waited* — for the attendants to finally open the door. I don't pray frivolous, complaining prayers, but I remember praying deeply, *Please, Lord, have them open the door before we freeze.*

When the door finally swung open, passengers rushed the stairs, scrambling and tussling to get inside the plane as quickly as possible. I was so glad to finally be seated and to begin to warm up from the chill that by this time had permeated me to my core.

Soon the flight attendant brought us some hot coffee, and I was never so thankful for a cup of coffee to help me get warm! But within just minutes of our settling in, we heard an attendant's voice over the intercom: "Please exit the plane at once. There is a problem with the door of the aircraft."

Why did we have to exit the plane in order for the crew to fix a problem with the door? As it turned out, the plane was so overloaded after we had all boarded that it had descended into the stairs, jamming the door of the plane. Passengers had to exit to lighten the plane so the stairs could be pried away from its jammed position with the door of the plane.

So along with everyone else, my associate and I descended the airplane stairs back into the freezing temperatures to cheer on in our hearts the crew who were trying to pull the jammed stairs from our now-damaged plane door — the *same* crew who'd just put out a major fire on the last aircraft we were on.

As I stood outside the plane in those Arctic winds blowing from the north, I could see that the weight on the plane had caused it to sink into those stairs, where the bottom of the plane door was clearly jammed tightly into the metal stairs as if fused together. *And the bottom rim of the door was severely bent!*

*Oh no*, I thought as I braced myself for the announcement that the flight would be canceled. The entire bottom rim of that door and the airtight seal that stretched across it were seriously compromised.

One of the flight attendants who had also disembarked the plane was standing nearby, so I asked her, "What do you think they're going to do about that bent door and the broken seal around it?"

She coolly answered me, "Don't worry about it. They will figure out what to do." Then she said, "They just need to pry those stairs loose so we can re-board and be on our way to Moscow"!

My associate and I watched in disbelief as those airport workers *pulled and pulled and pulled* with all their strength to detach the stairs from that plane door. And the harder they pulled, the more warped and bent the bottom of that plane door became.

At last, they jerked the stairs free from the door, leaving us with our jaws dropped, *aghast* at what we were seeing. Again, I turned to the flight attendant to ask what they were going to do about the huge indentation in the door and the broken seal around the bottom. But I could barely get out the words before she answered again, "Don't worry about it. They will figure out what to do."

Well, that was the third time in one day I'd been told in so many words "not to worry about it" — twice from this attendant and once from my associate when I smelled smoke on our incoming flight. There's certainly a truth to not worrying; in fact, the Bible commands us not to worry about anything (*see* Philippians 4:6). But that verse also commands to pray about everything. So with all the faith I could muster, I *loosed* the promise of Luke 10:19 into my situation and thanked God for His Word that "nothing would — no, by no means — harm us."

I then watched as the airport workers brought two ladders from the terminal to the plane. Each ladder was leaned on opposite sides of the bent open door. While we were still standing in freezing temperatures, I watched two airport workers simultaneously ascend those ladders on each side of the door, each with a large hammer in hand, and they began pounding the broken bottom rim that had been disfigured by the jammed stairs. They were endeavoring to hammer the metal back into place — using ordinary hammers you would find in any toolbox — so that the door to the plane would close and the plane could fly.

Back on the plane, I was relieved by my praying the promise of God for protection, but still concerned about the condition of that door — especially as the plane would soon be climbing to higher and higher altitudes. So I asked the flight attendant, "Is the door fixed?" I immediately wished I'd not said a word when she replied to me, "We *think* it will hold until we get to Moscow."

I looked at my associate and said, "They *think* it will hold until we get to Moscow?" Fully expecting him to say, "Don't worry about it," I waited, and

I heard him say, "Pastor Rick, there are no other flights out of here for days. Let's just pray and believe everything will be all right."

Well, I *had* prayed and now I had to *believe* in God's promise that He would make His promise good. And, of course, He *did*.

When our flight arrived in Moscow later that day without incident, I was so thankful for our safety that the fact that our luggage didn't make it onto the plane seemed very minor. But I must tell you that I diligently prayed and thanked God *continually* during that flight. It was later that I learned from another commercial pilot how risky and dangerous it was to fly in such a condition. He said that situation could have easily resulted in our demise.

### A 'Grandmother' Swept the Snow and Ice
### From the Wings of Our Plane

While I'm telling you about airplane experiences, let me share another experience I'll never forget. Again, what I'm about to tell you happened in the earlier days when hundreds of emerging airlines were being operated with little money, manpower, or equipment to repair or maintain those older, rundown planes.

I had been in Saint Petersburg for ministry and needed to quickly fly to Kharkov in eastern Ukraine for more ministry there. Although I rarely travel alone, for various reasons, I had to fly alone on that particular trip. My plane was scheduled to stop in Moscow, where I would be connected to another flight to Kharkov. It was another cold, wintry day, and I arrived at the Saint Petersburg airport at about three o'clock in the morning, checked in, and waited to board my plane to Moscow. The flight was delayed, but eventually all the passengers boarded buses that transported us to the middle of the runway to where our plane awaited us.

Inside, I was seated next to a window, so I curiously looked outside — and when I did, I noticed the airplane wings were completely covered with ice and snow. There were no trucks anywhere with de-icing equipment, but I knew we would certainly not take off with all that snow and ice on the wings. I wondered how they were going to de-ice the plane before time for take-off.

The answer to my question came pretty quickly when I saw a grandmotherly type woman crawling up onto the wing of the plane with a primitive looking broom that looked like it was made from a long branch of a tree. In the place of normal whisks at the bottom that you'd normally expect to see on a broom, there were tiny broken-off tree branches and sprigs that had been bunched and tied together to form the whisks.

I watched in disbelief as she took that crude-looking broom and began to do her best to sweep the snow off the wings of that plane. Once the snow was removed, I watched as she turned the broom upside down and used the other end of it to forcefully beat the wings of the plane in an attempt to break the ice free so she could then sweep it off the wings and onto the runway.

Because I had gotten up so early to catch that flight, I was really tired and actually fell asleep in my seat while watching the elderly woman do her laborious job on the wings of the plane. But then something jarred the plane so abruptly that it woke me up and nearly knocked me forward in my seat. I wondered, *What just hit the plane?*

We hadn't taken off yet, so I looked out the window to try to see what had jarred the plane so hard. That's when I saw that a large truck had driven up to the front of the plane and the driver was literally ramming the truck into the front wheel in an effort to break the ice free that the little woman hadn't been able to remove with her broom. Over and over, the driver backed the truck up and then placed it in gear to ram the vehicle once again into the wheel of the aircraft to shake all the remaining ice from the plane.

When the plane finally took off, the front wheel of the plane couldn't be retracted into the airplane — I suppose, because it had been damaged by the truck — so our airplane flew all the way to Moscow with the wheel extended. It was one of the roughest flights I've ever experienced. When our flight landed in Moscow, it had changed routes and ended up at a different airport that didn't connect to my flight to Kharkov.

At the end of a very long day of traveling, I couldn't make my connection to Kharkov, so I got another short flight back to the airport near our home. When I arrived, I learned that my luggage was lost, but after a long, unforgettable day, I'd made it home with another rock-solid testimony about the protection God provides when He sends you on assignment.

Remarkably, my luggage showed up *months* later at our front door. It was the first luggage service that any of our friends and associates had ever heard of here in those days. But God was so involved in His promise of protection that He even saw to it that my luggage was safely delivered to me — even if it was months later!

## Shady Neighbors and a Surprise Attack on a Train

Especially in the earliest days of our TV ministry in the former Soviet Union, we hand-delivered TV programs and cash payments to TV stations all across the eleven time zones of the former USSR. Back in those days, we had a small army of full-time couriers who traveled more than three weeks in a month to deliver the teaching of God's Word to those stations for broadcasting.

After traveling for weeks at a time on planes, trains, and automobiles, those brave couriers would finally get back to our office just in time to regroup, pick up the next load of TV programs and cash to pay for the next round of broadcasts, and head out again for their next three-week mission. Those couriers were heroic for what they did month after month, but they did it with joy. We were all *gripped* with the knowledge that we were in a historic moment together when the Gospel and the teaching of the Bible was going via television into homes all over the former USSR.

That era was also a time of a very "mafia-infested world" in which people could have been killed for as little as a hundred dollars, so it was simply amazing that none of our couriers was killed. The truth is, for the amount of money they were carrying to pay for the broadcasts each month, any one of them could have been killed if it had been discovered they were carrying that much cash. The devil attempted to stop us, as I'll share about in the following paragraphs, but God miraculously hid us. We suffered a few skirmishes here and there, but we suffered no tragedies for the Gospel.

Talking among ourselves today as we look back on that time, we all agree that the situation was far more dangerous than we ever realized — but that we were never afraid because we were so focused on the mission. It is simply amazing to recall the divine protection that was upon us!

All travel was difficult in those days, but our couriers mainly traveled by train. Just as the airplane system today has become marvelous, the current train system in this part of the world today is fabulous — but in those early days, trains were so dirty that to go to the restroom, one nearly needed waders because of all the urine around the toilets. Trains were so filthy that Denise always slept in her clothes when we were traveling by train. I also told you in Chapter Twelve that gypsies regularly meandered the hallways of the train wagons to see what they could steal. Travelers learned to sleep with their shoes under their pillow and not put them on the floor near their bed because gypsies were renowned for picking locks and slipping into train cabins at night to steal travelers' shoes or whatever else they could find lying around while passengers were sleeping.

We sent a small team on a very long train trip each month to deliver TV programs and cash to TV directors in various cities. On one of those long trips by train, one that was particularly arduous and exhausting, members of our team had an ominous feeling about the train wagon they were traveling in. Our team members were all in one cabin, and on each side of them, in two separate cabins, were a number of sordid-looking, mafia-type figures. Our team did their best to avoid contact with those men, so they kept the door to their cabin closed except for when they needed to walk down the narrow hall to the common restroom. When they walked to the toilet, they quickly returned to their cabin in order to limit contact with those individuals who seemed highly questionable in their tired travelers' minds.

As the train pulled to a stop at a station in one major city, suddenly the members of our team heard screaming outside the train as it felt like a blast of some sort hit the side of the train. The force pounded the side of the car they were in so hard that every window exploded and *shattered*, with shards of glass flying like knives and splinters into each cabin in all directions. Passengers in other cabins screamed in terror. To protect themselves, our team dropped to the floor and took refuge under a small cabin table. They huddled together to protect themselves from the blast of pieces of glass that finally settled over most of the interior of their cabin.

Too stunned to grasp what was happening when the blast hit, they had dove for cover and shouted at the top of their lungs, "In the name of Jesus, we claim protection from this!"

But what was *"this"*? What happened to impact that train car so forcefully?

All of a sudden, Russian troops began barreling through the broken windows of the train. These particular law-enforcement troops were special forces trained to resolve serious conflicts. They were dressed in fatigues, wore bullet-proof vests, and carried guns and knives. Our team ducked out of the way as those forces invaded the train through the shattered windows and also through both doors at either end of the wagon.

Soon the troops were racing up and down the long hallway, violently banging on locked cabin doors and demanding that they be opened. When doors weren't opened quickly, they kicked in the doors to gain access to those cabins.

Remember that during that whole trip, our team said they'd had an eerie feeling about the mafia-looking passengers who were in the cabins to their immediate right and left. And when those soldiers commenced their full-scale attack, going from cabin to cabin, they forcibly removed from those two cabins the mysterious occupants, handcuffed them in the hallway, and dragged them from the train.

Our team watched in shock through their shattered window as their former next-door neighbors from the train were placed in armored vehicles, which then sped away.

That certainly wasn't an everyday occurrence, even on those dirty, old Soviet-era trains. Our team was shaken by the terror, screaming, and destruction all around them that now resembled a war zone. They had inwardly sensed that something was amiss with their neighbors on the train and knew to obey that hunch and to steer clear of them. Now they could see that they had been right all along. Apparently, those "neighbors" were such serious, fearsome criminals that those special forces had been dispatched to apprehend them. And apprehend them they did, nearly destroying a whole train wagon in the process. But they achieved their objective and took those criminals captive.

That day our team was reminded afresh of the powerful promise of Jesus to protect us when we are on a mission for His sake. Although our team was a bit shaken, no one was harmed, and they returned home with quite a story to tell. And just as Jesus promised, they were completely protected from the violent events of that day — events that came so close to them, but did not touch them.

## Risking Their Lives for the Sake of the Gospel

In those earliest days, there were no commercial banks in the former USSR, so it was impossible to wire money for TV payments to stations across the eleven time zones of the Soviet Union. That's why our couriers personally carried huge amounts of cash on their bodies. They needed to get to those TV stations to deliver our programs and pay for the broadcasts. As I noted, in the criminal world that existed after the collapse of the USSR, if anyone had discovered our couriers were carrying so much cash, our team could have been easily murdered.

Andrey Chebotarev, my long-term associate who was a courier in the early days, said, "To pay for TV time and to deliver the TV programs on time, we had to develop a courier system. The couriers were mainly young single guys, but there were a few girls too. We would all gather at the end of each month for our courier meetings. The office prepared all the TV programs and organized all the cash payments for each courier to carry. We carried big duffle bags that were really heavy with TV tapes. Not only that, but some of us carried really large amounts of cash — and that was at a time when you could have easily been killed."

Because there were no mobile phones in those days, we wouldn't hear from our couriers the entire time they were gone, so we never knew what they were encountering. But every day while they were en route to TV stations, we prayed for God's supernatural protection over them. We believed God would protect them, but when they would finally return from those long trips and we saw their faces as they came through the door to our offices, we always breathed a thankful sigh of relief. We were so enthusiastically thankful for Jesus' promise of protection!

Yuri Ruls, another leader in our ministry who began working on the team as a courier, said, "Any one of the couriers could have been killed in those days. But it was physically impossible to wire money because there were no banks. We had no choice but to carry all that cash to the TV stations each month. I carried big money and was in serious jeopardy a few times, but God faithfully protected me and also the cash.

We each knew that what we were doing was dangerous, but we didn't over-think it because we knew it was the right moment to do what we were doing. The door had opened for us to purchase TV time and to broadcast our programs. So we prayed for protection and went out every month in faith. God really protected us, but when I think back on what we did in those days — how much money we carried and how we had to carefully conceal it — that none of our couriers was killed is truly miraculous."

When I recall what we did in those days to get those TV contracts and then to make sure the tapes of the programs were delivered to the stations on time, I am even more amazed and grateful to God for how He preserved and protected us. We had *some* understanding of the dangers associated with our mission — of course we did; those days were almost like the wild, wild west, and no mode of transportation was dependable. But we can see much more clearly today the great risk involved in doing what we did to deliver the Word of God to those stations to be broadcast across the nations of the former USSR.

Our couriers were brave souls who didn't realize at the time how really brave they were! They didn't have much of a life outside of what they were doing, because what they did for the Gospel consumed their lives. They traveled on undependable transportation and lived in an environment of insecurity and uncertainty to achieve their goal. But they were willing to give their lives to do it so that those TV programs would be aired to reach millions of Russian-speaking souls.

### A Photo Album That Saved the Day

One of our most faithful TV couriers was a young Russian man from a central Asian republic. He was from a Muslim-dominated region that was becoming progressively hostile to Christianity. Life in that particular country was becoming more difficult all the time, but in spite of the growing opposition, God had miraculously opened a door for us to broadcast our TV programs on the largest TV network in that nation. But to get the TV programs and cash payments there each month would require a very special kind of courier who would be willing to risk his life month after month. And when I say "risk" his life, I am not exaggerating. Such a courier could have been killed as he fulfilled such an assignment in that region of the world.

We prayed for God to provide such a person, and God brought us the young man He had chosen to be the courier for that hostile region.

I'll never forget meeting him for the first time because he looked so *un-*Russian. But he was a young Russian man with blond hair, blue eyes, and tanned skin — he looked more like a surfer from California than a Russian from a Muslim-dominated region of the world. He was full of zeal and was excited to do something significant for Jesus. Every month, he showed up at our courier meetings to collect the TV programs and cash, usually with a story to tell of how God had protected him and the cash in his travels in the previous month.

For example, one month as he traveled his usual route, he inwardly felt alerted by the Holy Spirit that some kind of attack awaited him as he entered that area. He knew criminal-type people had been tracking him because he made that commute to Moscow and back every month, which was unusual for anyone from his particular nation at that time. But because he inwardly sensed something foul awaited him, he prayed for direction about how to protect himself and the immense amount of cash he was carrying on his body to pay the enormous TV bill in that nation.

It so happened that on that particular trip to Moscow, he had brought along several photo albums to show us his family and friends and various events he'd photographed at his home church in his country. As he prayed about how to conceal the cash he was carrying, he sensed the Holy Spirit telling him to place folded one-hundred-dollar bills behind the photos in those multiple photo albums. He painstakingly folded those hundred-dollar bills and slipped each one of them behind hundreds of photos in the albums he was taking with him back home from Moscow.

And just as the Holy Spirit had alerted him, as this courier entered that nation, he was suddenly entrapped by criminals who demanded that he turn over any cash that he was carrying with him! They searched him, looked through all his belongings, and threatened to take his life if he didn't give them whatever cash he was carrying.

When those interrogators asked to see the photo albums our courier was carrying, he calmly said, "I'd love to show my photos to you." He flipped page after page of one of the multiple photo albums, telling them all about the people in each photo and about all the events at his church. Those criminals turned several pages, peering into that album, not knowing the cash they were looking for was nicely folded behind every photo they were looking at with him.

Finally, they said, "We've had enough of seeing your photos. We thought you had cash, but you obviously don't." And with that, the criminals left as quickly as they had appeared. Our courier quickly grabbed his suitcase, the duffle bag filled with TV programs — and his precious money-filled photo albums, of course — and walked away that day without incident.

We were so thankful that this young man allowed the Holy Spirit to speak to him and lead him that day. Because he was spiritually sensitive, he circumvented an attack that could have proven very serious.

### The Holy Spirit — *the* Safest Guide Through Life

That event reminded me of John 16:13, where Jesus said that the Holy Spirit would "…shew you things to come." The word "shew" is a Greek word that depicts *a guide who shows a traveler the safest course through an unknown country.*

This means the Holy Spirit *wants* to be our Guide. He knows the way we should go and He understands how to avoid every trap and obstacle along the way. If we're going into an area where we've never been before or we're doing something that could pose danger, the Holy Spirit wants to show us how to take the safest route. He knows exactly how to get us safely to our point of destination. This is part of His ministry to you and me.

I want to encourage you that if the Holy Spirit tells you to do something specific, obey Him, as He knows what you should and should *not* do. As you listen to the Holy Spirit's leading, you'll have the wisdom you need to avoid attacks and to take the safest routes to where you need to go. As you stand on the Word of God, listen to the Holy Spirit, and obey whatever He tells you to do, you will experience God's supernatural protection. It will kick into action, and you'll soon find the divine protection that Jesus promised would operate in your life.

We must obey the Holy Spirit if we want to be assured of God's divine blessing and protection — *but we can do it!*

## A Divine Plan To Circumvent the Mafia

For many years, some of our leadership gathered monthly at a hotel in an unnamed city to meet with our couriers from all over the former USSR. In those meetings, we received their monthly reports and heard all about the challenges they faced to deliver the TV programs and the dangers they encountered carrying cash for the broadcast payments. They'd tell us about the local resistance to our programs, and we'd prayed for them before we sent them out with the next month's duffle bag full of programs and cash for TV payments. For years, we held the meetings on the same exact days of each month, and those monthly dates were set in stone and never changed.

But because of schedule conflicts, one particular month, we were unable to have our meeting on the same days that month. Many couriers were already there for our meeting, but due to circumstances beyond our control, we had to move the courier meeting to a few days later in that week.

We were disappointed to have to inconvenience our couriers by making them wait a few days longer for us, but unbeknown to us, God was intervening to save us from a bad situation. The God who knows everything was moving things around to circumvent a terrible attack that was waiting for us at our meeting that month. Like a Master Chess Player, He was moving the pieces of the game board around to make sure we won and the enemy failed in his strategy.

Although we didn't know it, the local mafia in the city where we met each month had somehow figured out that we disbursed a large amount of cash on the same exact days every month. Apparently, they had been making such serious surveillance of us that they even knew what floor we stayed on at the hotel and what times we met for our meetings. Their plan was to take us by surprise before our courier meetings began and steal all the cash for our TV-broadcast payments.

If that evil plot had succeeded, not only would it have been dangerous to our physical well-being, but it would have jeopardized the broadcasts themselves. If we didn't pay on time, the broadcasts would not have been televised, which would have been a massive strike against the impact we were making in the lives of millions of TV viewers. If those gangsters had seized all our cash, it would have been *crippling* to what we were doing.

But due to circumstances beyond our control, we had to delay our arrival. When we finally arrived a few days later, the hotel administrator said, "It's a good thing you didn't show up on time. There was a group of people here waiting for you this month and asking questions about you. It was a trap and they were planning to rob you. When you didn't show up on time and they figured you weren't coming, they gave up and left." A woman who worked in housekeeping on our floor corroborated his story. Without anyone's asking them to do it, it seemed the staff at the hotel were looking out for us. We were simply thankful to God we'd averted a close call and a potentially life-threatening situation.

As it turned out, we had good meetings with our couriers that month with no trouble and with grateful hearts that God had orchestrated events for us to show up late to our meeting. Romans 8:28 says, "And we know that all things work together for good to them that love God, to them who are the called according to his purpose."

We can all take heart in knowing that nothing takes God by surprise. He knows all things and can orchestrate events for His purposes. Ephesians 1:11 says God "...worketh all things after the counsel of his own will." That month, He changed our schedule because He was protecting us. Whereas I felt embarrassed that we were not showing up on time for that meeting, God was secretly working behind the scenes to protect us.

Often, we don't have the foggiest idea what God is doing, but He knows *everything,* and He is always working behind the scenes to help bring us into the fullness of all He has planned for our lives. Imagine the ways the Lord has protected you in times past and you weren't even aware of what He was doing at the time. Can you think of such times in your own life? If you can, I think it's important to remember them often because they are signposts for what the Lord wants to *continue* to do for you as you walk with Him.

That month, if we had been on time for our regularly scheduled meeting, we would have stepped right into a trap that the devil had set for us. We would have felt the strike of a devil-sent serpent and the sting of a demonic scorpion against our ministry. *God protected us when we didn't even know we needed to be protected.* But we had released our faith in Jesus' promise of divine protection, which belongs to "those who believe" — and that is what we received!

As you walk out your own Heaven-given assignment, it is imperative that you activate your faith in Jesus' promise of protection. If you'll engage your faith to believe in those promises of divine protection, God will engage His power to protect you even when you don't know you need protection. Those "exceeding great and precious promises" of divine protection are for *you*! (*See* 2 Peter 1:4.)

## When a Train Official Tried To Confiscate Ministry Money

We have always done our best to diligently obey the law, regardless of what land we were in at the time. But when the former USSR dissolved and new national borders were going up, laws were in a constant state of flux and we often didn't know about the "newest and latest laws" that were being enacted during that confusing time.

That means you could think you were in compliance with the law, but suddenly an unknown law could be reactivated, which would mean you were no longer in compliance, and you wouldn't even know it — you could become a "lawbreaker" in an instant.

At the time we arrived in this part of the world, the former USSR was coming out of seventy years of socialistic-communism. It takes time to transition from a socialistic-communist to a capitalist system. I am often stunned at the thinking of some who do not comprehend the time it takes for an entire society to move from socialistic communism to a capitalistic market. Our family has lived through many monumental changes since we moved here, and we can testify that it's an enormous process that can take a generation or more to become a reality. The changes we have witnessed have occurred at what feels like the speed of light — it is simply amazing how many advancements have occurred in the short time since the USSR officially dissolved on December 8, 1991.

But because laws were in a constant state of flux and inactivated laws could be suddenly activated that could put us in jeopardy, especially in the earliest days, we ended up hiring our own lawyer to try to help us stay on top of all the rapidly changing laws and regulations. *Ugh* — it was such a difficult time to do things right, for it really was a time when the right hand didn't know what the left hand was doing!

I was once traveling a lot with my assistant to conduct TV-ministry business in those days, and on one particular trip, we were on a train, along with another team member, and we were carrying a large amount of ministry cash that was designated for TV-broadcast payments. This event did not occur in Russia, but as far as we knew, we were in compliance with the law in that country in regard to the amount of cash we could legally carry with us. But I nevertheless asked my team member to conceal the cash as deeply in his suitcase as possible so no one would find it if we were searched. He assured me he had it well-hidden and not to give it a second thought.

Just as I suspected, our train cabin was checked, and when the train official opened that team member's briefcase — there lying in plain sight for all to see was the cash for our TV programs! I remember thinking, *So that is how you conceal cash in your suitcase?*

When the train official saw the cash, his eyes lit up with excitement, and I knew he would confiscate it because it was more money than he would have earned in many years at that particular time. Although we were sure we were in compliance with the law, the train official informed us of an inactivated law that had suddenly become activated, which he said put the amount of cash we were carrying in a category of "illegal" and he would have to confiscate it.

I watched his eyes get wider and wider as he began to count the cash. Then he put all that cash into his personal bag, turned around, walked out of our train cabin, and exited the train with all our money!

That team member looked at me and asked, "What are we supposed to do?" I said, "I don't exactly know what to do, but I can tell you what I'm *not* going to do — I'm not going to sit here while he walks away with God's money. We don't even know if an inactivated law has really been activated or if he's just walking away with the cash that has been provided by our partners for our TV programs."

He asked me again, "So what are we going to do?" I told him, "I'm following the cash to wherever he takes it. I'm not leaving without the money that was given to us by partners for TV!"

This team member sat dazed as I got up, along with my Russian-speaking assistant, and together we followed the train official to the building where he had gone with our cash. Deep inside, I knew we had not broken any law and that the official had just seized the opportunity to walk off with what looked to him like a mountain of cash. And I was determined he wasn't going to get away with it.

The whole time we followed the train official, my associate kept asking, "What do you think you're going to do to get that cash back? He'll never just give it to us!" I said, "I have no idea what I'm going to do, but I can tell you that he is going to be sorry he ever met me today because I will not leave this station until he gives every cent back. That is holy money meant for the TV broadcasts, and I'm not leaving without it."

When I got to the building where the official had gone with our money, I sat on a primitive looking wooden bench right outside the main door to the tiny building where he had disappeared inside. My assistant knocked on the door, and the official suddenly reappeared and asked, "What are you doing here? Get back on the train — I'm keeping your money!" The train official didn't know I understood Russian and comprehended everything that was being said between him and my assistant.

I heard my assistant tell him, "Sir, you have no idea what you're dealing with here. This American is crazy, and he will not leave until you give him the cash back. I'm telling you that he is not normal, and he'll sit right here until you give his money back to him."

At first, I couldn't believe that my assistant was telling the official I was *crazy*. But as I thought more deeply about it, my mind went to First Samuel 21:13 where it is recorded that King David feigned madness in the sight of the king of the Philistines in order to protect himself. There was nothing wrong with David mentally, but he acted crazy, nevertheless, in front of that king.

First Samuel 21:13 (*MSG*) says that David, "pounding his head on the city gate and foaming at the mouth, spit dripping from his beard." Achish the king said in response, "Can't you see he's crazy? Why did you let him in here? Don't you think I have enough crazy people to put up with as it is without adding another? Get him out of here!" (v. 15).

That is a pretty good description of what happened with me at the station that night. I didn't care what theatrical act I had to play, I was not leaving that station without the money because it was money dedicated for the Gospel.

So I let the theatrical act play out. When it was time for the train to leave and I refused to get up and leave, it terrified the train official because he didn't know what to do with me. He was so worried that he had a serious situation on his hands that he handed me the bag with *all* the cash and said, "Get back on the train right now. Get out of here!" And just as David managed to escape King Achish, I walked back onto that train with every cent of God's money that he had taken — and I was filled with rejoicing!

When I think back to that day, it seems hilarious, but if that man had kept all the money he'd tried to confiscate, it would have been a huge blow against our ministry's ability to broadcast our programs. And guess what? We finally found out that on that particular day, *no* inactivated law had been activated to make the amount of money we were carrying illegal, and we were in complete compliance with the law. That man simply wanted to walk away with a pile of money. It was a con job that went sour for him. But

I learned that like King David, sometimes you have to be wise in uncanny ways to circumvent the enemy's attacks.

But as in all the other countless cases in which we experienced divine protection, we once again saw the power of standing on Jesus' promises of protection in Mark 16:18 and Luke 10:19. Those promises really do work for anyone who activates them by faith!

## Victory in the Midst of Tests and Trials

I've always appreciated that the apostle Paul was forthright about the challenges and difficult moments he faced as he fulfilled his ministry calling. While he never glorified the difficult times he faced, neither did he gloss over them and give the impression that he never faced a battle. For a man of faith who did the amazing things we read about with a sense of awe, he was very intentional about being candid concerning the many challenging circumstances he faced along the way.

One example is in Second Corinthians 1:8 and 9, where Paul wrote, "For we would not, brethren, have you ignorant of our trouble which came to us in Asia, that we were pressed out of measure, above strength, insomuch that we despaired even of life: But we had the sentence of death in ourselves, that we should not trust in ourselves, but in God which raiseth the dead."

But notice Paul said, "We would not, brethren, have you ignorant...."

This means Paul wanted his readers, including you and me, to know that everyone endures challenging moments from time to time. *Even great spiritual leaders are confronted with potentially devastating situations that they must overcome for the sake of the call.* But Paul didn't write these verses to glorify those hard ordeals — he wanted us to know that if we remain committed to fighting where we stand, we will win the victory!

Paul went on to say, "For we would not, brethren, have you ignorant of our *trouble* which came unto us in Asia...."

That word "trouble" is a translation of the Greek word *thlipsis*, which was used to convey the idea of *a heavy-pressure situation*. It depicts one who is *in a tight place, under a heavy burden*, and *in a great squeeze*. And by using this word *thlipsis*, Paul was essentially saying, *"We were under an unbelievably heavy amount of stress and pressure. We were beneath a heavy load and trapped in very tight circumstances."*

Then he added, "...We were *pressed out of measure*, above strength, insomuch that we despaired even of life." The words "pressed out of measure" are a translation of the Greek words *kath huperbole*, which means *to throw something beyond*. It is used here to describe something *excessive* or *beyond the normal range that most experience*.

By using this phrase, Paul was saying, *"We were under an abnormal amount of pressure. It was far beyond anything we had ever previously experienced. It was excessive, unbelievable, unbearable, and far too much for any one human being to endure."*

Paul continued to describe his situation with the words "above strength." The word "above" is a translation of the Greek word *huper*, which conveys the idea of something *excessive*. It's almost as though Paul was saying, *"Normal human strength would never have been sufficient for this situation. This predicament required strength on a measure that I had never previously needed. It was beyond me!"*

Then Paul added, "...Insomuch that we *despaired* even of life." The Greek word for "despaired" is the word *exaporeomai*, which describes *a situation with no way out*. It was used to describe individuals who were *caught, pinned down, trapped, up against the wall, and utterly hopeless*.

Paul's situation in Asia was so life-threatening that in verse 9, he added, "But we had the *sentence* of death in ourselves...." The word "sentence" in Greek is the word *apokrima*, which speaks of *a final verdict*. What Paul meant was, *"It looked to us like the verdict was in, and we were not going to survive."*

When the meanings of all these different words and phrases are combined in these verses, the passage could be translated as follows:

**We would not, brethren, have you to be ignorant of the horribly tight, life-threatening squeeze that came to us while we were in Asia. With all the things we've been through, this was the worst of all. It felt like our lives were literally being crushed. No experience we've ever been through required so much of us. In fact, toward the end of this ordeal,**

we were so overwhelmed that it felt like we'd never get out. We felt suffocated, trapped, and pinned against the wall. We really thought it was the end of the road for us. It felt like the verdict was in, and the verdict said death....

Never forget that God's delivering power is yours! All God asks is that you stay at your post, refuse to give in to pressure, and determine that you are going to enforce Jesus' victory. *Refuse to let the devil win!* If you remain faithful to God's task, He will remain faithful to you as well — even when it feels like the odds are stacked against you!

## When Satan Tries To Hinder *You*

Once when the apostle Paul felt resisted by the devil's assault, he wrote, "Wherefore we would have come unto you, even I Paul, once and again; but Satan *hindered* us" (1 Thessalonians 2:18).

This verse has been so important to me and to our ability to overcome that I want to take a moment to elaborate on it. The word "hindered" is translated from a Greek word that describes *an impasse* — and it could also depict a runner who runs with all his might and energy as he presses forward toward the finish line. But as he runs toward his goal, another competing runner comes alongside him *to elbow him out of the race.*

This is exactly the word Paul used in this verse, and by using this word, Paul warned that when you are doing the will of God, Satan will try to create impasses to stop you and may even try to elbow you out of your race.

Believe me when I tell you that our family has experienced some of Satan's unfair tactics as he has tried to create impasses for us and to cut in on us to stop us from fulfilling our mission. Some of these attacks have taken us by surprise and some were self-inflicted. But we learned that if the devil tries to create an impasse to stop us — or if his elbow tries to strike us to force us off track — those moments can become opportunities to use our faith to slap the wits out of him and to get back on track if we've veered from the course!

We are promised in James 4:7, "...Resist the devil, and he will flee from you." The word "resist" demonstrates the attitude of one who is opposed to something and therefore determines that he will do everything within his power to resist it, to stand against it, and to defy its operation.

This means *we must be determined to stand against the work of the devil.* If he challenges us, we must dig in our heels, brace ourselves for a fight, and put our full force forward to drive him back and out of our lives with the authority of Jesus' name, His blood, His Word, and all the spiritual weapons He has given to us. Our stand against Satan must be firm, unyielding, and steadfast. James 4:7 promises that if we'll take that position, the devil will *flee* from us.

## We've Lived Under the 'Spell' of God's Grace

When I look back at all we have done — and all the dangers we have faced — it has been as if we've lived under a spell of divine grace that enabled us to do it all bravely and with no fear. This concept of grace is so important that I want to share a moment about the origins of the word "grace," so you'll understand why I refer to it as "the divine spell of God."

In the Greek language of the New Testament, the word "grace" is *charis.* Pages and pages could be written about the origins and the various nuances of meaning contained in this one word. But in history, the word *charis* sometimes denoted *special power that was conferred upon an individual or group of individuals by the gods.* Once this *charis* was conferred upon a person or group of people, it imparted to them *superhuman abilities.* In other words, it enabled them to do what they could not normally or naturally do in themselves. In some secular literature from the early New Testament period, the word *charis* was even used to denote individuals who had been placed under a "magic spell" that transformed their personalities and imparted supernatural abilities to them.

In the New Testament, the word "grace" is also occasionally translated as *favor* because a person who receives *charis* is *supernaturally enabled* as a result of receiving *favor* from God. So when we read of "grace" in Paul's writings, we can know that he was referring to God graciously imparting a special touch that *enables, empowers,* and *strengthens* the recipients. All of this aptly depicts the word "grace" and its effects on those who receive it.

*Grace is like a divine spell that comes upon an individual and transforms him, giving him the ability to do what he could not do before.*

When God's "grace" touches a person or a group of people, as it did our family and team, that divine impartation *enables, empowers, strengthens,* and *enhances* their personalities. It puts them under the divine "spell" of God that imparts supernatural abilities to them so they can do what they would never have been able to do by themselves. That is a *perfect* explanation for the ingenuity and boldness that came on me, Denise, our sons, and our whole team, including those couriers in our early days of TV broadcasting. We were all transformed by the grace of God to do what we would never have been able to do by ourselves.

The stories in this chapter are a microscopic taste of the many dangerous experiences we have encountered over many years of our ministry. But again and again, we have experienced the preserving, protecting, delivering hand of God. In response to it all, I must say in the words of the apostle Paul, "He that glorieth, let him glory in the Lord" (1 Corinthians 1:31).

To God alone be the glory for all that has been accomplished and for the divine protection He has provided for us through the years. And our faith *remains* activated as we expect Him to *continue* protecting us by His mighty hand. We have proven that He will see us through victoriously as we obey His every directive and plan, and He will never fall short in any area of need.

In the next chapter, I'll share accounts of how, in addition to protecting us, God divinely provided for us — supernaturally, beyond anything we were able to do for ourselves. That's the grace of God for me and my family — and it's the grace of God for you and your loved ones too.

# 16

# UNLIKELY, *TRUE* STORIES OF SUPERNATURAL PROVISION

I n Chapter Seven, I shared that Jesus appeared to me in a vision in 1985 and spoke about my future ministry and that He would provide for it. As I told you, after I'd spent time in prayer about finances for our new season in the teaching ministry, I found myself in another dimension and Jesus appeared before me. In that moment, the Lord began to speak to me about the anointing He had placed on my life and where His call would take us in the future — *to the ends of the earth.*

In that vision, I heard the Lord say, "Behold, I give you fullness of ministry — so much ministry that it is already amassing more ministry for your future." I understood that Jesus was giving us ministry that was already *amassing* — that's the word He used — more ministry. So I knew we were going to have *greater, greater,* and *even greater* responsibility in ministry in the future. But then I heard the Lord say, "And behold, I'm giving you finances

**Left:** *Soviet rubles, 1991.*

for your ministry. It is wealth on a measure that is already amassing more wealth for you to fulfill your ministry assignment."

Jesus was giving us finances that were already *amassing* — and, again, that's the word that He used — more finances. In an instant, I understood that God would provide for any assignment He ever entrusted to us. Even though we could not see or touch those finances at that moment, I knew Jesus told me He would provide finances that were already *amassing* more finances so that we could do any job He would ever give us to do.

Although we have witnessed greater ministry assignments and greater responsibility in ministry — along with the fullness of finances to pay for it all — I am still in *awe* at the level of divine provision God has supplied to cover the costs for everything He has ever put in our hearts to do. Don't misunderstand me — it hasn't always been easy in the middle of each assignment when we were believing for every cent needed to do the job. But what we've seen God provide over the years has exceeded my wildest imagination, and His provision has always faithfully come on time.

As I think of what God has done, my mind goes to Paul's words in Ephesians 3:20 and 21. It says, "Now unto him that is able to do exceeding abundantly above all that we ask or think, according to the power that worketh in us, unto him be glory in the church by Christ Jesus throughout all ages, world without end. Amen." Denise and I, our sons, and our team can testify that God has "exceeding abundantly" provided everything we have ever needed to do any job He has entrusted to us, and He has provided far over and above all that we ever dared to ask or think. As the *Amplified Bible Classic* renders it, He has gone "infinitely beyond our highest prayers, desires, thoughts, hopes, or dreams" and provided *everything* we've needed to fulfill our Heaven-given assignments.

God has indeed supernaturally provided everything we have needed through the giving of pastors, churches, businesses, organizations, and individual partners who have sacrificially given over and over through the years. God gave me the instruction concerning what we were to do, my family was willing to do whatever God was asking of us, and He provided the funds to do it all through the giving of those who also got behind us in the work.

In fact, it was our partners' giving that enabled us to go on television, to start the first Christian TV network in the former USSR, to start churches and establish permanent buildings and facilities, to build an association of pastors and churches, to provide for Denise to minister to tens of thousands of women, to conduct our Golden Age ministry, and to supply outreaches to the poor, needy, and destitute.

The list seems nearly endless of what we have seen God do. But all of it has been accomplished because of people all over the world who have come alongside us to help us. Like water channeled through a conduit, their resources have flowed through us to accomplish the tasks God assigned to us. And we have done our best to wisely steward every dollar God has graciously provided through our partners. We have been conscious that each financial gift is given from someone's hard-earned resources and that their gifts have been sacrificial and are holy to the Lord.

Those who have given to this ministry are such a vital, integral part of the amazing story of what God has done through RENNER Ministries. In this chapter, I want to share more in depth how God has used these precious men and women to help us fulfill our ministry assignments.

It takes every one of us doing our different parts — with God's blessing on it — for doors to open and harvests to be reaped. Divine connections are essential for completing any divine assignment. And respect for every person for the role he or she plays is so important.

And we must certainly include God and *His* role. Most of us realize that even if we all did our respective parts to make supernatural things come to pass, nothing of value would ever grow if God didn't provide His continuous blessing. So *all* the glory goes to Him for what is produced in our lives.

## A Mind-Boggling Supply

As part of my preparation for writing this chapter about God's divine provision, I asked my team to provide me with a report of how much money has flowed through our ministry since our official move to the lands of the USSR in October 1991. When I heard the total number, it was so enormous that I found myself asking them over and over, "Did I hear you right? Are you absolutely sure that number is correct?"

The accumulated amount God has provided through our partners since we moved to the former USSR is simply *mind-boggling*. It is stunning to me because I vividly remember what we *didn't* have when it all began. We were counting our pennies and saving rubber bands and paper clips to economize. But God has supernaturally provided everything needed to miraculously do every job assignment as we've helped establish the move of God in the lands of the former Soviet Union.

Over the years, I've heard people refer to George Müller's remarkable testimony of how God again and again provided for his magnificent missions work in remarkable ways. But I am convinced that our story is just as miraculous. In fact, when I study modern missions history, I suspect that what we have experienced may be one of the largest supplies of resources to ever flow through a single ministry family. The story of how God has provided for our ministry and those He has called us to reach and care for is as big a miracle as any testimony I have ever heard or read. I give God all the glory for involving Himself in our work in a mighty way, providing everything we've needed to fulfill our heavenly assignment.

### Pastors, Churches, and Individuals
### Who Obey Jesus' Great Commission

In the early years of our traveling ministry in the United States, Denise and I and our family traveled thousands of miles all over the country to conduct meetings in churches. Over time, we dotted the landscape of America with our meetings — and how we loved ministering to pastors and the people who attended our services in all those churches.

Because the big picture concerning our ministry hadn't been revealed to us during that time, we didn't realize that all of those meetings would be so vital to our future. God was directing every step as we built relationships with pastors, churches, individuals, businesses, and organizations that would stay with us, at our side, as we moved our ministry base to the other side of the world. In those years, God was teaching us that doing first things first is very important and that every step is vital to help you take your future steps successfully in His plan.

As a result, our ministry today has long-time partners who have been with us from those earliest days when we were traveling across America as a family in our little car. Those early days — the very inception of our teaching ministry from our Tulsa base — laid the foundation for building partnerships that have put financial fuel in the tank of our ministry so we could keep moving ahead without interruption.

Those in our partner family are really family to us, and we mean it sincerely when we call them *partners*. Without them and the part they have played all these years, we wouldn't have been able to do our part in the grand scheme of God's call on our lives. When we all stand before Jesus in the future, those who gave to support the work of God will be rewarded alongside those who actually went to the front lines!

I could write an entire book about the miraculous provision God has supplied for our ministry over the years. But His supernatural provision has primarily been delivered through the hands of men. This is the principal way God provides financial support for the work of the ministry. God uses people — those who work very hard at their jobs, who earn a living in their professions, who believe Him for promotions and bonuses, and who love Him so much that they consecrate a certain portion of their income or assets for the advancement of His Kingdom.

## Mary, Joanna, Susanna, and *'Many Others'* — Jesus Had Ministry Partners

In Luke 8:2 and 3, we find that Jesus had ministry partners who gave of their resources to support His ministry while He was on the earth. Those verses say, "And certain women, which had been healed of evil spirits and infirmities, Mary called Magdalene, out of whom went seven devils, and Joanna the wife of Chuza Herod's steward, and Susanna, and many others, which ministered unto him of their substance."

Luke 8:3 says that these women "…ministered unto him of their substance." The word "ministered" is the Greek word *diakoneo*, a Greek word that depicts *a servant whose primary responsibility is to serve food and wait on tables.* It presents a picture of a waiter who painstakingly attends to the needs, wishes, and desires of his or her client. It was these servants' supreme task to professionally please clients; therefore, the servants served honorably, pleasurably, and in a fashion that made the people they waited on feel as if they were nobility.

Luke uses this word to picture the attitude of the women who served Jesus by financially giving to Jesus' ministry. These women believed it was their God-given assignment to painstakingly attend to the needs, wishes, and desires of Jesus. Their supreme task was to provide what He and His disciples needed to fulfill their ministry without hindrance.

Furthermore, the tense used in the original Greek indisputably means that these women did this task *consistently* and *regularly*; in other words, they *habitually* donated money to Jesus' ministry. They were faithful *partners* on whom Jesus could rely.

But the verse goes on to say that these women ministered unto Him of their "substance," which is a translation of the Greek word *huparchontos*, the word for *goods, possessions,* or *property.* These women became partners with Jesus' ministry because they were so thankful for what He had done in their own lives.

But precisely who *were* these women who supported Jesus' ministry? Let's look very carefully at Luke 8:2 and 3 to see what we can find out about these women God used to financially support Jesus' work on the earth.

Luke 8:2 tells us about "…certain women, which had been *healed* of evil spirits and infirmities.…"

The word for "healed" here is the Greek word *therapeuo*, an old Greek word from which we get the word *therapy.* This carries the idea of *repeated actions, such as a patient who visits a physician over and over until the desired cure is obtained.* This seems to suggest that these women had been so severely demonized that although they were helped when they first came to Jesus, they had to keep coming back again and again until, finally, they were completely free. It may have been Jesus' constant, tender, compassionate attention that caused them to have such grateful hearts, producing in these women a firm commitment to support His ministry with their finances.

The verse also says that they were healed of "infirmities," which is a translation of the Greek word *astheneia*, which depicts *physical frailties, weaknesses, sicknesses, or a state of ill health*. The word "healed" (*therapeuo*) is applied both to the women's deliverance from demonic spirits and to their freedom from illnesses.

No wonder these women were such avid financial partners with Jesus' ministry. It was through His compassionate touch that they were set free from demons and restored to full health. It is simply a fact that the best partners in the world are those whose lives have been changed by one's ministry. These women are vivid examples of people with grateful hearts who wanted to do what they could financially so the ministry that helped them could touch others' lives as well.

After mentioning the first unnamed group of female supporters, Luke now gives the first recognizable name in this group of women. He says in verse 2, "…Mary called Magdalene, out of whom went seven devils."

Many tales have been told about Mary Magdalene's working in the prostitution business before she met Jesus. However, there isn't a single New Testament source that records Mary Magdalene as a former prostitute. One thing *is* clear, though: She was possessed with an entire infestation of demons before Jesus touched her life. Both Luke 8:2 and Mark 16:9 affirm that she had been delivered of seven demons.

When Luke tells us of Mary, he identifies her as one "…out of whom went seven devils." The Greek word for the phrase "out of whom went" is *exerchomai*, a compound of the word *ex*, meaning *out*, as *to make an exit*, and the word *erchomai*, meaning *to go*. But when these are compounded, forming the word *exerchomai*, it takes on the meaning *to go out, to drive out*, or even *to escape*. The word *exerchomai* implies that these demons may have been so entrenched in Mary that Jesus had to literally drive them out of her. It is possible that when these seven spirits left her body, they literally *fled* in order to *escape* the fierce pressure Jesus was exercising on them. Once they were gone, Mary was free.

The Bible has no concrete record of Mary's actual deliverance from these seven demons — only that it happened. But evidently Mary Magdalene used her money to financially support Jesus' ministry, for she is listed in Luke 8:2 and 3, along with the other women who gave out of their assets to support Jesus' ministry.

As Luke continues to name the women who financially supported Jesus' ministry, he tells us next of "...Joanna, the wife of Chuza Herod's steward..." (v. 3).

Luke informs us that Joanna was the wife of Chuza, who was the "steward" of Herod. The word "steward" signifies *a person who has been entrusted with the guardianship or supervision of another person's belongings.* This was no low-level servant; rather, Chuza was a high-level dignitary who had authority to make decisions on behalf of Herod in regard to his personal fortunes. One of the rare uses of this word in the Greek Old Testament Septuagint is where it is used to describe Joseph's oversight of Potiphar's household.

The fact that Chuza held such a prominent position in Herod's household tells us that he was highly educated and was accustomed to managing massive sums of money. As the chief manager of Herod's personal fortune, Chuza served as the king's chief advisor regarding his personal financial matters. No doubt, a man in this position had many opportunities to increase his own personal wealth as well, for he lived in the atmosphere of affluence and had many high-ranking political connections as Herod's steward. Some have speculated that Chuza may have been the nobleman of John 4:46-53 whose son was healed by Jesus.

Chuza's wife was Joanna — a woman whose life had been dramatically touched and changed by Jesus. If Chuza was the nobleman of John 4:46-53, as some suggest, it is easy to imagine how grateful Joanna would have been to Jesus for saving her child from death. Certainly a person so impacted would want to use her fortune to make sure others could receive the same touch of God.

The Bible doesn't tell us how Joanna made her first connection with Jesus, but it apparently changed her life. After that encounter, she began to give of her personal substance to financially support Jesus' ministry so that others could experience a life-changing encounter. Joanna was also with Mary Magdalene and the other women who visited and discovered the empty tomb after Jesus' resurrection (*see* Luke 24:10), which lets us know that she was faithful to Jesus to the very end.

After Joanna, this passage mentions Susanna, and this is the only reference to Susanna in the New Testament. We know nothing more of her except that she ministered to Jesus out of her resources. This implies that she was another woman who used her personal money to support Jesus' ministry.

In Luke 8:3, Susanna is listed with "many others" who supported the ministry of Jesus. The word "many" in Greek speaks of *a great quantity*. So in addition to these women Luke specifically names, there were also *many* others who supported Jesus faithfully with their personal finances. These were givers who considered it their responsibility, their service, and their assignment to make sure the needs of Jesus' growing ministry were financially supplied.

We rightly focus on Jesus and the great works He did while on earth. But think of the reward that is laid up in Heaven for Mary Magdalene, Joanna, Susanna, and all the others who gave of their substance so that those life-changing meetings could take place! Today these individuals are experiencing rich rewards because they gave of their personal income to help advance the earthly ministry of Jesus. They were His ministry partners — and in Heaven, they will share in the rewards for the results reaped in Jesus' ministry.

When God calls you to be a ministry partner, never forget that what you do is vitally important. The gifts you give from your personal income and assets can make an eternal difference in other people's lives. Please don't let it bother you if your name is never put on a building or if people never know that you were a big giver to a ministry. Instead, rejoice that you are among the "many others" who gave to Jesus' ministry, but were not mentioned by name. Most importantly, never forget that *Jesus* knows who you are and what you have done and that an eternal reward is awaiting you!

The names of pastors, churches, individuals, businesses, and organizations that are our partners are too many to list in a chapter, but I want you to know that they have formed the foundation for the Gospel advancements you have read about in this book.

In the following pages, I wish to share a few stories of how God used partners to help us continue moving forward by faith to fulfill God's plan, purpose, and design for RENNER Ministries. For each person we do list in the pages that follow — and for the thousands of others who are not discussed — Denise and I, our sons, and our team, are eternally *thankful*.

In addition to these partners' stories, I want to additionally share a few miraculous stories of how God took what we had in our own hands and multiplied it to become exactly what we needed it to be.

### A Precious Partner Who Gave One Dollar Every Week

When Denise and I were just getting started in the teaching ministry in the fall of 1985, we held our first public church meeting in Booneville, Arkansas, and many people were healed and others were strengthened by the teaching of the Word. At that time, we only had a handful of people who expressed an interest in supporting us financially.

Several weeks after that meeting, we received a letter in the mail from a man who had attended our meetings in Booneville and who was deeply touched by our ministry. His letter, in essence, said, "Your ministry deeply touched me when you were here. I've never been a partner with anyone before, but I want to become a partner with your ministry. I don't have a lot of spare money to give, but I promise that I'll be faithful to send one dollar every week to support what you are doing."

A one-dollar contribution may sound small, but it was huge to us because he was expressing his support of our work. And every week — on the same day of each week — his letter showed up in our mailbox with a check for one dollar. Denise and I were so thankful to God for him. We knew that his one dollar was a sacrificial gift. To write a check for one dollar, put it into the envelope, write our address on it, pay for the stamp, and always make sure it was mailed on time spoke volumes to us. That man's weekly letter and his faithfulness to keep his word was a huge source of encouragement to us as we were getting started.

I told you in Chapter One that as a young boy I was impacted by my Grandmother Bagley's sacrificial giving to Oral Roberts' ministry. Oh, I can still see her slipping a one-dollar bill into an envelope and holding it next to her heart as she prayed over it!

To others' eyes, my grandmother's gift may have looked small, but for her, it was a very sacrificial gift, as her resources were very small. So every week, when that man's weekly envelope appeared at our ministry from Booneville, I knew his giving was in that same sacrificial category.

That man's weekly one-dollar gift is so etched into my mind that I still know his name even though this occurred many years ago, and I still pray for him. That precious man, like many others, did his best to obey God, and it brought tremendous encouragement to a young Rick and Denise Renner who were just getting started in a new phase of ministry. That one dollar meant so much more than money to us. It was God's voice booming that He was with us and that He would raise up people to help us along the way!

## A Stranger on a Plane

On my first trip to the USSR in late April of 1991, my traveling companions and I were on an airplane flying from Riga to Moscow for my first experience in Russia's capital city. I was seated next to Dave Duell and Duane Vander Klok, the two friends who had "conned" me into going on that trip — a trip, as you know, that radically altered the course of my life and set us on a new trajectory.

As we flew to Moscow, Dave and I realized we were both out of money and the trip was only half over. As we sat in our seats talking, we both wondered how we would make it through the rest of the trip with no cash!

But soon our conversation switched to all the things we had seen and experienced in Jelgava that week. We recounted the miracles we had seen — the dangerously packed auditorium in Dobele, near Jelgava, where God did so many miraculous things right in front of us — and about what a great honor it was to minister to those brave students who had come from all over the USSR to study in the first aboveground Bible school since the Bolshevik Revolution. We got so lost recounting the goodness of God that we both forgot about our financial need.

Suddenly, an American man seated in the row in front of us turned around and said, "Forgive me, but I've been eavesdropping on your conversation. I'm amazed at what you guys saw God do. This is the USSR, and this is not supposed to happen here!"

We were taken aback that he had heard every word of our conversation, but then we heard him say, "I'm a backslidden Christian. I'm not living for God. But as I'm hearing what you guys are saying, I just want to be a part of it." Then he reached between the airplane seats to hand us five one-hundred-dollar bills. He said, "Please, take this as my gift and pray for me that I'll get my life back on track with God."

*"Amazing"* is the only word I could think of to describe that moment. Only about a half hour earlier, we were wondering how we'd exist that week in Moscow with no cash, but God touched the heart of a backslidden believer who had eavesdropped on our conversation — and through that brother, God supplied our need.

But that's not the end of the story.

We took the man's hand and prayed for him as he requested. Then as the flight continued, Dave and I continued sharing between ourselves more of the miraculous events we had seen that week and how unthinkable it was that God was working so mightily and miraculously in the USSR. All of a sudden, the same man in the row in front of us turned around again and said, "Hey guys, I'm still listening intently to your every word, and I just can't hold myself back any longer — I have to give you more money to help you with your ministry." And with that, he reached between the seats again to give us five more one-hundred-dollar bills!

When we boarded that airplane, we didn't have any cash for our expenses in Moscow that week — we didn't know how we'd pay for the hotel or food. But by the time we disembarked at Sheremetyevo Airport, we had $1,000, more than enough to cover all our expenses that week.

After that stranger gave us cash for our trip, I told my traveling companions, "I feel like Elijah when he was fed by ravens at the brook." That miraculous story of divine provision is recorded in First Kings 17:4-6. The Bible says God told Elijah, "And it shall be, that thou shalt drink of the brook; *and I have commanded the ravens to feed thee there.* So he went and did according unto the word of the Lord: for he went and dwelt by the brook Cherith, that is before Jordan. *And the ravens brought him bread and flesh in the morning, and bread and flesh in the evening....* "

I do not remember the name of the backslidden brother who handed us the cash that day, but I've never forgotten what he did and the timing of when it occurred. We literally didn't know how we would get by that week with no cash, but God "commanded" that brother to give us what we needed, just as God commanded the ravens to feed Elijah. We were completely sustained by this miraculous provision.

Actually, that exact juncture as we flew into Moscow was such a milestone in my life that I've reflected on *many* times. Over the years since that time when I didn't know where funds would come from to do what God was asking us to undertake, I went to that memory and recalled how God proved He would take care of us even when we had no idea where the money was going to come from. I learned that God was so committed to getting us the resources we needed to do the job that, if necessary, he would send ravens — or even a backslidden brother in Christ — to sustain us!

### A Gift That Encouraged Us To Move Ahead

When I planned to take Denise to Latvia for the first time in October 1991 to rent our first house, we didn't have funds to do everything we needed to do once we got there. We wanted to rent a house in preparation for our family's arrival and we also needed to purchase a car for our family that would be ready for us when we arrived on January 28, 1992, just a few months later. We had only enough cash to rent a house, and we had no clue where we'd get the cash to purchase a car. Getting a car would be difficult since there was a deficit of cars and waiting lists were long. And we knew that getting one would be expensive.

Also, going there for two weeks meant we'd be doing no meetings back in the U.S., which would result in a loss of income, and the trip itself was expensive. So where were we going to get the cash to purchase a car for our family?

In the week before Denise and I departed from Tulsa to Jelgava, I got a phone call from a brother in Christ whom Denise and I had known since our years as students at the university. He and his wife had been partners for years and had supported several projects, including helping pay for the first printing of my first published book called, *Seducing Spirits and Doctrines of Demons*. He said, "Rick, I hear you need to buy a car when you get to the USSR this week. I figured you could use some help, so my wife and I and another married couple have put together $5,000 so you'll have money to purchase a vehicle."

I'm sure he and his wife and that other married couple had no idea how powerful that act of generosity was in our lives. Again, it showed us that God was with us every step of the way — so involved in every step we were taking that He wanted to make sure we had the money to purchase a car for our family. It was a very sacrificial gift for those families to give at that time, but the impact was far greater than money. It was a Heaven-sent message that God was going to supply *all* our needs as we obeyed Him and moved our family to the lands of the former Soviet Union. It was a huge, life-altering step that we were about to take, but we were off to a good start, *confident* that God was with us as our lives were about to change so dramatically. And that confidence was really all we needed — that He was with us comforted us so much and meant *everything*.

On that first trip with Denise to Latvia, we rented our first house, which for me officially marks the date when we began our move to that part of the world. Then we went to the Rumbula car market to choose a car for our family. Rumbula was the site where Riga's Jewish community was executed in 1941 by German soldiers as a part of the Latvian holocaust. On November 30 and December 8 in 1941, the Jewish community was marched there to be shot and buried in mass burial pits.

But during the years that Latvia was incorporated into the USSR, a military airstrip had been constructed in that area. Now, as we were arriving, the airfield was abandoned and had been turned into a "black market" where cars could be purchased immediately rather than having to wait months and even years to try to receive one from a manufacturer.

Because the socialist-communist system was bottlenecked in terms of producing and providing products, it could normally take years to get a car even if you paid cash for it up front. But while systems were being formulated to transition to the new economy, and capitalism was trying to take root, it was possible to instantly purchase a car at this large Rumbula market. The choices were pretty sad, and there were only Soviet-made cars. Back in those days, there was hardly a foreign-made car on the streets. So since we only had the choice to purchase a Soviet-made car, we decided on a cherry-colored Lada for exactly the equivalent of the $5,000 that had been given for that purpose.

Before I left Latvia on that first trip with Denise in October 1991 — three months before the dissolution of the USSR on December 8, 1991 — we had successfully rented our first house and purchased a car for our family and ministry. We didn't know when we said yes to God how we were going to pay for any of it, but God knew what to do. He touched the hearts of two married couples who wanted to use their finances to do something eternal — and their combined gifts were exactly what we needed to purchase our first automobile in the former USSR.

God had used the man from Booneville, a backslidden brother on an airplane, and now those married couples to give us the message loud and clear that He was going to bless our obedience to follow Him to the ends of the earth. He let us know that he was going to amply provide everything we needed to do the job — *and* that He would always do it on time.

## A Miracle of 'Double' Right Before Our Eyes

The following is a true story about a miraculous provision of cash that our entire family witnessed in the spring of 1992. It is definitely "one for the books" in terms of a testimony of God's power to bless — and His *commitment* to do so — when you're following His plans and purposes with a willing heart.

When we arrived in Latvia on January 28, 1992, we moved with a very small amount of U.S. dollars to live on in the following months. At that time, a little money went a long way in that part of the world because of the collapsed economic system and almost laughable low costs of food products — that is, *when* we could find food products to purchase. So when we arrived, besides the money we gave that contractor to build our home, we came with about $1,000 in cash, which at that time was enough for our family of five, plus our nanny, to live on for about five months. There were no banks in those days where a person could go to make any kind of a cash withdrawal, so whatever we brought with us when we arrived was all we had and there was no ability to get more. So, in essence, our family was living on approximately $200 a month in those earliest months after our arrival in 1992.

After about four months, it was time for me to make my first trip back to the United States to speak in a series of churches and to give a report of what we were seeing God do in the lands of the former USSR. Because overseas travel was so difficult and expensive, Denise and the boys would remain in Jelgava while I went for this month-long ministry trip to the United States.

The night before my plane was to depart, I looked to see where our family was on our cash reserves, and I discovered that all we had left from our original stash was a one-hundred-dollar bill. My trip would be for a full month, so I knew this $100 would only be enough for about two weeks before my family would be out of cash in my absence.

As I prepared to leave that night, I called our family together to pray for my trip and also so I could pray the safety provisions of Psalm 91 over each of them. As a part of our prayer time, I expressed that I was concerned about leaving them for a full month with only a one-hundred-dollar bill. The boys excitedly asked if they could look at the large bill, so I pulled it out and handed it to them to see.

One by one our sons — Paul, eight; Philip, six; and Joel, three — took that hundred-dollar bill in each of their hands and examined it because they thought it was really big money and they wanted a closer look. They pulled it this way and that way and looked at it from every angle. I thought they would tear it to pieces as they handed it to each other, so finally I said, "Hey, that's enough. We only have one, so please don't tear it."

When I took it back, I said, "Let's lay hands on this bill and ask God to make it stretch to cover a full month of expenses. Normally we need $200, but I'm leaving you with only this single bill for a full month, and we really need the Lord to help make it stretch as far as possible to cover everything until I get back with more cash."

As a family, we prayed over my trip. I prayed for God's protection over each of them, and then all five of us pinched with our fingers a tiny part of that hundred-dollar bill so that we were all "laying hands" on it as we prayed for God to stretch it.

I prayed something like this, "Father, I am asking You to watch over my family while I am gone for this month. This $100 isn't enough to cover all their needs, so I am asking You to stretch this money and make it be enough until I get back with more cash."

When we finished praying, I handed the bill to Denise and said, "Denise, I know it's only enough for about two weeks, but we're believing that God will make it be enough for a full month."

As Denise took that one-hundred-dollar bill into her hand, suddenly a *second* one-hundred-dollar bill fell onto the ground. All five of us saw it — we were *astonished* as we watched that single hundred-dollar bill multiply right in front of our eyes into *two* hundred-dollar bills!

Well, we had prayed for God to stretch it, and God certainly did stretch it — right in front of us, *that instant*. That money multiplied to meet our exact needs, as we had prayed. It wasn't a mountain of money, but it was exactly what we needed, and it was indeed a miracle.

Someone may argue, "Well, there were probably two bills stuck together the whole time and you just didn't know it." That was emphatically *not* the case. As a husband and father concerned about his family's welfare in his absence, I guarantee you that I had examined that bill because I was so concerned about leaving Denise and the boys on such a tight budget. After I'd handled the bill, our sons had pulled it this way and that — it had definitely not been two bills stuck together. God had simply, *literally*, stretched the one bill — miraculously making it *two* — to exactly meet our need as we had asked Him to do. And I believe He did it the way He did so that all five of us could experience *together* His goodness in the manifestation of that miracle.

In John 6:11, we read the story of a boy who gave two small fish and five barley crackers to Jesus when a crowd of thousands needed to be fed.

Naturally speaking, those fish and crackers were so tiny in comparison to the crowd. Even thinking that small fare would be enough seemed silly. But when those tiny fish and barley crackers were placed in Jesus' hands, a miracle took place as He multiplied them to feed thousands that day.

When I think of that day when all five of us watched a one-hundred-dollar bill miraculously turn into *two* one-hundred-dollar bills, my mind goes to this story of Jesus, who is decidedly, undisputedly, the Lord of miraculous multiplication! Since He is the same yesterday, today, and forever (*see* Hebrew 13:8), why would we be surprised that He still has the miraculous power to multiply even meager amounts that we entrust to His hands.

### 'According to Your Faith'

In Matthew 9, we read that two blind men came to Jesus to ask Him to restore their eyesight. In verse 29, Jesus responded to their faith by telling them, "According to your faith be it unto you." In essence, Jesus told them they would receive *exactly* what they *believed* — thus, the two blind men received sight that day, according to their faith.

As I think back to our miraculous experience, I can see that we *exactly* prayed for God to somehow make that $100 have the buying power of $200 for the duration of my trip. And God did *exactly* what we believed.

I have often wondered, *What would have happened if we had believed for that $100 to have the buying power of $500?* Think of it — since God could make $100 miraculously become $200, couldn't He also make it become *more?* But our faith that day was for that $100 to have the buying power of $200, and we got exactly what we *believed.*

Never underestimate the power of your faith! And make sure you are thinking and believing correctly — because what you believe is *exactly* what you will receive!

Over the years when it seemed our reserves were not enough to do whatever God was asking us to tackle, I have often recalled that day in Jelgava when we witnessed the miracle multiplication of money. That event made an indelible impression on Denise and me and our three small boys — and each of us carries that amazing moment in our memories. But it also made me realize that when we have a need and ask God to do the minimum to meet it, maybe we need to take our faith up several notches to believe for bigger provision.

We were so thankful for what we saw God do that day, but we got exactly what we believed. So I feel I need to ask you — are you sure you're asking God for enough for your life? Jesus taught that we receive according to what we believe, so make sure you are believing for enough when you pray.

## Living and Giving for Eternity

As I've said, when God's call came to us years ago, He was similarly calling *others* who would become partners to support the work He was entrusting us to fulfill. Every person's role is essential in the Kingdom of God, and that is why when we all stand before Jesus, we will each receive our reward based on how well we did with the part that was entrusted to us.

But one of the greatest honors God ever gave Denise and me was when He sent Wally and June Blume as friends and partners into our lives. They have stood by us, believed with us, believed *in* us, and have truly been God-sent "cheerleaders" to encourage us to keep forging ahead in obedience by faith. In so many ways, they are family to us. The call on our lives and the call on their lives have been intertwined, and for that reason, I want to share with you in this section about *Wally and June Blume.* It would be impossible to overstate the important role this precious family has played in our ministry and our lives. Over the years, they have become enormously cherished friends and partners in the Gospel.

In 1988, I was invited to speak at a church in Michigan for several days, and the meetings were quite wonderful. In those days, I poured the Word of God into that congregation regularly, and the Holy Spirit moved marvelously in people's hearts. That was the beginning of a long-term relationship with that church that has lasted for many decades.

In those 1988 meetings was a couple named Wally and June Blume who attended along with their young son Jon. That week during the meetings, June told Wally, "I really feel that God wants us to be partners with this ministry. We don't have the excess funds to do it right now, but I believe God is going to help us find a way to start supporting Rick Renner Ministries every month with a gift of $25. It will be a challenge for us, but I believe we're supposed to do it."

Of course, Wally agreed and, in obedience to the Spirit's prompting, Wally and June began to send monthly offerings to our ministry, and they increased them from time to time as the Lord enabled them. My mother headed up our Partner Care ministry in those days, so she regularly called Wally and June to keep them updated about all the exciting things that were happening in our ministry in the former USSR. The Blume family came so on board with us as partners that even Wally's elderly mother became a partner with our ministry!

But God was working in ways none of us understood when this partnership relationship with the Blume family first began. God was supernaturally connecting *our hearts* and *their hearts* to become lifelong friends and partners in a Gospel adventure that has strengthened believers and reaped a massive harvest of souls for the Kingdom of God worldwide.

When Wally and June Blume first became partners with our ministry, they were professionals in the dairy industry. God saw their faithfulness in many different realms, and as God always does when He finds faithful people, He blessed them and eventually enabled them to become owners of their own company called Denali Flavors, an enterprise that over time became one of the nation's leading developers and marketers of innovative flavors for the ice-cream industry — including a marvelous chocolate-fudge flavor called *Moose Tracks*.

If you've never tasted Moose Tracks-flavored ice cream, I advise you to find out where it is sold and buy some of it because it's unlike any ice cream you've ever tasted! With every scoop, you'll savor a mind-blowing blend of ice cream filled with delicious hidden treasures that will *stun* your taste buds. It's a delectable combination of vanilla ice cream, and melt-in-your-mouth peanut-butter cups, mingled with famous Moose Tracks Fudge. *Whew* — it is just wonderful.

This one flavor became *so* wonderful, in fact, that it "morphed" into a national brand, with numerous iterations by other brands, and has become an iconic flavor in the world of ice cream. This flavor is top-selling in the national market. If you've ever tasted any variation of the original Moose Tracks, you know yourself why it has become one of the biggest-selling ice-cream flavors in the United States.

But before all those business developments occurred, when we were ministering at their home church in Michigan years ago, the Blumes had asked to meet with Denise and me so we could pray with them about an "idea" they had, which eventually became Denali Flavors. We prayed with them sincerely with a heart of faith in God's desire to bless and increase these precious partners — and *all* our partners — as they participated with the plan of God for their lives. Little did we know what God would bring forth from the idea He had planted deep within Wally and June that they then faithfully engaged in cooperation with Him.

But what is most important about Wally and June Blume is their love for Jesus Christ and their passionate desire to see the Gospel go into all the world. Over the years, Wally and June not only became significant partners with our ministry, but on a personal level, they also became significant friends to Denise and me. The four of us have traveled the world together to participate in various ministry outreaches. And though they live on a different continent, we see their "touch" everywhere we look in our ministry in this part of the world, and it feels as if they are spiritually with us all the time.

I have met many people who claim to have the supernatural gift of giving that the apostle Paul refers to in Romans 12:8. In that verse, Paul writes that when a person is gifted with the gift of giving, he feels compelled with all his heart to give because *that* is his assignment in the Kingdom of God. And this powerful gift amazingly enables the Gospel to move forward at a faster speed to reach more people. It causes funds to be released into the work of the Gospel to drive back darkness and to bring the transforming power of the Holy Spirit into people's lives. Denise and I have personally witnessed the multiple facets of this grace-given gift shine brilliantly in Wally and June Blume. It has been a "wonder" to watch how they have stewarded this divine grace that operates in their lives.

A large photo of the Blume family hangs on the wall in the Moscow church building in a room lovingly called "The Blume Room" in honor of their partnership. Their names are engraved alongside ours on two bronze plaques (one in English and one in Russian) that every person sees who enters our Moscow church building. On those plaques, we acknowledge that God used every partner, every church member, and the Blume family to help us build the permanent home for the Moscow Good News Church.

One day when Denise and I and Wally and June are in Heaven, those bronze plaques will still be hanging permanently on that wall to remind future generations that there was a precious couple named Wally and June Blume who sacrificially gave for the Gospel and for that house of worship to be constructed. All the glory goes to Jesus, as they would tell you themselves, but we are thankful that He used the Blume family to help us do what He put in our hearts to do for His Kingdom. They are among the most eternity-minded people I've ever met in my life, and we are thankful for their willingness and obedience to let the grace of giving work so mightily in them.

For all the years we've known the Blume family, they have shared what God has put in their hands to advance the Gospel. Regardless of the challenges they've faced in their own walk of faith, they have been yielded vessels that God has used, and *millions* of lives have been impacted by the Good News of the Gospel as a result of their giving.

I can't do justice to the eternal significance their giving has made. But one day in eternity, the enormity of what they have done will be revealed as Jesus gives them a magnificent soul-winner's crown. Denise and I cherish their friendship, partnership, and love — and we respect the godly example they are to us and to millions who have been impacted by the fruit of their lives.

## The Epitome of Partnership

On my first trip to the United States after moving to the former USSR, I stopped in New York City to speak at a small church filled with long-time friends that I dearly loved. It wasn't a large church, and some may have argued that I could have used my time more wisely to speak at a larger church somewhere else. But I felt strongly impressed that God was going to do something *very special* in the meeting that night and that I *had* to be there.

That mid-week service was held on an "off night," and the attendance was relatively small. Instead of teaching as I would normally do, the pastor asked me to testify about what we were seeing God do in the lands of the former Soviet Union in the short time we had been there. I was excited about what God was doing and enthusiastically shared the amazing things we were seeing. I testified that it felt like our family had stepped into the book of Acts — we were witnessing salvations and dramatic healings and miracles. Then I began to tell the remarkable story of how God had opened the door for us to go on television.

When that meeting was over, I was a bit perplexed about *why* I had felt so strongly impressed to stop in New York City to speak at that church. If God wanted to do something special in that meeting, I didn't know what it was because it seemed nothing extra special transpired that night. When I boarded my plane the next morning to fly to Tulsa, the nagging question inside was *why* the Holy Spirit impressed me that it was so important to be at that meeting in New York City.

Eventually I returned to Latvia to rejoin Denise and our sons. Later we scheduled another trip to the United States to minister, but this time my entire family would join me. As we prepared to go to America for that ministry trip, I received a phone call from Delaine Neece, Kenneth and Gloria Copeland's secretary at the time, from the headquarters of Kenneth Copeland Ministries just outside of Fort Worth, Texas.

Denise and I had always had a deep respect for Kenneth and Gloria Copeland. In Chapter Five, I told you that Denise came across Kenneth Copeland's radio program when she was living in Houston and singing for the Houston Grand Opera. She had been afflicted with cystic acne for years and never knew she could be healed. But as Denise listened to Brother Copeland day after day, faith began to rise in her heart for her healing.

She eventually received a dramatic miracle, but it actually began when she heard Brother Copeland declare that she was healed by the stripes of Jesus (*see* Isaiah 53:5; Matthew 8:17; 1 Peter 2:24).

Brother Copeland had also been a participant in Kenneth E. Hagin's Campmeeting in July 1974 in Tulsa, where I had received a dramatic physical miracle. My point is that Denise and I were both deeply grateful to Kenneth and Gloria Copeland for how their ministry had impacted us personally. They were an impressive couple to us — role models in the ministry and in their lives of faith in Christ and His Word.

But now I heard their secretary say, "Rick, Kenneth and Gloria want to personally meet you here at the ministry headquarters. Can you and Denise come here to meet with them? They would like to ask you to speak at our staff chapel service. They'd like you to share what you are seeing God do in the former USSR and then have lunch with them for a private conversation." Surprised at her request, I said, "I'm honored that they would want us to come to meet with them, but since we've never had any personal contact with Kenneth and Gloria before — how did they find out about us?"

Delaine's answer took me back to that meeting in New York City. I was about to find out *why* the Holy Spirit had impressed me to do that service there months earlier.

She answered, "A few months ago, you spoke at a church in New York. In that meeting, you shared your testimony about what you were experiencing in the former USSR. That night, one of our partners was in the meeting, and she was so moved by your testimony that she purchased the cassette tape of the service and sent it to our ministry. When the cassette tape arrived at our headquarters, it ended up on the desk of Mary Neece (Gloria's mother). Mary listened to the audiotape and felt Gloria would want to hear it. She passed the audiotape to Gloria, and when Gloria heard your testimony, she felt impressed that she and Kenneth needed to personally meet you and talk to you."

I remember thinking, *Wow. It is amazing in a ministry that huge that the leadership actually took the time to listen to an audiotape sent to them by a partner.* That remarkable attention to partners was my first personal impression of Kenneth and Gloria Copeland. But over many years since, I have seen over and over that Kenneth and Gloria are very in touch with those who support their ministry. That is one of the greatest hallmarks of their ministry.

But that day, I was also reminded that when the Holy Spirit leads us to do something, we must obey Him even if we don't understand His leading. I didn't know why the Holy Spirit wanted me to be in that church in New York City, but I knew He impressed upon me that something special would happen in that meeting. Now I understood He wanted me to be there because that partner would purchase the audiotape of the meeting and send it to Kenneth Copeland Ministries — and that it would make its way to Kenneth and Gloria. It is a profoundly amazing, mind-blowing thought to me that just one evening in New York City arranged by God would bring about a divine connection that would lead to a supernatural partnership to affect millions of lives over the coming years.

The Holy Spirit *knows* how to make God's plan for your life succeed if you will listen to Him and follow Him every step of the way concerning that plan!

Denise and I flew to Fort Worth to meet with Kenneth and Gloria Copeland. The first person to greet us was Barry Tubbs, a long-time associate of Kenneth Copeland. Barry led Denise and me to the speakers' room where we waited for the staff chapel service to begin.

Soon the door opened and in walked George and Terri Pearsons, who introduced themselves to us. George had been the Executive Director of Kenneth Copeland Ministries, but had recently become pastor of Eagle Mountain International Church. Terri, Kenneth's oldest daughter, had been the first TV producer for *Believer's Voice of Victory*. Now George and Terri were leading the church, but in that divine moment, God was connecting us to them as some of the dearest friends we've ever had in our lives.

Finally, Kenneth and Gloria arrived in the speakers' quarters, and our connection with them was instant. Denise and I were taken back by their humility and the way they welcomed us warmly as if we were already long-time friends.

At chapel that day, Denise sang and I shared what God was doing in the lands of the former USSR with a special emphasis on the remarkable doors that were swinging open for the teaching of the Bible on television. When chapel ended, Gloria asked Denise and me to join her for lunch in the ministry headquarters with George and Terri Pearsons, John Copeland, Kellie Copeland, and Jan Harbor, Gloria's sister. We talked and talked, and Gloria and the others wanted to hear every nitty-gritty detail about life in the former USSR and about our expanding TV work there.

Then Gloria said, "Well, we are so excited about what you're doing that we want our ministry to be your partners." With that, she pulled an envelope out of her Bible and handed it to us, and in it was a sizeable check made out to our ministry. Gloria said, "We are serious about partnership, and you can count on us to be behind you. We've been praying for years for God to work in the USSR, now He's doing it, and we're not going to miss an opportunity to be a part of it. We'll be sending this to you every month as a part of our getting behind what you're doing there."

Denise and I thanked her — shocked, almost not knowing how to respond because we were so overwhelmed by the gift they gave, as well as by the fact that they *really wanted* to be partners with our work.

Then Gloria added, "I have a few more things I'd like to ask you, but I want to ask Kenneth to join us, so let's go upstairs to his office to continue our talk." In a matter of minutes, we were seated on a sofa in Kenneth's office in the executive suite with him and Gloria seated across the table from us. That is when Gloria said, "Rick, it has been my dream for years to be on TV in the USSR. I've prayed and prayed for it to come to pass. Do you think there is anything you could do to help us get on television over there? I'm convinced our message would change people's lives, but we don't know how to do it. Could you help us?"

I heard myself answer, "Of course we'll help you. When we negotiate for our own TV programs to go on TV in stations all over that part of the world, we'll negotiate for *Believer's Voice of Victory* too. You can absolutely count on us to help you."

When I really *heard* what I'd just said, I shocked myself, because we were just learning how to get on TV ourselves in a land where no one had ever done it before — and now I had committed to get *Believer's Voice of Victory* on the air along with our programs. In that unexpected conversation in which I'd agreed to help them, God was giving me the supernatural courage to not only broadcast our own programs, but to start the first TV network in the former USSR that would carry our programs and the programs of other faith-based Bible teachers. That network, which functions today in that very capacity, broadcasts the messages of *many* U.S. ministers of the Gospel into the lands and the languages of the former Soviet Union.

But it all started right there, in that moment in Kenneth's office with a question from Gloria. The result was the creation of our own TV network on this side of the world.

That night, Pastors George and Terri asked Denise and me to minister in their Wednesday-night service. They had so recently taken the helm of the church that Denise and I were their first guest ministers for a Wednesday-night service since they'd become senior pastors. Kenneth and Gloria were right there on the front row in that meeting. Then after the meeting, Brother Copeland asked to fly Denise and me back to Tulsa in the ministry airplane so he could have more time with us. We were deeply touched by his kindness and marveled at his hunger for the things of God.

As we flew to Tulsa, Brother Copeland asked Denise all about her professional training as a singer and what she dreamed to do with it. Denise expressed her desire to record a new album and also let him know how much she loved the orchestration on his album called the *London Praise Collection*. Brother Copeland said, "Denise, I'll give you all the tracks from that album for you to use in any way you need. In fact, you can use them in your own recording." The open-heartedness of Kenneth and Gloria we experienced on that day was only a foretaste of the generosity they would show us and our ministry over many years that followed.

In the years since that time, Kenneth and Gloria — along with their children, grandchildren, and many of their team members — have become some of the dearest friends God has ever placed in our lives. We simply have no suitable words to communicate how much we love the Copeland family and their ministry. They received us like family, and our relationship with them all these years has been precious.

Kenneth and Gloria and Kenneth Copeland Ministries have been faithful partners of this ministry, and it has been our honor and joy to work hand-in-hand with them to get *Believer's Voice of Victory* to the Russian-speaking world. As a result of this divine connection, Russian-speaking believers have been *transformed* as they have received the ministry of Kenneth and Gloria by television and by way of their printed materials published in their own native languages. The impact of what has transpired simply cannot be exaggerated. This divine connection has affected millions and millions of lives.

Gloria really meant it when she said, "We are serious about partnership, and you can count on us to be behind you." They became *partners with us*, and we became *partners with them* on that day in 1993. Ever since that time, *Believer's Voice of Victory* has reached into homes of Russian-speakers without interruption and lives have been healed, restored, and radically changed as a result of their faith-filled message that upholds the honor of God's Word.

Their enormous financial contributions to our ministry have helped us do what God called us to do, but equally as important to Denise and me has been the personal support, friendship, and relationship that Kenneth and Gloria and their family have with us. Our relationship with them means more than we'll ever know how to express. As a result of this divine connection, the Kingdom of God has advanced and countless multitudes have been affected to move forward in their own callings and destinies.

On that surprise visit to the Copeland headquarters in 1993, God supernaturally connected us to the Copelands and their family. It is a God-given relationship — and Kenneth and Gloria and their ministry *personify* what it means to be a real partner!

### Committed To Taking the Gospel Around the World

In 1996, on another trip to America, Denise and I returned to our hotel room after ministering in a church one night, and I saw that the light was blinking on our phone. I called the front desk to see if there was a message waiting for us. The receptionist said, "Yes, someone named Dave Meyer from Joyce Meyer Ministries called while you were out and said he needs to speak to you." She then gave me the phone number I needed to return his call.

My first knowledge of Joyce Meyer Ministries came years before we moved to the former USSR. Back in those days, I had a growing daily radio program that was called *Power in the Word*. At the same time, Joyce Meyer had a daily radio program called *Life in the Word*. Not only were the names of our programs very similar, our "1-800" phone numbers were identical with the exception of one digit, and in many of the fifty-plus cities where my radio program was being aired, we were on the air either *right before* or *right after* Joyce.

As a result of similar program names and similar phone numbers, our Tulsa office frequently got phone calls from people who were trying to reach Joyce's ministry, so we would give them the right number so they could reach Joyce Meyer Ministries. Yet we'd never had an occasion to meet the Meyers personally. So when the receptionist said that I needed to call Dave, I wondered, *Why would Dave Meyer be trying to reach me?*

I dialed the number, and when Dave answered, I introduced myself, and he said, in summary, "Thanks for calling me back. Joyce and I really want to meet with you two. We've heard all about what you're doing in the USSR."

I asked, "How have you heard about what we are doing?" He answered, "A pastor of a large church who is your partner told us that if we ever wanted to get behind someone who is doing a great work, we should consider getting behind you. So Joyce and I have talked about it, and we want to know if you and Denise can fly to St. Louis to meet us for lunch."

About two weeks later, Denise and I boarded our flight to St. Louis, where we were to have lunch with Dave and Joyce Meyer. A member of their staff graciously met us at the airport and drove us to their ministry offices in Fenton, Missouri. We felt so honored that they wanted to have lunch with us. When we arrived at their offices, Dave and Joyce warmly welcomed us and showed us around their ministry. Afterward, we joined them in their car to drive to a nearby restaurant.

During lunch, Joyce looked across the table and said, "I'm sure you're wondering why we wanted to talk to you. We've heard a lot about what you guys are doing in the former USSR. It is amazing to me that you were bold enough to move your family there in the middle of all the crisis that was happening." Dave and Joyce expressed their thanks for what our family and ministry were doing.

Then Joyce said, "We've made a decision that we want to become partners with your ministry. You need to know that we are very serious about the people we support, and we do research about them before we become partners. We've done our due diligence to find out as much as we could about you before meeting with you today. We've talked to people who know you well, and we even did a credit check to see if you are stable with your finances. After all our research, we found that you are real examples in your relationships with people, and as far as we can tell, you are very good at handling ministry money. So today we and our ministry are becoming your partners."

Joyce reached across the table to hand us an envelope with a large check in it that was written out to our ministry. Denise and I were speechless. Then we heard Joyce add, "You can count on us to send this amount to your ministry every month. When we join someone as a financial partner, we are very serious about it. So when we say we want to be your partner, we really mean we want to *partner* with you and your ministry."

Then I heard Joyce say, "I don't know if it's possible, but if there is any way you can get us on television in the former Soviet Union, we'd like to go on the air there. I know there are a lot of broken people in that part of the world, and I believe my message would help them. If there is anything you can do to help us, please consider helping us get on television there."

Once again, as I'd said to Gloria Copeland, I "heard" myself answer, "I'd love to help you get your program on television all over the lands of the former Soviet Union."

As we all held that check and prayed over it together with Dave and Joyce, Denise told Joyce, "God has used your teaching to deeply impact me over the years. I'm overwhelmed with joy to think that God loves the precious Russian-speaking people so much that He would use Rick and me to bring your TV program to them." Joyce teared up and said, "It is amazing to think that God would use my teaching to touch anyone."

Dave and Joyce's request to go on the air in the former USSR was especially huge because they had never done a foreign broadcast up to that time. This meant they were asking us to help them do something they had never done before. Well, I understood something about stepping out into unknown territory for the advancement of the Gospel! We were doing it ourselves, and I could appreciate their willingness to step out beyond their comfort zone to fulfill God's dreams that He had placed in their hearts.

Today Joyce's TV program is aired around the world *in more than a hundred languages*, but all of those foreign-language broadcasts began at lunch that day when Joyce Meyer Ministries became a partner with our ministry.

It is *amazing* how God knows so well how to create divine connections for the advancement of the Gospel, and that is what He did that day when we met for lunch with the Meyers. Dave and Joyce and Joyce Meyer Ministries became *partners with us* — and we became *partners with them* to get Joyce's teaching to people who desperately needed it.

Joyce was correct that the people of the former USSR were very broken in those days and needed her message. The Soviet Union suffered more casualties in World War II than any other Allied nation — more than twenty-six million. That part of the world lost so many men to death in the war that women literally had to step up as heads of households and do jobs in the workforce that men would ordinarily do. Those women became leaders in their homes as well, and the problems of fatherlessness, through no fault of the fathers, of course, caused problems for sons and daughters who were bereft of their dads.

Many of those young people turned aimlessly to alcohol for comfort. The effects of alcoholism on whole societies and nations was huge as those addictions transcended *generations*, affecting their children, their grandchildren, and so on. Drug-and-alcohol hospitals were doing their best to help, but were struggling to stay afloat — the same was true for the plethora of orphanages that sprang up to try to care for orphaned and abandoned children. And so much of this could be traced back to the war more than half a century earlier.

Joyce possessed such insight about the hurting condition of the people, and her compassion and teaching gift were perfect for those who were struggling desperately to repair their lives and preserve their posterity. Her insight was impressive and her burden to help was even more impressive. Those of us who have been rescued by God from the inexplicable, unfair tragedies of life know that there are no lasting, heart-reaching answers separate from God's Word and the love of Christ.

But how will people experience that knowledge and that love firsthand unless someone pays the price to deliver the Good News to them in a language they can understand? I'm talking about the ability to translate Bible messages into the languages of the world, but I'm also talking about the language of deeds of kindness that satisfy people's physical needs for food and shelter — something that is also close to the heart of Dave and Joyce and their family and team.

When we returned to the former USSR after that meeting with Dave and Joyce Meyer, I began to negotiate for TV time to put Joyce on television all over the former Soviet Union along with our program and the *Believer's Voice of Victory*. The Meyer team also needed an office to handle the mountains of mail that would be coming in response to Joyce's program. So not only did we negotiate for TV time for them, but for years, we have served as their office in the former USSR and have been responsible for responding to their TV viewers and for the translation and printing of Joyce's books in multiple languages across the former USSR.

At lunch that day in 1996, a real God-created partnership began that has lasted for decades and has resulted in millions of lives being changed by the power of God's Word.

We are so grateful for Dave and Joyce's support and for the opportunity to serve them all these years. And not only are we ministry partners, but they and their children became our very close friends whom we love so deeply on a personal level. This is another example of how God brings people together for the sake of His Kingdom. Together, by the power of the Holy Spirit, our ministry and their ministry have swung our sickle wide and have witnessed an ingathering of eternal fruit that has surpassed even our earnest expectation of harvest. And I must add that what both Joyce Meyer Ministries and Kenneth Copeland Ministries have done in partnership with our ministry, they have also done for many other ministries that are fulfilling Christ's Great Commission to "go" into all the world.

In the first moments we had with Kenneth and Gloria Copeland and in our first moments with Dave and Joyce Meyer, Denise and I experienced an unwrapping of God's divine plan to touch millions of people with the transformative power of God's Word — to radically affect their lives and give them a home in Heaven for all of eternity.

We also witnessed a warm unwrapping of the love of God toward our family and ministry because of the belief these ministries had in us. It was a "shot in the arm" and an encouragement that strengthened us to the core more than I can express. We are eternally grateful for these ministries that

God has raised up in the earth to undergird His people and to gather as many who will come to be a part of God's growing family before that last sickle is swung and Jesus returns for His Church.

Denise and I were, and are, in *awe* at God's supernatural ability to bring all the needed pieces together for the spreading of the Gospel. For me, it has been a demonstration of Romans 8:28, where Paul declares, "And we know that all things work together for good to them that love God, to them who are the called according to his purpose."

Likewise, when *you* step out to do what God has told *you* to do, you can be sure that God knows how to connect you with the right people at the right time in the right place. He will supernaturally establish divine connections between you and others who are assigned to help you fulfill His will for your life. Those God-called partners will be a blessing to you, and you will be a blessing to them!

### A Pastor Who Heard From God

When our ministry purchased our first large office facility in the city of Moscow, we had one year to pay off the entire building or it would revert to the hands of the seller. We had paid a very large deposit, and by faith, we were believing to completely pay off the balance on time so we wouldn't lose our total investment. Denise and I had agreed that in our ministry travels in the U.S., we would not mention the exact amount we needed, but would trust God completely to meet the need.

Finally, the deadline for paying the balance approached. The Moscow church and our ministry partners had given generously, but we lacked what we needed to finish retiring the debt on the building. It was exactly at this time that God spoke to Richard Mallette, a pastor of a church in the United States, and told him, "You have money in your church bank account right now, and Rick Renner and his ministry are believing for the finances to pay off their building. What good is your money in this account when they need it in Moscow? If you'll give what I tell you to give, I'll multiply it back to you more times than you can even begin to imagine." And then He told him the exact amount we still needed to pay on the building.

In obedience to the Lord, Pastor Mallette met with his Board of Directors, and they unanimously voted to give a gift to help cover the outstanding debt for our office building. They had no idea that this was the exact balance owed on the building. The pastor purchased a plane ticket and was soon on his way to Moscow. The following Sunday, he stood on the platform in our auditorium and said, "The Lord has sent me here to give you a check to hopefully cover the remaining costs for your new church facility!" Then he handed us the check, still not knowing that he was handing us the exact amount needed to completely pay off the balance on the building.

I shared this account in great detail in Chapter Thirteen. The Holy Spirit had spoken to this precious pastor as I was ministering in his church. But what words could ever be sufficient to express how grateful we were to this pastor and his church for this phenomenal act of generosity?

And how can we ever appropriately thank *all* the partners who sowed to get us to where we were on the building — *every dime and dollar counted!* The truth is, *we can never adequately thank enough* all those who have sown their finances for so many years into the work of our ministry. But God will never forget it, and He can multiply their seed sown to meet their needs abundantly so they can continue to sow into the Gospel "unto every good work" (2 Corinthians 9:8).

My wife and I, our sons, and our team may be the ones who are doing the actual work we've been called to do on the front lines of ministry, but we can only do that work because of the resources entrusted to us by faithful partners. When we all stand before Jesus to be rewarded for what we have done for Him in this life, our partners will be as richly rewarded as those of us who worked on the front lines, for they financially empowered us to do the job!

## A Widow Mightily Used By God

In First Corinthians 16:9, Paul wrote about a great and effectual door that had opened to him and his ministry. One such door opened to us in the early years of our TV ministry in the former USSR — it would be one of many over the course of our ministry. The door to broadcast our TV programs on the largest channel in the nation of Ukraine literally *swung* open for us — but it was going to be expensive to pay the bill each month. I didn't know how we were going to do it, but I knew in my heart we were supposed to sign the contract and walk through that open door.

After reviewing the contract one final time, I took a pen in hand, gulped a deep breath, and signed that piece of paper. It was a huge leap of faith for me, but I had the awesome inward witness that we were about to experience the supernatural provision of God in a measure we had never seen before. God was going to show Himself strong to us and provide every cent that was needed to broadcast on this massive TV channel. As a result, *every person in every home* in that nation where there was a television would be able to hear rock-solid Bible teaching *every day of the week*!

In my heart, I knew it was the moment to seize this incredible opportunity. So a few minutes after I'd been offered the contract, I signed my name on the dotted line, and national television in Ukraine fell into our hands! Our programs would now be broadcast into the homes of more than fifty million people each week — *but I didn't have any idea where the money would come from to pay for it.*

At the exact time I was signing that contract, a ministry partner — a widow who had faithfully given smaller offerings to our ministry for many years — received surprise information that she had received a large inheritance. She had always told the Lord, "If You'll trust me with money, I'll use it to finance the preaching of the Gospel." God heard her, knew she was serious, and did exactly what she prayed for. He supernaturally put a large sum of money into her hands. When she received that inheritance, she said, "Lord, I'm going to help Rick Renner preach the Gospel in the former Soviet Union!"

When we later looked at the calendar and compared the times on both sides of the world — we discovered that at the exact moment I was signing that contract, this woman was receiving the knock on her front door informing her of her inheritance. The timing was exactly synchronized! As I signed the contract, literally *simultaneously*, God was putting the money to pay for it into the hands of a widow who had made Him a promise.

Before the first payment was due for that massive TV outreach, we had all the finances we needed to pay the bill. God had entrusted that widow with the money necessary to cover the cost of those first broadcasts — and she kept her promise to steward her finances for the preaching of the Gospel. Today this precious woman is in Heaven, but she supported our TV outreach for many years. Our Bible-teaching programs were going into *every* home in that nation *every* day. As a result of our obedience and her sacrificial giving, we received millions of letters from people who watched the programs, who gave their lives to Jesus Christ, and who began to regularly correspond with our ministry for help to further develop their lives in Christ.

As I think back on this experience, I see how every person always plays such a vital role for any miracle to be brought to pass. On that day, I signed the contract — but I didn't have the money to pay for it. God gave finances to a faithful widow — and she supplied the money to pay. Each time I ponder this experience, I am still amazed at how God can miraculously speak to every heart to get every assignment done *on time* according to Heaven's design.

### A Significant Gift in Due Season

Another significant financial encouragement occurred when we were building the Riga church building and needed an inflow of cash to continue the project. Just at the time we had run out of funds, I received an unanticipated phone call from a Board member of a renowned ministry in the Charismatic world. The Board member was a long-time friend of mine whom I had met years earlier in New York City. He said, "Rick, I need to talk to you for a few minutes."

That Board member was one of the most brilliant and intelligent people I had ever met, and he and I gravitated to each other and became friends over the years. But he had never placed an urgent call to me before, so I asked, "What's on your heart?" He proceeded to tell me that this leading minister and the Board of Directors of his ministry wanted to give a financial gift to help us pay for the construction of our church building in Riga. This minister had heard we were building the first new church building in Riga in almost six decades, and he wanted his ministry to give a significant gift to help us build it.

This older minister had always been kind to me, but I was stunned at what I heard, so I wanted to make sure I really understood my friend correctly. I asked, "He wants to give a significant gift to help pay for our new building in Riga?" The board member answered, "Yes, he wants to do it — and, furthermore, he wants to give it as soon as possible."

The words "as soon as possible" really got my attention because we had come to the end of our cash reserves. We were using our money as wisely as we knew how, but we had come to the end of it and needed money — big money — so the work would not come to a grinding halt. What timing!

Oh, how I needed encouragement at that moment. Yes, we needed the cash and were grateful for it, but the exact timing of the call let me know that Jesus was with us in the middle of our project!

We were facing so many battles to construct that building that I felt a lot like what is written in Nehemiah 4 where it's recorded that when the walls in Jerusalem were being rebuilt, the builders worked with a building instrument in one hand and a sword in the other hand. While they kept their eyes on the task, they also had to fight off the encroachment of their enemies who wanted to stop the work. We, too, were doing our best to stay focused on constructing the building while simultaneously fighting enemies on every side.

God used this leading minister and his ministry to help us keep that project moving forward so we could finish on time. Since 1998 when that building was dedicated, it has been used to touch inestimable numbers of people, and God will credit part of that fruit to this ministry for the seed they sowed into its completion. And in the years since that time, this minister has remained supportive of our ministry and has written endorsements for a number of books I have written. I am thankful to this man and his ministry for being God's *booming* voice in that moment when I needed encouragement to keep marching ahead in my assignment!

This intervention of God through this minister was another significant moment when He proved that divine provision will always show up for projects that Heaven authorizes!

## A Friend Who Loved at All Times

In Chapter Eight, I shared about the moment I'd called a friend the night I publicly announced I would be moving my family to the USSR. When I called him that evening, that friend, who was usually very encouraging, *terrified* me with his words. After my talk with him, I *vomited* the whole night because that talk upset me so much. He didn't *intend* to upset me, but he was genuinely concerned that I was making a mistake by moving my family to the USSR.

Of course, it would have been an expensive, costly, and dangerous move to make if God hadn't called me and my family to move there. I understood my friend's concerns. But the truth was, God *had* spoken. The call to relocate to the former USSR was a shock to my senses because it was so radically different from anything I'd envisioned for my life and ministry. But it was undeniably God. Nevertheless, my head was reeling, so my friend's words affected me negatively.

But over the years, that same man proved himself again and again to be a bona fide friend to me and to our ministry. In fact, when I think of him, my mind goes to Proverbs 17:17, which says, "A friend loveth at all times...." That man was Robb Thompson, who was pastor at that time of a church in Chicago and one who has proven himself to be a "friend that loveth at all times" over many years and in many different situations.

I'll never forget one night in 1998 when I needed a friend to talk to about an ordeal we were facing. As I related in Chapter Twelve, we had ordered the steel from Tennessee for our Riga Good News Church building because it was so much less expensive than to purchase it locally.

But now it was time to pay for it, and our ministry did not have the money needed to pay for it before the steel factory would load it into containers to ship to the other side of the world. Feeling overwhelmed with pressure, I called Robb late one night from Riga to open my heart to him about our situation and to seek encouragement.

I had not called him to ask for money, as it has never been my style to ask anyone for money. I was only seeking the ear of a friend to hear what I was facing and to pray with me. But after I poured out my heart that night, I heard Robb answer, "Rick, let us cover it. Our church will take care of that for you and the ministry there." The next morning, he and his church wrote a check and provided all the money to pay for tons of steel so it could be loaded into containers, placed on a ship, and sent overseas so our building would be completed on time!

Again, Proverbs 17:17 says, "A friend loveth at all times." Robb Thompson certainly fulfilled that verse at a critical moment and at other moments, too, and I will be forever grateful for the way he allowed God to use him and his church to advance the cause of the Gospel in that moment when so much was hanging in the balance for our ministry and for the Gospel in the lands of the former Soviet Union.

## Examples of Good Stewardship

Doug and Sharon Graham are two more examples of God's grace to provide funds for our ministry at critical junctures. These two are shining examples who have also flourished in the supernatural gift of giving that Paul refers to in Romans 12:8.

As a young man, Doug graduated from the U.S. Military Academy at West Point, where he earned a degree in Engineering. After graduation from West Point in 1981, Doug entered flight school and then served in the U.S. Army for eight years, where he attained the rank of Captain. In late 1989, Doug started and operated a small interstate trucking company, which he sold in 1993, and he then served as Executive Pastor for a small independent church in Olympia, Washington, for two years. But earlier in life, he met and married a wonderful girl named Sharon. Because the two of them were and are deeply committed to Christ, they determined that they would serve God and would use their resources to advance God's Kingdom and the Great Commission.

When I first met Doug and Sharon decades ago, they were still owners of the trucking business. Although they were getting established in their business, they were already so serious about their commitment to use their resources for the Kingdom of God that they gave sacrificially even in that early stage of their business. During the time they owned that business, I ministered at the church they were attending, and it was at that time that Doug and Sharon decided to become partners with our ministry. Even in that early moment, I was so impressed with them as individuals, and I was repeatedly stunned at their supernatural "knack" for knowing when our ministry was in financial need and when to send a special gift.

Because of their personal dedication to Christ, discipline in their business, and commitment to use their resources to advance the Great Commission, God's blessings flowed mightily in their business. In time, God enabled them to become owners of other businesses that also became tremendously successful. And for all these years, they have been a conduit of resources for the advancement of the Gospel through our ministry and through the ministries of others. I will be forever thankful to Doug and Sharon Graham for their heartfelt willingness to be vessels God can work through to touch the world.

## A Gift That Keeps on Giving

Another significant person God used to provide resources for our ministry was an Armenian businessman in Moscow whose name was Henry Barsigyan, a man who was radically converted to Christ in the days after the collapse of the USSR.

In those days after the collapse of the communist regime, Henry and his family became faithful viewers of our TV program in Smolensk, the Russian city where they lived at that time. One day, they "happened" upon the TV programs that we were broadcasting — and it also just so happened that when we later held a TV rally in Smolensk, they decided to attend that meeting. Henry and his wife, Anya, and their sons, came and sat on the very first row. They were so excited to meet Denise and me because we were becoming significant voices for the Bible in the newly emerging Christian community. It was at that time, in that meeting in Smolensk, that Henry and Anya became partners with our ministry.

Many years later, Henry and his family relocated to Moscow at approximately the same time our family relocated there to start the Moscow Good News Church. When he and Anya heard that we were starting the new church, they and their sons began to attend. From the church's inception, they became rock-solid members of our Moscow congregation.

Not only were Henry and Anya spiritually supportive of us and our Moscow church, they gave enormous financial gifts over the years to advance the work of the ministry. Henry was a serious businessman whose business was fabricating particle board from wood. But most importantly, Henry was a serious believer — and as such, he and Anya and their sons covenanted to give faithfully to the work of God. They even provided the finances to pay for the construction of the large stage in the Moscow Good News Church.

Though Henry is now in Heaven, he put the revelation of giving into the hearts of his sons, and today his sons continue to give generously to God's work through our church and ministry. And every time I step onto the large platform in our church auditorium — literally *every time* — I think of the gift that Henry and Anya and their sons gave so that we could stand on that stage and proclaim the Word of Truth to those in the auditorium and to those watching by various media around the world. Henry may be in Heaven today, but his gift remains and keeps on giving!

### The Movie-Theater King From the Far East

We decided to conduct a week of meetings in Vladivostok, a large port city in Russia's Far East, about 5,600 miles from Moscow. As was our custom, we conducted multiple daytime sessions for pastors in that huge far-eastern region and then held large public meetings in the evenings for the general public.

It was our first time in Vladivostok, so I didn't know the man who volunteered to drive us back and forth to all the various meetings that week. His name was Eduard Korin, and he was a businessman whose life had been deeply touched by God. And because my books and TV programs had impacted him over the years, he had volunteered to be our driver that week.

We were in the car quite a bit that week, so as Eduard drove us back and forth to our meetings, I asked him a lot of questions about his life and his conversion. He told me about his radical conversion to Christ in prison. In prison, he'd heard the Gospel from a prison ministry that was led by Pentecostal brothers. When eventually released from prison, he attended the underground church in Vladivostok that had been the base for that prison ministry.

Over time, Eduard became a leader in that church. And because God blessed him with a keen sense of business, he amazingly became the owner and operator of the largest chain of movie theaters in Vladivostok and in Russia's Far East. I nicknamed him the "movie-theater king" without realizing that *he really was* the movie-theater king in that far-flung part of the nation.

At the end of all the services that week in Vladivostok, I was exhausted from nonstop meetings, and doing those meetings had been a great financial sacrifice as well. We had invested a small fortune to get there with our team, and the cost of holding all those services and paying for the lodging of all the pastors who attended was also quite high.

In public TV meetings like that in the former Soviet Union, we *never* received offerings because such meetings were designed to attract our TV viewers, many of whom had never darkened the door of a church and many of whom were not saved. Thousands of unbelievers all over the former USSR watched my TV programs, and our public meetings were designed to be a net to catch them and bring in a haul for the Kingdom of God. For the majority of them, it was their first experience at a Christian meeting. The money we spent on such meetings was always seed we were sowing into the harvest field to reap souls who had been exposed to God's Word as a result of our TV programs. It had taken faith for us to pay for that trip and all those meetings, and as was always the case, I was trusting the Lord to help us cover all our expenses.

On the last morning, Eduard arrived at our hotel to pick us up and drive us to the airport for our flight back to Moscow. But before my team and I stepped out of his car to walk into the airport, Eduard said, "Brother Rick, I would like to say a final word to you." I leaned back into my seat and looked into his eyes to focus so I could hear what he had to say to me. Then he said, "God has totally turned my life around and has blessed me more than I could have imagined possible. When I repented in prison and gave my life to Christ, I could never have dreamed all the things God would do in my life. He has given me a wonderful family and has blessed me financially. And because He has used you in my life, I am asking you to please accept an offering from me as my seed to help with your ministry across the former USSR."

With that, he handed a large envelope to our team to take back to Moscow. Before he handed it to us, he said, "Let's pray." He laid his hands on it and began to powerfully pray in tongues. Inside that envelope was an enormous amount of cash that he wanted to give as an offering for our ministry to underwrite our expenses in the Far East.

Although I had never told anyone the amount we had invested in those meetings, what Eduard gave was precisely the amount of money we had spent to do that ministry in Vladivostok! I knew this was a man who knew the voice of the Holy Spirit. When he told me the amount that was in that envelope — the exact amount we needed to recoup all those expenses — once again, God's voice was booming loudly in our ears that He always pays for Heaven-authorized assignments!

On subsequent trips to Vladivostok, Eduard allowed our ministry to hold multiple pastors conferences in his movie theaters and underwrote much of our ministry in areas all over the Far East of Russia. Because he had renovated many movie theaters that he had purchased over the years, he even offered to fly to Moscow to look at buildings we were considering for purchase for the permanent home of the Moscow Good News Church. No one knew how to renovate buildings to accommodate a crowd better than Eduard Korin, so we were thankful for his willingness to fly all that distance from Vladivostok to counsel us.

But one day after we had purchased the building for our Moscow church, I was discussing with him the kind of chairs we should use for the new auditorium, and he said, "I want to purchase all the theater-type chairs for your new auditorium. So when it's time for you to order the chairs, let me look at them and make sure they're the best ones available, and I will pay for all of them. We'll choose them together, but I'll pay for them. I want to have seed in that auditorium and invest in the people who will sit in those seats year after year to hear the Word of God."

I was amazed at Eduard's offer because the cost of all the theater-style chairs needed to fill our auditorium was going to be enormous. I never dreamed Eduard would make such an offer, and it completely took me off guard. But when the day came for us to place our order for those beautiful chairs, Eduard kept his promise and covered the entire cost of the chairs *and* the cost of transporting them from the factory in South Korea to Moscow to be installed in our new building.

Since then, thousands upon thousands of people have sat in those beautiful theater-style chairs that were paid for by Eduard Korin. When I sit in them, I have often thought, *Year after year, people have sat in these chairs that were purchased by the sacrificial gift of Eduard Korin. They don't even know who paid for them, but they are receiving the benefit of his gift.*

Although Eduard lives far from Moscow, his presence and the impact of his gift are here with us every week. What a reward he will receive when he stands before Jesus!

*And think of it.* All of that started with a man saved in a prison — a man whose life was impacted by our ministry and who had volunteered to be our driver for a week in Vladivostok. As it turned out, Eduard and his wife have supported many wonderful ministries over the years. He is known far and wide in Russia for his generous heart. Because he was so grateful for what God did in his life, he wanted to reciprocate by giving of his finances to the work of God. How could I ever adequately express my thankfulness to God for Eduard and for his willingness to serve and advance God's Kingdom!

## An Over-the-Top Giver

Another person God has graciously used to supernaturally provide resources for our ministry is Irina Fomina, a wonderful woman who is one of the most remarkable givers I have ever met in my life. As I've noted, I have encountered several people with a true gift of giving, but Irina stands out as one of the most remarkable.

In the years before Irina repented and came to Christ, she entered the business world and became quite successful. At one early point in the history of our Moscow church, one of Irina's friends invited her to a special event at our church, and on that day, she committed her life to Jesus Christ. Since that time, she has become the embodiment of what it means to be "faithful."

I once asked her, "Irina, what motivates you to be so faithful." She told me, "I've been forgiven for so much that I did in my past — I want to show my thankfulness for the rest of my life by being faithful to Jesus and to His Church."

From time to time, Irina would bring lovely gifts to various members of our pastoral staff as an expression of her appreciation for what they were doing in the work of the ministry. The gifts were treasures that expressed her heart of gratitude. I didn't know a lot of details about her past life, but I could see how obviously deeply grateful she was for the work of God's grace that was upon her.

Irina was one of those people who expressed thankfulness for every message preached and for every person who was serving in any way. If she knew she was going to be away on a business trip or a trip for personal business, she'd let us know why she would be gone and would ask us to pray for her trip.

One day when Irina came to church, she asked to meet with me and our church administrator for a few minutes privately. We went into a private room at the church, where we asked, "Irina, what's on your heart?" She answered, "I realize you don't know a lot of personal details about my life, but God has enormously blessed me in the financial realm. Now it's time for me to be a blessing to Him and to this church." I could see Irina was physically trembling as she spoke to us about her desire to give a significant gift for a special project in our church.

She said, "I'm so thankful I can give an offering, and I've been waiting for this moment for weeks. I'm so relieved to give it!" The manner in which she gave that gift let me know that what she was about to do was a true act of worship. But that was only the first time Irina would give a sacrificial offering for various projects in Moscow. I have observed that her timing is amazing, as she has nearly always shown up with a special gift at a critical juncture when we were awaiting God's provision. Irina suddenly seems to appear right on time. For many years, I have seen her tremble as she has given from the depths of her heart in gratitude for what God has so marvelously wrought in her life.

Finally, a day came when several members of our team said, "We need to take Irina to lunch so we can hear more of her personal testimony." Denise and I and several members of our executive staff sat around the table and listened as she shared her stunning testimony about how God had transformed her life completely.

Irina Fomina is one of the most remarkable givers I have ever met. She has never asked for anything but prayer and that we would accept the precious seed she desires to sow into the work of God's Kingdom. Her story of God's grace continues to amaze us all, and she is a precious example of how God's grace can change a life and then give that life a genuine supernatural gift of giving.

## God Makes Promises To Those Who
## Use Their Money for His Work

As I look back over the years of our ministry, I can testify that, just as Jesus showed me in that vision in 1985, we have indeed experienced fullness of ministry and fullness of finances to do those ministry assignments. But even if I'd never had that vision, there is a mountain of Bible verses that indisputably promise God's provision to those who obey and who give their lives for the Great Commission.

As I said in the last chapter, in Matthew 28:18-20, Jesus made an astonishing promise to any believer, church, or ministry organization that will *go and keep on going* with the Gospel to reach those who are nearby and those who are abroad. Jesus said, "...And, *lo*, I am with you always, even unto the end of the world. Amen" (v. 20).

The word "lo" is actually an exclamatory promise that Jesus makes to anyone who will in any fashion "go" with the Gospel to the lost. In other words, the "lo" belongs to those who "go." In Greek, the word "lo" would better be translated, *"And, WOW, will I ever be with you — even to the ends of the earth!"* In this verse, Christ promises His powerful presence will be enjoyed and experienced by all believers who are totally committed to discovering their part by the direction of the Holy Spirit and then *going* to the lost with the message of salvation. That means if believers want to experience the power of God, they must act on what triggers its release.

Some cannot physically go, but they can use their resources to help others go, and that qualifies them for the promise in Matthew 28:20 where Jesus essentially says, "If you will go and keep on going — doing all you can in every way possible to preach and teach the Gospel — *WOW, I promise that you will experience My amazing presence in the doing of it!*"

It is sure that God's heart is deeply touched when people give sacrificially, and He responds magnificently to those who give for the work of the Gospel. This is why Paul wrote, "...My God shall supply all your need according to his riches in glory by Christ Jesus" (Philippians 4:19).

When the Greek words Paul used in Philippians 4:19 are interpreted to their fullest extent, Paul was essentially telling them:

**But my God will supply your needs so completely that He will eliminate all your deficiencies. He will meet all your physical and tangible needs until you are so full that you have no more capacity to hold anything else. He will supply all your needs until you are totally filled, packed, and overflowing to the point of bursting at the seams and spilling over!**

At the first of this chapter, I told you that I stand in awe at how God has supernaturally supplied everything we've needed to do everything He has ever put in our hearts to do. God's provision has exceeded our wildest imaginations. It is miraculous — and *unlikely* — that we would have been able to do it as I recall how little money we started out with when our family moved to the USSR three decades ago.

But we have learned that if we'll obey God and get into alignment with His plan, our obedience will work like a magnet to attract all that is needed to accomplish any God-given assignment. I can testify to God's faithfulness to do just that as we have seen Him miraculously provide the resources to do our own God-given outreaches, but also to sow into the lives of others who have committed *their* lives to the Gospel.

Over the years, we have received supernatural provision to pay for the following:

- starting new churches (not just our own, but many others) that are filled with people today.
- the construction of multiple church buildings for other churches that are home to cumulative thousands of church members who are growing in Christ.
- paying the bills of many former USSR-based pastors who were in desperate financial need.
- the expenses for sabbaticals for former USSR-based pastors who were in need of physical restoration.
- surgical procedures for pastors and their families (eye operations, hip-replacement operations, and open-heart surgeries), medical evacuations for missionaries with urgent health issues, multiple expensive prosthetics for pastors and their children, ongoing long-term medications for pastors who did not have the money to pay for them, hospital stays for pastors and their families, and other long-term medical care for pastors.
- monthly financial support for six hundred pastors over the course of many years — a massive outlay of money that empowered those pastors whose incomes were not sufficient to do their ministries.
- the expenses for massive evangelistic crusades and meetings all over the former USSR for all kinds of ministries and missions organizations in addition to our own meetings.
- the total expenses for large pastors' seminars and conferences for years that were attended by a cumulative thousands of pastors.
- the complete expenses for those thousands of pastors to travel to and from the meetings and for all expenses connected with food and lodging during those events.
- legal expenses for many pastors and churches in the territory of the former USSR.
- significant monthly financial support of other missionaries all over the former USSR and in other parts of the world.
- a long list of mission trips, projects, and outreaches sponsored by other ministries in the former USSR in addition to our own.

- the offerings and all travel expenses for all special speakers who have traveled to the former USSR to minister alongside us in various events.

- the expenses for large crusades and meetings we have conducted in the former USSR for three decades that have been attended by a cumulative hundreds of thousands of people.

- the expenses for young people from Latvia to attend Bible school in America — their tuition and room-and-board expenses.

- the costs for hundreds of students to attend our Bible school in Jelgava and Moscow.

- the entire costs of the first National Prayer Breakfasts in Russia.

- the enormous cost of our TV programs for decades — a mountain of money bigger than I have the guts to write on paper.

- the entire costs of starting three large churches in three different countries, in three capital cities, in three different languages.

- building two large church buildings that cost multiple tens of millions of dollars.

- the expenses to open, operate, and maintain six churches, including affiliate campuses, that are thriving today.

- TV and sound equipment given to other churches and ministries.

- chairs we have provided for other churches for their new church auditoriums.

- *millions* of books we've printed and distributed at no charge, including all the postage to get the books to those recipients.

- the enormous costs to write, edit, and publish books in multiple languages.

- the costs of all international ministry expenses to get to meetings around the world.

- the total expenses for our U.S.-based and our Russia-based ministry.

- the total costs for special events for thousands of handicapped children and their families and for other needy families in the community.

- tons of food for needy, poverty-stricken families and the homeless, including gifts of Bibles, Christian materials, personal supplies, and finances for rehabilitation centers.

- the costs of ministering to elderly people and providing them with vitamins, Bibles, Christian literature, and other necessities.

- tons of clothes to needy families along with clothes to people who live in war-torn regions.

As a result of all of this, we have seen thousands repent and come to Christ; pastors fed, nurtured, and trained in the Word of God; new churches started; workers trained to reach nations; Christian TV programs broadcast around the world; and Christian materials published and distributed to the multitudes.

*And the list goes on and on!* We also miraculously pay the monthly salaries of several hundred employees in multiple ministry offices around the world who help us do this work.

*None of this has been naturally possible!*

*All of this has been unlikely!*

*But God has miraculously done it all!*

Ephesians 3:20 and 21 says, "…Unto him that is able to do exceeding abundantly above all that we ask or think, according to the power that worketh in us, unto him be glory in the church by Christ Jesus throughout all ages, world without end…." As I told you earlier, Denise and I, our sons, and our team can testify that God has superabundantly provided everything we have ever needed to do any job He has entrusted to us. But He has primarily provided it through the giving of pastors, churches, businesses, organizations, and individual partners who have sacrificially given over and over through the years. It is *their* giving that has enabled us to do it all.

But we also realize that even if we *all* do our respective parts, growth only comes with God's participation. Truly He is building this house and keeping watch over it. Our labors are not in vain, but those "labors" hold eternal value in His eyes.

In response to all of this, I thankfully declare that *all* the glory goes to God for the remarkable provision He has manifested on our behalf to enable us to fulfill the vision He put in our hearts so that our "sound" can go out into all the earth (*see* Romans 10:18). Although it was naturally unlikely when we launched out by faith that any of it would happen, God has done the *unlikely* for us over and over again.

But lest you think it has all been easy, I want you to know that we've also faced what we felt were crushing, insurmountable challenges at times. Some seemed so overwhelming that it was *unlikely* we would survive and overcome them. But God not only brought us through — He brought us through with fresh vision for new barriers to cross in heralding the Gospel message to the ends of the earth. We were never delivered so we could rest or "plateau" on any mountain we'd conquered. God simply showed us new parts of our race He'd ordained for us yet to run.

Although we have been abundantly supplied as we've stepped out to do God's will — that's the reason for this chapter — we are still receiving fresh vision and direction for the ministry in this part of the world today. And we are still standing in faith for the resources we need to do each new job. In the next chapter, I share about the future of RENNER Ministries, because *the best is yet to come!*

# 17

# NEW FRONTIERS
# IN OUR
# PRESENT-DAY MINISTRY

Most people write their autobiography later in life, but I chose to write this part of our story at this juncture and not wait for "later." Many whom we needed to interview for this book were older and in the sunset years of their journeys — I wanted to capture their memories while I could. In fact, my own mother went home to Heaven during the writing of this book. I simply sensed that this was the time that "the breath of God" was upon me to write our story.

It has taken a lot of pages to tell just this small part of our story. In the years to come, I am certain much more will be added to the *unlikely* story of Rick and Denise Renner and how God has continued to use our *yes* to work His plan through us, our sons, our team, and the partners who support this ministry.

---

**Left:** *Illustration representing one of the satellites our network uses to broadcast the teaching of the Bible to Russian-speakers around the world.*

I have nothing negative to say about anyone who plans to retire at a certain age in life, but for us, there will simply be no retirement. In fact, this is "Part One" — just the beginning of our story! After gaining so much life experience, I believe it would be a grave mistake for us to move off the playing field to sit on the sidelines. One leader I deeply respect noted that God intends a person's *first* thirty years to be years of learning and preparation, the *second* thirty years to be a time to implement what he or she has learned, and the *third* thirty-plus years to impart what he or she has learned to others. *This is what I believe too!*

While God's plan is for each of us to go from strength to strength (Psalm 84:7), many struggle for various reasons to go further as they get older. But with God's help and by doing our part to pay attention to our spiritual lives and our physical health, Denise and I intend to run our race for many years to come. It has been a good run so far, but everything behind us, though *weighty* in eternal value and significance, is merely preparation for the next phases before us.

I am determined to run a long race — to stay spiritually vibrant, on track with God's Word and His Spirit, physically fit, and alert to my God-given relationships — with *Denise, my sons, my team, my partners,* and *my covenant friends.* Denise and I are determined to keep moving forward with the assignments God gives and not to veer from them. *We are just getting started, and before us is a God-designed future that will be even more exciting than the past!*

All around us, there is a cloud of contemporary witnesses who ran long races or who are still running strong. I'm talking about men and women like Oral Roberts, Kenneth E. Hagin, Lester Sumrall, Derek Prince, and Billy Graham, who have finished their respective courses and have gone on to glory. Among those who are still running strong are Pat Robertson, Marilyn Hickey, David Hathaway, Charles Stanley, Kay Arthur, Kenneth and Gloria Copeland, John Hagee, Joyce Meyer, Kenneth W. Hagin, Pat Harrison, James Robison, and many others who are serving *robustly* into years beyond what most consider "the norm." Due to their remarkable examples, I believe it is entirely possible to run a long, *strong* race and to become even more usable as we age with God's grace.

## The Parable of the Talents

Denise and I have learned and have proven time and time again that if we'll do whatever God asks us to do, it causes our abilities and capacities to grow. This makes me think of Jesus' teaching about talents that were distributed to three different servants in Matthew 25. This parable has greatly affected how we have lived our lives and conducted our ministry — it has played a significant role in our *unlikely* journey.

Let me take a moment to expound on what Jesus said in this important parable, because it is so relevant to the subject of stewardship and "making full proof" of the ministry or vocation to which we've each been called (*see* 2 Timothy 4:5).

In Matthew 25, Jesus told the parable of a master who distributed "talents" to various servants. A "talent" referred to *a specific measurement of money*. In early New Testament times, an average worker was paid *one denarius* for a full-day's wage. A talent was *six-thousand denari*. This means *one talent* was nearly the equivalent of *sixteen years' salary*.

In verse 15, Jesus said, "And unto one he gave five talents, to another two, and to another one...."

Since one talent is *six thousand denari* or nearly *sixteen years' worth of salary*, when the Bible says the master in this parable gave *five talents* to the first servant, it means he was giving him *thirty-thousand denari* or the equivalent of nearly *eighty-two years of salary*.

When the master gave the second servant *two talents*, he was giving him *twelve-thousand denari* or the equivalent of nearly *thirty-three years of salary*. Finally, the master gave the last servant *one talent*. That was *six-thousand denari* or the equivalent of nearly *sixteen years of salary*. All three of the servants were given great opportunities, and the master clearly expected that they would increase what he had entrusted to them.

Matthew 25:16 goes on to tell us, "Then he that had received the five talents went and traded with the same, and made them other five talents." This means he increased his *30,000 denari* into *60,000 denari* or nearly the equivalent of *164 years of salary*. It takes *hard work* to increase one's money on such a large scale! Proverbs 10:4 says that a diligent, hard worker will be richly blessed. It is clear that the first servant's willingness to work hard gave him the ability to increase what had been entrusted to him.

Matthew 25:17 tells us, "And likewise he that had received two, he also gained other two." Like the first servant, the second servant was a hard-working man who also increased what his master entrusted to him. He increased his *twelve thousand denari* to *twenty-four thousand denari* or nearly the equivalent of *sixty-six years of salary.*

Finally, we come to the third servant, who received *one talent* or *six-thousand denari,* which was the equivalent of nearly *sixteen years of salary.* Rather than put forth effort to increase it as the other servants had done, Matthew 25:18 tells us that the third servant dug a hole in the ground, hid his money, and put forth no effort to increase what his master had entrusted to him. The other two servants increased what their master had given them, but the third servant did not increase what his master placed in his care.

This scenario makes me wonder if the master had previous experience with the third servant's work and perhaps, based on his previous experience with this servant, the master didn't trust him with more than a single talent. But the text tells us the third servant did nothing to increase what he had received.

If the first two servants were capable of increasing what their master entrusted to them, the third servant could have done it too. *He could have turned his six thousand denari into twelve thousand.* But rather than do what was necessary to increase it, he did nothing to increase what had been committed to him by his master.

### The Lord Will Reckon With Us

Matthew 25:19 continues to tell us, "After a long time the lord of those servants cometh, and reckoneth with them." The word "reckon" in this verse is a bookkeeping term that means *to compare accounts.* It would be used to portray an accountant who is putting together a profit-and-loss statement for his boss. He is examining the books to determine the real financial status of a corporation.

In this parable, the master wanted to know how these three servants had fared with the gifts he had given them. The word "reckon" is so intense that it means the master wasn't satisfied to take a shallow look; he intended to search and dig until he obtained a full picture of the real situation. He intended to dig deep and make a thorough investigation of what each servant had done with what he had entrusted to his care.

Matthew 25:26 and 27 tells us that the master expected *increase* when he returned. That is why he told them, "...Thou knewest that I reap where I sowed not, and gather where I have not strawed: Thou oughtest therefore to have put my money to the exchangers, and then at my coming I should have received mine own with usury."

All three of these servants *knew* the master's expectations. They *knew* he expected them to increase what he had entrusted to them. This means the master would accept *no excuses* for a lack of increase. It didn't matter how difficult the situation, how many odds were against them, or how impossible it seemed — he expected them to bring some amount of *increase* to what he had given to them. All three servants *understood* that this was his expectation.

Matthew 25:21 tells us that when the master returned and discovered the first servant increased what he had entrusted to him, he said, "...Well done, thou good and faithful servant: thou hast been faithful over a few things, I will make thee ruler over many things: enter thou into the joy of thy lord."

In verse 23, the master likewise was thrilled to discover the second servant had increased what had been entrusted to him. That verse says, "His lord said unto him, Well done, thou good and faithful servant; thou hast been faithful over a few things, I will make thee ruler over many things: enter thou into the joy of thy lord."

These two servants had proven themselves faithful, so their master declared that a bright future lay ahead for both of them. He was ready to thrust them into even bigger assignments.

## The Non-Productive Servant
### Was '*Wicked, Slothful,* and *Unprofitable*'

The third servant ended up in a horrible predicament because his master discovered he'd done nothing to increase what had been entrusted to him. His master was so displeased that he said to him, "…Thou wicked and slothful servant…" (v. 26). These words are taken from a single Greek word that carries the idea of *one who has a do-nothing, lethargic, lackadaisical, apathetic, indifferent, lukewarm attitude toward life.*

But then the master also calls him an "unprofitable" servant. The word "unprofitable" is from a Greek word that means *useless*. A literal translation of this Greek phrase would be "a good-for-nothing servant." Like the other two servants, he had received an amazing opportunity, and his master expected him to faithfully do something with it. But because he did not increase what was entrusted to him — he did nothing to grow or multiply what had been given to him — even what he had was taken away.

In Matthew 25:29, Jesus summed up this teaching by saying, "For unto every one that hath shall be given, and he shall have abundance: but from him that hath not shall be taken away even that which he hath."

Maybe you think some have enough on their plate already, but when God finds someone faithful, He gives that person more responsibility because He knows He has finally found someone He can trust. You see, God gives bigger assignments to those who have been faithful with what has already been entrusted to them.

I have certainly not been perfect by any stretch of the imagination, but I have done my best to faithfully manage and increase what Jesus has entrusted to my care over the years. As a result, as I get older, not only has my capacity for more grown, but God has given me more to do and He has given me an anointed team to help me do it.

There are no words to exaggerate how deeply this teaching from Jesus in Matthew 25 has impacted my life. It lets me know that Jesus expects increase from whatever He has put in my hands — and it further lets me know that if I am faithful, assignments will not diminish as time goes by. The assignments will increase — they will *amass*!

### Going From Glory to Glory?

Over the years, I've noticed that when some are displeased with the current phase of their lives, they often claim a portion of Second Corinthians 3:18 in which the apostle Paul says we go "from glory to glory." Many make this declaration — that they're going "from glory to glory" — when they don't like the way life is going. But what they really mean is this: "I'm weary of the mess in my life, and I'm ready to leave it and go to something glorious — 'from glory to glory'"!

But this verse doesn't say we go from *a MESS* to *glory.* It says we go from *GLORY* to *glory* — in other words, from *a current glorious place* to *another, higher glorious place.*

This means you and I won't move into the next glorious phase until the phase where we presently live is *glorious.* The Bible never promises that we will go from *mess* to glory. It says we go "from *glory* to glory." So if we want to go upward into a more glorious stage of life, we first have to make *glorious* the place where we are living right now. Only then will God promote us to the next level of glory that He has planned for us!

So it's wise to ask:

- *Have I done all the Lord has told me to do?*

- *Have I really completed the assignment as God instructed me to do it?*

- *Have I done everything I can to make this present stage of my life a bright and shining example to others, or is this part of my life a dismal failure of which I'm embarrassed?*

- *Have I increased what the Lord has entrusted to me?*

- *Have I made this season of my life glorious?*

Second Corinthians 3:18 goes on to importantly say, "But we all, with *open face* beholding as in a glass the glory of the Lord, are changed into the same image from glory to glory, even as by the Spirit of the Lord."

Notice the first part of the verse talks about us having "open faces." The word "open" in Greek means *to unveil, to uncover,* or *to disclose.*

When I saw this, it let me know that we must be willing to remove the veil from our eyes, take an honest look, and truthfully acknowledge the condition of our present stage. A truthful recognition of our present situation is part of the process that removes the veil from our eyes so the Lord can correct us, change us, transform us, and prepare us to move into the next glorious phase for our lives.

Paul says if we'll be willing to be honest, the Holy Spirit will change us. The word "changed" in Second Corinthians 3:18 means *to transfigure or transform one's appearance.* It is the same word used in Matthew 17:2 and Mark 9:2 to describe the *transfiguration* of Jesus. This word "changed" lets us know the Holy Spirit can actually *change* our present appearance, our current status, for one that is more glorious. Denial of the truth just keeps us stuck in the same hard place for a longer period of time. To move upward into the next glorious phase of life, we must be willing to lift the veil from our eyes and acknowledge that we need to be transformed!

But the kind of change I'm describing is only initiated when you are willing to get honest with yourself and with God about your behavior, your attitudes, and the condition of every area of your life at this present moment. If you're willing to remove the veil from your eyes and let the Holy Spirit really show you the areas where you need to be transformed, He *will* change you. And as this kind of transformation begins to work in you, you will become more and more prepared to move into a more glorious phase in your life.

So if the stage of life you're in right now is *not* glorious, you need to know that you'll probably be stuck in that mess until you become willing to take off the veil, look honestly at your situation, and begin to make the changes required to make your present status more glorious. Once you've done that, you'll be ready to move onward to the next more glorious place you are longing to experience!

And never forget that while God wants to take you from glory to glory, He isn't bothered if He has to wait until you correctly finish your current phase. God has lots of time. He knows that when you get serious about making your present situation more glorious, that's when you qualify for the Holy Spirit to open the way for you to move into the next glorious phase God really wants you to experience.

## How We Finish Our Race Is Important

I'm very far from finishing my race, and I intend to keep running it for a long time to come. But as I age, I often think of what Dr. Bennett used to tell me when I was living in Fort Smith and serving as his personal assistant. He often said, "Rick, many people begin with a bang, but end with a fizzle."

Those words have stuck with me all my life. It's true that many start out well, but do not end well. Like Dr. Bennett said, many people start with a bang, but they end with a fizzle. Though they start with a vision from God, they somehow get distracted along the way and fall out of the race.

But at the end of my own race, I am determined to be able to say with the apostle Paul that "I was not disobedient to the heavenly vision" (*see* Acts 26:19). And neither do I intend to pass the baton to someone else until I can say with the apostle Paul, "I have finished my course" (*see* 2 Timothy 4:7).

I am very aware that a day is coming when we will stand before the Judgment Seat of Christ to give an account for what we have done with what He entrusted to our care (Romans 14:10; 2 Corinthians 5:10). Oh, how I long to hear Him say, "Well done, thou good and faithful servant"! Hearing words of commendation from the lips of Jesus is the driving motivation of my life and ministry.

Denise and I and our sons have lived with this at the forefront of our minds — and to the best of our ability, we have lived our lives with eternity ever in view. On that day when I look into Jesus' eyes, I know that I will give account for what I did with what He entrusted to me. He will not reckon with me for past sin that is forgiven and under the Blood, but He will examine me to see how faithful I was with the tasks He assigned to me.

What we are doing and how well we are faithfully obeying Jesus' expectations of us right now will determine much of our activities throughout eternity. All Blood-bought people will go to Heaven, but how faithful we are right now is what qualifies us for future usefulness in God's eternal plan.

Over the years, as our family has lived with eternity in view, we've done our best to obey what God has asked us to do. Our family ministry of five has grown to a team that includes hundreds of God-called members who work alongside us in this ministry in offices in Russia, the United States, Latvia, Ukraine, England, and Mongolia.

## Obedience and Its Rewards

It has been said that obedience is its own reward — and I can certainly attest to the truth of that statement. Rewards aren't just measured in the tangible blessings God bestows on those who are obedient, although Denise and I can tell you that we have definitely been blessed. God is faithful, and every hard place we endured to see His assignment come to pass has always been answered, in time, with His precious recompense of reward.

But the most significant reward of obedience comes with following God's instructions to achieve *Heaven's* outcomes — the fruitfulness that accompanies carrying out *His* plans with precision. Ultimately, I'm talking about the fruit of seeing men's and women's souls ransomed and changed by the power of His Word. Truly, that is a reward of eternal significance.

In Isaiah 53, we read that Jesus brought many sons to glory and that the will of God prospered in His hands. Christ was our Substitute, doing for us in His magnificent act of redemption what we could not do for ourselves. But He also lived as our *Example* — and as such, He showed us the way to *also* bring many sons to glory and to see God's will prosper in our own lives.

But perhaps the greatest reward of obedience is that, as we've passed through this life, we have longed to please the Lord with our faith — *our trust* — and our corresponding works that must accompany faith and submission to His will. Heaven will remember what we did in heartfelt obedience to Him, including keeping our hearts right and our motives pure in hard times so that we were never stopped, stuck, or detoured in our assignments.

Denise and I and our family have seen others become completely *derailed* from their callings through bitterness of soul that was left unchecked. We never wanted that to be our story. No one has a path that's free of all hardships and obstacles as we follow God's will for our lives. But we *can* walk His exact path without swerving — or we can get back on track if we do swerve. We can carry out His plans and experience the richest measure of His divine presence in this life *besides* our rewards in the life to come.

I entered the ministry in 1977, but as I especially reflect on the last thirty years of our ministry in the former Soviet Union, there have certainly been highs and lows as we've followed God's plan for our lives. But He has faithfully seen us through every single one of those low moments and has led us into places of blessing. In one of those moments as we were forging into new spiritual territory in the USSR, I cried out to the Lord, "WHY did You choose me?"

I will never forget His resolved and comforting response: *Because I knew You would obey Me and do what I asked you to do!*

At any angle or through any lens, obedience is its own reward indeed.


## Teaching You Can Trust

I know that God's call is for me to do my part to bring trusted teaching to hungry hearts all across the globe. In my book *How To Keep Your Head on Straight in a World Gone Crazy*[1], I clearly write about how disturbed I am by the departure from the faith that is so evident all around us. But we are living at the end of the age, and the Holy Spirit prophesied that we would witness this as we approached the culmination of the era. Nevertheless, there is a remnant that is crying out for teaching they can trust, and I am humbled that God is enabling our ministry to participate in a "revival of the Bible" in the hearts of His remnant everywhere.

While we have witnessed a manifestation of the Holy Spirit's outpouring, the Charismatic Movements — of which I am a part and of which I love so much — is in jeopardy because it has assimilated so many various theological positions. The Charismatic Movement is comprised of believers in nearly every denomination, every theological camp, and every eschatological belief. It includes those who could be described as seeker-friendly, traditional Pentecostal, Word of Faith, Third Wave — and every other spiritual "label" you can imagine. The Charismatic Movement has attracted millions of people from a myriad of faith backgrounds. This is beautiful in one respect because it signals the removal of barriers within the Body of Christ. However, theologically, it has muddied the waters.

Believers who identify as Arminian, Calvinistic, Baptist, Presbyterian, Methodist, Lutheran, Catholic, Episcopalian, Church of England, Assemblies of God, Word of Faith, and so on are all rubbing elbows together in worship. But all of these various groups who have received the baptism in the Holy Spirit and speak in other tongues are still on different pages theologically. The wide variety of believers who call themselves Charismatics have no central dogma to hold them together and to help determine what is or isn't sound doctrine. And this isn't even to mention the many "maverick" or fringe groups that have no recognized background or affiliation and have also introduced New Age and Spiritualism ideas and practices into the Charismatic Movement!

Like a mighty river, the Charismatic Movement is a movement that has many different streams flowing into it, so that it has become a conglomeration of doctrines, beliefs, practices, and styles — and a great deal of doctrinal confusion. Some of these practices and beliefs in certain sectors of the Charismatic Movement are so bizarre that people are seeking out leaders and ministries within the movement who can serve as "safe havens." In other words, many are in search of groups who offer an approach to the Spirit-filled life that anchors believers securely to the Word of God and to the pure stream of the Holy Spirit. This is a part of our ministry calling that we have been commissioned to fulfill.

### Life in the Spirit With Common Sense

Although many recognize and appreciate the multiple flavors of the Charismatic Movement, they nonetheless find it necessary to navigate toward specific groups where they feel safe. I am an example of this myself, for I have found my place within a spiritual company who hold fast with rock-solid commitment to the authority of Scripture, to the moving of the Holy Spirit, to biblical morality, and to walking in integrity before God and men — and, in the midst of it all, who demonstrate *common sense*.

I am a staunch believer in the Charismatic Movement and see it as a supernatural move of the Holy Spirit. But for this movement to accomplish all that God intends, it needs help to stay within its God-ordained banks. If the mighty river called the Charismatic Movement keeps rushing ahead in its present trajectory without cultivating a strong, broad foundation based in Scripture, it runs the possibility of growing so varied that it veers off course. And the further that river flows off its intended course, the more diluted it will become in its effectiveness to reap the end-time harvest of souls as God intends.

God is calling on Charismatic Christians to *wake up* and redirect their trajectory once more toward the foundational doctrines of His Word. If the believers who make up the Charismatic Movement today will hold fast to Scripture and form systems of accountability to keep its leadership on track, this movement will continue to grow into the strong, vibrant river of God's truth and manifested power that He has always intended it to be. The present-day state of affairs in the Charismatic Church worldwide needs *sound doctrine* and *solid Bible teaching*.

And as a part of God's calling to take the sound teaching of the Bible to the hearts of spiritually hungry people all over the world, I also hear the Holy Spirit clearly telling me to keep writing books. In June of 1978, the Holy Spirit told me, "Write, write, write, and I will prosper what you write." I have done my best to faithfully obey that call and commission for most of the years since I received it, but I am more committed to writing today than ever before. In fact, not a day passes in which I do not write. My heart is filled with books that I have yet to write, and I am committed to harvesting the insights from the Bible that the Holy Spirit has taught me and putting them into print.

Trusted teaching has become the heart cry of believers all over the world who have experienced the dissatisfaction and even the pain of shallow moti- vational messages and men's doctrine that have fallen short of providing them with the deep foundation they've needed in order to really build their lives. During my ministry in the former USSR, I witnessed tremendous vic- tories as people have become transformed by solid teaching from the Bible.

But I've also witnessed a few sad stories of the mistakes and even the failures of some Christian ministers who failed the transformation test in their own lives. These failures led not only to the weakening, and in some cases the *collapse*, of their ministries as well as tragedies in their families, but they also brought a lot of disappointment to believers, many of whom were new converts. That's why I have committed to do my best to make sound

Bible-based teaching as accessible as possible worldwide and to continue to spread "teaching you can trust" through numerous media forms and means.

In the Body of Christ, a minister's job as a teacher of the Bible is to establish sound beliefs for some and strengthen sound beliefs for others. We are also called upon to uproot and stop the dangerous spread of misconception and error that have unfortunately taken root in some churches and in the lives of believers — error that has wreaked much havoc and harm in people's lives.

While the Church at large is gifted with many God-anointed teachers who are doing their parts, I know my part among them is to bring the "meat and potatoes" of God's Word to those who hunger to dive into God's Word with me. In no way do I think my gift sparkles brighter than others, but I am sure of what God wants me to do in the end-time Church. He wants me to do my part to see that His people are anchored in the Bible while they simultaneously pursue a move of the Holy Spirit *with* common sense.

### Ministry in Media — the Internet

When God called my family of five to the former USSR, we thought it was for a one-year commitment. But God expanded the plan, and all three of our sons are married to beautiful, godly Russian girls; we have eight Russian-speaking grandchildren; and many in our Renner family are dual citizens of both the United States and Russia.

We also have ministry offices in other parts of the world that are reaching out to God's people worldwide by various media. Our offices in Russia, the United States, Latvia, Ukraine, England, and Mongolia are essential to our ability to minister to our precious partner family. Together, as a team, we are corporately working to carry out God's calling on our ministry.

It is impossible to overstate how important we believe our ministry is to our God-called partner family. In particular, our staff in Tulsa is committed to serving them, ministering to them, and praying for them. This kind of ministry to our partners is as important as any aspect of our ministry and is foundational to our ability to touch the world. When we call people "partners," we really mean they are partners. They serve alongside us with their finances, putting fuel into the ministry tank to help us take the teaching of the Bible to the ends of the earth in obedience to the Great Commission in Matthew 28:19,20.

From our earliest beginnings in 1992 when we first began to broadcast the teaching of the Bible across the former USSR, I *knew* my assignment was to do my part to help Russian-speaking believers learn and study the Bible — to help them get grounded and *stay* grounded in the Word of God. That assignment has never changed, but it now reaches other parts of the world as well.

Besides taking "Sunday School" into people's living rooms through our TV programs, another part of that assignment entailed starting three significant churches — in Riga, Moscow, and Kiev — in addition to helping many other churches get started and providing oversight to them as well.

The Moscow church is a significant-sized congregation with influence across the former USSR. But because Moscow is so large, and it is difficult for people to travel hours and hours to get to the church, we are committed to completing the vision of establishing satellite campuses of the Moscow Good News Church throughout the city.

We must also keep our hand to the plow of maintaining and growing the ever-expanding Internet church (our Internet Good News Church, or IGNC), through which we are providing pastoral care in every part of the world where Russian-speakers live. Just as a local pastor, or shepherd, must abide with his flock and maintain oversight of that local work or the flock will become scattered and uncared for, the pastoral care we provide to our Internet congregation is hands-on and personal. It's not self-operated Internet technology. Rather, it is a network of human hearts and hands positioned by our leadership all over the world to actually hear the cries of those reaching out to us and to respond to them personally. We want to let them know they have not escaped our notice *or God's* and that they are deeply loved.

The Internet Good News Church experienced its own days of small beginnings, but today, hundreds of thousands regularly participate with IGNC to learn about God and His Word and to grow in their relationship with Christ. This Internet church is growing *exponentially*, and today there are Russian-speaking believers on every continent of the world who look to me as their "pastor" and who look at our online church as their home church because they do not have local pastors to care for them or churches to attend where they live. While a physical church would be best, IGNC answers a need for Russian-speaking Christians all over the world, and their massive response lets us know that we have indeed met a serious need. At present, I am certain that IGNC is already the largest online church ministry available to the Russian-speaking world.

Again, Denise and I are not that smart — all that we have done throughout our adult lives and ministry to succeed in God's plan is to *seek* His plan for our lives, *find* it, and *engage* it — act on it — with our wholehearted *yes*. *Our willing obedience has been the key to any success we have experienced.* Of course, we all need accountability and a "multitude of counselors" (*see* Proverbs 11:14), but God has provided us with that too. We have leaned hard on those precious gifts He has sent into our lives as they add their supply of wisdom, experience, and encouragement to what God has called us to do.

As I previously shared, God doesn't do anything randomly — without deliberateness and intentionality. He investigates and makes a thorough search until discovery is made and He *finds* someone who will be faithful in the little things and the big things, obeying Him thoroughly and precisely without reserve.

With all our hearts, Denise and I and our sons have run hard toward the will of God for our lives where we've understood it — and oftentimes, we've run on the word "go" without all the understanding we would have liked to have had at the moment. But may He *continue* to find us faithful to His will and plan!

### 'Their Sound Went Into All the Earth' — the Renner Story Goes On

In First Kings 10:1, we read that the Queen of Sheba had heard so much about Solomon's kingdom that she traveled to Jerusalem to personally see if Solomon's story matched his widespread fame. First Kings 10:4-7 tells us that she was impressed by the greatness of it all. In fact, those verses say, "And when the queen of Sheba had seen all Solomon's wisdom, and the house that he had built, and the meat of his table, and the sitting of his servants, and the attendance of his ministers, and their apparel, and his cupbearers, and his ascent by which he went up unto the house of the Lord; there was no more spirit in her. And she said to the king, It was a true report that I heard in mine own land of thy acts and of thy wisdom. Howbeit I believed not the words, until I came, and mine eyes had seen it: *and, behold, the half was not told me....*"

What you've read in this book has only touched the surface of our experiences and the victories that have been wrought for the Kingdom of God and His people. Like the Queen of Sheba, I can also say *the half has not been told.* Our *unlikely* story is still unfolding before us. The story indeed goes on.

It is a challenge to communicate all that God has done through our ministry. Only eternity will reveal the full impact of the lives that have been touched and changed. We have been pastoring, broadcasting, teaching, training, and distributing books and other teaching materials free of charge for so long that today, there are pastors leading significant churches who got saved as children under our ministry, many as they watched me on television.

Of all the early missionaries who came to Russia when everything changed here, only a handful of the early ones are still in Russia. Our family has stayed for all these years, our children marrying Russian women and having Russian families. But when our family arrived in 1992 and we kissed the ground, God really put this part of the world in our hearts.

And because we were there at the end of the Union of Soviet Socialist Republics and the very beginning of the Russian Federation, God allowed me to know legendary Pentecostal leaders in the Soviet Union, many of whom are now in Heaven — leaders like Bishop Roman Ivanovich Bilas, who was bishop of the Pentecostals in the USSR, Bishop Emmanuel Prokopenko of Latvia, Bishop Nikolai Melnick of Ukraine, and Bishop Fyodor Kondratyevich Marchuk of Belorussia. Very few leaders today in the modern movement knew these godly men. But these underground spiritual leaders during the Soviet years were legends.

I am so humbled when I ponder how God has graciously used Denise and me and our sons in this way. It was so truly *unlikely* that a family from Oklahoma would play such a role in the history of Russia's emerging Church.

When Denise and I first began our traveling teaching ministry, God gave us Romans 10:18 to claim for our ministry. It says, "But I say, Have they not heard? Yes verily, their sound went into all the earth, and their words unto the ends of the world." In all these years, we've seen this verse fulfilled at every turn in our ministry. He has literally enabled our voice to go to the ends of the earth to reach millions of people with the Gospel and the clear teaching of the Bible. *And He's not done yet!*

## Ministry in Media — the Printed Page

Some people suggested that we would fail in our ministry in the former USSR or that people in the West would forget about us, but God has been and is so faithful to help us fulfill our heavenly assignment — *and we were not forgotten!*

But what is totally amazing to me is that in the midst of all that God put on our plates to do, He also enabled me to write books that have been distributed to millions of readers around the world. And He *continues* to grace me to write.

It was very *unlikely* that my books would be a success without my being in the Western world to promote them, but against the odds, God has blessed them and has prospered what I've written, just as He said He would do in June of 1978. I'm so thankful that God speaks through my fingers to teach and strengthen readers around the world.

Denise has written multiple books, and her list of titles is also growing as she continues to publish written materials to help transform lives. Many of our books have also been published in Russian, Ukrainian, Latvian, Polish, French, German, Spanish, Portuguese, Japanese, and one book has been translated into a language in a region of the world that is dangerous for Christians.

With all the millions of pieces of mail we've received — indicating the hearts that have been touched and their response to us — God has miraculously enabled us to provide much-needed answers for these precious souls by writing back to them and sending millions of books and other materials free of charge. Because God has given us wonderful partners in the work, we've been able to get these materials to people who so desperately need them. It has been a privilege to be able to feed them with God's Word through the printed page.

## Ministry in Media — TV

Also, in our first thirty years in the former Soviet Union, we broadcast 589,964 TV programs, which amounts to 294,982 hours of nonstop TV time, which is the equivalent of 24 hours a day of nonstop broadcasting for more than 33 years! I have written extensively about our TV ministry in this book, but over the years, we have broadcast programs in Russian, English, Ukrainian, Latvian, Estonian, Romanian, Armenian, Georgian, Azerbaijani, Uzbek, Tajik, Mongolian, Polish, French, and Portuguese. We not only broadcast our own programs to the territories of the former USSR and beyond, but we have been honored to translate and broadcast teaching programs for multiple ministries in many of the languages I just mentioned.

## Our Public Ministry

In addition to writing books and building a TV network, we have personally preached in 80 cities of the former Soviet Union. In those cities, I have ministered more than 1,500 times. And since our first trip there together in 1991, Denise and I regularly traveled back to the United States twice a year — and in those trips, we ministered more than 1,000 times in 650 churches in 50 states.

We've been on about 5,000 flights to get to all those meetings, and some of the locations were remote and hard to reach. And if we add to this list the times I have ministered in approximately 3,500 services in the Moscow church, it means that at the time of this writing, I've publicly ministered more than 6,000 times since 1992.

And in all these years, God has graciously allowed us to be guests (sometimes multiple times) on the 700 Club, the Daystar network, TBN, VICTORY Channel (*Believer's Voice of Victory*), *Life Today* with James Robison, Marilyn Hickey's program, *Enjoying Everyday Life* with Joyce Meyer, *It's Supernatural!*

With Sid Roth, *Jewish Voice Ministries*, Richard Roberts' TV program, the *World Harvest* network, *The Jim Bakker Show*, Glenn Beck's program, and many other TV and radio programs.

## Our Partners Heard the Call Too

None of what I'm sharing with you would have been possible without the God-called partners who also heard the call and responded by taking their places alongside us in this work — in their finances and in their faith and prayers.

Every day when we wake up, Denise and I hold hands and thank God for those He has called to stand with us. We literally feel the support and the belief our partners have in us to faithfully execute with precision every assignment God gives us in the ministry. And the continual prayers of Denise and me, our sons, and our teams around the world are that God will continue to bring a *revival of the Bible* in people's hearts across the planet.

And this is not the end! I really believe Ecclesiastes 8:4, which says, "Where the word of a king is, there is power...." The power in God's Word is changing people's lives, and we are so thankful that God chooses to use us to be a part. Denise and I knew that we were some of the most *unlikely* of candidates to be chosen by God, but as I've said from the beginning, God truly delights in choosing those who are unlikely to carry out His Kingdom business.

## *'Fighting, Finishing, Keeping'* — and Loving Christ's Appearing

By the time the apostle Paul wrote what we know as Second Timothy 4:6 and 7, he was coming to the end of his race. When he wrote that epistle, he knew it would be his last words. That's why he wrote, "For I am now ready to be offered, and the time of my departure is at hand. I have fought a good fight, I have finished my course, I have kept the faith" (v. 7).

But notice Paul said, "...I have fought a good fight...." The word "fight" is the Greek word *agonidzo*, which is where we get the word *agony*. By using this word, Paul was telling us that some of his ministry had been *pure agony — an unbelievably difficult contest.* But Paul never budged an inch when things got hard. No, he stayed in the fight and remained faithful to his call.

The Greek sentence structure is actually reversed, and Paul literally said, "*A GOOD FIGHT — I fought one!*" The emphasis was on *the fight.* These words are the sentiments of a man who had no regrets. Paul was proud of the contest he had been in, and regardless of all the others who dropped out of their fight along the way, he could joyfully declare, "*I stayed in there. A GOOD FIGHT — I fought one!*"

But then Paul continued to say, "...I have finished my course...." The word "course" is actually the Greek word *dromos,* which describes *a foot race* or *a running track.* Notice Paul personalized this by saying "my course." He knew his course and didn't attempt to run anyone else's course. He stayed right on track — true to God's call on his life. Although many others had fallen out of their race and canceled their fight, Paul could victoriously state, "*Not me! I didn't fall out! I finished my assignment!*" Again, the Greek structure is reversed. A better translation would be: "*MY RACE — I finished it!*"

Next, Paul proclaimed, "...I have kept the faith." The Greek word for "kept" is the word *tereo,* which conveys the idea of *a total commitment to protect something.* This shows that, spiritually, Paul was far ahead of the rest of the gang who were *not* keeping the faith. You see, there were others who were letting go of their faith in order to save their skin! But Paul could say, "*Not me! I kept the faith!*" Like Paul's preceding statements, the Greek actually reverses the structure of this phrase as well. It reads, "*THE FAITH — I kept it!*"

Paul's ministry may have been difficult — one that was fraught with seemingly insurmountable challenges — but *he didn't relinquish an inch to the enemy.* And in Second Timothy 4:8, he said, "Henceforth there is laid up for me a crown of righteousness, which the Lord, the righteous judge, shall give me at that day: and not to me only, but unto all them also that love his appearing." But notice what he said: "...which the Lord, the righteous judge, shall give me *at that day....*"

Paul was referring to the moment he would soon die and go to meet the Lord. Instead of fearing that moment, Paul was ready to go. He was a soldier who, at the end of his life, was proud of the fight he had *fought*, the race he had run and *finished*, and the faith he had *kept*. *He had absolutely no regrets!* And that is how I want to be when one day, I come to the end of my own God-given race!

I am nowhere near the end of my fight of faith and my spiritual race, but like Paul, I am living with eternity in view — for the day when I shall stand before the Lord to receive the rewards He will righteously give to *all* those "who loved His appearing" and who lived to fulfill the eternal plan of God for their lives. When I look into the eyes of Jesus, who at that moment will become my Righteous Judge, I believe He will reward me, Denise, our sons, our faithful ministry team, and our partners who gave to help us with a crown of righteousness!

### The 'Before and After' of *Unlikely*:
### Don't Quit Now — Keep Dreaming

Forgive me if you think I'm belaboring the fact that Denise and I each grew up in *really* small towns in northeastern Oklahoma — but it is a fact that nearly no one in such "off the map" places in the United States goes about his days as a child thinking he will live one day on the other side of the world!

Although Denise and I in our youth each dreamed of doing something big for Jesus one day, there were times when we became discouraged, wondering if our desires were "just dreams." We struggled with thoughts that our deep desires to serve the Lord were just grand visions that would remain frustratingly unfulfilled. We didn't understand that it was the call of God we were grappling with all along — a sure call that, if found and fulfilled, would *never* frustrate or disappoint. Well, we found it — *and each other* — and we are still fulfilling our calling today!

I think back to my birthday vacation to New York City with my sister Ronda, where I heard for the first time the song "Corner of the Sky" at the Broadway production of *Pippin*. The "deep" of God's Spirit cried to the deep inside of me that day when those lyrics hit my ears and gripped my entire being to the core. That's when I knew that the thoughts of my heart I'd wrestled with were right, after all — I *would* leave Sand Springs one day, and it would be God's doing.

My wonderful hometown was not my final destination, only my starting point. It would not be the "corner of the sky" that my spirit longed for but my mind could not yet see. How could I know that God's calling would lead me, with a family of my own, to the other side of the world?

But God was calling — that much I knew. And when I experienced that epiphany moment in New York City, it was a divine appointment for me in which I saw a splinter of revelation from the Holy Spirit to let me know I was on the right path and that I could trust Him with great confidence to get me to where I needed to be.

Although I, too, have endured many of the hardships the apostle Paul alludes to in his epistles, my journey has been a secure one with Jesus at the helm and the Holy Spirit right there with me to lead me along the path God has chosen for me. But along with the challenges, my family and I have witnessed Kingdom advancements beyond our wildest imaginations and, oh, the things He has enabled us to do and see!

Since leaving Oklahoma, God has also enabled me to travel to many countries within the former Soviet Union as well as to nations all over the world. In fact, God has sent me to minister in nearly one hundred countries in my lifetime so far. In all my travels to minister, research, and film as I've taught the Bible in all media forms, I've seen some pretty amazing places on this planet. I can't list them all, but I will mention some of them that have made quite an impression on me.

*In Egypt* — I've visited the Pyramids of Giza, the Egyptian Museum in Cairo, the Cave Church of St. Simon in Cairo, ancient and remarkable monuments at Saqqara, ruins at Memphis, and the ancient sites of Luxor, Karnak, Valley of the Kings, Colossi of Memnon, Mortuary Temple of Hatshepsut, and Mortuary Temple of Rameses II.

I've also seen sites along the Nile River that include: Kom Ombo, the Temple of Horus at Edfu, the Temple of Philae, ancient Esna, and Elephantine Island in Aswan. I've seen the unfinished obelisk near Aswan, and I've ridden on a camel through the Egyptian desert, toured the catacombs of

Kom El Shoqafa in Alexandria, and walked upon the ruins of the ancient Lighthouse of Alexandria.

*In Europe and Great Britain* — I've visited the Ishtar Gate of Babylon and the Altar of Pergamum at the Pergamum Museum in Berlin. I've been to the Louvre, the Cathedral of Notre-Dame, and the Eiffel Tower in Paris. In Italy, I've spent many hours studying in the Vatican Museum. I've also visited the Sistine Chapel, *Abbazia delle Tre Fontane* (the place of the apostle Paul's beheading), and in and around Rome, I've toured the catacombs of San Sebastiano, San Callisto, Priscilla, and Domitilla.

I've toured and researched many times at the Roman Colosseum and Pantheon, and I've taken extensive tours of ancient underground Rome that lies below modern-day Rome. I've seen the ancient ruins of Pompeii, the leaning tower of Pisa, the architectural wonders and statues of Michelangelo in Florence, and I've traveled by gondola the canals of Venice. In Greece, I've visited the Parthenon in Athens, the cities of Corinth, Delphi, Philippi, and Thessalonica, the monasteries of Meteora, and the tomb of Philip II of Macedon.

I've been to the Nazi ghetto of Warsaw in Poland and to the Habsburg Imperial Palace in Prague. I've wandered the streets of Copenhagen and have seen other wonderful sites in Europe that are too numerous to name. In England, I've seen St. Paul's Cathedral, Westminster Abbey, the Tower Bridge, the Tower of London, the British Museum, Buckingham Palace, the Houses of Parliament, Windsor Castle, Blenheim Palace, and other castles and unforgettable sites throughout England.

*In Israel* — I've been to the Wailing Wall, the Temple Mount, the Church of the Nativity, the Church of the Holy Sepulchre, the Mount of Olives, the Herodium (Herodian Fortress), the Dead Sea, Masada, Sepphoris (the "City on a Hill" about four miles from Nazareth), nearly every biblical site mentioned in the Gospels in Galilee, and a long list of other ancient sites from the south to the north of Israel.

*In Turkey* — I've seen the Hagia Sophia, the Hippodrome, the underground cisterns, and the Chora Church in or around Istanbul. In other parts of Turkey, I've spent significant time studying at the sites of ancient Ephesus, Smyrna, Pergamum, Thyatira, Sardis, Philadelphia, and Laodicea (the seven cities Jesus addressed in the book of Revelation), Aphrodisias, Miletus, Antioch, Tarsus, the Titus Tunnel (near the border of Syria), and the reputed fossilized remains of Noah's Ark in eastern Turkey near Iran.

*In Russia* — I've been to places in Moscow and St. Petersburg that I know practically *inside out*. I have numerous favorite places to visit in Moscow, including the Kremlin, Red Square, Tsaritsyno Palace, the Bolshoi theatre, and various world-class museums. And as I wrote in Chapter Fourteen, I'll never forget the experience my son Paul and I, shared together at the Pashkov House (Palace) on Vagankovsky Hill in Moscow, where we were honored to participate in the historical celebration of the five-hundredth anniversary of the Protestant Reformation.

In Saint Petersburg, I cherish every opportunity to visit the Hermitage, Peterhof, Chinese Palace, Catherine Palace, Pavlovsk Palace, New Michael Palace (Novo Mikhailovsky), Gatchina Palace, St. Isaac's Cathedral, and Church of the Savior on Spilled Blood. In other parts of Russia, I've person-ally been to the bottom of coal mines in Vorkuta, to multiple cities scattered throughout Siberia, and to the shipyards of Vladivostok. I've sailed on a private ship on the Sea of Japan off the coast of Vladivostok, and I've minis-tered on Russia's distant island of Sakhalin. I've been to the northern city of Murmansk, and God has enabled me to minister in other locations scattered all over Russia.

*In the other fourteen former Soviet countries* — Throughout Latvia, I've seen ruins of Nazi concentration camps from the Holocaust as well as Medi-eval and Crusader Castles and Imperial Russian palaces. I've walked the fairytale-like streets of Tallinn in Estonia, and I've toured the Hill of Crosses and the Nazi concentration camps in Lithuania, as well as concentration camps in Belarus. I've visited ancient churches, cathedrals, monasteries, "holy caves," and the Babi Yar holocaust site in Kiev. I've toured the catacombs near Odessa, and I've been to the depths of a nuclear missile silo in central Ukraine. I've been to the gorgeous snow-covered mountains above Almaty in Kazakhstan and walked through bright-red poppy fields in Kyrgyzstan. I have also personally visited nomads in their tents in the plains of Central Asia, and I've been to ruins of two-thousand-year-old buildings that remain from the Silk Road in Azerbaijan. I've visited so many other historical sites and landmarks that there is not enough space here to mention them all.

*In other countries* — I've seen the Teotihuacan Pyramids, the peaks of massive volcanoes, and the ancient Xochimilco canals near Mexico City. I've been to the coast of Costa Rica and seen the enormous crocodiles near Jaco. I've been to the Caribbean island of Puerto Rico and to Jamaica, Haiti, Grand Cayman, Antigua, Saint Martin (French and Dutch sides), Aruba, Curaçao, and the Bahamas. I've been to the Taj Mahal and to the Red Palace in Agra, India, and I've walked the top of the Great Wall of China. I've sailed on a Junk through the breathtaking Ha Long Bay in Vietnam. I traversed the dangerous ledges of the world-famous Victoria Falls in Zambia, and I have ministered in Reunion Island near the coast of Mauritius. I have also been on safaris on the Zambezi River that flows near Livingstone, Zambia, and in Chobe National Park in Botswana.

Before our family relocated to the former USSR, we traveled for years across the United States by car as we ministered all over the U.S. and Canada. As we traveled thousands of miles by car to preach, Denise and I tried our best to chart our trips so that we could include interesting places along the way to give our sons a respite from being trapped in our small car as we traveled nonstop to minister the Word of God in nearly every continental state and major city in the nation.

During those days and over the years, we saw many significant National Parks in the United States and Canada. A few of these National Parks made big impressions on us, including: Great Smoky Mountains, Rocky Mountains, Carlsbad Caverns, Grand Canyon, Petrified Forest, Saguaro, Badlands, Yellowstone, Grand Teton, Glacier, Mount Rainier, Olympic, Mount St. Helens, Crater Lake, Death Valley, the Redwoods, Mount Rushmore National Memorial, and Haleakala National Park in Maui — as well as especially impressive parks in Canada like Banff, Lake Louise, Canmore-Kananaskis, Yoho, and Red Deer. This is just a small list of amazing parks and significant historical places we have seen over the years in the United States and Canada.

All of these are unlikely places to see, indeed, for a small-hometown boy like me!

From the time the Southern Baptist Foreign Mission Board began sending me all those maps when I was a youth — *and even before* — I'd dreamed of traveling the world. But I never imagined I'd see *all* these places where God has enabled me to travel in my studies, research, and ministry.

But in retrospect, I see that when, with my wholehearted yes, I committed my life to Jesus Christ for Him to do with me as He pleased, He initiated a stream of unlikely encounters with unlikely people that I never would have experienced without having willingly answered the call. Had I refused to make the turn at *any* bend in the road where He was leading me, I could have missed something very important for my life and ministry that could have mattered in the eternal scheme of things.

But by God's grace, He enabled me to say *yes* and has put me in the ministry office I stand in today — and He has *kept* me here all these years. I am and will forever be grateful.

In Chapter Five, I told you that I left the university before I received my bachelor's degree because I believed God wanted me to learn at the feet of Dr. Bennett at First Baptist Church in Fort Smith, Arkansas. Although I never received my degree from the university I attended, over the years, I did earn a Bachelor's Degree, Master's Degree, and Doctor of Ministry at a Christian university in the United States. I rarely tell it to anyone, but, technically, it makes me Dr. Renner.

There's always a "before and after" of the unlikely situations we find ourselves in. *"Before,"* we may have thought our future was hopeless. But after we answer the call and determine obediently to stay with it, we see that God has a marvelous way of helping us run our race and to finish what needs to be finished *on time* (*see* Philippians 1:6). He brings us full circle to complete everything that needs to be completed — and He never forgets what we commit to Him.

In my youth, I was never the wisest, best-educated, strongest, or most popular among my peers. When I look at my life now, I am still the *least likely* to stand in my God-given role in the Kingdom of God. I grew up belittled by teachers, made fun of by many of my peers, misunderstood by friends, and simply *depressed* in my youth. Although it seemed unlikely I would ever be where I am today, God graced me to make every turn so that He could bring me, with my family, to the place He had destined for me to be.

*The word "unlikely" is an entirely appropriate word to describe my entire life!*

### A New Door Swung Wide Open for the Gospel

At this season, Denise and I, our family, and our ministry team continue to be stretched by the fresh *unlikely* vision God gives us. We are continually hearing the call of God beckoning us to take new territory and explore new frontiers to reach more souls for His Kingdom.

One of the greatest developments of our new-frontiers ministry occurred when we acquired the largest Russian-speaking Christian satellite channel in the world. By God's divine commission and grace, we are the owners and operators of a twenty-four-hour-per-day satellite network that reaches Russian-speakers around the globe.

Because Denise and I have been determined to obey God fully and have run with the vision He has given us, He has entrusted us with this assignment — another amazing —huge — door of opportunity!

### Nonstop Ministry and the Propagation of the Gospel — 'This Gospel Shall Be Preached'

Throughout this book, I've explained to the best of my ability our teaching ministry in the U.S., our call to the former USSR, our commission to take the teaching of the Bible into people's homes via television, our assignments to establish Good News churches in three nations, and our duty to mentor, encourage, strengthen, and support other God-called men and women who desire to obey His plans and purposes for their own lives.

But this large Christian satellite network that God put into our hands is singularly the biggest opportunity ever given to us to bring trusted teaching from the Bible to millions of Russian-speaking believers all over the world where our satellite signal can be detected. Twenty-four hours a day, seven days a week, *nonstop*, we are broadcasting via this satellite network to Russian-speaking Christians in large geographical regions worldwide.

This is so amazing to me that my mind still wrestles to grasp its reality — what an *unlikely* assignment *and responsibility* for two people who grew up in small towns in Oklahoma. It is all so remarkable, but remember — God delights in choosing the unlikely and in doing the remarkable through their yielded lives.

Because of the acquisition of this satellite network, we have been tasked almost as "gatekeepers" of trusted teaching and sound doctrine — guardians of truth and light — affecting approximately eighty-three nations of the world. Just as I became practically spellbound in God's presence as I stood in the first service of the Moscow Good News Church in our new permanent facility, I am awed all over again at the responsibility that lies before us — it is truly ministry that keeps *amassing*, even as Jesus said to me all those many years ago.

## It Takes Desire To Do Anything Significant

The will and plan of God is more than just "logistics" — being *where you need to be* and *with whom* and *at what time* — even though being at the right place at the right time, or being led by the Spirit of God, is absolutely critical in one's spiritual journey.

But I have learned that the Holy Spirit not only wants to go before you as the One who makes the crooked path straight — He wants to make "the crooked straight" *in your soul* so that when you get to the place you need to be in His plan, you have the wherewithal to *remain* there and bring God glory instead of "fizzling out," as my mentor Dr. Bennett so vividly explained.

So before I close this final chapter, I want to share one more story with you along this same vein that I think might be meaningful for your own life.

Many years ago, I saw a photograph taken from the summit of one of Canada's tallest mountains. It was the most beautiful photograph I had ever seen. In fact, it was such an amazing sight that I determined I would take a trip to Canada and climb to the top of that summit to see the view for myself, *in real life*!

Seeing that photograph stirred me to action. The more I thought about it, the more I desired to make it to the top of that mountain myself. A mental vision of my reaching the summit of that mountain *filled* my thoughts. For someone so averse to every sport I'd been exposed to growing up, I had, however, watched television programs about mountain climbing and had always been interested in that type of daring activity. Now I was no longer content just to think about it — I wanted to do it myself!

To get ready for the climb, I went on a diet and lost a lot of weight, and I read books about the Canadian Rockies mountain range. But a week before the climb, something happened to taint my misguided efforts to prepare for this momentous climb. A brother in the Lord came to me after a church service I was conducting in the state of Kansas. He gave me a giant hug and said, "Brother Rick, thank you for your ministry. God used you to change my life!" I was thrilled with his testimony, but the hug he gave me was so tight that he broke a rib in my left side!

The pain was excruciating. At night as I tried to sleep, I cringed every time I tried to roll from one side to the other. When I tried to lift a sack of groceries from the car to carry them into the house, the pain was horrific! Then as Denise and I drove across the states of Kansas, Colorado, Wyoming, and Montana on our way to Canada, where I was determined to make that mountain climb, she kept pleading, "Rick, you shouldn't try to make this climb with a broken rib!"

But no broken rib was going to stop me. I was so full of desire that I was determined to make it to the top of that mountain peak. With a broken rib, a minimally fit physique, and a backpack loaded with seventy-five pounds of supplies, I was ready to look to the top of that mountain and say, *"Here I come!"*

Finally, I made it to Canada, where I met with a group of men who would accompany me to the top of the mountain. The other men were avid climbers — I was not. They were in superb physical condition — I was not. To be honest, although I'd read books about it, I had no idea, *practically*, how difficult the journey was going to be to get to the top of that summit. But I had enough desire to keep me going and get me to my goal!

Soon our climbing party began the difficult ascent. It wasn't the most dangerous climb, but it *could* be dangerous to a person unfamiliar with mountain climbing. And it could be *very* dangerous to a person as physically unfit as I was! And the climb up this mountain was treacherous enough to have claimed the lives of several people through the years. In fact, just one day before our climb, two professional climbers tried to cross a patch of black ice at the same spot where we were headed and, suddenly, they disappeared out of sight as they *hurtled* down to their deaths on a glacier below.

Sharp ridges and steep cliffs were just a few risks connected with the climb. Altitude sickness was another risk — unfortunately for me, that was a risk I read nothing about in all of my reading and therefore hadn't considered.

I huffed, puffed, and pushed my way toward the top of that mountain. With each step, the weight of my backpack got heavier. I scrambled up ninety-degree inclines that led to what felt like even sharper inclines. Rocks tumbled under my feet. I fell. I rolled. I promised God that I would never attempt to do such a stupid thing again if I could just get to the top and back down alive!

At one point, as I held on to a ragged rock to keep from falling, I noticed a mountain goat watching me! It looked at me as if to say, "What in the world are you doing up here?" I wondered, *Do I look as stupid to that goat as I feel right now?*

What in the world *was* I doing climbing this mountain? It was a world-class climb — *and it was my first climb!* For all the studying and preparing I'd done, I wished I'd really known what I was getting into before I started.

Finally, I stood on the top of that mountain and looked out over the peaks of the Canadian Rockies. Spread out before me was a panoramic view of hundreds of incredibly beautiful mountain peaks. The sky was so clear, it looked like I could see for a hundred miles as I took into my sights peak after peak after peak. Then as the sun went down, I watched as orange, blue, and purple tones filled the sky so vividly, it nearly looked like those colors were dancing. I'd seen sunsets in California and Hawaii, but this sunset was gorgeous beyond words. *What a view!* As I suspected, the photograph I had seen paled in comparison to actually being there.

My exhaustion abated, and for a few minutes, I forgot about the hardships I had encountered to get to the top of the mountain. I had conquered that mountain! My heart was shouting!

But my great victory was about to be interrupted in a big way by altitude sickness. A few hours later, my victorious celebration ended as I began to feel nausea and dizziness come over me. It came fast and hard, wave after wave of nausea pounding against me until I was unable to stand. My eyes began to see black spots. My head seemed to spin round and round, and I started violently vomiting. I vomited and vomited until I had nothing left in my stomach to throw up. Even then, my body still convulsed with dry heaves.

Dehydrated and weak, I didn't know how I could physically make it through the night. All night long my body wrenched with dry heaves, even though my stomach was empty. I cried. I pleaded for help. I prayed. It was a sickness like nothing I had ever experienced in my life. The next morning, I was still sick and so physically weak that I had to work hard to muster the energy to take even a few steps.

The problem was that we had to start the trip back down the slopes to where we had begun the climb the day before. The other men didn't know how I was going to make it, but I was determined that this mountain wasn't going to conquer me. I'd made it up that mountain, and I was going to make it down that mountain successfully. My desire was stronger than my physical weakness.

I took one small step down the mountain. Then another small step. Then another and another. Each step was such an effort that I had to really focus and work up the nerve to take the next small step. A climber from another group who passed me on my way down saw how sick I was and contacted the Canadian Mounties to notify them about my condition. Unknown to me, upon receiving that call, mountain police began searching the mountain for the dehydrated climber — *me*!

When I reached the bottom, I was met by an officer of the Royal Canadian Mounted Police who had been searching the mountain for me. He took me by the arm, led me to a vehicle, and drove me straight to a hostel. On the way, the man made sure I was drinking plenty of fluids. Meanwhile, he lectured me on the dangers of mountain climbing. He let me know how stupid it was for me to attempt that climb without first preparing myself.

The other men in our group already knew the risks. They assumed that I knew them too. But I was uninformed and unprepared. If I had possessed that information, it wouldn't have made the climb much easier, but at least I would have understood what I was going to face. The lack of information meant I had to figure it all out on my own. That's always the hardest way to learn!

Why am I telling you this story at the very end of my autobiography?

Because I want you to know that as you step out to do the things God will call you to do, it will take *strong desire* for you to get you through the obstacles you will encounter along the way that you will often feel unprepared to face. No one but God knows what lies in your path. But when you face unexpected problems that seem impossible to overcome, remember:

- Any obstacle can be overcome.

- Any challenge can be conquered.

- Any mountain can be successfully climbed — *IF* you have the inward desire and motivation to achieve your goal.

- God is not unprepared, and He will help you.

As you read these final paragraphs, I want to tell you confidently that Jesus really is Lord over every situation you will ever face. If you're willing to obey Him and surrender to follow wherever He leads, your life will take on color as never before. Any monotony will leave and your life will become a thrilling and *unlikely* faith journey that exceeds anything you could ever imagine.

Ephesians 3:20 and 21 in the *Amplified Bible* says, "Now to Him who is able to [carry out His purpose and] do superabundantly more than all that we dare ask or think [infinitely beyond our greatest prayers, hopes, or dreams], according to His power that is at work within us, to Him be the glory in the church and in Christ Jesus throughout all generations forever and ever. Amen." When you surrender your life to God's plans and purposes, the drabness of life departs as God begins to do superabundantly more than you could ever dare ask or think, even infinitely beyond your greatest desires, hopes, or dreams!

But one last thing before you lay this book down. If you are still tempted to think you are too "unlikely" for God's remarkable call to come to you, remember the *RIV (Renner Interpretive Version)* of First Corinthians 1:26-28.

**For you see your calling, brothers, how not many of you were especially bright, educated, or enlightened according to the world's standards; not many of you were impressive; not many came from high-ranking families or from the upper crust of society. Instead,**

**God selected people who are idiots in the world's view; in fact, the world sees them as imbeciles, jerks, and real twerps. Yet God is using them to utterly confound those who seem smart in the world's eyes. God has chosen people whom the world finds laughable, and through them, He is confounding those who think they are so high and mighty. Low-class, second-rate, common, average, run-of-the-mill people — those so low that the world doesn't even think they're worth the time of day — these are the ones whom God has chosen....**

You see, God is looking for anyone who is willing to follow Him to fulfill his or her assignment until it is completed as He ordered it. So *if* you want to be used by God, it's time to quit thinking you are too unlikely to be used. God is simply looking for hearts that are willing to follow Him and are *un*willing to quit or give up on His plan. *So if you have that kind of heart, you are exactly the kind of person God wants to use!*

By choosing regular folks like you and me, God has made sure that when the victories, big or small, are won, everyone will know it was due to His grace. That's why the apostle Paul said, "...According as it is written, He that glorieth, let him glory in the Lord" (1 Corinthians 1:31).

I wonder...have *you* limited God because of your past, your upbringing, your status in life — your own "unlikeliness" to experience an adventure in God? I encourage you to take the limits off your thinking as you offer Him your wholehearted *yes*. It's time for you to surrender and say, "God, I am yours to use as You wish. Your plan may seem unlikely to me and to those who know me, but regardless of how unlikely it is, I'm surrendering right now for You to reveal to me Your remarkable will and plan for my life!"

## The Faith of Those Who Followed Me

I can't end this book without talking about the faith of those who followed me into the ministry with every bit of consecration and grit that possessed me when *I* said yes to the call — and that is my precious wife and my three sons.

Because of the nature of the spiritual barriers I would need to transcend to answer the call, and the challenges of darkness I would have to withstand, God spoke to me in visions and in words from Heaven so remarkable that I would have difficulty misunderstanding what He was asking me to do. I needed those experiences as memorials I could look to when my mind was under assault. I needed the security of those eternal words to bolster and undergird me so I could stem the tide of the fierce spiritual storms that regularly opposed me.

Don't misunderstand me — Denise hears from God and so do Paul, Philip, and Joel — but those remarkable directives from the Lord for our lives and ministry came to *me*. I had to communicate to my family the direction He was taking us, and they followed in faith and trust not only in God, to whom they'd given their hearts and lives, but in me as the leader of our home and our ministry.

I had the huge responsibility of obeying what I'd heard so authoritatively from the Lord. But my family took on that responsibility for themselves like soldiers ready for battle. They were and are some of the most stable, unflinching, capable, and committed soldiers for Christ that I know — I have no closer comrades-in-arms than these precious people God has given me to share our lives and destinies together.

Each time I have laid before Denise a new directive I've received from the Lord, one of her first responses to me has been that "God's track record with us has been good." That statement always "shoots" right through me as I stop to recognize and thank Him once again that He has *never* failed this Renner family — and has, in fact, come through for us in ways so big, the *memories* of those God-feats still stun me today.

As I further pondered Denise's brief but bold statement, "God's track record with us has been good," another thought comes to me, and that is, I've always endeavored to be stable and trustworthy so that my own track record with my family was good. When I communicate that I sense God is saying something to us, I don't use those words lightly. And over time, they have come to see that "wisdom is indeed known by her children" — by the fruit that is produced — and the seeds of what I've received and acted on from God have produced a harvest of fruitfulness time and time again.

There is another precious group of people whose faith is remarkably seen in our ministry, and that is our ministry partners. They didn't hear it when Heaven resoundingly issued the command and call for us to take the Gospel to the nations of the world. But they believed that *we heard it* — and they have not only seen the fruit that has been borne as a result of our obedience, but they hold that fruit in their own hands as a result of *their* obedience. It is laid up to their account, too, for participating with the call of God on our lives through their giving.

## Part Two of Our Story

You've been reading our unlikely story. As I've said, we plan to run this race for a long time, so "Part Two" is still ahead of us! And we fully anticipate that the next season will take us from glory to glory!

Walking with God and doing His will is always an unending adventure. In fact, as I come to the close of this last chapter, I have become aware of a new, unexpected development that will lead to a repositioning for even greater harvest in the next phase of our ministry. But I'll save that surprising development for *Part Two*. Whatever happens, Denise and I are committed to obey God's call to take His Word to the ends of the world. We are traveling onward in our remarkable, faith-filled journey to the ends of the earth!

Remember, when Jesus performed His first miracle of turning water into wine, the wine Jesus miraculously made was so good, it tasted like the finest aged wine (*see* John 2:10). Although Denise and I and our family refrain from drinking alcoholic beverages as a choice, we embrace the conviction that just as wine gets richer and fuller with age, God has saved the best part of our lives and ministry for the next part of our journey!

And now I want to encourage you…if you feel your life hasn't quite "hit the mark" of God's high calling that He has uniquely designed just for you, it's time for you to lay this book down and to start experiencing His grace and power. As you seek Him and engage your God-ordained calling, He will launch you into your own remarkable and *unlikely* journey. God bless you on your Heaven-ordained path.

# Photos Corresponding to Chapters 13-17

**Above:** In August 2000 when our family arrived by train in Moscow, our work in the Russian-speaking world was about to be multiplied on new fronts. We willingly brought our supply so that God could disperse it to the far-flung lands of the former USSR. Moscow would be the place from which He would gloriously enable us to do it!

**Above:** An apartment in Moscow that was leveled by a terrorist attack. In and around the time our family moved to Moscow was a horrific season when violent terrorist attacks were occurring there and across many parts of Russia. While most of the world was focused on the tragedy of 9/11 in America, Russia was also being rocked with attack after attack. Photo: © Sputnik / used by permission.

**Above:** The gargantuan Hotel Russia sat right on the edge of Red Square and was the site where the Moscow Good News Church was born in the power of the Spirit on Thursday, September 7, 2000. Who would have ever dreamed that we would start a church on the edge of Red Square! Photo: © Dreamstime.com / Grafff77

**Above:** Denise led worship, Paul played the drums, Philip played the trumpet, and Joel sang with the backup singers on the worship team. The small auditorium we'd rented in the Hotel Russia was a hall used for lectures and only seated 225 people. The first night, every seat was taken, with people standing around the perimeters of the room.

**Above:** On that first night, I welcomed everyone and asked how many of them had either seen us on television or read one of my books. Nearly every hand was raised in response to those questions. The evening was so anointed and Heaven-kissed that it was "magical." God was there, and we knew something magnificent was unfolding before our eyes right on the edge of Red Square.

**Above:** It was a historic night as we held our first meeting near the multi-colored domes of St. Basil's Cathedral and the golden domes of the Kremlin. It was simply surrealistic, but we were really there, and the church was born on that night.

**Right:** Our new location was the Kino Theater Mir, a movie house with 820 seats located in downtown Moscow on Tsvetnoy Boulevard — next door to Moscow's most famous permanent circus called the Nikulin Circus. Because this Moscow circus frequently had overflow crowds, they occasionally used the Kino Theater Mir next door to accommodate the overflow matinee audiences.

**Left:** This circus was known to all Muscovites, so it was easy to tell people the location of the church meetings. We simply told them, "We're meeting next door to the Nikulin Circus on Tsvetnoy Boulevard downtown." That location was so well-known that people didn't even need an address because they had all been to that circus when they were children. People regularly packed our new notable location, and they were saved, filled with the Spirit, delivered, and healed.

**Right:** At the circus, a troupe of bears would enter the ring to perform, and, incredibly, many of them did tricks like they were humans. On days the circus had overflow crowds at the Kino Theater Mir, there were times when we arrived at this location to set up for church, and our paths literally crossed with Russian brown bears that were being walked out the same doors of the building that we were entering to hold our services.

Photo: © Sputnik / used by permission.

**Left:** Pictured here are our sons walking to the Metro to go to school when we first arrived in Moscow. Denise and I watched our sons flourish in the ministry and in their new surroundings. They embraced Russia, its language, and its culture. Today Paul, Philip, and Joel are married to Russian women, they have Russian-American children, and they speak Russian fluently.

**Right:** This elegant old auditorium with a wraparound balcony became the new temporary home for the Moscow Good News Church. God blessed us there and we continued growing — the place was teeming with life! On some Sundays, the place was so full that it seemed people were practically hanging over the balcony. Every week, people walked the aisle to give their hearts to Jesus, and believers were filled with the Holy Spirit.

**Left:** That location was a historic auditorium that was the concert hall of a Russian university. The theater-style auditorium was built in 1936 as a cultural center for the students and employees of this higher-education transport institution. Over the years, famous opera singers, contemporary singers, and Soviet cinema stars performed on the stage in this concert hall.

**Above:** Once a year at this venue, we celebrated the fifty-five nationalities that regularly attended our church. On that day, many came dressed in costumes reflecting their nationality, and food from many nations was served between services. Even Denise and I dressed in costumes from a former Soviet republic to join in all the fun and festivities.

**Above:** My pulpit was right above a sealed orchestra pit. Hidden in storage in that pit was an immense bust of Vladimir Lenin that had been used at socialist-communist events there in days gone by. Our being there was a symbolic picture of the truth that God's power will always surmount evil and put it underfoot where His people yield to Him and obey His directives and plans.

Photo: © Sputnik/Alamy / used by permission.

**Photos:** Our church next moved to the Moscow Youth Palace (MDM), a famous location where millions of youth over many years had attended events. And because the Metro actually opened right into the building itself, it meant no one had to be exposed to the rain or snow — they could walk from the Metro right into the auditorium, which also helped contribute to growth.

**Above:** Our Golden Stars events were attended by thousands and thousands of senior citizens. We invited legendary performers from the Soviet years to perform for the senior citizens — names unfamiliar to Western readers, but very familiar to Russian citizens of this era. Over the years, we invited Mikhail Boyarsky, Zinovy Visokovsky, Valery Zolotukhin, Alexander Malinin, Elina Bystritskaya, Vasily Lanovoy, Vladimir Zeldin, Inna Makarova, Klara Luchko, Vera

Vasilyeva, Lyudmila Kasatkina, the Pyatnitsky Russian Folk Chorus, and others. Those events were *enthralling* as the Soviet legends those elderly people grew up watching and listening to now stood on a stage right in front of them — and those stars had come just for this massive group of elderly honorees.

**Above:** Vitamin Club was started after we held these concerts — monthly events at which we provided entertainment, vitamins, and teaching from the Bible to senior citizens. We saw *streams* of senior adults flood into our Vitamin Club meetings. Over the years, *tens of thousands* of senior citizens attended these events. Many gave their lives to Christ and have since stepped into eternity with Heaven as their home because of those concerts and this God-inspired outreach. Today this ministry is called Golden Age, and it has a membership of several thousand who participate each month.

**Right:** Denise was remarkably invited to perform "The Lord's Prayer" on stage at the Kremlin Palace. People were spellbound as her voice, with the orchestra, filled that massive auditorium. She stood so regally on that stage that had once been dedicated to socialist-communist ideology, and the crowd applauded over and over when Denise was finished. She prayed for God to be glorified on that legendary stage in the Kremlin Palace, and that is precisely what took place that night.

**Left:** God allowed us the joy of seeing Paul Renner step forward as one of the leaders in the Protestant movement in Russia. Today he is loved and respected by leaders of various denominations.

Photo: © RUCEF (Russian United Union of Evangelical Christians) / used by permission.

**Right:** Denise and I watched as Philip, too, began to step forward into his calling. Philip became the youth pastor for the Moscow Good News Church — then he began to write worship songs that are today sung in Russian-speaking churches all over the former USSR.

**Above:** On March 17, 2007, we officially started the Kiev Good News Church. More than 1,500 people packed into the auditorium where those first services were held, and many became part of the church. For nearly two full years, Denise and I went back and forth every week between Moscow and Kiev. Today a wonderful church is thriving in Kiev, led by a pastor who is doing a marvelous job leading that congregation. Pictured here is my pulpit that I regularly preached from in the Kiev Good News Church.

**Right:** Joel grew up working in our ministry and had *many* jobs in the ministry over the years. Today he is a tremendously gifted leader who faithfully discharges his duties as Chief Executive Officer of RENNER Ministries. Joel oversees our outreaches, records his own segments for our daily TV program, and often travels with me to film on location.

**Above:** For years on March 8, Denise has held a major event for women on Russia's Women's Day — a holiday comparable to Mother's Day in the United States except that it celebrates *all* women: mothers, sisters, grandmothers, and so on — at home and in the workplace. These events are packed to overflowing with women, music, special speakers, and seminars designed to minister to Russian-speaking women.

**Above:** Denise has a burgeoning online ministry to Russian-speaking women all over the world. At present, there are more than fifty thousand women involved in this specialized online ministry. In addition, we broadcast her daily TV program on our Russian-speaking satellite network.

**Above:** There are *tens of thousands* of women involved in Denise's women's ministry, and there is no end in sight as to how many more will eventually be involved. It all started with Denise's vision for women whose lives have been wounded to be healed and to become God's healing instruments to other women still struggling in their self-images and marriages.

**Above:** Moscow currently has eight million cars registered in the city and an unknown number of cars that come from elsewhere. A report by an automotive analytics company has dubbed Moscow the "world capital of traffic jams." Photo: © Sputnik / used by permission.

**Above:** The Moscow Metro (subway) is breathtaking in terms of its architectural design. It has 238 stations and its tracks run underground for 254 miles, making it the fourth longest in the world and the longest outside of China. It serves about 9,000,000 passengers daily, which equals an approximate cumulative number of 2,500,000,000 passengers every year. Photo: © Sputnik / used by permission.

**Above:** Within the official city limits of Moscow, there is a population of more than twelve million people at the time of this writing. If you were to add the "unofficial" unregistered people in the region of Moscow, the population exceeds twenty million. In a recent speech by Moscow's mayor, he said that on a daily basis, there are some thirty million people in transit in the city of Moscow — more people than in the whole state of Texas! Photo: © Sputnik / used by permission.

**Above:** Our church's next location was a smaller auditorium, which required us to do five services every weekend. It was physically strenuous, but it was what we needed to do at the moment as we searched the city for a building we could renovate to become a permanent home for the Moscow Good News Church.

**Left:** When we found the building for our Moscow church, the *exterior* was in terrible shape. Exterior tiles were falling off the sides of the building, but what we saw on the outside would seem *nice* compared to the mess we were about to find inside. The interior was *devastated*. All around me I saw broken floors, falling ceilings, and bare brick walls.

**Above:** In commemoration of this monumental victory, we placed two bronze plaques in the foyer of the Moscow Good News Church — one written in English and the other in Russian.

**Above:** When it was time to start demolishing walls in our new church building, we wanted to be the first to swing sledge hammers to start the whole project. So Denise and I came with Paul, Philip, and Joel, and together, as a family, we demolished the first wall that needed to be removed.

**Left:** On December 7, 2014, we held the grand opening and dedication of the permanent facility of the Moscow Good News Church. This was a historic event for the entire Protestant movement in Russia, which was recognized even at the federal, state, and local levels of government. Since the consecration of one of the largest, most beautiful, and modern church buildings in the country was taking place in the Russian capital, this event was not ignored by the officials of the Presidential Administration of the Russian Federation, the State Duma of the Russian Federation, and the Moscow city government.

**Above:** From December 7, 2014, to the present, the Moscow Good News Church has lived in its own permanent home, which has become a regularly used venue for the Protestant movement in Russia. It is impossible to exaggerate the significance of this "building victory" for our church and the Protestant movement in this nation. A building

represents stability and permanence and says *we are here for the long haul*. Our permanent facility was a visible declaration that our church family of believers was a credible part of the community. It was a victory indeed for which we were so thankful.

**Photos:** October 31, 2017, marked the five-hundredth anniversary of the Protestant Reformation. On that date, Paul Renner and I attended an event hosted by the Presidential Administration in the renowned Pashkov Palace that stands on Vagankovsky Hill in Moscow. Gathered to celebrate Luther's historic defining of the Christian faith were Protestant, Catholic, and Ortho-dox ministers; representatives of other religions; senior officials from the government of the Russian Federation, including the former Prime Minister and First Deputy Chief of Staff of the Presidential Executive Office, Sergey Vladilenovich Kiriyenko; members of the Presidential administration; and members of the State Duma.

Photos: © RUCEF (Russian United Union of Evangelical Christians) and Anton Kruglikov / used by permission.

**Photos:** On October 16, 2020, Paul Renner was ordained as Senior Pastor of the Moscow Good News Church, and I was ordained as Bishop of the Good News Association of Churches. Paul stepped into the position of Senior Pastor, and I would become the overseer of our group of churches and our ministry branches in multiple nations. Paul and Polina and Denise and I posed for a commemorative photo.

Photos: © RUCEF (Russian United Union of Evangelical Christians) / used by permission.

**Right:** Pictured here are Bishop Sergei Vasilyevich Ryakhovsky, Bishop Rick Renner, and Pastor Paul Renner at the ordination service on October 16, 2020 — three precious friends privileged to serve God together.

**Below:** The Internet Good News Church is growing *exponentially*, and today there are Russian-speaking believers on every continent of the world who look to me as their "pastor" and who look at our online church as their home church because they do not have churches to attend where they live and local pastors to care for them. While a physical church would be best, IGNC answers a need for Russian-speaking Christians all over the world, and their massive response lets us know that we have indeed met a serious need. At present, IGNC numbers 200,000-plus in regular attendance, and I am sure it is already the largest online church ministry available in the Russian-speaking world.

🌐 ignc.org

**Above:** A large part of our ministry has been to help the homeless and those who are in need of food and clothing. We particularly focus on families with larger numbers of children who need assistance. In addition, we have a major outreach to orphans and to homeless people that has gained a sparkling reputation for what it has done to help those who are disadvantaged.

**Left:** Over the last thirty years, our ministry has literally received tons of mail and hundreds of thousands of responses from TV viewers across the former USSR. Each letter has been answered, and free-of-charge teaching materials have been sent to meet the needs of spiritually hungry people.

**Above:** No one is more amazed than *me* to see how God has used my books and to see who reads them. But today my books have been distributed by the millions around the world in English, Russian, Ukrainian, Uzbek, German, French, Polish, Portuguese, Japanese, Chinese, Spanish, and other languages.

**Above:** Today our TV program is also broadcast in English all over the world. Our vision is to take the Gospel — and trusted teaching from the Bible — to our nearby world and to the ends of the earth. And one way we're doing that is through my daily television program, RENNER TV, through which we are helping to facilitate a *revival of the Bible* in the hearts of people everywhere.

**Above:** As a part of my daily TV program, I film on site with my team at historical locations to help make the message of God's Word more meaningful to those who are a part of my TV family. To do this, we regularly film in Turkey, Israel, Egypt, Greece, Italy, all over Russia and the former USSR, and in the United States.

**Above:** In addition to our daily TV program, Denise and I and our team film a daily online Home Group in English and in Russian that is broadcast via social media and has a worldwide audience of thousands that joins us daily.

Photo: © Daystar / used by permission.

**Above:** We have personally preached 1,500 times in 80 cities of the former Soviet Union. Since 1991, Denise and I have regularly traveled back to the United States — and in those trips, we have ministered more than 1,000 times in 650 churches in 50 states. To do it, we've flown on about 5,000 flights. If we add to this list the times I've ministered in the Moscow church services — about 3,500 times over the years — it means I've publicly ministered more than 6,000 times just in the years since we moved to the former USSR.

**Above:** One of the greatest developments of our ministry transpired when we acquired the largest Russian-speaking Christian satellite channel in the world. Today our ministry owns and operates a twenty-four-hour-per-day satellite network that reaches Russian-speakers in every part of the world. It is all so remarkable, *but remember,* God delights in choosing the unlikely and in doing the remarkable through their yielded lives. Photo: © Andrey Armyagov / Dreamstime.com

**Left:** Abbot Pass, viewed from the top of Mount Victoria, Alberta, Canada. When I reached this destination summit, spread before me was a panoramic view of hundreds of incredibly beautiful mountain peaks. The sky was so clear, it looked as if I could see for a hundred miles. God used that mountain climb to symbolically teach me that it takes strong desire to get through the obstacles we will invariably encounter along the way in life — obstacles we will often feel unprepared to face.

Rick and Denise Renner

Paul and Polina Renner with Cohen, William, Anya, and Abby (left to right)

Philip and Ella Renner with Mika and Mia (left to right)

Joel and Olya Renner with Daniel and Mark (left to right)

*To Be Continued…*

# ENDNOTES

## Chapter 1

[1] "Indian Removal Act," Kansas Historical Society, March 2013, https://www.kshs.org/kansapedia/indian-removal-act/16714

[2] Francis L. and Roberta B. Fugate. *Roadside History of Oklahoma*. Missoula, Montana: Mountain Press Publishing Company, 1991.

[3] Francis L. and Roberta B. Fugate. *Roadside History of Oklahoma*. Missoula, Montana: Mountain Press Publishing Company, 1991.

[4] David Edwin Harrell, Jr. *Oral Roberts: An American Life*. Bloomington, Indiana: Indiana University Press, 1985.

[5] Kathy Weiser, "Isaac Parker – Hanging Judge of Indian Territory," Legends of America, October 2019, https://www.legendsofamerica.com/ar-isaacparker/

[6] "Gallows of Hanging Judge Parker," Roadside America, https://www.roadsideamerica.com/story/21204

[7] "Oklahoma's Legendary Outlaws," Travel Oklahoma, https://www.travelok.com/article_page/oklahomas- legendary-outlaws

[8] "Judge Isaac C. Parker," National Park Service, August 29, 2017, https://www.nps.gov/fosm/learn/historyculture/judge-parker.htm

[9] Sabamya Jaugu, "Little Africa: Historical Lessons from 'the Black Wall Street,'" African Globe, June 26, 2012, https://www.africanglobe.net/featured/africa-historical-lesson-black-wall-street/.

[10] Alexis Clark, "Tulsa's Black Wall Street Flourished as a Self-Contained Hub in Early 1900s," History, https://www.history.com/news/black-wall-street-tulsa-race-massacre

[11] Scott Ellsworth, "Tulsa Race Massacre," Oklahoma Historical Society, https://www.okhistory.org/publications/enc/entry.php?entry=TU013

[12] W. David Baird and Danney Goble. *Oklahoma: A History*. Norman, Oklahoma: University of Oklahoma Press, 2008.

[13] "Tulsa: Oil Capital of the World and Thriving Metropolis," Energy HQ, https://energyhq.com/2017/05/tulsa-oil-capital-of-the-world-and-thriving-metropolis/

[14] Stan Hoig, "Land Run of 1889," Oklahoma Historical Society, https://www.okhistory.org/publications/enc/entry.php?entry=LA014

[15] Tory La Forge, "She'd Like to Make the Run Again, *Tulsa Tribune*, Wednesday, April 22, 1942

[16] Tory La Forge, "She'd Like to Make the Run Again, *Tulsa Tribune*, Wednesday, April 22, 1942

[17] Tory La Forge, "She'd Like to Make the Run Again, *Tulsa Tribune*, Wednesday, April 22, 1942

[18] Tory La Forge, "She'd Like to Make the Run Again, *Tulsa Tribune*, Wednesday, April 22, 1942

[19] Ryan Schleeter, "The Grapes of Wrath," National Geographic, April 7, 2014, https://www.nationalgeographic.org/article/grapes-wrath

[20] History.com Editors, "Pearl Harbor," History, February 21, 2020, https://www.history.com/topics/world-war-ii/pearl-harbor

[21][22][23] "History – Raised to the Sky," Philtower, http://philtower.com/history/

## Chapter 3

[1] "Charles Page," Voices of Oklahoma, https://www.voicesofoklahoma.com/interview/page-charles/
[2] Kirk McCracken, "It takes a village: Family Village offers hand-up not hand-out," Tulsa World, June 20, 2017, https://tulsaworld.com/it-takes-a-village-family-village-offers-hand-up-not-hand-out/article_98ea247b-3f1d-52bf-95a4-9c38c8619e74.html
[3] Bill Sherman, "T.L. Osborn recalls times with Oral Roberts," Tulsa World, February 23, 2019, https://tulsaworld.com/archive/t-l-osborn-recalls-times-with-oral-roberts/article_0004ae8a-24a4-5030-aa0d-2864258888e6.html
[4] "About Derek Prince," Derek Prince Israel, http://www.dpisrael.com/about-derek-prince/
[5] "About Derek Prince," Derek Prince Israel, http://www.dpisrael.com/about-derek-prince/

## Chapter 4

[1] The Editors of Encyclopedia Britannica, "Hippie," Britannica, June 16, 2005, https://www.britannica.com/topic/hippie
[2] Timothy Leary quotes, IMDb, https://m.imdb.com/name/nm0495276/quotes
[3] Jennifer Peltz, "Woodstock generation looks back, from varied vantage points," ABC News, August 10, 2019, https://abcnews.go.com/Entertainment/wireStory/woodstock-generation-back-varied-vantage-points- 64897898

## Chapter 8

[1] Vladimir G. Mavinich, "Revitalization Movements in Kievan Russia," https://www.jstor.org/stable/1384314

## Chapter 9

[1] The Associated Press, "Putin: Soviet collapse a 'genuine tragedy'," NBC News, April 25, 2005, https://www.nbcnews.com/id/wbna7632057
[2] The Editors of Encyclopedia Britannica, "Michael — tsar of Russia," Encyclopedia Britannica, July 19, 2020, https://www.britannica.com/biography/Michael-tsar-of-Russia
[3] John L.H. Keep, "Nicholas II — tsar of Russia," Encyclopedia Britannica, May 14, 2021, https://www.britannica.com/biography/Nicholas-II-tsar-of-Russia
[4] Felix Gilbert and David Clay Large. *The End of the European Era, 1890 to the Present (Fourth Edition)*. New York, New York: W.W. Norton & Company, Inc, 1991.
[5] "Great Reforms (Russia) / Encyclopedia of Modern Europe: Europe 1789-1914: Encyclopedia of the Age of Industry and Empire," Encyclopedia.com, March 16, 2021, https://www.encyclopedia.com/history/encyclopedias-almanacs-transcripts-and-maps/great-reforms-russia
[6] Edvard Radzinsky. *Alexander II: The Last Great Tsar*. New York, New York: Free Press, 2005.
[7] "Why Visit the Church of the Savior," Travel All Russia, https://www.travelallrussia.com/savior-on-blood
[8] Oleg Yegorov, "How the 'royal disease' destroyed the life of Russia's last tsarevich," Russia Beyond, August 21, 2018, https://www.rbth.com/history/329002-tsarevich-alexei-russia-house-romanov
[9] Felix Gilbert and David Clay Large. *The End of the European Era, 1890 to the Present (Fourth Edition)*. New York, New York: WW. Norton & Company, Inc., 1991.

¹⁰ The Editors of Encyclopedia Britannica, "October Manifesto," Encyclopedia Britannica, October 23, 2020, https://www.britannica.com/event/October-Manifesto

¹¹ Paul Gilbert, "Religion and the Church under Nicholas II," Nicholas II, February 7, 2019, https://tsarnicholas.org/2019/02/07/religion-and-the-church-under-nicholas-ii/

¹² "The February Revolution and the Abdication of Emperor Nicholas II," Heritage Museum, https://www.hermitagemuseum.org/wps/portal/hermitage/explore/history/historical-article/1900/The+February+Revolution+and+Emperor+Nicholas+IIs+abdication/?lng=

¹³ Yuri N. Maltsev, "The Russian Revolution and Terror of Marxism-Leninism," Independent Institute, November 1, 2017, https://www.independent.org/news/article.asp?id=9194

¹⁴ Roland Boer, "Stalin as a Theological Student," Political Theology Network, November 12, 2014, https://politicaltheology.com/stalin-as-a-theological-student/

¹⁵ "Stalin's Security Force," Crime Museum, https://www.crimemuseum.org/crime-library/international-crimes/stalins-security-force/

¹⁶ History.com Editors, "German-Soviet Nonaggression Pact," History, June 7, 2019, https://www.history.com/topics/world-war-ii/german-soviet-nonaggression-pact

¹⁷ Oleg Yegorov, "How many Soviet citizens died in World War II?," Russia Beyond, July 8, 2019, https://www.rbth.com/history/330625-soviet-citizens-died-world-war-statistics

¹⁸ "Victory Day Parade," Travel All Russia, February 12, 2020, https://www.travelallrussia.com/blog/victory-day-parade

¹⁹ Volker Wagener, "Leningrad: The city that refused to starve in WWII," Deutsche Welle, https://www.dw.com/en/leningrad-the-city-that-refused-to-starve-in-wwii/a-19532957

²⁰ Scott Peterson, "Jaded Hope: Russia 10 Years Later," *The Christian Science Monitor*, August 17, 2001, https://www.csmonitor.com/2001/0817/p1s1-woeu.html

²¹ Mark R. Elliott, "East-West Church and Ministry Report 20," East-West Church Ministry Report, 2012, https://www.eastwestreport.org/44-english/e-20-3/352-persecution-of-christians-in-tsarist-russia-and-the-soviet-and-post-soviet-union

²² L.D. Freedman, "Strategic Arms Reduction Talks," Encyclopedia Britannica, January 8, 2018, https://www.britannica.com/event/Strategic-Arms-Reduction-Talks

²³ The Editors of Encyclopedia Britannica, "Perestroika," Encyclopedia Britannica, January 10, 2020, https://www.britannica.com/topic/perestroika-Soviet-government-policy

²⁴ The Editors of Encyclopedia Britannica, "Glasnost," Encyclopedia Britannica, March 18, 2019, https://www.britannica.com/topic/glasnost

²⁵ The Editors of Encyclopedia Britannica, "Boris Yeltsin," Encyclopedia Britannica, January 28, 2021, https://www.britannica.com/biography/Boris-Yeltsin

²⁶ Bridget Kendall, "Moscow 1991: A coup that seemed doomed from the start," BBC News, August 18, 2011, https://www.bbc.com/news/world-europe-14579945

²⁷ Daniel Sandford, "Moscow Coup 1991: With Boris Yeltsin on the tank," BBC News, August 20, 2011, https://www.bbc.com/news/world-europe-14589691

²⁸ The Editors of Encyclopedia Britannica, "Collapse of the Soviet Union," Encyclopedia Britannica, August 11, 2020, https://www.britannica.com/event/the-collapse-of-the-Soviet-Union/Aftermath-of-the-coup

²⁹ Michael Dobbs, "Gorbachev resignation ends Soviet Era," The Washington Post, December 26, 1991, https://www.washingtonpost.com/archive/politics/1991/12/26/gorbachev-resignation-ends-soviet-era/00444c16-0fe3-4b35-96df-e514956ee354/

[30] New World Encyclopedia contributors, "KGB," New World Encyclopedia, April 10, 2018, https://www.newworldencyclopedia.org/entry/KGB

[31] Sonia B. Green, Language of Lullabies: The Russification and De-Russification of the Baltic States, 19 MICH. J. INT'L L. 219 (1997). Available at: https://repository.law.umich.edu/mjil/vol19/iss1/4

[32] Sonia B. Green, Language of Lullabies: The Russification and De-Russification of the Baltic States, 19 MICH. J. INT'L L. 219 (1997). Available at: https://repository.law.umich.edu/mjil/vol19/iss1/4

[33] "The Latvian Ruble verses the Russian Ruble," Latvijas Banka, January 1, 2013, https://www.bank.lv/en/your-profile/media/550-publications/3172-the-latvian-ruble-versus-the-russian-ruble

[34] "The Latvian Ruble verses the Russian Ruble," Latvijas Banka, January 1, 2013, https://www.bank.lv/en/your-profile/media/550-publications/3172-the-latvian-ruble-versus-the-russian-ruble

[35] Robert Wood, "Olympic Games Unified Team," Topend Sports, 2000, https://www.topendsports.com/events/summer/countries/unified-team.htm

[36] Robert Wood, "Unified Team at the Winter Olympics," Topend Sports, December 2016, https://www.topendsports.com/events/winter/countries/unified-team.htm

[37] OlyMADMen, "Unified Team," Olympedia, 2006, http://www.olympedia.org/countries/EUN

[38] "Beethoven's Ode to Joy Lyrics, Translation, and History," Live About, https://www.liveabout.com/beethovens-ode-to-joy-lyrics-history-724410

[39] Charles E. Ziegler. The History of Russia. Westport, Connecticut: Greenwood Press, 1999

[40] Trevor Buck, Igor Filatotchev, Peter Nolan, Mike Wright, "Different paths to economic reform in Russia and China: causes and consequences," Journal of World Business, Volume 35, Issue 4 (2000): 379-400.

[41] G. Smidchens, "Riga," Encyclopedia Britannica, April 10, 2019, https://www.britannica.com/place/Riga

[42] "Francesco Bartolomeo Rastrelli," Saint-Petersburg.com, http://www.saint-petersburg.com/famous-people/francesco-rastrelli/

[43] "Jelgava," Museum 'Jews in Latvia,' http://www.jewishmuseum.lv/en/item/126-jelgava.html

[44] Andrew Ezergailis. The Holocaust in Latvia, 1941-1944: The Missing Center. Latvia: Historical Institute of Latvia, 1996.

[45] Andrew Ezergailis. The Holocaust in Latvia, 1941-1944 : The Missing Center. Latvia: Historical Institute of Latvia, 1996.

[46] Vincent Hunt. Blood in the Forest: The End of the Second World War in the Courland Pocket. West Midlands, England: Helion and Company, Limited, 2017.

[47] "German Institute of Surrender," Totally History, https://totallyhistory.com/german-instrument-of-surrender/

## Chapter 11

[1] United States Holocaust Memorial Museum, Washington, DC, "Riga," Holocaust Encyclopedia, https://encyclopedia.ushmm.org/content/en/article/riga

[2] United States Holocaust Memorial Museum, Washington, DC, "Riga," Holocaust Encyclopedia, https://encyclopedia.ushmm.org/content/en/article/riga

[3] "The Rumbula Massacre," Virginia Tech Department of History, https://www.arcgis.com/apps/MapJournal/index.html?appid=399b93efdd234538936fefdf0ece27f3

[4] Peter Curry, "The Horror of the Rumbula Massacre," History Hit, October 2018, https://www.historyhit.com/the-horror-of-the-rumbula-massacre/

[5] Gerald Fleming. *Hitler and the Final Solution*. Berkeley, California: University of California Press, 1984.

[6] "Jewish Memorial, Bikernieki," Live Riga, https://www.liveriga.com/en/1587-jewish-memorial-bikernieki-fores/

[7] "The Riga Ghetto and Holocaust in Latvia Museum," Riga Ghetto Museum, http://www.rgm.lv/about/? lang=en

## Chapter 13

[1] Russian News Agency, "Moscow remembers victims of terrorist attacks," TASS, September 2, 2011, https://tass.com/archive/659657

[2] Mike Eckel, "Two Decades On, Smoldering Questions About the Russian President's Vault to Power," Radio Free Europe Radio Liberty, August 7, 2019, https://www.rferl.org/a/putin-russia-president-1999-chechnya-apartment-bombings/30097551.html

[3] Mike Eckel, "Two Decades On, Smoldering Questions About the Russian President's Vault to Power," Radio Free Europe Radio Liberty, August 7, 2019, https://www.rferl.org/a/putin-russia-president-1999-chechnya-apartment-bombings/30097551.html

[4] Paul Murphy. *The Wolves of Islam: Russia and the Faces of Chechen Terror*. Sterling, VA: Potomac Books, 2005.

[5] Barry Renfrew, "17 Dead, 115 Injured in Another Russian Blast," Washington Post, September 16, 1999, https://www.washingtonpost.com/wp-srv/inatl/daily/sept99/russia16.htm

[6] David Satter. *Darkness at Dawn: The Rise of the Russian Criminal State*. New Haven, Connecticut: Yale University Press, 2004.

[7] https://www.911memorial.org/911-Faqs

[8] "Gas Killed Moscow Hostages," BBC News, October 27, 2002, http://news.bbc.co.uk/2/hi/europe/2365383.stm

[9] Reuters Staff, "Timeline Bomb Attacks in Moscow," Reuters, March 29, 2010, https://www.reuters.com/article/idINIndia-47291020100329

[10] "Moscow Airliner Bombings," X-Ray Screener, https://www.x-rayscreener.co.uk/terrorism/moscow-airliner-bombings/

[11] CNN Editorial Research, "Beslan School Siege Fast Facts," CNN, August 13, 2020, https://www.cnn.com/2013/09/09/world/europe/beslan-school-siege-fast-facts/index.html

[12] Associated Press, "Explosion at Moscow Market Kills 10," Fox News, January 13, 2015, https://www.foxnews.com/story/explosion-at-moscow-market-kills-10

[13] Luke Harding and Mark Tran, "Moscow Metro Bombs Kill Dozens," The Guardian, March 29, 2010, https://www.theguardian.com/world/2010/mar/29/moscow-metro-bombs-explosions-terror

[14] Lee Ferran and Matthew Cole, "Moscow Airport Bombing: Chechen Militant Claims Credit," ABC News, January 24, 2011, https://abcnews.go.com/Blotter/moscow-airport-bombing-chechen-militant-claims-credit/story?id=12862235

[15] Adam Taylor, "The recent history of terrorist attacks in Russia," The Washington Post, April 3, 2017, https://www.washingtonpost.com/news/worldviews/wp/2017/04/03/the-recent-history-of-terrorist-attacks-in-russia/

[16] "Five killed in suicide bombing in Chechan capital," BBC News, October 5, 2014, https://www.bbc.com/news/world-europe-29498909

[17] "Russia: 'Active Phase' of Chechen Anti-Terror Operation Completed," VOA News, December 4, 2014, https://www.voanews.com/europe/russia-active-phase-chechen-anti-terror-operation-completed

[18] "Russian Plane Crash: What We Know," BBC News, November 17, 2015, https://www.bbc.com/news/world-middle-east-34687990

[19] Associated Press, "Russian Supermarket Explosion Injures at Least 13," NBC News, December 27, 2017, https://www.nbcnews.com/news/world/russian-supermarket-explosion-injures-least-10-n832931

[20] "Chechnya Profile," BBC News, January 17, 2018, https://www.bbc.com/news/world-europe-18188085

[21] Dyfed Loesche, Timeline of Major Terrorist Attacks Against Russian Targets," Statista, April 5, 2017, https://www.statista.com/chart/8812/timeline-of-major-terrorist-attacks-against-russian-targets/

**Chapter 14**

[1] "Moscow Population 2021," World Population Review, https://worldpopulationreview.com/world-cities/moscow-population

[2] "Moscow Population 2021," World Population Review, https://worldpopulationreview.com/world-cities/moscow-population

[3] "Moscow Wins International Transport Award, Moscow Mayor Official Website, May 19, 2016, https://www.mos.ru/en/news/item/13024073

[4] "Traffic Index 2020," TomTom Traffic Index, https://www.tomtom.com/en_gb/traffic-index/ranking/

[5] Georgy Manaev, "How Muscovites Commute to Work," Russia Beyond, June 2, 2019, https://www.rbth.com/lifestyle/330446-how-muscovites-commute-to-work

[6] "The 85th Anniversary of the Moscow Metro," Moscow Mayor Official Website, https://www.mos.ru/en/city/projects/mosmetro85/

[7] AMA Staff, "Moscow Is Now the World's Most Expensive City," American Management Association, January 24, 2019, https://www.amanet.org/articles/moscow-is-now-the-world-s-most-expensive-city/

**Chapter 15**

[1] "The Coldest Places on Earth," World Atlas, https://www.worldatlas.com/articles/what-is-the-coldest-place-on-earth.html

# GLOSSARY

**Abbot Pass Hut** – A mountain hut in Abbot Pass accessible by foot at an altitude of more than 9,500 feet in the Rocky Mountains in Alberta, Canada. The mountaineer hut was built in 1922 using stones from surrounding mountains and is situated in Banff National Park as the second-highest structure in Canada.

**Abbot Pass** – Landmark mountain pass in Canada that lies between Mount Lefroy and Mount Victoria in the divide between Lake O'Hara and Lake Louise.

**Abdication** – The act of renouncing or relinquishing a throne, rights, power, or responsibility, especially formally; in context, refers to the abdication of Nicholas Romanov (Nicholas II), the last emperor of Russia, in 1917 on the cusp of the Bolshevik Revolution, thus ending the Romanov Dynasty and the era of Russian monarchs.

**Aboveground Church** – As opposed to the Underground Church, believers in Christ who meet publicly in local meetings free from legal restraints imposed by a government hostile to Christianity. In context, "aboveground church" refers to the Church in the former USSR that met publicly before and after the collapse of Soviet communism.

**Age of Aquarius** – In context, a cultural expression depicting the Hippie Movement of the 1960s and 1970s.

**Alexander III** – Emperor or Czar (Tsar) of Russia, 1881-1894; succeeded by his son Nicholas II, the last of the Russian monarchs.

**Alexander II** – Emperor or Czar (Tsar) of Russia 1855-1881; known as Alexander the Liberator for emancipating Russian serfs in 1861; sold Alaska to the United States in 1867.

**Alexander I** – Emperor or Czar (Tsar) of Russia 1801-1825 who ruled during the Napoleonic War.

**Alexander Palace** – A former Imperial residence of the Romanovs about thirty miles south of Saint Petersburg; favorite residence of Nicholas II and his immediate family.

**Alexander the Great** – King of Macedonia (336-323 BC), Pharaoh of Egypt (332-323 BC), and King of Persia (330-323 BC); undefeated in battle, became known as one of history's greatest military minds; laid foundation for the Hellenistic Period that lasted up to the time of the Roman Empire.

**Alexandrian Greek** – The Greek language spread by the soldiers of Alexander the Great.

**All-American football player** – Specially selected member of the All-American football team; a title awarded to outstanding college players by a national selection committee.

**Allied forces** – Referred to the nations that fought together against Adolf Hitler and Nazi Germany in World War II. The most prominent five Allied nations in that war were the United States, the United Kingdom, France, Russia, and China.

**Annie Oakley** – An iconic American figure whose sharpshooting skills made her famous; starred in Buffalo Bill's *Wild West* show.

**Apache** – North American Native American tribe living chiefly in Oklahoma, Texas, New Mexico, and Arizona; native tribe of the legendary *Geronimo*.

**Apollo 8** – The first manned spaceflight to orbit the moon in 1968.

**Archaic Greek** – Period of language preceding Koine Greek, which became used widespread as the "common man's" language and the language of the New Testament.

**Aristophanes' Clouds** – Called *The Clouds*, a comedy written by the celebrated playwright Aristophanes mocking intellectual fashions in classical Athens.

**Atheism** – The doctrine or belief that there is no God.

**Ayatollah (Ruhollah) Khomeini** – Iranian revolutionary who introduced Islamic law across the country and founded the Islamic Republic of Iran. Arrested by the Shah of Iran in 1964 for his opposition to the pro-Western regime of the Shah. Leader of the 1979 Iranian Revolution that overthrew the last Shah of Iran.

**Azusa Street** – Street where the historical Azusa Street Revival took place in Los Angeles beginning on April 9, 1906. Led by African American preacher William J. Seymour, "Azusa Street" became synonymous in name with the renowned revival.

**Baltic Sea** – Semi-enclosed inland sea surrounded by Denmark, Germany, Poland, Lithuania, Latvia, Estonia, Russia, Finland, and Sweden.

**Baptism in the Holy Spirit** – Subsequent experience to the new birth in which the Holy Spirit empowers a believer for testifying of Christ; accompanied with speaking in tongues.

**Belle Grove Historic District** – Residential historic district north of the central business district of Fort Smith, Arkansas.

**Belle Starr** – Also known as the "Bandit Queen," she was an American outlaw associated with the James-Younger gang.

**Beverly Sills** – World-renowned American operatic soprano whose singing career peaked between the 1950s and 1970s. She became the general manager of the New York City Opera and, later, the chairwoman of the Lincoln Center and the Metropolitan Opera.

**Bikernieki Forest** – Largest mass-murder site of the Nazi terror victims in Riga, Latvia that now serves as a Holocaust memorial.

**Bishop Albert, Founder of Riga** – The third bishop of Riga (1215-1229), who founded Riga in 1201 and built the city's cathedral twenty years later.

**Black Market** – An illegal trade in controlled or scarce commodities that takes place outside government-sanctioned channels; in context, refers to a means of obtaining goods that became sparse or altogether unavailable after the collapse of communism in the USSR.

**Black Wall Street** – The district surrounding the affluent African American community in downtown Tulsa, Oklahoma, and destroyed in the Tulsa Race Massacre of May 31 or June 1, 1921; now known as the Greenwood district.

**Blue baby** – Syndrome in which an infant's skin may turn blue due to a decreased amount of hemoglobin in the blood; the condition can be genetic or a factor in premature births.

**Bob Mumford** – Member of the Fort Lauderdale Five, widely regarded as one of the foremost Bible teachers of the Charismatic Movement of the 1970s.

**Bob Yandian** – Pastored Grace Fellowship, one of the largest and most prominent American Charismatic churches of its time, for more than thirty years in his hometown Tulsa, Oklahoma, where he now leads his own ministry.

**Bolshevik Revolution** – One of the most explosive political events of the Twentieth Century in which the Bolsheviks, led by Vladimir Lenin, seized power and destroyed the tradition of czarist rule in Russia in 1917.

**Bonnie and Clyde** – An infamous American robbery duo responsible for a twenty-one-month-long crime spree from 1932 to 1934.

**Boris Yeltsin** – Served as the first president of Russia after the collapse of socialistic communism from 1991 to 1999.

**Boustrophedon** – An older form of Greek language to be read or written from right to left and from left to right in alternate lines.

**Boy Scouts of America** – One of the nation's largest and most prominent values-based youth-development organizations.

**Buckboard** – A four-wheeled wagon meant to be drawn by a horse or other large animal.

**Buddy Harrison** – Co-founder of the Faith Christian Fellowship International Church (FCF) who served as president of the organization until his passing in 1978; also founded Harrison House Publishing in Tulsa, Oklahoma.

**Buffalo Bill's Wild West Show** – Started by William F. "Buffalo Bill" Cody on May 19, 1883, in Omaha, Nebraska, it was an outdoor attraction that featured wild animals, trick performances, and theatrical reenactments that toured annually.

**Calvary International Ministries** – An international ministry organization that trains and equips believers for evangelism and church planting worldwide; in context, the missions organization that began the first aboveground Bible school in Jelgava, Latvia, since the time of czarist rule.

**Campus Crusade for Christ** – Interdenominational Christian parachurch organization committed to equip the Body of Christ for evangelism and discipleship through various creative approaches.

**Carol Brice-Carey** – American contralto opera singer who founded the non-profit Cimarron Circuit Opera Company in Oklahoma with her husband Thomas Carey. Brice-Carey began teaching at the University of Oklahoma in Norman in 1974.

**Carriage step** – A block of stone placed on the edge of the street near the front of a home that served as a stepping-stone for carriage passengers; used during the "carriage era" of the late Seventeenth Century to the early Twentieth Century.

**Catherine Palace** – Rococo palace (Russia Baroque style) just south of St. Petersburg; served as a summer home for many Russian czars.

**Catherine the Great** – Catherine II, empress of Russia from 1762-1796; wife of Peter III, she was Russia's longest-ruling female leader, who revitalized culture and made Russia a world power.

**Central Intelligence Agency (CIA)** – A principal foreign intelligence and counterintelligence agency of the United States government.

**Cessationist** – One who believes in a doctrine stating that spiritual gifts, such as speaking in tongues, prophecy, and healing ceased with the Apostolic age.

**Charisma Magazine** – A monthly Christian magazine led by publisher Stephen Strang, who expanded the magazine to serve the Charismatic Movement at large.

**Charismatic** – A charismatic Christian who emphasizes the work of the Holy Spirit, spiritual gifts, and modern-day miracles as an everyday part of a believer's life.

**Charismatic Movement** – Springing from classic Pentecostalism in beliefs and practices, this movement became formally recognized in the 1960s.

**Charles Carroll of Carrollton** – The last survivor of the signers of the Declaration of Independence; in context, a distant maternal relative of Rick Renner.

**Charles E. Page** – Prominent businessman and philanthropist who made an impact on the early history of Tulsa, Oklahoma, in his charity to widows and orphans; founder of Sand Springs, Oklahoma.

**Charles Lindbergh** – The first aviator to complete a solo transatlantic flight, from New York to Paris in 1927.

**Charles Simpson** – An internationally known author, Bible teacher, and pastor; one of a group of Charismatic teachers in the 1970s and 1980s, which was known as The Fort Lauderdale Five.

**Charlie Chaplin** – English comedian, writer, producer, director, and composer who rose to fame in the era of silent film; one of the most prominent figures in film history.

**Cherokee** – North American Indian tribe predominantly located in the southeastern United States, forcibly relocated from their homeland in the 1830s in the Indian Removal Act. They were among the tribes evacuated in the infamous Trail of Tears.

**Chicken Pox** – Viral infection that causes fever and itchy rash with spots all over the body.

**Choctaw** – Northern American Indian tribe in the southeastern United States that was one of the Five Civilized Tribes and the first to be forcibly relocated under the Indian Removal Act.

**Christian Broadcasting Network (CBN)** – An American evangelical Christian religious television network and production company founded in 1960 by Pat Robertson.

**Church on Spilled Blood** – Also known as the Church of the Savior on Spilled Blood; a Russian Orthodox Church in Saint Petersburg that now serves as both a church and museum.

**Civil War** – The American Civil War was a war that took place from 1861-1865 between the northern states loyal to the Union and the eleven southern states that formed the Confederate States of America.

**Classical Greek** – A language and culture spanning 200 years in the Fifth and Fourth Centuries BC. In context, the period and language Rick Renner first studied at a secular university that provided the foundation for his studies of the Greek New Testament.

**Coffeehouse ministry** – A type of ministry that began around the time of the Jesus Movement in the 1960s and 1970s and appealed predominantly to young adults.

**Collectivization** – Policy adopted by the Soviet government, pursued most intensively between 1929 and 1933 to transform traditional agriculture in the Soviet Union, bringing ownership and power to the state and thereby reducing the economic power of the individual, in particular, that of the kulaks (prosperous peasants).

**College and Career** – A category of people in the age range of eighteen to approximately thirty years of age.

**Committee for Interaction With Public Associations and Religious Organizations** – A central executive body that ensures implementation of the state policy in the field of religion, as well as with other public associations, including compliance with provisions of legislation and the coordination of activities of all such associations. In context, a Presidential consultative and advisory body that acts as a liaison between federal bodies and entities inside the Russian Federation.

**Communism** – A political and economic ideology that advocates for a classless society in which all property and wealth are communally owned by the state or its appointees, instead of by individuals.

**Communist Party** – A political party that seeks to realize the social and economic goals of communism.

**Concentration camps** – Internment centers for political prisoners and members of national, minority, or religious groups who are detained or confined, usually under harsh conditions and without regard to the legal norms of arrest and imprisonment and "due process." In context, refers to the Holocaust and the extermination of much of the Jewish population under the tyrannous reign of Adolf Hitler.

**Congress of People's Deputies** – The supreme government institution in the Russian Soviet Federal Social Republic (SFSR) and in the Russian Federation from approximately 1989-1991. Created by Mikhail Gorbachev as a part of his reform agenda, it was the highest body of state authority during that time.

**Continental Congress** – A series of legislative bodies that met in the British American colonies and the newly declared U.S. just before, during, and after the American Revolution.

**Contrabandists** – Smugglers who illegally trade or transport goods.

**Contraband** – Goods that have been imported or exported illegally.

**Council Oak Tree** – The Creek tribe's Council Oak Tree is a historic landmark where council leaders met after their expulsion from their native homelands; represents the founding of the city of Tulsa, Oklahoma, and is visibly present in downtown Tulsa today.

**Coup d'état** – A sudden, often violent, illegal seizure of power from a government.

**Coupons** – In context, government-issued coupons during the shortages in the former USSR on the cusp of the fall of socialistic communism to avert over-consumption of commodities in the marketplace.

**Creek** – North American Indian tribe, one of the Five Civilized Tribes and the largest tribe in the U.S. The Creek tribe was also infamously displaced on the Trail of Tears.

**Cuban Missile Crisis of 1962** – A direct and dangerous confrontation between the United States and the Soviet Union during the Cold War; the moment when the two superpowers came closest to nuclear conflict.

**Cult of Stalin** – A prominent feature of Soviet culture beginning on December 1929, after a lavish celebration of Joseph Stalin's fiftieth birthday. For the rest of Stalin's rule, the Soviet press presented him as an all-powerful, all-knowing leader, with the dictator's name and image appearing everywhere, thus promoting him as a cult personality.

**Cyrillic language** – A writing system for various languages across Eurasia and is used as a national script in Greece and Russia, as well as in various Slavic countries.

**Cyril** – In context, a patriarch in Alexandria and a theologian and a missionary to Greece who helped create the Slavic alphabet, the basis of the Russian language.

**Czar (also Tsar)** – A word derived from the Roman "caesars," a czar was an emperor of Russia before the Bolshevik Revolution in 1917.

**Dacha** – A country house in Russia, typically used as a second home or a vacation home.

**Dalton Gang** – A group of outlaws in the American Old West during 1890-1892.

**David Ingles** – Popular minister and Christian musician who emerged with the teaching revival of the 1970s and 1980s; head of David Ingles Ministries based in Broken Arrow, Oklahoma.

**December 8, 1991** – Marks the official end of socialist-communist rule in the Soviet Union and the dismantling of the conglomerate USSR to form independent nations and governments.

**Declaration of Independence** – A document approved by the Continental Congress on July 4, 1776, that announced the separation of thirteen North American British colonies from Great Britain to eventually form the independent United States of America.

**Deficits** – The amount by which something, especially a sum of money, is too small. In context, refers to the deficits of basic staples on the cusp of the fall of socialistic communism and for a time thereafter as new nations struggled to regain their economic footing.

**Deoxyribonucleic Acid (DNA)** – The molecule that contains the genetic code of all living organisms.

**Department of Religion** – The Ministry of Religious Affairs and Public Education is a government ministry directing all educational and scientific institutions, as well as the religious activities of all faiths, in the time of the Soviet Union and in many former USSR countries today.

**Derek Prince** – International Bible teacher and theologian whose daily radio program, Derek Prince Legacy Radio, is still broadcast around the world in various languages. He was a member of the Fort Lauderdale Five. His teaching ministry emerged in the 1970s and continues today through his radio podcasts, books, and audio and video teachings.

**Dewey Decimal System** – a proprietary library classification system.

**Dom Kultury** – A Russian cultural community center similar to an American-based civic center or center for cultural arts.

**Don Basham** – A teacher and writer in the Charismatic movement whose ministry spanned 48 years, and who was a member of the Fort Lauderdale Five.

**Dr. Bill Bennett** – A pastor, scholar, and theologian who pastored churches ranging in membership from eighty-five to eight thousand over the course of fifty years. His major pastorate was the First Baptist Church in Fort Smith, Arkansas, where he served for nineteen years. In context, one of Rick Renner's primary mentors.

**Draft-dodgers** – Those who deliberately avoid compulsory military service.

**Dual citizenship** – A legal status in which a person is concurrently regarded as a national, or citizen, of more than one country under the laws of each of those countries.

**Duma** – A legislative body in the ruling assembly of Russia and of some other republics of the former Soviet Union.

**Dust Bowl** – Name given to the Southern Plains region of the United States (Texas to Nebraska) that suffered severe dust storms during the draughts of the 1930s.

**Ed Dufresne** – International healing minister who dedicated more than four decades in ministry during the charismatic movement. Founded three churches and pastored for fifteen years.

**Electrolux** – A Swedish multinational appliance manufacturer; in context, a vacuum-cleaner line sold by Denise Renner's father as a career.

**Ellis Island** - An iconic immigration station opening in 1892 in Upper New York Bay and operating for more than sixty years until its closure in 1954. In context, port of entry where Rick Renner's grandfather immigrated to the U.S. from Germany.

**El Shaddai** – Hebrew word conventionally translated to English as God Almighty.

**Emancipation of Russian Serfs in 1861** – Liberal reform passed by Alexander II in 1861; proclaimed the emancipation of domestic serfs on private estates.

**Emergency Immigration (Quota) Act of 1921** – The first act to place numerical limits on the number of immigrants who could enter the United States annually.

**Emperor Charlemagne** – Known as the Father of Europe, a Medieval emperor who unified and ruled most of western Europe from 768-814 AD. Recognized as the first emperor to rule from western Europe since the fall of the Roman Empire, his rule spurred the Renaissance period, a time of cultural and intellectual revitalization in the Western Church.

**Empress Elizabeth** – Daughter of Peter the Great; served as the lavish Empress of Russia for twenty years (1741-1762).

**Enemies of the State** – Individuals accused of committing certain crimes against the state government resulting in the accusation or conviction of treason.

**Engels** – Friedrich Engels; co-author with Karl Marx of *The Communist Manifesto*.

**Epiphany** – An intuitive grasp of reality caused by something (usually an event).

**Ern Baxter** – A member of the Fort Lauderdale Five and a Canadian Pentecostal evangelist, whose ministry flourished for more than sixty years.

**Ethnic Russians** – Russians by ethnicity, many of whom were residents of newly demarcated, non-Russian nations immediately following the collapse of the former Soviet Union and who lost their citizenship in those nations and/or privileges associated with residency.

**Falls Creek Baptist Youth Camp** – A conference center and youth summer camp along Falls Creek in southern Oklahoma; Oklahoma's oldest church camp. In context, camp where Rick Renner faked a call to foreign missions as a youth.

**Father Frost** – Also known as **Ded Moroz**, an important figure in Russian culture. Similar looking to Saint Nicholas, he is fabled as bringing presents to well-mannered children in December and especially on New Year's Eve. His persona originates in Slavic mythology as wearing a long robe and carrying a magic stick.

**Federal Bureau of Investigation (FBI)** – Principal investigative and domestic intelligence agency of the United States.

**Ferrell and Ferrell** – A husband-and-wife duo who recorded several contemporary Christian music albums between 1977-1991.

**Fidel Castro** – A Cuban politician and revolutionary who served as the Prime Minister of Cuba from 1959 to 1976, the First Secretary of the Communist Party from 1961 to 2011, and President of Cuba from 1976 to 2008. He was ideologically Marxist-Leninist and established Cuba as a one-party communist state, the first in the Western Hemisphere.

**First Deputy Premier of the Soviet Union** – Deputy head of government in the years of the USSR, a title held by an individual or a committee, and a position responsible for policy over various strata of Soviet society, such as industry, agriculture, religion, etc.

**Five-year plans** – Government-issued plan for economic development over the following five-year period. The first five-year plan was inaugurated in the Soviet Union in 1928.

**Flower children** – Synonym for hippie; one who wears flowers as symbols of peace and love.

**Fort Chaffee** – Army base located in northwestern Arkansas. In context, military installment where Cuban refugees were housed at the time Rick Renner was an associate of the First Baptist Church in Fort Smith.

**Fort Knox** – A military installation in the United States known to house large deposits of gold and known for its unmatched security.

**Fort Lauderdale Five** – Referring to the five founders of the Shepherding Movement in the early days of the Charismatic Movement: Don Basham, Bob Mumford, Derek Prince, Charles Simpson, and Ern Baxter.

**Fort Sill** – U.S. Army post and historic landmark located between Lawton and Oklahoma City in Oklahoma. Geronimo died at the Fort Sill hospital as a prisoner of war.

**Fort Smith** – Located in Arkansas, Fort Smith is a city on the Arkansas River whose beginnings was a military base in the frontier era.

**Fortune-teller** – A person who can allegedly predict the future with the use of palmistry, a crystal ball, or other similar methods.

**Fortune cookie** – A thin, folded cookie containing a piece of a paper with a vague prediction, aphorism, or "fortune" written on it.

**Fred Price** – An American pastor, televangelist, and author who was based in Los Angeles, California, and contributed significantly to the Word of Faith teaching movement.

**Fred Tecumseh Waite** – An infamous member of Billy the Kid's gang-turned politician when he served as a legislator in the Chickasaw government and as its Attorney General.

**Full Gospel Businessmen's Fellowship International (FGBFI)** – A nonprofit organization of businessmen with a vision to inspire participation with the Gospel of Jesus Christ.

**General Secretary of the Central Committee (of the Communist Party of the Soviet Union)** – Office holder who wielded executive authority in matters of the Soviet Union.

**Geronimo** – An Apache leader who was known for his resistance to anyone, namely the U.S. and Mexico, who attempted to remove his people from their native lands. Hailed as a hero among tribesmen, his name became synonymous with that resistance movement and the fight for Native-American civil rights and autonomy.

**Girls Auxiliary (G.A.)** – Program through the Southern Baptist Convention that teaches young girls about the Bible, missions, and Baptist doctrine.

**Glasnost** – The policy or practice of more open consultative government and wider dissemination of information, initiated by leader Mikhail Gorbachev from 1985.

**Good News Association of Pastors and Churches** – A ministry outreach of RENNER Ministries in the former USSR, begun in 1998, as a collaboration of pastors and leaders committed to each other and the advancement of the Gospel.

**Good News Churches, Riga, Moscow, Kiev** – Churches founded by Rick and Denise Renner in the former Soviet Union (in the nations of Latvia, Russia, and Ukraine) in 1993, 2000, and 2006 respectively.

**Good News Church Online** – Also known as the Internet Good News Church, this online church reaches hundreds of thousands of Russian speakers across the former Soviet Union and beyond.

**Great Commission** – A command, or commission, of Christ in Matthew 28:16-20; the instruction of Jesus to His disciples then and now to herald the Gospel or Good News.

**Great Hall of the Kremlin Palace** – The six-thousand-seat auditorium in the Moscow Kremlin Palace; also one of the most prestigious theatrical and concert venues in the world.

**Greatest Tragedy of the Twentieth Century** – Refers to the unprecedented economic and social conditions that unfolded after the sudden fall of the USSR.

**Greenwood District** – Also known as "Black Wall Street," the Greenwood District is a historic district located in downtown Tulsa, Oklahoma; one of the most prominent concentrations of Black-owned businesses in the United States during the early Twentieth Century before the Tulsa Race Riots and Massacre of 1921.

**Guadalajara** – A city in western Mexico.

**Gulag** – A system of Soviet labor camps in the Soviet Union in 1930-1955.

**Hanging Judge** – A judge (specifically referring to Judge Isaac Parker of the early U.S. District Courts) who is renowned for sentencing criminals to death by hanging.

**Hanseatic League** – A commercial association of towns in North Germany formed in the Fourteenth Century to protect and promote commerce.

**Hardline communists** – Those who follow the Communist Manifesto with an unwavering and inflexible ideological stance.

**Harry F. Sinclair** – American industrialist and founder of Sinclair Oil.

**Heir-apparent** – A person who is in first order of succession and whose claim cannot be displaced by the birth of another.

**Hell on the Border** – The renowned jailhouse in Fort Smith run by the "Hanging Judge," Judge Isaac Parker.

**Hemophilia** – A disorder in which the blood does not clot properly, resulting in excessive bleeding after injury.

**Hippie Movement** – A countercultural youth movement from the 1960s that rejected the ways of the American mainstream life.

**Homer's Illiad** – The epic poem attributed to Homer and first published in the Eighth Century BC; tells of the war between the Greeks and the Trojans in the Battle of Troy. Homer's poem contained notable characters from Greek mythology, including *Athena*, *Hera*, *Hermes*, and *Poseidon* (on the Greek side); *Aphrodite*, *Apollo*, *Ares*, *Artemis*, and *Zeus* (on the Trojan side); and the warrior *Achilles*.

**Horseshoe kidneys** – Renal fusion; a condition in which the kidneys bind together during fetal development causing them to form a "U" shape.

**Hotel Russia** – A five-star international Soviet hotel overlooking the famous Red Square of Moscow; was once the largest hotel in Europe. Location of first services of the Moscow Good News Church in September 2000.

**House of Culture** *(Dom Kultury)* – The name for major club houses in the former Soviet Union; a center for recreational, cultural, and communal activities.

**House of Romanov** – The second and last reigning imperial house of Russia from 1613 to 1917, the time of the Bolshevik Revolution that overthrew imperialism and introduced communism to Russia and the republics of the Soviet Union.

**Houston Grand Opera** – An award winning, highly acclaimed opera company based in Houston, Texas, where Denise Renner went to work and study during her college years.

**Hurlbut's Story of the Bible** – A classic collection of 168 stories from the Bible, spanning from Genesis to Revelation, formatted in a child-friendly manner by Jesse Lyman Hurlbut.

**Illustrated Bible Stories** – A fully illustrated collection of stories from the Bible, retold for young readers.

**Indian Removal Act of 1830** – An act that gave the President permission to grant lands west of the Mississippi to Indian tribes that agreed to give up their homelands, resulting in the mass forced relocation of several Indian tribes.

**Indian Territory** – A region of the south-central United States, mainly in Oklahoma.

**Influenza** – Commonly referred to as the flu, influenza is a contagious respiratory virus that affects the nose, throat, and lungs.

**Informer** – One who informs on another to the police or authorities.

**Intensive Care Unit (ICU)** – A department of a hospital that is specialized in providing critical care and life support for critically ill and injured patients.

**Intermediate-Range Nuclear Forces Treaty (INF) and the Strategic Arms Reduction Treaty (START I)** – Treaty between the United States and the Soviet Union on elimination of short- and intermediate-range missiles (INF) and a treaty between the two nations on the reduction of strategic offensives arms (START I); the latter arms-control treaty set limitations on number of deployments.

**Interpol** – International Criminal Police Organization; an organization consisting of 194 member countries that facilitates worldwide police cooperation and crime control.

**Iranian Revolution** – A series of events beginning in January 1978 that culminated in the overthrow of the Pahlavi dynasty in February of 1979. Known as the Islamic Revolution, this revolution culminated with the replacement of an Islamic republic under the Ayatollah Khomeini.

**Iron Curtain** – A political boundary separating the former Soviet bloc and its dependent eastern and central-European allies from the West prior to the collapse of socialistic communism in eastern Europe in 1991.

**Ishmael** – The outcast son of Abraham and Hagar according to the book of Genesis; euphemistically, a social outcast, and in some Christian circles, anything produced outside of the will of God.

**ITAR-TASS** – During the Soviet era, the Information Telegraph Agency of Russia (ITAR-TASS); now called TASS, Russia's largest news agency and one of the largest news agencies worldwide.

**J. Harold Smith** – A Southern Baptist evangelist and founder of the popular Radio Bible Hour of the mid-1900s.

**J. Paul Getty** – Considered to be one of the wealthiest men in the 1950s and '60s, Jean Paul Getty was an American-born petrol industrialist and art collector.

**James Levine** – American conductor and pianist who served as the guiding maestro of the Metropolitan Opera for more than forty years.

**Jamie Buckingham** – Founder of the Tabernacle Church, editor of *Ministry Today* magazine, columnist for *Charisma* magazine, and author of forty-five books.

**Jeannie Wilkerson** – Notable intercessor, prophetess, and teacher predominantly on the subject of prayer. From Tulsa, Oklahoma, she especially taught on and prayed about the end-time Church and a last-days move of God.

**Jelgava** – A city in central Latvia just southwest of Riga. Where Rick and Denise began their ministry in the former USSR.

**Jerome Hines** – An American operatic bass and composer who performed in the Metropolitan Opera for forty-one years.

**Jesse James** – A notorious American outlaw, bank and train robber, and leader of the James-Younger Gang.

**Jesus Freaks** – Originally deemed as pejorative, a term referring to young people involved in the Jesus Movement of the 1960s. The term was later reclaimed as a positive self-identifier.

**Jesus Movement** – The resurgence of evangelical Christianity beginning on the West Coast of the United States spanning from the late 1960s to the late 1980s.

**Jesus People** – Another term used to describe those involved in the Jesus Movement.

**Jill Clayburgh** – Popular American actor known for her work in television, cinema, and the theater — in particular in the 1972 Broadway run of the musical *Pippin.*

**Jim Bakker** – An American televangelist most popular in the 1980s with his Christian broadcast *The Jim Bakker Show*, a program that has been revived in recent decades and airs from the Ozarks in Missouri.

**Jim Crow** – State and local laws that authorized the former practice of segregation between black and white people in the United States.

**Job-placement tests** – Tests designed to help determine what career paths are best suited for the tester based on a series of questions about personal traits, skills, and interests.

**John Adams** – Served as the first Vice-President (1789-1797) and second President (1797-1801) of the United States. He was one of the leaders of the American Revolution and is attributed as one of the Founding Fathers.

**John Hancock** – Leader of the American Revolution, one of the signers of the Declaration of Independence, and Governor of Massachusetts.

**Joseph Stalin** – Served as the socialist-communist ruler of the Soviet Union from 1927 to 1953 and as General Secretary of the Communist Party and Chairman of the Council of Ministers of the Soviet Union.

**Joyce Meyer** – American televangelist, Bible teacher, and bestselling author whose ministry began in 1985 and spans continents.

**Judge Isaac Parker** – An American politician and jurist; became infamously known as the "Hanging Judge" for his pronouncement of numerous death sentences in his courtroom in Fort Smith, Arkansas.

**Karl Marx** – A German philosopher and co-developer of the communist theory called Marxism. His most popular published title is the pamphlet *The Communist Manifesto.*

**Kathryn Kuhlman** – An American healing-evangelist and broadcaster most popularly known for hosting powerful healing services worldwide.

**Kathryn Thorne** – Spouse of American gangster Machine Gun Kelly; involved in bootlegging during the Prohibition era and in other criminal activity.

**Kenneth Copeland** – An American televangelist and founder of Kenneth Copeland Ministries in Fort Worth, Texas, he is a renowned Bible teacher in the Charismatic Movement.

**Kenneth E. Hagin** – American prophet and teacher known for pioneering the Word of Faith movement; he is the founder of Rhema Bible Training College.

**Kenneth W. Hagin** – American minister, president of Kenneth Hagin Ministries, and founding pastor of Rhema Bible Church since 1985.

**KGB (Komitet Gosudarstvennoy Bezopasnati)** – Committee for State Security, the KGB was the primary security agency for the Soviet Union.

**Kiev** – The capital of Ukraine and the seventh most populated city in Europe.

**Kino Theater Mir** – A movie house in downtown Moscow that served as a rented location of the Moscow Good News Church in the early years.

**Kiri Te Kanawa** – A New Zealand opera singer and internationally famed soprano; had three Top-40 albums in Australia in the mid-1980s.

**Koine Greek** – The common form of Greek spoken and written in the Hellenistic period, the Roman Empire, and the early Byzantine Empire; a universal language in which the New Testament was written and translated.

**Konstantin Chernenko** – A Soviet politician and former General Secretary of the Central Committee of the Communist Party of the Soviet Union.

**Kremlin Palace Stage** – Stage at the State Kremlin Palace consisting of sixteen elevating platforms with one rotating platform in the center that is almost fifty-six feet in diameter; one of the most prestigious concert platforms in Russia and the world.

**Kremlin** – Meaning "fortress," the Kremlin is a fortified complex in the center of Moscow that overlooks the Moscow River, Saint Basil's Cathedral, and Red Square and includes five palaces, four cathedrals, and the enclosing Kremlin Wall with Kremlin towers. The Kremlin serves as the official residence of the President of the Russian Federation.

**Labor camps** – Detention facilities in which inmates are forced to participate in penal labor as a form of punishment.

**Lada** – A brand of cars manufactured by the Russian company AvtoVAZ (formerly VAZ).

**Latvia** – One of the Baltic State nations that is located on the Baltic Sea, west of Russia, sharing a border with Estonia on the north, Lithuania on the south, and a partial border with Belarus on the southwest.

**Latvian Academy of Sciences** – A Stalinist-style building built in approximately 1946 that functioned as a center for scientists and various research institutes complete with a seventeenth-floor observation deck. In context, the site of the Riga Good News Church's first service on Orthodox Easter Sunday in 1993.

**Latvian Holocaust** – War crimes committed by Nazi Germany and their collaborators victimizing Jews during the German occupation of Latvia.

**Lenin's Mausoleum** – The final resting place of Soviet leader Vladmir Lenin located in Red Square in Moscow, Russia.

**Leonid Brezhnev** – former General Secretary of the Central Committee of the Communist Party of the Soviet Union, a position he held for eighteen years, second in duration during the time of the USSR only to Joseph Stalin's rulership.

**Leonid Iovich Gaidai** – Russian comedy actor and film director whose films were widely popular in the former Soviet Union.

**Leo Tolstoy** – Russian writer, repeat Nobel Peace Prize nominee, and regarded as one of the greatest authors of all time; Tolstoy is best known for his novel *War and Peace*.

**Linotype machine** – A typesetting system used for newspapers and magazines until it was replaced by phototypesetting and computer typesetting.

**Living Sound** – International music ministry founded in 1971 by Terry Law.

**Lutherans** – Those who subscribe to Lutheranism, a belief based on three principles: that humans are saved from their sins by God's grace alone, through faith alone, and on the basis of Scripture alone. Two more principles were added later: though Christ alone, and glory to God alone.

**Machine Gun Kelly** – Formally known as George Kelly Barnes, Machine Gun Kelly was an American gangster during the Prohibition era.

**Marlow Brothers** – Five brothers who were falsely accused of horse-stealing and imprisoned in Oklahoma. One brother escaped, and the four remaining encountered gunfire from a mob while in transport to a new prison facility. Two brothers survived, escaped to Colorado, and were upstanding citizens there as officers of the law.

**Martial law** – Temporary imposition of military government involving the suspension of ordinary law.

**Martin Luther** – A German theologian, Luther was one of the most significant figures in Christian history and in the Reformation of 1517. He is widely known for writing his *Ninety-Five Theses* and for purportedly nailing the theses to the door of the All Saints' Church in Wittenberg on October 31, 1517.

**"Marxist Communism"** – A social, political, and economic theory developed from the works of Nineteenth-Century German Karl Marx that focuses on the struggles between capitalists and those in the working class; the communist ideology officially adopted by the Soviet Union.

**Masonic Temple** – The basic organizational unit of Freemasonry; the meeting place of a Masonic Lodge.

**May 9** – Referred to as "Victory Day," a holiday in Russia that commemorates the surrender and defeat of Nazi Germany in 1945.

**Mayberry** – Refers generally to any small, idyllic hometown; specifically, it was the fictional community of Mayberry, North Carolina, from *The Andy Griffith Show*.

**MDM** - Moscow Youth Palace; a concert hall erected in 1982 in Moscow, Russia. Former rented location of the Moscow Good News Church.

**Methodius** – Saint Methodius of Olympus was a bishop, church father, and martyr.

**Metropolitan Opera (The Met)** – American opera company based in New York City. Founded in the 1880s, the Met is the largest classical-music organization in North America. Its performing company consists of a large symphony-sized orchestra, a chorus, children's choir, and many supporting and leading solo singers.

**Metro** – A mass rapid-transport system, also known as "heavy rail" or subway, is a type of high-capacity public transport generally found in urban areas.

**Miami Indians** – Native American tribe of Algonquian origins that lived in territory that is now parts of Indiana, Michigan, and Ohio. By 1846, they had been forcefully relocated to Indian Territory and are now federally recognized as the Miami Tribe of Oklahoma.

**Michael Romanov** – Michael I, "Michael of Russia," the first Russian czar of the House of Romanov, coronated in 1613.

**Mikhail Gorbachev** – Eighth and final leader of the Soviet Union and the General Secretary of the Communist Party of the Soviet Union from 1985-1991.

**Mine sweeper** – A small vessel designed to detonate naval mines.

**Ministry partners** – People who make a commitment to support financially and prayerfully a ministry and the vision God has given that ministry.

**Mitava** – Original name for Jelgava, a city in central Latvia twenty-five miles south of Riga.

**Mite (as in "two mites")** – The smallest Jewish coin used as currency in New Testament times. "Two mites" refers to the widow's sacrificial offering that Jesus noticed and commended in Mark 12 and Luke 21.

**Mononucleosis** – Also called "mono"; an infectious disease that causes flu-like symptoms that can last up to six months or even longer.

**Moscovites** – People who were born in or who live in Moscow, Russia.

**Moscow Metro System** – A public rapid-transit system that reaches nearly every part of the city in Russia's capital city, also referred to as *the Metro*.

**Moscow State University** – Built in 1755, the highest-ranked and first-ever university in Moscow.

**Moscow Youth Palace** – A large cultural center erected in 1982 filled with concert halls and lecture rooms, also referred to as MDM.

**National Guard** – A military reserve force composed of National Guard military units from each state and a select few territories.

**Nationalization of all church property, January 20, 1918** – Part of the legislation put in place by Vladimir Lenin that declared any and all property being utilized by a church or religious group would become government and public property.

**National Origin's Act of 1924** – Authorized the formation of the United States Border Control and allotted provisions for enforcement of deportation by providing funding and legal instructions to the courts. Associated with the Immigration Act of 1924, it restricted immigration by establishing national quotas from certain sectors of the world.

**National Register of Historic Places** – The U.S. government's list of districts, sites, buildings, structures, and objects deemed worthy of preservation for their historical significance.

**Neoplatonism** – A strand of Platonic philosophy that emerged in the Third Century AD and was developed by major Hellenistic philosophers in Roman Egypt, among them Ammonius Saccas, who is often referred to as one of the founders of Neoplatonism, and his student Plotinus, also a noted Hellenistic philosopher in Roman Egypt, whose philosophy was influential during Late Antiquity and the Middle Ages.

**New Age Movement** – A range of spiritual beliefs that grew with popularity among the occult and metaphysical communities in the 1970s.

**New Wine Magazine** – A pioneering publication for the Charismatic Movement published from 1969-1986.

**New Year's Day** – In many parts of the world, including Russia, New Year's Day celebrated on January 1, the first day on the Gregorian calendar. During the rule of communism in the former Soviet Union, it was the premier holiday of the year since Christmas had been outlawed.

**New York City Opera** – A renowned American opera company founded in 1943 in Manhattan in New York City.

**Nicholas and Alexandra, Olga, Tatiana, Maria, Anastasia, and Alexei** – The Romanov family of Nicholas II, his wife and five children, all of whom were detained under house arrest during the revolutions and eventually executed.

**Nicholas II** – The last Russian emperor whose disastrous military ventures led to the Russian revolutions and ultimately the fall of the monarchy in favor of atheistic communism.

**Nicholas Romanov** – Nicholas II, czar of Russia from 1894-1917.

**Nikita Khrushchev** – Leader of the Soviet Union as the First Secretary of the Communist Party of the Soviet Union from 1953 to 1964.

**No man's land** – A situation or area of activity in which there are no rules; an uninhabited, indeterminate, and undefined place.

**Nondenominational** – A person or group that is not restricted to any one organized or "mainline" denomination.

**Nordic Countries** – A region consisting of five sovereign states, including Denmark, Finland, Iceland, Norway, and Sweden, as well as three adjoining territories known as the Faroe Islands, Greenland, and Åland.

**Norvel Hayes** – A successful businessman, renowned Bible teacher, and founder of several Christian ministries in the United States.

**October Manifesto** – "The Manifesto on the Improvement of the State Order," issued in 1905 by Nicholas II, marked the end of unlimited autocracy and the beginning of constitutional monarchy in Russia.

**Oil Capital of the World** – A title associated with the city of Tulsa, Oklahoma, for most of the Twentieth Century as it played a major role in the American oil industry.

**Oil Capital Historic District** – An area located in downtown Tulsa, Oklahoma, designated by the National Register of Historic Places to commemorate the success of the oil business in Tulsa in the early Twentieth Century.

**Oklahoma Land Rush of 1889** – The event in which nearly fifty thousand settlers "rushed" to claim a plot of the 1.9 million-acre portion of "Unassigned Lands" of Indian Territory in Oklahoma.

**Oligarch** – A fabulously wealthy individual — often, but not always, a term used to refer to rapidly accumulated wealth during the era of Russian privatization in the aftermath of the dissolution of the Soviet Union in the 1990s.

**Oral Roberts University (ORU)** – A private Christian University in Tulsa, Oklahoma, founded in 1963 by televangelist Oral Roberts.

**Oral Roberts University Mabee Center** – A multi-purpose arena opened in 1972 on the Oral Roberts University campus. Named after philanthropists John and Lottie Jane Mabee, the Mabee Center can seat more than eleven thousand spectators.

**Oral Roberts** – American Charismatic Christian televangelist and founder of Oral Roberts University; considered to be the father of the modern-day Charismatic Movement.

**Otoe** – Otoe Indians are the original people of Nebraska, Missouri, and Iowa, but were forcefully relocated to a reservation in Oklahoma in the 1800s. In context, Denise Roberson Renner is of Otoe descent on her father's side of the family.

**P. T. Barnum** – Phineas Taylor Barnum was an American businessman, politician, and entertainer, most commonly known for his part in founding his widely popular traveling P. T. Barnum circus.

**Partners** – People who make a commitment to support a ministry and the vision God has given that ministry, also referred to as "ministry partners."

**Pashkov Palace** – A mansion erected in 1786 by nobleman Pyotr Pashkov that sits atop Vagankovo Hill across from the Kremlin in Moscow, Russia. In context, it was the venue of the celebration of the five-hundredth anniversary of Luther's Reformation attended by spiritual leaders worldwide, including Rick Renner and his son Paul Renner.

**Pat Robertson** – An American businessman, broadcaster, and author, who founded the Christian Broadcasting Network (CBN) in 1960 and Regent University in 1977.

**Paul and Jan Crouch** – Founders of Trinity Broadcast Network (TBN) in 1973.

**Pearl Harbor** – A surprise military strike on American soil by the Imperial Japanese Navy Air Service at the United States' Naval base at Pearl Harbor in Honolulu, Hawaii, on December 7, 1941.

**Pentecostal** – A style of Christianity that emphasizes a direct and personal experience with God through the supernatural work of the Holy Spirit.

**Perestroika** – The practice of restructuring or reforming the economic and political system within the Communist Party of the former Soviet Union; set in place by former President Mikhail Gorbachev.

**Peterhof** – A series of classical palaces and royal gardens in Saint Petersburg, Russia, commissioned by Peter the Great in 1703.

**Peter the Great** – Former emperor of Russia whose great reforms had a lasting effect on Russia and ushered the country into the modern age.

**Philmont Scout Ranch** – A ranch covering more than 100,000 acres in New Mexico donated by oil baron and philanthropist Waite Phillips to the Boy Scouts of America.

**Pitcher pump** – A shallow well pump with an open spout that is operated by hand, resembling a pitcher.

**Plato** – Athenian philosopher during the Classical period in Ancient Greece (424/423-348/347 BC), who founded both the Platonist School of Thought and the Platonic Academy ("the Academy"), which is viewed by many as the first institution of higher learning in the Western world; also credited as the founder of much of Western philosophy.

**Plato's Apology of Socrates** – Plato's Socratic dialogue of Socrates' speech to defend himself at trial for impiety and corruption.

**Plato's Crito** – A dialogue written by Plato depicting what some believe was a real conversation that had taken place between Socrates, who was awaiting execution in prison, and Crito, who was trying to rescue him.

**Politburo** – The executive policy-making committee of the Communist Party.

**Presidential Administration of Russia** – A federal executive body that is responsible for governmental services, managing property, overseeing Presidential executive decisions, and other acts prescribed by the Presidential Office.

**President Putin** — Vladimir Vladimirovich Putin, one of the most prominent political figures of our time, has led the largest country in the world, which also possesses powerful nuclear weapons, for more than twenty years. Vladimir Putin was born on October 7, 1952, in Leningrad (now Saint Petersburg). From 1977 to 1991, he served in the KGB. In August 1999, Putin was appointed Prime Minister of the Russian government. It was Putin whom Boris Yeltsin eventually chose as his successor to be the first President. Putin became the Russian Prime Minister in August 1999, the acting Russian President 1999-2000, the elected President in 2000 (he served two terms as President from 2000-2008), and Prime Minister from 2008-2012. Putin was re-elected to a third Presidential term lasting from 2012-2018 and was then elected to serve a fourth Presidential term in 2018.

**Pretty Boy Floyd** – Charles Arthur Floyd, an American bank robber who operated out of the west and central states in the 1930s.

**Prime Minister** – Title given to the head of government in parliamentary political systems.

**Protestantism** – A religious movement stemming from the Sixteenth Century Reformation, following biblical Christian doctrine as opposed to doctrine of the Catholic or Eastern Orthodox church. Protestantism has approximately eight hundred million to one *billion* adherents worldwide.

**Pskov** – One of the oldest Russian towns in west Russia, about twelve miles east of the Estonian border.

**Psychedelic drugs** – A group of hallucinogenic drugs that trigger non-ordinary states of consciousness and alter perception, mood, and several cognitive processes.

**Psychic** – An individual who purports to use extrasensory perception (ESP) to identify information hidden from the normal senses, particularly involving telepathy or clairvoyance; one who performs acts that are apparently inexplicable by natural laws and means.

**Quapaw** – Federally recognized as the Quapaw Nation, this Native American tribe was relocated to Indian Territory in 1834, and their tribal base today is in Ottawa County in northeastern Oklahoma.

**Queen Victoria** – Reigning Queen of the United Kingdom of Great Britain 1837-1901, a total of a little more than sixty-three years, making her the longest-reigning queen up to that date.

**Rastrelli** – Francesco Bartolomeo Rastrelli was an Italian sculptor and architect who worked mainly in Russia. His major works, among many others, include the Winter Palace in Saint Petersburg and the Catherine Palace in Tsarskoye Selo, which are famed for their extravagant luxury and opulence.

**Red Army** – Also known as the Workers' and Peasants' Red Army, it was the army and air force of the Russian Soviet Socialist Republics founded by Valdmir Lenin in 1918.

**Red Square** – Large open square in the heart of Moscow, Russia, surrounded by historic buildings in Moscow, such as the Kremlin, Lenin's Tomb, and St. Basil's Cathedral.

**Reformation** – Referring to Martin Luther's Reformation, the Reformation of 1517 marks the time in which Martin Luther sparked the rise of Protestantism.

**Revival meeting** – A service or series of services intended to inspire and create a renewed enthusiasm in the faith of those who participate.

**Rhema Bible Training Center (now Rhema Bible College)** – Currently an accredited Bible college located in Broken Arrow, Oklahoma, started by renowned American prophet and teacher Kenneth E. Hagin in 1974.

**RIA Novosti** – Sometimes referred to as RIAN or RIA, it is a Russian state-owned domestic news agency founded in 1941 and is headquartered in Moscow.

**Riga Opera House (Latvian National Opera)** – An opera house and opera company in Riga that occupies a stately neoclassical-style building, originally constructed as the Riga German Theatre in 1863.

**Riga** – Capital city of Latvia and is known as a cultural center and home to many museums and concert halls. In context, the city where Rick and Denise Renner constructed one of the first church buildings in that territory in almost six decades.

**Riga's Old Town** – A preserved historic neighborhood located in the heart of Riga, home to many historical churches and beautiful Nouveau architecture.

**Robert M. McFarlin** – An American businessman and successful oilman who struck fortune upon oil-drilling in Glenpool, Oklahoma. McFarlin was one of the many who helped establish Oklahoma as a center for the booming petroleum industry in the 1930s.

**Romanov Dynasty** – The longest-running and last imperial dynasty to rule over Russia from 1613 to 1917.

**Romanovs** – The Russian imperial family, frequently referred to as the House of Romanov, which held the reigning imperial house of Russia from 1613 to 1917.

**Royal Ambassadors** – A popular Southern Baptist missions and discipleship group for young boys founded in 1908.

**Ruble** – The form of currency used in many Eastern European countries, but most commonly associated with the economy of Russia.

**Rumbula** – A region in a suburb of Riga that is infamous for the Rumbula Massacre, an event in which approximately 25,000 Jews were killed in or on their way to the Rumbula forest in 1941.

**Russian-American Citizens** – A person who has citizenship in both Russia and the U.S.

**Russian Empire** – Founded in 1721, the Russian Empire consisted of tsarist autocracy, absolute monarchy, autocracy, and dual monarchy forms of government, which was eventually overthrown by the Russian Revolution in 1917.

**Russian Federation Building** – The House of the Government of the Russian Federation, also known as the Russian White House, it is a government building in Moscow that stands on the Krasnopresnenskaya embankment. The building serves as the primary office of the government of Russia and is the official workplace of the Russian Prime Minister.

**Russian Federation** – A country that spans from eastern Europe to northern and western parts of Siberia, making it the largest country geographically in the world.

**Russian Parliament** – Known as the Federal Assembly, which consists of a 628-member parliament divided into two chambers, the State Duma and the Federation Council.

**Russian Revolution of 1917** – Also referred to as the Bokshevik or October Revolution, a political and social revolution led by Vladimir Lenin in which the working class revolted against the government of Czar Nicholas II and the Russian monarchy.

**Russian ruble** – The form of currency used in today's modern Russia.

**Russo-Japanese War of 1904-1905** – A conflict between the Japanese Empire and the Russian Empire in which Japan forced Russia to abandon their expansion efforts in East Asia. The war inflicted humiliating defeats on Russia and contributed to domestic unrest already present in that nation, which was a catalyst to the revolution of 1905 in Russia.

**Ruth Carter Stapleton** – The sister of former U.S. President Jimmy Carter who was known as a spiritual healer.

**Saint Nicholas, Patron Saint of Russia** – Famous for his kindness to children, this patron saint would later inspire the legend of Saint Nicholas, or Santa Claus. He was the saint most cherished by Russian hearts prior to the Revolution of 1917. Later, all semblances of religion were outlawed in the USSR, along with Saint Nicholas and the Christmas holiday itself, replaced by New Year's Day as the Soviet Union's big winter holiday and by Father Frost, a figure associated with magic.

**Salaspils** – A small town in Latvia located just southeast of Riga. Notably commemorated as the location of a Nazi concentration work camp where children, especially, were used as "guinea pigs" and their blood used for wounded soldiers.

**Sandites** – A term self-given to citizens of the town Sand Springs, Oklahoma.

**Sand Springs Children's Home** – A home founded by Charles Page in 1908 that provides care to orphans and families in need.

**Sand Springs Widows' Colony** – A compound of homes in Sand Springs, Oklahoma, for widows with children funded by Charles Page.

**School of Cinderella** – An online program for Russian-speaking women taught by Denise Renner that consists of sixteen lessons with a counselor assigned to each woman who enrolls in the free online "school."

**Secret Security Services** – Intelligence services in the former Soviet Union once closely associated with the KGB; now known as the FSB or the Federal Security Bureau of the Russian Federation.

**Seminole** – A Native American people of the Creek confederacy originating from Florida, but most were forced to relocate to Oklahoma in the Nineteenth Century.

**Seneca** – The Seneca Nation of Indians, a group of indigenous Iroquoian-speaking people who historically lived south of Lake Ontario, one of the five Great Lakes in North America. In the Twenty-First Century, more than 10,000 Seneca live in the U.S., which has three federally recognized Seneca tribes, one of which (the Seneca-Cayuga Nation) is in Oklahoma, where their ancestors were relocated from Ohio during the Indian Removal.

**Sergei Vasilevich Ryakhovsky** – One of Russia's most revered spiritual leaders, an advisor to the President, and Bishop of the Centralized Religious Organization of the Russian United Union of Christians of Evangelical Faith (POCXBE)

**Shah of Iran** – A title of kingship given to each of the various monarchial rulers of Iran before they were surmounted by the revolutionary Shiite ayatollahs. Mohammad Reza Shah was the last Shah of Iran from September 16, 1941, until February 11, 1979, at which time he was overthrown in the Iranian Revolution.

**Shawnee** – A Native American Algonquian-speaking ethnic group, some of whom were relocated to Indian Territory (now Oklahoma) in the 1830s. Other Shawnee did not move to Oklahoma until after the Civil War. Today three federally recognized Shawnee tribes, made up of descendants of different historical and kinship groups, are all headquartered in Oklahoma.

**Siamese twins** – Also known as conjoined twins, Siamese twins are identical twins who are joined in utero and born physically connected to one another.

**Sickle and Hammer of the Soviet Union** – A symbol adopted during the Russian Revolution meant to represent a union between the working and peasantry classes. It became internationally recognized as the symbol of the USSR.

**Singing in the Spirit** – Also known as singing in tongues, singing in the Spirit is the act of worship through glossolalic song.

**Slavic languages** – A group of Indo-European languages spoken in most Eastern European countries, primarily by Slavic peoples. The Russian language has its origins in the Slavic languages.

**Snow Maiden** – A popular seasonal character in Russian folklore who is often said to accompany Father Frost on his visitations to young children during the Christmas and New Year seasons.

**Social Security card** – A card containing a person's unique nine-digit Social-Security number issued to U.S. citizens by the U.S. government.

**Southern Baptist Convention** – The official name for Southern Baptist churches that works cooperatively to impact the lives of many with the Gospel. Founded in 1845, the group has fourteen million members, making it the largest Baptist and Protestant organization in the world.

**Southern Baptist Foreign Missionaries** – The International Mission Board (IMB) of the Southern Baptist Convention.

**Soviet ideology** – Referring to the ideology of the Communist Party largely based on Marxism, focusing on a centralized command of the economy and political dictatorship.

**Soviet Republics** - The Union of Soviet Socialist Republics (USSR) that spanned most of Europe and Asia before its downfall in 1991.

**Soviet ruble** – Currency previously used throughout the fifteen republics of the former USSR.

**Soviet Union** – The USSR, a one-party socialist state governed by the Communist Party until 1991, with Moscow as its capital.

**Spelling bee** – Competition held in which contestants or teams are required to spell a selection of words, won by the member or members who spell the most words correctly.

**Spittoon** – A receptacle or pot with a funnel-shaped opening most commonly for spitting tobacco refuse into.

**Square meter** – A unit of area used for measuring rooms, houses, blocks of land, etc., a square meter is an area equal to a square that measures one meter on each side; the equivalent of 10.76 square feet.

**St. Basil's Cathedral** – Also known as the Cathedral of the Vasily Blessed, St. Basil's Cathedral is an Orthodox Church in the center of Red Square, a colorful, popular symbol of Russia's culture.

**St. Louis Cardinals** – A professional American baseball team that competes in Major League Baseball (MLB) and has been a member of the National League Central division of baseball since 1892.

**St. Peter and St. Paul Church, Riga** – The oldest Orthodox church in the capital of Latvia, founded in 1728, it fell into ruins during the rule of communism, but has since been magnificently restored.

**Stalingrad** – Now Volgograd, a city in southwest Russia famously known for the Battle of Stalingrad in which Germany and its allies rivaled against the Soviet Union for control of the city from August of 1942 to February of 1943. Russia's "dark horse" victory over those Axis troops helped turn the tides of WWII in favor of the Allies.

**Stalinism** – A political ideology implemented by Joseph Stalin in the Soviet Union from 1927-1953 that was greatly influenced by Marxism and Leninism.

**Stamps Musical Family** – The family of Denise Roberson Renner on her mother's side of the family. Denise's mother, Nora Stamps Roberson, was raised in a musical family that hailed from Texas and were innovative in the Gospel-music industry.

**State Duma** – The lower of the two chambers of the Russian Federation, the State Duma is tasked with adopting federal constitutions and laws.

**Statue of Liberty** – A colossal, copper statue on Liberty Island in New York Harbor that was a gift from France to the United States commemorating the U.S.'s independence on July 4, 1776. The statue is a figure of a robed Roman goddess that holds a torch above her head. A broken shackle and chain lie at her feet, commemorating the national abolition of slavery. After the statue's dedication in October 1886, it became an iconic symbol of freedom, welcoming immigrants arriving by sea.

**Stephanie Boosahda** – A musical artist and worship leader who was considered to be one of the greatest Christian singers and Christian recording artists of the 1970s and '80s.

**Sunday School** – A Bible-teaching class usually preceding a Sunday church service and traditionally geared toward children and teenagers.

**T. L. Osborn** – An American healing evangelist, teacher, and author whose ministry was based in Tulsa, Oklahoma.

**Tallasi** – "Old Town," the name given to modern-day Tulsa by the Creek Native American tribe before Oklahoma statehood, which was eventually adapted to the name Tulsa.

**TASS** – Russia's leading news company since 1904, at which time, during the Soviet era, it was called *ITAR-TASS*.

**Teotihuacan** – San Juan Teotihuacan is an ancient Mesoamerican city about thirty miles east of Mexico City filled with archaeological complexes such as temples and pyramids.

**Terry Law** – A Christian evangelist and humanitarian, Terry Law was the founder of World Compassion Ministries and considered to be one of the most influential ministers to countries infamously hostile to the sharing of the Gospel.

**Thomas Carey** – An American baritone who became an opera professor at the University of Oklahoma and founded Oklahoma's touring opera group called the Church Cirquit Opera, later renamed Cimmaron Circuit Opera company.

**Thomas Gilcrease** – American oilman, philanthropist, and art collector who founded the Gilcrease Museum, which contains a comprehensive collection of western American art.

**Thomas Jefferson** – Served as the third U.S. President from 1801 to 1809 and, previously, as Vice-President to John Adams from 1797 to 1801.

**Thought-control** – A practice used by a totalitarian government in an attempt to restrict certain ideas and impose others using censorship and control of curriculum.

**Tithe** – A gift or payment given to the local church in support, typically ten percent of one's earnings.

**Tongues** – Also termed *glossolalia.* the utterance of speech-like sounds used in prayer and worship, the meaning of which is often unknown to the speaker.

**Torah** – Religious text known as the first part of the Jewish Bible; the essential text of Judaism.

**Trail of Tears** – A path walked by approximately sixty thousand displaced American Natives in which they traveled more than five-thousand miles across nine states between 1830 and 1850.

**Training Union** – Also called Baptist Training Union, a ministry of the Baptist church whose purpose is to train its membership in Christian living, Baptist doctrine and history, and missionary service to equip, reinforce, and strengthen believers.

**The Grapes of Wrath** – An American realist novel written by John Steinback in 1939 that won a Pulitzer Prize. The novel was set during the Great Depression and focuses on a poor family of tenant farmers beset by drought, changes in the industry, the Dust Bowl, and bank foreclosures as they set out for California along with thousands of other Oklahomans seeking dignity and a future.

**Tulsa Race Riot (Tulsa Race Massacre, the Greenwood Massacre, Black Wall Street Massacre)** – The tragic events that took place between May 31 and June 1 of 1921 in which mobs of white residents attacked black people and destroyed their homes and black-owned businesses, resulting in hundreds of deaths and injuries and leaving many homeless.

**Tulsa** – A city in northeastern Oklahoma known for its Art Deco architecture downtown and its major role in the American oil industry in the Twentieth Century.

**Typesetter** – A person who prepares text into the format in which it is to be printed.

**U.S. Consulate** – A place that provides consular services, such as passports, visas, and birth certifications, etc. for U.S. citizens abroad or for visitors to the United States.

**U.S. Consul** – An official representative of the government of one country in the territory of another, there to serve and assist the citizens of the consul's country of origin.

**U.S. Marshals** – The United States Marshals is a federal law-enforcement agency operating under the authority of the Attorney General.

**Ukrainian coupons** – A unit of currency used in Ukraine immediately after the collapse of the USSR.

**Underground church** – A term used to describe Christian believers who gather to serve and worship in secret due to active persecution.

**Union of Soviet Socialist Republic of Latviskaya** – The Latvian Soviet Socialist Republic also known as Soviet Latvia, one of fifteen republics of the former Soviet Union.

**USSR** – Official abbreviation for the Soviet Union: Union of Soviet Socialist Republics.

**Vacation Bible School** – Often abbreviated to VBS, Vacation Bible School is a daily educational Bible-teaching program offered by churches for children most often during the summer months lasting up to a week at a time in duration.

**Vep Ellis** – A beloved singer-songwriter who was largely popular in the Southern Gospel genre and served as a Church of God minister for forty-nine years.

**Vicki Jamison-Peterson** – An American singer, evangelist, author, and founder of Vicki Jamison-Peterson Ministries. She was also a regular guest on Christian television during the 1970s and '80s.

**Victory Day** – The day of May 8, 1945 that commemorates the surrender of Nazi Germany and an Allied victory during World War II.

**Video Club** – A club started by Rick Renner for pastors and associates that included teachings and messages on video predating his Good News Association of Pastors and Churches.

**Vietnam War** – A war between North and South Vietnam often referred to as the Second Indochina War that caused conflict in Vietnam, Laos, and Cambodia from November 1955 until the fall of Saigon in April 1975.

**Villa Philmonte** – Formerly the summer home of Waite and Genevieve Phillips located just outside Cimarron, New Mexico, Villa Philmonte was deeded to be used by the Boy Scouts of America 1939.

**Vitamin Club** – A special outreach dedicated to the elderly population of Moscow, Russia, hosted by Rick and Denise Renner, RENNER Ministries, and their partners and associates.

**Vladimir Lenin** – The founder and former Premier of the Soviet Union and communist revolutionary often referred to as "Lenin" who founded the Russian Communist Party and led the Bolshevik Revolution.

**Vladimir Putin** – Vladimir Vladimirovich Putin, one of the most prominent political figures of our time, has led the largest country in the world, which also possesses powerful nuclear weapons, for more than twenty years. Vladimir Putin was born on October 7, 1952, in Leningrad (now Saint Petersburg). From 1977 to 1991, he served in the KGB. In August 1999, Putin was appointed Prime Minister of the Russian government. It was Putin whom Boris Yeltsin eventually chose as his successor to be the first President. Putin became the Russian Prime Minister in August 1999, the acting Russian President 1999-2000, the elected President in 2000 (he served two terms as President from 2000-2008), and Prime Minister from 2008-2012. Putin was re-elected to a third Presidential term lasting from 2012-2018 and was then elected to serve a fourth Presidential term in 2018.

**Vorkuta** – A coal-mining town belonging to the Komi Republic in Russia just north of the Arctic Circle founded in the year 1936 that was a remote location where Christian believers were forcibly sent to prison and to work in coal mines.

**W. K. Warren** – An American businessman and oil baron who founded the Warren Petroleum Corporation of Delaware in 1922 and specialized in the marketing and production of liquified petroleum gas. His headquarters was in Tulsa, and his philanthropic work included the establishment of the Saint Francis Healthcare system.

**Wagner Hall, The Richard Wagner** Opera Theater House – The first stationary opera house in Riga erected in 1782 that was the hub of cultural life in Riga for many years.

**Waite Phillips** – An American businessman, oilman, and philanthropist who played a large role in the successes of Tulsa businesses in the Twentieth Century.

**Walter Cronkite** – An American broadcaster, journalist, and lead anchorman of CBS News for nineteen years; named "the most trusted man in America."

**Wanderlust** – A strong inner desire or impulse to explore, travel, and wander to places all over the globe.

**Watergate** – The Watergate Scandal was a series of events taking place over the course of two years involving the break-in at the Democratic National Committee headquarters at the Watergate complex in Washington DC and its coverup by the U.S. President at the time Richard Nixon, eventually resulting in his resignation in 1974.

**Wells Hotel** – A historic hotel in the heart of Tulsa, Oklahoma, opening in February 1923, the lobby of which served as the unofficial office of early oil businessmen and later became a Sunday School building for Tulsa's First Baptist Church.

**White Army** – Also known as the White Movement, an anti-communist force that fought the Bolsheviks, otherwise known as the Red Army, in the Russian Civil War active from 1918 to 1923.

**White Space** – A concept in visual arts created by Frank Heaston that is referred to as a negative space or an area between elements, such as margins, gutters, and space between columns, lines of type, graphics, etc.

**William Skelly** – An American entrepreneur who played a major role in the oil business and in Tulsa's reputation for becoming the "Oil Capital of the World."

**Winter Palace** – A baroque-style palace that served as the official residence of Russian Emperors from 1732 to 1917 and is currently a large part of the Hermitage Museum in Saint Petersburg.

**Women's Day** – An international celebration of the political, socioeconomic, and cultural progress of women across Europe, celebrated on March 8 each year.

**Woodstock** – An iconic rock-music festival held over a period of days on a dairy farm in Bethel, New York, with a record attendance of nearly 400,000 people.

**World Action Singers** – A Christian musical group, led by Richard Roberts for many years, closely affiliated with Oral Roberts University in Tulsa.

**World War II** – A global war lasting from 1939 to 1945 that involved most of the world's countries; fought between two main opposing military alliances: the Allies and the Axis Powers.

**Yalta** – A resort city located in the Crimean Peninsula facing the Black Sea.

**Yolki** – Russian word meaning "fir tree" that was used to name the secular New Year's holiday in the former Soviet Union after Christmas festivities were banned.

**Yuri Andropov** – The sixth leader of the Soviet Union, once the head of the KGB, and General Secretary of the Communist Party.

**Zaks** – The marriage-registration office in Russia where all marriage unions are registered to be recognized by the state.

# PRAYER OF SALVATION

When Jesus Christ comes into your life, you are immediately emancipated — totally set free from the bondage of sin! If you have never received Jesus as your personal Savior, it is time to experience this new life for yourself. The first step to freedom is simple. Just pray this prayer from your heart:

*Lord, I can never adequately thank You for all You did for me on the Cross. I am so undeserving, Jesus, but You came and gave Your life for me anyway. I repent for rejecting You, and I turn away from my life of rebellion and sin right now. I turn to You and receive You as my Savior, and I ask You to wash away my sin and make me completely new in You by Your precious blood. I thank You from the depths of my heart for doing what no one else could do for me. Had it not been for Your willingness to lay down Your life for me, I would be eternally lost.*

*Thank You, Jesus, that I am now redeemed by Your blood. On the Cross, You bore my sin, my sickness, my pain, my lack of peace, and my suffering. Your blood has removed my sin, washed me whiter than snow, and given me rightstanding with the Father. I have no need to be ashamed of my past sins because I am now a new creature in You. Old things have passed away, and all things have become new because I am in Jesus Christ (2 Corinthians 5:17).*

*Because of You, Jesus, today I am forgiven; I am filled with peace; and I am a joint-heir with You! Satan no longer has a right to lay any claim on me. From a grateful heart, I will faithfully serve You the rest of my days!*

If you prayed this prayer from your heart, something amazing has happened to you. No longer a servant to sin, you are now a servant of Almighty God. The evil spirits that once exacted every ounce of your being and required your all-inclusive servitude no longer possess the authorization to control you or dictate your destiny!

As a result of your decision to turn your life over to Jesus Christ, your eternal home has been decided forever. Heaven will now be your permanent address for all eternity.

God's Spirit has moved into your own human spirit, and you have become the "temple of God" (1 Corinthians 6:19). What a miracle! To think that God, by His Spirit, now lives inside you!

Now you have a new Lord and Master, and His name is Jesus. From this moment on, the Spirit of God will work in you and supernaturally energize you to fulfill God's will for your life. Everything will change for you as you yield to His leadership in your life — and it's all going to change for the best!

# PRAYER TO RECEIVE
# THE BAPTISM IN THE HOLY SPIRIT

The baptism in the Holy Spirit is a free gift to *everyone* who has made Jesus Savior and Lord of his or her life (*see* Acts 2:39).

After you made Jesus your Lord at the time of the new birth, the Holy Spirit came to live inside you, and your old, unregenerate spirit was made completely new. This subsequent gift is the "baptism into," or *an immersion in*, the Holy Spirit.

The baptism in the Holy Spirit supplies the supernatural power of God for witnessing about Christ, for enjoying a deeper, more intimate relationship with the Holy Spirit, and for victorious Christian living.

Receiving this precious gift is easy. Before you pray to receive the infilling of the Holy Spirit, you might want to read and meditate on the Scripture references I provide on the next page. Then expect to receive what you asked for *the moment* you pray!

If you would like to be baptized in the Holy Spirit and speak with new tongues (*see* Acts 2:4), simply pray the following prayer and then act on it!

> *Lord, You gave the Holy Spirit to Your Church to help us fulfill the Great Commission. I ask You in faith for this free gift, and I receive right now the baptism in the Holy Spirit. I believe that You hear me as I pray, and I thank You for baptizing me in the Holy Spirit with the evidence of speaking with a new, supernatural prayer language. Amen.*

As a result of praying this prayer, *your life will never be the same*. You will have God's power working through you to witness, to operate in the gifts of the Holy Spirit, and to experience Jesus' victory as a living reality every day.

*Rick Renner*

**Scripture References for Study and Review:** Mark 16:17; Luke 24:39; Acts 1:4,5,8; 2:4,39; 10:45,46

# CONTACT RENNER MINISTRIES

For further information
about RENNER Ministries,
please contact the office nearest you,
or visit the ministry website at:
**www.renner.org**

**ALL USA
CORRESPONDENCE:**
RENNER Ministries
P. O. Box 702040
Tulsa, OK 74170-2040
(918) 496-3213
Or 1-800-RICK-593
Email: renner@renner.org
Website: www.renner.org

**MOSCOW OFFICE:**
RENNER Ministries
P. O. Box 789
101000, Moscow, Russia
+7 (495) 727-1470
Email: blagayavestonline@ignc.org
Website: www.ignc.org

**RIGA OFFICE:**
RENNER Ministries
Unijas 99
Riga LV-1084, Latvia
+371 67802150
Email: info@goodnews.lv

**KIEV OFFICE:**
RENNER Ministries
P. O. Box 300
01001, Kiev, Ukraine
+38 (044) 451-8315
Email: blagayavestonline@ignc.org

**OXFORD OFFICE:**
RENNER Ministries
Box 7, 266 Banbury Road
Oxford OX2 7DL, England
+44 1865 521024
Email: europe@renner.org

# BOOKS BY RICK RENNER

Build Your Foundation*
Chosen by God*
Dream Thieves*
Dressed To Kill*
The Holy Spirit and You*
How To Keep Your Head on Straight in a World Gone Crazy*
How To Receive Answers From Heaven!*
Insights on Successful Leadership*
Last-Days Survival Guide*
A Life Ablaze*
Life in the Combat Zone*
A Light in Darkness, Volume One,
    *Seven Messages to the Seven Churches* series
The Love Test*
No Room for Compromise, Volume Two,
    *Seven Messages to the Seven Churches* series
Paid in Full*
The Point of No Return*
Repentance*
Signs You'll See Just Before Jesus Comes*
Sparkling Gems From the Greek Daily Devotional 1*
Sparkling Gems From the Greek Daily Devotional 2*
Spiritual Weapons To Defeat the Enemy*
Ten Guidelines To Help You Achieve
    Your Long-Awaited Promotion!*
Testing the Supernatural
365 Days of Increase
365 Days of Power
Turn Your God-Given Dreams Into Reality*
Why We Need the Gifts of the Spirit*
The Will of God — The Key to Your Success*
You Can Get Over It*

*Digital version available for Kindle, Nook, and iBook.
**Note:** Books by Rick Renner are available for purchase at:
**www.renner.org**

# SPARKLING GEMS FROM THE GREEK 1

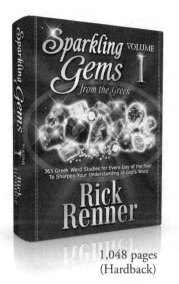

1,048 pages
(Hardback)

Rick Renner's **Sparkling Gems From the Greek 1** has gained widespread recognition for its unique illumination of the New Testament through more than 1,000 Greek word studies in a 365-day devotional format. *Sparkling Gems 1* remains a beloved resource that has spiritually strengthened believers worldwide. As many have testified, the wealth of truths within its pages never grows old. Year after year, *Sparkling Gems 1* continues to deepen readers' understanding of the Bible.

To order, visit us online at: **www.renner.org**

# SPARKLING GEMS FROM THE GREEK 2

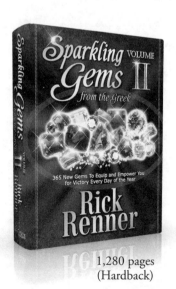

1,280 pages
(Hardback)

Rick infuses into **Sparkling Gems From the Greek 2** the added strength and richness of many more years of his own personal study and growth in God — expanding this devotional series to impact the reader's heart on a deeper level than ever before. This remarkable study tool helps unlock new hidden treasures from God's Word that will draw readers into an ever more passionate pursuit of Him.

To order, visit us online at: **www.renner.org**

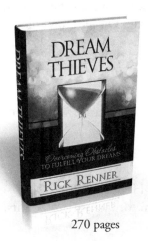

# DRESSED TO KILL
## A BIBLICAL APPROACH
### TO SPIRITUAL WARFARE AND ARMOR

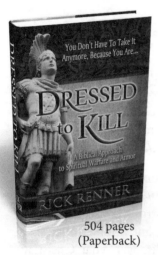

504 pages
(Paperback)

Rick Renner's book *Dressed To Kill* is considered by many to be a true classic on the subject of spiritual warfare. The original version, which sold more than 400,000 copies, is a curriculum staple in Bible schools worldwide. In this beautiful volume, you will find:

- 504 pages of reedited text in paperback

- 16 pages of full-color illustrations

- Questions at the end of each chapter to guide you into deeper study

In *Dressed To Kill*, Rick explains with exacting detail the purpose and function of each piece of Roman armor. In the process, he describes the significance of our *spiritual* armor not only to withstand the onslaughts of the enemy, but also to overturn the tendencies of the carnal mind. Furthermore, Rick delivers a clear, scriptural presentation on the biblical definition of spiritual warfare — what it is and what it is not.

When you walk with God in deliberate, continual fellowship, He will enrobe you with Himself. Armed with the knowledge of who you are in Him, you will be dressed and dangerous to the works of darkness, unflinching in the face of conflict, and fully equipped to take the offensive and gain mastery over any opposition from your spiritual foe. You don't have to accept defeat anymore once you are *dressed to kill*!

To order, visit us online at: **www.renner.org**

Book Resellers: Contact Harrison House at 800-722-6774 or visit **www.HarrisonHouse.com** for quantity discounts.

# LAST-DAYS SURVIVAL GUIDE

## A Scriptural Handbook
## To Prepare You for These Perilous Times

472 pages
(Paperback)

In his book *Last-Days Survival Guide*, Rick Renner thoroughly expands on Second Timothy 3 concerning the last-days signs to expect in society as one age draws to a close before another age begins.

Rick also thoroughly explains how not to just *survive* the times, but to *thrive* in their midst. God wants you as a believer to be equipped — *outfitted* — to withstand end-time storms, to navigate wind-tossed seas, and to sail with His grace and power to fulfill your divine destiny on earth!

If you're concerned about what you're witnessing in society today — and even in certain sectors of the Church — the answers you need in order to keep your gaze focused on Christ and maintain your victory are in this book!

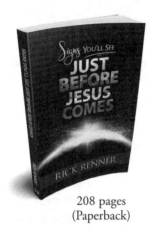

Connect with us on
Facebook @ HarrisonHousePublishers
and Instagram @ HarrisonHousePublishing
so you can stay up to date with news
about our books and our authors.

Visit us at **www.harrisonhouse.com**
for a complete product listing as well as
monthly specials for wholesale distribution.

# The Harrison House Vision

Proclaiming the truth and the power

of the Gospel of Jesus Christ with excellence.

Challenging Christians

to live victoriously,

grow spiritually,

know God intimately.

# Thoughts for Your Own Unlikely Journey

# Thoughts for Your Own Unlikely Journey

# Thoughts for Your Own Unlikely Journey

# Thoughts for Your Own Unlikely Journey

# Thoughts for Your Own Unlikely Journey

# Thoughts for Your Own Unlikely Journey

# Thoughts for Your Own Unlikely Journey

# Thoughts for Your Own Unlikely Journey

# Thoughts for Your Own Unlikely Journey

# Thoughts for Your Own Unlikely Journey

# Thoughts for Your Own Unlikely Journey

# Thoughts for Your Own Unlikely Journey

# Thoughts for Your Own Unlikely Journey

# Thoughts for Your Own Unlikely Journey

# Thoughts for Your Own Unlikely Journey

# Thoughts for Your Own Unlikely Journey

# Thoughts for Your Own Unlikely Journey

# Thoughts for Your Own Unlikely Journey